TRANSLATING RUSSIAN LITERATURE IN THE GLOBAL CONTEXT

Translating Russian Literature in the Global Context

Edited by
Muireann Maguire and Cathy McAteer

https://www.openbookpublishers.com

Digital material and resources associated with this volume are available at https://doi.org/10.11647/OBP.0340#resources

Version 1.1

ISBN Paperback: 978-1-80064-983-5
ISBN Hardback: 978-1-80064-984-2
ISBN Digital (PDF): 978-1-80064-985-9
ISBN Digital ebook (EPUB): 978-1-80064-986-6
ISBN DIGITAL ebook (HTML): 978-1-80064-989-7
DOI: 10.11647/OBP.0340

Cover Design: Jeevanjot Kaur Nagpal

This project has received funding from the European Research Council (ERC) under the European Union's Horizon 2020 research and innovation programme as part of the RUSTRANS academic project, 'The Dark Side of Translation: 20th and 21st Century Translation from Russian as a Political Phenomenon in the UK, Ireland, and the USA' (grant agreement no. 802437).

Contents

Acknowledgements

This book was originally envisaged as a volume of conference proceedings surveying the state of the field in Anglophone literary translation from Russian. When the Covid-19 pandemic caused that conference to be delayed and reconfigured as a non-academic event, we conceived this more ambitious (and also more logistically challenging) idea to recruit an even wider range of contributors to tell a bigger story about the worldwide circulation, reception, and influence of Russian literature in translation over the last century.

The editors would like to thank our families, for all their support during the preparation of this book; our contributors, for their unflagging enthusiasm; and the anonymous external readers of this book at manuscript stage, whose enthusiastic and insightful reviews buoyed our faith in the project. We thank Professor David Brandenberger and Dr Barbara Wyllie for their assistance with the verification of an elusive reference.

This project has received funding from the European Research Council (ERC) under the European Union's Horizon 2020 research and innovation programme as part of the RUSTRANS academic project, 'The Dark Side of Translation: 20th and 21st Century Translation from Russian as a Political Phenomenon in the UK, Ireland, and the USA' (grant agreement no. 802437).

Introduction: "The Greatest Gift"?

Muireann Maguire and Cathy McAteer

In a 2015 interview with an American professor of literature, conducted in the peaceful surroundings of a villa near Cumae in Italy, the writer Boris Akunin remarked: "Russian literature is the best thing to happen to my country; it is also the greatest gift Russia gave to mankind".[1] For well over a century, this attitude to Russian literature (or, more precisely, Russophone writing, incorporating all the regions of post-Soviet space) has been a truism in Western humanitarian circles: to read Russian literature was to acquire wisdom, unsparing psychological insight. Russian prose was also a powerful critique of totalitarianism and injustice—and a summons to the realisation of spiritual responsibility, whether you were reading Pasternak or Tolstoy. In April 2022, two months after the second Russian invasion of Ukraine, an essay by the celebrated Ukrainian novelist Oksana Zabuzhko targeted this complacent Western vision of the invader's literary field. Russian literature, she argued, was "one flesh" with Russian society (and its crimes); the mistake the West has made was to assume a separation between literature and state. "[T]he road for bombs and tanks has always been paved by books [...]. It is time to take a long, hard look at our bookshelves", she wrote in a blistering and widely cited *TLS* opinion piece.[2]

1 Boris Akunin in conversation with Stephen M. Norris, 'Interview with Grigorii Chkartashishvili (Boris Akunin)', in *The Akunin Project: The Mysteries and Histories of Russia's Bestselling Author*, ed. by Elena V. Baraban and Stephen M. Norris (Toronto: University of Toronto Press, 2021), pp. 30–41 (p. 36). Akunin (which means 'villain' in Japanese, a language from which he translates) is the pen name of Grigorii Chkartashishvili, an ethnic Georgian who is probably the world's most successful post-Soviet Russophone author; with the initial 'B' of 'Boris', the moniker refers playfully to the famous nineteenth-century Russian anarchist Mikhail Bakunin. Akunin openly rejects Vladimir Putin's regime; he left Russia in 2013.

2 Oksana Zabuzhko, 'No Guilty People In The World? Reading Russian Literature After Bucha', trans. by Uilleam Blacker, *Times Literary Supplement*, 22 April 2022,

 https://doi.org/10.11647/OBP.0340.00

The ability of Russian literature to inspire, or to acquire, hearts and minds has long been exercised through a wide range of 'soft power' strategies, as well as through coercive educational policies of Russification. This process has never been studied on a global scale or even on a comparative, multilingual basis. Its results have, however, been critiqued, not only by scholars from directly affected nations but by Western critics newly aware of the negative potential of Russian influence. Literature, traditionally seen as a critic of the Russian state, is now often regarded as its ally. Whether the great authors associated with the Russian canon, such as Pushkin, Dostoevsky, and Tolstoy, can genuinely be considered complicit with their nation's imperialist and militarist policy is arguably an anachronistic question. While some continue to debate the morality of funding the translation of contemporary Russian writers, the influence of the nineteenth-century 'classics'—and, especially in the Global South, of Soviet Socialist Realist prose—is already established and enduring. Their pre-eminence as models for emulation, whether creative or personal, and as vectors of philosophical and ethical enquiry, is a fact of global culture. The major questions explored by the essays in this volume include how this pre-eminence was achieved, and how Russian literary influence has evolved abroad during the twentieth and twenty-first centuries: as our contributors show, it has developed spontaneously, trans-creatively, and often (from the perspective of Russian or Soviet statecraft) counterproductively.[3]

From 1938 until its demise, the Soviet state funded the translation of Russophone literature into both globally prevalent and geographically peripheral languages, through several heavily subsidised publishing firms under the umbrella of the Foreign Languages Publishing House. This task, which employed hundreds of translators and censors (including many foreign nationals), was sustained over so many decades partly to honour a Leninist ideological commitment to the internationalisation of culture, but primarily as an exercise in soft power. (The mission of its literary-fiction-focused subsidiaries Progress and Raduga (Rainbow) has since been assumed by new Russian state-appointed organisations such as the

pp. 7–8 (pp. 7–8). https://www.the-tls.co.uk/articles/russian-literature-bucha-massacre-essay-oksana-zabuzhko/. For a more nuanced, but still cumulatively damning, treatment of the theme of imperialism in nineteenth-century Russian literature, see Ewa M. Thompson, *Imperial Knowledge: Russian Literature and Colonialism* (London and Westport, CT: Greenwood Press, 2000). See also Susan Layton, *Russian Literature and Empire* (Cambridge: Cambridge University Press, 1994).

3 An intriguing example of transcreation is the 2011 novel *Maudit soit Dostoïevski* by French-Afghan writer and director Atiq Rahimi, translated by Polly MacLean in 2013 as *A Curse on Dostoevsky*. The book recreates the events and characters of Dostoevsky's *Crime and Punishment* with a cast of young Muslims contending with corrupt and brutal police on the streets of Kabul in the recent past. Among other possible readings, the novel offers a satirical commentary on Russian interference in Afghan politics.

Russkii Mir Foundation, founded in 2007, and the Institute of Translation (Institut Perevoda, or IP), a non-profit organisation established in 2011.) Despite the scale of Progress's achievement, it has never been the subject of a full-length scholarly monograph in English (several essays in this volume offer windows on its activity in specific language areas).[4]

While the political impact of Progress proved negligible (and recent Russian soft power has proved similarly ineffective in terms of securing economic or political allegiance), the cultural penetration achieved by Russian literature in the twentieth century is incalculable, particularly in countries of the Global South where Soviet Communist classics were widely and almost freely distributed, and where Russian political influence was regarded sympathetically (although only in a few nations, like Cuba, was this opinion consistently held by the political mainstream).[5] Sometimes Russian literature failed to take root in the target culture (as in the case of Colombia: see the chapter by Anastasia Belousova and Santiago Méndez). Elsewhere, it thrived despite political suspicion (as in Greece or Brazil); the underfunding of translation and persecution of individual translators (as in Turkey); or ideological dissimilarities, as seen in the history of translating Dostoevsky in Buddhist Mongolia and Communist China respectively, in chapters by Zaya Vandan and Yu Hang. China's President since 2012, Xi Jinping, is a self-professed ardent reader of Russian literature; while he values Tolstoy (and *War and Peace*) highest of all, he has claimed that the Soviet-era writer Mikhail Sholokhov and particularly the nineteenth-century radical Nikolai Chernyshevsky provided important models for his own experience of privation and exile. Great Russian literature, translated via Soviet propaganda, is thus reinscribed as cultural capital in the public biography of China's leading politician: truly transcreation in action.[6]

This unpredictability of literary influence has led to an imbalance in academia: Western overemphasis on the reception of nineteenth-century Russian literature in Anglophone countries, and neglect—now beginning to

4 For an overview of Progress's achievements, see Rossen Djagalov, 'Progress Publishers: A Short History', in *The East Was Read: Socialist Culture in the Third World*, ed. by Vijay Prashad (New Delhi: LeftWord Books, 2019), pp. 83–93 (which in turn draws on Petr Petrov's Russian-language monograph, *K istorii izdatel'stva 'Progress'* (Moscow: Progress Publishers, 1987). Articles in our current volume which throw light on Progress include Nikolay Steblin-Kamensky's study of translation into Amharic and Anna Ponomareva's experience as a translator for Progress's Telugu section.

5 On the ineffectiveness of Russian cultural soft power, see Sergei Medvedev, 'In Search of Past Glory: Russia's Cultural Statecraft in the Age of Decline', in *Russia's Cultural Statecraft*, ed. by Tuomas Forsberg and Sirke Mäkinen (London and New York: Routledge, 2022), pp. 226–38.

6 See, for example, 'A Look at What's on President Xi Jinping's Shelves', *China Daily*, 18 October 2016, https://www.chinadaily.com.cn/china/2016-10/18/content_27093635.htm

be rectified by recent scholarship—of Russia's profound cultural influence on the rapidly evolving societies and politics of Latin America, Africa, and Asia. As one senior Latin American Slavic Studies scholar said, when the editors of the present volume mentioned their plans to produce the first global history of the translation and reception of Russian literature, "I have been waiting a long time for this book". *Translating Russian Literature in the Global Context* is the first scholarly anthology to describe not only the history of literary translation and translators from the Russian language since approximately 1900 (and in several cases, even earlier) in more than fifty countries across the world; it is also the first extended study to examine how translated Russian literature has influenced creative production in those nations, over the same timescale, up to the present day. By implication, these essays are also a map of Russian and especially Soviet soft power: our contributors on Scandinavia, Latin America, Africa, India, East Asia, and the formerly Communist nations of Eastern Europe demonstrate how funding for the transmission of Russian books (in terms of both physical export and intralingual transfer) has waxed and waned in harmony with both Soviet influence and internal political trends in the nations affected.

Despite its ultimate failure as a political entity, the Soviet Union achieved enduring moral authority over much of our planet's land surface, thanks in large part to the production and distribution of Russian literature in multiple languages through Moscow's Foreign Languages Publishing House and its worldwide network of translators. Our contributors on Finland liken this variable influence to the action of a pendulum.[7] By revealing the mechanisms of soft power and its extraordinary transnational reach, our volume is a useful model for future studies of how any nation can achieve political ascendancy through cultural appeal. At a time when Russia's geopolitical approach is changing again from soft power to hard conflict (currently in Ukraine, a country whose complicated cultural relationship with Russian literature is analysed in this volume), it is politically useful to be aware of the extensive groundwork laid by the former.

A further achievement of this volume is to demonstrate, yet again, how Translation Studies is "intimately linked" to Comparative Literature.[8] As this overlap has become increasingly obvious to academics and students in both

7 See Tomi Huttunen, Marja Jänis, and Pekka Pesonen, 'The Pendulum of Translating Russian Literature in Finland', in the present volume.

8 Susan Bassnett, 'Preface', in *Constructing Cultures: Essays on Literary Translation*, ed. by Susan Bassnett and André Lefevere (Clevedon, UK: Multilingual Matters, 1998), pp. vii-viii (p. viii). Although more than two decades have elapsed since Bassnett and Lefevere made this argument (Bassnett even suggesting "that Translation Studies should be seen as the discipline within which comparative literature might be located, rather than the other way round" (ibid.)), there is still considerable reluctance to admit the resonances between these two disciplines, perhaps especially in Slavic Studies.

disciplines, it has become almost impossible to study one effectively without some awareness of the methodology of the other. Some of our contributors (especially those writing about Western Europe, where Russian literature has been available in translation for at least two centuries and has therefore substantially influenced cultural imaginaries) have leaned towards comparative methodology, arguing for the influence of particular Russian writers on national literature at a specific moment. Hence, we have included essays about, for example, the influence of Tolstoy in translation on Turkish, Telugu, and Tamil literature; and about Dostoevsky's reception in Germany by Thomas Mann. Other contributors have opted for a historical approach, outlining the lives and cultural impact of specific translators of or advocates for Russian literature, such as Japan's Futabatei (from the first category), Spain's Emilia Pardo Bazán and France's Eugène-Melchior de Vogüé (from the second).

Each case study reinforces the message that the translator's importance transcends the sum of their word count. Microhistorical details such as translators' motivation, pay, and individual social contexts are clearly crucial, especially for sociologists and cultural historians; however, the enduring significance of the translator's function lies in their role as gatekeepers for the receiving cultures.[9] By translating (and in many cases adapting) Russian literature into their target languages, they opened up new literary subjects, techniques, and styles for other writers, introducing Dostoevsky's psychological realism (often with shocking effect in the target culture's critical ecosystem), but also the technophilic, self-annihilating aesthetic of interwar Socialist Realist production novels. As we unite in this volume multiple national histories of Russian literature in translation, we discover how integral translated Russian literature was for the great pre-modernist and early twentieth-century publishing houses offering cheap, mass-market literary fiction: Selzoff's Russian Authors Library in Brazil, Allen Lane's Penguin in Britain, Albatross and Tauchnitz in Germany, Govostēs Editions in Greece, the Shinchō paperback series in Japan, and Johan Sørensen's Norwegian 'Library for a Thousand Homes', to name some of those discussed by our contributors. Several publishers dedicated book series exclusively to Russian authors. All changed the cultural direction of popular reading in their home nations.

Compiling an edited volume of genuinely global scope is not without its challenges. Our global remit implied the need to recruit global scholars, for many of whom English is a second or third language; as editors, we worked

9 On microhistories, see Anthony Pym, *Method in Translation History* (London and New York: Routledge, 1998); on translatorial social contexts and personal histories (habitus and hexis), see Daniel Simeoni, 'The Pivotal Status of the Translator's Habitus' (*Target*, 10:1, 1998, pp. 1–39) and David Charlston, 'Textual Embodiments of Bourdieusian Hexis', *The Translator*, 19:1, 2013, pp. 51–80. On gatekeeping, see William Marling, *Gatekeepers: The Emergence of World Literature and the 1960s* (New York: Oxford University Press, 2016).

especially closely with these authors to reconcile them with unfamiliar academic style. We selected our contributors through a combination of direct invitation and advertisement, seeking out acknowledged subject experts in every field, not necessarily professional academics (and occasionally accepting more than one contributor to cover different aspects of the reception of Russian literature within a single language). Another challenge has been the regrettable gaps in our range: we were not able to commission essays offering a historical overview of the translation and reception of Russian literature in the US, Canada, the UK, France, Germany, much of the African continent including South Africa, Australia, or New Zealand (in the case of the last two nations, our chosen contributor was prevented from completing their essay by illness and overwork; most of the writing and editing for this volume was undertaken under the exceptional circumstances of a global pandemic).[10] At least four major world languages, each essential for the translation and mediation of Russian literature, are under-represented in this volume. On reflection, we find this omission less grave than it may seem. As explained below, our volume's contributions are organised geographically, with each 'continent' prefaced by a short essay prepared by the editors providing an overview of the reception of Russian literature since 1900 throughout that region. This allows us to briefly summarise the significance of omitted nations or translators and signpost to further and more specific research, as our extensive Bibliography already does and as we have encouraged all of our contributors to do.

In its current form, this volume includes essays on the French, German, and North American reception of Russian literature, dealing with individual critics (de Vogüé), authors (Fedor Dostoevsky and Thomas Mann; Andrey Kurkov and Alexey Nikitin), and specific historical moments (the evolving reception of Russophone Ukrainian authors in the West, for example). We also note two key points in defence of our omissions: first, that new studies of Russian literary transmission within the cultures we left out, including academic monographs, are already available or in preparation.[11] In some cases, such as French, these

10 Similarly, we lost our Israel contributor to academic precarity, while our Poland author, who works for a Polish university, withdrew almost immediately after the February 2022 invasion of Ukraine: apparently Polish University faculties would not tolerate any new research on a Russian theme, even the historical reception of Russian literature in Poland.

11 On France, see, for example, the following monographs and dissertation: Leonid Livak, *How It Was Done in Paris: Russian Émigré Literature and French Modernism* (Madison, WI: University of Wisconsin Press, 2003); F. W. J. Hemmings, *The Russian Novel in France: 1884–1914* (London: Oxford University Press, 1950); and A. McCabe, 'Dostoevsky's French Reception: from Vogüé, Gide, Shestov and Berdyaev to Marcel, Camus and Sartre (1880–1959)' (unpublished doctoral thesis, University of Glasgow, 2013). On Spain, see Lynn C. Purkey, *Spanish Reception of Russian Narratives, 1905–1939: Transcultural Dialogics* (Cambridge: Cambridge University Press, 2013). See also our Bibliography.

have been available for years (Hemmings's authoritative monograph was published in 1950). Second, the history of Russian influence on Anglophone literary culture has already been largely told, albeit piecemeal, through various articles and monographs published in recent decades; indeed, research on the Anglophone countries tends to monopolise study of the translation and reception of Russian literature. We therefore find it appropriate and perhaps even necessary that the history of the transmission of Russian literature into the Anglophone world, which has for so long been over-represented in academia, should be under-represented in our volume.[12] (On the other hand, the essays from the Global South which we have curated here do constitute—in some cases for the first time in English—their nations' history of cultural contact with Russia). Our overview of the absorption of Russian literature into the Anglophone intellectual everyday follows our section on the Americas, forming a coda to our volume.

Methodology

The chapters in *Translating Russian Literature* are both geographically diverse and chronologically broad, covering an eventful century of socio-political change: two world wars, the Russian Revolution and subsequent Cold War and mass migration, both of individuals and their literary influences. To instil theoretical and epistemological coherence we asked all our contributors to follow a clear methodological framework, derived primarily from Translation Studies (with some input from Comparative Literature). This interdisciplinary framework offers a useful set of theories to unite the many case studies of translators and translated literature in our volume. It conveniently accommodates strands of research that share space with (and often overlap) book history, comparative literature, sociology, microhistory, publishing, linguistics, diplomacy, and soft-power politics.

12 On the reception and translation of Russian literature in the UK, please see Rebecca Beasley's work (mentioned elsewhere here and also listed in our Bibliography). While the present volume does not cover the history of Russian translation in the US in detail, under the auspices of the same research project we plan to publish two monographs on this subject, both currently in preparation. Muireann Maguire's monograph, working title *Russian Silhouettes*, will provide an outline history of US-based literary translators active from the late nineteenth century to the present day, with particular focus on those translators who were also active as editors or publishers. Cathy McAteer's monograph *Cold War Women: Female Translators and Cultural Mediators of Russian and Soviet Literature in the Twentieth Century* (London: Bloomsbury Academic, 2024), will examine the careers of twentieth-century female translators who were also advocates for Russian culture and for Russophone writers.

The theorists whose key works we identify as particularly apposite here—Pascale Casanova and David Damrosch—have been credited with taking the field of Translation Studies in all these directions. Casanova's *World Republic of Letters* (1999, reprinted 2007) and both of Damrosch's texts *What Is World Literature?* (2003) and *Comparing the Literatures: Literary Studies in a Global Age* (2020) have equipped translation scholars with paradigms with which to investigate both broad and nuanced factors determining target/source culture relationships and underscoring the transnational circulation of texts.[13] Such research now commonly encompasses global perspectives, particularly the Global South, producing compelling case studies that define the cultural connection between national dominance and domination, the role of power in driving literary trends and carving epicentres of book production (and hence, of translation). Socio-political developments drive the movement of people and texts, unexpectedly propelling writers and translators into a new public domain, shaping literary canons, and forming new or cementing old (often lasting) impressions, alliances, and sometimes, resentments between nations.

Casanova's and Damrosch's discourses on European literatures extend as far east as Bulgaria, Romania, and the Czech Republic, to Marx, Kafka, Kundera, and Kiš; they travel beyond to China, Japan, Africa, Latin America, and India. They evidence political, literary, linguistic, and social conditions behind the circulation of texts and their trajectories from obscurity to the world stage. There is, however, one creation story (with the exception of a few fleeting references) that eludes their full attention and yet merits scrutiny: the Russian/Soviet paradigm. Casanova offers passing commentary in the course of the *World Republic* on the Russian/Soviet context, and Damrosch refers to Dostoevsky, Tolstoy, Nabokov and Russian formalists as part of a global tapestry of literary contributors, bit parts in a bigger, more complex picture. In each case, however, they resist the temptation to linger on and explore more fully the potential of what is a rich and fascinating case study, emerging from the Soviet desire to disseminate its literature (and political presence) around the world. Our edited volume, the first of its kind to address Russian literature in a global translatorial context, tracks the migration of the Russian literary canon across all continents, and its translation into local languages over the span of one century. It identifies the networks of agents who facilitated such literary migration, while evaluating the cultural impact of the Russian (and Soviet) canon on each receiving nation. We have therefore applied a number of versatile methodological strands to construct a macroscopic case study of each discrete literature, allowing us to find out exactly what drives the transmission of Russian book culture abroad.

13 See Casanova, *The World Republic of Letters*, trans. by Malcolm DeBevoise (Cambridge, MA: Harvard University Press, 1999; 2nd edn, 2007) and David Damrosch, *What Is World Literature?* (Princeton, NJ: Princeton University Press, 2003) and *Comparing the Literatures: Literary Studies in a Global Age* (Princeton, NJ: Princeton University Press, 2020).

Our volume asks the same sociological questions that have occupied major translation scholars (Casanova and Damrosch, but also Anthony Pym, Johan Heilbron and Gisèle Sapiro) over the past two decades. How has Russian literature arrived in neighbouring and not-so-near countries? Who has financed its journey (and why?)? Which social agents (publishers, editors, translators, ambassadors) have facilitated its publication, and how has it been received, by scholars, critics, and casual readers?[14] What were the principal pivot, or bridge, languages which carried Russian literature to nations such as Spain where few translators knew Russian, and how does the transmission of, for example, Pushkin or Gorky map onto pathways of colonial influence? Inspired by sociologist Pierre Bourdieu, whose ideas similarly challenge disciplinary boundaries, we have asked about Russian literature around the world: "Who are the discoverers, and what interest do they have in discovering these things?".[15] In the field of Russian literary translation studies, such prior enquiry has typically been directed at language-specific configurations rather than forming a synchronous image of Russian literature's global reception.[16] The ambitious historiography we have collated here constitutes a step-change in Slavic literary translation scholarship.

Other emerging trends in Translation Studies have facilitated our methodological choices. In the last decade, the entire field has experienced a theoretical shift towards sociological and archival research, a key example of which is Jeremy Munday's approach. Munday's microhistorical and Bourdieusian methodology, which validates the (often unnoticed) agency of translators and seeks to make them visible, has led to new scholarship in the field of Russian Translation Studies in, for example, Cathy McAteer's *Translating Great Russian Literature: The Penguin Russian Classics* (2021), and now here in this volume.[17] Munday advocates use of translators' notes, drafts and manuscripts,

---

14 Pym, *Method in Translation History*; Johann Heilbron and Gisèle Sapiro, 'Outline for a Sociology of Translation: Current Issues and Future Prospects', in *Constructing a Sociology of Translation*, ed. by Michaela Wolf and Alexandra Fukari (Amsterdam and Philadelphia, PA: Benjamins Translation Library, 2007), pp. 93–107.

15 Pierre Bourdieu, 'The Social Conditions of the International Circulation of Ideas', in *Bourdieu: A Critical Reader*, ed. by R. Shusterman (Oxford: Wiley-Blackwell, 1999), pp. 220–28.

16 On Anglophone translation, see Rachel May, *The Translator in the Text: On Reading Russian Literature in English* (Evanston, IL: Northwestern University Press, 1994); on Russo-Chinese translation, Mark Gamsa, *The Chinese Translation of Russian Literature: Three Studies* (Leiden and Boston, MA: Brill, 2008); and on Brazilian reception of Russian literature, see Bruno Barretto Gomide, *Da Estepe à Caatinga: O romance russo no Brasil (1887–1936)* (São Paulo, Brazil: Editora de Universidade de São Paulo, 2011).

17 Cathy McAteer, *Translating Great Russian Literature: The Penguin Russian Classics* (London and New York: Routledge BASEES Series, 2021), https://www.taylorfrancis.com/books/oa-mono/10.4324/9781003049586/translating-great-russian-literature-cathy-mcateer; https://doi.org/10.4324/9781003049586.

archived correspondence, and analysis of paratexts in order to understand the wider "role of translation in concrete socio-historical contexts".[18] This call for understanding reflects our own desire not only to identify the translators and their motivations for translating Russian literature around the world, but also to contextualise their activities in the wider literary community. The interconnected nature of agency in the literary field—a reliance on a complex network of facilitators—merits exploration beyond the scope of the translator alone, inviting comparable analysis of other types of facilitator. Only by surveying the spectrum of key agents and their socio-historical/socio-political contexts can Munday's aspiration "to uncover the power relations at work in the production of the literary text" be satisfactorily fulfilled.[19]

Thus, we have invited our contributors to draw on primary archival and paratextual material to construct microhistories of translators, publishers, and cultural mediators who have promoted Russian literature in foreign locations over the past century. In a further advancement, we have encouraged microhistorical explorations of any specific national writer, genre, or literary group within the target culture who translated, transmitted, or adapted aspects of Russian literature in their own literary production. In this regard, we honour Casanova's commitment to understanding world canon-formation, we extend Klaus Kaindl's, Waltraud Kolb's and Daniela Schlager's innovative line of enquiry into the sub-field of literary translator studies, and we complement the intricate socio-cultural research carried out by scholars like Rebecca Beasley and Peter Kaye in the field of transnational Russian studies.[20]

Outline

The thirty-seven essays in the present volume are divided into three sections, by continent, in rough chronological order of the major stages of diffusion of Russian literature abroad. Within each section, essays are arranged in alphabetical order by country name.

18 Jeremy Munday, 'The Role of Archival and Manuscript Research in the Investigation of Translator Decision-Making', *Target*, 25:1 (2013), 125–39.

19 Jeremy Munday, 'Using Primary Sources to Produce a Microhistory of Translation and Translators: Theoretical and Methodological Concerns', *The Translator*, 20:1 (2014), 64–80.

20 *Literary Translator Studies*, ed. by K. Kaindl, W. Kalb, and D. Schlager (Amsterdam and Philadelphia, PA: Benjamins Translation Library, 2021); Rebecca Beasley, *Russomania: Russian Culture and the Creation of British Modernism, 1881–1922* (Oxford: Oxford University Press, 2020); Peter Kaye, *Dostoevsky and English Modernism, 1900–1930* (Cambridge and New York: Cambridge University Press, 1999).

Europe

We begin in France, famous for the contribution of Eugène-Melchior de Vogüé to the reception of Russian literature with his vastly influential (and popular) *Le Roman russe* (1886). Elizabeth Geballe uses the writings of Rachel May and David Damrosch, in addition to existing scholarship on the history of Russian writing in French translation, to argue that de Vogüé was a uniquely influential figure in the process of 'transculturation' of Russian prose. As she writes, this celebrated mediator "shaped the expectations of the French reading public" through the metatexts he supplied for his own and others' translations of leading Russian writers. In their essay on 'Russian Literature in Estonia Between 1918 and 1940', Anne Lange and Aile Möldre show transculturation in action in another context: the influence of Russian literature (specifically Tolstoy and Dostoevsky) on the Socialist Realism of Estonian author and translator Anton Hansen Tammsaare (1878–1940). This is a particularly interesting case study, given the hegemonic influence of Russian culture on Estonian writers before and after the two-decade window of Estonian national independence. Similarly, Finnish writers have had to cautiously negotiate a balance between establishing their own national culture and language while determining the extent of influence from the literature of their vast and sometimes overweening neighbour, Russia. Tomi Huttunen, Marja Jänis, and Pekka Pesonen frame their study of the interrelationship between Russian and Finnish literature, 'The Pendulum of Translating Russian Literature in Finland' (from the late eighteenth century to the present day), as a deliberate attempt to *reverse* the traditional trajectory of Casanovian analysis. That is to say, rather than looking at how peripheral languages are translated into major global languages (as Casanova does in *The World Republic of Letters*), they analyse the reverse process: how Russian is translated into Finnish, and with what effect. They use the metaphor of the 'pendulum' to vividly illustrate the variations in the transmission of Russian literature according to political relations and cultural fashions. The remaining essays in this section discuss the influence of Russian literature on Germany's Thomas Mann (Elizaveta Sokolova), Greece (Christina Karakepeli on the Greek reception of Dostoevsky, and Niovi Zampouka on the translation and reception of Russian literature more generally), Hungary (Zsuzsa Hetényi provides an overview of the translation and literary influence of Russian writers in Hungary since the early nineteenth century, including her own activity as a translator of Bulgakov), Spain (Margaret Tejerizo on the impact of the populariser Emilia Pardo Bazán) and also Catalonia (Miquel Cabal Guarro), Ireland (Mark Ó Fionnáin focuses on Irish-language translations of Pushkin), Italy (with a general survey by Claudia Scandura following Ilaria Sicari's study of the important translator and advocate for Russian dissidents, Mariia Olsuf'eva), Scandinavia (Susan Reynolds documents reception in Norway and Sweden), Romania (Octavian Gabor on translation, philosophy, and political resistance), Scotland (James Rann on the Russian influence on twentieth-century Scots poetry), and finally, twentieth-century relations between Russian literature and Ukrainian culture, colourfully described by co-authors Lada Kolomiyets and Oleksandr Kalnychenko as resembling "the slow but increasingly deadly compression of a rabbit by a boa constrictor".

Africa and Asia

As mentioned above, this section is particularly revealing about the under-researched activities of the USSR's Foreign Languages Publishing House, an important instrument of Soviet soft power. Essays by Nikolay Steblin-Kamensky (Ethiopian translations in the Amharic language), Anna Ponomareva (the Telugu section of Progress Publishers), and others vividly illustrate both the reach and the diversity of Russian literature as cultural propaganda in the developing world during the second half of the twentieth century. We have also included essays describing the reception of Dostoevsky in China (Yu Hang) and Japan (Hiroko Cockerill), while Trang Nguyen contrasts the transmission of Russian literature and the reading habits of the public in North and South Vietnam, respectively. The exceptional complexities of reception, transmission, and translation in multilingual India are outlined in essays by Ranjana Saxena (overview), Guzel' Strel'kova (Hindi), Ayesha Suhail (Tolstoy in translation), and Venkatesh Kumar (Tolstoy in Tamil). Anna Ponomareva's contribution on translations into Telugu was mentioned above. The former Soviet republics in Asia are represented by Kazakhstan (Sabina Amanbayeva) and Uzbekistan (Benjamin Quénu), while Zaya Vandan describes the complex reception policy of Mongolia. Turkish reception is discussed in two essays: a historical overview from Hülya Arslan and a Pushkin-specific study by Sabri Gürses. In an appropriate parallel to Nikolay Steblin-Kamensky's essay on Gorky's Amharic reception history, Mukile Kasongo and Georgia Nasseh have co-authored an article about the 'spectre' of Gorky in Angolan writing. This Lusophone strand resonates with Bruno Barretto Gomide's essay on Brazilian reception of Russian literature in our 'Americas' section, which includes some of the same writers, translators, and publishers. Such confluences emphasise the interrelationships created in the reception of Russian literature through multiple intermediary languages and overlapping cultures. Finally, Russian prose in the Arab world—again, primarily translations of Gorky—is introduced by Sarali Gintsburg.

Americas

For the reasons explained above, we have included only one essay dealing directly with North American reception (although Muireann Maguire includes the US in her summary of Russian reception in the Anglophone world). Catherine O'Neil's essay focuses on Russophone Ukrainian literature in translation in the twenty-first century. However, our exploration of Russian literature in Latin America is both diverse and far-reaching. Bruno Barretto Gomide details the several stages in the transmission of Russian translations to Brazil, culminating in their consecration in university curricula, partially thanks to the work of the Russian-Jewish émigré scholar-translator, Boris Schnaiderman. Anastasia Belousova and Santiago Méndez present an interesting anomaly: the *lack* or failure of Russian literature in Colombia, which they ascribe to an absence of cultural curiosity or political stimuli. Damaris Puñales-Alpízar discovers echoes of late Soviet culture in Cuba, while Rodrigo García Bonillas traces the scholarly and cultural impact of Russian literature (including book series) in Mexico.

Conclusion

Translating Russian Literature in the Global Context aims to provoke new debate about the continued currency of Russian literature as symbolic capital for international readers, in particular for nations seeking to create or consolidate cultural and political leverage in the so-called 'World Republic of Letters'. These essays also benefit researchers aiming to examine and contrast the mechanisms of the translation and reception of Russian literature across the globe. We hope our contribution will inform and inspire students and scholars in the fields of both Slavic and Translation Studies, as well as book historians, and practitioners and researchers across the translation and publishing communities.

EUROPE

Russian Literature in Europe: An Overview

Muireann Maguire

The larger European languages, particularly French and German, have always acted as pivots for the transmission of Russian literature beyond the borders of the Russian nation. The complex relationship of cultural imitation, trade, and mutual conquest between the Russian Empire and the nations of Western and Central Europe created a dynamic whereby French and German (together with English, the dominant language of another close partner through trade, diplomacy and dynastic intermarriage) were typically the first foreign languages in which major works of Russian literature appeared.

The present volume includes case histories spanning the European continent from Norway to Catalonia. As in other sections, our contributors on Europe offer a variety of approaches: some offer a history of the reception and translation of Russian literature within a specific nation or region (Estonia; Finland; Hungary; Denmark and Norway); others examine the life of a single translator, writer, or other cultural advocate whose interaction with Russian authors altered his or her country's reception of Russian literature (France, Germany, Italy, Spain), while others follow the reception history of a particular Russian writer within a single cultural field (Catalonia, Ireland, Germany, Greece); still others combine overall reception history with a mix of these approaches (Greece, Hungary, Scotland, Italy again, Romania, Ukraine). We welcome this plurality of models, and in this brief introductory essay we will suggest why it is important to trace the reception history of Russian literature in Europe not only from a strictly chronological and geographical perspective, but also through the complex history of literary influence. While neither space nor expertise permit us to include an overview of every nation or region of Europe, we attempt here and elsewhere to point our readers to additional texts which offer more specific case histories, including studies of those major European nations whose reception history is not fully covered elsewhere in this volume.

 https://doi.org/10.11647/OBP.0340.01

The first reason to chart the European penetration of Russian literature is borne out by the later sections of this volume: precisely because of the unhappy history of European imperialism, the languages of Europe acted as pathways of transmission of Russian literature through each other's territories and, even more importantly from a world literature perspective, to their colonies across the globe. Hence, the Spanish reception of Russian prose (which, as our contributor Margaret Tejerizo informs us, was jump-started by the remarkable Emilia Pardo Bazán with a series of lectures delivered at the Madrid Ateneo during the late 1880s) went on to colour its Latin American reception, as discussed in the 'Americas' section of this volume. While we lack a direct contribution on the Portuguese-language reception of Russian writing, later chapters in this volume explore the influence of Russian writers on the culture of Brazil and Angola respectively, both former Portuguese colonies. The French diplomat and critic E.M. de Vogüé, who taught himself Russian while serving as secretary to the French Embassy in St Petersburg, later (through a series of articles and a book) persuaded not only his French contemporaries of the importance of the great Slav Realist authors, as Elizabeth Geballe shows in her essay, but at the same time facilitated the reception of nineteenth-century Russian prose in Spain, Portugal, and far beyond, thanks to translations of his criticism.[1] By retracing how European critics and writers interpreted Russian literature, we gain insight into how that same literature was re-translated and re-configured abroad, into other world languages.

A second reason is the fact that so many major European writers owe their inspiration to Russian literature. Some admittedly so, others more covertly. In the case of writers like Thomas Mann or Romain Rolland who openly advertise their debt to Russian writing, it is useful to know which translations they used; in the case of those writers who may have adapted Russian themes without acknowledging them, it is pragmatic (when building a case for influence) to know which translations they would have been able to access, or how Russian literature was evaluated in their culture at the time of writing. It is also helpful, from the cultural historian's standpoint, to understand which critical essays changed attitudes within a nation in favour of Russian influences (or indeed the reverse); a particularly complex task in the twentieth century, when reading of nineteenth-century Russian prose was impossible to extricate from the supposed Communist threat to national integrity (particularly in Spain or Greece, which were for many decades controlled by anti-Communist dictatorships).

It is remarkable how often Russian literature was perceived (by both critics and writers) as a completely fresh alternative to the materialist trends dominating European Realism; how frequently its aesthetic was welcomed as spiritual and philanthropic. (This idealistic reception would, in the long

1 See F.W.J. Hemmings, *The Russian Novel in France 1884–1914* (Oxford: Oxford University Press, 1950), esp. pp. 27–48.

term, undermine the commercial success of Russian literature, especially in Anglophone nations). This reputation for higher spirituality, ostensibly inherent to Russian literature, encouraged similar responses from its readers, as in the following analogy. Dostoevsky famously wrote from Siberian exile in 1854 to one of his benefactors, Natalia Fonvizina, that "if someone proved to me that Christ is outside the truth [...] then I should prefer to remain with Christ rather than with the truth".[2] A character in a 1914 short story by the Spanish author Miguel de Unamuno protested:

> My vision of Russia [...] arises from my reading of Russian literature [...]. My Russia is the Russia of Dostoevskij, and if that is not the real, true Russia of today, then all that I am about to say will lack any real practical value but not any other value. I vote for the triumph of the philosophy [...] that is to be found in Dostoevsky.[3]

In other words, where Dostoevsky stood for Christ against the truth, Unamuno's character stood for Dostoevsky's imagination against the truth of Russia.

This quotation highlights the importance of studying the history of the transmission of Russian literature to the nations of Europe: for many European writers, and for their readers, Russian literature represented a state of psychological and spiritual truth-telling which was not contingent on historical or political conditions. As fiercely as it might be criticised on aesthetic grounds, it remained—for many European critics—an enduring moral exemplar. Meanwhile, up to the present day, an uncountable number of European writers (and film-makers) are inspired directly or indirectly in their own creative work by reading 'the Russians'. Sometimes this influence can be traced through obvious parallels or the author's own admission, as in the essay on Thomas Mann and Dostoevsky in this section; often the influence is unacknowledged or unconscious. There is even a third category, consisting of writers inspired to write non-fiction about the Russians they admire, and/or to translate their work into their own language—like the French novelist Prosper Mérimée, who wrote articles for the *Revue des Deux Mondes* in the 1850s about Pushkin, Turgenev, and Gogol (and translated work by all three, not without some errors), or the case of André Gide's 1926 study of Dostoevsky.[4] And of course, there is a fourth

2 Cited by Joseph Frank in *Dostoevsky: A Writer in His Time* (Princeton, NJ: Princeton University Press, 2010), p. 220.

3 Cited by William B. Edgerton in 'Spanish and Portuguese Responses to Dostoevskij', *Revue de Littérature Comparée* 55:3 (1981), 419–38 (p. 423).

4 See Hemmings, *The Russian Novel*, p. 5, p. 7. On Mérimée's translations, see also John L. Chamberlain, 'Notes on Russian Influences on the Nineteenth Century French Novel', *The Modern Language Journal* 33:5 (1949), 374–83. Chamberlain reports that despite publishing his translation of Pushkin's 'The Queen of Spades' ('Pikovaia dama', 1833; 'La dame de pique') in 1849, Mérimée wrote to his Russian 'friend and mentor' Varvara Ivanovna de Lagrené (née Dubenskaia): "I wish that

category: philosophers and other creative intellectuals who found their thinking enriched by the experience of reading Russian literature in translation. Gide, for example, began his *Dostoevsky* with an epigraph from Nietzsche: "'Dostoevsky was the only psychologist from whom I had anything to learn: he belongs to the happiest windfalls of my life, happier even than the discovery of Stendhal.'"[5] The Norwegian author Knut Hamsun, whose reception of Dostoevsky is discussed in Susan Reynolds's chapter in the present volume, falls into several of these categories.

Not all discoveries of Russian literature were as happy as Mérimée's or Nietzsche's—nor as spontaneous. In the present volume, Lada Kolomiyets and Oleksandr Kalnychenko describe how Russian literary culture was forced on Ukraine through a combination of strategic rewards, political persecution, and mass state-subsidised translation. The history of Polish-Russian literary contact is at least equally fraught and complex; for every Polish scholar "fanatically enamored [sic]" with the work of a Russian author,[6] a multitude of ordinary Poles were compelled to study their uncongenial neighbour's prose canon in school. Although Poland did not lack skilled translators, including the prolific Seweryn Pollak (1907–87), Andrzej Stawar (1900–61), and the poet Julian Tuwim (1894–1953) whose translation of Pushkin's *Bronze Horseman* (*Mednyi vsadnik*, 1833; *Jeździec miedziany*, 1932) became the canonical Polish version, a 1947 reader survey showed that the majority of the Polish public had only ever heard of Tolstoy and Dostoevsky (that is, out of all Russian authors; yet they were familiar with over 150 other foreign writers). A decade later, more than half the books provided for schools, libraries, and book clubs in Poland were translations from Russian: but, in a seemingly odd decision by the Soviet authorities responsible for this unsubtle Russification of the Soviet literary field, few of these were nineteenth-century classics. Instead, Polish readers were treated to contemporary fiction by Mikhail Sholokhov, A.N. Tolstoy, Viktor Nekrasov and other, lesser luminaries of Soviet Socialist Realism: "millions of

---

I could tell you, madame, that I am making progress in the Russian language, but it seems to me, on the contrary, that the study of it becomes harder day by day. I can never find even one line of poetry which I can understand at once, without looking up one or two words." (p. 374).

5 André Gide, *Dostoevsky*, unknown translator (London and Toronto: J. M. Dent and Sons, 1925). https://archive.org/stream/in.ernet.dli.2015.169976/2015.169976.Dostoevsky-By-Andre-Gide_djvu.txt.

6 This is how Roman Jakobson described the attitude of the great Polish Pushkinist Wacław Lednicki (1891–1967) in 'Polish Scholarship and Pushkin', *The American Slavic and East European Review*, 5:1/2 (May 1946), 88–92 (p. 89). By Lednicki's own admission, other Poles (including the poet Adam Mickiewicz) viewed Pushkin more soberly, judging that his unwilling subservience to the Russian Tsar tainted the quality of his poetry. See Wacław Lednicki, 'Pushkin, Tyutchev, Mickiewicz and the Decembrists: Legend and Facts', *The Slavonic and East European Review*, 29:73 (June 1951), 375–401.

copies of the mediocre, dull novels that characterized Soviet fiction after the Zhdanov decrees of 1946".[7] As Seweryn Pollak reflected in a wry 1947 article on translation, a translator was rarely free to choose their texts on aesthetic grounds: political contexts took precedence.[8]

A third justification for our case studies is the light they shed on the lives and professional networks of dozens of translators who made the cultural exchanges described above possible, but who would otherwise be lost to history. These range from culturally peripheral figures like Juli Gay, the obscure Catalan translator of Dostoevsky, rediscovered by his twenty-first century successor (and our contributor) Miquel Cabal Guarro; or the Jesuit classicist Fr. Gearóid Ó Nualláin, whose early twentieth-century Irish-language adaptations of Pushkin and Tolstoy are touched upon by Mark Ó Fionnáin in his chapter in our volume. Several essays mention the importance of the German translations (of Pushkin, Turgenev, Lermontov and others) produced by Friedrich Martin von Bodenstedt (1819–92), a Hanover-born polyglot who taught himself Russian and Persian. As a professor of Slavonic Studies (and later of English literature) at the University of Munich, he translated Russian and Ukrainian poetry; despite his failings, his versions of these authors would be re-translated into Hungarian, Turkish, and other languages, as our contributors show, with lasting influence on the literatures of those nations. Genuine polyglots like Von Bodenstedt deserve re-evaluation today: what can we learn about their success as intercultural communicators in an age where resurgent populism and nationalism challenge the values of multilingualism and tolerance?

Similarly, major European translators of twentieth-century Soviet and dissident literature are in danger of being lost to history, apart from a few notes in the front matter of a paperback. There are casualties of the translator's infamous 'invisibility' in every national culture.[9] In France, significant twentieth-century translators include the Prague-born academic and translator of Pasternak,

7 Maurice Friedberg, 'Russian Literature in Postwar Poland: 1945–1958', *The Polish Review*, 4:1/2 (Winter-Spring, 1959), 33–45 (p. 35), https://www.jstor.org/stable/25776220. I am indebted to Friedberg's article for the statistics on Polish readers cited in this paragraph.

8 Cited by Friedberg, 'Russian Literature in Postwar Poland', p. 34. For the early modern history of Polish-Russian literary relations, see Paulina Lewin, 'Polish-Ukrainian-Russian Literary Relations of the Sixteenth-Eighteenth Centuries: New Approaches', *The Slavic and East European Journal*, 24:3 (Autumn 1980), 256–69, https://www.jstor.org/stable/307180. For more on the impact of Soviet literature behind the Iron Curtain, see the relevant articles on Poland, Hungary, the former Yugoslavia and other Eastern European nations in *Translation Under Communism*, ed. by Christopher Rundle, Anne Lange, and Daniele Monticelli (Cham: Springer/Palgrave Macmillan, 2022).

9 See Lawrence Venuti, *The Translator's Invisibility* (London and New York: Routledge, 1995).

Tolstoy, and Solzhenitsyn, Michel Aucouturier (1933–2017);[10] René Huntzbucler, the translator of Gorky (*Mother*, 1906; *La mère*, 1952), Vsevolod Ivanov, and Konstantin Simonov; Claude Ligny, first French translator of Bulgakov's *Master and Margarita* (*Le Maître et Marguerite* (Editions Robert Laffont, 1968)); Françoise Marrou-Flamant (1931–2015), whose widely acclaimed version of Bulgakov's novel was published by the prestigious 'Bibliothèque de la Pléiade' and Folio series in 2004 and 2017 respectively;[11] and Bruno de Schloezer (1881–1969), one of France's most eminent (and prolific) translators of Tolstoy.[12] As this incomplete list shows, Francophone translators include émigrés, academics, amateurs, authors, journalists, and some who filled more than one category (often at the same time). Their personal and professional networks are exceptionally rich in national and international historical resonances and cultural influences. France—like every other European nation—is overdue for an historical investigation of its heritage of literary translation (and not only from Russian).

One major French exception to the translator's usual obscurity is the 'Prix du Meilleur Livre Étranger'; this prestigious literary prize, established in 1948 and funded since 2011 by the hotel firm Sofitel, rewards both the author and translator of the best foreign novel translated into French during the previous year. In 1968, translations of Solzhenitsyn's novels *The First Circle* (*V kruge pervom*, 1968) and *Cancer Ward* (*Rakovyi korpus*, 1955–68) were honoured;[13] more recent Russophone laureates have included Vasilii Grossman (1984), Mikhail Shishkin (2005), Marina Tsvetaeva (2011), Guzel' Iakhina (2021), and Maria Stepanova (2022). The prize favours translations of contemporary fiction and essays: only once, in 1957, was a nineteenth-century Russian author honoured. This was Pavel Melnikov-Pecherskii's *In the Forests* (*V lesakh*, 1874; *Dans les forêts*, translated by Sylvie Luneau in 1957).[14] Analogously with the Anglophone International Booker Prize (which, since its establishment in 2004, splits its

---

10 For more biographical details, see Catherine Depretto, 'Michel Aucouturier (1933-2017), *Cahiers du monde russe* 59:1 (2018), 143–52, https://journals.openedition.org/monderusse/10292.

11 On translations of *The Master and Margarita* into French, see this French-language interview with the novel's latest translators: Annick Morard, 'André Markowicz et Françoise Morvan: '"Le Maître et Marguerite" est un acte de résistance en soi', *Le Temps*, 1 December 2020. https://www.letemps.ch/culture/livres/andre-markowicz-francoise-morvan-maitre-marguerite-un-acte-resistance-soi.

12 Schloezer was born in Vitebsk, now in modern Belarus, also the home-town of his near-contemporary Marc Chagall. Celebrated as a musicologist and a philosopher (and a devotee of Lev Shestov), Schloezer translated Tolstoy's *War and Peace* for Gallimard (*La Guerre et la Paix*, 1960). For more information, see B.J. Bisson, 'Boris Shlezer: paradoks perevodchika' ['Boris de Schloezer: A translator's paradox'], *Voprosy literatury*, 1:1 (2020), 220–30.

13 The French translations referred to here were *Le Premier Cercle*, by Louis Martine, and *Le Pavillon des cancéreux*, by Michel Aucouturier.

14 See 'Palmarès du prix du Meilleur Livre Etranger', http://www.lalettredulibraire.com/Palmarès-du-prix-du-Meilleur-Livre-Etranger

prize money equally between the author and translator), the Prix du Meilleur Livre Étranger bestows symbolic capital as well as publicity on both author and translator; recent awards to authors whose work is considered original, polemic, or at least interrogative (such as Shishkin, Stepanova and Iakhina) indicate a desire to encourage the dissemination of Russian literature abroad, although this may change post-2022 to align with the critical reaction against Russian culture in some Western countries.

A final reason for recovering national histories of translation, and of translators, can be applied even more generally. Any comparative and diachronic study of the reception history of Russia, such as we have attempted for Europe, helps scholars of cultural transmission to determine the most favourable conditions for this phenomenon to occur (if, indeed, these circumstances can be reliably categorised). As Hemmings notes in his history of France's reception of Russian literature between 1884 and 1914, there was no particular reason why this reception could not have taken off nationally well before the 1880s: translations were available, cultural contacts were extensive, the reading population was large. He points out that "a perfectly satisfactory translation of *War and Peace*" barely sold any copies in Paris in 1879 yet, "six years later the book was a best-seller".[15] It is difficult not to accept Hemmings' argument that Russian literature must have acquired during the 1880s a "special appeal" for French readers, produced by a collection of identifiable circumstances, which it did not possess earlier: what we might call a perfect storm of favourable conditions.[16] He lists the conditions applicable in the French case: France's need (since 1870) for a political ally against Prussia; the insidious appeal of popular romances set in Russia; the growth of critical interest in Russian literature, accompanied by the foundation of the first academic chairs in Russian Studies at French universities; and, not least, the critical discovery of Tolstoy and Dostoevsky by de Vogüé, which led the way for other writers to be translated and enjoyed.[17] Analogously, in this section on the European reception of Russian literature, and indeed in this book as a whole, we compare and discuss the conditions for that reception to work: to inspire emulation, to provoke debate, and to infiltrate a culture's imaginative categories. Can any such set of favourable circumstances be described? In the essays which follow this section, we will discover which conditions were necessary for Russian literature, in translation, to take root among its European neighbours.

---

15 Hemmings, *The Russian Novel*, pp. 2–3 (p. 3). He is referring to *La Guerre et la Paix, roman historique* (St. Petersburg, 1879), attributed to Princess Irène Paskévitch. Turgenev, then living in Paris, enthusiastically sent copies to French literary friends and critics, including Flaubert, Zola, and Daudet (see Hemmings, p. 20).

16 Ibid., p. 3.

17 Ibid., pp. 3–10.

Catalonia

More Than a Century of Dostoevsky in Catalan[1]

Miquel Cabal Guarro

Introduction

Since the first work by Fedor Dostoevsky appeared in Catalan in 1892, and, more significantly, since some of his most relevant titles appeared in that language (between the late 1920s and the late 1930s), this canonical Russian literary figure has been regularly disseminated within the Catalan publishing market. Two hundred years have passed since Fedor Dostoevsky's birth and more than a century since his irruption into the Catalan-language literary system. It is therefore time to address the circumstances specific to the Catalan publication of his works and to analyse the main achievements of Dostoevsky's Catalan publishing history.

This essay will focus on the unique factors determining the stages of Dostoevsky's dissemination in the Catalan cultural sphere. Firstly, I will tackle the emergence of Russian literature within the Catalan cultural milieu, particularly Dostoevsky's arrival on this scene. I will also examine the role of certain key characters involved in his reception, namely the translators Andreu Nin, Francesc Payarols, and Josep Maria Güell, as well as the writers Carles Soldevila and Joan Sales, all of whom made both qualitative and quantitative contributions to Dostoevsky's presence in the Catalan literary domain.

1 This work has been developed in the framework of the research project 'Francoist Censorship and Russian Literature (1936–1966)' (PID2020–116868GB-I00), funded by the Spanish Ministry of Science and Innovation /AEI/10.13039/501100011033.

 https://doi.org/10.11647/OBP.0340.02

Different Waves

The Rather Unplanned Emergence of Russian Authors in Catalan

Although Dostoevsky is my main topic here, I will briefly explain the conditions and factors specific to the arrival of Russian literature in Catalonia. In the last quarter of the nineteenth century, Russian literature was still an unknown and exotic domain for the Catalan cultural milieu. Echoes of this vast artistic field arrived mainly from French reviews and newspapers, arousing growing interest. Perhaps inevitably, the first Russian author to be printed in a Catalan publication was Aleksandr Pushkin.[2] The *Catalan Newspaper* (*Diari català*) was the first newspaper to be published in Catalan. During its short life (1879–81), it printed several articles relating to Russia; the editors tended to sympathise with subversive Russian movements of the time, namely Nihilism.[3] By virtue of the Spanish Press Law of 1879, criticism of any national monarchy had to be censored by the Spanish authorities, and the *Catalan Newspaper* was suspended for continually siding with the Russian Nihilist movement and claiming overtly that Nihilists were in a "struggle for freedom" against the criminal tsarist monarchy.[4] On 26 June 1879, the *Diari català* newspaper included one of Pushkin's 'Little Tragedies': *Mozart and Salieri* (*Motsart i Sal'eri*, 1832). This short play in two scenes was translated into Catalan by a certain 'P. R.', the same initials as Pere Ravetllat, one of the editors in charge of literary affairs at the *Diari català*.[5] The play was awkwardly subtitled 'Poema d'Alexandre Poucrkine'. This clumsy misspelling provides a significant piece of information: on the one hand, the transcription of the author's name is clearly French, so the source language

2 "Translations from Russian appear to have been an isolated phenomenon, rather than a planned activity with thematic uniformity. These texts were present in key French magazines of the time, and the work of writer-translators allowed for these snippets of Russian literature to enter the Catalan literary system. There was no consistency in the choice of the texts, and therefore the list of translated texts is eclectic and difficult to categorise". Noemi Llamas Gomez, 'Francesc Payarols and Andreu Nin, Agents of the Catalan Polysystem. Unmediated Translations from Russian in the 1930s: A Critical Overview' (unpublished doctoral thesis, University of Glasgow, 2018), p. 51, https://theses.gla.ac.uk/30794/.

3 On the construction of a cultural vision of Russian Nihilism in the liberal press of Spain as well as the flexible boundaries separating the press and the literary realm in the late nineteenth century, see Sandra Pujals, 'Too Ugly to Be a Harlot: Bourgeois Ideals of Gender and Nation and the Construction of Russian Nihilism in Spain's *Fin de Siècle*', *Canadian-American Slavic Studies*, 46 (2012), 289–310.

4 Josep M. Figueres i Artigues, *El primer diari en llengua catalana: 'Diari Català' (1879–1881)* (Barcelona: Institut d'Estudis Catalans, 1999), pp. 116–17.

5 Figueres i Artigues, *Diari Català*, p. 170; Manuel Llanas and Ramon Pinyol, 'Les traduccions en el *Diari Català*', *Anuari Verdaguer*, 12 (2004), 81–90 (p. 88).

of the Catalan version becomes indisputable; on the other hand, by confusing an upper-case H with an upper-case R, the typesetting probably indicates that nobody in the newspaper was aware that a poet named Pushkin actually existed. The editors must have admired the so-called 'tragedy' in its French form and translated it without making further inquiries. Whether the misspelling already existed in the French version lies beyond the scope of my present research.

The next translation into Catalan of an entire literary work of Russian origin appeared in 1886, with more noticeable consequences. The book *In Solitary Confinement: Impressions of a Nihilist* (*En cellule. Impressions d'un nihiliste*, 1879) by Isaak Pavlovskii (1852–1924), a Russian journalist, writer, and revolutionary activist who spent extended periods in Catalonia, France, and Spain, was translated from the French version by the renowned Catalan writer Narcís Oller (1846–1930), under the author's personal supervision.[6] In his preface to this volume, the translator describes the fortuitous nature of the birth of Russian-Catalan cultural relations. A group of Catalan literary representatives of the 'Renaixença' neoromantic movement were meeting at their usual café.[7] There they encountered Pavlovskii, with whom Oller later became close friends. Apparently, the Spanish novelist Benito Pérez Galdós had sent Pavlovskii to encounter Oller and his colleagues.[8] As Oller describes their meeting:

> Slightly more than a year ago the whole group of poets and writers at Cafè Pelayo struck up a strong and lasting friendship with a young man, a Russian national, who had just arrived in Barcelona aiming to seriously study our literature, our history, our traditions, and the way we live and think nowadays. That extremely observant young man, his very direct and instructive conversation, polite manners, and kind behaviour was Isaac Paulowsky [sic], the author of the *Memoirs* which form this book.[9]

6 Isaac Paulowsky, *Memorias d'un nihilista*, trans. by Narcís Oller (Barcelona: La Ilustració Catalana, 1886).

7 A clear and detailed explanation in English of the nature and leading actors of this movement can be found at Open University of Catalonia, *Lletra (Catalan Literature Online): La Renaixença (The Catalan Cultural Renaissance)*, https://lletra.uoc.edu/en/period/la-renaixenca/.

8 José Manuel González Herrán, 'Un Nihilista Ruso En La España de La Restauración: Isaac Pavlovsky y sus relaciones con Galdós, Oller, Pardo Bazán, Pereda', *Anales Galdosianos*, XXIII (1988), 83–105 (p. 84), http://www.cervantesvirtual.com/nd/ark:/59851/bmcpp153.

9 "No fa gayre més d'un any que tot l'esbart de poetas y escriptors del cafè de Pelayo entaulá fonda y perdurable amistat ab un jove, rus de nació, que venía á Barcelona disposat á estudiar en serio nostra literatura, nostra historia, nostras costums, nostre actual modo d'ésser y pensar. Aquell jove, en alt grau observador, de conversa discretíssima é instructiva, de finas maneras y de tracte per demés simpátich, era n'Isaac Paulowsky, autor de las *Memorias* que forman aquest llibret." Narcís Oller, 'Preface', in Paulowsky, *Memorias*, pp. 5–9 (p. 5).

Russian translations into Catalan and Catalan translations into Russian were probably triggered by this personal encounter, after which Pavlovskii and Oller ('deux frères', in Pavlovskii's own words) started to correspond, exchanging more than 160 letters over four decades.[10] Subsequently, Oller translated (from French) various works by Aleksandr Ostrovskii, Lev Tolstoy, Ivan Turgenev, and Pavlovskii, while Pavlovskii was responsible for translations into Russian of works by Oller and Àngel Guimerà, both extremely influential Catalan *fin-de-siècle* writers. Thus, the door was already open; Catalan interest in Russian literature was real. It was not long before more translations from Russian into Catalan appeared, finally including some of Dostoevsky's works.

The First (Relatively Shy) Stage: The Late Nineteenth Century

Translations from Russian spread through different European countries for very similar reasons. As the scholar and translator Carol Apollonio has written of the Anglophone world:

> Literary, cultural and political values tend to drive literary translation, particularly in the Russian case. [...] The interest in Russian literature [...] that began in the early [twentieth] century was inspired both by the reading public's fascination with Russian radical political movements and by the *fin de siècle* avant-garde. [...] The influx of political exiles [...] and the sensational developments of the Bolshevik Revolution contributed to the 'Russian craze'.[11]

Hence, in the last two decades of the nineteenth century, the main triggers for translating from Russian into Catalan were probably, in Apollonio's words, "the reading public's fascination with Russian radical political movements and the *fin de siècle* avant-garde".[12] The fact that the first translation from a Russian author appeared in a strongly libertarian newspaper like the *Diari català* seems to confirm this argument. The press and non-fiction literature (like Pavlovskii's book, mentioned above) might have been key factors for the so-called "Russian craze", as Sandra Pujals explains:

10 Anna Llovera Juncà, 'Correspondència d'Isaac Pavlovsky a Narcís Oller, 1907–1908. Presentació i edició', *Anuari TRILCAT: Estudis de Traducció, Recepció i Literatura Catalana Contemporània*, 2013, pp. 84–104 (p. 85), https://dialnet.unirioja.es/servlet/articulo?codigo=5803374.

11 Carol Apollonio, 'Dostoevsky: Translator and Translated', in *Dostoevsky in Context*, ed. by Deborah A. Martinsen and Olga Maiorova (Cambridge: Cambridge University Press, 2015), pp. 236–43 (p. 240).

12 Ibid.

> The evidence suggests that non-fiction literature and the press may have actually played a more significant role than fiction in the construction of collectively accepted cultural visions that would be later transformed into literature or as in the case of Spain's *fin de siècle* literary elite would give way to the mysterious fascination with Russian literature and its application as a model for modern literature in Spain.[13]

Since political and cultural contexts determine the production and reception of translations,[14] all of these socio-political elements conditioned the dissemination of Russian literature in Catalonia. Among them, there is one particularly important circumstance that influenced the Catalan cultural scene. Spain's political instability throughout the nineteenth century and its defeat by the US in 1898 strengthened the Catalan movement of national construction (Catalanism), whose policies clearly focused on language and culture, and which primarily supported republicanism and federalism.[15] But these same historical policies also fostered Spanish nationalism, which generally supported the monarchy and a centralised state and which in turn helped to provoke the Catalan nationalist reaction.[16]

Thus this rather agitational political environment might have aroused Catalan interest in the political convulsions afflicting Russian society at the same time and opened the field of international relations of exchange between Russia and Catalonia, specifically at the cultural level (of literature and translation) since, as Heilbron and Sapiro remind us, "translation has multiple functions: as an instrument of mediation and exchange it may also fulfil political or economic functions and constitute a mode of legitimation", in this case, of emergent Catalanism.[17] In the shadow of this movement, during the 1880s and 1890s a set of literary publications arose. These were directed towards building a complete and modern literary system which aimed to enlarge the linguistic-literary

---

13 Pujals, *Too Ugly*, pp. 292–93.

14 Johan Heilbron and Gisèle Sapiro, 'Outline for a Sociology of Translation. Current Issues and Future Prospects', in *Constructing a Sociology of Translation*, ed. by Michaela Wolf and Alexandra Fukari (Amsterdam and Philadelphia, PA: John Benjamins, 2007), pp. 93–107.

15 "From the middle of the nineteenth century, there had been a revival of Catalanist sentiment, of Catalan literature and of the language whose official use had been banned since the eighteenth century. This was intensified by the federalist movement from 1868 to the collapse of the First Republic. Nowhere was federalism as strong as in Catalonia." Paul Preston, *A People Betrayed: A History of Corruption, Political Incompetence and Social Division in Modern Spain 1874–2018* (London: William Collins, 2020), p. 50.

16 Borja de Riquer i Permanyer, 'La débil nacionalización española del siglo XIX', *Historia Social*, 1994, pp. 97–114.

17 Heilbron and Sapiro, *Outline*, p. 103.

capital of Catalan, a dominated language whose development was suspended, and which needed to be "recreated".[18]

This cultural operation encompassed the dissemination of the new aesthetic forms and subjects circulating across *fin-de-siècle* Europe, which the Catalan intelligentsia usually accessed through French publications.[19] These publications, which included Russian literary works, served as sources for the first indirect translations from Russian into Catalan via French.[20] Of this group of new Catalan publications, one proved unusually active in exploring unknown literary tradition. This was *The Renaissance* (*La Renaixensa*), a Catalanist and rather conservative biweekly magazine that, from 1892 to 1900, also published a literary supplement devoted to both Catalan and foreign novels. The magazine and its literary collection introduced foreign literature to the Catalan scene, including Russian titles. Catalan publications were trying hard to catch up with literary discussions elsewhere in Europe, and Russian authors were, of course, a point of interest since "one might remember that the mythification of the Russian novel was precisely one of the most prominent phenomena of the European turn of the century".[21]

Works by Tolstoy, Pushkin, Vladimir Korolenko, Nikolai Gogol, Turgenev, and finally by Dostoevsky featured in the pages of *La Renaixensa*.[22] Dostoevsky's first texts published in Catalan were the novellas *An Honest Thief* (*Chestnyi Vor*, 1848; *Lo lladre honrat*, 1892), and *The Landlady* (*Khoziaika*, 1847; *Un vell amant*, 1892).[23] *An Honest Thief* appears as an anonymous text in the magazine's year index, though the work is subtitled "a translation of Dostoevsky". There is no mention of the translator, which is unusually remiss for *La Reinaxensa*; the periodical generally credited the names of translators since they provided evidence of both cultural responsibility and literary intentionality. The translation of *The Landlady* is credited to Juli Gay. It therefore seems reasonable to credit Gay also as the translator of the unsigned *An Honest Thief*, since it would be odd for a periodical to publish two works by the same author within the same year and entrust two

18 Pascale Casanova, 'Consécration et accumulation de capital littéraire. La traduction comme échange inégal', *Actes de la recherche en sciences sociales*, 144 (2002), pp. 7–20.

19 Jordi Castellanos, 'La novella antimodernista: les propostes de *La Renaixensa*', in *Professor Joaquim Molas: Memòria, Escriptura, Història*, ed. by Rosa Cabré and others, 2 vols (Barcelona: Universitat de Barcelona, 2003), I (2003), pp. 215–328 (p. 315).

20 Ramon Pinyol i Torrents, 'Les traduccions de literatura russa a Catalunya fins a la Guerra Civil: esbós d'una bibliografia', in *Traducció i Literatura: Homenatge a Ángel Crespo*, ed. by Soledad González Ródenas and Francisco Lafarga (Vic: Eumo, 1997), pp. 247–64 (p. 248).

21 Castellanos, *La novella*, p. 324.

22 Pinyol i Torrents, 'Les traduccions de literatura russa', pp. 253–54.

23 Anonymous, 'Lo lladre honrat (Traducció de Dostoiewsky)', no translator credited, *La Renaixensa*, XXII/34–35 (1892), pp. 529–37 and pp. 545–50; Fedor Michailowitch Dostoiewski, 'Un vell amant', trans. by Juli Gay, *Novelas catalanas y extrangeras (fulletó de* La Renaixensa), I (1892), pp. 713–40.

different translators with the assignment. The translator Juli Gay is a rather obscure figure, deserving of further microhistorical research.[24]

Regarding the social context of the reception of Russian (or any other) literature in the late nineteenth-century Catalan cultural milieu (and in fact up to the present day, with some obvious major discrepancies), one must take into account the presence of the Spanish language in Catalonia. In the 1880s and 1890s, members of the urban, educated Catalan population were literate in Spanish. The Catalan population's degree of bilingualism at this period was extremely unequal, and dependent on several factors, including social class (the upper classes had a far better command of Spanish), and location (cities were much more receptive to foreign languages).[25] The cultural elite of the time could read the first mentions of Dostoevsky and other Russian authors in both Catalan and Spanish periodicals,[26] as well as the first translations of Dostoevsky's works into Spanish, which had appeared in 1890, slightly prior to the author's first Catalan translations.[27] Also, the first Dostoevsky novels to appear in Spanish

24 In my own research on this translator, I found out that eleven years before the first Catalan translation of Dostoevsky appeared, shortly after the latter's death, a child named Juli Gay won a prize in a costume contest in Barcelona dressed as a "Russian villager", as stated in the *Diari Català* (27 February 1881, p. 559). Such an early calling for Russian culture is both curious and revealing, and this Juli Gay is most likely the younger translator. He was probably connected to the composer Joan Gay Planella (1868–1926), but further research is ongoing.

25 Francesc Bernat, Mireia Galindo, and Carles de Rosselló, 'El procés de bilingüització a Catalunya en el segle xx a partir de testimonis orals', *Treballs de Sociolingüística Catalana*, 30 (2020), 97–111 (p. 100), https://doi.org/10.2436/20.2504.01.162.

26 "In fact the first few mentions of Dostoevsky's name in the Catalan press came from the serialisation of *Crimen y castigo* [*Crime and Punishment* in Spanish] in 1885, as mentioned earlier. This text, published in [the newspaper] *La Publicidad* over the course of a few months, is an interesting one: produced in the Catalan system for a Spanish-speaking audience, it sits too uncomfortably on the fence between systems for either milieu to have claimed it." Llamas, 'Francesc Payarols and Andreu Nin', p. 161.

27 The first Spanish translations of Dostoevsky were *A Hundred-Year-Old Woman* (*Stoletniaia*, 1876; *La Centenaria* (*Cuento ruso*), 1890) and 'A Christmas Tree and a Wedding' ('Elka i svad'ba', 1848; 'Cálculo exacto. Cuento ruso', 1890), both published in the magazine *Modern Spain* (*La España Moderna*), which also issued *Notes from the House of the Dead* (*Zapiski iz mertvogo doma*, 1862; *La casa de los Muertos. Memorias de mi vida en la cárcel de Siberia*, 1892). On the chronology and circumstances of the reception of Russian literature in the Spanish literary milieu, see Julia Obolenskaya, 'Historia de Las Traducciones de La Literatura Clásica Rusa En España', *Livius: Revista de Estudios de Traducción*, 1 (1992), 43–56; Jordi Morillas Esteban, 'F. M. Dostoievski En España', *Mundo Eslavo*, 10 (2011), 119–43; Dzhordi Moril'ias and Nataliia Arsent'eva, 'Ispanskoe Dostoevskovedenie: istoki, itogi i perspektivy', in *Dostoevskii. Materialy i issledovaniia*, ed. by Konstantin Barsht and Natalia Budanova (Saint-Petersburg: Institut Russkoi Literatury RAN, 2013), vol. XX, pp. 305–28.

were mainly issued by Maucci, a publisher from Barcelona, and translated from French versions.[28]

These nineteenth- and early twentieth-century French pivot translations from the Russian, especially of Dostoevsky's works, usually distorted the original. The Russian text was adapted to the translator's taste, excerpts (or even whole chapters) were deleted, names were changed, passages were freely rewritten, etc., so the result was drastically removed from the original, both in terms of substance and form.[29] These adaptations, although unacceptable today, were considered reasonable at the time. We should remember that:

> Canons of accuracy in translation, notions of 'fidelity' and 'freedom', are historically determined categories. [...] The viability of a translation is established by its relationship to the cultural and social conditions under which it is produced and read.[30]

The first justification for the 'free' French translations is the aim of making the foreign author familiar in the translated version, "to move the author toward the reader,"[31] a process which usually leads to "wholesale domestication of the foreign text."[32] This was common practice amongst almost all translators of that time from and into almost all European languages, with the possible exception of German translations.[33]

This 'abusive' form of adaptation was a general practice, but there seem to be other specific reasons in the early French versions for domesticating Dostoevsky's texts. In his influential *The Russian Novel* (*Le Roman russe*, 1886), Eugène-Melchior de Vogüé stated that "*The Idiot* and *The Possessed*, and especially *The Brothers Karamazov*, are spun out to intolerable lengths" ("dans l'*Idiot*, dans les

28 Moril'ias and Nataliia Arsent'eva, *Ispanskoe*, pp. 309–11.

29 Ivan Garcia Sala, 'Olga Savarin i altres històries de la traducció indirecta del rus al català al segle xx', in *Traducció indirecta en la literatura catalana* (*Actes del V Simposi sobre traducció i recepció en la literatura catalana contemporània*), ed. by Ivan Garcia Sala, Diana Sanz Roig, and Bożena Zaboklicka (Lleida: Punctum, 2014), pp. 145–68; Alexander McCabe, 'Dostoevsky's French Reception: From Vogüé, Gide, Shestov and Berdyaev to Marcel, Sartre, and Camus (1880–1959)' (unpublished doctoral thesis, University of Glasgow, 2013).

30 Lawrence Venuti, *The Translator's Invisibility. A History of Translation*, 2nd edn (London and New York: Routledge, 2008), p. 4.

31 "In my opinion, there are only two possibilities. Either the translator leaves the writer in peace as much as possible and moves the reader toward him; or he leaves the reader in peace as much as possible and moves the writer toward him." Friedrich Schleiermacher, 'On the Different Methods of Translating', trans. by Susan Bernofsky, in *The Translation Studies Reader*, ed. by Lawrence Venuti (London and New York: Routledge, 2012), pp. 43–63 (p. 49).

32 Venuti, *Invisibility*, p. 4.

33 Ibid., p. 5.

Possédés et surtout dans les *Frères Karamazof*, les longueurs sont intolérables").[34] Thus de Vogüé's authority on Russian literature could be invoked to justify omissions from and 'free' adaptations of Dostoevsky's texts over the next two decades, by blaming the excessive length of the original. André Gide's articles on Dostoevsky of 1908 and 1911[35] eventually drew attention to the inaccuracy of extant translations,[36] and explicitly suggested that the German versions (in particular) might have been more accurate. In Gide's words: "In Germany translations of Dostoevsky follow one upon the other, each an improvement in scrupulous accuracy and vivacity on the one before."[37]

When scrutinising these indirect translations, and recognising the differences between French and German versions, there is an important aspect to consider about the first Catalan translations of Dostoevsky. Comparison of the Catalan translation with Wilhelm Goldschmidt's German versions appeared in 1886,[38] and the degree of coincidence found in the solutions, omissions, and punctuation of both versions has led me to conclude that Dostoevsky entered the Catalan literary milieu through a German rather than a French filter. It seems clear that Gay used German translations by Goldschmidt as the source texts for his versions of Dostoevsky's novellas *An Honest Thief* and *The Landlady*. It is a remarkable fact, since French has been commonly assumed as the main or only source of Dostoevsky's titles not only for all the other Romance cultures, but even for other medium- and small-sized European languages, and this was also certainly the case for the vast majority of Catalan translations from Russian during this period. Hence this finding has dramatic implications for the study of the Russian author's earliest reception in the Catalan literary milieu and might inaugurate an illuminating new research trajectory.

There is another relevant element to consider when approaching early translations of Dostoevsky: the role of censorship in modelling the text, whether the original source text, the pivot translation, or the final version. In the Russian Empire, authors were subject to strict political and moral censorship, a pressure that was obviously applied to Dostoevsky from the very beginning of his career as a writer.

---

34 Eugène-Melchior de Vogüé, *Le Roman russe* (Paris: Libraire Plon, 1886), p. 255; English translation quoted from Eugène-Melchior de Vogüé, *The Russian Novel*, trans. by Colonel H. A. Sawyer (New York: Alfred A. Knopf, 1916), p. 250.

35 André Gide, 'Dostoïevsky d'après sa correspondance' (1908) and 'Les Frères Karamazov' (1911), in André Gide, *Dostoïevsky* (*articles et causeries*) (Paris: Libraire Plon, 1923).

36 Ivan Garcia Sala, 'Olga Savarin', p. 151.

37 André Gide, *Dostoevsky*, trans. by Louise Varèse (New York: New Directions, 1961), p. 170.

38 F. M. Dostojewskij, *Erzählungen* ('Die Wirtin', 'Christbaum und Hochzeit', 'Helle Nächte', 'Weihnacht', 'Der ehrliche Dieb') (Leipzig: Verlag von Ph. Reclam 'Universal-Bibliothek', 1886).

> By the time Dostoevsky began publishing in the mid-1840s, censorship requirements were an ever-present reality for writers. [...] Writing about censorship in the 1870s, Dostoevsky recalled that in the 1840s censors 'strictly suppressed' 'every new idea' and forbade 'almost everything'—even lines and dots were suspect as allegories or lampoons.[39]

From Dostoevsky's correspondence, it is clear that he feared the reactions of the official censors sufficiently to adapt his works to accommodate them, and that he was more than once compelled to cut, ameliorate, and rewrite many of his original texts. But censors aside, Dostoevsky's editors were also responsible for significant cuts and amendments: Stavrogin's confession in *The Possessed* (*Besy*, 1872) is one of the most infamous cases.[40] The original Russian text had already endured several levels of censorship by the time it reached Western European countries for translation into first French or German, and subsequently into other languages. But censorship did not end there for Dostoevsky, and even more agents were involved in the process of curtailing his texts.

> Along with Vogüé and the critics of this first period, those who proceeded to translate Dostoevsky deemed it necessary to 'protect' the public from certain subversive—if not 'unseemly'—aspects of his post-exile writings. [...] No further sign, preface or disclaimer alerted the reader as to the extent to which the translation deviated from the original in content.[41]

Beyond the abovementioned discrete levels of censorship that had already altered the original Russian text, Alex McCabe emphasises that French translators also modified Dostoevsky's texts for the sake of moral and political correctness. Besides the translators' self-censorship, it is reasonable to think that French editors might also have censored actively for the same reasons. Hence, at this point we may assume that Catalan translators and editors proceeded in the same manner as their French counterparts. The result of this multi-layered censorship was an extremely questionable and rather unreliable Catalan translation. There is much more research to be done regarding the ethical and aesthetic outcomes in early Catalan translations, by taking into account the layers of censorship that consecutively affected Dostoevsky's original works.

39 Irene Zohrab, 'Censorship', in *Dostoevsky in Context*, ed. by Deborah A. Martinsen and Olga Maiorova (Cambridge: Cambridge University Press, 2015), pp. 295–302 (p. 296).

40 Ibid.

41 Alexander McCabe, 'Dostoevsky's French Reception', p. 63.

The Second (Solid) Stage: From the Early 1920s to the Late 1930s

The debate over the accuracy and fidelity of French translations from Russian (and the fact that they were used as the source text for most Catalan translations which followed Gay's German-sourced texts) peaked in the early 1920s. Some notable representatives of the Catalan intelligentsia (like Gaziel, Carles Riba and Joan Estelrich)[42] were able to read German translations of Russian authors. It was probably this exposure, combined with perusal of André Gide's articles about the unreliable French versions, that confirmed to them that almost all indirect translations that had been published up to that moment were disastrous, and especially those of Dostoevsky's prose.[43] Moreover, the Russian Revolution of 1917 exponentially increased interest in Russian history, culture, *and* literature, consequently increasing translations of the latter. The first direct translation from Russian into Catalan was made by the Czech polyglot Rudolf J. Slabý in 1921: it was a volume of Pushkin's stories.[44] As Slabý was not a native Catalan speaker, his translations required intensive correction. This first instance of direct translation contributed to raising both editors' and other literary agents' awareness of the need to be more meticulous with Russian translations, whether direct or indirect. Nevertheless, after editing Slabý's second volume of Pushkin's prose, which included only *The Captain's Daughter* (*Kapitanskaia dochka,* 1836; *La filla del capità,* 1922), Estelrich declared in a letter to Riba, who had corrected the book, that the text types had to be re-set and that it was the last time he [Estelrich] would rely on "direct Slavic translations", since he preferred "re-translations

42 Gaziel was the pen name of Agustí Calvet (1887–1964), an influential journalist, writer and publisher; Carles Riba (1893–1959) was a skilled poet, writer and translator; Joan Estelrich (1896–1958) was a writer, publisher and politician. The three of them were active and prominent figures in the Catalanist movement until the Spanish Civil War (1936–39).

43 Ivan Garcia Sala, 'Olga Savarin', pp. 152–7.

44 Rudolf Jan Slabý (1885–1957) was a Czech linguist and translator who lived and worked in Barcelona from 1914 to 1926. He lectured in Slavic languages at the University of Barcelona and translated about sixty titles (fiction and non-fiction), working into Catalan and Spanish from Czech, Russian, German, Swedish, Ukrainian, Polish, Serbian and English (in his personal records, he also refers to translations from French, Danish, Italian, Slovak, Slovene, Sorbian, and Bulgarian, although these works have not been found). He also translated into Czech from Catalan, Spanish, and Portuguese (Llanas and Pinyol, 'Les traduccions en el *Diari Català*', p. 41). The first ever Russian-Catalan direct translation was a volume published in 1921 with Slabý's versions of *Dubrovsky* (*Dubrovskij*, 1841; *El bandoler romàntic*), *The Queen of Spades* (*Pikovaia dama*, 1834; *La dama de pique o El secret de la comtessa*), 'The Squire's Daughter' ('Baryshnia-krest'ianka', 1831; 'La pagesa fingida'), 'The Blizzard' ('Metel'', 1831; 'Temporal de neu'), and 'The Shot' ('Vystrel', 1831; 'Un tret') by Aleksandr Pushkin (Pinyol i Torrents, 'Les traduccions de literatura russa', p. 249).

from Italian or German".[45] It is worth noting that French pivot versions were not used on this occasion.

In 1923 a theatrical version of Dostoevsky's *The Brothers Karamazov* (*Brat'ia Karamazovy*, 1881; *Els germans Karamàzov*), adapted by Jacques Copeau and Jean Croué for the Théâtre des Arts de Paris,[46] was translated from French into Catalan by Josep Maria Millàs-Raurell.[47] The adaptation was staged in the Romea Theatre in Barcelona, where it was first performed on 10 March 1923. The première was widely advertised in print media and was preceded by a debate on its appropriateness, since it was assumed that the play would "clash too violently with the mindset" of the Catalan public.[48] *La Vanguardia*'s review of the play stated that "it is probably impossible to set on stage all the vigour contained in Dostoevsky's story" and that "the translation is maybe too rigid and literarily meticulous, not sufficiently touching."[49]

Dostoevsky's next title rendered in Catalan was an indirect translation from French of the short story 'The Beggar Boy at Christ's Christmas Tree' ('Mal'chik u Khrista na ëlke', 1876; 'El pobrissó a casa de Crist el dia de Nadal'), which was translated by David Jordi and appeared in the December 1924 issue of *From Here and There* (*D'ací i d'allà*), a cultural magazine. More indirect translations followed, such as *The Landlady* (*Khoziaika*, 1847; *La dispesera*, 1928), translated from French by Josep Carner Ribalta and published in the Biblioteca Univers collection. This collection was created and managed by the renowned writer and publisher Carles Soldevila (1892–1967), who was also in charge of the *D'ací i d'allà* magazine, and who was devoted to broadening and disseminating new (from the point of view of the Catalan tradition) literary styles and authors.[50] In fact, this book was preceded in the series by Lev Tolstoy's *The Kreutzer Sonata* (*Kreitserovaia sonata*, 1889; *La sonata a Kreutzer*, 1928).

Soldevila was a Russian literature enthusiast, and was especially interested in Dostoevsky.[51] Besides Tolstoy and Dostoevsky, the series which he edited also published works by Leonid Andreev, Anton Chekhov, Nikolai Gogol, Maksim Gorky, Aleksandr Kuprin, and Ivan Turgenev. Nine out of the forty-six titles published before 1936 were written by Russian authors (that is, 19.6%).[52] Only two of these books were translated directly from Russian (by Aleksei Markov,

45 Ivan Garcia Sala, 'Olga Savarin', p. 152.

46 Jacques Copeau and Jean Croué, *Les Frères Karamazov*, drame en 5 actes (Paris: Éditions de la Nouvelle Revue Française, 1911).

47 *Els germans Karamazov*, adaptation in five acts from Dostoevsky's novel by Jacques Copeau and Jean Croué, trans. by Josep M. Millàs-Raurell (Barcelona: Publicacions de l'Escola Catalana d'Art Dramàtic, 1923), Biblioteca Teatral.

48 Manuel Reventós, 'Notes Sobre Teatre. L'esforç d'enguany', *La Revista*, 1923, 24–25.

49 'Els germans Karamazov', *La Vanguardia*, 13 March 1923, p. 22.

50 Montserrat Bacardí, 'Carles Soldevila, socialitzador de la literatura', *Quaderns: Revista de Traducció*, 8 (2002), 51–66 (p. 57).

51 Ivan Garcia Sala, 'Olga Savarin', p. 156.

52 Pinyol i Torrents, 'Les traduccions de literatura russa', p. 250.

"the son of an exiled white Russian")[53] while the others were indirectly translated via French.[54] In November 1928, Soldevila's *D'ací i d'allà* published a well-documented article by Agustí Esclasans (a writer and journalist who had translated poetry by Valerii Briusov, Ivan Bunin, and Vladimir Maiakovskii from intermediate languages), claiming that Dostoevsky was an exceptional writer deserving of serious consideration: "What power Dostoevsky must have in his original language that, whether we read him in good or bad translations, he seizes us, controls us, and amazes us!"[55]

In December 1928, marking the centenary of Tolstoy's birth, an article by Alfred Gallard about Russian literature and its reception in Catalonia was more critical of Dostoevsky, suggesting also that Russian literature had stagnated since the ascension of the Soviets.[56] The contradictions between these articles illustrate a key moment in the reception of Russian literature in the Catalan cultural milieu. Interestingly, this period of efflorescence of Russian (and other foreign) literature coincided with the last years of Primo de Rivera's dictatorship (1923–30). Neither censorship nor the clearly anti-Catalan character of the regime had a discernible impact on the publishing industry. The number of translations and overall titles kept growing, and even *The Communist Manifesto* (*Manifest der Kommunistischen Partei*, 1848; *Manifest del partit comunista*, 1930), as well as various books about Lenin, were published during those years.[57]

Also in 1928, the debate about whether to avoid indirect translations became intense. In a long article about Russian literature in Catalonia, Josep Farran i Mayoral stated:[58]

> It is essential that translations are all direct from Russian and very accurate about and respectful of the expressive qualities and defects of the authors. Otherwise, as is often the case, we would offer Russian authors only a second- or third-hand interpretation; which actually means a falsification.[59]

---

53 Ibid., p. 249.

54 Montserrat Bacardí, 'Carles Soldevila', p. 57.

55 'Quina ha d'ésser la força de Dostoiewski en sa llengua original, si àdhuc llegit a través de bones o males traduccions, ens empunya, ens domina i ens admira!', Agustí Esclasans, 'La Força de Dostoiewski', *D'ací i d'allà*, 131, vol. XVII, November 1928, p. 387.

56 Alfred Gallard, 'Tolstoi (1828–1928)', *La Revista*, July-December 1928, pp. 99–102.

57 Jordi Chumillas i Coromina, 'Traducció i edició a Catalunya durant la primera dictadura del s. xx (1923–1930)' (unpublished doctoral dissertation, University of Vic, 2007), p. 81.

58 Josep Farran i Mayoral (1883–1955) was an essayist, a journalist and a translator.

59 'És indispensable que les traduccions siguin totes directes del rus i ben acurades i ben respectuoses envers les qualitats i els defectes expressius dels autors. Altrament, com s'ha fet sovint, no donaríem dels autors russos, sinó una interpretació de segona, o tercera mà; cosa que vol dir en realitat, una falsificació'.

But the very same year Dostoevsky's *Uncle's Dream* (*Diadushkin son*, 1859; *El somni de l'oncle*) appeared in the new world literature collection 'A Tot Vent' by Edicions Proa, translated from French by Prudenci Bertrana.[60] This series, directed by Joan Puig i Ferreter,[61] had previously published Tolstoy's *Resurrection* (*Voskresenie*, 1899; *Resurrecció*, 1928) and soon became a crucial agent in the popularisation of Russian authors in Catalonia: thirteen books out of the ninety-two which it published in the next eleven years were Russian titles (that is, 14.1%).[62]

Nevertheless, Puig i Ferreter soon also insisted on direct translations from Russian, since he assumed that the previous distortion of Dostoevsky's texts via intermediate language translations might afflict all translations from Russian. In the first catalogue of Proa's 'A Tot Vent' collection, he wrote: "regarding the Russians, the question of direct translations has been posed. We've been concerned about this for a long time. Today we can say it is solved".[63] So in this series, the first direct Catalan translations of Dostoevsky's works were to be published in 1929: *Crime and Punishment* (*Prestuplenie i nakazanie*, 1866; *Crim i càstig*) by Andreu Nin and *The Eternal Husband* (*Vechnyi muzh*, 1870; *L'etern marit*) by Francesc Payarols.

For their professional commitment and accuracy, Nin and Payarols are regarded as icons of literary translation from Russian into Catalan.[64] Born into a poor family, Nin (1892–1937) worked as a teacher and a journalist before starting his political career, through which he gained international visibility. He was a prominent member of different Communist and Anarcho-Syndicalist parties and organisations in Catalonia and abroad, including Soviet Russia, where he joined the Trotskyist movement. While in Moscow he began translating both fiction and non-fiction into Catalan for Proa and other publishing houses. Nin translated works by Boris Pil'niak, Nikolai Bogdanov, Mikhail Zoshchenko, Tolstoy, Chekhov, and Dostoevsky, amongst others.[65] His foreword to the Catalan version of *Crime and Punishment* contains valuable comments on the author's

Josep Farran i Mayoral, 'La literatura russa i nosaltres II', *La Veu de Catalunya*, 29 August 1928, p. 5.

60 Prudenci Bertrana (1867–1941) was a modernist novelist who developed his career outside the Catalan cultural mainstream.

61 Joan Puig i Ferreter (1882–1956), playwright and writer, was the editorial manager of this ambitious collection of Catalan and foreign literature. He was also involved in politics and exiled himself in France after the Spanish Civil War. His literary works were influenced by Dostoevsky.

62 Pinyol i Torrents, 'Les traduccions de literatura russa', p. 251.

63 Ivan Garcia Sala, 'Olga Savarin', p. 157.

64 An extended study about the contribution of Francesc Payarols and Andreu Nin to the Catalan literary system between 1928 and 1937, and about the specificities of the Catalan literary milieu at the beginning of the twentieth century can be found in Llamas, 'Francesc Payarols and Andreu Nin'.

65 Pinyol i Torrents, 'Les traduccions de literatura russa', pp. 256–7.

style and gives significant information on how Dostoevsky was read in early 1930s Catalonia.[66] In 1930, at the very beginning of Stalin's purges, he returned to Catalonia, where he continued his political and literary activities until he was killed by the Soviet secret services during the Spanish Civil War.[67]

Payarols (1896–1998) was also born to a working-class family. He trained as a teacher, later working as a bookkeeper while teaching himself German, English, and Russian. He improved his Russian with lessons from the daughter of a Jewish Russian émigré family living in Barcelona. This non-professional teacher later became his wife.[68] Payarols was offered his first translation commission from Russian by Puig i Ferreter in 1928. He translated into Catalan works by Chekhov, Mikhail Saltykov-Shchedrin, Tolstoy, Turgenev, and Dostoevsky.[69] Since he had taught Catalan to the Soviet consul, Payarols was briefly detained by the Francoists before the end of the Spanish Civil War. Afterwards he suffered financial problems due to a lack of work. He was finally hired as a high-school teacher and continued translating for years, mainly from German and into Spanish.[70]

During the 1930s, there appeared translations of *The Village of Stepanchikovo and its Inhabitants* (*Selo Stepanchikovo i ego obitateli*, 1859; *Stepàntxikovo i els seus habitants*, 1933) by Nin for the Proa publishing house;[71] and also of *White Nights* (*Belye nochi*, 1848; *Les nits blanques*, 1937), translated from French by Pere Montserrat Falsaveu for the 'Quaderns literaris' collection. A prospective translation of *Poor Folk* (*Bednye liudi*, 1846) was listed as *Pobra gent* in the 1934 catalogue of Soldevila's 'Biblioteca Univers', but never actually appeared. It is not clear which translator was assigned to it, or why it was never realised. Payarols claimed that he was originally commissioned by Puig i Ferreter to translate *The Brothers Karamazov*, but that after he had already translated three chapters Nin expressed his interest in taking on the project, to which Puig i Ferreter agreed.

66 Andreu Nin, 'Pròleg del traductor' ('Translator's Preface') to Fedor Dostoevsky, *Crim i càstig* (Badalona: Proa 'A Tot Vent', 1929), pp. 5–11 (pp. 10–11).

67 Judit Figuerola, *Andreu Nin, revolucionari i traductor* (Barcelona: Publicacions de l'Abadia de Montserrat, 2018).

68 Pilar Estelrich, 'Francesc Payarols, traductor', *Quaderns: Revista de Traducció*, 1 (1998), 135–51.

69 Pinyol i Torrents, 'Les traduccions de literatura russa', pp. 256–7.

70 Estelrich, 'Francesc Payarols', pp. 143–45.

71 This unusual choice is defended by Llamas in his doctoral thesis: "The only plausible explanation behind this choice is that whilst books such as *The Humiliated and Insulted*, *Notes from the Underground*, and *The Gambler* (among others) had been translated into Spanish, *The Village of Stepanchikovo and its Inhabitants* had not been at that point. [...] By translating a novel not previously available in Spanish, Proa took a risky bet in order to attract the public towards an exclusive text. This makes sense from a marketing point of view, as translating one of the novels mentioned above meant the Catalan text would have to compete with its Spanish version already in the market, as well as the French in some cases", pp. 177–78.

It seems that the chaotic months after Franco's coup halted this project, so the book was never translated by any of these outstanding translators. Not until the 1960s did *The Brothers Karamazov* appear in Catalan (see below).[72]

A theatrical version of *Crime and Punishment* was premièred in Barcelona on 29 November 1936, when the Francoist military uprising was already in progress.[73] The text was adapted by Josep Maria Jordà and Lluís Capdevila on the initiative of the Young Group of the Socialist Unified Youth of Catalonia, and was presented as a homage to the USSR in support of the anti-Fascist militias.[74] The director supposedly used a French version of Dostoevsky's book: rather surprisingly, as Nin's direct translation into Catalan had been available since 1929.[75] There are two key elements that can help to clarify the source choice for this adaptation. On the one hand, in November 1936 the Socialist Unified Youth of Catalonia, which had promoted the project, was in serious conflict with the Workers' Party of Marxist Unification, which was then led by none other than Andreu Nin.[76] On the other hand, Gaston Baty's theatrical adaptation of the same novel (as *Crime et châtiment*) had premièred in Paris on 21 March 1933, in the Théâtre Montparnasse. The *dramatis personae* of the French and the Catalan versions are very similar.[77] Further research is required to determine the concrete circumstances of this translation.

After Franco's victory in 1939, and during the harsh first decades of his dictatorship, literature and any other cultural expressions in Catalan were banned. In the 1960s, the Catalan cultural framework started timidly to recover, but political and moral censorship was always present as a threat to editors' and translators' projects.

---

72 Pilar Estelrich, 'Francesc Payarols, traductor', p. 142.

73 Josep M. Figueres i Artigues, 'Lluís Capdevila, corresponsal de guerra. Les cròniques al front d'Aragó (1936–1938)', *Gazeta*, 2, 2010, pp. 61–71 (p. 63).

74 *La Vanguardia*, 1 December 1936, p. 6.

75 Núria Camps Casals, 'Lluís Capdevila i Vilallonga: un traductor de l'època de preguerra entre la memòria i l'oblit', *Quaderns: Revista de Traducció*, 22 (2015), 181–92 (p. 184).

76 Josep Puigsech Farràs, 'Popular Front, War and Internationalism in Catalonia During the Spanish Civil War', *Bulletin for Spanish and Portuguese Historical Studies*, 37:1 (2012), 146–65 (pp. 154–55).

77 The Catalan version appears in Dostoievski, '*Crim i càstig*, drama en tres actes', adapted by Josep M. Jordà and Lluís Capdevila, *Catalunya teatral*, 95, 1936. The *dramatis personae* of Baty's version is listed in a note on the title 'Crime et châtiment' in *Les Célestins. Saison 1965–1966* (with no pagination). It is very likely that this list of characters is the same as that in 1933.

The Third Stage: The Lazy 1960s and 1970s, the Active 1980s and 1990s

The first book by Dostoevsky to be indirectly translated into Catalan after the Spanish Civil War was the aforementioned translation, previously cancelled because of that war: *The Brothers Karamazov* (*Brat'ia Karamazovy*, 1881; *Els germans Karamàzov*, 1961), indirectly translated from different languages by the prominent writer and editor Joan Sales.[78] Sales took as his main reference text the 1923 French translation by Henri Mongault and Marc Laval, but he also used Cansinos Assens's Spanish translation (in its fifth edition) as well as Italian and English versions.[79] Regarding possible problems with Francoist censors due to the nature of the book and the repression of Catalan cultural expressions during the Fascist dictatorship ruling Spain, on 21 October 1960 the head of the censorship section confirmed that the Catalan version of the book was permitted.[80] This text was the last indirect translation from Russian into Catalan to be published, though it was revised and amended by the translator Arnau Barios in 2014.

From the late 1960s to the late 1990s, Josep Maria Güell translated twenty-one titles into Catalan, by authors like Nina Berberova, Mikhail Bulgakov, Gogol, Ivan Goncharov, Gorky, Boris Pasternak, Iurii Trifonov, and, of course, Dostoevsky, amongst others.[81] Güell is one of the most prolific translators from Russian both into Catalan and Spanish. He combined a fondness for the Russian language with his own literary activity as an expression of his personal rebellion against Franco's dictatorship, and as an act of Catalan patriotism.[82] Güell translated into Catalan Dostoevsky's *The Idiot* (*Idiot*, 1869; *L'idiota*, 1982) for Edicions 62, *The Possessed* (*Besy*, 1872; *Dimonis*, 1987) for Edhasa publishing house and *The Adolescent* (*Podrostok*, 1875; *L'adolescent*, 1998) for Proa. In 1972, an

---

78 Joan Sales i Vallès (1912–83), writer, translator, and publisher, one of the renowned figures of the Catalan literary milieu under the Franco dictatorship. After fighting on the Republic side, Sales had to go into exile (France, the Dominican Republic and Mexico). Once he had returned to Catalonia in late 1940s, he founded Club Editor publishing house, where *The Brothers Karamazov* was to appear.

79 Cansinos Assens's translation was first published in 1935; its fifth edition appeared in 1953. Ivan Garcia Sala, 'Algunes observacions en l'anàlisi comparativa d'*Els Germans Karamàzov* de Joan Sales', in *La traducció i el món editorial de postguerra*, ed. by Sílvia Coll-Vinent, Cornèlia Eisner, and Enric Gallén (Lleida: Punctum, 2011), pp. 39–53 (pp. 40–1).

80 Lara Estany Freire, 'La censura franquista i la traducció catalana de narrativa als anys seixanta' (unpublished doctoral thesis, Universitat Autònoma de Barcelona, 2019), p. 112.

81 Figuerola, *Andreu Nin*, p. 245.

82 Xènia Dyakonova and José Mateo, 'El personatge obscè. Visita retrospectiva als traductors de la prosa russa al català', *Revista del Collegi Oficial de Doctors i Llicenciats en Filosofia i Lletres i en Ciències de Catalunya*, 2011, 63–80 (p. 76).

allegedly direct translation of *White Nights* (*Belye nochi*, 1848; *Les nits blanques*) by Francesc Pagès appeared for Editorial Selecta, together with a new version of *The Landlady* (*Khoziaika*, 1847; *La dispesera*).[83] Additional research is needed to clarify further details about the translator and the translation itself. In 1984, Laertes published Monika Zgustová's first Catalan version of *A Little Hero* (*Malen'kii geroi*, 1849; *El petit heroi*).

The Current Stage: 2000-present

In recent decades, the emergence of several independent Catalan-language publishers, as well as the programme of grants initiated by the Russian Institute for Literary Translation (Institut Perevoda) has established a new framework for the translation of both classic and contemporary Russian authors into Catalan. Moreover, the celebration of the bicentenary of Dostoevsky's birth in 2021 marked a milestone in the history of Catalan versions of his books. Many of the bicentenary translators are former students of Ricard San Vicente and Helena Vidal, two prominent figures within Russian studies in Catalonia; they co-founded the department of Slavic Studies at the University of Barcelona in the early 1990s. All of these factors have contributed to the creation of an ecosystem favourable to cultural interchange between Russia and Catalonia.

In this recent period, two translations of *Notes from Underground* (*Zapiski iz podpol'ia*, 1864) have been published: *Apunts del subsol*, by Miquel Cabal Guarro in 2002 for Llibres de l'Índex (revised in 2021 for Angle Editorial), and *Memòries del subsol*, by Raquel Ribó in 2004 for Destino. A theatrical adaptation by Carlota Subirós of Ricard Altés's translation of *White Nights* (*Belye nochi*, 1848; *Nits blanques*, 2002) was staged at the Teatre Lliure in 2003. A translation of *The Gambler* (*Igrok*, 1867; *El jugador*) by Reyes García Burdeus and Teresa Camañes appeared in 2006 for 3i4 Edicions. In 2008, Arola Editors published a translation of *The Grand Inquisitor* (*Velikii inkvizitor*, 1879; *El gran inquisidor*) by Anna Soler Horta and Nina Avrova. The selection *The Crocodile and Other Stories* (*El cocodril i altres narracions*) was elected, edited, and translated by Margarida Ponsatí-Murlà in 2010 for Accent Editorial.[84] The masterpiece *Notes from the House of the Dead* (*Zapiski iz mërtvogo doma*, 1862; *Memòries de la casa morta*) was translated into Catalan by Jaume Creus in 2011 for Adesiara. In 2015, Angle Editorial published

83 Editorial Selecta was founded in 1946; it was one of the first publishing houses permitted to print books in Catalan after the Spanish Civil War, including both translations and titles written originally in Catalan.

84 This volume includes 'A Nasty Story' ('Skvernii anekdot', 1862; 'Un episodi vergonyós'), 'Bobok' ('Bobok', 1873; 'Bobok'), 'Another Man's Wife and a Husband Under the Bed' ('Chuzhaia zhena i muzh pod krovat'iu', 1848; 'L'esposa d'un altre i el marit sota el llit'), and 'The Crocodile' ('Krokodil', 1865; 'El cocodril').

a new version of *White Nights* (*Belye nochi*, 1848; *Les nits blanques*) in my own translation.

In the year of the bicentenary of Dostoevsky's birth (2021), the following translations were issued: the compilation *The Dream of a Ridiculous Man* (*El somni d'un home ridícul*) by Marta Nin (a distant relative of Andreu Nin) for Comanegra,[85] a translation of *The Double* (*Dvoinik*, 1846; *El doble*) by Xènia Dyakonova for Quid Pro Quo, a new translation of *Crime and Punishment* (*Prestuplenie i nakazanie*, 1866; *Crim i càstig*) for Bernat Metge,[86] a translation of *A Gentle Creature* (*Krotkaia*, 1876; *Manyaga*) for Angle Editorial as well as the first Catalan version of *Poor People* (*Bednye liudi*, 1846; *Pobres*) for Cal Carré, all of them my own. In 2022, theatrical adaptations of my versions of *Crime and Punishment* and *A Gentle Creature* were staged.[87] Finally, in 2023 my translation of *Summer Notes on Winter Impressions* (*Zimnie zametki o letnikh vpechiatleniiakh*, 1863; *Notes d'hivern sobre impressions d'estiu*) was published by Angle Editorial and a first volume of Dostoevsky's selected letters (*Letters 1838–1867*; *Cartes 1838–1867*) was published by Edicions del Cràter.

Conclusion

Fedor Dostoevsky entered the Catalan literary scene on the back of aesthetic trends that arrived from France and Germany in the last decades of the nineteenth century. At that time, translations were in French and, to a much lesser extent, German, with the very first Catalan versions of Dostoevsky's works were apparently translated from German. Even after the 1917 Russian Revolution, translations from Russian were mostly indirect and translators still preferred to use French pivot versions. When the first direct translations of Dostoevsky's works were published in 1929 (*Crime and Punishment* by Nin and *The Eternal Husband* by Payarols), the notion arose that Dostoevsky's style was crucial and needed to be preserved in any translation. In the years that followed,

85 This volume includes *Novel in Nine Letters* (*Roman v deviati pis'makh*, 1847; *Una novel·la en nou cartes*), 'A Weak Heart' ('Slaboe serdtse', 1848; 'Un cor dèbil'), 'An Honest Thief' ('Chestnii vor', 1848; 'Un lladre honest'), 'A Gentle Creature' ('Krotkaia', 1876; 'Una noia dòcil'), and 'The Dream of a Ridiculous Man' ('Son smeshnogo cheloveka', 1877; 'El somni d'un home ridícul').

86 My translation of *Crime and Punishment* into Catalan was awarded the 2021 Barcelona City Prize for Translation, hugely increasing the book's visibility. It has proven to be a long-standing bestseller, and has made a major contribution to the revival of all Dostoevsky's works.

87 *Crim i càstig* (*Crime and Punishment*), adapted and directed by Pau Carrió, was staged in Barcelona at Teatre Lliure from 23 February 2022 to 3 April 2022; *Orgull* (*Pride*), adapted from *Manyaga* (*A Gentle Creature*) by Andreu Benito, Ramon Vila and Oriol Broggi, and directed by Oriol Broggi, was staged in Barcelona at Teatre la Biblioteca from 13 October 2022 to 13 November 2022.

only one more indirect translation appeared: Joan Sales's version of *The Brothers Karamazov* in 1961.

Since then, many of Dostoevsky's works have been rendered into Catalan, but some outstanding issues remain: while there are three direct translations of *White Nights*, two of *Notes from Underground*, and two of *Crime and Punishment*, it is still impossible to read a direct translation of *The Brothers Karamazov*, for example. Similarly, there is still no Catalan version of *The Humiliated and Insulted* (*Unizhennye i oskorblennye*, 1861) or of *Netochka Nezvanova* (1849), to name just a few of his well-known works. It would also be of special interest to translate both the fiction and non-fiction material contained in the different volumes of *A Writer's Diary* (*Dnevnik pisatelia*, 1873–81), since these texts would be both philologically and philosophically relevant to current Dostoevskian debates. The second and final volume of Dostoevsky's selected letters will be published in 2024–25, in my own translation.

In the near future, I hope to publish further research on the following topics: the reasons and circumstances behind the cancellation of *Poor Folk* in 1934; the original text for the theatrical version of *Crime and Punishment* in 1936; the life and times of the translator Francesc Pagès; and, last but certainly not least, an in-depth analysis of the source texts for the first Dostoevsky translations into Catalan (*The Landlady* and *An Honest Thief*), along with some biographical details about their translator, Juli Gay. Finally, in the context of the project on 'Francoist Censorship and Russian Literature (1936–1966)', I expect to develop a new research angle on the different levels of censorship that afflicted Dostoevsky's translations in Catalonia until 1966.

Estonia

Russian Literature in Estonia between 1918 and 1940 with Special Reference to Dostoevsky[1]

Anne Lange and Aile Möldre

Translation is "a cultural practice interacting with other practices in a historical continuum".[2] This definition by Theo Hermans foregrounds the need to understand translation as a social phenomenon dependent on its cultural and political environment, in both synchronic and diachronic perspectives. Our study of translations of Russian literature in Estonia between the two world wars originates from this premise.

Since Estonia had been part of Imperial Russia and therefore subject to its policy of Russification, Estonian intellectuals of the late nineteenth and early twentieth centuries received schooling in Estonia only in the Russian language. This period of Russification in Estonia has been conditionally defined as lasting from the second half of the 1880s until 1905.[3] It was aimed at unifying the Russian Empire and standardising administration, while also ending the autonomy of the Baltic provinces, which derived from the privileges of the Baltic-German nobility. Historian Toivo U. Raun has distinguished between administrative (e.g. judicial or police reforms) and cultural (linguistic, educational, or religious) changes.

1 The research for this chapter was supported by an Estonian Research Council Grant held by Prof. Daniele Monticelli at Tallinn University ('Translation in History, Estonia 1850–2010: Texts, Agents, Institutions and Practices' (grant no. PRG 1206), https://translationinhistory.tlu.ee/en/people/.

2 Theo Hermans, *Translation in Systems. Descriptive and System-oriented Theories Explained* (Manchester: St. Jerome Publishing, 1999), p. 118.

3 Ea Jansen, 'Aleksander III venestusreformid ja Eesti avalikkus' ['Russifying Reforms of Alexander III and the Estonian Public Opinion'], *Acta Historica Tallinnensia*, 3 (1999), 39–65 (p. 39).

 https://doi.org/10.11647/OBP.0340.03

Russification led to the introduction of Russian as the language of administration at all but the lowest levels and as the language of education at all levels, from primary schools to the University of Tartu, by the end of the nineteenth century.[4] Estonian-language private schools and elementary education were allowed only after the 1905 Revolution in Russia. While, before Russification, few Estonian intellectuals were Russophone, afterwards the Russian language was widely used, enabling Estonians to study in Russian universities, primarily in St Petersburg. Studying abroad fostered interest in Russian culture and stimulated translation from Russian.

After Estonia became an independent state in 1918, Estonian became the official state language. It was now used at all levels of the educational system. According to the 1934 law on public secondary schools, English, German, French, and Russian were taught as foreign languages. Secondary school students were supposed to learn two foreign languages.[5] While in the 1920s, German was usually the first foreign language of choice, secondary school language policy changed over the years and on 27 November 1936, English was decreed the first foreign language in secondary schools.[6] The Russian language, as an elective subject, held a rather marginal position. The 1934 census demonstrated that 17.5% of the 1,126,413 residents of Estonia knew the Russian language. This figure included ethnic Russians living in Estonia (8.1% of the total population).[7] Thus translations from Russian were needed because "the language of its masterpieces is not understood or not understood in its details".[8] Russian literature remained available in the original, as the contents of the public libraries of Tartu, the university town of Estonia, show. Even in 1939, after twenty years of national independence with Estonian as the state language, 43.4% of its literature was in Russian. The situation was different elsewhere: in Tallinn, the share of Russophone literature was only 23.5%, and in Paide, a small town in central Estonia, it was 2.3%.[9] The average percentage of

---

4 Toivo U. Raun, 'Part Four: The Estonians', in *Russification in the Baltic Provinces and Finland, 1855–1914*, ed. by Edward C. Thaden (Princeton, NJ: Princeton University Press, 1981), pp. 287–356.

5 'Keskkoolide seadus' ['Law of Public Secondary Schools'], in *Eesti rahvahariduse ja kultuuriala korraldus* [*Organisation of Estonian Public Education and Culture*], ed. by Aleksander Kurvits (Tallinn: Riigi Trükikoja Trükk ja Kirjastus, 1938), pp. 105–11.

6 *Riigi Teataja* [*State Gazette*], 98 (1936), p. 2078.

7 Kadri Koreinik and Tõnu Tender, 'Eesti keeltest rahvaloendustel' ['Languages of Estonia in Censuses'], *Emakeele Seltsi aastaraamat*, 59 (2013), 77–102 (p. 86), http://doi:10.3176/esa59.04.

8 August Annist, 'Meie iseseisvusaegne tõlkeklassika ja Eesti Kirjanduse Selts' ['Translations of Canonical Texts in our Years of Independence'], *Eesti Kirjandus*, 5 (1939), 198–221 (p. 199). All translations from non-English sources, including Tammsaare's fiction, are by the present authors unless otherwise indicated.

9 Aliide Tuisk, 'Avalikud raamatukogud' ['Public Libraries'], in *Eesti Statistika. Recueil mensuel du Bureau Central de Statistique de l'Estonie*, 221:4 (1940), 161–66 (p. 162).

literature in Russian in Estonian public libraries was 23.5% in towns and 4.0% in the countryside, where 95.1% of literature was in Estonian.[10]

This chapter will begin with a survey of translations of Russian literature made between 1918 and 1940. Our focus is on translations published as separate books. We will then discuss the impact of Fedor Dostoevsky on the poetics of Anton Hansen Tammsaare, a major Estonian prose author of the first half of the twentieth century and a translator of Dostoevsky. We view Tammsaare as an author and translator working in the interculture of his own artistic endeavours,[11] besides those authors he read and translated, who in turn influenced his own novels.

Translations of Russian Literature in 1918–40

The establishment of the independent Republic of Estonia in 1918 was followed by the War of Independence (1918–20), in which Estonians resisted invasion by Soviet Russia. The book market was empty after the war, creating a great need for diverse types of publication. Thus, state legislation and a financial support system from public funds set the preconditions for publishing activities. Many private publishing firms were established, and title production increased considerably. Although economic crises, especially the Great Crash of 1929, had a temporary negative impact on the publishing industry, annual growth continued throughout the period. Output increased from 658 titles in 1920 to 1660 titles in 1939.[12] This increase ensured a constant influx of new texts and re-prints. Adaptation to market fluctuations led to a decrease in print runs (that is, the number of copies of a book printed at one time) and a shift in the selection of texts for publishing. Smaller print runs increased printing costs and the nominal prices of books, which, in turn, also reduced the number of purchases. This effect can also be seen in the dynamics of publishing translations of literary fiction for adults. During the short, local economic crisis in the early 1920s, the number of translations decreased from ninety-five titles in 1924 to fifty-six in 1925. The publishing of translations quickly recovered, reaching 148 titles in 1929. Yet another economic crisis at the beginning of the 1930s led to a decline (seventy titles in 1933), followed by an increase during the economically stable second half of the 1930s when the number of translations increased to 140 titles in 1936.[13] Translation publishing was also affected by Estonia's signature of the Berne Convention in 1927, which complicated the process for obtaining

10 Tuisk, 'Avalikud raamatukogud', p. 163.

11 Anthony Pym, *Method in Translation History* (Manchester: St. Jerome Publishing, 1998), pp. 177–92.

12 *Eestikeelne raamat 1918–1940: Eesti retrospektiivne rahvusbibliograafia* [*Estonian Book 1918–1940: Estonian Retrospective National Bibliography*], ed. by Anne Ainz and Leili Tenno, 4 vols (Tallinn: Eesti Rahvusraamatukogu, 2012–13), I (2012), p. 102.

13 Aile Möldre, 'Ilukirjanduse tõlked 20. sajandi esimese poole Eesti ja Soome raamatutoodangus (1900–1940)' ['Translations of Belles-Lettres in the Book

translation licences; new royalty requirements could be challenging for smaller publishers.

In 1918–40, translations of literary fiction (excluding books for children) from the Russian language ranked fourth by number of titles (136), coming after translations from English (570), German (465) and French (199).[14] The publication of translations from Russian had been increasing in Estonia since the 1880s. In view of the predominantly peasant readership, preference was initially given to translations of folktales and a limited selection of works by canonical writers.[15] In the early twentieth century, attention turned to contemporary authors, such as Anton Chekhov, Maksim Gorky, and especially Lev Tolstoy. Although the aesthetic programme of the influential Young Estonia literary movement, established in 1905 with the aim of modernising Estonian culture, focused first and foremost on the French, Scandinavian, and Italian literatures, its members took an interest in new trends within Russian literature—primarily Symbolism—as national borders do not determine literature.[16] In the first decades of the twentieth century, these translations were not published as separate books but in collections or periodicals. For example, short stories by Fedor Sologub and Valerii Briusov were included in the collection of translations *Selected Pages* (*Valitud leheküljed*, 1912) by Friedebert Tuglas (1886–1971), one of the leaders of the Young Estonia movement. Translation of Symbolist authors was part of the Europeanising characteristic of Estonian literary development in the early twentieth century.[17]

The Republic of Estonia's relationship with Russian culture was ambivalent. On the one hand, the Russification experienced in tsarist Russia and the fight against the Bolsheviks during the War of Independence had provoked animosity towards anything originating in Russia. On the other hand, the Estonian intelligentsia, educated through the Russian language and often in Russian universities, was curious about the development of Russian literature and culture. The writer and translator Johannes Semper (1892–1970) argued in a 1922 article that, following independence, Estonian observers could compare and assess different cultural phenomena more neutrally. Estonia's position

Production of Estonia and Finland during the first half of the 20th Century (1900–1940)'], *Methis*, 9–10 (2012), 88–103 (p. 96).

14 The figures are calculated based on the Estonian national bibliography database ERB, available at: https://www.ester.ee/search~S95*est. In 1940, only books issued by the publishers from the independent Republic of Estonia during the first half of the year are included in the statistics.

15 Sergei Issakov, *Arhiivide peidikuist* [*From the Caches of Archives*] (Tallinn: Eesti Raamat, 1983), pp. 274–75.

16 Pascale Casanova, 'Literature as a World', *New Left Review*, 31 (2005), 71–90.

17 Lea Pild, 'Küsimus "vene mõjust" Friedebert Tuglase artiklis "Valeri Brjussov"' ['The Question of Russian Influence on Friedebert Tuglas' article "Valeri Brjussov"'], *Methis*, 1–2 (2008), 178–85 (p. 183), https://doi.org/10.7592/methis.v1i1-2.482.

between Europe and Russia obliges the nation to take an interest in successive Russian cultural trends.[18] The social context of translation has been discussed by Johan Heilbron and Gisèle Sapiro, who distinguish between political, economic, and cultural dynamics that affect the relations of exchange. Translation activity is dependent on the space of reception and social demand, as shaped by relevant intermediaries.[19] The Estonian case demonstrates the relative autonomy of cultural exchange from political factors, facilitated by various intermediary agents and readers' demand for Russian literature. Literary translations from Russian steadily began to appear. As a rule, the number of Russian titles issued per year corresponded to the total output of translated literary fiction, relative to the economic situation. For example, only one fiction book translated from Russian was published between 1933 and 1935, compared to thirteen such titles in 1939.

By examining the genres and authors published in translation, we can distinguish between literary trends in the 1920s and 1930s. Translations of plays accounted for more than half (57%) of all translations from Russian during the 1920s. The same applied to translations from German, but not so much to translations from English, French, and other languages. Thus, plays were primarily translated from historically dominant, familiar literatures. The repertoire of professional theatres, however, was quite varied and not focused solely on German or Russian plays. Theatrical activity thrived during this period: besides the seven professional theatres in Estonia at the time, there were also many amateur theatres. Numerous song and drama societies had already been established during the rise of Estonian nationalism in the second half of the nineteenth century and these activities increased during the years of independence, when the number of amateur theatrical associations exceeded 300.[20] Plays were performed during social events organised by societies in community centres and schools for the general public, often followed by dancing. Therefore, comedies and farces dominated the choice of plays that were also popular in professional theatres at that time. The most popular Russian author was Arkadii Averchenko, five of whose comedies were published in Estonian between 1918 and 1925. Plays were often translated by actors or directors, whose translations could be rather dilettante. It was customary to publish the scripts of plays performed in professional theatres, often as cheap mimeographed

18 J. Semper, 'Vene tulevasest kultuurist' ['About the Future Culture of Russia'], *Kirjandus-kunst-teadus: 'Päevalehe' erileht*, 23 March 1922, p. 97.

19 Johan Heilbron and Gisèle Sapiro, 'Outline for a Sociology of Translation: Current Issues and Future Prospects', in *Constructing a Sociology of Translation*, ed. by Michaela Wolf and Alexandra Fukari (Amsterdam and Philadelphia, PA: Walter Benjamins, 2007), pp. 93–107.

20 Jaak Rähesoo, *Eesti teater: ülevaateteos. 1, Üldareng: "Vanemuine", "Estonia" [Estonian Theatre: Overview. 1, General Development: The Theatres "Vanemuine", "Estonia"]* (Tallinn: Eesti Teatriliit, 2011), p. 219.

reproductions, enabling performances to be staged all over the country and to be read by wider audiences. The leading publisher specialising in plays was T. Mutsu Theatrical Publishing House, which also issued translations from Russian.

However, the list of drama translations was not confined to comedies. For example, the dramatisation of Fedor Dostoevsky's *Crime and Punishment* (*Prestuplenie i nakazanie,* 1866) by J. A. Delier, translated by the poet and theatre critic Artur Adson (1889–1977), was published by the Drama Theatre (Tallinn) in 1921. Adson was a literary adviser to the Drama Theatre in the early 1920s. He also translated Leonid Andreev's symbolist drama *The Life of Man* (*Zhizn' cheloveka,* 1906), published in Estonian in 1921 (re-printed in 1927). Comedies by Nikolai Gogol were translated by writer Richard Kullerkupp. During the 1930s, audiences' theatrical tastes changed, pivoting towards more serious drama. Meanwhile, new works by Estonian authors superseded the abundance of translated plays.

Prose translations were dominated by stories and novellas, although several Russian novels were also issued during the 1920s. Among the authors translated were Aleksandr Kuprin, Evgenii Chirikov, Mikhaíl Artsybashev, Ivan Bunin, and other émigrés from Russia. The few publications from Soviet writers included a collection of short stories by Panteleimon Romanov and Lev Gumilevskii's novel *Dog Alley* (*Sobachii pereulok,* 1926), both of which critiqued the supposed extinction of moral values during the social upheaval in the Soviet Union in the 1920s. Both writers were well known in Soviet Russia in the 1920s and 1930s but later condemned by official criticism and soon forgotten. They were not canonical Soviet authors who created highly politicised texts in accordance with the Communist Party line. The topic of moral conflict, different attitudes towards love and family were also treated in Nikolai Nikitin's novel *The Crime of Kirik Rudenko* (*Prestuplenie Kirika Rudenko,* 1927), which was published in Estonian by Loodus in 1933. Nikitin's later fate was different; he adopted the official Soviet line, receiving the Stalin Prize in 1951. Loodus also included works by Aleksei Tolstoy, Aleksandr Neverov, and Lev Nikulin in their fiction series after the early 1930s.

Reviewing the collection of feuilletons published under the cover title *Agitator* (*Agitaator*) by Mikhail Zoshchenko, issued in Estonian in 1928, the writer and translator Oskar Truu stated that in addition to his interesting characters, Zoshchenko's depictions of everyday life under Communist rule were politically relevant to Estonian readers.[21] Similarly, Russian emigrants read Soviet authors not only for aesthetic pleasure, but out of curiosity, or for informative-cognitive interest as the literary scholar Sergei Isakov put it.[22] Russian émigré-run

21 O. Truu, 'M. Zoštšenko: Agitaator' ['M. Zoshchenko: Agitator'], *Eesti Kirjandus*, 4 (1930), 200–01.

22 Sergei Isakov, *Kul'tura russkoi emigratsii v Ėstonii 1918–1940: Stat'i. Ocherki. Arkhivnye publikatsii* [*The Culture of Russian Emigrants in Estonia in 1918–1940:*

publishing houses in Latvia (such as Literatura, Knizhnaia Lavka Pisatelei, Zhizn' i Kul'tura, and M. Didkovskii), in addition to those Latvian publishers who issued books in Russian (e.g. Grāmatu Draugs), provided some of the channels through which Russian-language books reached Estonia. Zoshchenko, Romanov, and Il'ia Ehrenburg were the most popular Soviet writers for Russian-language publishers in Latvia, with the largest number of titles.[23] Their works also attracted the attention of established Estonian publishers of literary fiction like Loodus, Noor-Eesti, or Valik, who then commissioned translations into Estonian.

Some works by Soviet Russian writers were translated and produced by individuals who were interested in a particular author or subject. For example, the poet Jaan Kurn was among the first translators of Vladimir Maiakovskii in Estonia. The latter's Futurist poems inspired Kurn's own literary output, published under the pseudonym Ralf Rond. Kurn's translations of Maiakovskii's poems were published as *A Cloud in Trousers* (*Pilv püksten*, 1930), which included mainly pre-revolutionary lyrics by the poet. Reviewing this collection for an Estonian literary journal, the philologist Johannes Silvet criticised the quality of the translation, but welcomed the publication of Maiakovskii in Estonian.[24]

After the 1920s, the distribution of Soviet literature and Soviet-approved canonical Russian writings was organised by the All-Union Society for Cultural Relations with Foreign Countries, whose representative joined the Soviet Embassy in Estonia in 1927. Books and periodicals published in the Soviet Union were delivered to various Estonian cultural organisations as well as to several prominent intellectuals.[25] As an authority from a Communist country, its activities were politicised and ideological considerations left their mark on cultural exchange. The society also organised trips for Estonian writers to the Soviet Union; they brought back Soviet books, and published overviews of trends in Soviet literature and their travel impressions in Estonian literary journals. These imported books, however, did not stimulate translations of Soviet literature. The poet Johannes Vares-Barbarus (1890–1946), known for his leftist views, visited Moscow in 1928. In a letter to Johannes Semper, Vares-Barbarus admits that even the most popular works were quite boring and unattractive to readers, especially poetry "where I found very few eye-catching and heart-healing lines".[26]

Articles. Overviews. Archival Publications] (Tallinn: Aleksandra, 2011), p. 107.

23 Isakov, *Kul'tura russkoi emigratsii v Ėstonii*, p.110.

24 J. Silvet, 'Vl. Majakovski. Pilv püksten' ['Vl. Maiakovskii. A Cloud in Trousers'], *Eesti Kirjandus*, 10 (1930), 490–92.

25 Karl Martinson, 'Eesti kirjanike suhteid Nõukogude Liiduga kahel sõjaeelsel aastakümnel' ['The Contacts of Estonian Writers with the Soviet Union during the Two Pre-War Decades'], *Keel ja Kirjandus*, 12 (1972), 731–42 (p. 734).

26 Jaak Valge, *Punased. I.* [*The Reds*] (Tallinn: Tallinna Ülikooli Eesti Demograafia Instituut; Rahvusarhiiv, 2014), p. 278.

Several Estonian organisations (libraries, museums, scientific organisations) maintained direct contact with their Soviet counterparts and acquired Soviet publications through exchange or purchase. Some publishers had business contacts with the Estonian-language publishing houses that operated in the Soviet Union, issuing books for the more than 154,000 Estonians resident there. Although the trade focused on Estonian-language books, the Estonian publishers were also interested in Russian-language publications.[27] Following the shift to Socialist Realism during the 1930s, the monotonous new Soviet literature created under conditions of strict censorship remained distant and alien to Estonian readers. Thus, no such books can be found among the publications of established publishers. However, some notable works of Socialist Realism were issued by small, leftist publishing houses. For example, the publishing house Sõprus (Friendship), which issued publications by the Estonian Socialist Workers' Party and its youth organisation, brought out Gorky's novel *Mother* (*Mat'*, 1906) in 1936. It was translated by the writer and youth organisation leader Nigol Andresen; Gorky was one of his favourite authors. The text was acquired through the All-Union Society for Cultural Relations with Foreign Countries, and the Estonian print run of the book was significant (2000 copies), distributed mainly among the working class via cultural and other societies without the mediation of bookstores.[28] Another example is the novel *And Quiet Flows the Don* (*Tikhii Don*, 1928–32) by Mikhail Sholokhov, published in Estonian in 1936–37. Both volumes were translated by August Koit and issued by the publishing house Kalev; the latter had been founded in Tartu in 1936 by left-wing students aiming to translate and publish Soviet literature.

However, from the end of the 1920s and especially during the second half of the 1930s, the focus of translations of Russian literary fiction remained on nineteenth-century classic authors. By that time, living standards in Estonia and the level of education had risen, and readers' preferences shifted to novels. In order to study the wishes and expectations of its readership, Loodus conducted a survey in 1928 among readers of its fiction series *Looduse universaal-biblioteek* (LUB, 1927–31; Universal Library of Loodus). Just over two and a half thousand respondents named more than 700 writers whose works they wished to see included in the series. The five most popular authors were Knut Hamsun, Henrik Ibsen, Jack London, Lev Tolstoy, and Fedor Dostoevsky. Other Russian authors among the top forty were Maksim Gorky, Nikolai Gogol, and Ivan Turgenev.[29] Thus, the results demonstrate Estonian readers' demand for Russian literature.

27 Aile Möldre and Tiiu Reimo, 'Publishing Activities of Estonians in St. Petersburg before the Second World War (1918–1937)', *Knygotyra*, 50 (2008), 114–31 (pp. 124–26).

28 Nigol Andresen, 'Maksim Gorki ja Eesti' ['Maksim Gorky and Estonia'], *Looming*, 8 (1961), 12, 1227–245 (p. 1241).

29 J.K., '"LUBi" ankeedi tulemustest' ['Results of the LUB Survey'], *Kirjanduslikke Uudiseid*, 19 (1928), 3, 6–8 (p. 6).

These sought-after writers' works were afterwards published in various series by Loodus, as well as other literary publishers. The circle of published canonical writers was not limited to the favourite authors of the survey respondents, but also included Ivan Goncharov, Vladimir Korolenko, Anton Chekhov, Mikhail Lermontov, and Aleksandr Pushkin. A selection of Pushkin's poetry (published as *Valik luulet*, or *Selected Poems*, by the Estonian Literary Society in 1936) was compiled by the outstanding literary scholar Ants Oras (1900–82), who also translated most of the poems included. This collection was the only book of 'classic' Russian poetry published in the period 1918–40. The hundredth anniversary of Pushkin's death in 1937 was widely celebrated in Estonia both by Russian emigrants and Estonian cultural organisations, which arranged lectures, exhibitions, festive meetings, concerts, and other events.

Publications of Russian literature, however, culminated with the *Complete Works* (*Kogutud teosed*) of Dostoevsky in fifteen volumes, issued in 1939–40. Dostoevsky appealed to Estonian readers while enjoying popularity in the West. As literary scholar Lea Pild has stated, certain Russian classics were considered part of the Western European literary canon in the translation culture of the period. According to Iurii Lotman, introducing external cultural structures into the world of a given culture assumes the existence of a common language. For communication to occur, the receptive culture must 'interiorise' the image of the exterior culture within its own world. This process is inevitably dialectical and contradictory, with levels of meaning lost on both sides.[30] Pild argues that the modes of interiorisation of Russian classics gradually became established in Estonia and associated with the latter's 'native' heritage.[31]

This is in line with Maria Tymoczko's proposal to enlarge the concept of translation beyond its usage in ordinary speech (where it primarily means interlingual translation, the reproduction of a text in another language), to include the concept of transculturation.[32] The latter is broadly defined as the transmission of cultural characteristics from one cultural group to another, encompassing the spread of literary systems that are integrated with previous practices. The poetics of writing have always changed, everywhere, under the influence of texts written in another language. The world republic of letters (to use Pascale Casanova's formulation) enters into relation with national practices, since literature does not recognise the "political and linguistic boundaries

---

30 Iurii Lotman, *Culture, Memory and History: Essays in Cultural Semiotics*, ed. by Marek Tamm, trans. by Brian James Baer (Cham, Switzerland: Palgrave Macmillan, 2019), pp. 76–77.

31 Lea Pild, 'Tõlkimine kui interioriseerimine: Friedebert Tuglas Aleksei Tolstoi romaani "Peeter Esimene" tõlkijana' ['Translation as Interiorization: Friedebert Tuglas as Translator of the Novel *Peter the First* by Aleksei Tolstoy'], *Tõlkija Hääl*, 6 (2018), 136–48 (p. 136).

32 Maria Tymoczko, *Enlarging Translation, Empowering Translators* (Manchester and Kinderhook, NY: St. Jerome Publishing, 2007; repr. 2010, 2014), pp. 107–39.

of nations".[33] One author's technique ramifies and becomes a performative part of another's repertoire, 'transculturated' to the extent that it ceases to be perceived as alien. Verse metres, for example, whether learned from the original or a translation, become integrated within various literary cultures without having originated within them. Translation, understood as transculturation, is instrumental in shaping the receiving culture.

Tammsaare and Dostoevsky: Direct References

Transculturation is particularly relevant to the poetics of Fedor Dostoevsky in the work of Anton Hansen Tammsaare (1878–1940), who has always acknowledged the influence of Dostoevsky on his imaginary landscape. Born into a peasant family in central Estonia, Tammsaare attended local parish schools, then a private secondary school in Tartu, and later Tartu University, where he studied law. In 1911, he began to suffer serious health problems; he also started writing cultural criticism for Estonian periodicals while publishing his own fiction. From 1919, he was a professional writer. In 1928, interviewed on his fiftieth birthday, Tammsaare admitted that Dostoevsky, with his "excruciating" psychology, had convinced him that literature is capable of representing human realities beneath their overt manifestation.[34] In 1934, after completing his iconic pentalogy *Truth and Justice* (*Tõde ja õigus*, 1926–33), he expanded this statement in an interview with Elsa Heporauta, a Finnish writer and journalist. Here he attributed his decision to write a panoramic account based on the ideas that had both motivated and hampered the Estonian people during the late nineteenth and early twentieth centuries to his reading of *Crime and Punishment* (in Russian). He had been a student at the time (1898–1903) at the private Hugo Treffner School in Tartu (then known as Iurev). Reading the novel "depressed and shocked me," he told Heporauta. "I had never read a book like this before, and our own literature, in comparison with it, seemed suddenly trivial—it seemed so cold and careless about men and all living creatures."[35]

The seeds for Tammsaare's ambitious idea to encompass the mental landscapes of his people took another quarter of a century to mature before he began writing *Truth and Justice*. This fictional work had to be a pentalogy, Tammsaare had decided long before, "because we have to fight with four forces: land, God, society, and ourselves, and then comes surrender, resignation."[36]

33 Pascale Casanova, *The World Republic of Letters*, trans. by Malcolm DeBevoise (London and Cambridge, MA: Harvard University Press, 2004), p. xi.

34 Harald Tammer, 'A.H. Tammsaare juubeli eel' ['Before the Jubilee of A.H. Tammsaare'], *Päevaleht*, 26 January 1928, p. 6.

35 Elsa Heporauta, 'Huomattavinta elämässani?' ['Of Importance in my Life?'], *Suomen Kuvalehti*, 34 (1934), 1206–207.

36 Ibid., p. 1207.

The New York Estonian émigré magazine *Our Way* (*Meie Tee*) summed up Tammsaare's synopsis of the pentalogy thus:

> We begin like moles digging the earth and trusting in God. Gradually we unbind ourselves from land and God, construct a sophisticated society and, looking for personal happiness, build our houses even on sand or between winds and water so that they collapse next moment. People perish, cultures perish, and we begin again from land, trusting in God.[37]

The stimulus to translate Dostoevsky came to Tammsaare in November 1922 when the Estonian Writers' Union, acting with publisher Albert Org, announced a competition for the translation of world literature. Tammsaare signed a contract to translate *Crime and Punishment* by 1 July 1923. The translation was completed on time and Tammsaare won the competition, but the publisher went bankrupt. Only in 1929 was the manuscript issued by the Loodus publishing house, which had bought the rights. The only contemporary review of Tammsaare's translation in an Estonian daily, by novelist Albert Kivikas (1898–1978), stated that Russian literature had become remote from Estonian readers' experience. Kivikas listed three possible factors for this: boredom (since Russian had long been the main compulsory language in schools); political developments in Soviet Russia; and/or the then-fashionable cultural orientation towards Western literatures. The reviewer added, however, that Dostoevsky's novel, as "one of the most typical and deepest examples of Russian literature" is of greater importance for younger generations no longer exposed to Russification.[38]

Contemporary reviews are revealing sources for the context of translations. Kivikas' words demonstrate that Tammsaare was translating in a milieu not unanimously receptive of his work. But he had always been writing and translating against the tide, working not for the multitude but rather to advance artistic consciousness independently of capricious commercial fashions. Tammsaare's 1931 translation of Joseph Conrad's *Lord Jim* (1900) had also received guarded reviews, correctly predicting a limited readership. Yet Tammsaare, convinced that "a book can save many a moment from transience", used his introduction to *Lord Jim* to urge readers towards authors who re-create the moral and emotional atmosphere of a specific place and a time.[39] Tammsaare, a polymath who read English, French, German, and Russian, effectively inhabited Casanova's titular "world republic of letters". He wished "to patiently retie the threads that link these two universes [the world and literature], which otherwise are condemned

---

37 Andres Pranspill, 'Tammsaare "Tõde ja õigus"' ['Tammsaare's *Truth and Justice*'], *Meie Tee*, 12 (1934), 5–6 (p. 5).

38 Albert Kivikas, 'F.M. Dostojevski Kuritöö ja karistus' ['F.M. Dostoevsky's *Crime and Punishment*'], *Päevaleht*, 27 June 1929, p. 4.

39 A. H. Tammsaare, 'Midagi ilust ja "Anna Holmist"' ['On Beauty and "Anna Holm"'], *Vaba Sõna*, 1 (1914), 39–42 (p. 39).

to exist in parallel without ever meeting each other".[40] As the above-mentioned readers' survey by Loodus indicates, he was not alone in his quest; Estonian audiences wanted more translations of Ibsen, Tolstoy, and Turgenev.

Many authors have been compared to Tammsaare (Shakespeare, Goethe, Nietzsche, Oscar Wilde, Joseph Conrad, and Knut Hamsun, among others) but Dostoevsky remains his preeminent influence. In 2014, Mihkel Mutt, a contemporary Estonian cultural critic and novelist, published an article entitled 'Tammevsky and Dostosaare' examining the similarities between these two writers.[41] Both, he argues, wrote about a cross-section of their respective societies with emphasis on the middle classes; their narratives share common motifs, which Tammsaare had gained from reading Dostoevsky. For example, in Tammsaare's 1917 story 'Shades' ('Varjundid'), a character (significantly called Sonia, like *Crime and Punishment*'s Sonia Marmeladova) reads Dostoevsky's *The Insulted and the Injured*. As Sonia is dying of tuberculosis, she admits that she should not read a depressing text like this, "but—I want to [...] A few pages here or there—I have read it before—and I am already intoxicated".[42] There are also thematic parallels with Dostoevsky in Tammsaare's *Truth and Justice*: Tiina, a character who arrives in the second volume of the pentalogy, is crippled like Liza Khokhlakova in *The Brothers Karamazov* (*Brat'ia Karamazovy*, 1881). Thanks to an apparent miracle, she stands on her feet. There are further parallels between Tiina and *Crime and Punishment*'s Sonia, who share a deep and innocent faith in God, Christ, and angels. Yet another analogy: a major character in Tammsaare's pentalogy has a troubled daydream about the eyes of a beaten dog, just as the eyes of a beaten horse trouble Raskolnikov in his dream. Although these references to Dostoevsky are overt, all Tammsaare's sentences are undeniably his own. The recycling of Dostoevskian motifs does not impinge on Tammsaare's stylistic autonomy. Tammsaare must have perceived his own homage to Dostoevsky as excessive, since he removed from his initial manuscript of *Truth and Justice* a scene where Indrek Paas, the main hero of the second volume, reads *Crime and Punishment* with a reaction similar to Sonia's response to a different novel of Dostoevsky in 'Shades'. This deleted passage can be found in Tammsaare's draft manuscript, which is preserved at the Estonian Literary Museum in Tartu.

The *Weltanschauungs* of Dostoevsky and Tammsaare are still not easily compatible. "Even a great mind of worldwide significance like Dostoevsky becomes boring when he starts advocating his only remedy that can redeem us, and forgets to depict, to create", Tammsaare wrote in 1914.[43] His admiration for Dostoevsky was limited to the latter's poetic devices; he distanced himself from

40 Casanova, *World Republic*, p. 348.

41 Mihkel Mutt, 'Tamjevski ja Dostosaare'. https://www.looming.ee/artiklid/tamjevski-ja-dostosaare.

42 A. H. Tammsaare, *Kogutud teosed* [*Complete Works*], ed. by Eerik Teder, 15 vols (Tallinn: Eesti Raamat, 1978–93), III (1979), p. 72.

43 Tammsaare, *Kogutud* XV (1986), p. 300.

the Russian author's religious and nationalist views.[44] "History has shown that the human race is somehow or other progressing in every sphere", Tammsaare stated in 1906.[45] His own optimistic convictions did not prevent his characters from struggling with highly Dostoevskian questions about the presence of God, or their nation's destiny. However, being born into similar circumstances and equivalent milieus, Dostoevsky and Tammsaare both went on to experience analogous psychological phenomena and social turmoil, which each writer reflected through his characters. We will discuss this textual reflection of reality in the next section.

Dostoevsky and Tammsaare: Poetic Similarities

Since he translated *Crime and Punishment* in 1923 before beginning *Truth and Justice* in 1925, Tammsaare was well versed in Dostoevsky's literary devices, including that "completely new type of artistic thinking" which Bakhtin called polyphony.[46] This multi-voiced metaphor of composition is also apt for describing Tammsaare's poetics, although the latter could not possibly have encountered Bakhtin's ideas, nor did he later read the initial 1929 version of Bakhtin's essay on Dostoevsky.[47] Tammsaare distilled his own literary technique from reading and translating Dostoevsky.

When reading Dostoevsky and Tammsaare side by side, one is struck by the carnivalisation of dialogue in their novels. Complete strangers with vastly different social backgrounds engage in lengthy conversations to clarify their understandings of prevalent discourses, often conflicting with conventional hierarchies. These conversations relativise established mental and behavioural patterns by bringing together ideas from various spheres of life, relevant for each character at that moment in the plot. Dostoevsky's characters inhabit an eccentric and elevated atmosphere of scandal: "Dostoevsky takes much dramatic licence, employing chance encounters and messengers, eavesdropping, and accelerated action".[48] The wild party in the cellar flat of a caretaker in the second volume of Tammsaare's *Truth and Justice*, where people come together "by pure chance" is no different: there are seamstresses, shop-assistants, students from a nearby

44 Ilmar Vene, 'Tammsaare ja Dostojevski. Maailmapiltide kõrvutus' ['Tammsaare and Dostoevsky. Comparison of their Weltanscahuungs'], *Keel ja Kirjandus*, 5 (2007), 345–56.

45 Tammsaare, *Kogutud*, XV (1986), p. 91.

46 Mikhail Bakhtin, *Problems of Dostoevsky's Poetics*, ed. and trans. by Caryl Emerson (Minneapolis, MN and London: University of Minnesota Press, 1984; repr. 1999), p. 3.

47 For this information we are indebted to Maarja Vaino, a leading Tammsaare scholar, who is also the director of the A. H. Tammsaare Museum in Tallinn.

48 Victor Terras, *A History of Russian Literature* (New Haven, CT and London: Yale University Press, 1991), p. 349.

private school, and its headmaster, too. The narrator of the novel comments: "[A] human being is sometimes like a thunderstorm: it is coming and coming to flood us, and we all wonder from where it is coming, and then it turns aside for some reason and there is no rain anymore even if we need it, no rain at all. Why? No one knows".[49]

The characters in the private school (in *Truth and Justice*) where most of the action takes place include people who have moved to Estonia from elsewhere in tsarist Russia. They spend their time in an inebriated atmosphere outside the confines of ordinary life. The discussions between two teachers at the school (Voitinskii, a Pole, and Slopashev, a Russian) verge on bathos as they debate profound questions over vodka: "But when we all are eternal, me, you, Goethe, Schiller, Gogol, Pushkin, well, if the two of us, these two creatures of God, the dogs of God, are eternal like God himself, why should we then believe in God and his angels, and why couldn't God and his angels believe in us?"[50] The most carnivalesque character in the novel is Maurus, the private school's Estonian headmaster. He, like Porfirii Petrovich from *Crime and Punishment*, cannot stand still; he runs up and down the classroom, talking and gesticulating constantly. His thoughts jump hectically from one subject to another; he goes off on tangents when speaking to his students and staff: "A young man must be always polite, always deferential," he tells Indrek, the protagonist of the novel, at their first meeting:

> Therefore always—Herr Headmaster, Herr Maurus, Herr Lehrer. In Herr Maurus's house everyone is polite, Herr Maurus has a polite house. But wait, wait! Where can we put you to bed? Where can we find you a room? Yes, polite, deferential. Latin and politeness, these two govern the house of Herr Maurus. Latin! Romans loved space; they loved a lot of space. Herr Maurus is teaching Latin, but he has not so much space as a Roman had.[51]

This is as erratic as Porfirii Petrovich's discourse in *Crime and Punishment*. For example, having asked Raskolnikov to pardon him his pedestrian habits (Part 4, Chapter 5), Porfirii Petrovich adds: "I suffer from my sedentary life... I always intend to join a gymnasium; they say that officials of all ranks, even

49 A. H. Tammsaare, *Tõde ja õigus. II jagu* [*Truth and Justice. Part 2*] (Tartu: Noor-Eesti Kirjastus, 1929), p. 415. We will use this volume for our examples in order not to introduce too many unfamiliar storylines, and because its action takes place in a city and at a time when Estonia was still part of tsarist Russia, and thus closest to Dostoevsky's settings.

50 Tammsaare, *Tõde ja õigus*, p. 144.

51 Ibid., p. 28.

Privy Councillors, may be seen skipping gaily there; there you have it, modern science... yes, yes ..."[52]

Maurus, who established his private school to offer Estonian boys secondary education (in Russian, the only possible language of instruction under Russification), is well aware that he is "living in a foreign country, living in Germany that is situated in Russia [...] speaking a foreign language because [he does not] have a language that [he] can use".[53] The German teacher's description in the novel of life under Russification for Estonians living in the late nineteenth and early twentieth centuries aptly expresses the atmosphere that Tammsaare is trying to capture. As mentioned above, Maurus is depicted mostly through his conversation, always addressed to others, reacting randomly to momentary ideas. "Herr Maurus does not want to become famous for having killed God", he says in the novel after Indrek publishes a blasphemous pamphlet, renouncing God. Maurus expels Indrek from his school:

> [... B]ecause he knows that he cannot resist God. Herr Maurus is old, he knows. But [Indrek] Paas is tall and dumb like a rock, he does not know. He trusts his height like the Philistine giant who was slaughtered by little David. Herr Maurus knows: God will tell the inspector, the inspector the director, the director the curator, the curator the minister, and the minister the tsar that He will be killed. And then the tsar tells the minister, the minister the police and the gendarmes that gods are being slaughtered at Herr Maurus's. Tell me now, can old Maurus fight the tsar and his police and gendarmes! Can he fight the lightning and angels of God once they come? Therefore, the tall Paas with his fame must go. Go and live where there is neither tsar nor faith. Go to France with its president and revolution. Go there. But Herr Maurus will stay in Russia, under the generous wings of the Russian eagle, because an Estonian loves his tsar and his eagle.[54]

Tammsaare's characters are not spokespersons for their author; in keeping with Bakhtinian polyphony, they possess their own words and voices, often dissonant from their author's. The consciousness of his characters is presented as remote from Tammsaare's; they encounter each other at events where they interact but remain emotionally and intellectually separate.

Maurus's student Indrek Paas undergoes several important influences: discussing Darwin, Nietzsche, and Marxism with his fellow students, a life-changing lesson on cosmography, and, most decisively, the death of the girl he loves. He subsequently shares his belief in the death of God in the school

52 Fedor Dostoevsky, *Crime and Punishment*, trans. by Constance Garnett. https://www.gutenberg.org/files/2554/2554-h/2554-h.htm#link2HCH0025.

53 Tammsaare, *Tõde ja õigus*, p. 206.

54 Ibid., p. 566–67.

newspaper *Truth*. He is then expelled from school by Maurus. Indrek sits on his suitcase in the street until Mrs Vaarmann, the caretaker, invites him into her cellar flat. Indrek explains to her the reasons for his expulsion, which her daughter, the crippled Tiina, overhears. Tiina, waiting for God's angels to heal her, breaks down in despair, and Indrek, realising the effect of his words on the girl, retracts them. He tells Tiina that she will get well, because God is living and will send his angels to cure her. At this point Tiina stands up and takes her first steps. The apparent miracle juxtaposes Indrek's newly adopted credo with the need to show compassion to the little girl. Thus, abstract dialectics fade from Indrek's consciousness because of his interaction with another mind, albeit one he barely understands:

> Indrek had renounced everything but now he was kneeling on the floor as if he were bowing down before the one whom he had recently renounced. But there was one thing he felt good about: he had conquered himself because of the crying little child. He forgot his own sorrow and pain; he gave up the truth born out of the blood of his heart to console the miserable and unhappy girl. What else could he have done? Even God could not do much more if he were there.[55]

Maurus's school accepts students and instructors regardless of age or nationality because not many Estonians can pay the fees. The school includes Russians, Germans, Poles, and Jews alongside Estonians; therefore, the multiple voices crowding Tammsaare's dialogues may appear chaotic. Only in the light of his artistic endeavour can one "begin to understand the profound organic cohesion, consistency, and wholeness" of his poetics—as might be said of Dostoevsky.[56] Tammsaare was not aiming to create generic character archetypes, but rather reactive personalities sensitive to both mental and social events. The extradiegetic narrator of *Truth and Justice* does not describe the characters from his own monologic point of view; instead, his imagination fosters dialogic interaction between numerous consciousnesses. This quotation from Bakhtin about Dostoevsky's poetics is equally applicable to Tammsaare: "The consciousnesses of other people cannot be perceived, analysed, defined as objects or things—one can only *relate to them dialogically*. To think about them means to *talk with them; otherwise they immediately turn to us their objectivized side*: they fall silent, close up, and congeal into finished, objectivized images" [original italics].[57] Tammsaare neither affirms nor denies the contradictory opinions of his characters; he simply integrates them into his narrative.[58]

The third aspect of poetics shared by Tammsaare and Dostoevsky (besides carnivalisation and polyphony) is their use of lexical repetition. 'Suddenly'

55 Ibid., p. 579.

56 Bakhtin, *Dostoevsky's Poetics*, p. 8.

57 Ibid., p. 68.

58 Arne Merilai, 'Tammsaare aga-ometi' ['Tammsaare's 'but-yet''], *Keel ja Kirjandus*, 5 (2015), 297–315 (p. 304).

(*vdrug*) is the most commonly reiterated word in *Crime and Punishment*; it is meticulously reproduced in Tammsaare's translation. The Estonian equivalent 'äkki' is also frequent in *Truth and Justice*, and its function is analogous: 'äkki' marks the seemingly unreasonable impulses of characters who suddenly realise they should do something or suddenly feel something without saying a word; 'äkki' is the adverb of intuitive understanding that establishes the psychological rhythm of the ideas that possess the characters.

A companion word to 'äkki' in Tammsaare's novels is 'aga' ('but'). It recurs to such an extent that the critic Arne Merilai has called Tammsaare's idiolect "an epic *but*-mantra" that hypotactically structures not only Tammsaare's syntax but also his philosophy. His characters repeatedly undergo abrupt or paradoxical insights or experiences that alter their previous decisions. Indrek, attending the funeral of an Estonian national hero with his headmaster Maurus, listening to the strange intonation of the pastor, and observing his always voluble headmaster silently kneeling, suddenly feels a tenderness he cannot explain.[59] Another example: on the journey home to his father's farm for the summer vacation, Indrek meets a neighbour his father has never tolerated, and to whom he has never talked. Surprising himself, he suddenly greets the man and has a conversation with him.[60] Intuitive reactions to events are of equal importance in plot development for both Dostoevsky and Tammsaare, and are often introduced by the adverb 'suddenly'.

Tammsaare's Translation of *Crime and Punishment*

Tammsaare's translation of *Crime and Punishment*, first published in 1929, was reissued in 1939, 1958, 1987, 2007, and 2020. The translation has stood the test of time; no retranslation has yet been commissioned. Sensitive to the internal rhythm of Dostoevsky's text, Tammsaare's translation preserves the original arrangement of sentences and their rhythmic punctuation. In Tammsaare's version, form is as important as content because structural equivalence (linguistic differences excluded) was the established norm of translation in Estonia during the 1920s and 1930s. "In its essence, a piece of art is an organism that cannot be divided," Gustav Saar, an Estonian cultural critic, wrote.[61] He continued:

> Form in art is not the surface [...] but the sensual cover of animated ideas, the visible part of mental activities, and its rules depend on its dynamic relationship with the subject matter [...]. Destroying the outward form cannot keep intact the inward one, the feel of life of the work, because the content floods in only with the lava of the form.[62]

59 Tammsaare, *Tõde ja õigus*, p. 244.
60 Ibid., p. 277.
61 Gustav Saar, 'Kunstipärasest tõlkest' ['On Artistic Translation'], *Looming*, 8 (1927), 751–57 (p. 754).
62 Ibid., pp. 754–55.

Estonian translation practice during this period thus recoded the formal plane of the source text as closely as possible, and since Estonian word order is flexible, the syntax of other languages can be reproduced, resulting in texts with a barely perceptible foreign intonation. Translators and editors at this time did not strive for idiomatic and fluent Estonian, unlike now.

Comparing two Estonian translations of Dostoevsky's *The Brothers Karamazov* (Aita Kurfeldt's 1939–40 version and Virve Krimm's 2015–16 text), we reach a similar conclusion: Kurfeldt "follows [word-for-word] a Dostoevsky phrase or his long syntactic construction, even preserving his word order."[63] This literalism, the same critic continues, is not a symptom of the translator's 'dilettantism' but can be viewed as her attempt to reproduce the "broken accent of the narrator of *The Brothers Karamazov*."[64] The same can be said of Tammsaare's translation of *Crime and Punishment*—its clumsy phrases do not violate the rules of Estonian grammar *per se*. Instead, they draw attention to the incompleteness and uncertainty of Dostoevsky's fictional world. As the translation preserves the conceptual poetics of Dostoevsky, there has been no need for retranslation.

Although Tammsaare's text has never been replaced, it has been edited. The 1939 edition was not sent to him for revisions, even though Tammsaare was still alive. Instead, it was edited by a proof-reader from Loodus who changed the spellings of Russian names, in line with modified transliteration norms. The 1958 edition, which included redactions and notes based on the 1957 Soviet version of the original with critical apparatus, replaced certain lexical items then perceived as archaisms. Vello Tarnaste (1929–99), the editor of this edition, had himself translated numerous books from Russian. The 1958 edition of Tammsaare's translation included a translation of a new afterword by the contemporary Soviet critic Boris Riurikov. The lengthy paratext acknowledges the realistic depiction of the life of humiliated classes in ruthless capitalist society but sees Dostoevsky's inability to believe in the revolutionary socialist ideas of his time as "the greatest tragedy of his life".[65] The readers of *Crime and Punishment* are encouraged to distance themselves from the reactionary religious teaching of the novel that is "alien to us, [...] the fighters, workers, builders [...] who incessantly battle with the forces of the old world and build a bright future".[66]

The 1987 edition updated Tammsaare's lexis once again and expanded the critical apparatus, now based on translations of notes from the 1970 Soviet

63 Lea Pild, 'Jutustajateksti muutlikkus Fjodor Dostojevski romaani "Vennad Karamazovid" eestikeelsetes tõlgetes' ['Variations in the narration in the Estonian translations of Fedor Dostoevsky's *The Brothers Karamazov*'], *Methis. Studia humaniora Estonica*, 25 (2020), 68–94 (p. 70).

64 Ibid.

65 B. Rjurikov, 'F. M. Dostojevskist ja tema romaanist "Kuritöö ja karistus"' ['On F.M. Dostoevsky and his novel *Crime and Punishment*'], in Fjodor Dostojevski, *Kuritöö ja karistus* (Tallinn: Eesti Riiklik Kirjastus, 1958), pp. 560–82 (p. 563).

66 Ibid., p. 582.

edition of Dostoevsky's novel. This time the afterword, entitled 'Love and Mercy', was penned by Peeter Torop, an Estonian Slavist scholar and Dostoevsky specialist, then lecturing on Dostoevsky at Tartu University. The 2007 reprint appeared in a series for classical novels from world literature; it reproduced the 1958 redaction while omitting the redactions made in 1987, the notes, and Riurikov's afterword. The latest edition, in 2020, updated the vocabulary and spelling again but refrained from tampering with the general style of the text out of respect for Tammsaare's poetics of translation, as the editor says in his preface.[67] As we can see, every new edition of Tammsaare's version of *Crime and Punishment* has conformed to evolving contemporary usage of Estonian as well as to Russian transliteration practices; editing was motivated by the wish to add available paratexts so that *Crime and Punishment* could be used in schools (where it is a compulsory part of the literature curriculum).

Mihkel Samarüütel, a contemporary Estonian author, has carefully compared Tammsaare's original translation with the edited 1987 version in his blog *Lottery* (*Loterii*). Acknowledging that languages do change within decades, he concludes that "a publishing house could think of reissuing the old *Crime and Punishment*, the examples given here leave an impression that the initial version [of the translation] is more alive [...]. The [1987] redaction has impoverished the language or perhaps centralized it? [...] The first translation is more poetic, more sensitive; the later version more pedagogical and straightforward, seeking clearer formulations".[68]

Aare Pilv, a researcher, author, and translator who redacted the latest edition of Tammsaare's translation and collected information on previous editions for his *Acta nubis* blog entry on *Crime and Punishment*, highlighted some lexical changes in the 2020 text in personal correspondence with us, relevant to Raskolnikov's inner dialogue. In the penultimate paragraph of Chapter 7 (Part 6), Dostoevsky—and Tammsaare, following him—presented this as free indirect speech (in both the first and third person).[69] Fearful of confusing readers, in later editions these passages are in the first person. The mingled narrative technique must have also perplexed Constance Garnett, whose translation is purely in third-person free indirect speech (deictics in bold):

> He fell to musing by what process it could come to pass, that **he** could be humbled before all of them, indiscriminately—humbled by conviction. And yet why not? It must be so. Would not twenty years of continual

67 Aare Pilv, 'Redigeerija kommentaar' ['Editor's Comment'], in Fjodor Dostojevski, *Kuritöö ja karistus* (Tallinn: Helios, 2020), pp. 5–6 (p. 6).

68 See Mihkel Samarüütel's blog post, 'Feodor/Fjodor Dostojevski—Kuritöö ja karistus I (1929/1987)', 29 August, 2009. https://loterii.blogspot.com/2009/08/feodor-fjodor-dostojevski-kuritoo-ja.html.

69 For the original, see F. M. Dostoevsky, *Prestuplenie i nakazanie*, in *Sobranie sochinenii v piednadtsati tomakh* (Leningrad: Nauka, 1988–96), V (1989), p. 493.

> bondage crush **him** utterly? Water wears out a stone. And why, why should **he** live after that? Why should **he** go now when **he** knew that it would be so?[70]

Richard Pevear and Larissa Volokhonsky use both persons:

> He fell to pondering deeply by what process it might come about that **he** would finally humble himself before them all without reasoning, humble himself from conviction? But, after all, why not? Of course, that is how it should be. Won't twenty years of unremitting oppression finish **him** off completely? Water wears away stone. But why, why live in that case? Why am **I** going now, if **I** know myself that it will all be precisely so, as if by book, and not otherwise![71]

In Tammsaare's initial translation, the passage relies on both first- and third-person pronouns:

> Deeply thought **he** about the question:—How could the process look like that **he** would be tamed in front of them all without any discussion, tamed in **his** convictions! But so what, why not? Of course, it must be like that. Wouldn't twenty years of incessant suppression smash **you** finally? Water wears out even a stone. But why, why to live then, why am **I** going now when **I** know that it all will be exactly like this, as by the book and not otherwise!
>
> [Sügavasti mõtles **ta** [he] küsimuse üle järele:—Missuguse arenemise kaudu võiks nõnda sündida, et **ta [he]** lõpuks kõigi nende ees ilma igasuguse arutamiseta taltsub, oma veendumustes taltsub! Aga mis siis, miks mitte? Muidugi, nõnda see peabki olema. Kas kahekümneaastane vahetpidamatu rõhumine ei rusu **sind** [you] lõplikult? Vesi sööb kivissegi augu. Aga milleks, milleks siis elada, milleks **ma** [I] siis praegu lähen, kui ise tean, et see kõik tuleb nimelt nõnda, nagu kirja järele, mitte teisiti!][72]

Of interest here is the fact that Tammsaare also used a second-person deictic pronoun ("Wouldn't twenty years of incessant suppression smash **you** finally?") that is absent in the original Russian text, and Pilv has kept this pronoun:

70 Fedor Dostoevsky, *Crime and Punishment*, trans. by Constance Garnett (London: Heinemann, 1914). https://www.gutenberg.org/files/2554/2554-h/2554-h.htm#link2HCH0038.

71 Fedor Dostoevsky, *Crime and Punishment*, trans. by Richard Pevear and Larissa Volokhonsky (London: David Campbell Publishers, 2002), p. 520.

72 F.M. Dostojevski, *Kuritöö ja karistus*, trans. by A.H. Tammsaare (Tartu: Loodus, 1929), p. 647.

> **He** [ta] deeply thought about it: 'What could be the process with the help of which **I** [ma] will be finally tamed in front of all of them without any discussion, convincingly! But why not? Of course, it must be like that. Wouldn't twenty years of incessant suppression smash **you** [sind] finally? Water wears out even a stone. But why, why to live then after that, why am **I** [ma] going now when **I** know myself that it all will be exactly like this, as by a book and not otherwise'.
>
> [**Ta** [he] jäi sügavalt mõtlema selle üle: „Milline on see protsess, mille kaudu **ma** [I] lõpuks kõigi nende ees juba ilma igasuguse arutamiseta taltsaks saan, veendunult! Aga miks siis mitte? Muidugi, nõnda see peabki olema. Kas kahekümneaastane vahetpidamatu rõhumine ei rusu **sind** [you] lõplikult? Vesi uuristab kivissegi augu. Ent milleks, milleks siis elada pärast seda, milleks **ma** [I] siis praegu lähen, kui ise tean, et see kõik tuleb nimelt nõnda, nagu kirja järgi, mitte teisiti!"]

The comparison shows that translators and editors tend to modify the narrative technique of the original if they find it uncustomary themselves or believe their readers may be unfamiliar with it. This is one of the "trials of the foreign" that all translations have to face.[73]

Pilv mentions one other significant amendment to the latest edition of the translation. He points to Dostoevsky's subtle hint regarding the association of Raskolnikov's name with the *raskolniki,* schismatics dissenting from the Russian Orthodox Church. In Chapter 2 of Part 6 of *Crime and Punishment,* Porfirii Petrovich says of Mikolka, the man who confesses to the murder he did not commit, "A izvestno li vam, chto on iz Raskolnikov [...]" ; in Garnett's translation "And do you know he is an Old Believer [...]?"; in Pevear and Volokhonsky's, "And do you know he's a schismatic?".[74] In Tammsaare's original translation, 'raskolnik' ('*раскольник*') became 'vanausuline' ('Old Believer'); while in the 2020 redacted version, Pilv simply transliterates the word 'raskolnik', thus using the Russian loan word already present in the Estonian lexicon. Pilv explains: the word has its role in the texture of the novel. Porfirii Petrovich, already knowing the real culprit, still plays his cat-and-mouse game and continues "but not because he is a raskolnik"[75] (in Tammsaare's translation "but not the true one"). Since etymologically, 'raskolnik' means 'one with a split head' or even 'a splitter of heads', the use of this word in the context of the fictional Raskolnikov's axe-murder is undeniably meaningful—as Dostoevsky's character names often are.[76]

---

73 Antoine Berman, *L´épreuve de l'étranger: Culture et traduction dans l'Allemange romantique* (Paris: Gallimard, 1984).

74 F.M. Dostoevsky, *Prestuplenie i nakazanie*, p. 429. See also Dostoevsky, *Crime and Punishment* [online], trans. by Constance Garnett; and Dostoevsky, *Crime and Punishment*, trans. by Richard Pevear and Larissa Volokhonsky, p. 454.

75 F.M. Dostoevsky, *Prestuplenie i nakazanie*, p. 429

76 See Aare Pilv's blog 'Acta nubis', especially the post 'Fjodor Dostojevski "Kuritöö ja karistus"', 12th Dec. 2012. http://aarepilv.blogspot.com/2020/12/

This is the essence of Hermans' idea of literary interactions within a "historical continuum", as we cited at the start of this essay.

Conclusion

Although the quantity of individual books translated from Russian was relatively modest, translations of Russian literature were represented consistently in Estonian book production between 1918 and 1940. Besides numerous plays (predominantly comedies) printed in the 1920s, the selection of translations also included prose by contemporary Russian writers, both émigré and Soviet. Works by Soviet authors introduced new topics and literary styles to Estonian readers. The official attitude towards Soviet Russia might have been cautious, but Soviet cultural developments intrigued those adult Estonians who had been educated in tsarist Russian times. During the later 1930s, readers turned to nineteenth-century Russian literary classics. It was considered important to introduce the best examples of world literature to the young generation of Estonians who, having studied no Russian at school, relied on translations. At the same time, major works of Socialist Realism were published by leftist organisations primarily for distribution among the working class. Thus, the output of translations from Russian was quite diverse, combining entertaining and educational books. Publications of intellectual interest and political propaganda were targeted at different strata of readership, whether issued by established commercial publishers or other organisations.

According to studies of the reading public, the most renowned and widely known Russian classics—Tolstoy and Dostoevsky—also appealed to wider audiences. While the impact of Russian classics on the general public in pre-Second World War Estonia cannot be accurately established, the impact of Dostoevsky on the poetics of Anton Hansen Tammsaare, the classic Estonian novelist, is discernible in the latter's public statements and literary work. Tammsaare's use of carnivalesque and polyphonic dialogue, his adoption of 'suddenly' as an adverb of intuitive recognition, and the many motifs in his fiction which pay homage to scenes in Dostoevsky's novels are all clear tokens that Tammsaare and Dostoevsky belong together in the "world republic of letters".

fjodor-dostojevski-kuritoo-ja-karistus.html?m=0.

Finland

The Pendulum of Translating Russian Literature in Finland

Tomi Huttunen, Marja Jänis, and Pekka Pesonen

Introduction

The title of this article indicates how steeply the quantity of translations of Russian literature published in Finland has varied over time. Proximity to Russia has shaped Finnish history, including the arts, literature, and cultural activities; it is a factor that cannot be neglected in understanding Finland's past, present, and its future. The publication of translations of Russian literature has been most intensive when Finnish-Russian relationships are tranquil, and has declined markedly at times of conflict. Since the Russians are neighbours of the Finns, Russian literature has answered Finnish questions such as: what is Russia? What are the Russians like, and how can we understand Russian history? Few educated Finns have mastered the Russian language, so those individuals who did have played an important role as mediators and translators. This role has proven to be particularly crucial when Finnish-Russian relations have cooled or become hostile.

Pascale Casanova's *The World Republic of Letters* (2004) deals with the inequalities of the international literary space, always dominated by literatures with a long history from widely known languages, and with the difficulties faced by literatures in a language with a very limited readership.[1] Finnish obviously belongs to the latter category, and thus literary translation has played a substantial role in the development of Finnish literature. Although Casanova discusses the role and work of translators, her scope is limited, and is primarily

1 Pascale Casanova, *The World Republic of Letters,* trans. by M.B. Debevoise (Cambridge, MA: Harvard University Press, 2004).

 https://doi.org/10.11647/OBP.0340.04

concerned with the translation of literary works from the cultural periphery into the languages of the centre.[2] This article considers translation in the opposite direction, that is, into peripheral languages.

Finnish Language, Finnish Literature, and Translation in the Grand Duchy

For more than a century (1809–1917), Finland was an autonomous Grand Duchy within the Russian Empire. Previously, it had been the Eastern province of Sweden; Swedish was the language of education, administration, and culture. As a Grand Duchy, during the nineteenth century, Finnish language and cultural identity were reinforced, partly due to the separation from Sweden and partly because Russia initiated a new distance from Swedish language and influence. Another significant factor was the popularity of European nationalist ideas among educated Finns.[3] The Finnish language advocates were called *Fennomans*; they were devoted to making Finnish language, spoken by the majority of the people, into a fully-fledged medium of administration, education, and culture. Ironically, most of the Fennomans spoke Swedish as their mother tongue.

Two Swedish-speaking Finns, Eric Gustaf Ehrström (1791–1835) and Carl Gustaf Ottelin (1792–1864), were Fennoman intellectuals who emphasised the importance of the Finnish language in Finland. They were the very first Finnish university students to receive a scholarship to study Russian in Moscow, which they did in 1812.[4] During their stay in Russia, which coincided with the dramatic historical events of Napoleon's invasion and the burning of Moscow, they studied and actively practiced Russian. They even made the first-ever translations of Nikolai Karamzin's poetry into Swedish without using any bridge language.[5]

2 Casanova, *The World Republic of Letters*, pp. 142–46.

3 Pascale Casanova mentions the 'Herder effect' in connection with nineteenth-century demands to create or revive a national language in many smaller European countries. She mentions Finnish as an example of a language that existed almost entirely in oral form. Her ideas about the role of writers and intellectuals in constructing a national identity in adherence to emergent national norms can be applied to Finland; see Casanova, pp. 28–29.

4 Kari Ketola, *Ryssän koulussa. Suomalaiset Venäjän stipendiaatit autonomian aikana 1812–1917* [*In the Russian School: Finnish Scholarship Students in Russia during the Autonomy 1812–1917*] (Helsinki: Finemor, 2007), pp. 23–25. The system of the Moscow scholarships had an enormous impact on Russian language studies in Finland during the nineteenth century.

5 See Nils-Åke Nilsson's introduction in *Från Karamzin till Trifonov. En bibliografi över rysk skönlitteratur i svensk översättning av Märta Bergstrand* [*From Karamzin to Trifonov: A Bibliography of Russian Literature in Swedish Translation by Märta Bergstrand*] (Stockholm: Almqvist & Wiksell, 1985), pp. 11–17. There were several Swedish translations of Karamzin prior to Ehrström's and Ottelin's, all effected via French or German versions.

Returning to Finland, they published the first grammar of Russian language in Swedish, and Ehrström also taught Russian at the Royal Academy of Turku (now the University of Helsinki). Among his students was the exceptionally talented young Elias Lönnrot (1802–84), who would later compile the Finnish national epic, the *Kalevala*. As a student of Ehrström's, Lönnrot translated one of Karamzin's poems into Swedish in 1824. Karamzin was thus well positioned to become the very first Russian writer translated into Finnish; one of his short stories, rendered by an unidentified translator, appeared in 1830.[6]

The conflict between proponents of Finnish and of Swedish as Finland's official language was heated, but the Fennomans slowly strengthened their position. Swedish became, and remains today, the second official language. The Finnish Literature Society was established in 1831 by a group of young scholars and writers, among them Elias Lönnrot and the Finnish-Swedish poet J.L. Runeberg (1804–77). Its bold programme aimed to promote Finnish literature by: (a) collecting existing Finnish-language literature, (b) collecting and publishing Finnish folklore, and (c) promoting the production of Finnish literature and of translations into Finnish (both fiction and non-fiction).[7] The society recommended that foreign literary works chosen for translation into Finnish should include both classics and contemporary literature.

Besides the Swedish-speaking Fennomans' initiatives, others sought to familiarise Finnish speakers with Russian literature through translation. Many translators of Russian literature came from families that had lived in St Petersburg after Finland became a Grand Duchy in 1809. Among the first literary intellectuals in Finnish St Petersburg was Thomas Friman (1821–86), who spent his life in the capital of the Russian Empire. Friman was a notable individual in the city's Finnish literary life, a teacher in the Finnish school and Theological Academy, and a newspaper editor. As early as the 1840s, he made several translations for Finnish newspapers, rendering texts by Iakov Grot, Nestor Kukol'nik, or Vladimir Odoevskii, for example. Grot, who was the first full Professor of Russian language and literature at the Imperial Alexander University (of Helsinki), became personally familiar with some leading Finnish writers (e.g. Runeberg and Lönnrot) and served as a key mediator between the literatures.

In St Petersburg, the descendants of Finnish artisans, servants, and traders also learned Russian while attending the city's Finnish school, and some became translators of Russian literature. One was Samuli Suomalainen (1850–1907), son

6 The short story 'Peasant Flor Silin' was published on 26 June 1830 in the newspaper *Turun Wiikko-Sanomat*.

7 Irma Sulkunen, 'Finnish Literary Society as a Promoter of Literary Translation in the 19th century' ['Suomalaisen Kirjallisuuden Seura ulkomaisen kirjallisuuden käännättäjänä 1800-luvulla'], in *Suomennoskirjallisuuden historia* [*History of Translation in Finland*], ed. by H.K. Riikonen and others, 2 vols (Helsinki: SKS, 2007), I (2007), pp. 127–29 (p. 127).

of a Finnish goldsmith, who studied under the above-mentioned Thomas Friman. Thanks to his background, Suomalainen was considered a suitable mediator for the "strange world" of Russian literature.[8] His first published translation from Russian to Finnish was Pushkin's *The Captain's Daughter* (*Kapitanskaia dochka*, 1836; *Kapteenin tytär*, 1876). However, even earlier in 1876, the short story 'The Inn' ('Postoialyi dvor', 1852) by Ivan Turgenev had appeared as an independent volume. The following decade proved to be a golden age for literary translation into Finnish. Many works by Gogol, Turgenev, Pushkin, Dostoevsky, Tolstoy, and Ivan Goncharov were translated for the first time during the last decades of the nineteenth century. Suomalainen's translation of Nikolai Gogol's *Dead Souls* (*Mertvye dushi*, 1842) as *Kuolleet sielut* (1882) is a classic among Finnish translations of Russian literature; it has been republished several times, with the latest edition appearing in 2008.

Translations of Gogol's works by Samuli Suomalainen were read aloud in a literary salon (named the Elisabet Circle, after its central figure) in the town of Kuopio in Eastern Finland. The history of this salon makes for an interesting case study in the popularity of Russian literature in Finland. It was led by Elisabet Järnefelt (1839–1929), daughter of the celebrated sculptor Peter Clodt von Jürgensberg, who retired to his Finnish estate after enjoying a distinguished career in St Petersburg. Elisabet married Alexander Järnefelt, a Finnish army officer educated in Russia, later a high administrative officer in the Grand Duchy and a provincial governor.[9] In her salon, she inspired contemporary young Finnish writers to discover and admire Russian literature, particularly Tolstoy, by reading aloud existing translations; she even shared works not yet available in Finnish by translating them aloud on the spot. Elisabet Järnefelt greatly admired Russian Realism; she introduced her young followers, among them the novelist, playwright, and early supporter of women's rights Minna Canth, to Vissarion Belinskii's concept of types as the basis of Realist literature. Elisabet Järnefelt's literary salon, however, rejected the emergent school of Modernism.

Finland established a network of public libraries in the 1880s; translations of Russian literature amounted to 13% of all acquisitions of foreign literature.[10] Dostoevsky's *The House of the Dead* (*Zapiski iz mertvogo doma*, 1862), Gogol's *Dead Souls*, and Turgenev's *A Nest of the Gentry* (*Dvorianskoe gnezdo*, 1859) and *First*

---

8 This is a quotation from an article in *Aamulehti* on 21 December 1886. Cited by Outi Paloposki and Sari Kivistö, 'Samuli Suomalainen', *Suomennoskirjallisuuden historia*, I, pp. 207–11 (p. 208).

9 The children of Alexander and Elisabet Järnefelt also became prominent figures in the history of Finnish culture: Armas Järnefelt was a composer, Eero Järnefelt a painter, and Arvid Järnefelt a writer, the most prominent follower of Lev Tolstoy's ideas in Finland. Their daughter Aino married the composer Jean Sibelius.

10 In the 1860s, Finnish state authorities recommended that municipal and rural schools open libraries, not only for use by pupils. This was the origin of Finland's public library system; by the 1880s, libraries were subsidised by municipalities and the state.

Love (*Pervaia iubov'*, 1861), with two collections of short stories by Lev Tolstoy, were among these acquisitions.[11] *Arvosteleva kirjaluettelo* (*The Critical Catalogue of Books*),[12] the main source for determining Finnish libraries' acquisition policy, distinguished between works appropriate for less educated readers using rural libraries, and those that required "a more sophisticated readership". Recommendations for acquiring translations of Russian literature followed these guidelines. For instance, Lev Tolstoy's *Childhood, Boyhood and Youth* trilogy (*Detstvo, otrochestvo, iunost'*, 1852–56) and *War and Peace* (*Voina i mir*, 1869; translated as *Sota ja rauha* by Iivari Wallenius in 1905) were recommended "primarily for public libraries of more developed regions".[13]

'Icy Times' and 'Oppression'

While Finnish was now firmly established as Finland's principal language, the attempt to make Russian an official national language had failed. Finland had become a well-organised society with thousands of schools where the language of the empire was not taught.[14] Political turmoil in Europe and unrest in Russia's peripheral regions hardened Russian attitudes towards Finland's autonomy within the Empire. In 1899, Nikolai Bobrikov, the newly appointed Finnish Governor-General, declared in his February Manifesto that imperial state legislation should be enacted in Finland. Finnish people saw this decision as an end to their autonomy. It was followed by a language manifesto in 1900: Russian should become the official language of administration. The February Manifesto led to widespread demonstrations in Finland, although Tsar Nikolai II forbade protests. The period from 1899 to 1905 is known as 'Icy Times' ('*routa-aika*') and even the 'Oppression' ('*sortokausi*') in Finnish historiography.[15] The newly 'icy' attitude to Russia, including its literature and language, now made compulsory in secondary schools, affected translation policy. However, the works of Russian writers considered anti-tsarist, such as Lev Tolstoy and Maksim Gorky, were

11 Eija Eskola collected data of acquisitions of translated literature in six municipal libraries in 1880–1890. Eija Eskola, *Rukousnauha ja muita romaaneja. Suomennetun kaunokirjallisuuden valinta yleisissä kirjastoissa 1880–1939* [*The Rosary and Other Novels: Selection of Literature, Translated into Finnish, for Public Libraries in 1880–1939*] (Jyväskylä: Jyväskylän yliopisto, 1991), p. 12.

12 *The Critical Catalogue* was established in 1902 to assist in acquiring books for public libraries. The critical comments were given in short articles, written by librarians, teachers, literary critics, and others. The catalogue had no board of editors or editor-in-chief, only a secretary responsible for its compilation. It served librarians, especially those not professionally trained, and was not well known among literary circles or readers.

13 Eskola, *Rukousnauha*, p. 44.

14 David Kirby, *A Concise History of Finland* (Cambridge: Cambridge University Press, 2006), p. 123.

15 Kirby, *Concise History*, p. 130.

translated and published widely. Tolstoy's didactic and social writings were translated into Finnish earlier than his great novels, and he had devoted followers in Finland—the most active of them was Arvid Järnefelt, the son of Alexander and Elisabet Järnefelt. Gorky supported the Finnish people's fight against tsarist oppression and received a triumphant welcome when he visited Finland to see the performance of his play *The Lower Depths* (*Na dne*, 1902; translated as *Pohjalla* by Iisakki Lattu) at the Finnish National Theatre in Helsinki in 1903.

During the 1910s, the view of Russia as an oppressor continued to weaken interest in Russian literature. Among the few exceptions were Eino Kalima (1906–72), a former student of Konstantin Stanislavskii at the Moscow Arts Theatre, who later ran the Finnish National Theatre. Kalima is known for his translations of Tolstoy and Chekhov (and for his productions of the latter's plays). He stated bitterly in his memoirs that there was hardly any other civilised European country, where "splendid Russian literature" was as ignored and under-valued as in Finland.[16] His first Finnish translation of Tolstoy's *Anna Karenina* (1878), published in 1910–11, was met with contempt by V.A. Koskenniemi (1885–1962), an influential poet and cultural figure, who wrote: "Tolstoy's characters lack the higher intellectual life. [...] They do not possess the balance between activity and passivity, reason and heart, which is significant to Western cultural ideals".[17]

In the 1910s, no novels or plays by Russian authors were listed as favourites by readers using public libraries.[18] Yet it was only a few hours by train from St Petersburg to the Karelian isthmus and Eastern Finland. Many holiday resorts and summerhouses (*dachas*) were visited by Russian writers and artists in the early 1900s. Kornei Chukovskii's dacha 'Chukokkala' in Terijoki was a gathering place for artistic and literary circles from St Petersburg in 1912–17.[19] However, Finnish writers were apparently not invited to these gatherings, although some young enthusiastic Swedish-speaking Finnish writers did obtain and share information about Russian Modernism.[20]

16 Eino Kalima, *Sattumaa ja johdatusta* [*Accidents and Guidance*] (Helsinki: WSOY, 1962), pp. 270–71.

17 V.A. Koskenniemi, '*Anna Karenina*. Oriens an Occidens', in *Aika* [*Time*], 12 (1912), pp. 15–25.

18 Eskola, *Rukousnauha*, p. 78.

19 Lidiia Chukovskaia lists, among the visitors to Kornei Chukovskii's dacha, the prominent writers and poets Maksim Gorky, Vladimir Maiakovskii, Viktor Shklovskii, Leonid Andreev, Anna Akhmatova and Nikolai Gumilev. See Merja Suomi, *Metamorphoses of a Text within Stalinist Context: Kornei Chukovskii's 'A High Art' in the 1930s* (Tampere: Juvenes, 2016), p. 9. See also Natalia Baschmakoff, 'Avant-Garde Encounters on Karelian Bedrock (1890s-1930s)', in *A Cultural History of the Avant-Garde in the Nordic Countries (1900–1925)*, ed. by Hubert van den Berg, Irmeli Hautamäki, and others (Amsterdam and New York: Rodopi, 2012), pp. 351–70.

20 See Ben Hellman, Tomi Huttunen, Tintti Klapuri and Lauri Piispa, 'Finlandssvenskarna som förmedlare av rysk kultur på 1920- och 30-talen'

Independent Finland

After heated debates about how and whether Finland should remain part of Russia, now ravaged by strikes and revolutions, the Finnish Head of State, Pehr Evind Svinhufvud, travelled to Petrograd in December 1917 to negotiate and confirm Finland's sovereign independence from the Council of People's Commissars. But there was no agreement between opposing political parties in Finland, and thus a Finnish civil war broke out in January 1918. The Reds (Socialists) were defeated, and the Whites, supported by German troops, celebrated their victory in early May.[21] The existing negative attitude towards Russia, including Russian culture and literature, primarily provoked by the tsarist regime's oppressive politics towards Finland at the beginning of the century, was aggravated by the new situation. Soviet Russia represented the ideology that had triggered the Civil War in Finland and revolutions elsewhere in Europe. Russian culture was rejected in the newly independent Finland. The closed border made it impossible to follow developments on the Soviet side. This negative attitude towards Russian literature was reflected in the acquisition records of public libraries. In the 1910s, translations of Russian literature comprised 11% of all acquisitions, but in the 1920s their share fell to 2%. In the 1930s no translations of Russian literature were listed among readers' favourites.[22]

Russian Modernism

In Finland, not much was known about the avant-garde forms of literature, arts, theatre and cinema in Soviet Russia after the revolution and the early 1920s, even though Russian printing presses had been sending legal-deposit

['Finnish Swedes as Mediators of Russian Culture in the 1920s and 30s'], *Finsk Tidskrift*, 3–4 (2017), 75–78, http://www.finsktidskrift.fi/wp-content/uploads/2018/01/ft_3417_paino.pdf.

21 The leaders of the defeated Reds fled across the Eastern border to Soviet Russia, accompanied by many ordinary workers who found it difficult to re-establish themselves in Finland after participating in the Civil War. The Finnish language played a significant role in the linguistic situation of Soviet Karelia, necessitating the translation of both personal documents and fiction from Russian into Finnish. This continued in the 1920s and early 1930s, but when Stalinist repression intensified in the mid-1930s, it lost its position. Translation into Finnish was resumed in the 1960s, and translations of Russian literature were again distributed and read in Finland also. See Marja Jänis and Tamara Starshova, 'Cultural and Political Contexts of Translating into Finnish in Soviet/Russian Karelia', in *Domestication and Foreignization in Translation Studies*, ed. by Hannu Kemppanen and others (Berlin: Frank & Timme, 2012), pp. 189–207.

22 Eskola, *Rukousnauha*, p. 55, p. 61.

copies—among them many Futurist rarities—to the Helsinki University Library.[23] Regarding Russian literature, the Finnish press published mainly 'bad' or sad news from Bolshevik Russia, such as information about the tragic deaths of the poets Aleksandr Blok and Velimir Khlebnikov. Word about new and interesting literary developments came via various routes, often dependent on certain active individuals, very often with a transnational identity. The journalist Rafael Lindqvist (1867–1952) was a Swedish-speaking Finn who translated major works by Tolstoy, Gorky, and many Russian and Soviet poets, also Modernists. His translations, although into Swedish, were published in Finland. His ideological views were Suecophile, i.e., he was a member of the pro-Swedish movement in Finland. He also became known as an anti-Semite (he translated the Protocols of the Elders of Zion into Swedish). As we know today, Modernism in Swedish literature was initiated not in Sweden, but among Finland's Swedish-speaking minority.[24] Thus it is not surprising that Russian Modernism was mediated into Swedish not only by Lindqvist, but also by a Swedish-speaking Finnish poet, Edith Södergran (1892–1923). A notable translator of Igor Severianin's poetry, she was born and educated in St Petersburg.[25] Another transnational mediator, Antti Tiittanen (1890–1927), an Ingrian Finnish refugee,[26] was an exceptionally active journalist and writer who published articles about Russian literature and theatre. He also translated poems and short stories. His main influences were Aleksandr Blok and Nikolai Evreinov. Tiittanen's fate remains unknown; he disappeared during his daily walk in Helsinki in January 1927. The Finnish newspapers suspected that right-wing political activists kidnapped him. Another highly active mediator was Henry Parland (1908–30), who also died young, aged just twenty-two. From a multi-lingual family in Vyborg and educated partly in St Petersburg, Parland succeeded in introducing contemporary Russian Modernism to Finland, especially within Finno-Swedish cultural circles. While living in Kaunas, the interim capital of Lithuania, he acquainted himself with local poets and with Russian avant-garde authors, like Iurii Olesha and Anatolii Mariengof. Their writing influenced his own unfinished experimental novel project titled *Sönder* (*To Pieces*), published posthumously in 1932.

23 Tomi Huttunen and Tapio Pitkäranta, 'The Futurism Collection at the National Library of Finland in Helsinki', in *International Yearbook of Futurism Studies*, ed. by Günther Berghaus and others (Berlin: de Gruyter), 9 (2019), 297–308.

24 Lars Kleberg, 'The Advantage of the Margin', in *Swedish–Polish Modernism: Literature—Language—Culture*, ed. by Małgorzata Anna Packalén and Sven Gustavsson (Stockholm: KVHAA / Almqvist & Wiksell International, 2003), pp. 56–89.

25 Hellman and others, 'Finnish Swedes as Mediators of Russian Culture in the 1920s and 30s', pp. 76–78.

26 Ingrian Finns are descendants of the seventeenth-century Finnish-speaking, predominantly Lutheran settlers on the South-Eastern shore of the Gulf of Finland; after 1918 until 1922, a considerable number of so-called 'tribe refugees' (Ingrians and East Karelian people) fled Soviet Russia for Finland.

Contemporary Russian poetry was described in Finnish in an article by the young literary critic Olavi Paavolainen (1903–64) in his 1929 volume of essays *In Search of Modern Times* (*Nykyaikaa etsimässä*). According to Paavolainen, Aleksandr Blok, Vladimir Maiakovskii, and Sergei Esenin represented the trinity of 'Faith, Hope and Love' amid the tragedy of the revolution. Paavolainen describes Blok's 1918 poems 'The Scythians' ('Skify') and 'The Twelve' ('Dvenadtsat') as examples of irresistible poetic power, breaking the political wall which rose around Russia after the revolution.[27] Maiakovskii introduced Futurism in good time: nowhere else than in revolutionary Russia has Futurism been more intensely developed. For Esenin, Paavolainen argued, the revolution was a tragedy, since it denied Russia's essential status as a peasant country. *In Search of Modern Times* was widely disseminated and influential.[28]

Translations of the Classics

While a negative attitude towards contemporary Russian literature tended to prevail, the prominent Finnish publishing house Werner Söderström (founded in 1878) nonetheless launched a project to translate Russian classics. Since the first translations of Russian literature had appeared, mainly during the 1880s, their importance had changed; and so had the Finnish literary language. When these translations were first published, they represented contemporary foreign writing; but by the 1920s, they were classics of world literature. All Dostoevsky's major works were now translated into Finnish. Some translators, like V.K. Trast (1878–1953) and Ida Pekari (1894–1986), were descendants of Finns who had lived in St Petersburg. Tolstoy's radical thoughts on equality made some readers suspicious that his work might have partly incited the Russian Revolution. Arvid Järnefelt, son of Elisabet Järnefelt and a prominent follower of Tolstoy's ideas in Finland, questioned these thoughts in his article 'Should Tolstoy be Considered the Father of the Russian Revolution?'.[29] The quantity of both published literatures originally written in Finnish and of translations into Finnish declined in the 1930s. From 1900 to 1929, these were at parity, but the proportion of translations fell in the 1930s, remaining at a lower level

27 Olavi Paavolainen, *Nykyaikaa etsimässä* [*In Search of Modern Times*] (Helsinki: Otava, 1929, reprinted 1990), pp. 196–225 (p. 196).

28 For a survey of Russo-Finnish literary interactions in the early twentieth century, see also E.G. Soini's *Vzaimoproniknovenie russkoy i finskoy literatury v pervoj polovine XX veka* [*The Permeation of Russian and Finnish Literature in the First Half of the 20th Century*] (Moscow: IaSK, 2017), 2nd edn, esp. Chapter One, 'Vospriiatie russkoi literatury v sisteme kontaktnykh sviazei' (pp. 46–90), which has a subsection on Rafael Lindqvist.

29 Arvid Järnefelt, 'Onko Tolstoi pidettävä Venäjän vallankumouksen isänä?' ['Should Tolstoy Be Considered Father of the Russian Revolution?', published in the literary periodical *Sininen kirja* [*Blue Book*], 8 (1928), 7–17.

until the 1950s.[30] Many factors have been cited to explain this, such as Finland's signature of the Berne Convention in 1928, forcing publishers to pay royalties for acquiring translation rights; nationalistic tendencies and isolationism, also noted in many other newly independent states in Central and Eastern Europe; and the Finnish government's promotion of patriotism, the agrarian lifestyle and the Lutheran church as the essential values of Finnish life.[31] New radical currents in contemporary European literature as well as interesting tendencies from Soviet literature, however, were discussed in several liberal and left-wing cultural publications in both Finnish and Swedish.

When publishers were accused of neglecting to publish translations, they resorted to commissioning anthologies. 'Golden Books' from several literatures—anthologising the Scandinavian, German, English, French, Italian, and Spanish and Portuguese classics—were issued in the 1930s.[32] Russian literature comprised one third of *The Golden Book of Slavic Literatures* (1936). In his Editor's Introduction, V.K. Trast called Ivan Turgenev the foremost master of style, and Tolstoy the greatest thinker. He claimed that in Russian literature, ideologies and social questions are more important than artistic aspirations and aesthetic perfection; Trast credited Vissarion Belinskii with this hierarchy.[33] In 1943, the librarian Helle Kannila, who was primarily responsible for developing the Finnish public library system, published an overview of translations of literature in the first half of the twentieth century. Kannila concluded her article by observing that Russian literature was well represented in translation before World War I, but that Soviet Russian literature understandably failed to resonate with Finnish readers.[34]

New Kinds of Contact, New Kinds of Translation

After the short 'Winter War' (1939–40) between Finland and the Soviet Union, and following Finland's involvement in World War II as an ally of Germany

30 Erkki Sevänen, ['Ikkunat auki, ikkunat kiinni! Suomennoskirjallisuuden asema ja luonne 1920—ja 1930—luvuilla' ['Open the Windows, Close the Windows! The Position and Character of Translated Literature in 1920s and 1930s'], in *Suomennoskirjallisuuden historia*, I, pp. 382–93 (p. 384).

31 Ibid., p. 382.

32 The series editors were prominent literary critics Rafael Koskimies and Martti Haavio; each anthology had its own dedicated editor.

33 V.K. Trast, 'Venäjän kirjallisuus' ['Russian Literature'], in *Slaavilaisten kirjallisuuksien kultainen kirja* [*The Golden Book of Slavic Literatures*], ed. by V.K. Trast (Helsinki: WSOY, 1936), pp. 2–30 (p. 30).

34 Helle Kannila, 'Tällä vuosisadalla ilmestyneen kaunokirjallisuuden suomennoksista' ['Translations of Literature during this Century'], in *Kirjallisuudentutkijain seuran vuosikirja VII* [*Yearbook of the Society of Scholars of Literature VII*], ed. by Rafael Koskimies and others (Helsinki: SKS, 1943), pp. 79–110 (p. 106).

from 1941 to 1944, the country managed to withdraw from conflict in September 1944. What followed can be described as the "problematic early years of a new relationship with the Soviet Union".[35] As a condition for ending hostilities, Finland had to allow the presence of a Control Commission formed by the Allies, but led by Soviet politicians. This regulated internal politics. Political parties with far-left ideologies, including the Communist Party (prohibited since the Civil War ended in 1918), were allowed to function openly. In March 1945, a coalition of far-left parties managed to attract nearly a quarter of the votes in the parliamentary election. Attitudes towards Russian culture and literature changed in many ways. Anti-Soviet literature could no longer be published. Conversely, publications of both Soviet classics and new Soviet literature were encouraged. What followed was a short but astonishing efflorescence of translations from Russian in 1945 and 1946, when about 20% of all new literary translations were from that language. A new, openly far-left, publishing house called Kansankulttuuri (People's Culture), commissioned most of these translations. Maksim Gorky's *Mother* (*Mat'*, 1906) was published for the first time in book form in Finnish in 1944 and received substantial attention. Among the authors to be translated in the 1940s were Mikhail Sholokhov, Vasilii Grossman, Nikolai Ostrovskii, Leonid Leonov, Aleksei Tolstoy, Konstantin Simonov, Il'ia Ehrenburg, and Konstantin Paustovskii. Ehrenburg and Paustovskii became very popular among Finnish readers when their respective memoirs came out in the 1960s.

The first anthology of Russian poetry in Finnish, *The Russian Muse* (*Venäjän runotar*), appeared in 1946. Its editors described the history of Russian poetry and poetic language from Pushkin to the Soviet poets in their foreword.[36] This anthology was not fully comprehensive, since it neglected Russian Modernism, but it did include a wide variety of Russian poetry and poets. The editors claimed that Russian poetic metre had returned to traditional forms, as if Modernist experimentation had ended.[37] Some contemporary poets to feature were Aleksandr Tvardovskii and Evgenii Dolmatovskii, whose poems were linked to the 'Winter War'. The editors wrote: "We can say that Tvardovskii, and especially Dolmatovskii, who participated in the Taipale River battles, write poems with a truly human message, where along with the heroism of Soviet soldiers, the tough resistance of Finnish soldiers and the majestic austerity of the war is described".[38]

The radical turn towards interest in Soviet culture and literature was short-lived, and it did not affect literary institutions like publishing houses, the press, or cultural foundations. Interest in classic Russian literature persisted among

35 Kirby, *A Concise History of Finland*, p. 206.

36 Lauri Viljanen and Valentin Kiparsky, 'Johdanto' ['Preface'] in *Venäjän runotar* [*The Russian Muse*], ed. by L. Viljanen and V. Kiparsky (Helsinki: WSOY, 1946), pp. 5–19.

37 Ibid., p. 15.

38 Ibid., p. 16.

Finnish readers, however, and during the 1950s new editions of translations of Russian classics were regularly issued.[39] In 1947, the Soviet Union and Finland signed a treaty of friendship, co-operation, and mutual assistance, which differed from Eastern European mutual assistance treaty models and thus assured relative freedom to Finland, for instance via entry into the Nordic Council and the United Nations. However, the Soviet Union maintained firm control over Finland, occasionally affecting the latter's cultural life as well.

The Thaw and Afterwards

Interest in Soviet literature was enhanced by irregular dramatic changes. 'The Thaw'—the time after Stalin's death, named after Ehrenburg's novel (*Ottepel'*, 1954; published in Finnish as *Suojasää* in 1963 in Ulla-Liisa Heino's translation)—led to looser control over cultural politics and the emergence of new styles in Soviet literature. Vladimir Dudintsev's novel *Not by Bread Alone* (*Ne khlebom edinym*, 1956; *Ei ainoastaan leivästä*, 1957) was a sensation in Finland as well as in other countries but is now almost forgotten. It was translated by Juhani Konkka (1904–70), who also translated Gogol, Dostoevsky, and Pasternak (among others) into Finnish. Another sensation—both in Finland and elsewhere—was the Nobel Prize given to Boris Pasternak, author of *Doctor Zhivago* (*Doktor Zhivago*, 1957), in 1958. In the same year, Juhani Konnka's translation of the novel (*Tohtori Živago*) appeared and became a bestseller. Later, Pasternak's poetry was also translated and published, both in anthologies and as a separate collection. Gorky's selected writings were published in Finnish in four volumes in the 1950s, an honour given to few world writers. Translations of Mikhail Sholokhov's *Quiet Flows the Don* (*Tikhii Don*, 1926–40) and *Virgin Soil Upturned* (*Podniataia tselina*, 1932) were also popular among Finnish readers.

Only a few collections of Russian poetry were published in Finnish between the 1950s and 1970s. An exception was Vladimir Maiakovskii's poetry, translated by the Finnish poet Arvo Turtiainen (1904–80), and now considered a classic example of poetry translation into Finnish. In the 1960s and 1970s, Evgenii Evtushenko's poetry was widely translated and enjoyed by Finnish readers. His fame at that time was almost phenomenal, surpassing most other poets in Finnish translation. Paradoxically, during the late Soviet period, Evtushenko

39 Jarl Hellemann, the head of the publishing house Tammi, writes about the strong traditions of Russian literature in Finland: when Finnish readers are asked about their favourite writers, they mention Tolstoy, Dostoevsky, Chekhov and Gogol, whereas Scandinavian writers have lost the position they acquired at the turn of the nineteenth century and the early twentieth. Jarl Helleman, 'Käännöskirjallisuuden vuosisata' ['Century of Translated Literature'] in *Kirjan rantaviiva* [*The Beachline of Literature*], ed. by Jussi Nuorteva (Helsinki: Gaudeamus, 1988), pp. 84–95 (p. 92.)

was a famous and sensational poet because he discussed problematic topics, but his fame dwindled when those topics ceased to be relevant.

Interest in Russian Modernist prose and, later, also in Modernist poetry started in the 1960s. Some works by Andrei Belyi, Isaak Babel, Boris Pil'niak, Iurii Olesha, and Evgenii Zamiatin were translated. Mikhail Bulgakov's *The Master and Margarita* (*Master i Margarita*, 1940) was translated as *The Devil Comes to Moscow* (*Saatana saapuu Moskovaan*, 1969). The Finnish title was initially credited to the translator, Ulla-Liisa Heino (1934–2023), but in fact—as she has shown—it was the publisher's idea. Bulgakov's novel has since been reprinted several times and remains the most popular twentieth-century Russian novel in Finland. It has also been staged in numerous Finnish theatres. Not even Aleksandr Solzhenitsyn's works have achieved success on the scale of Bulgakov's novel.

Solzhenitsyn began to be translated in the 1960s, a significant process for Finnish translation and publishing policy. *One Day in the Life of Ivan Denisovich* (*Odin den' Ivana Denisovicha*, 1962; *Ivan Denisovitšin päivä*, 1963) was swiftly translated into Finnish by Markku Lahtela (1936–80), immediately after the original text appeared in the Soviet Union. Solzhenitsyn's next works were published outside the Soviet Union. Finnish translations of *Cancer Ward* (*Rakovyi korpus*, 1968; *Syöpäosasto*, 1968) and *The First Circle* (*V kruge pervom*, 1968; *Ensimmäinen piiri*, 1970) were issued in large print runs. Both were translated by Esa Adrian (1939–2007), who specialised in translating Russian Modernism and dissident literature for Finnish readers. They became popular bestsellers, selling tens of thousands of copies. The Soviet Embassy in Finland tried to prohibit the translation and publication of Solzhenitsyn's works but succeeded only in persuading Finnish authorities at the last minute to stop the release of *The Gulag Archipelago* (*Arkhipelag Gulag*, 1973–78; *Vankileirien saaristo*, translated by Esa Adrian) by the Tammi publishing house. Tammi had published all previous Finnish translations of Solzhenitsyn's works. The first volume of *Archipelago* was then published by a small publishing house in Sweden instead (Wahlström & Widstrand in Stockholm), but it could still be bought and read freely in Finland.[40] Solzhenitsyn's works were very popular in the 1960s and 1970s in Finland (and internationally), but interest in them has since faded. However, new editions of his major works have been republished in Finland, most recently *The Gulag Archipelago* in 2012.[41]

Very few works by Russian emigrant and dissident writers were published in Finland in the 1960s and 1970s, and far fewer than in other Western countries, where interest in contemporary Russian literature was largely supported by

40 The fact that although *The Gulag Archipelago* was not published by a Finnish publishing house, the Finnish translation of the book published in Sweden could be freely distributed, read and discussed, demonstrates the Finns' relative freedom and self-determination from Soviet authorities.

41 Aleksandr Solzhenitsyn, *The Gulag Archipelago* [*GULAG: Vankileirien saaristo*], trans. by Esa Adrian (Helsinki: Silberfeldt, 2012).

the writings of dissident and emigrant authors. 'Finlandisation'[42] affected the translation policy of Soviet literature, particularly in the 1970s, when translations of contemporary Soviet literature were published more than ever before. Several Finnish publishing houses joined forces to launch a new publishing project, 'Soviet Literature'; books published in this series had a standardised cover design and logo. Eventually, eighty-four titles were issued over ten years. Four volumes of poetry called *Soviet Lyrics* (*Neuvostolyriikkaa*) were published in this series between 1975 and 1986; they introduced classics of Russian poetry from the beginning of the twentieth century, starting with Symbolists and ending with contemporary poets, most of them appearing for the first time in Finnish. Later the poetry of these authors—Anna Akhmatova, Osip Mandel'shtam, Boris Pasternak, and Iosif Brodskii—was published separately, translated by Finnish poets. Dissident or unofficial Russian literature has not been widely published in Finland. Vasilii Grossman's *Life and Fate* (*Zhizn' i sudba*, 1960; translated by the prolific Esa Adrian as *Elämä ja kohtalo* in 1984), depicting the 1930s and the wartime Soviet Union, was much discussed, as was Vladimir Voinovich's *The Life and Extraordinary Adventures of Private Ivan Chonkin* (*Zhizn' i neobychainye prikliucheniia soldata Ivana Chonkina*, 1969; *Sotamies Ivan Tsonkinin seikkailut*, 1979, translated by Riitta Pyykkö (b. 1953)) and its sequels. Fiction by Nikolai Gogol, Fedor Dostoevsky, Lev Tolstoy, and Anton Chekhov has been published in new translations in recent decades—and this is a continuing trend. Chekhov's correspondence, published in three volumes with detailed commentaries, has attracted much attention from Finnish readers.

After the Soviet Union

During perestroika, many translations of Russian books popular in the Soviet Union appeared, but they attracted few readers in Finland and were quickly forgotten. This cannot be said of translations of prose by the Absurdist writer Daniil Kharms whose stories were first issued in Finnish in 1988 in a collection of short stories entitled *Hazards* (*Sluchai*). This collection has been republished many times, included on school curricula, and staged in many theatres. In the 2000s, more collections of Kharms's work were translated.

Included among authors whose works have been translated into Finnish in recent decades are later avant-garde, dissident, and postmodernist Russian

42 This term was first applied by commentators and politicians outside Finland to warn about certain measures of Soviet control. After the collapse of the Soviet Union, when the Treaty of Friendship, Co-operation and Mutual Assistance was buried, it has been adopted in Finnish discussions of recent history to assess the extent to which Finns conceive themselves as having practised self-control in their relationship towards Russian interference in Finnish political and cultural life. See Kirby, *A Concise History of Finland*, p. 245, p. 272.

writers such as Evgenii Popov, Vladimir Sorokin, and Viktor Erofeev. Andrei Bitov's *Pushkin House* (*Pushkinskii dom*, 1987; *Puškinin talo*, 1983) and Venedikt Erofeev's *Moscow-Petushki* (*Moskva-Petushki*, 1973; *Moskova-Petuški: runoelma*, 1990)[43] have been treated as classics of contemporary Russian literature; both were translated into Finnish by Esa Adrian. The author (and former head of Finnish PEN) Jukka Mallinen (b. 1950), who participated actively in the cultural and literary exchange between post-Soviet Russia and Finland, made many of the translations of 1990s prose and poetry. However, apart from publications in periodicals, the 1990s witnessed very few translations of Russian literature until the appearance of such best-selling writers as Viktor Pelevin. The translation of his novels into Finnish was obviously motivated by his prior success across Europe. This shows that the market economy has become influential in Russian-Finnish literary relations, which were traditionally governed by bilateral developments.

Two Russian prose writers have proved exceptionally popular among readers in the 2000s. Aleksandra Marinina's detective novels have become extraordinary best-sellers, while Boris Akunin's historical detective fiction has also dominated sales. Both are constant record breakers in the Russian literary market. Meanwhile, it has become obvious that more popular and internationally successful Russian contemporary fiction is now being translated into Finnish. Thus, Russian literature is no longer seen by Finns as consisting solely of psychological realism, or of religiously, philosophically, or intertextually challenging texts. This is reflected in the recognition of the fantasy novel series by Sergei Luk'ianenko and Dmitrii Glukhovskii, for example. Meanwhile, prose by women writers has gradually gained visibility in contemporary Russian fiction. Following the success of Tat'iana Tolstaia's and Liudmila Petrushevskaia's short stories, it is obvious that Liudmila Ulitskaia, Dina Rubina, and Elena Chizhova have acquired many devoted readers in today's Finland. Sergei Dovlatov, whose prose had already become immensely popular in Russia during the 1990s, enjoyed a more recent spike in readers. Two books translated by the poet and scholar Pauli Tapio (b. 1986) in 2012—*The Suitcase* (*Chemodan*, 1986; *Matkalaukku*) and *Ours* (*Nashi*, 1983; *Meikäläiset*)—initiated a series of exceptionally best-selling translations which at the time of writing comprises five titles. The current trend for autofiction, along with the high quality of these translations, may have encouraged this phenomenon.

Conclusion

The recent history of Finnish translations of Russian literature vividly demonstrates that, during the 1990s, the few works translated were most often

43 Also translated into English with the title *Moscow to the End of the Line* by H. William Tjalsma (Evanston: Northwestern University Press, 1994).

chosen according to and as a result of their success in the European book market. This also remained the case in the early 2000s, when the number of translations remained rather small. However, the situation changed rapidly in the 2010s, when translation activity suddenly became much more intense than in the previous decades. This may reflect the fact that Russia and its turbulent political situation were constantly present in newsfeeds, as during the so-called 'winter of demonstrations' of 2012–13 and, even more so, after the annexation of Crimea and the beginning of the war in Ukraine in 2014. On the other hand, this was perhaps merely a reflection of a new generation of translators making their debuts in the publishing arena.

For 2015, the Helsinki Book Fair had chosen Russia as its theme country. While this decision was not accepted unanimously in Finnish society, more than thirty contemporary Russophone writers still came to advertise their oeuvres at the Book Fair—legitimately representing the diversity of Russian-language literature both ideologically and aesthetically. This achievement naturally encouraged Finnish publishing companies to have new Russian authors' works translated and thus further boosted translation activity. New names were identified during Book Fair discussions, and Finland soon began to increasingly publish—along with other Nordic countries—new Russian literature. Consequently, Finnish translations of Guzel Iakhina's *Zuleikha* (*Zuleikha otkryvaet glaza*, 2015; *Suleika avaa silmänsä*, 2016, translated by Kirsti Era), Mariia Stepanova's *In Memory of Memory* (*Pamiati pamiati*, 2017; *Muistin Muistolle: Romanssi*, 2020, translated by Mika Pylsy) and Oksana Vasiakina's *The Wound* (*Rana*, 2021; *Haava*, 2023, translated by Riku Toivola) constituted the very first translations of these novels outside Russia. Typically for the cultural periphery, these examples show that individual translators' cultural sensors are still evidently the most important factor influencing the translation of Russian literature in Finland, as was the case at the very beginning of Russian-Finnish translation history in the early nineteenth century, or in the 1920s, for example. At the same time, Russia's escalation of military aggression in Ukraine has initiated many discussions of ethics within Finnish publishing companies, which will most probably lead to a decrease in translation activity in the future.

To return to Casanova's idea of the world republic of letters, we emphasise the importance of examining events on the periphery of any literary space. Translating literature from many different major languages into less widely spoken languages has played a remarkable role in making the periphery aware of the developments in the international literary space. In small literary and linguistic spaces like Finland, translators are not just a minority of benevolent polyglots. They are a choir of masters of many languages and cultures, including their own. In Finland, translations have played a crucial role in the development of Finnish literature. This article has examined just one aspect of literary translation in Finland: that of works from Russia, the country's largest neighbour.

France

"May Russia Find Her Thoughts Faithfully Translated": E. M. de Vogüé's Importation of Russian Literature into France

Elizabeth F. Geballe

Introduction

Eugène-Melchior de Vogüé (1848–1910), a French diplomat, literary critic, travel writer, archaeologist, and philanthropist is known primarily in the Slavic intellectual community for bringing the pantheon of nineteenth-century Russian writers to French and then to West European attention. After acquiring first-hand knowledge of Russia, and of Russian, as a diplomat in Saint Petersburg, and marrying a Russian (Aleksandra Annenkova), de Vogüé turned his attention to literature.[1] His *Le Roman russe* (*The Russian Novel*), published in 1886 and translated immediately into English and German, was both epoch-making and canon-forming.[2] It offered biographies of Aleksandr

1 For a more detailed summary of de Vogüé's introduction to Russian culture and language, see Anna Gichkina, *Eugène-Melchior de Vogüé, ou comment la Russie pourrait sauver la France* (Paris: L'Harmattan, 2018), esp. Chapter IV, pp. 77–94.

2 The study comprised five articles that had been published in the *Revue des Deux Mondes* between 1883 and 1886 and one article, on Pushkin, that had appeared in the *Revue bleue* in 1886. Although several studies of Russian literature were published in the years preceding de Vogüé's book—including Ernest Dupuy's *Les Grands maîtres de la literature russes au dix-neuvième siècle* (1885) and Charles Turner's *Studies in Russian Literature* (1882)—neither achieved the widespread relevance that *Le Roman russe* did. In *Russomania,* Rebecca Beasley explains that "while Dupuy and Turner provided straightforward introductions to the novelists,

 https://doi.org/10.11647/OBP.0340.05

Pushkin, Nikolai Gogol, Ivan Turgenev, Fedor Dostoevsky, and Lev Tolstoy, while also summarising their plots, sketching their relationships to Realism, and generalising about the Russian character. Ostensibly designed to redirect the trends of French Naturalism, de Vogüé's study cast Russian literature as "the great alternative, a paragon of decency and truthfulness with a moral edge, qualities calculated to warm the hearts of the late Victorians."[3] Though many of these chapters had been published in previous years, in slightly different forms, they cemented de Vogüé's reputation. Even in the current edition of France's Larousse literary encyclopaedia, de Vogüé is credited with having "discovered for French audiences" the major works of Russian literature.[4]

For the purposes of this essay, I acknowledge de Vogüé's achievements as a critic and cultural ambassador who set the expectations of the French reading public, but I grant more importance to his role as a translator. In the final sentence of *Le Roman russe*, de Vogüé expresses his hope that Russia will find in his study a sincere expression of its national virtues: "May she find her own thoughts faithfully translated, and recognize, without too much disparagement, the image of herself, ever before my eyes" [*"Puisse-t-elle y retrouver sa pensée fidèlement traduite et se reconnaître, sans trop y mécomptes, à l'image qu'elle m'a laissé dans les yeux"*].[5] Metaphorical as his 'translation' may be here, de Vogüé's oeuvre—when it concerned Russia—persistently grappled with both practical and theoretical issues of translation. Though a version of Tolstoy's 'Three Deaths' ('Tri smerti', 1859) was the only complete translation published by the French scholar ('Trois

---

they stopped short of arguing for the contemporary significance of the Russian novel. In contrast, Vogüé argued that the Russian novel offered a moral and spiritual corrective to the materialism of French literature." See Rebecca Beasley, *Russomania* (Oxford: Oxford University Press, 2020), p. 15.

3 Rachel May, *The Translator in the Text* (Chicago, IL: Northwestern University Press, 1994), p. 21.

4 Larousse, *Eugène Melchior, vicomte de Vogüé*, https://www.larousse.fr/encyclopedie/litterature/Eug%C3%A8ne_Melchior_vicomte_de_Vog%C3%BC%C3%A9/171945. F.W.J Hemmings, although he believed French audiences would have discovered the splendours of Russian literature without de Vogüé's help, credits the French author with establishing the feverish cult of Dostoevsky and Tolstoy: "The prestige of the periodical in which he was writing, his own eloquence, and evident sincerity—all these must be allowed to have given great impetus to the rapid popularisation of Tolstoy and Dostoevsky in France after 1886". See F.W.J. Hemmings, *The Russian Novel in France 1884–1914* (Oxford: Oxford University Press, 1950), p. 30.

5 In the course of this essay, I cite French passages from de Vogüé's original text: Eugène-Melchior de Vogüé, *Le Roman russe* (Paris: Librarie Plon, 1886). English translations are from Eugène-Melchior de Vogüé, *The Russian Novel*, trans. by Colonel H. A. Sawyer (London: Chapman and Hall, 1913). The lines cited here are from p. 347 of *Le Roman russe*, p. 332 of Sawyer's translation. In cases where Sawyer did not translate the French passage cited—his translation is slightly abridged—I provide my own translations. All other translations are my own, unless otherwise indicated.

Morts', 1882), he translated all the quotations scattered throughout *Le Roman russe* and used the latter study—and a separate article in the *Revue des Deux Mondes*—as a platform to evaluate the work of other translators.[6] It would be misleading to suggest that de Vogüé introduced the French public to Russian literature for the first time, since other translators preceded him. By 1886, the French public could access, among other texts, translations by Prosper Mérimée (1803–70) of Pushkin's 'The Queen of Spades' ('Pikovaia dama', 1834), 'The Hussar' ('Gusar', 1833), and 'The Bohemians' ('Tsygany', 1827), Gogol's 'The Inspector General' ('Revizor', 1836) and *Dead Souls* (*Mertvye dushi*, 1842); a translation by Victor Derély (1840–1904) of Dostoevsky's *Crime and Punishment* (*Prestuplenie i nakazanie*, 1866); translations by Louis Viardot (1800–83) of Pushkin's *The Captain's Daughter* (*Kapitanskaia dochka*, 1836) and of Gogol's 'Taras Bulba' ('Taras Bulba', 1835) and other stories; translations by Charles Morice (1860–1919) of Dostoevsky's *The Brothers Karamazov* (*Brat'ia Karamazovy*, 1880) and of other works by the same author; Tolstoy's *War and Peace* (*Voina i mir*, 1867) translated by Princess Irène Paskévitch (1835–1925); translations by Ernest Charrière (1805–65) of Gogol's *Dead Souls* and Turgenev's *A Sportsman's Sketches* (*Zapiski okhotnika*, 1852); and translations by Ely Halpérine-Kaminsky (1858–1936) of Tolstoy's 'The Death of Ivan Il'ich' ('Smert' Ivana Il'ycha', 1886), 'Three Deaths', 'Kholstomer' ('Kholstomer', 1886), Andrei's death in *War and Peace*, and Nikolai Levin's death in *Anna Karenina* (*Anna Karenina*, 1878), grouped in a collection enticingly called *Death* (*La Mort*, 1886).[7] By including translated extracts from all these authors, including Maksim Gorky, however, de Vogüé's survey covers most ground. Indeed, as Jean-Louis Backès points out in a recent article on *Le Roman russe*, if one were to collect de Vogüé's translated citations, "one could compile an interesting anthology of 19th-century Russian literature".[8]

My choice to single out de Vogüé from the above list of translators has less to do with the volume of his output than with the authority which he was granted

6 Eugène-Melchior de Vogüé, 'Les Livres russes en France', *Revue des Deux Mondes*, 78 (1886), 823–41.

7 Vladimir Boutchik helpfully divides this group into three categories. The first consists of translators like Irène Paskévitch, née Irina Vorontsova-Dashkova—Russian aristocrats who had mastered French and who were motivated by national pride. The second group includes Mérimée and Charrière—French writers who had lived in Russia and were perhaps inspired to translate by a desire to improve their Russian language skills. The third group—a generation removed from the first two and including Halpérine-Kaminsky, Morice, Derély, and Neyroud—consisted of more professional translators, though they varied in their fidelity to the original texts. See Vladimir Boutchik, *La Littérature russe en France* (Paris: Honoré Champion, 1947), pp. 13–34.

8 Jean-Louis Backès, 'Eugène-Melchior de Vogüé et *Le Roman russe*', in *L'Appel de l'étranger: Traduire en langue française en 1886*, ed. by Lucile Arnoux-Farnoux, Yves Chevrel, and Sylvie Humbert-Mougin (Paris: Presses Universitaires François-Rabelais, 2015), pp. 213–28 (p. 219), https://doi.org/10.4000/books.pufr.11309.

by editors and the reading public at large. In his *Method in Translation Theory* (1998), Anthony Pym, focusing especially on translations into French at the end of the nineteenth century, remarks that by those years "translation had become just one of several methods for the transmission of knowledge".[9] De Vogüé, who had served at the French Embassy and written for the *Revue des Deux Mondes* and was soon to be elected to the Académie Française, was what Pym might refer to as an "active efficient cause"—an individual translator who acquires enough power and influence to intervene in literary history.[10] Such power allowed de Vogüé to determine and shape processes of literary transculturation that are often addressed in the passive voice. In *What Is World Literature?* (2003), David Damrosch, for example, submits that "works of literature take on a new life as they move into the world at large, and to understand this new life we need to look closely at the ways the work becomes reframed in its translations and in its new cultural contexts".[11] In too many cases, such "reframing" is a hazy historical process, shaped by translators, editors, publishing pressures (the Franco-Russian alliance of the early 1890s creating a higher demand for Russian literature, for example), the literary marketplace, and the cultural zeitgeist. This case study, however, tracks what could almost be considered a one-man show of canon formation, and the 'reframing' can easily, though not solely, be credited to de Vogüé. The latter was a mediator who sacrificed the time he might have spent translating to focus on the critical [re]framing of Russian novels: in addition to his books and articles, he penned prefaces to Dostoevsky's *Notes from the House of the Dead* (*Zapiski iz mertvogo doma*, 1861) and *The Idiot* (*Idiot*, 1869), to Tolstoy's *War and Peace*, to Nikolai Nekrasov's poetry, to works by Ivan Krylov, Denis Fonvizin, and Fedor Tiutchev. Unlike Constance Garnett, who was far more prolific than her French counterpart but by and large refused to write prefaces to her English translations, de Vogüé shaped the expectations of the French reading public in his non-fiction.[12] In the following microhistorical case study, I will track the interventions de Vogüé made in *Le Roman russe*, his translation of Tolstoy, his reviews of other contemporary translations, and his prefaces to translated Russian works. Taking into account de Vogüé's highly personal and idiosyncratic motivations, I focus primarily on how, as a literary critic, he defined the otherness of Russian literature and how, as a translator, he modelled a reaction to it.

9 Anthony Pym, *Method in Translation History* (London and New York: Routledge, 1998), p. 174.

10 Pym, *Method in Translation History*, p. 161.

11 David Damrosch, *What Is World Literature?* (Princeton, NJ: Princeton University Press, 2003), p. 24.

12 Constance Garnett (1861–1946) was by far the most prolific translator of Russian literature in the U.K. Translator of some seventy volumes of Russian literature, Garnett made available—often for the first time—works by Gogol, Dostoevsky, Chekhov, Tolstoy, Turgenev, and Goncharov.

Anguish, Despair, Hangovers: The Language of Moral Suffering

The animating force behind de Vogüé's articles, and, as I hope to show, his translations, is his dissatisfaction with *fin-de-siècle* French Naturalism. Concentrating on what the Russian realists can teach their French counterparts, de Vogüé dismisses Russian poets from his canon, using translation as a convenient excuse to do so: "Russian poets are not and will never be translated" (*"Les poètes russes ne sont et ne seront jamais traduits"*).[13] He turns instead to prose writers like Gogol, Turgenev, Dostoevsky, Tolstoy, and later, Gorky, to demonstrate how they document human suffering. Though de Vogüé has a soft spot for the landscapes evoked in Russian literature, the passages he chooses to translate are by and large accounts of physical torment and bodily deterioration: from Gogol he highlights the execution of the Cossacks in 'Taras Bulba' ('Taras Bulba', 1835); from Turgenev, the half-dead hag attempting to sing in 'A Living Relic' ('Zhivye moshchi', 1874); from Dostoevsky, the death of Mikhailov in *Notes from the House of the Dead* and of the student in *Poor Folk* (*Bednye liudi*, 1846); from Tolstoy, Prince Andrei's battlefield injury and the carnal reality of war in *War and Peace*. In an essay called 'Russian Books in France' ('Les Livres russes en France') for the *Revue des Deux Mondes* in 1886, which was not included in *Le Roman russe*, de Vogüé—though he jokes that nervous people will hesitate to enter libraries full of macabre Russian titles—admits that Halpérine-Kaminsky beat him to the idea of grouping Tolstoy's death tales into one collection.[14] Taken together, de Vogüé's translation choices—and I include his version of 'Three Deaths'—suggest that he was trying to put these scenes in dialogue with the morbid trend in French literature that was, in his view, initiated by Stendhal and perfected by Gustave Flaubert.[15] By demonstrating the deficiencies of French Naturalism, de Vogüé hoped to facilitate the welcoming of Russian literature by French readers.

De Vogüé can be as hard on the mercilessness of the Russian realists as he is on his own compatriots; Tolstoy's 'The Death of Ivan Il'ich' makes him want to turn away, as if from the "last convulsions of a dying animal" (*"dernières convulsions d'une bête mourante"*).[16] However, de Vogüé rejoices that their prose generally combines laboratory-style Realism with "moral intention" (*"intention morale"*)

13 De Vogüé, *Roman russe*, p. 36. De Vogüé later furthers this thought: "I remember having seen a firefly brought home between two leaves of a small copy of *Onegin* by a young girl just returned from Naples. It was an infinitesimal particle of a glorious Italian night, but all the charm of its luminiferous light departed the moment it had been touched. Thus would perish Russian poetry were I to transpose it in these pages" (ibid., p. 45).

14 De Vogüé, 'Livres russes en France', p. 838; p. 829.

15 De Vogüé, *Roman russe*, p. xxxvi.

16 De Vogüé, 'Livres russes en France', p. 829.

or "moral inspiration" ("*inspiration morale*").[17] In his preface to *Notes from the House of the Dead* (*Souvenirs de la maison des morts*, 1886), de Vogüé welcomes the salutary effects of "moral suffering"'—something he cannot find in French literature.[18] It is a point that other contemporaneous translators make as well: in his preface to *La Mort*, Halpérine-Kaminsky insists that the physical deaths depicted therein are attended by "moral suffering" ("*les souffrances morales*");[19] Charrière, in his preface to a French translation of Turgenev's *A Sportsman's Sketches*, speaks of the "moral suffering" ("*souffrance morale*") of both characters and readers.[20] The moral dimension of Russian Realism encourages, according to de Vogué, a feeling of charity and pity in readers: "Realism becomes odious when it ceases to be charitable" ("*Le réalisme devient odieux dès qu'il cesse d'être charitable*").[21] For de Vogüé, the characters that populate Russian literature—especially those in Dostoevsky and Tolstoy—are meant to inspire "that mystical feeling of compassion towards an unfortunate being" ("*cet état mystique de compassion près d'un être malheureux*").[22]

However, it is precisely the language of moral suffering that de Vogüé finds nearly impossible to translate. Over and over again, as he attempts to display the inner life of fictional characters, the French scholar questions the very possibility of cross-cultural understanding. In the context of Gorky, '*toska*' becomes the impediment, just as '*poshlost*' did for Nabokov in his book on Gogol.[23] De Vogüé recognises that '*toska*'—roughly translated as 'anguish' or 'yearning'—is the "national variety of the oldest human evil" ("*variété nationale du plus vieux mal humain*"), while emphasising its untranslatability.[24] Translating into French, he repeatedly italicises 'toska', revelling in its foreignness: "But where does this *toska* come from?" ("*Mais d'où vient cette* toska?"); "Suddenly *toska*, like a bullet to the head" ("*Tout de suite la* toska, *comme une balle dans le front*").[25] In Dostoevsky and Tolstoy, the verbal culprit is 'otchaianie' : "that state of mind for which I try in vain to find an equivalent into French" ("*cet état de coeur et d'esprit pour lequel je m'efforce vainement de trouver un equivalent dans notre langue*").[26] Noting that the

17 De Vogüé, *Roman russe*, p. xxxix.

18 Th. Dostoievsky, *Souvenirs de la Maison des Morts*, trans. by M. Neyroud (Paris: Librarie Plon, 1886), pp. i-xvi (p. viii).

19 *La Mort*, ed. by M. E. Halpérine (Paris: Librairie Académique Didier, 1886), pp. i-viii (p. vii).

20 Ivan Tourgéneff, *Mémoires d'un Seigneur Russe*, trans. by Ernest Charrière (Paris: Librarie Hachette, 1883), pp. v-xix (p. xi).

21 De Vogüé, *Roman russe*, p. 45. De Vogüé also accuses Gustave Flaubert of having forgotten that moral infirmity, just like physical infirmity, "is worthy of compassion" ("*est digne de compassion*") (p. xxxiii).

22 Ibid., p. 25; de Vogüé, *Russian Novel*, p. 246.

23 Vladimir Nabokov, *Nikolai Gogol* (New York: New Directions, 1961), pp. 63–64.

24 Eugène-Melchior de Vogüé, 'Maxime Gorky: L'oeuvre and l'homme', *Revue des Deux Mondes*, 4:3 (1901), 660–95 (p. 676).

25 Ibid.

26 De Vogüé, *Roman russe*, p. 227; de Vogüé, *Russian Novel*, p. 225.

term generally means 'despair' (*désespoir*), de Vogüé complains that this word too is 'untranslatable' (*intraduisible*) and that:

> [...] the dictionary is a poor money changer at any time, and never gives the exact value, handing over the foreign coins in return for yours without reference to their own intrinsic fiscal value. As a matter of fact, to give that word its true value, one ought to smelt down twenty others, such as: despair, fatalism, savagery, asceticism and what not. [...] It is the allurement and the terror of the country where reigns sheer madness, where the excesses of life are preferred, where everything can be borne except the average lot, where the people, for choice, desire annihilation rather than moderation. Poor Russia![27]

De Vogüé finds that the Russians have much more complex ways, "a whole rich vocabulary" ("*tout un riche vocabulaire*"), to express "the nausea on days after drinking" ("*la nausée des lendemains d'ivresse*"), for which the French only have the vulgar "j'ai le mal aux cheveux" (literally 'my hair hurts').[28] Underlying de Vogüé's dwelling on the untranslatability of such forms of suffering as depression, melancholy, and even hangovers is the fear that compassion—the hallmark of Russian Realism—might be beyond French audiences.[29]

This spectre of untranslatability is woven through *Le Roman russe*, giving rise to larger problems. "In truth, I am in despair when I think of trying to explain these people to our own" ("*En verité, le désespoir me prend quand j'essaye de faire comprendre ce monde au nôtre*") de Vogüé laments, referring to Dostoevsky's characters.[30] The critic's 'despair', however, functions to preserve the foreignness of the original texts that is lost in so many translations of the period. In an essay on the analytics of translation, French translation theorist Antoine Berman describes translation as "the trial of the foreign" ("*l'épreuve de l'étranger*"), where 'the foreign' is a manifestation of cultural otherness that can be either domesticated or preserved in translation.[31] Advocating for a foreignising approach—for "open[ing] up the foreign work to us in its utter

---

27 De Vogüé, *Roman russe*, pp. 291–92; de Vogüé, *Russian Novel*, pp. 281–82. Anna Gichkina, in her monograph on de Vogüé, notes that the French critic was the first specialist on Russia to try to explain the emotion. She finds in his journals evidence that he explained *'otchaianie'* to himself as "a consecration of oneself to ennui," the refined pleasure of combating oneself. See Anna Gichkina, *Eugène-Melchior de Vogüé*, p. 83.

28 De Vogüé, 'Maxime Gorky,' p. 679.

29 Hemmings goes so far as to suggest that de Vogüé was fooling himself in his search to find compassion in Tolstoy, who "never himself sheds tears over the fate of his characters" (*Russian Novel in France*, p. 46).

30 De Vogüé, *Roman russe*, p. 238; de Vogüé, *Russian Novel*, p. 235.

31 Antoine Berman, 'Translation and the Trials of the Foreign' in *The Translation Studies Reader*, ed. by Lawrence Venuti (London and New York: Routledge, 2012), pp. 240–53 (p. 240).

foreignness"—Berman argues that in the Western tradition, the individual essence of foreign texts is "radically repressed".[32]

I would suggest that de Vogüé, in calling attention to the untranslatable, is effectively exposing the foreign.[33] Adopting in his essays all the strategies that, according to Berman, foreignising translators would use—italicisations, footnotes, in-text commentary—de Vogüé disturbs the deceptively fluid currents of cross-cultural transmissions.[34] Anticipating Berman and other proponents of foreignising translations in his preface to 'Trois Morts', de Vogüé addresses the violence that foreign texts should wreak on the translating language. Justifying his 'servile' translation, de Vogüé asserts: "one shouldn't hesitate to abdicate the genius of one's own language, to de-ossify it in a way, in order to adapt it to the skeleton of another language" (*"il ne faut hésiter, je crois, à abdiquer le génie de sa propre langue, à la désosser, en quelque sorte, pour l'adapter au squelette de la phrase étrangère"*).[35] In thus guiding the public's taste, de Vogüé was also responsible for popularising other translations that emphasised the foreignness of Russian literature. In 1879, he ended his admiring review of the first French translation of *War and Peace* (accomplished by Princess Irène Paskévitch) with a warning, which reads almost like an endorsement, that "no French reader, in reading these pages, could doubt that he owes them to a foreign pen" (*"nul Français, en lisant ces pages, ne pourra se douter qu'il les doit à une plume étrangère"*).[36] In 1886, de Vogüé remarked in 'Les Livres russes en France' that Halpérine-Kaminsky, in translating Turgenev's *On the Eve* (*Un Bulgar à la Veille*, 1886), had managed to

---

32 Berman, 'Translation and the Trials of the Foreign', pp. 240–41.

33 Elsewhere, de Vogüé asserts that the translator "must remain enslaved to foreign thought" (*"doit rester esclave de la pensée étrangère"*). See de Vogüé, 'Livres russes en France', p. 839.

34 De Vogüé's 1888 review of a performance of Tolstoy's 'The Power of Darkness' ('Vlast' t'my', 1886), is perhaps where his pessimism about the possibility of translation reaches its apex. In it, he laments the translation of Tolstoy's title, dialogue, idioms, and genre, reminding his readers that translations are not clothes that can be tailored to fit the same thought. See Eugène-Melchior de Vogüé, 'La Puissance des Ténèbres', *Revue des Deux Mondes*, 86 (1888), 426–50 (p. 430).

35 Léon Tolstoi, 'Trois Morts', trans. by E. M. de Vogüé, *Revue des Deux Mondes*, 52 (1882), 913–25 (p. 913). De Vogüé was occasionally resigned about the inability of the French tongue to accommodate the nuances of Russian literature. In his essay on Maksim Gorky, he promises several translated quotes from the author, only to offer the following caveat: "These quotes will only give an approximate idea of the original. I translate and our old language, with its sharp contours, is desperate when forced to render the chaotic richness, the spontaneous liberty, the nuances and the blur of the evolving idiom that each Russian writer kneads at his will" (*"Elles ne donneront qu'une idée approximative de l'original: je traduis et notre vielle langue aux contours si nets est désespérante, lorsqu'on veut lui faire rendre la richesse désordonnée, la liberté primesautière, les nuances et le flou de l'idiome en formation que chaque écrivain russe pétrit à sa guise"*). See de Vogüé, 'Maxime Gorky,' p. 673.

36 Eugène-Melchior De Vogüé, 'Essais et notices', *Revue des Deux Mondes*, 33 (1879), pp. 972–74.

"impart to our language a little of the master stylist's magic" (*"faire passer dans notre langue un peu de la magie du maître styliste"*).[37] And in his preface to Charles Neyroud's translation of Dostoevsky's *Notes from the House of the Dead*, de Vogüé muses that:

> There is one means of taming the public and we use it all too frequently: that of strangling the translations of foreign works in order to 'adapt' them to our tastes. We have ruthlessly discarded several of these helpful fantasies and awaited a version of *Notes from the House of the Dead* that is at least a faithful version of the Russian text.[38]

De Vogüé's exaggerated angst about untranslatability in *The Russian Novel* could be read as a performance of his own mastery of Russian. But, taken together with his reviews, his non-fiction essays propose that Russian literature should challenge its readers. The foreignisation model in general, and the foreignisation of moral suffering in particular, requires that French readers not only be aware of their linguistic distance from Russian texts, but also gauge their own emotional capacity to respond to the characters in those texts. I turn to this aspect of transculturation next.

Translation and Compassion

In the face of all this foreignness, which he admirably embraces, de Vogüé resolves to foster understanding for characters whose moral/spiritual constitution defies translation. His individual translations, while preserving the foreignness outlined above, deviate from their originals when they insist upon the humanity of those who might otherwise be too foreign for pity. In 'Trois Morts', this impulse towards compassion manifests itself in contrasting references to the same character: where Tolstoy drily refers to "the invalid" (*"bol'noi"*), de Vogüé writes *"l'homme"* ("the man").[39] When he translates an excerpt from *Notes from the House of the Dead*, the same impulse has de Vogüé report that a prisoner "was *atoning* in prison for an irreparable crime" ("expiait *en Sibérie un crime irremissible*") while Dostoevsky's narrator says merely that he was sent to Siberia "for an extremely important crime" ("за чрезвычайно важное преступление").[40] And when Raskolnikov tells Sonya that he is bowing down before "human suffering" ("страдание человеческое"),

37 De Vogüé, 'Livres russes en France', p. 840.

38 Dostoievsky, *Souvenirs de la Maison des Morts*, p. xiv.

39 Tolstoi, 'Trois morts', p. 920; Lev Tolstoi, *Polnoe sobranie sochinenii*, 90 vols (Moscow: Gosudarstvennoe Izdatel'stvo 'Khudozhestvennaia Literatura,' 1928–1964), V (1931), p. 59.

40 De Vogüé, *Roman russe*, p. 229, my emphasis; F. M. Dostoevskii, *Polnoe sobranie sochinenii*, 30 vols (Leningrad: Nauka, 1972–1990), IV (1972), p. 33.

de Vogüé has him prostrate himself before "the suffering of humanity" ("*la souffrance de l'humanité*").[41] I would argue that in each of these cases, de Vogüé is accomplishing one of the goals that he sets out in *The Russian Novel*: to restore the etymological meaning of compassion, which he defines as "to suffer with and through another" ("*souffrir avec and par un autre*").[42] While in theory de Vogüé celebrated the Russian national forms of moral suffering—so foreign to Western audiences—in practice he needed to make such forms globally available for empathy. The tension between de Vogüé's theoretical interest in foreignisation and his practical turn to what one might call 'emotional domestication' reaches its apex in the Dostoevsky chapter. De Vogüé's approach for most of *Le Roman russe* is thoroughly estranging—he mulls over 'otchaianie', fumbles while trying to explain Dostoevsky's characters, and struggles with Dostoevsky's "terrible realism" ("*réalisme terrible*")[43]—but in the final pages the French critic finds himself compelled to take a different approach. In his culminating meditations on the author, he invokes a claim Dostoevsky made once to him: "We are blessed with all the talents of the whole world—even more—that of Russia; therefore we are able to understand you, but you are incapable of understanding us" ("*Nous avons le génie de tous les peuples et en plus le génie russe; donc nous pouvons vous comprendre et vous ne pouvez nous comprendre*"). Disgruntled and challenged by what he sees as Dostoevsky's arguments in favour of the supremacy of the Russian race, de Vogüé accepts the challenge: "May his shade forgive me, for I am now going to show the contrary" ("*Que sa mémoire me pardonne; j'essaye aujourd'hui de lui prouver le contraire*").[44] He thus implies that none of the preceding pages—in which he discusses the novels, *otchaianie*, and Dostoevsky's personality—were part of his project to 'understand' the Russian author. Instead, he offers in his last five pages descriptions of Dostoevsky's two funerals: the private one in the author's home and the public procession in the streets of Saint Petersburg. Structurally, de Vogüé's essay implies that Dostoevsky is only interpretable—and therefore translatable—in death.[45]

---

41 Dostoevskii, *Polnoe sobranie sochinenii*, VI (1973), p. 246; de Vogüé, *Roman russe*, p. 251.

42 De Vogüé, *Russian Novel*, p. 246; de Vogüé, *Roman russe*, p. 250. Compassion is also what drives de Vogüé's critical evaluations. He finds that Nikolai Levin's death in *Anna Karenina* is far more touching than the death of Ivan Il'ich because Konstantin Levin, serving as intermediary, promotes readers who "think and tremble with him" ("*pense et tremble avec lui*"). See de Vogüé, 'Livres russes en France', p. 330.

43 De Vogüé, *Roman russe*, p. 230; de Vogüé, *Russian Novel*, p. 228.

44 De Vogüé, *Roman russe*, p. 270; de Vogüé, *Russian Novel*, p. 263.

45 And in fact, there is a hint of this assumption in the Tolstoy essay too, when de Vogüé declares that writing about the living author is too difficult: "How can one write of greatness before the last pinch of dust has rotted away, or before the individual has been transformed into an abstract image [...]? It is difficult; but I see him before me so great that I believe him dead". De Vogüé, *Russian Novel*, p. 273.

I would suggest that in the final paragraphs of de Vogüé's study, the 'foreign body' of literature is literalised, and Dostoevsky's corpse becomes the text that needs to be translated. Confronted by Dostoevsky's dead body, de Vogüé struggles to judge the author's "moral value" (*"valeur morale"*) just as he struggled to find the *'valeur morale'* of *Crime and Punishment*.[46] However, in the context of the funerals, de Vogüé is able to make the dead Dostoevsky—that is, the moral suffering he represents—translatable in two ways. First, unconsciously or not, he draws on a pre-eighteenth-century definition of 'translation' that existed in both English and French. The word 'translation'—from the Latin 'translatio' ('to carry across')—referred to the transfer of bodies between two sites, and usually implied the remains or relics of a saint being transferred from one monastery or church to another.[47] I turn to this medieval definition of translation partly because Dostoevsky—as described by de Vogüé—is characterised as a secular saint: de Vogüé refers to the author's final "apotheosis" (*"apotheose"*), the mourners take the flowers alongside his body as "relics" (*"reliques"*), and when the lights sputter and go out in the room where the corpse is being visited, "there only remained the uncertain light given by the small lamp hanging before the holy images of the Saints" (*"il ne resta que la lumière de la petite lampe appendue devant les images saintes"*).[48] Carried like a saint to his place of burial, Dostoevsky is, in de Vogüé's conception, translated more easily than his oeuvre ever could be.

Secondly, de Vogüé uses both funerals to emphasise the pity that the Russian author inspired from his public: "He had spent himself for this people and evoked in them feelings of pity [...]" (*"Il avait épanché sur ce people et réveillé en lui de la pitié* [...]").[49] As if afraid that he himself will not be able to muster this pity and charity in himself—and therefore, in his own eyes, fail Dostoevsky's challenge—de Vogüé turns, in his final lines, from literary criticism to translation: "I could find no other words of farewell than those the student addressed to the young girl, words which summed up Dostoyevsky's faith and now come back to him, 'It is not before thee I kneel—I prostrate myself before the sufferings of all humanity'" (*"Je ne trouvai d'autre adieu que les mots de l'étudiant à la pauvre fille, les mots qui résumaient toute la foi de Dostoïevsky et devaient lui revenir: 'Ce n'est pas devant toi que je m'incline; je me prosterne devant toute la souffrance de l'humanité'"*).[50] In this case, de Vogüé merges to such an extent with a fictional

---

46 De Vogüé, *Roman russe*, p. 277.

47 Cecilia Feilla, who writes about this particular meaning in the letters of Abelard and Héloïse, points out that the saint's body was often accompanied by an official 'letter of translation'. See Cecilia Feilla, 'Translating Communities: The Institutional Epilogue to the Letters of Abelard and Heloise', *The Yale Journal of Criticism* 16.2 (2003), 363–79.

48 De Vogüé, *Roman russe*, pp. 273–74; de Vogüé, *Russian Novel*, pp. 265–66.

49 De Vogüé, *Roman russe*, p. 277; de Vogüé, *Russian Novel*, p. 269.

50 De Vogüé, *Roman russe*, p. 277; de Vogüé, *Russian Novel*, p. 270.

character that he becomes a radical example of Lawrence Venuti's "invisible" translator, completely abandoning his role of mediator.[51] Moreover, borrowing Raskolnikov's words, and using his own translation rather than Derély's more literal rendering, de Vogüé universalises Dostoevsky's suffering. His linguistic and contextual translation of *Crime and Punishment* provides the ultimate means of judging Dostoevsky, of pitying him, and, therefore, of understanding him. Translation, in other words, facilitated compassion where criticism had failed.

Conclusion

As de Vogüé's fellow critic and translator, Téodor de Wyzewa, noted in 1887, "De Vogüé profoundly sensed the French public's unconscious desire for a restoration of spiritual life".[52] Thanks to his social standing, linguistic skill, and travel experiences, de Vogüé's restoration of spiritual life was most famously achieved in the realm of literary criticism. "With *The Russian Novel,*" Gichkina writes, "the richness of the Russian literary tradition was, for the first time, presented to the French public in a way that was both accessible and captivating".[53] The appearance of de Vogüé's collection of essays in 1886, which had been tantalisingly heralded for the preceding three years in the *Revue des Deux Mondes* and the *Revue bleue,* and which offered quality translations of key passages in Russian literature, spawned a Russian fever. Gichkina cites the example of *War and Peace,* which had sold 550 copies within five years of its first French translation in 1874. After de Vogüé's study of Tolstoy was published in 1884, however, over two thousand copies of the same translation were printed for each of the next four years.[54] *The Russian Novel* itself received rave reviews, one hailing it as "a masterpiece of French criticism".[55]

But the 'restoration of spiritual life' anticipated by de Vogüé was not to be accomplished through literary criticism, as influential as his essays were. From the pen of a cultural ambassador who had captured public attention through his essays and novels, de Vogüé's translations ultimately did far more than introduce the French reading public to the spectrum of Russian realist authors, and, in fact, actively contradicted his theoretical views. De Vogüé maintained that "the task of the translator is to place clear glass, invisible if possible, between our eyes and the unknown landscape" (*"le souci du traducteur doit être d'interposer une vitre*

51 See Lawrence Venuti, *The Translator's Invisibility* (London: Routledge, 1995), pp. 1–34.

52 Téodor de Wyzewa, 'Les Russes, notes', *La Revue Indépendante*, 2 (1887), 65–91 (p. 69).

53 Gichkina, *Eugène-Melchior de Vogüé*, p. 174.

54 Ibid., p. 166.

55 André Hallays, '*Le Roman Russe* par le vicomte E.-M. de Vogüé', *Journal des débats politiques et littéraires*, Sept. (1886), p. 3. See Gichkina, *Eugène-Melchior de Vogüé*, pp. 177–81, for a more complete summation of reviews garnered by *The Russian Novel.*

limpide, invisible s'il se peut, entre nos yeux et le paysage inconnu").[56] It has been my contention that de Vogüé revelled in the blurriness of this window, highlighting the impossibility of understanding the Russian character. As a practising translator, however, he promoted compassion as a means of overriding that impossibility. As a literary critic and amateur translation theorist, he objected that the word 'otchaianie' is untranslatable. As the translator of 'Three Deaths', however, he did translate the term—as "despair" ("*désespoir*"), apparently finding it adequate for capturing pathos.[57] And as a critic, he applauded the French translations produced by Halpérine-Kaminsky, Morice, and Derély. But as an active translator, he proffered his own versions of key passages from Russian novels. When France, and on its heels Western Europe, suddenly became infatuated with the nineteenth-century Russian novel, it was because de Vogüé had glorified literary suffering. But it was also because his translations and metatextual commentaries gave French readers the language to empathise with that suffering.

56 De Vogüé, 'Livres russes en France', p. 840.
57 Tolstoi, *Sobranie sochinenii*, V, p. 61; Tolstoi, 'Trois morts', p. 921.

Germany

Mann's View of Dostoevsky and Tolstoy in Times of War and Peace: *Doctor Faustus* (1947)[1]

Elizaveta Sokolova

Russian culture was truly meaningful to Thomas Mann (1875–1955), the celebrated German writer (laureate of the 1929 Nobel Prize for Literature), who lived in exile in the USA from September 1938 onwards, and who undoubtedly belonged to Pascale Casanova's list of "great cosmopolitan intermediaries" who determine the world literary canon and its development in their time.[2] Mann significantly "surpassed the other German writers of his generation" in "the fullness of his spiritual connections with Russian literature".[3] Reflections of the creative thought and biographies of many Russian writers are clearly distinguishable in his work, to the extent that some scholars emphasise the essential and even 'salvific' role of Russian literature in Mann's own development as a great writer of the twentieth century, "a holy literature indeed".[4]

1 Some elements of this article previously appeared in Russian in E. V. Sokolova, '"Povorot k Dostoevskomu" u Tomasa Manna: "Doktor Faustus" (1947)', in *Vestnik kulturologii*, 4: 99 (2021), 96–113, https://doi.org/10.31249/hoc/2021.04.06.

2 Pascale Casanova, *The World Republic of Letters*, trans. by Malcolm DeBevoise (Cambridge, MA: Harvard University Press, 2004), p. 21.

3 Tamara Motyleva, *Tomas Mann i russkaia literatura* (Moscow: Znanie, 1975), p. 6. Here and below, unless otherwise indicated, all translations into English from Russian and German are my own.

4 "[...] aus die anbetungswürdige russische Literatur, die so recht eigentlich die heilige Literatur darstellt [...]": Thomas Mann, *Gesammelte Werke*, 12 vols (Berlin: Aufbau-Verlag, 1955), IX, p. 232. See also Mann, XI, p. 575. On the 'salvific' role of Russian literature for Mann see Aleksei Zherebin, 'Tomas Mann i "Iunosheskii mif russkoi literatury"', in *Izvestiia Rossiiskoi Akademii Nauk. Seriia literatury i iazyka*, 72 (2013), 45–51.

 https://doi.org/10.11647/OBP.0340.06

Mann's acquaintance with Russian literature began in his early youth, made possible by the increasingly positive reception of Russian literature in Germany in the 1880s. He read Russian authors in German translations, which had just begun proliferating.[5] Certain Russian writers contributed significantly to this trend, including the bilingual Karolina Pavlova (1807–93), one of the first translators of nineteenth-century Russian literature into German; Ivan Turgenev (1818–83), who called Germany his "second homeland",[6] and later, in the early twentieth century, Dmitri Merezhkovskii (1865–1941), a noted Russian philosopher who settled in Paris in 1920, where he remained an important Russian literary influence abroad, a connoisseur and a populariser of Russian thought in Europe.[7] Among the first translators of Turgenev, Dostoevsky, and Tolstoy into German, Jürgen Lehmann singles out Wilhelm Wolfsohn (1820–65), who "facilitated" the reception of Russian literature for readers brought up on German classical philosophy and aesthetics.[8] Lehmann also acknowledges translations by Friedrich von Bodenstedt (1819–92)—who produced an edition of Turgenev's short stories—although he considers von Bodenstedt less gifted than Wolfsohn.[9] From the mid-1880s, translators of Russian literature into German increased rapidly in number, thus we cannot always determine whose translations introduced Mann to a specific text. He evidently read Tolstoy and Turgenev in different translations. Tolstoy's works, for example, were translated by Raphael Löwenfeld, August Scholz, and Frida Rubiner.[10] Mann is known to have read *The Brothers Karamazov* (*Brat'ia Karamazovy*, 1880) in Karl Nötzel's translation, and Dostoevsky's remaining novels mostly in Hermann Röll's versions.[11] He may also have been familiar with other translations including *Raskolnikow* (1882), a version of *Crime and Punishment* (*Prestuplenie i nakazanie*, 1866) by Wilhelm Henckel (1825–1910).[12] This was the very first translation of a Dostoevsky novel in Western Europe, preceding Victor Derély's 1884 French *Le Crime et le châtiment* by two years. Henckel's translations may also have introduced Mann to the work of Anton Chekhov.

5 Jürgen Lehmann, *Russische Literatur in Deutschland* (Frankfurt: Metzler, 2015), pp. 63–64.

6 Lehmann, *Russische Literatur*, pp. 31–34. On Turgenev's influence on Mann see, for example, Georg Wenzel, 'Ivan Sergeevič Turgenev in Aufzeichnungen Thomas Manns', in *Zeitschrift für Slawistik*, 28 (1983), 889–914; Horst-Jürgen Gerigk, 'Turgenjew unterwegs zum Zauberberg', in *Thomas Mann Jahrbuch*, 8 (1995), 53–69.

7 Lehmann, *Russische Literatur*, p. 65.

8 Ibid., p. 40.

9 Ivan Turgenev, *Erzählungen*, 2 vols, trans. by Friedrich von Bodenstedt (München: Rieger'sche Unversitätsbuchhandlung, 1864–65).

10 L. N. *Tolstoj, Sämtliche Werke*, 33 vols, trans. by R. Löwenfeld (Leipzig: Diederichs, 1901–07); Lehmann, *Russische Literatur*, p. 65.

11 Michael Wegner, 'Zu den Teufelsgestalten bei Thomas Mann und Fedor Dostojewski', in *Dostojewski Studies*, 9 (1988), 34–43 (pp. 35–36).

12 Fjodor Dostojewski, *Raskolnikow*, 3 vols, trans. by Wilhelm Henckel (Leipzig: Wilhelm Friedrich, 1882).

Russian literature occupies an important place in Mann's own critical writings. He wrote three essays on Tolstoy;[13] one on Dostoevsky,[14] in which he compares the latter with Nietzsche; and another on Chekhov, as its title clarifies (*Versuch über Tschekhov*, 1954).[15] He was well acquainted with Merezhkovskii's *Tolstoy and Dostoevsky* (*Lev Tolstoi i Dostoevskii*, 1901), published in Berlin in 1919 in Carl von Gütschow's German translation.[16] Mann owed Merezhkovskii not only the idea of contrasting Tolstoy (as a "seer of the flesh") with the "seer of the spirit" Dostoevsky, but also the notion that "the greater are an artist's creative powers, the more precisely he is able to summon the contents of his imagination into both the reality of his life and that of his works".[17] This informed Mann's admiration for Tolstoy as the embodiment of such powers. We should also mention Maksim Gorky, whose *Memories of Leo Nikolaevich Tolstoy* (*Vospominaniia o L've Nikolaeviche Tolstom*, 1919), according to Mann, his best book,[18] served the latter as a reliable source of information about the life and personality of the "great writer of the Russian lands".[19] The first critical views on Mann's assessments of Russian literature and his expression of Russian motifs in his work were offered by Alois Hofmann in German or Tamara Motyleva in Russian.[20] More recently, Aleksei Zherebin also lends profound insight into Mann's perception of Russian literature as a whole.[21] Intertextual connections with Russian literature in Mann's work have been studied globally, showing that, while the universe of Mann's Russian influences accommodated numerous writers, Tolstoy and Dostoevsky were crucial among them.[22]

Despite his own "rather sceptical attitude" towards Tolstoy's moralising and to some of his pedagogical ideas, Thomas Mann always found in his work "the

---

13 Mann, *Gesammelte Werke*, X, *Goethe und Tolstoi. Fragmente zur Problem der Humanität*, pp. 157–73; *Anna Karenina. Einleitung zu einer ameikanischen Ausgabe von Leo Tolstoi*, pp. 274–92; XI, *Tolstoi. Zur Jahrhundertfeier seiner Geburt*, pp. 185–90.

14 Mann, X, *Dostojewski—mit Maszen*, pp. 617–35.

15 Mann, XI, *Versuch über Tschekhov*, pp. 311–40.

16 Dmitri Mereschkowski, *Tolstoi und Dostojewski. Leben—Schaffen—Religion* (Berlin: K. Voegel, 1919).

17 Aleksei Zherebin, 'Nemetsko-russkaia utopiia Tomasa Manna ("Gete i Tolstoi")', in *Novyi filologicheskii vestnik*, 48 (2019), 273–81 (p. 279).

18 'Maxim Gorki hat nach Tolstoi's Tode ein kleines Buch der Erinnerungen an ihn veröffentlicht–sein bestes Buch, wenn ich urteilen darf', from Mann, X, *Goethe und Tolstoi*, p. 162.

19 Mann, X, *Dostoewski—mit Maszen*, p. 618.

20 Alois Hofman, *Thomas Mann und die Welt der Russischen Literatur* (Berlin: Akademie Verlag, 1967); Motyleva, *Tomas Mann*.

21 Aleksei Zherebin, *Interpretatsiia literaturnogo proizvedeniia v inokul'turnom kontekste* (Sankt-Peterburg: Knizhnyi Dom, 2013; 'Nemetsko-russkaia utopiia...' (2019); 'Tomas Mann i "Iunosheskii mif russkoi literatury"' (2013).

22 Georgy Fridlender, '"Doktor Faustus" T. Manna i "Besy" Dostoevskogo', in *Dostoevskii. Materialy i issledovaniia*, 14 (1997), 3–16; Motyleva, *Tomas Mann*; Lehmann, *Russische Literatur*, pp. 111–29.

highest example of epic art".[23] While working on *Buddenbrooks* (1897–1901), he kept Tolstoy's portrait on his desk as a "mythical mentor" in the genre of the epic.[24] Some scholars identify Tolstoyan traits in Leo Naphta, the mystically inclined Jesuit in Mann's *The Magic Mountain* (*Der Zauberberg*, 1924), who preaches "Byzantine-Asian anarchist despotism" and hence opposes the Italian scholar Lodovico Settembrini with his codes of "classical" European humanism.[25] Solomon Apt, the Russian translator of Mann's *Joseph and His Brothers* (*Joseph und seine Brüder*, 1933–43) and *Doctor Faustus* (*Doktor Faustus*, 1947), likens Tolstoy to Mynheer Peeperkorn, another *Magic Mountain* character who represents Mann's "ideal of a vital solar unconsciousness" and an alternative way of life for the novel's protagonist, Hans Castorp.[26] Apt identifies the kinship between the majestic Dutchman Peeperkorn and Tolstoy in an episode from the last chapter of Mann's novel, where Peeperkorn urges his listeners to look at the sky, pointing out a soaring eagle. "'*Jupiters Vogel*' [Jupiter's bird], says Peeperkorn, 'flies high, sees wide and pursues its natural prey [...]'".[27] Apt finds a corresponding episode from Tolstoy's life in Gorky's *Memories of Leo Nikolaevich Tolstoy* (*Vospominaniia o L've Nikolaeviche Tolstom*, 1919), arguing that the symbolism of the eagle shows the significance of Tolstoy's personality to Mann.[28] Peeperkorn seems to overshadow both Settembrini and Naphta in their "fighting for the soul" of the future (in the person of Castorp) by "the very fact of his being there, the inexplicable magic of his life force, victorious naturalness and integrity".[29] Almost the same could have been written by Mann about Tolstoy, Apt insists.[30] Describing the set of tropes to which Mann "confines his stylised image of Tolstoy", Zherebin also notes "Herculean strength", "unrestrained sensuality"

---

23 Solomon Apt, *Nad stranitsami Tomasa Manna* (Moscow: Sovetskii Pisatel, 1980), p. 118.

24 Solomon Apt, *Tomas Mann: Biografiia* (Moscow: Molodaia gvardiia, 1972), p. 118.

25 Lehmann, *Russische Literatur*, p. 117.

26 Igor Ebanoidze, 'Tomas Mann', in *Istoriia literatury Germanii XX veka*, 2 vols (Moscow: IMLI RAN, 2016-), I [Part 2] (2018), pp. 17–55 (p. 44).

27 Mann, II, *Der Zauberberg*, p. 838: "Er kreist gerade über uns im Blauen, schwebt ohne Flügelschlag in grossartige Höhe zu unseren—und späht gewiss aus seinen mächtigen, weitsichtigen Augen unter den vortretenden Brauenknochen—Der Adler, meine Herrschaften, Jupiters Vogel, der König seines Geschlechtes, der Leu der Lüfte!"

28 Apt, *Nad stranitsami Tomasa Manna*, p. 120.

29 Ibid., p. 121.

30 Illustrating Mann's attitude towards Tolstoy, Apt also quotes the author's own words, uttered, according to Mann's daughter Erica, on 2 August 1914, after he learned of the outbreak of World War I: "It's a strange thing, but if the old man were still alive—he would not have to do anything, just be in the world, just be in Yasnaya Polyana—and the disaster would not have happened, would not have dared to happen" (ibid., p. 123).

and "wisdom of the ancient sorcerer", bestowed by "the mysterious connection of a child of nature with life in general" stimulating "mystical awe".[31]

At the same time, Mann's attitude towards Tolstoy was not unambiguous. In his article 'Tolstoy: On the Centenary of His Birth' ('Tolstoi. Zur Jahrhundertfeier seiner Geburt', 1928),[32] Mann portrayed the Russian writer as "an ally in his [Mann's] own struggle against irrationalism, [...] that ideological dope having intoxicated the whole of Europe while making Germany more and more defenceless before the Nazis".[33] But in the early 1930s, in the second version of his essay 'Goethe and Tolstoy', "*der grosse Dichter des Russenlandes*" ("the great writer of the Russian lands") was clearly opposed to the idealised figure of Johann Wolfgang von Goethe.[34] According to Mann, the latter had successfully completed the synthesis of nature and spirit in his life and work, and therefore still remains a true educator of the German nation, leading it towards humanity. In contrast, Tolstoy, as a native of the "element of Sarmatian savagery", failed in a similar task.[35] Apt emphasises that Mann, though admiring Tolstoy's vitality and power, questioned his spirituality. The German writer seems to be unable to completely overcome a deep inner prejudice against what he saw as Tolstoy's alignment with the physical in the conflict of "vitality" and "spirit", writing: "What a blessed life! But so tragically, even tragicomically, blessed with power not spirit".[36]

Precisely this antithesis underlies the distinction which Mann perceived between Tolstoy and Dostoevsky. In 'Dostoevsky—with Moderation' ('Dostojewski—mit Maszen', 1945–46) Mann opposes one dyad, Goethe and Tolstoy, to another pair—Nietzsche and Dostoevsky—in analogy to health (both physical and spiritual) versus illness.[37] In other words, the Tolstoy-Dostoevsky contrast embodies for Mann the antithesis of spirituality to the natural creative gift (like the contrast between sickness and wellness). This opposition is central for *Doctor Faustus*, where the title character Adrian Leverkühn personifies the problematic relationship between genius and illness in the historical context of the two wars waged by Germany against the rest of the world. At the same time, Leverkühn illustrates how the "integral ideal of an artist of genius and a humanist intellectual" can split into antinomic pairs—"spirit and life, life and art, art and spirit".[38]

31 Zherebin, 'Nemetsko-russkaia utopiia...', p. 275.
32 Mann, XI, *Tolstoi. Zur Jahrhundertfeier seiner Geburt*, pp. 185–90.
33 Apt, *Nad stranitsami Tomasa Manna*, p. 144.
34 Mann, X, *Goethe und Tolstoi*, p. 162
35 Ibid., p. 230.
36 Mann, XI, *Tolstoi. Zur Jahrhundertfeier seiner Geburt*, p. 189.
37 Mann, X, *Dostojewski—mit Maszen*, p. 617.
38 Ebanoidze, 'Tomas Mann', p. 51.

Unsurprisingly, therefore, while working on *Doctor Faustus* (May 1943-January 1947)[39]—including the last two years of World War II—Mann admitted his own "decisive preponderance of interest in Dostoevsky's grotesque-apocalyptic world of suffering" over "a usually deeper attraction to Tolstoy's epic gift".[40] The correlation between crises in world history and Mann's interest in Dostoevsky was already revealed by many authors. Georgii Fridlender points out Mann's turn toward Dostoevsky during World Wars I and II,[41] while Ekaterina Barinova identifies three such periods: the 1890s and the First and Second World Wars.[42] Mann studied Dostoevsky's novels between 1938 and 1943, mainly reading the 1921 twenty-five volume edition of his collected works in German.[43] In his diaries and letters, he mentions repeatedly "reading" and "re-reading" *Uncle's Dream* (*Diadiushkin son*, 1859), *The Eternal Husband* (*Vechnyi muzh*, 1870), *The House of the Dead* (*Zapiski iz mertvogo doma*, 1862), *Notes from Underground* (*Zapiski iz podpol'ia*, 1864), *The Village of Stepanchikovo* (*Selo Stepanchikovo i ego obitateli*, 1859), *The Gambler* (*Igrok*, 1867), *The Idiot* (*Idiot*, 1869), *Crime and Punishment*, *Demons* (*Besy*, 1872), and *The Brothers Karamazov*.[44]

The edition of Dostoevsky which Mann was reading, with an introductory article by Stefan Zweig, includes all Dostoevsky's novels in German translations by Karl Nötzel (*The Brothers Karamazov*) and Hermann Röll (the remaining novels). Thus we know that Mann's *Doctor Faustus* was influenced by the style of Karl Nötzel (1870–1945), author of numerous books on the history of Russian literature and translator of Tolstoy, Gogol, and Nikolai Leskov, as well as Dostoevsky. Michael Wegner postulates that in 1938 Mann was already deeply impressed by the scene from Chapter IX of Book Eleven of *The Brothers Karamazov*, where the dialogue between Ivan Karamazov and the devil occurs; later, he repeatedly re-read it.[45]

In his major essay *The Story of a Novel: The Genesis of Doctor Faustus* (*Die Entstehung des Doktor Faustus. Roman eines Romans*, 1949),[46] Mann mentions having read only *The Brothers Karamazov*, *Uncle's Dream* and *The House of the Dead* by that time.[47] Besides the war, a practical reason had arisen for Mann to re-read Dostoevsky in the mid-1940s: the American publisher Dial Press had invited

39 Mann, XII, *Die Entstehung des Doktor Faustus*, p. 333.

40 Ibid., p. 261.

41 Georgy Fridlender, '"Doktor Faustus" T. Manna i "Besy" Dostoevskogo', in *Dostoevskii. Materialy i issledovaniia*, 14 (1997), 3–16 (p. 5).

42 Ekaterina Barinova, *'Russkie kontsepty' v tvorchestve Tomasa Manna v 1890–1920-kh godakh* (unpublished doctoral thesis, University of Nizhnii Novgorod, 2007), p. 11.

43 Fjodor Michailowitsch Dostojewski, *Sämtliche Romane und Novellen*, 25 vols, trans. by Hermann Röll and Karl Nötzel (Leipzig: Insel, 1921).

44 Lehmann, *Russische Literatur*, pp. 117–18; Wegner, 'Zu den Teufelsgestalten bei Thomas Mann', 35.

45 Wegner, 'Zu den Teufelsgestalten bei Thomas Mann', 36.

46 Mann, XII, *Die Entstehung des Doktor Faustus*, pp. 178–335.

47 Ibid., p. 228, p. 261, p. 329.

him to write an introduction for a proposed new edition of Dostoevsky (*The Short Novels of Dostoevsky*, 1945). According to the chronology given in *The Story of a Novel*, Mann turned to the scene with the devil from *The Brothers Karamazov* while working on Chapter XIV of *Doctor Faustus*, where the starting point of his protagonist Adrian Leverkühn's "turn towards the devil" is to be found. At the conclusion of that chapter, Mann's narrator Serenus Zeitblom expresses his confidence in Adrian's imminent departure from the Theological faculty.[48] Mann confessed that he was studying this particular scene from Dostoevsky at that time "with detached mindfulness", much as he had explored Flaubert's *Salambo* before commencing work on *Joseph and his Brothers*.[49]

Indeed, Chapter XXV of *Doctor Faustus*, which features Leverkühn's conversation with the devil, turns out to be the climax of the whole novel, where the storyline of Adrian's renunciation of God also culminates. Soon after finishing that viscerally troubling chapter on 20 February 1945,[50] Mann re-read *Uncle's Dream*.[51] But only much later, already working on the ending of his own novel, did he immerse himself in Dostoevsky's *Notes from the House of the Dead*.[52] Meanwhile, Leverkühn suffers a stroke after an unsuccessful attempt at public confession and remains depressed for the next ten years until his death (like Nietzsche in Turin). We thus find three main points in the "spirit degradation storyline" central for Mann's novel, namely its exposition (in Chapter XIV), culmination (Chapter XXV) and the denouement (in Chapter XLVII). These stages correlate with Mann's records of his "reading and rereading" of Dostoevsky's works in *The Story of a Novel*.

Another correlation is also striking: Mann wrote Chapters XIV–XXV (which chronicle Leverkühn's spiritual decline) soon after the tide turned for Germany in World War II, as the Soviet army finally started to advance westwards. Just as he was working on Chapter XIX (where Adrian's ultimately fatal contact with "the hetaera" Esmeralda takes place), several important cities surrendered to the Soviet army: Minsk, Lviv, Brest-Litovsk, the "river", which "was forced incredibly quickly", all of which Mann cites in one sentence.[53] It is notable, therefore, how much was surrendered to the "demonic forces" at exactly the "point" in *The Story of a Novel* which corresponds chronologically to Chapter XIX: as if all the debts that had not been collected in time (in previous chapters,

48 Mann, VI, *Doktor Faustus*, p. 172.

49 Mann, XII, *Die Entstehung des Doktor Faustus*, p. 228. For comparison of this scene from *The Brothers Karamazov* to the conversation with the devil from Chapter XXV of *Doctor Faustus* see, for example, Wegner, 'Zu den Teufelsgestalten bei Thomas Mann', pp. 34–43; J.N.K. Sugden, *Thomas Mann and Dostoevsky: A Study of* Doctor Faustus *in Comparison with* The Brothers Karamazov (unpublished doctoral thesis, University of Cambridge, 1982).

50 Mann, XII, *Die Entstehung des Doktor Faustus*, p. 250.

51 Ibid., p. 261.

52 Ibid., p. 329.

53 Ibid., p. 233.

where Adrian's own decline was only implied) were suddenly called in. From that point, both "declines" (that of Adrian and of Fascist Germany) develop in parallel and with increasing speed. Only two pages later, the Russians are already "near Warsaw, threatening Memel".[54] And as in Chapter XXI, Leverkühn (to the horror of the humanist Zeitblom) opposes "art" to "truth", identifying art with cold and rational cognition, thereby striking a devastating blow to the ideals of "holy Russian literature" in attacking Dostoevsky. It is no coincidence that the paragraph announcing in *The Story of a Novel* the completion of Mann's work on the "conversation with the devil" (20 February 1945) says also that the "Russians" are already thirty miles from Berlin and are gathering forces for the final blow.[55] The next paragraph mentions the Yalta Conference (the new world order) and "the end" of Germany.[56] *The End* was also the title of the article Thomas Mann wrote at that time for the American press about the German catastrophe.[57] Recovery from a catastrophe on this scale takes a lot of time, and a three-month-long pause in the work on *Doctor Faustus* followed the completion of its climactic chapter (XXV). By that time, the deadline for the introduction about Dostoevsky had arrived, and in July 1945, shortly after the celebration of the victorious Independence Day, a "chilled and tired" Mann, "issued 24 pages in 12 days" so that "in the last third of the month", having finally turned the tide of his disease, he could "return to Faustus again".[58]

'Dostoevsky—with Moderation' is the title of the article, which Mann ends by quoting his unnamed friend: "When I told a friend of my intention to provide a preface for three volumes he said laughing: 'Be careful! You will write a book about him!' I was careful", announces Mann in conclusion before returning to his own Faustus.[59] However, despite all Mann's "caution", Dostoevsky (besides Nietzsche and Schoenberg) is often suggested as a prototype for Adrian Leverkühn.[60] In the above-named article, Mann likens Nietzsche's syphilis to Dostoevsky's epilepsy and places this "holy disease" at the centre of the Russian writer's personality, in which sense, Mann's Leverkühn mirrors not only Dostoevsky but also Nietzsche.[61] Paying minimal attention to the continuity of ideas between Dostoevsky and Nietzsche, Mann still calls these two "brothers in spirit", viewing their diseases—Dostoevsky's epilepsy and Nietzsche's

54 Ibid., p. 235.

55 Ibid., p. 250.

56 Ibid., p. 251.

57 On the 'national catastrophe' of Hitlerism Mann wrote an essay 'Germany and the Germans' ('Deutschland und die Deutschen', 1945) that may be considered a revised version of the above-mentioned text. See ibid., p. 574, p. 575.

58 Ibid., p. 265.

59 Thomas Mann, 'Dostoevsky—with Moderation', in *The Short Novels of Dostoevsky. With an Introduction by Thomas Mann* (New York: Dial Press, 1945), pp. 8–51 (p. 51).

60 Lehmann, *Russische Literatur*, p. 118.

61 Mann, X, *Dostojewski—mit Maszen*, p. 618.

progressive paralysis—as almost the main reason for such brotherhood.[62] Mann speculates that each of them at least partially owed their breakthroughs into the sphere of the spirit (or at least beyond the limits of human morality) to the diseases they suffered.

Scholars quite often draw parallels between *Doctor Faustus* and Dostoevsky's *The Brothers Karamazov* while focusing on the conversations with the devil in each text.[63] Summarising their conclusions, Jürgen Lehmann notes many similarities in the demonic visions (or encounters) of Ivan Karamazov and Adrian Leverkühn.[64] In both cases, the devil is depicted as both a double of the protagonist and as an allegorical expression either of excessive intellectualism coloured by mental illness (in Dostoevsky) or of illness as a source of creative productivity (in Thomas Mann). Both Ivan Karamazov and Adrian Leverkühn seem to have been expecting the devil's visit. At first, they try to convince themselves that what they are seeing is mere delirium; each feels sick and weak while speaking with their devil. Both devils express the innermost thoughts of their interlocutors: Ivan Karamazov's doubts about the existence of God; Leverkühn's guesses about the connection between illness and creativity (much as this topic is treated in Mann's 'Dostoevski with Moderation') as well as his reflections on the essential mediocrity of modern culture and its inevitable end. The course of each conversation, each outwardly bland demonic interlocutor, and even certain details of their clothing (caps, chequered patterns) echo the end of mediocre modernity in the other text. And although Karamazov, unlike Leverkühn, does not reach a deal with his devil, the bargain made by the latter diverges from the 'classical' Faust-context: by giving up his soul to the devil (or to his illness), Adrian receives in return a "dangerous gift of guaranteed genius"[65] (within a fundamentally unoriginal culture), agreeing at the same time to the absence of love and intimacy from his life. The main difference between these two demonic conversations seems to lie in their respective degree of spirituality: Ivan Karamazov is concerned with issues of a higher order (theodicy, the limits of human freedom), while Leverkühn does not leave the field of the Apollonian and Dionysian rupture in art (remember Nietzsche again).

Doctor Faustus is compared to Dostoevsky's *Demons* almost as often as to *Brothers Karamazov*. For example, Georgii Fridlender identifies significant similarity between Leverkühn and Stavrogin, "perhaps mysteriously the most compelling character in all of world literature" according to Mann.[66] The life of Stavrogin, "the denier of the spirit", with the "fatal consequences" of his nihilism for "himself, the surrounding people and social life as a whole", unfolds

---

62 Ibid., p. 619.

63 See Sugden, *Thomas Mann and Dostoevsky*; Wegner, 'Zu den Teufelsgestalten bei Thomas Mann'.

64 Lehmann, *Russische Literatur*, pp. 119–20.

65 Ebanoidze, 'Tomas Mann', p. 50.

66 Mann, X, *Dostojewski—mit Maszen*, p. 623.

in *Demons* much as the life and the fate of Adrian Leverkühn unfold in *Doctor Faustus*.[67] And the spiritual nihilism (the resistance to the spirit) shown in both novels as "a tragic phenomenon threatening all the foundations of human life" is grounded in the loss of faith in "living life" and in God (by Dostoevsky) and in "universal values of humanism, unshakable moral principles" (by Mann).[68] Parallels may be drawn between Adrian Leverkühn and Aleksei Kirillov (who describes his own epileptic aura in *Demons*) or even the postal official Liamshin in the latter novel—particularly through the latter's style of playing music.[69] *The Adolescent* (*Podrostok,* 1975) has also been mentioned in connection with *Doctor Faustus*—by none other than Mikhail Bakhtin.[70]

Yet Dostoevsky is named just once in *Doctor Faustus,* and even then indirectly: Saul Fitelberg (in Chapter XXXVII) refers to Hugo Wolf's "perplexing" statements about him.[71] However, this is adequate proof that the Leverkühn was intended to be aware of the Russian writer but not necessarily of Arnold Schoenberg or Friedrich Nietzsche whose fates, ideas, and creative achievements were also "appropriated" by Mann's protagonist, although they are never named in the novel. But if Schoenberg's involuntary contribution to the artistic level of the novel is indirectly confirmed by Mann in the refutation at its conclusion (added later at the insistence of the composer himself), then Nietzsche's contribution remains anonymous: despite his ideological and biographical overlaps with Adrian, he is never mentioned in the novel—as if he had never existed in Leverkühn's world. Could this imply that Adrian Leverkühn plays a Nietzsche-like role in the global catastrophe described in Mann's novel? If so, it looks as if Mann had some burning questions for Nietzsche by the mid-1940s.

Salvation from "spiritual death" came to Thomas Mann in his youth via two phenomena: Nietzsche's rebellious philosophy and the "essence of the Russian soul" known to him through "holy Russian literature", as he confirmed again, already middle-aged, in his introduction to the *Russian Anthology* (*Russische Antologie*, 1921), a special issue of the German journal *Süddeutsche Monatshefte,* ((18), February 1921), which he co-edited with the translator Alexander

67 Fridlender, "Doktor Faustus" T. Manna i "Besy" Dostoevskogo', p. 16.

68 Ibid., p. 16.

69 See Elizaveta Sokolova, 'Vserossiiskaia nauchnaia konferentsiia "Teksty i konteksty": "Doktor Faustus" T. Manna (23–24 iiunia, 2021, MGU). (Obzor dokladov)', in *Sotsial'nye i gumanitarnye nauki. Otechestvennaia i zarubezhnaia literatura. Seriia 7. Literaturovedenie*, 4 (2021), 129–46 (p. 135).

70 Mikhail Bakhtin, *Problemy poetiki Dostoevskogo*, in *Sobranie sochinenii*, 7 vols (Moscow: IMLI RAN; Russkie slovari; Iazyki slavianskoi kul'tury, 1996–2010), VI (2002), p. 249 (footnote 1).

71 Mann, VI, *Doktor Faustus*, p. 549. 'Nonsense about Dostoevsky' was discovered by Thomas Mann in a letter by the Austrian composer Hugo Wolff (1860–1903), see Mann, XII, *Die Entstehung des Doktor Faustus*, p. 190.

Eliasberg.[72] But in the 1940s, the "German spirit" as a whole seemed to have come very close to death—both through fascism and by its reflection in the fate of the "German composer" Adrian Leverkühn. So, in his final great novel, *Doctor Faustus*, Mann symbolically called upon both his former "saviours"—Nietzsche and "holy Russian literature" (now personified by Dostoevsky more than anyone)—for help, or perhaps to be held accountable. And Dostoevsky came to the rescue.

72 Mann, XI, *Russische Antologie*, p. 575; Zherebin, 'Tomas Mann i "Iunosheskii mif russkoi literatury"', pp. 45–46. The selection, chosen and introduced by Mann, included works by and extracts from L. N. Tolstoy, A.N. Tolstoy, Dostoevsky, Leskov, Chekhov, Lermontov, Turgenev, Sologub, Kuzmin, and Gorky, among others. See Andre von Gronicka 'Thomas Mann and Russia', *The Germanic Review: Literature, Culture, Theory*, 20:2 (1945), 105–37 (pp. 108–10), https://doi.org/10.1080/19306962.1945.11786230.

Greece

Two Translation Periods in Dostoevsky's Canon Formation in Greece (1886–1900 and 1926–54)

Christina Karakepeli

Introduction

This chapter will examine the role of translation in Fedor Dostoevsky's reception in Greece: a largely smooth and successful process, ever since his introduction to Greek readers at the end of the nineteenth century.[1] Within the Modern Greek literary field, Dostoevsky's translations may be used as a case study for how the reception of Russian literature has developed diachronically, and how (re) translations and the agents involved in the translation process (translators, publishers, editors) have contributed to Dostoevsky's canonisation in Greek culture. I will argue here that the act of translation adds to the symbolic value of a literary work and can be a means of canonisation for a foreign author

1 In this article, I have followed Library of Congress transliteration rules for both Modern Greek and Russian with some adjustments for ease of reading. For example, Dostoevsky's name, if transliterated from its Greek version, would be radically foreignised as Phiontor Dostogiephski. I have therefore chosen to back-translate Dostoevsky from Greek as 'Dostoevskii', with minor exceptions (e.g. when transliterating the titles of articles or monographs), and to use Dostoevsky otherwise, as elsewhere in this volume. The publisher Govostēs and his firm Govostēs Editions should technically be transliterated as Gkovostēs; however, on their own international publicity materials, they used both forms inconsistently. I have therefore used 'Govostēs' in the main text and 'Gkovostēs' only in footnote references.

 https://doi.org/10.11647/OBP.0340.07

being introduced to a receiving culture.[2] Translations and retranslations can be studied as an index to measure the successful reception of a particular author within a foreign culture.[3] The success of the canonisation process depends on the power of consecration that the agents involved in the translation process hold—namely, the translators, publishers, editors, and advisors—and on the discursive strategies they adopt when presenting the work of a foreign author to the national readership.[4]

The systematic productions of (re)translations of Dostoevsky's work that continue with the same, if not higher, frequency today have sustained this author's visibility for more than a century in different socio-cultural contexts of the Modern Greek literary field. In this chapter, I will focus my analysis on two critical periods in the reception of Dostoevsky in Greece: namely, the last two decades of the nineteenth century when the writer was first translated into Greek, and the interwar and postwar period when Dostoevsky's collected works were first published in that language. To enable my assessment of the reception of Dostoevsky through translation in these historical periods, I will examine the socio-cultural factors that shaped translation and publishing choices; how the socio-cultural context affected readers' reception of Russian literature and Dostoevsky; and how publishers and translators reacted to these changes.

I will suggest that Dostoevsky was introduced to Greek readers in the late nineteenth century as an author of canonical status, and that he has retained his position at the centre of the foreign literature canon in Greece largely thanks to the work of Greek translators. Among Dostoevsky's numerous Greek translators in the nearly 150 years since he was first introduced to Greek readers in 1886, two names stand out: Alexandros Papadiamantēs (1851–1911) and Arēs Alexandrou (1922–78). Papadiamantēs, an author often characterised as the 'Greek Dostoevsky', wrote the first translation of *Crime and Punishment* into Greek in 1889. Alexandrou's translations of Dostoevsky—made in the 1940s and 1950s—are considered the best available in Greek, enjoying the status of standard editions.

---

2 See Lawrence Venuti, 'Retranslations: The Creation of Value', *Bucknell Review*, 47: 1 (2004), 25–38; Françoise Massardier-Kenney, 'Toward a Rethinking of Retranslation', *Translation Review*, 92:1 (2015), 73–85; Piet Van Poucke, 'Retranslation History and Its Contribution to Translation History: The Case of Russian-Dutch Retranslation', in *Perspectives on Retranslation*, ed. by Özlem Berk Albachten and Şehnaz Tahir Gürçağlar (New York and London: Routledge, 2019), pp. 195–211.

3 Anthony Pym, *Method for Translation History* (Manchester: St Jerome, 1998), p. 79.

4 Pascale Casanova, 'Consécration et accumulation de capital littéraire. La traduction comme échange inégal', *Actes de la recherche en sciences sociales*, 144 (Sept. 2002), 7–20 (p. 18); Pierre Bourdieu, *The Rules of Art: Genesis and Structure of the Literary Field*, trans. by Susan Emanuel (Stanford, CA: Stanford University Press, 1996), p. 51 and p. 224.

This essay will argue that Papadiamantēs's consecration and the popularity of Alexandrou's translations contributed to the canonisation of Dostoevsky in Greek culture. The work of these two translators reveals the historical importance of translation in the development of a national literary field and demonstrates how translators—especially when they are credited—create literary value by making foreign authors part of the receiving culture.

Nineteenth-century Translations of Dostoevsky

First Translations in Greek Periodicals (1886–99)

Greek translations of Russian literature were first published in Greek periodicals during the second half of the nineteenth century.[5] The main distributors of these translations were newspapers and literary journals. These newly established periodicals followed European literary trends by primarily publishing French authors and their *romans populaires*, a preference which waned as the century came to a close.[6] During the last decades of the century, critics' and readers' fatigue with French popular literature (which some saw as superficial and morally detrimental)[7] and a move from Romanticism towards Naturalism in Greek literature, created the need for a new literary model that could appeal to the late nineteenth-century Greek reader. This literary vacuum was filled by translations from 'Northern' literatures—Russian and Scandinavian writing—a trend which gained momentum in the twentieth century.[8] Production of translated Russian literature picked up from the 1880s, with the number of

---

5 See Sonia Ilinskagia, *Ē rōsikē logotechnia stēn Ellada. 19os aiōnas* [*Russian Literature in Greece. 19th century*] (Athens: Ellēnika Grammata, 2006), p. 27.

6 French *romans populaires* ('popular novels') were long novels often published in serialised form (as *feuilletons*) intended to appeal to a wide audience. Although they were classified as paraliterature, many authors of *romans populaires* are now considered canonical, like Alexandre Dumas and Victor Hugo. See Kōnstantinos G. Kasinēs, *Vivliographia tōn ellēnikōn metaphraseōn tēs xenēs logotechnias, 1801–1900* [*A Bibliography of Greek Translations of Foreign Literature, 1801–1900*] (Athens: Syllogos pros Diadosin Ōphelimōn Vivliōn, 2006).

7 The Russophile journalist Theodōros Vellianitēs, in an 1889 speech on Russian literature, referred to French literature as a "literary cholera" that had "no psychological or logical basis" (I will discuss Vellianitēs's speech, which later appeared as an article in the journal *Parnassos*, later in this chapter). See Theodōros Vellianitēs, 'Synchronos Rōssikē Philologia', *Parnassos*, 6 (1889), 253–74.

8 Kōnstantinos G. Kasinēs, "Ē neoellēnikē 'voreiomania': Ē rēksē me to romantiko parelthon" ['The Modern Greek "North-mania". A Rupture with the Romantic Past'], in *Synecheies, asynecheies, rēkseis ston ellēniko kosmo (1204–2014: oikonomia, koinōnia, istoria, logotechnia)* [*Continuities, Discontinuities, Ruptures in the Greek World (1204–2014): Economy, Society, History, Literature*], ed. by Kōnstantinos A. Dēmadēs (Athens: European Society of Modern Greek Studies, 2015), pp. 119–38.

Russian authors translated increasing with each year.[9] Despite a common misconception that nineteenth-century Greek translators relied on French intermediate translations, a large percentage of translations, as my research has clarified, were from the original Russian and written by Russian-speaking translators.[10] The authors most frequently translated into Greek during the nineteenth century were Ivan Krylov, Aleksandr Pushkin, Ivan Turgenev, Lev Tolstoy, and Mikhail Lermontov.

The rising popularity of Russian authors with Greek readers from the 1880s onwards was due in part to the positive influence of French criticism, particularly the work of Eugène-Melchior de Vogüé (1829–1916).[11] France was "the chief place of consecration in the world of literature", exporting literary works to the rest of the world after "impressing them with the stamp of *littéralité*".[12] In his study *Le Roman russe* (1886), de Vogüé recognised the literary value of Russian authors, effectively elevating them to canonical status within the world literary field. De Vogüé's *Le Roman russe* was well-known to Greek critics, who disseminated his work in Greece.[13] As French-speaking intellectuals, many of whom had studied and lived in France, they carefully followed literary movements as they were exported from Paris, "the capital of the literary world".[14] The consecration of Russian authors by French critics, who had the power to define and legitimate the literary and the modern, was enough to warrant the positive reception of Russian authors in Greece. It could be argued that Russian writers' canonisation in Greek was almost instant; their consecration initially established by French criticism and then disseminated in Greece firstly by French-speaking intellectuals and secondly by Greek critics who, as we shall see further on, saw in the works of Russian authors a model for their own national literature.

The first translations of Dostoevsky into Greek were published in the late 1880s. The first Greek translation was the short story 'A Christmas Party and a Wedding' ('To dendron tōn Christougennōn kai gamos') ('Elka i svad'ba',

9 Ilinskagia, *Russian Literature in Greece*, p. 43.

10 Ibid.

11 On the French reception of Russian literature and the role of de Vogüé, see also Alexander McCabe, 'Dostoevsky's French Reception: From Vogüé, Gide, Shestov and Berdyaev to Marcel, Camus, and Sartre (1880–1959)' (unpublished doctoral thesis, University of Glasgow, 2013), http://theses.gla.ac.uk/id/eprint/4337.

12 Pascale Casanova, *The World Republic of Letters*, trans. by M.B. DeBevoise (Cambridge, MA: Harvard University Press, 2004), p. 78 and p. 127.

13 Sophia Makrē, in her dissertation on the influence of French literary criticism on the early reception of Dostoevsky in Greece, has demonstrated how most late nineteenth-century and early twentieth-century Greek critics recycled passages from de Vogüé's *Le Roman russe*, often obscuring the source. Sophia Makrē, 'Ē proslēpsē tou Dostoevskii stēn Ellada 1886–1940' ['The Reception of Dostoevskii in Greece 1886–1940'] (unpublished doctoral dissertation, Aristotle University of Thessaloniki, 2018). See also Elizabeth Geballe's essay in this volume for more on De Vogüé's influence.

14 Casanova, *The World Republic of Letters*, p. 127.

1848), published on the front page of the Athenian newspaper *Akropolis* on Christmas Eve 1886.[15] It was translated by Theodōros Vellianitēs (1863–1933), a Russian-speaking journalist and translator, who was among the first Greek critics to advocate for Russian literature. Vellianitēs had studied in Russia and later travelled across the country writing reports on the latest news for the Greek press.[16] When he returned to Athens, Vellianitēs took upon himself the role of introducing Russian literature to Greek readers either through his own translations from Russian or in articles for newspapers and literary journals. In an 1889 article entitled 'Modern Russian Literature', Vellianitēs made the case for importing Russian literature into Greece as a factor in "invigorating [...] [the] dwindling Greek literature".[17] Vellianitēs praised Russian literary works for their "originality" and "national colour", writing that:

> In Russian writers, the life and actions of a young and spirited nation shines through. The Russian writer does not seek to add anything foreign to Russia. He depicts traditions, desires and feelings that are inherently Russian, and he depicts them so faithfully that his books can be considered mirrors reflecting the nation's life [...]. The Russian writer does not have literary prejudices, nor does he follow rules set by others. He has his own manner of writing and his own aesthetic values.[18]

Vellianitēs's emphasis on the national character of Russian literature had particular weight at a time when Modern Greek literature was still emergent. After its recognition as an independent state in 1831, Greece was trying to re-imagine itself as a modern European nation after four hundred years under Ottoman rule. Part of constructing the national identity involved envisioning what Modern Greek literature should look like: what its goals, language, style, and themes should be. Literary critics dismissed national literature produced in the first decades after Greece's independence as a passive mimesis of European literary models, which failed to reflect the realities of Greek society in the nineteenth century.[19] According to Vellianitēs, for national literature to distinguish itself from the "wrinkled" and "exhausted" literatures of European nations without becoming a bad copy of the "literary cholera" that was French literature, it should emulate Russian authors; rely on inspiration from folk

15 *Akropolis*, 24 December 1886, pp. 1–2.

16 Ilinskagia, *Russian Literature in Greece*, p. 57.

17 Vellianitēs, 'Synchronos Rōssikē Philologia', pp. 253–74.

18 Ibid., p. 256.

19 Anna Dialla, 'Epaneksetazontas tē dichotomia Dysē-Anatolē: ta pollapla prosōpa tēs Rōsias ston ellēniko 19o aiōna' ['Re-examining the East-West Dichotomy: The Many Faces of Russia in the Greek 19th Century'], in *Ē Ellada tēs Neōterikotētas. Koinōnikē krisē kai ideologika dilēmmata (19os-20os aiōnas)* [*Greece in Modern Times. Social Crisis and Ideological Dilemmas (19th-20th Century)*], ed. by K. Arōnē-Tsichlē, S. Papageōrgiou and A. Patrikiou (Athens: Papazēsēs, 2014), pp. 53–72.

traditions and the everyday lives of common people in order to create their own, Herderian model of literature: a mirror reflecting the nation's life.[20]

Vellianitēs translated one more of Dostoevsky's short stories in the next decade, 'The Beggar Boy at Christ's Christmas Tree' ('To paidion para to dendron tou Christou') ('Elka u Khrista', 1876) in 1889. However, he had neither the linguistic skills nor the literary depth to undertake the daunting task of translating Dostoevsky's novels into Greek. That person was Alexandros Papadiamantēs (1851–1911).

Roidēs's 'Dostoevsky and his Novel "Crime and Punishment"'

In 1889, Papadiamantēs, an emergent writer in his thirties, was working as a translator from French and English for Greek periodicals.[21] In 1889, he translated *Crime and Punishment* (*Prestuplenie i nakazanie*, 1866) for the newspaper *Ephēmeris*. The translation was serialised in 106 instalments over four months, published on the front and second page of the newspaper following the format of French newspaper literary supplements (*feuilletons*).[22] The writer and critic, Emmanouēl Roidēs (1836–1904), who worked for *Ephēmeris*, encouraged the newspapers' editors to print this translation of *Crime and Punishment*.

A day prior to its publication, the novel was introduced by Roidēs in an article titled 'Dostoevsky and his Novel "Crime and Punishment"', which became a seminal text in the reception of Dostoevsky in Greece.[23] Roidēs, an author and critic who had lived and studied in Europe, suggested to the editors of *Ephēmeris* that they publish Dostoevsky's novel in order to, as he put it, finally "eradicate the quite widespread belief that literary works are divided into those that can be enjoyed by all and those that are appreciated by few". Roidēs, echoing the negative reception of French authors by critics of that period, wrote that "if Zola [...] and Maupassant remove from their heroes and heroines the clothes—and sometimes the undergarments—then Dostoevskii removes the

20 Theodoros Vellianitēs, 'Synchronos Rōssikē Philologia', p. 256.

21 Phillipos Pappas, 'Pros Vioporismon: Anaplaisiōnontas ton metaphrastiko kosmo tou Papadiamantē ston ēmerēsio kai periodiko typo' ['To Make a Living: Contextualizing Papadiamantēs's Translations in Newspapers and Journals'], *Praktika G' Diethnous Synedriou gia ton Alexandro Papadiamantē* [*Proceedings of 3rd International Conference on Alexandros Papadiamantēs*] (Athens: Domos, 2 (8–7 October 2011)), 329–45.

22 Eugenia Makrygiannē, 'Epimetro' [Afterword] in Fedor Dostoevsky, *To Enklēma kai ē Timōria*, trans. by Alexandros Papadiamantēs (Athens: Ideogramma, 1992), pp. 501–10.

23 Emmanouēl Roidēs, 'Dostoevsky and His Novel "Crime and Punishment"', *Ephēmeris*, 13 April 1889, p. 2 (p. 2). This text was reprinted to introduce the annotated 1992 Ideogramma edition of Papadiamantēs's translation.

skin". He presented Dostoevsky as an author of universal appeal who had a "gift bestowed by God" to "depict what is felt by everyone but which no one who had come before him, had described as faithfully and clearly". Drawing parallels to Euripides and Aeschylus, Roidēs identified Dostoevsky as a writer of *mythographia* (fable-writing), someone who had the power to "accurately interpret the sentiments that are nested in our hearts". He claimed that the Christian character of Dostoevsky's works was evident in "the apotheosis of pain, humility, dysmorphia of the body and spiritual bankruptcy". Finally, Roidēs called on readers to approach *Crime and Punishment* as a "moral parable", a work whose moral value was equal to its artistic virtues.

Roidēs's views on Dostoevsky were of great consequence to Dostoevsky's reception in Greece.[24] Roidēs was already a well-respected writer and critic by the time he provided his preface for the translation of *Crime and Punishment*. His insights about Dostoevsky's fiction anticipated major trends in how the author would be understood and studied in the Greek context, drawing parallels to Ancient Greek tragedy, establishing psychological analysis as an integral component of his fiction, employing Dostoevsky's biography as a tool of literary analysis, and recognising Christian morality as the main tenet of his philosophy. By giving such a strong endorsement of Dostoevsky and his fiction in one of the first Greek-language introductory texts on that author, Roidēs made Dostoevsky valuable in the eyes of nineteenth-century Greek readers. He thus became the first *consecrator* of Dostoevsky in Greece; he was an author with enough prestige and recognition—symbolic capital—in Greek culture to determine and legitimise Dostoevsky's literary value.[25] As Pascale Casanova has written on the relationship between translation and consecration: "the characterization of a text by a great consecrator as a text 'that has to be translated' is enough to consecrate it as a great work of literature".[26]

Alexandros Papadiamantēs's *To Enklēma kai ē Timōria*

Roidēs might have been a well-known writer when he introduced *Crime and Punishment*, but the translator of the novel was not, in 1889, yet well-known. Although *Crime and Punishment* was quite popular with readers of *Ephēmeris*,

24 Makrē, in 'Ē proslēpsē tou Dostoevskii stēn Ellada', has argued that Roidēs's introduction and his overall decision to suggest to *Ephēmeris*' editors the translation of *Crime and Punishment* was influenced in part by his having read de Vogüé's study. While it is true that Roidēs's analysis of Dostoevsky's work follows certain aspects of de Vogüé's, I argue in this chapter that Roidēs's introduction is important for the reception of Dostoevsky not because he disseminated de Vogüé's ideas on Dostoevsky in Greece, but because of his power of consecration as an established author within the Modern Greek literary field.

25 Casanova, *The World Republic of Letters*, p. 22.

26 Pascale Casanova, 'Consécration et accumulation', p. 18.

its translator was never named, which was usual practice at the time.[27] In 1905, Vellianitēs identified him as the writer Alexandros Papadiamantēs.[28] Papadiamantēs would later be recognised as Modern Greece's "national prose-writer".[29] Although little-known beyond Greek borders, at home Papadiamantēs's novels and short stories are considered a landmark in the development of Greek national literature.[30] During his lifetime, Papadiamantēs had minor commercial success as an author and supported himself by translating European literature for newspapers and journals, using his knowledge of English and French.

Papadiamantēs's *Crime and Punishment* was entitled *To Enklēma kai ē Timōria* (*The Crime and the Punishment*); his addition of definite articles to both nouns mirrored the title of the French translation—*Le Crime et le Châtiment*, translated by Victor Derély (1884)—obliquely indicating its own indirect source. Derély's French translation was the intermediate text for many European translations of *Crime and Punishment*, among them the first translation of the novel in English by Frederick Whishaw published in 1886 by Henry Vizetelly.[31] After its serialisation in *Ephēmeris*, Papadiamantēs's *To Enklēma kai ē Timōria* was not republished in book form, making the first translation of *Crime and Punishment* into Greek unavailable to readers for at least a hundred years. A critical edition of the translation was published for the first time in 1992, when academic interest in Papadiamantēs's translations rose.[32]

Once his translation had been reissued, scholars of Papadiamantēs were able to appreciate the author's idiosyncratic style and the creative liberties he

27 A few days after publishing the first instalment, *Ephēmeris* informed readers that it had to reprint the issue due to high demand. Eugenia Makrygiannē, 'Epimetro', p. 501.

28 In a footnote under the 'Dostoevskii' entry in his translation of Alexander Skabichevskii's *History of Modern Russian Literature* [*Istoria Noveishei Russkoi Literatury*, 1840–1890], Vellianitēs credited Papadiamantēs as the first Greek translator of *Crime and Punishment*. See A. Skabichevskii, *Istoria tēs rōssikēs logotechnias* [*History of Russian Literature*], trans. by Theodōros Vellianitēs (Athens: Vivliothēkē Maraslē, 1905), p. 601.

29 David Ricks, 'In partibus infidelium: Alexandros Papadiamantēs and Orthodox Disenchantment with the Greek State,' in *The Making of Modern Greece: Nationalism, Romanticism, & the Uses of the Past (1797–1896)*, ed. by Roderick Beaton and David Ricks (Farnham: Ashgate Publishing, 2009), pp. 249–59 (p. 249).

30 The following works by Papadiamantēs are available in English: *The Murderess*, trans. by Peter Levi (New York: New York Review of Books Classics, 1983) and *The Murderess: A Social Novel*, trans. by Peter Constantine (Limni: Denise Harvey, 2011); *The Boundless Garden. Selected Short Stories*, multiple translators, 2 vols (Limni: Denise Harvey, 2007–19); *Tales From a Greek Island*, trans. by Elizabeth Constantinides (Baltimore: Johns Hopkins University Press, 1994); *Love in the Snow*, trans. by Janet Coggin & Zissimos Lorenzatos (Athens: Domos, 1993).

31 See McCabe, 'Dostoevsky's French reception'.

32 The 'translation turn' in Papadiamantēs Studies culminated in the publication of his translations in annotated editions for the first time in the 1990s.

took when translating from the French intermediate.[33] Papadiamantēs's Greek remained faithful to Derély's text at the macro-textual level. He deviated from the French version with micro-textual level adjustments to the style and register, taking full advantage of Greek intralinguistic variations within the diglossia of Modern Greek.[34] Papadiamantēs translated the descriptive parts of the novel in *katharevousa*, an archaic variant of Modern Greek, and the dialogic parts in *demotic*, the vernacular form. Within dialogues, he also alternated between higher and lower registers to render the idiolect and the social background of the speaker. The result was a stylistically rich translation reflecting the entire history of the Greek language from Homeric epithets to Modern Greek colloquialisms. In a way, it could be argued that Papadiamantēs intuitively sensed the polyphony of the original, rendering it into a stylistically rich idiolect of Modern Greek. Papadiamantēs would revisit *Crime and Punishment* almost ten years later in his novella *The Murderess*, which was inspired by Dostoevsky's novel.

The Murderess (1903)

For many years, Papadiamantēs's most widely known connection to Dostoevsky was not his 1889 translation *To Enklēma kai ē Timōria* , but his novel, *The Murderess* (*Ē Phonissa*, 1903), a work strongly influenced by *Crime and Punishment*. *The Murderess* follows a series of murders on a small island community in mid-nineteenth-century Greece. The titular murderess is Frankogiannou (named, as was customary in small village societies, after her husband's surname), a woman in her sixties, who starts murdering infant girls in the firm belief that she is releasing their parents from the economic burden of raising a female child. The realistic depiction of the murderess's inner turmoil as she commits these crimes, including her attempts to rationalise her actions, led Greek critics to compare *The Murderess* to *Crime and Punishment* from the novel's first publication. They soon characterised Papadiamantēs as "Greece's Dostoevsky". The novel's psychological realism, its treatment of social and moral issues, and Papadiamantēs's rich language, make it one of the most representative texts of Modern Greek literature, still relevant today.

---

33 Nikos Triantaphyllopoulos, review of Fedor Dostoevsky, *To Enklēma kai ē Timōria*, trans. by Alexandros Papadiamantēs (reprinted 1992), *Papadiamantika Tetradia*, 2 (1993), 193–203.

34 Greek diglossia was the coexistence of an artificially created 'purist' language—the *katharevousa*—based on Ancient Greek syntax and vocabulary that was used for official and formal purposes; and the *demotic*, the language of the people (= *dēmos*), a more colloquial variant used in everyday life. Diglossia lasted for more than a century and was finally abolished in 1976, when the demotic was established as the official language of the state. See Peter Mackridge, *Language and National Identity in Greece, 1766–1976* (Oxford: Oxford University Press, 2009).

Comparisons between Dostoevsky's and Papadiamantēs's fiction were drawn even before *The Murderess* was published.[35] However, it was in *The Murderess* that Greek critics and scholars traced Dostoevsky's direct influence. Beyond the central theme of murder/sin and punishment/redemption shared by both novels, similarities have been noted in the narrative structure—the use of an omniscient third-person narrator—and the authors' social commentary on the motives for crime.[36] Despite these similarities, Papadiamantēs's *The Murderess* was not considered an attempt to passively mimic Dostoevsky's prose style. It was perceived rather as a creative transformation—transcreation—of Dostoevsky's themes and poetics into the Greek literary tradition. Translating *Crime and Punishment* was Papadiamantēs's "intellectual education", an "incentive" for Papadiamantēs to produce original fiction in Greek.[37] The hypothesis that translated foreign literature can function as an accumulation of literary resources with the momentum to transform original literary production proved right in Papadiamantēs's case.[38] That the latter used his translations as a creative exercise for his own fictional writing illustrates how translated literature can "fulfil the need of a younger literature put into use its newly founded (or

35 One of the earliest mentions of Papadiamantēs as 'the Greek Dostoevskii' is a notice advertising Papadiamantēs's upcoming short story *Ōch Vasanakia* (1894) in the newspaper *Akropolis* (6 January 1894, p. 2), nine years before the publication of *The Murderess* in 1903 and just five years after his translation of *Crime and Punishment*. See Sophia Bora, 'O Papadiamantēs kai oi anagnōstes tou: zētēmata istorias tēs proslēpsēs tou ergou tou (1879–1961) ['Papadiamantēs and his Readers: Historical Issues in the Reception of his Work (1879–1961)'] (unpublished doctoral thesis: National and Kapodistrian University of Athens, 2008).

36 According to literary critic Kōstēs Papagiōrgēs, Papadiamantēs wrote *The Murderess* in "dual narration"—having an omniscient third-person narrator describe both the events taking place and the innermost thoughts of the protagonist—following the narrative structure of *Crime and Punishment*. See Kōstēs Papagiōrgēs, *Alexandros Adamantiou Emmanouēl* (Athens: Kastaniōtēs, 1998), p. 188. *The Murderess* was published with the subtitle "a social novel", alluding to possible social causes of the crimes described in the novel such as prevailing social conditions in nineteenth century Skopelos—and similarly in Raskolnikov's nineteenth-century St. Petersburg—where murder could be considered a viable solution to social inequality. The subtitle "a social novel" further disclosed Papadiamantēs's real-life inspiration: a series of 'secret infanticides' reported in his natal island of Skopelos allegedly prompted by the economic burden of daughters on families (who would struggle to provide them with dowries). See Guy Saunier, *Eōsphoros kai Avyssos: O prosōpikos mythos tou Papadiamantē* [*Lucifer and the Abyss: Papadiamantēs's Personal Myth*] (Athens: Agra, 2001), p. 277.

37 Angelos Terzakēs, 'Ē zoē tōn grammatōn. Epimetro' ['The Life of Letters. Afterword'], *Neoellēnika Grammata*, 30 (26 June 1937), p. 2.

38 Itamar Even-Zohar, 'The Position of Translated Literature Within the Literary Polysystem', in *The Translation Studies Reader*, ed. by Lawrence Venuti (London and New York: Routledge, 2000), pp. 192–97; Pascale Casanova, 'Consécration et accumulation', pp. 7–20.

renovated) tongue for as many literary types as possible in order to make it serviceable as a literary language".[39] The translation of *Crime and Punishment* by an author at the centre of the Modern Greek canon and its role in inspiring the novel *The Murderess*—which would become a canonical text of Modern Greek literature—sealed Dostoevsky's literary fate in Greece from his very first contact with Greek readers. His positive reception in Greece established, Dostoevsky would continue to captivate the interest of Greek readers: albeit in a different socio-historical context, as we shall see next.

Twentieth-century Translations

1900–25: The Impact of the Russian Revolution

During the first two decades of the twentieth century, Greek readers' turn to Russian literature continued to fuel translation production which increased pace with each year. Soon, Russian became the third most translated language, after English and French.[40] The Russian Revolution of 1917 gave new momentum to the dissemination of Russian literature in Greece and its reception, profoundly changing reading habits and translated literature production.[41] Up until the 1920s, the majority of Greek readers interested in Russian literature were the "socially privileged part of society [...] that travelled to study at the [European] capitals", spoke foreign languages and had access to French or German translations of Russian works.[42] After the Russian Revolution of 1917 and the creation of the KKE (the Communist Party of Greece) in 1922, which laid the foundations for the Communist movement in Greece, Russian literature's readership expanded to

39 On Papadiamantēs's translations as creative exercise, see Stesē Athēnē, 'O Papadiamantēs Metaphrastēs. Sta entypa tou Vlassē Gavriēlidē' ['Papadiamantēs the Translator. In Vlassēs Gavriēlidēs's Printing Press'], in *Praktika G' Diethnous Synedriou gia ton Alexandro Papadiamantē*, II [*Proceedings of 3rd International Conference on Alexandros Papadiamantēs*] (Athens: Domos, 8–7 October 2011), 29–53; Zohar, 'The Position of Translated Literature'), p. 194.

40 Kōnstantinos G. Kasinēs, *Vivliographia tōn ellēnikōn metaphraseōn tēs xenēs logotechnias, 1901–1950* [*A Bibliography of Greek Translations of Foreign Literature, 1901–1950*] (Athens: Syllogos pros Diadosin Ōphelimon Vivliōn, 2013), p. x.

41 Phillipos Pappas, 'Logotechnikē metaphrasē kai Aristera: entypa, tomes, repertorio (1901–1950)' ['Literary translation and the Left: Publications, Innovations, Repertoire (1901–1950)'], in *Zetēmata neoellēnikēs philologias, metrika, yphologika, kritika, metaphrastika* [*Issues of Modern Greek Philology, Metric, Stylistic, Critical, Translational*] (Thessaloniki: Aristotle University of Thessaloniki, 2016), 603–11 (p. 605). For more detailed discussion, see Niovi Zampouka's chapter in this volume.

42 Angelos Terzakēs, 'Dēmosthenēs Voutyras', *Nea Estia*, 190 (15 November 1934), 1015–22 (p. 1015).

include a new group of readers from the lower-middle class;[43] "the student from the countryside with a meagre income, the intellectual young worker overcome by unexpected new aspirations to become a social hero".[44] Authors like Maksim Gorky (doyen of Socialist Realism) gained in popularity, while nineteenth-century Russian authors—among them Dostoevsky—were re-introduced to Greek readers through the lens of Socialist aesthetics.[45]

The shift in tone in how Russian literature was discussed was evident in Greek critical discourse of that period; the notions of 'proletariat' and 'Socialist Realism', endowed with positive meaning, entered the vocabulary of critics who discussed Russian authors, even nineteenth-century ones like Dostoevsky. One such example can be found in a 1930 text written by author Nikos Kazantzakēs in his *History of Russian Literature*, the first book on the subject by a Greek writer.[46] Kazantzakēs had long been fascinated by Russian culture. He had visited the country on several occasions and was an early advocate of Socialist and Communist ideology. In the chapter on Dostoevsky, Kazantzakēs described him as a writer who from the very start emerged as "a visionary of the urban proletariat, the poet of the maniacs, the ridiculous, the scorned and the sick"; he was "a petty-bourgeois, suffering all his life in poverty, sickly, his nervous system struck by any slight change in his soul, a neuropath proletarian of the metropolis".[47] In Dostoevsky's works, Kazantzakēs noted, the reader did not find the family sagas of the Russian aristocracy which Tolstoy wrote about; instead, his heroes were the "spiritual proletarians that wander in the streets of the great metropolis; who stumble on the border of crime, insanity and hunger".[48] The harsh social reality depicted in Gorky's and Dostoevsky's novels provoked "the interest and the sympathy of young people" who saw in their writings a reflection of their own lives.[49] The writer and critic Angelos Terzakēs, who lived through that period, describes how young idealists like him

43 Giōrgos Michailidēs, 'Translating Russian Literature in Interwar Greece: The Example of Maxim Gorky', *Syn-Thèses*, 6 (2013), 38–57 (p. 42).

44 Terzakēs, 'Dēmosthenēs Voutyras', p. 1015.

45 Giōrgos Michailidēs, 'Translating Russian Literature in Interwar Greece: The Example of Maxim Gorky'. According to Kasinēs, between 1900 and 1950, Gorky was the third most translated Russian author in Greek, after Dostoevsky and Tolstoy. See Kōnstantinos G. Kasinēs, *Vivliographia tōn ellēnikōn metaphraseōn tēs xenēs logotechnias, 1901–1950* [*A Bibliography of Greek Translations of Foreign Literature, 1901–1950*] (Athens: Syllogos pros Diadosin Ōphelimōn Vivliōn, 2013).

46 Nikos Kazantzakēs, 'Theodōros Dostoevskii' in Kazantzakēs, *History of Russian Literature* (Athens: Eleutherouthakēs, 1930), pp. 87–98.

47 Ibid., p. 90 and p. 94.

48 Ibid., p. 89.

49 Christina Dounia, *Logotechnia kai politikē: Ta periodika tēs Aristeras sto Mesopolemo* [*Literature and Politics: The Journals of the Left in the Interwar Period*] (Athens: Kastaniotēs, 1996), 34.

"imagined themselves one of Gorky's or Dostoevsky's heroes".[50] The connection with Dostoevsky's work was instant, "a connection of the soul":

> It is impossible for me to describe the emotions of this generation, when they encountered Dostoevsky for the first time. His novels spread throughout Greece to the most isolated village. The connection was instant. A connection of the soul [...] We loved him instantly. There is an [reading] audience. It is up to us to come closer to him. He is waiting for us.[51]

The fact that Russian authors were mostly available in poor-quality translations from French did not deter readers who "avidly consumed badly printed newspapers with translations or hurried summaries of foreign sociological articles, volumes of selected literary works slyly chosen to serve the propaganda [of the movement] but also to serve temporary publishing interests".[52] The rush to print Russian works to keep up with the growing readership is reflected in the lack of order or any coherent plan for producing translations between 1900 and 1925. Although new translations of Dostoevsky's works—both major and minor—appeared regularly, there was neither a single unified publishing effort to translate the author's remaining untranslated works, nor were the same translators employed by publishing houses to preserve consistency in translation style. Early twentieth-century translations depended usually on French versions and translators were unaware of previous versions. In 1912, Stelios Charitakēs (the first translator of *Crime and Punishment* into the demotic variant of Modern Greek), expressed in his translator's note his disappointment that "Dostoevsky's works are unknown in Greece"; seemingly, he had no knowledge of either Papadiamantēs's or Vellianitēs's existing translations.[53] The general dissatisfaction with the quality of Greek translations of Dostoevsky's works was voiced by writer and translator Petros Pikros in an introduction to the first Greek translation of *The House of the Dead* (*Zapiski iz mertvogo doma*, 1861) published in 1921.[54] While Pikros approved of the "surprisingly warm reception" of Dostoevsky by Greek readers, he was highly critical of available translations in Greek. He criticised translators for using French intermediate translations and denounced any such translation as "lacking" in style and "inadequate" in

50 Terzakēs, 'Dēmosthenēs Voutras', p. 1015.

51 'Ta synchrona provlēmata tēs pneumatikēs mas zōēs', interview with Angelos Terzakēs in *Neoellēnika Grammata*, 24 (22 September 1935), p. 3.

52 Ibid.

53 Fedor Dostoevsky, *To Enklēma kai ē Timōria* [*The Crime and the Punishment*], trans. by Stelios Charitakēs (Chania: Gorgias Phortsakēs, 1912).

54 Petros Pikros, 'The Man and the Work "The Deadhouse"', in Fedor Dostoevsky, *Anamnēseis apo to spiti tōn pethamenōn* [*The House of the Dead*], trans. by 'Miss A.K.' (Athens: Athēna, 1921), pp. 3–16.

terms to the original. Tellingly, the translator of the novel was credited only with her initials— 'Miss A.K.'—and was not mentioned once by Pikros.

Despite the overall positive reception of Russian literature, it was becoming increasingly clear that available translations of Russian works, while sufficiently numerous to satisfy high market demand in the short term (and provide economic profit for publishers), fell short of readers' literary standards.

Govostēs Editions

The breakthrough in translating Dostoevsky into Greek came in 1926 when twenty-two-year-old Kōstas Govostēs (1904–58) founded the Publishing Company Anatole in Athens, later renamed Govostēs Editions. Govostēs saw himself as a publisher promising to "present something completely new".[55] Govostēs, writing on the reception of Russian literature in Greece, expressed his disapproval with what he saw as opportunism from publishers and editors who sought to profit from readers' appetite for "everything Russian" and a superficial interest from a large part of the readership.[56] Govostēs talked of the complete lack of "translation conscientiousness" by publishers and editors who hired "anyone who knew a couple of French words" and was willing to work for the lowest rates to translate Russian works from intermediate translations; "poor Russians arrived in Greece, some via Berlin, others via Paris; others were collected shipwrecked in Italian waters".[57] As for Greek readers, he distinguished between those who read Russian literature to keep up with literary trends and not appear old-fashioned ("the snobs"); and those like himself, whose interest in Russian culture was genuine and who believed that "Russian thought has influenced to such a great degree humanity's progress and holds in its hand its historical fate".[58] Govostēs's target audience would not be the wider public that read to "kill time", but those who sought a deeper and wider understanding of Russian culture; the sophisticated readers.[59]

The first book published by Govostēs was *Dream of a Ridiculous Man* (*To oneiro enos geloiou*) ('Son smeshnogo cheloveka', 1877), "a small masterpiece [...] by the greatest Russian writer" translated by Geōrgios Semeriōtēs.[60] The translation was to be part of a series on "small masterpieces of World Literature"

55 Kōstas Govostēs, 'The Publication of the History of Russian Literature', in *History of Russian Literature*, ed. by Louis Léger and trans. by Ad. D. Papadēma (Athens: Gkovostēs Editions, 1929), pp. vii-xi.

56 Govostēs, 'Publication', p. vii.

57 Ibid., p. ix.

58 Ibid., p. x.

59 Ibid.

60 Introduction by Kōstas Govostēs to Fedor Dostoevsky, *To oneiro enos geloiou* [*Dream of a Ridiculous Man*], trans. by Geōrgios Semeriōtēs (Athens: Anatolē, 1926). No page numbers.

by authors like Dostoevsky, Maksim Gorky, Alexander Dumas, Henrik Ibsen, Honoré de Balzac, Victor Hugo, Lev Tolstoy, Luigi Pirandello, Anton Chekhov, and Knut Hamsun. Introducing the edition, Govostēs set his publishing house's goals and aspirations: to publish "the most beautiful works of World Literature" in "colourful" translations, in well-curated editions and affordable prices in order to "disseminate literature and make it accessible to everyone".[61]

Govostēs benefitted from the upsurge in demand for Russian literature in the 1920s.[62] His newly founded publishing house filled a gap that existed in Greek publishing for good-quality translations from Russian. Govostēs Editions's attractive editions and coherent book series satisfied both older readers, accustomed to the standards of European publishing houses, and new readers who sought in his editions an introduction to Russian literature. Besides Russian writing, Govostēs Editions ran a number of book series on philosophy, sociology, and Communism. As part of the 'Socialist Library' series, he published works by Leon Trotsky, Vladimir Lenin, Joseph Stalin, and Nikolai Bukharin. For Govostēs, the publication of these texts was "invaluable" and "necessary" at a time "when the communist movement in Greek was still struggling".[63]

In 1936, Iōannēs Metaxas, a former army general, became dictator of Greece on the pretext of safeguarding the country from the threat of Communism. In one of its first decrees, Metaxas's regime outlawed the Communist Party and banned the publication of Communist texts and any work that ran counter to the country's "national interests".[64] Govostēs was targeted by the regime as a publisher of Communist and Marxist texts. His offices and bookshop were looted, and the books were confiscated and burned in public. Govostēs himself was sentenced to several months in prison.[65] When he was released, he realised that for his publishing house to survive under a hostile regime, he needed to change course. He stopped publishing explicitly political texts and shifted his focus towards literary fiction—translated and national. Govostēs Editions now

61 Ibid. For studies on book series which responded to European modernism and the commercialisation of 'high' literature see, for example, Lise Jaillant, *Cheap Modernism: Expanding Markets, Publishers' Series and the Avant-Garde* (Edinburgh: Edinburgh University Press, 2017).

62 Pappas, 'Logotechnikē metaphrasē kai Aristera', p. 606.

63 The quote comes from an advertisement for an edition of Lenin's writings in the back matter of Leon Trotsky, *O Emphylios Polemos* [*The Civil War*], trans. by K. Papadopoulos (Athens: Gkovostēs Editions, 1929).

64 Giannēs Gklavinas, 'Eph' oplou "psalidi": O kratikos mēchanismos epivolēs logokrisias kai to pedio epharmogēs tou tēn periodo tēs Diktatorias tēn Syntagmatarchēn (1967–74) mesa apo to archeio tēs Genikēs Grammateias Typou kai Plērophoriēn', in *Logokrisia stēn Ellada* [*Censorship in Greece*], ed. by Pēnelopē Petsinē and Dēmētrēs Christopoulos (Athens: Rosa Luxemburg Foundation Greek Branch, 2016), pp. 167–76 (p. 168).

65 Kēstas Chatziotēs, *Vivliopēleia kai ekdotikoi oikoi tēs Ellados* [*Bookstores and Publishing Houses of Greece*], 3 vols (Athens: Municipality of Athens, Cultural Committee, 2000–2006), I (2000), pp. 113–17.

printed novels, poetry collections, and dramas by foreign and Greek authors as well as titles on literary theory and psychology. In 1939, the publishing house became active again. Govostēs's decision to focus on literature was vindicated; Govostēs Editions quickly recovered and became profitable. By 1950, it was the second most productive publishing house in Athens, having published more than 135 titles in its 24 years of existence.[66] Govostēs hired new translators and gathered a team of editors and advisors, spearheaded by the poet Giannēs Ritsos (1909–90), to supervise all manuscript editing and ensure the quality of the final product.[67] Govostēs published Ritsos's poetry collections and maintained a lifelong friendship with the poet, now considered a towering figure of the Greek Left. The inclusion of Ritsos, with his deep linguistic and literary knowledge, showed Govostēs's care for the quality of translations.

As part of the renewed effort to concentrate on translated literature, Govostēs started publishing the collected works of classic authors such as Fedor Dostoevsky, Lev Tolstoy, William Shakespeare, Émile Zola, Oscar Wilde, and many others. He began publishing Dostoevsky's collected works in 1940 in new translations by Athēna Sarantidē and Koralia Makrē (made directly from Russian). All editions now included on the cover the caption 'translated from Russian'. By 1944, he had published new translations of *The Gambler* (*O paiktēs*) (*Igrok*, 1867), *Notes from Underground* (*To ypogeio*), *Netochka Nezvanova* (*Nietotska Niesvanova*) (*Netochka Nezvanova*, 1849), *The Eternal Husband* (*O aiōnios syzygos*) (*Vechnii muzh*, 1869), and *The Humiliated and Insulted* (*Tapeinōmenoi kai Kataphrōnemenoi*) (*Unizhennye i oskorblennye*, 1861). In 1942, with the addition of Arēs Alexandrou (1922–78), a young Russian-born translator, to the team, Govostēs was able to complete Dostoevsky's collected works in Greek.

Arēs Alexandrou

Alexandrou was hired on Ritsos's recommendation; the latter had read and admired Alexandrou's prior translations from Russian.[68] The two men moved in the same political and literary circles, both active members of the Communist Party (Alexandrou had joined the youth section of the party when he graduated). Alexandrou was thus an ideal candidate to fulfil the job of house translator from Russian. His father was an ethnic Russian-Greek from the city of Trabzon on the East Black Sea, and his mother was Russian–Estonian. Alexandrou's birth name was Aristotelēs Vasileiadēs; his pseudonym, by which he remains best-known, was suggested by the poet Giannēs Ritsos when Alexandrou began translating

66 Kasinēs, *Vivliographia* (2013), p. xxxiv.

67 'The Publishing House Govostēs and its Founder, 1926–2016', promotional leaflet to commemorate ninety years since Govostēs Editions's foundation, https://www.govostis.gr/spaw2/uploads/files/timokatalogos_2016%20lres.pdf.

68 Dēmētres Rautopoulos, *Arēs Alexandrou o Exoristos* [*Arēs Alexandrou The Exile*] (Athens: Sokolē, 2004), p. 100.

for Govostēs.[69] After the revolution of 1917, the Vasileiadēs family left for Greece where they had relatives since they struggled to make a living under the new Soviet regime. Alexandrou, then six years old, spoke only Russian and had to learn Greek at school. He quickly showed aptitude for languages and literature. Besides Russian, he was fluent in English and French, and had a basic knowledge of Italian and German. In his last years of high school, Alexandrou translated into Greek Pushkin's *Eugene Onegin* and the novella *The Captain's Daughter* (*Kapitanskaia dochka*, 1836) as a personal translation challenge. It was Alexandrou's translation of *Eugene Onegin* that convinced Ritsos to introduce him to Govostēs.

Alexandrou's first translation for Govostēs Editions was from English: D.H. Lawrence's *The Woman Who Rode Away* (1925), published in Greek in 1944.[70] Alexandrou's name featured on the cover as the translator above that of the author of the introduction, Aldous Huxley. Govostēs's decision to include Alexandrou's name on the cover on his first translation was both a sign of support for the young translator and a tacit acknowledgement of translation's contribution to importing foreign literature into Greece. In the same year, Govostēs published Alexandrou's first translation of Dostoevsky, *The House of the Dead* (*Anamnēseis apo to spiti tōn pethamenōn*, 1944), written during the Nazi Occupation (1941–44) of Athens. Alexandrou—who took part in the Resistance against the Nazis—later wrote that he thought of this translation as "an act of resistance":

> I was taking a sort of stand—since this was a Russian novel—against labour camps, like the one the author described and where he had been sent to be punished for harbouring libertarian ideas. Dostoevsky didn't say this clearly, but the informed reader would pick up on it. Dostoevsky was taking a stand against the authoritarian tsarist regime and by extension I, as his translator, encouraged resistance against the Germans.[71]

During the Greek Civil War (1946–49) and the politically fraught period that followed—a time of strong anti-Communist sentiment in Greece—Alexandrou spent ten years (1948–58) in exile on island prison camps, where thousands were held by the right-wing postwar government, for his involvement with the Communist Party. Throughout his life, Alexandrou translated many

69 Ritsos acted as Alexandrou's "spiritual father" and mentor throughout the latter's career. See Giannēs Ritsos, *Trochies se diastaurōsē: Epistolika deltaria tēs exorias kai grammata stēn Kaitē Drosou kai ton Arē Alexandrou* [*Trajectories at Cross-Roads: Epistolary Cards from Exile, and Letters to Kaitē Drosou and Arēs Alexandrou*], ed. by Lizy Tsirimōkou (Athens: Agra, 2008), p. 100.

70 D.H. Lawrence, *Ē Gynaika poy ephyge me t' alogo* [*The Woman Who Rode Away*], trans. by Arēs Alexandrou (Athens: Gkovostēs Editions, 1944).

71 Arēs Alexandrou, *O Dramatourgos Dostoevskii* [*Dostoevskii the Dramatist*] (Athens: Gkovostēs Editions, 2012), p. 28.

Russian and Soviet authors, including Nikolai Gogol, Lev Tolstoy, Anton Chekhov, Maksim Gorky, Vladimir Maiakovskii, Anna Akhmatova, and others. Alexandrou's translations of Dostoevsky, written during the years of the Nazi Occupation and between his imprisonments, stand out as one of the most successful translation efforts to introduce the works of a foreign author in Greek. Beginning with *The House of the Dead* (1944), Govostēs published the following novels in Alexandrou's translations: *Crime and Punishment* (*Enklēma kai Timōria,* 1951–52), *Demons* (*Besy,* 1872; *Daimonismenoi,* 1952–53), *The Idiot* (*Idiot,* 1869; *O Ēlithios,* 1953), and *Brothers Karamazov* (*Brat'ia Karamazovy,* 1880; *Oi Aderphoi Karamazov,* 1953–54). Govostēs also published Alexandrou's translations of shorter works, posthumously (not all Greek publication dates can be established definitively): *The Village of Stepanchikovo* (*Stepnachikogo i ego obitateli,* 1859; *To chōrio Stepanchikovo*), *Poor Folk* (*Bednye liudi,* 1846; *Oi Phtōchoi*), 'Dream of a Ridiculous Man' ('Son smeshnogo cheloveka', 1877; *To Oneiro enos geloiou*), *White Nights* (*Belye nochi,* 1848; *Leukes nychtes*), and 'A Gentle Creature' ('Krotkaia', 1876; *Mia glykia gynaika*).[72] Alexandrou, besides his professional career as a translator from Russian, English and French, was an author in his own right; he published poetry collections, dramas, and the novel *Mission Box* (*To Kivōtio,* 1974), a semi-allegorical, Kafkaesque novel on the Greek Civil War. It is considered a seminal text of Modern Greek postwar fiction.[73]

Alexandrou's translations were promoted by Govostēs Editions as a "restoration" of the Russian text, a major improvement from previous translations that had, in their view, "abused" the Russian original.[74] Govostēs implicitly challenged the validity of previous translations, promoting translations from his firm as superior and authentic. "Dostoevskii in our editions is the Real Dostoevskii [...]", always translated from the original by translators like Arēs Alexandrou, he claimed.[75] Alexandrou's biographer also referred to Alexandrou's translations as "restoring" and "reconstructing" Dostoevsky's text:

> What distinguishes [Alexandrou's translations] is their faithfulness, neither typical or lexical; it is their faith to the ethos and the spirit of the foreign work [...]. True fidelity does not entail solely technical competence and ethos, but something more. What was it in Alexandrou's case?

72 Govostēs Editions is quite inconsistent in its in-house records of publication dates. Most of its editions are dated incorrectly, as proven by my own research in the publishing house's catalogue.

73 Alexis Argyriou, 'The End of a Vision', *The Times Literary Supplement,* 14 November 1976, p. 1368.

74 The quote is from an advertisement for his forthcoming version of *Brothers Karamazov* in the back matter of Alexandrou's translation of *Crime and Punishment*). See Fedor Dostoevsky, *Enklēma kai Timōria* [*Crime and Punishment*], trans. by Arēs Alexandrou, 3 vols (Athens: Gkovostēs Editions, 1951–52), I (1951).

75 Advertisement by Govostēs in the literary journal *Diavazō,* 131 (1985), p. 7.

> What I see in his translations is pleasure, or if you will, reconstruction. Unexpectedly, he found a common link between linguistic sense and his own need for creation in this back-and-forth between his mother tongue and his adopted language; from the language he was forced to abandon...[76]

Alexandrou's translation work has been described as operating on the principles of "faithfulness to the original and respect to the Greek [text]".[77] Alexandrou himself described his effort to write "the crooked way [Dostoevskii] would have done in Greek, but without being told that it [the translated text] is crooked in Greek".[78] He confessed that:

> I used to interfere with the text, for had I left it the way it was, I would have been branded a sloppy translator. I had thus to balance on a tightrope, to intervene on the text in a way that the reader would think that I had altered nothing, and that that was how Dostoevsky himself would have written in Greek; that is, that he would have written neglecting style, piling phrases on paper, as if the text was raw material to be refined later.[79]

Alexandrou's success as a translator lies in his ability to render the Russian text in a Greek language that was and still is accessible and familiar to the Greek reader. Alexandrou in his translations chooses to "move the writer towards the reader" and not the reader toward the writer.[80] He moves Dostoevsky towards a Greek audience, the Dostoevskian text towards the linguistic expectations of the Greek reader. Another reason for the success of Alexandrou's translation was the rigorous editing that his text underwent by the editing team Govostēs had gathered, led by Ritsos and Govostēs himself; all translations were read, discussed, and edited to ensure the linguistic coherence of the final product. In many editions, Govostēs included special dedications, where he described the publication of the translations as the result of "collaborative labour", thanking "invisible collaborators-editors" without whom the completion of this work would have been impossible.[81]

---

76 Rautopoulos, *Arēs Alexandrou o Exoristos*, p. 13.

77 Alexandra Iōannidou, 'Metaphrasē ōs "metempsychōsē": Arēs Alexandrou-Leo Tolstoy' ['Translation as Reincarnation: Arēs Alexandrou-Leo Tolstoy'], *The Athens Review of Books* (February 2013), 21–25 (p. 22).

78 Alexandra Iōannidou, 'An Interview with Kaitē Drosou', *Panoptikon*, 22 (June 2017), 61–79 (p.73).

79 Arēs Alexandrou, *O Dramatourgos Dostoevskii*, p. 26.

80 Jeremy Munday, *Introducing Translation Studies: Theories and Applications* (London and New York: Routledge, 2016), p. 48.

81 The dedications can be found in the back matter of first editions of Alexandrou's *Demons* and *Crime and Punishment*, Fedor Dostoevsky, *Daimonismenoi* [*Demons*], trans. by Arēs Alexandrou, 3 vols (Athens: Gkovostēs Editions, 1952–3), III (1953), and Fedor Dostoevsky, *Enklēma kai Timōria* [*Crime and Punishment*], trans.

Together, Govostēs's publishing and editing decisions in terms of book format and pricing, and Alexandrou's literary language made Dostoevsky's works accessible—commercially and linguistically—to the Greek reader at that time. Alexandrou's translation style, with Govostēs's effective publishing strategy, combined to gain his translations the status of Greek standard editions. Alexandrou's literary recognition as an author and poet, which grew posthumously, further enhanced the legitimation and visibility of his translations; he soon eclipsed in popularity all other translators, with the exception of Papadiamantēs, a canonical Modern Greek author by that time. Since then, the majority of Greek readers have been introduced to Dostoevsky's oeuvre in Alexandrou's translations by Govostēs Editions. The many reprints of Alexandrou's translations since their publication in the 1950s are an index of their popularity—commercial and cultural—and of Alexandrou's visibility as a translator. Characteristic of that visibility is his commemoration in many studies and special volumes on Dostoevsky published in Greek.[82]

In the back matter of the first edition of Alexandrou's translation of *Brothers Karamazov* (1954) that marked the completion of Dostoevsky's collected works in Greek, Govostēs described the completion of this effort as an undertaking of "immense importance both for the colossal literary value of [Dostoevsky's] works and its [...] dissemination in our language" that "established the undeniable cultural and literary value of Greek translation".[83]

Conclusion

If we consider Dostoevsky's position within the global literary field to be at the centre of the world literature canon, Greek translations of his novels can reveal how the work of this Russian author became World Literature. David Damrosch describes a process of "double refraction, whereby":

> works become world literature by being received into the space of a foreign culture, a space defined in many ways by the host culture's

by Arēs Alexandrou, 3 vols (Athens: Gkovostēs Editions, 1951–2), III (1952). Alexandrou's wife, Kaitē Drosou, has also talked about the collaborative character of translations, referring to Ritsos as the "rewriter" of the text. See Alexandra Iōannidou, 'An Interview with Kaitē Drosou', *Panoptikon*, 22 (June 2017), 61–79 (p. 72).

82 In his introduction to an edited volume published in 1982 to commemorate the centenary of Dostoevsky's death, Alexandrou is mentioned in the introduction as "the man who offered us so many translations of Dostoevskii and who was himself a 'Dostoevskian hero' in his tortured life". Panagiōtēs Drakopoulos, 'Introduction', in *Spoudē ston Dostoevskii* [*A Study on Dostoevskii*], eds. by Th. Tampakē-Geōrga and M. Dēmopoulou (Athens: Imago, 1982), pp. 5–7 (p. 7).

83 See back matter in Dostoevsky, *Aderphoi Karamazov* [*Brothers Karamazov*], trans. by Arēs Alexandrou, 4 vols (Athens: Gkovostēs Editions, 1953–54), IV (1954).

> national tradition and the present needs of its own writers. Even a single work of world literature is the locus of a negotiation between two different cultures.[84]

Since translation is the point of contact between two cultures, World Literature becomes "writing that gains in translation".[85] The "double refraction" in Damrosch's definition concerns both the formation of a wider supra-national field and of national literary fields. Within the receiving culture, the study of translation history allows for an examination of how "a culture has changed through contact with another culture".[86] Translations that successfully render a foreign author's work in the receiving culture's literary tradition, as I have argued that both Papadiamantēs and Alexandrou accomplished in their domesticating translations of Dostoevsky, have the power to establish the literary value of his work within a national literary field (thus making it a fact of the target culture),[87] as well as, cumulatively, within the world literary field.

Given that Modern Greek national literature was at a formative stage when Russian literature was first imported at the end of the nineteenth century, this essay has shown how Russian fiction introduced new themes and a new poetics to the Modern Greek literary field. Translation acted as a force for innovation that provided Modern Greek authors with literary resources; as an "accumulation of literary capital".[88] Papadiamantēs's *The Murderess*, written after his translation of *Crime and Punishment*, testifies to that momentum. Alexandrou's retranslations, written half a century later, consolidated Dostoevsky's central position in the Greek canon of foreign literature. Alexandrou's retranslations "actualized the potential contained" in Dostoevsky's literary text and helped provide a space for it within Greek culture and language.[89] The publisher Govostēs's decision to prioritise literary over commercial motives in publishing the collected works of Dostoevsky in Greek—evident in his choice of professional translators and editors—added to the literary value of the Greek literary language, further consecrating Dostoevsky in Greek culture.

---

84 David Damrosch, *What Is World Literature?* (Princeton, NJ: Princeton University Press, 2003), p. 283.

85 Ibid., p. 288.

86 Pym, *Method in Translation History*, p. 19.

87 Gideon Toury, *Descriptive Translation Studies—and Beyond* (Amsterdam: John Benjamins, 1995), p. 29.

88 Pascale Casanova, 'Consécration et accumulation', p. 19.

89 Françoise Massardier-Kenney, 'Toward a Rethinking of Retranslation', *Translation Review*, 92:1 (2015), 73–85 (p. 73, p. 78).

Greece

The Reception of Russian and Soviet Literature in Interwar and Postwar Greece

Niovi Zampouka

The Greek reception of Russophone literature during the twentieth century has been mainly restricted to two categories of literature: the most prominent nineteenth-century classics and the classics of Socialist Realism. In this chapter, I will attempt a historical overview of the main stages, aspects and tendencies of the Greek translation and publication of Russian and Soviet literature, focusing on the socio-political context that shaped it within the broader comparative perspective of Greek-Soviet literary entanglements. Further, I will briefly discuss the Greek appropriation of Socialist Realism, drawing on three representative case studies. Finally, I will elaborate on why Modernist voices are missing from the Greek canon of Russian literature.

The Greek 'Northern Obsession'

The most important figures of nineteenth-century Russian literature were introduced in Greece, albeit fragmentarily and unsystematically, mainly during the last quarter of the nineteenth century, through periodicals.[1] This occurred

1 On the reception of Russian literature in nineteenth-century Greece see Sonia Ilinskagia, *Ē rōsikē logotechnia stēn Ellada (19os aiōnas)* (Athens: Ellēnika grammata, 2006), as well as Christina Karakepeli's essay in the present volume. For a bibliographical overview of translations in the nineteenth century, see Kōnstantinos Kasinēs, *Vivliographia tōn ellēnikōn metaphraseōn tēs xenēs logotechnias ITH'-K' ai.*, 2 vols (Athens: Syllogos pros diadosin ōphelimōn vivliōn, 2006–13), I (2006).

 https://doi.org/10.11647/OBP.0340.08

partly through translations from Russian undertaken by Russian-speaking Greeks living in Russia or having close ties to it, and partly through Western languages (French, English, or German). From the mid-1890s onwards, the field of Greek literary translations documents a gradual decline in translations of French literature, which had dominated during the nineteenth century,[2] and a sharp increase in the number of translations from Russian, English, German, and the Scandinavian languages, peaking during the interwar period (1919–38). The noticeable preference for these literatures, which contemporary literary critics called the "northern obsession" (in Greek, *voreiomania*),[3] reflected a broader shift from Romanticism to Realism within the Greek literary field during the first quarter of the twentieth century. It was characterised by a strong preoccupation with social questions and a growing interest in Socialist ideas. As a well-known critic from that period, Aimilios Chourmouzios, notes:

> [...] a time came, which I can place between 1915 and 1930, during which Greece aspired to become a Russian or at least a northern province. That was the time during which we discovered the Russians and the Scandinavians (from 1915 up to 1920). The periodicals made them accessible to the literary audience and from 1920 onwards, a real publishing frenzy begins, characterized by an astonishing plurality of translations of Russian and Scandinavian works, novels and short stories).[4]

According to statistics in Kōnstantinos Kasinēs's *Bibliography of Foreign Literature in Greek Translation 1901–1950*,[5] Russian literature vastly increased its share in the total production of translated literature during the first half of the twentieth century (by comparison with the nineteenth). With sixty-two and fifty-one translated titles respectively, Fedor Dostoevsky and Lev Tolstoy occupy the third and fourth places (in that order) among the twenty most translated foreign authors in Greece, after William Shakespeare and Jules Verne. Maksim Gorky

---

2 Cf. Kōnstantinos Kasinēs, *Vivliographia tōn ellēnikōn metaphraseōn tēs xenēs logotechnias ITH'-K' ai.*, 2 vols (Athens: Syllogos pros diadosin ōphelimōn vivliōn, 2006–13), I (2006), p. 29.

3 For additional information about the origin and emergence of the term, see Kōnstantinos Kasinēs, 'Ē neoellēnikē „voreiomania". Ē rēxē me to romantiko parelthon', in *Continuities, Discontinuities, Ruptures in the Greek World (1204–2014): Economy, Society, History, Literature: 5th European Congress of Modern Greek Studies of the European Society of Modern Greek Studies: Proceedings*, ed. by Kōnstantinos Dēmadēs, 5 vols (Athens: Eurōpaikē Etaireia Neoellēnikōn Spoudōn, 2015), III, pp. 119–38 (p. 127).

4 Aimilios Chourmouzios, 'Logotechnikē alētographia', *Nea Estia*, 313 (1940), 40–43 (p. 41).

5 Kōnstantinos Kasinēs, *Vivliographia tōn ellēnikōn metaphraseōn tēs xenēs logotechnias ITH'-K' ai.*, 2 vols (Athens: Syllogos pros diadosin ōphelimōn vivliōn, 2006–13), II (2013). The statistics provided here refer to book translations only.

holds (with forty-five books) sixth place, with Leonid Andreev in thirteenth (with twenty-eight books). In addition to these four most-translated Russian authors, another forty-six—the vast majority of them belonging to the nineteenth or early twentieth centuries—were translated during this period. These include Ivan Turgenev, Aleksandr Pushkin, Anton Chekhov, Mikhail Lermontov, Nikolai Gogol, Mikhail Artsybashev, Vsevolod Garshin, Aleksandr Kuprin, Vladimir Korolenko, and others. After French and English, Russian was the third most common translated foreign literature (accounting for approximately 13% of all translated literature),[6] the novel being the predominant genre. Most works were translated from the original, while French and German served occasionally as bridge languages.[7] The publishing house Govostēs Editions founded by Kōstas Govostēs (a former literary translator from Russian) in 1926, was the main distributor of translated Russian literature; however, many other major as well as short-lived publishers from across the political spectrum were also active in this field.[8] The fact that, seeing the economic benefit, several publishing houses were retranslating and/or republishing the same titles within very short periods of time, indicates the popularity which Russian classics enjoyed during this period.

The Cult of Gorky

The October Revolution gave even greater impetus to the translation of pre-revolutionary Russian literature. It led to the foundation of Greece's Socialist Labour Party in 1918.[9] At the same time, the dynamic artistic landscape of post-revolutionary Russia encouraged the leftist intelligentsia to discuss proletarian literature, Marxist aesthetics and the purpose of art. Describing the spirit of the highly productive interwar period with regard to the publication and reception of Russian literature, the well-known Greek author Angelos Terzakēs wrote:

6 Kōnstantinos Kasinēs, *Vivliographia*, p. 29.

7 Little or no background information is available regarding three of the most productive translators of the interwar period working directly from Russian. Koralia Makrē translated over twenty works of Russian authors, Athēna Sarantidē translated twelve works of Russian literature in the period 1919–46 and the Egypt-based polyglot Kōstas Trikoglidēs translated works by Dostoevsky, Gorky and Andreev. Prevalent translators of the interwar and postwar period were the novelist and poet Arēs Alexandrou (1922–78), well-known to this day for his translations of Dostoevsky, Maiakovskii, Ehrenburg and of Akhmatova's *Requiem* (*Rekviem*, 1963) as well as the left-wing author Petros Pikros (1894–1956), who also translated Gorky, Dostoevsky and other Russian classics directly from Russian. See Christina Karakepeli's essay in this volume for more on Alexandrou.

8 For statistics on publishing houses of this period, see Kōnstantinos Kasinēs, *Vivliographia*, pp. 36–38.

9 In 1924 the Party adopted its current name: the 'Communist Party of Greece'.

> Imperative messages of the biggest social revolution in the world were coming from the North. [...] While a small, socially privileged, group continued the tradition of turning to the West, [...] another group, more numerous and invisible, was rising up from the popular underground [...]. It was then, that Russian authors triumphantly invaded Greece. In the literary undergrounds, a wind of wild admiration for the heroes of misery and rebellion was blowing. Short-lived literary magazines were competing to promote any short story by a revolutionary writer translated from Russian and literary novices without a future were copying these exaggeratedly for their mental emancipation. They were wearing flat caps on uncombed hair, growing beards like those of persecuted writers of the tsarist era and falling platonically in love with prostitutes like Dostoevsky's, Gorky's and Andreev's protagonists.[10]

Within this context, Gorky constituted one of the leading figures among translated Russian authors in interwar Greece, not only in terms of circulation—approximately thirty-five of his works were translated by more than twenty-five translators during the first half of the twentieth century[11]—but mostly in terms of popularity and productive appropriation on various levels of intertextuality. Since he was perceived not only as a writer but also as a literary theoretician and critic, Gorky enjoyed a multifaceted reception, acquiring—also by means of his own 'eventful' biography—virtually mythological status. As the leftist writer and literary critic Petros Pikros (his pen name 'pikros' meaning 'bitter' in Greek, just like 'gor'kii' in Russian)[12] noted in 1928: "We all know that Gorky [...] has always been the most popular writer of all the Russians here [...] even when the French were very popular, even when the Scandinavians were totally in fashion [...] Gorky found himself to be the most well-known, the most read".[13] Gorky was praised regularly as the "spiritual father" of revolutionary literature by father figures of the Greek Left such as the poet Kōstas Varnalēs and the Marxist theoretician Dēmētrēs Glēnos,[14] and was appreciated as a realist writer by established liberal literati such as Kōstēs Palamas, Stratēs Myrivēlēs, and others. Left-wing writers related to him directly through the dedication of

10 Angelos Terzakēs, 'Dēmosthenēs Vouturas', *Nea Estia*, 190 (1934), 1015–22 (p. 1015).

11 Works such as *Mother* (*Mat'*, 1907), *The Lower Depths* (*Na dne*, 1902) and *The Philistines* (*Meshchane*, 1902) were retranslated and republished several times. See Kōnstantinos Kasinēs, *Vivliographia*, p. 27.

12 His real name was Giannēs Gennaropoulos (1894–1956).

13 Petros Pikros, 'Gyrō apo to iōvilaio tou. O Gkorky s' emas edō', *Nea Epitheōrēsē*, 5 (1928), 129–36 (p. 131).

14 See for instance Varnalēs' text 'Pōs gnōrisa ton Gorki' ['How I Met Gorki'], *Rizospastis*, 28 June 1936, pp. 3–4.

poems[15] or inscriptions, as well as intertextually by adopting specific Gorkian motifs such as the eponymous 'Mother', Pelageia Nilovna, from his 1906 novel,[16] or the figure of the Vagabond (the latter inspiring the titles of short stories and poems or even pen names).[17] While the appropriation of Gorky's critical realism and/or revolutionary romanticism by Realist writers can be argued in regard to social protest novels and proletarian novels of Greek leftist literature (at least two canonical Greek authors—Dēmosthenēs Vouturas and Menelaos Lountemēs—have been called the 'Gorky of Greece' in different periods of time), Gorky's 'vagabond' characters triggered, especially among young writers of the interwar period, a great wave of imitation, forming a distinct literary trend, much discussed by interwar critics.[18]

The Introduction of Socialist Realism

These domestic literary needs of Russophone literature were motivated by historical and cultural ties between Greece and Russia and by the development of Greek Socialist thought, which examined how Russians had reflected on the socio-political and moral-spiritual situation in their country on the eve of the revolutions, as well as by corresponding West European literary trends. The book market's major focus lay thus on Russian writers of the late nineteenth and the early twentieth century, whereas post-revolutionary Russian literature, though gradually presented to the public by leftist periodicals, held an insignificant market share until the end of the Second World War. The diversity of viewpoints regarding the forms of revolutionary art, depicted in the Greek leftist literary journals in the first decade of the interwar period and reflecting to a large extent the literary controversies of the Soviet 1920s as well as Western European Marxist positions, indicate an openness to avant-gardist approaches. Notwithstanding, periodicals of translated literature clearly focused on those writers and poets who embraced the revolution, some of the most widely published being Gorky,

15 See for instance Giannēs Ritsos's poem 'Ston s. Gkorki' ['To c. Gorki'] in *Neoi Prōtoporoi*, 7 (1935), pp. 254–55, or Teukros Anthias's poem 'Gorky—teacher, brother, father!' as cited in Iannis Mochos, 'Traditsii Maksima Gor'kogo v grecheskoi literature', in *Gor'kii i sovremennost'*, ed. by Vladimir Shcherbina (Moscow: Nauka, 1970), pp. 388–93 (pp. 389–90).

16 For instance by Giannēs Ritsos in his poem *Epitaphios* (1936) or by Melpō Axiōtē in her novel *The Twentieth Century* (*Eikostos aiōnas*, 1946).

17 See for instance Dēmosthenēs Vouturas's short story *The Vagabonds* (*Oi alaniarēdes*, 1921) or Teukros Anthias's poem cycle *The Whistles of the Vagabond* (*Ta sfyrigmata tou alētē*, 1929), which allude to Greek publications of Gorky's short story collections that adopted the French edition's title *Les vagabonds* (first published in 1901 by Mercure de France in Ivan Strannik's translation).

18 For a more detailed analysis of Gorky's reception in Greece, see Giōrgos Michaēlidēs, 'Translating Russian Literature in Interwar Greece: The Example of Maxim Gorky', *Syn-Thèses*, 6 (2013), 1–19, https://doi.org/10.26262/st.v0i6.5306.

followed by Vladimir Maiakovskii, the poet of the Revolution *par excellence*, and Dem'ian Bednyi, very popular in the 1920s and 1930s.[19] Modernist writers and poets like Anna Akhmatova, Boris Pil'niak, Boris Pasternak, and others were not unknown to interwar literary criticism, but remained largely untranslated and thus obscure to the public; or else known exclusively for the romantic-revolutionary aspects of their work. For instance, Aleksandr Blok's poem 'The Twelve' ('Dvenadtsat'', 1918) was reprinted multiple times due to its thematic affinity to the revolution, while the rest of his work received almost no attention.[20] From the early 1930s onwards, this relative openness was gradually replaced by a canonical, party-regulated conception of literature. The programme of Socialist Realism, launched in Moscow at the First Congress of Soviet Writers in 1934, also drew a line under domestic left-wing critical reflection on aesthetics. The principles of Socialist Realism were imported to Greece directly after their official consolidation through the important Greek leftist literary magazine *New Avant-gardists* (*Neoi Prōtoporoi*), which devoted a September 1934 special issue to the Congress, with translations of the major keynote speeches by Gorky, Andrei Zhdanov, Karl Radek, and Nikolai Bukharin. Later issues listed the charter of the Soviet Writers' Union. From this point onwards, Socialist Realist postulates were adopted by left-wing literary critics, becoming common currency among them.[21] Polemics against 'bourgeois literature', naturalism, and formalism intensified while the representation of reality in its 'revolutionary development', the positive hero, and linguistic simplicity were strongly promoted. Gorky's glorification of folklore encouraged the Marxist Greek intelligentsia's interest in folk culture and oral storytelling traditions while the number of translations of Soviet literary theoretical articles elaborating on the concept of Socialist Realism increased.[22]

Public disputes, especially about Socialism, were interrupted by anti-Communist repressions under the dictatorial Metaxas regime (1936–41), followed by the outbreak of World War II and the Axis occupation of Greece (1941–45). Significantly fewer translations were published in this period; most were reprints, with some new translations of Russian nineteenth-century classics (Tolstoy, Dostoevsky, Pushkin, Gogol, Chekhov, Andreev, and Gorky),

19 See, for example, the contents of the magazine *Neoi Prōtoporoi* in *Neoi Prōtoporoi (1931–1936)*, ed. by Maria Sakellariou (Thessalonika: University Studio Press, 1999).

20 After the war, at least three editions of Blok's 'The Twelve' were published: by Petros Kolaklidēs (Athens: n.pub., 1945); by Giannēs Ritsos (Athens: Kedros, 1957); and in 1964, by Kōstas Tambakēs (Athens: n.pub.). This poem also appeared in several literary journals, including *Epitheōrēsē technēs*, 34 (1957).

21 See Christina Dounia, *Logotechnia kai politikē: Ta periodika tēs aristeras sto mesopolemo* (Athens: Kastaniōtēs, 1996).

22 The amount of aesthetic theory and literary criticism translated from Russian and published in leftist literary magazines exceeds that translated from other languages over the entire interwar period. See Dounia, *Logotechnia kai politikē*, pp. 504–5.

and a few works of contemporary Soviet war literature (e.g. Aleksandr Bek and Vasilii Grossman). Russian and Soviet literature published in 1945—the year of liberation—exhibited a sharp turn to twentieth-century Russian literature, showcasing the diversity of literary trends (together with the plurality of interests) that might have eventually prevailed in the publishing field if the Greek Civil War had not broken out. In parallel with Socialist Realist Bildungsromans such as Nikolai Ostrovskii's *How The Steel Was Tempered* (*Kak zakalialas' stal'*, 1932/1934) and Il'ia Ehrenburg's *Without Pausing For Breath* (*Ne perevodia dykhaniia*, 1935), other prominent genres of Soviet literature of the 1920s such as Aleksei Tolstoy's utopian science-fiction novel *Blue Cities* (*Golubye goroda*, 1925) and Il'ia Il'f's and Evgenii Petrov's satirical novel *The Twelve Chairs* (*Dvenadtsat' stul'ev*, 1928), two narratives clearly incompatible with the officially promoted literature of the Zhdanov era—Isaak Babel's banned *Red Cavalry* (*Konarmiia*, 1926) and *The Man from the Restaurant* (*Chelovek iz restorana*, 1911) by the Russian émigré writer Ivan Shmelev—demonstrated an alternative aesthetic and political approach that, without being polemically anti-Soviet, took a critical stand against the dogmatism of the Soviet literary canon. Despite the explicitly antidogmatic rhetoric of the editions' prefaces—which Gérard Genette famously considers "a zone not only of transition but also of transaction: a privileged place of pragmatics and a strategy, of an influence on the public"[23] —both the last-named works were framed by their Greek publishers as highly popular in the Soviet Union without mentioning their authors' fates, such as Babel's arrest or the execution of Shmelev's son by the Bolsheviks, causing Shmelev to exile himself in Paris.

Soviet Literature as Role Model

After the Communists lost the Greek Civil War (1946–49), which erupted (following the end of the Axis occupation) between the Communist-dominated leftist forces and the government forces from the political right, Greek Communists shifted their activities to the so-called 'ideological front'. Printed propaganda produced during the partisan warfare by means of portable hand-printing presses in the mountains was transferred to new settlements in the Eastern Bloc countries,[24] where the outlawed Communist Party (KKE) and

23 Gérard Genette, *Paratexts: Thresholds of Interpretation* (Cambridge: Cambridge University Press, 1997), p. 2. For the ideological use of paratexts and their relevance for translated literature, see also Caroline Summers, 'What Remains: The Institutional Reframing of Authorship in Translated Peritexts', in *Text, Extratext, Metatext and Paratext in Translation*, ed. by Valerie Pellatt (Newcastle upon Tyne: Cambridge Scholars Publishing, 2013), pp. 9–32.

24 Mainly in Bulkes (now Maglić) and Belgrade in the former People's Republic of Serbia, in Bucharest and Dej in the Romanian People's Republic and in Borovets in the People's Republic of Bulgaria.

Greek political exiles sought refuge. The main goal of their 'ideological struggle', steered by the Communist Party's quest for political influence, was political indoctrination and popularisation of the Party line among the masses. As far as publishing was concerned, this translated into the circulation of works that:

> contribute to the increase of the Marxist-Leninist and ideological-theoretical level of Party members and people's fighters in general; to the creation of politically and theoretically trained combat cadres in Greece, and active and cultivated fighters of socialist construction abroad.[25]

Anna Matthaiou and Popē Polemē have shown how the Party used literature to make a targeted contribution to Communist enlightenment and education. Authors living in political exile, as well as domestic left-wing writers, were prompted to compose patriotic works inspired by the people's heroic struggles for resistance and liberation, which vividly depicted the 'New Man' of Socialist culture and cultivated optimism and belief in victory along with hatred for Fascism, war, and pessimism. Soviet literature's function as a role model for this process was accentuated by explicit references in the left-wing press and in Party speeches of the time; it was reflected in the book production of the exile publishing houses in their first years of operation (1947–54). The publication of translated Soviet literature during this time exceeded that of native Greek literature many times over.[26] The General Secretary of the Communist Party of Greece, Nikos Zachariadis, announced in 1949:

> We have published a few dozens of the best works of Soviet literature, mostly dealing with the heroism, the achievements and exploits of the Soviet people during World War II. For us, these works contain, among other things, a rich and very valuable war experience. So we need to make sure that all of our male and female fighters familiarize themselves with these in order to learn from them.[27]

In parallel with Soviet theoretical texts on Socialist Realism, the Greek Communist Party's printing houses outside of Greece published during these years Greek translations of Aleksandr Bek's *Volokolamsk Highway* (*Volokolamskoe shosse*, 1947); Petr Vershigora's *People with a Clear Conscience* (*Liudi s chistoi sovest'iu*, 1947); Vasilii Grossman's *For a Just Cause* (*Za pravoe delo/Stalingrad*, 1952); Boris Polevoi's *Story of a Real Man* (*Povest' o nastoiashchem cheloveke*,

25 According to a report by the KKE politburo from 1951 as cited in Anna Matthaiou and Popē Polemē, *Apo to vouno stēn yperoria: Ē ekdotikē peripeteia tōn Ellēnōn kommounistōn, 1947–1968* (Athens: Vivliorama, 2003), p. 62.

26 This picture emerges from the evaluation of the publications catalogue provided in Anna Matthaiou and Popē Polemē, *Apo to vouno stēn yperoria*.

27 Nikos Zachariadēs' speech in the Central Committee's fifth plenary session (1949), cited in Anna Matthaiou and Popē Polemē, *Apo to vouno stēn yperoria*, p. 24.

1947); Petr Ignatov's *Partisans of the Kuban* (*Zapiski partizana*, 1944); Nikolai Ostrovskii's *Born of the Storm* (*Rozhdennye burei*, 1936); Dmitrii Furmanov's *Chapayev* (*Chapaev*, 1923); Mikhail Sholokhov's *They Fought For Their Country* (*Oni srazhalis' za rodinu*, 1943); Aleksandr Fadeev's *The Young Guard* (*Molodaia gvardiia*, 1946) and *The Rout* (*Razgrom*, 1927), besides numerous other classics of Soviet war literature, most of which were illegally exported to and circulated in Greece. These works were considered important for boosting fighters' morale. In their backpacks—as one can read in the Party's newspaper *Neos Kosmos*—"while bread was unlikely to be found, books like *Volokolamsk Highway*, *How the Steel Was Tempered* and *Story of a Real Man* one would definitely find".[28] Literary figures such as Furmanov's Klychkov or Polevoi's Vorob'ev were used as role models for the political commissars of the Democratic Army of Greece (KKE's military branch), while literary representations of battles served as guidelines for war reports: "In the description of the battle the man should be shown with his emotions, his feelings (as this is done in *Volokolamsk Highway*)".[29] At the same time, Socialist Realist classics were meant to function as a preparatory 'proto-canon'—a textual reservoir providing, in Pascale Casanova's sense of the phrase, the "literary resources" for Greek "progressive" literary production.[30]

From the mid-1950s onwards, the publication of translated Soviet literature by the Party's printing houses in exile decreased considerably in favour of contemporary left-wing Greek literature. According to an article in *Neos Kosmos* after the Second Congress of Soviet Writers (1954), "Soviet literature, its humanistic ideals, its patriotism and internationalism had a great and beneficial impact, not only on the readers, but also on the writers of Greece".[31] The vast majority of Greek literary works that can be identified as appropriations of Socialist Realism, as defined by the widely accepted typologies of Katerina Clark, Hans Günther, Evgeny Dobrenko, and others, belong to postwar and resistance literature.[32] They primarily address the Greek resistance movement and Greek social reality in the aftermath of the Civil War (and also, in later years, resistance to the Greek military junta of 1967–74). The Civil War itself is

---

28 Kōstas Bosēs and Apostolos Spēlios, 'To 2o synedrio tōn sovietikōn syngrapheōn. (Didagmata gia tēn ellēnikē patriotikē logotechnia)', *Neos Kosmos*, 3 (1955), 63–74 (p. 64).

29 From the instructions directed to radio correspondents in 1948 as cited in Anna Matthaiou and Popē Polemē, *Apo to vouno stēn yperoria*, p. 25.

30 Pascale Casanova, *The World Republic of Letters* (Cambridge, MA: Harvard University Press, 2007), p. 235.

31 Bosēs and Spēlios, 'To 2o synedrio tōn sovietikōn syngrapheōn'.

32 See Katerina Clark, *The Soviet Novel: History as Ritual* (Chicago: University of Chicago Press, 1981); *Sotsrealisticheskii kanon*, ed. by Chans Giunter and Evgeny Dobrenko (St Petersburg: Akademicheskii proekt, 2000); Hans Günther, *Die Verstaatlichung der Literatur. Entstehung und Funktionsweise des sozialistisch-realistischen Kanons in der sowjetischen Literatur der 30er Jahre* (Stuttgart: Metzler, 1984).

implicitly present, represented by the disappointed, and therefore less positive, hero of leftist post-civil-war literature. It is largely absent as a central theme or setting, both because of the Communist defeat, which makes it a delicate issue of literary negotiation, and because of this period's party line on literature.[33] In general, Greek appropriations of Socialist Realism correspond to the concept of the "prototypical plot" defined by Katerina Clark in *The Soviet Novel: History as Ritual* (1981), which outlines the typical young Soviet hero's "rite of passage" from relative spontaneity to political consciousness. Assisted in his quest by an older, more 'conscious' mentor figure, the hero overcomes obstacles and achieves his goal through social integration and gradual development of collective identity.[34] Beyond the structural elements of the master plot, these works share most of the Socialist Realist novel's tropes and literary paradigms: Gorky's Mother-figure; Ostrovskii's portrait of physical suffering and paralysis as constitutive characteristics of a true hero; the prioritisation of the collective over the personal; expressive focus on machines and agricultural labour; criticism and parody of bourgeois culture; female emancipation and collective action; and explicit philo-Soviet references. However, Greek Socialist Realism primarily differs from the Soviet version by the intensity of its expression of Party spirit (*partiinost'*), a difference explicable by the respective transformations of the canon within the Greek literary field.

Greek Appropriation of Socialist Realism

A brief comparison of three exemplary cases demonstrates the main tendencies of the Socialist Realist canon's appropriation by Greek leftist literature. The

---

33 Despite its reorientation and alleged openness to scepticism and criticism in light of Khrushchev's secret speech (1956), the Party recommended restricting the Civil War as a literary theme in favour of anti-Nazi resistance topics. This served the interests of both the Party, which sought to establish a broad patriotic front in Greece and therefore benefit from emphasis on the resistance movement instead of the one-sided portrayal of Communist guerilla fighters (which risked providing additional pretexts for anti-Communist state propaganda); and of politically exiled authors themselves, whose concerns for amnesty and repatriation were bound up with Civil War memory. See Venetia Apostolidou, 'The Politics of Memory in the Fiction of Greek Political Exiles in Eastern Europe', in *Greek Diaspora and Migration Since 1700: Society, Politics and Culture*, ed. by Dimitris Tziovas (Burlington: Ashgate, 2009), pp. 215–28 (pp. 222–23); and Venetia Apostolidou, *Trauma kai mnēmē: ē pezographia tōn politikōn prosphygōn* (Athens: Polis, 2010), p. 65.

34 Katerina Clark, *The Soviet Novel: History as Ritual*, pp. 159–76. For the key features and periodisation of Socialist Realism see also Hans Günther, 'Die Lebensphasen eines Kanons–am Beispiel des sozialistischen Realismus', in *Kanon und Zensur. Beiträge zur Archäologie der literarischen Kommunikation*, ed. by A. Assmann and J. Assmann, 3 vols (Munich: Fink, 1983–1999), II (1987), pp. 138–48.

first is *The Twentieth Century* (*Eikostos aiōnas*, 1946) by Melpō Axiōtē (1905–73), which appeared in Athens shortly before its author's long-term exile in Paris and East Berlin. Axiōtē, whose innovative earlier works employed surrealistic techniques, converted to Marxist ideology and joined the Greek Communist Party in the mid-1930s. Her novel describes the sacrifice of a modern Polyxena. This is the name of the protagonist, a young woman from a middle-class family, who after joining the Greek resistance on the Communist side, finds herself spending her last night in a prison cell awaiting execution. Here she reflects on her life, which has been closely intertwined with major socio-political events of the early twentieth century.[35] Despite fulfilling every aspect of the Socialist Realist master plot, including Gorky-esque motifs, and showing an explicitly philo-Soviet spirit, Axiōtē's novel is far from conventional in the strict, dogmatic sense of the canon. The novel features several modernist literary devices as well as a highly controversial depiction of the October Revolution, described in an eyewitness report by Russian refugees as a bloody event orchestrated by violent and ruthless Bolsheviks.

Published in the same year and prior to its author's exile variously in Hungary, Romania, and East Berlin, the novel *Fire* (*Fōtia*, 1946) by Dēmētrēs Chatzēs (1913–81) addresses, through the experiences of a peasant family, Greek national resistance against occupying German troops. *Fire* offers a vision of a Greek People's Republic. Following a young woman's character development from naivety to emancipation and ideological consciousness, the novel is characterised by heroic self-sacrifice, the cult of labour, collective optimism, and Party-driven sentiment. Due to its modernist poetics and subversively negative depiction of the October Revolution, Axiōtēs' novel is situated on the periphery of Socialist Realist style, while Chatzēs' novel represents an ideal realisation of Stalin's well-known formula "national in form, socialist in content".[36] Having been composed during the phase of full implementation of the canon[37] and also on the eve of the Civil War without knowledge of its outcome, both novels communicate—despite their differences in style—explicit optimism, an enthusiastic bond with the Communist Party, and clear political conviction.

Different again is the dilogy by Mētsos Alexandropoulos (1924–2008), *Nights and Dawns* (*Nychtes kai auges*), published by the Greek Communist Party's printing house in Romania in 1961–63, during the author's exile in the Soviet

35 In Greek mythology Polyxena was the youngest daughter of King Priam of Troy and his queen, Hecuba, who—according to one variation of the myth—was sacrificed by the Greeks on the tomb of Achilles after the fall of Troy in order to appease his ghost and thus raise winds to take the Greek ships home.

36 Iosif Stalin, 'O politicheskikh zadachakh universiteta narodov Vostoka: Rech' na sobranii studentov KUTV. 18 maia 1925 g.', in *Sochineniia*, 18 vols (Moscow and Tver': Gosudarstvennoe izdatel'stvo politicheskoi literatury, 1946–2006), VII (1952), pp. 133–52 (p. 138).

37 For the key features and periodisation of Socialist Realism see for instance Hans Günther, 'Die Lebensphasen eines Kanons'.

Union. The novel, which was originally written as a graduation thesis at the Maksim Gorky Literature Institute, discusses partisan fighting during the Axis occupation of Greece. This work preserves the master plot and positive hero, however—like many other politically engaged novels to emerge in the aftermath of the Civil War and during the period of decanonisation—its political position is significantly more reserved, albeit clear, with elements of leftist self-criticism. Within the context of the Soviet Union's "largest more or less coherent project of translation the world has seen to date",[38] these three novels—along with many other works of Greek left-wing writers—were translated and introduced as "progressive literature" into the Soviet literary field of the 1950s and 1960s, where they underwent further canonisation and Sovietisation through paratextual framing, ideological translation, and censorship.[39] Gorky's (and occasionally Dostoevsky's) 'influence', or any kind of thematic affiliation with his work, is regularly accentuated in the translations' paratexts (often written by Greek authors and philologists in Soviet exile), serving as a legitimisation of the publication and indicating the father role of the Russian literary tradition. Most of these authors, including those discussed above, would eventually distance themselves from Socialist Realist aesthetics.

Revisionist Tendencies and Repression

Within the domestic Greek literary field of the 1950s and 1960s, literary production and publishing operated in a climate of extreme political polarisation under conditions of repression and fear. The 'Emergency Law 509' of 1947, ostensibly created to discourage violent coups but essentially a bulwark against Communist propaganda, had provided for harsh penalties such as imprisonment, internal exile, or execution. It was not repealed until after the end of the Greek junta in 1974.[40] In the mid-1950s, Gorky's *Mother* (*Mat'*, 1907),

38 Susanna Witt, 'Between the Lines: Totalitarianism and Translation in the USSR', in *Contexts, Subtexts and Pretexts: Literary Translation in Eastern Europe and Russia*, ed. by Brian James Baer (Amsterdam and Philadelphia, PA: John Benjamins, 2011), pp. 149–70 (p. 167).

39 On Greek appropriation of Socialist Realism and Greek literature reception in the Soviet Union see my published dissertation, *Sozialistischer Realismus erzählen und übersetzen: Von der Sowjetunion nach Griechenland und retour* [*Narrating and Translating Socialist Realism. From the Soviet Union to Greece and Back*] (Berlin and Boston, MA: De Gruyter, 2023), pp. 158–75, https://www.degruyter.com/document/doi/10.1515/9783111026534/html?lang=en.

40 For in-depth accounts of the Greek Civil War and Greek political and social reality after the liberation from Nazi occupation, see for instance *After The War Was Over: Reconstructing the Family, Nation, and State in Greece, 1943–1960*, ed. by Mark Mazower (Princeton, NJ: Princeton University Press, 2000); Roderick Beaton, *Greece: Biography Of A Modern Nation* (London: Allen Lane, 2019); and Mark Mazower, 'Policing the Anti-Communist State in Greece, 1922–1974', in *The Policing*

Dostoevsky's *Poor Folk* (*Bednye liudi*, 1846), Gogol's *Dead Souls* (*Mertvye dushi*, 1842) and Il'ia Ehrenburg's *The Fall of Paris* (*Padenie Parizha*, 1941), among other world literature classics, were banned; many Greek left-wing writers, poets, publishers and artists were put on trial and sent to internal exile on prison islands. In this hostile context for the publication of Soviet literature, translation work and relatively diverse publishing activity continued. Besides new editions of old translations and new translations of Russian nineteenth-century classics and of Gorky's works, contemporary Soviet writers who enjoyed multiple translated publications included Aleksei Tolstoy, Il'ia Ehrenburg, Valentin Kataev, and Aleksandr Blok. From the mid-1950s onwards, revisionist trends, as well as close monitoring of the publishing activity abroad, become more and more apparent. Although not published by the Communist Party, Ehrenburg's *The Thaw* (*Ottepel'*, 1954) appeared in 1955 with an anonymous preface summarising both Soviet criticism of the novel during the Second Congress of Soviet Writers (1954) and Ehrenburg's response. It was subsequently republished in four editions and re-translated three times by 1960.[41] The 1958 Greek translation of Boris Pasternak's *Doctor Zhivago* (*Doktor Zhivago*, 1957), imported debates surrounding the 'Pasternak affair' into the Greek field of literary criticism. In 1959, Vladimir Nabokov's *Lolita* (1955) appeared; in 1963–64, Aleksandr Solzhenitsyn's *One Day in the Life of Ivan Denisovich* (*Odin den' Ivana Denisovicha*, 1962) was published.[42] Revisionist tendencies seeking to liberate Socialist Realism from the absolute dominance of tropes like the positive hero and the absence of conflict (*bezkonfliktnost*), short of abolishing the canon, were still subject to Party control. Thus, the publication of Daniil Granin's novella *A Personal Opinion* (*Sobstvennoe mnenie*, 1956) by the important revisionist literary journal *Epitheōrēsē technēs* in 1959, a work which had already drawn criticism from Soviet Party bureaucrats and even from Nikita Khrushchev, led to an

of Politics in the Twentieth Century: Historical Perspectives, ed. by Mark Mazower (Providence, MA: Berghahn Books, 1997), pp. 129–50.

41 Two translations of the book—one from Russian by the journalist and left-wing resistance fighter Lampros Sekleiziōtēs (Athens: Kerkēs) and one by Moursella Pierakopoulou (Athens: Arkadia)—appeared in 1955. Sekleiziōtēs' translation was republished in 1956 (Athens: Pyxida), while a third version by K. Ch. Angelidis also appeared around this time (Athens: Parisianos, n.d.). Very little is known today about these translators and publishers. Due to inadequate bibliographical information, common with older editions, and the frequent use of pseudonyms because of political repression, their identities often prove elusive. More generally, the field of the Greek reception of Russian literature from the perspective of sociology of translation and actor–network theory remains largely unexplored.

42 Based on its paratexts, the year 1964 is the *terminus ante quem of* this publication. Soviet dissident literature such as Solzhenitsyn's *One Day in the Life of Ivan Denisovich* or other officially banned literary works such as Mikhail Bulgakov's *The Master and Margarita* (*Master i Margarita*, 1967) would be (re-)published under the Greek military junta, often with an explicitly anti-Communist framework.

informal Greek Communist Party trial. As a result, the journal editors resigned, and the journal was forced to change course.[43]

Conclusion

The editorial decision to publish a story depicting the dark side of the Soviet state and Party apparatus by a journal, which only two years before had been prosecuted for publishing an issue dedicated to the fortieth anniversary of the October Revolution,[44] not only manifests a conscious attempt to expand, modernise, and rationalise the Zhdanovian conception of the canon, but also highlights a broader problematic of the reception of Russian literature in Greece. Elaborating on the conditions that determine the transnational circulation of literature in translation, Johan Heilbron and Gisèle Sapiro cite politics as a determining and also—depending on the "degree of politicisation"—constraining factor.[45] Due to prevailing political conditions in Greece from the interwar period until the mid-1970s—also substantially responsible for the delayed institutionalisation of Slavic studies in Greece[46]—the primary reception and subsequent introduction of twentieth-century Russian literary production in Greece took place largely through leftist ideological channels—organised mainly around the Communist Party—through which only officially-approved Soviet literature was imported.[47] As a consequence of this extreme political polarisation, as well as the continuous conflict, repression, and exile endured by the Greek Left for most of the twentieth century, the very limited attempts observed to import nonconformist, controversial, or stigmatised works were necessarily also politically inflected. In other words, the dissemination of Russian literature in Greece during the period I have discussed was not primarily

43 See Alexandra Iōannidou, *Ypothesē Gkranin: Ē logotechnikē kritikē sto edōlio* (Athens: Kastaniōtēs, 2008).

44 See *Epitheōrēsē technēs*, 34 (1957). The publication by the same journal of an issue devoted to Soviet literature in 1962 (96) provoked this time a Soviet reaction because of its promotion of 'modernist' texts. See Popē Polemē and Dēmētrēs Dēmētropoulos, 'Dēmētrēs Spathēs (1925–2014): o theatrologos', *The Books' Journal* (29 December 2014), https://booksjournal.gr/synenteykseis/774.

45 Johan Heilbron and Gisèle Sapiro, 'Outline for a Sociology of Translation: Current Issues and Future Prospects', in *Constructing a Sociology of Translation*, ed. by Michaela Wolf and Alexandra Fukari (Amsterdam: Benjamins Translation Library, 2007), pp. 93–107 (p. 97), https://doi.org/10.1075/btl.74.07hei.

46 The first purely philological department of Slavic studies was founded only in 2007.

47 Another factor to be considered is the absence in Greece of big Russian diasporic communities, as in Paris, Berlin or the United States, which could possibly form an additional channel for the dissemination of dissident literature. See also Alexandra Iōannidou, 'Political Aspects of Russian Literature Reception in Greece: Aris Alexandrou and Mitsos Aleksandropoulos', *Slavica Gandensia*, 32 (2005), 67–79.

motivated by aesthetic value nor by the philological consciousness of a specific foreign literature; rather, it fulfilled broader ideological purposes. For reasons linked to the political history of Greece, many of the most important Russian novelists and poets such as Aleksandr Blok, Anna Akhmatova, Marina Tsvetaeva, Sergei Esenin, Osip Mandel'shtam, Nikolai Gumilev, Boris Pil'niak, Iurii Olesha, Andrei Siniavskii, Iosif Brodskii, and many others, remained largely inaccessible to Greek readers until the mid- to late-1970s, emphatically confirming, in the case of Greek reception of twentieth-century Russian literature, Gideon Toury's definition of translations as "facts of target cultures".[48] Interestingly, some of those Greek authors in Soviet exile, who had embraced Socialist Realism and/ or used their status as translators or literary critics to introduce official Soviet aesthetics to Greece, repositioned themselves during the late Soviet period as mediators of Russian culture and formerly banned Russian literature.[49]

48 Gideon Toury, *Descriptive Translation Studies—and Beyond* (Amsterdam: John Benjamins, 1995), p. 29.

49 Two of the most widely published Greek writers in the Soviet Union—Mētsos Alexandropoulos and Alexēs Parnēs—are characteristic examples of such authorial repositioning. For a more detailed analysis of these strategies see Niovi Zampouka, *Sozialistischer Realismus erzählen und übersetzen.*

Hungary

"Russia has so far given humanity nothing but samovars": On the Reception of Russian Literature in Hungary from the Beginning to Nabokov and Beyond

Zsuzsa Hetényi

Dionýz Ďurišin (1929–97) was the first scholar to categorise literary translation as a form and genre of comparative literature, drawing attention to the important distinction between direct and indirect relations in mediation.[1] Ďurišin considers literary translation the most complex form of cultural transfer. He points out that research into mediation plays an extremely important role in the study of patterns of world literature as a whole; it is particularly important in countries with isolated languages, like Hungary. Initially, very few Hungarian translators knew Russian: therefore, until the 1870s, most Russian works reached Hungarian audiences primarily through intermediary (or bridging) translations. My essay aims to describe the main trends in the Hungarian reception of translated Russian literature from the beginning, in the nineteenth century, up to the twentieth. I will provide deeper insight into the problems of the Socialist era by finishing with three brief case studies (from my own direct experience as a translator) on the translation of censored Russian authors and samizdat.

The evolution of nineteenth-century literature in Central and Eastern Europe differs in many respects from its development in Russia because of the huge difference in geo-literary space: smaller nations' cultural progress was defined

1 Dionýz Ďurišin, *Theory of Literary Comparatistics*, trans. by Jessie Kocmanová (Bratislava: Slovak Academy of Sciences, 1984), p. 12.

 https://doi.org/10.11647/OBP.0340.09

by their devotion to strengthening national consciousness.[2] In a phenomenon Pascale Casanova has described as the 'Herder effect', Croatians, Serbs, Czechs, Slovaks, Serbs from Vojvodina, and also Hungarians, attached great importance to the study of folk poetry that enriched their national culture and to themes drawn from their (often idealised) national past.[3] Hence in Central and Eastern Europe, this Romantic literary tendency prevailed much longer than it did in Russian literature.[4] In Hungary, in the 1850s and 1860s, during the heyday of the Russian Realist novel, poetry remained the principal genre, while the historical and romantic novels of Mór Jókai (1825–1904) continued to play a leading role in prose.[5] That is why Aleksandr Pushkin's 1832 *Evgenii Onegin*, translated in 1866 by Károly Bérczy (1821–67), not only found its place in this verse-oriented literary mainstream but influenced a popular new genre: novels in verse proliferated in Hungary.[6] Itamar Even-Zohar has argued that "the very principles of selecting the works to be translated are determined by the situation governing the (home) polysystem".[7] Thus, Russian literature apparently did not provide new patterns or topics for peripheral Hungary's literary development until the last decades of the nineteenth century.

From Mediated to Direct Translations: Three Periods in the Nineteenth Century

The period between 1820 and 1840, when sporadic translations from Russian literature were published in German or mediated through German translations, brought not only Pushkin and Lermontov (whose *Hero of Our Time* or *Geroi nashego vremeni*, 1839–41 was translated very roughly by János Kriza in 1840), but also Vladimir Odoevskii and Nikolai Gogol to Hungarian audiences. They were accompanied by their contemporary Russian critics, including essays by Faddei Bulgarin and Vissarion Belinskii, translated via German. The main mediators of this process during this first period (the so-called Age of Reforms) were the

2 Zsuzsa Zöldhelyi, *A külföldi közvetítés szerepe az orosz irodalom magyar fogadtatásában (XIX. század)*, ed. by Zsuzsa Hetényi (Budapest: ELTE BTK Műfordító Műhely, series *Dolce Filologia*, 2008).

3 Pascale Casanova, *The World Republic of Letters*, trans. by Malcolm DeBevoise (Cambridge, MA: Harvard University Press, 2004).

4 István Fried, 'A kelet-középeurópai romantika jellegzetességeiről', *Filológiai Közlöny*, 2 (1980), 153–68.

5 István Sőtér, 'A verses regény és a regény (Az Anyegin és a magyar irodalom)', in Sőtér, *Az ember és műve* (Budapest: Akadémiai Kiadó, 1971), pp. 310–19.

6 Bérczy started working from Friedrich von Bodenstedt's German translation but, enchanted by Pushkin's novel in verse, he learned Russian in order to translate it directly.

7 Itamar Even-Zohar, 'The Position of Translated Literature within the Literary Polysystem', in *The Translation Studies Reader*, ed. by Lawrence Venuti, 2nd edn (London: Routledge, 2004), pp. 192–97 (p. 197).

language-reformer Ferenc Kazinczy (1759–1831); Ferenc Toldy (1805–75), the author of an overview titled *Russian Poetry* (1828);[8] and the literary translator and Member of Parliament, Gábor Kazinczy (1818–64).

In 1844, seven years after Pushkin's death and three years after Lermontov's, Ferenc Toldy (then still Ferenc Schedel; Toldy was a pseudonym) noted in his foreword inaugurating a new series of 'Foreign Novels' (*Külföldi regénytár*) published by the Kisfaludy Society (a literary association founded in 1836 by leading Hungarian writers) that it would be challenging to present to Hungarian readers works from such minor (!) literatures as Dutch, Swedish, Polish, or Russian.[9] Only after the 1840s, however, did translation become more faithful. During and even before the era of Classicism (from the late eighteenth century to 1820), authors' names could be omitted and substituted with the translator's instead, especially if the original text was heavily adapted. As early as 1787, the poet János Batsányi became the first to publish a study (consisting of three essays) on the theory and principles of literary translation, well before such theoretical considerations became a scholarly topic.[10]

Between 1850 and 1870, a considerable time lag developed in the translation of contemporary Russian literature. From the end of the 1850s, more and more information emerged about conditions in Russia, most probably thanks to the two figures who acted as catalysts for mediation in Western Europe, Aleksandr Herzen (1812–70) and Ivan Turgenev (1818–83), based in London and France respectively. Lermontov's *Hero of Our Time*, translated first from German in 1855 and then from Russian in 1879, was received critically.[11] This novel suffered on account of its unlikable protagonist and loose narrative structure; critics queried whether it could even be considered as a single integral work.[12] In 1855, the poet János Arany (1817–82), translator of Gogol's 'The Overcoat' via German ('Shinel'', 1842; 'A köpenyeg', 1860) advised one of his former students to read Pushkin

8 Based on poems including Adolf Müllner's version of Petr Pletnev's original anthology.

9 Külföldi Regénytár, *Kiadja a Kisfaludy-társaság. Szerkeszti Nagy Ignác* (Pesten: Hartleben Konrád Adolf, 1843–44).

10 János Batsányi, 'On Translation' ('A fordíttásról', 1788), *Magyar Museum*, II (1790). This journal, under Batsányi's editorship, was printed after two years' delay. See also *Batsányi János Összes Művei* [*Collected Works of János Batsányi*], ed. by Dezső Keresztury and Andor Tarnai, 4 vols (Budapest: Akadémiai Kiadó, 1953–67), II: *Prózai Művei* [*Collected Prose*] (1960), esp. pp. 101–07.

11 Mihail Lermontov, *Korunk hőse*, trans. by Zsigmond Falk and János Vajda and serialised in the daily newspaper *Magyar Sajtó* in 1855, issues 88–144. The retranslation from Russian in book form, also under the title of *Korunk hőse*, was by Ruby Miroszláv and Iván Timkó (Budapest: Athenaeum, 1879).

12 Ferenc Zsigmond, 'Orosz hatások irodalmunkban' ['Russian Influences on our Literature'] in Zsigmond, *Értekezések a nyelv és széptudományi osztály köréből* (Budapest: MTA, 1945), p. 21.

and Lermontov (in translation).[13] Arany's remark highlights his intellectual tolerance and his ability to distinguish Russia's politics from its literature (a perennial complication of the reception of Russian culture in Hungary). After 1848, the negative perception of Russia in Hungary was reinforced by Tsar Nikolai II's cruel repressions and by the Russian Army's alliance with Austria, Hungary's traditional oppressor. Even the popular romantic novelist Mór Jókai (much admired by the élite of Victorian-era England) followed this trend for a while, as an active participant in the revolution of 1848.[14] However, his hostility towards everything Russian relaxed in the 1860s, when he expressed solidarity with those Russians who resisted absolutism, like the Decembrists; Pushkin became for him an emblematic figure of the fight for freedom against absolute rulers.[15] Jókai's name is closely linked to the reception of Russian history in Hungary; he visualised Russia as an exotic space and a source for romantic plots. Jókai's *Freedom under the Snow* (*Szabadság a hó alatt*, 1879) focuses on Pushkin and the noble Decembrist rebels of 1825. The Decembrist theme emerged in Russian literature after the return of the last exiled member from Siberia in 1856, but Jókai did not know Russian. His manuscript notes allow us to trace his use of German and French sources like Alexandre Dumas or Alfred de Vigny.[16]

From the 1870s onwards, the primary intermediary language for Russian translations after German (where Friedrich von Bodenstedt's translations dominated as pivot texts) was French, used for the 1868 Hungarian translation of Tolstoy's *War and Peace* (*Voina i mir*, 1867) and for Turgenev's novels. But this new wave of translated literature often lacked politically meaningful details. For example, Vera Pavlovna's famous Fourth Dream of a utopian future society in Nikolai Chernyshevskii's *What Is To Be Done* (*Chto delat'*, 1863; *Mit tegyünk?*, 1877) was omitted by Ármin Sasvári, who translated the novel from French.[17] For similar political reasons, some Turgenev novels, like *Virgin Soil* (*Nov'*, 1877) or *Fathers and Sons* (*Ottsy i deti*, 1862), which launched debates elsewhere in Europe and in Russia on Nihilism and the populist *narodnik* movement, were

13 The name of the student is unknown. See Aladár Komlós, 'Puskin a magyar irodalomban', *Filológiai Közlöny*, 3 (1955), 333–52. Quoted by Zöldhelyi, *A külföldi közvetítés*, p. 15.

14 Lóránt Czigány, 'Jókai's Popularity in Victorian England', *The New Hungarian Quarterly*, 60:16 (1975), 186–92.

15 Mór Jókai, 'Kivel szövetkezzünk', *A Hon* [*The Homeland*], issues 200, 201, 202 and 205 (1867), p. 1 (in every issue).

16 See Zöldhelyi, *A külföldi közvetítés*, p. 40.

17 The same omission of Vera Pavlovna's fourth dream occurred with the first (1886) English-language translation of this text, produced via French by the American radical Socialist, Benjamin R. Tucker, as *What's To Be Done? A Romance*. For commentary on this and subsequent English translations of Chernyshevskii's novel, see Michael R. Katz, 'Review of English Translations of *What is to be Done?*', *Slavic Review*, 46:1 (1987), 125–31, https://doi.org/10.2307/2498628. Ármin Sasvári's translation of the novel appeared in Budapest in 1877.

also translated after a time lag, too late for their social content to be topical.[18] Only two decades later could these issues be freely debated; ensuring that Alphons Thun's German-language study *The History of the Russian Revolutionary Movements* (*Geschichte der revolutionären Bewegungen in Russland*, 1883) was immediately translated into Hungarian in 1884 under a new, high-sounding title, *The Nihilists* (*Nihilisták*).[19] The translator's foreword notes that the obvious parallel between resistance to the Tsars' absolutist regime and to the Habsburg monarchy invites sympathy from Hungarian audiences.

Next to Pushkin's *Onegin*, Turgenev's novels had the most enduring influence on Hungarian literature. Russia and Hungary shared many common tropes of fading nobility, with their neglected country houses and declining traditional rural culture. The idleness and procrastination personified in the titular hero of Ivan Goncharov's *Oblomov* (1859) also struck a chord with the Hungarian mentality, echoed in the Hungarian poet Sándor Petőfi's poem 'Pató Pál', a mock-folkloric song where the narrator (Pató Pál) choruses, "'Oh, we have plenty of time ahead to do it later'".[20] At this period, a new generation of literary translators emerged, working without pivot languages. They offered new foci of interest to the Hungarian readers, as well as translating, for the first time, Russian authors of an earlier period, such as Ivan Krylov and Vasilii Zhukovskii. But they also translated the work of Nikolai Nekrasov, Fedor Dostoevsky, Mikhail Saltykov-Shchedrin, Vsevolod Garshin, and Anton Chekhov. Two outstanding figures of this new generation were Dezső Ambrozovics (1864–1919) and Endre Szabó (1849–1924). The breadth of Hungarian awareness of Russian literature by the end of the nineteenth century is demonstrated by the list of entries in the Great Pallas Encyclopaedia (Pallas Nagy Lexikon, 1893), compiled by Endre Szabó. These entries included Vissarion Belinskii (vol. 3), Chekhov (vol. 4), the Decembrists, Dostoevsky ('uniting mystical ideas with realism', vol. 5), Griboedov (vol. 8), Herzen (vol. 9), Nihilism (as a synonym of propaganda and terror, vol. 13), and an overview of Russian language and literature (vol. 12)—with their first names domesticated (for example, Pushkin's forename became Sándor instead of Aleksandr, Elek replaced Aleksei for A. K. Tolstoy, and so

18 As Zsuzsa Zöldhelyi has pointed out, an article by the Russian 'narodnik' thinker Petr Lavrov (1823–1900) which appeared in an English newspaper (*Athenaeum*) was translated without the name of the author. This Hungarian version was heavily redacted, having been filtered (re-translated) from the original Russian through English and then German. See Zöldhelyi, *A külföldi közvetítés*, p. 37.

19 Alfonz Thun, *A nihilisták* (*Az orosz forradalmi mozgalmak története*), trans. by Rezső Szentgyörgyi Vörös (Budapest: Athenaeum R. Társulat, 1884).

20 Sándor Petőfi (1823–49), poet and revolutionary, considered Hungary's national poet. He was a key figure in the Hungarian Revolution of 1848. He died in the last battle for liberation from the Austro-Hungarian Empire, aged only twenty-six; ironically, he may have been killed fighting Russian troops who had intervened on the side of the ruling Habsburg dynasty.

on).[21] By 1900, Russian literary influence was already detectable in Hungarian prose narrative patterns, even explicitly referenced in dialogue. Among such Russian-influenced writers were István Petelei with his Turgenevian tonality (1852–1910), and the Chekhovian short stories of István Tömörkény (1866–1917).

The Twentieth Century: Cataclysms

In the first decades of the twentieth century, the main new arrival in Hungarian letters was Maksim Gorky,[22] followed by Leonid Andreev and Aleksandr Kuprin. Gorky swiftly shared the place of honour afforded to Chekhov, Gogol, Tolstoy, Dostoevsky, and Turgenev; all were mentioned not only in reviews, commentaries written by translators, and newspaper articles, but also in the correspondence of major Hungarian writers (including Endre Ady, Dezső Kosztolányi, Gyula Juhász, Tóth Árpád, Nagy Lajos, and Frigyes Karinthy). Karinthy was famous for his literary parodies; his spoof of Mikhail Artsybashev's *Sanin* (1907; translated in 1912)[23] shows the popularity of the latter work at the time. Endre Szabó's translation of *Sanin* had appeared in four editions in 1909 and two lesser-known translators undertook alternative versions of the text that same year. Arkadii Averchenko was also popular: his work appeared in the newspapers *Élet*, *A Hét*, and *Új Idők* from 1916 onwards. In 1911, Chekhov was the subject of an important scholarly analysis by the noted scholar György Lukács.[24] The influence of Russian literature persisted in Hungarian prose: Gyula Krúdy (1878–1933) with his Oblomovian-Oneginian hero Szindbád,[25] and Benő Karácsony with his Oblomovian *Piotruska* (1927), are some of those who represented Russian connections for their readers.

---

21 My main source for the history of literary translation is Sándor Kozocsa's bibliography is *Az orosz irodalom magyar bibliográfiája*, ed. by Sándor Kozocsa (Budapest: Országos Széchényi Könyvtár, 1947).

22 Dezső Ambrozovics, 'Gorky Makszim', *Új Idők*, 26 (23 June 1901), p. 557.

23 Frigyes Karinthy, *Így írtok ti* [*So write you*] (Budapest: Athenaeum, 1912), pp. 144–53. For an overview of Artsybashev's shocking novel's *succès de scandale*, see Nicholas Luker, 'Scandalous "Sanin" Revisited: A Literary Re-Assessment,' *New Zealand Slavonic Journal* (1999), 193–202 ; and Otto Boele's monograph *Erotic Nihilism in Late Imperial Russia: The Case of Mikhail Artsybashev's* Sanin (Madison, WI: University of Wisconsin Press, 2009).

24 György Lukács, *A modern dráma fejlődése* [*The Development of Modern Drama*] (Budapest: Kisfaludy-Társaság, 1911).

25 Krúdy's Sindbad stories were collected in one volume in 1944, uniting *The Travels of Sindbad* (1912), *The Resurrection of Sindbad* (1916), and *The Youth and Grief of Sindbad* (1917). See Gyula Krúdy, *Szindbád* [*The Adventures of Sindbad*], comprising *Szindbád utazása*, *Szindbád feltámadása*, and *Francia kastély* (Budapest: Új Idők, 1944).

The echo of the revolutions of 1905 and 1917 in Russia was amplified during the 133-day lifetime of the Hungarian Soviet Republic in 1919.[26] However, geographical distance also led to misinterpretations, such as the misrepresentation of Sergei Esenin as a revolutionary poet. His poems were translated only after his tragic death in 1925, appearing in weeklies and journals (such as *Literatúra*, *100%*, *A Hét*, and *Korunk*). Here is a typical left-wing poem by Imre Forbáth (1898–1967), a former contributor to the famous Constructivist journal *MA* (*Today*).[27] The poem summarises Russian literature through images and types:

Imre Forbáth
A Russian Portrait Gallery

Leaden tears fell from Gogol's eye onto sad Russia.
And long wrinkles on Herzen's forehead: the path of the exiles to Siberia.
Turgenev's nose: the ladder on which the titans walked.
Pushkin's words: a glacier, glittering with cold stars;
From Dostoevsky's mouth the cold reeks as if from a morgue.
Tolstoy's beard is a frowning forest, where wondrous wise owls sit on the branches.
Blok a dim window through which heavy raindrops run down.
On Esenin's lips hangs sadness like pale blue roses.
But Lenin's forehead is a battering ram that broke through the cordon of the Past,
From the brain of Stalin the locomotives of History are humming.
Maiakovskii's gigantic throat trumpeted the horn of revolution,
And in the bosom of Gorky, Gorky smoldering, beats the heart of humanity![28]

While between 1920 and 1945, Hungarians maintained consistent interest in classical nineteenth-century Realist Russian literature, it is intriguing to note what contemporary new Soviet culture reached Hungary, and how. An example of Russian cultural mediation in Berlin is Lajos Kassák's article 'For the Russian

26 The Hungarian Soviet Republic (or Hungarian Councils' Republic) was a short-lived Socialist–Communist rump state (active 21st March–3rd August 1919).

27 *MA* was a Hungarian literature and arts magazine founded in 1916 in Budapest by the avant-garde poet Lajos Kassák, who continued to publish it after 1919 in exile in Vienna until 1925. It was launched after a previous journal *A Tett* (*The Action*). Forbáth published a poem there entitled 'A költő' ['The Poet'], dedicated to Briusov. *MA*, 1 February 1922, p. 46. See also footnote 30 below.

28 In Imre Forbáth, *Panasz és remény* [*Complaint and Hope*] (London: Hungarian Club, 1942), p. 8. All translations are my own, unless otherwise indicated.

Exhibition in Berlin' ('A berlini orosz kiállításhoz', 1922).[29] Blok became celebrated only after his death, in 1921. Symbolist writers like Aleksei Remizov and Andrei Belyi arrived belatedly; Ivan Bunin was recognised only in 1933, the year he won the Nobel Prize for Literature. It was mainly left-wing intellectuals who turned to contemporary Soviet literature and news, such as work by Maiakovskii (from 1921) and Isaak Babel (from 1926), but Valentin Kataev's production novel (*Time, Forward!* (*Vremia, vpered!*, 1935)) and the satires of Il'ia Il'f and Evgenii Petrov (as well as those of Mikhail Zoshchenko) also found a place in the press and on the bookshelves of liberal intellectuals. Russian religious philosophy was represented only by Vladimir Solov'ev and Nikolai Berdiaev, and primarily in secondary criticism rather than in translation. Some writers' popularity exceeded their merits: arguably including Dmitry Merezhkovskii (who was not translated until the 1920s, but then in quantity), and Mikhail Sholokhov. Two volumes of the latter's *The Quiet Don* (*Tikhii Don*, 1933; *A csendes Don*, 1935–36) appeared in Hungarian as early as 1935; but Sholokhov's full pentalogy only appeared in Hungarian during the Second World War, from the publisher Imre Cserépfalvi. Ironically, at this point Soviet and Hungarian soldiers were fighting against each other on that same Don, which was anything but quiet. Il'ia Ehrenburg's works (such as *Julio Jurenito*, 1924) were also read in German editions by Budapest natives whose mother tongue was German. Ehrenburg's *The Stormy Life of Lazik Roitshvanets* (*Burnaia zhizn' Lazika Roitshvanetsa*, 1927), translated in 1933, was censored: the Vatican chapter was omitted.[30] While this chapter re-appeared in the appendix in the reprinted edition published in 1988,[31] a different chapter (on the visit to the Kremlin and the dialogue with Lenin) was omitted. The most prominent literary journal between the two wars was the intellectual *Nyugat* (*The West*) which regularly reported on Russian literary news. For example, in 1926 it published Sándor Bonkáló's long essay on Boris Pil'niak, whose novella *Ivan Moscow* (*Ivan-Moskva*, 1927) became the longest work in the *Nyugat*-published 'Contemporary Russian Decameron' anthology (1936).[32] This anthology was

29 Lajos Kassák, 'A berlini orosz kiállításhoz', *MA*, 25 December 1922, 2–3. Kassák was the editor-in-chief of the journal. When Miklós Horthy's terror defeated the Hungarian Soviet Republic, the journal's editors had to emigrate to Vienna after unwisely organising a 'Russian Evening' (on 20 November 1920). Some members of this *MA* circle, like Sandor (Aleksandr) Barta, his wife Erzsébet Újvári, and the painter Béla Uitz, co-editor of *MA*, emigrated to the Soviet Union. Barta was executed in 1938, Újvári died in 1940, Uitz was arrested but released for providing his monumental frescos. He returned to Hungary in 1970, two years before his death.

30 Ilja Ehrenburg, *Lasik Roitschwantz mozgalmas élete*, trans. by Gábor Goda (Budapest: Cosmos, 1933).

31 Ilja Ehrenburg, *Lasik Roitschwantz mozgalmas élete*, trans. by Gábor Goda (Budapest: Téka, 1988).

32 The contents (with many misspelled names): Isaac Babel: 'Probuzhdenie' ['Awakening']; Maxim Gorkii: 'Byk' ['The Bull']; Leonid (nb. not Vasilii) Grossmann: 'V gorode Bredicheve' ['In Berdichev']; Ilya Ilf and Evgenii Petrov: 'Chudesnyie gosti' ['The Wondrous Guests'], 'Kak rodilsa Robinzon' ['How

part of a series of foreign-literature anthologies, starting in December 1934 with a French volume, continuing through American, German, and English volumes in 1935, and concluding with the Russian and Japanese volumes in 1936. This series demonstrates that translations from Russian, viewed quantitatively, did not occupy a special place compared with other languages and cultures: focus on Russian literature was only rarely excessive. The turn of the twentieth century was one such intensive period and the half-decade around the fall of the Soviet Union (1987–92) would constitute a second, as we shall see below.

The production of the Russian-focused *Nyugat* anthology was the result of extensive correspondence mediated by the Soviet Embassy, and probably initiated by Gyula Illyés (1902–83), a poet and novelist with left-wing convictions. He had spent two months in the Soviet Union by invitation of the Soviet Writers' Union, participating in its first Congress in 1934. Even though Illyés had previously spent the years 1922 to 1924 in Paris and knew the literary historian Vladimir Pozner and had read Mark Slonim,[33] he compiled his anthology exclusively using texts recommended by Soviet authorities within the newly formed Soviet Writers' Union. Illyés even maintained contacts with the Soviet Embassy in Hungary. In a letter to his commissar in Moscow, the Russian ambassador to Hungary Aleksandr Bekzadian advocated building a lively cultural relationship. As noted by his secretary Semion Mirnyi, he complained that "in Hungary, there is no Russian-language press or Russian books at all [...] so far we do not have a library or even a single book package. When I visited the Press Department of the [Hungarian] Ministry of Foreign Affairs, I promised the head of the department that we would regularly provide [it] with materials and data on our development".[34] All the texts included in Illyés's *Nyugat* anthology were translated by Hugó Gellért (1890–1937), who had learned Russian during

Robinson was born']; Vsevolod Ivanov: 'Ditë' ['The Kid']; Iurii Olesha: 'Liubov' ['Love']; Konstantin Paustovskii: 'Doblest' ['The Heroic Deed']; Boris Pilniak: 'Ivan Moskva' (70 pages); Nikolai Tikhonov: 'Vechnyi tranzit' (translated as 'The Eternal Chase'); Mikhail Zoshchenko: 'Vory' ['Thieves'], 'Slabaia tara' ['Weak Wrappage'], 'Krizis' ['Crisis'].

33 Mark Slonim (1894–1976) was a controversial figure among the Russian émigré community: a politician, a literary scholar, and the editor of the Prague-based journal *Volia Rossii.* It is probable that Illyés used the following books as sources for the texts in his anthology: *Anthologie de la prose russe contemporaine*, ed. by Vladimir Pozner (Paris: Émile Hazan & Cie Éditeurs, 1929) and *Anthologie de la littérature soviétique 1918–1934*, ed. by Marc Slonim and George Reavey (Paris: Gallimard, 1935). Both can be found in Gyula Illyés's archive at the Manuscript Archive of the Hungarian Academy of Sciences, folders IGY 5585 and 5586. See more in Erzsébet Schiller, 'A *Mai orosz dekameron* szerkesztése (1935–1936)', *ItK Irodalomtörténeti Közlemények* 4 CXVIII (2014), 547–60 (p. 556).

34 Attila Seres, 'A budapesti szovjet követség jelentései, 1934–1935', *Lymbus Magyarságtudományi Forrásközlemények* (2007), 225–92 (p. 246). Ambassador Aleksandr Bekzadian cited by Schiller in 'A *Mai orosz dekameron* szerkesztése', p. 548.

the First World War as a prisoner of war in Russia.[35] Bitterly and paradoxically, the historical cataclysms of the twentieth century produced translators with knowledge of the Russian language and culture, because they had been exiled, forced to emigrate, made prisoners during both world wars, or held captive in Gulag camps. This was why, in the twentieth century, direct translations from Russian to Hungarian became increasingly common.

The Pushkin Memorial Year in 1937 (marking the centenary of Pushkin's death) was commemorated by the greatest Hungarian writers, among them Mihály Babits, Illyés, and Sándor Márai. The book sensation of 1941 was Antal Szerb's three-volume essayistic, meandering *History of World Literature* (*A világirodalom története*), which prominently featured portraits of Russian writers. Well-informed about the literature of the Soviet era, Szerb explored the tensions between literature and politics, using the Futurists as examples of politically engaged writers, mentioning the *poputchik* (fellow-traveller) phenomenon, innovation in the theatre, and the Five-Year Plans, as well as some new literary names, including Boris Pasternak who is mentioned here for the first time in Hungary.[36] Szerb's chapter on 'Contemporary Soviet Literature' was censored—not only in 1941 but also in the later (posthumous) 1945 and 1947 editions: an especially cruel gesture as Szerb, who was of Jewish origin, was killed in 1945 by Hungarian Fascists. The chapter on Soviet literature was rewritten by Sarolta Lányi in such ardently pro-Soviet propagandistic terms that later, Kádár-era editions (1956–89)[37] were printed without it.[38] One sentence by Szerb was partially deleted from all postwar editions: namely, the 'samovars' clause in the following question: "But what will Russia, which has so far given humanity nothing but samovars, teach Europe?"[39]

35 The translator Hugó Gellért (born Hugó Goldmann), mentioned here, should not be confused with his better-known namesake and co-eval, the Hungarian-American artist and pro-Communist propagandist Hugo Gellert (born Hugó Grünbaum, 1892–1985). Both were born in Budapest, but Gellert emigrated to New York in 1906.

36 Antal Szerb, *A világirodalom története* [*History of World Literature*], 3 vols (Budapest: Révai, 1941), III (1941), pp. 395–406.

37 János Kádár (1912–89) led the Communist Party and Hungary itself for thirty-two years, after the failed anti-Soviet Revolution of 1956 (when he played an actively pro-Soviet role). After six years of terror, an amnesty was announced. From 1962, the regime started liberalising society and the economy, permitting (within strict guidelines) some freedom of speech and freedom to trade on the open market, so that Hungarians enjoyed arguably the highest standard of living in the Eastern bloc.

38 Chapters dealing with culture within the new Soviet bloc (Serbia, Slovenia, Bulgaria) were also eliminated in all postwar editions.

39 This phrase inspired the title of this chapter. See Szerb, *A világirodalom története:* "But what will Russia, which has so far given humanity nothing but samovars, teach Europe?" ("De mire fogja megtanítani Európát Oroszország, amely eddig még a szamováron kívül nem adott semmit az emberiségnek?"), p. 627.

The genre of Russian literature noticeably absent from this period was poetry. But at the end of the Second World War in 1945, as a quick welcoming gesture to the arrival of the Soviet army, an anthology of poetry was compiled including one poem by Anna Akhmatova, three by Nikolai Gumilev, three by Osip Mandel'shtam, and three by Marina Tsvetaeva. The gesture may strike us as paradoxical, given that the last three had fallen victim to the Soviet totalitarian regime. It is worth noting that Russian works translated into Hungarian were also published in Moscow, by and for the Hungarian Communist émigré community. This applied only to books with strong propaganda content, like Aleksandr Fadeev's *The Rout* (*Razgrom*, 1926), published by the meaningfully titled Sarló és Kalapács (Hammer and Sickle) Publishers: the book appeared under a completely different Hungarian title, *Tizenkilencen* (*Those Nineteen*, 1932). Oleksandr Dovzhenko's story about a heroic deed during the war, 'The Mother' ('Mat'', 1943; *Az anya*, 1943), was published in Hungarian by the Idegennyelvű (Foreign Language) Publishers in Moscow.

The post-1945 era was a new departure in every way, with several distinct phases following a short period of pure enthusiasm which died away after 1947.[40] The head of the new Communist cultural policy was the Party ideologue József Révai (1898–1959), who during his Moscow exile in the 1930s, had already outlined a Hungarian version of national Bolshevism. He relied extensively on the work of György Lukács, after the latter's return from the Soviet Union. As Szegedy-Maszák has suggested elsewhere, "Since Révai supervised several areas in domestic politics, it was Lukács who took over a leading role in the press campaign against bourgeois culture, a role he played until around the turn of 1948–49."[41] A sharp dividing line was of course the anti-Soviet uprising in 1956. This period (called the 'Rákosi years' after the Communist politician Mátyás Rákosi) brought comparatively less relief than the Soviet Thaw did within the USSR, where there was a slight relaxation following Stalin's death. The main function of literary translation during the difficult 1950s, in Hungary as in the USSR, was to support unpublished writers, who resorted to translation and writing children's stories for income. A good example is László Németh's 1951 translation of Tolstoy's 1878 novel *Anna Karenina* (the fourth Hungarian translation of this text since 1887); Németh, a conservative nationalist thinker

40 On 31 August 1947, during the infamous 'blue-ribbon elections', the Hungarian Communist Party manipulated the balloting to win power. Despite this, they received only 22% of the vote; but in this political climate, the will of the electorate was no longer decisive. Hungary's period as a Socialist dictatorship began in 1948.

41 Mihály Szegedy-Maszák, 'The Introduction of Communist Censorship in Hungary: 1945–49', in *History of the Literary Cultures of East-Central Europe: Junctures and Disjunctures in the 19th and 20th Centuries*, ed. by Marcel Cornis-Pope and John Neubauer (Amsterdam: Benjamins, 2007), pp. 120–24 (p. 120).

who was not allowed to publish his own writing, learned Russian purely to be able to translate the prose of Russian authors.[42]

The Kádár era began in 1956, with a brief ideological thaw followed by the renewal of totalitarian sanctions. The public and cultural climate did not alter again until 1962, when a general amnesty released many Hungarian writers (and translators) who had been arrested and imprisoned since 1956.[43] Árpád Göncz, who later became Hungary's first democratically elected and non-Communist president (1990–2000), learned English during the six years he spent in prison; after his release, he worked as a literary translator (translating William Faulkner, Thomas Wolfe, and even J. R. R. Tolkien into Hungarian). The first Kádár-era reforms began in 1962, with a significant shift occurring after 1968. This was because, although the so-called 'new economic mechanism' (decentralisation of the economy) was not yet introduced officially, Hungary was allowed exceptional freedoms from Soviet control, because the Hungarian leadership argued that a second 1956-style revolution must be avoided. This strategy created opportunities that made Hungary, in the parlance of the time, the most cheerful barracks in the Socialist camp.

During the Kádár era, Hungary's only literary journal of world literature, *Nagyvilág* (its Soviet equivalent would have been *Inostrannaia literatura* (*Foreign Literature*)) was launched in 1956 and soon became the leading monthly of its type, widely read by intellectuals. It published translations of Russian and Soviet literature regularly and on a compulsory basis but did not favour them more than translations from other languages. This balanced situation, by failing to prioritise Soviet-Russian literature, may have spurred on the cultural powers of

42 Németh was censored because he belonged to the nationalist wing of so-called '*népi*' writers (meaning, literally, 'of the people'). This politically and ideologically heterogeneous group (often opposed to the 'urbanist' writers) was deeply rooted in the social ethnography of the 1930s. See Balázs Trencsényi, *The Politics of 'National Character': A Study of Interwar East European Thought* (New York: Routledge, 2012), p. 93. For more on Hungarian translations of *Anna Karenina*, see Albert Sándor, 'Az Anna Karenina magyar fordításairól', *Fordítástudomány*, XIV:2 (2012) 2, 80–92, https://www.epa.hu/04100/04125/00016/pdf/EPA04125_forditastudomany_2012_2_080–092.pdf. Németh's translation had many mistakes and was not always accurate, so a new translation was recently completed by László Horváth (*Anna Karenyina* (Budapest: Európa, 2021)). Horváth (b. 1950), who published his translation of *War and Peace* (*Háború és béke*) with the online Hungarian publisher 21. Század Kiadó in 2022 and is now working on Tolstoy's final novel *Resurrection* (*Voskresenie*, 1899; *Feltámadást*), told an interviewer that after more than a thousand days of living daily with Tolstoy's novels, he doubts that any other translator has succeeded in translating these three great novels in succession. See 'Gy. Horváth László: A szerző nagy gonddal komponált mondatait fordítjuk' ['Gy. László Horváth: We translate the author's carefully composed sentences'], Liter@, 2 February 2023, https://litera.hu/magazin/interju/gy-horvath-laszlo-a-szerzo-nagy-gonddal-komponalt-mondatait-forditjuk.html.

43 For example, the writers Tibor Déry and István Eörsi.

Brezhnev's Soviet Party line to create the Moscow-based literary journal, *Soviet Literature*, in 1975, with national versions translated into the language of every Socialist country.[44] The journal's Hungarian version was *Szovjet Irodalom*. Most of its content was edited centrally in Moscow (at Kutuzovskii Prospekt 1/7), but local editorial committees in Socialist countries were allowed autonomy over the remaining materials (approximately 10% of the journal content). In Hungary, this space was allocated to essays and translations by Hungarian writers and translators. Of course, the editor-in-chief and his deputies were carefully selected from 'reliable' but also skilled cadres. (One curious detail was that the two editors, István Király and Pál E. Fehér, never met; they did not even speak, so deep was their loathing for each other. They visited the office only once a year, on a date announced well in advance.)[45]

In Hungary, the establishment created a special system whereby cultural discourse was monitored according to the so-called 'three T's' system, from the Hungarian words meaning 'supported', 'tolerated', and 'prohibited' (*támogatott, tűrt, tiltott*). The principle was derived from Kádár's famous slogan: "anyone who is not against us is with us".[46] Since Hungary had no written censorship regulations, rules had to be devised and guessed on the basis of previous experience or international exemplars (as provided by neighbouring Socialist countries). Although in Hungary, dislike of everything Russian was a logical consequence of the forty-year Soviet occupation, interest in formerly prohibited

44 For more on *Inostrannaia literatura* and other Soviet translation initiatives, see Emily Lygo, 'Between Ideology and Literature: Translation in the USSR during the Brezhnev Period', *Perspectives*, 24:1 (2016), 48–58, https://doi.org/10.1080/0907676X.2015.1032311. See also Samantha Sherry, 'Better Something Than Nothing: The Editors and Translators of *Inostrannaia literatura* as Censorial Agents', *Slavonic and East European Review*, 91:4 (Oct. 2013), 731–58, https://doi.org/10.5699/slaveasteurorev2.91.4.0731; and Brian J. Baer and Susanna Witt, 'Introduction: The Double Context of Translation', in *Translation in Russian Contexts*, ed. by Brian Baer and Susanna Witt (Abingdon: Routledge, 2017), pp. 1–16 (pp. 9–12).

45 István Király (1921–89) was a Hungarian literary historian, a Member of Parliament (from 1971), and a member of the Hungarian Academy of Sciences. Pál E. Fehér (1936–2013) was a Hungarian journalist, editor of several Party-ruled journals and newspapers as well as many anthologies of Soviet poetry, prose, and essays between 1961 and 1981. He was a controversial personality, linked both to senior Party members in Moscow and to oppressed or outcast individuals.

46 This statement of Kádár's became official policy at the Ninth Hungarian Communist Party conference in 1966. The 'three T's' system was developed by György Aczél; for more on his role as Hungary's "main censor", see Raija Oikari, 'Discursive Use of Power in Hungarian Cultural Policy during the Kádár Era', *Hungarologische Beitrage*, 2 (2000), 133–62. See also István Bart, 'Transition and Privatization in Publishing', *The Hungarian Quarterly*, 140 (Winter 1995), 36–45; Mátyás Domokos, *Leletmentés. Könyvek sorsa a „nemlétező" cenzúra korában, 1948–1989* (Budapest: Osiris, 1999); István Bart, *Világirodalom és könyvkiadás a Kádár-korszakban* (Budapest: Scholastica, 2000); and László Lator, 'My Life as Editor', *The Hungarian Quarterly*, 165 (2002), 64–74.

Russian literature (not only contemporary prohibited or émigré tamizdat, published in Russian by Western publishing houses or journals) but also in earlier Russian texts (by Symbolist, avant-garde, and absurdist writers) was still extremely high during the 1980s and the early 1990s. One might even speak of a boom. In perestroika Russia, after seventy years of censorship, a vast fund of unpublished writings was rescued from the proverbial drawer to flood the market. Here the keyword is 'market', because as a simultaneous cause and consequence of socio-political change, the Russian book market was transformed: the profit-oriented approach replaced the value-oriented one. Hence the paradox arose that authors who had resisted the Soviet system, sometimes even risking their liberty or life, now that their long-sought freedom was finally realised, could not be published for fear that their work would not be commercially viable.

Paradoxically enough, while the Russian language was obligatory during the Communist era, there was no real public interest in 'official' Russian literature. Hungarian translators and publishing houses were obliged by the unwritten rules of censorship to publish only those books which had already appeared in the USSR. Nevertheless, they constantly tried to obtain the best literary works, staying well-informed about prohibited, illegal, or Western tamizdat publications. Such works, which attacked the Soviet social and political regime and thus influenced contemporary Russian oppositional thinking, helped to prepare Hungarian readers for the fall of the Soviet Union. Since this change of regime brought freedom of expression to the former Soviet bloc, formerly controversial Russophone authors like Aleksandr Solzhenitsyn, Venedikt Erofeev, Mikhail Bulgakov, Osip Mandel'shtam, Andrei Platonov, and Evgenii Zamiatin regained their reputation in their homeland and consequently could now be published abroad.[47]

Three Cases from the Kádár Era: Evtushenko, Nabokov and Bulgakov

Evgenii Evtushenko's 'Babii Iar'—The 1960s

When compiling an anthology of twentieth-century Russian literature during the 1990s, I recalled a scandal from three decades earlier, provoked by Evgenii

47 On changes in the book market and its commercial context in the 1990s, see György Kókay, *A könyvkereskedelem Magyarországon* (Budapest: Balassi Kiadó, 1997) and Pongrácz Sennyey, 'Book Publishing in Hungary, After a Decade of Changes', *Slavic & East European Information Resources*, 4 (2001), 29–39. The article reviews the major changes that affected book publishing in Hungary in the 1990s.

Evtushenko's taboo-shattering poem 'Babii Iar'.[48] It was the first Russian poem to address the massacre of Jews near Kyiv on the Jewish New Year in September 1941. Thirty-four thousand people were killed that day, and another hundred thousand died during the following years.[49] Evtushenko indicted the Ukrainian collaborators who were jointly responsible with the Nazi invaders for this extermination, which was a forbidden subject under Soviet censorship. Although I remembered hearing a Hungarian translation of Evtushenko's poem read onstage at my university, I could not find this text. Through many chains of professional acquaintances, I eventually located its translator (Ágnes Ágai). But she could not tell me where the poem had been published; she even doubted whether it had ever appeared in print. I failed to find the poem in any anthology of Evtushenko's verse. When I asked a librarian to search back issues of *Nagyvilág*, Hungary's world literature periodical, from between 1960 and 1970, he found the poem on his second attempt: hidden within a short, unsigned nineteen-line article, not even included in the table of contents.[50] Nor did Evtushenko's name appear in the contents list, apparently as a precaution against censorship. This sophisticated camouflage could have caused the translation to be permanently lost (had I not tracked it down to complete my anthology)...

Vladimir Nabokov's Road to Publication in Hungary (1966–87)

Vladimir Nabokov (1899–1977) arrived in Hungarian translation surprisingly late, during the fifth decade of his literary career.[51] The first Nabokov short story appeared in Hungarian as part of a 1968 anthology of American short stories, followed by another nineteen-year silence. Hungarian translators and editors constantly schemed to bypass censorship, and the simplest method was to hide problematic authors in anthologies.[52] The first Soviet publication of Nabokov was concealed within *The Chess Review* (*Shakhmatnoe obozrenie*, 8 (1986)), for example.

48 *Én—nem én. Modern orosz irodalmi antológia. A MűMű—Műfordítói Műhely (ELTE BTK) fordításai*, ed. by Zsuzsa Hetényi (Budapest: Dolce Filologia VI, 2008).

49 Anatoly Kuznetsov also wrote what he called a "documentary novel" on this subject, with the same title, published in Russia in a heavily censored form in 1966.

50 *Nagyvilág*, 1 (1962), 140–41.

51 An earlier version of this section on Nabokov was published as Zsuzsa Hetényi, 'Nabokov's Art as a Juggler's Act': Vladimir Nabokov's Road to Publication in Hungary', *Anzeiger Für Slavische Philologie*, 44 (2016), 9–14. It is republished with permission, for which I thank the journal editor, Prof. Renate Hansen-Kokoruš.

52 Vladimir Nabokov, 'Becsületbeli ügy' ['An Affair of Honour'], trans. by Á. Réz in *Autóbusz és iguana*, ed. by Géza Ottlik (Budapest: Európa, 1968), pp. 31–58. The editors may have noted this story's previous appearance in Dmitri Nabokov's translation in *The New Yorker*, 3 September 1966, 36–66.

Hungarian law subserviently emulated Soviet censorship practice, but this was only one reason for the delay in Nabokov's Hungarian debut. One can only wonder why Nabokov was not noticed among Russian émigré writers earlier, even as soon as the 1920s, since Hungarian intellectuals usually oriented themselves in contemporary Russian literature by following their publications in Berlin and Vienna. *Mary* (*Mashen'ka*, 1926), Nabokov's first novel, was translated into German, but its title in that language *Sie kommt—kommt sie?* (*She comes, does she come?*, 1928) was confusing.[53] A second reason to overlook Nabokov was his relative unpopularity in the German book market. A third explanation could be that the Hungarian intellectuals of the interwar period were more interested in what they considered "new" Russian (rather, Soviet) literature than that produced by Russian émigrés. Nabokov's lyrical and philosophical voice was not even heard among the choir.

The only Russian émigré writer from Berlin widely published in Hungary between the two wars was Mark Aldanov (1886–1957), but his historical novels had already appeared in Paris in the 1930s. Aldanov's *The Ninth Thermidor* (*Deviatoe termidora*, 1923) was translated in the same year (1930) from the Russian original.[54] Eight of his novels appeared in several Hungarian editions between 1930 and 1944. Paris, the most significant centre of Russian emigration after 1925, seemingly received more attention from Hungary than Berlin. French sources were used for information about cultural news and trends, as the Hungarian interest in Merezhkovskii and Bunin (both Paris residents) reveals. Both writers were translated into Hungarian significantly earlier than the Berlin-based Nabokov, even though the latter's work regularly appeared alongside theirs in the most important Parisian Russian émigré journal, *Sovremennye zapiski* (*Contemporary Notes*).

Nabokov's name was first mentioned in a Hungarian periodical in 1961 in a short review of *Lolita* (1955).[55] Its author, a young writer called Mihaly Sükösd (1933–2000), framed his review with reference to Graham Greene, the first critic to praise *Lolita* (in 1955), thus saving that controversial book from oblivion. Graham Greene was an 'accepted' writer in the Soviet bloc because of his Cuba-related novels, which were published even in the Soviet Union. Moreover, Greene's 1955 novel *The Quiet American*, published in English for Russian readers by a Moscow publishing house, was also printed in Hungary.[56]

53 Wladimir Nabokoff-Sirin, *Sie kommt—kommt sie?*, trans. by Jakob Margot Schubert and Gregor Jarcho (Berlin: Ullstein, 1929). It was followed by a second novel in German translation: Wladimir Nabokoff-Sirin, *König, Dame, Bube. Ein Spiel mit dem Schicksal*, trans. by Siegfried von Vegesack (Berlin: Ullstein, 1930).

54 Márk Áldánov, *Thermidor kilencedike*, trans. by Károly Piroska (Budapest: Világosság Ny., 1930).

55 Mihály Sükösd, 'Lolita', *Nagyvilág*, 7 (1961), 1085–86.

56 Graham Greene, *Tikhii amerikanets* [*The Quiet American*] (Moscow: Izdatel'stvo inostrannoi literatury, 1959). For more on Greene's relationship with the Soviet

Thus, I speculate that the Hungarian book business was well-informed about those authors considered acceptable by Soviet censors. There might be an even simpler explanation for the extended gap between *Lolita*'s publication in 1955 and 1961 (the year of the review): the failed 1956 Hungarian Revolution, which made this period inhospitable for the reception of a scandalous foreign novel.

In the first Hungarian review of *Lolita*, the five-year time lag in reception was concealed by the absence of the book's publication date. Sükösd described *Lolita* as boring, superficial, and lightweight but playful. It was an ironic, picaresque, essayistic novel with undeveloped characters: in short, a piece of decadent elegance. Before the political changes of 1989 introduced press freedom, very little more was published on Nabokov's fiction: just three short introductory essays written by the translators of *Lolita* and *The Enchanter*, and an excerpt from *Other Shores* (*Drugie berega*, 1954).[57] One reasonably scholarly review did appear in a popular literary weekly under the title 'The Aesthetic Evil' by Ferenc Takács.[58] Takács was the first advocate for publishing *Lolita*, in a series of unpublished 'reports' commissioned by Hungary's world literature publishing house, Európa. The only essay translated into Hungarian in this period about Nabokov was a somewhat unanalytical but charming piece by the half-Hungarian Yugoslav writer, Danilo Kiš, whose review reflected his own feelings on exile and emigration.[59]

Internal Reports on Nabokov (1966–87)

The debates and controversies paving Nabokov's pathway to publication can be traced in the reviews written for the Európa publishing house by specialists on American literature, now held in the library of Petőfi Museum of Literature (PIM). This is a closed collection accessible only by special permission. The reasons for this precaution are not only potential copyright issues afflicting these reviews, which were often written by well-known individuals seeking extra income, but also because the ideological subservience of the reports would embarrass their authors if printed today. (Hence, I only identify names below with permission from the writers or from their heirs.)

bloc, see Duncan White, *Cold Warriors: Writers Who Waged the Literary Cold War* (London: Harper Collins, 2019).

57 These essays were as follows: Pál Békés, 'Ismeretlen szerző a huszadik századból' ['An Unknown Writer from the 20th Century'], *Nagyvilág*, 1 (1987), 82–83; János Széky, 'Nabokov kisregénye elé', *Nagyvilág*, 3 (1988), 386; Zoltán Vargyas, 'Az orosz Nabokov' ['The Russian Nabokov'], *Nagyvilág*, 8 (1989), 1234–36. On 31 March 1989, the Central Committee of the Socialist Party loosened restrictions on media ownership, effectively ending the state's media monopoly.

58 Ferenc Takács, 'Az esztétikai gonosz (Nabokov: *Lolita*)', *Élet és Irodalom* 13 (XXXII, 25 March 1988), 11.

59 Danilo Kiš, 'Nabokov, avagy a nosztalgia', trans. by Marietta Vujicsics, *Nagyvilág*, 8 (1989), 1118–21.

When evaluating which books to publish, Európa commissioned two independent reviews for every proposal. Theoretically, two positive opinions were needed for a publication to go ahead. If one was positive and one negative, a third opinion was requested. In Nabokov's case in 1966, the first opinions submitted were negative, on both *Invitation to a Beheading* (*Priglashenie na kazn'*, 1936), and *Despair* (*Otchaianie*, 1934). The reviewer of the latter was overtly horrified by this novel; he missed the irony and grotesque playfulness of *Lolita*. He considered the plot inexplicable, the language "pompous babble, stuck-up, proud"; the whole book "either nonsense or of no interest", because "[Nabokov's] distasteful, ranting, worn-out style quickly becomes tiresome". Strikingly, this reveals how widely *Lolita*, although in practice forbidden, was read in Hungary at the time. In the Soviet Union, one could be arrested and sentenced for possessing or discussing forbidden books. *Lolita* must therefore have featured on official Hungarian lists for confiscation.

The next confidential reviews were commissioned for *Lolita* in 1969, during Hungary's post-1968 Thaw. The year 1968 held dual symbolism for Hungary: it was marked by both enthusiasm for the Paris-centred European student movements, and the shame of having participated in the invasion of Czechoslovakia, for which the Soviet Union had rewarded Hungary with a modicum of freedom and limited economic reforms. That year Európa published Mikhail Bulgakov's *The Master and Margarita* (*Master i Margarita*, 1940; *A Mester és Margarita*, 1969, trans. by Klára Szőllősy), even including a few pages censored from the Soviet journal edition of 1966–67 (no book edition appeared in the Soviet Union until 1973).[60] The positive 1969 evaluation nevertheless finds *Lolita* to be "art as a juggler's act" ("bűvészkedés a művészetben"), while the negative review considers it a dull novel about "a literary person who has nothing better to think of than a girl's roundish figure". The next reviewer was a well-regarded poet, Otto Orbán, who was evidently irked by the material differences between his life in early-1970s Hungary and Nabokov's descriptions of luxury in Swiss hotels and mountains in *Transparent Things* (1972). Thus, despite his admiration for Nabokov's style, his irony leads him to a negative conclusion.[61]

In 1975, *Look at the Harlequins!* (1974) was judged negatively by a translator and a screenwriter. In 1980, *Speak, Memory* (1967) was rejected (for translation) on the grounds that:

> [...] the author failed to answer the real question of his readers; because of his social situation and age he has no memory of or message about the revolution [...] he hates Bolsheviks inexorably and extremely [...] and cannot see any difference between Lenin and Stalin [...], he is a passionate and blindfold anti-Communist.

60 Mikhail Bulgakov, *Master i Margarita* (Moscow: Khudozhestvennaia literatura, 1973).

61 I name Ottó Orbán with permission from his widow, Julia Orbán.

These words did their job: not only was this book not even given to another reviewer, but it was sent back to the foreign editor. As if it were contagious, the fact of returning is noted on the review with an exclamation mark. In the same year, *Pale Fire* (1962), despite garnering two positive reviews (1980, 1981), was not commissioned for translation. Surprisingly, even the *Lectures on Literature* (1980), based on Nabokov's university courses about Dickens, Austen, Stevenson, Proust, Kafka, Joyce, and Flaubert, were rejected in 1983. They were considered anti-intellectual, too direct, lacking the terminology of literary theory, and too self-reflective. But a breakthrough had already occurred in 1981 when a new and thoughtful seven-page evaluation of *Lolita* was submitted to Európa, warmly supporting its publication, and further endorsed by another positive review that year. Both reviewers were specialists in American literature, well-placed to emphasise Nabokov's status as an outstanding modernist writer, a dominant figure in American literature. Yet, despite the positive reviews of 1981 and 1982, Európa published *Lolita* only in 1987, in a translation by the author and actor Pál Békés (1956–2010). 1989 marked a Nabokov boom of sorts; from this date on, there were only positive reviews of Nabokov texts (although in 1989 one editor was still hesitating to commission *Speak, Memory*), and translations of his early Russian novels dominated. A Hungarian edition of Nabokov's collected works (novels and short stories) was published by Európa between 2006 and 2015.[62]

Bulgakov's *Heart of a Dog*: The 1980s

Mikhail Bulgakov's *Heart of a Dog* (*Sobach'e serdtse*), a satire on the Soviet New Man, was written in 1925 in the Soviet Union, and immediately confiscated and banned (until 1987). From the 1960s onwards, it was circulated in the West in so-called tamizdat (Russian-language unofficial editions), so that very few people in Eastern Europe could read it. It was not known even among those with access to sources of clandestine literature under the Kádár regime. This situation changed slightly when the Slovak journal *Svetová Literatúra* published a Slovak translation in 1978. The polyglot Hungarian writer György Spiró then read the novel—strangely enough, upon the recommendation of the notoriously hardline cultural journalist, Pál E. Fehér, mentioned above as the "ghost-editor" of the journal *Szovjet Irodalom*. Spiró, who had begun working in 1981 as a dramatist at the Csiky Gergely Theatre in Kaposvár, a city in South-Western Hungary, decided to adapt *Heart of a Dog* for the stage on Fehér's suggestion; he asked me to translate it. I had already finished my translation (based on the 1969 Paris edition of the book, which Spiró had lent to me) when the planned staging was banned. My (now officially illegal) Hungarian translation *Kutyaszív* (literally *Heart of a Dog*) was filed at the archive of the Institute of Theatre in Budapest.

62 The Nabokov Estate contracts oblige translators to use the English version of Nabokov's works, even for those novels originally published in Russian.

A second attempt to stage the work was made in 1986, but again the authorities intervened. My Hungarian translation, however, was published in the same year by one of the smaller samizdat (illegally printed and distributed) publishers, Katalizátor Iroda. It was printed on the clandestine stencil machine of a samizdat journal located in an artist's workshop. Thus, illegal Western tamizdat became Hungarian samizdat. At my request, as I had small children, the translator's identity was not mentioned. Moreover, I did not want to cause any trouble for my father, then Hungary's Minister of Finance. This new translation was noticed by the political police in January 1987, when one of their agents visited the samizdat workshop and bought a copy. Katalizátor Iroda was then targeted by the secret police and dissolved. One year later, in 1988, my translation was legally published by Európa Publishing House.

The three examples above (Evtushenko, Nabokov, and Bulgakov) show how unclear the dividing lines were between permitted and prohibited texts. Totalitarian terror relied on this uncertainty. Thus, it is difficult to establish exactly when totalitarian censorship ended, since its decline was gradual and took different forms in each country it affected.[63] The end of totalitarianism in Eastern Europe is often dated to 1989, but in Hungary, censorship was weakening long before that date. The last bastion of the collapsing fortress, defending the culture of Socialist Hungary, was the translation of Russian literature.[64]

---

63 On the connection between translation and censorship from a multidisciplinary perspective, see 'Translation Studies Forum: Translation and Censorship', in *Translation Studies*, 3 (IV, 2011), 358–73, https://www.tandfonline.com/doi/pdf/10.1080/14781700.2011.589657. For a Polish comparison, see the Polish case: John M. Bates, 'From State Monopoly to a Free Market of Ideas? Censorship in Poland, 1976–1989', in *Censorship and Cultural Regulation in the Modern Age*, ed. by Beate Müller (Amsterdam: Rodopi, 2003), pp. 141–67.

64 Mikhail Gorbachev banned censorship in the Soviet Union on 1 August 1990. The censorship authority itself was abolished; the federal government found its continued operation unnecessary.

Appendix

Below are some translations of Russian Literature in Socialist and post-Socialist Hungary. The first date is the publication year of the Hungarian translation. The second date (in parentheses) is the year of the first full-text publication in the Soviet Union (or Russia).

Controversial Soviet-Era Fiction

1962 (1962) Aleksandr Solzhenitsyn, *One Day in the Life of Ivan Denisovich* (*Odin den' Ivana Denisovicha*) (*Iván Gyenyiszovics egy napja*), trans. by László Wessely (Budapest: Európa, 1962).

1969 (1966–67) Mikhail Bulgakov, *The Master and Margarita* (*Master i Margarita*) (*A Mester és Margarita*), trans. by Klára Szőllősy (Budapest: Európa, 1969).

1979 (1922) Boris Pil'niak, *The Naked Year* (*Golyi god*) (*Meztelen év*), trans. by Péter Kántor (Budapest: Európa, 1979).

Glasnost' Period

1985 (1910) Aleksei Remizov, *Sisters of the Cross* (*Krestovye sestry*) (*Testvérek a keresztben*), trans. by Péter Kántor (Budapest: Európa, 1985).

1985 (1913) Andrei Belyi, *Petersburg* (*Peterburg*) (*Pétervár*), trans. by Imre Makai (Budapest: Európa, 1985).

1986 (1907) Fedor Sologub, *The Petty Demon / The Little Demon* (*Melkii Bes*) (*Undok ördög*), trans. by Imre Makai (Budapest: Európa, 1986).

1988 (1926) Boris Pil'niak, *Tale of the Unextinguished Moon* (*Povest' nepogashennoi luny*) (*A kiolthatatlan hold története*), trans. by Pál Misley (Nagyvilág 5., 1988).

1988 (1987) Anatolii Rybakov, *Children of the Arbat* (*Deti Arbata*) (*Az Arbat gyermekei*), trans. by Elli Nikodémusz (Budapest: Magvető, 1988).

1988 (1988) Boris Pasternak, *Doctor Zhivago* (*Doktor Zhivago*) (*Zsivago doktor*), trans. by Judit Pór (Budapest: Európa, 1988).

1989 (1987) Andrei Platonov, *The Foundation Pit* (*Kotlovan*) (*Munkagödör*), trans. by Zsuzsa Király, Erzsébet Vári (Budapest: Európa, 1989).

1989 (1988) Andrei Platonov, *Chevengur* (*Chevengur*) (*Csevengur*), trans. by Mária Szabó (Budapest–Uzsgorod: Magvető–Kárpátia, 1989).

1989 (1989) Varlam Shalamov, *Kolyma Tales* (*Kolymskiie rasskazy*) (*Kolima*), trans. by Ágnes Gereben, László Maráz, Ágnes Osztovits, Judit Osztovits, Zsuzsa Rab (Budapest: Európa–Szabad Tér, 1989).

1989 (1989) Vasilii Grossman, *Forever Flowing* (*Vsio techot*) (*Panta Rhei*), trans. by György Enyedy (Budapest: Magvető, 1989).

1990 (1987) Mikhail Zoshchenko, *Before Sunrise* (*Pered voskhodom solntsa*) (*Napfelkelte előtt*), trans. by László Bratka (Budapest: Európa, 1990).

1990 (1987) Nikolai Erdman, *Plays* (*Piesy*) (*Drámák*), trans. by Éva Harsányi, Rimma Dalos (Budapest: Európa, 1990).

1990 (1988) Evgenii Zamiatin, *We* (*My*) (*Mi*), trans. by Iván Földeák (Budapest–Pozsony: Európa–Madách, 1990).

1990 (1990) Aleksandr Solzhenitsyn, *The First Circle* (*V kruge pervom*) (*A pokol tornáca*), trans. by Imre Makai, Mária Szabó (Budapest: Magvető, 1990).

1990 (1990) Aleksandr Solzhenitsyn, *Cancer Ward* (*Rakovyi korpus*) (*Rákosztály*), trans. by Mária Szabó (Budapest: Árkádia, 1990).

The Post-censorship Era

1992 (1985) Tat'iana Tolstaia, *Hunting the Woolly Mammoth* (*Okhota na mamonta*) (*Mamutvadászat*), trans. by Zsuzsa Rab (Budapest: Európa, 1992).

1993 (1989) Aleksandr Solzhenitsyn, *The Gulag Archipelago* (*Arkhipelag GULAG*) (*A GULAG szigetvilág*), trans. by András Soproni (Budapest: Európa, 1993).

1993 (1990) Isaak Babel, *1920 Diary* (*Dnevnik 1920*) (*Napló, 1920*), trans. by Zsuzsa Hetényi (Budapest: Pesti Szalon, 1993).

1994 (1989) Konstantin Vaginov, *Goat Song, Harpagoniada, Works and Days* (*Kozlinaia pesn', Garpagoniana, Trudy i dni*) (*Harpagoniáda*), trans. by László Bratka (Budapest: Osiris–Századvég, 1994).

1994 (1989) Venedikt Erofeev, *Moscow-Petushki* (*Moskva-Petushki*) (*Moszkva-Petuski*), trans. By Erzsébet Vári (Budapest–Pécs: JAK–Jelenkor, 1994).

1994 (1992) Andrei Siniavskii, *Strolls with Pushkin* (*Progulki s Pushkinym*) (*Séták Puskinnal*), trans. by Katalin Szőke (Budapest: Európa, 1994).

1999 (1992) Viktor Pelevin, *Omon Ra* (*Omon Ra*) (*A rovarok élete*), trans. by Zsuzsa Király (Budapest: Park, 1999).

2001 (1990) Sergei Dovlatov, *Pushkin Hills* (*Zapovednik*) (*Puskinland*) / *Ours* (*Nashi*) (*Ezek vagyunk mi*), trans. by Miklós M. Nagy—Erna Páll (Budapest: Európa, 2001).

2002 (1994) Vasilii Aksionov, *Generations of Winter* (*Moskovskaia Saga*) (*Moszkvai történet*), trans. by András Soproni (Budapest: Európa, 2002).

2002 (1998) Boris Akunin, *The Winter Queen* (*Azazel*) (*Azazel*), trans. by Ibolya Bagi (Budapest: Európa, 2002).

2003 (2000) Liudmila Ulitskaia, *The Kukotsy Enigma* (*Kazus Kukotskogo*) (*Kukockij esetei*), trans. by Edit V. Gilbert, József Goretity (Budapest: Európa, 2003).

2004 (2000) Tat'iana Tolstaia, *Kys* (*Kys*) (*Kssz!*), trans. by Miklós M. Nagy (Budapest: Ulpius-ház, 2004).

2005 (1988–89) Vladimir Voinovich, *The Life and Extraordinary Adventures of Private Ivan Chonkin* (*Zhizn i neobychaynyie prikliucheniia soldata Ivana Chonkina*) (*Ivan Csonkin közlegény élete és különös kalandjai*), trans. by Zsuzsa Hetényi (Budapest: Gabo, 2005).

2009 (1999) Sasha Sokolov, *A School for Fools* (*Shkola dlia durakov*) (*Bolondok iskolája*), trans. by Rita Haffner (Budapest: Napkút, 2009).

2010 (2005) Dmitrii Glukhovskii, *Metro 2033* (*Metro 2033*) (*Metró 2033*), trans. by Márton Bazsó (Budapest: Európa, 2010).

2012 (1989) Vasilii Grossman, *Life and Fate* (*Zhizn'i sud'ba*) (*Élet és sors*), trans. by András Soproni (Budapest: Európa, 2012).

Ireland

Alastar Sergedhebhít Púiscín, the Séacspír of Russia: On the Irish-Language Translations of Pushkin

Mark Ó Fionnáin

Introduction

In the early years of the Gaelic revival after the founding of *Conradh na Gaeilge* (The Gaelic League) in 1893, the Irish language was finding its feet again after centuries of neglect, despite the continuing fall in the number of native speakers and its ongoing retreat in the face of English. With this revival of interest, there also appeared the need to produce reading material in Irish for the newly literate Irish-speaker, whether they be native or second-language speakers, material which—apart from poetry and folk songs—had never been much cultivated in recent times. Translation was thus one of the easiest, and most obvious, ways to produce it quickly. As Pascale Casanova notes:

> For an impoverished target language, which is to say a language on the periphery that looks to import major works of literature, translation is a way of gathering literary resources, of acquiring universal texts and thereby enriching an underfunded literature—in short, a way of diverting literary assets.[1]

Whilst this was indeed true in the case of Irish, there was also the related issue of showing Irish speakers how to create those forms of literature that had not existed before in the language, due to its marginalised status and lack of literate

1 Pascale Casanova, *The World Republic of Letters*, trans. by Malcolm DeBevoise (London and Cambridge, MA: Harvard University Press, 2007), p. 134.

 https://doi.org/10.11647/OBP.0340.10

speakers and potential readership. This is a point also mentioned by Erich Prunč in the context of the Austro-Hungarian Empire for the same era; whilst 'non-serious' literature did exist in Slovenian and Croatian, it was only in the late nineteenth-century that 'serious' works began to be translated, and with a specific focus on "the representative function of language, not on the bi- or multilingual competence of the audience, and the aim was to provide translated scripts to help develop theatre as a national institution".[2] Whilst theatre might have been the goal in the Austro-Hungarian Empire, in the Ireland of the British Empire, and the case of Irish, it was the aim of developing not only theatre, but also short stories, novels, and every other form of literature that had bypassed the language to date.[3] Irish, indeed, at that time fulfilled all three of Itamar Even-Zohar's criteria for the centrality of translation to a given literature: Irish-language literature was young, weak and facing a vacuum, i.e. a lack of any established norms or practices. As Even-Zohar observes:

> Through [...] foreign works, features (both principles and elements) are introduced into the home literature which did not exist there before. These include possibly not only new models of reality to replace the old and established ones that are no longer effective, but a whole range of other features as well, such as a new (poetic) language, or compositional patterns and techniques.[4]

And so, from those early decades of the revival, alongside first native attempts at producing plays, novels, and short stories, we also have extant translations into Irish of English-language material as varied as Charles Dickens, George Moore, and Daniel Defoe. Translators were not just concerned with bringing English works to an Irish-language audience; international authors also appeared in a Gaelic guise. Jules Verne, Hans Christian Andersen, Omar Khayyam, Thomas Mann, Plutarch, and others were all Gaelicised, but whilst some might have

---

2 Erich Prunč, 'Priests, Princes and Pariahs: Constructing the Professional Field of Translation', in *Constructing a Sociology of Translation*, ed. by Michaela Wolf and Alexandra Fukari (Amsterdam and Philadelphia, PA: Benjamins Translation Library, 2007), pp. 39–56 (p. 46).

3 For a more detailed look at the issue of translations into Irish, see the relevant chapters in Philip O'Leary's monographs, namely: *The Prose Literature of the Gaelic Revival, 1881–1921: Ideology and Innovation* (University Park, PA: Penn State University Press, 1994); *Gaelic Prose in the Irish Free State, 1922–1939* (Dublin: University College Dublin, 2004); *Writing Beyond the Revival: Facing the Future in Gaelic Prose, 1940–1951* (Dublin: University College Dublin, 2011).

4 Itamar Even-Zohar, 'The Position of Translated Literature within the Literary Polysystem', in *The Translation Studies Reader*, ed. by Lawrence Venuti (London and New York: Routledge, 2000), pp. 192–97 (p. 193).

been rendered from the original German, French, or Latin, it is more likely that others from further afield were translated via the medium of English.[5]

Such a rapid growth in the field of translation into Irish also gave rise to the appearance of several Russian authors in a Gaelic milieu, although the same caveat needs to be applied regarding the original language of the work in question; it is unlikely that many would have known enough Russian—if any—in Ireland at the turn of that century to have translated from an original Cyrillic text. Thus, whilst Lev Tolstoy, Anton Chekhov, and others did appear in Irish from the original language, as rendered by Gearóid Ó Nualláin, Liam Ó Rinn, and Maighréad Nic Mhaicín, for example, other translators most likely worked from an English text, although they were frequently coy when admitting to this. Such renditions tended to be ambiguously subtitled, for example, "*Sgeul on Ruisis: aistriú é seo ar Sgeul Rúisise do cheap Anton Tchehov*" (A story from the Russian: this is a translation of a Russian story composed by Anton Chekhov),[6] "[...] *do chuir Gaedhilg air*" (Translated into Irish by [...]) or "*Tolstoí na Rúise do scríobh*" (Tolstoy of Russia wrote it).[7] Furthermore, whilst the initial numbers in those early heady days might look impressive—Tolstoy apparently had eleven stories and two plays translated—on closer examination the results lose some of their lustre. Two of the stories by Tolstoy were each translated three times, and one of these—'What Men Live By'—was adapted into English for the stage by the English actor and dramatist Miles Malleson as *Michael* in 1917, and this was, in turn, translated into Irish as *Mícheál* in 1933. And it was into this *mélange* of various translations from varied sources, and with an equal variety of reasons behind them, that Aleksandr Pushkin made his appearances in Irish.

Whilst an in-depth analysis of the translations of Pushkin is beyond the scope of this short essay, the aim here is to present in brief those translations that were done of Pushkin into Irish, and to justify their production against the background of the growing cultural, linguistic, and political awareness of the time.[8]

5 For example, Tadhg Ó Donnchadha's rendition of Khayyam explicitly states on the inside cover page that he translated it 'from Edward FitzGerald's English translation' ['ó aistriú Bhéarla Éadbhaird Mhic Gearailt'], *Rubáiiát Omár Caiiám Ó Naíseápúr* (Áth Cliath: Mártan Lester, Tta [Ltd], 1920).

6 All translations from the Irish are by the author of this chapter.

7 Mostly the English pivot text is not mentioned. One rare case is that of Chekhov's *The Proposal* by Muiris Ó Catháin [*Cúrsaí Cleamhnais*, Baile Átha Cliath: Oifig Díolta Foillseacháin Rialtais, 1933], where it is stated that it has been rendered from "Mrs. Garnett's translation of the original Russian".

8 For a more detailed look at translations from Russian into Irish in general, see, for example, Mark Ó Fionnáin, 'Na Ceithre Máistrí: Chekhov, Turgenev, Tolstoy and Pushkin and the Translation of Russian into Irish', in *Representations and Interpretations in Celtic Studies*, ed. by Tomasz Czerniak, Maciej Czerniakowski and Krzysztof Jaskuła (Lublin: Wydawnictwo KUL, 2015), pp. 267–82; 'Opportunities Seized: From Tolstóigh to Pelévin', *Studia Celto-Slavica*, 9 (2018), https://doi.org/10.54586/JMAU5002. See also Muireann Maguire, 'From Dostoevsky to

Translations of Pushkin

'The Snowstorm' ('Metel'')

Pushkin made his first appearance in Irish in Fr. Gearóid Ó Nualláin's (1874–1942) book *God, Devils and People* (*Dia, Diabhail agus Daoine*),[9] which came out in 1922 and where we find both Pushkin and Tolstoy amongst several of Ó Nualláin's own original works. It is described as consisting of "Seven Short Stories, dealing with modern life. With Explanatory Notes", and thus was clearly aimed not just at an Irish-language readership, but also at learners of the language. This book has been erroneously described as having been "*aistrithe ó shaothar Rúisise Leo Tolstoy*" (translated from Lev Tolstoy's Russian work),[10] with no mention of Pushkin or of Ó Nualláin's own compositions, although on the inside cover we are told that the story by Pushkin is 'The Snowstorm' (titled in Irish '*Síon agus Sneachta*', meaning 'Bad Weather and Snow'), and Tolstoy's contribution is 'What Men Live By' ('The Visitation' or *An Fiosrú*) (Ó Nualláin, *Dia*, vii). Unlike most of the aforementioned translators of works into Irish, Ó Nualláin did know the original language of the text. In his autobiography, Ó Nualláin relates how he was encouraged in his younger days to learn some Russian by Fr. Risteárd Ó Dálaigh, head at the time of the Irish-language college Coláiste na Mumhan, to which end he learnt an amusing story from a book. He was then persuaded to meet a young Russian to whom he related the story and who laughed upon hearing it, praising both the story and Ó Nualláin's pronunciation. This simple recollection finishes with "*Is oth liom a rádh gur éirigheas as an Rúisis ó shoin*" (I regret to say that I have given up Russian since then).[11] Ó Nualláin thus knew

---

Yeltsin: Failed Translations and Russian Literary Landings in the Irish Language', *RUS* 11:17 (2020), https://doi.org/10.11606/issn.2317-4765.rus.2020.178520.

9 Gearóid Ó Nualláin, *Dia, Diabhail agus Daoine* (Baile Átha Cliath: Comhlucht Oideachais na hÉireann, 1922).

10 It is thus described in the biography of Ó Nualláin by Diarmuid Breathnach and Máire Ní Mhurchú, *Ó Nualláin, Gearóid*, http://ainm.ie/Bio.aspx?ID=217.

11 Gearóid Ó Nualláin, *Beatha Dhuine a Thoil* (Baile Átha Cliath: Oifig an tSoláthair, 1950), p. 225. Unfortunately, this recollection appears in a chapter towards the end of the book titled 'Other Occasional Memories' ['Cuimhíntí Fánacha Eile'], made up of such reminiscences, and as such are unaccompanied by any particular dates. Thus, it is unknown for how long Ó Nualláin's relationship with Russian lasted; he merely says 'ar feadh tamaill fadó' ['for a while, long ago']. After his tale about the story, he goes on to mention the fact that if a person can speak Irish, then Russian sounds should not pose a problem, and mentions that the Cyrillic alphabet has thirty-six letters (it has thirty-three). Based on this, his knowledge of Russian would seem to have been pre-Revolutionary. Moreover, Ó Nualláin states that Ó Dálaigh (1865–1930) was Professor of Russian in University College, Cork, at that time, although no such chair existed, and it is more likely that Ó Dálaigh

(some) Russian, and it is likely that 'Síon agus Sneachta' (and the Tolstoy story) were both translated from the original Cyrillic text.

Ó Nualláin was well known in Irish-language circles for his four-volume *Studies in Modern Irish*, a series that analysed the grammar of Modern Irish in painstaking detail. Thus, he seized the opportunity offered to him to provide his Irish-language readership with copious endnotes containing a wealth of knowledge on the life and customs in Russia at that time, including food and drink, accommodation, units of measurement, clothing, and linguistics. Indeed, his translation of Pushkin takes up twenty pages and is accompanied by six pages of detailed notes on both Irish grammar and Russian culture, whilst his rendition of Tolstoy takes up thirty-four pages and also has six pages of detailed explanatory notes. Ó Nualláin's multiple pages of notes and comments can somewhat distract from the joy of reading Pushkin in Irish, a feeling that is echoed in Muiris Ó Droighneáin's later comment on other compositions of Ó Nualláin's that there is "*mar a bheadh iarracht d'fhuairneamh fhir an ghraiméir agus na laoighice ar mhéireanna an ughdair agus an aistrightheora*" (a trace of the coldness of the man of the grammar book and of logic on the fingers of the author and translator).[12]

'The Coffin-Maker' ('Grobovshchik')

Pushkin further appeared in the short story collection *The Mouth of the Grave and Other Stories* (*Béal na hUaighe agus Sgéalta Eile*)[13] by León Ó Broin (1902–90), alongside some original works, several translations from French, and a rendition of 'The Man Who Did Not Believe in Luck' by Jerome K. Jerome. The story in question is 'Grobovshchik' ('The Coffin-Maker' or 'The Undertaker'), and whilst it was not produced with a didactic goal in mind, but merely to provide reading material, there is a brief biographical note at the end of the volume (*Béal*, 145–46). This note lauds Pushkin's talents as a writer of various genres, but it also encourages Irish speakers by suggesting that they should examine Pushkin's writings carefully, since, in Pushkin's era, Russian literature, music, and art were in a comparable state to that of contemporary Irish: "*faoi smacht ag meon iasachta agus ag cultúr iasachta*" (under the control of a foreign mentality and a foreign culture). Whilst not as overt as Ó Nualláin's didactic goal, the subtle message here is clear; Pushkin absorbed the foreign literary conventions prevalent in Russia at that time and reinvented them in an authentically Russian

was employed part-time. For more on Ó Dálaigh, see Breathnach and Ní Mhurchú, *Ó Dálaigh, Risteard*, https://www.ainm.ie/Bio.aspx?ID=200.

12 Muiris Ó Droighneáin, *Taighde i gComhair Stair Litridheachta na Nua-Ghaedhilge ó 1882 anuas* (Baile Átha Cliath: An Gúm, 1936), p. 166.

13 León Ó Broin, *Béal na hUaighe agus Sgéalta Eile* (Baile Átha Cliath: Thom i gcomhar le hOifig an tSoláthair, 1927). For Ó Broin's life, see Breathnach and Ní Mhurchú, *Ó Broin, Leon*, https://www.ainm.ie/Bio.aspx?ID=1625.

format, thus inventing modern Russian literature. Ó Broin is implying that this is what Irish-language authors should also aim to do, instead of mimicking foreign ways.

The importance of Pushkin to the development of Russian literature is also highlighted in Liam Ó Rinn's (1884–1943) translations from the Russian of Ivan Turgenev, titled *Prose Poems* (*Dánta Próis*).[14] This anthology is prefaced by a sixteen-page introduction in which Ó Rinn traces the development of Russian literature (*Dánta*, 9–25). Regarding Pushkin's role in this, Ó Rinn also notes (*Dánta*, 18–19):

> Deirtear gurb é do bhunaigh litríocht nua-aimseartha na Rúise [...]. Do shaor sé litríocht na Rúise ó gach ní bhí á cosc ar labhairt amach ina guth féin [...]. Isé Pús[h]kin a thug an nós réalaisteach isteach i litríocht na Rúise (i gcuid dá úrscéalta) mar an gcéad uair, i bhfad sarar dhein Balzac amhlaidh sa bhFrainc agus innstear dúinn gur do réir tréithe na n-úrscéal so dfás an úrscealaíocht sa Rúis ina dhiaidh sin.
>
> (They say that it was he who established the modern literature of Russia [...]. He freed Russian literature from everything which was stopping it from speaking out in its own voice [...]. It was Pushkin who introduced realism into Russian literature (in some of his novels) for the first time, long before Balzac did so in France, and it is said that that it was according to the traits of these novels that the Russian novel developed afterwards).

As did Ó Broin, Ó Rinn indicates the importance of Pushkin to Russian literature in general, whilst urging that modern Irish-language literature should also take inspiration from Russian authors—Casanova's 'literary assets', as it were. Furthermore, in Ó Rinn's opinion, Irish authors should not be afraid of translating from other languages into Irish at the expense of trying to develop a native, natural literature. Ó Rinn felt that the Irish language had nothing to fear from translating, since translations into Russian had not diminished the essential 'Russianness' of Russian literature itself. Another issue at that time was the purity of the Irish lexicon after centuries of linguistic contact and influence from English and the widespread use of loan words. Ó Rinn, therefore, also takes the opportunity to express his opinion regarding those who felt that Irish should remain pure and unsullied by foreign influences, especially in relation to the coinage of new words and neologisms. He notes that Russian authors were not averse to borrowing words. If such practice was good enough for them, Irish-language writers therefore had nothing to fear. Thus, in the case of

14 Liam Ó Rinn, *Dánta Próis* (Baile Átha Cliath: Oifig Díolta Foillseacháin Rialtais, 1933). For Ó Rinn, see Breathnach and Ní Mhurchú, *Ó Rinn, Liam*, https://www.ainm.ie/Bio.aspx?ID=106.

Ó Broin and Ó Rinn, Pushkin was not only meant to be enjoyed as fiction, but also to guide budding Irish-language writers and revivalists in both literary and linguistic matters.

'The Queen of Spades' ('Pikovaia dama') and 'The Stationmaster' ('Stantsionnyi smotritel'')

The first Irish attempt at 'Pikovaia dama' saw print in 1925 in an edition of the journal *An Branar*, by Domhnall Ó Mathghamhna.[15] It is a very reduced version, even for a small journal, and one does not need to look far to find abridgements: as one brief example, Chapter II of the story—the conversation in the Countess's bedchamber—is omitted altogether, and it takes only four lines for Lizaveta and Hermann to become friends after seeing each other for the first time:

> Two days after the social evening in Naroumoff's lodgings, Lisabéta saw the young officer Hermann out on the street looking up in her direction. It seems that he had decided to pretend that he was in love with the girl, and it was not long before the two were very friendly with each other.[16]

A further attempt at 'Pikovaia dama' made an appearance in 1932, this time serialised over two weeks in the newspaper *The Examiner*, in a version by Mícheál Ó Cionnfhaolaidh.[17] As might be expected from a version in print in a newspaper, it is also somewhat truncated, although not to the same extent as Ó Mathghamhna's. But it does not take long to find abridgements here, either: for example, in Tomskii's initial description of the Countess in Paris and her eventual financial salvation, references to Richelieu and Casanova are omitted, and the Countess's husband just refuses to pay her debts point-blank—no timid mouse he, nor does he receive a box on the ears as a reward for his refusal.[18]

---

15 Domhnall Ó Mathghamhna, 'An Bhainríoghan Spéarthaid', *An Branar*, March 1925, 7–18. This was later reproduced with some slight changes in Ó Mathghamhna's *Slabhra Nóiníní* (Baile Átha Cliath: Comhlucht Oideachais na hÉireann, 1934), a collection of Irish translations of some major European works.

16 'Dhá lá i ndiaidh na sgoruidheachta a bhí i lóisdín Naroumoff, do chonnaic Lisabéta amuich sa tsráid an t-oifigeach óg Hermann, agus é ag féachaint suas 'n-a treo. Is amhlaidh a bhí beartuighthe aigesean a leogaint air go raibh sé i ngrádh leis an gcailín. D'eirigh leis i ndiaidh ar ndiaidh, agus níor bh'fhada go raibh an bheirt ana-mhór le n-a chéile.' (*An Branar*, p. 10).

17 Mícheál Ó Cionnfhaolaidh, 'Bainríoghain Speireat', *The Examiner*, 30 July-6 August 1932.

18 The reasons for such abridgements are unknown. They might include the question of space, the opinion that Irish-language readers might be uninterested in long, descriptive passages, or other factors. The issue of censorship should not be ignored; see, for example, the refusal of Nic Mhaicín's translation of Leskov by An Gúm in Máirtín Coilféir, 'Tsechobh, Túrgénebh agus Púiscín na Gaeilge: Nótaí ar Mhaighréad Nic Mhaicín, Aistritheoir', *Comhar*, 76:9 (2016), 18–19.

In both cases, a truncated 'Queen' might be better than no Queen at all, but it was only in 1955 that a full version of the text—and the first to be rendered from the original Russian—appeared, in a miscellaneous collection simply titled *Stories from the Russian* (*Scéalta ón Rúisis*).[19] This contained two short stories by Pushkin, and one each by Tolstoy and Turgenev. Pushkin's contribution was 'Pikovaia dama', translated by Maighréad Nic Mhaicín,[20] and 'Stantsionnyi smotritel'' ('The Stationmaster') by the by-now late Fr. Ó Nualláin. 'The Queen of Spades' is here given in its full glory, including Richelieu, Casanova, the box on the ears, and Hermann's courtship of Lizaveta. Nic Mhaicín goes further than most of the previous translators, in that she Gaelicises the names as well; after all, if one of the points of a translation into Irish is to show that not everything needs to be conveyed via the medium of English, then why should names be an exception? Thus, the Irish-language reader is presented with the following variants, amongst others: Pushkin himself becomes *Puiscín*, Lizaveta Ivanovna *Lisabheta Ibhanobhna*, Chekalinsky *Tsecalínscaidh*, Tomskii *Tomscaidhe*, and so forth. In his 'Stationmaster', which is unaccompanied by any didactic footnotes, Ó Nualláin adheres more to the traditional English spelling (Vyazemsky, Minski) but also offers some somewhat schizophrenic versions: the stationmaster's daughter Dunia is simply called *Dunia*, whilst her full formal form is *Avdotya Semeonobhna* (a combination of both Irish and English orthography),[21] and *Vanka*, the young boy who shows the narrator where the stationmaster is buried, is fully Gaelicised in the rendition as *Seáinín* (Johnny). This issue of names helps illustrate—in a somewhat minor way—the nature of one of the questions Irish was facing at the time, and which had been addressed earlier by Ó Rinn: that of foreign borrowings and names in the language, and how to render them.[22]

'The Prisoner of the Caucasus' ('Kavkazskii plennik')

The first Gaelicisation of Pushkin's name had actually appeared earlier, when some of his poetry had finally seen the light of day in what is possibly the first rendition of original Russian poetry into Irish. In 1947, in the Irish-language cultural journal *Comhar*,[23] Seán Ó Maoilbhrighde (1919–83)[24] gave a brief

19 Maighréad Nic Mhaicín and Gearóid Ó Nualláin, *Scéalta ón Rúisis* (Baile Átha Cliath: Oifig an tSoláthair, 1955).

20 For more on Nic Mhaicín, see Breathnach and Ní Mhurchú, *Nic Mhaicín, Máighréad*, https://www.ainm.ie/Bio.aspx?ID=0450; Máirtín Coilféir, 'Nótaí'; Alan Titley, 'Eastward Ho! Aspects of Eastern European Writing Translated into Irish', *VTU Review: Studies in the Humanities and Social Sciences*, 5:1 (2021), and Maguire 'From Dostoevsky to Yeltsin', 32–34.

21 The patronymic is an erroneous transliteration of 'Samsonova'.

22 See Ó Fionnáin (*Opportunities*) for a closer analysis of such Gaelicisation of names.

23 Seán Ó Maoilbhrighde, 'Puiscin: An Fear agus an File', *Comhar*, 6:2 (1947), 1–2.

24 For Ó Maoilbhrighde (Ó Maolbhríde), see Breathnach and Ní Mhurchú, *Ó Maolbhríde, Seán*, https://www.ainm.ie/Bio.aspx?ID=1915.

biography of one 'Alastar Sergedhebhít Púiscín', who, he notes, is widely described as '*Séacspír na Rúise*' (the Shakespeare of Russia), but who, he feels, is actually more akin to '*Bíoróin*' (Byron) on account of the subjects he chose to write about. Ó Maoilbhrighde gives a brief list of Pushkin's major works, both prose and poetry, and then offers *sleachta* (sections) of 'Kavkazskii plennik', rendered into quite successful rhyming verse. This might have been merely an unbiased attempt at introducing Russia's major poet to an Irish-language audience, but Ó Maoilbhrighde was a fully paid-up member of the Communist Party of Ireland, and, after moving to Birmingham, he joined the British Communist Party. He resigned only after the Soviet invasion of Czechoslovakia. He was thus not averse to promoting the virtues of Russia and the Soviet Union—the following year, in the same journal, he wrote an article extolling the joys of Soviet literature, and lamenting the fact that it is not well-known outside of the USSR.[25] He also claimed, possibly correctly, to have been the first Irishman to visit East Germany officially in 1960, as part of a delegation of teachers from England to help run an international summer school for teachers in Erfurt, an event he also described in *Comhar*.[26]

'Yevgeny Onegin' ('Evgenii Onegin')

As the enthusiasm and availability of state funding for translations into Irish diminished, the overall number of translations into Irish fell. It is only in more modern times that Pushkin has again appeared in Irish, in the collection *Stories from Russia* (*Scéalta ón Rúis*) by Risteárd Mac Annraoi.[27] This is part of Mac Annraoi's single-handed attempt to produce major works of European literature in Irish; his *Scéalta* consists of excerpts from various Russian authors, for example Nikolai Gogol, Fedor Dostoevsky, Evgenii Zamiatin, etc. Mac Annraoi takes the opportunity to re-present Nic Mhaicín's translation of 'Pikovaia dama' in a more standardised, rather than dialectal, version. He also includes Ó Rinn's section on Pushkin from his history of Russian literature mentioned above, and Mac Annraoi's own translation of sections of 'Evgenii Onegin': Part 1 of Canto 1 in verse, and a selection of other stanzas rendered in prose (*Scéalta*, 101–37). Like Nic Mhaicín and Ó Maoilbhrighde, Mac Annraoi eschews the use of traditional English spelling in Irish works, producing examples such as 'Eivgéiní Oinéigin' and 'Alacsandar Suirgéivits Púiscin', in contrast to the earlier

25 *Comhar*, 8:5 (1949), 6–7.

26 *Comhar*, 20:2 (1961), 11–14.

27 Risteárd Mac Annraoi, *Scéalta ón Rúis* (Baile Átha Cliath: FÁS, 2016). For more on Mac Annraoi, see Maguire, 'From Dostoevsky to Yeltsin'. The linguistic wordplay (and honesty) should be noted here: Mac Annraoi's translations are not rendered directly from Russian, hence the title 'stories from Russia', whilst Nic Mhaicín and Ó Nualláin's 1955 collection is titled 'stories from the Russian [language]', hence implying they have been translated from the original Cyrillic text.

'Puiscín' and 'Púiscín', further illustrating the fact that there is still no standard way of presenting Russian names in a Gaelicised form.

Conclusion

In the general scheme of translation into Irish, six translations of Pushkin (including three of the same short story ('Pikovaia dama'), two of which were heavily abridged) may not appear too impressive, although the scarcity of Pushkin's output compared to that of authors such as Chekhov, as well as their suitability for inclusion in collections of short stories or newspapers, would have had some influence on the works chosen. However, despite the unorthodox approach to some of the renditions, it can only be said that Irish literature is better off for having had such works translated. The overall aim of the whole translation movement in general was both cultural and literary. It aimed to provide material for the newly literate Irish speaker, and also to show the aspiring Irish-language writer models and forms of short stories or novels which they could then draw on as inspiration for their own works, as evidenced by Ó Broin's and Ó Rinn's comments on Pushkin. However, those who translated Pushkin were also concerned with bringing to their audience a work from the original source language, and thus were making, consciously or not, a political and cultural statement that not everything foreign had to be received through the medium of English. This can be seen in Ó Nualláin's endnotes, and in Nic Mhaicín's, Ó Maoilbhrighde's and Mac Annraoi's attempts at Gaelicising names (and in the case of Ó Maoilbhrighde, English names too), moving a further step away from receiving everything through the filter of English—why have the text in Irish if the names themselves are in English? Further to this, there were Ó Nualláin's didactic goals, Ó Maoilbhrighde's pro-Communist sympathies and Ó Rinn's outward-looking (for the time) approach to the issues of translation and borrowings in relation to Irish. As Casanova observes:

> Because the linguistic battle involves the creation of a literature that itself is subject to political criteria and the judgment of political authorities, it is at once an essential moment in the affirmation of a national difference and the starting point for the constitution of an independent heritage.[28]

Casanova wrote this in relation to the emergent English-language literature in Ireland at the turn of the 1900s, but it can equally be applied to the linguistic battle and motivations involved in producing a literature in Irish as one of the ways of establishing national differences and an independent heritage. As such, the renditions of Pushkin are not only translations, but also cultural and political statements of the era in which they appeared.

---

28 Casanova, *Republic*, p. 139.

Italy

Mariia Olsuf'eva: The Italian Voice of Soviet Dissent or, the Translator as a Transnational Socio-Cultural Actor[1]

Ilaria Sicari

The Translator of Samizdat as Socio-cultural Actor

In the wake of the "cultural turn",[2] in recent decades the field of Translation Studies has witnessed the emergence of a sociological approach which considers any translation as a "socially regulated activity",[3] namely, a cultural product "necessarily embedded within social context".[4] In this perspective, all the human agents involved in the different phases of a translation—i.e. selection, production, and dissemination—started to "be accounted for not only as professionals but

1 This article is the outcome of a broader research project – *Transnational Book Diplomacy beyond the Cultural Cold War: Towards a Socio-Cultural History of Tamizdat* – sponsored by the EU with a postdoctoral Marie Sklodowska-Curie fellowship (HORIZON-MSCA-2022-PF-01, 101109157, TAMIZDAT). Views and opinions expressed are however those of the author only and do not necessarily reflect those of the European Union or MSCA. Neither the European Union nor the granting authority can be held responsible for them.

2 Susan Bassnett and André Lefevere, 'Introduction: Proust's Grandmother and the Thousand and One Nights: The "Cultural Turn" in Translation Studies', in *Translation, History and Culture*, ed. by Susan Bassnett and André Lefevere (London: Pinter, 1990), pp. 1–13. See also Susan Bassnett, 'The Translation Turn in Cultural Studies', in *Constructing Cultures: Essays On Literary Translation*, ed. by Susan Bassnett and André Lefevere (Clevedon: Multilingual Matters, 1998), pp. 123–40.

3 Theo Hermans, 'Translation as Institution', in *Translation as Intercultural Communication*, ed. by Mary Snell-Hornby, Zuzana Jettmarová and Klaus Kaindl (Amsterdam and Philadelphia, PA: John Benjamins, 1997), pp. 3–20 (p. 10).

4 Michaela Wolf, 'Introduction: The Emergence of a Sociology of Translation', in *Constructing a Sociology of Translation*, ed. by Michaela Wolf and Alexandra Fukari (Amsterdam and Philadelphia, PA: John Benjamins, 2007), pp. 1–36 (p. 1).

 https://doi.org/10.11647/OBP.0340.11

as socialized individuals".[5] When considering the translator as a socialised individual, one should take into account not only that "[t]he habitus of a translator is the elaborate result of a personalized social and cultural history",[6] but also that "[t]he actors' plural and dynamic (intercultural) habitus therefore forms a key concept for understanding the modalities of intercultural relationships".[7] The translation itself is then conditioned to a certain extent by "the agents involved in the translation process, who continuously internalize the aforementioned structures [such as power, dominance, national interests, religion or economics—*IS*] and act in correspondence with their culturally connotated value systems and ideologies".[8] Consequently, it is possible to contextualise the social dimension of the translation and its relative reception only if the agency of the translators is also taken into account. In this analytical framework, the translator should be perceived not only as the linguistic and cultural mediator of the source text and as co-creator of the target text, but also as a socialised individual who acts and, consequently, makes choices according to his/her personal experiences; his/her political, religious, and ideological beliefs, and, not least, his/her relationships with other socio-cultural actors involved in the selection, production and diffusion of translations.[9]

In the specific case of translating samizdat, the modalities and dynamics of intercultural relationships implemented by the translator working across the Iron Curtain had a transnational dimension. The unofficial flow of cultural objects across and beyond the Iron Curtain—a geopolitical and ideological boundary that was permeable[10] to the point of being defined by György Péteri as a transparent

5 Reine Meylaerts, 'Translators and (Their) Norms', in *Beyond Descriptive Translation Studies*, ed. by Anthony Pym, Miriam Shlesinger and Daniel Simeoni (Amsterdam and Philadelphia, PA: John Benjamins, 2008), pp. 91–102 (p. 91).

6 Daniel Simeoni, 'The Pivotal Status of the Translator's Habitus', *Target*, 10:1 (1998), 1–39 (p. 38).

7 Meylaerts, 'Translators and (Their) Norms', p. 91.

8 Michaela Wolf, 'Introduction: The Emergence of a Sociology of Translation', p. 4.

9 An interesting sociological study of this type was recently published by Cathy McAteer, who, focusing her attention on the 'social identity' of certain Russian-to-English translators in the twentieth century, highlighted their personal contribution in the reception of translated literature abroad. See Cathy McAteer, *Translating Great Russian Literature. The Penguin Russian Classics* (London and New York: Routledge BASEES Series, 2021), esp. Chapter 2, 'David Magarshack: Penguin Translator Becomes Translation Theorist', pp. 43–87, https://www.taylorfrancis.com/chapters/oa-mono/10.4324/9781003049586-2/david-magarshack-penguin-translator-becomes-translation-theorist-cathy-mcateer?context=ubx&refId=d79d056f-bf7a-4602-ab6c-b13b0fc7af92.

10 On the Iron Curtain's "permeability", see Friederike Kind-Kovács, 'Crossing Germany's Iron Curtain. Uncensored Literature from the GDR and the Other Europe', *East Central Europe*, 41 (2014), 180–203 (p. 180) and Friederike Kind-Kovács and Jesse Labov, 'Samizdat and Tamizdat. Entangled Phenomena?', in

"Nylon Curtain"[11]—was primarily composed of two kinds of texts, both of which constitute "a specific form of socio-cultural practice":[12] samizdat and tamizdat. A transnational cultural cross-border transfer such as the smuggling of uncensored Soviet texts in both directions—samizdat from Eastern to Western Europe and tamizdat, the other way around—was possible only thanks to the cooperation and collaboration of different cultural actors (editors, translators, literary agents, critics, journalists) and social agents (such as human rights activists, dissidents, diplomats, political, and religious figures) involved in the production, diffusion, and reception of those texts on both sides of the Iron Curtain. Consequently, samizdat and tamizdat were the result of a complex process of negotiation and bargaining by a varied group of individuals forming a "transnational community".[13] Thus, this "transnational socialization of texts"[14] was made possible thanks to the personal contribution—at different levels and with different functions—of social and cultural agents who acted not only as professionals, but also as socialised individuals. The translation of samizdat as a social practice and the role of the translator as a transnational socio-cultural actor responsible for the socialisation of these texts between the two sides of the Iron Curtain will be illustrated by the case of one of Italy's major translators of samizdat: Mariia Olsuf'eva. As I show below, several factors make her case emblematic for this volume.

By examining the archive of Mariia Olsuf'eva's personal papers[15] as well as archival documents of the publishing houses Mondadori and Il Saggiatore,[16] I aim to reconstruct her activity in terms of what Jeremy Munday calls the "micro-history of translators", meaning the reconstruction of the social and cultural history of translators. As "personal papers [...] give an unrivalled insight into the working conditions and state of mind [...] of the originator of the papers

Samizdat, Tamizdat and Beyond: Transnational Media During and After Socialism, ed. by Friederike Kind-Kovács and Jesse Labov (New York: Berghahn, 2013), pp. 1–23.

11 György Péteri, 'Nylon Curtain–Transnational and Transsystemic Tendencies in the Cultural Life of State-Socialist Russia and East-Central Europe', *Slavonica*, 10:2 (2004), 113–23.

12 Olga Zaslavskaya, 'Samizdat as Social Practice and Communication Circuit', in *Samizdat: Between Practices and Representations*, ed. by Valentina Parisi (Budapest: Central European University, 2015), pp. 87–99 (p. 87), https://ias.ceu.edu/sites/ias.ceu.edu/files/attachment/article/421/valentinaparisisamizdat.pdf.

13 Friederike Kind-Kovács, 'Tamizdat: A Transnational Community', in F. Kind-Kovács, *Written Here, Published There: How Underground Literature Crossed the Iron Curtain* (Budapest and New York: Central European University Press, 2014), pp. 83–208.

14 Valentina Parisi, 'Viaggio nella vertigine di Evgenija Ginzburg come esempio di socializzazione transnazionale dei testi', *eSamizdat*, IX (2012–13), 77–85.

15 Olsuf'eva's personal papers are stored at the Contemporary Archive 'Alessandro Bonsanti' of the Gabinetto G. P. Vieusseux (ACGV) in Florence, Italy.

16 The archival funds of the publishing houses Mondadori and Il Saggiatore are stored at the Arnoldo and Alberto Mondadori Foundation (FAAM) in Milan, Italy.

and the social activity in which he or she is engaged",[17] through the analysis of these documents, I will delineate a complex picture of the exchanges and transnational relations that Olsuf'eva conducted with the various socio-cultural actors involved in the production, circulation, and dissemination in Italy of uncensored Soviet literature (*nepodtsenzurnaia literatura*). In particular, I shall address her role in the reception of samizdat and tamizdat in Italy; explore her position within the transnational community as an enabler of their circulation between Eastern and Western Europe; and, last but not least, I shall examine the functions of her socio-cultural activity and activism.

Mariia Olsuf'eva: A Transnational Socio-cultural Actor

Mariia Olsuf'eva's transnational position is evident even in her identity card: she was a Russian born in Italy, with dual Italian and Swiss citizenship. Russian was her mother tongue, but she also spoke Italian, into which she translated and interpreted. Daughter of the tsarist colonel Vasilii Alekseevich Olsuf'ev and descended from an ancient Russian noble family, Mariia Olsuf'eva was born in Florence in 1907, where she spent the first four months of her life before moving to Russia, her home until the age of eleven.[18] Every year she holidayed at her parents' Florentine villa, thus maintaining a deep bond with the Tuscan city.[19] The outbreak of the October Revolution found her in the Caucasus with her family: by travelling through Batumi and Constantinople, after a daring journey on an English military ship, they managed to take refuge in Italy in 1919, settling permanently in Florence.[20] In 1926, Mariia Olsuf'eva married a Swiss-Italian agronomist, Marco Michahelles, and thus acquired Swiss citizenship. However, Florence remained her adopted city; she died there in 1988.

---

17 Jeremy Munday, 'Using Primary Sources to Produce a Microhistory of Translation and Translators: Theoretical and Methodological Concerns', *The Translator*, 20:1 (2014), 64–80 (p. 73).

18 See Stefania Pavan, *Le carte di Marija Olsuf'eva nell'Archivio Contemporaneo Gabinetto G. P. Vieusseux* (Rome: Edizioni di storia e letteratura, 2002), p. 7; Mariia V. Olsuf'eva-Mikaėllis, 'Moim detiam', in D. A. Olsuf'ev, *Vechnyi kover zhizni: Semeinaia khronika*, ed. by M. Talalaia (Moscow: Indrik, 2016), pp. 369–84 (p. 369, p. 372).

19 Mariia V. Olsuf'eva-Mikaėllis, 'Moim detiam', p. 376.

20 Enrico Romero, 'Intervista a Maria Olsufieva', *Incontri. Fatti e personaggi del nostro tempo*, Radio-Televisione della Svizzera Italiana (RSI), 29 September 1975.

Fig. 1 A page from the family album that portrays Mariia Olsuf'eva (first on left) with her father, Vasilii Alekseevich Olsuf'ev, sisters (Dar'ia, Aleksandra and Ol'ga), and brother, Aleksei, in Batumi, en route to Italy, 1919. The dates and stages of the journey are marked at the bottom right. Courtesy of Daria Bertoni.

Fig. 2 Mariia Olsuf'eva (first on the right) with her mother, Ol'ga Pavlovna Shuvalova, sisters and brother in Italy, 1921. Courtesy of Daria Bertoni.

Mariia Olsuf'eva often said that Russia was the country where she felt she had her roots.[21] Throughout her life, she maintained this bond with her motherland by translating numerous Russian writers into Italian, weaving a series of contacts with the Russian intelligentsia in exile, forging lasting and deep friendships with leading Soviet dissidents and, importantly, acting as starosta of the Orthodox church of Florence.[22] Her support for Florence's large Russian community soon led her to welcome the exiles of the so-called third wave of immigration (1960–80) arriving from the Soviet Union.[23] Olsuf'eva did not only offer support to exiled Russians, but also actively worked in favour of Soviet dissidents and activists within the USSR. She made their voices heard beyond the Iron Curtain not only by translating their works into Italian, but by sharing their appeals in national and foreign newspapers and by promoting various initiatives in their favour. A member of Amnesty International, she was among the founders of its Florentine section, launching national and international campaigns in support of different dissidents—including Andrei Sakharov, Elena Bonnėr, and Aleksandr Solzhenitsyn—with whom Olsuf'eva was also linked by a deep friendship. Due to her activism, her work as a translator of many samizdat and tamizdat texts, and her material contribution to the circulation of Soviet clandestine manuscripts, in 1973 she was declared persona non grata by Soviet authorities.[24] She died in Italy, unable to return to Russia, thus paying dearly for her life choices.

In an interview broadcast in 1975 on Swiss-Italian radio and television (RSI), she commented:

> Of course, I regret that I will not be able to go back [to Russia]. On the other hand, I prefer to have translated Solzhenitsyn, this is also a choice. If I were faced with this choice, to translate Solzhenitsyn or to be able to get my visa back to Russia, I would choose to translate Solzhenitsyn. Being Solzhenitsyn's voice in Italy is a tremendous honour for me.[25]

---

21 Ibid.

22 Grazia Gobbi Sica, *In Loving Memory: Il cimitero degli allori di Firenze* (Florence: Leo S. Olshki, 2016), p. 97, p. 283.

23 See Romero, 'Intervista a Maria Olsufieva'; Pavan, *Le carte di Marija Olsuf'eva*, p. 8.

24 Sakharov's widow Elena Bonnėr wrote in her memoirs that Mariia Olsuf'eva, her niece Elena Borghese and her friend Nina Kharkevich used to visit the Sakharovs in Moscow twice a year, from 1968 until 1973, when Mariia and Nina were stopped at Soviet customs with a "load of samizdat" and, consequently, were banned from the USSR. See *Andrei Sakharov, Elena Bonnėr i druz'ia: zhizn' byla tipichna, tragichna i prekrasna*, ed. by B. Al'tshchuler and L. Litinskii (Moscow: AST, 2020).

25 Romero, 'Intervista a Maria Olsufieva'. Unless otherwise indicated, all translations are my own. Olsuf'eva is still "Solzhenitsyn's voice in Italy": her translation of *The Gulag Archipelago* is the only Italian version of this key work by the Russian writer, and it is still in print. See, for example, the latest reprint of Olsuf'eva's translation in a revised and supplemented version by Maurizia Calusio, published

To the journalist Enrico Romero, who asked her if translating Solzhenitsyn was "a kind of posthumous revenge"[26] for the exile into which she had been forced, Olsuf'eva replied:

> No. It is not a revenge. It is simply that I consider him such a great writer and [*The Gulag Archipelago*] is such an important work for all of us, and it is an honour for me to translate it. I do not know how to express it otherwise. For me, it is the highest point a translator can reach.[27]

Fig. 3 A frame from Romero's interview with Maria Olsuf'eva, released in 1975. Courtesy of RSI.

In a 1974 letter to Solzhenitsyn (responding to his concern that her translation of the first volume of *The Gulag Archipelago—Arkhipelag Gulag*, 1973–75—was made too hastily, thus compromising textual fidelity), Olsuf'eva expressed even more frankly and resolutely her reasons for translating his work:

> I have no doubt that here and there another translator would change a comma, an adjective, etc. but I have fulfilled what I considered and still consider much more important: to give Italy, especially in such a politically difficult moment for this country, the possibility of knowing

in Mondadori's 'I meridiani' series as A. Solženicyn, *Arcipelago Gulag*, trans. by M. Olsuf'eva (Milan: Arnoldo Mondadori Editore, 2001).

26 Ibid.

27 Ibid.

> as soon as possible the whole truth, that truth which A. D. Sakharov, in transmitting to me by telephone his *Appeal from Moscow* [*Moskovskoe obrashchenie*, 1974], said was needed by all men on earth.[28]

These few lines clearly show that Olsuf'eva saw her task more as a mission than as a purely literary activity. That mission was not only cultural but markedly social and political, a side which she considered "much more important" than all the rest: her goal was to spread the voice of Soviet dissent in Italy (and throughout the world), thereby contributing to the struggle for civil rights that was being fought in the USSR and, through the translations of prohibited books, to attract the interest of international public opinion on these issues.

Cultural Activity

Olsuf'eva started translating from Russian into Italian in the 1950s, initially while teaching at the Higher School for Interpreters and Translators in Florence and later collaborating with some of the main Italian publishing houses for about forty years.[29] Her first translation, published in 1957, was Vladimir Dudintsev's *Not by Bread Alone* (*Ne khlebom edinym*, 1956).[30] Her translation activity therefore coincided with the years of the so-called Thaw (*ottepel'*), which marked, in the Soviet cultural field, phases when the easing of censorship gave hope for a liberal turning point and the restoration of freedom of speech—ultimately to be bitterly betrayed by increased control over the cultural life of the country. Despite the continuous fluctuation of Soviet cultural policies during those years (1956–66), Olsuf'eva consistently strove to give a voice to authors who could not be legally printed in the USSR. The long list of titles translated by her and published in Italy consists primarily of works that arrived clandestinely beyond the Iron Curtain (samizdat) or were printed abroad (tamizdat). She penned the first Italian translations of writers such as Andrei Platonov,[31] Andrei

28 Pavan, *Le carte di Marija Olsuf'eva*, p. 144.

29 Antonella d'Ameliia, 'Olsuf'eva Mariia Vasil'evna', *Russkoe prisutsvie v Italii v pervoi polovine XX veka. Entsiklopediia*, ed. by A. D'Ameliia and D. Ritstsi (Moscow: ROSSPĖN, 2019), pp. 490–91 (p. 490).

30 V. Dudincev, *Non si vive di solo pane* [*Ne khlebom edinym*], trans. by M. Olsuf'eva (Firenze: Centro internazionale del libro, 1957). The novel also appeared in the US and London that same year in Edith Bone's English translation, with E.P. Dutton and Hutchinson respectively.

31 Andrej Platonov, *Nel grande cantiere* [*Kotlovan*, 1969], trans. by M. Olsuf'eva (Milan: Il Saggiatore, 1969); Andrej Platonov, *Il villaggio della nuova vita* [*Chevengur*, 1972], trans. by M. Olsuf'eva (Milan: Mondadori, 1972). Olsuf'eva's translation preceded the first English translation by Thomas Whitney by four years. Published by Ardis in 1973, Whitney's translation was succeeded in 1975 by Mirra Ginsburg's version for E.P. Dutton.

Siniavskii,[32] Valerii Tarsis,[33] Aleksandr Solzhenitsyn,[34] Andrei Sakharov,[35] Eduard Kuznetsov,[36] and Vladimir Maksimov,[37] to name only a few. However, she also translated official authors such as Andrei Voznesenskii,[38] Iurii Bondarev,[39] and even recipients of the Stalin Prize for Literature such as Veniamin Kaverin[40] and Vera Panova.[41] Various factors contributed to the disproportion between the official and unofficial Soviet texts translated by Olsuf'eva: the dynamics of the Italian publishing market as well as her personal involvement and interests, determined this imbalance.

From the publication of the first Italian tamizdat in 1957—Boris Pasternak's *Doctor Zhivago* (*Doktor Zhivago*, 1957) published by Feltrinelli—a stream of

---

32 Andrej Sinjavskij, *La gelata* [*Fantasticheskie povesti*, 1961], trans. by M. Olsuf'eva (Milan: Rizzoli, 1962).

33 Valerij Tarsis, *La mosca azzurra* [*Skazanie o sinei mukhe*, 1963], trans. by M. Olsuf'eva, (Milan: Rizzoli, 1964).

34 This was *Divisione cancro* [*Rakovyi korpus*, 1968], trans. by M. Olsufieva (Milan: Il Saggiatore, 1968) and ostensibly authored by 'Anonimo sovietico'. This was the same year that Lord Nicholas Bethell's and David Burg's translation of *Cancer Ward* appeared in English, published by The Bodley Head. Other Solzhenitsyn translations which she completed include Aleksandr Solženicyn, *Vivere senza menzogna* [*Zhit' ne po lzhi*, 1974], trans. by M. Olsufieva (Milan: Mondadori, 1974); A. Solženicyn, *Arcipelago Gulag*, vol. 1 [*Arkhipelag GULAG*, 1973], trans. by M. Olsufieva (Milan: Mondadori, 1974); A. Solženicyn, *Lettera ai dirigenti dell'Unione Sovietica* [*Pis'mo vozhdiam Sovetskogo Soiuza*, 1974], trans. by M. Olsufieva (Milan: Mondadori, 1974); A. Solženicyn, *Arcipelago Gulag*, vol. 2 [*Arkhipelag GULAG*, 1974], trans. by M. Olsufieva (Milan: Mondadori, 1975); A. Solženicyn, *La quercia e il vitello: saggi di vita letteraria* [*Bodalsia telёnok s dubom*, 1975], trans. by M. Olsufieva (Milan: Mondadori, 1975); A. Solženicyn, *Arcipelago Gulag*, vol. 3 [*Arkhipelag GULAG*, 1975], trans. by M. Olsufieva (Milan: Mondadori, 1978). Thomas Whitney's English translation of *The Gulag Archipelago* (New York: Harper and Row, 1973) appeared only a year before Olsuf'eva's.

35 Andrei Sacharov, *Il mio paese e il mondo; Progresso, coesistenza e libertà intellettuale* [*O strane i mire*, 1975; *Razmyshleniia o progresse, mirnom sosushchestvovanii i intellektual'noi svobode*, 1968], trans. by M. Olsufieva and C. Bianchi (Milan: Euroclub, 1976); A. Sacharov, *Un anno di lotta di Andrej Sacharov* [*Trevoga i nadezhda: Odin god obshchestvennoi deiatel'nosti A. Sakharova*, 1978], trans. by M. Olsoufieva (Milan: Bompiani, 1977).

36 Eduard Kuznetsov, *Senza di me: diario da un lager sovietico 1970–71* (*Dnevniki*, 1973), trans. by M. Olsufieva and O. Michahelles (Milan: Longanesi, 1972).

37 Vladimir Maksimov, *La quarantena* [*Karantin*, 1973], trans. by M. Olsufieva and O. Michahelles (Milan: Rusconi, 1975).

38 Andrej Voznesenskij, *Scrivo come amo* [*Pishetsia kak liubitsia*], trans. by M. Olsoufieva and M. Socrate (Milan: Feltrinelli, 1962).

39 Iurii Bondarev, *Il silenzio* [*Tishina*, 1962], trans. by M. Olsoufieva (Milan: Rizzoli, 1962).

40 Veniamin Kaverin, *Sette paia di canaglie* [*Sem' par nechistykh*, 1962], trans. by M. Olsoufieva (Milan: Rizzoli, 1962).

41 Vera Panova, *Sergio* [*Serezha*, 1955], trans. by M. Olsoufieva (Milan: Mondadori, 1965).

uncensored Soviet literary texts began to flow clandestinely yet unstoppably from the USSR into the catalogues of Italian publishing houses. Indeed, Italy was one of the European countries where the publication of tamizdat flourished. This phenomenon involved both the main Italian publishing houses—like Mondadori, Einaudi and Il Saggiatore—and others founded at that time which specialised in the publication of uncensored Soviet literature, such as La Casa di Matriona and Jaca Book. Besides this specifically Italian impetus, another key factor was Olsuf'eva's personal interest and direct involvement in the selection of translations. Thanks to her contact with numerous Soviet dissidents, she was able to pitch these texts to Italian publishers, often mediating between the latter, Soviet authors, and various transnational socio-cultural actors.

Her activity as a mediator and, not infrequently, as a literary agent for dissident writers intensified after her first institutional visit to Moscow at the invitation of Viktor Shklovskii, several of whose works she had translated for the De Donato publishing house.[42] In December 1967, she wrote excitedly to Giampaolo Dossena—a Mondadori editor—that she would spend New Year in Moscow.[43] Olsuf'eva often recalled that trip as a turning point in her professional and private life when she encountered several leading exponents of the Soviet intelligentsia:

> I just happened, at the beginning, to meet Shklovskii [...] and through him I met the first writers right at our home[44] during a New Year's party,

42 Viktor Shklovskii, *Una teoria della prosa* [*O teorii prozy*, 1929], trans. by M. Olsufieva (Bari: De Donato, 1966); V. Shklovskii, *Viaggio sentimentale* [*Sentimental'noe puteshestvie*, 1923], trans. by M. Olsufieva (Bari: De Donato, 1966); V. Shklovskii, *La mossa del cavallo* [*Khod konia*, 1923], trans. by M. Olsoufieva (Bari: De Donato, 1967); V. Shklovskii, *Majakovskij* [*O Maiakovskom*, 1940], trans. by M. Olsufieva (Milan: Il Saggiatore, 1967); V. Shklovskii, *Il punteggio di Amburgo* [*Gamburskii schët*, 1928], trans. by M. Olsoufieva (Bari: De Donato, 1969); V. Shklovskii, *Marco Polo* [*Marko Polo razvedchik*, 1931], trans. by M. Olsufieva (Milan: Mondadori, 1972); V. Shklovskii, *Tol'stoj* [*Lev Tol'stoi*, 1963], trans. by M. Olsufieva (Milan: Il Saggiatore, 1978).

43 Florence, Archivio Contemporaneo 'Alessandro Bonsanti' Gabinetto G. P. Vieusseux (ACGV), Marija Olsuf'eva, OL.3.15.

44 Here Olsuf'eva refers to the fact that, by a curious chance, the House of Writers (Dom Literatorov) in Moscow, where all the official ceremonies of Soviet literati took place (including New Year celebrations which she herself attended several times) had its headquarters in Povarskaia Street, in the very building which had been the Olsuf'ev Palace before they fled Russia. Olsuf'eva repeatedly mentioned the toast that Shklovskii dedicated to her during the celebrations of 1 January 1968, calling her "the landlord", and how, as soon as word got out that the granddaughter of the old owner (Count Olsuf'ev) was present in the room, everyone raised their glasses in greeting: "I spent in that house three New Years, always invited by fellow writers of the Union [of Soviet Writers]. And it is funny

> where I also met Sakharov's wife [Elena Bonnėr] [...]. And since then, one thing leading to another, it has been a string of acquaintances that have given me a lot.[45]

Thanks to her friendship with the Sakharovs, her circle of acquaintances in Russia greatly expanded, soon including several groups of dissidents, especially Muscovites. Thanks to their intercession, when Solzhenitsyn signed a contract with Mondadori in 1974 for the first volume of *The Gulag Archipelago*, he requested that the translation be entrusted to her. The book caused quite a stir in the Italian press and public opinion,[46] and Olsuf'eva gave several interviews explaining why Solzhenitsyn chose her as his Italian translator:

> I don't know Solzhenitsyn personally. I know him through the friends we have in common. First of all, the scientist Andrei Sakharov [...]. It was Sakharov who told me about Solzhenitsyn during my visit to Moscow. [...] Previously I had translated *Cancer Ward*, so I think that's why Solzhenitsyn trusted me.[47]

This trust was later confirmed by the writer himself, as Olsuf'eva mentioned in a 1975 interview:

> I personally met him [Solzhenitsyn] only in September, when he returned. He knew about me, I asked him why and with a smile he told me 'when I was still allowed into the House of Writers, which as you know is your home, I heard about you and your translations and so I wanted you to be the translator of my works'. Needless to say, this gave me immense pleasure.[48]

Over time, the professional relationship between Olsuf'eva and Solzhenitsyn turned into friendship, thanks to the support that she offered the Soviet writer. Their closeness is evidenced not only by their correspondence, but also by

---

that every time, as soon as word got around that the old owner was present [...] a line of people would form in front of me, with full mugs, to greet me joyfully, to toast my health, as if indeed for a moment they were once again the guests of an Olsuf'ev. Funny, isn't it?". Claudio Serra, 'Solgenitsin ha voluto lei', *L'Europeo*, 7 February 1974, 48–51 (p. 48).

45 Romero, 'Intervista a Maria Olsufieva'.

46 On the reception in Italy of Solzhenitsyn's *The Gulag Archipelago*, see: A. Reccia, 'Narrazione del silenzio e dibattito nella prima ricezione di *Arcipelago Gulag* in Italia', in *Lo specchio del Gulag in Francia e in Italia*, ed. by Luba Jurgenson and Claudia Pieralli (Pisa: Pisa University Press, 2019), pp. 323–42.

47 Mario Pancera, 'Intervistata a Firenze la signora russa che ha tradotto "Gulag"', *Corriere d'informazione*, 13 February 1974, p. 3.

48 Romero, 'Intervista a Maria Olsufieva'.

the numerous letters that she received from editors and various Italian and international cultural personalities requesting her to act as an intermediary with Solzhenitsyn. Among Olsuf'eva's personal papers is one particularly interesting letter from Giorgio Mondadori on 22 February 1974, ten days after Solzhenitsyn had been expelled from the USSR. The publisher offered his hospitality to the writer in his house near Verona, in order to show support at such a fraught moment. Giorgio Mondadori asked Olsuf'eva—then translating *The Gulag Archipelago*—to communicate his invitation to Solzhenitsyn.[49] On 3 March, Olsuf'eva wrote to Solzhenitsyn attaching her Russian translation of the letter she received from Mondadori.[50] The film director Franco Zeffirelli, in the days immediately following the expulsion of the Soviet writer from the USSR, also felt the need to express his solidarity by sending a telegram to Olsuf'eva's Florentine address, in which he asked her, as a friend of the writer, to transmit his message of solidarity to Solzhenitsyn.[51] Olsuf'eva's friendly relations with other leading Soviet dissidents were also known outside Italy; for example, Patricia Blake, an American Slavic scholar specialising in dissident literature, wrote to her on 29 August 1971 requesting an interview about Solzhenitsyn (on whom Blake was writing a biography).[52] Olsuf'eva told Blake that she had not yet had the pleasure of meeting the writer personally, but that she could help by sharing anecdotes she had heard from mutual friends. However, she asked Blake to keep her identity strictly confidential and not name her in the book as a source.[53]

Olsuf'eva's international fame as a personality close to the circles of Soviet dissent increased further in 1975, the year when Sakharov was awarded the Nobel Peace Prize. The physicist could not personally collect the award because the Soviet authorities had denied him permission to go abroad. His wife Elena Bonnėr—who, when he was proclaimed the winner of the Nobel Prize, was in Florence as Olsuf'eva's guest to undergo an eye operation—went to Oslo in his stead. She chose Olsuf'eva to accompany her to the ceremony and interpret.

49 ACGV, Marija Olsuf'eva, OL. 3.12.19.

50 ACGV, Marija Olsuf'eva, OL. 3.12.21.

51 ACGV, Marija Olsuf'eva, OL.2.3.9.

52 Pavan, *Le carte di Marija Olsuf'eva*, pp. 135–36. A footnote to Blake's review of Solzhenitsyn's *The Gulag Archipelago* informed the reader that "[Blake herself] is writing a biography of Solzhenitsyn" (*New York Times Book Review*, 26 October 1975, 1). However, no trace of this volume has been found either in Blake's bibliography, or in the general bibliography on Solzhenitsyn: probably, the book remained unpublished, although Blake had worked on it for several years.

53 Pavan, *Le carte di Marija Olsuf'eva*, pp. 136–37.

Fig. 4 King Olav V, M. Olsuf'eva and E. Bonnèr at the Nobel Prize ceremony, December 1975. Courtesy of Elena Bonnèr's heirs. ©Norsk Telegrambyrå.

Fig. 5 M. Olsuf'eva sitting in the stalls during the Nobel Prize ceremony, December 1975. Courtesy of E. Bonnèr heirs. ©Norsk Telegrambyrå.

Fig. 6 E. Bonnèr at the Press Conference with M. Olsuf'eva in the background, December 1975. Courtesy of E. Bonnèr heirs. ©Norsk Telegrambyrå.

Olsuf'eva's personal papers contain invitations to the official award ceremony and to the gala dinner;[54] a signed typewritten copy in Russian and English of Sakharov's *lectio magistralis* (*Mir, progress, prava cheloveka—Peace, Progress, Human Rights*); a copy of the speech given on that occasion by Elena Bonnėr; and a series of congratulatory letters and telegrams, including a letter from Nikita Struve congratulating Bonnėr and Olsuf'eva on their global celebrity, referring to the fact that the international press had published the official photographs of the awards ceremony in which both were portrayed alongside King Olav V of Norway.[55]

Thanks to her contacts with numerous Soviet dissidents (Sakharov, Bonnėr, Solzhenitsyn, Roy Medvedev, Andrei Amal'rik, Vladimir Bukovskii, and Natalia Gorbanevskaia, to name but a few) and with some of the most influential intellectual Russian émigrés in the West (including Nikolai Struve, Marc Slonim and Zhores Medvedev), Olsuf'eva soon became a key contact for anyone seeking to contact Soviet dissidents at home or abroad. Italian publishers interested in samizdat wrote to her, as did journalists, intellectuals, and politicians. On 30 January 1974, for example, the journalist Enrico Romero—author and director of a series of interviews dedicated to Soviet dissidents, broadcast by the Swiss-Italian radio and television station (RSI)—wrote mentioning Medvedev's willingness to be interviewed if Olsuf'eva acted as an interpreter and mediator.[56] Olsuf'eva's work with RSI is evidenced not only by this correspondence with Romero, but also by an interview with Bonnėr that aired in February 1976, in which Olsuf'eva is filmed with Bonnėr. In fact, the interview took place in Olsuf'eva's house in Florence.

Fig. 7 Frame from E. Romero's interview with E. Bonnėr (on the left), accompanied by M. Olsuf'eva (on the right), 1976. Courtesy of RSI.

54 The following references are located in ACGV. For the invitations Olsuf'eva received to attend the award ceremony, see OL.2.2.16, and for the gala dinner OL.2.2.18. For the signed copy of Sakharov's *lectio magistralis*, see OL.2.2.20 and Bonnėr's speech OL.2.2.19. For examples of congratulatory letters and telegrams, see OL.2.2.24.

55 See, for example: *Russkaia mysl'*, December 1975; *Herald Tribune*, 11 December 1975.

56 AGCV, Marija Olsuf'eva, OL.2.4.9.

Further proof of Olsuf'eva's activity as a cultural intermediary is found in her correspondence with Sergio Jacomella—the director of a Swiss-Italian socio-cultural cooperative—who, between 1974 and 1977, organised in Lugano a series of meetings with major Soviet dissidents. Jacomella praised her "invaluable mediation" and "precious collaboration" in meetings with Aleksandr Galich and others.[57] Olsuf'eva also corresponded with Giovanni Volpe—publisher and founder of the Gioacchino Volpe Foundation—who wrote to her seeking contact details for dissidents whom he wished to invite to the conference 'Order and Disorder' ('Ordine e disordine'), which was to be held in Rome in April 1979.[58] In her reply, Olsuf'eva suggested inviting the poets Natalia Gorbanevskaia and Naum Kozhavin; she furnished Volpe with their addresses, as well as Vladimir Bukovskii's.[59] Even Ronald Reagan resorted to Olsuf'eva to contact Soviet dissidents directly: when he first stood for the presidency of the United States (1975), he tasked Senator James Buckley with sending an article about Sakharov to Bonnėr via Olsuf'eva's Florentine address.

These close friendships with Soviet dissidents allowed Olsuf'eva to play a fundamental role in the circulation and diffusion of samizdat in Western Europe, not only pitching the translation of their works to Italian publishers, but also often acting as their literary agent, representative, and copyright protector. Several times Olsuf'eva took the initiative of pitching the translation of books that interested her or of samizdat manuscripts that had come into her possession to different publishing houses, as in the case of Anatolii Marchenko's *Testimonies* (*Moi pokazaniia*, 1969), which she introduced to Il Saggiatore thus:

> Following the telephone conversation of 20 February [1969] with Miss De Vidovich [editor of Russian literature], I hasten to send you the typescript (photocopied) of the book, unpublished in the USSR, Anatolii Marchenko's *Testimonies*, which I received from Nikita Struve in Paris. [...] if the book rights have not yet been acquired by some other publisher, I would deem it appropriate and urgent to translate it.

However, her proposal was rejected by the publishing house on the grounds that the work had "a more scandalous than literary nature". In 1977, she pitched to the Florentine publishing house Editoriale Nuova two non-fiction books by Valerii Chalidze (*The Legal Situation of Workers in the USSR* and *Criminal Russia: Essays on Crime in the Soviet Union*): the editorial director Giampaolo Martelli thanked her and requested the original manuscripts in order to submit them

57 ACGV, Marija Olsuf'eva, OL. 2.4.19.

58 ACGV, Marija Olsuf'eva, OL. 2.4.47a. Given that papers by Soviet dissidents were not published in the conference proceedings (*Ordine e disordine. Settimo incontro romano, 1977*, Roma: Giovanni Volpe Editore, 1980) and none is mentioned in the list of participants (*Ordine e disordine*, p. 217), one might reasonably assume that the Soviet dissidents did not take part in the conference sessions.

59 ACGV, Marija Olsuf'eva, OL. 2.4.47b.

to his editorial consultants, a request that Olsuf'eva satisfied by sending the manuscripts in her possession. Martelli's letter reveals his keenness to stay updated about "the most significant books by Soviet authors who turn to you for the publication of their works in Italy", while demonstrating how editors held Olsuf'eva's collaboration in high esteem.

One of the authors who benefited most from Olsuf'eva's intermediation was undoubtedly Eduard Kuznetsov; their substantial correspondence (1972–80) attests to their friendship.[60] In 1972, Olsuf'eva personally undertook to publish Kuznetsov's diary of his years of imprisonment in a labour camp in Mordovia. Olsuf'eva's 1972 translation for the publisher Longanesi, as *Without Me. Diary of a Soviet Concentration Camp, 1970–1971* (*Senza di me. Diario di un campo di concentramento sovietico, 1970–1971*), was a world première. Her correspondence with Longanesi clearly shows that the proposal was pitched by Olsuf'eva herself.[61] The most interesting aspect of this correspondence is Olsuf'eva's role as the author's literary agent, providing the publishing house with detailed information on the remuneration to be paid to the author through her:

> We agreed that as copyright fees for publishing the work, you will pay me the lump sum of 1,000,000 lire. This amount includes my translation into Italian and any amount due on the work up to 10,000 copies of your edition. Beyond this amount, you will pay me an 8% stake on the cover price of each copy sold. For any other use of the work, in any language and any form, you will reserve for me 50% of the net revenue.[62]

Olsuf'eva frequently reiterated the need to protect the rights of Soviet authors, well aware of the difficulty experienced even by officially approved writers in receiving copyright fees across the Iron Curtain. She often acted as their guarantor, offering to personally collect their fees and to send them on to the recipients, sometimes even advancing money out of her own pocket.[63] One such example is her correspondence with Bulat Okudzhava, several of whose poems she translated: Okudzhava, through his wife, asked her to help him obtain his copyright fees.[64] Olsuf'eva repeatedly used his fees to buy and send on garments for the Okudzhavas; she also personally brought his money to Russia.[65]

60 The following references concerning Olsuf'eva's mediation with Soviet dissidents are located at ACGV. For more on President Reagan, Senator Buckley and Olsuf'eva, see OL. 2.2.14a and OL.2.2.14b. For more on Olsuf'eva's Marchenko pitch to Il Saggiatore, see OL. 3.15.70, and regarding the publisher's rejection of the work as more scandalous than literary, see OL.3.15.73. For correspondence between Martelli and Olsuf'eva, see OL. 3.7.1. and OL. 3.7.2. On Olsuf'eva's friendship with Eduard Kuznetsov, see OL.3.28.

61 ACGV, Marija Olsuf'eva, OL.3.11.30.

62 Ibid.

63 Pavan, *Le carte di Marija Olsuf'eva*, p. 30.

64 Ibid., p. 78.

65 Ibid., p. 79.

Confirming Olsuf'eva's helpfulness, a 1977 letter from Bonnėr's son-in-law, Efrem Jankelevich, mentions that Bonnėr hoped to be able to travel to Italy using the fee for the translation of an article by Sakharov.[66]

Olsuf'eva also carried out an important role as an intermediary between Soviet authors and their Western literary agents, as evidenced by a letter sent on behalf of Bonnėr to the literary agent Eric Linder.[67] Here Olsuf'eva was passing on a request from Bonnėr to the agent: since the Garzanti publishing house had rejected Sakharov's *My Country and the World* (*Il mio paese e il mondo*, 1975), Bonnėr wanted another firm, Rusconi, to option it.

Another relevant aspect of Olsuf'eva's cultural activity was her commitment to disseminating samizdat and tamizdat works not only in Italy, but abroad. By exploiting her personal acquaintance with numerous cultural agents, Olsuf'eva was able to advertise the tamizdat publication of Kuznetsov's *Diary* which, as we have seen, was first published thanks to her mediation. In a letter to the publisher Mario Monti on 25 November 1972, Olsuf'eva proposed sending this tamizdat work to *Time* correspondent Patricia Blake and to the editors of the *Nouvel Observateur*, who were keen to run a review of Kuznetsov's work.[68]

I have shown that Olsuf'eva's agency as a cultural actor was not limited to translation, but also included various editorial activities, such as pitching texts to publishers on her own initiative and offering to mediate with and on behalf of Soviet authors about copyright issues, as well as promoting tamizdat works in the national and international press. Another significant side of her commitment as a social actor was her work for Amnesty International, which facilitated her representation of Soviet dissidents in Italy. As such, Olsuf'eva exemplified the role of a "gatekeeper".[69]

Social Activity and Activism

From the late 1960s onwards, Mariia Olsuf'eva was committed to defending human rights in the USSR: she helped promote a series of international campaigns and mobilisations supporting political prisoners and other victims of Soviet authorities. In 1968 she became the spokesperson for an initiative promoted by Marc Slonim to support Solzhenitsyn at the Mondadori publishing house.[70]

66 Ibid., p. 98; ACGV, Marija Olsuf'eva, OL.2.2.25.

67 The letter is stored in the archive of the International Literary Agency (Agenzia Letteraria Internazionale, ALI) at the Fondazione Arnoldo e Alberto Mondadori (FAAM) in Milan. FAAM, Agenzia Letteraria Internazionale–Erich Linder, Serie annuale 1975, b. 54, f. 10 (Maria Olsufieva).

68 ACGV, Marija Olsuf'eva, OL.3.11.34.

69 William Marling, *Gatekeepers: The Emergence of World Literature and the 1960s* (Oxford and New York: Oxford University Press, 2016).

70 FAAM, Archivio storico Arnoldo Mondadori Editore, Area Editoriale Marco Polillo, Solženicyn, serie non-ordinata, 32b.

Slonim's letter, translated into Italian by Olsuf'eva and enclosed with her own message,[71] was a last-ditch attempt to stop the oppression to which Solzhenitsyn was subjected in the USSR: Slonim proposed to send, on the occasion of Solzhenitsyn's fiftieth birthday (11 December 1968), a series of telegrams from writers, translators, professors, editors and any other cultural actors in Europe and the United States to the Writers' Union and to the *Literaturnaia gazeta*. It was hoped that this show of European intellectuals' genuine commitment to Solzhenitsyn and his protection could not fail to impress the Party leaders.[72] Thanks to mediation by Olsuf'eva and by the literary agent Eric Linder,[73] the Mondadori Director of the Foreign General Secretariat Glauco Arneri and the Editorial Directors Donato Barbone and Vittorio Sereni joined the initiative.[74]

In 1980, Olsuf'eva personally promoted an international protest campaign against the escalation of the persecutions suffered by the Sakharovs, now in internal exile in Nizhnii Novgorod, the birthplace of Gorky. On 19 February, Olsuf'eva sent three telegrams from her Florentine address to, respectively, Iurii Andropov,[75] the Soviet Minister of Foreign Affairs Andrei Gromyko, and the Procurator-General Roman Rudenko. The first two cables, in Italian, were sent on behalf of the Florentine branch of Amnesty International, which she had helped found in 1977; the third, in Russian, was signed personally by her. A few days later, Olsuf'eva began collecting signatures, campaigning for the Sakharovs. This campaign soon involved several Italian MPs, as shown by letters exchanged with the Christian Democrat member of parliament Gianni Cerioni and his assistant, Giuseppe Fortunato. On 23 February, on behalf of Cerioni, Fortunato sent Olsuf'eva several documents with official Italian Chamber of Deputies headers, to be used for messages signed by the Italian MPs; on 25 February, Olsuf'eva sent to Cerioni three letters she had written (in Italian and Russian) to be addressed to Gromyko, Anatolii Aleksandrov (the President of the Academy of Sciences of the USSR), and Iurii Khristoradnov (the First Secretary of the CPSU Gorky City Committee). She also promoted this campaign with Italian editors: one letter from

71 FAAM, Archivio storico Arnoldo Mondadori Editore, Area Editoriale Marco Polillo, Solženicyn, serie non-ordinata, 32c.

72 Ibid.

73 FAAM, Archivio storico Arnoldo Mondadori Editore, Area Editoriale Marco Polillo, Solženicyn, serie non-ordinata, 32a.

74 A copy of the cable sent by Vittorio Sereni on that occasion is stored at the Arnoldo Mondadori Foundation: FAAM, Archivio storico Arnoldo Mondadori Editore, Direzione Letteraria Vittorio Sereni, Solzhenitsyn, 26/20. See also: FAAM, Archivio storico Arnoldo Mondadori Editore, Area Editoriale Marco Polillo, Solženicyn, serie non-ordinata, 32; 32b.

75 The archival references relevant to this paragraph are all located at ACGV. For Olsuf'eva's telegram to Andropov, see OL.2.2.56; to Gromyko, see OL.2.2.55; to Rudenko, see OL.2.2.54. For Fortunato's documents to Olsuf'eva, see OL.2.2.57. Olsuf'eva's letters to Gromyko via Cerioni are found at OL.2.2.61; her letters to Aleksandrov are found at OL.2.2.60; and her letters to Khristoradnov are at OL.2.2.59. The letter from Città Armoniosa can be found at OL.3.5.24a.

the publishing house Città Armoniosa reported that "about Sakharov we filled out a lot of the sheets that you sent to us. About 500 signatures". In those years, she also collaborated with Amnesty regularly as a translator and interpreter.[76]

As with her cultural activity, Olsuf'eva's varied work as a social actor and human rights activist kept her occupied on several fronts simultaneously. On 15 February 1974, the British newspaper *The Guardian* published Sakharov's 'Appeal from Moscow', in which he protested against the arrest of Solzhenitsyn and requested the publication of *The Gulag Archipelago* in the USSR. Olsuf'eva was mentioned in the article because Sakharov had dictated the text of his appeal to her over the phone, so that it could be disseminated in the West.[77] The Italian press also mentioned Olsuf'eva, quoting her in numerous articles relating to human rights in the USSR, or publishing photographs that portrayed her in the company of important Soviet dissidents and human rights activists. On 13 September 1977, during Bonnėr's second stay in Florence, *La Nazione* reported on her meeting with the city's mayor, Elio Gabbuggiani, publishing a picture of the two in Olsuf'eva's company alongside its article.[78] She was once again interpreting, having also organised the meeting.

On 22 March 1978, *La Nazione* wrote about an institutional visit to Florence by the General Secretary of Amnesty International, Martin Ennals: Olsuf'eva was present on that occasion too, not only as an interpreter, but as a member of Amnesty International and co-founder of its Florentine Group.[79] In 1977, she also committed herself to protecting the families of political prisoners in the USSR, launching an international aid campaign. Among the papers relating to her activity as a member of Amnesty International are two letters with the names and addresses of the families of political convicts which request the recipients (other Amnesty co-ordinators) to deliver staple goods via tourists visiting the USSR and other occasional travellers.[80] The list of desired goods, which Olsuf'eva received from Bonnėr, contained shoe and clothing sizes for the Russian end users.[81] She therefore aimed to provide support to Soviet dissidents and their families via every possible route, promoting international campaigns in their favour so as to raise public awareness, as well as offering pragmatic material help, such as clothes parcels and other goods.

76 In January 1980, Olsuf'eva wrote to Leoni that she was working on an urgent translation of Amnesty International's annual report on the USSR (ACGV, Marija Olsuf'eva, OL.3.5.21); on another occasion, she also mentioned her participation as an official interpreter in the Sakharov Hearings, which were held in Washington in 1979 (ACGV, Marija Olsuf'eva, OL.3.5.20).

77 William L. Webb, 'Dissidents Challenge the Kremlin', *The Guardian*, 15 February 1974, https://www.theguardian.com/theguardian/2013/feb/13/alexander-solzhenitsyn-arrest-1974-archive.

78 'Elena Sakharova dal sindaco', *La Nazione*, 13 settembre 1977.

79 'Il rapporto annuale sui diritti dell'uomo', *La Nazione*, 22 marzo 1978.

80 ACGV, Marija Olsuf'eva, OL.2.1.3; ACGV, Marija Olsuf'eva, OL.2.1.4.

81 ACGV, Marija Olsuf'eva, OL.2.4.50.

Conclusion

Olsuf'eva's case exemplifies "the active and often physical contribution"[82] made by individuals involved in the cross-border flow of samizdat and tamizdat, a transnational community composed of many émigrés from different waves of the Russian diaspora. Their role has been described thus by Kind-Kovács:

> The role of émigrés was one, if not *the* most crucial element in the initiation and maintenance of cross-cultural literary entanglements. While the community across the "Other Europe" was one of discourses and ideas, through the West this virtual community developed into a tangible collective. The long-term presence of émigrés created the foundations for cross-border communication.[83] [original italics]

As we have seen, in fact, it was also thanks to Olsuf'eva's network of contacts from the different waves of Russian emigration to Europe and the United States that she was able to obtain manuscripts smuggled out of the USSR, which she then pitched to Italian publishing houses and, ultimately, translated. Therefore, besides her roles as a translator and intercultural mediator, she was actively involved in the production, dissemination, and reception of samizdat and tamizdat and, last but not least, as an activist defending human rights in the USSR.

In the transnational distribution of uncensored Soviet literature (*nepodtsenzurnaia literatura*), the translator's role was not limited to linguistic and cultural mediation. In the case of samizdat and tamizdat, we have seen that the translator was often one of the main actors within that 'transnational community' which enabled the circulation of cultural goods and ideas on both sides of the Iron Curtain. Thus, when considering the production, dissemination and reception of the 'other literature' between the 'two Europes', it is important to rethink the role of the translator, as a transnational (non-state) actor of cultural diplomacy.[84] Reframing the translator's role in this way would moreover enrich the field of cultural Cold War studies, which has often

82 Friederike Kind-Kovács, *Written Here, Published There*, p. 220.

83 Kind-Kovács, *Written Here*, p. 155.

84 See, for example, Giles Scott-Smith's essay 'Opening Up Political Space: Informal Diplomacy, East-West Exchanges and the Helsinki Process', in *Beyond the Divide. Entangled Histories of Cold War Europe*, ed. by Simo Mikkonen and Pia Koivunen (New York and Oxford: Berghahn, 2015), pp. 23–43; and various essays in *Entangled East and West: Cultural Diplomacy and Artistic Interaction during the Cold War*, ed. by Simo Mikkonen, Giles Scott-Smith and Jari V. Parkkinen (Berlin and Boston: De Gruyter, 2019).

wrongly regarded translators as marginal to the production, dissemination and reception of unofficial Soviet culture across the Iron Curtain.[85]

85 On the cultural Cold War, see *The Cultural Cold War in Western Europe 1945–1960*, ed. by Giles Scott-Smith and Hans Krabbendam (Portland: Frank Cass, 2003); *Across the Blocs. Cold War Cultural and Social History*, ed. by Rana Mitter and Patrick Major (Portland: Frank Cass, 2004); and *Divided Dreamworlds? The Cultural Cold War in East and West*, ed. by Peter Romijn, Giles Scott-Smith and Joes Segal (Amsterdam: Amsterdam University Press, 2012). See also Esmaeil Haddadian-Moghaddam and Giles Scott-Smith, 'Translation and the Cultural Cold War. An Introduction', *Translation and Interpreting Studies*, 15:3 (2020), *Special Issue: Translation and the Cultural Cold War*, 325–32.

Italy
Russian Literature in Italy: The Twentieth Century

Claudia Scandura

Between 1905 and 1945

This paper aims to map the history of Russian literary translation in Italy in the twentieth century and to reflect on how politics influenced publishers' and translators' choices. Literary exchange is an important vehicle for intercultural knowledge and understanding. Through this lens, translation, as the interpretation of verbal signs in one language by means of verbal signs in another, represents a particularly complex and sophisticated process of communication involving different recipients, both in terms of individual people and of specific social contexts.[1] According to Giovanni Maver's speech at the First Congress of Slavonic Studies held in Prague in 1929, translation highlights the relationships between different languages, cultures, and peoples.[2] If we understand, with Maver, translation as a "linguistic and literary tool" that starts from a precise model and transfers it into a different culture, there are many investigative angles for study. By comparing the original with its translated version, we find many valuable elements through which to study the evolution of literary language. The translation enables communication between cultures or individuals while being open to analysis and comparison, because it lacks the sacral quality that

1 George Steiner, *After Babel: Aspects of Language and Translation* (Oxford: Oxford University Press, 1998), pp. 18–50.

2 Giovanni Maver, 'Lo studio delle traduzioni come mezzo d'indagine linguistica e letteraria' ['Linguistic and Literary Research through the Study of Translations'], in *Recueil des travaux du 1er Congrès des philologues slaves à Praha en 1929*, ed. by J. Horak, M. Murko and M. Weingart (Prague: Orbis, 1932), pp. 177–83 (p. 177).

 https://doi.org/10.11647/OBP.0340.12

distinguishes the original. The concept of 'restitution', of the restoration of equilibrium between the original text and its translation, an equilibrium made vulnerable by translation itself, raises ethical questions of extreme complexity. The transcendence of a merely inter-textual problematic that is centred on the relation between an original and its translation leads to a series of specifically sociological questions about the stakes and functions of translations, the space in which they are situated, and the constraints, both political and economic, that circumscribe them.

In the twentieth century, the growth in technology and the development of communications produced a sharp increase of translations. The *Index Translationum*, created in 1932 as an initiative of the League of Nations International Committee on Intellectual Cooperation, is an international bibliography of translations. Founded as a quarterly catalogue of books translated in fifteen countries, it was taken over by UNESCO after World War II. Throughout recent decades, the Index has progressively transformed itself into a large database capable of producing statistics on the flow of global translation, providing figures on the most-translated books and authors, as well as the languages from which and into which literature is translated. In the period from 1948 to 1970, the total number of translations increased four and a half times, while Russian was the second most widely translated literature.

To understand the reason for this centrality of Russian culture, we must consider several aspects of the conditions of transnational circulation of cultural goods: firstly, the structure of the field of international cultural exchanges; secondly, the types of constraint—political and economic—that influence these exchanges.[3] The prestige and power gained by the USSR had implications for the status of the Russian language and related translation activity. The increase of Russian literary translation into Italian is linked to the strong interest Italians have maintained for Russia since the eighteenth century, and to a reception process unique among European literatures.[4] The rise of the overall cultural level and the politics of the publishing industry in the twentieth century in Italy have had important consequences. Multi-volume editions of the works of major Russian authors were published, demonstrating the lively interest Italians took in the culture of this country. A bibliography of Italian translations of Russian literature gives interesting and objective information on the choices made by Italian cultural circles, on the contribution of intellectuals to the development of publishing, and on the progressive transformation of the critical-literary world. Moreover, it sheds light on the important but often under-examined role

3 Johan Heilbron and Gisèle Sapiro, 'Outline for a Sociology of Translation: Current Issues and Future Prospects', in *Constructing a Sociology of Translation*, ed. by Michaela Wolf and Alexandra Fukari (Amsterdam and Philadelphia, PA: Benjamins Translation Library, 2007), pp. 93–107.

4 For more on this subject, see Claudia Scandura, *Letteratura russa in Italia. Un secolo di traduzioni* (Rome: Bulzoni, 2002).

of the translator, especially their understanding and sensibility, details which ultimately ensure the success or failure of a work. Unscrupulous exploitation of translators' work was, however, not infrequent. It suffices to mention the relationship between a prominent writer, critic, and editor such as Elio Vittorini (1908–66) and Lucia Rodocanachi (1901–78), the wife of the painter Paolo Rodocanachi, who conducted a literary and artistic salon in Arenzano, near Genova. A writer herself and a polyglot (she spoke English, French, Spanish, and German), Rodocanachi effectively became a ghostwriter for Vittorini, who sold her translations (from English) as his own work.[5] Vittorini's silence about Rodocanachi's contribution to his literary translations from English is unfortunately a common form of misconduct, encoded in literary practice: the translator traditionally occupies a marginalised position.

In the twentieth century, Russian literature became increasingly familiar to Italian readers, for various reasons. The failed Russian Revolution of 1905 brought various exiles to Italy, most famously Maksim Gorky, who arrived in Naples in October 1906 from the United States aboard the steamship *Princess Irene*. The Neapolitans welcomed him warmly. Tommaso Ventura, a journalist from the newspaper *Roma*, greeted him in Russian; the entire Italian press announced his arrival. The Socialist newspaper *Avanti!* wrote:

> We warmly welcome our Gorky. He symbolizes the revolution, its intellectual principle. He represents fidelity to ideas and now the fraternal souls of proletarian and socialist Italy are looking at him. Long life to Maksim Gorky! Long live the Revolution![6]

In the streets of Naples, a joyful crowd cheered Gorky's arrival; a party in his honour was organised at the Labour Union. As a writer and as a revolutionary, Gorky was lionised in Italy. Following his arrest in Riga two days after the 'Bloody Sunday' incident in St Petersburg in 1905, protests were voiced in the Italian Chamber of Deputies, and both the media and the general public expressed support for Gorky. His fame as a great writer owed much to Italian translations of his works, largely printed by Neapolitan publishers. Among these were the Società Editrice Partenopea, a company that, in the years immediately before World War I, published popular Socialist literature; and Bideri, established in 1876 in Naples by Ferdinando Bideri (1850–1930), which mainly published Modernist literature. The principal translators at this time were the young Socialist, Cesare Castelli (1871–1940), and the writer and journalist Federico Verdinois (1844–1927), who taught Russian language and

---

5 Elio Vittorini, *Si diverte tanto a tradurre? Lettere a Lucia Rodocanachi 1933–1943* [*Do You Enjoy Translation So Much? Letters to Lucia Rodocanachi*] (Milan: Archinto, 2016).

6 Angelo Tamborra, *Esuli russi in Italia dal 1905 al 1917* (Bari: Laterza, 1977), p. 16. All translations, unless otherwise indicated, are my own.

literature at the Oriental Institute in Naples and authored many translations of works by Dostoevsky, Gogol, Gorky, Pushkin, and Tolstoy. Castelli was the Milan representative of the Ladyzhnikov publishing house, based between Russia and Berlin. It held the rights for translations of Leonid Andreev's works, among other Russian writers; it collaborated with Mondadori, a Milanese publishing house established in 1907 by Arnoldo Mondadori (1889–1971). However, according to the scholar Ettore Lo Gatto, Castelli did not know Russian and therefore translated from German versions. Nevertheless, his contract with Mondadori lasted ten years (1922–32). However, from 1927 his translations were co-signed with Raissa Olkienizkaia Naldi (1886–1978), who sometimes appears under the pseudonym Raissa Folkes, or with Ossip Felyne (1882–1970), both Russian emigrants who settled in Italy after the October Revolution. Later, Mondadori's chief translator from Russian would be Erme Cadei, former employee of the publishers Treves and Bietti.

Titles for Italian translations can be quite arbitrary, and barely related to the original title. For example, Gorky's novel *Foma Gordeev* (1899) was translated by Nino De Sanctis as *Life Is a Foolishness* (*La vita è una sciocchezza!*, 1904), and one can deduce the Russian title only by back-translating the characters' Italianised names ('Ignazio Gordeieff' is the protagonist). This characterised many pre-Second World War Italian translations. Gorky lived in Capri until 1913, returning to Italy several years after the October Revolution, officially for health reasons. He stayed in a beautiful Sorrento villa, 'Il Sorito', from 1922 to 1928 (departing permanently for Moscow in 1932). This period played an important role in the development of Russian-Italian relations, thanks to Gorky's cultural heft, and to the large number of writers and artists who visited him and enjoyed his generous 'Russian' hospitality.

After the October Revolution, other Russian exiles, including Evgenii Anagnine (1888–1965), Mikhail Osorgin (1878–1942), and Olga Resnevich (1883–1973), chose Italy as their second home. There they tried to propagate their culture and values, binding their lives to the history of Italian culture. The most important of these was the poet Viacheslav Ivanov (1866–1949), who lived in Rome from 1924 until his death, aloof and disengaged from émigré life and politics. However, he played an important role in the translation of Russian poetry in Italy. Thanks to his encouragement, the first rhymed Italian translation of Aleksandr Pushkin's *Evgenii Onegin* appeared (as *Eugenio Oneghin*, 1937). The translator was the celebrated scholar Ettore Lo Gatto (1890–1983), who rendered Russian verse (nine-syllable lines) in Italian hendecasyllable, which Ivanov praised in his introduction as "faithful, artistic, straightforward Italian".[7] Thanks to Lo Gatto, known as the 'father' of Slavic Studies in Italy, Italian culture

7 Venceslao Ivanov, 'Introduzione' (1937), in Aleksandr Pushkin, *Lirica*, ed. by Ettore Lo Gatto (Florence: Sansoni, 1968), pp. 681–87 (p. 687).

was actively involved in the debate between Russia and Western Europe.[8] He was the first to grasp and satisfy Italian social demands for better knowledge of Russia. Friendly with the many Russian and Slavic intellectuals circulating in Europe after the October Revolution, Lo Gatto, with his wife Zoia Voronkova (1892–1963), was a very active translator of Russian literature of all genres.

Russian literature appealed to Italian intellectuals commensurately with their enthusiasm for social transformation. In 1936, the poet Giuseppe Ungaretti (1888–1970), knowing no Russian, translated two poems by Sergei Esenin, 'Requiem' ('Sorokoust', 1920; as 'Requiem') and 'The Ships of the Mare' ('Kobyl'i korabli', 1919; as 'Le navi delle cavalle') to "understand why Russian rural masses opposed the Soviet regime".[9] If this was his reason, Esenin was not the most appropriate poet to choose; his poems, written under the influence of Imaginism, one of many poetic movements that flourished in Russia after the Revolution, could not be read as historical documents. Esenin's poetry relies on arresting and unusual images that privilege hyperboles and metaphors. Ungaretti's translation, probably made via a French bridge text, is also powerfully expressive; he became the first translator to circulate Esenin's poetry in Italy.

Another poet, Clemente Rebora (1885–1957), deeply concerned with moral and ethical problems, produced his own versions of Gogol's 'The Overcoat', Leonid Andreev's *Lazarus* (*Eleazar*, 1906) and Tolstoy's *Family Happiness* (*Semeinoe schast'e*, 1859). Rebora empathised with these predominantly pessimistic works, characterised by passive acceptance of life. His translation of Gogol's short story, one of the most popular texts chosen by Italian translators, merits some discussion. Formalist critics such as Boris Eichenbaum have identified Gogol's narrative technique here, with its alternating grotesque and pathetic declamations, as "skaz", which reproduces the forms of oral communication, including grammatical mistakes, pauses, repetitions, and dialectal variations.[10] Gogol's use of long, complex sentences, rare or invented character names, comical puns, and bizarre sound combinations both challenge and attract translators. His texts are insidious in their apparent simplicity. Rebora's version of 'The Overcoat' (as 'Il Cappotto', 1922), masters Gogol's subject and accentuates the text's capacity for nonsense, while Tommaso Landolfi's later translation of the same story

8 Lo Gatto was Secretary of the Institute for Eastern Europe from 1921, and in 1922 he was appointed Professor of Russian Literature at the Universities of Naples, Padua and Rome. He authored many works on Russian culture, still fundamental, such as *A History of Russian Literature* [*Storia della letteratura russa*, 1942], *A History of the Russian Theatre* [*Storia del teatro russo*, 1952], *The Myth of Petersburg* [*Il mito di Pietroburgo*, 1960], *Pushkin: The Story of a Poet and His Hero* [*Pushkin: storia di un poeta e del suo eroe*, 1954].

9 Iginio De Luca, *Tre poeti traduttori. Monti-Nievo-Ungaretti* (Florence: Olschki editore, 1988), p. 229.

10 Boris Eichenbaum, 'The Structure of Gogol's "The Overcoat"', *Russian Review*, 22:4 (Oct. 1963), 377–99.

as 'Il Mantello' (1941) aims to reproduce as faithfully as possible the original text, not only its appearance but also its inconsistencies, vexing constructions, redundancies, and punctuation. Landolfi (1908–79) was a translator and writer whose aesthetic sensibility resembled Gogol's. As each translator found his own equivalent of 'The Overcoat', multiple Italian versions appeared under titles such as 'The Uniform', 'The Cloak', or simply 'The Coat'. Recently (in 2018), a new version of Gogol's so-called 'Petersburg Tales' appeared, translated by the writer Paolo Nori (1963). Nori, who has also translated Venedikt Erofeev's 1973 samizdat novel *Moskva-Petushki* with the title *Mosca-Petuski: Poema ferroviario* (*Moscow-Petushki: A Railway Poem*, 2014) and Daniil Kharms' 1933 short-story cycle *Sluchai* (*Disastri*, 2003), privileges the surreal and grotesque elements of these stories. His translations of Gogol's *Dead Souls* as *Anime morte* (2013) and of the short story 'Diary of a Madman' ('Zapiski sumasshedshego', 1835; 'Memorie di un pazzo'), included in his 2014 anthology *Gogol, Dostoevskij, Tolstoj: tre matti* (*Three Madmen*, 2014), together with his translations of Dostoevsky and Tolstoy, show his love of Russian literature. In his lively version of Gogol's short stories, which include dialectal terms from his regional idiom (*emiliano*), Nori captures both the innovative and disruptive character of the Russian writer's prose and the ambiguity that enhances Gogol's relevance today.[11]

From the early 1920s until the mid-1930s, publishing activity flourished in Italy. In 1933, in Turin, a group of friends who shared a belief in the values of cultural freedom and civil commitment, founded the publishing house Einaudi, wishing to create an Italian class of intellectual readers. Their company soon became "a wellspring of fine literature, intellectual thought and political theory".[12] Giulio Einaudi (1912–99), son of Luigi Einaudi (1874–1961), the future second president of the Italian Republic, was the entrepreneurial soul of the group, but Leone Ginzburg (1909–44), of Russian-Jewish origin, was the first editorial director. Thanks to Ginzburg's work as a critic and translator, Italy received the first complete editions of many Russian masterpieces, including Tolstoy's *Anna Karenina* (1878) and major works by Gogol, Turgenev, Pushkin, and others. During the later 1930s, when Italy allied itself with Nazi Germany, Russian titles for translation were carefully curated by publishing houses. Works by White émigrés and other critics of the Soviet Union were preferred.[13] There are always vested interests involved in choosing texts for publication; care and prudence in the selection of reading materials for the masses were considered crucial for social control. To fulfil the political functions of Italian Fascist culture, selections were based on the positions of both translated authors and translators.[14]

11 For more on Paolo Nori's active translation work, including his use of *Emiliano*, see his regularly updated blog: https://www.paolonori.it/.

12 Luisa Mangoni, *Pensare i libri. La casa editrice Einaudi dagli anni Trenta agli anni Sessanta* (Turin: Bollati Boringhieri, 1999), p. 403.

13 Pierre Bourdieu, *The Field of Cultural Production* (Cambridge: Polity, 1999), p. 222.

14 Pascale Casanova, 'From Internationalism to Globalization', in *The World Republic of Letters*, trans. by M. B. De Bevoise (London and Cambridge, MA: Harvard

After World War II

Following World War II, Italians identified Russian literature with the Soviet Union and thus the reading public and literary critics preferred texts with a socio-political focus. Interest in Soviet-Russian culture, which had been banned in Italy in the final years of fascism, grew under the Government of National Unity (established in 1946). The Italian Communist Party (PCI), founded and led by Palmiro Togliatti (1893–1964), who had returned to Italy in 1944, after almost twenty years of exile spent mainly in Moscow, participated in that government. This political situation, even more than editorial or cultural considerations, produced a real flowering of pro-Soviet publications. Desire for social control and moral education were the building blocks of the editorial system in the second half of the twentieth century.[15] Moreover, the ideological and symbolic value that Soviet culture has traditionally held in Italy should be emphasised. For this reason, from the postwar period until at least the late 1970s, the choice of topics for public discussion in both the Italian press and in PCI cells was almost exclusively dependent on the editorial and cultural institutions of the left. This monopoly may have been pragmatically justified, since obtaining a copy of a Soviet book was extremely difficult, almost impossible, if not achieved through institutional channels such as the PCI and its organs.

Editori Riuniti

Until the early 1950s, the Einaudi publishing house dominated this sector uncontested, as the sole firm with both the political support and the economic means necessary to tackle a programme of translations and the widespread dissemination of Soviet-Russian work. However, Einaudi's owners manifested little interest in the ideological discourse that these publications inevitably entailed. Other firms with stronger political views lacked the funds to support their own imprint in the nascent Italian publishing market. There was therefore no serious competition for Einaudi until the appearance of two other publishing houses: Editori Riuniti in 1953 and Feltrinelli in 1955 (both discussed below). Editorial competition in a politically strategic sector, such as Soviet literature, was a genuinely new feature of the Italian cultural landscape. In addition, Khrushchev's Thaw had brought relative freedom for Italian intellectuals to enter Russia and engage in cultural exchanges with their Soviet counterparts or with Soviet editorial offices and publishing houses. This meant publishers could potentially obtain manuscripts which had not been filtered through the

University Press, 1999; repr. 2007), pp. 164–70.

15 See Gian Carlo Ferretti, *Il mercato delle lettere* (Milan: Il Saggiatore, 1994), pp. 69–86 and pp. 209–52.

Soviet Embassy or the PCI. In the postwar period, publishing rights for Soviet works had to be granted by the Embassy of the USSR. This posed a practical problem with significant political and economic implications. The question of rights alone certainly explains little. Yet it helps to understand that in Einaudi's business plan, their alliance with the PCI, which was known to be indispensable, but not binding, assumed strategic importance. Similarly, the Communist Party, still lacking their own printing press, had focused on an external cultural agency, a publishing bookshop (Libreria editrice del Partito comunista d'Italia) established in 1921. Through such subtle social alliances, the publishing industry appeared to bend to the will of the Party.

But other smaller publishers also took an interest in Soviet literature. Macchia (in Rome) edited (from 1947 to 1950) a book series called 'The Stalin Prizes' (Premi Stalin), which included novels by Aleksandr Fadeev, Aleksandr Grin, Il'ia Ehrenburg, and Aleksei Tolstoy, to mention only the most important names, as not all Stalin Prize-winners were included. In 1948, two small publishing firms, Rinascita and the Edizioni di cultura sociale, appeared: the first favoured works by Marxist theorists, the second leant towards current affairs. Their publishing business was impractical when it came to distribution and marketing. Edizioni di cultura sociale did all of its editing, proofreading, and advertising in a room in Via delle Botteghe Oscure (Rome), which was also the headquarters of the PCI. In March 1953, Rinascita and Edizioni di cultura sociale combined to form a new publishing house, Editori Riuniti, thus allowing the PCI a market outlet. Editori Riuniti was a modern publisher, with a very wide-ranging catalogue, attentive to political and trending texts and rich in foreign literature series, of which many were Soviet-Russian titles. Hence Editori Riuniti soon became one of Einaudi's main competitors, even forcing the latter to abandon important plans, such as the projected publication of Vladimir Maiakovskii's *Letters* (1958) (*Perepiska*), or Il'ia Ehrenburg's *Uomini Anni Vita* (published in Italy 1960–65) (*Liudi, gody i zhizn'*, 1956–60). It was Editori Riuniti who, between 1956 and 1960, published Gorky's *Collected Works* (*Sobranie sochinenii*) in Italian in twenty volumes, and also Maiakovskii's eight-volume *Works* (*sochinenii*) in 1958. Its series 'Le opere e i giorni' (Works and Days) and 'Scrittori del realismo' (Realist Writers) were devoted exclusively to Soviet-Russian literature. Italian readers discovered Soviet authors through these cheaply produced editions, which were sold everywhere from bookshops to newspaper kiosks, often with primitive graphics and at low prices.

1956 marked a turning point, when Khrushchev's cultural Thaw transformed the intellectual environment in the Soviet Union. A period of détente in international diplomatic relations and revisions to internal policies followed. The important process of rehabilitating victims of Stalin's repression in the Soviet Union led to the publication there of previously banned works; persecuted and censored authors could now be discussed. The world followed Thaw literature attentively, and Editori Riuniti published a series titled 'Scrittori sovietici' ('Soviet Writers' (1961–65)), which set works by contemporary authors alongside newly rehabilitated 1920s writers. Ehrenburg's memoirs, so controversial at home, were published by Editori Riuniti in six volumes; so, too, were poems by Evgenii Evtushenko (*Babii Iar,* 1961) and Andrei Voznesenskii (*Antimiry,* 1961). Prose translations included Isaak Babel's *Red Cavalry* (*Konarmiia,* 1926), Nikolai Zabolotskii's 'Columns' (*Stolbtsy,* 1929), Aleksandr Grin's *Scarlet Sails* (*Alye parusa,* 1923), Vsevolod Ivanov's *Armoured Train 14–69* (*Bronepoezd 14–69,* 1927), Bulat Okudzhava's *Good-bye, Schoolboy!* (*Bud' zdorov, shkoliar!,* 1961), and the epic novel by the 1965 Nobel Prize laureate, Mikhail Sholokhov, *And Quiet Flows the Don* (*Tikhii Don,* 1928–32).

The 1960s saw Editori Riuniti gradually gain autonomy from the Communist Party as it became increasingly professionally structured and economically viable. In the 1970s, two new series appeared, the 'David', which showcased contemporary fiction (including emerging talents Valentin Rasputin, Vasilii Aksenov, Vasilii Shukshin and Iurii Trifonov), and the 'Universale', which consisted of paperback reprints. The mid-1980s marked the onset of a crisis for Editori Reuniti, which had traditionally focused on social issues, with economic problems forcing it to reduce its fiction output. The collapse of old ideologies and the dissolution of the Soviet Union changed the traditional market; Editori Riuniti underwent many changes in ownership. It seems reasonable to say that the Communist Party had established the publishing house Editori Riuniti because of its failure to ally itself politically with Einaudi. This project, so attractive on Liberation Day (25 April 1945), collapsed during the Cold War. Soviet and Russian writing (not confined to literary fiction) had represented both a strategic node and a weak point in that internal pact that the Italian Left made with the publishing industry. Italy's left-leaning publishers had conferred value and legitimacy on the Soviet Union in its incessant struggle for international power.[16]

Einaudi and Feltrinelli

Russian literature played a fundamental role in Einaudi's later development, as well as that of the ill-fated Riuniti. After World War II, the publishing house had welcomed twentieth-century Russian writers, thanks to Ettore Lo Gatto, Tommaso Landolfi and Angelo Maria Ripellino (1923–78), whose high-quality translations had revealed to Italian audiences the existence and aesthetic value of Russian poetry and prose. Pietro Zveteremich (1922–92), a translator and literary critic, played a significant role in liaising between the Communist Party and Einaudi. In 1945, he was summoned to Turin by the publishing house as their main consultant for Soviet writing. From this point onwards, his editorial

16 Pascale Casanova, 'The Small Literatures', in *The World Republic of Letters,* pp. 175–90.

decisions were politically informed, aimed at a convergence between Party goals and publishing activity. A member of the Communist Party, Zveteremich was also editor-in-chief of *Cultura sovietica*, the journal of the Italian Society for Cultural Relations with the USSR. He immediately prepared a rich programme of translations, which included little-known modern Russian and Soviet literature, such as Konstantin Simonov's novel *Days and Nights* (*Dni i nochi*, 1944).[17] However, many of the proposed books were not translated: Zveteremich's list was sharply criticised by Elio Vittorini, who had helped to connect him with Einaudi. Vittorini felt that Zveteremich's choice of authors was influenced by the latter's links with the Soviet Embassy.[18]

The need to contain the influence of the Communist Party led Einaudi to supplement Party loyalists with his own 'internal' intellectuals. Zveteremich's work was overseen by writers such as Giovanni Nicosia, the translator of Il'f and Petrov's novel *One-Storied America* (*Odnoetazhnaia Amerika*, 1936) as *The Country of God* (*Il paese di Dio*, 1947), and Cesare Pavese (1908–50), the poet, novelist, and literary critic, who was employed by Einaudi as an editor and translator (from English). The publishing house also worked with freelance literary agents and translators, as with Franco Venturi (1914–94), the historian and author of the important monograph *Il populismo russo* (*History of Russian Populism*, 1952), and resident in Moscow since 1947. From Moscow, Venturi reported on intellectual debates and literary developments to Felice Balbo (1914–64), manager of Einaudi's philosophy series, Giuseppe Berti (1901–79), Secretary of the Italy-USSR Association, and Emilio Sereni (1907–77), a writer and PCI member. Venturi's insider input allowed Einaudi to bypass the PCI's advocacy for the publication of specific Soviet works. In fact, difficult relations with the Party pushed Einaudi to distance the press from the former's influence, especially in strategic, politically sensitive sectors. This is the context of the affair surrounding *The Flower of Russian Verse* (*Il fiore del verso russo*),[19] a 1949 poetry anthology edited by Renato Poggioli (1907–63). This publication aroused the ire of PCI leaders because of the editor's decision to include 'decadent' poets, such as Blok, Akhmatova, and Mandel'shtam, and his critical approach to Soviet poetry. The anthology was problematic on both a cultural and political level; it was assessed on a political basis as defiant of the Soviet Union. Poggioli, a Florentine scholar of Russian studies, also a Jew with strong anti-Fascist views, had in 1938 emigrated to the USA, where he became a professor at Brown University (and later at Harvard). Italian critics, insisting on interpreting the anthology in terms of Soviet and anti-Soviet opposition, accused him of choosing

---

17 Konstantin Simonov, *I giorni e le notti* [*Days and Nights*] (Turin: Einaudi, 1946).

18 Luisa Mangoni, *Pensare i libri: la casa editrice Einaudi dagli anni trenta agli anni sessanta* [*Thinking about Books, Einaudi Publishing House from the Thirties to the Sixties*] (Turin: Bollati Boringhieri, 1999), pp. 214–18, pp. 328–29.

19 *Il fiore del verso russo: Da Pushkin a Pasternak un secolo di poesia*, ed. by Renato Poggioli (Turin: Einaudi, 1949).

yesterday's poetry. The furore over this anthology caused a crisis within the Einaudi publishing house, exposing its relationship with the Communist Party. The Party's Secretary, Palmiro Togliatti, Minister of Justice from 1945 to 1946 and a member of the Constituent Assembly of Italy, decided to withdraw his own collected works from Einaudi as a result of the controversy. Poggioli's anthology had exposed the failure of Einaudi's agreement with the Communist Party regarding the publication of Soviet works, and the Party's control over left-leaning cultural production was seriously challenged.

Zveteremich, who would later harshly criticise *The Flower of Russian Verse* (he even referred to Akhmatova as "a limited parlour poetess"), left Einaudi two years after its publication. In 1953, the year of Stalin's death, Vittorio Strada (1929–2018) joined Einaudi's editorial staff in Milan. Keenly observant of cultural changes in the USSR, he soon proposed the translation of a novel which had provoked intense controversy in the Soviet press. Its title would christen the entire era: *The Thaw* (*Ottepel'*) by Il'ia Ehrenburg. This novel had been published in 1954 in Moscow and by January 1955, *The Thaw* was already available in Italian translation from Einaudi.[20] After its appearance, Strada's work became more complex and structured. Thanks to his private contacts, he could suggest other titles related to the new Soviet cultural atmosphere. In 1958 he moved to Moscow, where he began the ultimately unsuccessful project of translating Evgenii Zamiatin's dystopian novel *We* (*My*, 1924), which the Soviet government had refused to publish in 1921. *We* had been published in 1955 (translated by Ettore Lo Gatto) by a small publishing house (Minerva Italica), but only in 1963 would the novel enjoy wide circulation, thanks to Feltrinelli's reprint of this edition. New translations appeared only as recently as 2013 (by Alessandro Niero, for Voland) and 2021 (by Alessandro Cifariello, for Fanucci).

However, while increased competition enhanced readers' access to literary texts, it did not guarantee publishers exclusive rights. The USSR was not a signatory to the Berne Convention, which regulated the transfer of rights within Europe. This created tempting opportunities for economic profit, since the first publishing house to publish any Soviet work within thirty days of its release in the USSR gained exclusive European rights to that publication. On the other hand, the potential for commercial gain from Soviet fiction provoked ruthless competition that was resolved more than once with the publication of duplicate translations. For example, Viktor Nekrasov's novel, *In the Hometown* (*V rodnom gorode*, 1955), which criticised the Soviet bureaucratic system, was translated in the same year as its release under two different titles by both Strada (*Nella città natale*) and Zveteremich (*Nella sua città*), which had been commissioned by Einaudi and Feltrinelli respectively.

---

20 Ilja Ehrenburg, *Il disgelo*, trans. by C. C. (Torino: Einaudi, 1955). Clara Coisson (1896–1981), the translator, started working for Einaudi in 1949.

For both Feltrinelli and Einaudi, Soviet literature was a key element of their 'editorial strategy'; Zveteremich's appointment to the latter was a factor in their competing ambitions. The Nekrasov affair and the need to outdo Einaudi induced Feltrinelli to hire Sergio D'Angelo (1923–2023), a journalist from Radio Moscow, as a literary talent scout in Russia. Famously, D'Angelo received the manuscript of Boris Pasternak's novel *Doctor Zhivago*, published for the first time in any language by Feltrinelli in 1957 in Zveteremich's translation. Competition for this book even extended beyond the border, forcing the translator to deliver the Italian version within a few weeks, in order to snatch the rights from Gallimard. This fortunate and even unscrupulous negotiation that allowed Giangiacomo Feltrinelli (1926–72), a small Milanese publisher specialising in political works, to secure the world rights to a famous novel, has been reconstructed thanks to numerous archival materials recently published in Russia.[21] The uproar resulting from its publication, followed by the award of the Nobel Prize to Pasternak in 1958, was a huge success for Feltrinelli, and *Doctor Zhivago* is still a significant part of the firm's cultural capital. Pasternak's novel, censored in the USSR, stimulated very heated debate in Italy, where the Left-leaning 'intelligentsia' vented still-unresolved issues from the discussions of 1956, when the Soviet invasion of Budapest had caused deep internal rifts in the international Communist bloc. The leadership of the PCI was called upon to intervene by Khrushchev himself—in vain. The publisher and the translator defended *Zhivago* against any censorship attack. Later, Zveteremich was marginalised by the Party, but continued to work as an editor and translator and, from 1972 until his death, he taught Russian literature at the University of Messina. In 1957, in addition to *Zhivago*, he translated Chekhov's notebooks (*Zapisnye knizhki doktora Chekhova*, 1899)[22] and planned (but never completed) an anthology of contemporary Russian poets (his riposte to *The Flower of Russian Verse*). Feltrinelli, however, secured another world première in 1958 with the publication of Boris Pasternak's *Autobiography* (*Biograficheskii ocherk*, 1956; *Autobiografia e nuovi versi*) along with the poet's last poems, translated by Sergio D'Angelo.

It was probably the competitive pressure exerted by Feltrinelli that pushed Einaudi to appoint a scholar to manage its Russian literature titles. On the advice of Renato Solmi (1927–2015), a Marxist historian who had worked from 1951 to 1963 as an editor for Einaudi, Angelo Maria Ripellino (1923–78), a university professor and a fine connoisseur of classical and early twentieth-century Russian literature, joined the editorial staff. Called upon to judge Strada's proposals, he might have helped the latter to continue translating Thaw literature, but their

21 *Doktor Zhivago: Pasternak, 1958, Italia, Antologia* [*Anthology*], ed. by Stefano Garzonio and Alessandra Reccia (Moscow: Reka vremen, 2012).

22 Anton Chekhov, *I quaderni del dottor Cechov. Appunti di vita e letteratura di A. P. Cechov* [*Dr. Chekhov's Notebooks. Notes on Life and Literature*] (Milan: Feltrinelli, 1957).

interests diverged sharply. Whereas Einaudi already had plans for translating Soviet-Russian publications of both literature and theoretical criticism, Ripellino was heavily invested in the dissemination of classical authors and works, such as the then almost unknown Nikolai Leskov or Pushkin's narrative poems and *Little Tragedies* (*Malenkie tragedii*, 1830), as opposed to those by Modernist and avant-garde poets. Although, due to the USSR's political heft in Italy at the time, Soviet-Russian works were generally very successful, the public showed little interest in Pasternak's poems (edited by Ripellino) just weeks before *Zhivago* appeared.[23] The most complete collection of Pasternak's poetry in Italian was thus lost in the raucous debate over his novel. As an esteemed author of critical essays about the Russian avant-garde, Ripellino was intellectually close to the 'Einaudian school', distinguished by the rigour and care he put into his work and the erudition and aptitude with which he pursued his project of popularising Russian literature. But Strada's and Ripellino's roles in the diffusion of Soviet-Russian culture were very different. Strada, like Zveteremich before him, helped to connect Soviet literature to Europe's moments of complex political transition between 1956 and 1989. Ripellino, however, can without exaggeration be said to have determined the public and academic image that we still have today of classical and modern Russian literature.

Italy's special bond with Russia was once again evident in 1964 when Anna Akhmatova obtained permission to travel abroad for the first time since the 1917 Revolution. Her first trip was to Italy, including Rome and Sicily. In the latter, she was awarded the Etna-Taormina Literary Prize. During this trip the poetess met Carlo Riccio (1932–2011), a scholar of Russian literature, to whom she gave the complete typescript of her poems *Requiem* (*Rekviem*, 1935–40) and *Poem Without a Hero* (*Poema bez geroiia*, 1940–60). Based on these manuscripts and notes, Riccio drafted a translation which Akhmatova read and approved. Thus, these poems were released for the first time, together with the Russian text of her final draft, by the publisher Einaudi in 1966.[24]

The failure of left-wing intellectuals' post-1945 cultural plan was already clear by the late 1950s, with cultural issues relegated to the publishing industry and political policies entrusted to the Party. This polarisation increasingly pushed discourse on Russian and Soviet literature into academia or drowned it with the "background noise" of political debate.[25] In Italy, many publishing houses helped to popularise Russian literature. Eridano Bazzarelli (1921–2013), a professor of Russian literature at the State University in Milan, edited a new 'Scrittori sovietici' series for Mursia, between 1972 and 1988. This series introduced Italian readers to more contemporary authors, such as Chinghiz Aitmatov, Valentin Rasputin, Vasilii Belov, Iurii Trifonov, and Bulat Okudzhava.

23 Boris Pasternak, *Poesie* [Poems], ed. by A. M. Ripellino (Turin: Einaudi, 1957).
24 Anna Akhmatova, *Poema senza eroe e altre poesie*, ed. by Carlo Riccio (Turin: Einaudi, 1966).
25 Casanova, *The World Republic of Letters*, pp. 180–212.

An ideologically distinct approach, critical of official Soviet culture, was formulated by the 'Russian Gateways' (Propilei russi) series edited from the late 1970s onwards by the publishing cooperative La Casa di Matriona (Matriona's Place), the editorial branch of a Catholic organisation named after Aleksandr Solzhenitsyn's novella (*Matrionin dvor*, 1963).

From the mid-1980s onwards, Russian literature gradually lost its centrality to Italian translation publishing, which was overwhelmed by the collapse of the Soviet Union. Nevertheless, in 1994 the small publishing house Voland appeared in Rome; its name derives from the Satanic villain of Bulgakov's novel, *The Master and Margarita* (*Master i Margarita*, 1928–40). Voland intended to publish authors from Eastern European countries exclusively, but the publisher was soon forced to acknowledge market demand and to include other authors in its catalogue. Thanks to the success of its translations of novels by the Belgian writer Amélie Nothomb, Voland avoided bankruptcy and has continued to publish Slavic authors (including Evgenii Zamiatin, Valerii Briusov, Konstantin Vaginov, Aleksandr Kuprin, Aleksandr Sharov, Vladislav Otroshenko, Zakhar Prilepin, Marina Stepnova, the Bulgarian Georgi Gospodinov and many others).

Translating Eugene Onegin

The history of Italian translations of Pushkin's novel in verse *Evgenii Onegin* stretches back to a version created in 1856, by an Italo-French poet, Luigi Delâtre (1815–93), with the aid of Pushkin's friend Petr Viazemskii (1792–1878). The most recent translation (Milan: Oscar Mondadori, 2021) is by Giuseppe Ghini (b. 1957), a professor at the University of Urbino, who has tried to restore the rhythm and linguistic density of the original. Delâtre insisted upon the translator's right to diverge from the original text in order to clarify obscure points, remove unnecessary details, and so on (a not untypical view for his era). Delâtre's version occasionally eliminates epithets, explicates the author's ideas (!), deletes descriptions which he felt impeded the narration, and even shifts the chapter order when it violates his notion of logic. We can only imagine how readers responded to this revised *Evgenii Onegin,* as there are no reviews. Luckily, many other translations followed, including the first in verse format (non-rhyming hendecasyllable) in 1906, by Giuseppe Cassone. The hendecasyllable, the classic metre of Italian poetry, was also selected by Ettore Lo Gatto for his 1937 verse translation of Pushkin's poem, as mentioned above. Lo Gatto's translation was praised by Viacheslav Ivanov, Mikhail Osorgin (1878–1942), and numerous scholars. Republished in 1950 by Einaudi, this version is considered definitive and was often reprinted. Despite the flattering reviews, Lo Gatto, evidently wishing to make *Onegin* more appealing to Italian readers, published a prose version of Pushkin's poem (Milan: Mursia, 1959), which was lexically not very different from the verse one. Critics failed to show much interest in his *Onegin* dialectics. Other translations have appeared over the years, but none was more controversial than the 1975 version by the poet Giovanni Giudici (1924–2011). During his first visit to Russia in 1966, Giudici decided to translate Pushkin's poem into Italian verse. He did not know the language very well, so he worked with Giovanna Spendel, a professor of Russian literature at Milan's State University, to co-produce an edition of Pushkin's poems with the publisher Mondadori.[26] His first translation of *Evgenii Onegin* appeared in 1975 (Milan: Garzanti). Keen to reproduce the original iambic tetrameter, Giudici preferred lines of nine rather than eleven syllables since he considered the former metrically equivalent to the Russian form. Scholarly reception was harsh. Many Slavists soon pointed out mistakes, oversights, and various imperfections in Giudici's translation. This criticism did tend to unfairly ignore the positives of the translation, as noted by outstanding specialists in Italian culture, such as Gianfranco Folena (1920–92) and Gianfranco Contini (1912–90), and poets like Franco Fortini (1917–94) and Giovanni Raboni (1932–2004). Despite the critical response, Giudici continued to revise his translation for several years, and new editions appeared in 1983 and in 1984 (Milan: Garzanti), which he then re-published in a new version in 1990 and reviewed once again in 1999.[27]

Conclusion

When we analyse the flows of translations in the light of power relations between languages, we facilitate better understanding of historical change. A country's loss of prestige or power, and the resulting diminution of its language's status, has consequences for the level of translation activity. After the collapse of Soviet Communism, the international position of the Russian language underwent this kind of abrupt change: the number of translations from Russian in Italy dropped very sharply, and this drop was accompanied by a sharp rise in the number of foreign translations published in Russia.[28] In 1991, the collapse of the Soviet Union and the transformation of the Italian Communist Party into a social-democratic 'Democratic Party of the Left' had, among many other consequences, the effect of stripping Russian literature of its protected status. There were no longer any special channels or funds for translating Soviet authors, and Russophone writers had to compete for their place in the book market just like everyone

26 Aleksandr Pushkin, *Viaggio d'inverno e altre poesie*, ed. by Giovanni Giudici and Giovanna Spendel (Milan: Mondadori, 1985).

27 Giovanni Giudici, *Eugenio Onieghin di Aleksandr S. Pushkin in versi italiani* (Turin: Fogola Editore, 1990; Milan: Garzanti, 1999). Gianfranco Folena contributed the Introduction.

28 Johan Helbron and Gisèle Sapiro, 'Translation: Economic and Sociological Perspectives', in *The Palgrave Handbook of Economics and Language*, ed. by Victor Ginsburgh and Shlomo Weber (London: Palgrave Macmillan 2007), pp. 373–402, https://doi.org/10.1007/978-1-137-32505-1_14.

else. Canonical writers such as Tolstoy kept their consolidated place while new authors had to fight for the chance to be read.

Dostoevsky's bicentenary in 2021 and the many new translations which appeared to mark it, including his *Letters* (the most complete edition published outside Russia),[29] show how, thirty years after the end of Communist ideological influence, and despite Russia's increasing isolation from the European cultural space, Russian authors can still inspire readers today with their talent for psychological revelation and original insights on the meaning of human existence. The success of Paolo Nori's autofictional *It's Still Bleeding* (*Sanguina ancora*, Milan: Oscar Mondadori, 2021), winner of the Campiello literature prize (Premio Campiello 2021), a biography of Dostoevsky that also describes Paolo Nori's own life, exemplifies this inspiration. Russian authors continue to symbolise both the anguish of being human, and the courage of survival.

Poetry, which traditionally has a narrower market than prose, has maintained its prestigious position within the Italian publishing tradition. However, the texts proposed for translation have changed: for example, after a period of obscurity, Maiakovskii's love lyrics (but not his political poems) have re-appeared in bookshops. In recent years there have been new editions of authors previously regarded as of elite interest only, such as Marina Tsvetaeva, whose poems of the 1920s, 'Tsar Girl' ('Tsar' devitsa') and 'The Demesne of the Swans' ('Lebedinyi stan'), were translated, as well as her final lyrics (1938–41);[30] or Osip Mandel'shtam, a great connoisseur of Italian culture and language, whose essay, 'Conversation about Dante' ('Razgovor o Dante', 1967) was published in a joint edition by three different publishing firms as *Discorso su Dante* in 2021 to celebrate 130 years since the poet's birth; or Boris Pasternak, whose entire poetic oeuvre has now been commissioned by the publishing house Passigli. Other poets such as Velimir Khlebnikov, Nikolai Zabolotskii, Daniil Kharms, and Boris Slutskii, who avoided "Aesopian language" in their depictions of Soviet Communism, are now accessible to Italian readers, as are the latest generation of Russophone poets, among them Maria Stepanova, Sergei Stratanovskii, Timur Kibirov, Elena Schwartz, Mikhail Aizenberg, Dmitrii Prigov, Sergei Gandlevskii and many others. Thus, poetic currents that formed in Russia at the beginning of the twentieth century—such as Symbolism, Acmeism, and Futurism—have unexpectedly re-emerged in the twenty-first century as a new poetic triad: Metarealism, Presentism, and Conceptualism. Without Russian literature, Italy's literary heritage would be irredeemably impoverished.

29 Fedor Dostoevskij, *Lettere*, ed. by Alice Farina, trans. by Giulia De Florio, Alice Farina and Elena Freda Piredda (Milan: Il Saggiatore, 2020).

30 Marina Cvetaeva, *La principessa guerriera*, ed. by Marilena Rea (Rome: Sandro Teti editore 2020); *Il campo dei cigni*, ed. by Caterina Graziadei (Milan: Nottetempo, 2016); and *Ultimi versi 1938–1941*, ed. by Pina Napolitano (Rome: Voland, 2020).

Norway and Sweden

"The mysteries of the nerves in a starving body": Knut Hamsun and Dostoevsky

Susan Reynolds

Introduction

In *The World Republic of Letters,* Pascale Casanova, surveying "world literary space", discusses how the influence of French literary culture within Scandinavia provoked a rebellion against the German cultural ascendancy of the nineteenth century.[1] She describes the significance of Georg Brandes in bringing back to Denmark the Naturalism which he had discovered during his years in Paris. As the founder of *Det moderne Gennembrud* (the 'modern breakthrough'), Brandes hoped to launch a national literature capable of tackling social, political, and aesthetic questions in opposition to German idealism. His books *Eminent Authors of the Nineteenth Century* (*Hovedstrømninger i det 19. Aarhundredes Litteratur*, 1871) and *The Man of the Modern Breakthrough* (*Det moderne Gjennembruds Mænd*, 1883) presented the possibilities that Paris had revealed by modelling such changes. In the chapter that follows, I propose to survey the influence of Russian literature in translation on Scandinavia in the late nineteenth and early twentieth centuries, with a particular focus on Norway and especially Knut Hamsun's relationship with Dostoevsky's work. For purposes of comparison, I will begin by briefly considering the situation in Sweden, since different cultural and linguistic factors have influenced the translation and reception of Russian literature in Sweden and Norway.

1 Pascale Casanova, *The World Republic of Letters*, trans. by Malcolm DeBevoise (London and Cambridge, MA: Harvard University Press, 1999; repr. 2007), p. 158.

 https://doi.org/10.11647/OBP.0340.13

Sweden

The Linguistic Filter: Pivot Languages and Popularity

As a new century approached, another literature began to gain currency throughout Scandinavia: that of Russia. One of the earliest authors to achieve popularity (not least because his cosmopolitan lifestyle raised his profile on the wider European stage) was Ivan Turgenev.[2] Next came Nikolai Gogol, whose psychological insights into the loneliness and alienation of the individual in the city and picturesque depictions of rural life transcended their immediate setting. The importance of French as a medium for the transmission of Russian literature made sense in Turgenev's case, but by the time that Dostoevsky and Tolstoy appeared on the Swedish publishing scene, German had become the most widely spoken second language (at least for Swedes). Indeed, the Swedish publisher Albert Bonnier 'discovered' Tolstoy through a German translation of *Anna Karenina*. The translator, Walborg Hedberg, a member of a well-known Stockholm theatrical family and daughter of the playwright Frans Hedberg, subsequently learned Russian, but the majority of her translations were made from German.[3] In Finland, Dostoevsky, Gogol, Tolstoy, and Turgenev were first translated into Swedish rather than Finnish, not surprisingly, in view of the increasing strength of Swedish publishing houses and the growing number of Swedish translators of Russian.[4] From the late 1860s to the mid-1880s, translated literature actually predominated on Finnish publishers' lists over that written originally in Swedish, with Russian literature occupying a central position.[5]

2 See Jørgen Erik Nielsen, *Fra Neva til Øresund. Den dansk modtagelse af russisk litteratur 1800–1856* [*From Neva to Øresund. The Danish Reception of Russian Literature 1800–56*] (Copenhagen: Museum Tusculanums forlag, 1998). See also Karl Tiander, *Turgenjev i dansk aandsliv* (Copenhagen: Gyldendal, 1913); Johan Fjord Jensen, *Turgenjev i dansk åndsliv. Studier i dansk romanskunst 1870–1900* (Copenhagen: Gyldendal, 1961) and Ivan Malinovski, *Russiske bøger i danske oversættelser* (Copenhagen: Borgens forlag, 1953).

3 Walborg Maria Hedberg (1859–1931) published her translation of *Crime and Punishment*, *Raskolnikow* (later known as *Brott och straff*) to great acclaim in 1883. She subsequently translated *Anna Karenina* and *War and Peace* in 1885 and 1886 respectively, working from a French translation of the latter.

4 For more on the Finnish reception of Russian literature, see the chapter by Tomi Huttunen, Marja Jänis, and Pekka Pesonen in this volume.

5 For an analysis of the Swedish publishing market and its role in disseminating Russian literature in translation, see Nils Håkanson, *Fönstret mot Öster: rysk skönlitteratur i svensk översättning 1797–2010 med en fallstudie av Nikolaj Gogols svenska mottagande* (Uppsala: Ruin, 2012), esp. his notes on pp. 27–28 for further reading on the translation and reception of Russian literature in Scandinavia.

The Neighbour to the East: The Changing Image of Russia in Swedish Culture

Russophobia was widespread in Sweden during the 1840s; in the reign of Oscar I (1844–59), Sweden distanced herself from St Petersburg. The Swedish national and liberal movements became strongly anti-Russian, exacerbated by the outbreak of the Crimean War and reinforced by the Polish uprising of 1863. After the Crimean War, however, Russia gradually became less demonised in Sweden; increased trade and economic progress encouraged cultural exchanges and a closer acquaintance between the countries. This in its turn created a growing respect for Russia as a nation of high culture, with the dissemination of Russian literature and music, and the establishment in the 1880s of departments of Slavonic Studies at the universities of Uppsala and Lund.[6]

Nils Håkanson has identified a first (1863–90) and a second (1890–1917) phase in the breakthrough of Russian Realism in Sweden. These followed a period (1797–1863) when translations of Pushkin, Gogol, and Lermontov, together with novels by largely forgotten authors such as Mikhail Zagoskin, Aleksandr Bestuzhev-Marlinskii, and Faddei Bulgarin were in vogue; the Finnish-Swedish translator Otto Adolf Meurmans, for example, published his translation of Pushkin's *The Captain's Daughter* (*Kapitanskaia dochka*, 1836) in 1841, and in 1849 the Swedish journal *Tiden* printed 'The Queen of Spades' ('Pikovaia dama', 1834) as a feuilleton. Meurmans and his publisher Thomson were almost entirely responsible for this surge in translations of Russian authors. Thus, when their collaboration ended, Russian literature disappeared from publishers' lists in Sweden for a quarter of a century (1843–68). This resulted in a long gap between the Russian publication of works by authors such as Dostoevsky, Tolstoy, Turgenev, and Mikhail Saltykov-Shchedrin in the 1840s and their appearance in Swedish twenty or thirty years later. Håkanson also notes that out of eighteen translations issued by Swedish publishers, eight were made directly from Russian and the rest from secondary languages (chiefly French and German).[7]

As the new century progressed, the number of translations from Russian in publishers' lists decreased, so that by the end of its first decade only a few were appearing every year. For a while, Tolstoy and Dostoevsky disappeared, to be replaced by a new generation of writers—Chekhov, Leonid Andreev, Gorky, and Dmitrii Merezhkovskii. Håkanson suggests that this marked fall in publications may be explained by a "monoculture" or fixation on individual

6 This was considerably in advance of the situation in Britain, where it was not until 1900 that William Richard Morfill became Professor of Russian and Slavonic Languages at Oxford, the first to be appointed at any British university; Russian was only accepted as a degree subject at Oxford in 1904.

7 Nils Håkanson, *Fönstret mot Öster*, pp. 27–28.

personalities.[8] By the early twentieth century, all of Turgenev's works had been translated, but after *The Kreutzer Sonata* (*Kreitserova sonata*, 1889) appeared in 1890, Swedish publishers had to wait nearly ten years to publish another book by Tolstoy. Swedish translations of both Dostoevsky and Tolstoy declined in the late nineteenth and early twentieth centuries. No Swedish publisher brought out a single translation of Dostoevsky between 1891 and 1905, and nearly all the earlier translations vanished from print during this period. However, a new trend arose in the early 1900s, when most of his major works were (re-) translated. This coincided with reawakening interest in Russian radicalism, even though Dostoevsky could no longer be regarded as the voice of "young Russia".[9] Instead, it was the philosophical and psychological aspects of his writing which attracted attention in Sweden, just as they did in England and Germany; these themes of universal interest made him equally accessible to international and Russian readers.[10]

Two trends emerged in the translation of Russian authors in Sweden after the turn of the century. In contrast to the first wave of enthusiasm for Russian literature, the channels of communication between source and target cultures were maintained and widened. More translations of authors who were still alive and active—including Leonid Andreev, Vladimir Solov'ev, and the prose writers Nikolai Oliger (1882–1919) and Georgii Erastov (1875–1918; born Heinrich Edelman to German and Polish parents living in Finland)—were appearing. Notable among translators with an anti-militaristic and anti-tsarist stance was Erik Gustaf Nordenström, who brought out an anthology in two volumes entitled *Free Words from the Land of Tyranny* (*Fria ord från tyranniets land*, 1901–02). A further indication of diminishing distance between the cultures of Russia and Sweden is the marked difference between the more sensationalist and exoticising fascination with Nihilism before 1890 and the newly-awakened interest in Russian radicalism after 1900. While the former arose at a time when awareness of Russian culture was limited, the second occurred during

8 Ibid., pp. 29–30.

9 Incidentally, the only Scandinavian country which Dostoevsky visited was Denmark. In October 1865 he spent ten days in Copenhagen as the guest of his friend Baron Aleksandr Wrangel, who was secretary to the Russian Embassy there. He arrived on Friday 13 October after a stormy passage lasting four days, shortly after finishing *Crime and Punishment* (*Prestuplenie i nakazanie*, 1866). He visited the Assistens Cemetery, where both Hans Christian Andersen and Søren Kierkegaard were buried. On 3 November 2019, a monument to Dostoevsky created by the Russian sculptor Andrei Tartishnikov was unveiled there at a ceremony including musical and dramatic performances in the presence of the Russian ambassador to Denmark: see 'Dostojevskij Monument Unveiled in Copenhagen', *Daily Scandinavian*, 12 November 2019, https://www.dailyscandinavian.com/dostojevskij-monument-unveiled-in-copenhagen/.

10 Håkanson, *Fönstret mot* Öster, p. 91. See also Bengt Rur, *Björck & Börjesson. Ett antikvariat med historia*, https://www.yumpu.com/sv/document/view/19925985/bjorck-borjessons-ett-antikvariat-med-historia-av-bengt-rur-pa-.

a period when closer acquaintance left less room for stereotypes. Increased social, economic, political, and scientific contacts between Sweden and her Eastern neighbour, and the international respect accorded to the great Russian Realists, promoted a similar regard within the Swedish literary world. There were also direct contacts between Swedish and Russian authors; in the early 1900s Tolstoy's son Lev, Georgii Erastov, and Valerii Briusov were among those who visited or resided in Sweden. Nordenström's anthologies and the Swedish left-wing press demonstrated a sense of solidarity with groups in Russia whose experiences were regarded as relevant to conditions in Sweden; Gorky's work acquired considerable significance as Swedish workers' literature.[11]

The principal left-leaning Swedish publishing house was Björck & Börjesson, whose distinctive political character became particularly evident around 1905. In 1904 it launched the series 'The Free Word' ('Fria ord'), which began with Tolstoy and continued with Algot Ruhe's *Maxim Gorky—Agitator. His Life and Literary Activity* (*Maxim Gorkij—upprorsmannen. Hans lif och litterära verksamhet*, 1905), an anonymous text entitled *The Tsar* (*Tsaren*, 1905), claiming to be the work of "a high Russian official", and *Russia in Revolution* (*Ryssland i revolution*; 1905), a compilation of political texts by Tolstoy, Kropotkin, and Cherkasov. Among its other publications in 1904 were Swedish versions of revolutionary Sergei Stepniak-Kravchinskii's novel *En nihilist* (first published in London in 1889 as *The Career of a Nihilist*) and of Dostoevsky's *Crime and Punishment* (translated as *Raskolnikow* by David Hector) and *The Insulted and Injured* (*Unizhennye i oskorblennye*, 1861). In 1905, Gorky's *Prison* (*Tiur'ma*, 1905) was translated by Rafael Lindqvist. Lindqvist, a Finland-based Swedish translator, also translated Gorky and Dmitrii Mamin-Sibiriak for Bonnier and Söderström, and compiled anthologies of contemporary and earlier Russian poetry. In general, the Russian authors whose works appeared in Sweden were also published in Swedish in Finland, with certain significant differences. In the period from 1863 to 1914, it was not Tolstoy but Turgenev who was the most frequently published Russian author in Finland, possibly because of difficulties with the Russian censors who moderated Finnish literature. Swedish translations of earlier Russian authors ranked higher on Finnish publishers' lists than they did in Sweden; in the years 1863–1914, six out of nine translations into Swedish of works by Aleksei Tolstoy appeared in Finland, thirteen out of twenty-five translations of works by Lermontov, and thirteen out of forty translations of works by Pushkin. Probably because of the closer proximity to St Petersburg, a higher percentage of Swedish translations of Andreev appeared in Finland than in Sweden; in the 1900s Andreev, Erastov, and other Russian authors were also discovering Finland as a holiday destination. In the 1890s, there was a rise in the number of translations of Russian literature into Finnish, with a further increase in 1905–14.

11 See Stig-Lennart Godin, *Klassmedvetandet i tidig svensk arbetarlitteratur* (Lund: Lund University Press, 1994), p. 25, p. 147, p. 156, and Håkanson, *Fönstret mot Öster*, p. 91.

Norway

It is instructive to compare the cultural, linguistic, and literary context of translations of Russian literature at this time in Sweden (which had the advantage of an established literary language) and in Norway. The situation in Norway is of particular interest within the field of Translation Studies, as potential translators had the opportunity to make a statement by choosing to work in either Danish or Norwegian. Until 1814, Norway existed within the state of Denmark-Norway, in which Denmark was the dominant partner. Danish was the officially recognised language used by church, state, and nobility, while Norwegian, with no such recognition, existed mainly as a spoken language within Norway. This situation was succeeded by a 'personal union' with Sweden which lasted until 1905. Following a plebiscite, Norway then became an independent monarchy. As Jeremy Munday indicates, Translation Studies frequently illustrate power disparities between languages, both in postcolonial translation theory and other ideological contexts.[12] Thus the choice to translate authors of international significance into a target language which was gradually emerging as a literary medium constituted a bold political statement. As a growing nationalistic movement sought to establish a Norwegian purified of Danish influences, Ivar Aasen (1813–98), a self-taught Norwegian linguist, travelled throughout the country collecting local dialects as the basis of what he named Landsmål, a form of Norwegian which he developed between 1848–73 using the language of ordinary rural speakers, in contrast to Riksmål, a Danish-Norwegian form of the language used for official purposes.

With special reference to Dostoevsky's reception in Norway, Martin Nag records eleven translations of his fiction between 1883 and 1890. He notes in particular the popularity of two stories whose themes made them especially appropriate for publication in a number of Christmas issues of periodicals such as *Aftenposten* and *Christiania Intelligentssedler*: 'A Christmas Tree and a Wedding' ('Elka i svad'ba', 1848) and 'The Heavenly Christmas Tree' ('Mal'chik u Khrista na ëlke', 1876), whose similarity to Andersen's *The Little Match-Girl* may have made it especially appealing to Scandinavian readers (it appeared in two Norwegian translations and one in Danish between 1884 and 1899).[13] He

12 Jeremy Munday, *Introducing Translation Studies: Theories and Applications* (London and New York: Routledge, 2016), pp. 207–16. See also Munday, 'Using Primary Sources to Produce a Microhistory of Translation and Translators: Theoretical and Methodological Concerns', *The Translator*, 20:1 (2014), 64–80.

13 Martin Nag, *Dostojevskis gjennombrudd i Norge. Rapport fremlagt på symposiet 'Ryssland och Norden i skjønlitteraturen', Sandberg Slot, 5.-11. Oktober 1975* (Oslo: Slavisk-baltisk avd., 1977). He lists the translations, with details (where available) of the translators: Winter-Hjelm's translation of *Crime and Punishment*, discussed below, was followed by 'A Gentle Creature' ('Krotkaia', 1876) in 1885, a collection of four stories: 'The Landlady' ('Khoziaika', 1847), 'A Christmas Tree and a

does not, however, specify the reasons as to why new translations of *Crime and Punishment* and *The Brothers Karamazov* appeared comparatively soon after the first Norwegian versions.

The first Norwegian translation of *Crime and Punishment*, published by Albert Cammermeyer in 1883 under the title *Raskolnikow*, was made by Kristian Winter-Hjelm from a German version.[14] Martin Nag suggests that Hamsun first became acquainted with Dostoevsky's work in the spring or summer of 1884, when he was acting as secretary to the Unitarian pastor and poet Kristofer Janson in Minneapolis and had access to his extensive library; Janson, a great admirer of Russian literature, possessed a copy of the Winter-Hjelm translation.[15] In November 1882, Winter-Hjelm had written to Dostoevsky via Cammermeyer asking permission to translate the novel; the fact that he was unaware that the author was already dead indicates Dostoevsky's relative obscurity in Norway at that time. Dostoevsky's widow Anna granted permission by return of post, and the translation appeared the following July.

Wilhelm Henckel's 1882 German translation of *Crime and Punishment*, used by Winter-Hjelm as the basis of his version, appeared fifteen years after the novel's publication in Russia. This delay may be attributable to the negative reviews of the original text in the *Magazine for Foreign Literature* (*Magazin für die Literatur des Auslandes*);[16] however, Henckel's translation achieved immediate success, and provided a basis for the first three Norwegian versions. In 1887, the wholesaler Johan Sørensen set up the first publishing house in Norway to produce cheap editions, *Bibliothek for de tusen hjem* (*Library for a thousand homes*), offering literature in translation at low cost. It was strongly supported by the radical left as a means of making such literature readily available to the working classes. Holger Sinding (1853–1929) was a member of Sørensen's circle; originally trained in chemistry, he came from Gothenburg, edited the newspaper *Stavanger Amtstidende* (1877–78), wrote novels and plays, and in 1889 published his own translation of *Crime and Punishment*, the second to appear in Norwegian, once again based on Henckel's.

Wedding' ('Ëlka i svad'ba', 1848), *White Nights* (*Belye nochi*, 1848) and 'The Honest Thief' ('Chestnyi vor', 1848) in 1886, 'A Faint Heart' ('Slaboe serdtse', 1848) in 1887, two versions of *White Nights* in 1888, *The Brothers Karamazov* (*Brat'ia Karamazovy*, 1878–80), *The Gambler* (*Igrok*, 1866) and another translation of *Crime and Punishment* (as *Raskolnikow*, by H. Sinding), and a further *Brothers Karamazov* in 1890.

14 *Raskolnikow* (1882), translated by the German bookseller, translator and publisher Wilhelm Henckel (1825–1910).

15 See Martin Nag, *Geniet Hamsun—en norsk Dostojevskij?* [*Hamsun the Genius—a Norwegian Dostoevsky?*] (Oslo: Solum, 1998). For Janson's enthusiasm for Russian literature, see his memoirs *Hvad jeg har oplevet. Livserindringer* (Kristiania and Copenhagen: Gyldendal, 1913), p. 118.

16 Geir Kjetsaa, '*Forbrytelse og straff* i samtidens kritikk', in *Dostojevskijs roman om Raskolnikov*, ed. by Geir Kjetsaa (Oslo: Aschehoug, 1973), p. 138.

In 1908, Olav Hammer published the first and only translation of this novel into Landsmål (known after 1929 as Nynorsk), which since 1885 has been one of two officially approved written forms of the Norwegian language. Unfortunately, Hammer's *Crime and Punishment* remained incomplete as the entire print run of the third volume was destroyed in a fire in 1911. It was not until 1929 that the first Norwegian translation made directly from the Russian was published by Carl Olaf Fosse (1860–1940). All these translations bore the title *Raskolnikow*; it was not until 1975 that the novel appeared as *Forbrytelse og straff*, a calque of the Russian title (in his preface, Sigurd Fasting explains that Henckel had feared that the sophisticated public of the 1880s would have taken *Crime and Punishment* for a moralising *roman à these* or a cheap tract).[17] In her survey of Norwegian translations of the novel from 1883 to 1972, Anne Ragnhild Berteig notes that two Danish versions by Ejnar Thomassen (1921) and Georg Saurow (1943) were also widely read in Norway. Examining the specific challenges of rendering Dostoevsky into Norwegian, she concludes that, of the secondary versions, Winter-Hjelm's remains the best and most faithful. As such, it dominated the market until new translations made directly from Russian became available. Sinding's version is fair but less reliable, while Sturla Kvam's 1972 version, based on an English translation, deviates so far from the original text as not to be acceptable as a translation at all.[18]

These translations achieved Friedrich Schleiermacher's aim of bringing the reader and the original author closer together in time to meet a particular cultural need.[19] As Norwegian developed as an independent literary medium, liberating itself from German cultural and Danish linguistic domination, Kristiania was described by Edvard Munch as a "Siberian town" requiring its own Dostoevsky to depict it.[20] The author who rose to this challenge was Knut Hamsun:

> I could, so help me, create a whole world about desperate states of mind. But if people look on Dostoevsky as mad, then I am not likely to get anywhere. For the kind of oddities Dostoevsky has written about in the

17 For analyses of these and three later translations of *Crime and Punishment* into Norwegian, see Anne Ragnhild Berteig, *Norske oversettelser av Dostojevskijs* Forbrytelse og straff (Oslo: Universitetet i Oslo, Slavisk-baltisk avdeling, 1993). She does not mention which English translation Kvam used as the basis of his version (*Forbrytelse og straff*; Oslo: Solum, 1972).

18 Berteig, *Norske oversettelser*, p. 45.

19 Friedrich Schleiermacher, 'On the Different Methods of Translating' in *The Translation Studies Reader*, ed. by Lawrence Venuti (London and New York: Routledge, 2012), pp. 43–63.

20 Pola Gauguin, *Edvard Munch* (Oslo: Aschehoug, 1933), p. 15. Quoted in Sue Prideaux, *Edvard Munch: Behind The Scream* (London: Yale University Press, 2005), p. 71. Munch was also profoundly influenced by Dostoevsky; he was reading *Devils* on the day of his death in 1944 (see Alexandra Guzeva, 'How Dostoevsky Influenced Edvard Munch', *Russia Beyond*, 19 April 2019, https://www.rbth.com/arts/330262-dostoevsky-influenced-edvard-munch).

> three books by him I have read—and I haven't read more—is something I live through daily. I only have to take a walk down Gothersgade to find far more peculiar things. Alas![21]

On Boxing Day 1888, in a letter from Copenhagen, Knut Hamsun addressed these words to the Danish author Erik Skram, who had introduced him to the city's literary scene. At that time the twenty-nine-year-old Hamsun had recently returned from America, pawned his raincoat to rent an attic room, and presented himself to Edvard Brandes, editor of the magazine *Politiken*, with a thirty-page story which he hoped Brandes would publish. When Hamsun returned the following day, he was informed that although it was too long for *Politiken*, Brandes had recommended that Carl Behrens should publish it in the November issue of *Ny Jord* instead. Within three days, it had sold out, winning the author a contract for publication of the entire work and making his name—although it was published anonymously. Born Knut Pedersen, he experimented with various pseudonyms until *Hunger* (*Sult*, 1890) finally appeared under the name of Knut Hamsun.

By the time Hamsun finished the novel, he had moved back to Kristiania. He had been commissioned by the Danish publisher Philipsen to write a book on culture in America, based on two lectures which he had given drawing on his own experiences and impressions while living there (1882–84 and 1886–88). *On the Cultural Life of Modern America* (*Fra det moderne Amerikas Aandsliv*, 1889) presented a view very different from the optimistic visions of Henrik Ibsen, who had never been there, or of the Norwegian Nobel laureate Bjørnstjerne Bjørnsen, whose lecture tours had made him a celebrity. Hamsun's experiences in Chicago and Minneapolis as an agricultural worker, train conductor and labourer as well as a journalist had exposed him to a far harsher reality, which continued when he moved to Copenhagen, an existence of poverty, hunger, and rootlessness. Throughout his life he retained a distrust and dislike of urban life. Yet the novel which established his reputation—the first section published, as he readily admitted, for the sake of the money—owed its existence to his bitter periods of destitution in Kristiania during the winters of 1880–81 and 1885–86.

The material could not, as Hamsun himself observed, have taken its final form without the influence of one of the three figures whom he identified as the greatest influences on his younger self—Nietzsche, Strindberg, and Dostoevsky. Writing to his second wife Marie in 1910, he would state that "Dostoevsky is the only writer from whom I have learned anything; he is the greatest of the Russian giants".[22] This was shortly after he had received a copy of Vasilii Perov's 1872 portrait of Dostoevsky from a Russian admirer, Mariia Blagoveshchenskaia, who had translated his novel *Victoria* (1898). According to Hamsun's son Tore, the

21 Knut Hamsun, *Selected Letters*, ed. by Harald Næss and James McFarlane, 2 vols (Norwich: Norvik Press, 1990–98), I: *Selected Letters 1879–98* (1990), p. 82.

22 Martin Nag, *Geniet Hamsun*, p. 195.

portrait, framed in black, accompanied him to his homes in Nordland, Larvik, and Nørholm, where it hung over his bed, "the finest and most soulful face of an epileptic in the world".[23] He would later declare that he was completely ignorant not only of the Russian language but even of its alphabet—not surprising in a man whose education had been so sparse that in his first year at school (1868) he received a mere eleven days' schooling, leaving school altogether aged just fourteen in 1873. How, then, did he become acquainted with Dostoevsky's writings, and which translations were available to him? Why, too, was he so vehement in denying that during one particular period of his early career he had had any knowledge whatsoever of a specific work by Dostoevsky?

Hamsun's first awareness of Russia came through stories told by the men who came to supply Russian grain to the village mill. In 1899, shortly after his first marriage, he and his wife Bergljot set off from Finland, where they had lived for a year, on a trip to the Caucasus via Moscow and St Petersburg. From there they continued to Batumi and Baku. He later recorded this journey in *In Wonderland* (*I Æventyrland*, 1903), an account of his travels which also includes his appraisals of Russian authors including Tolstoy and Dostoevsky.[24] He describes Russia's people, landscapes, architecture, and bizarre characters in a style that at times recalls Mark Twain's travel writings in its detailed portrayals of quaint incidents (his search for a tailor in Moscow to replace a missing button, or the misunderstandings which resulted from his use of mime). In other passages, he tends to idealise the people of a country which he had glimpsed through the lens of its literature:

> Some distance away a number of good old people are chatting and eating, and their faces aren't ugly and ravaged like those of old people generally, but open and strong, and they have all their thick hair. Slavs, I think to myself as I look at them, the people of the future, conquerors of the world after the Teutons! Only in such a people can a literature like that of Russia well forth, endless and heaven-defying, flowing in eight thick, warm streams from its eight creative giants.[25]

This was to be Hamsun's only visit to Russia; ten years later, writing to his Russian translator Peter Emanuel Hansen, he sighed, "How I longed to come to Russia—properly, for a long time, to stay there for a year or so. But it is so fearfully expensive there. And then there is the language. [...] So I remain stuck."[26] Writing to Dagny Kristensen, a friend with a good knowledge of Russian, in December 1900, Hamsun exclaimed:

---

23 Tore Hamsun, *Knut Hamsun som er var. Et utvalg af hans brev* (Oslo: Gyldendal, 1956), p. 144.

24 Knut Hamsun, *In Wonderland*, trans. by Sverre Lyngstad (Brooklyn, N.Y.: lg publishing, 2004).

25 Ibid., p. 29.

26 Quoted by Martin Nag, *Geniet Knut Hamsun*, p. 304.

> It must be wonderful to know Russian. Oh God—how I wish I knew it! I have been in Petersburg and Moscow—I shall never experience a more powerful and beautiful adventure, especially the journey from Vladikavkas over the mountains to Tiflis. [...] It's another world—more handsome people, redder wine, higher mountains. And I believe that God lives around Mount Kasbek all year long.[27]

It was in Tbilisi that Hamsun paused to consider Russian writers who had visited the city, from Griboedov and Pushkin to Lermontov and Tolstoy, and to make his own pronouncements on them: "Russian literature is, everything considered, very large and very difficult to get a hold on", which he attributes to the "wide expanses of the Russian land and the expansiveness of Russian life". In his view Turgenev was "a European, a Frenchman, at least as much as a Russian", a calm mediocrity in direct contrast to Dostoevsky, "as torn and disproportionate as his characters" and possessed of a Slavophilism "rather too hysterical to be deep", but in a class of his own: "Never has human complexity been dissected as by him; his psychological sense is overwhelming, clairvoyant. Appraising him, one lacks the measure to mete with; he is in a category of his own".[28]

For Hamsun, then, Russia remained largely a 'wonderland' in the sense of a country of the imagination, experienced through the medium of literature in translation; *In Wonderland* contains a chapter in which he sets forth his views on Russian literature. Unlike the translations of his own works into Russian by Hansen,[29] many of the translations of Dostoevsky which Hamsun would have read were not made directly from the original at all. The one work by Dostoevsky which he mentions by name in this chapter, the story 'A Gentle Creature', first appeared in Norwegian in 1885, translated by Gerhard Gran from a French version and published in Bergen.[30] Nag traces the influence of this story and especially of Dostoevsky's remarks in the preface about his use of the first-person narrative, on Hamsun's own preface to his story *Sin* (*Synd*, 1886), and his construction of a similar "monological world"—a new universe of psychological insights—in *Hunger* and *Mysteries* (*Mysterier*, 1892).[31] In 1890,

27 Quoted by Martin Nag, *Myter! Myter!* (Kveldsbel-eika: Martin Nags forlag, 2001), p. 30.

28 Hamsun, *In Wonderland*, pp. 145–47.

29 Peter Emanuel Hansen (1846–1930) was born in Copenhagen, trained as a telegraphist, and in 1871 went to work in Siberia in that capacity. From 1881 to 1904 he was the director of a school of telegraphy in St Petersburg. Here he met and married his Russian wife Anna (1869–1942), with whom he collaborated on Russian translations of Scandinavian authors, including Hamsun.

30 For a detailed analysis of the novella and its reception in Norway, see Ingvild Broch, 'F.M. Dostoevskijs fortelling *Krotkaja*' in *F.M. Dostoevskij 1821–1881–1981: fire forelesninger*, ed. by Ingvild Broch, Jan Brodal, and Erik Egeberg (Tromsø: Universitetet i Tromsø, 1982), pp. 68–86.

31 Nag, *Geniet Knut Hamsun*, pp. 184–85.

a new literary review, *The Present Day* (*Samtiden*), appeared, edited by Jørgen Brunchorst and Gerhard Gran, the translator of 'A Gentle Creature'. The first issue contained Hamsun's own manifesto:

> What if literature were now to become more concerned with states of mind, and less with marriage plans and dances and trips to the country and other misfortunes like that? We would learn a bit about the disorderly confusion of our senses [...] the endless boundless journeys of our hearts and minds, the mysterious operation of the nervous system, the whisperings of our blood, the prayers of our bones: the whole subconscious life of the soul.[32]

In following Dostoevsky by revealing the invisible subtext as narrative and addressing similar existentialist issues, Hamsun dispensed with plot in favour of exposing and analysing his characters' interior lives by means of a stream of consciousness which laid bare the state of mind of the dispossessed—a condition in which Hamsun knew all too well.

While in America, Hamsun had been commissioned to write and edit articles for various Norwegian-language periodicals including the Minneapolis temperance magazine *Battle Cry* (*Felt Raabet*). Under the subtitle 'Marmeladov, or Cause and Effect', he presented two extracts from *Crime and Punishment* in this publication in 1887:

> This faithful representation of the misery of drunkenness is taken from the Russian author F. M. Dostoevsky's novel `Raskolnikov', which appeared in 1883 in a translation by K. A. Winter-Hjelm, published by Alb. Cammermeyer. Raskolnikov is the book's main character [...].[33]

The first passage is headed 'What drink did to him and his' and consists of Raskolnikov's encounter with Marmeladov in the tavern while the second, 'How it ended', describes how Marmeladov is run over while drunk and subsequently dies.

In 1929, when the Swedish professor John Landquist was working on a biography of Hamsun, he asked the latter about an episode early in his career. The author Arne Garborg, whom Hamsun had approached with *Pa Tourné* (*On Tour*), an account of Hamsun's unsuccessful Norwegian lecture tour in 1886, had rebuffed the young writer with the criticism that his work was too strongly influenced by Dostoevsky. Hamsun claimed that this was wrong; rather, he was trying to apply Dostoevsky's concept of style to Norwegian material. However, he acknowledged that when Georg Brandes had remarked that the younger Hamsun's *Mysteries* had been "infected" by Dostoevsky, that was true: "at that

32 Hamsun, `The Unconscious Life of the Soul' in *Samtiden*, I (1890), quoted in Prideaux, *Edvard Munch*, pp. 122–23.

33 Nag, *Geniet Knut Hamsun*, p. 184.

time I read all the translations of Dostoevsky that I could get, and this reading infected me..."[34]

There was, however, one work by Dostoevsky that Hamsun strenuously claimed not to have read at this time. Shortly before Christmas 1889, he encountered a newly published Norwegian translation of *The Gambler* (*Igrok*, 1866). He had just had his story *Hazard* (*Hazard*, 1889) accepted for publication in the periodical *The Way of the World* (*Verdens Gang*). In view of the similarities between Dostoevsky's story and his own text, he asked the editor Olaf Thommessen to return the manuscript, but it was already too late; the story was scheduled to take up three pages of the eight-page Christmas edition. Despite Thommessen's reassurances that, if necessary, he could testify that Hamsun's story owed nothing to Dostoevsky, accusations of plagiarism emerged some years later. In the summer of 1892, Hamsun was puzzled not to hear from Marie Herzfeld, who had translated *Hazard* and agreed to translate *Mysteries* into German. The letter that finally arrived contained a cutting from the Berlin periodical *Free Stage* (*Freie Bühne*), in which *Hazard* had appeared, where Felix Holländer openly accused Hamsun of plagiarism. As his German publisher Samuel Fischer also oversaw *Freie Bühne*, this was especially disastrous. On 25 June, he replied at length to Herzfeld; the story, he alleged, had been drafted during his time in America and expanded and revised when he had an opportunity to publish it. He also claimed that Thommessen would vouch for him as promised and urged Herzfeld to translate the whole letter for Holländer to read.[35] In the meantime, however, Hamsun had antagonised Thommessen by his aggressive dismissal of Ibsen. Not only did Thommessen fail to defend Hamsun; he published a review of *Mysteries* in *Verdens Gang*, which scornfully declared that Hamsun was no more than a pitiful but opportunistic imitator of Russian literature writing about a mentally unbalanced protagonist remarkably similar to Hamsun himself. In addition to the hostile reviews in the Norwegian press, the Danish critic Edvard Brandes sneered at the "childish" impression created by the novel and the crippled Minutten, "a very Russian character". It was against this background that Hamsun wrote to Albert Langen, the German publisher of *Mysteries*, from Paris on 10 February 1894 in fractured English, explaining the situation and urging him to do all he could to prevent attacks on Holländer in *Freie Bühne*:

> I fear there are certain persons standing behind Holländer, persons which I will not name. The question is: if he conferred with other persons, and who these persons were. [...] At present I can do nothing for anybody. I wish I could leave Paris today and go to Germany and live there. I feel myself only as a *Germanish Soul*, not as a Romanish, and these feelings are

34 Hamsun, *Selected Letters*, I (1990), pp. 157–59.
35 Ibid., pp. 196–97.

> increasing the longer I remain here. [...] And so you will kindly try to see the Kritiker of *Mysterien* before it gets too late.[36]

It could certainly be argued that Hamsun had no need to resort to plagiarism when writing a story about gambling; in his letter to Herzfeld he admitted, "If I could go through certain papers I have—material for a novel which, between you and me, consists of personal experiences at the roulette table—I could easily explain a good deal of the similarity there is between Dostoevski and me in our gambling stories." His penchant for gambling would, like Dostoevsky's, reach dangerous levels, and contributed to the breakdown of his first marriage. Early in 1901, he hoped to resolve his financial difficulties by taking off for Belgium to try his luck at the tables. He spent several weeks at the Hotel D'Harscamp in Namur, shuttling back and forth between casinos there and in Ostend and losing heavily at both. Ironically, in view of the fact that his flight had been precipitated by his guilt at living off Bergljot's money, he gambled away much of her dowry. In a letter to her he inveighed against God, claiming that he had had recourse to prayer "not just once, but on my knees, in the middle of the night in the Ostend streets for a month, or was it five weeks—and He heard me the way He hears everyone. Now I spit in his face for the rest of my life. He gave me this mind, it's His responsibility."[37]

While it is plausible that Hamsun had not read the Norwegian translation of *The Gambler* while writing the first draft of *Hazard*, an English version of the former had been published in London in 1887 by Vizetelly & Co. Translated by Frederick Whishaw directly from the Russian, it appeared as part of the 'Celebrated Russian Novels' series at the time when Kristofer Janson, Hamsun's employer in Minneapolis, was building up his library of Russian literature. Pages 244–45 of the English text contain a meticulous explanation of terms such as *pair, impair, manque, passe* and *zero*, and bear a clear similarity to the passage in *Hazard* where Hamsun explains precisely the same expressions. In 1993, Nag suggested to Tore, Hamsun's son, that his father considered using Dostoevsky as the basis of his portrayal of the psychology of gambling as a legitimate modus operandi rather than plagiarism. The latter suggested that his father could well have noted down a few lines immediately after reading *The Gambler* (he was in the habit of keeping such notes folded and pinned together), and subsequently forgotten where they had occurred.[38]

In Thomas Mann's estimation, Hamsun was the most distinguished of Dostoevsky's 'pupils', not only in Norway, but in Russia itself. Having disposed of the question of plagiarism, and of Georg Brandes' sneer at Hamsun as a mere epigone, it remains to be seen what Hamsun took from the author who "felt as

36 Ibid., pp. 197–98.

37 See Robert Ferguson, *Enigma: The Life of Knut Hamsun* (London: Hutchinson, 1987), pp. 189–90.

38 Nag, *Geniet Knut Hamsun*, pp. 201–203.

I do—I realise it now—and even in some ways thought as I do, only infinitely richer and better and greater, because he is the greater writer", as he wrote in his letter of 1892 to Marie Herzfeld. Sixty years later, his contempt for the Naturalist school, already evident in his distaste for Ibsen, was as strong as ever; Zola and his contemporaries, he declared, had "no use for a psychology of nuance", but dealt in people whose behaviour was dominated by a "ruling characteristic" (as in Zola's Rougon-Macquart series, where the characters' lives are largely controlled by heredity): "Dostoevsky—and others—taught all of us something different about people".[39]

These words come from the report on Hamsun's psychological state following his confinement to a hospital in Grimstad after being detained by the police on 14 June 1945. His meetings with Hitler and Goebbels, his support for Germany during the war, his loathing of England, and his outspoken admiration of Hitler, whom he described in an obituary as "a warrior for mankind", led him to be tried for treason. Only his advanced age saved him from an even more severe penalty than the fine of 325,000 kroner eventually imposed on him. He had pleaded ignorance—an attitude which chillingly recalls his words in reply to the accusation of plagiarism: "I never reply to attacks on myself—why should I do it now?"[40] It is, however, possible to trace qualities throughout his writings which, taken to extremes, contributed to this attitude, and among these are certain features which, it can be argued, may derive from Dostoevsky.

Recurring throughout Hamsun's work is the figure of the exceptional individual who regards himself as existing outside the norms and limitations of conventional society. Living in conditions of profound and humiliating poverty in his early years and later in America and Copenhagen, he personally experienced the hallucinatory effects of hunger and physical suffering. Like Ekaterina Marmeladova, he suffered from tuberculosis in his youth, and was warned that he might not survive. These traits were reflected in the heroes of *Hunger*, *Mysteries* and *Pan*; the refusal to conform and compromise with society's expectations, the development of a moral code on one's own terms (deliberately depriving oneself to offer food to hungry children, stealing but subsequently confessing to the crime) link them directly to Raskolnikov with his generosity towards the Marmeladov family and his final public acknowledgement of his guilt. These are the acts of characters who refuse to accept the tight-lipped morality of the 'unco guid'—the rigidly righteous—citizens progressing through Munch's *Evening on Karl Johan Street*, but identify with the solitary figure walking in the opposite direction, treading a path supported by its own bizarre logic. As Raskolnikov develops the arguments which justify his crime and lead him to overthink himself into possibly the most irresolute murderer

39 Gabriel Langfeldt and Ørnulv Ødegård, *Den rettspsykiatriske erklæring om Knut Hamsun* (Oslo: Gyldendal, 1978), p. 82.

40 Tore Hamsun, *Knut Hamsun som er var*, pp. 138–44.

since Hamlet, they too operate, like Ivar Kareno in Hamsun's dramatic trilogy, as 'supermen', unrestricted by the rules applicable to ordinary mortals. Tellingly, Hamsun himself noted that reading *The Insulted and Injured* "just about murdered" him,[41] leaving him shattered and shaking after the long walk which he took on closing the book. To demonstrate the evolution of such ideas required a narrative technique and subtle psychological exposition equal or, at the very least, closely related to Dostoevsky's.

Shortly after the events of 22 July 2011, when Anders Breivik caused the deaths of seventy-seven people in Oslo and on the island of Utøya, the Danish author Klavs Birkholm published an article on 'Nihilism in Norway—and Denmark'.[42] Here, Birkholm describes the plot of *Devils* and the murder of a young student at the Moscow School of Agriculture which inspired Dostoevsky to explore the motives of Sergei Nechaev and his anarchist cell, presenting a whole gallery of Nihilists including Nikolai Stavrogin, perhaps the most extreme. Like Raskolnikov, Stavrogin makes a confession—that of raping a twelve-year-old girl, who is later driven to suicide which he fails to prevent. But Tikhon, the holy recluse who hears Stavrogin's confession, immediately recognises its emptiness and falsity, expressed with the arrogance of an accomplished narcissist *avant la lettre*.

Birkholm draws parallels between the Nihilism which Dostoevsky feared would leak out of Russia and lead to a general disintegration of society, and his depiction of the inner emptiness characteristic of those capable of committing such acts. This vacuum, and the attempts to fill it by developing a means of justifying their actions, are equally present in Hamsun's solitary figures. A study of his writings may not enable us to pardon them, but can at least assist us in developing some measure of understanding.

41 Hamsun, *Selected Letters*, I (1990), pp. 157–59.

42 Klavs Birkholm, 'Nihilismen i Norge—og Danmark', *Klavsbirkholm.dk*, 7 August 2011, https://www.klavsbirkholm.dk/2011/08/07/nihilismen-i-norge-og-danmark/. See also Frederik Strand, 'Den danske Raskolnikov', *Weekendavisen*, 12 January 2022, https://www.weekendavisen.dk/2022–2/ideer/den-danske-raskolnikov, which discusses the 1890 murder in Copenhagen of an elderly debt collector, Johan Meyer, by Adolph Philipsen. The Danish translation of *Crime and Punishment* (1884) had made a powerful impression on Philipsen, who was condemned to death for the murder. His motive was never explained. However, the sentence was commuted, and after fourteen years in prison Philipsen was released to start a new life in Canada.

Romania

Dostoevsky in Romanian Culture: At the Crossroads between East and West

Octavian Gabor

Introduction

Alexandru Paleologu (1919–2005), Romanian writer and scholar, describes Fedor Dostoevsky as "Russian to the core". However:

> Dostoevsky was just as much a "European", through his culture but also his radical structure as a townsman, a devourer of daily news; his critique of the West stems from a conscience that is essentially involved in the West's destiny.[1]

Paleologu's words are cited in the afterword to the most comprehensive study of Dostoevsky's reception currently available in Romanian, Dinu Pillat's (1921–75) *Dostoevsky in the Romanian Literary Conscience* (*Dostoievski în conştiinţa literară românească*, 1976).[2] Dostoevsky's reception in Romanian culture exists, like the writer himself, at the crossroads between two civilisations, a mystical East and a rational West. Constantin Noica (1909–87), one of the most important Romanian philosophers of the twentieth century, describes the Romanian ethos thus: "in

1 Alexandru Paleologu, 'Afterword or: A Postponed Discussion' ['Postfață sau: O discuție amânată'] in Dinu Pillat, *Dostoevsky in Romanian Literary Conscience* [*Dostoievski în conștiința literară românească*] (Bucharest: Cartea Românească, 1976), pp. 136–70 (p. 186). Unless otherwise noted, all translations from Romanian are my own.

2 I will return to Pillat's volume later in this chapter. Much of this essay is indebted to Pillat's careful and thorough analysis.

 https://doi.org/10.11647/OBP.0340.14

their encounter, two massive worlds enclose a community which, instead of being crushed by them, as at a crossroad, can open itself towards them and, especially, open them toward each other".[3] This struggle between East and West, and also the geographical and cultural similarity between the Romanian and Russian cultures (both share important Orthodox Christian influences and traditional views on society, combined with a sense of belonging to the European cultural space) has led Romania to welcome Dostoevsky's thought. In addition, one other aspect of Dostoevsky's reception is quite specific to Romania: the country's domination, at the end of the Second World War, by the political descendants of the fictional terrorists Dostoevsky imagined in his novel *Demons* (*Besy*, 1872). As we shall see, the Russian author's reception began under the influence of politics and continued to be more or less impacted by Romania's own government and its political culture.

This chapter focuses on the history of Dostoevsky's academic and intellectual reception in Romania. While translations of the Russian writer's work into Romanian are not the primary subjects of this essay, a focus on how the work of an author changes as it moves from one political system to another shows a different kind of 'translation'. The discussion will begin with the pre-Communist period, in a milieu dominated by nationalist and religious ideas. I will then move to the Communist period, when, after a couple of decades where Dostoevsky is virtually absent, a series of scholars wrote essays in praise of him, creating robust scholarship. I will then examine how literary and theological interpretations of Dostoevsky changed after the fall of the totalitarian regime. This chapter will conclude with an overview of Romanian philosophical approaches to the author.

The two most influential studies of Dostoevsky's influence upon and reception in Romanian culture are Dinu Pillat's monograph, mentioned above, and Elena Loghinovski's *Dostoevsky and the Romanian Novel* (*Dostoievski și romanul românesc*, 2003). Indeed, one cannot venture to discuss Dostoevsky's reception in Romanian culture without paying homage to Pillat's well-documented and carefully crafted study. Although incomplete, due to the author's premature death, Pillat's book provides a comprehensive account of Dostoevsky's reception in Romania until 1974. In its three sections—'Discovering Dostoevsky (1881–1920)', 'Understanding Dostoevsky (1920–1944)', and 'Reconsidering Dostoevsky (1944–1974)'—Pillat's volume explores translations from the Russian author's work and the reception of his novels, as well as his influence upon Romanian novelists. Like Pillat, I begin here with Dostoevsky's first mention in the Romanian press. *The Telegraph* (*Telegraful*), a Bucharest newspaper, announced the writer's death (on 20 February 1881)

3 Constantin Noica, *The Romanian Sentiment of Being* [*Sentimentul Românesc al ființei*], trans. by Octavian and Elena Gabor (Santa Barbara, CA: Punctum Books, 2022), p. 22, https://punctumbooks.com/titles/the-romanian-sentiment-of-being/

as "the most significant event in the life of the Capital of the Tsar".[4] As Pillat observes, even this first mention was thus politically inflected; as I will show, this would prove typical of much of Dostoevsky's Romanian reception. In this first article, Dostoevsky's work was evaluated "exclusively from the perspective of nihilist circles".[5] He is criticised as "a completely reactionary author" who became "an enemy of the young generation, which fought against obscurantism, autocratic traditions, and despotism".[6] Pillat suggests that this critical tone is unsurprising, since the author of the article had participated "in the formation of a revolutionary committee as a student at the Military Academy of Surgery in Petersburg, together with the nihilist Sergey Nechaev, based on whose legal case Dostoevsky [would] later write *Demons*".[7] This essay is heavily indebted to Pillat's work for much of the timeline and many of the facts regarding the Romanian reception of Dostoevsky, as outlined below.

The first Romanian literary analysis of Dostoevsky was published four years after the writer's death. It appeared in 1885 as an introduction to several extracts translated from *The Insulted and the Injured* (*Unizhennye i oskorblennye*, 1861) in the journal *The Romanian* (*Românul*). Despite his own Socialist sympathies, its author, Constantin Dobrogeanu-Gherea (1855–1920), one of the country's most important nineteenth-century literary critics, did not reject Dostoevsky's work on the basis of the latter's politics. On the contrary, Dobrogeanu-Gherea returned to Dostoevsky after this first commentary in an article entitled 'What We Must Translate', where he assessed *Crime and Punishment* (*Prestuplenie i nakazanie*, 1866) as the "climax" of Dostoevsky's "creative force", the equivalent of *Madame Bovary* (1856) for Flaubert and *The Red and the Black* (*Le rouge et le noir*, 1830) for Stendhal.[8]

During the first two decades of the twentieth century, the reception of Dostoevsky's works remained very limited, likely owing to the scarcity and poor quality of translations.[9] Those who did read Dostoevsky accessed his writing through other languages. Octavian Goga (1881–1938), for example, the Romanian poet, playwright, and translator of several books from Hungarian to Romanian, read *Crime and Punishment* in German, in an edition translated as *Rodion Raskolnikoff*.[10] He claimed that the novel inspired him to undertake

4 See Pillat, *Dostoevsky*, p. 7.

5 Ibid.

6 Zamfir Arbore, 'From Russia' ['Din Rusia'], *Telegraful*, 20 February 1881. See also Pillat, *Dostoevsky*, p. 8.

7 Pillat, *Dostoevsky*, p. 8.

8 Ibid., p. 11.

9 Ibid., p. 21.

10 This was probably the 1908 translation by the Estonian-born Elisabeth Kaerrick (1886–1966) under the pseudonym of E.K. Rahsin. Her versions of Dostoevsky's novels in 22 volumes, originally edited by her brother-in-law, the German historian and nationalist thinker, Arthur Moeller van den Bruck (1876–1925), were

a "revision of moral problems" and "a change of world view".[11] Although interest in Dostoevsky intensified between the two world wars, Pillat notes that Romanians continued to read him through intermediary languages. The educated preferred French translations. The relatively few and unreliable Romanian translations were used by casual readers. Pillat's brief summary of these translations is as follows:

> *Memoirs from the House of the Dead* (1862) appeared in a version by A. Iacobescu, in two editions, one in 1926, the other in 1944. *Crime and Punishment* was issued in four editions, starting with the version by S. Avramof in 1922; the last was by Ion Pas in 1939. *The Brothers Karamazov* (1879) was printed in 1921 and again in 1929, in a scandalously abbreviated version by an unscrupulous translator, George B. Rareș. N. Dașcovici published his translation of Book X of *The Brothers Karamazov* under the title *The Precocious Ones* [*Precocii*] in 1923 [...]. *The Idiot* (1869) was translated for the first time by Zizica Pătrășcanu, with a sinister cover image, just as for *The Brothers Karamazov*. Although a masterpiece such as *Demons* remains untranslated, [... Romanians, surprisingly, benefited from] two translations of the chapter known as 'Stavrogin's Confession': one attributed to a certain R.D. in 1925, the other by the industrious George B. Rareș in 1928.[12]

Pillat concludes that "[w]e cannot consider Dostoevsky fully naturalized in Romanian as long as there is no complete edition of *The Brothers Karamazov* and no translation of *Notes from Underground* (1864), *The Adolescent* (1875), or of *Demons*".[13]

A significant step in the reception of Dostoevsky prior to the Second World War was a course taught by Nichifor Crainic (1889–1972), a prominent writer and politician who held office in the pro-Fascist government between 1940 and 1941. Prior to his political career, Crainic taught his own Dostoevsky course, first at the Faculty of Theology in Chișinău in 1926, and later at the University of Bucharest in 1933.[14] Crainic called his course 'The History of Religious Literature' and justified his focus on Dostoevsky by calling the latter "one of the greatest literary geniuses that humankind [had] to offer. He is on the same level as Homer, Vergil, Dante, Goethe, Milton [...]".[15] Crainic claimed that Dostoevsky's

published between 1906 and 1919 by the publisher Reinhard Piper and gradually became the canonical German editions of Dostoevsky.

11 Octavian Goga, 'Autobiographical Fragments' ['Fragmente autobiografice'] in *Talks* [*Discursuri*], (Bucharest: Cartea Românească, 1942), p. 17.

12 Pillat, *Dostoevsky*, pp. 30–31.

13 Ibid., p. 32.

14 Ibid., pp. 52–53.

15 Nichifor Crainic, *Dostoevsky and Russian Christianity* [*Dostoievski și creștinismul rus*] (Sfinții Martiri Brâncoveni, 2013), p. 21. This volume is the second edition of

stature precluded his elimination by the cultural police of the new Communist power in Russia:

> While many other Russian writers were excluded, ranked among forbidden literature, by the Bolshevik censorship and thus cast off by the Communist state from the new culture that pretended to be established, Dostoevsky remained an undeniable good. My words are paradoxical: we are in the presence of a genius who was accepted by two fundamentally mutually exclusive worlds. If the Russians of the former empire accepted him with imperial honours, the Russia that was born from the collapse of the Tsarist Empire accepts him as well, although with different honours. The paradox is, however, only apparent when you know Dostoevsky's works deeply [... then] you understand why such a complex genius can be claimed by a Christian Russia as well as by a Communist, deeply anti-Christian Russia.[16]

Crainic's words resonate with events that would transpire in Romania just over a decade later. When the Communist Party seized power there in 1946, Dostoevsky almost disappeared for a decade. When his works did return, critics had to re-package them for compatibility with their new political masters' ideological demands.

The history of Crainic's lecture course is relevant to us because it indicates how Dostoevsky was greeted alternately with veneration and disregard: both forms of reception were exaggerated, corresponding to whatever ideology was identified with authority at any given time. Between the wars, Crainic's thinking was ultra-conservative, and this was then reflected in his reading of Dostoevsky.[17] Reasonably for a course about modern *religious* literature, he chose to focus on the Russian writer's Orthodoxy. Crainic's analysis is robust. He engages with the important problems of Dostoevsky's works, from the opposition between Westernisers and Slavophiles to the question of universal guilt, where Crainic finds clear evidence of Dostoevsky's "religious, specifically Orthodox thinking".[18] Crainic's course came to be published much later, after the fall of Communism in 1989. The person responsible for its rediscovery was Bartolomeu Anania (1921–2011), the former Archbishop of Cluj.

Anania credits Crainic's course as the source for his own interest in Dostoevsky. With other adolescents from the Central Seminary in Bucharest, Anania formed a literary group in 1938 because the curriculum did not fulfil

---

the course that was first published in 1998, if we do not include the lithographed version.

16 Ibid., p. 21.

17 Crainic's political views were simultaneously ultra-conservative, anti-Semitic, and pro-Fascist.

18 Crainic, *Dostoevsky and Russian Christianity*, p. 169.

their thirst for culture.[19] Their group was mentored by a theology student, Ion Bârlănescu, "who began speaking about Dostoevsky, a new name for us, not even mentioned by our professors of literature".[20] Bârlănescu discussed "[Dostoevsky's] heroes, their deeds and inner turmoil, and so, slowly, for two years, strange and mysterious silhouettes were travelling through our thoughts: Raskolnikov, Sonia, Prince Myshkin, Stavrogin, Dmitry, Ivan, and Alyosha Karamazov, the *starets* [wise man] Zosima, but also the tall, sober, and frightening shadow of the Great Inquisitor".[21] Much later, Anania realised that Bârlănescu was aware of these characters as a former student of Crainic at the University of Bucharest. The latter's "course about Dostoevsky had become famous not only because different generations shared it verbally, but also because of the aura of mystery [conferred by the circulation of notes] in very few copies [...]".[22] One such rare copy was offered to Anania by the Archimandrite Grigorie Băbuş (1915–2007), who had been imprisoned by the Communists between 1959 and 1964 for belonging to *The Burning Bush* [*Rugul Aprins*] cultural organisation.[23] The Archimandrite kept a copy of the course in his cell. After the fall of Communism, he entrusted this copy to Anania, who eventually published it under the title *Dostoevsky and Russian Christianity*.

Dinu Pillat, completing his Dostoevsky monograph under Communism in 1976, mentions Crainic's course, but his analysis of the latter's thought is drawn from his pre-war published articles. Pillat begins in a critical tone, despite citing Crainic abundantly. Crainic's principal opinion, which he sketched in his lectures, was predicated on the claim that, to understand Dostoevsky's ideas, one must start with the doctrine of the Elder Zosima in *The Brothers Karamazov*: "the universalism of love is opposed to nihilist individualism".[24] At the end of his account of Crainic, Pillat reveals his implicit sympathy with Crainic's view: "Regarding Dostoevsky's work, Nichifor Crainic's judgment as an essayist leaves no space for errors of interpretation".[25] But this emphasis by Crainic and others on religious aspects of Dostoevsky's thought disappeared after the end of the Second World War, when Christian spirituality was critiqued by Romania's new political regime. The presence of the Soviet army and the Communist seizure of power enforced a national decline in Dostoevsky's reception. Many intellectuals were imprisoned as enemies of the regime. Atrocities occurred both

19 Anania's memory appears as a short introduction to Crainic's *Dostoevsky*, pp. 3–4.

20 Anania, 'Argument', in ibid., p. 3.

21 Ibid. According to Anania, Bârlănescu himself was a political prisoner of the Communist regime.

22 Crainic, *Dostoevsky*, p. 4.

23 For details on the Burning Bush, see Andrei Scrima, *The Time of the Burning Bush* [*Timpul Rugului Aprins*] (Bucharest: Humanitas, 2012), pp. 123–204.

24 Nichifor Crainic, 'Dostoievski' in *Gândirea*, February 1931, 49–53. See also Pillat, *Dostoevsky*, p. 55.

25 Dinu Pillat, *Dostoevsky*, p. 57.

in and out of prisons.[26] In this context, Dostoevsky could only be interpreted as a reactionary against the Communist Revolution, someone who forsook the Socialist ideals of his youth on account of the persecution that he experienced and his subsequent fear of the tsarist regime. Thus, critical literature from this period attempting to re-evaluate Dostoevsky sounds either pathetic or comical, couched in the wooden formulae of Socialist dogma then current.

Among the first such unsuccessful attempts was Mihai Novicov's (1914–92) 1956 article, marking the seventy-fifth anniversary of Dostoevsky's death.[27] Novicov, a proponent of Socialist Realism, produced a typically uninspired text. Dinu Pillat, although also bound by Communist-era restrictions, singled out Novicov's "narrowness of spirit".[28] Novicov attributed Dostoevsky's genius to his investigation of existential angst, adding however, that Dostoevsky's "solutions are almost always mistaken, because his reactionary ideology is manifested in them through violence".[29] Nor was Novicov alone in using scholarship to court political power—such actions were widespread. Similar ideas appear in the writings of the scholar George Călinescu, one of the most widely cited Romanian literary critics, and in important monographs like Albert Kovács's *Dostoevsky's Poetics* (*Poetica lui Dostoievski*, 1987) and Ion Ianoşi's work, which I will discuss below. Despite their indisputable academic quality, all of these occasionally manifest ideas that were designed to appease the Communist censors. These ideas are purely superficial elements, mandatory tributes to an authority that refused to consider freedom of thought. In treatments of Dostoevsky from the early Communist period, the authors' claims are blatantly false, and written in typically clichéd language. To illustrate this impoverished, partisan analysis, I will cite a 1963 essay by Valeriu Ciobanu, a pioneering scholar of Dostoevsky's Romanian reception. He explains how Dostoevsky was received before the country became Communist:

26 For an account of this historical period, see Dennis Deletant, *Romania under Communist Rule* (Bucharest: Civic Academy Foundation, 2006); Romulus Rusan, *The Chronology and the Geography of the Repression in Communist Romania. Census of the Concentration Camp Population (1945–1989)* (Bucharest: Civic Academy Foundation, 2007), *Romania during the Cold War: A Short Chronology of Events, Institutions and Mentalities (1945–1989)*, ed. by Romulus Rusan (Bucharest: Civic Academy Foundation, 2008), and Robert D. Kaplan, *In Europe's Shadow. Two Cold Wars and a Thirty-Year Journey through Romania and Beyond* (New York: Random House, 2016). Noica's *Pray*, mentioned above, is a philosophical description of life in prison (and at liberty).

27 Mihai Novicov, 'Marking 75 years since F. M. Dostoevsky's death' ['La 75 de ani de la moartea lui F. M. Dostoievski'] in the volume *Studies of Universal Literature* [*Studii de literatură universală*] (Bucharest: Societatea de Stiinţe Istorice și Filologice, 1956), pp. 177–88.

28 Pillat, *Dostoevsky*, p. 94.

29 Ibid., p. 93.

> During this period, when the reactionaries in capitalist countries who were worried about the success of the Revolution in Russia attempt to falsify the correct perception of Russian literature, the contradictions in Dostoevsky's work appear more obvious in our country, by their insistence on their negative aspects [sic–*OG*] which the mercenaries of the bourgeoisie emphasize. In general, there is no critical attitude toward the weaker parts of his works. On the contrary, it is precisely these parts that are brought to light, with emphasis on their mystical, obscure parts, denoting mistrust in man. [...] To such unilateral and also mystifying echoes from the Romanian press were added contributions from French newspapers and journals infiltrated by notorious reactionaries, such as Merezhkovskii and Berdiaev.[30] These articles and notes disfigured Dostoevsky's image by emphasizing certain features and neglecting others, precisely the positive ones. They were not published in the clearly reactionary media only, but, at times, even in media that pretended to be on the left but was in fact eclectic.[31]

One can see in this text how the author tries to redeem Dostoevsky, making him meaningful to a dogmatic society. To do so, he blames all the "dangerous" elements of his writings on the "faulty" interpretation of the "reactionary" society that preceded Communism. While Ciobanu wrote in the bureaucratic style of the time, he may have intended this text as a subtle path for the rehabilitation of Dostoevsky's work, which as he seems to argue, should not be dismissed. Instead, we should reject reactionary interpretations of Dostoevsky so that we can discover the 'real' writer.

1965 brought a short but welcome period of relaxation in Romanian culture. The Communist Party no longer interfered with publishers' plans. Consequently, the 1970s witnessed perhaps the most fertile period in Dostoevsky scholarship

30 To understand the context of this political era, one must recall that in the late 1940s and throughout the 1950s, Romanian intellectuals filled political prisons. Some of them died and were disposed of in common graves; others survived to eventually be released in 1964, during a general amnesty. Dinu Pillat and Nichifor Crainic both spent time in prison. Pillat was tried in the same group as Constantin Noica, a Romanian philosopher whose prison diary appeared in English as *Pray for Brother Alexander,* trans. by Octavian Gabor (Santa Barbara, CA: Punctum Books, 2016). Dostoevsky's "presence" in Communist political prisons is also attested to in Nicolae Steinhardt's *Diary of Happiness* [*Jurnalul fericirii*] (Rohia: Mănăstirea Rohia, 2005). Steinhardt mentions, for example, a moment when a priest is upset by Dostoevsky's distinction, in *The Brothers Karamazov*, between non-salvific suffering and suffering as a holy spectacle. While Communist political prisons were dungeons of terror, there were times when imprisoned intellectuals could offer lectures to each other in their respective fields. See Noica's *Pray for Brother Alexander.*

31 Valeriu Ciobanu, 'F.M. Dostoievski in Romania', *Studii şi cercetări în istorie literară şi folclor*, 1–2 (1963), 105–106. See also Pillat, *Dostoevsky*, p. 101.

in Romania up to that point. Prior to Pillat's book, which I have already cited extensively, four remarkable scholarly monographs analysing Dostoevsky appeared: Ion Ianoşi's *Dostoevsky: 'The Tragedy of the Underground'* (*Dostoievski: 'tragedia subteranei'*, 1968), Liviu Petrescu's *Dostoievski* (1971), Valeriu Cristea's *The Young Dostoevsky* (*Tânărul Dostoievski*, 1971), and Alfred Heinrich's *The Temptation of the Absolute: Character and Composition in Dostoevsky's Works* (*Tentaţia absolutului: Personaj şi compoziţie în opera lui Dostoievski*, 1973). Immediately after the publication of Pillat's book in 1976, Ion Ianoşi produced *A Story with Two Strangers: Dostoevsky and Tolstoy* (*Poveste cu doi necunoscuţi: Dostoievski şi Tolstoi*, 1977). I will begin by discussing the last of these, as an unusual example of scholarship.

The Romanian word for 'strangers' (*necunoscuţi*), may suggest either that Dostoevsky and Tolstoy are strangers to each other, since they never met, or else that both are unknown to the reader, because aspects of their work and characters still need to be revealed. Ianoşi's book plays on this double meaning. At one level it is a playful analysis of both authors' works based on their accounts of each other's writings and memoirs by common friends. But Ianoşi's book also reveals new aspects about each of these two major writers: not by presenting previously unknown biographical details, but rather by interpreting their historical interconnections on a personal level. Occasionally repetitive, Ianoşi's analysis is nonetheless refreshingly written, making original links between ideas. It reads like a novel rather than a work of scholarship, citing the two authors' diaries and letters without references to precise page numbers or editions. This approach deliberately creates the impression of sitting in a coffee shop, listening to a friend's knowledgeable and sophisticated account of parallels in the lives of two literary giants. Yet this innovative book pays lip service to Romania's political context and the requirements of Communist ideology. Ianoşi (1928–2016) was himself an intellectual with Socialist ideas. Nevertheless, his references to Lenin and his judgment of Dostoevsky's betrayal of the ideas of his youth should be read as obligatory prepared statements.

Ianoşi wrote a more traditionally academic analysis of Dostoevsky's work ten years prior to the publication of *A Story with Two Strangers*. In 1968, he had published *Dostoevsky: 'The Tragedy of the Underground'* (*Dostoievski: 'tragedia subteranei'*), a study of the "characters from the underground", as he calls them: namely, Raskolnikov, Ippolit, Stavrogin, Versilov, and Ivan Karamazov. Ianoşi wrote, "The 'Idiot' Myshkin, Makar Ivanovich Dolgorukii, or Alyosha Karamazov are examples of a Russian Don Quixote, while Hamlet has the face of 'the man from the underground', Raskolnikov, Ippolit, Stavrogin, Versilov, or Ivan Karamazov".[32] This is, in my estimation, one of the best analyses of Dostoevsky's writings, placing the Russian author in the context of international

32 Ianoşi, *Dostoevsky: 'The Tragedy of the Underground'* [*Dostoievski: 'tragedia subteranei'*] (Bucharest: Editura pentru Literatură Universală, 1968), p. 9.

literature and demonstrating the considerable openness of Romanian society towards the West.[33]

Ianoşi situates each 'negative' character from Dostoevsky's novels within the context of world literature, analysing his work in connection with Friedrich Nietzsche, Albert Camus, Nikolai Berdiaev, and Thomas Mann. Thus, he inserts Dostoevsky, and indirectly Romanian scholarship, into "the world republic of letters" described by Pascale Casanova, where Russian characters take their place beside international fictional heroes.[34]

Three years after Ianoşi's scholarly volume, two more monographs appeared: *Dostoevsky* by Liviu Petrescu (1941–99) and *The Young Dostoevsky* by Valeriu Cristea (1937–99).[35] Petrescu's short book is an excellent essay that tackles Dostoevsky's problem of man's solidarity with nature, with the universe, which is in an "extremely precarious state, under the menace of being destroyed at any instant, either by the loss of faith, or by an unprepossessing character of the laws of nature".[36] The opposite of "mystical union with the universe" is "human revolt, chaos, and the freedom that is unbridled by anything, the affirmation of individuality".[37] Dostoevsky's hero is placed, Petrescu says, "before a tormenting alternative, which he cannot bypass or avoid; [...] he is forced to choose between supreme freedom and supreme depersonalization".[38] The use of the latter term is confusing, but it should be understood as de-individualisation. This dichotomy emphasises the stark choice posed by Dostoevsky between freedom of action which Ivan Karamazov professes, and loss of individuality as is accepted by, for example, Markel, Fr. Zosima's brother.

This is how Dostoevsky depicts the metaphysical drama of humanity, Petrescu writes:

> Tragic lucidity is always to be preferred to gross disappointments, to which those who are easily impressionable consent with joy; one of the most efficacious forms of disappointment is represented—in the author's view—by a society organized after a totalitarian model, because in such an organization man will hide from himself his duty of being free.[39]

33 In 1968, Romania was the only Eastern bloc country not to support the Soviet repression of the Prague Spring in Czechoslovakia. Nicolae Ceaușescu gained in popularity after condemning the USSR's invasion. Nevertheless, after visiting North Korea in 1971, his approach changed, and he became one of the most ruthless dictators in Eastern Europe.

34 See Pascale Casanova, *The World Republic of Letters*, trans. by Malcolm DeBevoise (Cambridge, MA: Harvard University Press, 2004), p. 83.

35 According to Paleologu's 'Afterword', Dinu Pillat was planning on continuing his reception studies with an analysis of Ianoşi's and Petrescu's works (p. 136).

36 Petrescu, *Dostoevsky* [*Dostoievski*] (Cluj: Editura Dacia, 1971), p. 15.

37 Ibid., p. 19.

38 Ibid., p. 22.

39 Ibid., pp. 26–27.

Reading such a phrase in a book published in Romania would have been impossible even six years earlier than 1971.

Cristea's *The Young Dostoevsky*, published the same year, is regarded as another high-quality academic work.[40] The author studies Dostoevsky's earliest works, but in an original way: as a 'reversed lecture', in which the early characters are analysed through the lens of the later, major writings. "By dwelling on a theme or an epic situation, we will try to show how it was transformed and in which subsequent creations it appears".[41] Cristea is convinced that there is no internal hiatus in Dostoevsky's work between the period prior to his 1849 imprisonment and the decades after his return to European Russia; and that the major works are derived not exclusively from Dostoevsky's prison experiences, but rather his earliest literary beginnings.

The last major work from this period of intense scholarship is Heinrich's 1973 *The Temptation of the Absolute: Character and Composition in Dostoevsky's Works* (*Tentaţia absolutului: Personaj şi compoziţie în opera lui Dostoievski*). Heinrich focuses on Dostoevsky's psychological realism, moving from the early works to the complex characters of *The Brothers Karamazov*. Among various intriguing insights, he believes that Dostoevsky's characters cannot be interpreted in terms of their psychological traits only. His explanation, though, does not seem justified by the text. He says:

> They are not individualized by their psychological traits, nor by the contradictions of their internal worlds. Some impulse was required to kick-start their psychology. For Dostoevsky, the engine of psychic life is constituted by a character's ideology, as expressed in his 'ideas'. He acts under the impulse of an idea that mobilizes all his forces and all his possibilities, concentrating them into a single point.[42]

Heinrich's work remains, however, a significant moment in Dostoevsky's reception in Romania.

Thus, the period bookended by Ianoşi's two monographs, *Dostoevsky: 'The Tragedy of the Underground'* (1968) and *A Story with Two Strangers: Dostoevsky and Tolstoy* (1978), is, I believe, the golden decade of Dostoevsky's reception in Romania, in which Universal Literature Press (Editura pentru Literatură Universală, 1966–74) published a translation of his collected works into Romanian in eleven volumes. The first volume included a robust introductory essay by Tudor Vianu (1898–1964), one of the most gifted literary critics of his time. The next two volumes include meticulous critical apparatus by Tamara

40 Cristea also published *The Dictionary of Dostoevsky's Characters* [*Dicţionarul personajelor lui Dostoievski*] in two volumes (1983 and 1995).

41 Cristea, *The Young Dostoevsky* [*Tânărul Dostoievski*] (Bucharest: Editura Cartea Românească), p. 21.

42 Alfred Heinrich, *The Temptation of the Absolute* [*Tentaţia absolutului: Personaj şi compoziţie în opera lui Dostoievski*] (Timişoara: Facla, 1973), p. 96.

Gane, while the remaining eight were edited by Ion Ianoşi. The final volume, containing extracts from Dostoevsky's *A Writer's Diary*, was translated and edited by Leonida Teodorescu, with an introduction by Ion Ianoşi. The volumes have different translators.

The tradition of careful and remarkable Dostoevsky scholarship continued with Ileana Mălăncioiu's splendid short monograph *The Tragic Guilt: The Greek Tragedians, Shakespeare, Dostoevsky, Kafka* (*Vina tragică: Tragicii greci, Shakespeare, Dostoievski, Kafka*, 1978) and two studies by Albert Kovács, who would remain an influential scholar in the field even after the fall of the Communist regime. His two volumes, *Dostoevsky's Poetics* (1987) and *Dostoevsky: Quo Vadis Homo?* (2000) are remarkable, Bakhtin-influenced analyses.

After the fall of Communism, the study of Dostoevsky's Christian spirituality was reprised in two substantial monographs, the Archimandrite Paulin Lecca's *Divine Beauty in Dostoevsky's Work* (*Frumosul divin în opera lui Dostoevschi*, 1998) and Ion Mânzat's *The Christian Psychology of the Depths: F.M. Dostoevsky against S. Freud* (*Psihologia creştină a adâncurilor: F.M. Dostoievski contra S. Freud*, 1999). We should note that Nichifor Crainic's lecture series was also first published at this time as *Dostoevsky and Russian Christianity* (2013).

Lecca (1914–96) believed that Dostoevsky should be understood through the figure of Jesus Christ. His thinking resembles the twentieth-century Romanian theologian Andre Scrima's theory of "apophatic anthropology", which combined elements of Christian anthropology with Eastern Orthodox mysticism. Scrima believes that the problem of understanding other humans begins with Christ, who has two indivisible natures, divine and human as the Council of Chalcedon stated.[43] Humans also have two natures, according to Scrima, but the split between them is inchoate: we have lost our divinity and we are journeying toward recovering it. To understand who we are, we need to understand both our divinity and our humanity. Scrima emphasises in his 1952 monograph *Apophatic Anthropology* that "[t]he problem of man can be formulated in its plenitude only in the light of a theandric idea".[44] Lecca seconds Scrima's formulation and attributes a similar view to Dostoevsky. By so doing, Lecca reopens the study of Dostoevsky's connection with Christianity, a field which had lapsed during the forty-five years of the Communist regime. To examine the problem of understanding human motivations, Lecca analysed Dostoevsky's ideas by interpreting the author's fiction through his biography. For Lecca, every character of the writer's novels is an expression of Dostoevsky's life. His characters were developed with the purpose of answering the question of what man is. While Mânzat's book, discussed

43 The Council of Chalcedon was the fourth ecumenical council of the Christian Church. It took place in 451 AD, and it established the two natures of the person of Christ.

44 Andre Scrima, *Apophatic Anthropology*, trans. by Octavian Gabor (Piscataway, NJ: Gorgias Press, 2016), p. 44.

below, scrutinises Dostoevsky's psychology, *Divine Beauty in Dostoevsky's Work* starts from the Russian writer's own confession that he was not a psychologist but rather a realist attempting to portray the depths of the human soul—as Heinrich did in *The Temptation of the Absolute*.

As an archimandrite, Lecca was one of relatively few ordained clergy to engage with Dostoevsky's fiction.[45] His formal role within the Church naturally inflects his work. He frequently brings Dostoevsky into *rapprochement* with the Church Fathers, as well as with his own ideas. Near the end of *Divine Beauty*, Lecca returns to what he considers the key element in the interpretation of Dostoevsky's novels: the figure of Christ. He says, "According to Dostoevsky, beauty is Christ, He is the saint, the spiritual man, everything that is uplifting, generous, good, and pure".[46] To find beauty, Lecca says, Dostoevsky labours to reveal its source in Christ. Lecca's writing makes no pretence to be scholarly, although it abounds in references to other scholars. Sometimes he juxtaposes citations in order to convey his own view. Regardless of whether he cites from Dr A. Stocker or Konstantin Mochulsky,[47] perhaps his two primary sources, his own view is clear. Lecca summarises Dostoevsky's core notion thus: "each one of us, being guilty before all, can bring the Kingdom of Love on Earth only by taking the sins of our brothers upon us, just like Christ himself did on Golgotha".[48]

Lecca's dialogue with Dostoevsky is not limited to this monograph. He often returns to him in his other, specifically theological writings. In his *Spiritual Diary* (*Jurnal duhovnicesc*, 2013), he refers to Dostoevsky as often as he does to the Church Fathers, as if they were equally valid spiritual authorities. For example, he says that "Dostoevsky, the only one who writes the truth, shows in *The Brothers Karamazov* that hell is man's inability to love any more".[49] Lecca does not focus in this book on Dostoevsky's writing, but rather on ordinary human beings who "have a basement, as Dostoevsky said, where worms, toads, snakes, and even dragons live. [...] Often, when I contemplate all these crawling things, more or less dangerous and poisonous, I am overtaken by horror".[50] It is no wonder that he perceives that the solution to all of this terror is beauty: "Perhaps this is the meaning of Dostoevsky's claim that humankind can live without bread, but it

45 Lecca's analysis is not the only study by a Romanian priest. Pillat mentions two others active before the Second World War: Clement Bontea, author of the short 1926 study, *F. M. Dostoevsky: His Life and His Works* [*F.M. Dostoievski: Viaţa şi operele lui*] and Stefan Dobra's 1938 examination of 'Christian pedagogy' in Dostoevsky: *Dostoevsky and the Youth* [*Dostoievski şi tineretul*]. Pillat criticises both works for lacking personal vision (see Pillat, *Dostoevsky*, pp. 57–60).

46 Lecca, *Divine Beauty in Dostoevsky's Work* [*Frumosul divin în opera lui Dostoevschi*] (Bucharest: Discipol, 1998), p. 212.

47 Lecca cites Konstantin Mochulsky's *Dostoevsky: His Life and Work* (1947) and A. Stocker's *Ame Russe: Réalisme psychologique des Frères Karamazov*.

48 Lecca, *Divine Beauty*, p. 330

49 Lecca, *Spiritual Diary* [*Jurnal duhovnicesc*] (Bacău: Editura Studion, 2013), p. 27.

50 Ibid., p. 130.

cannot live without beauty. And beauty, according to Dostoevsky, belongs to Christ the Saviour".[51]

The fact that a theologian cites Dostoevsky in defence of his professional views is relevant to how some Romanian scholars persist in seeing the Russian writer as a significant religious figure. While focusing on the soul and Christianity, both Lecca and Crainic stay away from psychology. This is 'corrected' by Ion Mânzat in his thorough analysis, *The Christian Psychology of Depths: F.M. Dostoevsky against Sigmund Freud* (*Psihologia creştină a adâncurilor: F.M. Dostoievski contra S. Freud*, 2009). Mânzat begins with a claim similar to Lecca's: "Dostoevsky developed a psychology of suffering throughout his entire work, which sprang from his life. Suffering is an experience lived in spirit, with beneficial and malefic effects on self-knowledge and self-realization. Suffering guards us against mediocrity, increases our dignity; suffering strengthens the spirit which thus finds its Self".[52]

Mânzat discusses whether Dostoevsky's views influenced Freud. One of the points of comparison is the dichotomy between tender love and sensual love, which Mânzat applies to *Crime and Punishment*. He concludes however that:

> [...] psychoanalysts' competent comparisons and analyses are incomplete and partially artificial, since they did not take into consideration the third kind of love, one which proved definitional for Dostoevsky and his characters. This is the mystical love of Christ, love between a human being and divinity, as a metaphysical form of knowledge and communication between a human and divinity.[53]

In comparing what he calls the psychoanalytic approaches of Freud and of Dostoevsky, Mânzat considers the author of *The Brothers Karamazov* superior, because of his profound Christian sensitivity. This passage expresses Mânzat's view in essence:

> Freudian psychoanalysis acknowledges that it has limits; it feels defenceless before the subtleties and refinements of artistic creation (Sigmund Freud's own testimony). On the contrary, Dostoevsky's Christian psychoanalysis of the depths has no limits of time and space, because its premise and its result represent the relation of the human spirit with divinity; God and the spirit have no limits.[54]

51 Ibid., p. 311.

52 Mânzat, *Christian Psychology* [*Psihologia creştină a adâncurilor: F.M. Dostoievski contra S. Freud*] (Bucharest: Univers Enciclopedic Gold, 1999), p. 23.

53 Ibid., p. 90.

54 Ibid., p. 104.

In a somewhat surprising conclusion, Mânzat claims that "Freud is identified more with Moses, while F.M. Dostoevsky with Christ".[55] His book thus engages with major themes of Dostoevsky's work from a psychoanalytic perspective, exploring both atheistic and Christian approaches to the novels. This unusual study certainly deserves more thorough analysis than this chapter can offer.

One of the most recent volumes dedicated to Dostoevsky is Ciprian Iulian Toroczkai's *Nihilism in Dostoevsky's Work* (*Nihilismul în opera lui Dostoievski*, 2014). This monograph is yet another theological interpretation. Often modelling his arguments on Lecca's, Mânzat's, and Ianoşi's previous works, Toroczkai engages with the problems of nihilism as Dostoevsky described them before indicating tools to cure what he calls this "nihilist malady": the word of Scripture, suffering, love, and beauty.[56]

* * *

A short note about Dostoevsky's influence on Romanian novelists: Pillat states that, prior to the Second World War, many novelists referred to the Russian author:

> [...W]e don't have a notable writer, regardless of the generation [...] that would not feel the need to say what he believes about Dostoevsky. Having become a cardinal point of reference even for Romanian culture, the author of *The Brothers Karamazov* does not, however, constitute a point of influence as well.[57]

Loghinovski's aforementioned volume on reception, *Dostoevsky and the Romanian Novel*, is useful on this topic. She continues Pillat's work, focusing primarily on Romanian novelists' responses to Dostoevsky's writings. Her book discusses three great Romanian novels: Liviu Rebreanu's *Ciuleandra* (1927),[58] Gib Mihăescu's *The Russian Woman* (*Rusoaica*, 1933), and Marin Preda's *The Most Beloved of Earthlings* (*Cel mai iubit dintre pământeni*, 1980). But after the Second World War, Dostoevsky no longer seemed to preoccupy Romanian writers. From 1944 to 1974, the period analysed by Pillat, only a few explicitly mention Dostoevsky. Pillat does not attempt to explain this situation; perhaps it was self-evident that the Orwellian conditions of Communist society precluded references to novels of this type. After the fall of Communism, Dostoevsky has appeared in new and unexpected interpretations. I will mention here only Mihail Gălăţanu's novel, *The Last Karamazov* (*Ultimul Karamazov*, 2014), which is framed as a continuation

55 Ibid., p. 105.

56 Ciprian Iulian Toroczkai, *Nihilism in Dostoevsky's Work* [*Nihilismul în opera lui Dostoievski*] (Sibiu: Astra Museum, 2014), p. 129.

57 Dinu Pillat, *Dostoevsky*, p. 89.

58 'Ciuleandra' is the name of a folk dance from Muntenia, the Southern part of Romania. It has a progressively accelerated rhythm.

of Dostoevsky's famous book, as penned by the youngest Karamazov brother, Mikhail. This character does not appear, of course, in Dostoevsky's original.

* * *

One cannot write about Dostoevsky's reception in Romania without touching upon how the Russian author was received by philosophers. The three giants of twentieth-century Romanian philosophy, Lucian Blaga (1895–1961), Constantin Noica (1909–87), and Emil Cioran (1911–95), each took a different path, recalling Romanian culture's diverse approaches to Dostoevsky. Lucian Blaga found inspiration in the Orthodox tradition; thus, he cited Dostoevsky to support his own views. Constantin Noica's thought evolved within the framework of traditional Western metaphysics, focusing on Greek and German philosophy, and therefore he was silent about Dostoevsky. But Noica does mention the Russian author in a 1934 article, listing translations into Romanian from Russian literature.[59] Here he observes that "Dostoevsky has over twenty translations, while Lev Tolstoy almost *one hundred*"[60] (his own emphasis). Emil Cioran, a philosopher who did not merely discuss, but who viscerally experienced the despair and absurdity of life, could hardly remain impassive to Dostoevsky's troubled characters or to the problem of suffering. Nor did he—but I will turn first to Lucian Blaga. In the second volume of his *Trilogy of Culture* (*Trilogia culturii*), *The 'Mioritic' Space* (*Spaţiul mioritic*, 1936),[61] Blaga used 'the wedding at Cana' scene from *The Brothers Karamazov* to illustrate Orthodox spirituality. As we have seen in the theological approaches outlined earlier in this chapter, Dostoevsky's works often serve to provide insight into the meaning of Orthodox thought. Blaga discusses what he calls bipolar spiritualities within three strands of Christianity: Protestantism, Catholicism, and Orthodoxy. When discussing the conflict between the transcendent and the temporal, he uses Dostoevsky to illustrate the Orthodox view. Blaga refers to the scene when Alyosha enters the room where Fr. Zosima's corpse is laid out and a monk reads the Gospel of the wedding in Cana. Alyosha has a vision of Zosima as one of the guests. Blaga says:

> Overtaken by tears of joy, Alyosha comes out of the room in the night. Above, he sees the starry heaven and the Milky Way; at that moment, without knowing why, he falls down [...] and kisses the earth crying. In this moment of ecstasy, the earth becomes an equivalent of heavens for him. The reality of death is transformed into a vision of life, this eternal

---

59 Published in *Faith* [*Credinta*], 70 (27 February 1934), p. 3. See Constantin Noica, *Between Soul and Spirit* [*Între suflet şi spirit*] (Bucharest: Humanitas, 1996), p. 302.

60 Noica, *Between Soul and Spirit*, p. 302.

61 The term *mioritic* designates an ethos that Blaga finds uniquely characteristic of Romanian culture. I cannot find a precise English equivalent. It derives from a term of endearment, *mioara*, meaning literally a 'lamb'.

> wedding at Cana. Alyosha kisses the earth crying as it is a great keeper of life. The organic, with all of its aspects and values, is crowned with the diadem of the Milky Way.[62]

Blaga's conclusion is that Dostoevsky was more than an analyst of the dungeons and sanctuaries of the human soul, or an Orthodox dialectician; he was also "a lyrical poet of the Orthodox experience".[63]

Whereas Blaga focuses on the Orthodox spirituality of Romanian culture and so finds in Dostoevsky illustrative examples because of this common Orthodox trend, Emil Cioran's perspective was different. Preoccupied with dissolution and despair, Cioran was drawn to Dostoevsky's treatment of suffering.[64] The son of an Orthodox priest, Cioran left Romania prior to the Second World War and moved to France. His Romanian writings before his departure for France show his attraction to Dostoevsky's themes, without accepting the Russian author's ideas. This struggle continued in Cioran's books published in French. I mention here one passage from his *History and Utopia* (*Histoire et utopie*, 1960), written after he had settled in France. In his typically exalted style, Cioran writes:

> Suffering, in its early stages, counts on the golden age here on earth, seeks a basis for it, attaches itself to it, in a sense; but as suffering intensifies, it withdraws, attached only to itself. Once an accomplice of utopian systems, it now rises against them, discerning in them a mortal danger to the preservation of its own pangs, whose charms it has just discovered. With the voice of Dostoevsky's *Notes from Underground* it will plead in favour of chaos, rise up against reason, against '"two and two equals four", against the "crystal palace", that replica of the phalanstery.[65]

Cioran continues for several pages to recount different scenes from Dostoevsky's novel, dialoguing with the author's "hostility to utopia".[66]

* * *

Who is Dostoevsky, in Romanian culture? Some scholars say that translation has a dialogical nature: translators must attempt to live in two cultures at the same

62 Blaga, *The Mioritic Space* [*Spaţiul mioritic*] (Bucharest: Humanitas, 1994), pp. 35–36.

63 Ibid., p. 36.

64 For an excellent article about Cioran's life and work, see Costică Brădăţan's 'The Philosophy of Failure: Emil Cioran's Heights of Despair', in *Los Angeles Review of Books*, 28 November 2016, https://lareviewofbooks.org/article/philosopher-failure-emil-ciorans-heights-despair/

65 Emil Cioran, *History and Utopia*, trans. by Richard Howard (New York: Seaver Books, 1987), p. 111.

66 Ibid., p. 112.

time, transferring their way of being from one to another.[67] Ideas do not live in a vacuum; rather, they are embodied in languages and cultures. Translators, interpreters, and adapters of Dostoevsky enter into dialogue with him from whichever space they inhabit. Thus, Dostoevsky gains meanings and flavours relative to the culture or society that his writings inform. It can be challenging to exclude politics from any text. Dostoevsky's reception in Romania certainly proves this statement. His own political and religious views made him attractive for some and problematic for others. But the Romanian experience shows that genuine philosophical value transcends political interests. Dostoevsky's consistently positive and thoughtful reception among scholars in the turbulent history of Romania gives reason for hope that, regardless of political affiliation, people can always find a way to communicate if they focus on what is valuable. Dostoevsky's great novels provide such a space for potential opponents to encounter each other peacefully.

67 See Eugenio Refini, *The Vernacular Aristotle. Translation as Reception in Medieval and Renaissance Italy* (Cambridge: Cambridge University Press, 2020).

Scotland

Russian Poetry and the Rewilding of Scottish Literature: 1917 to the Present

James Rann

Introduction

In recent years, a popular response to Scotland's dwindling biodiversity has been to encourage 'rewilding' projects in which plants and animals are brought in from overseas to kickstart moribund ecosystems. In this endeavour, however, ecologists have a lot to learn from poets, since a similar regeneration programme, replenishing the resources of Scotland with an injection of new life from abroad, has been going on in literature, and especially poetry written in Scots, for the past hundred years—"a period unprecedented in the history of Scots-language writing in the quantity of work and the range of languages and genres translated".[1] Perhaps surprisingly, in this literary rewilding, one of the 'keystone species', the crucial imports that catalyse the wider process, has been the difficult, distant poetry of Russian Modernism. Poets like Aleksandr Blok, Boris Pasternak, and Vladimir Maiakovskii "have dominated a strand of 20th-century translations into Scots", providing poets with both "a wider range of voices" and "desperately needed cultural connotations".[2] In this chapter, I will trace the evolution of these voices and connotations across three distinct

1 Bill Findlay, 'Editor's Introduction', in *Frae Ither Tongues: Essays on Modern Translations into Scots*, ed. by Bill Findlay (Clevedon: Multilingual Matters, 2004), pp. 1–14 (p. 1). The author is grateful to Professor Alan Riach for his comments on a draft of this chapter.

2 John Corbett, *Written in the Language of the Scottish Nation: A History of Literary Translation into Scots* (Clevedon: Multilingual Matters, 1999), p. 140. By my estimation, based on a limited survey, at least fourteen individuals have translated from Russian to Scots since 1917.

 https://doi.org/10.11647/OBP.0340.15

periods, in connection with changes both in the Scottish literary landscape and in the global standing of Russian culture. This case study will also, in so doing, demonstrate the usefulness of 'rewilding' as a paradigm able to express overlooked nuances in systems of global cultural interaction, and especially the unique role of Russia therein.

Such wider relevance notwithstanding, as with all translation histories, the development of Russian poetry in Scots is a product of the complexities of the local linguistic ecosystem. Between the late medieval decline of Norman French and Latin and the recent efflorescence of languages brought by migrants, Scottish speech and writing has been carried along by the troika of Gaelic, English, and Scots. Scottish Gaelic is a Celtic language descended from Old Irish; in the Middle Ages it was used in the courts of kings as well as in homes across much of the country, but now it thrives in only a handful of Hebridean communities. This decline is largely a result of the dominance of English, which has become ever more ubiquitous since the union of the Scottish and English crowns in 1603. This same Anglophone hegemony has also forced Scots—our focus here—to the margins. Scots, which has also variously been known as Lallans, Doric, and Braid Scots, is a descendant of Northern varieties of Old English and it has, despite three centuries of subordination to its Southern sister-tongue, maintained a distinct literary tradition and persisted as a diverse spoken idiom across Southern and Eastern Scotland.[3] Its common origin and significant overlap with standardised and officially sanctioned English has led to Scots being classed by some linguists not as a distinct language but as a dialect or language variety.[4] Instead of relitigating these debates, I want here to emphasise how the absence of a hard border between English and Scots has allowed Scottish translators both to reach heights of creativity and to call into question assumptions about Britain as a target culture and about English as a global language.[5]

3 Fittingly for a language that has never been standardised, Scots has gone by many names. Initially it was often termed 'Inglis', to distinguish it from Gaelic, before distinction from English became more important. The name 'Doric', taken by analogy from the dialects of Ancient Greek, is now used to refer only to the Scots of Aberdeen and the North-East of Scotland. The term Lallans, derived from the 'Lowlands' in which Scots has been most actively spoken, is sometimes used to refer to Scots as a whole and sometimes to 'synthetic Scots'—an artificial poetic language that is discussed at length in this essay. 'Braid Scots' simply means 'broad Scots', that is Scots as a consistent language variety distinct from English.

4 For an overview of the different definitions of the status of Scots, and their contexts, see Johann Wolfgang Unger, *Discursive Construction of the Scots Language: Education, Politics and Everyday Life* (Amsterdam: John Benjamins, 2013), pp. 88–97.

5 The exploitation of the continuum between Scots and English has been an evergreen feature of Scottish literature, present in the eighteenth-century poetry of Robert Burns and in contemporary prose. On Burns, see Robert Crawford, *Devolving Scottish Literature*, 2nd edn (Edinburgh: Edinburgh University Press,

Although translations by Scottish writers from Russian into English are plentiful and often excellent and although there is even some Russian verse in Gaelic, these bodies of work do not constitute coherent traditions in the same way that translations into Scots do. This influence is reciprocated in the large corpus of Russian versions of Robert Burns, which largely do not distinguish his "Scottish dialect" from "standard" English.[6] This absence of clear water between Scots and English has not stopped Scottish writers or translators from delineating between the two when explaining their practice. Since the seventeenth century, writing in Scots has nearly always been a political act, a pointed refusal of English by people who are well capable of using it but who wish instead to underline the particularity of local voices and perspectives.[7] This has led to a comparative dearth of prose in Scots in comparison to drama and especially poetry, with their emphasis on oral expression and smaller audience—a situation that is reflected in translated texts. But the need to define Scots against English has also fostered an unusually active translation tradition: to use Scots for translation reinforces the rejection of English in a way that more locally oriented writing does not, since the translator ostentatiously spurns a wider readership in favour of strengthening the autonomous body of Scottish literature by enlarging its repertoire, by appropriating the prestige of foreign classics, and by demonstrating an independent connection to cultures beyond these islands.[8]

2000), pp. 103–04; on contemporary fiction see Scott Hames, *The Literary Politics of Scottish Devolution* (Edinburgh: Edinburgh University Press, 2019), p. 240.

6 Christopher Whyte has translated Anna Akhmatova into Gaelic. See Anna Achmàtova, 'Marbhrann 1935–1940', trans. by Crìsdean Whyte, *Gairm*, 125 (1984), 74–83; Anna Akhmatova, 'Bho Stikhi i Proza (Leningrad 1976)', trans. by Crìsdean Whyte, *Gairm*, 135 (1986), 239–42. For an analytical history of Russian translations of Burns, which largely overlook the distinctiveness of his poetic language, see Natalia Kaloh Vid, *Ideological Translations of Robert Burn's Poetry in Russia and the Soviet Union* (Maribor: Filozofska fakulteta, Mednarodna založba, Oddelka za slovanske jezike in književnosti, 2011).

7 Of the close and contentious relationship between English and Scots, Derrick McLure has written: "It might be predicted that such a language conflict, in which the less prestigious form was so closely related to its rival as to be readily assimilable to it and was, if at all, only weakly supported by the patriotic loyalty attaching to a national language, would result in a quick and easy victory for the incoming tongue. This has not happened." One reason for this, he continues, is "a literary resistance movement", beginning with Allan Ramsay (1686–1758), Robert Fergusson (1750–74) and Robert Burns (1759–96) that has eschewed standard English in order "to employ their native speech in a conscious and determined attempt to raise its literary prestige". Other, more recent examples will be discussed below. See J. Derrick McClure, *Scots and its Literature* (Amsterdam: John Benjamins, 1995), pp. 10–11.

8 See Corbett, *Written in the Language of the Scottish Nation*. There has also been, of course, translation between Scotland's languages.

In this regard, translation into Scots appears to accord with the description in Itamar Even-Zohar's polysystem theory of 'peripheral' literatures that use translation to grow in scope and status.[9] Nevertheless, the case of Scotland and Russia gives us reason to question this centre/periphery model, not least because it problematises Even-Zohar's equation of Western "peripheral literatures" with "the literatures of smaller nations".[10] In the words of the poet Edwin Morgan (1920–2010), who, along with Hugh MacDiarmid (1892–1978), will be the major figure in our story, Scotland is one of those "untidy places" where "linguistic and national boundaries [...] refuse to coincide": not only is it home to multiple 'native' languages with their own power relations to each other, but it is also entangled in decidedly non-peripheral supranational entities like the United Kingdom and the British Empire.[11] This ambivalent position, which is not unique to Scotland, is one reason to take our metaphors from ecology, which is inherently non-hierarchical and tolerant of complexity—qualities which have been identified as lacking in the concentric, economics-based models of world literature proposed by Even-Zohar, Franco Moretti, and Casanova, among others.[12]

Furthermore, presenting translation as an act of rewilding allows us to extend another of Translation Studies' staple frameworks: Lawrence Venuti's celebrated distinction between "domestication" and "foreignization", whereby the former "maintains the status quo, reaffirming linguistic standards" in the translated text, while the latter "carries the potential to challenge the dominant, as well as the cultural and social hierarchies that structure the receiving situation" by "drawing on marginal resources".[13] John Corbett and Stewart Sanderson have questioned the relevance of these popular concepts to translation into Scots.[14] On

9 Itamar Even-Zohar, 'The Position of Translated Literature within the Literary Polysystem', *Poetics Today*, 11 (1990), 45–51. On the case of Scots as a peripheral literature, see Stewart Sanderson, 'Poems Chiefly in the Scottish Dialectic: Scots Poetic Translation and the Second Generation Modern Scottish Renaissance (c.1940–1981)' (unpublished MPhil thesis, University of Glasgow, 2012).

10 Even-Zohar, 'The Position of Translated Literature', p. 48.

11 Edwin Morgan, 'Registering the Reality of Scotland', in Edwin Morgan, *Essays* (Cheadle: Carcanet, 1974), pp. 153–57 (p. 154).

12 See Alexander Beecroft, *An Ecology of World Literature: From Antiquity to the Present Day* (London and New York: Verso, 2016), pp. 7–21.

13 Lawrence Venuti, *The Translator's Invisibility: A History of Translation*, 3rd edn (Routledge: New York, 2017), p. xiv.

14 Corbett, *Written in the Language of the Scottish Nation*, p. 185 and Stewart Sanderson, '"Order and Adventure": Sydney Goodsir Smith's Translations', in *Sydney Goodsir Smith, Poet*, ed. by Richie McCaffery (Brill: Leiden, 2020), pp. 103–17 (p. 115). Debates about the relevance of 'foreignisation' and 'domestication' in regard to minority literatures have also been held in, for instance, the Italian context: see Elisa Segnini, 'Global Masterpieces and Italian Dialects: Eduardo de Filippo and Luigi Meneghello's rewritings of Shakespeare', *Journal of World Literature*, 2 (2017), 236–54 (p. 246).

the one hand, written Scots has never been standardised or widely disseminated, and so it can occasionally seem "not unlike a foreign language to many Scottish people", offering the sort of "resistancy" and estrangement that Venuti values in foreignising translations.[15] On the other, for Scottish readers Scots "is a language that is nominally 'theirs'" and, furthermore, given its exclusion from official discourse, it is one particularly associated with the familiar and the "homely".[16]

Venuti is not using "domestic" to mean "homely"', however, and he has also rightly pushed back against any characterisation of "foreignization" and "domestication" either as binary opposites or as "discursive strategies".[17] This clarification notwithstanding, Corbett and Sanderson are still correct to suggest that neither concept is entirely adequate in the case of Scots. First, although Venuti by no means assumes the existence of a single, uniform, and stable English, his polemic against "the hegemonic English-language nations" does not make sufficient allowance for the fact that these nations are themselves multiple, divided, and contested, with translators and readers able to align themselves with competing norms, both marginal and dominant, at the same time.[18] Second, as a term if not as a concept, "foreignization" does not fully capture the ambivalent feeling of simultaneous estrangement and rootedness that arises when reading these Scots translations, especially out loud. Many of these words may look unusual, but they sound familiar, even to monolingual English speakers, who will recognise their shape, sound, and effect even if ignorant of their dictionary meaning. And in poetry, as MacDiarmid says, "It's soon' no' sense, that faddoms the herts o' men".[19]

It is in order, therefore, to tweak Venuti's terminology for the Scottish situation (and potentially that of other "untidy places") that I interpret domestication ecologically, as an act of taming or cultivation—a contribution to the promotion of

15 Corbett, *Written in the Language of the Scottish Nation*, p. 185; Venuti, *The Translator's Invisibility*, p. 18.

16 Corbett, *Written in the Language of the Scottish Nation*, p. 185. On the 'homeliness' of Scots in translations see Brian Holton, 'Wale a Leid an Wale a Warld: Shuihu Zhuan into Scots', in *Frae Ither Tongues*, ed. by Findlay, pp. 15–37 (p. 15).

17 Venuti, *The Translator's Invisibility*, p. xiii.

18 Ibid., p. 120. Venuti expressly states in this passage that foreignisation is "based on the assumption that [...] communication is complicated by cultural differences between and within linguistic communities".

19 "It's sound not sense that fathoms the hearts of men." Hugh MacDiarmid, 'Gairmscoile' in *Complete Poems*, ed. by Michael Grieve and W. R. Aitken, 2 vols (Manchester: Carcanet, 1993-), I (1993), pp. 72–73 (p. 73). MacDiarmid continues by explaining that his Scots will affect even those who do not know the language: "E' en herts that ha'e nae Scots 'll dirl richt thro' / As nocht else could—for here's a language rings / Wi' datchie sesames, and names for nameless things" ["Even hearts that have no Scots it will pierce right through / As naught else could—for here's a language that rings / With penetrating discoveries and names for nameless things"].

superficially productive but ultimately sterile and unsustainable monocultures.[20] The antonym of such domestication is thus rewilding—an ethical intent, if not always an effect, to undo cultural impoverishment by reasserting linguistic diversity, favouring complexity over comprehension and difficulty over utility. Such rewilding obviously overlaps with foreignisation as described by Venuti, with its valorisation of the puzzling and the marginal, but it also shifts the emphasis from international to intranational politics and foregrounds an idea of the recovery of something inherent thought to be lost.

What is more, unlike Venuti's enthusiastic advocacy of foreignisation, I would not characterise such rewilding as unambiguously positive. As our example will show, in translation as in ecology, rewilding can be criticised for overemphasising charismatic big beasts at the top of the food chain (in this instance, almost all male poets), for a nostalgic and/or utopian indifference to lived experience, and for potentially concretising a dangerous distinction between native and non-native.[21] Nevertheless, the idea of translation-as-rewilding can help to unsettle the longstanding (and justified) association between translation, imperialism, and extractive cash-crop agriculture as related instruments of domination and exploitation. This interrelation between control of language and control of land, which is signalled by the etymological connection between culture, cultivation, and colony, has long had relevance in Britain and Ireland, since, before the global expansion of the coordinated project of colonialism, it was trialled here and elsewhere on the fringes of Europe. In the sixteenth century, Edmund Spenser talked of "translatinge" Irish speakers by "planting" among them English speakers; similar processes were inflicted on Scottish Gaeldom, where land enclosure and forced migration were potent catalysts for language death.[22] To treat translation as a force not of taming but of rewilding can, therefore, serve to disrupt conventional pictures of centripetal

---

20 A similar reading is suggested by Kaisa Koskinen: see her 'Domestication, Foreignization and the Modulation of Affect', in *Domestication and Foreignization in Translation Studies*, ed. by Marja Jänis, Hannu Kemppanen and Alexandra Belikova (Berlin: Frank & Timme, 2012), pp. 13–32 (p. 15). The same reading is also implied in one of the possible Russian translations of the term, *odomashnivanie*, which is somewhat rarer than *domestikatsiia*. Indeed, neither is common due to the relative indifference to Venuti displayed by Russian translation studies scholars: see Alexandra Borisenko, 'Fear of *Foreignization*: "Soviet School" in Russian Literary Translation', in *Domestication and Foreignization in Translation Studies*, ed. by Marja Jänis and others, pp. 177–88 (p. 177).

21 For a summary of debates around rewilding from a sociological perspective, see John Bone, 'Rediscovering the "Noble Savage": The Rewilding Movement and the Re-Enchantment of the Scottish Highlands', *Scottish Affairs*, 27 (2018), 465–85.

22 On the relationship between translation and colonialism see Susan Bassnett and Harish Trivedi, 'Introduction: Of Colonies, Cannibals and Vernaculars', in *Postcolonial Translation: Theory and Practice*, ed. by Susan Bassnett and Harish Trivedi (Routledge: London, 1999), pp. 1–19 (p. 4). The quotations from Spenser are taken from a longer discussion of this passage by Laura O'Connor

power dynamics, allowing the 'periphery' unexpected agency. Rewilding translations can perhaps even be seen as prefiguring the future for translation desired by Walter Mignolo and Freya Schwiy, in which "the 'lower end' of the colonial difference would no longer be the place of shame and ignorance but of epistemic potential".[23]

Of course, neither Scotland nor Russia is situated at that 'lower end' of colonial difference. Rather, any unsettling of assumptions is made possible by the fact that, both on their own and as a pair, these countries do not fit easily within any dichotomous system of coloniser and colonised, centre and periphery. Thanks to Scotland's role as both a partner in empire and, in linguistic terms in particular, an object of colonisation, Scottish literature has displayed "a dual relationship of congruence and conflict centred on the form of the British empire" and as such often shares with strands of postcolonial writing the tendency to critique "the jurisdiction of the imperial mode of British state culture", including the aptly named King's English.[24] Russia too was an imperial power, at least from 1721 to 1991 but arguably for much longer, and one with only sporadic and limited tolerance for the languages and traditions of others. Nevertheless, like their counterparts in Scottish literature, in recent years scholars such as Heekyoung Cho, Jeanne-Marie Jackson, and Rossen Djagalov have successfully argued that neither influential discourses of postcolonialism nor the predominating planetary models of intellectual traffic have truly come to terms with the position of Russian culture. It presents a problem both in its internal complexity, with its much-agonised-over liminality between Europe and Asia, and in its sudden rise from relative obscurity to worldwide influence in the early 1900s.[25] For much of the subsequent century, Russia seemed to many, both at home and abroad, to be a counter-hegemonic force undercutting the cultural dominance of Western Europe and America through a series of unusual provocations: the hectic spirituality of Fedor Dostoevsky, the exoticism of the

in her *Haunted English: The Celtic Fringe, the British Empire, and De-Anglicization* (Baltimore, MD: Johns Hopkins University Press, 2006), p. 1.

23 Walter D. Mignolo and Freya Schiwy, 'Translation/Transculturation and the Colonial Difference', in *Beyond Dichotomies: Histories, Identities, Cultures, and the Challenge of Globalization*, ed. by Elisabeth Mudimbe-Boyi (Albany, NY: State University of New York Press, 2002), pp. 251–86 (p. 251).

24 Michael Gardiner, 'Introduction', in *Scottish Literature and Postcolonial Literature: Comparative Texts and Critical Perspectives*, ed. by Michael Gardiner and Graeme MacDonald (Edinburgh: Edinburgh University Press, 2012), pp. 1–12 (p. 3, p. 1).

25 Heekyoung Cho, *Translation's Forgotten History: Russian Literature, Japanese Mediation, and the Formation of Modern Korean Literature* (Cambridge, MA: Harvard University Asia Center, 2016); Jeanne-Marie Jackson, *South African Literature's Russian Soul: Narrative Forms of Global Isolation* (London: Bloomsbury Academic, 2015); Rossen Djagalov, *Internationalism to Postcolonialism: Literature and Cinema between the Second and the Third Worlds* (Montreal: McGill-Queen's University Press, 2020). See also Steven S. Lee, *The Ethnic Avant-garde Minority Cultures and World Revolution* (Columbia University Press: New York, 2015).

Ballets Russes, the experimentalism of the Modernist avant-garde, and, after 1917, the Soviet Union's self-appointed role as a champion of decolonising movements and their cultural output.

For poets writing in Scots, already predisposed to reject orthodoxies, it was this apparent insurgent force above all that made Russia appealing, both as a rebuke to the complacency and conservatism of Anglophone literature and as a role-model. Here, it seemed, was another semi-peripheral place which, while never powerless politically, had nonetheless undergone a rapid transformation from cultural backwater to trendsetter. As MacDiarmid put it in 1933: "the little known language of Russian [...] has since [the turn of the century] been the paramount force in *welt-literatur* [*sic*]".[26] After the Revolution, it became impossible to disentangle this unexpected cultural pre-eminence from the appeal of the Soviet Union as a political project, especially for writers looking for a new society and a popular, socially motivated literature to go with it. Writers like MacDiarmid and Sydney Goodsir Smith adopted a policy of emulation resembling that of Socialist organiser John Maclean, who believed that "we can make Glasgow a Petrograd".[27] This is not to say, however, that Russian verses in Scots are the devotional texts of Communist true believers: while most of the translator-poets under discussion were at least sympathetic to the Soviet cause, this admiration largely derived from their notion of Russia as an alternative to the constrictive status quo, rather than conformity to the Party line.[28] Consequently, the poets most frequently translated in Scotland have not been propagandists (with the honourable exception of Maiakovskii), but simply those whose work

26 Hugh MacDiarmid, 'The Case for Synthetic Scots', in *At the Sign of the Thistle: A Collection of Essays by Hugh MacDiarmid* (London: Stanley Nott, 1934), pp. 177–96 (p. 194).

27 William Knox, *Scottish Labour Leaders 1918–1939: A Biographical Dictionary* (Edinburgh: Edinburgh University Press, 1984), p. 187.

28 MacDiarmid, typically confrontational, would occasionally describe his output as 'propaganda' but he followed only his own directives and was twice expelled from the Communist Party in the 1930s. Scott Lyall surmises that the poet "undoubtedly did not produce agitprop in the service of the Party" and cites MacDiarmid's fairly astute self-description as a *pre-revolutionary* Bolshevik, a dissident in waiting: "For I am like Zamyatin. I must be a Bolshevik / Before the Revolution, but I'll cease to be one quick / When Communism comes to rule the roost". See Scott Lyall, 'MacDiarmid, Communism and the Poetry of Commitment', in *The Edinburgh Companion to Hugh MacDiarmid*, ed. by Scott Lyall and Margery Palmer McCulloch (Edinburgh: Edinburgh University Press, 2011), pp. 68–72 (p. 76, p. 81). The quotation is from Hugh MacDiarmid's 'Talking with Five Thousand People in Edinburgh', in *The Complete Poems of Hugh MacDiarmid*, II (1994), pp. 1155–158 (p. 1158). For his part, Morgan has been described as an "engaged if lower-case sympathiser" with Communism and was certainly never a Party member. See Matt McGuire and Colin Nicholson, 'Edwin Morgan', in *The Edinburgh Companion to Contemporary Scottish Poetry*, ed. by Matt McGuire and Colin Nicholson (Edinburgh: Edinburgh University Press, 2009), pp. 97–111 (p. 98).

has enjoyed the best reputation in the West—Pushkin, Blok, and Pasternak in the first half of the twentieth century, Evtushenko and Voznesenskii in the latter.

Even working within a slim canon, however, the treatment of Russian poetry in Scots has evolved. Retrospectively, this development can be said to consist of three periods that correspond with the regnant mood and personalities in Scottish literature. The first is the 'Scottish Renaissance' of the Modernist 1920s, which was spearheaded by MacDiarmid and thus informed by his passionate interrogations of and prescriptions for national identity and language; the second is the 1960s and 1970s, when Modernism slipped into Postmodernism and when the presiding figure was the prolific and playful Morgan; finally, there is the period between the fall of the Soviet Union and the present, in which no single figure or explicit ideology has dominated, except perhaps for a growing concern with the promotion of minority identities as an end in itself.

Hugh MacDiarmid and the Scottish Renaissance

In his masterwork *A Drunk Man Looks at the Thistle* (1926), Hugh MacDiarmid appeals to Dostoevsky, asking his Russian forebear to lend him some of his "appallin' genius" as MacDiarmid must "address a similar task"—that is to say, to use literature, and the single charismatic figure of the writer, to revitalise a nation and resolve its internal tensions.[29] In the words of Peter McCarey, Dostoevsky serves as "a character and an artist who helps the drunk man [the poet's alter ego] look for the sense of life in the depths of the psyche".[30] In the poem, which is sprinkled with allusions to Dostoevsky's work, MacDiarmid treats the Russian writer sometimes as an untouchable idol—"As bairn at giant at thee I peer"—and at other times as an equal, including in matters of linguistic competence—"I ken no Russian and ye ken nae Scots".[31] Just as Dostoevsky's ignorance of Scots has not hindered his reputation, neither MacDiarmid's lack of Russian nor his output of fewer than a dozen translations from that language prevent him from being the indispensable figure in our story. Without him, subsequent generations would not have been so drawn to Scots, nor to contemporary European literature and its translation, nor to Russia. Nevertheless, these founding achievements require contextualisation, not least because, for all his cussed individualism, MacDiarmid was in many ways an exemplar of the ambitions and modus operandi of global Modernism.

29 Hugh MacDiarmid, 'A Drunk Man Looks at the Thistle', in *Complete Poems*, I (1993), pp. 81–170 (p. 138–45).

30 Peter McCarey, *Hugh MacDiarmid and the Russians* (Edinburgh: Scottish Academic Press, 1987), p. 22. See also Catherine Kerrigan, 'Underground Men: Dostoevsky in the Work of Hugh MacDiarmid', *The Journal of Narrative Technique*, 17 (1987), 45–50.

31 Hugh MacDiarmid, 'A Drunk Man Looks at the Thistle', in *Complete Poems*, I (1993), p. 111, p. 145, p. 151.

In the 1920s, MacDiarmid set a new agenda for Scottish poetry with his programme for a so-called "synthetic Scots", a literary language derived not from any single spoken vernacular but from dictionaries and historic texts as well as speech. Synthetic Scots was part of MacDiarmid's self-proclaimed Scottish Renaissance, which was intended to reinvigorate a Scottish culture shackled by foreign rule and local pettiness, returning its lost linguistic patrimony and unleashing hidden sensory forces. There were backward- and inward-looking aspects to this renaissance, which sought to restore continuity with medieval and early modern Scottish writing, but it was also a conscious contribution to Modernist experiments in remaking word and world. In 1933, about a decade in, MacDiarmid described his ambitions for synthetic language as transcending Scots:

> By the synthetic use of a language, then, I mean 'the destruction of a toothless ratio'—'freedom of speech' in the real meaning of the term—something completely opposed to all our language habits and freely utilizing not only all the vast vocabulary these automatically exclude, but illimitable powers of word formation in keeping with the free genius of any language [...]. I go further and agree with Joyce in regard to the utilization of a multi-linguistic medium—a synthetic use, not of any particular language, but of all languages.[32]

In this vision, global and local unite. MacDiarmid shares with other Modernists a utopian optimism about the malleability of language and its world-changing power: the reference to "the destruction of toothless ratio", for instance, is taken from a description of the Russian Futurist agenda.[33] But his initial attempts to actualise this planetary potential are grounded in his own 'peripheral' locality and in usage that is counterposed to the assumed stability and pre-eminence of the 'standard' English that was itself a nascent global lingua franca. In this he recalls not only Joyce, but also Pound and Yeats—other exponents of what scholar Robert Crawford has described as "provincial modernism".[34]

The way in which MacDiarmid's synthetic Scots aspires to bridge the national and the international is replicated in his concurrent project to re-establish Scotland's connections with Europe—also held to have been severed by the Union—through translation and other cultural exchanges. MacDiarmid himself

32 Hugh MacDiarmid, *The Letters of Hugh MacDiarmid*, ed. by Alan Bold (London: Hamilton, 1984), p. 771.

33 See Babette Deutsch and Avrahm Yarmolinsky, 'Introduction', in *Modern Russian Poetry: An Anthology*, edited and trans. by Babette Deutsch and Avrahm Yarmolinsky (New York: Harcourt, Brace and Co., 1921), pp. xi-xix (p. xviii).

34 Crawford, *Devolving Scottish Literature*, p. 217. MacDiarmid criticised English for being too international and cosmopolitan; see MacDiarmid, 'Case for Synthetic Scots', p. 181. He would later go on to write in 'synthetic English', notably in *Stony Limits and Other Poems* (1934).

presented this in ecological terms, quoting with approval the sentiment that: "If pigeon fanciers are too exclusive, and refrain from all exchange of eggs, their stock will weaken and ultimately die out. A like fate [...] awaits the literature of any country which is preserved from all foreign intercourse".[35] In the early 1920s the "foreign intercourse" MacDiarmid desired was increasingly accessible thanks to a boom in literary journalism, which made of him first a voracious reader and then a serial founder of small magazines.[36] This new publishing reality was itself driven by a general appetite, in selected circles, for thought-provoking new writing, an important part of which was an explosion of interest in Russia. This trend was sufficiently widespread and influential, especially in bohemian London, as to constitute what Rebecca Beasley has called a "Russophile modernism", the practitioners of which found English and French writing enervated and unambitious in comparison to Russian prose.[37] The Russians, with Dostoevsky foremost, seemed to offer "a model to renew and update the project of romanticism: it was read as a literature confident of its ability to express national identity, and thereby able to imagine and potentially achieve political change."[38]

MacDiarmid, always an outspoken critic of the British state, could not but be galvanised by the Russian example, especially at a time when empires appeared to be crumbling.[39] His Herderian programme for a new Scottish literature in Scots is thus framed as an emulation of a Russian culture that is the quintessence of continental vanguardism and the antithesis of English mediocrity:

> The Scottish Vernacular is the only language in Western Europe with those uncanny spiritual and pathological perceptions alike which constitute the uniqueness of Dostoevsky's work, and word after word Doric establishes a blood-bond in a fashion at once infinitely more thrilling and vital and less explicable than those deliberately sought after by writers such as D. H. Lawrence in the medium of English which is inferior for

35 Hugh MacDiarmid, 'Swatches o' Hamespun', in *Contemporary Scottish Studies*, ed. by Alistair McIntyre (Edinburgh: Scottish Educational Journal, 1976), pp. 82–84 (p. 83).

36 See Margery Palmer McCulloch, *Scottish Modernism and its Contexts 1918–1959: Literature, National Identity and Cultural Exchange* (Edinburgh: Edinburgh University Press, 2009), pp. 11–52.

37 Rebecca Beasley, *Russomania: Russian Culture and the Creation of British Modernism, 1881–1922* (Oxford: Oxford University Press, 2020), p. 28. Beasley acknowledges that the specifics of the Scottish Modernist reception of Russian literature are beyond the scope of her study and in need of further research (p. 33).

38 Ibid., p. 433.

39 Scott Lyall has identified this post-imperial or late-imperial moment as an important context for Scottish translations of German literature, including those of MacDiarmid. See Scott Lyall, 'Minor Modernisms: The Scottish Renaissance and the Translation of German-language Modernism', *Modernist Cultures*, 14 (2019), 213–35 (p. 213).

> such purposes. [...] The Scottish Vernacular is a vast storehouse of just the very peculiar and subtle effects which modern European literature in general is assiduously seeking and [...] the resumption of the Scots Vernacular into the mainstream of European letters [...] is inevitable.[40]

By translating modern European literature into Scots, MacDiarmid could both match Scotland with Europe and demonstrate that this would be a marriage of equals, in terms of both ambition and erudition. Just as MacDiarmid treats Dostoevsky variously as mentor and mate, so he occasionally elides Russia's head start on the path out of semi-peripheral semi-obscurity in order to emphasise a bilateral "Russo-Scottish parallelism", in which the two nations' location at opposite ends of Europe empowers them to reverse the decline of the West recently diagnosed by influential German historian Oswald Spengler.[41] This essentialist underdog story is inextricable from both the rejection of (the) English and utopian aspirations for language, as the poem *To Circumjack Cencrastus* (1930) suggests:

> If we turn to Europe and see
> Hoo the emergence o' the Russian Idea's
> Broken the balance o' the North and Sooth
> And needs a coonter that can only be
> The Gaelic Idea
> To mak' a parallelogram o' forces,
> Complete the Defence o' the West,
> And end the English betrayal o' Europe.
> (Time eneuch then to seek the Omnific Word
> In Jamieson yet.
> Or the new Dictionary in the makin' noo,
> Or coin it oorsels!)[42]

---

40 Hugh MacDiarmid, 'A Theory of Scots Letters', in *Selected Prose*, ed. by Alan Riach (Manchester: Carcanet, 1992), pp. 16–33 (p. 22). Although MacDiarmid's conscious bypassing of Western Europe here contradicts the Gallocentric model proposed by Pascale Casanova, the close link he implies between language and nation can be seen as evidence of what Casanova calls "the Herder effect", a trend throughout Europe, initiated by the German philosopher, for "the language of the people" to be seen as "the instrument of emancipation and means for defining a distinctive national character". See Pascale Casanova, *The World Republic of Letters*, trans. by Malcolm DeBevoise (London and Cambridge, MA: Harvard University Press, 1999), p. 78.

41 MacDiarmid, 'A Theory of Scots Letters', p. 29.

42 Hoo: how; eneuch: enough; noo: now; oorsels: ourselves. Hugh MacDiarmid, 'To Circumjack Cencrastus', in *Complete Poems*, I (1993), pp. 179–296 (pp. 222–23). Although unable to write in Gaelic, MacDiarmid was a consistent supporter of Gaelic culture as a repository of an authentic Scottish identity that transcended any Highland / Lowland division.

MacDiarmid's grandiose pronouncements on Russian and Scottish identity have led one observer to suggest that his mooted parallelism is nothing more than "a vague and overblown sense of racial affinity".[43] The same critic also makes the reasonable argument that, because of his linguistic limitations and especially because of his preference for secondary criticism over original works, MacDiarmid's knowledge of Russian culture never went beyond name-dropping, even in the case of oft-cited authorities such as Dostoevsky, Vladimir Solov'ev, and Lev Shestov.[44]

That said, it is not necessary to appreciate the intricacies of literary history to take something profound from your reading and other scholars have given more generous assessments of the autodidact MacDiarmid's motives and "magpie methods" regarding Russia.[45] Neither a mediated image of Russia nor a tendency to generalisation were unusual at the time. As Beasley argues, following Donald Davie, what Russia offered British writers at this time was not so much new content or even new forms, but rather "a challenge".[46] MacDiarmid rose to this challenge with considerable vim and, in so doing, created a legacy of enviable durability. His reliance on literary criticism, and particularly upon the work of D.S. Mirsky, in preference to translated primary texts in fact allowed MacDiarmid to look beyond the perennial touchstone of Dostoevsky and find common cause with contemporary experimentalists.[47] In making the case for synthetic Scots he cites as inspirations the *skaz* of Aleksei Remizov (translated into English in 1924) and the *zaum'* of the as-yet-untranslated Futurists, who had exploded into notoriety a decade earlier.[48] And, although misunderstandings and misspellings sometimes expose his reliance on limited sources, MacDiarmid really did have a lot in common with these writers, especially the Futurists: he too relished the articulatory jouissance of words-in-themselves and took it as the starting point in a bold bid for a more expressive language; he too combined a certain naive internationalism with a chauvinistic desire to return to a past made remote by foreign intervention; he too frequently fired off essays full of

43 Alexander Mackay, 'MacDiarmid and Russia Revisited', in *Beyond Scotland: New Contexts for Twentieth-Century Scottish Literature*, ed. by Gerard Carruthers, David Goldie and Alastair Renfrew (New York and Amsterdam: Rodopi, 2004), pp. 59–93 (p. 81).

44 Ibid., p. 66, p. 73.

45 McCulloch, *Scottish Modernism and its Contexts*, p. 107. For comprehensive analyses of MacDiarmid's relationship with Russian literature, see Patrick Crotty, '"Like Pushkin, I": Hugh MacDiarmid and Russia', *Studies in Scottish Literature*, 44 (2018), 47–89, and McCarey's *Hugh MacDiarmid and the Russians*.

46 Beasley, *Russomania*, p. 7.

47 MacDiarmid's interest in twentieth-century Russian literature was quite rare among British Modernists. See ibid., p. 353.

48 MacDiarmid, 'The Case for Synthetic Scots', p. 185.

truculent disdain for peers and predecessors.[49] Nothing could be more Futurist in spirit than MacDiarmid's iconoclastic claim that Velimir Khlebnikov was of more value to the future of Scottish letters than the sainted Burns.[50]

Nevertheless, this reliance on mediation also meant that, despite citing them as authorities, MacDiarmid probably never read a word of the Futurists Khlebnikov, Aleksei Kruchenykh, or, until years later, Maiakovskii. These poets did not feature among the translations by Babette Deutsch and Avrahm Yarmolinsky in *Modern Russian Poetry* that served as the basis for MacDiarmid's own Scots versions, such as Blok's 'The Unknown Woman' ('Predchuvstvuiu tebia...', 1901) and 'The Lady Unknown' ('Neznakomka', 1907), Dmitrii Merezhkovskii's 'The Last Trump' ('Trubnyi glas', 1901) and Zinaida Gippius's 'Psyche' ('Ona', 1905). Deutsch and Yarmolinsky instead dismiss the Futurists in their introduction and say, not without reason, that they "resist translation", forcing MacDiarmid to turn to more formally uncomplicated material.[51]

There is some irony in the fact that, in order to perform an avant-garde experiment in poetic language, MacDiarmid had not only to make use of less experimental poetry but also to submit himself to the limiting bottleneck of other translators' choices. Blok's 'I have a presentiment of you...' ('Predchuvstvuiu tebia...', 1901), for instance, gives no hint of the addressee's gender: MacDiarmid's title for it, 'The Unknown Goddess', is a direct consequence of Deutsch's and Yarmolinsky's 'The Unknown Woman'. Furthermore, we see that for all his disdain for English, MacDiarmid was nearly entirely reliant on it, seemingly vindicating Moretti's contention that "movement from one periphery to another (without passing through the centre) is almost unheard of".[52] These ironies should not be read as deficiencies, however. First, as previously suggested, nearly all writing in Scots automatically activates in the reader a consciousness of the English that is *not* being used. For MacDiarmid's synthetic Scots this is especially true: not only do his essays—written in English!—constantly reassert the ascendancy of English while bemoaning its inadequacy, but, since his words are unmoored from any specific Scottish speech community in order to profit

49 For instance, in 'The Case for Synthetic Scots', cited above, MacDiarmid misinterprets the adjective *zaumny* (relating to *zaum'* poetry) as a noun, a mistake that he reprised in the long poem *In Memoriam James Joyce* (1955). See Hugh MacDiarmid, 'In Memoriam James Joyce', in *Complete Poems*, II (1994), ed. by Michael Grieve and W. R. Aitken (Manchester: Carcanet, 1994), pp. 737–805 (p. 745).

50 Hugh MacDiarmid, 'Towards a Synthetic Scots' in *Contemporary Scottish Studies* (Edinburgh: Scottish Educational Journal, 1976), pp. 117–118 (p. 117).

51 Deutsch and Yarmolinsky, 'Introduction', p. xviii. MacDiarmid complained about the omission of Maiakovskii: see Hugh MacDiarmid, 'Básníci Revoluchího [*sic*] Ruska—Breiz Atao', in *The Raucle Tongue: Hitherto Uncollected Prose*, I, ed. by Angus Calder, Glen Murray and Alan Riach (Manchester: Carcanet, 1996), pp. 196–98 (p. 196).

52 Franco Moretti, 'More Conjectures', *New Left Review*, 20 (2003), 73–81 (p. 76).

from "the free genius of any language", the reader is invited to make linguistic connections and comparisons where she finds them, including, naturally and easily, with English.[53]

Second, MacDiarmid's willingness to rework existing translations without understanding the source text was shared by contemporary "provincial modernists" like Ezra Pound, W. B. Yeats, and James Joyce.[54] Like MacDiarmid (and Samuel Beckett too), these writers were conscious of their position at once inside English and outside it, or at least outside its notional centre. Accordingly, as Daniel Katz argues, they turned to translation, even when it was not readily available to them, because it could help prove their wider point that "there is no 'English' but only 'a series of Englishes'".[55] MacDiarmid might have baulked at having his Scots reduced to a subspecies of English, but, whatever its name, the destabilising effect is the same: the centre cannot hold; in fact, the centre might not even exist.[56]

Whereas Pound chose to describe his verses in *Cathay* as "translations" from Chinese, MacDiarmid not only avoided this term, using coy formulations such as "suggested by the Russian", but also omitted all mention of intermediaries and integrated his versions of Blok and Gippius into *A Drunk Man* almost seamlessly.[57] In comparison with Pound, therefore, MacDiarmid's appropriations might appear at first to be a less effective subversion of translation norms. Nevertheless,

---

53 On the relationship of MacDiarmid's Scots poetry to English, see Matthew Hart, *Nations of Nothing But Poetry: Modernism, Transnationalism, and Synthetic Vernacular Writing* (Oxford: Oxford University Press, 2010), p. 10: "its undeniable Scottishness has to be read [...] against the spectral body of English: the language that remains unseen, that the phonemic riches of Scots exceeds, and yet—like the Derridean supplement—that it cannot help referring to and, referring to, affirm".

54 See Steven G. Yao, *Translation and the Languages of Modernism: Gender, Politics, Language* (New York: Palgrave MacMillan, 2002), pp. 10–11 and Venuti, *The Translator's Invisibility*, pp. 164–78.

55 Daniel Katz, 'Ezra Pound's Provincial Provence: Arnaut Daniel, Gavin Douglas, and the Vulgar Tongue', *Modern Language Quarterly*, 73 (2012), 175–99 (p. 181).

56 Not without good reason Casanova treats Irish writers working in English like Yeats, Joyce and Beckett as paradigmatic of the "rupture with the literature of the centre" and a "model of the possibilities contained in outlying spaces". Her analysis has, however, been criticised for a narrow conception of Irish literature and an overemphasis on the importance of the capital of her 'world republic', Paris—a place that MacDiarmid's engagement with Russia, like Pound's engagement with China, entirely bypasses. As such, our example lends weight to Michael Malouf's proposal to "salvage her theory for inter-peripheral comparativism, not by taking the cent out of her system, but rather, by redirecting her system of literary networks as they function through and around a multiplicity of centers)", amongst which, for MacDiarmid, not only London but also Moscow must feature. Michael Malouf, 'Problems with Paradigms: Irish Comparativism and Casanova's "World Republic of Letters"', *New Hibernia Review / Iris Éireannach Nua*, 17 (2013), 48–66 (p. 62).

57 See, for instance, Hugh MacDiarmid, 'The Last Trump', *Complete Poems*, I (1993), p. 29.

MacDiarmid's light touch in reworking his precursors' ponderous English into lively memorable Scots—and the versions have been described as "virtually identical"—can be seen as equally radical since it shows how far the short step from English to Scots can take us.[58] A comparison of stanzas from 'The Lady Unknown' ('Neznakomka', 1907) can demonstrate both this derivativeness and this deviation.

Deutsch and Yarmolinsky	*MacDiarmid*
I guard dark secrets' tortuosities.	*I ha'e dark secrets' turns and twists,*
A sun is given me to hold.	*A sun is gi'en to me to haud,*
An acrid wine finds out the sinuosities	*The whisky in my bluid insists,*
That in my soul were locked of old.	*And spiers my benmaist history, lad.*[59]

MacDiarmid achieves the kind of equivalence that Deutsch and Yarmolinsky lack: not of meaning or even tone—Blok's original is less spirited and demotic—but of poetic impact. Furthermore, much of the force of Blok's poem comes from the juxtaposition of a longing for sublimity with semi-squalid suburban setting. Likewise, MacDiarmid's use of minoritised Scots, and its inclusion in *A Drunk Man*'s longer stream of whisky-fuelled philosophising, grounds the narrative of his poem, and its philosophical allusions, in a locality (albeit an unspecific 'Scottish' one) and a less than refined milieu.[60]

The success of MacDiarmid's translations inspired other poets in the 1920s and 1930s and their versions of Russian verse exhibit a similar blending of the foreign and the familiar. In 'Poem' William Soutar lights on the contrast of urban and rural in Sergei Esenin's 'Yes, now it is decided. Without return…' ('Da, teper' resheno. Bez vozvrata…', 1922) to tell a very Scottish story of forced migration and the ruination of the countryside, using distinctive terms of landscape and cityscape that fix both the location and the subaltern perspective:

58 J. Derrick McClure, 'European Poetry in Scots', in *Scotland in Europe*, ed. by Tom Hubbard and R. D. S. Jack (Leiden: Brill, 2006), pp. 89–104 (p. 93). Fuller analyses of this translation, including its similarities to the intermediary, can be found at McCarey, *MacDiarmid and the Russians*, pp. 72–76; O'Connor, *Haunted English*, pp. 138–40; Crotty, '"Like Pushkin, I"', pp. 55–57; Catherine Kerrigan, *Whaur Extremes Meet: The Poetry of Hugh MacDiarmid, 1920–1934* (Edinburgh: Mercat Press, 1983), pp. 116–18.

59 "I have dark secrets' turns and twists, / A sun is given to me to hold, / The whisky in my blood insists, / And questions my innermost history, lad." Russian: "Glukhie tainy mne porucheny, / Mne ch'e-to solntse vrucheno, / I vse dushi moei izluchiny / Pronzilo terpkoe vino". Aleksandr Blok, *Polnoe sobranie sochinenii i pisem*, ed. by M. L. Gasparov and others, 20 vols (Moscow: Nauka, 1997-), II (1997), 122–23 (p. 123).

60 According to Alan Bold, "Much of the tension of *A Drunk Man* derives from the conflict between the physical and the metaphysical aspects of humankind." Alan Bold, *MacDiarmid: Christopher Murray Grieve, A Critical Biography* (London: Murray, 1988), p. 200.

> The fower thackit wa's I was born in.
> Are stanes on a brae:
> And here in the yowtherin' vennel.
> I am weirded to dee.[61]

As befits a narrative poem about a world-historical event, Goodsir Smith's 'The Twal'' (1959), his version of Blok's 'The Twelve' ('Dvenadtsat'', 1918), preserves more of the specifics of the Russian setting. Nonetheless, his use of Scots and its marked vocabulary—the atheistic refrain "Eh, eh, no cross!" ("Ekh, ekh, bez kresta!") becomes "Nae Kirk for me!"—compels us to reimagine the Revolution as a Scottish affair in a way that neutral, international English never could. Here is Mclean's desired Scoto-Russian revolutionary parallelism in reverse: Petrograd has become a Glasgow.[62]

We see in these examples how synthetic Scots translations frustrate a clear distinction between foreignisation and domestication. These versions, all mediated by an unseen English, have a foreignising effect for speakers of English by estranging our language, using 'marginal resources' to challenge hierarchies. At the same time, despite MacDiarmid's forays into the recherché and the fantastical, these translations use language that projects an image of anti-elitist authenticity, in so doing achieving a certain 'domesticity', not in the sense used by Venuti of replicating hierarchies but rather by promoting the local and 'homely' over the standardised and official. What is more, by combining subversion and 'provincial' familiarity in this way, these translations sublate their own marginality. Far from being the province of unlettered peasants, Scotland is shown to possess a language and a people capable of thinking the thoughts of distant Russian geniuses as their own and even of reincarnating a revolution. Within these translations, Scotland is anything but the periphery of

---

61 "The four thatched walls I was born in / Are stones on hillside: / And here in the reeking alleys / I am fated to die." William Soutar, 'Poem', in *European Poetry in Scotland: An Anthology of Translations*, ed. by Peter France and Duncan Glen (Edinburgh: Edinburgh University Press, 1989), pp. 18–19 (p. 18). Soutar compresses the first two stanzas of the Russian: "Yes! Now it is decided. Without return / I have quit my native fields. / No longer, with winged foliage / Will the poplars ring over me. / My low house stoops over, / My old dog has long since died. / On the windy streets of Moscow, / Know, God has fated me to die." ["Da! Teper' resheno. Bez vozvrata / Ia pokinul rodnye polia. / Uzh ne budut listvoiu krylatoi / Nado mnoiu zvenet' topolia. // Nizkii dom bez menia ssutulitsia, / Staryi pes moi davno izdokh. / Na moskovskikh izognutykh ulitsakh / Umeret', znat', sudil mne Bog."] Sergei Esenin, *Polnoe sobranie sochinenii*, ed. by Iu. L. Prokushev, 7 vols (Moscow: Nauka-Golos, 1995–99), I (1995), pp. 167–68 (p. 167).

62 Sydney Goodsir Smith, 'The Twal'', in *European Poetry in Scotland*, ed. by France and Glen, pp. 64–73 (p. 67); Blok, *Sobranie sochinenii*, ed. by Gasparov and others, V (1999), pp. 7–20 (p. 11). This same poem has also been translated into Scots by Frances Robson: see Alexander Blok, *The Twelve, Owerset Intae Scots*, trans. by Frances Robson (Edinburgh: Mossrig, 2017).

Europe and still less of Britain; instead, it is in direct and equal communion with a great power that itself has become a new global centre.

Nevertheless, in transcending Scotland's marginality, synthetic Scots and MacDiarmid especially could be said to be guilty of 'domestication' in the Venutian sense of concretising hierarchies, since they risk undermining both Scotland's particularity and its internal heterogeneity—the different dialects that people actually speak—in favour of the poet and his exalted, holistic vision. Emulating Dostoevsky, the unifying figure of *A Drunk Man's* protagonist smooths over Scotland's conflicts and contingencies ("and I in turn 'ud be an action / To pit in a concrete abstraction / My country's contrair qualities, / And mak' a unity o' these") and, with tongue in cheek, reveals even its most distinctive-sounding localities to be avatars of a global *Geist* ("I wad ha'e Scotland to my eye / Until I saw a timeless flame / Tak' Auchtermuchty for a name, / And kent that Ecclefechan stood / As pairt o' an eternal mood").[63] Just as MacDiarmid's synthetic Scots treats minoritised lexis as the nucleus of a world language, so his remaking of Russian poetry in Scots as a deliberate manifestation of the hidden kinship of the two nations can be seen as an attempt to expedite a universal state of oneness uniting humanity. In this longing for transcendent connection, MacDiarmid deliberately echoes Dostoevsky's famous address at the opening of the Pushkin monument in 1880, which was quoted at length both in Alexander Brückner's *A Literary History of Russia,* which came out in English in 1908, and in Janko Lavrin's *Dostoevsky and His Creation* (1920).[64] The Russian author then proposed an altogether more mystical model of intercultural contact than that proposed by Casanova and co.: one in which through the agency of a poet of genius equipped with a unique cosmopolitan sympathy and the capacity to be "reincarnated in the spirit of another nation", along with his God-bearing (in the sense of '*narod bogonosets*') people (be they Scots or Russians), all nations may be translated into one.[65].

Edwin Morgan and Mid-century Modernism

While it has become a central pillar of not only MacDiarmid's personal canon but that of twentieth-century Scottish literature, with annotated editions and extensive scholarship, *A Drunk Man* was initially a commercial and critical failure, with fewer than 100 copies of an initial print run of 500 sold in its first year. From the early 1930s MacDiarmid turned away from both Scots and from translation, but in his long search for inspiration and expression he

63 MacDiarmid, 'A Drunk Man Looks at The Thistle', p. 145, p. 144.

64 Alexander Brückner, *A Literary History of Russia*, ed. by Ellis H. Minns, trans. by H. Havelock (New York: Scribner's, 1908), pp. 407–08. See also Crotty, '"Like Pushkin, I..."', p. 56. On Lavrin see Bold, *MacDiarmid*, p. 201.

65 Fedor Mikhailovich Dostoevskii, 'Pushkin (Ocherk)', in Dostoevskii, *Polnoe sobranie sochinenii*, ed. by V. G. Bazanov and others, 30 vols (Moscow: Nauka, 1972–86), XVI, pp. 136–49 (p. 146, p. 147).

never gave up on Russia or the revolutionary possibilities which it offered and which its Caledonian counterpart seemed continually to spurn. One of these wishes did come true, however, although perhaps not as he had hoped. In 1926 MacDiarmid said that "A Scottish Mayakovsky would be a godsend"; in 1972, he got one—with the publication of Edwin Morgan's *Wi' the Haill Voice*, a collection of twenty-five Maiakovskii poems in Scots.[66]

In some ways, Morgan was heir to MacDiarmid's Russophile tradition: not only did he use a dictionary-derived Scots in a significant minority of his translations from Russian, but he also saw in the translation of Russian poetry a chance to unsettle Anglophone complacency. In other ways, however, Morgan was very different: he was equivocal about the merits of synthetic Scots vis-à-vis both English and more localised Scots dialects—a debate that had become so rancorous by the 1950s that a young Morgan described it as an "incubus"—and in a long career of translation he took as his aim "conscientious faithfulness" to the original.[67] He could do this because, along with French, Italian, and German, he had a thorough knowledge of Russian.

The circumstances in which Morgan was working also differed. On the one hand, Modernism as a global literary movement had lost much of its impetus and the invasion of Hungary and revelations about Stalinism in 1956 had taken the gloss off the Soviet project for many (not MacDiarmid—his response was to rejoin the Communist Party).[68] On the other, for some Scots, the Cold War had made both Scottish nationalism and internationalism seem more urgently necessary than ever. Morgan explained the importance of his mission in the introduction to his *Sovpoems* (1961), a collection of translations of poets from the Communist world which featured his first published translations into Scots—of three Maiakovskii poems:

> These translations are issued with the desire to redress a balance—to open the door slightly on a world which political (and in part linguistic) considerations have kept too remote from Western writers and readers—to show, if not throw, a few of the lifelines that have been preserved within the European tradition: lifelines which are now as perilous to refuse as they have usually been thought naïve to accept.[69]

---

66 MacDiarmid, 'Towards a Synthetic Scots', p. 188.

67 Morgan, 'The Beatnik in the Kailyard', in *Essays*, pp. 167–76 (p. 172); Morgan, 'Introductory Note to *Rites of Passage*', in *Collected Translations* (Manchester: Carcanet, 1996), p. 185. On Morgan's language choices, see W. N. Herbert, 'Morgan's Words', in *About Edwin Morgan*, ed. by Robert Crawford and Hamish Whyte (Edinburgh: Edinburgh University Press, 1990), pp. 65–74 (p. 71); Peter France, 'Edwin Morgan and Russian Poetry', *Slavonica*, 25 (2020), 52–61 (p. 54); Colin Nicholson, *Edwin Morgan: Inventions of Modernity* (Manchester and New York: Manchester University Press, 2002), pp. 16–45.

68 Bold, *MacDiarmid*, p. 409.

69 Edwin Morgan, 'Introduction to *Sovpoems*', in *Collected Translations*, pp. 27–31 (p. 27). The translations from Maiakovskii are 'Whit mair?' ('What more?', 'Nu chto

Morgan distances himself from any political motivation—plausibly enough, considering he showed the same enthusiasm for American poetry. Rather, he is excited by the continued ingenuous Modernist optimism that he identifies in Russia's poets, as well as its architects and engineers, and that he hopes to reintroduce to Scotland. For Morgan, Maiakovskii in particular possesses an "unusual combination of wild / *avant-garde* leanings and flashes and something of central human concern".[70] Once again the antagonist is staid English literature, which is said to have lost whatever experimental spark it might have had. In his *Sovpoems* essay, Morgan compares Larkin unfavourably to Evtushenko and proposes that the long-dead Maiakovskii has more vitality than the still extant Eliot.[71]

For his own part, Morgan was more open to linguistic experimentation than his English contemporaries, and, although his poetry as a whole shows ample 'human concern', his most formally unconventional works, including his translations into Scots, exhibit a sort of playful, post-modern detachment that is rare in the almost monomaniacal mythopoesis of Maiakovskii and MacDiarmid. His choice of poems to translate into Scots, for instance, displays a wry awareness of the histories of English, Russian, and Scottish literature: among his first translations in the 1950s were excerpts from *Macbeth* and *Beowulf* in Scots and Burns in English.[72] Working from Russian, he uses Scots for a poem by Vladimir Solov'ev (a nod, surely, to the philosopher's great admirer MacDiarmid), for Pushkin's 'Twa Corbies' ('Two Crows', 'Dva vorona', 1828) itself a translation via French of a Scots ballad, and for Khlebnikov's 'Gaffin-cantrip' ('Laughing-incantation', 'Zakliatie smekhom', 1913), an etymology-obsessed *zaum'* poem. He also employs Scots for famous poems such as Blok's 'Nicht, causey, leerie, pothicar' ('Night, street, lamp, chemist...'; 'Noch', ulitsa, fonar', apteka...', 1912) and Pushkin's 'I loed ye' ('I loved you'; 'Ia vas liubil', 1830), as if deliberately

---

zhe?', 1927), 'Aye but can ye? ('A vy mogli by?', 1913) and 'Wi' the haill voice' ('With the whole voice', 'Vo ves' golos', 1930).

70 Morgan, 'Introduction to *Wi' the Haill Voice: 25 Poems by Vladimir Mayakovsky*', in *Collected Translations*, pp. 105–13 (p. 110). Original emphasis.

71 Morgan, 'Introduction to *Sovpoems*', p. 28. Morgan's negative assessment of the state of English literature is shared by his publisher, Michael Shayer, who in a letter of 5 December 1960 says of Morgan's translations: "there is the missing link!—this is what has been happening since Lawrence died, and Eliot became an English gentleman. This is what we can pick up from." Glasgow, University of Glasgow Archives and Special Collections, MS Morgan, E.7. In a later interview Morgan said that "[...I]n Russian Futurism, perhaps especially in Mayakovsky, there's a sense that the experiment in art—the modernistic experiment in art—is to be linked up with the future, not with the past, and I'm drawn more, in that sense, to European modernism, especially Russian modernism, than to the modernism of Eliot and Pound." Edwin Morgan, *Nothing Not Giving Messages*, ed. by Hamish Whyte (Polygon: Edinburgh, 1990), p. 106.

72 Glasgow, University of Glasgow Archives and Special Collections, MS Morgan, E.1.1 Translated Poems 1937–59.

testing Scots against the very best. Scots is used most commonly and most effectively, however, for poems with a comic or semi-comic sensibility, such as Maiakovskii's 'Maykonferensky's Anectidote' ('Prozasedavshiesia', 1922), or with a distinctive first-person perspective, like the same poet's 'Fiddle-ma-gidgin' ('Violin and a little nervous', 'Skripka i nemnozhko nervno', 1914).[73]

In *Wi' the Haill Voice*, Morgan argues that Scots is well suited to Maiakovskii's vital exuberance because its literature has historically possessed "a vein of fantastic satire".[74] Despite this appeal to literary tradition, however, Scottish and English readers agree that it is in the poet's evident delight in manipulating language as an oral and aural phenomenon that Morgan's versions best capture Maiakovskii's Russian, reproducing its dense consonantal texture and declamatory tone.[75] Indeed, by making the reader sound out unfamiliar words, Morgan's unfamiliar but richly expressive vocabulary resists quiet, contemplative reading and demands to be read aloud, achieving the orality, immediacy, and estrangement that Futurists considered fundamental to good poetry.[76] In fact, critics have suggested that Morgan's vivid text even "overshoots Mayakovsky's wordplay".[77] A related weakness is that, with the possible exception of 'A Richt Respeck for Cuddies' ('A Proper Respect for Horses', 'Khoroshee otnoshenie k loshadiam', 1918), Morgan's consistently boisterous Scots fails to replicate Maiakovskii's ability to juxtapose verbal fireworks with lines of childlike simplicity. Take, for instance, the opening of 'Forcryinoutloud' ('Poslushaite', 1913), in which Morgan's neologism "starnhuid" (starhood) is too elaborate for Maiakovskii's plangent and prosaic rhetorical question "Does it mean that someone wants them to be there?":

> Forcryinoutloud!
> The starns licht up—aa richt:
> does that prove some loon hud to hae it?
> Does it prove some loon mun want their starnhuid?[78]

---

73 Morgan, *Collected Translations*: 'The Wintry Loch o' Saimaa' ['Na Saime zimoi', 1894], p. 334; 'Twa Corbies', p. 325; 'Gaffin-cantrip', p. 335; 'Maykonferensky's Anectidote', pp. 129–31; 'Fiddle-ma-gidgin', pp. 115–16.

74 Morgan, 'Introduction to *Wi' the Haill Voice*,' p. 113.

75 McClure, 'European Poetry in Scots', p. 99; George Hyde, 'Mayakovsky in English Translation', *Translation and Literature*, 1 (1992), 84–93.

76 Maiakovskii explains the importance of spoken performance to his poetry in his manual 'How Verses Are Made' ['Kak delat' stikhi']. See Vladimir Maiakovskii, *Polnoe sobranie sochinenii*, 13 vols (Moscow: Khudozhestvennaia literatura, 1955–61), XII (1959), 81–117 (p. 113).

77 France, 'Morgan and Russian Poetry', p. 53. See also Stephen Mulrine, 'Mayakovsky and Morgan', in *Frae Ither Tongues*, ed. by Findlay, pp. 146–79 (p. 156).

78 "For crying out loud! / The stars light up—all right: / does that prove some wrong had to have it? Does it prove some rogue must want their starhood?" Russian: "Poslushaite! / Ved', esli zvezdy zazhigaiut—/ znachit—eto komu-nibud'

For Morgan as for MacDiarmid, English plays the part of unspoken intermediary and interlocutor: he translated 'A Proper Respect for Horses' into English some fourteen years before its publication in *Wi' the Haill Voice*.[79] But the fact that Morgan is using Scots in a playful search for equivalence, not, like MacDiarmid, as a way of inaugurating a new literary epoch, means that he is less dismissive about English, both using it within his Scots versions to ventriloquise negative characters or pastiche hackneyed poetry and acknowledging that, for much of his audience, it is the norm. Both *Sovpoems* and *Wi' the Haill Voice* were published in England and featured glosses of Scots vocabulary (although so did the first edition of *Drunk Man*).[80] Indeed *Wi' the Haill Voice* served as the foundation for a long and fruitful relationship with the poetry press Carcanet (based first in Oxford and then Manchester) and its publisher Michael Schmidt, who would later acknowledge Morgan's considerable contribution to the press's survival and success.[81] One sign of the collection's influence and enduring popularity (amongst a select readership) was its reissue in 2016, to positive notices in *The Guardian* and elsewhere.[82]

In his willingness to speak to both English and Scottish audiences in this way, Morgan could be said to anticipate in part the instrumental adoption of vernacular modes in Scottish fiction of the 1990s, which often "ducks the question of separateness (from English/English literature), to cultivate linguistic and literary difference as a flexible end in itself".[83] But the slipperiness of Scots in relation to Venutian foreignisation and domestication also has a different, if no less significant, function for Morgan. First, writing in Scots allows him to remain true to his professed "sense of close and deep obligation" to the original (a sympathy to the source text that Venuti would scorn) while still producing poetry that effects a Modernist estrangement of its own.[84] Given Morgan's willingness to translate Maiakovskii's later, less verbally experimental

nuzhno?" Maiakovskii, *PSS*, I, pp. 60–61 (p. 60). A more literal rendering of the full Russian quotation would be: "Listen! / So, if the stars light up / Does it mean that someone needs that? / Does that mean someone wants them to exist?"

79 Glasgow, University of Glasgow Archives and Special Collections, MS Morgan E. 1.1.1—Translated Poems 1937–59. Most of the poems published in *Wi' the Haill Voice* were translated between 1959 and 1961 (not coincidentally, the peak of Soviet success in the space race). See Nicholson, *Edwin Morgan*, p. 66.

80 Morgan argued unsuccessfully for the glossaries to be omitted when his Maiakovskii translations were reprinted in *Collected Translations*, describing such annotations as "fussy information-bytes [that] take away from the poetry". Quoted in Robyn Marsack, 'Publishing Edwin Morgan', *Scottish Literary Review*, 4 (2012), 35–52 (p. 47).

81 Marsack, 'Publishing Edwin Morgan', p. 51.

82 'Poem of the week: "Aye but can ye", by Vladimir Mayakovsky, *The Guardian*, 16 October 2017, https://www.theguardian.com/books/2017/oct/16/poem-of-the-week-ay-but-can-ye-by-vladimir-mayakovsky.

83 Hames, *Literary Politics*, p. 248.

84 Morgan, 'Introductory Note to *Rites of Passage*', p. 185.

verse, one might even object that by "outmaiakovskii-ing Maiakovskii" Morgan creates complexity where there is none in the Russian.[85] But in this way Morgan, who frequently cited the Futurists as inspiration for his own poetry, can display fidelity not only to the literal meaning of Maiakovskii's words but also to the Russian avant-garde's commitment to linguistic innovation and the disruption of convention.

In accordance with the Futurist preference, readers of *Wi' the Haill Voice* are encouraged by the strangeness of the words on the page to read them aloud and get a sense of the poem by ear alone. They have another option too, however: they can also use the glossaries diligently to decode its mysteries. In both cases, the reader acts just as a language-learner would. In this way, as Peter McCarey observes, Morgan "gives us not Mayakovsky as the ideal Russian reader would understand him, but Mayakovsky as Morgan found him—full of strange invention, glinting with unfamiliar words."[86]

For a moment, Morgan's Scots allows even monolingual English-speakers, used to understanding and being understood, to experience both the discomfort of incomprehension, or near-comprehension, and its potential rewards. Although this dislocation effect is achieved by much difficult poetry, the cross-cultural context adds further complexity. Morgan's Scots could be compared to the imaginative use of language by writers in 'English' from Africa and the Indian subcontinent and be ascribed to Rey Chow's category of "the xenophone", that is writing that emerges from the experience of colonisation and which embraces its divergence from 'standard' English to form "a creative domain of languaging [...] that draws its sustenance from mimicry and adaptation and bears in its accents the murmur, the passage, of diverse found speeches" and which as such produces "linguistic multiplicities" that serve "as unmistakable clues to a collective refashioning of that mass experience known as postcoloniality".[87]

What is more, by refusing to treat equivalence with 'native speaker' perceptions as the gold standard in translation, Morgan not only frees the reader from the narrow confines of English, but also liberates Maiakovskii from Russia. This deterritorialisation is fitting for a poet who, thanks to his close relationship with the Soviet project, became a global export. Far from making a Scottish Maiakovskii, in fact, Morgan's Scots allows the English-speaker to see the true face of the multinational Maiakovskii revered by non-Russians—the

85 Mulrine, 'Mayakovsky and Morgan', p. 156.

86 Peter McCarey, 'Edwin Morgan the Translator', in *About Edwin Morgan*, ed. by Crawford and Whyte, pp. 90–104 (p. 101).

87 Rey Chow, *Not Like a Native Speaker: On Languaging as a Postcolonial Experience* (New York: Columbia University Press, 2014), p. 59, p. 60. For a discussion (that shares with Chow a sensitivity to global power relations) of the potential benefits of failing to understand, see Alison Phipps, 'Linguistic Incompetence: Giving an Account of Researching Multilingually', *International Journal of Applied Linguistics*, 23 (2012), 329–41.

revolutionary soul who inspired Julia Kristeva, Diego Rivera, and Frank O'Hara; the anti-racist icon translated by Langston Hughes; the gnomic sage encountered by William Carlos Williams in New York intoning "words that could be felt, if not understood, and that could cross cultural and linguistic divides".[88]

The Post-Soviet Period

The prominence of MacDiarmid and Morgan can obscure the fact that "synthetic Scots", their inventive invented language, was not the only game in town for translators into Scots. Alongside it was the work of speakers of Scots who brought international poetry into local idioms such as Shetlandic, Doric, and Glaswegian. By analysing the work of poets such as Robert Garioch, Tom Scott, and William Tait, Sanderson has shown that the triadic model of Scottish literature "has to be rewritten slightly, acknowledging the plurality, as opposed to the singularity, of the Scottish 'minor' utterance"—a plurality that runs counter to the risk inherent in the synthetic Scots agenda that local linguistic diversity might be suppressed and that an anti-colonial linguistic project might metamorphose into a "quasi-colonial situation, in which individuals continue to find themselves in an unsatisfactorily peripheral relation to the new centre".[89] Until the twenty-first century, these localised versions seem to have been less popular when working from Russian but something of their effectiveness—and their distance from the exuberance of Morgan's Maiakovskii—can be found in the translations of Alastair Mackie (1925–95). As in his own verse, Mackie makes use of the "inspiredly plain authenticity of his own working-class, or perhaps lower middle-class, Scots utterance" to capture the simplicity and occasional solemnity of poets Osip Mandel'shtam, Fedor Tiutchev, and Anna Akhmatova.[90]

This embrace of diversity within Scots has become increasingly prominent with the waning of MacDiarmid's influence since the 1970s. Accordingly, dialectal variety represents one of the more salient trends in translation from Russian in the past thirty years (although translations into English still predominate), as a number of recent initiatives show. A sonnet exchange in 2016–17 organised by the British Council, in which Scottish and Russian poets translated each other's work (via a bridge translation) showcases Christine De Luca's distinctive Shetlandic, although it does not announce it as such.[91]

88 Quoted in Lee, *Ethnic Avant-garde*, p. 52.

89 Stewart Sanderson, 'Poems Chiefly in the Scottish Dialectic', p. 53. See also Stewart Sanderson, 'Peripheral Centre or Central Periphery: Two Approaches to Modern Scots Translation', *Comparative Critical Studies*, 11 (2014), 93–108.

90 Roderick Watson, 'Scottish Poetry 1987–1989', *Studies in Scottish Literature*, 25 (1990), 218–45 (p. 223); for Mackie's translations, see *European Poetry in Scotland*, ed. by France and Glen, pp. 129–37.

91 A description of this event may be found here: https://literature.britishcouncil.org/blog/2016/to-russia-with-poets-sonnet-exchange/.

Another collaborative Russo-Scottish production, also making use of bridge translations—a practice that is still the norm, if not the rule—was 2014's *After Lermontov: Translations for the Bicentenary*, which, as MacDiarmid had once done, used the Russian Romantic's Scottish roots as a point of departure for closer connection between the two countries.[92] Here too the numerous Scots translations interspersed among the English are presented as "Scots", but their varied lexis and orthography reflect both the translator's personal preference (an inevitability in an unstandardised language) and, at times, their different regional origins, for instance in the Ayrshire Scots of Rab Wilson.[93] Many of the Scots poets featured in these collections (as well as this author) also took part in a 2020 event, 'Dr Chekhov's Prescription', in which the playwright—who, as a staple of the English stage is perhaps the Russian classic most thoroughly domesticated in Britain—was thoroughly defamiliarised by versions in Gaelic and in regionally specific varieties of Scots from Fife, Ayrshire, and the North-East (Doric).

The diversity of dialect has been accompanied by a slight broadening of generic range in the past thirty years. Like poetry, drama has been more frequently translated into Scots and Scotticised English than prose, particularly in the latter part of the twentieth century.[94] In the Russian context, while broadly 'in English', versions of Anton Chekhov's *Three Sisters* (*Tri sestry*, 1901) by Liz Lochhead and John Byrne, as well as Byrne's version of Nikolai Gogol's *The Government Inspector* (*Revizor*, 1836) have used Scottish settings and accompanying linguistic touches in part as a way of interrogating Anglo-Scottish relations.[95] Even narrative prose has made an appearance, with Colin Donati's translation of a chapter of *Crime and Punishment* (*Prestuplenie i nakazanie*, 1866)—a somewhat inevitable choice, perhaps, given the importance of Dostoevsky in Scots-language Russophilia.

Increasing dialectal diversity is a product not only of the fading influence of synthetic Scots, but also of related changes in Scotland's cultural politics. New authorities have emerged with new ways of expressing Scotland's specificity—its singularity in Britain and the world, as well the internal variation between classes and regions. Among others, the poets Liz Lochhead and Tom Leonard and the prose writers James Kelman and Irvine Welsh have catalysed the wider shifts in thinking about language and national identity that have accompanied

92 Peter France, 'Introduction' in Mikhail Lermontov, *After Lermontov: Translations for the Bicentenary*, ed. by Peter France and Robyn Marsack (Manchester: Carcanet, 2014).

93 See Lermontov, 'Ma Kintra', trans. by Rab Wilson, in *After Lermontov*, p. 105. The author is grateful to Dr Tom Hubbard for private correspondence related to regional variations in this volume.

94 A good overview of twentieth-century translations of classical drama into Scots is available in *Frae Ither Tongues*, ed. by Findlay.

95 See Ksenija Horvat, 'Scottish Demotics and Russian Soul: Liz Lochhead's Adaptation of Chekhov's *Three Sisters*', *Studies in Scottish Literature*, 44 (2018), 29–36.

the rise of Scottish nationalism as a political force and, consequently, devolution as a constitutional reality and the 2014 independence referendum as a historical moment. The complexities of these changes are beyond the scope of this essay, but one can see how translation from Russian, in its gradual move away from the separatist (but internationalist) project of a single synthetic Scots and towards a celebration of internal diversity, coincides with the emergence in Scottish literature of what scholar Scott Hames has called "a new idiom of national subalternity combining the demand for autonomy with the recognition of difference". This celebration of "authenticated marginality" is also evident in the Scottish National Party's promotion of a multiracial, multilingual civic nationalism and, Hames argues, shares with the politics of devolution a willingness to accept representation instead of actual power.[96]

Hames contextualises this self-confident but ineffectual marginality within two global trends: "the postmodern valorisation of 'difference' and marginality" and a post-Cold War shift in "the nationalism of the stateless", in which "stateless nations and regions came to be identified with the modern and even post-modern".[97] This new valence was itself partly precipitated by the break-up of the Soviet Union, an event which terminated any lingering sentimental connection between the Russian language and emancipatory politics, not least because the emergence of (more or less) linguistically autonomous states out of the former USSR made obvious the extent to which in its own region, despite its association with revolution and with anti-hegemonic internationalism, Russian had continued to be a language of imperial domination. Historically, many Scottish writers have chosen to overlook the awkward fact that, in geopolitical terms, Russian's closest linguistic counterpart is English, not Scots.[98] This may now be changing, as Scottish translators begin to find more compelling parallels with nations whose political and linguistic sovereignty has been infringed by Russia and Russian. In 2021, for instance, an event at the StAnza poetry festival in St Andrews featured translations into English, Gaelic, and Shetlandic of poetry written in Ukrainian and the related language/dialect Hutsul (we note the characteristic attentiveness to intranational diversity). While Russian here is, for good reason, ignored, the opposite is true of *Alindarka's Children* (2021) (*Dzetsi Alindarki*, 2014) by the Belarusian author Alhierd Bacharevič, a complex tale of linguistic and cultural oppression and resistance in which Russian is used for the dominant *iazyk* and Belarusian for the forbidden *mova*. In their recent

96 Hames, *Literary Politics*, p. 267, p. 295, p. 271.

97 Michael Keating, 'Nationalist Movements in Comparative Perspective', in *The Modern SNP: From Protest to Power*, ed. by Gerry Hasan (Edinburgh: Edinburgh University Press, 2009), pp. 204–18 (p. 206).

98 This observation is also made in Mackay, 'MacDiarmid and Russia Revisited', p. 67. Steven Lee uses the example of Maiakovskii to explore Soviet-era tensions between Russian linguistic chauvinism and internationalism. See Lee, *Ethnic Avant-Garde*, p. 55.

translation of this novel, Jim Dingley and Petra Reid replicate this relationship, using English as the *lingo* and Scots as the minoritised *leid,* interlarding the text with quotations from Scots poetry, including MacDiarmid's *Drunk Man.*[99] In some ways, indeed, this translation marks a return to the cultural and linguistic inclusivity of synthetic Scots, if not its universalist ambitions: Reid, who was responsible for the Scots elements of the translation, describes her omnivorous approach to the language as "MacDiarmid lite".[100]

These recent developments show a welcome tendency to engage with Russia and Eastern Europe as real, untidy places, rather than as ideological caricatures. As such, we can see the potential , as yet largely untapped, for a bilateral process in which translation helps to rewild Russia—revealing its internal diversity and supranational entanglements, to foreign and domestic audiences. They also show that the meaning of Russia has changed. In Scotland as elsewhere, Russia's role as an abundant source of wild rebukes to conventional taste—Lermontov's fusion of "romantic imagination and stern reality", Dostoevsky's "confused, diffuse, tumultuous" soulfulness, Maiakovskii's optimistic Socialism—belongs to history.[101]

Nevertheless, translation involves borrowing from the past as well as from other cultures, and these living fossils, can, like their descendants, still find new niches in Scotland's changing literary ecosystem, if translators do their job right. And, as *Alindarka's Children* suggest, the Scots translations of the twentieth century have left behind a strong legacy. First, as with *Wi' the Haill Voice* and Carcanet, a small publisher can have a big impact: *Alindarka's Children* was one of only five books released by Edinburgh's Scotland Street Press in 2020, but it won an English PEN award for translation and was reviewed in the *New York Review of Books.* Second, all the texts discussed above have shown that wildness comes not just from *what* you translate, but *how* you do it, and that a translator sensitive to her linguistic environment can transform it: not only by nurturing endangered diversity, but also by challenging the 'naturalness' of assumptions about languages' boundaries and capabilities. This has profound implications

---

99 *Iazyk* is Russian for 'language', like *mova* in Belarusian, *leid* in Scots, and 'tongue' in English.

100 Petra Reid, 'A Note from the Scots Translator', in Alhierd Bacharevič, *Alindarka's Children (Things Will Be Bad)*, trans. by Jim Dingley and Petra Reid (Edinburgh: Scotland Street Press, 2020), pp. xiii-xiv (p. xiii). Reid says she wants "to explore 'Scots' in different cultural contexts by moving freely between centuries and genres". See also blog post XI at https://scotlandstreetpress.com/alindarkas-children-blog/.

101 Virginia Woolf, 'The Russian Point of View', in Woolf, *Collected Essays*, ed. by Leonard Woolf, 4 vols (Hogarth Press: London, 1966), I (1966), pp. 238–46 (p. 242); Hugh MacDiarmid, 'Lermontov: A Scoto-Russian Genius', in *The Raucle Tongue: Hitherto Uncollected Prose*, ed. by Angus Calder, Glen Murray and Alan Riach, 2 vols (Manchester: Carcanet, 1996), I (1996), pp. 60–64 (p. 60). MacDiarmid is here quoting Maurice Baring.

for ongoing debates about language and identity in Scotland—and beyond. The standard English that was attacked by MacDiarmid and then slyly undermined by Morgan is now, in its internationalised form, more dominant, more 'central', than ever. The example of Russian poetry in Scots tells us that a creative attentiveness to overlaps and intersections both between distant cultures and between contiguous tongues can, on paper at least, help to redraw global maps of influence and make the whole wild world an untidier place.

Spain

Countess Emilia Pardo Bazán (1851–1921): The Single-handed Populariser of Russian Literature in Spain

Margaret Tejerizo

What am I working on just now? I am in the heart of Russia. I want to make a study of that strange and curious literature [...] I think that I am one of the few people in Spain who can look at what is happening abroad.

Emilia Pardo Bazán, 1886.[1]

Look, daughter, we men are very selfish, and if they ever tell you that there are things that men can do which women cannot, tell such people that it is a lie, because there cannot be two sets of morality for the two sexes.[2]

Con esta intención salí / de Moscovia... [I left Muscovy / With this intention....

Pedro Calderón de la Barca, 1636.[3]

1 ["¿En qué trabajo ahora? ... Estoy en el corazón de Rusia. Quiero hacer un estudio sobre esa extraña y curiosa literatura. [...] En España creo ser una de las pocas personas que tiene la cabeza para mirar lo que pasa en el extranjero."] From a letter by Bazán to the Catalan writer (and her childhood friend) Narcís Oller (12 October, 1896), cited by Isabel Burdiel in her monograph *Emilia Pardo Bazán* (Barcelona: Penguin, 2019), p. 267. Unless otherwise attributed, all translations from Spanish are my own.

2 ["Mira, hija mía, los hombres somos muy egoístas, y si te dicen alguna vez que hay cosas que pueden hacer los hombres y las mujeres no, di que es mentira, porque no puede haber dos morales para dos sexos."] Sara Herran, who coordinated a special non-paginated supplement (to mark the anniversary of Pardo Bazán's death) of the women's magazine *Glamour* (Madrid, June 2021) quotes these words, spoken by Pardo Bazán's father to his daughter.

3 Calderón de la Barca, *La vida es sueño/Life is a Dream*, ed. by María del Mar Cortés Timoner (Barcelona: Austral, 2014), p.64.

 https://doi.org/10.11647/OBP.0340.16

Two Monumental Endings... And a New Beginning.

A certain vague notion of 'Russia'—as a distant, snow-covered and exotic land—may have entered Spanish sensibilities as early as 1636 with the publication of Pedro Calderón de la Barca's (1600–81) tragedy *Life is a Dream* (*La vida es sueño*, 1636), in which one of the main 'dramatic locations' mentioned is the fantastically distant "Moscovia" (Muscovy).[4] In today's Madrid, however, certain monuments and memorial plaques offer 'unspoken tributes' to the four people who, speaking figuratively, laid the foundations for a much deeper cultural relationship between Russia and Spain. This new awareness began, albeit slowly and hesitantly at first, to flourish in the later nineteenth century.[5] A statue of politician Emilio Castelar (1832–99), whose 1881 study *Contemporary Russia* (*La rusia contemporánea*) was crucial for establishing greater political and social understanding of Russia in Spain, towers over a main road junction.[6] A beautiful statue of Aleksandr Pushkin (1799–1837) stands in pensive mode in one of Madrid's small parks, positioned directly opposite his Spanish 'counterpart', the Romantic poet Gustavo Adolfo Bécquer (1836–70), as though the two were engaged in some profound poetic dialogue.[7] Indeed, setting aside the earlier 1832 Spanish translation of Gavrila Derzhavin's 1784 poem 'God' ('Bog'), 'Metel'' ('The Blizzard'), one of Pushkin's *Tales of Belkin* (*Povesti Belkina*, 1830) has the honour of being the first work of Russian literature to be translated into Spanish (as 'El turbión de nieve'). It was not a direct translation from the Russian; French was the medium for the rather flat and lifeless Spanish version of the vivacious original.[8] A statue to novelist Juan Valera (1824–1905) stands in the Paseo de Recoletos; Valera's *Letters from Russia* (*Cartas desde Rusia*, 1856) was one of the first Spanish-language works to describe direct personal experience of life in Russia. Finally, not far from Valera (although, in life, they

4 Calderon's play is likely to have been introduced into Russia early, by Polish Jesuits. The latest Russian translation was done by Russian poet Natalia Vanjanen in 2021; this version was performed in Moscow in the autumn of that year. It is a verse translation which clearly attempts to build creative and literary bridges between the two cultures by subtly referencing works by Pushkin, Griboedov and Nadezhda Durova.

5 2012 was designated as a special year for the celebration of Russian and Spanish cultures. Many new translations of Russian literature were made in that year.

6 For more details about Castelar's work, see Margaret Tejerizo, *The Influence of Russian Literature on Spanish Authors in the Nineteenth and Twentieth Centuries: Reception, Translation, Inspiration* (Lewiston: Edwin Mellen Press, 2007); hereafter, *Influence*. These details can be found in various sections of the first two chapters.

7 See, for example, Margaret Tejerizo, 'Lo exótico se trastoca en familiar: La presencia de la literatura rusa en la Generación del 98 con especial hincapié en páginas escogidas de Miguel de Unamuno', in *1898: Entre la crisi d'identitat i la modernització*, ed. by Joaquim Molas and others, 2 vols (Barcelona: L'Abadia de Montserrat, 1998), II (2000), pp. 395–401.

8 Ibid.

were literary rivals), stands a statue of Countess (doña) Emilia Pardo Bazán, whose single-handed role as the major populariser of Russian literature in Spain is the main topic of this essay. Pardo Bazán also enjoys a memorial plaque at 33 Calle Princesa and another at 35 Calle San Bernardo, each noting (somewhat implausibly) that she died in that location in 1921![9] Important threads connecting Spanish-Russian literary and cultural relations between Spain and Russia have been left dangling for many years. There are, of course, numerous reasons for this—including the vast geographical distances that separated the countries, linguistic and religious differences, and their harsh political regimes. Yet often, on closer inspection, one finds that these two countries have more cultural similarities than differences. Much as Russia did, Spain relied on France for cultural and intellectual inspiration; as mentioned above, Russian literature first entered Spain via French as a pivot language.

It must be stressed that Pardo Bazán was not a translator of Russian literature; she was, nonetheless, an excellent linguist who knew French, Italian and indeed German well enough to translate Heine into Spanish—besides being bilingual in Castilian Spanish and in her native Galician.[10] However, her three lectures and her later essays on Russian culture and literature almost immediately inspired a new wave of interest in her subject, not only in Spain but in the wider Hispanic world. By the time her essays were published, the major novels of Lev Tolstoy (1828–1910), Fedor Dostoevsky (1821–81), and Ivan Turgenev (1818–83) had made their way into Spain (largely as French translations); not until the early 1890s did the first direct translations of Russian writers begin to flourish. Inspired by her great love of Russian literature, Countess Emilia Pardo Bazán shared with her fellow Spaniards and also with the much wider Spanish-speaking reading public in Spanish America an excellent survey of the history, culture and literature of Russia—first of all in spoken form, through her lectures, and then later with their publication as essays—and she did so with great humility, aware that she was reading in translation and that she had never visited Russia.

At best, Pardo Bazán's work has been undervalued by her fellow Spaniards; at worst ignored. But by a curious quirk of fate, Isabel Burdiel, at the very start of her recent biography of Pardo Bazán, makes a link between the latter and Russia when she relates how the Russian-Jewish author and journalist Il'ia Ehrenburg, after leaving Odesa in 1908 for South America, accidentally encountered one of her books in his first 'home' in Santiago de Chile:

9 See Burdiel, *Emilia Pardo Bazán*, p. 15.

10 Among her many other achievements and ground-breaking literary works, she was the first Spanish woman to write detective fiction; as will be noted, she greatly admired Dostoevsky's depictions of the 'criminal' mind. A full scholarly study of the possible impact of Dostoevsky's writings on Pardo Bazán's own fiction is long overdue. Likewise, an examination of Dostoevsky's potential influence on some of her detective stories would be a fruitful academic exercise.

> [H]e could not [...] even read Spanish but he tried his best [...] and [...] for him it was a strange world yet at the same time a familiar one. He was surprised that the author was a woman. He did not discover until later that she was also a passionate admirer of the Russian novel.[11]

This contribution will re-read some of Pardo Bazán's contributions to this field and re-evaluate their importance.

Where It All Began: 1921 to 2021...

On 12 May 1921, the well-known Spanish writer, essayist, champion of women's rights and literary critic Countess Emilia Pardo Bazán died in her home at 27 Calle Princesa, today one of Madrid's busiest streets. She had lived and worked there for the last four years of her life. A little further down Calle Princesa, opposite her last dwelling-place, stands a large statue erected to Countess Pardo Bazán in 1995, engraved from 'The Women of Madrid and Argentina'. Although Pardo Bazán was born in La Coruña, Galicia on 16 September 1851, her adulthood was spent mostly in Madrid. Her prosperous parents encouraged her, unusually for girls of that period, to study and develop her talents. She thus gained self-confidence from an early age. Reading and writing were always her favourite pastimes. Throughout her long life she dedicated herself to literary and intellectual activities, swiftly establishing herself as a successful novelist, essayist, and advocate of women's freedoms in Spain; in addition, she was one of the first writers in Spain to use a typewriter, and Spain's first female university professor (at the Central University of Madrid). Exceptionally for women of those times, she frequently travelled unaccompanied beyond Spain—she notes in the opening section of her volume of lectures and essays on Russian culture that she greatly envied "the daughters of Great Britain" (*"las hijas de la Gran Bretaña"*) since they were able to travel freely.[12] Paris was one of her favourite destinations and it was during a visit to the French capital in winter 1885 that her great, lifelong passion for Russian culture began—specifically, after reading Dostoevsky's *Crime and Punishment* in French.[13] Pardo Bazán's close relationship

11 ("[N]i [...] leía español, pero se esforzó [...] y [...] le resultó un mundo al tiempo extraño y familiar. Le asombró que el autor fuese una mujer. Hasta más tarde no supo que era también una apasionada de la novela rusa.") Burdiel, *Emilia Pardo Bazán*, p. 15.

12 Emilia Pardo Bazán, *La revolución y la novela en Rusia : (lecturas en el Ateneao de Madrid)* (Madrid: Tello, 1887), p. 11, http://dbooks.bodleian.ox.ac.uk/books/PDFs/300893789.pdf. This edition was personally approved by Pardo Bazán.

13 "I recall that it was in March 1885 that a Russian novel fell into my hands, which produced a profound impression upon me: Dostoevsky's *Crime and Punishment* [...]." ("Recuerdo que fué cuando cayó en mis manos una novela rusa, que me produjo impresió muy honda: *Crimen y castigo*, de Dostoyeusky [...].") Pardo Bazán, *La revolución y la novela*, p. 3.

with Spain's most popular and well-known novelist of that era, Benito Pérez de Galdós (1843–1920), placed her securely at the centre of literary developments (and polemics) of those times. Undoubtedly Galdós's own admiration for the works of Tolstoy and Turgenev derived in great part from his contacts with Pardo Bazán.[14] She was also well acquainted with one of the other outstanding authors of that period, Leopoldo Alas, known as 'Clarín' (1852–1901), as discussed below.[15] But not all male authors of that time condoned Pardo Bazán's daring literary ventures beyond the Spanish frontier; the novelist Juan Valera was one of her harshest critics, as will be seen below.

Many events were held in Spain during 2021 to mark the centenary of Pardo Bazán's death, including major exhibitions, dramatisations of some of her works, journalism, and academic articles. And yet one of her greatest achievements has barely been mentioned: the transmission of Russian culture and literature to Spain and the Hispanic world. Even Isabel Burdiel's biography seems almost to dismiss Pardo Bazán's carefully constructed, well-researched, and original work as a cultural intermediary between Spain and Russia as possessing little more than "historical interest" (*"interés histórico"*) for contemporary readers.[16] Doña Emilia accomplished her wide-ranging critique of Russian culture single-handedly, despite opposition from male contemporaries who judged her endeavour to be, at best, inappropriate. As I will discuss below, she delivered three polished, stimulating, and informative lectures on Russian culture in April 1887, which were later published in essay form. All of her main written sources for this work are listed in the bibliography accompanying the published lectures; in the spoken version, she repeatedly mentioned how her personal encounters with intellectuals and scholars (mostly in Paris) had inspired and encouraged her. Sadly, even during Pardo Bazán's centenary, no separate edition of these lectures was available for purchase in any of Madrid's main bookstores, although new editions of her other works were published to mark this anniversary.[17]

---

14 Benito Pérez de Galdós admitted to having acquired a great admiration for Dostoevsky and Turgenev after the publication of Pardo Bazán's essays. His own novel *Doña Perfecta* (1876) has certain similarities with Turgenev's *Fathers and Children* [*Ottsy i deti*, 1862] with the interesting difference that the older generation in Galdós's novel is represented by a woman. I discuss this in more detail in *Influence* (esp. Chapter Four).

15 Alas was accused of plagiarism as his novel *The Regent's Wife* (*La Regenta*, 1885) was considered too close to Tolstoy's *Anna Karenina* (1878). It is one of the great nineteenth-century 'novels of adultery' and both protagonists are called Anna/Ana; but there, in my opinion, the similarity ends.

16 Burdiel, *Emilia Pardo Bazán*, p. 269.

17 It was surprising that in the bookshop of the Spanish National Library which had acquired many editions of her work to sell during its exhibition 'The Challenge of Modernity' ('El reto de la modernidad'), which was planned to mark Pardo Bazán's centenary in 2021, lacked a copy of these essays.

On 6 September 1921, four months after Pardo Bazán's death, the writer Carmen Laforet, whose award-winning novel *Nothing* (*Nada*, 1944) broke new ground for women's literature in post-Civil War Spain, was born in Barcelona (the centenary of Laforet's birth was also celebrated throughout Spain in 2021). Pardo Bazán and Laforet, besides their remarkable contributions to enhancing the position and esteem of women writers at two different critical points in Spanish history, are linked in two further and perhaps somewhat unexpected ways: firstly, by a so-called 'university', the Madrid Athenaeum (Ateneo) in the Calle del Prado, and secondly by Dostoevsky. In the Madrid Ateneo, over three nights in April 1887 (13, 20, and 27 April) Pardo Bazán delivered her lectures on Russian literature and culture, published later that year as *The Revolution and the Novel in Russia* (*La revolución y la novela en Rusia*, 1887). This volume became the first informed, organised, and thorough Spanish-language presentation of Russian literature and culture. Pardo Bazán was the second woman ever to address the Ateneo, and eighteen years later, in 1905, she became its first female member. Still later, in the library of the Madrid Ateneo, Carmen Laforet would write her novel *Nothing* almost in a single sitting. Pardo Bazán claimed that Dostoevsky, whose novels she had read in French translation during her visit to Paris in the winter of 1885, had inspired her ever-increasing passion for Russian literature. Laforet's *Nothing*, with its disturbing, claustrophobic house and irrational, disturbed characters, set in the dark, winding and sinister streets of Barcelona, has long deserved a detailed comparative study alongside Dostoevsky's vision of St Petersburg.[18] (Dostoevsky's *Crime and Punishment* was translated into Catalan directly from the Russian by Andreu Nin in 1929; only in 2021 did Miquel Cabal Guarro complete a new version.)[19] Today, Emilia Pardo Bazán is the only woman commemorated in the Ateneo with a portrait, among the vast gallery of male politicians, writers, and public figures. I shall now turn to examine her contribution to the popularisation of Russian literature in Spain and in the wider Hispanic world.

Russian 'Literary Wars'—And Some Alliances

> She had a remarkable memory, a curiosity that knew no bounds, a superb intelligence and a hot temper: she fought with most of her colleagues for her own rights and for women's rights in general [...].[20]

18 A detailed study of the presence of Dostoevsky in the fictional world of Carmen Laforet is long overdue.

19 There was an excellent discussion about the Nin version and a presentation of the latest translation in the Spanish daily newspaper, *ABC*, 22 May 2021, p 8. On the translation of Dostoevsky into Catalan, see Miquel Cabal Guarro's chapter in the present volume.

20 "Tenía una memoria prodigiosa, una curiosidad infinita, una inteligencia portentosa y mucho genio: se peleó con casi todos sus colegas, por sus derechos

Although Emilia Pardo Bazán was born in Galicia, she moved to Madrid as soon as possible in the hope of establishing herself as a writer. The plaque above her first Madrid residence (35 Calle San Bernardo) notes that she hosted many important literary salons, bringing together major intellectuals of the period. When her marriage (to her childhood friend José Quiroga) ended in 1886 after sixteen years, Pardo Bazán was able to support herself from family legacies and via her profession as a novelist and essayist. Unusually and fortunately for a woman at that time, she could lead an almost fully financially independent life in the capital. By 1887, she had already become known as a novelist and critic. Her frequent journeys to Paris consolidated her cultural authority. While the importance of France as a cultural reference for Spain was noted above, by the late nineteenth century Spain was seeking to discard the sense of French intellectual supremacy. While the philosopher José Ortega y Gasset (1883–1955) would later describe Spain and Russia as "two 'pueblo' races, ("dos razas 'pueblo'") races where the common people predominate—that is, races that suffer from an obvious and continuous lack of eminent individuals". When Pardo Bazán began her work in 1887, Spain was at the very start of what I have elsewhere called the second era of its reception of Russian culture—following a rocky first era earlier in the nineteenth century.[21] I date the end of this second era to the advent of the so-called 1898 Generation, many of whose members were profoundly influenced by Russia and her literature, and also by specific authors like Tolstoy and Dostoevsky. I have in mind particularly the great philosopher and writer Miguel de Unamuno (1864–1936) and the novelist Pío Baroja (1872–1956), about both of whom much more could be said in this regard.[22] Spain lost a potentially important populariser of Russian culture in the early years of the twentieth century with the suicide of Angel Ganivet (1865–98) in Riga; he had accepted the post of Spanish Consul in Latvia, then part of the Russian Empire. Ganivet produced several short studies on Russia, including his famous *Letters from Finland* (*Cartas finlandesas*, 1898) and a short essay titled 'Spain and Russia' ('España y Rusia', 1898).[23]

However, by 1887 Pardo Bazán had made one important literary enemy, the prominent Spanish novelist Juan Valera who, unlike any of his contemporaries, had spent several years in Russia as part of a Spanish diplomatic mission, during which he compiled his *Letters from Russia* (*Cartas desde Rusia*, 1856–57).[24] These

y por los de las mujeres [...]." Cited by Sara Herran in the special anniversary supplement of *Glamour* (Madrid, June 2021).

21 José Ortega y Gasset, *Invertebrate Spain*, trans. by Mildred Adams (New York: Howard Fertig, 1974), p. 71.

22 French cultural dominance in Spain was analogous to its influence over Russia. For further discussion, see Chapter One in Tejerizo, *Influence*.

23 See Tejerizo, 'Lo exótico', p. 395.

24 See Tejerizo, *The Silence Between Two Worlds* for more discussion of Valera and his *Cartas desde Rusia*.

letters barely refer to Russian literature which, as Valera noted, was closed to him because of the difficulty of the language; he only briefly mentions the current state of culture in Russia, instead prioritising his observations on and encounters with members of the Russian aristocracy. Valera openly accused Pardo Bazán on many occasions of "promoting the foreign" ("extranjerismo"), that is, of focusing on cultures beyond Spain's frontiers while neglecting "our own" ("lo nuestro"). He also charged her with displaying "a blind desire for novelties" ("un afán ciego de novedades").[25] Valera frequently suggested that Pardo Bazán should concentrate on analysing her own native Galician literature; her focus on strange, remote, and exotic Russia was not at all necessary or useful for her readers. The Russian language was seen as yet another barrier; Leopoldo Alas, or 'Clarín', suggested that it would pose insurmountable difficulties for her work. Pardo Bazán's response to Clarín, clarifying her views on reading literature in translation, is instructive:

> I do not know a word of Russian either and it is clear that in Russian literature as in all translated literatures, I resign myself to losing the pleasure of the form but there always remains for my literary curiosity knowledge of what lies underneath which is, in that virgin and semi-barbarian literature, that which is most interesting.[26]

Clarín also sought to undermine her lecture preparations by observing that "we all already have been reading our Gogol and our Tolstoi [...]" ("ya hemos leído todos a nuestro Gogol y a nuestro Tolstoi [...]").[27] However, because of her close acquaintance with her fellow, almost exclusively male, authors, including perhaps the most famous of them all, Pérez Galdós (their correspondence has been well documented),[28] she was able to understand their hostility and defend herself accordingly. Interestingly, after her lectures (which the contemporary press praised as intellectually outstanding) and their subsequent appearance in print, several of these male writers admitted the importance of Russian authors and even assimilated their work within their own writings. Critics have observed potential Tolstoyan influence on some of Galdós's later works, including *Reality* (*Realidad*, 1892);[29] Turgenev, whose great admiration for Spain and Spanish

---

25 For my analysis of this critique, see Tejerizo, *Influence*, esp. Chapters Two and Three.

26 "Yo tampoco sé una palabra de ruso, y claro está que en *ésa*, como en todas las literaturas traducidas, me resigno a perder el placer de la forma, pero siempre resta a mi curiosidad literaria el conocimiento del fondo, que es acaso, en esa literatura virgen y semibárbara, lo más interesante." Cited by Burdiel, *Emilia Pardo Bazán*, p. 267.

27 Ibid.

28 See, for example, Emilia Pardo Bazán, *Cartas a Benito Pérez Galdós 1889–1890*, ed. by Carmen Bravo Villasante (Madrid: Turner, 1975).

29 See, for example, George Portnoff's article 'The Influence of Tolstoy's *Ana* [sic] *Karenina* on Galdós' *Realidad*', *Hispania* 15:3 (1932), 203–14, https://doi.

literature has been well documented, corresponded with Galdós, although sadly their letters have been lost. Three of Spain's most famous writers, Miguel de Unamuno, Pío Baroja and Federico García Lorca (1898–1936), all engaged at important levels with Russian culture, possibly as a direct result of having read Pardo Bazán on this subject.[30] Moreover, not long after her essays appeared, the quality of Spanish translations of Russian literature began to improve; many were now made directly from Russian into Spanish, avoiding French entirely.

From the Spoken to the Written Text

May God spare me from becoming a prophetess [...]

("Libreme Dios de meterme a profetisa [...]")[31]

As we have seen, Pardo Bazán introduced Madrid audiences to Russian literature in three separate lectures, each offered a week apart, in Madrid's Ateneo. (Pardo Bazán, as Isabel Burdiel notes, was only the second woman to deliver lectures in the Ateneo; the first was the poet and dramatist Rosalía de Acuña, three years earlier in April 1884.)[32] Burdiel stresses that Pardo Bazán's topic "highlighted [...] the fact that the speaker was both a studious and an erudite woman" ("enfatizaba [...] su autora como estudiosa y erudita").[33] For the purposes of this essay, I have cited Pardo Bazán's own approved text of these lectures, published as *The Revolution and the Novel in Russia.* A careful examination of these lectures as texts that were originally spoken creates quite an impression even on the modern reader. At the very outset of the first lecture, Pardo Bazán admits her own "great inner perturbation" ("gran turbación interior"), making it clear that she is fully aware of her "insufficiencies" ("mi insuficiencia"), which are exacerbated by her femininity: this reflects her lucid awareness of the place of women in Spanish society at that time. She describes her efforts to gain insights into Russian culture as a "new, exotic, arduous and extremely vast" ("nuevo, exótico, arduo y vastísimo") experience.[34] She observes that Russian literature was all the rage in Paris, where people were reading Turgenev, Tolstoy, and Dostoevsky; not, she continues, merely as a caprice of upper-class Parisians, but as a fact of urban daily life. She notes her own interest in Russia's historical, social, and political problems of Russia as well as in Russian writers. She swiftly addresses the issue of translation: "I need something indispensable for this venture, namely the Russian language" ("me falta algo indispensable

org/10.2307/331955.

30 Lorca professed great love for Russian culture. See also Tejerizo, *Influence*, Chapter 5.

31 Pardo Bazán, *La revolución y la novela*, p. 23.

32 Burdiel, *Emilia Pardo Bazán*, p. 268.

33 Ibid.

34 Pardo Bazán, *La revolución y la novela*, p. 1.

tal vez para mi empresa: la posesión del idioma rusa").[35] However, it is worth noting here again that Pardo Bazán received an excellent linguistic education at her French school; she knew many other languages very well. With honesty and humility, she comments that she has always striven to "make up for what I lack" ("suplir lo que me falta") through extensive research and reading, and by consulting the intellectuals she had befriended in Paris.[36]

Pardo Bazán refers to the French diplomat and critic Eugène-Melchior de Vogüé (1829–1916) but her lectures cannot be regarded in any way as a plagiarism or as a mere recasting of the former's *The Russian Novel* (*Le Roman russe*, 1886).[37] Her work has its own clear agenda; her lectures and later essays were intended to inform and inspire her Spanish readers, by creating meaningful connections between Russian and Spanish literature. Each of the three lectures was organised around a clear, logically argued topic. There was no chance of improvisation but, rather the opposite—one senses that Pardo Bazán made careful choices in order to provide a well-formed and interesting text, serving both to introduce Russian culture to her public in the Ateneo and later to suggest an anthology of representative Russian authors and themes. Lecture 1 introduced the topics of 'Nature', 'Race', 'Agrarian Communism', 'Social Classes', and 'Serfdom' ('la servidumbre'). Through this varied content, Pardo Bazán obviously aimed to centre her listeners in the new and exotic terrain of Russian culture, offering as much relevant historical and social information as possible.[38] Gogol is introduced briefly in this lecture, where she also remarks on Russia's relative youth (as a nation) compared to the countries of Europe. Elsewhere she makes what must have struck her audience and later her readers as an extraordinary comparison between the sense of apathy found in Ivan Goncharov's *Oblomov* (1859), and the "sense of sadness and longing" ("morriña") characteristic of her native Galicia. Lecture 2 covered the following topics:

> The Word *nihilism*,—Origins of the Revolution.—Women and the Revolutionary family.—*Going to the People*.—Hertzen and Bakunin—The Nihilist Novel.—The Terror.—Police and Censorship. —Origins of Russian Literature: Romanticism.—The Lyric Poets: Realism: Nicolás Gogol.[39]

35 Ibid., p. 9.

36 Ibid., p. 12.

37 Ibid., p. 13, p. 23, pp. 439–30.

38 Ibid., p. 1.

39 "La palabra nihilismo.—Orígenes de la revolución.—La mujer y la familia revolucionaria.—Ir al pueblo—Hertzen y Bakunine.—La novela nihilista.—El Terror.—Policía y Censura.—Orígenes de las letras rusas.—El romanticismo: los poetas líricos.—El realismo: Nicolás Gogol." Pardo Bazán, *La revolución y la novela*, p. 153. For mention of Goncharov's '*Oblomoff*' [sic] as "a tender Russian novel" ("una delicada novela rusa"), see Pardo Bazán, p. 50.

This second lecture included a short history of Russian women as well, for the first time in Spanish letters, as an organised presentation of both Gogol and Turgenev. There was even a short critical description of Turgenev's character Bazarov: "disobedient, bad-mannered, unbearable and he is the very personification [of Nihilism]" ("díscolo, mal criado é inaguantable que personifica el tipo").[40] In her brief survey of Russian women, she notes that, previously "women's condition in Russia [has been] more bitter and humiliating than in the rest of Europe: [...] beatings and imprisonment in the home turned her into a beast of burden".[41] Happily, however, at the time of writing, "[e]verything has changed, [there are] new ideas [...] and today the Russian woman has most equality with men, she is the most free, the most intelligent and the most respected in Europe".[42] Mikhail Lermontov (1814–41) is introduced as "the Russian Byron" ("el Byron ruso"), "the great Romantic poet [...who complained] about the moral inferiority of women in his country [...]" ("el gran poeta romántico [...q]uejaba de la inferioridad moral de la mujer en su patria [...]").[43] Concluding this lecture, Pardo Bazán referred briefly to the important critics (also authors) Aleksandr Herzen (1812–70), Vissarion Belinskii (1811–48), Ivan Goncharov (1812–91), Nikolai Chernyshevskii (1828–91), and Nikolai Karamzin (1766–1836), before mentioning Pushkin as the "the demigod of Russian poetry" ("semidiós del verso ruso").[44] When introducing Aleksandr Griboedov (1795–1829), she refers generously to her so-called "enemy", Juan Valera, observing that the title of the latter's novel *Being too Clever* (*Pasarse de listo*, 1878) could also serve as the title of Griboedov's play *Woe from Wit* (*Gore ot uma*, 1825), "the pearl of the Russian theatre" ("la perla del teatro ruso").[45] Her third lecture covered exclusively literary topics:

> The Poet and Artist Turgenev.—*Oblomovism*: Slav lassitude—Dostoevsky, the psychologist who hallucinates; Count Tolstoy, the nihilist and mystic;—French naturalism and Russian naturalism.[46]

In these lectures on literature, Pardo Bazán always attempts to give as much relevant background on each writer as possible; sometimes, she also ventures a short original critique of his main works. These lectures would have had

40 Pardo Bazán, *La revolución y la novela*, p. 165.

41 "el estado de la mujer en Rusia [ha sido] más amargo y humillante que en el resto de Europa: [...] el palo y el encierro la hicieron bestia de labor", ibid., pp. 168–69.

42 "[t]odo ha cambiado, las ideas nuevas [...] y hoy es la mujer rusa la más igual en condición al hombre, la más libre, la más inteligente, la más respetada de Europa..." Ibid., p. 169.

43 Ibid., p. 170.

44 Ibid., p. 243.

45 Ibid., p. 257.

46 "El poeta y artista Turguenef.—Oblomovismo: la pereza eslava—El psicólogo y alucinado Dostoyuevsky: El nihilista y místico conde Tolstoi:—Naturalismo francés y naturalismo ruso." Pardo Bazán, *La revolución y la novela*, p. 313.

enormous impact, delivered as they were in the splendid surroundings of the Ateneo. Unsurprisingly, as witnessed by the praise of many of Pardo Bazán's contemporaries, they were regarded as the most important intellectual event of the times. Pardo Bazán succeeded admirably in uniting Russian history and literature, giving a chronological overview of early times in Russia up to the 'modern' era. Her lectures end with a finely tuned study of the works of Tolstoy, Dostoevsky, and Turgenev. She paced her talks cleverly, in order to retain audience interest. Lecture 1, for example, introduces Gogol to counterbalance the extensive historical content; Lecture 2 balances a history of Russian women with a focus on female characters in Turgenev and Tolstoy—hardly surprising given Pardo Bazán's interest in and sympathies with feminism. Lecture 3 invites her audience into the fictional worlds of Russia's greatest writers, from Pushkin to Dostoevsky. Dostoevsky was presented to his future Spanish 'audience' as "the psychologist who hallucinates" ("el psícólogo y alucinante Dostoyeuski [sic]").[47] Intriguingly, much later Pío Baroja, a trained psychologist as well as an author, would seize on this description to produce an excellent yet little-known essay 'Psychological Doubling in Dostoevsky' ('El desdoblamiento psicológico de Dostoievski', 1938).[48]

To conclude, from this brief examination of Pardo Bazán's lectures, we can see that their rhetorical skill would easily have captured audiences; they were well prepared, widely researched and apparently delivered with genuine humility, i.e. via admissions of the speaker's lack of knowledge of the Russian language or of first-hand experience of Russia. The published essays include a full bibliography, which emphasised their utility as a gateway to Russian culture for Spanish readers, and this continues to be true even today. Her closing words demonstrate her honesty and sense of adventure:

> As my farewell, a sincere confession [...]. Above all, Russia is an enigma; let others resolve this as best they can; I could not. The Sphinx called me; I looked into her eyes, deep as an abyss: I felt the sweet vertigo of the unknown, I asked questions [...]. I am waiting, without much hope, for the sound of the sea swell to bring me an answer.[49]

---

47 Ibid.

48 For more information about the impact of Russian literature on the works of Pío Baroja, and for a discussion of his long essay on Dostoevsky, see Tejerizo, *Influence* (esp. Chapter 4). Baroja was a physician with a keen interest in psychiatric medicine.

49 "Para despedida, una confesión sincera [...]. Rusia es, ante todo, un enigma; otros lo resuelvan si a tanto alcanzan: yo no pude. Me llamó la esfinge: puse mis ojos en los suyos hondos como el abismo; sentí el dulce vertigo de lo desconocido, interrogué [...] aguardo, sin gran esperanza, a que el rumor del oleaje me traiga la respuesta." Pardo Bazán, *La revolución y la novela*, p. 445.

Conclusion: 'Making the exotic familiar?'

I have already queried Isabel Burdiel's suggestion that Pardo Bazán's essays on Russia might hold merely historical interest for the modern reader. Even my brief survey of these texts argues that the reverse is true. While Pardo Bazán was indisputably hampered by the fact that she read Russian literature through translations, she was still able to capture the essence of these great literary works and to convey her excitement for them—initially to her Ateneo audiences on three April nights in 1887, and later to readers of her essays. Her enthusiasm and her creative attempts to bridge cultural barriers and connect the literary traditions of Spain and Russia should be applauded and more prominently acknowledged in her oeuvre.

Many scholars and anthologists of Russian culture in Spain have judged the latter as slow to acquire information about Russian authors and literature. Careful re-examination of Pardo Bazán's essays, and a re-evaluation of her lectures, should disprove this view. Her lectures and essays marked a new stage in the transfer of Russian culture to Spain and elsewhere in the Hispanic world—we should note Pardo Bazán's great popularity in countries such as Chile and Argentina (her Madrid memorial was funded by women in both Spain and Argentina). Although Spain had no equivalent of Britain's Constance Garnett to translate Russian literature, Pardo Bazán's work as a creative intermediary between Spain and Russia has been unjustifiably neglected. Many scholars have pointed to the slow reception of Pushkin in the Hispanic world, seemingly forgetting that Pushkin was, in fact, the first Russian prose writer to be translated into Spanish.[50] Pardo Bazán provided ample information on Pushkin while bringing him to life in her own words as a crucial Russian author, naming most of his key works. A wave of new translations of Russian literature into Spanish, some of which were direct translations, followed shortly after the publications of her essays, thus heralding a new era for Spanish readers.[51] Pardo Bazán remains to this day the greatest intermediary between Russian and Spanish cultures, the outstanding populariser of Russia in Spain.

50 See Tejerizo, *Influence* (esp. Chapter 1), for a discussion of these early translations; and see the bibliography in the same volume for suggested further reading on this topic. Another helpful summary and source of further reading is Jordi Morillas, 'Dostoevsky in Spain: A Short History of Translation and Research', *Dostoevsky Studies*, XVII (2013), 121–43, https://core.ac.uk/download/235190384.pdf.

51 Pardo Bazán was well-acquainted with two of the best translators from Russian of her era, the Catalan Narcís Oller and the Spanish poet (and translator of Dostoevsky) Rafael Cansinos-Asséns.

Postscript

In the small but bustling Eugenio Trías Library, almost hidden away in Madrid's Retiro Park, a table displaying works by Pardo Bazán has been set up to mark her centenary. At its centre lies a copy of a Spanish translation of Dostoevsky's *Crime and Punishment*—a small detail suggesting that, after all, Pardo Bazán's achievement as a mediator of Russian culture may not have been completely forgotten.[52]

52 This small library maintained its exhibition of Pardo Bazán's writings throughout her entire centenary year (2021), hosting both lectures and workshops to commemorate her life and work.

Ukraine

Translating Russian Literature in Soviet and Post-Soviet Ukraine

Lada Kolomiyets and Oleksandr Kalnychenko

> [....] the Russians have been the first modern people
> to practice the political direction of culture consciously
> and to attack at every point the culture of any people
> whom they wish to dominate.
>
> T. S. Eliot, *Notes Towards the Definition of Culture*[1]

Introduction

This paper portrays Russian literature in Ukrainian translation from the early 1920s to the early 2020s. Our critical framework is Iurii Lotman's theory of cultural dialogue. As Lotman argues, "in a broad historical perspective, the interaction of cultures is always dialogical".[2] It enables a given receiving culture to take in the experience of other cultures, their literary forms, or philosophical, political, and scientific ideas; it incorporates the culture into international cultural and creative exchange, thereby helping it to advance. But sometimes, where cultural potential depends on the stronger influences of another culture, translation practices may hazardously destabilise the originality of a source

1 T.S.Eliot, *Notes Towards the Definition of Culture* (London: Faber and Faber, 1948), p. 93.

2 Iurii Lotman, 'Problema vizantiiskogo vliianiia na russkuiu kul'turu v tipologicheskom osveshchenii' ['The Issue of the Byzantine Empire's Impact on Russian Culture in the Typological Interpretation'], in *Izbrannye stat'i v trekh tomakh*, I (1992), *Stat'i po semiotike i tipologii kul'tury* [*Selected Articles in Three Volumes: (I) Articles on the Semiotics and Typology of Culture*] (Tallinn: Alexandra, 1992–93), pp. 121–28 (p. 122), http://yanko.lib.ru/books/cultur/lotman-selection.htm#_Toc509600919.

 https://doi.org/10.11647/OBP.0340.17

culture's spiritual manifestations. All these features are clear in the dramatic collisions of the Ukrainian-Russian coexistence within the so-called 'shared cultural space'.[3]

Lotman's remark that "the dialogue of cultures is accompanied by the growing hostility of the recipient towards the one who dominates him"[4] helps us to puzzle out the complex relationship between Russian and Ukrainian cultures through translation. It enables us to understand why their dialogue has sometimes become strained, as it did in February 2014 after the Russian Federation annexed Crimea and began sponsoring a proxy war in Donbas, or broke down entirely, as from February 2022 with the expansion of Russia's war against Ukraine. To evaluate the current trends, it is enough to read the thoughts of leaders of public opinion in Ukraine, such as Oksana Zabuzhko, a popular Ukrainian novelist, essayist, and poet, who recently denounced all Russian classical literature as imperialist: "In many ways, it was Russian literature that wove the camouflage net for Russia's tanks".[5] According to Lotman, "an acute struggle for spiritual independence is an important typological feature".[6] Dialogue between Russian and Ukrainian cultures in the field of translation from and through Russian, as a mediating language, from the mid-1930s to the mid-1950s, was more like the slow but increasingly deadly compression of a rabbit by a boa constrictor. When in the post-Stalin era, this suffocating grasp partly relaxed, an entire school of translation emerged inflected against Russification. Its chief theorists included well-known translators of Russian prose such as Oleksa Kundzich, Stepan Kovhaniuk, and Maksym Rylsky, among others.

Considering translation "a deeply ambivalent concept and practice", Naoki Sakai pinpoints its functional duality ("translation always cuts both ways: at once a dynamism of domination and liberation, clarification and obfuscation, commerce and exploitation, concession and refusal to the 'other'").[7] This feature is particularly important to recall while surveying the inherently ambivalent role of translation in Russo-Ukrainian cultural dialogue. Sakai's inference that translation "can always be viewed to a larger or lesser degree

3 See, for example, Rostyslav Dotsenko, 'Pereklad—dlia samozbahachennia chy samoobkradannia?' ['Translation: for Self-Enrichment or Self-Robbery?'], in Rostyslav Dotsenko, *Krytyka. Literaturoznavstvo. Vybrane* [*Criticism. Study of Literature. Selected*] (Ternopil: Bohdan, 2013), pp. 103–12.

4 Lotman, 'Problema vizantiiskogo vliianiia', p. 123.

5 Oksana Zabuzhko, 'No Guilty People in the World? Reading Russian Literature after the Bucha Massacre', *Times Literary Supplement*, 22 April 2022, https://www.the-tls.co.uk/articles/russian-literature-bucha-massacre-essay-oksana-zabuzhko/.

6 Lotman, 'Problema vizantiiskogo vliianiia', p. 123.

7 Naoki Sakai, 'The Modern Regime of Translation and Its Politics', in *A History of Modern Translation Knowledge. Sources, Concepts, Effects*, ed. by Lieven D'hulst and Yves Gambier (Amsterdam and Philadelphia, PA: John Benjamins, 2018), pp. 61–74 (p. 61).

as an ethico-political manoeuvre of social antagonism"[8] also works well with Russian-to-Ukrainian translation. As part of the historiographic description of Russian literature in Ukrainian translations, the authors of this article will examine reprints and retranslations alongside the first translated editions. Our study also incorporates translator biographies and their individual voices in paratexts. Our investigation of literary translators' and editors' self-concepts, their (multi)positionality, teloi, and goals, along with institutional attitudes and approaches, primarily draws on microhistorical methodology and terminology.[9]

Throughout our research, we refer to one of the key texts underlying this volume, Pascale Casanova's 2004 monograph *The World Republic of Letters*, which represents the history of world literature as incessant struggle, competition, and rivalry.[10] Casanova's important premise that literary value "circulates and is traded"[11] helps illuminate the ideology-based market and the shifting character of the Soviet canon of classical Russian and foreign literature. The processes of Soviet politicisation of the language of translation constitute an important aspect of our research. Having discerned in the politicisation of language "the ambiguity and paradox that govern the very enterprise of literature itself", Casanova adds, "since language is not a purely literary tool, but an inescapably political instrument as well, it is through language that the literary world remains subject to political power".[12] For postcolonial literary spaces (such as both Soviet and post-Soviet Ukrainian literature) she suggests "a more sophisticated model" of language that "would take into account a peculiar ambiguity of the relation of literary domination and dependence, namely, that writers in dominated spaces may be able to convert their dependence into an instrument of emancipation and legitimacy".[13] Furthermore, in Casanova's viewpoint, "literature itself, as a value common to an entire space, is not only part of the legacy of political domination but also an instrument that, once reappropriated, permits writers from literarily deprived territories to gain recognition".[14]

Given the ambivalent role of the national writer and translator in colonial literature, it is crucial to ascertain the cultural positions from which translations of Russian-language literary works were carried out at different stages of the

8 Ibid., pp. 61–62.

9 Our sources include *A History of Modern Translation Knowledge. Sources, Concepts, Effects*, ed. by Lieven D'hulst and Yves Gambier (Amsterdam and Philadelphia, PA: John Benjamins, 2018); *What is Translation History? A Trust-Based Approach*, ed. by Andrea Rizzi, Birgit Lang, and Anthony Pym (Cham, Switzerland: Palgrave Macmillan, 2019); *Literary Translator Studies*, ed. by Klaus Kaindl, Waltraud Kolb, and Daniela Schlager (Amsterdam and Philadelphia, PA: John Benjamins, 2021).

10 Pascale Casanova, *The World Republic of Letters*, trans. by M. B. De Bevoise (Cambridge, MA and London: Harvard University Press, 2004).

11 Ibid., p. 13.

12 Ibid., p. 115.

13 Ibid., p. 116.

14 Ibid.

USSR and after it. In this regard, an important concept for our research is that of the national writer, discussed by Casanova,[15] the meaning of which we specify for the context of Ukrainian literature and extend to literary translation, using the term 'writer-translator'. Defined by Casanova as "conventional" and "outmoded" in the literary models he reproduces, a national writer finds himself relegated "to political dependence, aesthetic backwardness, and academicism" by anti-national writers who reverse the polarity of the space, as it were, by belonging to autonomous literary (sub)spaces.[16] Anti-national writer-translators appeared in the Ukrainian literary field only in the late 1980s (the iconic figure is Iurii Andrukhovych), and in Ukrainian émigré literature in the West twenty years earlier (like Ihor Kostetsky).

The traditional self-identification of Ukrainian translators as *national writers*, united by the idea of literature and translation as a nation-building function, provides a national framework for the study of translations, particularly those from Russian (as a closely related language) and, in general, for the scrutiny of selections in the repertoire of translated literature in Soviet Ukraine.[17] Ukrainian writer-translators of the Soviet period faced political repression, persecution for "nationalism", accusations of "nationalistic wrecking in translation",[18] arrests and executions, while their translations were either destroyed or ruthlessly edited linguistically and ideologically, and many of them even several times. The method of genetic criticism,[19] applied, for instance, to edited reprints and retranslations of Nikolai Gogol's works, demonstrates the gradual approximation of the formal lexical and structural texture of the originals during the period from the mid-1930s to the mid-1950s. This trend covers even the early works of Gogol, from his so-called 'Ukrainian cycle', where this shift towards literality becomes particularly noticeable and devastating in aesthetic and stylistic terms. When their own life, or at least freedom, was at stake in Stalinist times, Soviet writer-translators often publicly criticised the work of their contemporaries or nearest predecessors, praising their own or somebody else's subsequent retranslations and trying to adapt to ideological slogans that

15 "The national writer has a national career and a national market: he reproduces in the language of his nation models that are not only the most conventional but also the most consistent with commercial—which is to say national, universally outmoded criteria", ibid., p. 279.

16 Ibid., p. 193.

17 Maksym Strikha, *Ukraïns'kyi khudozhnii pereklad: Mizh literaturoiu i natsiietvorenniam* [*Ukrainian Literary Translation: Between Literature and Nation-Making*] (Kyiv: Fakt/ Nash Chas, 2006).

18 This term meant the distancing of the Ukrainian language from Russian at the grammatical, lexical and syntactic levels; 'wrecking' in translation was equated to 'wrecking' in any other sphere of Stalin's national economy; 'the wreckers' were blamed for all the small and big troubles and failures in Soviet industry, collective farming, education, and even communal services.

19 A detailed comparison of successive versions of a text. See *What Is Translation History?*, ed. by Rizzi et al., esp. the glossary on pp. 113–16.

were imposed by the Kremlin. Under the circumstances, psychological factors, apart from socio-political stimuli and ideological reasons, played an important role in the evaluation and editing of translations at that time. Purely aesthetic motives came last on the agenda if they did not disappear completely.[20]

It is important to remember that Ukrainian culture itself has been toxic to its natives both in the Russian Empire and the Soviet Union, and that translations into Ukrainian bore constant danger for their creators. As Vitaly Chernetsky has concisely outlined:

> The implication for local Ukrainian culture, during both the tsarist and the Soviet period, was 'a syndrome of dependence and derivativeness', according to which the best and the brightest were either coerced or encouraged to shed attachments to Ukraine. [...] Often, especially during the years of Stalinist terror, such flights from Ukraine and distancing from Ukrainian culture by members of the Ukrainian intelligentsia were essentially attempts (often unsuccessful) at physical survival.[21]

Thus, our study will also address the psychology of the translators' social behaviour in terms of their attitude to predecessors, competitors, and rivals, especially in a repressive social system. Following Rakefet Sela-Sheffy, we supplement the study of the translators' "personae" with our research on their editors and reviewers, while observing how translators treat their competitors in a stressful social situation complicated by state-imposed terror.[22] While seemingly seeking to gain the upper hand and eliminate their rivals by hurrying to expose so-called 'wrecking' translations, translators in Soviet Ukraine in the majority of cases were actually trying to defend their own lives and the lives of their families by criticising their fellow translators' work. We believe that the translators' non-linear and seemingly paradoxical psycho-behavioural reactions to the direct challenges and threats of the totalitarian Soviet system are an important part of Ukraine's microhistory of translation, along with objective (and in many cases tragic) biographical data. The microhistorical scale of a particular psychological state, action, or event may seem insignificant, and individual circumstances inconspicuous against the broad background of mass processes across the state, but a holistic view of translation history, as of any generalised history, is based on microhistorical elements.

---

20 In particular, a group of young researchers of literature, mostly members of Pylypenko's Literary Association, whose journal was known as *Plough*, were also arrested (accused of belonging to a counterrevolutionary organisation) and executed in December 1934.

21 Vitaly Chernetsky, 'Russophone Writing in Ukraine: Historical Contexts and Post-Euromaidan Changes', in *Global Russian Cultures*, ed. by Kevin F. Platt (Madison, WN: University of Wisconsin Press, 2019), pp. 48–68 (p. 56, p. 57).

22 Rakefet Sela-Sheffy, 'The Translators' Personae: Marketing Translatorial Images as Pursuit of Capital', *Meta*, 53:3 (2008), 609–22.

Literary Translations from Russian in the 1920s and 1930s

As early as 1930, the literary critic Elizaveta Starynkevych, in a Russian-language review of books translated into Ukrainian in 1929–30, argued that in comparison with the pace of translation of canonical Western authors, the rate of translating Russian masterworks was unsatisfactory because many big names in the genres of prose and drama were still waiting for Ukrainian publishers to fill the gap.[23] From the early 1930s, this gap was quickly filled.[24] By the late 1930s, the Ukrainian dynamics for publishing translated books revealed a significant predominance of Russian and Russian-language literature. This tendency is better understood if we adapt Casanova's concept of soft power as domination over other nations' literatures.

The critics and editors of that time paid special attention to stylistic peculiarities of translating canonical Russian authors of the nineteenth and early twentieth centuries with Ukrainian backgrounds and/or whose writings were stylistically close to Ukrainian linguistic patterns or topics. First and foremost, among them were Gogol, Anton Chekhov, and Nikolai Leskov, whose works contain significant Ukrainian elements, both stylistic and thematic. A literary critic of the early Soviet period, Volodymyr Derzhavyn singled out these authors as belonging to both Russian and Ukrainian literature. Gogol was the most frequently translated author, although Pushkin—the number one classic in the official canon of Russian literature in the USSR—outstripped him by the number of separate publications. Various works by Gogol appeared in separate Ukrainian editions each year from 1926 to 1937. Works translated in the early 1920s were re-translated during this period. In the 1930s, several separate publications appeared each year. More than two dozen translators, including prominent writers and skilled stylists, were involved in the Gogol (known in Ukrainian as Mykola Hohol') translation 'industry'. In commemoration of Gogol's *Evenings on a Farm near Dikanka* (*Vechera na khutore bliz Dikan'ki*, 1829–32), the Ukrainian publishing house Knyhospilka scheduled the first five-volume Ukrainian collection of Gogol's works (*Tvory*) to appear between 1929 and 1932. The team of translators included recognised authors, Rylsky and Mykola Zerov

23 Elizaveta Starynkevych, 'Problemy i dostizheniia v iskusstve perevoda. (K itogam ukrainskoi perevodnoi literatury za 1929–1930 gg.)' ['Problems and Achievements in the Art of Translation. (Towards the Results of Ukrainian Translated Literature in 1929–1930)'], *Krasnoe slovo*, 3 (1930), 111–18.

24 From the 1850s onwards, both anthologies and individual Russian classics in Ukrainian translation were also published in Western Ukraine (Lviv and Kolomyia); Russian poetry and fiction appeared in Western Ukrainian periodicals as well.

among them. However, only three of the planned five books emerged—the first, second, and fourth volumes.

Chekhov's short story 'Kashtanka' was first published in Ukrainian translation in 1923, in a version by Serhiy Efremov (reprinted in 1928 and 1929). Efremov was a principal figure in the Ukrainian Academy of Science at the time.[25] Knyhospilka's publication in 1929–30 of Chekhov's *Selected Works* (*Vybrani tvory*)[26] under Vasyl Ivanushkin's and Rylsky's editorship became an outstanding event in Ukrainian Chekhoviana.[27] In 1930, a volume of Chekhov's *Comedies* (*Komedi̇̈*) appeared from Ukraine's State Publishing House (Derzhavne Vydavnytstvo Ukraïny, abbreviated as DVU), as well as several other editions of Chekhov's stories in various translations. The 1935 edition of Chekhov's *Short Stories* (*Opovidannia*), edited by Zinaida Yoffe, did not credit its translators. By the time the extended 1937 edition of *Short Stories* appeared, Yoffe herself, wife of the executed linguist and translator Borys Tkachenko, had been sentenced to five years in a labour camp. Hence this expanded edition mentioned neither its editor nor any translators.

Prose works from classical Russian literature began to be translated extensively in the 1930s. Tolstoy's prose appeared first from various publishing houses, in particular, *Khadzhi Murat* (written c. 1904) from DVU in 1924; *Childhood, Boyhood, and Youth* (*Detstvo. otrochestvo. iunost'*, 1852–56) from Knyhospilka (*Dytynstvo, khlop'iatstvo I yunatstvo*) and *The Cossacks* (*Kazaki*, 1863) by Rukh publishing house (*Kozaky*), both in 1930. From the mid-1930s onwards, the State Publishing House of the Ukrainian SSR (UkrSSR) monopolised all subsequent publications, producing the first book of *Anna Karenina* (1878) in a translation by the well-regarded writer, poet, and editor, Oleksiy Varavva (1935). This was followed by various short stories ('A Landlord's Morning' ['Utro pomeshchika'] and 'Master and Man' ['Khoziain i rabotnik']), all of *War and Peace* (*Voina i mir*, 1869) (*Viina i myr*), and the *Sevastopol Sketches* (*Sevastopol'skie rasskazy*, 1856) (*Sevastopolski opovidannia*) in the late 1930s, translated by the eminent journalist and editor Antin Kharchenko.[28] Ivan Turgenev's works were also widely (re) translated. For example, his cycle of short stories *A Sportsman's Sketches* (*Zapiski okhotnika*, 1852) was published in 1924, 1930, and 1935 (*Zapysky myslyvtsia*) by several publishing houses and in different translations, often without mentioning the translator(s).[29]

25 After Efremov's arrest in 1930 (he was sentenced to ten years in prison, dying in captivity in 1939), 'Kashtanka' was re-translated by Borys Tkachenko and published together with the short story 'Van'ka' in 1935.

26 This was intended as a three-volume collection: but, similarly to the truncated collection of Gogol's *Works* [*Tvory*] planned by the same publisher, only two of three projected volumes were produced.

27 Tragically, Ivanushkin was shot dead on 13 July 1937.

28 That very year, 1936, Kharchenko was arrested.

29 Ukrainian editions of Turgenev's *Selected Works* [*Vybrani tvory*] appeared in 1935 and 1937. Further separate editions in Ukrainian of the works by Turgenev

In 1936, crucial works from the Soviet canon of classical Russian literature appeared in Ukrainian: Nikolai Chernyshevsky's novel *What is to be Done?* (*Chto delat'?*, 1863) (*Shcho robyty?*), Aleksandr Griboedov's comedy *Woe from Wit* (*Gore ot uma*, written 1823) (*Hore z rozumu*), and Ivan Goncharov's *Oblomov* (1859). Aleksandr Ostrovsky's plays were printed in 1936 in Kharchenko's translation, and Mikhail Saltykov-Shchedrin was also well-represented by successive translations of his major works: *The History of a Town* (*Istoriia odnogo goroda*, 1870 [*Istoriia odnoho mista*, translated 1930]), *A Tale of How One Man Fed Two Generals* (*Povest' o tom, kak odin muzhik dvukh generalov prokormil*, 1869 [*Povist pro te, yak odyn muzhyk dvokh heneraliv prokormyv*, 1938]), and the novel *The Golovlev Family* (*Gospoda Golovlevy*, 1880) (*Pany Holovliovy*, 1939).

A Zone of Permanent Political Turbulence: Soviet Russian Prose and Dramatic Works in Translation

The most popular Soviet author was Maksim Gorky, whose novel *Mother* (*Mat'*, 1906/1922), translated by Varavva and edited by Serhiy Pylypenko, was first published in Ukrainian translation (*Maty*) in 1928. *My Universities* (*Moi universitety*, 1923; *Moï universytety*), translated by Mykhailo Lebedynets under the editorship of Pylypenko, also appeared that year. It was retranslated by Maria Pylynska and Ivan Dniprovsky in 1933, with only Pylynska named as translator when the translation was republished by the same publisher in the following year.[30] 1928 also saw the publication of Gorky's *Foma Gordeev* (1899), translated by Lizaveta Kardynalovska (sister of Pylypenko's wife, Tetiana Kardynalovska) and reprinted in 1935. Gorky had opposed the translation of his works into Ukrainian, considering it a "Little Russian" rather than a fully-fledged language. Gorky's imperialist prejudice is clear from his 1927 letter to Oleksa Slisarenko, editor-in-chief of the Knyhospilka publishing cooperative, declining permission to translate his novel *Mother* into Ukrainian and thrice referring to that language as a "narechie" (dialect).[31] However, Slisarenko eventually managed to persuade Gorky to agree to the translation.

---

appeared in different translations and publishing houses, e.g., the short story 'Mumu' (1852) in 1928 and twice in 1934, the novel *Fathers and Sons* [*Ottsy i deti*, 1862] in 1929 and 1935 [*Bat'ky i dity*], the novel *Rudin* (1855) in 1935 and 1937. 'Bezhin Meadow' ['Bezhin Lug'] was published in 1930 under the editorship of Rylsky ['Bizhyn Luh']. The novels *Home of the Gentry* [*Dvorianskoe gnezdo*, 1858], published in 1936 [*Dvorians'ke hnizdo*], and *On the Eve* [*Nakanune*, 1860], published in 1936 [*Naperedodni*], reprint 1937, were translated by Volodymyr Svidzinsky.

30 From 1934 to 1956, the writings of Dniprovsky, who was Pylynska's husband, were banned, as was any mention of his name.

31 Maksym Strikha, *Ukraïns'kyi khudozhnii pereklad: Mizh literaturoiu i natsiietvorenniam*, pp. 208–09.

Gorky's main argument against translating into Ukrainian was that an average Ukrainian reader can read any work of Russian literature in the original. His personal conviction contradicted the general policy of the ruling Communist Party of the Soviet Union, which aimed at indigenisation, and in the case of Ukraine, Ukrainisation: the use of the Ukrainian language in education, culture, literature, science, and office work in order to establish Soviet ideological slogans in Ukrainian mass culture. By way of a counterargument to Gorky's reasoning, we cite a 1928 article by N. Gavrashenko (this is most likely a pseudonym). It appeared in the Russian-language literary and art journal of the All-Ukrainian Union of Proletarian Writers, *Red Word* (*Krasnoe slovo*). This article justified the need for Ukrainian translations of Gorky and other Russian writers thus:

> It is true, of course, that the Ukrainian reader can read any work of Russian literature in the original. But it also matters for the ordinary reader's perception whether this work, in terms of its intimacy, greater proximity, and hence effectiveness, is being perceived in Russian, which sounds foreign, or in the intimately close and native Ukrainian language.[32]

In the late 1920s, *Krasnoe slovo*, where Gavrashenko's article had appeared, served as a propaganda platform for promoting the idea of Ukrainian translations of Russian literature. In 1929, it published a review article, 'Translated Literature in Ukraine', by the philologist Oleksandr Biletskii. The author of the article argued that the main priority when commissioning translations for a Ukrainian readership was to offer as many translations into Ukrainian as possible—both from Russian and direct translations from other foreign languages—to develop a Ukrainian canon of world literature. Moreover, Biletskii compared reading world literature in Russian rather than Ukrainian translation to consuming a surrogate that "upsets the natural growth and development of thought, which is [...] inseparable from words, is being formed by words".[33] The critic Derzhavyn had also called for the formation of a Ukrainian canon of world literature. Arguments in favour of Ukrainian translations from Russian prevailed and Gorky's works continued to be published in abundance.[34] From 1928 to 1966,

32 N. Gavrashenko, 'Maksim Gorky v ukrainskikh perevodakh' ['Maksim Gorky in Ukrainian Translations'], *Krasnoe slovo*, 5 (1928), 151–53 (p. 152).

33 Aleksandr Beletskii, 'Perevodnaia literatura na Ukraine' ['Translated Literature in Ukraine'], *Krasnoe Slovo*, 2 (1929), 87–96. Reprint in Oleksandr Kalnychenko and Yuliana Poliakova *Ukraïns'ka perekladoznavcha dumka 1920-kh–pochatku 1930-kh rokiv: Khrestomatiia vybranykh prats' z perekladosnavstva do kursu 'Istoriia perekladu'*, pp. 376–91 (p. 386). All translations of quotations from the Russian and Ukrainian languages throughout this chapter are by Lada Kolomiyets, unless otherwise indicated.

34 For more details see Lada Kolomiyets, *Ukraïns'kyi khudozhnii pereklad ta perekladachi 1920–30-kh rokiv: Materialy do kursu 'Istoriia perekladu'* [*Ukrainian Literary Translation and Translators in the 1920s–1930s: Materials for the Course 'History of Translation'*] (Vinnytsia: Nova Knyha, 2015), p. 41.

his writings in Ukrainian translation totalled 186; Chekhov, for comparison, had eighty-three; Gogol, seventy-seven; Tolstoy, seventy-six; Turgenev, thirty-nine; and Lermontov, thirteen.[35]

The Ukrainian language proved capable of meeting the demands placed on it by the subject matter and style of the translated works; the expenditure of effort and money on translating Russian canonical writings fully justified itself. The rapid appearance of numerous translations became a living refutation of the idea of the uselessness and futility of translations from Russian into Ukrainian, and the business of Russian-to-Ukrainian translation developed relatively smoothly until 1934. That summer, a conference of translators and editors of Gorky's works was held at the Central Committee of the Ukrainian Communist Party. Subsequently, the Ukrainian-language *Literary Newspaper* (*Literaturna hazeta*) published an article which severely criticised recent translations of Gorky's works into Ukrainian, accusing them of deliberately avoiding homophones common to Russian and Ukrainian.[36] It announced that Gorky's books would be retranslated using a different, more literal strategy. This rapprochement with the Russian language extended to translations of other authors, for instance, including those of the Socialist Realist author Mikhail Sholokhov.[37] In the spirit of combatting "nationalistic wrecking", a devastating critique of Pylypenko's translation of Sholokhov's *Virgin Soil Upturned* (*Podniataia tselina*, 1932) appeared in *Literary Newspaper* on 20 August 1934,[38] four months after Pylypenko was executed on 3 March (he had been arrested on 29 November 1933, accused of "distorting national policy, ideological instability and conciliatory attitude towards bourgeois-nationalist elements").[39] Whether

35 *Presa Ukraïns'koï RSR, 1917–1966: stat. dovidnyk* [*The Press of the Ukrainian SSR, 1917–1966: Statistical Reference Book*] ed. by Mykola A. Nyzovy, Maria I. Brezghunova, and Yuri B. Medvedev (Kharkiv, n.p., 1967), pp. 72–73.

36 Andriy Paniv, 'Tvory O.M. Gorkoho ukraiins'koiu movoiu: Pro potrebu novykh perekladiv, vilnykh vid "natsionalistychnykh" perekruchen' ['O.M. Gorky's Works in Ukrainian: On the Exigency of Retranslations Free from "Nationalistic" Distortions'], *Literaturna hazeta*, 12 August 1934, p. 1. For more details see Oleksandr Kalnychenko and Nataliia Kalnychenko, 'Campaigning against the "Nationalistic Wrecking" in Translation in Ukraine in the Mid-1930s', in *Translation and Power*, ed. by Lucyna Harmon and Dorota Osuchowska (Berlin: Peter Lang, 2020), pp. 53–60.

37 For a further example of destructive editorial journalism, see Oleksandr Kalnychenko and Lada Kolomiyets, 'Translation in Ukraine during the Stalinist Period: Literary Translation Policies and Practices' in *Translation under Communism*, ed. by Christopher Rundle, Anna Lange, and Daniele Monticelli (Basingstoke: Palgrave MacMillan, 2022), pp. 141–72 (p. 158), https://doi.org/10.1007/978-3-030-79664-8_6.

38 Yevhen Kasianenko, 'Yak Pylypenko perekruchuvav Sholokhova' ['How Pylypenko Distorted Sholokhov'], *Literaturna hazeta*, 20 August 1934, p. 2.

39 Tetiana Yelisieva, 'Ukrainskyi literator na tli radianskoi doby', in *Reabilitovani istoriieiu. Kharkivska oblast* (Kyiv; Kharkiv: Red.-vydav. hrupa Kharkiv. tomu ser. 'Reabilitovani istoriieiu', 2008. Book. 1, Part. 2), pp. 111–19 (p. 118).

or not the author of the article, Yevhen Kasianenko,[40] knew at the time of writing that Pylypenko was no longer alive, remains unclear.[41] Shortly before his arrest, Pylypenko had submitted his translation of *Virgin Soil Upturned* in manuscript to the Literature and Art publishing house, then part of the State Publishing Association of Ukraine (Derzhavne vydavnyche ob'iednannia Ukraïny, DVOU). However, in March 1934 DVOU was liquidated, and its constituent publishers were reorganised in order to subordinate them more closely to the relevant people's commissariats (the Literature and Art publishing house was thus subordinated to the People's Commissariat of Education of the Ukrainian SSR). A well-known writer, translator, scientist, editor, and a member of the Bolshevik Communist Party since 1919, Pylypenko sat on the editorial board of the DVOU. Therefore, after his arrest and the reorganisation of the DVOU, all the members of the Literature and Art editorial board were exposed. At that time, the other well-known translator, journalist, and editor, Kasianenko, was working with this publishing house. It is likely that the editorial board of Literature and Art deliberately asked Kasianenko for a devastating review of Pylypenko's translation to pre-empt further repression. Prior to Pylypenko's arrest, Kasianenko had collaborated with him as a co-editor of the former's journal *Plough* (*Pluh*); the two men were certainly not ideologically opposed. Yet Kasianenko re-translated Sholokhov's highly popular Soviet novel *Virgin Soil Upturned*, which he eventually published in Literature and Art in 1934 (*Pidniata tsilyna*), when the publishing house withdrew Pylypenko's previously submitted translation.

This dramatic story shows how tightly intertwined personal motives and psychological attitudes were with allegedly political decisions and actions, particularly when the translator's ego turns out to be the main trigger of political accusations of one's literary predecessors and rivals. Even assuming that Kasianenko knew about Pylypenko's execution before publishing his denunciatory article, he did not seem concerned about how his defamatory remarks would affect the lives of Pylypenko's family and followers. The publishing microhistory of Ukrainian translations of Sholokhov's works, which includes paratexts and biographical data about translators, is very revealing for the whole process of Russian-to-Ukrainian Soviet translation. Sholokhov's

40 Yevhen Kasianenko (1889–1937) was a Ukrainian public and political activist, aircraft designer, journalist, translator, and a prominent literary editor. He was arrested on 11 July 1937 and executed on 31 December 1937 by the verdict of the military commission of the Supreme Court of the USSR. See Mykhailo Zhurovsky, 'Braty Kasianenky: polit kriz' morok chasu' ['The Kasianenko brothers: A Flight through the Darkness of Time'], *Kyivs'kyi politekhnik*, 1–4 (2011), https://kpi.ua/kasianenko.

41 Kasianenko and Pylypenko lived next door, in the same Slovo Building which accommodated Ukrainian writers and poets, in Kharkiv; Kasianenko's family resided in apartment 18, while Pylypenko's family occupied apartment 20.

epic novel in four volumes *And Quiet Flows the Don* (*Tikhii Don*),[42] translated by Semen Kats and edited by Yevhen Pluzhnyk (*Tykhyi Din*), was printed in two editions by Literature and Art—first in 1931 (books 1 and 2) and later, between 1932 and 1934 (books 1, 2, and 3). In 1935 all three books of the novel (in the same translation) reappeared in print from the State Publishing House of the UkrSSR.[43] After the Soviet authorities stopped trusting Kasianenko, the novel *Virgin Soil Upturned* appeared in a new translation by Stepan Kovhaniuk (*Pidniata tsilyna*, 1935). Kasianenko was arrested on 11 July 1937 (and executed on 31 December of the same year).

Translations of Russian Literature from World War II to the Collapse of the USSR

Only a few Ukrainian writer-translators from Russian survived Stalin's purges and remained active: Rylsky, Tychyna, Mykola Bazhan, Mykola Tereshchenko, Leonid Pervomaiskyi, Natalia Zabila, besides Volodymyr Sosiura, Andriy Holovko, Iurii Ianovskyi, Andriy Malyshko, and some others. However, translations from Russian increased rapidly. From 1946 to 1955, translations into Ukrainian totalled 310 volumes of Russian pre-Soviet classics and 413 books by modern Russian writers.[44] Ukrainian publishing houses printed translations of prose works by 180 Russian authors in the postwar period, including twenty-eight classics. The total circulation of these translations was about 25 million copies.[45]

Stepan Kovhaniuk estimates that in the mid-1950s, fifty-eight people translated Russian classics, including thirty writers and twenty-eight professional translators. This group can be further narrowed to about thirty writers and professional translators who were engaged in translation constantly, with at least a dozen translations to their credit.[46] Of those thirty writers, Kovhaniuk names only five leading translators: Rylsky, Tychyna, Mykhailo

---

42 The first three volumes were written from 1925 to 1932 and published in the magazine *Oktyabr* in 1928–32, and the fourth volume was finished in 1940 and published in the magazine *Novy mir* in 1937–40.

43 Book 4 of *And Quiet Flows the Don*, translated by Stepan Kovhaniuk [*Tykhyi Don*], appeared in print in 1941 from the State Publishing House of the UkrSSR.

44 Oleksa Kundzich, 'Stan khudozhnioho perekladu na Ukraïni' ['The State of Literary Translation in Ukraine'] in *Pytannia perekladu: z materialiv respublikans'koï narady perekladachiv (liutyi 1956)* [*Issues of Translations: Proceedings of the All-Ukrainian Meeting of Translators (February 1956)*] (Kyiv: Derzhlitvydav, 1957), pp. 5–54 (p. 6).

45 Stepan Kovhaniuk, 'Pereklad khudozhnioï rosiis'koï prozy na ukraïns'ku movu' in *Pytannia perekladu: z materialiv respublikans'koï narady perekladachiv (liutyi 1956)* (Kyiv: Derzhlitvydav, 1957), pp. 55–75 (pp. 55–56).

46 Ibid., p. 56.

Stelmakh, Kundzich, and Holovko.[47] Having defined a "perfect translation" as "a translation when the reader forgets about the translator and does not see him in the text", Kovhaniuk points to Rylsky, whose translations "could be unconditionally called perfect and exemplary in this respect". He specifically refers to Rylsky's Gogol translations, 'May Night, or the Drowned Maiden' ('Maiskaia noch' ili utoplennitsa', 1831; 'Mais'ka nich, abo Utoplena', 1929) and 'The Tale of How Ivan Ivanovich Quarrelled with Ivan Nikiforovich'[48] ('Povest' o tom, kak possorilsia Ivan Ivanovich s Ivanom Nikiforovichem', 1835; 'Povist' pro te, iak posvaryvsia Ivan Ivanovych z Ivanom Nykyforovychem', 1930).[49] Thus, the translator's invisibility is guaranteed, in Kovhaniuk's view, by the fluency of the "cultivated" translating language (in Berman's terms).[50]

Among new translations, which fall short of 'exemplary' status, Kovhaniuk mentions Stelmakh's and Holovko's 1954 translations of Pushkin's *The Tales of the Late Ivan Petrovich Belkin* (*Povesti pokoinogo Ivana Petrovicha Belkina*, 1831; *Povisti pokiinoho Ivana Petrovycha Bielkina*) and 'Roslavlev' (1831) respectively, Ostap Vyshnia's 1952 version of Gogol's *The Inspector General* (*Revizor*, 1836), Kundzich's 1951 version of Lermontov's *A Hero of Our Time* (*Geroi nashego vremeni*, 1841; *Heroi nashoho chasu*), and Maria Rudynska's 1954 translation of Chekhov's 'The Grasshopper' ('Poprygun'ia', 1891) ('Vitrohonka').[51] On the one hand, by the mid-1950s, "Ukrainian writers had already made all the best works of Russian artistic and philosophical thought the spiritual heritage of the Ukrainian people", as Kundzich, both a practitioner and theoretician of Russian-to-Ukrainian translation, summarises.[52] However, the problem of insufficient quality of most postwar translations arose in the mid-1950s. The ban on translations published during the 1920s and early 1930s (this period went down in history as the decade of Ukrainian national revival) gave rise to the appearance on a massive scale from the mid-1930s of the so-called "edited translations", while the names of translators who were arrested and executed completely disappeared from printed editions, as if they had never existed. A repressed person's translations underwent ruthless and repeated editing and had to be published without the translator's name—only with the label "translation edited by such and such", or even with an abbreviated version of the label: "edited translation".

The role of literary editor was reduced to transforming the Ukrainian literary language into a pale shadow of the Russian language:

---

47 Ibid., p. 57.

48 Also known in English as 'The Squabble'.

49 Kovhaniuk, 'Pereklad khudozhnioï rosiis'koï prozy', p. 58.

50 Antoine Berman, 'Translation and the Trials of the Foreign' (1985), trans. by Lawrence Venuti, in *The Translation Studies Reader*, ed. by Lawrence Venuti, 2nd edn (New York and London: Routledge, 2004), pp. 276–89.

51 Kovhaniuk, 'Pereklad khudozhnioï rosiis'koï prozy', p. 60.

52 Kundzich, 'Stan khudozhnioho perekladu na Ukraïni', p. 27.

> If you take a closer look at the translations of 1946–1950, you can see that they are ALL [*original capitals*—L.K.] marked by the heavy seal of all-binding literalism. It was, so to speak, a sign of the time, a period of editorial arbitrariness, when the translator sometimes could not recognize his translation after the book was published. The editor's pen would mercilessly and consistently cross out any living word that 'deviated from the original', i.e., was not a calque.[53]

Kovhaniuk, whose corrected complete translation of Sholokhov's novel *And Quiet Flows the Don* in four volumes appeared in 1955 (and was reprinted in 1961), experienced this editorial insistence on literalism. As a speaker at a formal meeting of Ukrainian translators in Kyiv on 16 February 1956, Kovhaniuk focused his speech 'The Translation of Russian Literary Prose into the Ukrainian Language' ('Pereklad khudozhnioï rosiis'koï prozy na ukraïns'ku movu') around the painful and urgent issue of literalism in translations from or via Russian. This critic-translator called the literalist strategy "a depressing copyism", "a gramophone that will never replace a living voice", and "the most dangerous enemy of translated literature" that bears "the stillborn fruit".[54] In his keynote speech 'The State of Literary Translation in Ukraine' ('Stan khudozhnioho perekladu na Ukraïni') at the same meeting, Kundzich denounced literal translations from Russian and their disastrous impact on the Ukrainian literary language.[55] Kundzich labelled the literalist strategy as "slavish copying", "the spoilage of literary language", and "a clerical style" (as opposed to artistic literary style).[56] The danger of such a strategy, displayed in the multi-volume editions of Russian classics and the hundreds of works of Soviet literature, was that it exerted great influence on the Ukrainian literary language. As Kundzich maintained, the language of translations had overwhelmed Ukrainian literary language.[57] Through mass publications of these translations, despite their impoverished and monotonous lexis severed from the vital source of folk speech, the artificial translation style was replacing native Ukrainian literary style.

However, concerted opposition by Ukrainian translators (Kovhaniuk, Kundzich, Borys Ten, and others) to slavish literalism in translations from Russian stimulated Rylsky to develop a theory of translation. In his article 'Problems of Literary Translation' ('Problemy khudozhn'oho perekladu'), first circulated in 1954 and later included in Rylsky's 1975 volume *The Art of*

53 Kovhaniuk, 'Pereklad khudozhnioï rosiis'koï prozy', p. 60.

54 Ibid., pp. 61, 62, 63.

55 This meeting took place just a week before Nikita Khrushchev's secret report, vilifying Stalin, 'On the Cult of Personality and Its Consequences', was made at the Twentieth Congress of the Communist Party (25 February 1956).

56 Kundzich, 'Stan khudozhnioho perekladu na Ukraïni', p. 8, p. 10.

57 Ibid., p. 5.

Translation (*Mystetstvo perekladu*), the author attempted to break free from the dictates of literalism with the help of this theory.[58] The writer-translator warned against calquing from a closely-related language (read: from Russian) because of the threat of misusing words similar in sound but different in meaning, and of the interlingual homonyms that trip up translators. While denouncing extremely literal translation, Rylsky simultaneously warned against its opposite, the temptation to excessively domesticate (here, Ukrainianise) foreign-language texts.[59] Rylsky's resilient opposition to the unofficial literal norm of translating from Russian was organised into a clear list of the main threats and difficulties awaiting the translator, namely: (1) noun gender, rarely identical in the Russian and Ukrainian languages; (2) false friends, or interlingual homonyms; (3) the danger of either subordinating the native language to a foreign-language structure, or, conversely, over-identifying the target language in specifically national colouring; (4) discrepancies between life depicted in the original and in the target culture; and (5) foreign-language borrowings in the original text.[60]

Through the Russian language and translations from Russian (in Ukraine and other Soviet Republics), a Soviet cultural space was established, which proved to be deliberately isolated from the world cultural space and which was intended to supplant the latter. We recall Casanova's comment on the danger of omitting translations of world literature from closed literary spaces, which seems relevant for translations in the USSR at that time: "By contrast with autonomous literary worlds, the most closed literary spaces are characterized by an absence of translation and, as a result, an ignorance of recent innovations in international literature and of the criteria of literary modernity".[61] Thus, the period of late Stalinism (from the mid-1930s to mid-1950s) witnessed a decline in Ukrainian translation tradition, characterised by multiple retranslations and revisions of previously published works as well as the mass phenomenon of indirect translation via Russian mediation. After the campaign against "translator-wreckers", as Ukrainian scholar and translator Maksym Strikha maintains, publishers began to shun those translators active during the first Soviet decades. From 1937, these disappeared from publishing houses.

The translators of the new conscription who came to replace those executed or exiled to the GULAG camps were often individuals of much lower culture and professionalism, who had no command of foreign languages other than Russian. Moreover, the translations published in the UkrSSR since the late 1930s mainly belonged to the Russian and partly European classics (but only to those authors who were considered 'progressive') as well as 'the fraternal

58 Maksym Rylsky, 'Problemy khudozhn'oho perekladu' ['Problems of Artistic Translation'], in *Mystetstvo perekladu* [*The Art of Translation*], ed. by Maksym Rylsky (Kyiv: Radians'kyi pys'mennyk, 1975), pp. 25–92.

59 Ibid., pp. 51–52.

60 Ibid., p. 56, p. 57, pp. 58–59, p. 63.

61 Casanova, *The World Republic of Letters*, p. 107.

literatures of the peoples of the USSR' (later also the literatures of 'people's democracies', of 'Socialist camp', and of 'peoples struggling for liberation from colonial oppression'). However, those translations of European classics and the literature of the peoples of the USSR were already carried out from Russian translations.[62]

On the eve of World War II, a notorious 'translationese' began to develop, flourishing in the first postwar decade. This was when Russian classics were most widely published. The mass-produced Ukrainian-language editions of Chekhov (1949), Leskov (1950), Lermontov (1951), Gogol in three volumes (1952), Pushkin in four volumes (1953), and Chekhov in three volumes (1954) are a good case in point. Chekhov's 1949 volume did not name any translators. Gogol's three volumes contained several translations (unrecognisably distorted) by repressed translators whose identities were disguised under circumlocutions such as "translation edited by I. Senchenko" or "translation edited by P. Panch", which only named the most recent editor. Translations included in these volumes were subject to linguistic revision characterised by editors' efforts to eliminate so-called "archaisms" (references to national history), and to purify the Ukrainian language from European elements not found in Russian, which should be replaced by specifically Russian words and structures. Translations played the dominant part in this process.[63] In 1952–53, Kundzich published his four-volume translation of *War and Peace* (the first two volumes had been published in 1937 in Varavva's translation; as he had now emigrated to the West, his name and works could not be mentioned, and therefore Kundzich retranslated them). Translations of works by "proletarian" writers, primarily Gorky, remained obligatory.[64] For example, between 1952 and 1955, sixteen volumes of Gorky's works appeared in Ukrainian. Translations of other contemporary Soviet Russian authors abounded.

Soviet versus Anti-Soviet Translation (Late 1950s-Late 1980s)

During the early postwar years, there was a tendency to translate writers from other Soviet ethnic groups, as well as other foreign authors, only via Russian. Later any publication of texts in Ukrainian not yet extant in Russian translation was closely monitored, and Ukrainian translations were scrupulously compared with Russian versions of the originals to ensure that the latter remained

62 Maksym Strikha, *Ukraïns'kyi pereklad i perekladachi: mizh literaturoiu i natsiietvorenniam* [*Ukrainian Translation and Translators: Between Literature and Nation-Building*] (Kyiv: Dukh i litera, 2020), p. 246.

63 Bohdan Nahaylo and Victor Swoboda, *Soviet Disunion: A History of the Nationalities Problem in the USSR* (London: Hamish Hamilton, 1990), p. 78.

64 Maksym Strikha, *Ukraïns'kyi pereklad i perekladachi*, p. 261.

authoritative. The practice of 'translation from translation', almost exclusively from Russian translation, now became widespread. As Ukrainian translator and literary scholar Rostyslav Dotsenko argues, "translations from Russian have served for years as an easy 'fishing trip' for ungifted authors of local significance, who managed to produce whole piles of translated socialist-realist low-quality 'wastepaper', including even the masterworks of 'fraternal republics', mutilated by awkward translations".[65] Moreover, the detrimental effect of literalism in Ukraine replicated the enormous scope of translation practice in all its branches—in the press and radio, in the compilation of dictionaries and in scholarly and political publications. The intrinsic bias towards Russian literature of the ostensible Soviet 'commonwealth' of literatures clearly created a monological Russian dominance in Ukraine's cultural space, rather than fraternal dialogue.

The publication of Russian literary classics was prioritised in Ukraine: by the year 1967, almost four million copies of Pushkin's works, for example, had been published; over five million copies of Tolstoy, nearly three million copies of Gogol, and many millions of copies of books by Vladimir Korolenko, Dmitrii Mamin-Sibiriak, Nikolai Nekrasov, Saltykov-Shchedrin, and Chekhov.[66] Concurrently, cohorts of Soviet Ukrainian scholars developed the concept of the Russo-Ukrainian literary 'interaction', 'commonwealth', 'unity', as well as 'linguistic relations' and the 'brotherhood of cultures',[67] which all essentially sustained a Russian totalitarian monologue based on censorship and state control of book production.[68] Daniele Monticelli terms this cultural situation, where translations take a large share of book production and "only one source language and culture is absolutely hegemonic among translations" as "totalitarian translation".[69] Such translation is characterised by erasure of the previous national legacy through censorship and destruction of books and by repressing the living writer-translators, making their creative individuality invisible. In the USSR, translations from Russian served to fill in the blanks caused by the erasure of national memory, enabling the Communist rewriting of Ukraine's cultural heritage. However, Ukrainian translators and translation scholars of the 1950s (Kundzich, Kovhaniuk, Rylsky, Mykola Lukash, and their

---

65 Rostyslav Dotsenko, 'Pereklad—dlia samozbahachennia chy samoobkradannia?', pp. 105–06.

66 Viktor M. Skachkov et al., ed., *Spivdruzhnist' literatur: bibliohrafichnyi pokazhchyk (1917–1966)* [*The Commonwealth of Literatures: Bibliographic Index (1917–1966)*] (Kharkiv: Knyzhkova Palata UkrSSR, 1969).

67 Ibid., p. 8.

68 On the layers of the historicity of translation see Daniele Monticelli and Anne Lange, 'Translation and Totalitarianism: The Case of Soviet Estonia,' *The Translator*, 20:1 (2014), 95–111.

69 Daniele Monticelli, '"Totalitarian Translation" as a Means of Forced Cultural Change: The Case of Post-war Soviet Estonia' in *Between Cultures and Texts: Itineraries in Translation History*, ed. by Antoine Chalvin, Anne Lange, and Daniele Monticelli (Frankfurt: Peter Lang, 2011), pp. 187–200 (p. 190).

ilk) challenged literalism as a means of Russifying the Ukrainian language. They contributed to the rise of a dissident movement in the 1960s.[70] Not only the textual praxis of translation but also the paratexts, or commentaries on translations, "became a site of resistance to official Soviet culture and values".[71]

In contrast to the 'Soviet translation project', 'anti-Soviet' translation also developed at that time, mainly in Ukrainian émigré literary circles.[72] Ukrainian translators in the West often deliberately aimed to translate authors *not* published in the USSR, including Russian and Ukrainian authors writing in Russian.[73] Oksana Solovey translated Russian dissident writers, including excerpts from Solzhenitsyn's novel *The First Circle* (*V kruge pervom*, 1968) (*V koli pershomu*, 1969), short stories from Varlam Shalamov's collection *Kolyma Stories* (*Kolymskie rasskazy*, 1978) (*Iz 'Kolyms'kykh opovidan''*, 1972),[74] both appearing in the Munich Ukrainian émigré journal *Modernity* (*Suchasnist'*). Ukrainian émigré poet, prose writer, and literary scholar Igor Kaczurowsky, a prolific translator of Russian poets into Ukrainian (particularly of Silver Age poetry), also translated Solzhenitsyn's Nobel Prize Lecture (1972)[75] (*Nobelivs'ka lektsiia z literatury*, 1973) and two Shalamov stories, published in the journal *Suchasnist'* in 1981.

Meanwhile, in Soviet Ukraine, classics of Russian literature continued to be retranslated and reprinted during the 1970s and 1980s, although on a smaller scale. During the period 1965–90, Soviet Russian Village Prose (*derevenshchiki*) became popular, mostly in the original language, but also in translation. In the 1980s, Fedor Abramov's novels *The Wooden Horses* (*Dereviannye koni*, 1970; *Derev'iani koni*, 1982), and *The Swans Flew By* (*Proletali lebedi*, 1989; *Prolitaly lebedi*, 1989), as well as the collection of Abramov's *Works* in two volumes (*Tvory: V 2 tomakh*, 1989), appeared in Ukrainian translation. Vladimir Tendriakov's books—*A Topsy-Turvy Spring: Stories* (*Vesennie perevërtyshi*, 1973; *Vesniani pereverty*, 1978), *Atonement: Novellas* (*Rasplata*, 1979; *Rozplata*, 1986) and *Assassinating Mirages* (*Pokushenie na mirazhi*, 1987; *Zamakh na mirazhi*, 1990)—were also published.

70 Taras Shmiher, *Istoriia Ukraïns'koho perekladoznavstva XX storichchia* [*The History of Ukrainian Translation Thought of the 20th Century*] (Kyiv: Smoloskyp, 2009).

71 Brian James Baer, 'Literary Translation and the Construction of a Soviet Intelligentsia', *The Massachusetts Review*, 47:3 (2006), 537–60 (p. 537).

72 The majority of the most talented Ukrainian translators in the USSR silently opposed the regime—despite declarations of political loyalty and occasional fulfilment of politicised state commissions, such as the Ukrainian version of the USSR National Anthem.

73 For example, Ivan Koshelivets' translations of Viktor Nekrasov's essays on America, *Both Sides of the Ocean* (*Po obe storony okeana. V Italii — v Amerike*, 1962) (*Po obydva boky okeanu*, 1964), and Aleksandr Solzhenitsyn's *One Day in the Life of Ivan Denisovich* [*Odin den' Ivana Denisovicha*, 1962; *Odyn den' Ivana Denysovycha*, 1963].

74 *Kolyma Stories* were translated into Ukrainian almost in parallel with foreign publications in Russian.

75 Aleksandr Solzhenitsyn was awarded the Nobel Prize for literature in 1970. The text of his Nobel speech appeared in 1972, and once in exile he received the Nobel insignia in person in 1974.

Vasilii Shukshin's famous collection of short and movie stories *Snowball Berry Red* (*Kalina krasnaia*, 1973; *Kalyna chervona*, 1978, 1986) appeared in Ukrainian translation by the well-regarded prose writer, Hryhir Tiutiunnyk (1931–80). The best Russian novellas of the 1970s were anthologised in the translated collection *Contemporary Russian Novellas* (1983), which featured works by Viktor Astafyev, Shukshin, Valentin Rasputin, Irina Grekova, Vyacheslav Shugayev, and Iurii Trifonov. One more anthology, *Russian Soviet Stories* in two volumes (1974–75), deserves separate mention. It primarily comprised Russian authors who wrote outside the official framework of Socialist Realism and were therefore semi-disgraced (Andrei Platonov, Iurii Kazakov, Vasilii Aksenov, Sergei Zalygin, Abramov, and Shukshin, among others). The third issue (1987) of the book series 'Novels and Novellas' published monthly by the Dnipro Publishing House consisted of translations of Iurii Bondarev's novel *The Game* (*Igra*, 1985; *Hra*), Rasputin's novella *Fire* (*Pozhar*, 1985; *Pozhezha*), and Astaf'ev's novel *The Sad Detective* (*Pechal'nyi detektiv*, 1986; *Pechal'nyi detektyv*). One more contemporary strand of Russian literature popular in Ukrainian translations was 'lieutenant prose' (*leitenantskaia proza*), or Second World War 'trench truth' (*okopnaia pravda*), reflecting the reality of war experience, stripped of all bravado (such as the prose of Viktor Nekrasov, Grigorii Baklanov, and Konstantin Vorobev).

The Market for Translated Russian Literature in Post-Soviet Ukraine

With Ukraine's independence in 1991, a new stage of cultural dialogue with Russian literature began: put more precisely, existing exchanges went on hold because of structural and economic transformations in the Ukrainian book market. During the first two post-Soviet decades, translations of modern Russian prose were extremely rare, mainly in the genre of children's literature. The publication in Ukrainian of the satirical novel *The Life and Extraordinary Adventures of Private Ivan Chonkin* (*Zhizn' i neobychainye prikliucheniia soldata Ivana Chonkina*, 1969 Russia/1975 Paris editions) by Russian dissident writer Vladimir Voinovich (*Zhyttia i nadzvychaini pryhody soldata Ivana Chonkina*, 1992) is a happy exception to the rule—the book appeared in print in Ukrainian translation even earlier than its separate edition in Russia in 1993. As reported by UNESCO *Index Translationum*,[76] very few Russian authors were translated in the years from 1992 to 2010 (these included Boris Akunin and Viktor Suvorov).[77] Among canonical

76 UNESCO *Index Translationum*, https://www.unesco.org/xtrans/bsresult.aspx?lg=0&sl=rus&l=ukr&c=UKR&from=1992&to=2003&fr=20.

77 The total number of publications (forty-three titles) may be underestimated, probably due to sporadic data submission by Ukraine (2004 was the last year of data submission). However, compared to the 2,080 titles reported for the period 1979–91, the difference in the number of publications is striking.

Russian authors, Gogol maintained his appeal for Ukrainian readers, but he was regarded as a Ukrainian writer.

Oversaturation with Russian products, primarily Russian-language translations, characterised the book market in independent Ukraine in the 1990s and 2000s.[78] During the first twenty years of independence, the number of translations from Russian has slowly declined; since 2014, with the onset of the Russo-Ukrainian war, translations from Russian reduced sharply. And with the start of Russia's full-scale invasion of Ukraine on 24 February 2022, any cultural exchanges with the Russian Federation, including translation, came to a halt. In addition, the Ministry of Education and Science of Ukraine has removed all texts belonging to the Russian literary canon from foreign literature programmes in Ukrainian secondary and higher education institutions, a political decision that will last until the end of the war.

After the book publishing crisis of 1993, when economic and political instability distracted Ukrainian readers, Ukrainian publishers flooded the market with Russian-language translations of popular literature, targeting local readers and even Russian book markets. Thus, between 1993 and 2000, almost all translations into Ukrainian were made thanks to foreign grants (from the International Renaissance Foundation and other Western European charitable funds). This fact partly explains the growing disinterest in Ukrainian translations of Russian-language fiction or poetry. Funding, and hence the attention of book publishers, was primarily directed towards translations of the works which disseminated Western European cultural values and thus contributed to the intellectual development and formation of civil society. The Russian Federation has not funded Ukrainian translations, with very few exceptions: in 2013 the International Sholokhov Committee supported the Kyiv publishing house, Friendship of Peoples, with its new translation of Sholokhov's *And Quiet Flows the Don* within the book series 'Library of V. S. Chernomyrdin'.

It is important to note that the Ukrainian-language book market began developing separately from the Russian market at the turn of the twenty-first century, namely, in 1999, after the Russian economy defaulted.[79] For commercial survival, some independent Ukrainian publishing houses, which had appeared in the 1990s and specialised in translations into Russian (which they even exported to Russia), were forced to rebrand their products as Ukrainian-language translations (not neglecting covert or overt translations from

78 Kostiantyn Rodyk, *Pereklady na ukraïns'ku, 1992–2012: Rezul'taty doslidzhennia perekladiv na ukraïns'ku movu, opublikovanykh u period 1992–2012 rokiv* [*Translations into Ukrainian, 1992–2012: Results of a Study of Translations into Ukrainian Published in the Period 1992–2012*] (Book Platform: Attribution-NonCommercial-ShareAlike), http://www.bookplatform.org/en/activities/50-translations-into-ukr-en.html.

79 Interview with Oleksandr Krasovytsky, a Ukrainian publisher, 9 July 2017, https://www.ukrinform.ua/rubric-culture/2261781-oleksandr-krasovickij-ukrainskij-knigovidavec.html.

Russian as the intermediary language) when copyright laws came into force in Russia. Meanwhile, statistics provided by Kostiantyn Rodyk demonstrate that translations from foreign languages in 1999 accounted for 28.9% of new publications in Ukraine, of which more than a third were from Russian.[80] A significant number of these translations were guides, horoscopes, leisure, office manuals, and children's books. In the period 2002–12, translations from Russian took second place after those from English, accounting for about 16% of all translated publications.[81] However, fiction is outnumbered by nonfiction texts, and mostly consists of children's works by Russian authors.

Serial editions have resumed since the early 2000s, including the 'Library of World Literature' series, which publishes Ukrainian-language translations of classic foreign works (both new versions and edited Soviet ones), but there has been no mass retranslation of Russian classics. Other publishing projects include, for example, the 2003 edition of the book *Sorochyn Fair on Nevsky Prospekt: The Ukrainian Reception of Gogol* as part of the Kyiv publishing house Fakt's series 'Text+Context'. Gogol occupies a special place in post-Soviet Ukraine, because he is perceived as a Ukrainian writer and has been among the most frequently translated writers in Ukraine from 2002 to 2012 by number of publications (thirty-three editions, overtaking Shakespeare).[82] Interestingly, translations of fiction by Russophone Ukrainian writers, including the spouses Maryna and Serhii Dyachenko, who worked in the science-fiction genre, have also been produced in large numbers. Impressively, between 2005 and 2017 the Dyachenkos' twenty-seven novels, more than fifteen collections of stories, and up to a dozen children's books have been translated and published separately. In the period 2017–20, the Kharkiv publishing house Folio printed a Ukrainian-language collection of the Dyachenkos' collected works in twenty-six volumes.[83]

For obvious reasons, the translation of Russian literature into Ukrainian has been rather limited in the 2010s, and not only due to the conflict raging during this period, or even the widespread Ukrainian-Russian bilingualism in Ukraine.[84] With the beginning of the Russo-Ukrainian war in February 2014—as a consequence of the Euromaidan protests and the Revolution of Dignity, as well as Russia's annexation of Crimea, inciting and sponsoring the military conflict in Donbas—and Ukraine's subsequent restrictions on the "shared informational space", i.e., a ban on certain Russian Internet resources and sites, Russian-to-Ukrainian translation has drastically changed, although it has not disappeared completely. It became clear that the book market is not only a component of the

80 Rodyk, *Pereklady na ukraïns'ku*, p. 13.

81 Ibid., p. 21.

82 Ibid., p. 22.

83 For more on English-language translations of Russophone Ukrainian authors, see Catherine O'Neil's article in this volume.

84 Despite the fact of numerous self-translations in both directions and covert translations from Russian as a relay language.

country's outward-facing market system, but also interwoven with its cultural integrity. The tendency towards political and cultural dissociation from the 'Russian world', accompanied by reorientation from 'East' (Russia) to the 'West' (the Euro-Atlantic cultural space), as expressed in the slogan 'Ukraine is Europe', has been normalised in Ukraine since Russia annexed Crimea and launched hostilities in the Donbas. Unlike the Soviet past, contemporary Ukraine has no writer-translators translating and/or retranslating Russian authors on a large scale. Their absence can be explained by the growing desire for distantiation from Russian political hegemony: "For writers from countries that have long been under colonial domination, [....] bilingualism (defined as 'embodied' translation) is the primary and indelible mark of political domination".[85] In the wake of rising patriotic sentiment in Ukraine, demand for books in the Ukrainian language (including translated editions) has increased, but this trend does not apply to translations from the classical Russian authors.

During the 2010s, multicultural dialogue emerged in the field of Ukrainian literary translation, based on translations of the works by contemporary Russophone authors from the former Soviet republics. The best-known of these include Svetlana Alexievich (from Belarus) and her books *Chernobyl Prayer* (*Chernobyl'skaia molitva*, 1997), translated by the prominent writer and public intellectual Zabuzhko (*Chornobyl: khronika maibutnioho*, 1998) and *The Unwomanly Face of War* (*U voiny ne zhenskoe litso*, 1985), translated by acclaimed writer Volodymyr Rafeyenko in 2016 (*U viiny ne zhinoche oblychchia*), among other titles. The Armenian artist and writer Mariam Petrosyan's famous novel, *The Gray House* (*Dom, v kotorom*, 2009) was translated by the prize-winning Ukrainian poet and author Marianna Kiyanovska (*Dim, v yakomu*) in 2019. The Georgian journalist and writer Oleg Panfilov is represented in Ukrainian translation by his books *Anti-Soviet Stories* (*Antisovetskie istorii*, 2016; *Antyradianski istorïi*, 2016), *A Conversation with a Vatnik* (*Razgovor s vatnikom*, 2017; *Rozmova z "vatnykom"*, 2017), and other texts. Since hostilities began, only those contemporary Russian writers who openly condemn the Kremlin's policy towards Ukraine (such as Liudmila Ulitskaia, Boris Akunin, Viktor Erofeev) or who parody Putin's regime (Vladimir Sorokin) have been translated. For example, translations of Sorokin's satirical novels *Day of the Oprichnik* (*Den' oprichnika*, 2006) and *Sugar Kremlin* (*Sakharnyi kreml'*, 2008) (*Tsukrovyi Kreml'*) were both published as separate editions by Folio (Kharkiv, 2010) in translation by Sashko Ushkalov.

Since 1 January 2017, a new law has impeded the import into Ukraine of Russian books, including translations into Russian published in the Russian Federation.[86] On 30 March 2021, the Verkhovna Rada of Ukraine adopted a

85 Casanova, *The World Republic of Letters*, p. 258.

86 In December 2016, the Verkhovna Rada of Ukraine adopted the Law 'On Amendments to Certain Laws of Ukraine Concerning Restrictions on Access to the Ukrainian Market of Foreign Printed Products of Anti- Ukrainian Content', which came into force on 1 January 2017. This law introduced a procedure limiting

resolution on the escalation of the Russo-Ukrainian conflict, which officially recognised that Ukraine was at war with the Russian Federation—an aggressor country.[87] Arguably, intra-national translation now prevails in the current field of Russian-to-Ukrainian translation, where 'intra-national' refers to Russophone Ukrainian writers. These writers identify themselves as Ukrainian authors writing in Russian, with a pro-Ukrainian worldview and a sense of patriotism towards the Ukrainian state. They are unafraid to 'Ukrainianise' their Russian lexis. For the most part, Russophone Ukrainian authors produce commercially successful genre literature, such as detective stories (Andrii Kurkov, Iryna Lobusova), science fiction (Maryna and Serhii Dyachenko, Andrii Valentynov, Yan Valetov, Volodymyr Vasylyev, H. L. Oldie—the pen name of science fiction and fantasy writers Dmytro Hromov and Oleh Ladyzhenzkyi), mysticism (Lada Luzina), and drama (Natalia Vorozhbyt). Twenty detective novels by Kurkov, for example, have already been translated into Ukrainian. Some authors who previously wrote in Russian have now switched to Ukrainian (Kurkov, Rafeyenko, Vorozhbyt, and others).

Conclusion

A sharp decline in the number of translations from Russian literature since the Revolution of Dignity, the Maidan Revolution (February 2014), and the beginning of the Russo-Ukrainian war testifies to the Ukrainian culture's resistance to the expansion of hegemonic Russian culture. As the prominent Ukrainian dissident writer Ivan Dziuba notes, the history of Ukrainian culture in the twentieth and twenty-first centuries shows that its interaction with Russian literature and culture was two-sided. One side is receptive to the humanistic and aesthetic impulses of Russian culture, while the other reacts defensively, by developing its own alternative cultural space.[88]

Translations of canonical Russian literature during Ukraine's National Renaissance period (from the 1920s to the early 1930s) corresponded to the

the importation of printed matter from Russia to Ukraine: Russian-produced publications could legally enter Ukraine only after assessment by the expert council of the State Committee for Television and Radio Broadcasting.

87 "Russia, as a party to the international armed conflict, must recognize its responsibility for unleashing armed aggression against Ukraine and make every effort to resolve the conflict" (from the 'Resolution on the Escalation of the Russo-Ukrainian Armed Conflict', adopted by the Verkhovna Rada of Ukraine on 30 March 2021), https://zakon.rada.gov.ua/laws/show/1356–20#Text.

88 Ivan Dziuba, 'Ukraïna–Rosiia: Protystoiannia chy dialoh kul'tur?' ['Ukraine–Russia: Confrontation or Dialogue of Cultures?'] In *Ukraïna—Rosiia: kontseptual'ni osnovy humanitarnykh vidnosyn* [*Ukraine–Russia: Conceptual Foundations of Humanitarian Relations*], ed. by Oleh P. Lanovenko (Kyiv: Stylos, 2001), esp. Chapter Five, pp. 265–333.

receptive view of Russian culture. From the mid-1930s to the mid-1950s, and again from 1972 until the late 1980s, Ukrainian culture and its national figures were repressed and translation from Russian was a strategy employed in the Russification of Ukrainian culture. Ukrainian translators have tried to oppose this function of Russian-to-Ukrainian translations throughout Ukraine's shared history with Russia: both as part of the Russian Empire (the first translations into Ukrainian appeared in the nineteenth century) and later as part of the Soviet Union. The national function of Ukrainian translation—to protect the Ukrainian language and culture despite externally imposed bans and repressions—always opposed Russification. While Russian culture has mostly been perceived by Ukrainians as the culture of an ethnically and linguistically related people, it also represents, today more than ever, an imperial and destructive force with a clear political goal. According to Dziuba's vision, the dominance of Russian culture in Ukraine will naturally decrease, thanks to the growing potential and influence of Ukrainian national culture in society, and due to the growing assimilation of global culture by Ukraine itself.[89]

From 24 February 2022, the barbaric actions of Putin's Russia became visible to everyone and broke the natural course of events for the distancing of Ukrainian culture from Russian, as predicted by Dziuba. All cultural ties had to be interrupted after the revelation of such atrocities as the Bucha massacre. Today, most Ukrainian writers and leaders of public opinion consider Russian literature complicit in the crimes of Russians in Ukraine. As Zabuzhko writes in her denunciatory essay, "it barely needs pointing out that Putin's offensive on 24 February owed much to Dostoevskyism".[90] She views and understands the invasion through this prism: "literature is of one flesh with the society for which and about which it writes".[91] Therefore, according to some Ukrainian humanitarian thinkers, literature is also responsible for infusing those who have committed war crimes in Ukraine with a feeling of absolute impunity and long-suppressed hatred and envy ('Why should you live better than us?' is the challenge apparently being voiced by some Russian soldiers to Ukrainians).[92] Total rejection and condemnation of Russian literary production is now, for many Ukrainian writers and critics, not just an aesthetic choice in a long-running struggle for cultural identity, but an existential necessity. Before the 2014 and 2022 invasions, much of the world did not notice that the landscape of Russian culture was predominantly imperial, or that Russian cultural heritage, with its canon of 'classical Russian literature', was sometimes absorbed or co-opted from other nations (mostly Ukraine), or complicit in spreading an imperialist, often racist and militarist, mythos (this applies even to iconic figures like Pushkin, Dostoevsky, and Tolstoy). As one recent *Economist* journalist has clarified for

89 Ibid.
90 Oksana Zabuzhko, 'No Guilty People in the World?'.
91 Ibid.
92 Ibid.

outside observers: "For Ukrainians, the stakes are higher. The Kremlin denies the existence of a discrete Ukrainian history and identity. That makes culture a matter of survival."[93] A nation's culture is not only about entertainment; it embraces its values and identity. Culture has no right to remain silent. Sadly, 'Russian culture', except for certain isolated voices, has been silent on its politicians' treatment of Ukraine.

93 'Why an American Novel Set in Russia Was Pulled from Publication', *The Economist*, 26 June 2023, https://www.economist.com/the-economist-explains/2023/06/26/why-an-american-novel-set-in-russia-was-pulled-from-publication.

AFRICA AND THE MIDDLE EAST

Russian Literature in Africa: An Overview

Cathy McAteer

In their work on global literatures, Pascale Casanova and David Damrosch each chart key moments, definitive for African writers and for their contributions to the evolution of modern Africa's literary canon. Casanova traces Africa's journey from oral tradition to the formation of, specifically, Nigerian and Kenyan literature (occasionally in translation) and beyond, onto the world scene. She explores a chronology of significant contributions, including works from Nigeria's Daniel Olorunfemi Fagunwa (writing in Yoruba) and the internationally known English-language author Ben Okri, Algeria's Kateb Yacine (writing in both French and Arabic) and Kenya's English- and Kikuyu-language novelist Ngũgĩ wa Thiong'o. Their writings, Casanova argues, were decisive both in creating new literary spaces and reinventing "a national language distinct from the language of colonization".[1] Damrosch identifies African writers—Nigeria's Chinua Achebe and South Africa's J. M. Coetzee—among placeholders in a so-called "hypercanon" of postcolonial literature.[2] He also notes the less conventional case of Egyptian Nobel Prize winner Naguib Mahfouz, whom, as a "major writer in a peripheral country",[3] Damrosch describes as languishing "in the minor category, despite their seminal importance in the literary histories of their countries and their entire regions".[4] Several of these writers, notably Mahfouz, were heavily influenced by their reading of Russian literature, often the novels of Gorky, Dostoevsky, or Tolstoy.[5] Each of these theorists examines

1 Pascale Casanova, *The World Republic of Letters*, trans. by M. DeBevoise (London and Cambridge, MA: Harvard University Press, 2004), p. 228.
2 David Damrosch, *Comparing the Literatures: Literary Studies in a Global Age* (Princeton, NJ: Princeton University Press, 2020), p. 229.
3 Ibid., p. 227.
4 Ibid.
5 For an interesting if incomplete analysis of Dostoevsky's influence on Mahfouz and two other Egyptian writers, see Jihan Zakarriya, 'Dostoevsky's Philosophical Justice and Moral Dilemma in the Egyptian Novel', 20

 https://doi.org/10.11647/OBP.0340.18

to varying degrees, therefore, the significance of the successful circulation of African literature, given the continent's predominantly oral literary tradition and its many minority languages, beyond its borders to the historic centres of world literature. But Damrosch and Casanova show little, if any, awareness of Africa's other literary feat: its assimilation of world literature through translation. Neither analyses Africa's reception of foreign literature, let alone the specific case of Russian literature.

For a continent comprising fifty-four countries, some of which enjoyed close political links with Moscow during the Soviet years, there is surprisingly scant scholarship even within the field of Russian Studies on the reception and influence of Russian literature in Africa and on African writers directly influenced by their relationship with the Russian literary canon. Much as research on Asia's relationship with Russian literature fails to correspond to the continent's size and scope—as explained in the introduction to the Asia section of this volume—the absence of scholarship on Africa's relationship with Russian literature is equally striking. Only a few researchers are active: Jeanne-Marie Jackson, Rossen Djagalov, Monica Popescu, and the South African novelist, essayist, and academic, Imraan Coovadia. Discrete areas of interest define the research that has so far been conducted by scholars in this field. These include the connection between South-African born writer J.M. Coetzee and classic Russian writers; the role of Progress Publishers in disseminating Russian and Soviet literature across parts of Africa; and the significance to Nelson Mandela, as Coovadia asserts, of Tolstoy's devotion to non-violence (which echoes the case of Tolstoy's influence on Gandhi, explored extensively by our various Indian contributors in the Asia section).

Jeanne-Marie Jackson's academic monographs *South African Literature's Russian Soul: Narrative Forms of Global Isolation* (2015) and *The African Novel of Ideas: Philosophy and Individualism in the Age of Global Writing* (2021) explore the links between nineteenth-century Russian and modern African literatures, which she describes as fraught in their relations with the wider world.[6] *The African Novel of Ideas* presents more broadly a "major transnational exploration of African literature in conversation with philosophy", yet even here, Jackson invites comparisons with Russian literature. Her fourth chapter, for example, analyses the significance of Fedor Dostoevsky's *Demons* (*Besy*) and the motif of suicide in Zimbabwean author Tendai Huchu's *The Maestro, the Magistrate, and the Mathematician* (2014), and in Coovadia's *Tales of the Metric System* (2016).

June 2022, 'Bloggers Karamazov', the blog of the North American Dostoevsky Society, https://bloggerskaramazov.com/2022/06/20/dostoevskys-philosophical-justice-and-moral-dilemma-in-the-egyptian-novel/.

6 See Jeanne-Marie Jackson, *South African Literature's Russian Soul: Narrative Forms of Global Isolation* (London and New York: Bloomsbury, 2015); and also her *The African Novel of Ideas: Philosophy and Individualism in the Age of Global Writing* (Oxford and Princeton, NJ: Princeton University Press, 2021).

Opening with an epigraph from J.M. Coetzee's *Diary of a Bad Year* (2007)—"In South Africa, as in Russia, life may be wretched, but how the brave spirit leaps to respond!"[7]—Jackson's *South African Literature's Russian Soul* states from the outset the premise that unites her research: "the propensity of many of Russia's notable 19th-century thinkers to take a despairing view of their homeland provides a clear bridge to this book's South African context".[8] Jackson does not aim to reveal "how writers construct new versions of reality" in South Africa inspired by the Russian literary canon, but rather to "show how it is that similarly problematic realities yield new constructions".[9] She cites scholar Monica Popescu when highlighting the versatility of Communist Moscow as a model of progress for South Africa according to Alex La Guma (author of the 1978 travelogue *A Soviet Journey*), and La Guma's fellow critics of late-twentieth-century Afrikaner authoritarianism.[10] Chapters in Jackson's book triangulate Nadine Gordimer, J.M. Coetzee and Ivan Turgenev, and Lev Tolstoy, Coetzee and Marlene van Niekirk. Elsewhere, she explores rewritings of Chekhov's major drama in the contemporary Afrikaans playwright Reza de Wet's play *Russian Trilogy*;[11] and finally, she draws comparisons between Vladimir Nabokov's *Speak, Memory*, and Lewis Nkosi's *Mandela's Ego*. Her monograph presents a compelling case study of Russia's influence over modern South African literature.

Rossen Djagalov's chapter 'The Afro-Asian Writers Association (1958–1991) and its Literary Field' examines cross-cultural interaction between Soviet and African and Asian writers during the mid- to late-twentieth century.[12] His research, enhanced by rare, archived photographs that visually capture the collaborative mood of the Afro-Asian Soviet programme, illustrates the particular significance of the 1958 Tashkent Congress (and, during the same year, of a special reception of writers from the United Arab Republic at the Kremlin Palace hosted by Khrushchev). At this event:

> over a hundred writers from Asia and the emerging African nations descended onto Tashkent [...]. Among the list of participants we find the nonagenarian W.E.B. Du Bois, who had just flown from Moscow, having persuaded Nikita Khrushchev to found the Institute for the Study of Africa. In Tashkent, he was joined by the major figures of the 1930s literary left outside of Europe or the Americas: the modernist Turkish poet Nazim Hikmet, the Chinese polymath Mao Dun, as well as the founding figures of the Popular-Front-era All-India Progressive Writers

7 Jackson, *South African Literature's Russian Soul*, p. 1.

8 Ibid., p. 2.

9 Ibid., p. 14.

10 Ibid., pp. 18–19.

11 Ibid., p. 130.

12 Rossen Djagalov, *From Internationalism to Postcolonialism: Literature and Cinema between the Second and Third Worlds* (Montreal and Kingston, London and Chicago, OH: McGill-Queen's University Press, 2020), pp. 65–110.

> Association—Mulk Raj Anand and Sajjad Zaheer. Though poorly known at the time, some of the younger delegates at that meeting would go on to become the leading literary figures of their countries: the Indonesian Pramoedya Toer, the Senegalese novelist soon-to-become filmmaker Sembene Ousmane, the poet and one of the founders of Angola's Communist Party Mario Pinto de Andrade, and his Mozambican counterpart—the poet and FRELIMO politician Marcelino dos Santos.[13]

Djagalov's research on the inauguration and legacy of the Afro-Asian Writers Association, including its role as a counterweight to the Congress of Cultural Freedom (a literary outreach project sponsored by the CIA), offers valuable insight into the routes through which the Kremlin achieved collaboration and favourable political relations between non-capitalist nations. Djagalov describes the effort as an attempt to create what he calls "a Soviet Republic of Letters";[14] he emphasises the movement of African and Asian literature into Russian translation as a means by which the Soviet Union strove to consolidate this phenomenon. Djagalov's chapter, though mainly focused on the Soviet reception of Asian and African literature within the Soviet Union, also elaborates (as do many of the chapters in this edited volume) on the role played by Progress Publishers in Africa. In exploring the dissemination of Russian and Soviet literature to what Damrosch and Casanova call peripheral territories, Djagalov reveals the extent of Progress's sphere of influence. In the case of Africa and Asia, he notes that the Afro-Asian Writers Association, the "main organizational vehicle of the Soviet engagement with postcolonial literatures" directly supported Progress's work.[15] According to Djagalov, study of the organisation's official transcripts "would only confirm [...] suspicion of the Association as a propaganda vehicle for Soviet, Chinese, Egyptian, and even Indian foreign policy":[16]

> The diverse agents of the Afro-Asian literary field—writers, cultural bureaucrats, publishers, critics, and readers—intuitively shared with contemporary dependency theorists such as Samir Amin, Raul Prebisch, and Walter Rodney an understanding of how they could escape their peripheral position within world literature: by delinking from the larger (literary) world-system, which kept them in a subordinate position; by developing their (literary) resources through interconnections; and by setting the terms of their own presence on the world (literary) stage. The Afro-Asian Writers Association represented just such an attempt

13 Ibid., p. 65.

14 Ibid., p. 71.

15 Rossen Djagalov, 'The Afro-Asian Writers Association and Soviet Engagement with Africa', *Black Perspectives* (2 November 2017), https://www.aaihs.org/the-afro-asian-writers-association-and-soviet-engagement-with-africa/.

16 Djagalov, *From Internationalism to Postcolonialism*, p. 81.

> to gain some autonomy from Paris and London and their interpretative authority.[17]

In this regard, the Soviet policy of soft power through cultural diplomacy created an emerging literary space for Afro-Asian writers that proved instrumental in propelling them towards global recognition. Djagalov observes that:

> The Afro-Asian Writers' Association also sought to consolidate Third World literature as a coherent field through the Lotus Literary Prize, modeled after the World Peace Council's Lenin Peace Prize of the early Cold War. Envisaged as the Afro-Asian Nobel for literature, the Lotus Prize helped produce a veritable contemporary Afro-Asian canon: the Palestinian poet Mahmoud Darwish (1969) and the South African prose writer Alex La Guma (1969), the novelists Sembene Ousmane (1971) and Ngugi wa Thiongo (1973), the Nigerian novelist Chinua Achebe (1975), and his compatriot, the poet, graduate of Moscow's Literary Institute, and future President of the Union of African Writers Atukwei Okai (1980). Many of the recipients received the award well before they acquired a significant literary reputation among Western publics.[18]

Monica Popescu's monographs—*South African Literature Beyond the Cold War* (2010) and *At Penpoint: African Literatures, Postcolonial Studies, and the Cold War* (2020)—also explore (and frame in Casanovan terms) Africa's relationship with Russian cultural soft power.[19] In *At Penpoint*, the most recent of her publications, she poses a valuable rhetorical question:

> If Pascale Casanova wrote the intellectual history of world literature with paths that weave in and out of Paris, how do we do justice to the stories of Ibadan, Kampala, Freetown, Dakar, and Johannesburg, as cities where writers forged alternative aesthetics and set up cultural solidarity networks with other marginalized artists' communities?[20]

Three previously unpublished case studies in the present volume answer Popescu's appeal for more stories to reinforce the notion of an African Republic of Letters. These case studies explore the circulation of Russian literature in Angola (Mukile Kasongo and Georgia Nasseh), Ethiopia (Nikolai Steblin-Kamensky), and in several Arabic nations (here, Egypt, Syro-Palestine, and Iraq are overviewed by Sarali Gintsburg). At the time of writing, Russian interests in

17 Ibid.

18 Djagalov, 'The Afro-Asian Writers Association'.

19 Monica Popescu, *South African Literature Beyond the Cold War* (London and New York: Pan Macmillan, 2010); and *At Penpoint: African Literatures, Postcolonial Studies, and the Cold War* (Durham, NC and London: Duke University Press, 2020).

20 Popescu, *At Penpoint*, p. 2.

Africa, as in Asia, are assuming new, post-Soviet significance: geopolitical lines are being revised in response to Russia's invasion of Ukraine. This development will have an inevitable impact on Russia's cultural diplomacy in the region. According to Isaac Antwi-Boasiako, Russia has replaced promulgating Soviet-Communist ideology in the twentieth century by its desire in the twenty-first "to improve global perceptions of Russia".[21] To further this aim, Russia promotes itself as "the protector of the 'free world'" and of "traditional family values".[22] As Antwi-Boasiako asserts, "[m]any non-Western countries, especially in Africa, welcome these two narratives as convincing".[23] (The effectiveness of Russia's diplomacy campaign in Africa since the 2000s can perhaps best be illustrated by the number of African leaders who chose "not to condemn Russia for the war in Ukraine in 2022".)[24] During October 2022, Moscow hosted its own international conference, 'Past, Present and Future of Russian-Arabic and Arabic-Russian Translations', at the Centre for Arab and Islamic Studies at the Institute of Oriental Studies in Moscow.[25] In November 2022—immediately following the Frankfurt Book Fair, from which Russia was banned—Sharjah's 41st International Book Fair in the Emirates admitted Russian publishers and literary agents among the ninety-five attendant countries.[26] Under the theme of 'Spread the Word', the Sharjah Book Fair focused on literature in the Arabic language. If, against the backdrop of war in Ukraine, Russia's status persists for the foreseeable future as *persona non grata* in the Global North, we may reasonably assume that this status will steer Russian literature in translation decisively towards Africa and the Middle East.

21 Isaac Antwi-Boasiako, 'The Quest for Influence: Examining Russia's Public Diplomacy Mechanisms in Africa', *South African Journal of International Affairs 2022*, Vol. 29, (4) (12 May 2022), 463–82, https://doi.org/10.1080/10220461.2022.2153728.

22 Ibid.

23 Ibid.

24 Ibid.

25 Schedule of the Institute of Oriental Studies Russian Academy of Sciences' conference 'Past, Present and Future of Russian-Arabic and Arabic-Russian Translations', https://www.ivran.ru/en/announc?artid=210593..

26 Sumit Arora, '41st Edition of the Sharjah International Book Fair Fall Inaugurated at the Expo Centre', *Adda247 Current Affairs* (3 November 2022), https://currentaffairs.adda247.com/41st-edition-of-the-sharjah-international-book-fair-fall-inaugurated-at-the-expo-centre/.

Angola

The Spectre of Maksim Gorky: The Influence of *Mother* on Angola's Geração *Cultura*

Mukile Kasongo and Georgia Nasseh

In November 1957, the first issue of *Cultura*—a cultural bulletin edited by the Sociedade Cultural de Angola—was published in the Angolan capital of Luanda, then under Portuguese colonial rule. Its aim was to provide "[os] homens de Angola, e sobretudo [a] sua juventude, [com] um meio de abordar quantos problemas atormentam o seu espírito" ("the men of Angola, and especially its youth, with a means of addressing whatever problems plague their spirit") and to contribute to the "gestação de uma cultura angolana, nacional pela forma e pelo conteúdo, universal pela intenção" ("development of an Angolan culture, national in its form and content, universal in its intention").[1] It might, therefore, come as a surprise that the inaugural issue of *Cultura*, on its single double-page spread, and among such pieces as the Angolan author José Luandino Vieira's ode 'Canção para Luanda', featured a Brazilian Portuguese translation of Maksim Gorky's short story 'The Conclusion' ('Vyvod', 1895), under the title 'Acompanhamento'.[2] The Russian author's story—first published in the *Samarskaia gazeta* on 26 February 1895, and later republished in a revised version in the *Krest'ianskaia gazeta* on 8 March 1935—recounts the events of 15 July 1891, which the author himself witnessed in the village of Kandybovka, in

1 'Editorial', in *Cultura*, 8 (June 1959), pp. 1–2.

2 Máximo Górki, 'Acompanhamento', *Cultura* 1 (November 1957), pp. 6–7. While the translator of 'Acompanhamento' is not named in the first issue of *Cultura*, it is likely that the translation published therein is the work of Ukraine-born Brazilian translator Boris Schnaiderman. An earlier translation of 'Vyvod' was published under the title 'A Surtida' on 12 August 1902, in *Pacotilha*. For more on Schnaiderman's Brazilian career, see Bruno B. Gomide's essay in this volume.

 https://doi.org/10.11647/OBP.0340.19

modern-day Ukraine: the public punishment of a woman accused of infidelity towards her husband.[1]

Yet, in its material context, Gorky's sketch of 'bytovaia kartina, obychai' (a picture from life, a custom) of nineteenth-century Ukraine speaks to the values—ethical and aesthetic—of Angola's nascent independence movement, which found intellectual expression in such spaces of 'conscienlização política nacionalista' (nationalist political consciousness) as the Sociedade Cultural de Angola.[2] On the double-page spread of the first issue of *Cultura*, the story 'Acompanhamento', which spans the lower half of both pages, is interrupted by a poem entitled 'Simples: poema aos meus irmãos' ('Simple: Poem to my brothers') by the Angolan poet João Abel. While the decision to print Gorky's story in itself suggests intercultural dialogue between Angola and Russia (then the Soviet Union) in the late 1950s, the fact that the story functions as a visual accompaniment—indeed, an 'acompanhamento'—to Abel's poem further invites the reader to consider the texts in relation to one another. When read together, Abel's poem seems to address, through the use of the intimate second-person pronoun 'tu', the punished woman of the Russian author's sketch:

1

Dá-me a tua mão,

E anda comigo à rua
a mostrar a toda a gente
que podemos andar no mundo de mãos dadas.[3]

(Give me your hand,

And walk with me through the street
that we may show everyone
that we can walk in the world hand in hand.)

The "rua"—or "street"—invoked in the opening stanza of Abel's poem parallels the "rua da aldeia, entre as casas brancas de taipa" ("village street, between rows of white-plastered cottages"), along which marches an "estranha procissão" ("strange procession"), described in Gorky's story.[4] Indeed, the speaker of

1 'Vyvod', *Samarskaia gazeta*, 44 (26 February 1895); 'Vyvod', *Krest'ianskaia gazeta* 35–36 (8 March 1935).

2 Fernando Tavares Pimenta, 'Representações políticas da cultura colonial dos brancos de Angola', *Estudos do Século XX*, 8 (2008), 293–304 (p. 302).

3 João Abel, 'Simples: poema aos meus irmãos', in *Cultura*, 1 (November 1957), pp. 6–7 (p. 6, ll. 1–4). All translations are our own unless otherwise indicated.

4 Górki, 'Acompanhamento', *Cultura*, 1 (November 1957), pp. 6–7 (p. 6); Maxim Gorky, 'The Exorcism', in *Orlóff and his Wife: Tales of the Barefoot Brigade*, trans. by Isabel F. Hapgood (New York: Charles Scribner's Sons, 1901), pp. 187–92 (p. 189).

the Angolan's poem, through their use of imperatives pervading the first four stanzas—"Dá-me a tua mão,/ E anda comigo à rua" ("Give me your hand,/ And walk with me through the street"), "Ouve.../ Não te cales sob a violência/ nem grites a tua inocência./ Reaje." ("Listen.../ Do not silence yourself in the face of violence/ nor scream out your innocence./ React.")—seemingly reaches out, across the printed page, to the woman described in 'Acompanhamento'.[5] The decision to print the Russian author's short story and the Angolan author's poem side by side is evidence of intertextual *and* intercultural dialogue. Their publication in the inaugural issue of *Cultura* illustrates the broader history of the transmission of Gorky's writing in mid-twentieth-century Angola. This transmission underpinned, crucially, the development of a *littérature engagée* during the country's struggle for independence from the Portuguese Empire in the late 1950s and early 1960s.

This chapter seeks to determine the ways in which Gorky's work influenced, through processes of translation, transmission, and adaptation, a critical moment in the emergence of an Angolan national literary culture. Through a case study of José Luandino Vieira—one of the most widely celebrated members of the Geração *Cultura*, a generation of writers committed to promoting an Angolan national identity, or *angolanidade*—drawing on extant scholarship of translation and ideology, this chapter analyses the "degrees of mediation" between Gorky's *oeuvre* and its instrumentalisation by the 1950s generation of Angolan authors through a comparative analysis of works by Gorky and Luandino Vieira.[6] The "degrees of mediation" traced in this paper fall into two main categories: first, both the translation of the Russian author into Brazilian Portuguese—with particular emphasis on his novel *Mother* (*Mat'*, 1906)—and its transnational dissemination across the Atlantic; second, in light of the translations then available to Angolan authors, the adaptation of aspects of Gorky's novel in the early writings of Luandino Vieira (*A Cidade e a Infância*, 1954–57; *A Vida Verdadeira de Domingos Xavier*, 1961; *Vidas Novas*, 1961–62).

Angola is a fruitful case study of Soviet entanglements in the African continent—a significant aspect of the Soviet Union's policy of anti-imperialist internationalism. According to Christopher Stevens's evaluation: "Angola is unique in the history of Soviet involvement in Africa. Never before has the USSR assisted an African liberation movement on such a grand scale".[7] The Soviet Union's investment in Angola—and, more specifically, in the People's Movement for the Liberation of Angola (MPLA)—increased considerably during the Angolan Civil War (1975–2002). However, previous links between

5 Abel, 'Simples: poema aos meus irmãos', in *Cultura*, 1 (November 1957), 6–7 (p. 6, ll. 1–2, ll. 5–8).

6 Basil Hatim and Ian Mason, *The Translator as Communicator* (London and New York: Routledge, 1997), p. 122.

7 Christopher Stevens, 'The Soviet Union and Angola', *African Affairs*, 75:299 (April 1976), 137–51 (p. 137).

the two countries dating back to the late 1950s meant that literary affiliations at the start of Angola's nationalist movement were inevitably measured alongside political affiliations. As the dates reveal, the development of these affiliations was contemporaneous with the formation of the MPLA and the outbreak of the anti-colonial struggle. The party's early history was deeply imbricated with the policies and influence of the Soviet Union. Poet and 'father of Angolan nationalism' Mário Pinto de Andrade (1928–90), for example, visited the USSR during his stint as president of the MPLA (1959–62). In August 1960, he travelled to Moscow to take part in the International Congress of Oriental Studies, "as [a] guest of the Soviet Writers' Union"; he returned to the USSR a year later with other MPLA leaders "at the invitation of the Solidarity Committee".[8] Similarly, in 1963, Agostinho Neto (1922–79), Pinto de Andrade's successor as president of the MPLA (1963–75, 1975–79) and first president of Angola (1975–79)—embarked on a tour of the Soviet bloc with the intention of publicising "o estado da luta contra a soberania portuguesa em Angola" ("the state of the struggle against Portuguese sovereignty in Angola").[9] That Neto would later win the Lenin Peace Prize for 1975–76, and indeed the fact that he died in the Soviet Union, attests to the inter-relationship between Angola and the Soviet Union. According to Rossen Djagalov, "[t]he appeal of Soviet anti-imperialism indirectly helped the stature of Russo-Soviet literature with readers and writers from the (semi-)colonial world".[10] It is this relationship that underpins the interest Angolan authors had in Russian literature in the decades leading up to independence, and helps to explain why they sought out both political and aesthetic affiliations with the USSR.

A new chapter in the history of the Portuguese-language transmission of Gorky's work, and of Russian literature more generally, remains to be written: one in which these texts' (often clandestine) circulation throughout Portuguese-speaking Africa, in either Brazilian or European translations, whether from the French or directly from the Russian, might more thoroughly be traced. That project extends beyond the scope of this present chapter, which nevertheless aims to begin work in this direction. For our purposes, it suffices that, on both shores of the Atlantic, Portuguese-speaking writers with emancipatory aspirations saw opportunities for political and aesthetic affiliation in Gorky's works. Therefore, the remainder of this chapter will compare Gorky and Luandino Vieira, foregrounding the transposition of aspects of Gorky's *oeuvre*, and the novel *Mother* in particular, into the Angolan author's early writings. What emerges,

8 W. Martin James, *Historical Dictionary of Angola* (Lanham: Scarecrow Press, 2004), p. 6; Vladimir Shubin, *The Hot 'Cold War': The USSR in Southern Africa* (London: Pluto Press, 2008), pp. 7–8.

9 Carlos Alberto de Jesus Alves, 'Política externa angolana em tempo de guerra e paz: colonialismo e pós-colonialismo' (unpublished doctoral thesis, Universidade de Coimbra, 2013), pp. 44–45.

10 Djagalov, *From Internationalism to Postcolonialism*, p. 36.

then, not only serves to confirm Djagalov's suggestion that "Moscow's realpolitik [...] did not straightforwardly translate into the imaginaries of leftist cultural producers" in the Third World, where "the vast majority of such intellectuals took the October Revolution and the Soviet cultural production it inflected and turned them into gigantic canvases onto which to project their own aspirations", but also to provide an opportunity to trace how material histories of translation, however *un*straightforward, have intersected with this projection.[11]

Reading Gorky in Angola

The influence of Gorky's work on the generation of Angolan writers active in the 1950s and 1960s has been explicitly acknowledged. In a 1977 interview, for instance, Luandino Vieira remarks that a close acquaintance, fellow poet António Jacinto, "pôs-nos a sua biblioteca à disposição e nós lemos muito" ("placed his library at our disposal and we read a lot").[12] Luandino Vieira proceeds with a description of Jacinto's private library and the volumes held therein:

> Ele tinha uma biblioteca muito boa, quero dizer: de muitos livros maus quanto ao papel, eram edições populares que naquele tempo circulavam nos anos 30, alguns mesmo eram edições de cordel, publicadas em fascículos. [...] Lembro-me que li o Górki em caderninhos, publicados em fascículos.[13]
>
> (He had a very good library: that is to say, with many volumes in cheap editions, they were popular editions that circulated at the time in the 1930s some were even serialised editions, published in fascicles. [...] I recall that I read Gorky in small notebooks, published in fascicles.)

Of particular significance among the volumes held in Jacinto's private library were Brazilian translations of "o que, na altura, chamávamos de literatura revolucionária, como a *Mãe* do Górki" ("what we, at the time, called revolutionary literature, such as Gorky's *Mother*").[14] Attesting to the pervasive influence of Russian literature and of Gorky's works, in particular on Angolan intellectuals of the 1950s and 1960s, other prominent writers of the period report similar

11 Ibid., p. 12.

12 'Encontro de 6 de abril de 1977', in *Luandino: José Luandino Vieira e a Sua Obra (Estudos, Testemunhos, Entrevistas)*, ed. by Michel Laban (Lisbon: Edições 70, 1980), pp. 11–29 (p. 15).

13 Ibid., p. 15.

14 Débora Leite David and Susanna Ramos Ventura, 'Conversa com o escritor angolano José Luandino Vieira, que gentilmente nos recebeu na tarde do dia 27 de fevereiro de 2006, em sua casa no Convento de San Payo, Vila Nova de Cerveira', África: *Revista do Centro de Estudos Africanos* 27–28 (2006/2007), 175–97 (p. 175).

experiences to that of Luandino Vieira.[15] In a 1984 interview, Pinto de Andrade echoes Luandino Vieira's account:

> Foi o romance russo que verdadeiramente me formou. Em traduções brasileiras, comecei a ler, muito cedo, com dezasseis anos, [...] Gogol, Górki e Tolstói. *A Mãe* foi um dos primeiros romances revolucionários—e de que maneira—que li. Recordo-me muito bem do exemplar, num péssimo papel, e da capa da versão brasileira.[16]
>
> (It was the Russian novel that truly shaped me. In Brazilian translations, I began reading, at a very early age, at sixteen [...] Gogol, Gorky, and Tolstoy. *Mother* was one of the first revolutionary novels—and how revolutionary it was—that I read. I remember the copy well, printed on awful paper, and its cover that of the Brazilian edition.)

The two Angolan writers' accounts share similarities that merit further consideration. While Pinto de Andrade notes the significance of the encounter with "o romance russo" ("the Russian novel") to his intellectual development, he emphasises, in a manner similar to Luandino Vieira, the pre-eminence of *Mother* specifically mentioned by both Angolans. Pinto de Andrade, moreover, highlights that he read Gorky's novel in a Brazilian edition, printed on "péssimo papel" ("awful paper"), recalling Luandino Vieira's earlier description of the "muitos livros maus quanto ao papel, [...] edições populares que naquele tempo circulavam" ("many volumes in cheap editions, [...] popular editions that circulated at the time"), of which the Portuguese-language *A Mãe* was one.[17]

---

15 In the preface to the 1980 illustrated edition of poet and first president of Angola Agostinho Neto's *Náusea*, Antero Abreu describes it as "[u]m conto de escritor 'engagé'" ("a committed writer's story"), listing "os neo-realistas portugueses e de outros países europeus, e Gorki, e Jorge Amado, e Graciliano Ramos" ("the Portuguese neo-realists as well as those from other European countries, and Gorky, and Jorge Amado, and Graciliano Ramos") as significant influences. See Antero Abreu, 'Prefácio', in Agostinho Neto, *Náusea/O Artista* (Lisbon: Edições 70, 1980), p. 14. Similarly, according to Rubens Pereira dos Santos, writer Eugénia Neto considered her encounter with Gorky's work the most important consequence of her travels to the Soviet Union. See Rubens Pereira dos Santos, 'Gorki e Luandino Vieira: Relações Literárias', in *De* Luuanda *a Luandino: Veredas*, ed. by Francisco Topa and Elsa Pereira (Porto: Edições Afrontamento, 2015), pp. 111–20 (p. 112).

16 Mário Pinto de Andrade, *Uma entrevista dada a Michel Laban* (Lisbon: Edições Sá da Costa, 1997), pp. 33–34.

17 The seemingly idiosyncratic remark is, nevertheless, revealing of these editions' intended readerships. According to Bruno Barretto Gomide, Gorky's works, often printed by publishers associated with "intelectuais e gráficas de esquerda" ("left-wing presses and intellectuals"), were also read in Brazil, almost exclusively in cheap editions. Bruno Barretto Gomide, *Dostoiévski na Rua do Ouvidor: A Literatura Russa e o Estado Novo* (São Paulo: Edusp, 2018), p. 17, p. 29.

Pinto de Andrade expounds, albeit briefly, on this process of transmission: in Brazil, he observes, "[e]stava-se na época de Getúlio Vargas, uma época liberal, em que se traduzia muito, e vamos encontrar mais tarde diversas versões brasileiras dos clássicos marxistas, que foram distribuídos em Angola" ("it was the time of Getúlio Vargas, a liberal time, during which much was being translated, and later we will encounter several Brazilian editions of the Marxist classics, which were distributed in Angola").[18]

The clandestine nature of the distribution of such "clássicos marxistas" ("Marxist classics") during the decades leading up to independence in 1975 has unfortunately resulted in sparse, although still illuminating, accounts of the history of the transmission of Russian literature (often by way of Brazil) in Angola. In a 2006 interview, Luandino Vieira remarks that due to "ligações mais ou menos clandestinas" ("more or less clandestine connections") between the two Portuguese-speaking countries, "todo o material de natureza política, a formação política [...] veio do Brasil" ("all material of a political nature, all political development [...] came from Brazil").[19] This reflects the situation Pascale Casanova has described, whereby Brazil's influence—in particular its establishment of alternative centres of literary production to Lisbon—"made it possible for writers in other parts of the Portuguese-speaking area, less endowed in cultural and literary resources, to look to the São Paulo pole in attempting to overturn traditional political and literary norms".[20] Indeed, Angolan writers during this period "rel[ied] upon Brazilian literary resources", ranging from national Brazilian literature to Brazilian translations of literature from other national canons, "in order to counteract the influence of European models and to create their own literary genealogy and history"[21]

The translation and circulation of Russian literature in Brazil can be traced back to the late nineteenth century. However, the vast majority of these translations, Iulia I. Mikaelyan notes, did not use Russian originals as source texts, but rather what Mikaelyan terms "European" translations, particularly in English and—in the case of Brazil—French.[22] The 1930s, under President Getúlio Vargas (1930–45), saw the number of translations of Russian literature increase, as the first years of the decade were characterised by a "febre de eslavismo".[23] Significantly, however, there was also a rise in the number of direct translations

18 Andrade, p. 34.

19 David and Ventura, p. 176.

20 Pascale Casanova, *The World Republic of Letters*, trans. by M. B. DeBevoise (Cambridge, MA: Harvard University Press, 2007), p. 123.

21 Ibid., pp. 123–24.

22 Iu. I. Mikaelian, 'Rossiia v Brazilii: vzaimodeistvie kul'tur (opyty perevoda)', *Kontsept: filosofiia, religiia, kul'tura* 3 (2017), 95–100 (p. 97). For more on the Brazilian reception of Russian literature in the late nineteenth century, see Bruno Barretto Gomide, *Da Estepe à Caatinga: O Romance Russo no Brasil (1887–1936)* (São Paulo: Edusp, 2011).

23 Gomide, *Dostoiévski na Rua do Ouvidor*, p. 17.

from the Russian: the consequence, according to Bruno Barretto Gomide, of a "forte cruzamento entre política, imigração e tradução de textos russos" ("strong overlap between politics, immigration, and the translation of Russian texts"), which took place during the period.[24]

The publication of Gorky's *oeuvre* in Brazil attests to this shift. If the earliest translations of Gorky to appear in Brazilian publications date to the first years of the twentieth century, it was in the 1930s and 1940s that interest in the Russian author's work became evident. Let us take *Mother* as an example. The first Portuguese translation of Gorky's novel was published in Brazil in 1931, under the title *A Mãe*, by the publishing house Marisa;[25] that same year, the translation (revised by Renato Travassos) was also published as an instalment of Companhia Editora Americana's Collecção de Obras Celebres. In 1932, another Brazilian edition of *A Mãe* was published, now by José Calvino Filho—founder of Calvino Filho Editor (later Editorial Calvino Limitada) and publisher of a number of 'clássicos marxistas' ('Marxist classics') in alleged response to such 'fenômenos sociológicos' ('sociological phenomena') of the time as the USSR. Still more editions followed: in 1935, *A Mãe* was published by Civilização Brasileira as part of their Collecções Econômicas SIP; in 1944, by the Brazilian Communist Party-affiliated Editorial Vitória; also in 1944, by Editora Pongetti, in a new translation by Araújo Neves. As suggested by the accounts of such Angolan writers as Luandino Vieira and Pinto de Andrade, it is likely that these editions were among those circulated clandestinely in pre-independence Angola. Increased politicisation has been shown to influence the circulation of symbolic goods.[26] In the Angolan case, this politicisation conditioned the reception of Gorky's *Mother* from the USSR to Angola via Brazilian translations. A question nevertheless remains: in what ways did Angolan intellectuals 'translate' Russian literature, and the work of Gorky in particular, in the 1950s and 1960s?

The emphasis within Translation Studies on the relationship between ideology and translation, and, in particular, the concept of mediation, is important here. Anthony J. Liddicoat argues that, in the context of Translation Studies, 'mediation' is often understood in two ways. First, as "an interpretive act", a "cognitive process that is central to the translator's coming to understand a text

24 Bruno Barretto Gomide, 'Estado Novo, José Olympio e Dostoiévski: por que uma "coleção" de obras completas?', *Anais do 38º Encontro Anual da Anpocs [Associação Nacional de Pós-Graduação e Pesquisa em Ciências Sociais]* (27–31 October 2014), 1–28 (p. 3). https://anpocs.com/index.php/papers-38-encontro/gt-1/gt28-1. See also Gomide's essay in the current volume.

25 No translator was named in any of the earlier editions.

26 Johan Heilbron and Gisèle Sapiro, 'Outline for a Sociology of Translation: Current Issues and Future Prospects', in *Constructing a Sociology of Translation*, ed. by Michaela Wolf and Alexandra Fukari (Amsterdam: John Benjamins, 2007), pp. 93–107 (p. 97).

and representing it for a new audience".[27] Second, as a consequence of the fact that a "translator is an intermediary intervening in texts to achieve meaningful communication", and therefore occupies a position "between languages and cultures".[28] At the heart of this dual concept of mediation is Basil Hatim and Ian Mason's understanding of translation as "an act of communication which attempts to relay, across cultural and linguistic boundaries, another act of communication (which may have been intended for different purposes and different readers/hearers)", and their view of the translator "as a processor of texts" who "filters the text world of the source text through his/her own world-view/ideology, with differing results".[29] Hatim and Mason stress both the "degrees of mediation" that intervene between source text and target text, and the role of the translator as mediator. Translation emerges from their analysis as a complex communicative function by which a text is processed, by which new ideological content is incorporated into it, and by which it is made to communicate with new audiences.[30]

The Influence of *Mother*

Maksim Gorky's novel *Mat'* was written in 1906 while the author was abroad, evading the threat of arrest in Russia following the events of 1905.[31] It was first published in (English) translation in the United States in seven instalments in *Appleton's Magazine* under the title *Mother* (1906–07); it finally appeared, with revisions, in Russian in 1907.[32] The novel has since been canonised as the first work of Socialist Realism—and its author as "the acknowledged 'father' of Soviet literature".[33] However, this classification has not elicited critical consensus. While critics such as Andrei Siniavskii have argued that *Mother* has been "rightly considered in Soviet historiography as the first example of socialist realism" ("spravedlivo priniatyi v sovetskoi istoriografii kak pervyi obrazets sotsialisticheskogo realizma"), others, like Evgeny Dobrenko, have more recently foregrounded the "artificial" nature of the endeavour to trace

27 Anthony J. Liddicoat, 'Translation as intercultural mediation: setting the scene', *Perspectives*, 24: 3 (2016), 347–53 (p. 348).

28 Ibid.

29 Hatim and Mason, p. 1, p. 122.

30 Ibid., p. 122.

31 Barry P. Scherr, *Maxim Gorky* (Boston, MA: Twayne Publishers, 1988), pp. 8–9.

32 Sara Pankenier and Barry P. Scherr, 'Searching for the Ur-Text: Gorky's English "Mother"', *Russian Language Journal*, 51:168–170 (1997), 125–48 (p. 125); Richard Freeborn, *The Russian Revolutionary Novel: Turgenev to Pasternak* (Cambridge: Cambridge University Press, 1982), p. 45.

33 Scherr, p. 19.

the "origins" of Socialist Realism to Gorky's novel.[34] Earlier critics, moreover, have associated Gorky with Critical Realism (*kriticheskii realizm*)—an important precursor of Socialist Realism, which, unlike the latter, does not necessarily pose Socialism as the solution to the issues it analyses.[35] It is nevertheless the case that *Mother*, on the basis of both its narrative structure and its dominant themes, became "a prototype for future socialist realist novels"—an ethical and aesthetic model seized upon by Angolan writers of the 1950s and 1960s.[36]

The novel depicts the process of revolutionary awakening among workers in tsarist Russia, balancing both a portrayal of the lives of ordinary people and an account of a transformative encounter with Socialism. It is divided into two parts: in the first, one of its two protagonists, Pelageia Nilovna Vlasova—a forty-year-old woman, mother to Pavel Vlasov—is depicted as a passive witness to unfolding events. Having suffered years of abuse from her late husband, Mikhail Vlasov, she clings desperately to her son Pavel, supporting him when he joins a group of Socialists. In the second part, Nilovna participates actively in the revolutionary struggle. She is transformed by contact with Pavel and his comrades, becoming an exemplary revolutionary and heroic figure. Both the novel's setting—a workers' settlement—and its privileging of working-class characters and issues, find echoes in the themes and settings of Luandino Vieira's early works. Many of the Angolan author's texts draw attention to locations—such as the "musseques" or the "sanzala", the Angolan cultural equivalents of the "slobodki" of Gorky's fictional world—associated either with labour or labourers, depicting characters that live at the margins of colonial society.

34 Andrei Siniavskii, 'Roman M. Gor'kogo *Mat'*—kak rannii obrazets sotsialisticheskogo realizma', *Cahiers du monde russe et soviétique*, 29:1 (January–March 1988), 33–40 (p. 34); Evgeny Dobrenko, 'Socialist Realism', in *The Cambridge Companion to Twentieth-Century Russian Literature*, ed. by Evgeny Dobrenko and Marina Balina (Cambridge: Cambridge University Press, 2011), pp. 97–114 (p. 103).

35 A. Lavretskii, 'O sud'be literaturovedcheskogo termina' [About the Literary Term], *Izvestiia Akademii nauk SSSR*, 16:1 (1957), 34–38 (p. 35).

36 The debate between 'Critical Realism' and 'Socialist Realism' has also featured in studies on Angolan literature. Soviet literary critic and translator of Angolan literature Elena Aleksandrovna Riauzova, noting a change in the literary methods and topics featured in Angolan literature between the 1950s and 1970s, argues that Angolan writers of this period used mostly Critical, as opposed to Socialist, Realism, as they sought to analyse social inequalities, urban and village experiences, and conflicts between social groups. Nevertheless, despite Aleksandrovna's accurate evaluation of texts like Luandino Vieira's *A Cidade e a Infância*, close attention to the development of his style more generally across his early career evidences a growing tendency to favour the themes and techniques of Socialist Realism. See Elena Aleksandrovna Riauzova, *Roman v sovremennykh portugaloiazichnykh literaturakh* (*problemy tipologii i vzaimodeistviia*) (*The Novel in Contemporary Portuguese Literatures: Problems of Typology and Reciprocal Action*) (Moscow: Nauka, 1980), p. 185.

While the similarities between Gorky's novel and Luandino Vieira's early works are clear, it is important to note that the Angolan author's portrayal of the "musseques" and the "sanzala" differs from Gorky's "slobodki" as a result of the racial dynamics that characterises these spaces. In *A Vida Verdadeira de Domingos Xavier* (*The Real Life of Domingos Xavier*), for instance, the "musseques" and the "sanzala" are where the "operários e trabalhadores negros" ("black workmen and labourers"), such as Domingos Xavier, live. This location is contrasted with the "camaratas de alumínio" ("aluminium dormitories")—where the "operários brancos" ("white workmen") live—as well as the houses inhabited by the "empregados superiores da empresa" ("senior staff of the construction company"). The workers' settlement is, for members of the anti-colonial struggle, a site of racialised differences. This racial dimension is, of course, absent from Gorky's novel, where class represents the dominant means of social striation. Yet, both authors demonstrate how, in their respective contexts, characters begin to organise their discontent towards authoritarian regimes into meaningful collective action. The different emphases in each author's works do not obfuscate what is immediately comparable about the experiences and struggles of their characters. For instance, Angola, under Portuguese colonial rule, much like tsarist Russia, was characterised by political repression, censorship, arbitrary arrests, and torture. Whereas the Russians were subjected to the Okhrana, the Angolans were subjected to Portugal's International and State Defense Police (PIDE)—the colonial police—which was responsible for the arrests of those the regime deemed dangerous to its rule. While both authors depict struggles that take place in environments characterised by repression, both nevertheless depict the beginnings of struggles for liberation, which would eventually culminate, respectively, in the Russian Revolution of 1917 and Angolan independence in 1975.

Within these contexts of repression, characters undergo important transformations. Nilovna and Pavel begin as passive victims of oppression and develop into heroes of revolutionary agency. According to Rufus Mathewson:

> *Mother* contains two formulas often found in later Soviet fiction: the conversion of the innocent, the ignorant, or the misled to a richer life of participation in the forward movement of society; and the more important pattern of emblematic political heroism in the face of terrible obstacles. The first theme is embodied in the figure of the mother, whose life is transformed by affiliation with the revolutionary movement, and the second in the grim figure of her son, Pavel.[37]

These two formulas are, however, harder to separate than Mathewson suggests. The politicisation of Nilovna through contact with her son and his comrades

37 Rufus W. Mathewson, Jr, *The Positive Hero in Russian Literature* (Stanford, CA: Stanford University Press, 1975), p. 167.

produces, beyond a mere "conversion", its own "pattern of emblematic political heroism". For instance, Nilovna's ability to take the revolutionary struggle forward after Pavel's arrest implies that the distribution of agency and exemplary behaviour between Mathewson's "two formulas" is more complex. What is clear, however, is the importance of the figure of the hero, of exemplary lives and actions, to the socially engaged literature read by Angolan intellectuals in the context of the struggle for national independence. As Emmanuel Nagra argues, speaking here of the African novel in general, "[s]ocialist realism is [...] orientated towards the future, towards the building of a happy, successful and socialist society", and this orientation is frequently concentrated in the action of characters like Nilovna and Pavel—characters who exemplify the manifold processes of conversion, participation, and political heroism Mathewson describes. These processes are, as Gorky himself suggests in a speech delivered at the first Soviet Writers' Congress in 1934, in accordance with Socialist Realism's mythic qualities:

> Myth is invention. To invent means to extract from the sum of a given reality its cardinal idea and embody it in imagery—that is how we got realism. But if to the idea extracted from the given reality we add—completing the idea by the logic of hypothesis—the desired, the possible, and thus supplement the image, we obtain that romanticism which is at the basis of myth and is highly beneficial in that it tends to provoke a revolutionary attitude to reality, an attitude that changes the world in a practical way.[38]

Gorky here proposes an artistic scheme in which Mathewson's "two formulas" operate in conjunction: both the educative extraction of the "cardinal idea" of a given situation, producing a realism capable of converting "the innocent" and "the ignorant" by the force of its representation; and the infusion into this "reality" of "the desired, the possible", a "pattern of emblematic political heroism" which might provoke admiration and imitation.

The Making of Heroes

This combination of social critique and the 'romanticism' of heroism is essential to the political purposes of Luandino Vieira's writing. For instance, 'Quinzinho', one of the ten pieces included in Luandino Vieira's first collection of short stories, *A Cidade e a Infância*, tells—through a second-person address to Quinzinho—of

38 Maksim Gorky, 'Soviet Literature', in *Soviet Writers' Congress 1934: The Debate on Socialist Realism and Modernism in the Soviet Union* (London: Lawrence and Wishart, 1977), pp. 25–69 (p. 44).

the eponymous character's death at the hands of a factory machine.[39] Referred to as a "poeta do trabalho" ("poet of labour"), Quinzinho, we learn, has been "[d]espedaçado pela máquina que te escravizava e que tu amavas" ("torn apart by the machine that enslaved you and that you loved").[40] At the funeral, the narrator states:

> Eu também aqui no meio dos teus amigos. Mas eu não vou triste. Não. Porque uma morte como a tua constrói liberdades futuras. E haverá outros a quem as máquinas não despedaçarão, pois as máquinas serão escravas deles, que as hão-de idealizar, construir.[41]
>
> (I am here, too, among your friends. But I am not sad. No. Because a death like yours constructs future freedoms. And there will be others whom the machines will not tear apart, because the machines will be their slaves, who will envision them, construct them.)

Written on 8 February 1957—the same year in which the inaugural issue of *Cultura* was published—the short story gestures to concerns that will be considered in greater detail in subsequent works by the Angolan author, such as *A Vida Verdadeira de Domingos Xavier* and *Vidas Novas* (*New Lives*). While Russell G. Hamilton, in his pioneering 1975 study on the literatures of Portuguese-speaking Africa, *Voices from an Empire*, notes that, in *Vidas Novas*, we are met with the (recognisably Gorkian) "idea of the hero or of the hapless victim who becomes the hero of the people", it is nevertheless the case that such heroic trajectories feature not only in Luandino Vieira's 1962 collection, but also in his earlier works.[42] Here, Quinzinho's death—at the hands of both a literal and, indeed, metaphorical 'máquina' ('machine'), the word's connotations extending past its immediate context (that is, the factory), towards what was often referred to as the 'máquina colonial' ('colonial machine') of Portuguese administration under António de Oliveira Salazar—functions much like Pavel's arrest in *Mother*. Quinzinho's death is regarded as a means through which other workers—"outros a quem as máquinas não despedaçarão" ("others whom the machines will not tear apart")—might develop class consciousness, enabling the construction of "liberdades futuras" ("future freedoms"). The future-oriented stance of 'Quinzinho', like that of *Mother*, can be seen to permeate much of Luandino Vieira's *oeuvre*.

This is particularly true of the novella *A Vida Verdadeira de Domingos Xavier*. The protagonist, Domingos Xavier, is a tractor driver, husband to Maria and

---

39 José Luandino Vieira, 'Quinzinho', in *A Cidade e a Infância* (Lisbon: Edições 70, 1977), pp. 147–53 (p. 149).

40 Ibid., p. 150.

41 Ibid.

42 Russell G. Hamilton, *Voices from an Empire: A History of Afro-Portuguese Literature* (Minneapolis, MN: University of Minnesota Press, 1975), p. 138.

father to Bastião—a man described as "muito amigo, nunca faltando com seu ordenado" ("very affectionate, never missing his wages"), a detail that serves to underline his sense of responsibility; a man described, moreover, as someone "[que] nunca fez mal a ninguém" ("who never did anyone any harm").[43] An ordinary man who, in a manner similar to *Mother*'s Pelageia Nilovna, undergoes a process of revolutionary awakening through his conversations with Silvestre, the white engineer stationed at the construction site. For this, Domingos Xavier is arrested, tortured, and killed by agents of the PIDE, transformed into a "corpo martirizado" ("martyred body"); into an "herói mítico angolano" ("mythical Angolan hero"), an ideal of national liberation.[44] Mussunda, in the novella's closing speech, proclaims:

> — Irmãos angolanos. Um irmão veio dizer mataram um nosso camarada. Se chamava Domingos Xavier e era tractorista. Nunca fez mal a ninguém, só queria o bem do seu povo, e da sua terra. Fiz parar esta farra só para dizer isto, não é para acabar, porque a nossa alegria é grande: nosso irmão se portou como homem, não falou os assuntos do seu povo, não se vendeu. Não vamos chorar mais a sua morte porque, Domingos António Xavier, você começa hoje a sua vida de verdade no coração do povo angolano...[45]
>
> (— Angolan brothers. A brother came to say that they have killed one of our comrades. He was called Domingos Xavier and he was a tractor driver. He never did anyone any harm, he only wished for the good of his people, and of his land. I have stopped our festivities, not to put an end to them, for our joy is great, but to say this: our brother carried himself like a man, he did not talk about the affairs of his people, he did not sell himself. We will no longer cry over your death because, Domingos António Xavier, today you begin your real life in the heart of the Angolan people...)

Here, the future-oriented stance of the short story 'Quinzinho' is once more made manifest. In both works, life does not end with death. Just as Quinzinho's death marks less an end than it does a starting point for "liberdades futuras" ("future freedoms"), that of Domingos Xavier marks the beginning of his "vida de verdade" ("real life"). Both narratives subscribe to the "formulas" Mathewson identifies in *Mother*, adapting them for Angolan audiences. If, in the former, we see Quinzinho (however inadvertently) become consecrated as a representative of the "emblematic political heroism" embodied by Pavel, in the latter we see the

43 Luandino Vieira, *A Vida Verdadeira de Domingos Xavier*, p. 35, p. 128.

44 Ibid., p. 104; Heleno Godoy, 'Dizer/não dizer: por que é verdadeira a vida de Domingos Xavier?', *Scripta*, 1:1 (1997), 196–203 (p. 196).

45 Luandino Vieira, *A Vida Verdadeira de Domingos Xavier*, p. 128.

"innocent" Domingos Xavier—and other characters, such as the "misled" Xico Kafundanga—undergo a "conversion [...] to a richer life of participation in the forward movement of society", following, like Quinzinho, "the more important pattern of emblematic political heroism in the face of terrible obstacles".[46] Both works, like much of Luandino Vieira's early writings, contain a "general presentation of an awakening consciousness within previously ignorant people", a "depiction of the seemingly inexorable growth of the revolutionary movement", and an "ending, which in one sense is a defeat [...] but also contains the seeds of future victories".[47] Barry Scherr's evaluation of Gorky's novel is also a surprisingly adequate description of the Angolan writer's texts.

Gendered Revolutions

While the narrative trajectory popularised in *Mother* finds expression in *A Vida Verdadeira de Domingos Xavier*, Luandino Vieira adapts this trajectory—or the agent of this trajectory—to the expectations of an Angolan readership. Scherr's phrase, "seeds of future victories", is particularly evocative of the generative potential of Nilovna as "mother". Many critics have commented on the relationship between gender and revolutionary agency in Gorky's novel. Angela Brintlinger has argued that "[b]y naming the novel after his secondary character, the mother Nilovna [...], Gorky offers a generative model for future revolutionary action."[48] Indeed, Nilovna extends the support she offers Pavel to other characters, particularly Andrei Onisimovich Nakhodka, her son's Ukrainian comrade. In a sense, she becomes a mother to Andrei, and adapts a maternal role to encompass extra-familial support and care. As the novel progresses, Nilovna is transformed into the "Mother" of the revolutionary movement. She considers all fighters her children: as she herself points out, "Voistinu, vse vy—tovarishchi, vse—rodnye, vse—deti odnoi materi—pravdy!" ("In very truth we are all comrades, all kindred spirits, all children of one mother, who is truth!").[49] Gender plays an essential role in this transformation. By reconfiguring motherhood, Nilovna discovers a revolutionary vocation. As Brintlinger says: "'Mother' with a capital *M* defines Gorky's attitude toward revolution: not only can the older generation be reformed, but they can 'give birth' to more and more youth willing to work and fight for changes in society."[50]

46 Mathewson, *The Positive Hero in Russian Literature*, p. 167.

47 Scherr, *Maxim Gorky*, p. 47.

48 Angela Brintlinger, *Chapaev and His Comrades: War and the Russian Literary Hero Across the Twentieth Century* (Boston: Academic Studies Press, 2017), p. 39.

49 Maksim Gor'kiĭ. *Mat'* (Moscow: Detskaia literatura, 1936), p. 171; Maxim Gorky, *Mother*, trans. by Margaret Wettlin (Moscow: Progress Publishers, 1980), p. 377.

50 Brintlinger, p. 39.

Yet, women in pre- and post-independence Angolan literature are rarely—if, indeed, ever—portrayed as heroes.[51] Despite Angolan "[w]omen's involvement in the struggle for independence [in] response to the ideals of the MPLA to fight for the 'equality of all Angolans, regardless of ethnicity, religion, regional origin and sex'", and despite the active participation of the Organization of Angolan Women (OMA)—the women's wing of the MPLA—in this struggle since its establishment in 1962, women have largely been sidelined in narratives, both fictional and official, of national liberation.[52] As such, the models of heroism available in *Mother* are adapted to reflect the MPLA's ideological line. As we learn from Mussunda's speech, Domingos Xavier's perceived heroism is attributed to the fact that "nosso irmão se portou como homem" ("our brother carried himself like a man"). This is echoed in the story 'O Exemplo de Job Hamukuaja', written in 1962 and included in the collection *Vidas Novas*. The story concerns two characters, ultimately deemed "dois bons angolanos" ("two good Angolans"): Job Hamukuaja, a man being tortured by agents of the PIDE, accused of having "entregado o pacote com os panfletos para distribuir na 'industrial'" ("delivered the package with the pamphlets to be distributed in the industrial zone"); and Mário João, a comrade who, unable to withstand torture, reveals Job's name.[53] On realising that Job is steadfast in his silence, Mário João smiles: "Sabia bem que ia aguentar, o companheiro tinha-lhe mostrado como fazem os homens de verdade."[54] ("He knew he would be able to bear it, his comrade had shown him how real men carry themselves.")

Once more, a masculinised image of heroism is invoked. Here, the term "real man"—"nastoiashchii muzhchina"—is reminiscent of the longstanding Soviet model of hegemonic masculinity.[55] The translation of the gender associated with the "seeds of future victories" represents one important degree of mediation in the reception and circulation of Russian writing in Angolan contexts. Indeed, in portraying the gender politics of pre-independence Angola, Luandino Vieira

51 For a more extensive discussion on the erasure of women in Angolan literature, see Dorothée Boulanger, *Fiction as History: Resistance and Complicities in Angolan Postcolonial Literature* (Cambridge: Legenda, 2022).

52 Henda Ducados, 'An all men's show? Angolan women's survival in the 30-year war', *Agenda* 16:43 (2000), 11–22 (p. 15).

53 José Luandino Vieira, 'O Exemplo de Job Hamukuaja', in *Vidas Novas* (Lisbon: Edições 70, 1976), pp. 139–54 (p. 143).

54 Ibid., p. 154.

55 Elena Zdravomyslova and Anna Temkina note that, in the early Soviet period, "a real man was first and foremost someone who participated in the industrialisation of the country and in the Great Patriotic War, and his image was replicated in Soviet movies, literature, and art as a positive socio-anthropological type". They note, moreover, that "[h]eroism was a substantial trait" of such "real men", whose "vocation [...] was to serve his motherland"—a service which, as seen in *Domingos Xavier*, "was well rewarded by his heroization". See Elena Zdravomyslova and Anna Temkina, 'The Crisis of Masculinity in Late Soviet Discourse', *Russian Studies in History*, 51:2 (2012), 13–34 (esp. pp. 21–22).

translates the "formulas" popularised in *Mother* in accordance with the MPLA's expectations regarding the participation of women in the struggle for national liberation.

The Pedagogy of Example

These heroic figures, moreover, convey a sense of pedagogical purpose central to both *Mother* and Luandino Vieira's early writings, in terms of an investment in the representation of exemplary lives, and also in explicit forms of teaching and instruction. For Vladimir Lenin, the "importance" of Gorky's *Mother* is bound up with its educative function: "many workers," he suggests, "who have joined the revolutionary movement impulsively, without properly understanding why, will begin to comprehend after reading" it.[56] Lenin's enthusiasm reflects a much broader faith in the transformational power of fiction—a faith that modulated Soviet interest in cultural movements across the African continent. "Down to its very bureaucracy," Djagalov notes, "the Soviet state, as an heir to the 19th-century Russian intelligentsia, believed in the power of literature and culture to change hearts and minds, heavily invested in this belief, and projected it onto societies, including postcolonial ones, structured very differently from its own".[57] In this context, it is hardly surprising that aspects of Luandino Vieira's writing reflect the themes and tropes of Gorky's. In *Mother*, for instance, Pavel's encounter with Socialism allows him (and his mother) to escape the influence of his alcoholic and violent father; an educative exposure to new ideas is central to the novel's narrative.

A similar mentoring relationship is expressed in Luandino Vieira's *A Vida Verdadeira de Domingos Xavier*. Xico Kafundunga follows a comparable trajectory:

> Com essas conversas de sábado à tarde ou domingo de farra no clube, Xico foi verificando que a vida não é só de calça estreita, brilhantina avulso, camisa americana. E mais tarde, num dia de grande chuva de Abril, amigo Mussanda tinha falado umas conversas que lhe abriram nos olhos: mostrou que não havia branco, nem preto, nem mulato, mas só pobre e rico, e que rico é inimigo do pobre porque quer ele sempre pobre.[58]

> (Through their conversations on Saturday afternoons or at the Sunday festivities, Xico started to understand that life wasn't only tight-fitting trousers, oil-slicked hair, and American shirts. And later, on one of those days during the heavy April showers, his friend Mussunda said things

56 Boris Bursov, 'Preface', in Gorky, *Mother*, trans. by Margaret Wettlin, pp. 5–11 (p. 10).

57 Djagalov, *From Internationalism to Postcolonialism*, p. 11.

58 Luandino Vieira, *A Vida Verdadeira de Domingos Xavier*, p. 46.

> that had opened Xico's eyes: he showed him that there weren't whites, blacks, or mulattos, but only the poor and the rich, and that the rich were the enemies of the poor because they wanted the poor to remain poor.)

This sense of didacticism—emphasised by the use of verbs like "mostrar" ("to show"), "abrir" ("to open"), "verificar" ("to verify")—reflects themes and intentions conventionally attributed to Socialist Realism, which Hamilton associated with Luandino Vieira's early writings. For Hamilton, "Luandino has adopted an artistic technique and a stylistic approach appropriate to the didactic optimism of the social reformer".[59] This combination of "artistic technique" and social reform is nowhere clearer than in the blurring between the speech of the novella's characters and the stances of the MPLA. For instance, Mussunda, the tailor, educates his comrades and fellow workers, like Xico Kafundunga, stressing the importance of overcoming racial divisions and adopting instead political opposition along economic lines. The relegation of racial politics to the background of this ideology—a relegation the novella encourages, as one of the main agitators is a white engineer—helps to advance a model of Socialism that remains in accordance with the MPLA's line.

What connects Gorky's novel with Vieira's, then, is their sensitivity to the ways in which an individual life can—as a result of an educative encounter—begin to correspond to, and influence, collective social forces and political movements. Both texts foreground these encounters alongside an effort to represent lives that are politically and socially exemplary, lives which carry over the effect of educative encounters between characters into the encounter between text and reader. Individuals are confronted with collective questions within these narratives, just as the reader is confronted with the collective significance of the heroic activity and behaviour of specific characters. As Maria Lúcia Lepecki argues, this stress on the collective is at the heart of the narrative's force. "Em todas as suas páginas," she observes, "a narrativa da vida verdadeira de um e de muitos Domingos Xavier transporta a vitalidade funda que ultrapassa, de muito, a experiência colectiva e individual do lugar onde foi escrita"[60] ("In all its pages the narrative of the real life of one and many Domingos Xavier transmits the deep vitality that greatly surpasses the collective and individual experience of the place where it was written). The same applicability to experiences beyond "the place where it was written" characterises *Mother*, in which we are told that "the life of working people was the same everywhere", and in this sense it is the universality of the heroic trajectory of Nilovna that provides a model to Angolan writers narrating the anti-colonial struggle—a narrative that itself "ultrapassa, de muito, a experiência colectiva e individual do lugar onde foi

59 Hamilton, *Voices from an Empire*, p. 134.

60 Maria Lúcia Lepecki, 'A Vida Verdadeira de Domingos Xavier, ou o sinal da verdade', in *Sobreimpressões: Estudos de Literatura Portuguesa e Africana* (Lisbon: Editorial Caminho, 1988), pp. 165–173 (p. 167).

escrita" ("greatly surpasses the collective and individual experience of the place where it was written").[61]

Conclusion

According to M. Keith Booker and Dubravka Juraga, "the Russian writers whose historical situation most resembles that of postcolonial African writers are not nineteenth-century figures such as Pushkin and Dostoevsky, but post-Revolutionary Socialist writers such as [Maksim] Gorky, [Mikhail] Sholokhov, and Alexei Tolstoy. After all, Soviet literature is itself in a sense postcolonial".[62] Though a contentious claim, this strong sense of affiliation between postcolonial and post-revolutionary writing goes some way to explain why Angolan writers in the 1950s and 1960s, in precisely the decades leading up to independence, found attractive models of literary expression in such works of Socialist Realism as Maksim Gorky's *Mother*. For Angolan authors like José Luandino Vieira, these works constituted—to recall the title of Gorky's short story, published in translation in the first issue of *Cultura*—a vital "*acompanhamento*" ("accompaniment") to the developing struggle for national liberation, and, as in *Cultura*, they suggested the possibility of a mutually enriching dialogue, a relationship of engagement and imaginative response, capable of simultaneously accentuating what is universal about this struggle, and stressing what is particular to it. As such, they provide a means of answering the editors of *Cultura*'s call for the "gestação de uma cultura angolana, nacional pela forma e pelo conteúdo, universal pela intenção" ("development of an Angolan culture, national in its form and content, universal in its intention").[63]

This dual emphasis—on what is shared internationally and on what distinguishes the local contexts in which works like *A Vida Verdadeira de Domingos Xavier* were written—is reflected in the two aspects of Russian literature's influence in Angola discussed above. First, the material channels—acts of translation, transmission, and adaptation connecting transnationally agents in Russia, Brazil, and Angola—which underpinned the efforts of writers like Luandino Vieira to develop a *littérature engagée* are capable of both inspiring resistance to colonial rule, and dramatising alternatives to it. Second, the degrees of mediation that characterise Luandino Vieira's translation and adaptation of Gorky's techniques and themes into the terms of an anti-colonial struggle. Indeed, for Luandino Vieira, as well as for Angolan intellectuals more generally, Gorky's *Mother* represented, in the words of Djagalov, a "gigantic [canvas] onto which to project

61 Gorky, *Mother*, trans. by Margaret Wettlin, p. 17; Lepecki, p. 166.

62 M. Keith Booker and Dubravka Juraga, 'The Reds and the Blacks: The Historical Novel in the Soviet Union and Postcolonial Africa', *Studies in the Novel*, 29:3 (Fall 1997), 274–96 (p. 284).

63 'Editorial', in *Cultura*, 8 (June 1959), pp. 1–2.

their own aspirations" of national liberation.[64] But it also came to represent this only by virtue of specific histories of translation, transmission, and adaptation, by virtue of significant places, such as the library of António Jacinto, and by virtue of the widespread enthusiasm for Russian literature, and in particular its models for the production of radical and socially-engaged narratives, in the wake of 1917.

64 Djagalov, *From Internationalism to Postcolonialism*, p. 42.

The Arabic-speaking Peoples

Maksim Gorky and Arabic Literature: From *The Thousand and One Nights* to Contemporary Classics

Sarali Gintsburg

> Gorky is the writer who belongs to all the unfortunate and oppressed on the entire surface of the Earth, backways and sideways—that is, to the overwhelming majority of humankind.
>
> Ra'īf al-Khūri[1]

> Travel! and thou shalt find new friends for old ones left behind;
> Toil! for the sweets of human life by toil and moil are found:
> The stay–at–home no honour wins nor aught attains but want;
> So leave thy place of birth and wander all the world around.
>
> *The Thousand and One Nights*[2]

Introduction: Arabic Literature in the Twentieth Century, the Role of Russian Literature in its Revival, and the Place of Gorky

In Western literary scholarship, the development of Arabic literature throughout the twentieth century is traditionally linked to the influence of Western literature, principally French and English. The role of Russian and early Soviet

1 Ra'īf al-Khūri, "Ghūrki allathi faqadathu al-insānīya', *aṭ-Ṭalī'a*, 2:6, 548–55. All translations are my own, unless otherwise indicated.

2 'Tale of Nur ad-Din and his Son', *The Thousand and One Nights*, trans. by Richard Burton, 9 vols (Burton Club, 1885–86), I (1885), p. 122.

 https://doi.org/10.11647/OBP.0340.20

writers often remains underestimated. This pro-Western approach is true up to a certain point. Indeed, from the end of the nineteenth through the first third of the twentieth century, the educated Arabic reader would often encounter foreign literature, encompassing Russian and early Soviet literature, mainly through English and French translations. The very first known translation of Russian literature into Arabic was a prose version of Ivan Krylov's fables—themselves a transcreation from Lafontaine and Aesop—produced in 1863 in St Petersburg by Khaleba Abdullah, also known as Fedor Ivanovich Kelsey (1819–1912), and adapted and re-published four years later in London (still in classical Arabic) by the Syrian journalist Risqallah Hassun (1825–80).[3] But such English and French translations form only a small fragment of the history of Russian and Soviet literature in the Arab world which, during the twentieth century, became very influential among Arab readers. In the late nineteenth and early twentieth centuries, Arabic literature began to assimilate influences from Western literature. The British Arabist scholar Hamilton Gibb, for instance, mentioned that during this period in Egypt, a group of Modernist literary critics and writers emerged who saw it as their mission to revive Arabic literature by abandoning the traditional classical Arabic canon, which they replaced with canons borrowed from Western literatures.[4] Gibb also noted that these plans for literary revival were partly inspired by literary nationalism, since the ultimate goal of the Modernist movement was not to blindly copy foreign literature, but to improve their own. During this period, although public interest was only mild, Arabs perceived Russian culture as exotic. Ignatii Krachkovskii, a key figure in Russian and Soviet Arab Studies, wrote that the relatively few Arabic books that mentioned Russian culture depicted Russia as an imaginary, almost fictional place.[5] Only after the Russian Revolution of 1905, and primarily in the

3 Lina Kandakzhi, 'Nekotorye aspekty literaturnykh vzaimodeistvii Rossii i Sirii' in *Problemy lingvistiki, metodiki obucheniia inostrannym iazikam i literaturovedeniia v svete mezhkul'turnoi kommunikatsii: Materialy II Mezhdunarodnoi nauchno-prakticheskoi konferentsii 24–25 marta 2011*, editor unknown (Ufa: Izdatel'stvo BGPU, 2011), pp. 146–48 (p. 146), https://www.ippo.ru/historyippo/article/nekotorye-aspekty-literaturnyh-vzaimodeystviy-ross-200499.

4 Hamilton Gibb, *Studies in Contemporary Arabic Literature*. Vol III Egyptian modernists (London: University of London, 1929).

5 Ignatii Krachkovskii (1883–1953) was a leading scholar in global Arab Studies. Krachkovskii wrote on a wide range of topics related to Arabic language and literature, history, medieval literature, Arab Christian literature, Semitology, and so on. Krachkovskii spent his entire academic career as a professor of Arabic language at St Petersburg (later Leningrad) State University; his scholarly achievements were acknowledged not only in the Soviet Union but throughout the Arab world and in the West. He was so well-regarded that Western Arabists commonly studied Russian just to read Krachkovskii's publications on their field. For more on the Lithuanian-born Krachkovskii's fascinating career and internationally recognised achievements, see his former student Anna Arkadievna Dolinina's biography (in Russian), *Nevol'nik dolga* (St Petersburg:

Levant and Egypt, did Russian literature, or indeed Russian culture, start to attract greater attention.[6]

New Russian-influenced literary trends first developed in Arabic poetry. This was because, in the early twentieth century, the prose genres of Arabic literature lacked the flexibility to allow for innovation and change.[7] Although until the First World War, the Arab world in general still knew very little about Russia and Russians, a region already existed where the two cultures could mingle without any intermediary. This was the Syro-Palestinian region, or Levant, where, in the 1890s, the Imperial Orthodox Palestine Society founded several Russian Orthodox schools for the local Arab Orthodox population.[8] Several students at one such school, in Nazareth, would become famous Arab writers, as well as future literary translators. Among these graduates of the Nazareth seminary was one of the most prominent Russian-Arabic literary translators of the epoch, Selim Qob'eyn (1870–1951), a Palestinian-born Egyptian writer and journalist who was drawn to Tolstoy's teachings as much as to his fiction.[9] In 1901, Qob'eyn released an Arabic translation of Tolstoy's autobiographical and non-fiction writings, later also translating *The Kreutzer Sonata* (*Kreitserova sonata*, 1889). Another graduate of the Nazareth pedagogical seminary, the Palestinian Khalil

---

Sankt Peterburgskoe vostokovedenie, 1994). Mikhail Rodionov describes the political repression of Krachkovskii and other leading Soviet Arabists in 'Profiles under Pressure: Orientalists in Petrograd/Leningrad, 1918–1956', in *The Heritage of Soviet Oriental Studies*, ed. by Michael Kemper and Stephan Conermann (London: Routledge, 2011), pp. 47–65; a useful overview is provided in Michael Kemper, 'Introduction: Krachkovskii and Soviet Arabic Studies, or: *What* is *not* in *Among Arabic Manuscripts*', in *I.Y. Kratchkovsky, Among Arabic Manuscripts: Memories of Libraries and Men*, ed. by Michael Kemper (Leiden: Brill Classics in Islam, 2016), pp. 1–24.

6 For detailed discussion of these novels, see Ignatii Krachkovskii,'Otzvuki revoliutsii 1905 goda v arabskoi khudozhestvennoi literature', *Sovetskoe Vostokovedenie*, 3 (1945), 5–14.

7 For more information see A.A. Dolinina, *Voskhodi lun na stoiankakh veselyia* (Leningrad: Khudozhestvennaia literatura, 1983); and Mike Baynham and Sarali Gintsburg, 'Tar or honey? Space and time of Moroccan migration in a video sketch comedy 'l-kāmīra la-kum', in *Narrating Migrations from Africa and the Middle East: A Spatio-Temporal Approach*, ed. by S. Gintsburg, R. Breeze and M. Baynham (London: Bloomsbury, 2022), pp. 157–74.

8 On the activities and the role this society had in the Middle East, see Aleksandr Grushevoi, 'Plany razvitiia obrazovaniia v russkikh shkolakh na Blizhnem Vostoke pered Pervoi mirovoi voinoi', *Khistianstvo na Blizhnem Vostoke*, 4 (2020), 37–56.

9 For more on Qob'eyn's role in the history of translating Russian and early Soviet literature into Arabic, see Ignatii Krachkovskii's various essays on 'Russko-Arabskie literaturnie sviazi' in I. I. Krachkovskii, *Izbrannye sochineniia*, ed. by V. A. Gordlevski, 6 vols (Moscow and Leningrad: Izadatel'stvo Akademii Nauk SSSR, 1955–60), III, pp. 267–311. On his translations of Tolstoy, see Kirill Gordeev, '"Velikii moskovitskii mudrets" i ego arabskie pochitateli' (2004), https://www.ippo.ru/historyippo/article/velikiy-moskovitskiy-mudrec-i-ego-arabskie-pochita-200423.

Beidas (1874–1949), translated Pushkin's *The Captain's Daughter* (*Kapitanskaia dochka*, 1836; *Ibnat al-Kubtan*, 1898) and various stories by Gogol and Tolstoy, early in his distinguished career as an educator, author and translator.[10] Despite widespread interest in Tolstoy, Krachkovskii identified Gorky as one of the most widely read Russian authors in Arabic translation, closely followed by Anton Chekhov and then Fedor Dostoevsky.[11]

Curiously, in Soviet Russia, Gorky was effectively hostage both to his personal popularity and the politicisation of almost everything he would do, say, or write. He was frequently represented as the precursor of Socialist Realism which, as other authorities insist, is simply not true.[12] Numerous parks, cultural centres, theatres, libraries, streets and even towns and cities were named after him. Curiously, this disproportionate attention to Gorky has caused fatigue and even satiety among Russian readers. By contrast, in the Arab world, Gorky, whose image was not so much politicised as romanticised, became an almost legendary hero, a survivor who rose from the depths of his society, overcoming difficulties along the way to finally attain a metaphorical Olympus. For Arabs, Gorky acquired the glamour of the fighter and became a very popular writer, remaining so even today. In the Arab world, a popular myth circulated about Gorky's supposed Eastern connection; as one of the authors and propagators of this myth, Selim Qob'eyn, suggested, the writer may have had Oriental ancestors. Rumours also spread that the first book the youthful Gorky ever read was a Russian translation of *The Thousand and One Nights*.[13] Gorky's influence on Arabic literature is difficult to underestimate: he was one of the few writers to influence the minds and philosophy of several generations of Arab writers and intellectuals. This influence manifests both directly, through obviously similar plots, and more discreetly, by (for example) echoes in Arabic literature of Gorky's humanist concerns.

In this chapter, to show the extent of Gorky's impact on the literary life of the Arab world,[14] I first briefly introduce the history of translation of Russian

---

10 Kandakzhi, 'Nekotorye aspekty literaturnykh vzaimodeistvii Rossii i Sirii', p. 146. Intriguingly, Beidas was a cousin of the noted Palestinian scholar, Edward Said.

11 For more detailed discussion on Gorky's influence in the Arab world during the first half of the twentieth century, see Ignatii Krachkovskii's essay 'Gor'kii i arabskaia literatura', in Krachkovskii, *Izbrannye sochineniia*, III (1957), pp. 271–311; and S. Areshan, 'Gor'kii i literaturnyi vostok', *Sovetskoe vostokovedenie*, 3 (1945), 177–82.

12 See, for instance, Genrikh Mitin, 'Evangelie ot Maksima: zametki o rannem romane A. M. Gor'kogo *Mat'*,' *Literatura v shkole*, 4:99 (1989), 48–65.

13 Krachkovskii notes how this myth developed: in fact, Gorky wrote the preface to the first direct Arabic to Russian translation of *The Thousand and One Nights* in 1929 (see Krachkovskii, 'Russkaia literatura i arabi v proizvedeniiakh Gorkogo', in *Izvestiia Akademii Nauk Soiuza SSR*, 5 (1), p. 47.

14 The term 'Arab world' refers to the twenty-two countries whose primary language is Arabic. Arabic-speaking countries are located in: Africa, particularly the north;

literature into the Arabic language in the twentieth century. I then briefly discuss the history of translations of Maksim Gorky's works, including aspects specific to his Arab reception, including the mythologisation of his personality. Next, I present two case studies which demonstrate how motifs and ideas from Gorky's novels and plays were understood and implemented in the literary works of two different Arabic writers from Egypt: Khairy Shalaby (1938–2011) and Albert Cossery (1913–2008). I will conclude by summarising my most important findings.

Russian Literature in Arabic Translation: Egypt, the Levant, Iraq and the USSR

Focus on Gorky

As Damrosch and other researchers maintain, once any national literature starts circulating outside its linguistic and cultural homeland, moving into the sphere of world literature, it inevitably undergoes transformations conditioned by the linguistic and cultural norms of its new home.[15] Gorky's afterlife in Arabic confirms this statement. The Arab world presupposes a different cultural background and literary tradition, which for quite some time had been developing independently from Western and Russian literatures. As a Semitic language, Arabic is linguistically remote from European languages, whether Germanic, Romance, or Slavic. Therefore, the process of translating literature from or into Arabic almost always poses difficult choices for its translator, often necessitating extensive domestication and/or adaptation of the text to suit the target readership.[16]

During the first half of the twentieth century, three regions could be considered major centres of cultural and literary life in the Arab world: the Levant, consisting of modern Lebanon, Syria, Jordan and Palestine; Egypt; and Iraq.[17] The first Arab literary translators to work directly with Russian texts

West Asia; and the Arabian Peninsula. These regions are referred to collectively as the Arab world or Arab nations.

15 David Damrosch, *What Is World Literature?* (Princeton, NJ and Oxford: Princeton University Press, 2003).

16 See Sarali Gintsburg, '"Ne smeshno!" Osobennosti perevoda arabskoi iumoristicheskoi literatury na russkii iazyk', in *Miri literaturnogo perevoda*, ed. by A. Ia. Livergant, 2 vols (Moscow: Institut Perevoda, 2018), I (2018), pp. 336–39.

17 In this chapter, I use the words 'centre' and 'periphery' only in the sense of sequences of cultural and literary activities noticeable by outsiders rather than in Casanovan terms. The Arab world is a complex construct currently comprising twenty-two countries and it would be naive to argue that the relationship between these twenty-two countries is driven by anxiety or based on the centre-periphery

came from the Syro-Palestinian region, followed slightly later by those from Egypt, while Iraqi translators emerged during the 1930s. Other Arab nations were not yet ready to take the lead in the cultural sphere.[18] Arab literature, like translations of literary works by European and Russian writers, was usually published in cultural journals and newspapers which played, at that time, an extremely important role in facilitating the cultural, religious, and literary transformation of Arab society.[19] Among these newspapers and journals were *al-Manār* (Beirut), *al-Murāqib* (Beirut), *an-Nafā'is* (Haifa), *aṭ-Ṭalī'a* (Damascus), and *as-Siyāsa* (Cairo).

Texts translated in the pages of these publications usually had an explanatory preface, where the translator or editor would outline for the reader the main topics arising.[20] Such prefaces varied in length: Selim Qob'eyn typically wrote two pages, as discussed below; Antun Ballan, a Syrian translator, would provide just a few lines. Among the first Russian writers to be discussed by Arab intellectuals and translated into Arabic were Tolstoy, Dostoevsky, Pushkin, Chekhov, and Gorky. However, the history of literary translations of Russian and early Soviet writers into Arabic is poorly documented and often rather unreliable: Krachkovskii's accounts tend to be anecdotal rather than systematic. It can be difficult to deduce who translated Gorky, or when and where Arabic versions were produced. My research resonates with Jeremy Munday's call to take into account microhistories of translators, with the difference, however, that in the case of the Arab world, we have no means of restoring their life stories, or, in some cases, even knowing their names.[21] An additional complication is the fact that such translations would often appear in part only in newspapers and journals, frequently without the author's name. Finally, the Arab world lacked a system for registering and cataloguing literary production. Thus today, when we discuss the history of translating Gorky into Arabic, the most reliable source of information remains the data collated by Krachkovskii in his 1956 article 'Gorky and Arabic Literature' ('Gorkii i arabskaia literatura').[22]

According to Krachkovskii's article, the first Arabic translator of Gorky was Ibrahim Faraj, a Lebanese immigrant who settled in Brazil. Faraj translated three short stories into Arabic, published in São Paulo in 1906, although their Arabic

---

principle. Later in this essay I will address the difficulties of applying Casanova's approach to the Arab world.

18 On the development of Arabic literature in the Arab world in late 1800s and early 1900s, see Krachkovskii, *Izbrannye sochineniia*, III (various essays).

19 See Sabry Hafez, 'Cultural Journals and Modern Arabic literature: a Historical Overview', *Alif: Journal of Comparative Poetics*, 37 (2017), 9–49.

20 Although this was not a unique practice, I believe that the analysis of such prefaces and paratexts allows us to better understand the reception of literary works in foreign cultures.

21 See Jeremy Munday, 'Using Primary Sources to Produce a Microhistory of Translation and Translators: Theoretical and Methodological Concerns', *The Translator*, 20:1 (2014), 64–80.

22 See 'Gorkii i arabskaia literatura', in *Izbrannye sochineniia*, III, pp. 271–311.

titles make it impossible to determine the original texts: 'Insane' ('Majānūn'), 'The Devil' ('Šayṭān') and 'A Lie' ('Kithb').[23] In 1907, Selim Qobe'yn translated and published four journalistic articles by Gorky: 'The King Who Holds the Flag High' ('Korol', kotoriii vysoko derzhit svoe znamia', 1906), 'One of the Kings of the Republic' ('Odin iz koroleii respubliki', 1906), 'Magnificent France' ('Prekrasnaia Frantsia', 1906), and 'On the Jews' ('O evreiakh', 1906). Qob'eyn's preface presented his personal view of Gorky as a freedom fighter and a rebel. Gorky is shown as a writer who openly criticised censorship in tsarist Russia and whose pen was sharper than the proverbial sword. Although Qob'eyn had never visited Russia, Gorky's personality seemed so familiar and his thoughts so pertinent to Arab reality, that he described Gorky as part Oriental, at least psychologically. Other translations of Gorky's works also appeared at this time, often translated via French, English or German. We know that in this period a number of Gorky's fundamental works were translated and published for Arab readers, among them: *Mother* (*Mat'*, 1907, extracts only), *A Confession* (*Ispoved'*, 1908, extracts only), and *My Childhood* (*Detstvo*, 1913, abridged).

From the 1930s onwards, Iraq joined Egypt and the Levant as a key centre of literary translation and book publishing in the Arab world. Gorky's *Chelkash* (*Chelkhash*, 1895) was published in 1932 (in a translation by the Iraqi translator Abdalla Jaddawi).[24] It would be tempting to define the literary situation as a kind of Arab Republic of Letters, following Casanova. But this would oversimplify the complex and multidirectional processes that existed in the Arab sphere at that time. It might also imply an element of elitism. Several attempts to apply the notion of the Republic of Letters to the Arabic context have subsequently been criticised.[25] Moreover, in the Arab world, the literary processes that unfolded during the first half of the twentieth century were characterised by a strong nationalist drive—each Arab country sought to follow its own national path without becoming peripheral. Krachkovskii, for instance, termed this phenomenon "particularism".[26]

23 In this chapter, I do not touch on the topic of translating the titles of Gorky's books into Arabic. This would have led me too far away from the main focus of my contribution. I also want to avoid confusion with titles in Russian and English, although, I admit that analysis of Arabic translations of titles would be an exciting topic for research.

24 See Mohammed Qasim Hassan Al-Mas'ud, *Retseptsiia proizvedenii Gorkogo o russkoi revoliutsii v literaturakh stran arabskogo vostoka* (Voronezh: Voronezhskii Gosudarstvennyi Universitet, 2014).

25 See for instance, Reuven Snir's response to Muhsin Musawi's *The Medieval Islamic Republic of Letters: Arabic Knowledge Construction* (Notre Dame, IN: University of Notre Dame Press, 2015): Reuven Snir, 'World Literature, Republics of Letters, and the Arabic Literary System: The "Modernists" in the Defendants' Bench—A Review Article', in *Mamlūk Studies Review*, XXII (2019), 137–92.

26 See Ignatii Krachkovskiii's essay 'Novoarabskaia literatura', in *Izbrannye sochineniia*, III, pp. 65–85 (specifically pp. 69–79).

A new phase started after the Second World War, when literary translation was concentrated in Egypt, Syria, Lebanon, and Iraq, but also in the USSR, where three new publishing houses with the express aim of translating Russian and Soviet literature into foreign languages were founded: Progress, Raduga, and Znanie. From the 1950s to the 1980s, new translations of Gorky appeared at an increased rate: many were works previously unknown to the Arab reader, such as *Foma Gordeev* (*Foma Gordeev,* 1899) and *The Artamonov Business* (*Delo Artamonovykh,* 1925).[27] Others were new, supposedly improved retranslations of known works such as *Mother*, *The Lower Depths* (*Na dne*, 1902; translated by Abdelhalim al-Bashlun, published in 1962 in Cairo),[28] and *A Confession* (1968, translated by Naofal Niof). New retranslations continue to appear even today—since 2019 the Canadian publishing house Masaa has published the latest Arabic translations of *My Childhood* and *Among People* (*V ludiakh,* 1915), which were completed by Ahmad ar-Rahbi, an Omani translator based in Moscow.

We have seen that the first translators of Gorky represented him as a symbol of the fight for freedom and individual rights, a kind of "stormy petrel", the famous epithet for an independent and revolutionary character drawn from Gorky's poem 'The Song of the Stormy Petrel' ('Burevestnik', 1901). This image coincided with a widespread Arab ideal during this period, as many dreamed of overthrowing their Turkish rulers and, later, Western colonisers. Other themes highlighted by Gorky, such as the role of women in society, or the lives of the poor and oppressed, resonated with Arab concerns and made Gorky one of the most influential and widely read Russian and Soviet writers in the Arab world. His persona thus acquired almost legendary status. It is also important to remember that besides his reputation as the founding father of Socialist Realism, Gorky was also famous as a Romantic writer. Some of his early Romantic works were translated into Arabic and warmly received because Arabic literature was then undergoing its own Romantic period.[29] These early works included *The Old Man*

27 Later, these novels were published several times in different translations. For instance, Dolinina mentions that during the period between 1954–68 the novel *Mother* was published in five different translations. See A.A. Dolinina, 'Iz istorii arabskikh perevodov romana M. Gorkogo "Mat"', *Vestnik Leningradskogo universiteta,* 4:20 (1980), pp. 59–64 (p. 59).

28 Although I was unable to establish whether there were any earlier translations of *The Lower Depths* into Arabic, it is certain that by the 1920s, educated Arabs could already access English and French translations of the novel: this 1902 play had by 1907 already been translated into English and published in New York. In France, at least two different translations were published, in 1904 and 1905. See Yuliya Bystrova, 'Iz istorii russko-frantsuzskikh kulturnikh sviazey v nachale XX veka (populiarnost rannego tvorchestva M. Gorkogo vo Frantsii', *Vestnik SGTU,* 1 (2007), https://cyberleninka.ru/article/n/iz-istorii-russko-frantsuzskih-kulturnyh-svyazey-v-nachale-xx-veka-populyarnost-rannego-tvorchestva-m-gorkogo-vo-frantsii.

29 See the texts discussed in *Arabskaia romanticheskaia proza XIX-XX vekov*, ed. by Anna Dolinina and Galina Bogolyubova (Leningrad: Khudozhestvennaia literatura, 1981).

(*Starik*, 1915, translated into Arabic in 1906), and *Song of a Falcon* (*Pesnia o Sokole*, 1899, translated and published in 1914 in *as-Sā'iḥ*, an Arabic literary journal published by members of the Arab immigrant community in New York). This is why the theme of the storm appears in works by several Arabic Romantic writers of that era, notably the Lebanese-American novelist Kahlil Gibran (1883–1931), author of *The Prophet* (1923) and Mikhail Naimy (1889–1988), another graduate of the Russian Orthodox seminary in Nazareth. Finally, I emphasise that, within the Arab world, literary translations could circulate freely: a book published, for instance, in Cairo, was also accessible in Jordan, Tunis, Morocco, or Algeria.

Even after a national literature has begun to circulate in translation in a new culture, its direct influence can be traced within the ultimate target language. This is certainly true of early translations of Gorky into Arabic, which, as I have mentioned, were sometimes made not from the Russian original, but by means of French or English pivot translations. And as we have seen, the records of the history of the translation of Gorky (and other Russian authors) into Arabic are fragmented. This makes it difficult to determine which translations, and even which intermediary languages, were used. Nevertheless, I will attempt to demonstrate that despite these complex trajectories, Gorky's influence on Arabic writing can still be traced. It is important to note that in the context of Arabic literature (and indeed other literatures), it is almost always difficult to establish with absolute certainty which literary work has been influenced by which writer(s). My criteria for identifying Gorky's influence are twofold. Firstly, Gorky, together with Tolstoy, Chekhov, and Dostoevsky, was considered by Arab writers to be among the most influential writers of the twentieth century in the Arab world. Therefore, Gorky, his ideas, and his mythology contributed to shaping the values of several generations of Arabic writers from the 1920s onwards. Secondly, I am guided by the views of readers themselves.

Gorky's immense popularity as a writer and as an almost legendary personality can be explained by a number of factors, as I have mentioned above, including the relevance of his topics to Arab readers and his rejection of glib answers or interpretations. Finally, in the course of his career as a writer, Gorky's works evolved from Romantic, to Realist, and by the end of his life he was known as the founding father of Socialist Realism. His work thus possessed the potential to adapt to the settings and norms of other cultures, thereby being subsumed into other national literatures. Moreover, the anti-hero, or vagabond, one of the most recognisable of Gorky's protagonists, contributed to the positive reception of his literary production in the Arab world. A huge number of novels, stories, and plays written by Arabic writers in the course of the twentieth century were inspired by the motifs, issues, and questions they encountered in Gorky's fiction. Among these writers were the Nobel Prize-winning Egyptian author Naguib Mahfouz (1911–2006, who was also influenced philosophically and thematically by Dostoevsky), Mikhail Naimy, the Syrian Social Realist novelist Hanna Mina (1924–2018), Ghaib Furman (1927–90), and many others.

To illustrate the scale of Gorky's influence, I have chosen two Egyptian writers whose life trajectories, besides their writing styles and even languages, were strikingly different. The first, Khairy Shalaby (1938–2011), spent his whole life in Egypt and wrote in Arabic, while the second, Albert Cossery (1913–2008), the so-called 'Voltaire of the Nile', was born and raised in Egypt but spent most of his long life in France and wrote exclusively in French. Despite these differences, both Shalaby and Cossery did have access to Gorky's books in Arabic, English, and/or French translations.

At this point, I should emphasise that in no way are my case studies meant to imply that these two writers were not creatively independent, nor to suggest that Gorky was their sole literary influence. This would be erroneous. What I would like to demonstrate, instead, is Gorky's significant and undeniable *influence* on several generations of Arab writers, including Shalaby and Cossery.

Maksim Gorky and Khairy Shalaby: The Rogues, the Women, and Rebellion against the Oppressor

Khairy Shalaby (in Arabic Khayri Shalabi) was a famous Egyptian writer and author of over seventy books, mostly novels and collections of short stories. Among his best-known books are *The Time-Travels of the Man Who Sold Pickles and Sweets* (*Rahalāt at-turši al-halwaji*, 1990), *The Lodging House* (*Wikālat 'Aṭṭīya*, 1999), *The Hasheesh Waiter* (*Sāliḥ Haiṣa*, 2000), and *The Tent Peg* (*al-Watad*, 2003). Shalaby, who was born in rural Egypt, called himself "the singer of the Egyptian street"[30] and, indeed, most of his literary works revolve around the lives of everyday Egyptians, including street people. In his interviews, Shalaby usually emphasised the importance of studying canonical Egyptian and Arabic literature; he was opposed to blindly following Western literary fashions. For Shalaby, *The Thousand and One Nights* sufficed as reading material. On the other hand, he repeatedly named among his literary influences Naguib Mahfouz, Yahya Haqqi (1905–52), and Yusuf Idris (1927–91), who were themselves clearly influenced by Russian literature and specifically by Chekhov, Dostoevsky, and/or Gorky.[31] Shalaby's literary affiliation might be best defined as Middle Eastern Magical Realism, interweaving Egyptian oral traditions and magic tales with

30 ar-Riwā'i Khairy Šalabi: adabi yanba'u min aš-šāri', *Al-Bayān*, 28 December 2008, https://www.albayan.ae/paths/books/2008-12-28-1.823074.

31 On the influence of Russian literature on Yahiya Haqqi, see Miriam Cooke's 'Yahya Haqqi As Critic and Nationalist', *International Journal of Middle East Studies*, 1:1, 21–34. On the influence of Russian literature, principally Gorky and Chekhov, on Yahiya Haqqi and Yusuf Idris, see Elmira Ali-Zade, 'Chekhov v arabskikh stranakh', in *Chekhov i mirovaia literatura* (Moscow: IMLI RAN, 2005), III (2005), pp. 228–52.

a Western style.[32] Below, I list some of Shalaby's more Gorky-esque motifs and themes.

The Rogue as Anti-Hero and Protagonist

Shalaby, perhaps partly due to his own early life experiences, appears drawn to rogues, regularly featuring them as protagonists in his novels. This is exemplified by one of his most acclaimed novels: the autobiographical *The Lodging House* (1999). The protagonist strikingly evokes Gorky's public persona: a young man with a very poor village background. Thanks to an unlikely coincidence, this young man becomes a student at the local pedagogical institute. Like Gorky, he is an avid reader who also dreams of becoming a writer. Also like Gorky, he seeks justice, and his quest to achieve it leads him to encounter a local group of Muslim Brothers. Just as Gorky did, this man rebels against unjust treatment and, as a result, gets expelled from the institute. Thus, even at the very beginning of the novel, the main protagonist becomes a rogue (*ṣa'lūk* in Arabic or *bosiak* in Russian), Gorky's archetypal protagonist, also popular in classical Arabic literature. Often witty and charming, rogues are the heart of the story. Even today, the rogue continues to play an important role in oral Arabic narratives.[33]

The "Oppressive Horrors" of Egyptian Life[34]

Describing the lives of all kinds of rogues and vagabonds from the depths of society, and the routine manifestations of cruelty accompanying their lives is a prominent but not central theme of Shalaby's writings. We find numerous descriptions of such lives in *The Lodging House*, *The Hashish Waiter*, and *Time*

32 Casanova notes this trend in Algerian (as well as South American and African) literature, defining it as a manifestation of anxiety experienced by writers from literary peripheries: "the quest for political independence brings with it a need to display and increase the nation's literary wealth and adaptation for the stage of the tales and legends (as well as novels) that constituted the heritage" (p. 227). Adopting this approach, however, would effectively deny Arabic literature the opportunity to explore its own literary canons. On my interpretation of Shalaby's literary style, see Gintsburg (forthcoming), 'Khairy Shalaby's novel *The City of the Dead*: Egyptian Prison Literature with a Russian Twist', *Comparative Literature and Culture*, 26:1 (2024).

33 See Baynham and Gintsburg, 'Tar or Honey?', pp. 157–74.

34 Here I refer to the famous passage from Gorky's *My Childhood*, much cited by Russian speakers to characterise the suffering of the poorest in society, to refer to the meaningless and cruel life of people from the lowest rungs of society: "svintsovye merzosti nashei dikoi russkoi zhizni" ("the oppressive horrors of our wild Russian life"). See Maksim Gor'kii, *Detstvo* (Moscow: Shkol'naia biblioteka, 1955), p. 204; for the translation here I have used Gertrude M. Foakes' English translation, *My Childhood* (London: T. Werner Laurie, 1915), p. 346.

Travellings. *The Lodging House* is structured around a run-down caravanserai called Attiya and its dwellers, all from the social underworld: criminals, prostitutes, the unemployed, and so on. Interestingly, similarities between the protagonists of Gorky's famous play *The Lower Depths* and *The Lodging House* are easy to establish: Amm Shawadfi, the mean landlord from *The Lodging House* resembles Kostylev, who is equally grasping and ruthless. Both landlords are portrayed as cynical, cruel, and greedy, although Amm Shawadfi exhibits more humane qualities: he tries to help the main protagonist from time to time, although his help is always self-interested. Another apparently similar character dyad is Aleshka from *The Lower Depths* and Mahrous from *The Lodging House*, both young, hard-working boys, forced to grow up too fast but fond of fun, dancing and, in Aleshka's case, playing the accordion. Mahrous likes to improvise poetry. But both youngsters are already addicts: Aleshka is addicted to alcohol, while Mahrous is addicted to smoking hasheesh. Depictions of everyday cruelty, like the "oppressive horror" portrayed by Gorky a century earlier, also feature prominently in Shalaby's later fiction. In *The Lodging House*, lengthy passages describe acts of cruelty that were routinely committed by the *inglīz*, i.e., the British (in this case, British soldiers) toward Egyptian people during colonial times. Such descriptions echo the police brutality described in Gorky's novel *Mother*, and also in his trilogy of memoirs, which opens with the well-known *My Childhood*. However, unlike Gorky, Shalaby does not seem to call his readers to rebel against injustice and cruelty.

Women as Central Protagonists

Women characters play an important role in Gorky's writing. Gorky's most popular work is almost entirely about a woman: Pelageia Nilovna Vlasova in *Mother*. Largely because of this novel, Gorky achieved mythological status both in Russia and the Arab world. In Soviet Russia, thanks to *Mother*, Gorky was considered the 'founding father' of Socialist Realism. In the Arab world, both *Mother* and *Foma Gordeev* were consulted for discussion of women's rights and the role of women in society. This work clearly influenced Shalaby's writings about women as well: in his novel *The Tent Peg*, he portrays a strong-willed woman from an Egyptian village, a true mother, who will do anything to protect her large family. In his short story 'Food for Children' ('Akl l-'ayāl', 2009),[35] Shalaby again introduces a woman who will make any sacrifice to provide for her children. His depiction of such strong female protagonists raises the issue of women's roles in Egyptian society, but the questions of moral choices and spiritual growth that are central for Gorky do not appear relevant for Shalaby's protagonists.

35 Khairy Shalaby, 'Akl al-'ayyāl', in Shalaby, *Ma laysa yadmunuhu ahadu: majmū'a qisasįya* (Cairo: Kātib al-yawm, 2019), pp. 141–48.

Maksim Gorky and Albert Cossery: Despair, Oppression, Rebels, and Objectified Women

Albert Cossery (in Arabic Albēr Quṣeyri) was a celebrated Franco-Egyptian writer, who referred to himself as "an Egyptian writer who writes in French".[36] Cossery's biography has been poorly studied because the author liked to surround himself with mutually contradictory rumours. We do know that he was born in Cairo, into a Christian family, presumably of Syro-Palestinian origin, and educated at a French school. At the age of eighteen, Cossery left Egypt and in the 1930s settled in Paris, where he spent the rest of his life. He wrote only eight books, all in French and all set in Cairo, as if he had never left his natal city.[37]

Two of Cossery's best-known works are *Men God Forgot* (*Les hommes oubliés de Dieu*, 1941), and *The House of Certain Death* (*La Maison de la mort certaine*, 1944). Interestingly, most of his books, including these two, have been translated into Arabic and even made into films in that language. The Egyptian journalist and writer Mahmud Qasim, who has translated four of his novels into Arabic, insists that Cossery is clearly an Arabic writer because, despite their original language, his novels abound in peculiarly Arab sentiments. Qasim even suggests they were written in Arabic and later translated into French.[38] Albert Cossery would make an interesting subject for Casanova's examination of the insecurities of Francophone Arab authors from the European periphery, which includes, from Algeria, the works of Kateb Yacine, Mouloud Feraoun, Mouloud Mammeri, and Rachid Boujedra. Casanova views their writing from a clearly Francocentric perspective, classifying them as "dominated and peripheral" and their writing style as "the general adoption of a narrative model that, in fact, only reproduced the French academic tradition of *belle écriture*".[39] This might be true if we look at Arabic literature through the prism of French culture, as Casanova does. However, her approach strips Arabic literature of its own rich heritage and conceals its complex interactions with other cultures and literatures, as Albert Cossery's case demonstrates.

36 Robyn Cresswell, 'Undelivered: Egyptian Novelists at Home and Abroad', *Harper's* (February 2011), 71–79 (p. 78).

37 Several researchers note that Cossery's written French included numerous idioms and terms that are more typical of the Arabic language. See, for instance, F. Lagrange, 'Albert Cossery écrit- il arabe?' in *Savants, amants, poètes et fous: Séances offertes à Katia Zakharia*, ed. by Catherine Pinon (Beyrouth: Presses de l'Ifpo, 2019), pp. 133–57. See also Cresswell, 'Undelivered'.

38 See Mahmud Qasim, *Al-adab al-'arabi al-maktūb bi-l-lugha al-'arabīya* [*Arab Literature Written in the French Language*] (Cairo: al-Hey'a al-miṣrīya al-'āmma li-l-kuttāb, 1996).

39 Pascale Casanova, *The World Republic of Letters*, trans. by Malcolm DeBevoise (Cambridge, MA: Harvard University Press, 2004), p. 176, p. 343.

Nowhere in any interviews did Cossery ever mention Gorky, although he did admit that, as a youth, he had read Russian literature, especially the works of Dostoevsky.[40] However, other readers and critics have repeatedly emphasised the obvious influence of Gorky on some of Cossery's writings.[41] His friend, the novelist Henry Miller, wrote in his preface to Cossery's first collection of stories, *Men God Forgot*, that "he touches depths of despair, degradation and resignation which neither Gorky, nor Dostoyevsky has registered".[42] We should not be surprised that Cossery never publicly mentioned Gorky because, as even his biographer notes, Cossery was a hoaxer and a mystifier, and so his descriptive anecdotes can hardly be considered reliable sources of information.[43] Below, I will briefly outline the motifs and ideas from Cossery that appear to owe something either to Gorky's persona or his writings.

Rogues, Oppressors, and Revolutionaries

Like Shalaby, Cossery was clearly drawn to the lowest rungs of Egyptian society, and thus he chose rogues and criminals as the protagonists of almost all of his books. Often, Cossery uses the contrast between rich and poor, or the powerful and the helpless, to emphasise the dark side of life for Egyptian outcasts. In the collection *Men God Forgot*, the author introduces his readers to a gallery of impecunious characters, whose poverty and despair is comparable to that of Gorky's protagonists in *The Lower Depths*. In the story 'The Barber Killed his Wife' ('Le coiffeur a tué sa femme'), Chaktour, a poor, unemployed carpenter, explains to his young son that they are poor because God forgot about them. He adds that if God forgets about someone, this cannot be rectified. In the same story, Cossery introduces the policeman Goloche, who is described as a naturally cruel person with a glare like an angry beast, ready to kill any living creature. If we make allowances for Cossery's tendency to hyperbole, common in Arabic literary style, this mean-natured policeman from a Cairo slum will immediately call to mind the figure of Abram Medvedev, another cruel policeman, this time

40 Shaker Nouri, '"I do not like to talk in the present tense": Interview with Albert Cossery', *Banipal* 4 (1999), http://www.banipal.co.uk/selections/18/179/albert-cossery/.

41 See, for instance, John Taylor, 'Drooping Eyelids, a Farcical World (Albert Cossery)', in *Paths to Contemporary French Literature*, ed. by John Taylor, 3 vols (London and New Brunswick, NJ: Transaction Publishers, 2004–2011), III (2011), pp. 118–21; or Stephen Murray, 'More Albert Cossery fiction', *Japanese Culture Reflections Blog* (2017), https://japaneseculturereflectionsblog.wordpress.com/tag/albert-cossery/.

42 Reprinted as Henry Miller, 'The Novels of Albert Cossery', in Miller, *Stand Still Like the Hummingbird: Essays* (New York: New Direction Books, 1962), pp. 181–84 (p. 181).

43 Frédéric Andaru, *Monsieur Albert: Cossery, une vie* (Clichy: Editorial Éditions de Corlevour, 2013).

from *The Lower Depths*. Both Gorky and Cossery see these policemen, ostensibly meant to symbolise law and order, as elements of the lower depths, among those, as Cossery put it, forgotten by God. This juxtaposition of the rogues and vagabonds with more powerful individuals is also in line with the classical Arabic tradition I mentioned earlier, in which vagabonds and rogues are often given centre stage. Cossery's novel *The House of Certain Death* is set in one of the poorest Cairo neighbourhoods, where several families inhabit an old, extremely dilapidated house. In vain, they ask their landlord to repair it: nothing happens, and they keep living in misery. In this regard, their greedy landlord, Si Khalil is of special interest. Cossery used the image of the avaricious landlord again in *The House of Infamy* (*Les couleurs de l'infamie*, 1999). This cruel landlord figure echoes Kostylev from *The Lower Depths* and also Shalaby's Amm Shawadfi in *The Lodging House*. Toward the end of *The House of Certain Death*, Cossery openly calls for social change.

Clearly, both Cossery and Gorky share certain views. Gorky described these desperate situations without proffering solutions, while Cossery carefully describes them before unequivocally demanding change. The majority of both writers' protagonists live as if in a dream, but in key texts by each, one character becomes aware, in order to protest the existing, unjust order of things. This is, for instance, the case with Abdel Al from *The House of Certain Death*, or Serag in *Laziness in the Fertile Valley* (*Les fainéants dans la vallée fertile*, 1948). The Vlasovs, mother and son, from Gorky's *Mother* are the obvious Russian counterparts, or inspirations, for these Egyptian activists *malgré soi*. Interestingly, Mahmud Qasim terms the attitude of Cossery's protagonists "revolutionary" ("mawqif thawri"), which brings Cossery's writings ideologically even closer to Gorky's.[44] Despite the revolutionary sentiment typical of Cossery's writing, his female characters are undeveloped, and are always assigned secondary roles. Mahmud Qasim concludes bluntly that women in Cossery's novels are merely objectified.

Idleness that Leads to Death

As both Western and, more interestingly, Arab critics have emphasised, one of Cossery's central themes is laziness, or passivity. This is the lifestyle adopted by Cossery himself but is also, as Mahmud Qasim points out, a lifestyle typical of the poor, because efforts on their part generally are not justified by results. This suggests an interesting parallel with Gorky's depiction of those in the depths of society, who similarly inhabit a world without meaning or purpose. Throughout his writing career, Cossery was drawn to themes of death and dying; Gorky, too, often dwells in detail on his characters' deaths, such as those of Anna, Kostylev, and the Actor in *The Lower Depths*, and Natalia in *My Childhood*. It was obvious for Gorky that a meaningless, inert life inevitably leads to decay and

44 Mahmud Qasim, *Al-adab al-'arabi*, pp. 35–36.

an early death. Similarly, Cossery felt that living in everlasting hopelessness led to lethargic sleep (which is why so many of his characters sleep excessively) and, consequently, to death. *The House of Certain Death* derives its title from this theme: its characters inhabit a strange, unchanging world in a crumbling house which they can neither leave nor repair. The inevitable destruction of the house envisioned by its landlord at the very end of the novel stands for the metaphorical death of everything meaningless.

Conclusion

In this chapter, I have demonstrated some of the complex trajectories of influence followed by Maksim Gorky's writing in the Arab world, as well as the transformations of his ideas and persona facilitated by the translation of his books into Arabic. This has led to the emergence of a number of Arabic literary works demonstrably influenced both by Gorky's writings and the myths surrounding his personality. These trajectories are comparable, to some extent, to the global circulation of *The Thousand and One Nights*; their travels confirm Damrosch's contention that, once national literature is translated into a foreign language, it commences an independent life in the target culture. To describe the complex life of world literature, Damrosch uses the term "elliptical approach", where the original literary work and the reader's perception of the same work in translation represent two foci connected by an ellipse.[45] This image of numerous interconnected foci with overlapping ellipses reflects the interrelatedness of Gorky's legacy with the literary works of two Egyptian writers: Khairy Shalaby, who lived his whole life in Egypt and wrote in Arabic, and Albert Cossery, who left Egypt for France and wrote in French, but set all his novels in Cairo. Hence, Gorky's Arabic afterlife enjoyed, in Cossery's case, an even more convoluted trajectory: his influence extended to French and subsequently returned to Arabic via translations of Cossery's fiction.

Almost ninety years since his death, Gorky remains an influential writer, consistently retranslated and reprinted. Completely new translations have been produced by the Omani Ahmad ar-Rahbi and the Iraqi Munther Kathem Husseyn (e.g., the latter's version of *Tales from Italy* (*Skazki ob Italii*, 1923) published by the Lebanese publishing house ar-Rafideyn in 2018). In 2020, the same publishing house released Gorky's *The Spy: The Story of a Superfluous Man* (*Shpion: Zhizn' nenuzhnogo cheloveka*, 1910) in a translation by Ayman Ibn Masbah al-Uwaisi, from Oman. New and old Arabic translations of Gorky's works continue to be downloaded from free online libraries and reviewed by Arab readers. As of late 2023, *The Lower Depths* had been rated 3,428 times and reviewed 139 times, *Selected Works* had been rated 6,921 times with 391 reviews, and *Mother* had been

45 Damrosch, *What Is World Literature?*, p. 133.

rated 16,490 times.[46] Moreover, adaptations of Gorky's plays remain popular in Arab theatres: for instance, in 2017 *The Lower Depths* was performed four times by a Palestinian student cast with the 'ASHTAR' Theatre in the West Bank city of Ramallah. Gorky's importance as an intellectual and cultural inspiration to the Arab world persists in the twenty-first century.

46 For these specific statistics, see: https://www.goodreads.com/book/show/13493339 and https://www.goodreads.com/book/show/15729096 respectively. Both pages are in Arabic.

Ethiopia

A Handbook of the Socialist Movement: Gorky's *Mother* in Ethiopia[1]

Nikolay Steblin-Kamensky

Introduction

From 1961 to 1991, the Ethiopian book market experienced a significant flow of literature in both English and Amharic which had been published in, and imported from, the USSR. In these three decades, more than 350 titles were translated into Amharic: the total number of copies printed exceeded four million. Books were translated both directly from Russian and through the medium of English; curiously, the role of the latter was never acknowledged in those Soviet publications. Because of this circumstance, I choose to call this phenomenon the Soviet project of translations into Amharic without specifying the source language. The reference to the USSR also rightly frames it as a part of that state's soft-power operation, which Susanna Witt calls "the largest more or less coherent project of translation the world has seen to date—largest in terms of geographical range, number of languages (and directions) involved and time span; coherent in the sense of ideological framework (given its fluctuations over time) and centralized planning".[2]

1 I would like to express my sincere gratitude to Saada Mouhammed, Hiwot Tefera, Aboneh Ashagrie, Ambachew Kebede, A.P. Renzhin, M.L. Volpe, Kebru Kefle, Nikolaus Vitzthum and the family of Ge'ezan Yemane. Thank you for your support and insights! My deep appreciation also goes to the anonymous reviewers and editors of this volume for their comments and suggestions.

2 Susanna Witt, 'Between the Lines', in *Contexts, Subtexts and Pretexts: Literary Translation in Eastern Europe and Russia*, ed. by Brian James Baer (Amsterdam: John

 https://doi.org/10.11647/OBP.0340.21

Most Soviet Amharic publications were from Progress Publishers, established in 1963 to succeed the Foreign Languages Publishing House. Officially tasked with publishing classics of Marxism-Leninism, including textbooks and fiction; statutes of the Communist Party; and speeches by high officials, it was probably the least autonomous of all Soviet state-reliant publishing institutions. It might appear that this translation project's statist and pragmatic nature makes it less interesting for a scholarly inquiry. Yet, following Pierre Bourdieu, we can challenge the idea of the literary field as independent from the social world. Progress Publishers was certainly the opposite of a purely aesthetic operation. The state selected books for translation, instructed, paid, and supervised translators, then printed and distributed Progress publications. This highly controlled situation might seem to augur limited success, if not failure, for the Soviet translation project. My own interest in Progress emerged from one simple question: how could a state-run enterprise with open political bias spark such excitement and creativity and leave an enduring legacy? Thus, my research will attempt to assess the Soviet project of translations into Amharic in light of its egalitarian appeal and its pragmatic agenda.

This chapter utilises two consecutive strategies to examine this project and its reception in Ethiopia. The first outlines the history of the Soviet-Ethiopian relationship, placing the translations in that context. My point here is to show that the selection of titles and number of publications corresponded smoothly to political circumstances. My statistics come from the *Annals of Books* (*Knizhnaia letopis'*, since 1906)—a monthly Russophone bibliographical index. Due to the centralised nature of the Soviet publishing industry, it is likely that every translation was registered in the index, but we should keep in mind that some translations were carried out independently in Ethiopia. The *Annals of Books* record typical bibliographical information, including the number of copies published. In rare cases, it also identified translators.[3]

My second strategy is a detailed case study of Maksim Gorky's *Mother* (*Mat'*, 1906), based on my readings of translations and on personal interviews with its readers. A closer look at *Mother*'s Amharic translations and Ethiopian reception reveals that prominent translators succeeded in engaging with the text creatively despite the rigid rules set by Progress. My microhistorical, personality-focused perspective on the Progress translation project counters the view fostered by the Soviet state itself, namely, that it was the sole cause of the translations. As Anthony Pym argues, causation of translations is plural in its very nature and thus, as I will attempt in this essay, the limits of state control over translation

Benjamins, 2011), pp. 147–70 (p. 167).

3 For detailed data collected from *Annals of Books* and selected bibliography of fiction translated into Amharic, see Nikolay Steblin-Kamensky, 'Literature of "Progress": History of Soviet Translations into Amharic', in *Proceedings of the 20th International Conference of Ethiopian Studies*, ed. by Mitiku Gabremedhin and others (Mekelle University, forthcoming 2024).

projects must be examined.[4] A few words by way of context about the position of the Amharic and English languages in Ethiopia: Amharic has been the dominant language of the Ethiopian ruling elites since at least the thirteenth century A.D., and early Amharic texts date back to the sixteenth century. But prior to the reign of Menelik II (1889–1913), its position as a written medium remained incidental, overshadowed by Ge'ez—the language of the Ethiopian Orthodox church taught by the clergy—which had a kind of diglossic relationship with Amharic.[5] In the late nineteenth century, the need for modern education and literacy was recognised and Amharic developed into the national language of Ethiopia. Amharic was taught within the school curriculum and its role as a medium of education grew slowly from the first two grades (in the 1940s) to six grades (in the 1960s). As for the English language, it was established as the medium of secondary and higher education in 1941, and subsequently, many Anglophone teachers were invited to Ethiopia from India while the curriculum was shaped with the help of British advisors.

An Overview of Soviet Publications in Amharic: Ideological Intervention or Literary Aid?

Amharic literature is very young, although it constitutes one of the earliest literary spaces in African vernacular languages.[6] The first Amharic novel, *A Heart-Born Story* (*Lebb wallad tarik*, 1908) by Afework Gebreyesus (1868–1947)[7] was published in Rome in 1908, where a printing press with Ethiopic letters was already available (the first official Ethiopian printing house would be founded in 1917). It would take another twenty years before fiction became an established genre among educated Ethiopians.[8] In Casanova's 'world republic of letters', the Amharic literary space would certainly count as underdeveloped.[9] Casanova shows how the French and German literary spaces initially accumulated their

4 Anthony Pym, *Method in Translation History* (Abingdon: Routledge, 2014), p. 158.

5 J. Fellman, 'The Birth of an African Literary Language: The Case of Amharic', *Research in African Literatures*, 24:3 (1993), 123–25.

6 Albert X. Gérard, 'Amharic Creative Literature: The Early Phase', *Journal of Ethiopian Studies*, 6:2 (1968), 39–59.

7 The title *Lebb wallad tarik* literary means 'a story born in the heart', that is, an invented tale. This title coined the Amharic term for 'fiction'. Please note that all translations from Amharic or Russian in this essay are, unless otherwise indicated, my own. In this essay, Ethiopians are referred to by a first name followed by a patronymic or by a first name alone. This is the standard form of address in Ethiopia used by most scholars in Ethiopian studies.

8 Denis Nosnitsin, 'Amharic Literature' in *Encyclopaedia Aethiopica*, 1 (2003), 238–40 (p. 239).

9 Pascale Casanova, *The World Republic of Letters*, trans. by Malcolm DeBevoise (Cambridge, MA: Harvard University Press, 2004).

capital through extensive translation work, which required certain economic and social conditions. Should we therefore see the Soviet translation project as a genuine contribution to the Ethiopian literary space? And how did the Soviet government view its commitment?

Brian Baer suggests that the Soviet Union celebrated literary translation as a political vehicle serving internationalism and the "friendship of peoples", constantly recreating the illusion of brotherhood among its republics and ethnicities.[10] Katerina Clark similarly observed that "the translation project was not only about Soviet aggrandizement or hegemonic aims but also about creating a common cultural universe of the like-minded, creating a common tradition that superseded the local".[11] Another fact which hints at the non-intrusive nature of Progress is that the Ethiopian side actually asked for books. In 1946—two years after an official diplomatic relationship between Ethiopia and the USSR had been established—the Ethiopian Minister of Foreign Affairs entered into talks with a Soviet diplomat, expressing the former's needs in aviation and education. Among other things—mostly technical assistance—he requested "Russian books" from VOKS.[12] We do not know exactly what kind of books were sought, but it was most probably educational material.

The first period of the translation project, prioritising educational texts, lasted from 1961 to 1974, when the Emperor Haile Selassie I—a member of the Solomonic dynasty, which had ruled Ethiopia since at least the thirteenth century A.D.—was overthrown and a military junta known as the Derg took power. Under Haile Selassie I, Ethiopia had been a major ally of the USA in the Horn of Africa, providing a military base in the Red Sea, while the Emperor was a convinced anti-Communist. Despite significant progress in the Soviet-Ethiopian relationship, marked by Haile Selassie's visit to the USSR in 1959, Moscow had to make large-scale efforts "to overcome Ethiopian animosity toward the Soviet system, to detach Ethiopia from the West and, if possible, to win ultimately its exclusive friendship".[13] A cultural agreement was signed in January 1961, which led to various cultural activities and scholarships for

10 Brian J. Baer, 'Literary Translation and the Construction of a Soviet Intelligentsia', *The Massachusetts Review*, 47:3 (2006), 537–60 (p. 541).

11 Katerina Clark, 'Translation and Transnationalism: Non-European Writers and Soviet Power in the 1920s and 1930s', in *Translation in Russian Contexts: Culture, Politics, Identity*, ed. by Brian James Baer and Susanna Witt (London: Routledge, 2017), pp. 139–58 (p. 143).

12 *Rossiia i Afrika: dokumenty i materialy, XVII v-1960 g.*, ed. by A.B. Davidson and S.V. Mazov (Moscow: Institut vseobshchei istorii RAN, 1999), p. 49. VOKS (Vsesoiuznoe Obshchestvo Kul'turnoi Sviazi s Zagranitsei)—the All-Union Society for Cultural Links with Abroad—was an organisation which distributed Soviet materials throughout the world, arranged cultural exchanges, and helped found friendship societies in various countries.

13 Sergius Yakobson, 'The Soviet Union and Ethiopia: A Case of Traditional Behavior', *The Review of Politics*, 25:3 (1963), 329–42 (p. 332).

Ethiopian students. During this period, the Soviet Union could not distribute any explicit Socialist propaganda in Ethiopia. Therefore, Communist translation powers were channelled into the domain of Russian fiction and children's books, but the print runs remained very low.

In this fourteen-year period, the print run for each book ranged from one to three thousand. Altogether, only 116,600 Amharic-language books were printed in the USSR, but they included canonical texts such as Dostoevsky's *Poor Folk* (*Bednye liudi*, 1846) and *White Nights* (*Belye nochi*, 1848), Pushkin's *Dubrovsky* (*Dubrovskii*, 1841) and *The Belkin Tales* (*Povesti pokoinogo Ivana Petrovicha Belkina*, 1831), Gogol's 'Taras Bulba' ('Taras Bul'ba', 1835), Tolstoy's 'After the Ball' ('Posle bala', written 1903), Chekhov's 'The Lady with the Dog' ('Dama s sobachkoi,' 1899), Mikhail Sholokhov's novella *The Fate of a Man* (*Sud'ba cheloveka*, 1956), and even science-fiction stories such as Aleksandr Beliaev's ever-popular *The Amphibian Man* (*Chelovek-amfibiia*, 1928). Besides texts originally written in Russian, the Chukchi writer Iurii Rytkheu's *The Happiness of My People* (*Schast'e moego naroda*, 1964), the Tuvan politician and writer Salchak Toka's *The Word Arata* (*Slovo Arata*, 1951), three novels by the Kirghiz writer Chinghiz Aitmatov and various short stories by Georgian writers were also translated into Amharic. I suggest two reasons for selecting such non-ethnically Russian (but Russophone) authors. First, some Soviet republics were seen as showcases of Socialist development, and leaders of the Third World countries were regularly invited to observe the success of such non-Russian republics. Secondly, they demonstrated the inclusiveness of Soviet culture and stressed its egalitarian appeal. But in reality, Russian was the manifest centre of the Progress Amharic project. It was the only source language indicated on any of these titles (even if the original language of the text was not Russian). This reveals a hidden hegemonic ambition on the part of the state, for, as Johan Heilbron and Gisèle Sapiro argue, the number of books translated from any language indicates its relative power in the international literary field.[14] Thus, Progress's translations were also an investment in the symbolic capital of the Russian language.

While I have found little explicitly Socialist propaganda among those first Amharic translations (apart from an awkward children's book about Lenin at a New Year party and some self-congratulatory books about Soviet public health care and education), the USSR was secretly promoting Socialism through the dissemination of Progress titles. Kebru Kefle—currently a bookshop owner in Addis Ababa—recalls how, in the 1960s, he bought boxes of cheap books from the Soviet Embassy to sell them secretly on the streets.[15] These publications were known as 'red books' because of their red covers and they were in high demand among radical students. Ideological books were also secretly distributed by

---

14 Johan Heilbron and Gisèle Sapiro, 'Outline for a Sociology of Translation', in *Constructing a Sociology of Translation*, ed. by Michaela Wolf and Alexandra Fukari (Amsterdam: John Benjamins, 2007), pp. 93–107 (p. 102).

15 Endalegeta Kabbada, *Ma'eqab* [Ban] (Addis Ababa: Etafzer, 2018), p. 247.

the Soviet Centre of Science and Culture, which encouraged its visitors to take books. Endalegeta Kabbada in his *Ban* (Ma'eqab, 2018) provides the following memory:

> An individual who used to frequent the Center told me: 'when we entered the Russian [i.e. Soviet] Centre to read fiction, they would encourage us to take a political book. When we were about to leave, an Ethiopian librarian would approach us, whispering a piece of advice: 'Just take it and go, hide it behind your back'.[16]

The period from 1975 to 1978 might be considered transitional, since, despite the Ethiopian Revolution of 1974, the Soviet Union remained reluctant to welcome the Derg or accept its revolutionary credentials. Somalia was emerging as the Soviet Union's major ally in the Horn of Africa.[17] But growing interest in Ethiopian affairs was revealed by the rapid increase of Amharic literary production: these four years saw an equal number of new translations as in the previous fourteen years and a six-fold increase in the print run. Fiction remained a sizeable part of book production, with books by authors such as Dostoevsky, Aitmatov or even Beliaev reprinted in runs from ten to twenty thousand copies. Lermontov's *A Hero of our Time* (*Geroi nashego vremeni*, 1840) and Gorky's *My Universities* (*Moi universitety*, 1923) both appeared in Amharic at this time. The translation of ideological literature into Amharic began, mainly Vladimir Lenin's writings; soon it would flood the Ethiopian book market.

The years from 1979 to the end of the project in 1991 were marked by a scarcity of fiction, which was dwarfed by ideological literature. Fifty-three titles by Lenin and twenty titles interpreting his writings were translated and printed in huge runs (the total amount of Lenin's books alone was almost one million). A 1988 account of book publishing in Ethiopia, by a former director of the Addis Ababa University Library, noted with disapproval the ideological imbalance in translated literature available at this time. She stated that "the bookshops stock small quantities of cheap, well-produced translations into English of Russian and Soviet classics and into Amharic of Russian children's literature".[18] By then Amharic translations of Russian fiction had almost ceased. Gorky's *Mother* is one of the few exceptions during this period. Interestingly, the new ideology of perestroika and glasnost was also reflected in translations into Amharic, as

16 Endalegeta Kabbada, *Ma'eqab*, p. 248.

17 Richard Pankhurst, 'The Russians in Ethiopia: Aspirations of Progress', in *Africa in Russia, Russia in Africa: Three Centuries of Encounters*, ed. by Maxim Matusevich (Trenton: Africa World Press, 2007), pp. 219–38 (p. 230). See also Robert G. Patman, *The Soviet Union in the Horn of Africa: The Diplomacy of Intervention and Disengagement* (Cambridge: Cambridge University Press, 2009), p. 181.

18 Rita Pankhurst, 'Libraries in Post-Revolutionary Ethiopia', *Information Development*, 4:4 (1988), 239–45 (p. 240). Pankhurst was the library's director between 1968 and 1975.

Mikhail Gorbachev's *Perestroika: New Thinking for Our Country and the World* (*Perestroika novoe myshlenie dlia nashei strany i vsego mira*, 1987)[19] appeared besides a publication celebrating the millennium of the Russian Orthodox Church.[20]

Initiated by the Soviet state, the Progress translation project shared its fate. In March 1991, an ominously titled article, 'Progress Publishing House: All [Staff] Dismissed and Lenin No Longer Printed' appeared in the newspaper *Kommersant*.[21] The financial manager of Progress, Aleksei Ershov, declared that this drastic new policy was primarily necessitated by the huge losses in publishing Soviet political literature for export. The post-Soviet government had refused to cover those expenses, forcing Progress to dismiss more than half of its employees. Its ambitious project to publish literature in forty-seven languages was no longer viable.

What made the Soviet project of Amharic translations unique was the literature translated during its earliest years. Unlike other Soviet translation projects in African languages (including Swahili, Hausa, and Somali) in Amharic, a wide selection of Russian classics was made available to the target readers. Although Hausa and Somali were quite insignificant branches of the translation industry, the number of titles translated into Swahili exceeded the number of translations into Amharic (but with smaller print runs). However, Progress translated no pre-revolutionary Russian fiction into Swahili apart from Pushkin's *Belkin Tales* and some children's stories by Lev Tolstoy. As we have seen above, considerably more pre-Soviet fiction appeared in Amharic. The Ethiopian case was different because it was not merely a function of the USSR's foreign policy, but a product of the Soviet-Ethiopian relationship, where Ethiopia under Haile Selassie I managed to work with both superpowers and keep the Soviet friendship tamed.

The seemingly egalitarian nature of the Soviet translation project was also manifest in translations of Ethiopian literature from Amharic (sometimes via English) into Russian. But an overview of those translations discloses the hierarchical Soviet approach to such translations.[22] Michael Volpe, a translator

19 Mikhail Gorbachev, *Perestroika: addis astasasab lahagaracenna lamalaw alam* (Moscow: Progress, 1989).

20 This translation was not found. According to the *Annals of Books*, it was published in 1988 by Novosti Press Agency, translated by Lobachev and Pravotvorov, *Tysiacheletie russkogo pravoslaviia* [*The Millennium of Russian Orthodoxy*]; unfortunately, neither the initials of translators nor the author of the source text are stated in the *Annals of Books*.

21 'Izdatel'stvo "Progress": vsekh uvolim i Lenina pechatat' ne budem', *Kommersant Vlast*, 13 (1991), https://www.kommersant.ru/doc/265485.

22 Maurice Friedberg also notes that "no manifestations of obsequious literalism were tolerated in translations into Russian, that the same literalism was actually encouraged in translations from Russian into the languages of the minorities." See Friedberg, *Literary Translation in Russia: A Cultural History* (University Park, PA: Penn State University Press, 1997), p. 184.

from Amharic into Russian himself, argues that Russian translators had to "improve" Amharic fiction, they had to be creative and "practically always Russian translations were shorter, more expressive and had more accentuated plots vis-à-vis their Amharic originals".[23] Original titles were almost obsessively altered, for apparently no practical reason other than the explicit imposition of authority.[24] At the same time, translators into Amharic (most often recruited from Ethiopian students) worked in drastically different settings: they had to follow a rigid, literalist paradigm under the watchful eye of a Russian editor trained in Amharic. The very hierarchy between literalistic and assimilative modes shaped the assumed value of those translations. As Volpe puts it: "original Russian texts have been more or less diligently put into Amharic so as one could follow the plot and get a fairly clear idea about the content. At the same time more often than not the artistic impression, to my mind, is not high enough".[25] This attitude on the part of Progress is suggested by the fact that in the list of major translations into Amharic the names of translators were not even mentioned.[26] Was it because, unlike assimilative translations into Russian, these literal versions were perceived as less deserving? In fact, the work carried out by Ethiopian translators was quite impressive. Not only did they translate prose fiction with little or no professional experience, the scarcity of materials and strictly imposed literal aesthetic must have posed a constant creative challenge.

Gorky's *Mother* in Ethiopia

My outline of Soviet Amharic-language publishing policy has shown that it was less egalitarian than it wanted to appear. But whatever the general policy, there were many agents involved with their own interests, lending the project its multifaceted nature. To examine the identities of two of those agents, I shall move to my case study: Gorky's novel *Mother* in Amharic translation.

Maksim Gorky (1868–1936) was a visionary of a renewed and united humankind; he was a leading advocate of the idea of World Literature. The history of *Mother*'s dissemination, as a novel written abroad and first published in English translation, exemplifies such literature.[27] Although Gorky himself

23 Michael L. Volpe, 'An annotated bibliography of Ethiopian literature in Russian', *Rassegna di Studi Etiopici*, 32 (1988), 171–93 (p. 173).

24 This is why Taye Assefa and Shiferaw Bekele, apparently unaware of Soviet translation practice, were puzzled by the Russian titles and suggested that the translators lacked expertise in Amharic. See Taye Assefa and Shiferaw Bekele, 'The Study of Amharic Literature: An Overview', *Journal of Ethiopian Studies*, 33:2 (2000), 27–73 (p. 53).

25 Volpe, 'Annotated bibliography', p. 185.

26 Ibid., pp. 185–90.

27 Olga V. Shugan 'M. Gorkii i kontseptsiia mirovoi literatury', in *Mirovoe znachenie M. Gorkogo*, ed. by L.A. Spiridonova (Moscow: IMLI RAN, 2020), pp. 172–98.

became disillusioned with Marxism, and Soviet literary policy failed to embody the utopian dreams of its founders, the egalitarian message of *Mother* persisted, shaping the novel's reception around the world. After all, framed by Marxist class optics, it appealed to readers of all nations and ethnic backgrounds, especially those who felt unjustly oppressed. The first variant of the novel survives only in an anonymous translation (probably by the Russo-American translator and editor Thomas Seltzer), which was serially published in *Appleton's Magazine* in the US in 1906 and reissued in book form in 1907.[28] Most of the early translations in other languages were based on that version. Gorky revised *Mother* repeatedly; in 1922 it was published for the first time in the USSR, with stylistic and structural changes. In 1949, Margaret Wettlin (1907–2003)—a US-born teacher of English and translator who lived in the USSR from 1934 to 1980—translated this 1922 version, which became the standard version for translation and distribution abroad by Soviet publishers. It was thus in Wettlin's translation that the novel was first introduced to Ethiopia in the 1960s.

By this time, most Ethiopian intellectuals had become discontented with the modernisation policy imposed by Haile Selassie's government and with the USA as its major ally;[29] such scepticism was expressed by Socialist rhetoric which targeted both the so-called out-dated monarchy and 'American imperialism'. It is worth noting that leftist ideas entered Ethiopia not only from the East, but from the West as well, where many young African intellectuals were educated.[30] Randi Balsvik argues that during the 1960s the Soviet Embassy actually did little to engage with Ethiopian students. Despite concerns among Western residents of Addis Ababa about the effect of Soviet propaganda upon university students through the Soviet reading room and information centre, the United States Information Agency (USIA)[31] was much more popular.

Mother reached Ethiopia just as the country was seeking to define its own modernism, and thus establish its place among other 'progressive' nations. In other words, Socialism appeared the right strategy for maintaining national dignity under threat of 'backwardness', now dangerously associated with Ethiopia's supposedly 'feudal' system of government. Thus, "after the upheavals on the West of the late 1960s virtually every Ethiopian took up Marxism".[32] In his eloquent description of the Ethiopian revolution, Donald Donham stresses the

28 See Sara Pankenier and Barry P. Scherr, 'Searching for the Ur-text: Gorky's English "Mother"', *Russian Language Journal / Русский Язык*, 51:168/170 (1997), 125–48.

29 Randi Rønning Balsvik, *Haile Selassie's Students: The Intellectual and Social Background to Revolution, 1952–1977* (Addis Ababa: Addis Ababa University Press, 1985), p. 200.

30 Donald L. Donham, *Marxist Modern: An Ethnographic History of the Ethiopian Revolution* (Berkeley, CA and Oxford: University of California Press, 1999), p. 126.

31 The USIA was an American public relations organisation which served to highlight the views of the US while diminishing those of the Soviet Union. It was active in about 150 different countries.

32 Donham, *Marxist Modern*, p. 126.

importance of previous revolutionary narratives, particularly for the instigators, to make their own revolution meaningful: "it sometimes seems that the ancestral spirits of other great upheavals—from Marx to Lenin to Mao—presided over Ethiopian events like Greek gods".[33] *Mother*, with its realist appeal stressed by the paratext which introduced Pavel Vlasov's prototype,[34] was a perfect text for adapting the Soviet revolutionary narrative to the Ethiopian uprising.

Indeed, if Gorky had hoped to establish a new kind of literature (one that might even substitute for the Bible), *Mother*'s Ethiopian reception probably came close to obtaining that status. In her autobiography, Hiwot Teffera—then a radical student, later a member of the Ethiopian People's Revolutionary Party—recalls: "Maksim Gorky's *Mother* was actually the one that gave me an idea of what I would be doing in the underground organization. Pavel Vlasov became a model revolutionary to me. More than anything else, I was inspired and moved by the story of his mother".[35] In an interview with me, she specified that the novel "was a handbook for those who were involved in the socialist movement". In her opinion, the book was seminal for inspiring revolutionary zeal among the young generation in Ethiopia of the 1970s.[36]

The playwright and scholar Aboneh Ashagre (born in 1951) recalls that he, too, read *Mother* in English in 1969. The book was recommended to him by a "radical friend"; almost all young people of his circle read the novel at that time. Interest in Gorky's novel inspired him to explore other works by Russian writers.[37] Similarly, the journalist Meaza Birru (born in 1958) in an interview with the writer Endalegeta Kebbede recalled that, for her generation, *Mother* was an inspiration to serve others and help the oppressed.[38] These testimonies serve to hint at the novel's enthusiastic reception in Ethiopia.

Ge'ezan Yemane's Translation

The Amharic translation of *Mother* appeared relatively late, in 1981, and was published only in 1770 copies. Within two years, an additional 3000 were printed, and in 1986, fifteen thousand were issued. My own copy is one of the third editions. I bought it at 'Meshaf tera' (a second-hand bookstore in Addis Ababa) in 2015. Its well-worn binding has been neatly refurbished with a strip of denim. Paratexts

---

33 Ibid, pp. i-xxvi (p. xvii).

34 The dust jacket of *Mother*, published by Progress in 1967, contains a blurb linking the plot to real historical events: "The book deals with events which actually took place at Sormovo on the Volga in the early years of this century".

35 Hiwot Teffera, *Tower in the Sky* (Addis Ababa: Addis Ababa University Press, 2012), p. 105.

36 Hiwot Teffera, online interview with author (18 March 2021).

37 Aboneh Ashagre, from email exchanged with author (6 August 2021).

38 Endalegeta Kabbada, interview with Meaza Berru on Radio Sheger FM, programme 'Yechewata Engida' (25 June 2016).

include an introduction by Boris Bursov, which depicts Russian literature as an evolutionary progression with Gorky at the top, and an anonymous afterword where the history of the novel is explained.[39] The translation is attributed to Ge'ezan Yemane (1940–97), the fourth of eight children of a senior clergyman at Harar's Trinity Church. His father, Aleqa Yemane Mariam, encouraged Ge'ezan to pursue religious education, which made him proficient in the Ge'ez language. Growing up in the diverse city of Harar, Ge'ezan acquired fluency in Harari and Afaan Oromo languages as well. Ge'ezan completed his primary education at Ras Mekonen School and his secondary education at Medhanealem School in Harar before moving to Addis Ababa to attend Haile Selassie's University. A few years into his studies, he was awarded a Soviet scholarship to study at the University of Kyiv. There, he graduated with a Master's degree in Philosophy. After briefly returning to Ethiopia in the mid-1970s, Ge'ezan relocated to the USSR (Moscow) and worked for Progress Publishers. He has translated at least five other books, most of them non-fiction: Lenin's *The Land Question and the Fight for Freedom* (*Vopros o zemle i bor'ba za svobodu*, 1906) and *On Peaceful Coexistence* (*O mirnom sosushchestvovanii*); Viktor Grigor'evich Afanasiev's *Fundamentals of Philosophical Knowledge* (*Osnovy filosofskikh znanii*, 1977) and *Fundamentals of Scientific Communism* (*Osnovy nauchnogo kommunizma*, 1967); and A.N. Tolstoy's *The Garin Death Ray* (*Giperboloid inzhenera Garina*, 1927).

I limited my word-by-word analysis of Ge'ezan's translation to the first ten chapters. Though this approach inevitably does not provide a complete picture, it has proved sufficient to identify the characteristics of the text and to define its primary source. Ge'ezan's translation exemplifies the literalist mode of translation encouraged by Progress. The text includes many culture-specific Russian words such as "samovar", "Tsar", "verst" (a measure of distance), "pirog" (pie), "berezka" (birch tree), "osina" (aspen) and others, which he transliterated rather than explaining or domesticating. A character who pronounces unstressed 'o', which is common in some dialects of Russian, is described awkwardly in Amharic as somebody who adds an unnecessary 'o' sound to his utterances. These features, apart from the tree names, are also characteristic of Wettlin's English translation. As we shall see, Ge'ezan mostly relied on her translation, while the Russian version of 1922 was his constant reference point. He did not follow Wettlin in transliterating the Ukrainian term "nen'ko" (an affectionate word for 'mother'), which he replaced with the similarly tender Amharic "emmeye". This spared him a footnote (unlike Wettlin), but he did provide explanatory notes elsewhere. Words like "berezka" he explained with a gloss in the main text, with formulations such as "trees named birch" ("[illegible] [illegible] [illegible]").[40] Other footnotes introduce historical or ethnic concepts such as "Tatar", "Dukhobortsy" (a religious group), and

39 Maksim Gorkiy, *'Enat*, trans. by Ge'ezan Yemane (Moscow: Progress, 1981).

40 Ibid., p. 69.

"raznochinets" (a term for a class of people). Although very concise, these footnotes encourage a particular kind of reading by framing the fictional text as both educational and realistic.

The influence of Wettlin's English translation is clearly seen in certain places, most vividly in the way Ge'ezan Yemane rendered the phase "these are the best people on the earth" ("eto luchshie liudi na zemle"), which in Amharic (similarly to Wettlin's version) gained a biblical tone: "they are the salt of the Earth" ("☒☒☒ ☒☒☒☒☒☒ ☒☒ ☒☒☒").[41] Wettlin's translation tended to be over-determined by the literalist aesthetic of Progress, complicating my effort to determine whether her text or Gorky's original was the major source for the Amharic version. But the following examples convince me that Wettlin's work shaped many of Ge'ezan's decisions. The Russian insult "svoloch'", for example, was translated by Wettlin as "son of a bitch"; when addressed to a woman, she renders it as "bitch".[42] Similarly in Amharic, Ge'ezan has "☒☒☒ ☒☒" and "☒☒☒ ☒☒", which respectively translates as "son of a dog" and "you (fem.) dog".[43] The Amharic translation often splits Gorky's long sentences in precisely the places where Wettlin's text does. The Russian phrase "long work" ("dolgaia rabota") in both translations becomes "hard work". Another example is the description of the painting of Christ on the road to Emmaus, which marks an important stage in the enlightenment of Gorky's title character: both English and Amharic versions say that the figures in the painting are "*deep* in conversation" ("☒☒☒☒☒ ☒☒☒☒☒☒☒"), while in Russian they are only talking.[44] Wettlin's idiomatic "go to bed", used instead of the literal Russian imperative "sleep!", is reproduced in the Amharic ("☒☒☒☒☒ ☒☒").[45] There are many other similar examples.

While Wettlin's translation may have served as Ge'ezan's primary text, it was certainly not the only source of the Amharic version. It may have been easier for Ge'ezan to translate from English—a language which he had learned in school—but nevertheless he never ignored the Russian original. His translation conveys details absent in Wettlin's version. For example, Ge'ezan is very attentive to names and forms of address. While in Wettlin's translation the relation between Pavel and Pasha was left unexplained, he provides an explanatory footnote: "Pasha is an affectionate form for Pavel. When the mother

---

41 Maksim Gorkii, *Mat'; Vospominaniia* (Moscow: Khudozhestvennaia literature, 1985), p. 17. Gorkiy, *'Enat*, trans. by Ge'ezan Yemane, p. 45; Maxim Gorky, *Mother*, trans. by Margaret Wettlin (Moscow: Progress, 1967), p. 17. A reference to the Book of Matthew, 5.13.

42 Gorky, *Mother*, pp. 8–9.

43 Gorkiy, *'Enat*, trans. by Ge'ezan Yemane, pp. 26–27.

44 Gorky, *Mother*, p. 14. Gorkiy, *'Enat*, trans. by Ge'ezan Yemane, p. 37; Gorkii, *Mat'; Vospominaniia*, p. 13.

45 Gorky, *Mother*, trans. by Margaret Wettlin, p. 17. Gorkiy, *'Enat*, trans. by Ge'ezan Yemane, p. 45; Gorkii, *Mat'; Vospominaniia*, p. 17.

uses it for her son, it resembles the tender 'my so-and-so'".[46] This footnote does not simply explain the Russian diminutive, but also relates it to the Amharic system of affectionate naming by adding a possessive suffix. Wettlin refers to the character Sashen'ka (a diminutive of Aleksandra) as Sasha throughout her text, but Ge'ezan introduces her as Sasha (a departure from the original, which again suggests the importance of the English version for this translation), then switches to Sashen'ka with a similar footnote.

At the end of Chapter Eight, touched by Andrei's love story, the title character, Pelageia, unconsciously addresses him as Andryusha (another affectionate moniker) instead of his full name, Andrei Onisimovich.[47] Wettlin translated this part as follows: "She had never before called the *khokhol*[48] anything but Andrei Onisimovich but today without noticing it she said Andryusha".[49] The Amharic translation here uses a gloss to explain the Russian system of formal names, again relating it to the similar Ethiopian custom of using a first name followed by a patronymic: "The mother had used to call the khokhol by his full name in respectful form, Andrei Onisimovich, which was his name with his father's name. But today without noticing she said only his first name in an affectionate form".[50] The affectionate form did not require clarification as Ge'ezan Yemane was using the Amharic system: thus, instead of Andryusha, in Amharic we have the equivalent Andreyye. Also, unlike the Russian text, in Amharic Pelageia uses the informal second-person singular addressing Andrei.

Amharic possesses an elaborate system of formal pronouns, both for the second and for the third person. Ge'ezan Yemane seems to have tried to convey the Russian respectful 'you' (the second person plural form 'vy'), which has no equivalent in the English translation. Gorky often explicitly comments about formal and informal pronouns. For example, one sentence reads: "He called her 'Mother' and used the 'ty' [familiar] pronoun, which he did only when he felt drawn to her".[51] Wettlin's translation runs as follows: "He called her 'Mummy', and his tone was the one he used when he felt drawn to her".[52] But the Amharic translation is: "He said not 'antu' but 'anchi' and called her mother. He used this way of naming only when they were particularly close and he felt her spiritual

46 '[illegible]—[illegible] [illegible].' Gorkiy, *'Enat*, trans. by Ge'ezan Yemane, p. 39.
47 Gorkii, *Mat'; Vospominaniia*, p. 42.
48 'Khokhol' is a derogatory Russian term for Ukrainians. Both Ge'ezan's and Wettlin's translations keep this term with a brief footnote.
49 Gorky, *Mother*, trans. by Margaret Wettlin, p. 39.
50 "[illegible]..." Maksim Gorkiy, *'Enat*, trans. by Ge'ezan Yemane, p. 89.
51 "Он сказал ей 'мать' и 'ты', как говорил только тогда, когда вставал ближе к ней." Maksim Gorkii, *Mat'; Vospominaniia*, p. 53.
52 Gorky, *Mother*, trans. by Margaret Wettlin, p. 48.

affinity".[53] Ge'ezan actually could not reflect Russian pronouns consistently, because the systems of polite speech are different in Russian and Amharic. While Russian 'vy' often reflects formal politeness between equals, the Amharic 'antu' recognises a semantic hierarchy of power. Thus, Pavel's comrades could not use 'antu' to each other (although in the Russian, they used 'vy'). But Ge'ezan's translation does appear to have attempted to extend the norms of the Amharic system of politeness.

My final point here about Ge'ezan's translation is that, despite the enforced literality, he took care to contextualise his writing and even to embed a particular message. For example, when Gorky's character Andrei affirms the brotherhood of all tribes (*plemena*) and nations (*natsii*),[54] in Amharic Ge'ezan used terms which arguably localise the issue for Ethiopia: tribes are still tribes (⌧⌧), but nations become kin groups (⌧⌧).[55] Many other small deviations from the Russian text (and from Wettlin's translation) are connected to religion. "Two icons in the corner" ("dve ikony v uglu") in Amharic became "two icons to which one prays in the corner" ("⌧⌧⌧⌧⌧⌧⌧ ⌧⌧⌧⌧ ⌧⌧⌧⌧⌧");[56] "she knelt and prayed quietly" became "she knelt and prayed quietly and absorbed";[57] "if you honour Christ, why do not you go to the church?" became "if your love to Christ is so great, why do not you go to the church?"[58] Some Russian exclamations invoking God, which are epigrammatic in Gorky's text, in Amharic resemble brief prayers. For example, "Oh, God!" ("o, gospodi!") was rendered as "Lord Christ have mercy on us" ("⌧⌧⌧⌧ ⌧⌧⌧⌧ ⌧⌧⌧⌧⌧").[59] Minor in themselves, these deviations arguably constitute a pattern of domestication and explicitation, which might have favourably influenced the novel's reception. I give one example below of the novel's continuing importance for contemporary Ethiopian authors.

Sa'ada Mahamad (b. 1980)—an Ethiopian writer and playwright—read Ge'ezan's translation of *Mother* when she was in the equivalent of fifth grade. She describes it as her first major experience of reading, even before she discovered prominent Amharic writers like Haddis Alemayehu and Baalu Girma. Even though she could not then understand the full story, *Mother* remained one of

53 "⌧⌧⌧ ⌧⌧⌧⌧ ⌧⌧⌧ ⌧⌧⌧ ⌧⌧⌧⌧ ⌧⌧ ⌧⌧⌧ ⌧⌧⌧⌧ ⌧⌧⌧⌧ ⌧⌧⌧⌧⌧ ⌧⌧⌧⌧⌧⌧ ⌧⌧⌧ ⌧⌧⌧ ⌧⌧⌧ ⌧⌧⌧⌧⌧ ⌧⌧⌧⌧ ⌧⌧⌧⌧⌧⌧⌧ ⌧⌧ ⌧⌧ ⌧⌧⌧." Maksim Gorkiy, *'Enat*, trans. by Ge'ezan Yemane, p. 107.

54 Gorkii, *Mat'; Vospominaniia*, p. 36.

55 Gorkiy, *'Enat*, trans. by Ge'ezan Yemane, p. 78.

56 Gorkii, *Mat'; Vospominaniia*, p. 11; Gorkiy, *'Enat*, trans. by Ge'ezan Yemane, p. 34

57 "... она молча опустилась на колени перед образами." Gorkii, *Mat'; Vospominaniia*, p. 11.
"⌧⌧⌧⌧ ⌧⌧ ⌧⌧⌧⌧⌧⌧ ⌧⌧⌧⌧⌧ ⌧ ⌧⌧⌧ ⌧⌧ ⌧⌧⌧⌧⌧ ⌧⌧ ⌧⌧⌧⌧ ⌧⌧⌧⌧⌧⌧⌧." Gorkiy, *'Enat*, trans. by Ge'ezan Yemane, p. 33.

58 "Христа почитаешь, а в церковь не ходишь." Gorkii, *Mat'; Vospominaniia*, p. 13s'⌧⌧⌧⌧⌧⌧ ⌧⌧⌧⌧⌧ ⌧⌧⌧⌧⌧ ⌧⌧⌧ ⌧⌧⌧⌧⌧⌧ ⌧⌧⌧⌧ ⌧⌧⌧ ⌧⌧ ⌧⌧⌧⌧⌧⌧ ⌧⌧⌧⌧⌧?" Gorkiy, *'Enat*, trans. by Ge'ezan Yemane, p. 37.

59 Gorkii, *Mat'; Vospominaniia*, p. 18; Gorkiy, *'Enat*, trans. by Ge'ezan Yemane, p. 47.

her favourite pieces of writing. After briefly emigrating to Saudi Arabia for a year and a half, she returned to Ethiopia and wrote her first novel, *Thorny Gold* (*Eshohamma warq*, 1999). A story about Ethiopian girls in Jidda, it combines a catchy plot with almost ethnographic observations of migrants' everyday life. When the book was published, Saada Mouhammed—then just nineteen—gained immediate national recognition. Her novel was read on Radio Ethiopia. She has said that she considers the Russian writers, whom she has read in Amharic translations, as her teachers in literature: "translations of Russian literature have shown me, how similar Russian and Ethiopian lives were, and thus they taught me, how to describe my own society through fiction".[60]

Yohannes Kifle Dadi

The 1981 Amharic translation of *Mother* launched by Progress was not the first to be made. In 2020, an adaptation of a translation from the late 1970s was published, with a cover inscription stating that it was "translated by Yohannes Kifle Dadi together with his cellmates". The book opens with a one-page biography of the translator, followed by the translator's acknowledgments and a thirty-seven-page introduction entitled 'The Square of Sorrow: Memoirs of Yohannes Kifle, Prisoner of the Derg. How Could This Translation Happen?' ('[illegible] : [illegible]?'). Yohannes Kifle (1939–2020) was born in Kenya. Aged four, he moved with his parents to Ethiopia, and later spent five years of his adolescence in England. After gaining a degree in political sciences from Addis Ababa University College in 1963, he completed a master's degree in journalism in 1965 (University of Iowa). When the Derg seized power, Yohannes was managing the sales department for Ethiopian Airlines. He was arrested on apparently trumped-up charges in 1977 and spent four and a half years in prison.

The introduction describes Yohannes's arrest and imprisonment in detail. The horrifying atrocities of the Derg are interspersed by amusing and touching anecdotes about support given to the author by other prisoners and his family, supplemented by illustrations. Only the last page mentions translation, in the following context:

> One day I was sitting in the sun about to start reading when another prisoner, Tesfaye Assefa, approached me and said: 'Yohannes, could you please order a dictionary for me? I want to translate Gorky's *Mother* because its main character reminds me of my own mother so much'. I agreed and asked my wife to send me *Webster's Dictionary* which we had in our home. After two or three days Tesfaye asked me to read what he had translated and give him some feedback. I did not really like it. It

60 Saada Mouhamed, phone interview with author (15 June 2021).

> was a word for word translation, but it did not transmit the mood and feelings of the book. I took the novel and translated about ten pages to give him an idea of what he should try to do. Less than one hour later Tesfaye and our friend Hailemelekot Mewael (the future author of the novels *Yewediyanesh* and *Gunun*) approached me and scolded: 'Why do you waste your time reading those useless novels, if you are so skilled, you must translate *Mother*'.[61]

Yohannes Kifle's major concern was that his Amharic was insufficiently fluent because of his many years abroad, but he submitted to his friends' persuasion. Helped by a guard, they obtained sufficient pencils, pens, and paper. Yohannes worked for two hours every day, writing his translation on tissue paper, while another young prisoner copied it into a notebook. Hailemelekot Mewael, later an acclaimed author himself, revised the text four times. After the translation was finished and transcribed into eight notebooks, it was read aloud to entertain the other prisoners. Hailemelekot Mewael rewrote Yohannes's translation as a play and later smuggled the play out of the prison.[62] Hailemelekot and Yohannes Kifle tried to publish their translation, but Kuraz (a publishing house established with Soviet assistance in the late 1970s, primarily to assist with the ideological education of the Ethiopian public)[63] would not accept it, ostensibly because an Amharic translation (that is, Ge'ezan's) already existed.

The two versions of *Mother* differed significantly. Yohannes Kifle, unlike Ge'ezan Yemane, emphatically tried to domesticate his translation for Ethiopian readers. In his text "Tsar" is "negus" (the Ethiopian term for a monarch), "verst" becomes "kilometre", "Mikhail" is "Mikael", and a birch tree is a "juniper", to evoke local tree cover. Most surprisingly, he changed the stereotypically Russian samovar into a "jebena"—the coffee pot which enjoys a key place in the Ethiopian culture of hospitality and leisure. Later in the text, this became the more puzzling "tea jebena" finely to be replaced with a "tea boiler" ("☒☒ ☒☒☒☒").[64] Yohannes was apparently seeking dynamic equivalence, which "aims at complete naturalness of expression, and tries to relate the receptor to modes of behaviour relevant within the context of his own culture".[65] He thus refrained from overloading the text with incomprehensible foreign words and

61 Yohannes Kifle Dadi, 'The Square of Sorrow: Memoirs of Yohannes Kifle, Prisoner of the Derg. How Could This Translation Happen?', in Maksim Gorki, *'Enat*, trans. by Yohannes Kifle Dadi (Addis Ababa: Central Printing Press, 2020), pp. 5–42 (pp. 41–42).

62 Endalegeta Kabbada, *Ma'eqab*, pp. 69–74.

63 Kate Cowcher, 'From Pushkin to Perestroika: Art and the Search for an Ethiopian October', in *Red Africa: Affective Communities and the Cold War*, ed. by Mark Nash (London: Black Dog Publishing, 2016), pp. 52–67 (p. 53).

64 Gorki, *'Enat*, trans. by Yohannes Kifle Dadi, p. 78.

65 Eugene Nida, 'Principles of Correspondence,' in *The Translation Studies Reader*, ed. by Lawrence Venuti (London: Routledge, 2000), pp. 126–40 (p. 129).

he did not use footnotes. Nor did he imitate Gorky's heavily descriptive style, already polished by Wettlin's translation. He often split sentences and shortened descriptions. Generally, his Amharic is more colloquial than the original. For example, while Ge'ezan Yemane routinely translated "worker" ("rabochii") with a compound designated to mean proletarian ("⊠⊠ ⊠⊠⊠", literally, "one who goes to bed sweaty from work"),[66] Yohannes Kifle uses a more casual term ("⊠⊠⊠⊠").

In Yohannes Kifle's translation, the Amharic system of politeness is fully observed, and the form of address is non-reciprocal between Pelageia and her son's comrades (for example, she uses the informal second-person pronoun towards them, but they use the formal pronoun towards her). In the scene, where Pavel's home is searched, an officer addresses Pelageia rudely: "Answer, old woman!" ("Starukha,— otvechai!"), while she responds respectfully "you [formal] are still a young man" ("Vy eshche molodoi chelovek").[67] While Ge'ezan keeps these forms of address, which may sound even harsher in Amharic, Yohannes, who could not consult with the original, reverses the characters' attitudes. In his version, Pelageia exhorts the officer familiarly: "you [informal] are still a child!" ("⊠⊠ ⊠⊠ ⊠⊠"). Yohannes Kifle developed an ingenious solution to replace the rather unreadable transliterations of Russian patronymic names with the appropriate Amharic respectful title followed by that character's first name. Thus Gorky's "Pelageia Nilovna" becomes "Mrs (⊠⊠⊠⊠) Pelageia". My reading of Yohannes Kifle's translation shows that while he almost never fails to convey the meaning of the original, he both simplifies and domesticates Gorky's text for Ethiopian readers.

Conclusion

This overview of Soviet translations into Amharic, with its case study of Gorky's *Mother*, shows the limits of state control over the Progress translation project. Though the range of books and the number of copies were under direct control, translators could pursue their own agenda within limits, and the target culture enjoyed the authority over whether to accept or reject a piece of writing. The Russian classics, although disseminated in smaller quantities, overshadowed mass-produced propaganda literature in terms of their influence. This trend ultimately led to the bankruptcy of the Progress publishing house.

Ge'ezan Yemane, whose translation was supervised by a Russian editor, certainly encouraged a particular political reading of the text. Yet some non-Socialist features, like Ge'ezan Yemane's emphasis on religion and his contextualisation of debate over tribes and nations, are absent from the earlier

66 *Marksawi-leninawi mazgaba qalat* [Dictionary of Marxism-Leninism] (Addis Ababa: Kuraz 'asatami dereget, 1978), p. 400.

67 Gorkii, *Mat'*; *Vospominaniia*, p. 51.

translation by Yohannes Kifle, whose work had no constraints but prison bars. In fact, the literalist translation aesthetic enforced by Progress probably made those small adaptations even more persuasive, since translations are generally read as copies of the original. Thus, Ethiopian readers received a foreign text with elements they could nevertheless recognise and appreciate. A fascination with similarity and bonding between the Russian and Ethiopian cultures was one of the messages conveyed by these translations.

Progress's translations made a tangible contribution to Amharic literary space, despite the fact that Soviet officials did not promote them heavily. No less important is the fact that the work of Progress encouraged some Ethiopians to become writers or translators. Just one book like *Mother*, as we have seen, can inspire one person to engage in translation (like Yohannes Kifle), or another to create a play based on it (like his fellow inmate, Hailemelekot Mewale). My intention has not been to track these potentially multifarious creative interpretations of Russian original texts, but to challenge the optics which depict the Soviet state as the sole agent of a failed ideological enterprise. Indeed, as Heilbron and Sapiro suggest, while production of cultural goods under Communism was highly politicised, they transcended purely political functions (just as they cannot be reduced to market commodities).

It is important to note, that many educated Ethiopians became fascinated with Socialism before the Soviet Union set out to educate them about it. Since its introduction to Ethiopian readers in the late 1960s, *Mother* found a well-prepared readership. Young, romantic, truth-seeking bibliophiles immediately recognised themselves in Gorky's characters. *Mother* promised membership in a worldwide society of true Socialists, and despite the devastation of that promise by the reality of Soviet policy, this imagined community for a certain time persisted in Ethiopia. This shows how World Literature can create groups which imagine themselves as elements in a global community. In the hierarchical system of world literature, Ethiopians' high esteem for Russian fiction barely registers. Perhaps Gorky's fame in Russia would not have been overshadowed by the figures of Dostoevsky and Tolstoy had not the majority of his admirers been "unknown proletarians" in India, the Arab world, and Africa.[68]

68 For the Arabic and Indian cases see, Al'-Masud Mohammed Kadim Hassun, 'Ob arabskikh perevodakh romana M. Gor'kogo "Mat'", *Vestnik Voronezhskogo Gosudarstvennogo Universitata*, 2 (2012), 131–34; Megha Pansare, 'A Target-Oriented Study of Maksim Gorky's *Mother* in the Marathi Polysystem', in *Istoriia perevoda: mezhkulturnye podhody k izucheniyu*, ed. by N. Reinhold (Moscow: RGGU, 2012), 255–73; and relevant chapters on these regions in the present volume.

ASIA

Russian Literature in Asia: An Overview

Cathy McAteer

The task of mapping the modern circulation of Russian literature in Asia, identifying the agents and motivations behind its dissemination, has never been tackled as a geographical whole. This is primarily due to Asia's sheer extent as a continent which, according to the United Nations, comprises forty-eight countries. If we had been able to allocate each an individual chapter, Asia would require a volume in its own right. Instead, the eight case studies in this section provide a far-ranging and diachronic examination of Russo-Asian translation-publishing relations during the twentieth century. Our authors have contributed chapters on China, India, Japan, Kazakhstan, Mongolia, Turkey, Uzbekistan, and Vietnam. Besides consolidating and advancing existing scholarship (on China and Japan in particular), this section includes the first English-language studies of our topic, including five new essays on India's multilingual relationship with Russian literature within one composite chapter, co-written by five different subject experts.

Several scholars have researched discrete geographical contexts within Asia. Challenging his own assertion that Anglophone research on the reading of Russian literature in China is "limited in scope and has rarely so far ventured beyond tracing the influence of Russian stories and novels on the creative work of Chinese writers",[1] Mark Gamsa has produced several comprehensive works on the dissemination of Russian literature in China.[2] Heekyoung Cho has researched the reception history of Russian literature in Korea and more broadly

1 Mark Gamsa, *The Reading of Russian Literature in China: A Moral Example and Manual Practice* (New York: Palgrave Macmillan, 2010), p. 5.

2 Besides *The Reading of Russian Literature in China*, Gamsa is the author of *The Chinese Translation of Russian Literature: Three Studies* (Leiden: Brill, 2008), https://doi.org/10.1163/ej.9789004168442.i-430.2; *Harbin: A Cross-Cultural Biography* (Toronto: University of Toronto Press, 2020).

 https://doi.org/10.11647/OBP.0340.22

in East Asia.[3] For Cho, analysis of East Asia's interactions with Russian literature reveals "common cultural denominators in China, Japan, and Korea that do not necessarily surface when we approach East Asian modern literatures vis-à-vis 'the West'".[4] Cho refutes the Eurocentric approach that she attributes to Pascale Casanova and Franco Moretti. Instead, Cho focuses her attention on the semi-peripheral zones that exist alongside centres of world literature and produce their own literary activity. The earliest Russian craze in Korea—from 1900 and peaking in the 1920s—was roughly synchronous with Britain's so-called 'Russomania', but in Korea's case, Cho infers a Casanovan, or specifically Herderian, interest on the part of Korean writers to create "a new type of literature for the modern era".[5] She emphasises that Russian enjoyed greater popularity than other world literatures, and not only among Koreans; it was the most popular of the Western literary canons among Chinese and Japanese readers too:

> In the late nineteenth and early twentieth centuries, East Asian cultures avidly translated and imported foreign texts in the process of creating a new type of literature for the modern era. In Korea, translation of foreign literature started in the 1900s and reached its peak in the 1920s. Essays by Korean writers show that they eagerly sought out Russian literature, which was the most favoured of all foreign literatures. For example, Yi Hyosŏk recalls that during high school in the early 1920s, he and his friends 'also read English and French literature such as Hardy and Zola, but nothing could compete with the popularity of Russian literature'.[6]

Zaya Vandan, in this volume, endorses a similar view of Russian literature's significance to Mongolian culture, asserting that its influence "on the formation and history of Mongolian literature is impossible to measure". Cho explains four possible reasons for the impact of Russian literature on such cultures:

> [...] geographical proximity; political and military events, including the Russo-Japanese War and the Russian revolution; and the availability of translations of Russian literature in multiple languages, especially in English and Japanese. It is also very likely that writers in Japan, China, and Korea felt a strong sympathy with Russian writers and with the

---

3 Heekyoung Cho, *Translation's Forgotten History: Russian Literature, Japanese Mediation, and the Formation of Modern Korean Literature* (Cambridge, MA and London: Harvard University Asia Center, 2016), https://doi.org/10.2307/j.ctv47w7v7; Heekyoung Cho, 'World Literature as Process and Relation: East Asia's Russia and Translation', in *The Cambridge History of World Literature*, ed. by Debjani Ganguly (Cambridge: Cambridge University Press, 2021), pp. 566–84, https://doi.org/10.1017/9781009064446.031.

4 Cho, 'World Literature as Process and Relation', p. 571.

5 Ibid., p. 569.

6 Ibid.

> characters described in their works. Literature takes on a special role as a voice of social conscience in societies in which the state controls political speech. The tsarist regime in Russia, the strong state in modern Japan, and the Japanese colonial government in Korea all controlled public speech and blocked politically dangerous messages.[7]

This evaluation of East Asia's motivations for incorporating a Russian literary canon in translation resonates with Johan Heilbron's and Gisèle Sapiro's definition of the transnational movement of texts elsewhere in the world and the local gains that emerge as a result:

> We have already mentioned, with respect to translations into Hebrew in the 1920s, the role of translation in the constitution of national cultures. Brazil and Argentina built their national identities through competing cultural exchanges in which translations of Brazilian works into Argentinian Spanish played an important role throughout the 20th Century (Sora 2002; 2003). This use of symbolic goods can also be observed in the construction of social identities, of religious identity, genre identity, local identity (regionalism), and the identity of a social group (proletarian literature) [...].[8]

The fact that great Russian works depicted the lives of ordinary people set the Russian canon apart from other world literatures for the Asian readership and resulted in the shaping of national writers in the twentieth century whose own literary contributions forged new canons. Both pre-Revolutionary Russia and the Soviet Union, with their rejection of European cultural models, offered an acceptable template for imitation by East Asian writers, where there was a desire to avoid excessive dependence on Western literary approaches in the formation of their own national canons. Futubatei Shimei, identified by our contributor Hiroko Cockerill as the founder of the modern Japanese novel, assumes a key position as a modern, literary-canon builder in Japan with his Turgenev-inspired *The Drifting Cloud* (*Ukigumo*, 1889). In China, the arrival of Russian literature was comparatively delayed, eventually replacing the earlier Chinese craze for British literature. According to Gamsa, by 1920 the absolute majority of titles translated into Chinese were by English-language writers. Russian literature trailed far behind the second most-translated Western literature: French. With British and American missionaries living in China at the start of the century, English was predominantly the pivot or bridge language for transmitting French literature there. The translator Lu Xun, whom Yu Hang describes in our chapter on China,

7 Ibid.

8 Johan Heilbron and Gisèle Sapiro, 'Outline for a Sociology of Translation: Current Issues and Future Prospects', in *Constructing a Sociology of Translation*, ed. by Michaela Wolf and Alexandra Fukari (Amsterdam and Philadelphia, PA: Benjamins Translation Library, 2007), pp. 93–107 (p. 104).

helped engineer the shift towards reading Russian authors. In 1918, influenced by the Russian novelists he had read in German and Japanese translations while a student in Japan, Lu Xun produced his own Gogol-inspired 'A Madman's Diary'. This work is perceived as China's first modern short story, published at a time when, according to Gamsa, "the rise of interest for Russian literature was inseparable from the political victory of the Russian revolution".[9] As with Cho's assessment of Korean interest in Russian literature, Gamsa maintains that in China:

> Russian, and then Soviet, literature [...] was identified with real life, its fictional characters with living men and women and its authors with teachers. This equation [...] was applied to Russian literature more than to any other in the Chinese perception not merely out of political considerations but because [...] of the shared, or similar, postulates in the understanding of literature in both cultures. It was an equation responsible for the inspirational power of Russian literature in China, as for much of the brainwashing done in its name.[10]

Cho credits the Korean author Yi Kwang-su, who considered literature to be "a fundamental force which determines the rise and fall of a nation",[11] with introducing the Russian classical canon to Korean readers through his own literary influences. Kwang-su's *Heartless* (*Mujeong*), written in 1917, is regarded as his most famous work and as the first modern Korean novel. Much as Indian writers recognised in Tolstoy a crystallisation of the peaceful resistance to colonialism that inspired Mahatma Gandhi (as Ranjana Saxena and Ayesha Suhail assert in our India chapter), Cho explains that Korean intellectuals took as their model "not the author who wrote aesthetically excellent works but the activist who engaged with the problems of contemporary society through literature".[12] Korean and Chinese readers distinguished Russian literature from the European canon because the former pursued societal reform, adopting a "literature for life" rationale that appealed to the East Asian reader's political aspirations more than the ubiquitous European literary slogan of "art for art's sake". Thus "East Asian writers' passionate engagement with Russian literature was related to their own desire for an active role for literature in their specific sociopolitical situations".[13] In the early 1920s, Korean intellectuals interpreted Tolstoy, Dostoevsky, Gorky, and even Turgenev as Socialists and as a source of inspiration for Korea's proletarian writers.[14]

---

9 Gamsa, *The Reading of Russian Literature in China*, p. 4.

10 Ibid., p. 12.

11 Cho, 'World Literature as Process and Relation', p. 570.

12 Ibid.

13 Ibid., p. 571.

14 Cho, *Translation's Forgotten History*, p. 132.

Many of the case studies in this section show how Russian literature informed both literary ideas and political aspirations in the receiving countries of several Asian nations. Notable examples are India, where the influences of Tolstoy and Maksim Gorky, in particular, reinforced and fuelled revolutionary sentiments already rooted in the national independence movement, while serving as creative inspiration for national writers such as Rabindranath Tagore and Premchand, as discussed in our India chapter. In conflict zones, like North Vietnam, Russian literature (translated from both French and Russian) directly reinforced Soviet ideology (as Trang Nguyen asserts in the present volume). In Western Asia, our two chapters on the Turkish reception of Russian literature (by Sabri Gürses and Hülya Arslan, both translators from Russian themselves) show how the newly founded Republic of Turkey in 1923 correlated the promotion of foreign literature in translation to the country's modernisation projects. Translated Russian literature was particularly influential on the early career of the Nobel Prize-winning author Orhan Pamuk (as Hülya Arslan recalls in her essay). Other case studies in this section, however, exemplify a collision course between a nation's creative inspiration and Soviet politics. Benjamin Quénu's chapter highlights the phenomenon in post-Stalinist Uzbekistan of weaponising the professional act of translation against Uzbek translators by enforcing tight Soviet controls; he argues that literary translations from Russian resulted in a Soviet-controlled redefining of the Uzbek language. Similarly, Sabina Amanbaeva's essay uses the changing profile of turn-of-the-twentieth-century Kazakh writer Abai Kunanbaiuly to explore the extent to which power relations between Soviet and post-Soviet Kazakhstan and Russia, and between Kazakhstan and the West, play a key role in determining the shape of Kazakh national literature.

As the chapters in this section demonstrate, the aim of Soviet literary translation policy in Asia during most of the twentieth century—keeping Asia within the sphere of Soviet political influence—faded following the collapse of the USSR. Russia, however, has renewed efforts to expand its geographical influence by bolstering cultural links with Asia even after the invasion of Ukraine and the subsequent imposition of Western sanctions. Unlike the major 2022 European book fairs (London in April and Frankfurt in October), which had banned Russian delegates from participating, India's Kolkata book fair (on 1 March 2022) did not exclude the Russian pavilion it had already agreed to host (albeit with the added precaution of a police presence at the door in case of political protest).[15] Later in 2022, Russian publishers and writers continued to be welcome at other high-profile Asian book promotion events, including Ulaanbaatar in Mongolia in May; Baku, Azerbaijan during October; and in

15 Souvik Ghosh, 'Book Lovers' Enthusiasm over Russian Literature in Kolkata Book Fair Unperturbed by Ukraine War', *India Blooms*, 6 March 2022, https://www.indiablooms.com/life-details/LIT/6402/book-lovers-enthusiasm-over-russian-literature-in-kolkata-book-fair-unperturbed-by-ukraine-war.html.

Turkey, Russian delegates attended Istanbul's 'Week of Russian Literature and Translation' (*Nedelia russkoi literatury i perevoda*), also in October. In Hanoi, Vietnam, the annual Russian Language Week went ahead as planned, on 6 June 2022. At this event, Nguyen Thi Thu Dat, the head of Hanoi's Pushkin Institute, was quoted as saying: "In Vietnam, not only Vietnamese translators, poets and writers translate Pushkin poems into Vietnamese, but also entrepreneurs, soldiers, and students. This proves that Pushkin's poetry has touched the hearts of the Vietnamese, bringing Russian culture closer [to them]."[16]

Twenty-first century Korea is witnessing new directions in the translation of Russian literature, which continues to entertain and to influence Korean writers and translators. Seung Joo-Yeoun, who studied Russian language and literature in St Petersburg, is one of a new generation of translators to channel their excitement about this subject into the creation and promotion of Korean translations of contemporary Russian writing. In 2018, her translation of Viktoriia Tokareva's *One of Many* (*Odna iz mnogikh*, 2007) was published, followed by Alisa Ganieva's *Offended Sensibilities* (*Oskorblennye chuvstva*, 2018) in 2019 and Eugene Vodolazkin's *The Aviator* (*Aviator*, 2016) in 2021. In 2020, *Offended Sensibilities* was nominated for the 'Short List' of the fifth *Read Russia* Award for 'Works published after 1990'. Joo-Yeoun's translations of Liudmila Ulitskaia's *Big Green Tent* (*Zelenyi shater*, 2011) and Guzel Iakhina's *My Children* (*Deti moi*, 2021) were scheduled to be published in the first half of 2023.[17] Nor is Joo-Yeoun the only female Korean advocate for Russian literature in Korea. The Seoul-born, award-winning author and translator Bora Chung is a graduate of Russian Studies at Yale University with a doctorate in Slavic Literature from Indiana University. She cites Andrei Platonov and Liudmila Petrushevskaia, among others, as her key literary influences. She teaches Russian language and literature and science-fiction studies at Seoul's Yansei University and translates modern Russian and Polish fiction into Korean. Chung's short story collection, *Cursed Bunny* (2017), translated into English by Anton Hur, was awarded an English PEN/Heim translation grant in 2020, published in 2021, and was subsequently shortlisted for the 2022 International Booker Prize. *Cursed Bunny* is described as "genre-defying", with lines that blur "between magical realism, horror, and science fiction" (Booker Prize Foundation, 2022), a fusion influenced, inevitably, by her personal connection with Russian culture.[18] Like Korea, other Asian nations are developing a vital, (trans) creative relationship with Russian literature, as we hope the following chapters will show, which has transcended the one-way influence of the Soviet period.

16 Rosie Nguyen, 'Week of Russian Language Launched in Hanoi', *Vietnam Times*, 18 June 2022, https://vietnamtimes.org.vn/week-of-russian-language-launched-in-hanoi-42766.html.

17 'Seung Joo-Yeoun Profile: Translator Profile' in *K-Book Trends*, 6 December 2021, https://www.kbook-eng.or.kr/sub/info.php?ptype=view&idx=884&page=&code=info&total_searchkey=YA.

18 'Bora Chung', profile page on 'The Booker Prizes' website, https://thebookerprizes.com/the-booker-library/authors/bora-chung.

China

The Reception of Dostoevsky in Early Twentieth-Century China[1]

Yu Hang

Introduction

The reception of Russian literature in China dates back to the early twentieth century: the first Chinese translation of Russian literature was three fables by Ivan Krylov published in 1900 in *A General Examination of Russian Politics and Customs* (*Eguo zheng su tong kao*), translated and edited by Ren Tingxu and Lin Lezhi. This book was intended to inform Chinese intellectuals about their Russian neighbour. Three years later, an abridged translation (made via Japanese as a pivot language) of Aleksandr Pushkin's *The Captain's Daughter* (*Eguo qing shi: Simishi Mali Zhuan* or *Hua xin die meng lu*, 1903) appeared.[2] This initial stage of Chinese acquaintance with Russian literature lasted until the late 1910s, a period encompassing the fall of the Qing dynasty and the ensuing years of political chaos. The most important Chinese translation of Russian literature at this time was the 'nihilist'/'anarchist' novels translated by those sympathetic to political reform, describing late nineteenth-century Russian radical politics, which reflected some Chinese intellectuals' aspiration to overthrow imperial power. During this period, translations from Russian literature compared neither in quality nor scale to those from other European literatures, such as English and French. However, during the second stage (1919–49), a new tide in the translation of Russian literature began with the 'literary revolution' of the May

1 This article is an output of the case study, 'A Study of Dostoevsky's Thoughts of Modernity' within National Social Science Fund project No. 21FWWB012.

2 *The Captain's Daughter* (*Eguo qing shi:Simishi Mali zhuan* or *hua xin die meng lu*, 1903) was translated by Ji Yihui and published by Da Xuan Bookstore.

 https://doi.org/10.11647/OBP.0340.23

Fourth Movement.[3] On this day in 1919, a large student demonstration in Beijing overflowed into violent protest against the humiliating conditions imposed on China by the Treaty of Versailles, as well as their acceptance by the Chinese government. May Fourth was based on the student-led New Culture Movement, impelled by intellectuals newly returned from abroad, all of whom expressed themselves strongly in favour of a new cultural orientation. They advocated for a 'New Literature' which would use colloquial instead of classical language, rebel against the Confucian value system, and allow curiosity about Western literature. Active translators of Russian literature in the first half of the twentieth century included Qu Qiubai (1899–1935), Wei Suyuan (1902–32), Cao Jinghua (1897–1987), and Geng Jizhi (1899–1947), of whom Qu Qiubai and Geng Jizhi were proficient in Russian and therefore able to translate Russian literary works directly from the original. At this time, major academic contributions to the study of Russian literature included Li Dazhao's 'Russian Literature and Revolution' ('Eguo Wen xue yu ge ming', 1918), Zheng Zhenduo's *A Brief History of Russian Literature* (*Eguo wen xue shi lue*, 1924) and Qu Qiubai's *Russian Literature Before the October Revolution* (*Shi yue ge ming qian de Eguo wen xue*, 1927). The early Chinese translation, transmission and interpretation of Dostoevsky occurred in this context of growing intellectual and political curiosity.

This chapter will begin with an overview of the translation of Russian literature and of Fedor Mikhailovich Dostoevsky (1821–81) in particular; followed by a focus on two translators, Geng Jizhi and Lu Xun, who respectively demonstrate the value of a microhistorical methodology in Translator Studies (Geng Jizhi) and the difficulty of assimilating Dostoevsky's philosophy to the Chinese cultural mode (Lu Xun). In the first half of the twentieth century, Dostoevsky's reception in China, including the publication and introduction of his short stories in newspapers, grew gradually. Originally, English translations, mainly by Constance Garnett, were the primary intermediary for Dostoevsky's works in China.[4] The first direct translation from Russian was not completed until October 1940. In the process of accepting Dostoevsky, Chinese scholars and readers creatively misread some of his ideas, and their adaptations of the Russian writer were influenced by their own social status and cultural milieu. A debate about the purpose and the essence of literature in China's unique social conditions, at a time of national crisis, ensued. One camp believed the essence

3 The May Fourth Movement in Beijing on 4 May 1919 was dominated by students, joined by citizens from other classes, who led demonstrations, petitions and strikes against the Northern Warlord government. In January 1919, the Allied powers decided to allocate Germany's former holdings in Shandon to Japan. China was one of the victorious countries that participated in the declaration of war on Germany, but the Chinese government accepted this decision. This diplomatic failure triggered the May Fourth Movement.

4 Ding Shixin, 'Tuosituoyefusiji yu er shi shi ji er shi nian dai de Zhongguo' ('Overview of Dostoevsky and China 1920s'), *Journal of Changan University* (Social Science Edition), 2 (2011), 82–86 (p. 83).

of any literature was the representation of real life; hence, literature should be used to arouse patriotism.[5] Others put more emphasis on the artistic function of literature. Though both camps had their supporters, the argument that literature should aim for verisimilitude finally won more support.

There is reason to believe that in early twentieth-century China, most readers considered that the main purpose of literature was to represent the reality of life rather than to showcase artistic skills or reveal transcendental value. Therefore, the dominant theme of literature during this period was gritty realism. Dostoevsky's reception in China originally developed in this context. Thus, he was positioned as "a realist writer depicting the reality of life",[6] and Chinese translators' choices served the very urgent principle of national salvation. Although many writers and scholars admired Dostoevsky's artistic talents, the acceptance, evaluation, and promotion of his works by the important Chinese author Lu Xun (1881–1936, pseudonym of Zhou Shuren) played a crucial role in the reception of Dostoevsky's works in twentieth-century China. His articles 'An Introduction to *Poor Folk*' (first published 1926)[7] and 'Something about Dostoevsky' (1926) laid the foundation for Chinese Dostoevsky research for a very long time.[8] Even today, Lu Xun dominates research on the reception of Dostoevsky, especially his famous discussion of Dostoevsky's "cold" artistic skills in response to the literary critic N.K. Mikhailovskii's famous 1882 essay 'A Cruel Talent' ('Zhestokii talant'),[9] which still deeply influences contemporary Chinese scholars' research on Dostoevsky.

5 Literature for the sake of life can be simplified as 'literature for life' which represented the ideological position that the main purpose of literature is to depict reality, not an ideal world or the transcendental sphere. 'Literature for life' can be seen as the Realist literature which prevailed in nineteenth-century China due to people's preoccupation with social conditions.

6 See Nikolai Konstantinovich Mikhailovskii, *Literary Criticism and Articles on Russian Literature from the Nineteenth Century to the Early Twentieth Century*, ed. by E. Melnikov (Leningrad: Khudozhestvennaia literatura, 1989), pp. 151–234.

7 Lu Xun, 'An Introduction to Poor Folk' ['Qiong ren xiao yin', 1926], in *Ji Wai Ji*, ed. by Lu Xun (Beijing: People's Literature Press, 1976), pp. 85–87. As *Ji Wai Ji* is a widely cited and authoritative version of Lu Xun's texts, I have cited Lu Xun's 'Introduction' and 'Something about Dostoevsky' from this source for convenience.

8 Lu Xun, 'Something about Dostoevsky' ['Tuosituoyefusiji de shi', 1936], in *Qiejieting Zawen Erji*, ed. by Lu Xun (Beijing: People's Literature Press, 1976), pp. 162–64. See note 7 above on source texts.

9 Zhou Zuoren, 'Russia and China in Literature' ['Wen xue zhong de Eguo yu Zhongguo'], in *Art and Life*, ed. by Zhou Zuoren (Shi Jiazhuang: Hebei Education Press, 2002), pp. 67–76 (p. 73).

The Early Reception and Translation of Dostoevsky in Twentieth-century China

Compared with that of other nineteenth-century Russian literary giants such as Aleksandr Pushkin, Nikolai Gogol, Lev Tolstoy, and Ivan Turgenev, the translation and reception of Dostoevsky in early twentieth-century China was long overdue. Apart from sporadic translations of some chapters from Dostoevsky's novels in newspapers and magazines, Wei Congwu's 1926 translation of *Poor Folk* (*Bednye liudi*, 1846), published by the Weiming She (Unnamed Society) in Beijing, was the first single-volume translation of Dostoevsky's works in China. Wei Congwu (1905–78), an Anhui-born graduate of Yanjing University (the predecessor of Peking University), was a member of the Weiming She, established in 1925 with the help of Lu Xun. This important literary society, which intensively promoted the New Culture Movement, focused primarily on translating and introducing foreign literatures. The New Cultural Movement played a significant role in the importation and reception of Dostoevsky;[10] and Wei Congwu's translation was warmly greeted by Lu Xun, one of the movement's key leaders, who wrote a brief introduction to it.[11] His text was based on Constance Garnett's version in William Heinemann's Modern Library edition. It was not until 1940 that the first direct translation of Dostoevsky's works from the Russian language was completed by the well-regarded translator Geng Jizhi (1899–1947). In the first half of the twentieth century in China, English was the main medium for transmitting Dostoevsky's works. *Zui Yu Fa* (1931) (*Crime and Punishment*; *Prestuplenie i nakazanie*, 1866) by Wei Congwu and *Beiwurude Yu Beisunhaide* (1931) (*The Humiliated and Insulted*; *Unizhennye i oskorblyonnye*,1861) by Li Jiye were both translated from Garnett's versions, although they were proofread by scholars proficient in both Russian and Japanese. In fact, the translation and reception of Dostoevsky's works in early twentieth-century China was carried out with Garnett's English translation as the primary intermediary text. Among these English translations, those translated by Garnett were most respected and frequently chosen by Chinese translators. Since these translations were not directly translated from the original, some errors were inevitable. However, translators proficient in the English language checked their versions against Garnett's, compensating for this shortcoming.

---

10 In September 1915, Chen Duxiu founded *Xin Qingnian* (*New Youth*) in Shanghai, marking the start of the New Culture Movement. Initiated by intellectuals, the New Culture Movement was an ideological liberation movement against feudalism. Its basic slogan was to support 'Mr. De' (Democracy) and 'Mr. Sai' (Science). Advocates of the New Culture Movement supported individual freedoms, criticised Confucianism, vigorously advocated new ethics while opposing the old ones and favoured new literature over classical Chinese works.

11 Lu Xun, 'An Introduction to *Poor Folk*', in *Ji Wai Ji* (Beijing: People's Literature Press, 1976), pp. 85–87.

Dostoevsky's *The House of the Dead* (*Zapiski iz mertvogo doma*, 1860–62) deserves special mention here. Although seldom discussed by researchers, this book gained a significant reputation in early twentieth-century China. In May 1920, when the first translation of Dostoevsky's 'An Honest Thief' ('Chestny vor', 1848) was serialised as 'Zei' in a supplement to the newspaper *Guomin ribao* (*National Daily*) in Shanghai, its translator Qiao Xinying listed in the foreword Dostoevsky's Gogolesque works, including *The House of the Dead*. In 1936, this novel was published in full in Chinese as *Siwu shouji* (published by Pinghua Cooperative and translated by Liu Zunqi), and was accompanied by another version, *Xiboliya de qiutu* (*Prisoner of Siberia*, published by Shanghai Modern Book Company), translated by Liu Man. As for other works by Dostoevsky, the translation of *Notes from the Underground* (*Zapiski iz podpol'ia*, 1864) by the left-wing writer Hong Lingfei was published in the 1930s as part of the 'World Literary Classic Translation Collection' organised by the Shanghai Hufeng Publishing House, which was established in 1931 as the publishing organisation of the League of Left-Wing Writers. Soon after, Hong translated *Du tu* (*The Gambler; Igrok*, 1866) for the same series, and his version was later republished by the Shanghai Fuxing Book Company in April 1937.

In the 1940s, although the Anti-Japanese War of Resistance (known in the West as the Second Sino-Japanese war) hindered progress in the translation field, the translation and publication of Dostoevsky's works continued resolutely. During this period, the Russophone literary translator Geng Jizhi made a huge contribution to Dostoevsky's Chinese translations. His most important achievement was *The Brothers Karamazov*, translated directly from Russian. In August 1940, Shanghai Liangyou Fuxing Book Printing Company published the first volume of this book as *Xiong di* (*Brothers*). Another achievement that should be mentioned in this period is Shao Quanlin's *Beiwurude Yu Beisunhaide* (1943–44) (*The Insulted and the Injured; Unizhennye i oskorblennye*, 1861). Although it had been translated via English, it gained great popularity in the 1940s and 1950s; by 1956, his translation had been reprinted in six editions. Shao used a highly emotional lexis, appealing to the tastes of Chinese readers. Shortly thereafter, the Pacific War broke out and Shanghai was captured, leading to the suspension of translation projects.

The choice of a mediating, or pivot, language for translations of foreign literature (including Dostoevsky's works) into Chinese was closely related to social conditions in China. In the early twentieth century, Japan had already embarked on an ultimately successful course of political and cultural transformation, aided by Western technology and by the absorption of Western thought in the Meiji reforms of 1868. During the 1910s, Chinese educated society was making its first steps towards the discovery of Western literature. Steadily increasing numbers of Chinese students went to Japan in pursuit of Western learning, relying on the mediation of a language they found relatively easy to master. Japanese soon became the second most common intermediary language for translations. With the deterioration of Sino-Japanese relations and the success of the October Revolution in Russia, left-leaning Chinese intellectuals began to learn from another neighbouring country, Russia. The establishment of the League of Left-Wing Writers in February 1930 signalled the domination of Communism over a growing strand of Chinese literature. Many young people went abroad to Russia and as a result, more literature was directly translated from that language.

Among this younger generation, Geng Jizhi, a pioneer in translating Dostoevsky's works directly from Russian, played a significant role in the 1940s. He was the most prolific translator of Dostoevsky's works before 1949. When Mao Dun recommended *Xiong di* to Chinese readers, he remarked, "[this book] was translated from the original by Mr. Geng Jizhi. It is definitely a milestone in Chinese literary circles in recent years".[12] Geng's interest in Dostoevsky can be traced back to the late 1920s and early 1930s, when he submitted his translation of *Crime and Punishment* to the Shangwu Yinshuguan (Commercial Press) for publication. Sadly, however, both the Commercial Press and the manuscript were destroyed by fire during the Battle of Shanghai. Therefore this translation was never seen by readers. In the 1940s, however, Geng's efforts bore fruit as he completed his translations of *Xiong di* (1940) (*The Brothers Karamazov*; *Brat'ia Karamazovy*, 1879), *Bai chi* (1946) (*The Idiot*; *Idiot*, 1868), *Siwu shouji* (1947) (*The House of the Dead*; *Zapiski iz mertvogo doma*, 1860–62), and *Qing nian* (1948) (*The Adolescent*; *Podrostok*, 1875), all of which were selected for the 'Enlightened Literature and Art Translation Collection' book series. Geng's translation style was precise and literal. He aimed for meticulous fidelity to the original, while also making sentences appealing to Chinese readers.

Jeremy Munday underlines the value of archives, manuscripts, translator papers, and interviews—which used to be treated as mediated testimonies and seen as inherently unreliable by some historians—and the creation of microhistories of translators.[13] This method can be profitably applied to the study of the first translations and translators of Dostoevsky's works in China. Considering the huge difference between the Chinese and Russian languages and cultures, those primary sources can effectively reveal the vivid process of text conversion. Another reason is that early Dostoevsky translations in China coincided with a period of political turbulence: thus, my examination of primary sources from Chinese translators can locate the history of translation within a wider social and historical environment. As Munday points out, a microscopic analysis links the individual case study with the general socio-historical context. "If we are interested in finding out about the working and living conditions of a particular translator and relating this to a translating community, then

12 Xuan, 'Brothers' ['Xiong di'], *Sketches and Notes*, 6 (1941), 26–30. Xuan (玄) is another pseudonym of Shen Dehong (Shen Yanbing), who was mostly known as Mao Dun. He signed this article as Xuan.

13 Jeremy Munday, 'Using Primary Sources to Produce a Microhistory of Translation and Translators: Theoretical and Methodological Concerns', *The Translator*, 20 (2014), 64–80.

accessing and expressing the minutiae of the toils and tribulations of everyday life is important".[14]

The microhistory of Geng Jizhi can be partly pieced together from memoirs written by his wife, Qian Fuzhi, and some of his friends. In her memoir of Geng, Qian writes, "[w]hen translating, [Geng Jizhi] always strives to be faithful to the original, and makes the sentences fluent and convenient for reading by the majority of readers in China. I often see him pondering over a sentence or even a word."[15] She offers an extremely detailed picture of Geng's dedication to translation when Shanghai was occupied by Japanese armies between 1937 and 1941. According to Qian, late in 1937, the Kuomintang (Chinese Nationalist Party) troops withdrew from Shanghai, and then the entire city fell except the "orphan island" of the Anglo-French concession, and an atmosphere of terror enveloped even this island. As a relatively celebrated intellectual, Geng had to avoid being recruited by the Japanese puppet government; he "did not have a fixed place for working. However, no matter where he went, he never put aside his translation and literary research, for instance Gorky's *Russian Wanderlust* and *Family Affairs* (*Eluosi lang you san ji*) and Dostoevsky's *The Brothers Karamazov* (*Kalamazhufu xiong di men*) were translated by him in this extremely harsh environment".[16] She also mentioned his persistence in translating despite suffering constant illness, including high blood pressure and heart disease. Since Geng was a professional translator, rather than a writer or a scholar, very little research about him exists. Therefore, microhistorical study of existing primary materials helps us to compose a relatively complete picture of early Dostoevsky translation in China. Moreover, a microhistorical study of Geng's translating activity would yield valuable information about intellectual life in Shanghai during the Japanese occupation. Without such microdata, the details of working conditions of pioneers such as Geng would be lost.

In the three decades between the 1920s and the late 1940s, the Chinese translation of Dostoevsky's works experienced two surges. The first of these occurred in the early 1930s following the commemoration of the fiftieth anniversary of Dostoevsky's death in 1931; the second came within three years of victory in the Anti-Japanese War of Resistance. These surges resulted in the production of both *The Complete Works of Dostoevsky* (*Tuosituoyefusiji quan ji*, 1947) and *The Selected Works of Dostoevsky* (*Tuosituoyefusiji xuan ji*, 1946–48) by the Zhengzhong and Wenguang Publishing Houses. Shangwu Yinshuguan, established in Shanghai in 1897, played a very important role in the early

14 Munday, 'Using Primary Sources', p. 75.

15 Qian Fuzhi, 'Reminiscing about Geng Jizhi during the Dormant Period' ('Hui yi gu dao shi qi de Geng Jizhi'), in Qian Fuzhi, *Memoir of Literature of Isolated Time in Shanghai* (Beijing: China Social Science Press, 1984), pp. 340–61 (p. 358).

16 Qian Fuzhi, 'Reminiscing about Geng Jizhi at a Time of Isolation', *Social Science*, 2 (1981), 119–21 (p. 119). *Russian Wanderlust* and *Family Affairs* (*Eluosi lang you san ji*) was published by Shanghai Kaiming Bookstore in 1943. *The Brothers Karamazov* (*Kalamazhufu xiong di men*) was published by Liangyou Fuxing Bookprinting Company in 1940.

dissemination of Dostoevsky's works in China. It published translations in series such as the 'Russian Literature Series' and the 'World Literature Series'. These translations were usually based on English intermediary texts. Thus, Dostoevsky's works first entered China primarily through the medium of English translation, with the exception of Geng Jizhi's work.

Generally speaking, at the beginning of the twentieth century, there was no systematic academic study of Dostoevsky in China, and there were merely paratexual commentaries that accompanied translations. At this time, the evaluation of Russian literature and Russian writers was related solely to literary content, but intended also to facilitate an understanding of Russian politics and national character. Research on Dostoevsky supplemented the latter. The aesthetic qualities of Dostoevsky's works were not fully understood at this time, for various reasons. Firstly, there is a marked continuity between his gloomy and tedious style and a Chinese cultural characteristic that promotes gentleness and generosity in the form of aesthetics. Readers with some personal writing experience tend to draw a more nuanced interpretation. In this case, although Zhou Zuoren (1885–1967), Lu Xun's younger brother, an essayist and literary scholar, affirmed Dostoevsky's artistic achievements, he admitted himself "a little in awe... [that] I have never been able to read it easily, so Dostoevsky remains distant".[17] Likewise, although Lu Xun keenly observed Dostoevsky's revelation of the brilliance hidden behind the dark side of human nature, he thought that, for readers who preferred a warm style, Dostoevsky's work was too cruel—echoing Mikhailovskii's verdict.

Additionally, the reader's spiritual attitude often affects their aesthetic evaluation of literary works. Therefore, the Chinese preference for "writing for the sake of life" made Chinese readers and scholars elevate the practical content of Dostoevsky's works, while relegating his artistic skills. In fact, the reason for this reception, or lack of reception of Dostoevsky's aesthetic qualities, is that the reception of foreign literature in China at this time mainly served a pragmatic function. In other words, literature was regarded as an important means of social transformation. Thus, since Dostoevsky's reception in China at this time of great change coincided with the literature of the May Fourth Movement, his works came to be valued primarily for their portrayal of reality.

Still another reason for the partial neglect of this author is that the religious awareness crucial to Dostoevsky is relatively absent in the Chinese cultural framework. Put simply, the Chinese belief system is considerably removed from Western Christianity. Without this cultural background, Chinese readers struggled to understand the transcendence and redemptive spirit in Dostoevsky's works. Chinese traditional culture replaces religiosity with moral

17 Zhou Zuoren, 'European Literature' ('Ouzhou wen xue'), in *The Residual Light of Greece*, ed. by Zhong Shuhe (Changsha: Hunan People's Press, 1998), pp. 341–43 (p. 342).

feelings. Lu Xun used "ethics" instead of "religion" in 'An Introduction to *Poor Folk*' to interpret Dostoevsky's analysis of the human soul. This substitution illustrates how Chinese culture puts more emphasis on education about and regulation of reality, while distancing itself from Christian concepts such as sin, redemption, and kenosis. This difference in cultural worldviews problematises the Chinese reception of religious sentiment in Dostoevsky. Yet his religious thinking forms a key source for his aesthetic, especially his love for Orthodox iconography, based on the Byzantine tradition. Unfortunately, this gap between cultural aesthetics and psychology caused a certain dislocation in the early Chinese reception of Dostoevsky.

Social and Cultural Conditions Impacting Dostoevsky's Reception, Transmission, and Misreading in China

As mentioned earlier, compared with other literary masters of Russian literature, Dostoevsky's works were translated comparatively late in China. An undeniable fact here is that Chinese readers were far less interested in Dostoevsky than in other writers of the same era such as Tolstoy, Turgenev, and Anton Chekhov. Moreover, most of the translated works and fragments of works of Dostoevsky won the hearts of translators and readers mainly because of the theme of poverty. In contrast, the other genres written by Dostoevsky, such as his more fantastic work, were neglected. For example, *Er chong ren ge* (*The Double*; *Dvoinik*, 1866) was not translated (by Zhong Jue) until 1958 (when it was published by Xinwenyi Chubanshe's New Literature and Art Press), and *Qun mo* (1978) (*Demons*; *Besy*, 1871) was not translated in full until the 1970s.

From the above analysis, we can see that Chinese translators were selective about Dostoevsky's works, and mainly influenced by their contemporary social and cultural context. His fiction entered China as part of the dissemination of Russian literature, especially nineteenth-century Russian Realism, which was particularly influential. Specifically, on one hand, certain characteristics of Dostoevsky's art strongly influenced Chinese readers, and played a certain role in promoting the development of a Chinese "literature for the sake of life". On the other hand, the utilitarian needs inherent in the development of Chinese New Literature enabled the common characteristics of Russian Realist literature to conceal some of Dostoevsky's other unique artistic characteristics, thus strengthening his status as a realist writer. 'Dostoevsky the Realist' is still a widely accepted and understood reference point in China.

Therefore, Dostoevsky was represented as a writer dedicated to describing the realities of life. In the minds of Chinese readers, Dostoevsky seemed better-qualified than Tolstoy, Turgenev, Ivan Goncharov, and other aristocratic and wealthy writers to act as a spokesperson for the so-called lower classes.

It was Dostoevsky's social realism that resonated with Chinese readers. For instance, the critic Zhou Zuoren has noted that "we can see that [Dostoevsky's] characteristics are society- and life-oriented. Russian literary critics from [Vissarion] Belinsky to Tolstoy mostly advocate the art of life".[18] Elsewhere, he adds: "Russian literature is always a kind of ideal realism, which is because the relationship between the environment and temperament of the Russians cannot be set aside from social problems [...] we call it the literature of life".[19] This view was popular among Chinese readers. Many other pioneers of the New Literature Movement also agreed, and for a time the aim of depicting life and propaganda such as "the cry for life"[20] became synonymous with Russian literature, and its connotations included literary (but not dark psychological) realism. In this context, Russian writers of various styles, such as Dostoevsky, Tolstoy, and Turgenev, all belonged to the same 'for life' type in the eyes of Chinese literary circles. Consequently, their unique artistic characteristics, ideological tendencies, and artistic techniques were largely overlooked.

Let us take Dostoevsky's *The House of the Dead* as an example. Translator Liu Zunqi wrote in his preface to *Siwu shouji* (Pinghua Cooperative, 1936) that this book was based on Dostoevsky's five-year confinement in a Siberian prison camp. Other translators and critics also regarded it essentially a documentary, overlooking its fictional elements. In other words, *The House of the Dead* was generally accepted as "literature for the sake of life" in early twentieth-century China. This reception aligns with the general historical and social context of Dostoevsky's introduction in China. French sociologist Pierre Bourdieu (1930–2002) felt strongly that literature should be contextualised holistically for maximum comprehension of an author's contribution.[21] As we have seen, Dostoevsky was first translated and accepted in China during the May Fourth Movement in 1919, and thanks to the national spirit of "seeking new voices from other countries", he received the support of the New Cultural Movement. Translations and introductions of foreign literature in the first few issues of *New Youth*, an important magazine in the New Cultural Movement, occupied an important position. Moreover, Russia's 1917 October Revolution made the influence of Russian critical realism on China's New Culture Movement stand out from other European literatures. As a Communist revolutionary and literary critic, Li Dazhao (1889–1927) emphasised in his article 'Russian Literature and Revolution' (1918) that the characteristics of Russian literature were "a wealth

18 Zhou Zuoren, 'Russia and China in Literature', p. 73.

19 Zhou Zuoren, 'The Requirement of New Literature' ('Xin wen xue de yao qiu'), in *Art and Life*, ed. by Zhou Zuoren (Shi Jiazhuang: Hebei Education Press, 2002), pp. 18–24 (p. 19).

20 The propaganda of "the cry for life" aims to expose the darkness of real life and advocates the artistic technique of shaping typical characters.

21 See Pierre Bourdieu, 'Principles for a Sociology of Cultural Works', in *The Field of Cultural Production: Essays on Art and Literature*, trans. by Claud DuVerlie (Columbia, NY: Columbia University Press, 1993), pp. 176–91 (p. 181).

of social concern" and a "development of humanism", both of which could increase the momentum of the revolutionary trend.[22] It was in this general environment that the reception of Dostoevsky in China was ultimately achieved. Lu Xun once aptly summarised Chinese readers' common understanding of Russian literature: "Russian literature, since the time of Nicholas II, has been 'for life', no matter whether its doctrine is exploring or solving [problems], or falling into mystery and decadence, the main undercurrent is still for life".[23]

From a historical perspective, a work entering another cultural context risks encountering regional differences, as well as 'dislocation' across historical time and space. History constitutes a prerequisite for understanding a text and produces the foundations for bias and misunderstanding. Because of its strong humanist insights, *The House of the Dead* was interpreted as a prophecy of the 1917 October Revolution in Russia by Chinese scholars and readers.[24] For example, a promotional advertisement for the version translated as *Prisoners of Siberia* (*Xiboliya de qiutu*) believed that it "analyses the psychology of the prisoners, presents the cruelty of the rulers, and exposes traditional class differences".[25] The editor's notes to the Wenguang Bookstore's edition claimed that it "finally saw that people who were cut off from society are no worse than those outside prison, and most of them are innocent victims of a corrupt political society".[26]

Contemporary Dostoevsky scholars, however, often consider Dostoevsky's idea of the brilliance of human nature in convicts as more related to his religious thinking, especially kenosis. Precisely because they are closer to traditional culture, the convicts can retain traditional Russian virtues that Westernised intellectuals lose. Besides his empathy, Dostoevsky's description of political prisoners in this novel reflects their separation from the foundation of the traditional Russian religious culture. Therefore, the interpretation of 'corrupt political society' in China can be described as a misunderstanding based on the acceptance system of Chinese culture. However, this misunderstanding offered

---

22 Li Dazhao, 'Russian Literature and Revolution', *People's Literature*, 5 (1979), 3–8 (p. 3). In this article, Li Dazhao emphasised two characteristics of Russian literature, namely, its strong social concern and its humanism. He argued that the prohibition of people's political activities and the deprivation of people's freedom of speech by the authoritarian system make Russian literature pay special attention to social issues. Meanwhile, the Russian religious tradition also affected the humanitarian sentiment in literature. This article was originally intended for publication in the magazine *New Youth*, but was withheld by the editor Hu Shi, and did not appear (in the journal *People's Literature*) until May 1979. The manuscript is currently in the collection of the Institute of Modern History of the Chinese Academy of Social Sciences.

23 Lu Xun, 'The Preface of *Harp*' ('*Shu qin* xu'), in *Nan Qiang Bei Diao* (Beijing: People's Literature Press, 1973), p. 13.

24 See Tie Qiao, 'Cold Eyes' ('Leng yan'), in *Oriental Magazine*, 17 (1920), 100–05 (p. 103).

25 *Tsinghua Weekly*, 42 (1934), 1–5.

26 'Editor's notes', in F. M. Dostoevsky, *Xiboliyade qiutu* (*The Prisoner of Siberia*), trans. by Wei Congwu (Shanghai: Wenguang Bookstore, 1950), p. 2.

many Chinese readers a new way to understand the social environment of tsarist Russia as portrayed in *The House of the Dead*.

Thus, Dostoevsky's humanism attracted numerous Chinese readers, many of whom were famous writers in the history of modern Chinese literature. For instance, the nationally renowned writer Ba Jin (formerly Li Tangrao, 1904–2005) described himself as the one Chinese writer most influenced by foreign literature, especially Russian literature. It was widely believed that Ba Jin had composed his pseudonym from the first syllable of the name 'Bakunin' and the last in 'Kropotkin'. In his collection of essays, *Memoirs* published in 1936, Ba Jin singled out three great writers who, as he put it, had helped him become "a real human being".[27] They were Tolstoy, Dostoevsky, and Mikhail Artsybashev—writers whom Ba Jin ranked higher than Shakespeare, Goethe, and Dante.[28] Nevertheless, Dostoevsky's humanism was not the kind typically advocated by scholars and readers at that time; most preferred to attribute the roots of suffering and misfortune to socio-economic and political structures. In their opinion, misery and misfortune was often caused by poverty, oppression, bullying, and ignorance. But Dostoevsky feels that suffering and misfortune have a broader and deeper meaning, rooted in the paradox of human existence. Dostoevsky believes that it is impossible for humans to end poverty and ignorance by increasing material wealth, or to end suffering and misfortune with the creation of paradise on earth. As far as human nature is concerned, people might even prefer to indulge in suffering, rather than rationally pursuing happiness, as optimistic and superficial advocates of utilitarianism propose. Only by questioning the mystery of man in the mysterious relationship between man and God can the power of salvation be found through individual rather than social efforts. However, most Chinese readers at that time missed this line of thought, or struggled to concede this point about human experience. Therefore, for a long time, Dostoevsky's humanitarian spirit unfortunately remained absent from the Chinese cultural sphere.

The Role of Lu Xun and his Acceptance and Representative Evaluation of Dostoevsky

Generally speaking, in the early twentieth century, only Lu Xun, Yu Dafu (1896–1945), Ba Jin, and a very few others had an entirely literary relationship with Dostoevsky's thoughts and art. The most important of these figures is Lu Xun (formerly Zhou Shuren). An eminent writer, he was also a reader and translator

27 Ba Jin, *Memoirs* (*Hui yi lu*) (Shanghai: Wenhua Shenghuo Press, 1936), p. 172.

28 Mark Gamsa, *The Chinese Translation of Russian Literature: Three Studies* (Leiden and Boston, MA: Brill, 2008), p. 136. Also see Olga Lang, *Pa Chin and His Writings: Chinese Youth Between the Two Revolutions* (Cambridge, MA: Harvard University Press, 1967), pp. 232–33.

of foreign literature, most notably Russian literature. Due to his early experience of studying in Japan, he translated Russian literature primarily via Japanese. For instance, in 1931, he used a Japanese bridge text to translate Aleksandr Fadeev's *The Rout* (*Razgrom*, 1926). Lu Xun's close acquaintance with the blind Ukrainian poet Vasilii Eroshenko (1890–1952) is also a popular story in the history of Sino-Russian literary relations. In 1922, Eroshenko came to Beijing, taught Esperanto at Peking University and lived in the Badaowan residence of the Zhou brothers. During Eroshenko's time in China, he and the Zhou brothers established a sincere friendship. In the mid-1920s, Lu Xun translated many children's tales by Eroshenko, including those published as *A Collection of Eroshenko's Fairy Tales* (*Ailuoxianke tong hua ji*, 1922).

Lu Xun had extensive access to Dostoevsky's works and to critical literature about the writer. According to his own diary, he bought a Japanese copy of *Crime and Punishment* on 8 August 1913. According to *Lu Xun's Handwriting and Collection Catalogue* (compiled and printed by the Lu Xun Museum in Beijing), he not only collected many German and Japanese versions of Dostoevsky's original works, but acquired European books on the study of Dostoevsky in Japanese translation too, such as André Gide's *Dostoevsky* and Dmitri Merezhkovskii's *Tolstoy and Dostoevsky*.[29] He edited many journals that published translations of Dostoevsky. The first Chinese version of *Poor Folk* was completed with his support and participation. Not only was he funded to compile this translation as part of the Weiming Series, but he also compared the Japanese translations by Bai Guang himself, and distinguished many ambiguities. According to Mark Gamsa:

> One of the books in the Weiming series, a pioneering translation of Dostoevsky's *Poor Folk* by Wei Suyuan's younger brother Wei Congwu, had been rendered from the English (of Constance Garnett), but was only allowed into print in June 1926 after Lu Xun had checked it against a Japanese translation and Suyuan had compared the manuscript with the original Russian.[30]

Lu Xun's methodology of translation had a great impact at that time. Nevertheless, later in the 1920s, he was criticised for so-called 'Ouhua' ('Europeanised language') translation, which he preferred to call "direct", or even "hard/stiff" translation ("zhiyi" or "yingyi"). Lu Xun and his followers in the 'direct translation' camp chose to reproduce the "strangeness" of the foreign text, and even the word order of the English or German sentence. As he himself explained, his translations displayed complete fidelity to the source text because

29 According to Lu Xun's diary, he wrote, "On December 13, 1924, I went to the East Asia Company to buy *Tolstoy and Dostoyevsky*." See Lu Xun, *Lu Xun's Diary* (Beijing: People's Literature Press, 1976), p. 448.

30 Gamsa, *The Chinese Translation of Russian Literature*, p. 284.

of his commitment to preserving its "original atmosphere" and his refusal to domesticate, or Sinicise, it by using a more fluent and idiomatic language. Gamsa has convincingly pointed out that there were far more ideological than aesthetic factors behind Lu Xun's choice. As many literary reformers argued, vernacular Chinese needed to be enriched with the capacity for precision that classical Chinese lacked (but which European languages possessed). For "the lack of precision in our language proves the lack of precision in our way of thinking—we are muddle-headed".[31] While this process might be painful (Lu Xun acknowledged that readers of his "hard" translations were bound to become "frustrated, disgusted and outraged"),[32] the reader ought to admit that the linguistic revolution was being undertaken for their own benefit. "For better or worse, written Chinese underwent substantial 'Westernization' in the course of the twentieth century, a process on which the translation of Western literature, as practiced and promoted by Lu Xun, made an undeniable impact".[33]

The well-known translator Geng Jizhi's translations of Dostoevsky's works echo Lu Xun's above-mentioned views on hard translation. Geng knew that only by introducing expressions from Western languages could the development of Chinese be promoted; hence his translations of Dostoevsky also reflected this trend. His translation in *Bai chi* (*The Idiot*) is an example. The original text reads "уж как это к тебе не идет, говорит, если б ты знал, как к корове седло".[34] Geng translated it as "You have to know that this method is not very suitable for you, just like a saddle on a cow."[35] In Chinese, the corresponding idiom would mean "Donkeys' lips are not right for a horse's mouth". Even if the translator's idiom remains opaque to Chinese readers, they can still guess the meaning from the first half of the sentence. Therefore, Geng succeeded in producing a literal translation while retaining the original cultural connotation. Here, by preserving the 'strangeness' of the original by rendering it into an idiom half-way between that of the author and his own language, the translator enriches the target language with a new manner of perceiving the world. Geng translated this novel in the early 1940s, when the cultural exchange between China and Western countries (including exchange of languages) had been going on for a

31 Lu Xun, 'A reply to Qu Qiubai (1931)', trans. by Leo T. H. Chan, in *Twentieth-Century Chinese Translation Theory: Modes, Issues, Debates*, ed. by Leo Tak-hung Chan (Amsterdam and Philadelphia, PA: John Benjamins, 2004), pp. 158–61 (p. 159).

32 Gamsa, *The Chinese Translation of Russian Literature*, p. 154.

33 Ibid., p. 168.

34 Fedor Dostoevsky, *Polnoe sobranie sochinenii*, ed. by V. G. Bazanov, 17 vols (St Petersburg: Nauka, 2019), VIII (2019), p. 194. An equivalent English translation is, "This really doesn't become you at all, if you only knew, it's like a saddle on a cow." See Fedor Dostoevsky, *The Idiot*, trans. by Alan Myers (Oxford: Oxford University Press, 1992), p. 221.

35 Fedor Dostoevsky, *Bai chi* [*The Idiot*], trans. by Geng Jizhi (Shanghai: Kaiming Bookstore, 1946), p. 272.

long time. In Geng's case, combining the translation methods of foreignisation and domestication infused his translation with a mixed characteristic. It was precisely because of the combination of the two languages and even the two cultures that his new form of language had a stronger expressiveness and vitality. Expressing a deep understanding of this phenomenon, the linguist Wang Li has commented: "[t]he most dramatic changes have taken place in Chinese society during the past hundred years, mainly due to our contact with Western civilisation. [...] In the wake of new things have followed a great number of new words and new ideas [...]. Many new ways of organising statements have been added [to our Chinese language]".[36]

Lu Xun wrote 'An Introduction to *Poor Folk*' to accompany Wei Congwu's translation of the novel; it was one of many articles on Dostoevsky he wrote during the inter-war period. Lu Xun also wrote an article titled 'Something about Dostoevsky' for the popular edition of the *Complete Works of Dostoevsky*, printed by the Mikasa Bookstore in Japan. Lu Xun mentions Dostoevsky or his works at least fifty times throughout his critical writings, letters, and diaries. He also showed a strong interest in Dostoevskian literary styles. He once said: "My novels are all about dark things. I have admired Dostoevsky for a while. From now on, my novels will probably still be about dark things. What can be bright in China?".[37] The Russian Silver Age writer Leonid Andreev (1871–1919), whose works Lu Xun particularly admired, was also influenced by Dostoevsky. Lu Xun was Andreev's first Chinese translator, and he attributed to him an influence on many of his own stories such as 'Yao' ('Medicine').[38] Lu Xun's two articles on Dostoevsky, however, played a pivotal role in the history of Chinese Dostoevsky studies. They demonstrate the resonance between these two cultural giants of China and Russia as well as their dialogues across time and space. In the next section, I will focus on 'An Introduction to *Poor Folk*'.

In this essay, with remarkable intuition and inspiration, Lu Xun grasped the main preoccupation of all Dostoevsky's fiction, namely, the profundity of human nature. He dialectically and progressively analysed how Dostoevsky shows both the good and evil sides of the human soul. He writes:

> The interrogator lists the convict's crime in the court, and the convict states his own morality. The interrogator exposes the corruption in the soul, and the convict clarifies the hidden brilliance in the exposed filth. So in the very deep human soul, there is no such thing as cruelty, let alone compassion.[39]

36 Wang Li, *Essentials of Chinese Grammar* (*Zhongguo wen fa yao lue*) (Shenyang: Liaoning Education Press, 2002), p. 5.

37 See Lin Xianzhi, *Lu Xun In His Life* (Hefei: Anhui Education Press, 2004), p. 571.

38 Chen Jianhua, *Sino-Russian Literary Relations in the 20th Century* (*Er shi shi ji Zhong E wen xue guan xi*) (Beijing: Higher Education Press), p. 67.

39 Lu Xun, 'An Introduction to *Poor Folk*', p. 86.

Many of Dostoevsky's characters are in a state of conflict, internal or external, like Raskolnikov in *Crime and Punishment* and Ivan Karamazov in *Brothers Karamazov*. Therefore, even criminals have their own morality, and likewise the limited and emotional soul of man has its own sacredness. Lu Xun vividly refers to the dual structure of man's mind as described by Dostoevsky in his statement that "putting men and women in unbearable situations to test them, not only strips away the whiteness on the surface and tortures out the sin hidden underneath, but also tortures out the true whiteness hidden under the sin".[40] He believed that this exemplified Dostoevsky's famous concept of "realism in the higher sense".[41]

Since Dostoevsky believed that evil was an integral part of human beings, it follows that evil and pain originate within us. Therefore, to eliminate them, we must first face and admit our own sins. This spiritual journey was recognised by Lu Xun. As he remarked (drawing perhaps on Mikhailovskii's notion of Dostoevsky as a "cruel talent"), "digging through the depths of the soul, people have suffered mental torture and wounds, and from the wounds and healings, they discard their suffering and embark on the road of recovery".[42] Moreover, Lu Xun realised that the spiritual torture experienced by the characters in Dostoevsky's works was a reflection of the author's personal experience. He commented that even as a young man, Dostoevsky had begun the process of wilful mental self-torture that would last his whole life.[43] However, it is not certain whether Lu Xun had read Dostoevsky's very famous letter of February 1854 to a benefactress, N. D. Fonvizina, in which he undertakes, given the choice between Christ and the truth (*istina*), to choose Christ over truth if they differ.[44]

Lu Xun also examined the aesthetic psychology of Chinese readers at length. He used his own reactions as a model for their mentality, noting that when reading Dostoevsky, although admiring his greatness, "they often want to discard the book".[45] In addition to explaining the negative aesthetic characteristics of Dostoevsky's works such as tediousness and gloominess, Lu Xun also mentioned key cultural and psychological factors in Chinese readers' reception and processing of Dostoevsky, writing that "as a Chinese reader, I am still not familiar with Dostoevskian tolerance and obedience, which is true tolerance with sudden adversities. In China, there is no Russian Christ. In China,

40 Ibid.

41 In notes for his *Writer's Diary* (*Dnevnik pisatelia*) in 1881, Dostoevsky famously refers to himself as "lish' realist v vyshchem smysle, to est' izobrazhaiu vse glubiny dushi chelovecheskoi" ("[I am] only a realist in a higher sense, that is, I depict all the depths of the human soul"). See Fedor Dostoevskii, 'Dnevnik pisatelia: 1881', in Dostoevskii, *Polnoe sobranie sochinenii*, ed. by V.G. Bazanov and others, 30 vols (Leningrad: Nauka, 1972–90), XXVII (1984), pp. 5–174 (p. 65).

42 Lu Xun, 'An Introduction to *Poor Folk*', p. 86.

43 Ibid., p. 87.

44 Fedor Dostoevskii, 'Pis'mo N.D. Fonvizinoi, February 1854', in Dostoevskii, *Polnoe sobranie sochinenii*, XXVIII [I: Pis'ma 1832–59], (1985), pp. 175–77 (p. 176).

45 Lu Xun, 'An Introduction to *Poor Folk*', p. 87.

the dominant idea is 'rituality', instead of God".[46] He added, "When a person only has moderation, it is true that he has no danger of falling into hell, but he may not enter the kingdom of heaven either".[47] Specifically, the Chinese cultural tradition (which is dominated by Confucianism) lacks the Christian concept of sin or belief in the immortality of human souls. As we saw earlier, this makes some religious concepts in Dostoevsky's works unfamiliar or even inaccessible to Chinese readers.

Lu Xun's attitude towards Dostoevsky in the article he published a decade later, 'Something about Dostoevsky' (1936), was very different, and reflected a shift towards admiration, and even joy, as if he were welcoming an old friend. He not only acknowledges the greatness of Dostoevsky's "interrogation of the soul", but also fully considered the Russian author's thoughts on Christian brotherhood. Lu Xun concludes: "How pure the love is, and how the heart was disturbed by the curse! Given that the author was only twenty-four years old at the time, it is particularly amazing. The heart of a genius is indeed broad".[48] However, he remained dissatisfied with Dostoevsky's Christianity. Not only did he admit that he "[could not] love" Dostoevsky's practice of "torturing the soul", he also believed that even if "endurance and obedience" exist, "Dostoevskian in-depth exploration, I am afraid, is still hypocritical".[49] At the same time, he ruthlessly stated the potential damage caused to society by "Dostoevskian obedience": "hypocrisy is evil to the oppressed, but moral to the oppressor".[50]

This kind of emotional alienation is closely related to Lu Xun's own ideological transformation in 1927. Many scholars have shown that after 1927, Lu Xun shifted his personal views to fit in with the new political environment. Chiang Kai-shek's massacre of Communists made him soberly aware of the realities of Chinese social conflict, and led him to prioritise a utilitarian approach. This made him a leader in left-wing literary circles. Owing to these factors, his literary stance became more politicised and pragmatic, while his sensitivity to psychological realism was attenuated. Inevitably, he came to interpret Dostoevsky's art and thought from the perspective of sociological and Marxian class theory. In the postscript of *Qiejieting Essay*, Lu Xun stated his original intention in writing the article: "'Something about Dostoevsky' fulfilled a commission by the Mikasa Bookstore, and it was an introductory article written for new readers, but I am here to explain that the oppressed are either slaves or enemies to the oppressor. They must never become friends. Therefore, the morals of each other are not the same".[51]

46 Lu Xun, 'Tuosituoyefusiji de shi' ('Something about Dostoevsky'), in *Qiejieting Zawen Erji* (Beijing: People's Literature Press, 1973), p. 163.

47 Ibid., p. 164.

48 Lu Xun, 'An Introduction to *Poor Folk*', p. 86.

49 Lu Xun, 'Something about Dostoevsky', p. 163.

50 Ibid.

51 Lu Xun, 'Postscript to *Qiejieting Zawen*' ('*Qiejieting Zawen* Hou ji'), in *Qiejieting Zawen Erji* (Beijing: People's Literature Press, 1973), p. 196.

Conclusion

The central argument of this article is that Dostoevsky's reception in early twentieth-century China was greatly impacted by the cultural system, national psychology, and social historical context of his Chinese readers. Three areas of analysis were chosen to reflect the extent of his impact, namely, the basic situation of translation and research of Dostoevsky's works at that time, the social and cultural conditions impacting Dostoevsky's reception, transmission, and misreading in China, and finally, Lu Xun's reception of and commentaries on Dostoevsky and his role in the study of Dostoevsky in China.

Dostoevsky's Chinese reception is a very complicated phenomenon. This article has attempted a detailed analysis of that process from the 1920s to the 1940s, investigating the translation, publication, and transmission of Dostoevsky and his influence on Chinese writers' works. I have also examined where and in what format Dostoevsky's works were published in China during the 1920s and 1930s. The reception of Dostoevsky became intertwined with the contemporary historical background, the particular cultural moment in China, and several competing literary ideological trends there. As we know, the victory of the October Revolution in 1917 came as an unprecedented shock in Chinese society. Central to the introduction and reception of Russian literature in China was the idea of "learning from Russia". Since the early twentieth century, Chinese intellectuals, following the revolutionary developments in Russia, had become intent on overthrowing imperial power in their own country. When Chinese intellectuals turned from European literature to Russian writing, they focused on the description of social reality and humanism to be found in the latter, as Li Dazhao explains in 'Russian Literature and Revolution'.[52] Most twentieth-century Russian literature reflected Socialist Realism. Chinese readers recognised Dostoevsky sympathetically as a Socialist Realist *avant la lettre*. By accepting his fiction as "literature for the sake of life", they appreciated some essential parts of his works, while overlooking his Christian ideology and misreading his deep, complicated, and paradoxical revelations about the human soul. I hope this discussion will inspire and even facilitate deeper exploration of Dostoevsky's reception in China.

52 Li Dazhao, 'Russian Literature and Revolution', *People's Literature*, 5 (1979), 3–8.

India

Preface

We invited five leading scholars to comment on the interpenetration of Russian culture within the literature of the Indian subcontinent. Ranjana Saxena's opening essay traces the history of literary translation in India, and its centrality to this nation's diverse and multilingual culture; while adapting the concept of the 'imaginary of translation' to recent original creative responses by Indian writers to Russian literature. Guzel' Strelkova's essay focuses on the translation of Russian literature into Hindi, a language with over six hundred million speakers which is also a key intermediary for other Indian languages. Strelkova also provides short biographies of key Hinduphone translators, such as Premchand (India's first major translator of Tolstoy) and Madan Lal Madhu, who worked for over fifty years with the Foreign Languages Publishing House in Moscow. Anna Ponomareva, who also worked for this crucial department of Kremlin soft power, offers a snapshot of the work of Raduga and Progress Publishers specifically with translations into Telugu. Ayesha Suhail surveys why Tolstoy was so influential and popular in the Indian cultural sphere, with an overview of the main translators involved in spreading a message that, she argues, was as effectively ideological as literary. Venkatesh Kumar closes our section with a reflection on the history of Tolstoy's translation into Tamil.

Translation as a Cultural Event, a Journey, a Mediation, a Carnival of Creativity: A Study of the Reception of Russian Literature in Colonial and Postcolonial India

Ranjana Saxena

Translation in India: An Introduction

Although it is a multilingual space with diverse cultural practices, India's languages are connected by a common cultural thread. When reflecting upon the reception of Russian literature amongst India's reading public, we must remember that India is a multi-confessional, linguistically pluralistic country. Today's multilingualism emanates from an ancient tradition of linguistic pluralism. Thus, from Kashmir in the North to Kerala in the South, India enjoys multiple, highly developed literary cultures. As Avadesh K. Singh observes:

> present Indian multilingualism is a direct descendant of the linguistic pluralism of antiquity. Since Indians have been living with this pluralism for long, they are natural unconscious translators, who translate without caring for a methodology or theory of translation. Indians with multiple languages could shift simultaneously from one linguistic system to another with ease.[1]

In support of this, one might name Dayaram (1777–1853), the great Gujarat poet who also wrote in Hindi. Bhartendu Harishchandra (1850–85), a major

1 Avadesh Kumar Singh, 'Translation in/and Hindi Literature', *Translation Today*, 3:1 & 2 (2006), 206–27 (p. 208), https://www.academia.edu/38914808/Translation_Today_Vol_3_Issue_1_and_2.

 https://doi.org/10.11647/OBP.0340.24

Hindi author, described himself as a poet of Sanskrit, Hindi, and Urdu; he even composed in Gujarati. In this sense, Indian consciousness is essentially a process of constant translation. Despite their cultural and linguistic diversity, Indians share a common past. The existence of regional variants of the Indian epic *Ramayana* emphasises this fact. Prominent retellings of this text include the *Kamba Ramayanam* in Tamil (a text from the twelfth century), the *Saptakanda Ramayana* in Assamese (fourteenth- or fifteenth-century), the *Bhavarth Ramayana* in Marathi (sixteenth-century), the *Ramcharitamanas* in Awadhi (also sixteenth-century), and many more. Besides its twenty-two official languages, Indian literature exists in hundreds of dialects. In this context we may endorse V.K. Gokak's view that all regional and dialectal literatures share

> [a] unique quality of Indianness [...] stemming from a cultural tradition which is five thousand years old. [...] It is noted that the earliest works of Buddhist literature were written in Pali [...]. Rabindranath Tagore and Saratchandra, Premchand and Jaisankar Prasad, Bharati, Karanth, Bendre and Thakazhi Shivashankar Pallai and of Sri Aurobindo, to name only a few, are all of a piece, in that they present a view of life and ethos which are essentially and perennially Indian.[2]

Translation, in the Western sense, was far from unknown. Early, particularly medieval, translations are better understood as retellings or adaptations of their originals. Santosh Sareen writes that, as the modern Indian languages emerged from the eleventh century onwards:

> Sanskrit technical/cultural texts began to get transferred into those languages (including Assamese, Maharashtri, Kannada, and Telugu) as a method of preserving those texts through diffusion. At the same time translations began to be made into Persian. Zain-ul-Abedin (1420–1470), the enlightened ruler of Kashmir, established a translation bureau for renderings between Sanskrit to Persian. [...] In the [late] seventeenth-[early] eighteenth century, the Sikh guru Guru Govind Singh Ji set up a translation bureau and had a large number of Sanskrit texts translated into Persian.[3]

The first professional translations emerged in the early modern period (the seventeenth century) after a 'Maktab Khana' (Translation Bureau) was established in the late 1500s by the Moghul emperor of India, Akbar.[4] Religious

---

2 Jagbir Singh, Kapil Kapoor and Michel Danino, 'Literatures in India', *Knowledge, Traditions and Practices of India* (Delhi: Central Board of Secondary Education, 2012), p. 4, http://cbseacademic.nic.in/web_material/Circulars/2012/68_KTPI/Module_3_1.pdf.

3 Santosh Sareen, 'Translation in India: History and Politics', *Tradução & Comunicação*, 20 (2010), 77–87 (p. 78).

4 Mohammad Asaduddin, 'Translation and Indian Literature: Some Reflections', *Translation Today*, 3:1 & 2 (2006), 1–19 (p. 3), https://www.academia.

texts such as the *Mahabharata*, the *Ramayana* and the *Yog Vashisht* were officially translated from Sanskrit into Persian to facilitate better mutual understanding of the cultural codes of rulers and subjects. Some critics may also consider the re-narration in Sanskrit of texts originally composed in the sacred language of the clergy into lay language as translations. Avadesh Singh writes that the "poets of the Bhakti period (1100–1700) were translators in a different and loose sense, as they strove to translate ancient Indian knowledge and wisdom manifested in different treatises through Sanskrit by appropriating it in various *bhashas* (native languages)".[5] During this period, the poet-saints of the Bhakti movement democratised knowledge of elite Sanskrit texts.

The Translation of Russian Literature in India

Russian literature was extensively translated into the languages of India. The Indian intelligentsia's first real encounter with Russian literature followed Indian independence from the British Empire in 1947. Russian literature initially came to post-independent India on a high tide of nationalistic fervour, marked by hopes for a new, egalitarian society. The works of Lev Tolstoy, Ivan Turgenev, Fedor Dostoevsky, Anton Chekhov, and Maksim Gorky enjoyed great popularity in postcolonial India. Among that section of the Indian intelligentsia inclined towards Socialism, Russia inspired sympathy. In 1941, an organisation called 'Friends of the Soviet Union' was formed as an immediate response to Germany's attack on Russia. Its patron was the first non-European to receive the Nobel Prize for Literature, Rabindranath Tagore (1861–1941).

Tagore was a great Bengali polymath, a towering early twentieth-century figure, described as the "most compelling voice of Modernism in India".[6] We can safely assume Tagore's familiarity with Russian literature. As his biographer A.P. Gnatyuk-Danil'chuk writes:

> Tagore's favourite Russian writer was Ivan Turgenev [...]. In 1911, a friend of Tagore translated into Bengali, on his request, Turgenev's *Triumphant Love* [*Pesn' torzhestvuiushchei liubvi*, 1881]. Tagore himself read all he could find of Russian literature in English translation, while encouraging translations into Bengali. [...] Tagore read a lot of Russian literature in the years of the birth of the new Russia.[7]

---

edu/38914808/Translation_Today_Vol_3_Issue_1_and_2.

5 Singh, 'Translation in/and Hindi Literature', p. 209.

6 Partha Mitter, *The Triumph of Modernism: India's Artists and the Avant-garde 1922–1947* (New Delhi: Oxford University Press, 2007), p. 226.

7 A.P. Gnatyuk-Danil'chuk, *Tagore, India and Soviet Union, A Dream Fulfilled* (Calcutta: Firma KLM Private Limited, 1986), pp. 194–96, *Internet Archive*, https://archive.org/details/dli.bengal.10689.12744/page/n127/mode/2up?view=theater.

A leading Bengali periodical, *Bharati*, published by Tagore's acquaintance Satyendranath Datta, issued translations of Aleksandr Pushkin, Mikhail Lermontov, Afanasy Fet, and Nikolai Nekrasov into Bengali between 1878 and 1924. In an 1889 letter, Tagore mentions Tolstoy's *Anna Karenina* (1878). Although Tagore never translated any Russian literature, its impact on his writing should not be underestimated. Mention of Tolstoy recalls another Bengali writer deeply influenced by the great Russian critical realist. One cannot ignore the thematic similarities between *Anna Karenina* and Sarat Chandra Chattopadhyay's *The Home Ablaze* (*Grihadaha*, 1920). The latter's creative and critical writings were deeply informed by Tolstoy's views.[8]

Gnatyuk-Danil'chuk mentions Tagore's admiration for Gorky, noting that the female protagonist of Tagore's novel *Last Poem* or the *Farewell Song* (1928) is shown reading Gorky's *Mother* (*Mat'*, 1906).[9] Gorky may be the Russian writer most widely translated into the languages of India, and *Mother* the single most widely translated novel, beginning with the Marathi translation in the early 1940s.[10] This book influenced an entire generation who came of age in the early 1960s; *Indian Literature*, the journal of the Sahitya Akademi (India's National Academy of Letters) published a five-page list of Gorky's works translated into Indian languages, naming the translators of each.[11] Megha Pansare mentions six translations of *Mother* (from English) by different translators, published in 1932, 1941, 1945, 1956, 1959 and 1968 respectively. While analysing the salient features of these translations in the context of the Marathi polysystem, Pansare reviews the context for Russian literature's emergence in this language.

The translation of *Mother* in colonial India, which was already experiencing a phase of pro-Independence nationalistic fervour, further fuelled the sentiments of literate Indians with revolutionary ideas. Well-known progressive Marathi writer Anant Kanekar wrote in his obituary on Sinclair that "Maksim Gorky from Russia and Upton Sinclair from America have become our Gods; their novels and their stories have become our scriptures".[12] *Mother*'s immense popularity in India prior to Independence can be explained in terms of contemporary socio-political exigencies of the times. It was translated multiple times into Indian languages, including Malayalam. Thus, where the reception of Gorky's *Mother* and his other writings is concerned, we may say that for Indian critics

8 See Ranjana Banerjee, 'Leo Tolstoy and Saratchandra—A Comparative Study of Their Works', *JNU*, 4–5 (2003–04), 55–66.

9 Gnatyuk-Danil'chuk, *Tagore, India and Soviet Union*, p. 196.

10 R.K. Dasgupta, 'Maxim Gorky in Indian Languages', *Indian Literature*, 11:1 (New Delhi: Sahitya Akademi, 1968), 68–73 (p. 68).

11 Ibid.

12 See Sunil Sawant, 'Revolutionary Struggle as a Counterpoint to Colonial Domination: Marathi Translations of Upton Sinclair and John Steinbeck', *Translation Journal*, 13:4 (Oct. 2009), http://www.translationjournal.net/journal/50politics.htm.

and writers the author's views on the nature and purpose of literature were as important as the literary value of his work.

The Reception of Russian Literature in Colonial and Postcolonial India

Following the 1857 Sepoy Mutiny, direct British rule was imposed in India, forcing the subcontinent into the 'Great Game', a term often used to define the political and diplomatic confrontation between Britain and Russia that endured throughout the nineteenth century. Its main agenda was control over Central Asia and the Near East. Both Britain and Russia suspected each other's political designs. Russia supposedly envied Britain's conquest of India, while Britain viewed every movement by Russia towards Central Asia as a threat to her own future plans. Meanwhile, Russia saw British expansion along the northwest frontier of India as a threat to her borders. British rulers tried to camouflage "expansionist British aims in India, and, beyond the Indian frontier [...]".[13] On the other hand, Russia's forays into Central Asia provided grounds for concern. There was general, mutual distrust between India's British rulers and the Russian Empire. Notwithstanding this ambiance of mistrust, two visionary humanist philosophers from India and Russia respectively, Mohandas (Mahatma) Karamchand Gandhi (1869–1948) and Lev Nikolaevich Tolstoy (1828–1910) forged a spiritual alliance, upholding the banner of universal peace and justice. They both resisted authority in order to support the liberation of the common people, the exploited masses. Bhisham Sahni (1915–2003), a celebrated Indian writer who was also a translator of Tolstoy into Hindi, attested that British administrators feared the spread of Russian writers' ideas into Indian territory. According to Sahni, novels by Gorky were smuggled into India from Sri Lanka, and had to be read secretly.[14] Consequently, colonial India did not see much translation activity involving Russian literature into Indian languages. However, in 1923 Munshi Premchand (pseudonym of the prominent Hindi writer Dhanpat Rai Srivastava (1880–1936)), a pioneering author of Urdu and Hindustani realist social fiction, translated some of Tolstoy's short stories, which he chose for their moral content and simple style. Also at this time, Aleksandr Kuprin, Gorky, Turgenev, and Tolstoy were translated into Marathi. Gorky's works appeared in Tamil and Hindi.

13 M.A. Yapp, 'British Perceptions of the Russian Threat to India', *Modern Asian Studies*, 21:4 (1987), 647–65 (p. 647), https://doi.org/10.1017/S0026749X00009264.

14 See Nair K. Govindan, 'The Influence Of Maxim Gorky On Malayalam Novels between 1930 and 1960' (unpublished doctoral dissertation, University of Kerala, 1985), http://shodhganga.inflibnet.ac.in:8080/jspui/handle/10603/176953?mode=full.

Thus, the popularity of Russian literature in postcolonial India can be explained by many factors. Firstly, Indian independence facilitated free engagement with Russian literature; secondly, in a country afflicted until recently by foreign rule, by the just-abolished *zamindari* system of landholding and taxation, and by the caste system (the category of 'untouchable' was not abolished until 1955), the revolutionary ideas of freedom and equality for all raised the hopes of many for a just, humane society. As Rabindranath Tagore, the Bengali poet and admirer of Pushkin and Gorky, wrote following his 1930 visit to the Soviet Union:

> I had long nourished a deep repugnance for the business of *zamindari*, now it has become sordid. This time in Russia I have seen with my own eyes the shape of things I had dreamed of so long. That is why I feel so ashamed about the *zamindari* business. My mind has today left the upper seat and taken a place below. I feel sad that since my childhood I have been brought up as a parasite [...] the lavish material possessions are a barrier to my self-respect.[15]

And, thirdly, many believed that the time for literary change was overdue.

It was none other than the great doyen of Hindi literature, the so-called 'Indian Gorki' Munshi Premchand,[16] who became the beacon for the "socially-engaged, purposive literature [...] that was beginning to take shape in the 1930s", according to Rakshanda Jalil. I quote at length below from the same passage in her recent article about Premchand:

> When a group of Young Turks in London drew up a *Manifesto* of what would soon become the Progressive Writers' Movement, he published it (albeit in a slightly watered-down version) in his influential Hindi journal *Hans* in October 1935. And when the progressives decided to hold an ambitious first-of-its-kind meeting of the All-India Progressive Writers' Association (PWA) on April 9, 1936 at the Rifah-e Aam Hall in Lucknow, Premchand rose to the occasion with everything at his command as a writer. Not only did he give his whole-hearted support to this fledgling association, but his presidential address would, in later years, become a manifesto of sorts for a literary movement unlike any other in the history of this country, a movement that would shape the responses of a whole generation of Indian intelligentsia.[17]

---

15 See K. K. Khullar, 'Influence of October Revolution on Urdu Literature', *Indian Literature*, 24:3 (May-June 1981), 124–39 (p. 125).

16 A moniker given by Shyam M. Asnani, 'An Indian Gorki', *Indian Literature*, 18:2 (April-June 1975), 62–72 (p. 62).

17 Rakhshanda Jalil, 'For Premchand, Good Literature Was About Truth and Humanity', *The Wire*, 31 July 2017, https://thewire.in/books/

A fourth factor in the Indian preference for translating Russian literature may have been the generally pro-Socialist temperament of the intelligentsia (especially in the 1960s and 1970s). Awadesh Singh rightly remarks that in this period, the focus of literary translation changed: "translation into Hindi moved further away from England and America to Central and Eastern European countries such as Czechoslovakia, Yugoslavia, Hungary, Poland and Russia. Through the choice of source texts, this constituted indirect resistance to American hegemony".[18] As Khullar has noted, the Urdu poet Iqbal was inspired by the sensibilities of the Russian Revolution to praise manual workers and to urge the "insulted and injured" of India to resist exploitation. Similarly Premchand, who began his career as an Urdu writer, used his short story 'The Shroud' ('Kafan', 1936) and his 1936 novel *The Gift of a Cow* (*Godaan*):

> to amply illustrate the awareness that every human being has a right to carve a better life for himself. Premchand was at the forefront of the 1936 conference of Progressive Writers. Most of what he wrote after 1936 has a stamp of Russian literature. His last unfinished novel [promotes] the aura of revolution, demand for social justice and the elimination of what Tagore called 'the vulgar conceit of wealth'.[19]

Not only did the ideas behind the Russian Revolution hugely influence progressive Indian intellectuals, Russian literature of the pre- and post-Revolutionary period became the preferred reading matter of the Indian public. Many Russian literary works were translated into Marathi between 1932 and 2006. Most are works by Soviet authors (Gorky, Kuprin, Nikolai Ostrovskii, Aleksandr Fadeev, Fedor Gladkov, Vasilii Grossman, and Mikhail Sholokhov), but some are by pre-Soviet Russian authors such as Pushkin, Nikolai Gogol, Turgenev, Dostoevsky, and Tolstoy. 'Taras Bulba' (1835), Gogol's romantic account of a Cossack warrior, was translated four times by different Marathi translators. Russian literature was also extensively translated into Bengali, Malayalam, Tamil, Marathi, Hindi, Punjabi, and many other languages.

Many people whose childhood and/or youth were touched by Russian books, magazines, and children's literature fondly remember those days. Free magazines such as *Soviet Land* were widely shared.[20] New translations of Soviet literature, produced by the Soviet publishers Raduga and Progress, were popular throughout India. Even today, one can still experience an almost palpable nostalgia for Russian literature in India. Several cultural meeting points attest to

premchand-hindi-literature. Jalil also notes that Premchand was influenced by both Gandhi's teachings and the Russian Revolution.

18 Singh, 'Translation in/and Hindi Literature', p. 222.

19 Khullar, 'Influence', p. 127.

20 The magazine was published for Indian readers in thirteen languages including Marathi, Bangla, Hindi, Tamil, Telegu, Kannada, Urdu, and English, by Progress Publishers and Raduga Publishers.

such a phenomenon. Situated in Kolkatta, Manisha Granthalaya—a bookstore-cum-publishing house—is one such example.[21] It was launched by the Indian Communist Party in 1964 to sell and translate Russian books into Bengali. None other than the glorious Bishnu Dey, "the 'rebel' poet and harbinger of modernism in Bengali verse", gave the store its name.[22] This bookshop became a meeting place for Bengali intellectuals. Such was the influence of the progressive idealism emanating from Soviet Russia. "Here booksellers are familiar with Tolstoy, Gogol, Gorky, Dostoevsky, and Chekhov. Tell them what you are looking for and they will whip it out from the towering stacks. Most are by Raduga and Progress Publishers".[23] Another such treasure trove is situated in the misty valleys of Wayanad, Kerala.[24] This is an amateur venture by a couple who still cherish their childhood love of Soviet books. Their desire to pass on this legacy to future generations led them to set up this bookstore.[25] Reminiscing about her grandfather's collection of Russian books, Deepa Bhashthi writes that she continues to be intrigued by the "reach of these distribution networks, down to the smallest of towns".[26] She adds:

> I grew up in a village in the hills, a blip on the map of South India. To this day we do not have a bookstore in town, except for the newspaper vendor who stocks select pulp-fiction titles alongside gossip tabloids and the day's newspapers. And when I was growing up, there were no online marketplaces to log on to, of course. But there was Grandpa and his books from Russia. [...] I hear these books are now fast becoming collectibles. For a generation that came of age at the cusp of that very strange period in India when socialism ended and capitalism was becoming wholeheartedly embraced, these books remain a kind of sentimental paraphernalia.[27]

21 The Hindi word 'Manisha' stands for intellect/decisive wisdom in the English language. 'Granthalaya' can be translated as 'a library'.

22 Anon., 'Manisha Granthalaya The Bookstore Which Still Sells Russian Books', *Get Bengal*, 31 January 2022, https://www.getbengal.com/details/manisha-granthalaya-the-bookstore-which-still-sells-russian-books.

23 Anuradha Sengupta, 'Let's Talk Pushkin', *The Hindu*, 20 May 2017, https://www.thehindu.com/society/lets-talk-pushkin/article18508547.ece.

24 K.P. Aswini, 'Wayanad's Odd Library is a Wonder World of Soviet Books', *Mathrubhumi.com*, 8 May 2019, http://englisharchives.mathrubhumi.com/features/web-exclusive/wayanad-s-odd-library-is-a-wonder-world-of-soviet-books-1.3780560.

25 Divya Sreedharan, 'How Soviet Children's Books Became Collectors' Items in India', *Atlas Obscura*, 14 April 2021, https://www.atlasobscura.com/articles/soviet-childrens-books-in-india.

26 Deepa Bhasthi is a writer and blogger based in Madikeri/ Bangalore, Karnataka, India. She can be contacted at deepabhasthi@gmail.com.

27 Deepa Bhasthi, 'Growing Up with Classic Russian Literature in Rural South India', *Lithub*, 28 February 2018, https://lithub.com/growing-up-with-classic-russian-literature-in-rural-south-india/.

Such "passion projects", driven by nostalgia for Soviet-era books, point towards the fact that Russian literature, for numerous reasons, was well received in India. On the afterlife of literary works, Walter Benjamin wrote, "[j]ust as the manifestations of life are intimately connected with the phenomenon of life without being of importance to it, a translation issues from the original—not so much from its life as from its afterlife".[28] Russian literature is surely experiencing just such an afterlife in India.

Reception of Russian Literature: The "Imaginaries of Translation"[29]

Translation Studies are replete with "theoretical works that focus on the work of individual translators, but accounts of translators' histories are often structured in an anecdotal and descriptive fashion, and constitute records of accomplishments or, frequently, discussions of translation 'errors' and infelicitous decisions".[30] However, more recent scholarship is "increasingly addressing the complexities of the role and legacy of the translator".[31]

The literature of one country may influence the literary processes of another in many ways. The act of translation is not a linear process; rather it produces a multilayered impact on the consciousness of the translator. Translation thus provides ground for real or imagined cultural encounters, which in turn produce new creative writing: translation is an inherently creative activity. These meetings, whether real or imaginary, may lead to the production of new fiction that reflects the activity of translation or imaginary dialogues between the translator and the translated—a concept which has been labelled the "Imaginary of Translation", acknowledging "the subjectivity of translators, their psychological activities and their imaginary production".[32] This concept can be used to understand the dynamics of a different kind of literary reception, one mediated by the translator and touched by his or her imagination. To illustrate this point, I will briefly discuss below pertinent texts from the Marathi, Malayalam, and Hindi languages.

---

28 Walter Benjamin, *Selected Writings (1926–1931)*, ed. by Michael W. Jennings et al., 4 vols (Cambridge, MA and London: Belknap Press, 2020), p. 254.

29 Christina Bezari, Riccardo Raimondo and Thomas Vuong, 'The Theory of the Imaginaries of Translation', special issue of *Itinéraires*, 2/3 (2019), https://doi.org/10.4000/itineraires.5077.

30 Maria Constanza Guzmán, 'Towards a Conceptualization of the Translator's Legacy', *Forma y Funcion*, 22:1 (June 2009), 181–201, https://www.researchgate.net/publication/237029944_TOWARDS_A_CONCEPTUALIZATION_OF_THE_TRANSLATOR'S_LEGACY.

31 Ibid.

32 Christina Bezari et al, 'The Theory of the Imaginaries', paragraph 16.

A Carnival of Cultural Mutualities

Rajendra Yadav (1929–2013) was a well-regarded Hindi writer active in post-independence India. He participated in the 'Nayi Kahani' ('New Story').[33] movement that emerged in Hindi literature between 1954 and 1963. Yadav translated Russian writers including Lermontov, Turgenev, and Anton Chekhov. His very intense engagement with Chekhov (he studied the Russian author's biography and personal philosophy as well as his literary texts) led him to create an imaginary dialogue with the author, set in Moscow just before the latter's death. This was Yadav's 'An Interview with A. P. Chekhov—An Interview That Was Delayed By Fifty Years' (1955).[34] This fictitious interview covers various personal details of Chekhov's life, such as his difficult and lonely childhood; his love life and marriage to Olga Knipper, his relationship with Gorky and Tolstoy, his views on Turgenev's "unreal women characters", and so on. Finally, Chekhov narrates his journey to Sakhalin, offering virulent criticism of the Tsar's policies. Yadav's information was sourced from letters to and from Chekhov's contemporaries, as well as the text of *Sakhalin Island* (*Ostrov Sakhalina*, 1893); he also consulted the work of Chekhov's later, Western biographers, such as David Magarshack.

Ganesh Prabhakar Pradhan's *Letters to Tolstoy* is another example of the reception of Russian literature in India through the "imaginary of translation".[35] Pradhan (1922–2010) was a follower of Gandhi who participated in India's struggle for independence. He also taught English literature; Tolstoy was his idol. The *Letters* were initially written in 2006 in Marathi, and translated into English a year later. Unsurprisingly, as a professor of literature, Pradhan's epistolary novel manifests his own deep critical understanding of Tolstoy's creative oeuvre and its context. Pradhan's dialogue with Tolstoy is informed by his exhaustive grasp of both Indian and Russian politics and society, as well as of Russian literature. Pradhan also comments on relations between Tolstoy and his peers Turgenev, Dostoevsky, and Chekhov. He highlights the mutual appreciation between these writers despite their profound differences of opinion on socio-political and literary issues. In his *Letters*, Pradhan advises Tolstoy to complete his unfinished novel, *The Decembrists*, which he argues would have helped the

33 For more information about 'Nayi Kahani' ('New Story'), see Nikhil Govind, 'Nayi Kahani', in *The Routledge Encyclopedia of Modernism* (Taylor and Francis, 2016), https://doi.org/10.4324/9781135000356-REM673-1. Madhu Singh, 'Altered Realities, New Experiences: Bhisham Sahni, Nirmal Verma, and the "Nayi Kahani" Movement', *Comparative Literature Studies*, 53:2 2016), 312–33, https://doi.org/10.5325/complitstudies.53.2.0312. Raghuvir Sinha, 'Social Change in Contemporary Hindi Literature Indian Literature', *Indian Literature*, 17:3 (New Delhi: Sahitya Akademi, 1974), 9–22.

34 Rajendra Yadav, 'An Interview with A.P. Chekhov—An Interview That Was Delayed by Fifty Years', *Internet Archive*, https://archive.org/download/in.ernet.dli.2015.522559.

35 Ganesh Prabhakar Pradhan, *Letters to Tolstoy* (Mumbai: Popular Prakashan, 2008).

Indian youth to choose the correct path for social transformation. Pradhan asks Tolstoy whether, in the absence of a truly just system of government even in the twenty-first century, injustice can be resisted non-violently. *Letters* also contains an essay describing imaginary conversations in heaven between Gandhi and Tolstoy.

The 2021 commemoration of the bicentennial of Dostoevsky's birth increased awareness of his work and of his reception to date in India. Here, I will introduce Perumbadavam Sreedharan (b. 1938), a well-known Malayalam writer from the South Indian state of Kerala. He has been a prolific author of fiction. *Like a Psalm* (*Oru Sankeerthanam Pole*, 1993) is his most famous and critically acclaimed novel, for which he received the prestigious Vayalar Award for outstanding Malayalam fiction in 1996. This novel was inspired by Perumbadavam's love for Russian literature and for Dostoevsky in particular. As we have seen, Russian literature was widely distributed in India in the 1960s and 1970s, including in Kerala; arguably, "Soviet influence in the state in the 1960s and 70s [...] shaped the perspectives and sensibilities of generations of youngsters".[36] Perumbadavam's own reading of *Crime and Punishment* inspired his subsequent engagement with Russian literature, as the quotation below reveals. As the contemporary Malayalam author K. R. Meera comments, "Perumbadavam's book can be read as a Russian book [...]".[37] *Like A Psalm* novelises Dostoevsky's difficult life, narrating his affair with his stenographer Anna Snitkina, who later became his wife. This kind of manifestation of admiration for Dostoevsky can happen only when a writer has deeply internalised the life and works of the writer. *Like A Psalm* is set in St Petersburg, even though Perumbadavam had never visited the city. In recent years, the novel has been adapted for the screen as a docu-fiction named *In Return: Just A Book*. Perumbadavam himself described his work thus:

> When I first read the translation of *Crime and Punishment* as a 16-year-old, I was taken to a different world. I read it again and again like a holy text. I read more of [Dostoevsky's] works in Chennai and here in Thiruvananthapuram, especially at the Public Library. I realized that of all the characters he had created, he himself is the best. Call it my stupidity or my pride; I decided to write a novel about him.[38]

Like A Psalm has sold nearly three hundred thousand copies to date.[39]

---

36 Anjuly Mathai and Vaisakh E. Hari, 'How Soviets Invaded an Indian State, Two Decades Before it Collapsed', *The Week*, 8 December 2017, https://www.theweek.in/webworld/features/society/how-dostoevsky-reincarnated-kerala-century-after-his-death.html.

37 Ibid.

38 M. Athira, 'A World of His Own', *The Hindu*, 31 March 2017, https://www.thehindu.com/society/author-perumbadavam-sreedharan-on-his-workspace/article17749857.ece.

39 Kalyanee Rajan, 'Redeeming an Awkward Dostoevsky', The Pioneer, 3 June 2018, https://www.dailypioneer.com/2018/sunday-edition/redeeming--an-awkward--dostoevsky.html.

Conclusion

Indian and Russian intellectuals have been engaged in meaningful dialogue for a long time. This dialogue continues, facilitated by translators. Translators of Russian literature into Malayalam, Marathi, Hindi, Urdu, Panjabi, Tamil, Kannada, Bengali, and many more literatures played a pivotal role in creating this space for communion. In Pascale Casanova's words, the translator is "an indispensable intermediary for crossing the borders of the literary world, is an essential figure in the history of writing".[40]

40 Pascale Casanova, *The World Republic of Letters*, trans. by Malcolm DeBevoise (London and Cambridge, MA: Harvard University Press, 1999; repr. 2007), p. 142.

The Translation of Russian Literature into Hindi

Guzel' Strelkova

As one of the most widespread Northern Indian languages, with more than six hundred million speakers, Hindi plays a crucial role not only in the reception of translated foreign literature, but in its mediation for other Indian languages and cultures. The translation of Russian literature into Hindi was facilitated by one of the founders of modern Hindi and Urdu prose, Munshi Premchand (the pen name of Dhanpat Rai Srivastava (1880–1936), and author of over three hundred original short stories and fourteen novels in Hindi and Urdu). Premchand was also a noted translator of Tolstoy. As we have seen in the previous section, other Hindi writers like Bhisham Sahni and Rajendra Yadav also contributed. Their translations remain popular today, and are constantly updated by new generations of translators.

Premchand was born in a small village near Benares into a Hindu family, and received his early education in a madrasa (a school of Islamic theory and law), a term with multiple origins including Urdu. As a result, he wrote in both Urdu and Hindi, although scholars today regard him as the founder of modern Hindi literature. His realist style and focus in his own fiction, which represented the everyday life of ordinary people, was revelatory for his contemporaries. His translation of twenty-one stories, published under the title *Stories by Tolstoy* (*Taalstay kee kahaaniyaan*, 1923), was probably mediated via English as a bridging language as Premchand did not know Russian, and was immediately popular on its release.[1] Some of the stories were partly adapted to an Indian context: for example, the action was transferred from Russia to India and some characters received Indian names. Premchand's choice to translate Lev Tolstoy was probably inspired by the Russian sage's correspondence with the widely venerated Mahatma Gandhi. This example encouraged other writers to experiment with a more Realist style.

1 See Donatella Dolchini, 'Premchand's Encounter with Tolstoy', *Cracow Indological Studies*, XVII (2015), 164–65, https://doi.org/10.12797/CIS.17.2015.17.09.

 https://doi.org/10.11647/OBP.0340.25

Jainendra Kumar (1905–88), Premchand's admirer and younger contemporary, was also impressed by the talents of Tolstoy and Dostoevsky; some of the female characters in his fiction resemble Dostoevsky's heroines. Perhaps this similarity is one reason why Jainendra Kumar is considered a leading author of psychological prose in Hindi. But he also translated Tolstoy, notably the 1957 collection *God is with Love: A Collection of Stories by Tolstoy* (Hindu title *Prem men Bhagvaan. Tolstoy Granthaavalee*). The title was based on Tolstoy's short story 'Where Love Is, There God Is Also' ('Gde Bog, tam i liubov'', 1884). This anthology was published in New Delhi by the significantly named 'Society of Cheap Literature' (Sastaa saahitya manDal) in 1957, the term 'cheap' referring to affordability rather than quality. Jainendra Kumar, a follower of Jainism who was at this time undergoing a deep, spiritual crisis provoked by the recent war and India's complex political situation, had published nothing between 1938 and 1952, so this anthology marked a personal revival for him. As a Jain, Kumar rejected all violence; Tolstoy's pacifism would therefore have resonated with him.

Other nineteenth-century Russian writers and playwrights like Nikolai Gogol, Ivan Turgenev, and Anton Chekhov were also very popular in India, most probably because of adaptations of their work on the Indian stage, such as Gogol's *Inspector General* (*Revizor*, 1836), which was performed in the state of Maharashtra as *Amaldar*. It was a *roopaantar* performance (adapted to local characters and conditions), written by the very popular Marathi playwright P. L. Deshpande.[2] Later, the play was also translated into Hindi; it continues to be staged today.

Many prominent contemporary Hindi writers, like Krishna Baldev Vaid (1927–2020), Mridula Garg (b. 1938), and Kunwar Narain (1927–2017), have described how Russian literature influenced their work. For example, K. B. Vaid sometimes jokingly called himself "Krishna Oblomov", after the titular protagonist of Ivan Goncharov's *Oblomov* (1859); while Mridula Garg has claimed that everyone in her family read the Russian classics in translation.[3] The well-known poet Kunwar Narain, who visited Eastern Europe and crossed the Soviet Union by train in 1955, was familiar with Russian literature, especially poetry; he particularly admired Arsenii Tarkovskii, Osip Mandel'shtam, Anna Akhmatova, and Marina Tsvetaeva. Both the works of the most quintessential Soviet author, Maksim Gorky, and Mikhail Bulgakov's parody of Soviet culture *Master and Margarita* (*Master i Margarita*, 1967) have been translated into Hindi—the latter novel twice, in 2010 and again in 2016 (the second time with the financial support of Russia's Institute for Literary Translation).

---

2 *A Poetics of Modernity Indian Theatre Theory, 1850 to the Present*, ed. by Aparna Bhargava Dharwadker (Oxford: Oxford University Press, 2019).

3 Private conversation on 8 March 2023 between Garg and Strelkova (in the latter's capacity as Garg's translator from Hindi into Russian of her third novel *Cobra of My Mind* (*Chittakobara*, 1979)).

In the second half of the twentieth century, the USSR's Foreign Languages Publishing House (founded in 1946) became active. In 1963 it was subdivided into two firms, 'Progress' and 'Mir'; in 1982 'Progress' created its own subdivision, the 'Raduga' ('Rainbow') Publishing House. Each had its own specialisation: Progress was dedicated to social and political literature and popular science, Mir was for academic literature, while Raduga published translations of Russian literature into many foreign languages, including several Indian languages. These translations were undertaken by skilled professionals, many of whom were novelists or poets themselves, like the prominent Hindi writer Bhisham Sahni (1915–2003). Sahni is often considered to be Premchand's successor in realist Hindi prose (and as a translator of Tolstoy). Of his various writings, his novel *Darkness* (*Tamas*, 1974) is considered one of the most significant Hindi novels of the twentieth century. Sahni lived and worked in Moscow between 1957 and 1963 as a translator for the Foreign Languages Publishing House. He translated Tolstoy's *Resurrection* as *PunaruThaan* (Hindi for 'New Life') for Raduga in 1974. He was the General Secretary of the Progressive Writers' Association of India (1975–85). Translations such as these—including Rajendra Yadav's translations of Chekhov and Lermontov—were popularised in programmes produced by Radio Moscow's World Service Indian department, which up to the 2010s broadcast in twelve Indian languages.[4] These broadcasts were popular with Indian listeners. The majority of Indian translators employed by Radio Moscow also worked for Soviet publishing houses, translating Russian literature into their native languages. Those Russian editors who worked with Indian translators on these projects had an excellent knowledge of Hindi or other Indian languages, which enabled them to edit and improve the translations (primarily made via English as an intermediary language).

Some Indian translators spent their lives in the USSR. One such translator was the prolific Madan Lal Madhu (1925–2014), who translated into Hindi more than one hundred works of Russian prose and poetry, including Tolstoy's *War and Peace* (*Yudhh aur Shanti* in Hindi), published in 1988, *Anna Karenina* in 1981, and Aleksandr Pushkin's *Evgenii Onegin* in 1999. Having spent several years in the Soviet Union, Madhu was probably one of the first of very few translators who could translate directly from Russian without an English intermediary. This made his version of *Anna Karenina* more literally correct than S. N. Agarwal's 1955 translation into Hindi of the same novel. In all, Madhu translated more than a hundred works of fiction, including prose by Lermontov, Dostoevsky, Chekhov, poems by Pushkin, and children's literature by Kornei Chukovskii and Samuil Marshak. In 2012, Madhu published his memoirs, *Foggy-Bright Faces of Memories* (*Yadoon ke Dhundle Ujale Chehre*), in two volumes. The first volume describes his childhood up to 1956 when Madhu, then teaching in a college, received an official invitation on behalf of the USSR's Ministry of Foreign Affairs to work in

4 Rajendra Yadav, *Kathaa shikhara* (New Delhi: Pravin Prakashan, 1994).

Moscow as a translator and editor. This occurred after the Indian Prime Minister Jawaharlal Nehru visited the Soviet Union in 1955. The second volume carries the sub-heading 'Fifty-Five Years in Moscow' ('Masko men pachpan varsh') and offers a vivid overview of relations between India and Russia. It focuses on Madhu's literary and translation networks and activities from the 1950s up to the early twenty-first century. One of the most interesting sections throws light on the work of the Indian department at Moscow's Foreign Languages Publishing House, directed by Petr Vasilevich Gladyshev, a committed Stalinist and head of the Hindi section from 1957 to 1976. Brajesh Singh, a close relative of the Indian Foreign Minister, was appointed to this department, possibly because of nepotism as (according to Madhu) he was not very skilled.[5] He did, however, catch the eye of Svetlana Allilueva, Stalin's daughter, and the couple were married (Madhu's own wife Tatiana was also an editor in the department). Although Madhu's memoir is entertaining and illuminating on the processes and relationships within this department, he does not give any details about translation or his own philosophy of translation.

Relations between Russia and India were at their closest and most productive between the 1950s and 1980s, when Russian classics were not only widely translated, but in many cases re-translated. For example, Tolstoy's *Resurrection* (*Voskresenie*, 1899) was translated twice. As we have seen, Bhisham Sahni's full-length version appeared in 1974; but an abridged version by Shitala Sahay had previously appeared in the early 1950s (the specific year of publication is not stated) as *Punarjeevan* (*Regeneration*). Sahay's version contained errors, including mistranscriptions of personal names into the Devanagari alphabet, so that Nekhliudov became "NekhleeDoo" and Maslennikova became "Mesleneekaf". *Anna Karenina* also appeared in two Hindi versions. The first, as mentioned above, was Suraj Narayan Agarwal's 1955 translation, abridged and essentially retold by the translator, unlike Madan Lal Madhu's more literal version, published sometime in the 1950s (again, the exact year is not given). Tolstoy's *The Cossacks* (*Kazaki*) was also published twice by different Soviet publishing houses, in versions by different translators.[6] Later and contemporary generations of Indian translators have sought out less officially approved Russian authors for translation, from authors of the 'Village Prose' movement such as Vasilii Shukshin or Viktor Astaf'ev, to the poetry of Osip Mandel'shtam and Boris Pasternak, or the fantastic realism of Mikhail Bulgakov and Evgenii Vodolazkin.

5 Madan Lal Madhu, *Yadoon ke Dhundhle Ujale Chehre* (Delhi: Medha Books, 2012), pp. 188–89.

6 The first version was translated by Narayan Das Khanna (for whom, sadly, there are no available biographical details). It was published by the Foreign Languages Publishing House in 1959 in their series 'Library of the Best Works in Russian Literature' ('Sarvottam roosee pustakmaalaa'). The prominent Russian graphic artist and painter Dmitri Bisti illustrated it. In 1979, Raduga produced a second version translated by Yogendra Nagpal (1948–2020) who had worked there for many years and translated many works of Russian literature into Hindi.

The Visibility of the Translator: A Case Study of the Telugu Section in Progress Publishers and Raduga

Anna Ponomareva

Introduction

Lawrence Venuti's book *The Translator's Invisibility* opened a new era in Translation Studies by emphasising the importance of translators in the creation of literature in translation.[1] Jeremy Munday's ideas on microhistory have also contributed to this turn.[2] His translator works in a particular social and historical environment. Gengshen Hu, a scholar from China, offers a bird's-eye view of translation and the translator. His book *Eco-Translatology: Towards an Eco-paradigm of Translation Studies* provides a wider context for the translator by considering the publishing industry, cultural policies, and readers' expectations as formative aspects of his environment.[3] Both theories allow me to analyse my experience of working in the Telugu sections of Progress and Raduga, the biggest publishing houses to specialise in literature in translation in the USSR, between 1979 and 1991.

I will present my recollections as a microhistorical case study in which several era-specific elements are explored: the inner workings of the publishing houses, the translators and translation teams, and the importance of their collaboration with each other. Additionally, the voices of our Telugu readers will be heard,

1 Lawrence Venuti, *The Translator's Invisibility: A History of Translation* (London and New York: Routledge, 1995).

2 Jeremy Munday, 'Using Primary Sources to Produce a Microhistory of Translation and Translators: Theoretical and Methodological Concerns', *Translator Studies in Intercultural Communication*, 20:1 (2014), 64–80, https://eprints.whiterose.ac.uk/84279/1/Munday%20microhistory%202014.pdf.

3 Gengshen Hu, *Eco-Translatology: Towards an Eco-paradigm of Translation Studies* (Singapore: Springer Singapore, 2020).

 https://doi.org/10.11647/OBP.0340.26

and I shall conclude my study by pointing to the impact of Russian literature in translation on readers.

Translation as Ideology

Progress Publishers (formerly Foreign Literature Publishing House) was established in 1931 as another attempt to re-invent Maksim Gorky's World Literature (*'Vsemirnaia literatura'*) project, the first publishing house in Soviet Russia (1918–24).[4] Later, in 1956, Progress Publishers formed its Telugu section. Then, in 1980, this section was divided when Progress was split into two publishing houses, Progress Publishers (specialising in literature of philosophy, social sciences, and politics) and Raduga (which focused on various types of fiction and children's literature). Both publishing houses were funded by the Soviet government, and their role could easily be categorised as a form of soft power. Soviet translated books helped the authorities to create the image of a progressive and peaceful state which supported other countries in developing their literature by spreading leftist ideas and introducing their young readers to education by reading good quality books.

In 2011, the CIA released a sanitised copy for publication online of its 1985 report, *The Soviets in India: Moscow's Major Penetration Program*.[5] The report has a chapter which, in the spirit of the Cold War period, is called 'Soviet Propaganda and Disinformation Activities' (pp. 6–16). It includes a section dedicated to the publishing activities of the former USSR, one of which was the organisation of international bookfairs. Page 16 of the report reproduces a poster (Figure 1) that references the Indo-Soviet Treaty of Peace, Friendship and Cooperation (signed in August 1971) in its advertisement for an Indo-Soviet book fair in Chennai (formerly Madras) in 1984.

Fig. 1 Poster advertising Soviet books.[6]

4 *Izdatel'stvo Progress: 50* (Moscow: Progress Publishers, 1981).

5 CIA, *The Soviets in India: Moscow's Major Penetration Program: An Intelligence Assessment* (1985), https://www.cia.gov/readingroom/docs/CIA-RDP86T00586R000400490007-7.pdf.

6 Ibid., p. 16.

The report also names Mezhdunarodnaia Kniga as "the Soviet agency that organizes bookfairs in India and distributes books at cut-rate price through USSR bookstores and Indian book-stalls".[7] Earlier in the text, in a section titled 'The Two Communists Parties' (in the chapter on 'Funding Political Parties and Politicians'), the exact figure of this cut-rate price is named as "a 60- or 65-percent discount which was offered to People's Publishing House (PPH), an Indian company wholly owned by CPI".[8]

The abbreviation CPI stands for the Communist Party of India, one of several Communist parties in the country. Chandra Rajeswara Rao (1914–94) was the General Secretary of this party for many years, from 1964 to 1990. He was a Telugu native speaker. When he visited the Soviet Union, Comrade Rao always tried to find time in his busy schedule, in particular during CPSU party congresses in Moscow, to see his "Russian Telugu girls". He used this gender- and age-specific expression since, at the time when I worked there, both Telugu sections (at Progress and Raduga) were composed entirely of female staff.[9] These rare meetings with the general secretary of the CPI were perhaps the only opportunities for us to understand and maintain our ideological mission as part of the propaganda machine of the Soviet state. The rest of our time was dedicated to translation as a cultural and educational activity.

Translation as Publishing Business

The Telugu sections at Progress and Raduga were formed of teams of professional staff. Our in-house translators were all native Telugu speakers and Indian left-wing or progressive intellectuals. Some of them were literary figures in their own region. For example, Srirangam Srinivasa Rao (1910–83), popularly known as Sri Sri, an Indian poet and lyricist (and no relation to Comrade Rao), worked with us in the early 1970s. All of our chief editors were Russian native speakers who were also fluent in Telugu and English. We used the English translations of books originally written in Russian as our source texts. Svetlana Dzenit, the founder of the Telugu section and its first head, had a degree in English and studied Telugu with Telugu specialists who lived and worked in Moscow in the 1950s. According to her experience, in addition to two- to three-hour Telugu lessons with a native-speaking tutor on Sundays, all staff members were required to study independently. Dzenit writes: "There were the Arden grammar book, published at the beginning of the 20th century, and Telugu-English Dictionary

7 Ibid., p. 15.

8 Ibid., p. 4.

9 These so-called "Russian Telugu girls" will be more fully discussed later in my article.

by Professor P. Sankaranarayana".[10] Later, Dzenit published her own Russian-Telugu dictionary.[11]

Other senior colleagues, Olga Barannikova, Tamara Kovaleva, and Olga Smyslova, who were chief editors, studied Telugu at St Petersburg University with Nikita Gurov (1935–2009), who established the discipline of Telugu studies there in 1962. Their knowledge of Telugu helped them to communicate with native Telugu translators and participate actively in editing translators' drafts. They were translators themselves, and published their translations of Telugu novels and poetry into Russian. However, copy editors, such as Valeriia Kozlenko and Natasha Mikhnevich, did not have degrees in Telugu but learned the language on the job. They were responsible for maintaining the quality of publication standards, largely in terms of their technical requirements and terminology control, but not necessarily focusing on the linguistic or political peculiarities of the translated text.

The next group of colleagues were the youngest who, due to their age and experience, worked as copyists and proof-readers. They usually came to work immediately after finishing their high-school education. They spent a month or so familiarising themselves with the Telugu alphabet and then started to work by providing neat copies of translators' drafts. Neither publishing house had typewriters or computers equipped for Telugu script. In Raduga, Olesia Medvedeva, Tania Mramornova, and I copied by hand into Telugu many manuscripts which were translations of Russian and Soviet fiction (for example, novels by Lev Tolstoy, Fedor Dostoevsky, Maksim Gorky, and Chinghiz Aitmatov) and children's literature. Copyists worked side-by-side with editors. They also learned the language on the job. Later, after a year or two, they were given proof-reading tasks which largely required careful attention to detail and an excellent memory. My last transcriber's job was copying Rallanhandi's (who preferred to be called RVR) translation of Tolstoy's *Anna Karenina* into Telugu in 1990. This manuscript has never been published in Russia.

Our daily translation teamwork also included the maintenance of our own Russian/English/Telugu terminology lists through numerous visits to the publishing house library and consultation of encyclopaedias. Today, this work has been transferred from a paper format, such as card catalogue or filing-cabinet records, to CAT tools, building special terminology dictionaries in

10 Svetlana Dzenit and Anna Ponomareva, *The History of Telugu Section: Progress Publishing House, Moscow, USSR* (Vijayawada: Visalaandhra Publishing House, 2012). Telugu version: [illegible]& [illegible], [illegible] [illegible]. [illegible] [illegible] [illegible] [illegible](2012). The dictionaries cited above are: Albert Henry Arden, *A Progressive Grammar of the Telugu Language with Copious Examples and Exercises* (Madras: Society for Promoting Christian Knowledge, 1905) and Paluri Sankaranarayana, *An English-Telugu Dictionary*, 4th edn (Madras: P.K. Row Bros, 1900).

11 Svetlana Dzenit and Nidamarti Uma Radzheshvara Rao, *Russian-Telugu Dictionary* (*Russko-telugu slovar'*) (Moscow: Russkii iazyk, 1988).

machine-translation programmes. Our translation work in Moscow continued beyond the confines of Progress and Raduga. From 1969, the year in which Dzenit made her first business trip to India, we had regular contact and co-operation with Visalaandhra Publishing House. As our regional partner in India and our educator too, they sent us books in Telugu and their own newspaper, *Visalaandhra*, which provided good opportunities for us to read about events happening in Andhra. We also used their pool of staff members (or their recommendations) in order to select translators to invite to work with us in Moscow. Every book we translated contained a list of Visalaandhra branches where readers could purchase or order our other books. According to this list, written in Telugu, there were at least eight outlets: two offices in Hyderabad, and one office each in Vijayawada, Visakhapatnam, Warangal, Guntur, Tirupati, and Anantapur:[12]

మా ప్రచురణలు దొరికే చోట్లు:

విశాలాంధ్ర పబ్లిషింగ్ హౌస్
విజ్ఞాన్ భవన్,
4–1–435, బ్యాంక్‌స్ట్రీట్
హైదరాబాద్ – 500 001

విశాలాంధ్ర బుక్ హౌస్
11–1–37 గాంధీ రోడ
తిరుపతి – 517 501

విశాలాంధ్ర బుక్ హౌస్
ఏలూరు రోడ్డు
విజయవాడ – 520 002

విశాలాంధ్ర బుక్ హౌస్
సూపర్ బజారు ఎదుట
విశాఖపట్నం – 530 002

విశాలాంధ్ర బుక్ హౌస్
సుల్తాన్ బజారు
హైదరాబాదు – 500 001

విశాలాంధ్ర బుక్ హౌస్
హనుమకొండ
వరంగల్ – 506 011

విశాలాంధ్ర బుక్ హౌస్
కాలేజీ రోడ్డు
అనంతపురం – 515 004

విశాలాంధ్ర బుక్ హౌస్
అరండల్ పేట
గుంటూరు -- 522 002

Fig. 2. Contact details for all eight book outlets of Visalaandhra Publishing House in *Ukrainian Folk Tales*.[13]

In order to maintain correspondence with our readers and to obtain their opinions on our work, we also encouraged them to contact us in writing by using our official postal address. We used the Progress address during the

12 The addresses of the branches of Visalaandhra Publishing House can be found in the following publication: *Ukrainian Folk Tales* (Moscow: Raduga Publishers, 1988); in Telugu, ☒☒☒☒☒☒☒☒☒ ☒☒☒☒, p. 249, https://drive.google.com/file/d/0B07Gk0_NnBKiWWlYNElveVJXbWs/edit?resourcekey=0-NBTK-VwncQVhnD2VgkwR5Q.

13 *Ukrainian Folk Tales*, p. 247.

first couple of years of the establishment of Raduga, then moved to our own premises, a building located behind the Stalin skyscraper of the Ministry of Foreign Affairs, at 43 Sivtsev Vrazhek Lane. Our address was written in English; we received correspondence from readers in both English and Telugu. Answering questions or addressing requests expressed in these letters was part of everyone's workload. Sometimes, the head of the Telugu section would share reader feedback (including requests for specific books to be translated) with the head of the Department for Literature in Translation into Indian Languages. These discussions could result in plans to print more copies or prepare other editions of a particular publication.

Translation as Global Cultural Initiative

Before perestroika, only the heads of the Telugu sections could travel to India and visit our business partners there. After 1985, it became possible for other members of staff to go. These trips became more focused on expanding our horizons and studies of Telugu, in addition to maintaining our business contacts with Visalaandhra Publishing House. For example, I studied Telugu at the University of Madras from 1987–88. My visit to India was sponsored by the Soviet government: in addition to my studies, I actively participated in the Soviet-Indian friendship festival in 1987–88, organised under the joint initiative of Mikhail Gorbachev and Rajiv Gandhi. Among my official engagements were the following activities: delivering a speech titled 'The Importance of the October 1917 Revolution on the Development of Telugu Literature' in Telugu at the CPI's Congress in Vidjayawada; taking part in awards ceremonies organised by the journal *Soviet Land* and the regional branch of TASS (The Telegraph [News] Agency of the USSR); and working at the Soviet bookfair in Madras; and travelling freely, with the support of Vadim Cherepov, the Consul General of the USSR in Madras between 1979 and 1990, within the Southern state of Andhra Pradesh and Tamil Nadu. My experiences in Southern India enriched my knowledge of Indian culture and encouraged me to continue translating.

Concluding Remarks

I agree with Munday that "lived experience" has subjective elements, but I also hope that my own experience provides new perspectives on literary translation and its process. Out of the four advantages listed by Munday to applying a quantitative macro-social history approach,[14] my microhistory clearly illustrates the last one, i.e. that "it links the individual case study with the general socio-historical context". Moreover, it provides evidence on translation

14 Munday, 'Using Primary Sources', pp. 5 and 12.

as a collaborative activity in which the importance of team spirit and cultural enthusiasm rather than censorship and ideology is emphasised.

The impact of our translation work commissioned by Progress and Raduga on Telugu readers is difficult to overestimate. Today, when there is no literary tie between post-Soviet Russia and India on the level of state-sponsored publications, there remains great interest in our books among contemporary reading audiences in India. Young readers find them in the libraries of their parents and grandparents and use the platform of social media to read and discuss them. Divya Sreedharan (2021)[15] and Sai Priya Kodidala (2020)[16] provide several examples of various online sites, blogs and Facebook pages dedicated to the popularisation of this type of literature. Sreedharan also states:

> The Soviet literary heritage continues to exist in India. Many Indians who had been thrilled to read Soviet magazines and books some time ago, after becoming adults maintained their passion for the books of their childhood and even started to collect them.[17]

It seems that the process of creating world literature in translation, Gorky's famous initiative, continues in the twenty-first century.

---

15 Divya Sreedharan, 'How Soviet Books Became Iconic in India' ('Kak sovetskie knigi stali kul'tovymi v Indii') (2021), https://russkiymir.ru/publications/287073/.

16 Sai Priya Kodidala, 'From Moscow to Vijayawada: How Generations of Telugu Readers Grew up on Soviet Children's Literature', *Firstpost*, 14 September 2020, https://www.firstpost.com/art-and-culture/from-moscow-to-vijayawada-how-generations-of-telugu-readers-grew-up-on-soviet-childrens-literature-8809591.html.

17 Sreedharan, 'How Soviet Children's Books Became Collectors' Items in India'. AP's translation.

Tolstoy in India: Translating Aspirations across Continents

Ayesha Suhail

In the second half of the twentieth century, Soviet Russia found adherents to its anti-capitalist values within the Communist Party of India (CPI), founded in 1925. It became the third largest party in government by the 1952 elections.[1] While all members of the CPI supported the original vision of an international working-class movement, divisions emerged over support for the Soviet Union. In 1964, the party split into two factions, the Communist Party of India and the Communist Party of India (Marxist). Shortly after this rift, a shop was established in Kolkata by the Communist Party of India (Marxist).[2] The venture was assisted by India's National Book Agency, popularly known as the NBA, a Marxist publisher established in 1939 in Kolkata and still active today.[3] Until 1991, the shop was directly supplied with books printed in Moscow by Progress Publishers. Progress was previously known as the Publishing Cooperative of Foreign Workers, which was established in 1931, and whose literature section became Raduga Publishers in 1982.[4] These Russian books ranged from

1 For an overview of the history of the Indian Communist Party, see Valerian Rodrigues, 'The Communist Parties in India', in *India's Political Parties*, ed. by Peter Ronald deSouza and E. Sridharan (New Delhi: Sage, 2006), pp. 199–252 (esp. pp. 211–17).

2 Manisha Granthalaya is the name of the shop which still exists today in Kolkata's College Square near Gorky Sadan. For details regarding the books it sells, see *LBB*'s online article 'These Out-of-Print Books Came to India in 1982, All The Way From the USSR', lbb.in/Kolkata/books-russia.

3 The NBA was established on 26 June 1939 by the Communist leader Muzaffar Ahmad and his associates. They make Marxist publications accessible to the common reader. See www.nationalbookagency.com.

4 The literature section was one of four thematic series at Progress Publishers; it became the largest, and in 1982 evolved into the independent Raduga Publishers.

 https://doi.org/10.11647/OBP.0340.27

children's literature and beautifully illustrated folk tales, to novels by Pushkin, Gogol, Tolstoy, Dostoevsky, Gorky, and Soviet-era revolutionary writings. Today, the store still sells these books, but second-hand and at lower prices. They are remnants of a time when the newly realised dream of Socialism in Russia acted as a beacon to colonial India. Indian intellectuals, freedom fighters and the reading public were enthused by Vladimir Lenin's acknowledgement of the absolute injustice of British Imperialism in his article 'Inflammable Material in World Politics', published in August 1908.[5] However, within the movement for Indian independence, a large, pacifist faction responded to the writings of Lev Tolstoy.[6] This essay will consider Tolstoy's novels and their immediate resonance with Indian writers' styles and themes. This shared feeling is indicated by the many translations of Tolstoy's novels by leading Indian authors and translators, and their manifold references to Tolstoy's characters and works in their own dramas, short stories, and novels. I will also argue, with reference to György Lukács and Pierre Macherey, among others, that literature can transcend cultural and national borders by appealing to universal values of freedom and justice.

A vast ideological distance existed between Tolstoy's Russia, which was tsarist, and the Communist USSR, and a similar gap separated colonial India from independent India. However, the writings of the 'sage of Iasnaia Poliana' remained meaningful in both nations, under both circumstances. Tolstoy's most famous literary follower in India is probably Dhanpat Rai Srivastava (1880–1936), who wrote social fiction under the pen name of Munshi Premchand. His short stories, novels and plays written in the Hindustani language (i.e. Hindi-Urdu), dealt with the themes of caste hierarchies, the plight of women, and labourers in late nineteenth-century India. He was both influenced and impressed by Russian literature, particularly by Count Tolstoy's works. In a scene from his drama *The Struggle* (*Sangram*), written in 1923 and published in 1933, police search the house of a Swaraj landowner and arrest him for possessing a copy of Tolstoy's tales. A century later, in 2019, eerily similar events played out in the Bombay High Court when Indian human rights activist Vernon Gonsalves was asked to explain why he kept "objectionable material", including a copy of Tolstoy's *War and Peace*, at his home.[7] The Pune Police, who were probing the case, claimed

---

To find out more about the history of Progress Publishers see Rossen Djagalov, 'Progress Publishers: A Short History', *Leftword*, https://web.archive.org/web/20200410005445/https://mayday.leftword.com/blog/post/progress-publishers-a-short-history/.

5 Vladimir Lenin, 'Inflammable Material in World Politics', in *Lenin Collected Works*, 45 vols (Moscow: Progress Publishers, 1973), 15 (1908–09), pp. 182–88.

6 Tolstoy wrote his 'Letter to a Hindu: The Subjection of India—Its Cause and Cure' to Tarak Nath Das, editor of *Free Hindustan* on 14 December 1908. The letter was published in the Indian newspaper *Free Hindustan* and then reprinted in Mahatma Gandhi's South African newspaper *Indian Opinion* in 1909.

7 The incident is covered in the article by PTI (Press Trust of India), 'War and Peace at Home? "Explain", says Bombay High Court', *The Telegraph*, https://www.

that the book was part of the "highly incriminating evidence" it had seized from Mr. Gonsalves' house. The situation grew still more intriguing when, days later, Indian Prime Minister Narendra Modi, addressing an economic forum in Russia, said that Lev Tolstoy and Mahatma Gandhi had an "indelible effect" on each other and that India and Russia must take inspiration from them to strengthen bilateral ties.[8] Such contradictions and anxieties continue to manifest in the political imagination of the governments of both nations. Leaders often struggle to balance party politics with public veneration of these cultural and political giants. Tolstoy's and Gandhi's messages of non-violence and *ahimsa* ('noninjury', the ethical principle of not causing harm to any living thing), have been revered internationally. Moreover, Tolstoy's towering stature as a writer remains undisputed. Consequently, the conflict between the individual and the state, which celebrates these figures but does not always respect their non-violent convictions, continues to exist.

Writers like Premchand, Mulk Raj Anand (1905–2004), Jainendra Kumar (1905–88), and others welcomed Tolstoy's work when it began to appear in translation at the turn of the twentieth century. There were two primary reasons for the natural affinity the Indian public felt towards Tolstoy. First was his endorsement by Gandhi, who had publicly acknowledged Tolstoy as his spiritual master or guru. Gandhi claimed that Tolstoy's writings awakened within him the principles of the faiths of his own land, meaning Hinduism and Buddhism.[9] As a result, Gandhi's many followers were predisposed to trust Tolstoy. The second reason for Tolstoy's popularity was his literary aesthetic in *War and Peace, Anna Karenina, Resurrection* and the many short stories and novellas he wrote. The form and content evoked experiences familiar to the Indian sensibility. Tolstoy's realist style, along with the ideological image he chose to project, ranging from the agrarian and bucolic to his authoritative grasp

---

telegraphindia.com/india/war-and-peace-at-home-explain-says-bombay-high-court/cid/1701007. The statements made by Pune police can be found in the article by Vidya, 'Bhima Koregaon Case: Bombay High Court Questions Accused on Why He Read War and Peace', *India Today*, https://www.indiatoday.in/india/story/bhima-koregaon-case-bombay-high-court-questions-accused-on-why-he-read-war-and-peace-1592826–2019–08–28, para 4.

8 Translation of Prime Minister's speech in Plenary Session of 5th Eastern Economic Forum (5 September 2019), *Ministry of External Affairs, Government of India*, https://www.mea.gov.in/Speeches-Statements.htm?dtl/31798/translation+of+prime+ministers+speech+in+plenary+session+of+5th+eastern+economic+forum+september+05+2019, para. 11 of 11.

9 Tolstoy's reply to a letter from one of the editors of *Free Hindustan* was published in India with an introduction by Mahatma Gandhi wherein he said, "To me, as a humble follower of that great teacher whom I have long looked upon as one of my guides, it is a matter of honour to be connected with the publication of his letter, such especially as the one which is now being given to the world." Leo Tolstoy, 'A Letter to a Hindu: The Subjection of India—Its Cause and Cure', Introduction by M. K. Gandhi, https://www.gutenberg.org/files/7176/7176-h/7176-h.htm.

of war and the historical process, struck a chord with Indian readers. In fact, Tolstoy derived the themes of twenty-one of his *Twenty-Three Tales* written at Iasnaia Poliana from Indian mythology. As a youth, he took courses in Oriental Languages at Kazan University's Department of Oriental Studies in 1844. This piqued his interest in teachings of Moses, Mohammad, Socrates, Zoroaster, and Christ; and particularly in Buddhism and Hinduism. He read the Vedas and Upanishads and the two epics Ramayana and Mahabharata. Extracts from these teachings were included by him in his *Circle of Reading*.[10] In his later writings, Tolstoy adapted material from the *Panchatantra, Hitopadesha, Puranas, Kurals,* and the book of Buddhist ethics *Dhammapada,* the influence of these Hindu and Buddhist texts is visible in both his fictional and non-fictional writings—especially in stories where animals are the main characters—moral tales, and in his philosophy of passive resistance.[11] This process of adaptation came full circle when Premchand, as early as 1916, re-adapted and transposed Tolstoy's work, *Twenty-Three Tales,* into Hindi as *Talstāy kī kahāniyāṃ* (*The Tales of Tolstoy*).[12] Tolstoy's works have been translated into most Indian languages. Arun Som, a contemporary Russian-to-Bengali translator with forty years' experience, completed a four-volume translation of Tolstoy's *War and Peace* titled *Juddho aar Shanti,* and published by the Sahitya Akademi. Noni Bhoumik (1921–66), another Russian-to-Bengali translator, worked on *Anna Karenina* (as well as various works by Dostoevsky) for Progress. Mahatma Gandhi himself translated some of Tolstoy's short stories into Gujarati, including 'Ivan the Fool' (titled 'Moorakh Raja Ane Tena Be Bhaio') and 'How Much Land Does a Man Need', among many others. They were published in his South African newspaper *Indian Opinion* between 1911 and 1914. The Hindu novelist Jainendra Kumar (1905–88) translated Tolstoy's stories into Hindi in a 1961 collection, *Prem Mein Bhagwaan.*

Lukács claimed that a literary work of international influence can exist simultaneously as a stranger and as a native within a foreign culture.[13] Its acceptance is grounded in common qualities between the interacting cultures,

10 Around 1847, Tolstoy was admitted to a university hospital where he shared a ward with a Buddhist monk being treated for injuries received after refusing to retaliate during an assault. The encounter set Tolstoy on the path of discovering what the Indian religions of Buddhism and Hinduism said about nonviolence and passive resistance. Ajay Kamalakaran, 'The Influence of Buddhism and Hinduism on Leo Tolstoy's Life', https://www.rbth.com/arts/2014/10/14/the_influence_of_buddhism_and_hinduism_on_leo_tolstoys_life_39017.

11 Salahuddin Mohd Shamsuddin, 'Place of "Panchatantra" in the World of Literatures', *British Journal of Humanities and Social Sciences,* (Dec., 2013), https://www.academia.edu/6977957/Place_of_Panchatantra_in_the_World_of_Literatures, p.7.

12 John Burt Foster Jr., 'From Tolstoy to Premchand: Fractured Narratives and the Paradox of Gandhi's Militant Non Violence', *Comparative Critical Studies,* 10, https://www.euppublishing.com/doi/full/10.3366/ccs.2013.0113.

13 György Lukács, 'Leo Tolstoy and Western European Literature', *Studies in European Realism* (New York: Grosset and Dunlap, 1964), p. 242.

besides any influences the author may have drawn from the receiving culture. Both these factors facilitated the popularity of Tolstoy's writings in India. For European audiences, Tolstoy's realism may have felt dated by the mid-twentieth century; but in India, where Victorian novels had flooded school and college curriculums under colonial rule, his style was both familiar and welcome.[14] In this context, Tolstoy's form-defying style even appeared liberating.[15] It was proof that alternative expression within the realist novel was possible, that vast nations with scattered ethnicities and deep-rooted political and social problems (like both Russia and India) could find authentic representation within the form of the novel. It also helped that Tolstoy did not assume that capitalism was the only reality. Moreover, his attacks on the Greek Orthodox Church, and on the Church as an establishment in general, appealed to Indians who had been subjugated by the Empire in the name of Faith, the Crown, and Civilisation; three concepts which had become interchangeable under imperialism. As such, the spiritual values that Tolstoy offered, which drew nourishment from Eastern religions, resonated with the Indian temperament. Another point of similarity between Russia and India was the stratification of society in both nations into rigidly separated classes, accompanied by widespread injustice, inequity, and repression. When Tolstoy described social interactions, he insisted that empathetic mutual understanding between classes and change was possible. Tolstoy's characters modelled a way of being, often painfully achieved, where individualism was rejected in favour of duty towards others and society in general. This movement away from solipsism to resignation was expressed by characters like Konstantin Levin (*Anna Karenina*), or Nikolai Rostov and Natasha Rostova in *War and Peace*, or Katiusha Maslova and Prince Nekhliudov from *Resurrection*. Their sublimation of personal ambition was a potent means to negate the cycle of violence. In India, a very similar philosophy became the basis of Gandhi's Non-Cooperation Movement, which began on 4 September 1920.[16] The movement baffled the British establishment and shamed them

---

14 According to Priya Joshi, "The British novel of 'serious standards' was introduced in India in the nineteenth century as a means of propagating and legitimating Englishness in the colony", in 'Culture and Consumption: Fiction, the Reading Public, and the British Novel in Colonial India', *Book History*, I (1998), 196–220.

15 Tolstoy is quoted as saying, "*War and Peace* is 'not a novel, still less an epic poem, still less a historical chronicle'". See Courtney C. W. Guerra, 'Why Read War and Peace?', *Tableau* (Spring 2023), https://tableau.uchicago.edu/articles/2013/04/why-read-war-and-peace.

16 Gandhi's first reference to Tolstoy occurs in 1889 when, as a student in London, Gandhi visited Paris and reiterated Tolstoy's sentiments regarding the Eiffel Tower: that it was a "monument of man's folly". In another essay, 'Guide to London', Gandhi quoted from Tolstoy's *Why Do Men Stupefy Themselves?*. Gandhi's 'Satyagraha' movement (meaning 'truth force') was drawn from Tolstoy's 'soul force' or 'love force'. He also established a Tolstoy-inspired farm in 1910 in South Africa; the Sabarmati Ashram in Ahmedabad, India was based on the same model. Gandhi never denied the debt he owed to Tolstoyan thought and gave

simply by never retaliating against the state's brute force. In his 1908 'A Letter to a Hindu: The Subjection of India—Its Cause and Cure', Tolstoy advised the Indian nation against resorting to violence as a means to end the British rule. He argued that although violence might seem favourable from a short-term perspective, in hindsight, it was sure to beget further violence. Decades have passed since this opinion was brushed off by certain sections of Indian society as naïve. Indian Nationalism of the time was informed by many strains; some were unconvinced of non-violence as an effective political strategy. Revolutionaries, including readers of leftist thought, rejected Tolstoyan pacifism. Violence against the colonial establishment reached a peak during the early 1900s and the small group of activists who carried out these attacks was executed. They are revered as martyrs in independent India.[17] Tolstoy's fiction continued to inspire ordinary Indians, as well as writers like the Hindi novelist Amritlal Nagar, characters in whose 1964 novel *The Drop and the Ocean* (*Boond Aur Samudra*) responded directly to Tolstoyan inventions like Platon Karataev or Pierre Bezukhov from *War and Peace*, and *Resurrection*'s Dmitrii Nekhliudov.[18] These characters represented epochal and social struggles without losing their sense of optimistic innocence. Tolstoy's focus on Russian peasants earned him the title of "Mirror of the Russian Revolution" from Lenin and "Poet of the Russian Peasantry" from Lukács.[19] This focus was reflected partly in his portrayal of the naïve, patriarchal,

---

a memorable speech on the centenary of Tolstoy's birth (9 September 1928), in Gujarati at Sabarmati Ashram. The English version of his speech was published in *Young India* on 20 September 1928. See Y. P. Anand, 'The Relationship between Leo Tolstoy and Mahatma Gandhi—A Historical Review', *Dialogue*, 12:2 (2010), http://www.asthabharati.org/Dia_Oct%20010/y.p..htm.

17 The revolutionaries were Bhagat Singh, Sukhdev Thapar, and Shivram Rajguru. They vowed to avenge the assassination of Lala Rajpat Rai, who had succumbed to a lathi charge by the British Raj Police while carrying out a non-violent protest against the Simon Commission on 17 November 1928. The trio was hanged in Lahore Jail on 23 March 1931. Singh and Thapar were twenty-three while Rajguru was only twenty-two years old at the time of their hanging. For more on this, read Part One of Kama Maclean's *A Revolutionary History of Interwar India* (London: C. Hurst & Co., 2015).

18 On how Tolstoy influenced Amritlal Nagar, see Salim Arif's, 'Amritlal Nagar at 100: How a Simple Man Used Simple Language to Create Extraordinary Literature', *Swarajya*, 17 August 2016, https://swarajyamag.com/culture/amritlal-nagar-at-100-how-a-simple-man-used-simple-language-to-produce-great-literature. For how the characters of *The Drop and The Ocean* were inspired by Tolstoy, see Charumati Ramdas, 'Tolstoy and India: A Beautiful Bond', *Story Mirror*, https://storymirror.com/read/english/story/tolstoy-and-india-a-beautiful-bond/7nbtitpq?ref=/read/english/story/tolstoy-and-india-a-beautiful-bond/7nbtitpq, para 20 of 23.

19 Lenin wrote articles on Tolstoy's art between 1908 and 1911. These were grouped under the title *Leo Tolstoy: Mirror of Russian Literature*. See Vladimir Lenin's *Collected Works*, 45 vols (Moscow: Progress Publishers, 1963–80), 15 (1973), pp. 202–09. For Lukács's view, see György Lukács, 'Tolstoy and The Development of

and superstitious beliefs prevalent in the Russian countryside, which had their counterpart in the prejudices of Indian rural populations. Whether his characters were low- or high-status, domestic servants or libertines, serfs or masters, they embodied beliefs and values recognisable in Indian society just as well as in Russian Orthodox culture. Indian readers could readily relate to Tolstoy's portraits from feudal life, as conducted under an unpopular monarchy, with revolution impending. Tolstoy's fiction always centred the depiction of wars, romances and revolutions around Russia's perennial agrarian and economic problems. The betterment of the lives of the Russian peasants remained a primary theme. His heroes embodied these aspirations: consider Levin, Andrei Bolkonskii, Bezukhov, and Nekhliudov. All these fictional landowners were inspired by conscience to abandon their unethical and exploitative privileges and work instead to uplift the newly emancipated serfs. The abject poverty of the Russian serf was echoed in the condition of the Indian-bonded labourers, Harijans, and secluded tribes. Premchand, for one, was greatly moved by this mirroring of the common man in both the nations, emphasising that "[Tolstoy's tales are] written for ordinary people, who have neither money nor time".[20] Premchand felt Tolstoy had captured a universal pathos, transcending national and cultural conventions. In his third and last play *Prem Ki Vedi* (1933), the female protagonist, Jenny, is caught in an interfaith romantic dilemma with a Hindu man, Yograj.[21] Her inner turmoil makes her think of Anna Karenina. Premchand carried out a clever gender subversion in his play. When Jenny thinks of Anna, she is not worried that society's rejection of her and Yograj's love will push her to suicide; instead, she frets that it may push Yograj to that despair, since he, as a gentleman, a wealthy man, and an upper-caste Hindu, has more to lose. Thus, Jenny transcends the notion that harsher judgement of a woman in an interfaith affair is the major impediment.[22] At the end of the play, religious hypocrisies prevail over the lovers and they part ways.[23] Tolstoy may have rejected aggressive reactions to the injustices committed against the peasant class, but his realistic representation of their sentiments became a critique in itself of the social problems of the age. His ideology of resistance was

Realism', *Studies in European Realism* (New York: Grosset and Dunlap, 1964), p. 139.

20 Donatella Dolcini, 'Premchand's Enounter with Tolstoy', *Cracow Indological Studies*, 10:17 (2015), pp. 159–68 (p. 164).

21 Pushpal Singh, 'Upekshit Raha Premchand Ka Natya–Karm', *The Tribune*, 25 July 2010, https://www.dainiktribuneonline.com/news/archive/features/उपेक्षित-रहा-प्रेमचंद-का-नाट्य-कर्म-127359.

22 Munshi Premchand, *Prem Ki Vedi* (1933), *Hindi Kahani*, https://www.hindikahani.hindi-kavita.com/Prem-Ki-Vedi-Premchand.php (Act VI).

23 Madan Gopal, *Munshi Premchand: A Literary Biography* (Bombay: Asia Publishing House, 1943).

implicit in the text; it influenced Indian readers unconsciously.[24] Tolstoy's works contained their message of revolution, of impetus to change, in their careful silence, often misrepresented as negligent absences.[25] Macherey has called this dependence on the unspoken the unique characteristic of novelistic language.[26] The profound, often revolutionary impact of well-placed silence reminds one of Maksim Gorky's remarks on Tolstoy in his 1920 volume *Reminiscences of Leo Nikolaevich Tolstoy*, "I am deeply convinced that beyond all that he [Tolstoy] speaks of, there is much which he is silent about, even in his diary; he is silent and probably will never tell it to anyone".[27]

---

24 Pierre Macherey,'The Two Questions', *A Theory of Literary Production*, trans. by Geoffrey Wall (London: Routledge, 1978), p. 92, para 2.

25 For critiques of Tolstoy's passive resistance and rejection of revolutionary reactionism, see Roland Boer's, 'Lenin on Tolstoy: Between Imaginary Resolution and Revolutionary Christian Communism', *Science and Society*, 78 (January 2014), 41–60.

26 Pierre Macherey, 'Implicit and Explicit', in *A Theory of Literary Production*, trans. by Geoffrey Wall (London: Routledge, 1978), pp. 91–94.

27 Pierre Macherey, 'The Spoken and the Unspoken', in *A Theory of Literary Production*, trans. by Geoffrey Wall (London: Routledge, 1978), pp. 95–100. For the quote by Gorky, see Maksim Gorky, *Reminiscences of Leo Nikolaevitch Tolstoy*, trans. by S.S. Koteliansky and Leonard Woolf (Folcroft: Folcroft Publishers, 1977), p. 19.

Tolstoy Embracing Tamil: Ninety Years of Lev Tolstoy in Tamil Literature

Venkatesh Kumar

Rao Sahib K Kothandapani Pillai (1896–1979)

The earliest Tamil writer to take the initiative of translating Tolstoy's works into Tamil was Rao Sahib K Kothandapani Pillai, born in 1896 at Andalur Semmangudi village in South India, and, not entirely incidentally, my own grandfather. His version of three stories by Tolstoy was published in 1932 as *Kadhaimanikkovai* (*Stories from Tolstoy*), an academic textbook for primary-school children, and republished in 1948 as an edition for school-leavers. The three stories he chose were 'Two Old Men' ('Dva starika', 1885), 'How Much Land Does A Man Need?' ('Mnogo li cheloveku zemli nuzhno?', 1886), and 'A Lost Opportunity' ('Upustish' ogon'—ne potushish'', 1885). As a diplomat who read Tolstoy for pleasure, Kothandapani Pillai was well-placed to select and curate Tolstoy's texts in a way that would both appeal to, and inculcate Tolstoy's moral values in, Tamil readers. He probably worked from Aylmer and Louise Maude's English translations, supplemented by Munshi Premchand's Hindi version. The first edition of his *Stories* was a direct translation of Tolstoy's tales, but the revised 1948 version marked an intriguing departure in which

 https://doi.org/10.11647/OBP.0340.28

Kothandapani Pillai separated the stories into several fragments, interspersed with rhyming couplets from the oldest surviving work of Tamil literature, the long poem *Thirukkural* by Thiruvalluvar (who lived in the first century A.D.). By linking couplets from the *Thirukkural*—which expounds on politics, war, love, and pleasure—Kothandapani Pillai added to Tolstoy's prose, he transferred the native cultural capital of the former to the Russian writer's work, since both discuss moral problems and life experiences. By so doing, he made the Tamil reader's access to Tolstoy's message both direct, and unforgettable.[1] In addition to my grandfather's work, there were numerous other translations of Tolstoy into Tamil during the 1930s and 1940s. A new Madras-based publisher, Sakthi, even established their reputation by choosing Tolstoy's 'What Then Must We Do?' ('Ini naam seiya vendiyadhu yadhu'; 'Tak chto zhe nam delat'', 1886), translated into Tamil by Sri Brahmachari Vishwanathan, as their first publication, with Tolstoy's portrait as the cover image. Sakthi Publications continued publishing Tolstoy's other works in Tamil until the 1950s.

Front cover of *Sakthi Monthly Magazine* (November 1940) with an image of Tolstoy.

Later, during the 1960s and 1970s, Progress and Raduga Publishers (in Moscow) published numerous Tamil translations of works by Tolstoy, Maksim Gorky, Fedor Dostoevsky and Anton Chekhov. Progress commissioned fifty

1 A second volume of Kothandapani Pillai's Tolstoy translations, the 1930 *Stories* (*Kathaikkothu*), has regrettably been lost.

books by Russian writers in Tamil, while Raduga produced seventy-nine.[2] Other key Tolstoy translators include Narayanan Vanamamalai (1917–80), born in Tirunalveli in the district of South India, who translated the play 'The Power of Darkness' ('Irulin valimai'; 'Vlast' t'my', 1886) in 1942, for Sakthi; later he also translated the novella 'Family Happiness' ('Kudumba inbam'; 'Semeinnoe schast'e', 1859) into Tamil in 1951. K. (Kumbakonam) Pattabiramiyer Rajagopalan translated six more of Tolstoy's short stories into Tamil in 1941 as *Tolstoy Kadhaigal*, again for Sakthi Publications. Pattabiramiyer Rajagopalan (1902–44) was a journalist and translator born in Kumbakonam, South India. A writer who contributed to the Tamil reception of Russian literature in the 1980s and 1990s was Poornam Somasundaram (1918–81), whose translations (which included Pushkin and Gorky as well as Tolstoy) were published by both Progress and Raduga. Naturally, as Poornam Somasundaram's example shows, Tolstoy was not the only Russian to influence Tamil literature: others, however, arrived in translation only from the 1960s onwards. Pushkin first appeared in Tamil in 1968, Dostoevsky in 1964, Gorky in 1952, and Chekhov in 1957. Thus, Tolstoy made the first, and arguably profoundest, impact in the world of Tamil literature.

2 My statistics are derived from Pe. Govindasamy, *Thamizhil Soviet Ilakkiyangal* (Chennai: New Century Book House, 2018).

Japan
Translation from Russian in the Melting Pot of Japanese Literature

Hiroko Cockerill

Introduction

During the late nineteenth and early twentieth centuries, the Japanese literary language underwent radical transformation under the influence of translations from the literatures of European countries. Translations from Russian literature occupied a significant place among these. When translating from Russian to Japanese, nineteenth-century Japanese translators had to grapple with linguistic elements that did not exist in their own language. Japanese did not commonly use past tense verb endings or male and female third-person pronouns,[1] both of which are common in Russian literature and the literatures of other European languages. Komori Yōichi notes that Roland Barthes has identified the passé simple and third-person pronouns as markers of fiction in modern prose works.[2] However, when Barthes identifies the "preterite" (passé simple) and the "third-person" as markers of fiction in modern prose works, he limits this assertion to the Western novel.[3] If Barthes' assertion is correct, the question arises: how then could Japanese writers create modern prose works without the preterite or the third person? And how did translations from European literatures influence the

1 The Japanese literary language had a neutral third-person pronoun *kare*, which could indicate both male and female characters.

2 Komori Yōichi, 'Hon'yaku buntai ni okeru "ta" to "r(u)"' ['"Ta" and "r(u)" Forms in Translation Style'], in *Futabatei Shimei zenshū* [*Futabatei Shimei's Complete Works*], ed. by Shinsuke Tagawa and Ryōhei Yasui, 8 vols (Tokyo: Chikuma Shobō, 1984–93), III (1985), cited in the associated *Monthly Bulletin*, 3, pp. 3–4 (p. 3).

3 Roland Barthes, *Writing Degree Zero*, trans. by Annette Lavers and Colin Smith (New York: Hill and Wang, 1968), pp. 29–40.

 https://doi.org/10.11647/OBP.0340.29

creation of the modern Japanese novel? One of the most significant translators to influence the development of the Japanese literary language was Futabatei Shimei (1864–1909),[4] who was both a pioneering translator from Russian literature and the creator of the modern Japanese novel.[5] His novel *The Drifting Cloud* (*Ukigumo*) was published serially from 1887 to 1889. In 1888, he published translations of two of Ivan Turgenev's short stories under the titles 'The Tryst' ('Aibiki') and 'A Chance Encounter' ('Meguriai'), implying that his work on these translations overlapped with the composition of his novel.[6] A major innovation of Futabatei's translation style was the use of *-ta* verbal endings (also known as *-ta* auxiliary verbs) to convey the meaning of the past tense. It was left to a later translator from Russian, Nakamura Hakuyō (1890–1974), to establish the use of the male and female pronouns *kare* (he) and *kanojo* (she), two and a half decades later. Futabatei's use of *-ta* verbal endings as the past tense marker and Nakamura's use of Japanese male and female pronouns *kare* and *kanojo* were the result of their application of methods which, today, we would associate with Lawrence Venuti's concept of foreignisation. This chapter will examine how Japanese translators of Russian literature responded to the challenges of translating past tense verbs and third-person pronouns, and what impact this had on subsequent Japanese writers of fiction.

Creating Past Tense Forms (-ta Endings): Futabatei's Debut Translations, 'The Tryst' and 'A Chance Encounter'

Translations from Western literature began appearing in Japan after the nation opened its doors to the world in 1868. People were eager to learn about the West, and translators acted as mediators of Western culture. By 1888, when Futabatei published his versions of 'The Tryst' and 'A Chance Encounter', many European literary works by prominent authors had already been translated into Japanese, such as *A Marvellous Affair in Europe: A Springtime Tale of Blossoms and Willows* (*Ōshū Kiji: Karyū shunwa*, 1878), which was extracted from Edward Bulwer-Lytton's *Ernest Maltravers and Alice* (1837–38), and *A New Story: A Tour of the World in Eighty Days* (*Shinsetsu: Hachijū nichikan Sekai isshū*, 1878), from Jules Verne's *Around the World in Eighty Days* (*Le tour du monde en quatre-vingts jours*, 1872). Futabatei's two maiden translations differed markedly from the works of earlier translators. First, while the literary works translated prior to Futabatei's debut

4 With all Japanese names, surnames appear first and given names follow.

5 'Futabatei Shimei' was the pen name of Hasegawa Tatsunosuke.

6 Turgenev's original short stories are 'The Rendezvous' ('Svidanie') from the collection *A Sportsman's Sketches* (*Zapiski okhotnika*, 1847–52) and 'Three Meetings' ('Tri vstrechi', 1852).

were often politically inflected or adventure narratives, Futabatei chose two love stories. Secondly, while earlier translations were often abbreviated or adapted, Futabatei's debut works were painstakingly literal, word-for-word translations. Finally, the narratives of the two translations were written in the colloquial *genbun-itchi* style for the first time in Japanese translation history. *Genbun-itchi* literally means 'unification of the spoken and written language' and refers to the use of a style derived from spoken language in a written narrative. Prior to Futabatei's two translations, most literary translations employed the *kanbun kundoku* style, invented when Japanese monks tried to read Chinese Buddhist scriptures in the late eighth century. They converted Chinese sentences directly into Japanese sentences, retaining all the Chinese characters. They indicated word order by adding numbers to the original Chinese text, as the Chinese language typically observes a subject-verb-object sentence structure, while the sentence structure of the Japanese language is normally subject-object-verb. The Chinese characters were retained, unchanged, for nouns, verb stems, adjectives, and adverbs, while Japanese particles, Japanese verb and adjectival conjugations, Japanese adverbial endings, and Japanese auxiliary verbs were added to the original Chinese characters in the form of *katakana* (one of the two phonetic syllabaries used in modern Japanese, the other being *hiragana*). In this way, Japanese people were able to read Chinese sentences without knowing how Chinese characters were deciphered. This style was referred to as the male writing style and it continued to develop and be widely used until the Meiji era (1868–1912). Official documents and many scientific and technical texts were written or translated using this style during the early Meiji period. While previous translations of European literary works had usually been written with Chinese characters and *katakana*, Futabatei's debut translations were written with Chinese characters and *hiragana*.[7] The story translated by Futabatei as 'The Tryst' is taken from Turgenev's early work *A Sportsman's Sketches* (1847–52). The sportsman (who is out hunting) by chance witnesses a *rendez-vous* in a birch grove between an unfortunate peasant girl and an arrogant servant. The girl is heartlessly abandoned by the servant, who regards their liaison as only a casual affair. Futabatei's translation begins as follows:

> (A) <u>In autumn around the middle of September, there was a day when I sat in a birch grove.</u> From morning a fine rain had been falling, but from time to time there were intervals of warm sunshine; [it was] very unsettled weather. One moment fluffy white clouds spread in layers across the sky, and the next the sky suddenly cleared in parts, and from

7 For further details on this topic, see 'Japanese Tradition', in *Routledge Encyclopaedia of Translation Studies*, ed. by Mona Baker (London and New York: Routledge, 1998), pp. 485–94, and Donald Keen, *Dawn to the West: Japanese Literature of the Modern Era* (New York: Columbia University Press, 1998), esp. 'The Age of Translation', pp. 55–75.

> behind the clouds which had been parted, a bright and cheerful azure patch, like a beautiful and intelligent eye, was seen. (B) I sat, looked around and listened. The leaves rustled slightly above my head, and I knew the season just by listening.[8]

In his translation, Futabatei noted every text-based feature of the original. Later in 1908 he recollected how he worked on his early translations in a talk entitled 'Yo ga hon'yaku no hyōjun ('My Translation Norm')'.

> If you think solely of the meaning when translating a foreign language and attach excessive importance to it, you will take the risk of harming the original. I have always believed that you must saturate yourself with the rhythm of the original for some time, then transfer it to your own work. *In my attempt to use Russian rhythms in my translations, I did not omit a single comma or full stop. If the original contained three commas and one full stop, the translation also had three commas and one full stop.*[9] [my italics]

It is interesting to learn that Futabatei prioritised the rhythm of the original before meaning. His scrupulous efforts to reproduce the original style led him to create an unprecedented colloquial *genbun-itchi* style in his narrative. Although Futabatei could not completely adhere to the number of commas in the original, the number of full stops was meticulously reproduced. As a result, the five sentences in the passage quoted earlier match the five sentences in the original. Turgenev wrote his story as a first-person narrative. The narrator-sportsman recollects the *rendez-vous* he witnessed and the retrospective narrative point of view is fixed by consistent use of past tense verbs. Futabatei attempts to loyally convey the meaning of the past tense verbs in Turgenev's original by using *-ta* auxiliary verbs. Because in the Japanese language verbs usually come at the end

---

8 I. S. Turgenev, 'Aibiki' ('The Tryst'), trans. by Futabatei Shimei, in *Futabatei Shimei zenshū*, 8 vols (Tokyo: Chikuma Shobō, 1984–93), II (1985), pp. 3–16 (p. 5). All translations from Japanese in this text are my own unless otherwise indicated. Futabatei's original text is as follows:
秋九月中旬といふころ、一日自分がさる樺の林の中に座してゐたことが有ツた。今朝から小雨が降りそゝぎ、その晴れ間にはおりおり生ま煖かな日かげも射して、まことに氣まぐれな空ら合ひ。あわあわしい白ら雲が空ら一面に棚引くかと思ふと、フトまたあちこち瞬く間雲切れがして、無理に押し分けたやうな雲間から澄みて怜悧し氣に見える人の眼の如くに朗らかに晴れた蒼空がのぞかれた。自分は座して、四顧して、そして耳を傾けてゐた。木の葉が頭上で幽かに戰いだが、その音を聞たばかりでも季節は知られた。

9 Futabatei Shimei, 'Yo ga hon'yaku no hyōjun', in *Futabatei Shimei zenshū*, ed. by Yoichi Kōno and Mitsuo Nakamura, 9 vols (Tokyo: Iwanami Shoten, 1964–65), V (1965), pp. 173–77 (p. 174). I have used the English translation of this passage provided by Marleigh Grayer Ryan in her *Japan's First Modern Novel: Ukigumo of Futabatei Shimei* (New York and London: Columbia University Press, 1967), p. 120. This talk was addressed to the reading public, and it was published in the journal *Seikō* (*Success*) in 1906. Futabatei was interviewed among many other cultural celebrities, as he had begun producing many more translations in 1904 after the Russo-Japanese war broke out.

of the sentence, four of the five sentences quoted above end with *-ta*. The two underlined sentences in the passage quoted above clearly show the narrator's retrospective point of view:

> (A) Aki kugatsu chūjun to iu koro, hitohi **jibun** ga saru kaba no hayashi no naka ni zashite ita koto ga **atta**. [...] **Jibun** wa zashite shikoshite, soshite **mimi o katamukete ita**.
>
> (In autumn, around the middle of September, there **was** a day when **I** sat in a birch grove. [...] (B) **I** sat, looked around and **listened**.)

By using the first-person pronoun ***jibun*** (I) and the *-ta* endings: *at**ta*** (was) and *mimi o katamukete **ita*** (listened), Futabatei successfully reproduces Turgenev's retrospective narrative point of view. Futabatei's innovation is evident when we compare the colloquial *genbun-itchi* narrative style he created with the *kanbun kundoku* narrative style found in a translation made only five years earlier in 1883, *A Mysterious Story in Russia: The Story of a Flowery Heart Written by a Butterfly* (*Rokoku kibun: Kashin chōshi roku*). One would never guess from the title that this was a translation of Aleksandr Pushkin's *The Captain's Daughter* (*Kapitanskaia dochka*, 1836) and also the very first Japanese translation of a work of Russian literature. The translator, Takasu Jisuke (1859–1909), studied Russian at the same college as Futabatei.[10] However, Takasu changed the original first-person narrative into a third-person narrative. He also changed the main characters' names into English names, and his translation style contains a high degree of embellishment, identified by Antoine Berman as a deforming force causing inaccuracy in the translated text.[11]

> The mountains **are** winding endlessly like a flying dragon, and trees and plants **grow** thick to reach the valley. Although there **are** some wastelands covered with weeds, thorns **grow** everywhere and only a few paths **are** seen for the woodcutters. These **are** places for foxes and badgers to live, and for wild dogs and wolves to howl. Here we **find** a small village in the northern part of Russia called Siberia, and it is the most remote and poor place.[12]

---

10 Both Takasu and Futabatei studied Russian at the government institute *Tokyo Gaikokugo Gakkō* (Tokyo School of Foreign Languages). It offered six languages: English, French, German, Russian, Chinese, and Korean. Courses were usually completed in three to four years, and all subjects were taught in the language offered. Futabatei left the college several months before the graduation, as he opposed the amalgamation of the Russian department with the Tokyo School of Commerce.

11 Antoine Berman, 'Translation and the Trials of the Foreign', trans. by Lawrence Venuti, in *The Translation Studies Reader*, ed. by Lawrence Venuti, 2nd edn (London: Routledge, 2004), pp. 284–97 (p. 290).

12 A. S. Pushkin, *Rokoku kibun: Kashin chōshi roku* (*The Captain's Daughter*), trans. by Takasu Jisuke, in *Hon'yaku shōsetsu shū 2* (*The Selection of Translated Novels 2*); *Shin*

Takasu sets the story deep in the mountains, though no such mountains appear in Pushkin's original. He adds a stereotypical description of the place where the protagonist lives to produce an adaptation. His description has a grandeur reminiscent of Chinese scenery. Futabatei, on the other hand, painstakingly reproduced Turgenev's description of a Russian birch grove. The most obvious difference in the two descriptions of scenery is the choice of verb forms employed in each of them. The sentences in Takasu's *kanbun kundoku* style often end with the dictionary forms of verbs and auxiliary verbs, which are non-specific in regard to tense. In Futabatei's *genbun-itchi* style most sentences end with *-ta*. The emergence of *-ta* as a past tense marker creates a massive shift in narrative style. The Japanese grammarian Ōno Susumu explains it as follows:

> The modern Japanese auxiliary verb *-ta* [referred to in this chapter as the *-ta* ending] is nowadays used to express the meanings of both the past and the perfective, though it originally derived from the classic auxiliary verb *-tari*, which was used to express the perfective. This classic auxiliary verb *-tari* took the place of the other two auxiliary verbs *-ki* and *-keri*, and it has incorporated their meanings. Whereas *-ki* was used when one had a clear memory of the past, *-keri* was used when one became aware of things that had belonged to an unknown past. Thus *-keri* was often used in folklore as a marker for fiction.[13]

While the classic auxiliary verbs *tari* and *ri*, expressing the meaning of the perfective aspect, are often employed in the *kanbun kundoku* style, the classic auxiliary verbs *ki* and *keri*, expressing the meaning of the past tense, are hardly ever used. A story written in *kanbun kundoku* style is related as an incident unfolding before the readers' eyes, but Turgenev's story is related by a narrator-protagonist with a firm retrospective point of view and this viewpoint is reinforced by the consistent use of the past tense verbs. To reproduce these past tense Russian verbs, Futabatei consistently employed *-ta* auxiliary verbs, which were originally used to express the perfective aspect. The Japanese Slavist Kimura Shōichi praised Futabatei's debut translations 'The Tryst' and 'A Chance Encounter' for their loyal rendition of Turgenev's originals. He praised Futabatei's consistent use of *-ta* auxiliary verbs, writing that "Futabatei bravely used past tense form verbs consistently, despite the risk of creating monotony

---

nihon koten bungaku taikei: Meiji hen (*New Japanese Classic Literature Series during the Meiji Era*), ed. by Mitsutoshi Nakano, Shinsuke Togawa and others, 30 vols (Tokyo: Iwanami Shoten, 2001–13), xv (2002), pp. 291–348 (p. 295). Takasu's original text is as follows:
山脈蟠蜿万里似ニ亘リ　林樹蓊蔚幽谷ニ連リ　蕪蕪タル荒原アリト雖ドモ　荊棘、地ニ蔓シテ纔カニ樵蹊ヲ通ジ　狐狸ノ居ル処、豺狼ノ叫ブ処　此ハ是レ露国ノ北部即チシビリヤ地方ノ一村落ニシテ最モ寒陋僻鄙ノ境ナリ

13 Ōno Susumu, *Nihongo no bunpō o kangaeru* (*An Examination of Japanese Grammar*) (Tokyo: Iwanami Shoten, 1978), p. 129 and pp. 140–42.

in the narrative".[14] However, when Futabatei produced these translations, there was no past tense verb form in the colloquial Japanese language, so Futabatei's use of *-ta* auxiliary verbs as a past tense marker was a significant innovation occasioned by the act of translation. This is what can happen when a translator uses a foreignising translation method.

In *The Translator's Invisibility* (1955), Lawrence Venuti advocated for a foreignising translation method to overcome the Anglo-American translators' invisibility. Venuti cites the German theologian and philosopher Friedrich Schleiermacher's argument that only two translation methods exist. Either the translator leaves the author in peace as much as possible and moves the reader towards him; or he leaves the reader in peace and moves the author towards him. Venuti explains Schleiermacher's definition of these two opposing translation methods as follows:

> Schleiermacher allowed the translator to choose between a domesticating method, an ethnocentric reduction of the foreign text to target-cultural values, bringing the author back home, and a foreignizing method, an ethnodeviant pressure on those values to register the linguistic and cultural difference of the foreign text, sending the reader abroad.[15]

Futabatei's 'The Tryst' thus employed a foreignising strategy: he left Turgenev in peace and moved the Japanese reader towards him. As a result, the reader encountered an unprecedented colloquial narrative style that registered the linguistic difference of the Russian text through the novel use of *-ta* endings. However, the new translation style created by Futabatei in 'The Tryst' challenged his readers' relative ignorance. When 'The Tryst' was published, literary critics could not appreciate the new colloquial *genbun-ichi* narrative style; they criticised it as verbose, when it was, in fact, a loyal rendition of Turgenev's original. Some critics ridiculed the way that so many of his sentences ended in *-ta*. Bewildered by the readers' ignorant response, Futabatei suspended his literary activity for nearly eight years. Then, in 1896, he published revised versions of 'The Tryst' and 'A Chance Encounter' to break his literary silence. The most significant change in his revised versions was a reduction in the number of *-ta* endings. To break the monotony caused by the consistent use of *-ta* endings in the first versions, Futabatei changed some *-ta* endings to non-*ta* (mostly *-(r)u*) endings. Most *-ta* endings used to translate past tense imperfective verbs in the originals were changed to *-(r)u* endings, while *-ta* endings employed to translate past tense perfective verbs in the originals were left as they were. As a result, most

14 Kimura Shōichi, 'Futabatei no Tsurugēnefu mono no hon'yaku ni tsuite ('On Futabatei's Translations of Turgenev's Works'), *Bungaku* (*Literature*), (1956), 41–49 (p. 44).

15 Lawrence Venuti, *The Translator's Invisibility* (London and New York: Routledge, 1995), pp. 19–20.

-ta endings that remained in the revised versions conveyed a perfective aspect.[16] Futabatei continued to apply this method when translating Russian verbs until the end of his translation career, and the use of *-ta* endings for all past tense verbs in the first version of 'The Tryst' was buried and forgotten until younger writers of the naturalist school rediscovered it soon after the publication of the second version of 'The Tryst'.

The Emergence of the Third-person Pronouns *kare* (he) and *kanojo* (she) in Japanese Literary Works, In Spite of Futabatei's Apparent Aversion to Them

Considering all the effort Futabatei put into 'The Tryst' to create a new colloquial *genbun-itchi* narrative style, and how meticulous he was in translating Turgenev's original, it is rather puzzling that Futabatei did not directly translate any of the third-person pronouns found in the original. Although Futabatei translated the first-person pronoun 'I' (*ia*) used by the sportsman narrator, using the Japanese first-person pronoun *jibun* (I), the third-person pronouns 'he' (*on*) and 'she' (*ona*) referring to the arrogant servant and the hapless peasant girl are generally substituted either with their names (Viktor and Akulina become *Bikutoru* and *Akūrina*) or with the nouns *otoko* (a man) and *musume* (a girl). In the first version, Futabatei mostly relied on the personal names *Bikutoru* and *Akūrina*, while in the second version he primarily used the nouns *otoko* and *musume*. As a result, there is a greater emotional distance from the characters in the second version of 'The Tryst', as the personal names are mostly eliminated. We should note that in both versions Futabatei often consciously omitted to translate first- and third-person pronouns, especially when they are possessive pronouns. Futabatei adopted the same approach to the translation of third-person pronouns in 'A Chance Encounter' as he had already applied in 'The Tryst'. Turgenev's 'Three Meetings' ('Tri vstrechi'), the source for this text, is also written as a first-person narrative in which a sportsman recalls an inexplicable experience. By a strange twist of fate, he witnesses three encounters between a beautiful stranger (*neznakomka*) and a handsome man: one encounter in Italy and two in Russia. Finally, the narrator meets the mysterious woman at a masquerade and learns that she has been betrayed and abandoned by the handsome man. In 'A Chance Encounter' Futabatei again frequently employs the first-person pronoun '*jibun*' ('I') to translate the first-person pronoun 'I' ('*ia*') referring to the narrator; but he does

16 For a detailed examination of *-ta* forms in the two versions of 'The Tryst' and 'A Chance Encounter', see Hiroko Cockerill, *Style and Narrative in Translations: The Contribution of Futabatei Shimei* (Manchester: St. Jerome, 2006), pp. 30–72; and also my *Futabatei Shimei no Roshiago Hon'yaku* (*Futabatei's Translations from Russian*) (Tokyo: Hōsei University Press, 2015), pp. 17–49.

not directly translate the third-person pronouns 'she' (*'ona'*) and 'he' (*'on'*) referring to the beautiful stranger and her lover. These third-person pronouns are rendered by employing the nouns *'fujin'* ('a lady') and *'otoko'* ('a man') in the first version, and by *'onna'* ('a woman') and *'otoko'* ('a man') in the second version. In the original story, the couple whose encounters are witnessed by the narrator are presented as strangers, and the beautiful woman is indicated by the third-person pronoun 'she' (*'ona'*) throughout the story. Futabatei could not have failed to notice the use of third-person pronouns in Turgenev's original, especially the regular use of the female third-person pronoun 'she' (*'ona'*). Futabatei was thus confronted by a pressing need to find Japanese third-person pronouns equivalent to the Russian third-person pronouns, particularly 'she' (*'ona'*).

By the time Futabatei first translated 'A Chance Encounter' in 1888, many Japanese writers, including Futabatei himself, would already have been familiar with the male and female Japanese third-person pronouns *kare* ('he') and *kanojo* ('she'), through various grammar books describing Western foreign languages.[17] Another third-person pronoun widely employed in literary works at that time was the neutral *kare,* which could denote both male and female persons. Chongbo Li has charted the emergence of the Japanese third-person pronoun *kare*. He explains that *kare,* which is widely employed today as a male third-person pronoun, used to be a demonstrative pronoun. The first use of *kare* as a third-person pronoun was found in *Esopo no fables,* the Japanese translation of *Aesop's Fables,* in 1593. During the Edo period *kare* was frequently found in *yomihon* (books for reading) or *tsūzokumono* (popular books) which were translations or adaptations of colloquial Chinese novels. In the early Meiji period, *kare* was used as the third-person pronoun in *rakugo* (Japanese traditional comic storytelling) but these instances were rather rare.[18] *Kare* also continued to be used as a third-person pronoun in translations made in the *kanbun kundoku* style during the early Meiji period. For example, in *A Mysterious Story in Russia: The Story of a Flowery Heart Written by a Butterfly*, the translation of Pushkin's *The Captain's Daughter* quoted earlier, Takasu uses *kare* quite frequently. Another translator who often employed *kare* was Morita Shiken (1861–97), who created a meticulous *kanbun kundoku* translation style known as the *shūmitsu* (exhaustive) or word-for-word translation style. Yanagida Izumi, who made a comprehensive study of Japanese translation history during the Meiji era, considers that this *shūmitsu kanbun kundoku* style was the basis for Futabatei's colloquial *genbun-ichi* translation style found in 'The Tryst' and 'A Chance Encounter', pointing out

17 Yanabu Akira, *Hon'yakugo seiritsu jijō* [*Circumstances Surrounding the Establishment of Words Created by Translation*] (Tokyo: Iwanami Shoten, 1982), pp. 195–96.

18 Chongbo Li, '*"Kare" no goshi to sono shūhen: San'ninshō daimeishi ga seiritsu suru made no michisuji* (*The History of Japanese "kare" and its Related Phenomena: Up to the Establishment of the Third-person Pronoun*), *Dynamis*, 4 (2000), 1–33 (pp. 16–26).

that Futabatei was a keen reader of Morita's translations.[19] However, the fact that *kare* was used in the *kanbun kundoku* style may be the very reason that Futabatei did not use it himself. In a talk entitled 'Yo ga genbun itchi no yurai' ('The Origin of my *Genbun-itchi* Style'), Futabatei famously declared that he excluded any Chinese word that had not fully entered Japanese lexis from his colloquial *genbun-itchi* style.[20] When Futabatei made his debut translations, the third-person pronoun *kare* was a word used mainly in the *kanbun kundoku* style and was not fully recognised as Japanese. More than one Chinese character was used to denote *kare*. As well as 彼, which is widely used today, 渠 and 他 could denote male and female characters in the translations of Chinese literary works. While Takasu used 彼 and 他 in *A Mysterious Story in Russia: The Story of a Flowery Heart Written by a Butterfly*, Morita used 渠 in his translations. A careful reading of the two versions of 'A Chance Encounter' reveals that Futabatei uses *kare* only once, to denote the emancipated serf Luk'ianich, during a passage of dialogue. He used the Chinese character 彼 once in both versions, but the original Russian word is not 'he' (*on*) but 'that' (*eto*) and the reading Futabatei gives for it is not *kare* (he) but *are* (that). In this way, he avoided using the third-person pronoun *kare* in both versions of 'A Chance Encounter'. As for the female third-person pronoun *kanojo* (she), Futabatei did not use it at all in the first version of 'A Chance Encounter', and in the second version he uses the Chinese characters 彼女 (which today are read as *kanojo*) just once to denote the beautiful stranger, but the reading he gives them is *ano onna* (that woman). In this way, Futabatei completely avoided using third-person pronouns in his debut translations, even when it appeared that he could not escape using the third-person pronoun *kanojo* (she) if he was to translate the story accurately. So, who did initiate the use of the female third-person pronoun *kanojo* (she) in Japan, if not Futabatei? Surprisingly, the first instances of the Japanese third-person pronoun *kanojo*, as presented in various grammar books, were found not in translations but in literary works. The very first instance was detected in *The Character of Modern Students* (*Tōsei shosei katagi*, 1885–1886) written by Tsubouchi Shōyō (1859–1935), who was Futabatei's mentor in the late 1880s, when the latter was writing his novel *The Drifting Cloud*. Tsubouchi was a literary theorist who studied English literature and advocated realism in Japanese writing. *The Character of Modern Students* implemented Tsubouchi's own theory, and was published two years before Part One of *The Drifting Cloud* came out, in 1885. Subsequently Saganoya Omuro (1863–1947), who was Futabatei's friend and studied Russian in the

19 Yanagida Izumi, 'Meiji no hon'yaku bungaku kenkyū' ('A Study of Literary Translations during the Meiji Era'), in Yanagida Izumi, Hideo Nagata, Shōō Matsui, and others, *Nihon bungaku kōza* (*Lectures on Japanese Literature*), ed. by Giryō Satō, 15 vols (Tokyo: Shinchōsha, 1931–32), XII (1931), pp. 1–98 (p. 68).

20 Futabatei Shimei, '*Yo ga genbun-itchi no yurai*' in *Futabatei Shimei zenshū*, ed. by Kōno and Nakamura, 9 vols (Tokyo: Iwanami Shoten, 1964–65), V (1965), pp. 170–72 (p. 171).

same class, used *kanojo* in his novel *A Chrysanthemum at the End of a Field* (*Nozue no kiku*, 1889). However, neither Tsubouchi nor Saganoya made extensive use of the innovative word *kanojo*, with only one instance of the word in each work, and when Tsubouchi used it, he was hinting that the person in question was a prostitute. Okumura Tsuneya, who conducted thorough research into the establishment of the third-person pronouns *kare*, *kanojo* and *karera* ('they') during the early Meiji period, concluded that Saganoya introduced the use of *kanojo* into the works written in the *genbun-itchi* style but could not sustain its use.[21] During the period when Futabatei had suspended his literary activities (1889 to 1896), a new literary group emerged called *Ken'yūsha* ('Friends of the Ink Stone'), led by Ozaki Kōyō (1867–1903). They opposed the *genbun-itchi* movement and insisted on employing a classical style in narrative prose. Izumi Kyōka (1873–1939), a prominent member of this group, often selected mysterious and supernatural subjects for his stories. Izumi admired Morita's translations, and his classic style resembled Morita's *kanbun kundoku shūmitsu* style. He frequently employed *kare* in his stories (denoted by the Chinese character 渠) to refer to both male and female characters. In 1896, when Izumi was at his most popular, his former teacher Ozaki, who had stubbornly opposed the *genbun-ichi* movement, unexpectedly published his colloquial *genbun-itchi* novel *Tears and Regrets* (*Tajō takon*). Ozaki wrote the novel after being deeply impressed by a reading of *The Tale of Genji* (*Genji monogatari*, written in the early eleventh century by Murasaki Shikibu, who served as a lady-in-waiting to Empress Shōshi). *Genji* depicts a man grieving over the death of his beloved wife in a style close to a third-person narrative. In his own novel, Ozaki employed both the third-person pronoun *kare* and *-ta* endings, implying past tense, to express the omniscient narrator's voice. Ozaki also changed the Chinese character for *kare* from 渠 to 彼. Although the use of *-ta* endings was not as consistent as it needed to be, and the third-person pronoun *kare* referred not only to the heartbroken protagonist but also to other central male and female characters, Ozaki initiated a third-person narrative using the third-person pronoun *kare* together with a limited number of *-ta* endings carrying the meaning of the past tense. In the same year that Ozaki published his *genbun-itchi* novel *Tears and Regrets*, Futabatei added to his revised versions of 'The Tryst' and 'A Chance

21 Okumura Tsuneya, 'Daimeishi "kare, kanojo, karera" no kōsatsu: Sono seiritsu to bungo kōgo ('The Third-person Pronouns "he, she, and they": Their Establishment in Written and Spoken Languages'), *Kokugo Kokubun* (*National Language and National Literature*), 23 (1954), 63–78 (pp. 66–68). Hirota Eitarō has observed that the first instance of *kanojo* used in translations is found in *Bairai yokun* (*The Peach Buds and their Fragrance*) trans. By Ushiyama Kakudō from Walter Scott's *Ivanhoe* (1819). This translation was published in 1886, a year after the publication of Shōyō's *The Character of Modern Students*. See Ida Yoshiharu's article 'Yakugo "kanojo" no shutsugen to Sōseki no buntai ('The Emergence of the Translated Word "kanojo" and Sōseki's Writing Style'), *Eigakushi Kenkyū* (*History of English Studies*), 1 (1969), 68–78 (p. 68).

Encounter' the short novel *One-sided Love* (*Katakoi*), a translation of Turgenev's *Asya* (*Asia*, 1858). Young poets and Japanese naturalist writers such as Kunikida Doppo (1871–1908), Tayama Katai (1871–1930), and Shimazaki Tōson (1872–1943) were greatly impressed by Futabatei's translations of Turgenev's works. 'The Tryst' made such a strong impression on young writers that many of them referenced sentences from it, some quoting directly, and others writing similar sentences in their works.[22] Kunikida, in his early work *Musashino* (published in 1898, only two years after the publication of the revised versions of 'The Tryst' and 'A Chance Encounter'),[23] wrote the following sentence: "*Hayashi no oku ni zashite shikoshi, keichōshi, teishishi, mokusōsu*" ("I sit in the grove, look around, listen, cast my eyes down, and contemplate"). Kunikida was imitating the following sentence in 'The Tryst': "*Jibun wa zashite shikoshite, soshite mimi o katamukete ita*" ("I sat, looked around and listened"). What is surprising here is that the sentence imitated by Kunikida is taken not from the second version, just published, but from the first version, published ten years earlier. What is more, not only Kunikida, but all the other young naturalist writers described the strong impression that the first version of 'The Tryst' had made upon them. They felt the first-person narrator's voice more acutely in the first version.[24] Tayama and Shimazaki were the most enthusiastic readers of Futabatei's translations of Turgenev's works. They went on to read other translations Futabatei had made from Turgenev's originals. Then they too began writing original prose. The works by which they are remembered, including Shimazaki's *Spring* (*Haru*, 1908)[25] and Tayama's *The Quilt* (*Futon*, 1907) were written in near perfect third-person narrative with frequent use of the third-person pronouns *kare* and *kanojo* and consistent use of *-ta* endings.[26] Although the percentage of *-ta* endings found in their narratives did not exceed ninety percent, as in Futabatei's first version of 'The Tryst', almost seventy percent of their sentences ended with *-ta*. The third-person pronouns *kare* and *kanojo* were used to indicate

22 See Momiuchi Yūko, *Nihon kindai bungaku to 'Ryōjin nikki'* (*Japanese Modern Novels and 'A Sportsman's Sketches'*) (Tokyo: Suiseisha, 2006), pp. 343–47.

23 *Musashino* is the name of a district of Tokyo.

24 The poet Kanbara Ariake (1876–1952) recalled reading the first version of 'The Tryst' in these words: "Futabatei's *genbun-itchi* style, with its masterly use of colloquial language—that unique style—sounded so fresh, its echoes seemed to go on whispering endlessly in my ears. A nameless joy filled me. At the same time, I was so moved that something deep within me almost wanted to shout out. I just did not want to be spoken to so intimately." Ariake Kanbara, '"Aibiki" ni tsuite' ('About "The Tryst"'), cited in *Futabatei Shimei zenshū*, ed. by Kōno and Nakamura, I (1964), pp. 413–14 (p. 413).

25 Tōson began using *-ta* endings in *The Broken Commandment* (*Hakai*, 1906), though he employed only a few instances of third-person pronouns in the work.

26 A futon can mean either a quilt or a thin mattress. This is the first of a number of first-person confessional novels known as I-novels. The protagonist of *The Quilt* (modelled on Tayama himself) weeps into the futon used by his female disciple, after she rejects him.

all male and female characters respectively. Whereas Shimazaki used the relatively innovative Chinese character 彼 for *kare*, following Ozaki, Tayama used the rather old-fashioned Chinese character 渠. Both writers employed 彼女 for *kanojo*. The only deviation from the usual third-person narrative in *The Quilt* was that Tayama introduced the protagonist of the story using the third-person pronoun *kare*. Tayama initiated a distinctive use of the third-person pronoun *kare* to indicate a specific character, differing from the usage of third-person pronouns in Western novels.

Establishing a Distinctive Japanese Translation Style: Nakamura's Translation of *Crime and Punishment*

Futabatei ended his career as a translator when he departed for Russia as a foreign correspondent for the *Asahi Shinbun* newspaper in June 1908. Unfortunately, he fell seriously ill with pneumonia in St Petersburg and died on his return voyage to Japan in the following year. Although Futabatei had introduced works by major Russian writers such as Nikolai Gogol, Turgenev, and Lev Tolstoy into Japanese, he never translated anything by Dostoevsky.[27] The first Japanese person to translate Dostoevsky directly from Russian was the pioneering female translator Senuma Kayō (1875–1915).[28] She translated the diary of the female protagonist Varvara from Dostoevsky's debut novel *Poor Folk* (*Bednye liudi*, 1846), published in 1904 as a short story entitled 'A Poor Girl' ('Mazushiki shōjo'). Her translation style attempts to reproduce Dostoevsky's original accurately, but it occasionally deviates from this, especially when she translates the climactic scene, in which Varvara's first love, Pokrovskii, is dying. Her style is excessively emotional and verbose, almost pseudo-classical. Senuma was a disciple of Ozaki Kōyō, who had initially opposed the *genbun-itchi* movement before creating a third-person narrative form that incorporated the third person-pronoun *kare*

27 Futabatei translated nine works by Turgenev, five by Maksim Gorky, three by Gogol, two by Vsevolod Garshin, and one work each by Tolstoy, Leonid Andreev, and Ignatii Potapenko. He translated mostly short stories and novellas, and his translation of the novel *Smoke* (*Dym*, 1867) was left incomplete. Futabatei's most representative translations are *Rudin* by Turgenev (published in 1897), 'The Portrait' ('Portret', 1897) by Gogol, 'The Woodfelling' ('Rubka lesa', 1904) by Tolstoy, and *Melancholy* (*Toska*) by Gorky (published in 1906), with all dates referring to the Japanese translations.

28 The very first Japanese translation of Dostoevsky was Uchida Roan's partial translation of *Crime and Punishment* (*Tsumi to batsu*) from English. Uchida Roan (1868–1929), who was a close friend of Futabatei, read the English translation of *Crime and Punishment* with such enthusiasm that he was inspired to translate it. With Futabatei's help, Roan managed to translate the first half of the novel, which he published in 1892, but his translation remained unfinished.

and *-ta* endings indicating the past tense. Although Senuma did not pay much attention to the verb forms in the Russian original, she closely monitored the use of the third-person pronouns. She used the Chinese character 彼 to translate he (*on*), and the Chinese characters 彼女 to translate she (*ona*) with both彼 and 彼女 being read as *kare*. This use of third-person pronouns gave her translation a new style. Senuma next focused intensely on translating works by Anton Chekhov. At the same time, Nobori Shomu (1878–1958) began publishing his translations of works by old and new Russian writers such as Pushkin, Turgenev, Konstantin Bal'mont, Boris Zaitsev, Aleksandr Kuprin, Fedor Sologub, and Leonid Andreev. He produced three translation anthologies in 1908, 1910, and 1912 successively.[29] His translations were received enthusiastically by emerging Japanese writers, who regarded him as having ushered in a 'Shomu period' in the history of Japanese literary translation. Why did his translation style make such an impression on young writers? Nobori's predominant use of non-*ta* sentence endings was similar to Futabatei's usage following the 1896 revision of the debut translations, so that was not really an innovation. What probably most impressed young writers about Nobori's translations was this use of the third-person pronouns *kare* and *kanojo*. Nobori was the very first literary translator from Russian to Japanese to employ *kare* and *kanojo* in the same way as they are used in the present day. In his translations *kare* was used to translate he (*on*) and *kanojo* was used to translate she (*ona*), and the Chinese characters used for them were 彼 and 彼女 respectively. (Senuma had used the same Chinese characters, but imposed the same reading, *kare*, on both male and female characters.) In 1914, three Japanese translations of novels by Dostoevsky were published by the Shinchōsha publishing house as part of their paperback series (*Shinchō bunko*, 'the Shinchō paperback'), following the precedent of the German Reclam editions with their famous yellow Universal-Bibliothek paperbacks, launched in 1867. By selling the books in paperback form for the first time, Shinchōsha was able to provide Japanese readers with a wide range of foreign books translated directly from the original. Perhaps one of the reasons Futabatei did not translate Dostoevsky may have been the sheer length of the latter's novels. Futabatei and his publishers may have considered that long translations would not be accommodated by the book market at that time. One of the three 1914 translations of Dostoevsky's works for this paperback series was *The Humiliated and Insulted* (*Unizhennye i oskorblennye*, 1861) translated by Shomu under the title *The Humiliated People* (*Shiitagerareshi hitobito*). The other two translations

29 Nobori's first translation collection was *The White Night Anthology* (*Byakuya-shū*) which includes translations of works by Turgenev, Pushkin and Chekhov. His second anthology, entitled *Six Writers Anthology* (*Rokunin-shū*), includes the translations of the works by contemporary Russian writers such as Zaitsev, Kuprin, and Andreev, and his third anthology takes its name from a work by Sologub: *The Poisoned Garden* (*Doku no son*). It includes translations from Sologub, Bal'mont and Mikhail Artsybashev.

were of *Crime and Punishment* (*Prestuplenie i nakazanie*, 1866) and *The Idiot* (*Idiot*, 1868–69). The former was translated by Nakamura under the title *Crime and Punishment* (*Tsumi to Batsu*), and the latter was translated by Yonekawa Masao (1891–1965) under the title *Idiot* (*Hakuchi*). Both translators had graduated from the Tokyo School of Foreign Studies, where Futabatei had both studied and taught Russian. As new graduates, they worked hard on their translations and Nakamura even made a preliminary translation of *The Humiliated and Insulted* for Nobori, who was pressed for time.[30] Nakamura and Yonekawa both became prominent Russian translators and enjoyed long careers. Nakamura produced translations of Tolstoy's complete works, while Yonekawa translated Dostoevsky's complete works. After establishing himself as a renowned Russian translator, Nakamura commented on his translation method as follows:

> When we engage in literary translation, we must pay more attention to the style of the work than to its content. That is, it is more significant to pay attention to the way we translate than to what we translate. [...] We should not allow ourselves to freely change expressions in the original according to our own interpretation or understanding. For example, Dostoevsky is often criticized for his verbose and lengthy sentences. Is it right for a translator to cut short Dostoevsky's long sentences, or to cut them out completely, following his own judgement? I find great value in Dostoevsky's seemingly verbose long sentences. Without his lengthy and verbose style, Dostoevsky would not have achieved his artistic goal.[31]

Nakamura's translation method was almost identical with that of Futabatei. Both placed the original's style ahead of conveying its meaning, and both tried to reproduce the 'foreignness' of the text. In the opening two paragraphs of *Crime and Punishment*, Nakamura employed the same number of full stops (six out of six full stops are reproduced) and almost the same number of commas as Dostoevsky (seventeen out of eighteen commas are reproduced, though used in slightly different places). The punctuation marks mirrored the use in the original even more closely than in Futabatei's first version of 'The Tryst'. Nakamura meticulously reproduced the past tense form verbs in Dostoevsky's original employing *-ta* endings, just as Futabatei did in his debut translation. What is more, Nakamura carefully rendered the third-person pronouns found in the original using the third-person pronouns *kare* (彼) and *kanojo* (彼女). The number of such pronouns used in the two opening paragraphs of Nakamura's

30 Nakamura Hakuyō, *Koko made ikite: Watashi no hachijūnen* (*I Have Made It This Far: My Life of Eighty Years*) (Tokyo: Kawade Shobō Shinsha, 1971), pp. 174–75.

31 Nakamura Hakuyō, 'Hon'yakubun no hyōgen to shidō' ('Expressions and Guidance for Translated Sentences'), in *Nihon no hon'yakuron: Ansorojī to kaidai* (*Japanese Discourse on Translation: An Anthology with Commentary*), ed. by Yanabu Akira and Mizuno Akira (Tokyo: Hōsei University Press, 2010), pp. 267–77 (p. 268).

translation even exceeded those found in the original by one. Nakamura might have wanted to emphasise the third-person narrative form of the original, which Dostoevsky initially wrote as a first-person narrative. As a result, the third-person narrative in Dostoevsky's original was successfully conveyed in Nakamura's translation by the latter's consistent use of *-ta* endings indicating the past tense and the frequent use of third-person pronouns *kare* and *kanojo*. This was what Nakamura's foreignising method achieved.[32] By the time Nakamura had established this translation style, Japanese writers had already started using *kare* and *kanojo* at their own discretion. Nakamura, however, played a crucial role in paving the way for a distinctive Japanese translation style that made consistent use of *-ta* endings and the third-person pronouns *kare* and *kanojo*.

A Distinctive Translation Style in the Melting Pot of Japanese Literature

While the style developed by Nakamura became standard for Japanese translations, many Japanese writers kept experimenting with various narrative styles. When Futabatei produced two alternative versions of Turgenev's short stories, he unintentionally showed Japanese writers two narrative possibilities: one with the consistent use of *-ta* past tense endings and the other with mixed *-ta* and non-*ta* endings. Futabatei had also demonstrated that it is possible for Japanese writers not to employ third-person pronouns in their narratives, and thus it became optional for Japanese writers to do so. As a result, Japanese writers developed various narrative styles both with and without third-person pronouns, and with and without consistent *-ta* past tense endings. Perhaps we may divide Japanese writers into two groups: those who are/were conscious of the use of *-ta* endings and the third-person pronouns in their narratives and those who are/were not conscious of these things. I shall examine four representative Japanese writers who were highly aware of the effect brought by the frequent use of *-ta* endings and the third-person pronouns in their narratives: Natsume Sōseki (1867–1916), Akutagawa Ryūnosuke (1892–1927), Ōe Kenzaburō (1935–2023), and Murakami Haruki (b. 1949).

Natsume was a contemporary of Futabatei's. They both worked for the *Asahi Shinbun* newspaper, where their work was meant to be serially published (in turn). Due to Futabatei's sudden death, this plan was realised only once. When Natsume heard of Futabatei's death, he famously commented that Futabatei

32 Regarding Nakamura's translation of *Crime and Punishment*, please see my articles on this topic: 'Four Translations of *Crime and Punishment*', *The Dostoevsky Journal*, 8–9 (2007–2008), 53–62, and 'Stylistic Choices in the Japanese Translations of *Crime and Punishment*', in *The Palgrave Handbook of Literary Translation*, ed. by Jean Boase-Beier, Lina Fisher and Hiroko Furukawa (Cham, Switzerland: Palgrave, 2018), pp. 63–81.

had a clear idea of what he needed to do next in his literary activities.[33] By saying "a clear idea" Natsume may have hinted that Futabatei wished to write an authentic third-person narrative story in Japanese, and that Natsume would inherit his colleague's legacy. In fact, Natsume did not use any third-person pronouns in his early works, and the narratives of these early works were written in a mixture of *-ta* and non-*ta* endings, with non-*ta* endings predominating. It was in his novel *And Then* (*Sorekara*, 1909) that he began frequently using the third-person pronoun *kare,* together with predominant *-ta* endings.[34] He made regular and effective use of the third-person pronoun *kare* in his first-person narrative novel *The Heart* (*Kokoro*, 1914), the most widely-read modern Japanese novel in Japan. Here, Natsume examines the darkness within a man's heart. The protagonist confesses that he had betrayed his friend's trust, and caused his suicide, by marrying the girl whom the friend loved. Natsume uses the third-person pronoun *kare* mostly to refer to the protagonist's friend, called simply 'K'. In the protagonist's testament, the third-person pronoun *kare* serves to objectify his friend, allowing him to analyse his irreparable deed. Around this time, Natsume had begun reading Dostoevsky's novels, recommended to him by his mentee and future biographer, the novelist and translator Morita Sōhei (1881–1949).[35] Morita published translations of *Demons* (*Besy*, 1871–72) and *The Brothers Karamazov* (*Brat'ia Karamazovy*, 1879–80), made via English, in 1915. (The 1914 Dostoevsky translations by Nakamura and Yonekawa for Shinchō, mentioned above, were made directly from Russian.)

Natsume later wrote a fictionalised memoir, *Grass on the Wayside* (*Michikusa*, 1915). He openly revealed that he was analysing his own experience, while thoroughly objectifying that experience by employing *kare* to refer to himself, and by consistently using *-ta* endings which constituted the vast majority of all sentence endings in the book. In his final novel *Light and Darkness* (*Meian*, 1916), Natsume perfected the third-person narrative novel by employing the third-person pronouns *kare* and *kanojo* in reference to all characters without discrimination, and through his extremely consistent use of *-ta* endings (now the overwhelmingly dominant form). As a scholar of English literature, Natsume's literary theory was informed by his studies in England (he studied Shakespeare at UCL for two years). In his later novels, it is likely that he adopted the essential features of the Western third-person narrative form. However, it is also highly

33 Natsume Sōseki, 'Kanji no ii hito' ('A Pleasant Person'), in *Futabatei Shimei zenshū*, ed. by Shinsuke Tagawa, VIII (1993), pp. 294–95 (p. 295).

34 Kumakura Chiyuki, *Sōseki no takurami* (*Sōseki's Plot*) (Tokyo: Chikuma Shobō, 2006), pp. 275–79. Kumakura thoroughly researched the use of *-ta* endings in Sōseki's works and compiled a useful chart showing the percentage of *-ta* endings against all sentence endings. I have taken the percentages from this chart.

35 Morita recollected in his book *Natsume Sōseki Zoku* (*A Sequel to Natsume Sōseki*) (Tokyo: Kōchō Shorin, 1943), pp. 667–79, that he first recommended *Idiot* to Sōseki, and later, other works by Dostoevsky—presumably *Crime and Punishment*, *Demons* and *The Brothers Karamazov.*

possible that the translations made by Nakamura and Yonekawa influenced Natusme's decision to make such extensive use of third-person pronouns and *-ta* endings in his final novel.

One writer who inherited Natsume's literary legacy was Akutagawa Ryūnosuke, the former's most prominent disciple. Although Futabatei's name had gradually faded from young Japanese writers' memories, the translations made by Nobori were extremely popular among them, as I mentioned earlier. Akutagawa was one of those young writers who devotedly read Nobori's translations of various contemporary Russian writers. Acknowledging that he lacked an individual writing style, he may have tried to assimilate the many styles developed in Nobori's translations. Akutagawa's forte was the short story. He wrote short fiction with all sentences ending in *-ta*, and others with mixed *-ta* and non-*ta* sentence endings. Examples of the former are 'Princess Rokunomiya' ('Rokunomiya no himegimi', 1922) and 'Zenkaku sanbo' ('Zenkaku Sanbō', 1927). Akutagawa also wrote some short stories with no third-person pronouns. Such stories include 'The Nose' ('Hana', 1916), 'Hell Screen' ('Jigoku hen', 1918), 'The Death of a Disciple' ('Hōkyōnin no shi', 1918), 'Magic' ('Majutsu', 1919), and 'In a Bamboo Grove' ('Yabu no naka', 1922). Of these, 'The Nose' is the only story written from a third-person narrative point of view, though it has no third-person pronouns and uses a mix of *-ta* and non *-ta* sentence endings. Due to the obvious resemblance of the title and the theme of disappearance and reappearance of an unusually long nose, many critics have determinedly attempted to identify the influence of Gogol's 'The Nose' ('Nos') over the creation of Akutagawa's 'The Nose'. Wada Yoshihide has discovered that Akutagawa only read Gogol's work after completing his own short story. Akutagawa was thus more likely to have been influenced by Nobori's other translations.[36] Indeed, Akutagawa ingeniously exercised the four possible styles unconsciously suggested by Futabatei's works. It is no surprise that the literary prize named after Akutagawa Ryūnosuke later became the most prestigious literary prize in Japan for fiction by new writers.

Dostoevsky's influence upon Japanese writers became conspicuous during the Shōwa period (1926–89). Ōe Kenzaburō discussed the significance of Dostoevsky's works in twenty-first century Japan in his *In the Twenty-First Century, Dostoevsky is Coming* (*Nijūisseiki Dosutoefusukii ga yatte kuru*, 2007). Ōe, who considered Dostoevsky the most influential writer in the world, himself gained global status with the award of the Nobel Prize for Literature in 1994. He often wrote about political issues, structuring his narratives based on his childhood wartime experiences. His writing always uses third-person pronouns; having studied French literature at Tokyo University, Ōe was highly familiar with

36 Wada Yoshihide, *Roshia bungakusha Nobori Shomu and Akutagawa Ryūnosuke ronkō* (*Discussion on Russian Literary Scholars Nobori Shomu and Akutagawa Ryūnosuke*) (Osaka: Izumi Shoin, 2001), pp. 247–300.

Western literary style. He employed the Japanese third-person pronouns *kare* and *kanojo* just as third-person pronouns are used in Western literary works. In Ōe's works *kare* and *kanojo* never precede their antecedents, which are precisely articulated. Moreover, in his early story 'Unexpected Muteness' ('Fui no oshi', 1958), which describes the mysterious death of a Japanese interpreter working for the occupying American soldiers, Ōe replaced the Chinese character 彼 (*kare*) with the *hiragana* letters かれ (*kare*). Though Ōe retained the Chinese characters 彼女 for the female third-person pronoun *kanojo*, he consistently wrote *kare* (he) in *hiragana*. For Ōe the *hiragana* word かれ (*kare*/he) was no longer a foreign borrowing. For Ōe, his writing style emerged by itself as a requirement of his work and he did not have to invent a new style each time he initiated a new work.

Murakami Haruki may be the most frequently translated Japanese writer of all time. He has also translated many works by American writers into Japanese. Murakami has singled out three foreign novels which impressed him: F. Scott Fitzgerald's *The Great Gatsby* (1925), Raymond Chandler's *The Long Goodbye* (1953), and Dostoevsky's *The Brothers Karamazov*. Murakami has translated both American novels into Japanese, and he arguably adapts the detective element in *The Brothers Karamazov* in his own works. While many Japanese writers have admired Dostoevsky as a writer who portrays the deep mental struggles experienced by human beings, Murakami seems to be fascinated by the detective story aspect of Dostoevsky's fiction. Many of Murakami's stories involve elements from this genre, especially the need to solve a riddle. These are mostly first-person narratives, in which the narrator is denoted by the male first-person pronoun *boku* (I), and the other characters observed by the first-person narrator are usually signified by the third-person pronouns *kare* or *kanojo*. Murakami uses *kanojo* in his early works, where female characters are generally nameless and designated solely by that pronoun. As a writer and translator, Murakami does not arbitrarily deploy Japanese third-person pronouns. His use of the third-person pronoun *kanojo* to emphasise the anonymity and objectification of his female characters is intentional. This treatment of female characters changes when female anonymity becomes a focus in *The Wind-up Bird Chronicle* (*Nejimakidori kuronikuru*, 1994–95), his most successful detective story. Here, Murakami uses the third-person female pronoun *kanojo* masterfully in his opening, to refer to an enigmatic female stranger who phones the narrator protagonist, and who reappears throughout the novel. In the end, the protagonist realises that this woman is, in fact, his missing wife. Here the anonymity indicated by the third-person pronoun *kanojo* suddenly signifies the alienation that can exist in a close relationship. Murakami also experimented extensively in his novels with various sentence endings.

In retrospect, there was no standard literary style governing the use of third-person pronouns and *-ta* past tense endings through the course of the twentieth century. Third-person pronouns have been used more sparingly in original literary works than in translations. For the most part, Japanese writers employ a mixture of *-ta* and non-*ta* sentence endings in their narratives. As shown above, when Japanese writers do consistently use *-ta* past tense endings and combine this with frequent use of the third-person pronouns *kare* and *kanojo*, their narrative takes on a distinctive flavour, giving the text a 'foreign' feel, that is, achieving Schleiermacherian foreignisation.

Conclusion

Futabatei is mentioned in *Hon'yaku wa ikani su beki ka* (*How Translation Should Be Done*, 2000) by the renowned English-to-Japanese translator Yanase Naoki (1943–2016). In this work, Yanase quotes not only both versions of 'The Tryst', but also Futabatei's original work *The Mediocrity* (*Heibon*, 1907), noting the complete absence of third-person pronouns in all three. Yanase asserts that translators should refrain from the overt use of the third-person pronouns *kare* and *kanojo* in their works. He praises Futabatei's courage in deleting some *-ta* forms from the first version of 'The Tryst', and appears to advocate a domesticating strategy in Japanese translations.[37] Yanase's mentee Kōnosu Yukiko (b. 1963) practices the former's new translation norms of refrained use of third-person pronouns and mixed use of *-ta* and non-*ta* sentence endings in her translation of Andrew Miller's 1997 *Ingenious Pain* (*Kiyō na itami*, 2000).

A similar decline in the use of the third-person pronouns may be observed in new translations made from Russian. My own research reveals a gradual decline in the use of the third-person pronouns *kare* and *kanojo* in translations of Dostoevsky's *The Humiliated and Insulted*, *Crime and Punishment*, and *The Idiot* during the twentieth century, following Nakamura's establishment of a distinctive translation style.[38] Another feature of Nakamura's translation style—the frequent use of *-ta* past tense endings—proved remarkably stable during the latter half of the twentieth century. During the past two decades, translations of new Western literary works have struggled to gain popularity among Japanese readers. Many translations now sold in Japan are new translations of classic works. The Kōbunsha publishing house launched a new paperback series called *Koten shin'yaku bunko* ('New Translations of the Classics') in 2006, aiming to provide easy and readable translations of classics to young readers. When Kameyama Ikuo (b. 1949) published his new translation of *The Brothers Karamazov* as part of this series from 2006 to 2007, his five-volume translation sold more than a million copies in total. The publisher's strategy of placing readability above loyalty to the original appealed to young Japanese readers,

37 Yanase Naoki, *Hon'yaku wa ikani su beki ka* (*How Translation Should be Done*) (Tokyo: Iwanami Shoten, 2000), pp. 11–52.

38 See my 'Stylistic Choices', 63–81, and also Cockerill, *Futabatei Shimei no roshiago hon'yaku* (*Futabatei Shimei's Translation from Russian*), pp. 253–30.

drawing them back to Dostoevsky's forgotten classic. Kameyama made his translation more palatable by dividing long paragraphs and sentences into shorter ones, by increasing the font size, and, most importantly, by omitting many third-person pronouns. The translation norm has swung towards domestication in this regard. Though he retained the predominant use of *-ta* past tense endings, the number of third-person pronouns were cut to one-half or even one-third of those used in the original.

In summary, the narrative styles born of literary translations from Russian into Japanese have intertwined with mainstream Japanese literary styles over the course of the twentieth century. The predominant use of *-ta* endings invented by Futabatei to express the past tense has survived and become an established translation style, tending to foreignise the Japanese text. The third-person pronouns *kare* and *kanojo*, which Futabatei avoided, are growing less popular with translators, and are optional for writers of fiction. When they appear in Japanese writing, they foreignise it; Japanese people still consider *kare* and *kanojo* to be borrowed words which can even indicate a degree of disdain towards the person to whom they refer.

Kazakhstan

Abai Kunanbaiuly and Russian Culture: Changing Paradigms in Post-Soviet Kazakhstan

Sabina Amanbayeva[1]

Introduction

The connection of Abai Kunanbaiuly, the Kazakh poet and writer (1845–1904), to Russian culture is complex and multifaceted. Just as the relationship between Kazakhstan and Russia evolves, so does Abai's image and his importance for both Kazakh and Russian readers.[2] If, in the Soviet period, Abai was seen as essentially a Soviet writer who fought against both the colonial policies of tsarist Russia and the 'backwardness' of traditional Kazakh lifestyle, then in the new independent Kazakhstan, from 1991 onwards, Abai's image changed to accommodate post-Soviet realities. Now Abai is a symbol of Kazakh nationalism and of the uniqueness of Kazakh culture, on one hand; on the other, he is a 'world' writer, who helps to integrate Kazakhstan into 'world literature'. The present essay investigates Abai's status in modern Kazakhstan,

1 I would like to thank Aisulu Sailauovna Seisenbaeva, a specialist in Kazakh language employed at the ISL "Dostar" International School in Almaty, for her help locating Kazakh print and electronic editions of Abai's works. I also want to thank Gulnaz Abenovna Mashinbaeva, Senior Lecturer in Kazakh Language, Department of Language and General Education for International Students, Al-Farabi Kazakh National University in Almaty, for helping me elucidate some of the nuances of Abai's poetic language. Any errors are my own.

2 A note on names: Abai is the accepted way to refer to Abai Kunanbaiuly. He is referred to as 'Abai' in both scholarly publications and popular discourse. His last name is spelled either as 'Kunanbaiuly' (Kazakh version) or as 'Kunanbayev' (Russian version).

 https://doi.org/10.11647/OBP.0340.30

especially his role as a mediator between Kazakh and Russian-speaking cultures in Kazakhstan. Following Pascale Casanova's insight that national literatures are "constructed through literary rivalries, which are always denied, and struggles, which are always international", I will show that Abai's status is constructed partly in opposition to Russian culture.[3] The power relations between Kazakhstan and Russia and increasingly, between Kazakhstan and the West, play a key role in determining the shape of Kazakh national literature. In an article commemorating the 175-year anniversary of Abai's birth, celebrated in 2020, the then President of Kazakhstan, Kassym-Zhomart Tokaev, proclaimed:

> First of all, we must promote Abai as the cultural capital of our nation. Let's not forget that civilized countries value Kazakh identity, culture, literature and spirituality with the degree and popularity of outstanding personalities at the world level. Therefore, it is necessary to introduce Abai as the brand of the new Kazakhstan to the world community.[4]

Thus, Tokaev positions Abai as Kazakhstan's bid to enter Casanova's "world republic of letters", and in doing so, to distance Kazakhstan from its Russified, Soviet past. The present essay will trace Abai's status in Soviet and post-Soviet Kazakhstan, showing that the poet's value is inseparable from Kazakhstan's relationship with Russia and the West.

Abai was a poet and philosopher, most famous for his poems; for a collection of moral writings, *Words of Edification* (*Khara Sozder*, 1918; *Slova nazidaniia*, 1945) on how to live a good life; and for his translations of major Russian poets into Kazakh. Born in nomadic Kazakhstan in the mid-nineteenth century, Abai came from an aristocratic family of the Tobykty clan, where his father Kunanbai and grandfather Oskenbai occupied important positions as political and administrative leaders.[5] He received a Muslim education typical for boys of

3 Pascale Casanova, *The World Republic of Letters*, trans. by M. B. DeBevoise (Boston, MA: Harvard University Press, 2004), p. 36.

4 Tokaev also refers to Abai as a "brand" (in the original Kazakh: "жаңа Қазақстанның бренд"). See Kassym-Zhomart Tokaev, 'Memleket bacshysy Kasym-Zhomart Tokaevtyn "Abai zhane XXI gasydagy Kazakhstan" atty makalasy' (in Kazakh) ('Head of State Kassym-Jomart Tokaev's article entitled "Abai and Kazakhstan in the 21st century"'), *Akorda*, 8 January 2020, https://www.akorda.kz/kz/events/akorda_news/press_conferences/memleket-basshysy-kasym-zhomart-tokaevtyn-abai-zhane-hhi-gasyrdagy-kazakstan-atty-makalasy. All translations from Kazakh and Russian are my own, unless otherwise indicated.

5 The following summary of Abai's biography comes from the following two sources: Peter Rollberg, 'Abai: A Poet for All Seasons', *Abaicenter.kz*, 24 February 2020, https://www.abaicenter.org/abai-a-poet-for-all-seasons/, and the East-Kazakhstan Regional Library of Abai, '170 years since the birth of the great Kazakh poet-educator Abai (Imbragim) Kunanbayev (1845–1904)' ('170 let so dnia rozhdeniia velikogo kazakhskogo poeta-prosvetitelia Abaia (Ibragima) Kunanbaieva (1845–1904)'), *Semeylib.kz*, n.p., https://semeylib.kz/?page_id=4495&lang=ru/.

his status: after initially studying at home with a mullah, he went to a Muslim boys' school (madrasa) for five years, while also briefly attending the Russian school in the Kazakh city of Semipalatinsk. As an adult, Abai followed in his father's footsteps by becoming an administrator for the tsarist government in the region. At the same time, he read classical poetry from the Eastern canon as well as Russian poets, including Aleksandr Pushkin, Mikhail Lermontov, and Ivan Krylov. He began writing his own poetry, including 'Summer', the first poem to be signed with his own name, although it was not published until 1886 when Abai was already forty. Given that it was a questionable honour to be a poet at this time, most of Abai's poems were collected and published posthumously by his friends and Kazakh intellectuals. He is best known as a 'poet of enlightenment' (in Russian, *'poet-prosvetitel''*), who translated major Russian and European poets for the Kazakh people; he is also remembered for his poetic portraits of the Kazakh nomadic life at the end of the nineteenth century. He is often compared to Pushkin in terms of his importance for the development of national Kazakh literature. Abai's connection to Russian culture has gained and lost prominence as the political relationship between Kazakhstan and Russia has evolved.

Soviet Abai

During the Soviet period, critics positioned Abai as a proto-Soviet writer who spoke up for the rights of the working-class Kazakh people, resisting both the whims of the oppressive Kazakh aristocracy and the colonial policies of the Russian tsarist government. This representation of Abai as a Kazakh writer served the Soviet project of uniting the international proletariat: the elevation of a 'minority writer' from the periphery of the Soviet Empire who defends Soviet values demonstrates the extent and the importance of Soviet values for all. Abai's life story is famously retold in the form of an epic novel in four books in *The Path of Abai* (*Abai Zholy*, published in instalments between 1942–56) by the prominent Kazakh writer Muktar Auezov (1897–1961), who did more than anyone to popularise the life and works of Abai during the Soviet period. Auezov's book, still required reading in secondary schools in Kazakhstan today, presents a romanticised version of Abai's life, a coming-of-age story that retraces his boyhood in the Kazakh steppe, surrounded by his loving grandmother Zere (who nicknamed him 'Abai', rather than his official name 'Ibragim');[6] his

6 There are different theories as to why Ibragim Kunanbaiuly was named 'Abai'. One reason is phonetic. Baurzhan Myrzakul, a modern Kazakh poet and writer, argues that the Arabic name 'Ibrahim' would be shortened, pronounced by ordinary Kazakh speakers 'Ibraim', without the 'h' sound, and further, that 'r' would be elided in conversation to 'Ibaim'. Additionally, since 'Ibrahim' is the name of a Muslim prophet, to say it aloud would be considered disrespectful to the prophet. Finally, the word 'Abai', in Kazakh, means 'careful' or 'perceptive' and it is possible that the name reflected Ibrahim's character

loving mother Ulzhan and his stern father Kunanbai; his first love interests, his passion for books and folk stories; his growth as a poet; his relationship with the wider Kazakh community, and so on. This important biography is responsible for popularising and consolidating Abai's status as a national celebrity and contributing to Abai's mythologisation in Kazakhstan. The first two volumes of Auezov's *Abai Zholy* received the Stalin Prize in 1948; when all four books were completed, they were awarded a 1959 Lenin Prize as an outstanding example of Socialist Realism. Yet traces of what was unsaid or suppressed in the official Soviet propaganda of *Abai Zholy* as an example of a Socialist Realist novel can be seen in its introductions and interpretations written by Soviet critics. Here, for example, I cite the words of Mukamedzhan Karataev (1910–95), a prominent Kazakh academic, author of many textbooks on Kazakh literature, and the main editor of the *Kazakh Soviet Encyclopedia* (the first Kazakh-language encyclopedia, in twelve volumes, published between 1972–81) in his 1959 introduction to *Abai Zholy*:

> The Communist party and our Soviet society helped the writer [Mukhtar Auezov] overcome his ideological hesitancy, understand the essence of Socialist Realism, and thus contributed to his creative growth and development as a writer. [... Auezov] managed to create a vivid picture of a man who emerged from the exploitative class and then became a passionate defender of the common people—not an easy creative task.[7]

Karataev's reference to "overcoming ideological hesitancy" refers to Auezov's activism and his association with the Kazakh nationalist movement 'Alash Orda,' which lasted from 1917 to 1919. Auezov had repeatedly clashed with the Soviet authorities over important national issues, such as the Soviet collectivisation of privately owned Kazakh farmland, famine among formerly nomadic peoples, the marginalisation of the Kazakh language, and so on. Auezov, together with his colleague Zhusubpek Aimautov, briefly edited the journal *Abai*, which published many writers sympathetic to the Alash Orda movement—the journal was shut down after only eleven issues in November 1918.[8] In 1922, Auezov was

when he was growing up. See Baurzhan Myrzakul, 'Abai esimi–Ibrahimnim kyskargan turi' (in Kazakh) ('The name 'Abai' is a shortened version of Ibrahim'), *Azan.kz*, 27 October 2019, https://azan.kz/kz/maqalat/read/bauyirzhan-myirzaqul-abay-esimi-ibrahimnin-qyisqargan-tyri-11125.

7 Mukhamedzhan Karataev, 'Pevets naroda' ('The People's Poet'), in Mukhtar Auezov, *Abai zholy* (in Kazakh) (*The Path of Abai*), trans. by Mukhamedzhan Karataev (Almaty: Zhazushy, 1977), pp. 5–22 (p. 6).

8 The journal *Abai* was published after Abai's death in order to honour the writer and his works; additionally, to publish works on contemporary Kazakh literature and society. It featured many important Kazakh intellectuals of its day, many of whom were affiliated with Alash Orda and published their texts under a pseudonym. The history of the journal is told by Aizhan Baitanova, a Kazakh researcher, here: '"Abai": Zhurnalynyn shygu tarikhy' (in Kazakh) ('The History

expelled from the Communist Party for his involvement with Alash Orda and arrested in 1930. He then served two years in prison for activities summarised by his biographers as "conducting an underground struggle against the Soviet authorities, participating in preparations for the armed overthrow of the government; opposing the confiscation of property from the wealthy; helping form the national-bourgeois organization 'Alka'; and writing works that praise the pre-revolutionary lifestyle of the Kazakh people".[9]

The Soviet interpretation of Abai as a writer was largely based on Auezov's biography. Its focus was predictably limited, certainly as expressed by critics like Mukhamedzhan Karataev, whose introduction to *Abai Zholy* I cited above. Karataev focused on the class struggle between the allegedly Soviet-minded Abai and his own father, which the critics saw as an embodiment of the 'exploitative class.' *Abai Zholy* was read as a Socialist Realist work, within the only state-endorsed mode of Soviet literature from 1934 on. Karataev also praises Abai's "true fascination with the Russian people, with the Russia of Pushkin, Belinskii, Lermontov and Chernyshevskii" and the supposedly liberating role that Russian culture played for Kazakhstan, including "the building of cities and railroads in the Kazakh steppe" and the "collapse of the previous patriarchal structures of the nomadic auls or villages".[10] Just as Karataev's evaluation of Auezov's "ideological hesitancy" is a code phrase for disobeying Soviet authorities, Karataev's depiction of Soviet Kazakhstan is simply a convenient Soviet propaganda story that hides the vast human cost of collectivisation and city-building in nomadic Kazakhstan. Unsurprisingly, the Soviet Abai is described as a translator of Russian classics and even the author of a canonical Socialist Realist novel in Kazakh, *Abai Zholy*. Naomi Caffee traces the consolidation of Abai's status as the principal writer of Soviet Kazakhstan, an analogue of Russia's Pushkin, by critics like Karataev and most of all, Auezov.

In 1937, at the height of the Stalinist purges as well as the Union-wide Pushkin jubilee celebration, Auezov brought his renewed efforts to the Soviet

---

of the Publication of the Journal "Abai"'), *Abai.kz*, 19 May 2014, https://abai.kz/post/37635. *Abai.kz* is a portal dedicated to the study of the works of Abai.

9 Alash Orda was the first political party of Kazakhstan. It arose partly in opposition to the colonial Russian government and focused on prioritising Kazakh national autonomy. It formally became a party in November 1917. Alash Orda members opposed the Soviet government ('Reds') and supported the 'Whites' during the Civil War of 1918–21. Auezov worked closely with members of Alash Orda and founded the 'Youth of Alash' movement in the Kazakh city of Semipalatinsk. On Auezov, see 'Auezov M. O.', *East Kazakhstan: Famous Names*, East Kazakhstan Pushkin Regional Library, Pushkinlibrary.kz, 26 August 2020, http://imena.pushkinlibrary.kz/en/writers-and-poets/473-.html. See also the 'Alash Electronic Project' at East Kazakhstani Regional Universal Library, created in 2017 to commemorate 100 years from the founding of Alash Orda party in 1917, https://alash.semeylib.kz/?page_id=254&lang=ru.

10 Mukhamedzhan Karataev, 'Pevets naroda', p. 8.

reading public with an article strikingly titled 'How Tatiana Sang in the Steppe,' which featured Abai's translations of excerpts from Pushkin's *Evgenii Onegin* into Kazakh song form. Auezov portrayed these translations as the awakening of Kazakh culture to the majestic potential and universal appeal of Russian literature, as well as a watershed moment in the development of the Kazakh literary tradition.[11]

As Caffee notes here, besides the class struggle portrayed in Auezov's *Abai Zholy*, another feature commended by Soviet critics was Abai's translation of Russian literature. Between 1886 and 1898, Abai translated the Russian poets Pushkin, Lermontov, and Krylov, and European writers, such as Schiller, Goethe, Byron, Heine, and Adam Mickiewicz, into Kazakh. Soviet critics praised Abai's translations of Russian classics, while ignoring his far-ranging domestication and reworking of the original texts.

Changes to the Soviet Paradigm

Soviet critics were less apt to observe that Abai's translations of Russian poets served as a continuation of his own creative work, since he selectively translated only those poems (or excerpts from other poets' longer works) that resonated with his own sensibilities and allowed him to display his own talents and concerns. The continuity between Abai's satirical voice and his translation of the early nineteenth-century poet Ivan Krylov is telling. Ilyas Jansugorov, one of the founders of modern Kazakh literature and a member of Alash Orda, noted that the majority of Abai's poems are satirical and/or moralistic in their tone. Many of them teach readers correct social norms and attempt to point out and correct flaws in society through satire and ridicule.[12] Small wonder, then, that Abai decided to translate Krylov, famous for short parables that allegorise human failings. The moralistic satire of Krylov's poetry is consonant with Abai's own satirical tendency, fully exemplified in his own most famous prose work, *Words of Edification*, a collection of forty-five moral precepts and philosophical statements about the Kazakh people and their way of life.[13] Although Abai probably translated Krylov's poems prior to writing *Words of Edification*, his

11 Naomi Caffee, 'How Tatiana's Voice Rang Across the Steppe: Russian Literature in The Life and Legend of Abai', *Journal of Eurasian Studies*, 9 (2018), 12–19 (p. 14), https://journals.sagepub.com/doi/full/10.1016/j.euras.2017.12.002.

12 Ilyas Jansugurov, '*Abaidyn syoz ornegi*' (in Kazakh) ('Abai's Verbal Examples') (1934), in Ilyas Jansugurov, *Kop tomdyk shyghamalar zhinaghi* (*Collected Works*), ed. by M. Auezov, 10 vols (Almaty: Kazyghurt, 2004–19), IV (2005), page numbers unknown, https://abaialemi.kz/post/view?id=101.

13 Abai's satirical lines were recently translated into English and self-published by Simon Geoghegan as *Ghaklia: Words of Edification* (2022). The word 'Ghaklia' is the Arabic for 'word of wisdom' or 'proverb'.

preoccupation with satire and moral teaching is already evident in his Krylov translations.

For instance, one of Krylov's satirical poems, 'The Dragonfly and the Ant' (Krylov, 'Strekoza i muravei,' 1808; Abai, 'Shegirtke men Khumyrskha,' circa 1886–98) tells the story of a light-hearted "Dragonfly", who dances and plays all summer, and the hard-working "Ant" who works collecting food. When winter came, the Dragonfly begged the Ant for food and housing, but the Ant refused, pointing out that the Dragonfly had had all summer to prepare. Abai's translation exaggerates the Ant's role, apparently prefiguring the scourging voice of the narrator in the later *Words of Edification.* Abai adds sarcasm and irony absent from Krylov's original, as when the Ant mockingly pities the Dragonfly for being so busy during the summer that she had no time for work: "Poor one she had not time, / Being as she was a great poet and a great singer!" ("Kaitsyn, kholy timepti, / Olenshi, anshi esil er"). In Krylov's original lines, the Ant only makes a feeble reply upon discovering that the Dragonfly sang all summer, "Oh, and so you..." ("A, tak ty...").[14] Abai sharpens the satire in his translation of Krylov, so that readers can discern his familiar voice as a satirist of Kazakh behaviour.

Written in 1890, towards the end of Abai's creative career, *Words of Edification* strikes readers with a long list of moral failings supposedly characteristic of the Kazakh people: for instance, the third maxim asks, "Why are Kazakhs so hostile to each other, do not listen to each other, do not speak the truth, are quarrelsome and lazy?".[15] Recalling Krylov's emphasis on moral flaws, Abai devotes the majority of his treatise to explaining how the people fail and how they can learn to overcome their failings. In his sixth maxim, for example, he urges his people to devote themselves to "spirituality" over "material needs", asks people to care about education and knowledge (eighth maxim), learn science (eleventh maxim), seek constant self-improvement (twelfth maxim), and so on.[16] There is a strong continuity between Abai's creative and translation activities, as the latter seems to continue the themes and the narrative voice of his own poetry and prose.

Abai's relationship with other translated poems is similar. For instance, Jansugorov says of Abai's affinity for the Russian poet Mikhail Lermontov: "Abai translated into Kazakh a number of lyrical poems by his favourite Russian poet Lermontov. He selectively translates the poems that are most in tune with

14 I cite Abai's Kazakh translation ('Shegirtke men Khumyrskha') of Ivan Krylov's original Russian 'Strekoza i muravei' ('The Dragonfly and the Ant'). The former is available on the Abai Institute website (in Kazakh), https://abai.kaznu.kz/?p=750. Krylov's Russian text is available at https://rvb.ru/18vek/krylov/01text/vol3/01fables/070.htm.

15 'Abaidyn kara sozderi' (in Kazakh) ('Abai's Words of Edification'), *Abaicenter.kz*, 8 June 2009, https://abai.kz/post/6.

16 Ibid.

his own poetry, as can be seen in Abai's poems/translations '*Oi*' and '*Zhartas*'".[17] Abai's translations of Lermontov can be regarded as adaptations or even improvisations on the original theme. Nurghali Mahan, a contemporary Kazakh language teacher, compares Lermontov's originals against Abai's translations to argue that Abai re-works the source text in the context of the Kazakh steppe and Kazakh idioms. For example, Lermontov's poem 'The Cliff' ('Utes', 1841) describes a "golden cloud" ("*tuchka zolotaia*") that momentarily relieves the solitude of a lonely giant rock, but then "playfully" ("*veselo igraia*") sallies forth to continue her journey, abandoning the rock. Abai's translation is uniquely adapted to life in the Kazakh steppe, Mahan argues that the "golden" cloud, an unfamiliar trope in the Kazakh landscape, becomes "a young cloud"; the rock—an "old" or "elderly" rock (he uses "*kyari*", a respectful form of address to an older Kazakh), while the behaviour of the "young cloud" is conveyed through the Kazakh word "*oinaktap*", or "playful", connoting a young animal or child. Mahan remarks: "Only a young calf with a full stomach and no other space in his heart plays. Exactly the right word."[18]

In the final part of this chapter, I turn to Pushkin's *Evgenii Onegin*, which became one of Abai's most popular translations from Russian into Kazakh. Abai's method with Pushkin's text was far from systematic: he translated fragmentary extracts from *Evgenii Onegin*, usually the most emotional parts of the poem, which resonated with Abai's own love poetry. Abai translated eight excerpts, including Tatiana's famous letter to Onegin, Onegin's reply to Tatiana, and even (with respectful improvisation) Onegin's dying words. These love-themed sections from Onegin were translated by Abai as Petrarchan-style lyrics that discuss the alternating heat and cold of passion and focus on female beauty. Abai also embeds Tatiana in Kazakh culture. For example, Abai's version of Tatiana compares herself to a baby *saiga* (a type of steppe antelope native to Kazakhstan and parts of Central Asia) which barely survives its encounter with Onegin, whom she calls a wounded tiger.[19] Since Kazakhstan became independent, critics looking for non-Russian influences have noted that in many excerpts from the poem, Abai uses Eastern poetic forms characteristic of Persian poetry, such as the *ghazal* (aabaca) and the *rubaiyat* (aaba). Sergei Fomichev has noted that "[i]f one takes a close look, Abai's translations are hybrid works

17 Ilyas Jansugurov, 'Abai's verbal examples.'

18 Nurghali Mahan, 'Abaidyn Lermantovtan zhasagan' (in Kazakh) ('Abai's translations from Lermontov'), *Abai.kz*, 2 June 2020, https://abai.kz/post/113799.

19 In Abai's translation, this passage reads: "Sen zharaly zholbarys en,/ Men kiyktyn lahy em./ Tiri khaldym, olmey yaren,/ Khatty batty tyrnahyn." ("You are a wounded tiger, I am a fawn. I barely survived, I almost died, Your claws are sharp."). Abai translates Tatiana's letter to Onegin, which is in Chapter 3 of Pushkin's *Eugene Onegin*. Abai's text can be found at 'Abai Kunanbaev (Tat'iana sezi)' (in Kazakh) ('Abai Kunanbaiev (Tatiana's Word)'), *Zharar.com*, 18 June 2019, https://www.zharar.com/kz/olen/26403-abay.html.

that domesticate Pushkin's words in a multiplicity of contexts".[20] One of Abai's early poems 'Yuzi is a rose, her eyes are diamonds' ('Yuzi—raushan, kyozi—gauhar'), written in 1858–59, was inspired by medieval Eastern love poetry, such as the Persian poets Ferdowsi, Nizami Ganjavi, Saadi Shirazi, and Jami and the Turkic poet Navoi.[21]

With rising ethnic nationalism in independent Kazakhstan, critics have increasingly noted how Abai domesticated his translations and set them in the context of traditional nomadic Kazakh culture or incorporated Eastern and not simply European influences. For instance, Sheriazdan Eleukenov, a prominent Kazakh academic, shows that Abai's Onegin is a much more positive and sympathetic figure than Pushkin's. Moreover, Abai's depiction of the love story is more romantic and tragic, compared to the Russian tendency to praise Tatiana for rejecting the carefree and arrogant Onegin.[22] In this sense, Abai's translation is closer to traditional Kazakh stories of unhappy love, such as the popular folktale 'Enlik Kebek', first published in 1892. 'Enlik Kebek,' a folk tale from the eighteenth century, which exists in several versions, is a story of unhappy love between two lovers, Enlik and her beloved Kebek, from opposing clans, 'naiman' and 'argyn' respectively. Enlik is already engaged to be married to an older relative when she meets Kebek; she refuses her fiancé, and the lovers run away to the mountains. There they have a son, but eventually they are captured by Enlik's vengeful relatives who put both of them and their young son to death. This tragic story of doomed love is often seen as the Kazakh version of *Romeo and Juliet*; Abai's translation of Pushkin's love story *Evgenii Onegin* is closer to this tradition than to Pushkin's original, which is rather ambivalent about the depth of Onegin's and Tatiana's love. (In Pushkin's story, Tatiana rejects Onegin after marrying an older man following Onegin's refusal of her love, confessed to him as a young village girl.)

It is still relatively new to suggest that Abai's *Evgenii Onegin* reflects the encounter of two or more equal cultures, since the Soviet tradition of valuing Abai's Russian sources above his own creative work of translation and interpretation still persists. For instance, the website of the East Kazakhstan Regional Universal Library, the very library where Abai once studied Russian classics, now a major centre of Abai studies, features both Russian- and Kazakh-language versions of the same article on 'Abai and Russian Literature'. Curiously, the Russian-language version is much more outspoken and positive about the

20 Sergei A. Fomichev, 'Pushkin i Abai' (in Russian) ('Pushkin and Abai'), *Abai.kaznu.kz*, May 2013, https://abai.kaznu.kz/rus/?p=291.

21 On the influence of Eastern poetry on Abai, see S.A. Fomichev, 'Pushkin i Abai' and Ilyas Jansugurov, 'Abai's verbal examples'.

22 *'Tatiananyn khyrdahi yani'* (in Kazakh) ('Tatiana's song on the ridge'), in *Egemen Qazaqstan* [*Egemen.kz*], 23 September 2016, https://egemen.kz/article/105511-tatyananynh-qyrdaghy-ani.

vital role of Russian culture for Abai's own development. It echoes earlier Soviet critics, such as Karataev:

> He [Abai], the true spokesperson for the wishes of his people, saw the only correct way for the Kazakh steppe: the path of growing closer to Russia—the Russia of Lomonosov and Pushkin, Belinskii, Chernyshevskii, Tolstoy, and Shchedrin, the path of unification of the fortunes of Kazakh and Russian people. That is why Abai bravely entered into a single combat with everything that was inert, conservative, and reactionary, which hindered the social and cultural development of the region.[23]

The Soviet tradition of portraying Russian literature as "the only correct way for the Kazakh steppe" still exists, but scholars now tend to discuss Abai's works on their own terms, no longer in the shadow of Russian as, purportedly, the only true original text.

Today, critics apologise for Abai's strong pro-Russian views and his scathing critique of fellow Kazakhs in his *Words of Edification*. Satimzhan Sanbaev, who translated *Words of Edification* from Kazakh into Russian in 1970, wrote a preface for the new (2013) edition which tries to soften Abai's ostensibly anti-Kazakh critique. Sanbaev writes that Abai's "true genius is not limited by national characteristics"; that his works appeal to "universal human values" and that his *Words* are written for "people of different nationalities".[24] He even asserts that Abai "addresses himself to people through a code-word and in this case this code-word is 'Kazakh'".[25] Significantly, Sanbaev completely empties Abai's words of any ethnic referent, suggesting that the term 'Kazakh' is only a placeholder for individuals of any nationality. Indeed, Abai's critique of Kazakhs is scathing and difficult, despite Sanbaev's warnings, to separate from its historical context. The pendulum has swung back, as Kazakh writers try to purge Abai of his pro-Russian sentiment.

In *Words of Edification* Abai harshly criticises the Kazakh people, urging them to learn Russian. Thus, in his second maxim Abai writes that Kazakhs "used to laugh at others [he lists Kazakhs' ridicule of Tadzhiks, Tatars, and Russians], but we [Kazakhs] ourselves are worse than everyone, both in hard work, in faith, and in unity". In his third maxim, Abai recommends that "regional judges should be chosen from those people who received education in the Russian

23 East-Kazakhstan Regional Library of Abai, 'Abai i Russkaia literatura' (in Russian), *Semeylib.kz*, n.d., https://semeylib.kz/?page_id=1006&lang=ru.

24 Satimzhan Sanbaev, 'Predislovie' (in Russian) ('Introduction'), in Abai Kunanbayev, *Slova nazidaniia* (*Words of Edification*) (Almaty: Almatykytap, 2013), pp. 6–10 (p. 7), http://nabrk.kz/bookView/view/?brId=1117495&simple=true&green=1&lang=ru#.

25 Cited by Sanbaev, 'Introduction', p. 10.

language"; and perhaps most famously, in the twenty-fifth maxim Abai writes the following:

> One should learn the Russian language. Russian people have reason and wealth, progressive science, and high culture. The study of the Russian language, education in Russian schools, and mastery of Russian science will help us learn the best qualities of this nation and avoid its failings, because they, earlier than anyone, discovered the secrets of nature. To know the Russian language is to open one's eyes to the world.[26]

Abai's high praise for Russian culture has led some people to argue that *Words of Edification* may have been secretly edited or even wholly composed by Soviet critics. Zaure Bataeva caused a sensation and a scandal in Internet circles with her long blog post 'The Unknown Abai' ('Neizvestnyi Abai'), in which she identifies many "anti-nomadic" and "anti-Kazakh" statements in Abai's work before querying the authenticity of his authorship. Bataeva questions how a person raised in the steppe could know so much about European literature and philosophy or read Russian so easily.[27] Drawing a parallel with the anti-Stratfordian theory, which doubts the authenticity of Shakespeare as the true author of his plays and poems, Bataeva speculates that Alikhan Bukeihanov (1866–1937), one of the great Kazakh intellectuals and a leader of the 'Alash Orda' movement, is a better candidate for the authorship of Abai's works than the person claimed to be Abai. Bataeva's blog elicited vehement responses from Kazakh academics, though some commended her for raising the question of how little we really know about Abai from first-hand sources.[28] The highly negative reaction of Kazakh academics can perhaps be compared to another incident, when in 2012, Aleksei Navalnyi, the Russian opposition leader, off-handedly suggested to his supporters to meet at the statue of Abai in central Moscow, without realising who this statue represented and referred to the poet as the "unknown Kazakh" ("*neponiatnyi Kazakh*"). His tweet elicited negative feedback from the Kazakhstani public, many of whom felt that a part of their national identity had been compromised by this careless comment.[29]

---

26 Ibid., p. 102.

27 Zaure Bataeva, 'Zagadka Abaiia: velichaishii neizvestnyi poet Kazakhstana (I)' (in Russian) ('The Mystery of Abai: Kazakhstan's Greatest Unknown Poet (I)'), *Zerge blog*, *Zaurebatayeva.blog*, 19 July 2020, https://www.zaurebatayeva.blog/post/абай-кунанбаев-і-введение.

28 See for instance, Sultan Khan Akkuly, '"Gerostratova slava" Zaure Bataevoi' (in Russian) ("Herostratus' fame of Zaure Bataeva'), *Abai.kz*, 30 November 2020, https://www.abai.kz/post/124675.

29 The incident is described in detail in Dinara Kudaibergenova's article 'Misunderstanding Abai and the Legacy of the Canon', *Journal of Eurasian Studies*, 9 (2018), 20–29, https://journals.sagepub.com/doi/full/10.1016/j.euras.2017.12.007.

What these examples cumulatively suggest is that since Kazahstan's independence in 1991, Abai's dual role as an enlightenment figure for the Kazakh people (primarily by transmitting Russian literature) and as an ethnographer of the Kazakh lifestyle have shifted. Now, Abai is much more firmly identified as a Kazakh poet, while the influence of world literature on Abai's translations has been radically redefined. In 2020, Kazakhstan celebrated the 175th anniversary of Abai's birth, and the celebrations clearly indicated the nature of this shift. Perhaps the most revealing document was an article by the President of Kazakhstan, Kasym-Zhomart Tokaev, composed for the anniversary and entitled 'Abai and Kazakhstan in the Twenty-First Century'.[30] Tokaev's article identifies a number of national priorities: for Kazakhstan to "occupy leading positions" in the world in education and science; the study of "foreign languages", especially English; the popularisation, especially among young people, of their "native language" ("*ana tili*"), that is, Kazakh; the development of social solidarity given the worldwide "crisis of capitalism", to name some key priorities. Abai is crucial for all of these, as Tokaev emphasises by referencing his works, especially precepts from *Words of Edification*, in connection with each goal.

Surprisingly, Tokaev uses the twenty-fifth maxim, cited above (where Abai urges his compatriots to study the Russian language to "open one's eyes to the world") as a justification for simply learning "foreign languages", in his own ambiguous phrasing. Without ever naming Russian, the main language Abai mentions, Tokaev suggests instead that "we [Kazakhs] should develop and popularise the native language and increase its status" and "simultaneously with that, we should give priority to the study of the English language". By omitting Russian entirely and elevating Kazakh, Tokaev makes Abai a herald not of Russian culture, but an ethnic Kazakh icon and simultaneously a window to the world of progress and science, now identified with the English language. Moreover, in order to elevate Kazakhstan's standing in the world, Tokaev unabashedly proposes promoting and consecrating Abai as a symbol of "cultural capital" (in Kazakh, "*ultymyzdyn myadeni capitaly*") while turning him into a national "brand" ("*Kazakhstannyn brandy*"). Tokaev writes that just as every Kazakh wants to have a dombra ("*Yar kazakhtyn tyorinde dombyra tursyn*"), the traditional Kazakh instrument, he also needs a volume of Abai's works and his biography (Auezov's *Abay Zholy*, discussed above). Abai's present reinvention as a powerful Kazakh icon with the power to bestow prestige and legitimacy on the newly post-Soviet Kazakh nation may recall Bourdieu's interpretation of the social capital of symbolic goods.[31]

30 Kassym-Zhomart Tokaev, 'Abai zhane XXI gasyrdagi Kazakhstan' (in Kazakh) ('Abai and Kazakhstan in the XXI century'), in *Egemen Qazaqstan* [*Egemen.kz*], 9 January 2020, https://egemen.kz/article/217247-abay-dgane-xxi-ghasyrdaghy-qazaqstan.

31 See Pierre Bourdieu, *Distinction: A Social Critique of the Judgment of Taste*, trans. by Richard Nice (Cambridge, MA: Harvard University Press, 1987).

Tokaev's slippage between identifying Abai as an ethnic Kazakh and as an ideal citizen of Kazakhstan indicates a larger national confusion: is Abai a Kazakh or a Kazakhstani writer? In other words, is the poet a symbol of Kazakh ethnicity and pride ('Kazakh'), or is he the property of all citizens who live in Kazakhstan ('Kazakhstani'), regardless of their ethnic category? Tokaev seems to conflate the two identities, by referring to the poet's "native language" (meaning Kazakh, although many ethnic Kazakhs speak Russian as their native language), associating Abai with the traditional Kazakh dombra, and alternating interchangeably between the terms "Kazakhs" and "citizens". Confusingly, Abai represents Kazakhstan to the world, while apparently only speaking for ethnic Kazakhs. In his study of Kazakh nationalism, the sociologist Serik Bersimbaev considers the instability of the current policy of nation-building in Kazakhstan.[32] He discusses the weakening of the old Soviet paradigm of "double identification", by which a Soviet person belonged both to the nation and his ethnic group; he also notes the growth of an ethnic Kazakh identity in Kazakhstan. His conclusion is that 'Kazakh' identity remains mostly a birthright category lacking the kind of clear civic allegiance that could unite other ethnicities under a shared national heritage.

For many citizens of Kazakhstan, Abai remains an icon of traditional Kazakh culture. His music, such as the popular love song ('Kyozimnin Kharasy', literally, 'the eyes' blackness'), almost always features scenes from traditional nomadic life, such as Kazakh yurts, traditional Kazakh dresses, dombras, horses, and so on. On the other hand, Tokaev's efforts to popularise Abai as a global classic are mostly directed towards audiences outside of the country. Thus, for example, for Abai's 175th anniversary, Tokaev proposed an online 'challenge', where people from different places in Kazakhstan and around the world would recite Abai's works under the hashtag #Abai175. Prominent diplomats and public figures, from the US ambassador to Kazakhstan to the Chinese actor Jackie Chan, recited Abai's poems online; many school children and universities in Kazakhstan participated in the challenge. There is a concerted state effort to promote the cult of Abai in Kazakhstan. Meanwhile, Abai's work as a translator of Russian literature has been sidelined by the government's determination to promote Abai as an ethnic Kazakh symbol and as a worldwide Kazakhstani brand. In modern Kazakhstan, Abai's identity as a bridge between Kazakh and Russian cultures remains largely unexplored.

32 Serik Bersimbayev, 'Fenomen kazakhskogo natsionalizma v kontekste segodniashnei politiki: ot otritsaniia k ponimaniu' (in Russian) ('The Phenomenon of Kazakh Nationalism in the Context of Today's Politics: from Denial to Understanding'), *Soros.kz*, https://www.soros.kz/wp-content/uploads/2015/09/kazakh_nationalism.pdf.

Mongolia

Cultural Dialogue between Russia and Mongolia: Gombosuren Tserenpil and the Poetics of Translating Dostoevsky's Novels

Zaya Vandan

(Translated from Russian by Muireann Maguire)

> [T]here is not a single nation [...] which has developed culture in isolation.[1]

This essay will examine several facts from the history of the reception of Russian literature in Mongolia, allowing us to draw clear conclusions about how Russian and Soviet culture spread through this country, influencing its culture. I aim to complete the history of cultural dialogue between these two countries while providing insight into the history of Mongolian Translation Studies. In the case of the history of translation, as in the history of literature, there are pitfalls in developmental thinking. To avoid an evolutionary approach, I rely on the theoretical work of Jeremy Munday, which examines the dilemmas and possibilities of writing translation history and tries to construct a social and cultural history of translation by creating a microhistory of translators using extra-textual material.[2]

In the seventy-year historical relationship between Russia and Mongolia, the main creative drive was intercultural dialogue, within which translated

1 Johann Gottfried Herder, *Idei k filosofii istorii chelovechestva*, trans. by A.V. Mikhailov (Moscow: Tsentr gumanitarnykh initsiativ, 2013), p. 507.

2 Jeremy Munday, 'Using Primary Sources to Produce a Microhistory of Translation and Translators: Theoretical and Methodological Concerns', *The Translator*, 20:1 (2014), 64–80.

 https://doi.org/10.11647/OBP.0340.31

literature gained particular significance. The influence of Russian writing on the formation and history of Mongolian literature is impossible to measure. Translations of Russian works aided the development of the latest Mongolian literature in the broadest sense while assisting in the latter's interaction with global literature, or—as Pascale Casanova has defined international literary space—the *World Republic of Letters*.[3]

The first text to be translated from Russian into Old Mongolian was a Bible printed in St Petersburg in 1827.[4] Following the Mongolian People's Revolution in 1921, Russian became the main foreign language from which translations were effected, in all genres of written literature.[5] Translators' heightened interest in Russian literature can be explained by a range of facts, one of which was equivalence in alphabet.[6] Moreover, during the second half of the twentieth century, a new generation of Mongolian intelligentsia emerged: they were university-educated, spoke cultured Russian, and no less importantly from our perspective, took an interest in the theory and practice of translation. One of the first Mongolian scholars to turn his attention to the problem of literary translation was Rinchen Biamba (1905–77), an author, historian, literary scholar, and widely respected translator, who graduated from the Leningrad Institute of Eastern Languages with a degree in Oriental Studies. His excellent command of Russian and skill as a researcher was such that even in his earliest works, he broached issues related to Translation Studies, identifying concrete problems arising in the translation of literary fiction—particularly Russian and Soviet

3 Pascale Casanova, describing the formation and evolution of the international literary field, states that works and genres are distributed in the original language or translation, forming the World Republic of Letters. See Pascale Casanova, *The World Republic of Letters*, trans. by Malcolm DeBevoise (London and Cambridge, MA: Harvard University Press, 2004).

4 Irina Kul'ganek, 'Neizvestnaia rabota A.M. Pozdneeva o perevode Sviashchennogo Pisaniia (Iz arkhiva vostokovedov Sankt-Peterburgskogo filiala Instituta vostokovedeniia Rossiiskoi akademii nauk)', *Istoricheskii vestnik* 7 (2000), 111–31. About the now lost, earliest recorded translation of the Bible into Mongolian, see Staffan Rosén's study: 'The Translation History of the Mongolian Bible', *Mongolian Studies*, 30/31 (2008/09), 19–41.

5 By the mid-1950s, one thousand, seven hundred and seven works from thirty-nine countries had been translated and printed; of these, 84.5% were translations from Russian. See Onon Chinbayar, 'Izdanie proizvedenii russkikh pisatelei XX veka v Mongolii' (unpublished doctoral thesis, Moskovskii Politekhnicheskii Universitet, 2019), p. 31.

6 In 1941, efforts were made to replace the Old Mongolian script with the Latin alphabet, but a few months later, Mongolia began using the Cyrillic alphabet, a decision largely motivated by political factors. See Stéphane Grivelet, 'The Latinization Attempt in Mongolia', in *Historical and Linguistic Interaction Between Inner-Asia and Europe: Studia Uralo-altaica* (39), ed. by A. Bertalan and E. Horváth (University of Szeged, 1997), pp. 115–20 (p. 119).

classics—into the Mongolian language.[7] His ideas and theories, including those about the interdependence of Russian and Mongolian literature, would inform later studies. Nonetheless, in order to illustrate the nature and the stages of intercultural linkage reflected in the processes of translating Russian literature into Mongolian, rather than dwelling on Rinchen's work, we should turn to the achievements of a translator from a younger generation, the diplomat Gombosuren Tserenpil (born in 1943).[8] Gombosuren's contribution to the transmission of Russian literature in Mongolia has been (and continues to be) immeasurably great. His work, in my view, opens perspectives upon both the study of Mongolia's reception of Russian literature and the wider history of translation.

Gombosuren's life and career were closely connected with Soviet Russia and Russian culture generally; he first encountered the latter in 1961 as an eighteen-year-old youth matriculating at Moscow State University. After graduating, he worked for several years in the Mongolian Government Printing Department, returning in 1974 to Moscow to study political science. In 1976, he was appointed head of the Mongolian Department of Foreign Affairs, and from 1982 he served as deputy Minister of Foreign Affairs. In 1984, he returned to Moscow once again as an advisor and representative for the Mongolian ambassador to the USSR. After serving three years in this role, he was made deputy head of Mongolia's Department of Foreign Affairs, and in 1988 he became Foreign Minister. He held this position for two consecutive terms, during the democratic revolution of 1989 and subsequent events which profoundly altered Mongolian society and changed the course of its history. After his years in Moscow, Gombosuren spoke Russian perfectly. His spell in the printing department had allowed him to forge acquaintance with leading figures in contemporary literature and culture, including the writers and translators who directed Mongolian literary translation. This created an opportunity for him to start working as a translator.

The long-standing tradition in translated literature determined the direction of translation politics even in the Soviet era because literary texts for translation were allocated only to those whose skills were undisputed in the highest professional circles. To be allowed to translate professionally, the young Gombosuren had to pass an examination and translate ten pages from Alim Pshemakhovich Keshokov's novel *A Wonderful Moment* (*Chudesnoe mgnovenie*, 1964). His submission was evaluated by the well-known translator and editor

7 About Rinchen's literary translations, see N. G. Ochirova, 'Zhizn' i deiatel'nost' akademika B. Rinchena v kontekste kalmytsko-mongol'skogo nauchnogo vzaimodeistviia', *Mongolovedenie*, 4/1 (2007), 5–16 (p. 12). One of his important theoretical works on translation was *Mark Tvenii min' makhy n' idezh dee. Orchuulgyn tukhai*, ed. by Akim Gotov (Ulaanbaatar: Armiin Khevlekh uildver, 1991).

8 Hereafter referred to as Gombosuren, given that the first name is traditionally used in Mongolia.

Amar Gurbazar (1933–2016), who had translated several acknowledged masterpieces of Russian and world literature into Mongolian, including Johann von Goethe's *The Sorrows of Young Werther* (1774; *Zaluu Verteriin shanalan*, 1966), George Sand's *Consuelo* (1842; *Konsuelo*, 1981), and selected works by Fedor Dostoevsky (see below). As a result, Gombosuren was permitted to translate Keshokov's lengthy historical novel, which would occupy him for the next two years. His translation appeared in 1972 under the title *Gaikhamshigt egshin*. Thus, from the outset, Gombosuren's translation activity was closely linked to Russian literature. It is probable that his deep knowledge of the language and his familiarity, as a reader, with Russian literature predetermined his long and productive journey as a translator, interrupted between 1988 and 1996 by diplomatic service. In order to explore the stages and the nature of the reception of Russian literature in Mongolia, an essential feature of the intercultural exchanges between these two countries, I will examine Gombosuren's career as a translator from two perspectives: the Soviet and post-Soviet contexts of Mongolian history.

In accordance with the government's transformative aims, from the 1950s onwards Russian and Soviet literature were actively translated into other languages. A significant portion of such texts consisted of books spreading propaganda in favour of Soviet ideology and lifestyle. Gombosuren's earliest translations played a major role in popularising these concepts. Translations such as Keshokov's above-mentioned work, Vadim Mikhailovich Kozhevnikov's novella *The Special Section* (*Osoboe podrazdelenie*, 1969; *Ontsgoi salbar*, 1974), or Petr Andreevich Andreev's *A Story About My Friend* (*Povest' o moem druge*, 1979; *And nokhriin tukhai tuuzh*, 1983) all shared a common focus on the character and outlook of Soviet man. Collectively, they bore witness to the friendly relations between Mongolia and Soviet Russia and to the prevalence of propaganda on behalf of the latter's culture and way of life. In addition, a Mongolian-inflected strategy can be traced: when selecting works for translation, Mongolian translators favoured those which considered the national peculiarities of their own culture, aware that these books would exert enormous influence on the development of contemporary Mongolian literature. They thus favoured scenarios for resolving problems such as the retention of traditional national culture or the transmission of the ideas and achievements of other cultures.

Gombosuren's next translation, in 1982, also reveals the presence of this strategy. This was a translation of Viktor Petrovich Astaf'ev's *Tsar Fish* (*Tsar'-ryba*, 1976), describing the way of life, customs, and traditions of Siberian ethnic groups. The novella's main theme is the relationship between humans and nature, our unity with the environment, both notions which connect with traditional Mongolian conceptualisations. As a result of this theme and the poetic language Gombosuren used in the text of his 1982 translation (as *Khaan zagas*), his version became genuinely part of Mongolian culture. This is evidence that agreement between the themes and ideas in Soviet literature and the traditions and national features peculiar to the Mongolian people was one of the chief criteria in the selection of works for translation from Russian to Mongolian. This is confirmed by Anatolii Larionovich Builov's *The Great Nomadic Movement* (*Bol'shoe kochev'e*, 1982), which appeared in Gombosuren's translation (*Ikh nuudel*, 1989) and which describes the life of the Evenki, nomadic reindeer herders whose way of life resembles that of the nomadic Mongols.

Before beginning his diplomatic service, Gombosuren successfully translated an extract from Anatolii Naumovich Rybakov's novel *Children of the Arbat* (*Deti Arbata*, 1987; *Arbatiin khuukhduud*, 1989), which exposes truths about Stalin-era Moscow. The appearance of a text like this in the popular Mongolian journal *Literature and Art* (*Utga zokhiol urlag*) shows the extent of political change and the Mongolian government's intention to remove ideological links with Soviet power. At the end of the 1990s, a new, post-Soviet period began for Gombosuren. The Mongolian translation of Mikhail Bulgakov's *Master and Margarita* (*Master i Margarita*, 1967), a book which had by then become a global classic, demonstrates the translator's intention to expand the cultural experience of Mongolian readers by introducing them to works of worldwide importance. The translation came out in 1998 as *Master, Margarita khoer*. In 1999, the second volume in Rybakov's tetralogy, *Fear* (*Strakh*, 1990), appeared in Mongolian translation as *Aidas*. This was followed ten years later by the third book, *Dust and Ashes* (*Prakh i pepel*, 1994), as *Uns, chandruu* (2009). On the cusp of the new millennium, Gombosuren began making expanded and annotated translations of the works of early Soviet-era prose satirists Il'ia Il'f and Evgenii Petrov. Thus, *The Twelve Chairs* (*Dvenadtsat' stul'ev*, 1928) reached Mongolian readers in the year 2000 under the title *Arvan khoer sandal*, and a year later *The Golden Calf* (*Zolotoi telenok*, 1931) was published as *Altan tugal*. Over the next several years he translated Iurii Trifonov's novellas *The House on the Embankment* (*Dom na naberezhnoi*, 1976; as *Uiltei baishin*), *The Exchange* (*Obmen*, 1969; *Solio kholio*), and *Another Life* (*Drugiaia zhizn'*, 1975; *Ondoo am'dral*), which appeared as an anthology in 2015. Gombosuren's recent translations include a large number of masterpieces from Russian and world literature; for space, I will mention here only Ivan Bunin's *Life of Arsen'ev* (*Zhizn' Arsen'eva*, 1930; *Arsen'evyn am'dral*), which brought its author the Nobel Prize for Literature in 1933 and which appeared in Mongolian in 2017, and Nobel laureate Svetlana Aleksievich's *Chernobyl Prayer* (*Chernobyl'skaia molitva*, 1997; *Chernobyliin emgenelt zalbiral*, 2016). Gombosuren's repertoire of translations includes many other important books. One of his greatest achievements—in terms of the history of the reception of Russian literature as well as the Mongolian-Russian cultural exchange—was his translation of Dostoevsky's major works into Mongolian.

The appearance of Dostoevsky's novels in Mongolian translation marks an important recent cultural development. The Mongolian public began reading Dostoevsky in their own language only in the second half of the twentieth century when Navaan-Iunden Nasan-Ochir's (190885) translation of *Poor Folk* (*Bednye liudi*, 1846) appeared under the title *Yaduu khumuus* in 1956. It is interesting to speculate on what caused this remarkable delay. One of the reasons may have been the Soviet censors, who withheld approval from Dostoevsky's works until the Khrushchev Thaw not only on their own territory, but also in other countries within the Socialist camp. One might note the contrast with Dostoevsky's reception in their Southern neighbour: in China, translations of his novels were in print as early as 1918,[9] not to mention the many academic and informational works devoted to him, while in Mongolia there were still no translators with experience working from Russian. The novel *Poor Folk* was almost unknown to the public, nor did critics rush to evaluate it. In general, the popularisation of Dostoevsky in Mongolia was not a major priority for the country's cultural politics; he would not be translated again for almost thirty years. Finally, in 1983, the novel *The Insulted and the Injured* (*Unizhennye i oskorblennye*, 1861; *Dord uzegdegsed*) came out, followed two years later by *White Nights* (*Belye nochi*, 1848; *Tsagaan shono*, 1985), both translated by Amar Gurbazar. As mentioned above, Amar had evaluated Gombosuren's very first translation, and by approving it, launched Gombosuren's professional career as a junior translator. In this context, his translations of Dostoevsky's major novels may be considered as a natural follow-up, the continuation of what Amar had begun.

The next and most important stage in Dostoevsky's Mongolian reception is closely connected with Gombosuren. The first work he translated was the novel *Crime and Punishment* (*Prestuplenie i nakazanie*, 1866), published in 2003 as *Gem zem* by the Interpress publishing house. Although Gombosuren had had to resolve a host of problems during the translation process, linked to the difficulty of finding a Mongolian linguistic equivalent for Dostoevsky's idiolect,[10] the translation was highly praised by both critics and the general public;[11] it

9 Zhang Runmei, 'Osobennosti vospriyatiya idei F. M. Dostoevskogo v Kitae', *Vestnik Rossiiskogo universiteta druzhby narodov, Seriia: Filosofiia*, 21:3 (2017), 411–18 (p. 411). See also the essay by Hang Yu in this volume.

10 When collecting materials for this essay, I arranged an interview with Mr. Gombosuren, during which he responded to a range of my questions connected with translation practice and pointed out several problems which arose during the translation of *Crime and Punishment*: "Insofar as this translation represented my first experience with Dostoevsky's work, I came up against certain difficulties connected not only with his language and style but also with his system of thought. Therefore, I had to turn to Amar's translation of *The Humiliated and the Insulted*." This information shows that in order to resolve difficulties of idiosyncratic style, Gombosuren would study other texts by the same author, comparing the originals with previous translations to familiarise himself with the choices and strategies adopted by earlier translators, while at the same time refining his own practice. Please note that all translations from Russian and Mongolian are my own unless otherwise indicated.

11 The leading Mongolian Studies scholar Lidiia Grigor'evna Skorodumova, calling Gombosuren's translation "brilliant", wrote: "This book has become a significant event in the cultural life of our country. It is famously difficult to convey

immediately became prescribed reading for secondary school children. After this outstanding success, Gombosuren began translating *The Brothers Karamazov* (*Brat'ia Karamazovy*, 1880), which appeared in 2009 from the Monsudar Press as *Karamazovyn khovuud*. I have analysed the poetics of this text elsewhere in numerous articles, contending that Gombosuren's fundamental method—with several translational strategies at his disposal—was to preserve the atmosphere and spirit of the original, without violating the harmony of the Mongolian language.[12] After a short interruption, in 2015 Gombosuren published his version of *The Idiot* (*Idiot*, 1868), which appeared as *Soliot* from Monsudar. This third novel of the five translated by Gombosuren revealed him as a now-experienced translator of Dostoevsky's language; I will examine his treatment of Dostoevskian lexis separately below. Although Gombosuren had not planned to translate all of Dostoevsky's major novels early in his career, he soon started work on the outstanding volumes (of the five considered 'great'). *The Adolescent* (*Podrostok*, 1875; *Hovuun zaia*) appeared in 2016 from the publishing house Bolor Sudar, and the final novel, *The Devils* (*Besy*, 1872; *Albinguud*) reached Mongolian readers in 2018, again from Bolor Sudar. These translations are regularly re-issued, and while they are not currently the subject of much academic study, readers still—especially online—regularly discuss them, demonstrating a clearly marked need in Mongolian society to appreciate Dostoevsky's world.

In this chapter, I want to pause upon Gombosuren's translation of Dostoevsky's *The Idiot*, in order to analyse several examples of the use of cultural realia and the poetic/semantic formation of the original text, to indicate the aesthetic determination of the devices used by the translator.[13] In Lawrence Venuti's view, some so-called "ethnocentric violence" is inevitable in literary translation, since the process of translating texts and cultures always subjects them, to some degree, to reduction, omissions, homogenisation, and so on.[14]

Dostoevsky to the Mongolian mindset". See L. G. Skorodumova, *Mongol'skaia literatura XIX–XX vekov: Voprosy poetiki* (Moscow: RGGU, 2016), p. 154.

12 For more on this, see my 'Osobennosti peredachi kontsepta *bog* v mongol'skom perevode romana *Brat'ia Karamazovy* F. M. Dostoevskogo', in *Ad vitam aeternam. A Volume in Honour of the 70th Birthday of Professor István Nagy, Readings 6* (Budapest: ELTE BTK, 2017), pp. 313–19. In connection with the Mongolian translation of *Crime and Punishment*, see my 'Semantika i semantizatsiia *vechnosti* v romane *Prestuplenie i nakazanie* i ego mongol'skom perevode', *Mongolica*, XXIV:3 (2021), 33–40.

13 The problem of a translator's freedom is one of the most complex and disputed issues in translation theory. The many-sidedness of translation activity suggests that any analysis of the latter must account for the personality of the translator themselves, as they make subjective translation decisions. Pym holds this view, arguing for the necessity of "humanizing" translation and recommending that translation analysis focuses first and foremost on the identity of the translator and only secondarily on the text they create. See Anthony Pym, 'Humanizing Translation History', *Hermes*, 42 (2009), 23–48 (p. 32).

14 Lawrence Venuti, *The Translator's Invisibility: A History of Translation* (London and New York: Routledge, 1995), p. 310.

Does the essential difference in religion and culture signal the impossibility of fully realising a novel like *The Idiot*, so rich in subtexts, in Mongolian? It should be useful to examine the strategies selected by Gombosuren for translating those specifically Christian concepts unfamiliar to Mongolian readers.

My analysis reveals the translator's orientation towards reception, in this instance towards Mongolian culture. He resorts to a domesticating device more than once, showing his immediate substitution of Buddhist concepts for Christian ones.[15] Thus, the word "God" ("*Bog*") in the novel is translated as "*Burkhan*". In Constance Garnett's version: "Well, if that's how it is, [...] you are a regular blessed innocent, and *God* loves such as you" (p. 11),[16] while in Gombosuren's translation: "Za herev tiim bol, noën min', chi ëstoi khiitei khun bolzh taarakh n'. *Burkhan* cham shig khuniig khairladag ium" (literally, "Well, if that's how it is, sir, you're going to be filled with air. God loves people like you" (p. 25)).[17] There is no doubt that for the majority of readers of this translation, the concept of 'Burkhan', equivalent to 'God' for Mongolians, is very similar to 'Buddha' since the main Mongolian religion is Buddhism.[18] Nonetheless, in the given context this kind of device is acceptable for the achievement of reasonable accuracy, insofar as accuracy is measured in terms of equivalent emotional effect by the original and the translation. But, as a consequence of this domestication, readers of the translation miss out on the novel's important Christian connotations. An example of a meaningful passage from the original

15 The opposition between *domesticating* and *foreignising* translation has become a constant landmark in translation studies, originating with Friedrich Schleiermacher (1768–1834). According to his theory of translation, what we call *domestication* today brings the author's linguistic and conceptual world closer to the recipient, without any effort or interaction from the reader. Schleiermacher finds this unacceptable, on the basis that domestication inevitably distorts the author's concepts and thoughts. In his opinion, the translator should "leave the author in peace, as much as possible", and "move the reader towards him." Therefore, a translation should sound "foreign" enough to its reader, who "must always remember that the author lived in a different world and wrote in a different language." See Schleiermacher's 'On the Different Methods of Translating', in *Translation/History/Culture*, ed. by André Lefevere (London and New York: Routledge, 1992), p. 162. Despite Schleiermacher's rejection of the possibility of combining these two strategies (because they are mutually exclusive), I will argue that Gombosuren was able to create a translation that preserved foreignisation while involving the domestic assimilation of a foreign text.

16 All quotations from *The Idiot* are cited from the following text: F. M. Dostoevskii, *The Idiot*, trans. by Constance Garnett (London: Heinemann, 1913), with pages indicated in parentheses.

17 All quotations from the Mongolian translation of *The Idiot* are cited from: F. M. Dostoevskii, *Soliot*, trans. by Ts. Gombosuren (Ulaanbaatar: Bolor sudar, 2015), with pages indicated in parentheses.

18 For the problems of the Mongolian translations of the Bible, see Klaus Sagaster's study, which also covers the word 'Burkhan': K. Sagaster, 'Bible Terminology in Mongolian Translation', *Rocznik Orientalistyczny*, LXV:1 (2012), 171–79.

which becomes inaccessible to readers of the translation is the passage from Part One, Chapter Five of *The Idiot* where Myshkin recalls a donkey—immediately and consciously identified by him with the image of Christ. But to Mongolian readers, unfamiliar with biblical stories, these important analogies and symbolic values remain hidden or bereft of meaning. For such cases, Eugene Nida suggests adding some sort of explanatory note.[19] Gombosuren did not use notes, but there are other instances where he succeeds in compensating for similar losses. In the example above, the word 'blessed innocent' ('iurodivyi') became *'khiitei'*. The word *'khiitei'*, in literal translation, means 'filled with air' and is used to mean 'trusting, incautious, impulsive, boastful, insane', meanings which are far from compatible with the Russian 'iurodivyi'. But if we examine the etymology and semantics of this word, the translator's choice begins to make sense. The root *'hii'* refers to 'air', one of the five basic elements in the Buddhist understanding of the world. Not only air, but also its attributes—such as transparency and whiteness—are organically linked with the heavenly, or divine world, a connection reinforced by the Mongolian word *'Khiimor''* (literally, 'steed of the air'), which means 'the god of destiny' or 'the righteous part of the soul'. *'Khiimor''* is portrayed in the form of a horse with a blazing mane; it indicates the connection between fire and light, and in Mongolian thought, it is identified with the soul, fate, and fortune. On the etymological and semantic planes, the element of air and wind is identified with the word *'am''* ('life energy, the essentials of life, spirit'), from which words such as *'am'sgal'* ('breathing') and *'am'drakh'* ('to live') are derived.[20] *'Khii'* can be found in words such as *'delkhii'* ('world, universe').[21] In a semantic sense, *'khaki'* is cognate with words for transparency, light, and the colour white.[22] In *The Idiot*, whiteness is one of Prince Myshkin's consistent attributes that accompanies him from the very first pages of the novel (think of the insistent references to the Prince's *white*-blond curls and his bundle full of underclothes—known as *'whites'* (*'bel'e'*)) in

19 "But one does not do justice to the intention of the writer if he tries to 'ride the fence' in the case of those expressions which can have two or more meanings among which he cannot easily decide simply because he cannot reconstruct the cultural setting in which the writing first took place. In these instances, it is better for the translator to select the meaning which seems best supported by all the evidence and to put this in the text, while placing the other in a marginal note." Eugene Nida and Charles R. Taber, 'A New Concept of Translating', in *The Theory and Practice of Translation*, ed. by Eugene Nida and Charles R. Taber (Leiden: Brill, 1982), pp. 1–11 (pp. 7–8).

20 Skorodumova, *Mongol'skaia literatura*, p. 241.

21 Ibid., p. 233.

22 See Skorodumova, *Mongol'skaia literatura*: "The qualities of air are transparency, brightness, and white light. The moving fire-wind-air unites with our perception of the road, of the paths of fate" (p. 241). Thus, in the etymology of the Mongolian words *khii* and *delkhii* a semantic relationship emerges, much as exists between the Russian words *belyi* ('white'), *svet* ('light'), and *vselennaia* ('universe'), underlining the universality of these concepts.

Russian.[23] For readers of the original, well-versed in Christian culture, it is easy to interpret whiteness as a symbol of purity, chastity, and saintliness which leads on to the image of Christ. But how can a translation reformulate these allusions? Consider the following example (my italics):

> The owner of the cloak was a young man, also twenty-six or twenty-seven years old, above the average in height, with very fair thick hair, with sunken cheeks and a thin, pointed, almost *white* (*'sovershenno beloiu'*) beard. (Garnett, p. 2).

> Iudentei tsuvny ezen zaluu bas khorin zurgaa, doloo ergem nastai, dund zergiinkhees arai ondor gekheer chatstai, otgon gegchiin *tsav tsagaan* sevlegtei, ionkhoin khonkhoison khatsartai, barag tsagaan, shingekhen iamaan sakhaltai azh. (Gombosuren, p. 12).

The phrase 'very [white-]blond' (*'ochen' belokur'*) to describe Myshkin's hair colour is missing (!) from the English version; in Mongolian, it is translated as *tsav tsagaan* (literally, 'very white'), with the adverb 'completely' or 'perfectly' (*'sovershenno'*) omitted in relation to Myshkin's blond beard. This omission does not appear to overly influence the reception of the hero by readers of either translation, but in reality, this text suffers several losses of internal connotations. *'Sovershenno'*, via its link with 'completeness' or 'perfection' (*'sovershennost''*),[24] functions similarly to 'white', by emphasising the Prince's similarity to Christ. We have seen how some allusions to the text of the Bible are lost to readers of the translation. But how can the translator manage to create the same (equivalent) emotional effect upon readers as does the original? Gombosuren, as it will be seen below, consciously, or not, chose the method closest to Nida's concept of "dynamic equivalence", which has played a key role in the establishment of modern Translation Studies.[25]

23 The term *'belyi'* ('white') appears not only in constructing the image of the hero, but in the depiction of the Swiss countryside, thus interacting with the semantics of perfection, calm, and harmony: "At moments he dreamed of the mountains, and especially one familiar spot which he always liked to think of, a spot to which he had been fond of going and from which he used to look on the village, on the waterfall gleaming like a *white* thread below, on the *white* clouds and the old ruined castle. Oh, how he longed to be there now, and to think of one thing!—oh, of nothing else for his whole life, and thousand years would not be too long!" Dostoevsky, *The Idiot*, pp. 338–39.

24 Compare with these meanings: "the ideal, the conceptual image of the beautiful, worth, virtue, fulfilment", and so on. See *Tolkovyi slovar' russkogo yazyka*, ed. by D. N. Ushakov and others, 4 vols (Moscow: Gosudarstvennoe izdatel'stvo inostrannykh i natsional'nykh slov, 1940), IV (1940), p. 338.

25 In *dynamic equivalence*, translators concern themselves less with matching a target language message with a source language message and more with creating a dynamic relationship "between receptor and message that should be substantially the same as that which existed between the original receptors and the message".

In Mongolian culture, the word *'tsagaan'* ('white') is associated with purity; it is one of the most admired colours, used to represent the values of peace and the thinking of the people. It conveys the concept: "The first is the beginning of all".[26] The Mongolian language contains many widely used expressions that reflect the Mongolians' regard for the colour white. For example, New Year in Mongolia is traditionally called *'tsagaan sar'* (literally, 'the white month'), symbolising the beginning and the end of the year; *'tsagaan setgel'* (literally, 'the white soul') is a symbol of moral purity and a synonym of the word *'ariun'* (which literally means 'sacred, pure'). In Buddhism, many symbols and gods are referred to as 'white', showing that whiteness is also a symbol of sacrality. In this way, the textual codes of the original, implicitly linked with images of the Prince and of Christ, are reconstructed in the Mongolian text through the semantic link with *tsagaan* and *khiitei*, which connect to some of the most important Mongolian religious and mythological symbols. As a result of this, the symbolic composition of the Prince is supplemented by images analogous to those of the original. The translator's use of the word *khiitei*, while at first appearing strange, is justified by its links with Prince Myshkin, since he thoroughly expresses the essential qualities of the book's hero (a connection with the universe, with the divine world, with destiny, the soul, the beginning and the end, eternity and so on).[27] Thanks to this strategy, the extra-lingual context of the translation goes some distance to compensate for its inevitable losses.

Let me turn to one more interesting example. One inadequacy of the Mongolian version of the novel is the fact that the names of characters are not translated, even though they play an important role in communicating information and values. Providing equivalents to Dostoevsky's so-called 'speaking names' (for his characters) is clearly a complicated task for the translator, if not the most complicated task of all; so challenging, that so far it has not been possible to find a semantic match in Mongolian for any of the meaningful elements of personal names in the novel—for example for the syllables *'lev'* ('lion') or *'mysh''* ('mouse') in Prince Lev Myshkin's name—while retaining their national characteristics. To fully convey Dostoevsky's intentions, a translator must resort to notes or parenthetical glosses. Since Gombosuren has not done so, the Prince's name does not direct the reader towards deeper questions. But if he could rescue these connotations, which are contained in the

---

See Eugene Nida, *Toward a Science of Translating: With Special Reference to Principles and Procedures Involved in Bible Translating* (Leiden: Brill, 1964), p. 159.

26 Skorodumova, *Mongol'skaia literatura*, p. 223.

27 "In Buddhism, the god or gods are not separate from nature; there is no anthropocentrism. Unity (the absolute) emerges directly in the form of the individual, and the most profound reality is experienced as a result of unrealised being [...]. from which follows the disconnect between being and time, a total disregard of 'historicism'." See E. M. Meletinskii, *Srednevekovyi roman* (Moscow: Nauka, 1981), p. 67.

language itself, the interpretation of the most profound ideas of the translation could not be distorted or false by comparison with the original. When analysing the semantic peculiarities of the concept of *'tsagaan'* ('white'), the example of the phrase *'tsagaan sar'* (that is, 'New Year', literally 'white month') might return. The days of the 'White Month' depend on the phases of the moon (the word for moon in Mongolian—like the Russian *'mesiats'* ('month')—is *'sar'*). The lunar calendar, which Mongolians use, begins with *'am tsagaan khulgana'* ('the white-muzzled white mouse').[28] That means that some of the lost semantic content in Prince Myshkin's name is activated in the word *'tsagaan'*. One more concept related to the word *'tsagaan'* deserves our attention. That is *'tsagaach'* and *'tsagaachlakh'*, which contains the meaning of 'vagrancy, a person with no fixed home address', that is to say, rather like the Prince, who has neither a permanent home nor any means of survival (at least, at the time of his arrival in Petersburg).[29] In this way, thanks to the rich semantic associations of the word *'tsagaan'*, the text of the translation develops new connotations which not only expand its meaning, but are also included in the network of meanings making up the image of the Prince—without distorting the ideas of the original and, in fact, restoring them to the Mongolian text on the semantic and etymological levels.

According to Venuti, in the process of translation, the norms of the source language and culture are often severely distorted under the influence of target culture conventions—especially if the cultures in question are as widely separated as Russia and Mongolia. Meanwhile, my analysis indicates that the Mongolian translation of the novel *The Idiot*, together with this text's frequent use of devices for assimilation, generally exhibits effective transmission of the semantic and syntactic content of the origin. My view is that Gombosuren could not remain "invisible" when translating Dostoevsky's text, as while creating his version, he had to focus on the cultural identity of his target readers.[30] His crucial achievement, however, remains the wealth of conceptual images from the original, which, by making the most of the Mongolian language, he managed to transfer into a completely different linguistic system. His translation creates a new unity in cohesion with a new linguistic space: the internal form of the Mongolian words is restored, thus activating implicit meanings which correspond to the semantic world of the original.

The examples discussed above bear witness to Gombosuren's extraordinary inventiveness and poetic approach to the text. Thanks to his literary translations, the Mongolian public has been treated to an authentically global heritage; after all, the works of writers like Dostoevsky or Bulgakov belong to all humanity.

---

28 Mongolia, like several other Eastern and Central Asian countries, follows a lunar calendar on a twelve-year cycle (with years named after animals).

29 Skorodumova, *Mongol'skaia literatura*, p. 227.

30 Venuti uses this term ('invisibility') in order to determine the translator's ideal position in academia.

In this way, Gombosuren's labours as a translator have created a basis for dialogue not only between Russia and Mongolia; they stand as an intermediary in intercultural dialogue on a broader scale, transcending the development of literary language to play a role in the cultural and spiritual enrichment of the Mongolian people.[31]

31 Schleiermacher thinks of translation as a general cultural programme aimed at personal development and enrichment of language ("we should not fail to acknowledge that much of what is beautiful and powerful in our language has in part either developed by way of translation or been drawn out of obscurity by translation" ('On the Different Methods of Translating', p. 165)), where the goal is understanding. Translation thus becomes a "phenomenon influencing the whole evolution of a culture" (p. 159).

Turkey

Traces of the Influence of Russian Literary Translations on Turkish Literature of the 1900s

Hülya Arslan

The Nobel Prize-winning Turkish author Orhan Pamuk once said in an interview:

> My main interest is not politics, but literature. When people talk about Europe, Russia and St Petersburg, Dostoevsky immediately comes to my mind. Dostoevsky first taught me how similar our worries, everyday life, sorrows, and joys are. This writer from Petersburg not only told me how close the Russians and Turks are, but he also taught me to be human and tolerant. [...] [Dostoevsky] taught me to write.[1]

The Turkish novelist was a teenager, fond of literature and writing, when he first encountered Dostoevsky. In the same interview, he stated:

> I still clearly remember reading *The Brothers Karamazov*. I was eighteen years old, sitting alone in a room with windows facing the Bosporus. This was the first book that I read by Dostoevsky. Among the shelves of my father's library was a version of Dostoevsky's novel published in the 1940s that was translated into Turkish and another version of it that was translated into English by Constance Garnett. From the very first pages, I realised that I was not alone in this world, the reflections of the heroes seemed to echo my own thoughts. There were many acts and events that

1 Orhan Pamuk, 'Prorocheskii golos Dostoevskogo', *Gosudarstvennyi Ermitazh*, 24 (May 2017), 98–110, http://hermitage-magazine.ru/articles/orhan-pamuk-prorocheskiy-golos-dostoevskogo. All translations from Russian and Turkish are my own unless otherwise indicated.

 https://doi.org/10.11647/OBP.0340.32

> shook me—as though they had all happened to me for the first time. I only felt this way when I read great books.[2]

Not only Orhan Pamuk, but many other modern Turkish writers claim to have learned much from Russian literature. Many academic studies conducted in the field of comparative literature prove the same point. The above quote is, of course, crucial: there is a special cachet when a Nobel laureate credits a Russian writer's influence for the development of his own artistic inclinations. However, I am interested in another aspect of Pamuk's recollection. The translated novel, which Pamuk describes as "published in the 1940s", is the elaborate work of a "translation bureau", which played a remarkable role in the development of Turkish literature. The Westernisation trend, begun during the Ottoman reforming period known as the Tanzimat Era (1839–76), had gained considerable momentum with the establishment of the Republic of Turkey in 1923. As in many communities, fundamental changes in socio-cultural, economic, and political life occurred in Turkey through the translation of a diverse range of texts. The main reason behind this is undoubtedly a result of a series of translations: translation draws cultural values closer rather than merely transferring data from one language to another. Art, science, and schools of thought have been fed by translation throughout history. My aim in this essay is to explain in general terms the contribution of translations of Russian literary works to Turkish literary values, considered as a target culture. I use the concept of 'translation activity' to describe the entire process including the translator, the work, the translation decision, and the publication of the work.

Turkey has always favoured translation activities as a means to reinvent itself, like any other community on the verge of new discoveries. When educational reforms were needed, everyone's eyes turned to the West. Professor John Dewey, an American philosopher, social scientist, and educator, was invited to Turkey in 1924 to assess its education system. In his report, which was accepted as a reference on modernisation of schools and teacher training for years, Dewey emphasised how translations from foreign languages were essential for professional development in the field of education; he also added that the translations should meet students' expectations of good literature.[3] Dewey's emphasis on translation would prove significant for our topic. The first step towards establishing a new, secular national Turkish identity, able to take its place alongside world cultures, was the country's adoption of the Latin alphabet in 1928. In the first of many translation projects, a 'Delegation of Copyright and Translation,' appointed to translate books considered necessary for educational

2 Ibid.

3 Bahri Ata, '1924 Türk Basını Işığında Amerikalı Eğitimci John Dewey'nin Türkiye Seyahati', *Gazi Universitesi Gazi Eğitim Fakültesi Dergisi*, 3:21 (2001), 193–207.

use, was assembled in 1924 by the government of the new Turkish Republic.[4] But since the simplification of the Turkish language (by disclaiming the influence of Arabic and Persian), as well as the reconstruction of the educational system in conformity with secularism took precedence, translation activities remained in the background. However, by analysing relevant archives of the Ministry of National Education and the National Library today, we discover contemporary reports that reinforced the importance of translation for the country's development. These documents show that translation contributed to the modernisation of the Turkish language. As a result, the First Publication Congress was convened between 2 and 5 May 1939 under the leadership of the Ministry of Education to plan publications of the Republican period. The expression "invitation to a translation campaign", which Hasan Âli Yücel emphasised in his speech at the opening of the congress, drew attention. The main emphasis of the invitation was the necessity of carrying out the planning and execution of translations "under one roof", which consequently led to the formation of the Translation Bureau. A year after the congress, in 1940, the Translation Bureau was officially up and running.[5] The primary objective of its translation activities, which were intended to be carried out systematically by the government alone, was to mature the worldview of literate Turks and share the cultural capital of foreign literary works. This official cultural policy, spearheaded by the then Minister of National Education, Hasan Âli Yücel (1897–1961), is also called 'Turkish Humanism'. The campaign sought to ensure that all translation works holistically reflected a humanist perspective on the wider community. Although the translation activities that took place during this period caused ideological divisions between intellectuals, they undoubtedly had an outstanding impact on the development of Turkish literature, as well as on the social lives of literate Turks. One of the most notable decisions made at the abovementioned congress was the recruitment of "eligible persons for the selection and printing of integral literary works, including world classics, to be translated into Turkish".[6] In addition, a journal called *Tercüme* was initiated, and would publish eighty-seven issues from 1940 until its closure in 1966. Along with translations, translation theory, and criticism, readers of the journal could find articles on Russian literature. Within the scope of this forward-looking plan, a list of 1120 separate literary works was chosen for translation, eighty-eight of which were Russian classics.

For us, the most important aspect of these translation activities carried out by the Ministry of National Education is that the most influential writers and translators of the period worked voluntarily in this programme. Pre-Republican translations—made mostly from French or English as writers and translators

---

4 Taceddin Kayaoglu, *Türkiye'de Tercüme Müesseleri* (Istanbul: Kitapevi yayınları, 1998), p. 201.

5 See *Vakit Gazetesi*, 3 May 1939, p. 1.

6 Kayaoğlu, *Türkiye'de Tercüme Müesseleri*, p. 284.

interested in Russian literature generally did not know Russian—were during this period replaced by translations made directly from Russian. Some of the translators of these works were Russian citizens who had left their countries after the October Revolution, and others had lived in Russia for educational purposes or as officers of Foreign Affairs during the formation of the Turkish Republic. For example, Erol Güney (born in 1914 in Odesa; died in 2009 in Tel Aviv), whose birth name was Mikhail Rootenberg, immigrated to Turkey with his family and received his education there. As a philosophy student at Istanbul University, he met the poet Orhan Veli. This acquaintance brought him into Turkish literary circles, and as a result, he was actively engaged in translation during the 1940s. Erol Güney translated the works of Dostoevsky, Chekhov, and Molière into Turkish. He worked as a translator and journalist until he was deported, and his Turkish citizenship revoked, over a newspaper article he wrote in 1955, in which he suggested the Soviets wished to improve relations with Turkey. After living in France for a while, he eventually settled in Israel in 1956. In his last decade, he received a Turkish visa and started visiting the country again.[7] Another important translator, Oğuz Peltek (1908–56), who translated Russian classics directly from the original language in the 1940s, was born in Bulgaria. He moved to Istanbul to attend high school, and continued to live there after graduating. Like Güney, he studied philosophy at Istanbul University. He also worked as a journalist in Bulgaria and his articles defended the rights of Turks residing in Bulgaria. Peltek translated the works of Tolstoy, Chekhov, Pushkin, and Turgenev into Turkish. Nihal Yalaza Taluy (1900–68), who would eventually work in the Russian section of the Translation Bureau, is an important female translator of the period. Taluy, who was born in the Caucasus and immigrated to Turkey with her family after completing her high-school education, married Hayrettin Ziya Taluy, a novelist. She was known for translating thirty separate volumes from the canon of Russian classical literature.

The translator Hasan Ali Ediz (1905–72) was partly trained in Russia. After his Turkish university expelled him in 1923 for participating in political demonstrations (he was a medical student), Ediz went to the Soviet Union to receive an education there and to better understand the Socialist order. Many translators, writers, authors, and publishers of the same generation with an interest in Russian literature also had ideological aspirations. The same tendency is seen amongst intellectuals of the 1968–78 generation who were sympathetic to Socialism. Ediz was arrested when he returned to Turkey in 1929, but continued to work as a journalist and translator after his imprisonment. His translations of Gogol, Gorky, Dostoevsky, Pushkin, Tolstoy, Chekhov, and Ehrenburg were among the most successful Turkish publications of this period. Zeki Baştımar (1905–73), who had pursued his education in the USSR just like Ediz, studying social sciences at Moscow State University, started working in the Translation

7 See *Vakit Gazetesi*, 3 May 1939, p. 1.

Bureau after returning home. An active member of the undercover Communist Party of Turkey in 1947, he was arrested in 1951. After more than ten years in prison, he began to publish his work. Among his many translations, those of works by Tolstoy and Pushkin are the most widely read. Both Hasan Ali Ediz and Zeki Baştımar made innovative efforts to provide extra information about the authors whose works they were translating, in their paratextual synopses.[8] The oft-repeated catchphrase common to intellectuals born before the 1980s, roughly rendered as "we are a generation that grew up with Russian literature", was not just empty words. Besides the Russian works mentioned above, the growing list of translations also included Greek and Latin classics and works by German, Italian, Spanish, English, American, and French writers. As a result of all these studies, between 1940 and 1966 the Translation Bureau translated into Turkish 308 French texts, 113 German, 94 Greek, and 80 English (in addition to the 88 Russian texts mentioned above). The most-translated individual authors were Plato (with 30 works), Molière (27), Balzac (22), Shakespeare (22), Dostoevsky (14), Goethe (10), and Tolstoy (9). Introducing the World's Classics Series, in which these translations were printed, Hasan Âli Yücel emphasised the importance of translation in intercultural interactions and the exclusive role of Russian fiction in the development of Turkish literature:

> The first step in contemplating and perceiving the essence of humanism is internalising works of art, which are the foremost palpable interpretations of human existence. Of all the branches of art, literature is the richest in terms of expressing our voice and ideas. When a nation can reiterate other nations' works of literature in its native tongue, in other words, in its own mindset, that nation enlivens, enhances, and re-creates its own mentality and perception at an equal rate to those works of art. This explains why we deem translation activities significant and consider them effective assets for our cause of civilisation. Letters, the indelible tools to express ideas, and literature, their ultimate architecture, have such a deep impact that touches the very soul in all the nations that could turn thoroughly to every sort of such works of art. The fact that such an impact on both the individual and the community are identical, is, in fact, an indicator of robustness and scope transcending its immediate time and place.[9]

We should note that the statements commonly found in the first editions of this translation campaign (which was a direct intervention by the government

8 Altan Aykut, 'Türkiye'de Rus Dili ve Edebiyatı Çalışmaları Rus Edebiyatından Çeviriler 1884–1940 ve Rusça Öğrenimi 1883–2006', *Ankara Üniversitesi Dil ve Tarih-Coğrafya Fakültesi Dergisi*, 46:2 (2006), p. 17.

9 Hasan Âli Yücel, 'Onsoz', in *Dünya Klasikleri Dizisi* (Ankara: MEB Yayinlari), 23 June 1941, p. 1.

between 1940 and 1966) chime with Itamar Even-Zohar's 1990 article, which states: "[t]o say that translated literature maintains a central position in the literary polysystem means that it participates actively in shaping the centre of the polysystem. In such a situation it is by and large an integral part of innovatory forces, and as such likely to be identified with major events in literary history while these are taking place".[10] The truth of Even-Zohar's words had already been realised in Turkish society. Pascale Casanova explains the historical development of world literature similarly: "[f]or an impoverished target language, which is to say a language on the periphery that looks to import major works of literature, translation is a way of gathering literary resources, of acquiring universal texts and thereby enriching an underfunded literature—in short, a way of diverting literary assets".[11] Translation activities enormously enriched Turkish literature, as well as fostering artistic values in wider Turkish society. The development of short fiction changed the course of Turkish literature. Memduh Şevket Esendal (1883–1952), sent to Baku in 1920 as a representative of the first parliament, was a well-educated young man with a literary bent, and an author of short stories. He learned Russian during his four-year stay in Baku. He first encountered Chekhov's stories in the *Yeni Gazete*, which was published in Turkey and translated by the Turkologist Vladimir A. Gordlevskii (1876–1956).[12] Esendal's own stories, written in 1912 and published under a pseudonym, differed from the then-prevailing Turkish storytelling style. His laconic prose reveals his aptitude for observation, and researchers who have studied the emergence of this new style of Turkish short story have observed the aesthetic affinity between Esendal and Chekhov:

> We should note this: the works of most of our authors before Esendal, or of other contemporary literary movements, were under the influence of Western literature [...]. Although these works mentioned Turkey and its people, they conveyed a style, manner, and pattern of expression as if they had merely been translated or their authors had not belonged to this community. Esendal, who was content with adapting storytelling techniques from the West, did not convey any non-local touches in his works. These were the products of national literature, which described our own environment, our people, in our native language, and did not feel as if they had been translated.[13]

---

10 Itamar Even-Zohar, 'The Position of Translated Literature within the Literary Polysystem', *Polysystem Studies*, 11 (1990), 45–51 (p. 46).

11 Pascale Casanova, *The World Republic of Letters*, trans. by Malcolm DeBevoise (London and Cambridge, MA: Harvard University Press, 1999; 2nd edn, 2007), p. 134.

12 Hülya Arslan, 'Chehov v Turtsii', in *Dialog Kultur* (Kazan: Izdatel'stvo Yaz, 2012), pp. 50–52.

13 Cevdet Kudret, *Türk Edebiyatında Hikaye ve Roman—Meşrutiyetten Cumhuriyete Kadar*, 2 vols (Istanbul: Inkilap, 1967), p. 349.

Esendal did indeed create original literary works imbued with his own national values and cultural codes, but only by adapting techniques and inspiration learned from Chekhov. Esendal, known as 'our own Chekhov' in Turkey today, commented on his new aesthetic of storytelling and discussed the influence of Russian authors in a 1934 letter to his son:

> The writings I publish are not even among the ones I have endeavoured to write. I stumble upon new ideas written in this style for humanity. I work hard day and night to write a piece of original work, and I keep writing so much that I could write books with all that writing yet I tear them up in the end, while reading others' writings. [...] I do not remember when I felt like writing for the first time. I find myself reading carefully through some books to learn from them. And I read them several times over. I read Guy de Maupassant's *Une Vie* maybe ten times. Then I really liked Tolstoy. And I cannot let go of Doctor Chekhov recently. If one wants to tread the path to write in some way, they must absorb all the classics starting from the very first ones. In fact, you should still read them even if you do not wish to start writing. These books reveal new horizons every time you look at the world.[14]

Another of his letters from 1938 reveals, '"[t]he literary feelings within me awakened as I read the Russians [...]".[15]Although Chekhov claimed that he wrote in a cheerful manner, the concept of 'Chekhov's gloom' is often mentioned in Turkish letters today. Selim İleri (b. 1949), a contemporary author whose name is often mentioned in conjunction with Chekhov, exhibits traces of the latter's influence in his stories and novels. He even praises himself for having partially plagiarised his novel *This Summer Will Be the First Summer since the Split* (*Bu yaz ayrılığın ilk yazı olacak*, 2001) from Chekhov; in 2002 it won the prestigious Orhan Kemal Novel Award. İleri feels so close to Chekhov's style, in that he has borrowed the Russian author's famous gloomy evenings, unbearably sorrowful separations, and feuds with the past; even a character based on the faithful butler Firs from *The Cherry Orchard* (*Vishnevyi sad*, 1904) was integrated into his writing.[16] On the other hand, the film director Nuri Bilge Ceylan (b. 1959), the winner of the Golden Palm at the Cannes Film Festival in 2014, officially informed his audience that he was inspired by Chekhov's stories in the making of both *Once Upon a Time in Anatolia* (*Bir Zamanlar Anadolu'da*, 2011) and *Winter Sleep* (*Kıs uykusu*, 2014). Ceylan comments: "[h]owever much we write about

14 Memduh Şevket Esendal, *Oğullarıma Mektuplar* (Istanbul: Bilgi Yayınevi Bütün Eserleri -18, 2003), p. 73.

15 Ibid.

16 Hülya Arslan, 'Türk Yazın Dizgesinde Anton Pavloviç Çehov'un İzleri: Selim İleri', in *Prof. Dr. Altan Aykut'a Armağan: Rus Dili ve Edebiyatının İzinde*, ed. by Ayla Kaşoğlu (Istanbul: Çeviribilim yayınları, 2016), pp. 51–62.

Chekhov, we cannot feel him enough. He has contributed to almost all my films and he even taught me how to live beyond that".[17]

The influence of literary translations from Russian, which began in the early 1940s as a state-supported cultural repertoire to spread the understanding of 'humanism', was not limited to Chekhov. Dostoevsky's spiritual interrogations, Tolstoy's didactic prose, and Gogol's irony began to manifest themselves in contemporary Turkish literature during the following years as educational and social conditions improved. But translations from Russian literature did not merely influence literary genres. The purpose of such translation was not only to foster the development of new themes or new styles, but also to mature the broader outlook of Turkish artists and readers. In this context, Cemal Süreya (1931–90), one of the pioneers of modern Turkish poetry, claimed in an interview broadcast on television in 1986: "I was born in 1931. My mother died in 1937. I read Dostoevsky in 1944. I have had no peace since that day. That completes my biography". These translated texts reached more readers since they were completed after the alphabet reform of 1928. This is why I have focused here on the influence of Russian literary works translated into Turkish in the 1940s. Yet I would also like to note that the first book translated from Russian to Turkish in 1824 was Aleksandr Griboedov's *Woe from Wit* (*Gore ot uma*, 1833), by Mizancı Mehmet Murat, who emigrated from Russia to Turkey in 1873.[18] Between 1887 and 1900, at least twenty-seven poems were translated, including lyric poetry by Mikhail Lermontov and Aleksandr Pushkin.[19] In the early 1900s, Ol'ga Sergeevna Lebedeva (1854–19??) translated Pushkin and Tolstoy.[20] Tolstoy was increasingly translated into Turkish during this period, therefore enjoying greater influence, and is still one of the most-read Russian authors in Turkey today. *What Men Live by* (*Chem liudi zhivy*, 1885) is highly popular among twenty-first-century Turkish youth. Many countries' publishing policies are closely related to their national ideologies. A society's level of relative enlightenment is thus proportional to the framework through which culture is viewed, interpreted, and internalised. During the polarised global politics of the 1950s, officially approved Soviet literary figures such as Mikhail Sholokhov, Vladimir Maiakovskii, and Konstantin Simonov continued to be translated into Turkish and to inspire literary circles, although from an ideological standpoint, Turkey's politics were remote from those of the USSR. The Russian literary archetype of

17 Nuri Bilge, 'Kıs Uykusu Üzerine', *Altyazi*, 215 (2014), https://altyazi.net/soylesiler/nuri-bilge-ceylanla-kis-uykusu-uzerine.

18 Ismail Habib, *Avrupa Edebiyatı ve Biz* (Istanbul: Remzi Kitapevi, 1941), p. 267.

19 Altan Yakut, 'Turkiye'de Rus Dili Ve Edebiyatı Çalışmaları Rus Edebiyatından Çeviriler (1884–1940) Ve Rusça Öğrenimi (1883–2006)', *The Journal of the Faculty of Languages and History-Geography* (Ankara University), 46:2 (2006), 18–27, https://dspace.ankara.edu.tr/xmlui/handle/20.500.12575/65903.

20 Hülya Arslan, 'Kültürlerarası İletişimde Örnek Bir Çevirmen Kimliği: Olga Lebedeva' *Littera*, 16 (June 2005), 133–39. See also Sabri Gürses's essay in this volume for more on O. S. Lebedeva's translation career.

the 'little man', familiar from Gogol and Pushkin, influenced Turkish authors to begin creating (under the umbrella of Realism) portraits of characters oppressed by the political system; intellectuals, estranged from their communities, were targeted and criticised in Turkish society at that time, as illustrated by the attacks on Erol Güney after he published his article. Just as Maksim Gorky's *Mother* (*Mat'*, 1906) had inspired the Socialist youth of an earlier era, would-be revolutionaries in 1950s and 1960s Turkey read Mikhail Sholokhov's *And Quiet Flows the Don* (*Tikhii Don*, 1933). During this period, Turkish authors like Yaşar Kemal, Orhan Kemal, and Aziz Nesin visited the USSR at the special invitation of the Soviet Writers' Union, thus creating a direct cultural bridge between the two nations. The temporary stagnation in Russian literature after the dissolution of the USSR in 1991 briefly affected translations into Turkish. As it became more difficult to contact post-Soviet authors in order to acquire the rights to translate their works, publishers turned instead to authors banned during the Soviet era, with fiction by Aleksandr Solzhenitsyn and Mikhail Bulgakov commissioned by Turkish firms. Among the first modern Russian authors to be translated into Turkish in the late 1990s were Liudmila Ulitskaia, Viktor Pelevin, and Liudmila Petrushevskaia. Turkish translators who successfully translated classics as well as those authors mentioned above include Mehmet Özgül (b. 1936), who used to teach Russian at military schools; Ataol Behramoğlu (b. 1942), one of Turkey's most important poets, who also translated poems from Russian and has won many international literary awards; Ergin Altay (b. 1937); the poet Azer Yaran (1949–2005); Mazlum Beyhan (b. 1948); and Kayhan Yükseler (b. 1947). Since 2012, Russia's Institute for Literary Translation (Institut Perevoda), founded to promote the global translation of Russian literature, has begun to invite literary translators from Turkey to a biannual translation assembly in Moscow. This has brought a new dimension to Turkish literary translations from the Russian language. Turkish publishers and translators have been incentivised to produce new translations, and experienced greater recognition for doing so. My own direct translation of Boris Pasternak's *Doctor Zhivago* (1957) from Russian into Turkish was shortlisted in 2016 for the Institute's Read Russia Award. Moreover, it is a remarkable success that Sabri Gürses and Uğur Büke, the leading Turkish-language translators of contemporary Russian literature, jointly received the Literary Institute's 2020 Read Russia award for their *Complete Works of Tolstoy*, first published in 2019 in eighteen volumes. Since the 2010s, the impact on Turkish social life of Russian literary works translated into Turkish has reached a different dimension. As we analyse the communication tools of the twenty-first century, such as Twitter, Facebook, Instagram, etc., there are many Turkish social media accounts with names like Raskol'nikov, Svidrigailov, Rasputin, Doctor Zhivago, Woland, Lara, Onegin, and even Karenin—all borrowed from nineteenth- and twentieth-century Russian classics. Even this trivial illustration shows the relationship between the modernisation of Turkey and the growth of literary translation there. Translations from Russian and Western literature introduce new ideologies, philosophical ideas, and political trends. Influenced by literary translations from world languages, the margins of Turkish literature's cultural and linguistic formation expand. Damrosch states in his *What Is World Literature* that "[u]nderstanding world literature as writing that gains in translation can help us to embrace this fact of contemporary intellectual life and to use translations well, with a productively critical engagement". This statement allows us to conclude that translations have exceeded the limits of literary pleasure and revealed a richer world, both in terms of linguistics and of culture.[21] In this regard, although Russian literary works only began to be translated into Turkish a quarter of a century later than certain other languages, the influence of Russian fiction on the formation of a Turkish national literature has been both multifaceted and far-reaching.

21 David Damrosch, *What Is World Literature?* (Princeton, N.J.: Princeton University Press, 2003), p. 291.

Turkey
Pushkin's Journey through Turkish Translations

Sabri Gürses

The translator from Russian has long been a rarity and an outsider in Turkey; the same applies for academic study of Russian literature and philology. The most plausible explanation for this is the lengthy wars between Russia and the Ottoman Empire between the sixteenth and twentieth centuries (twelve wars in total), and during the second half of the twentieth century, Turkey's generally anti-Soviet political position. This also explains why there were few literary translators from Russian in Turkey until after the collapse of the Soviet Union, and why Lawrence Venuti's concept of the translator's invisibility hardly applies in the Turkish context: as outsiders, translators were almost painfully visible.[1]

Aleksandr Pushkin was the first Russian writer to visit Turkey, during his first and last foreign journey, long before he achieved canonical status. In 1829, during the Russo-Turkish War, he crossed the border with the Russian Caucasus Army and visited the occupied Turkish cities of Kars and Erzurum. He recorded his impressions and published them under the title *A Journey to Erzurum During the 1829 Campaign* (*Puteshestvie v Arzrum vo vremia pohoda 1829 goda*, 1836). At this time, both Russian literature and Pushkin were unheard-of in Turkey, despite gaining ground in Europe. The Russian army drove Napoleon back across Europe in 1814 and its march into Paris symbolically opened the way for Russian literature: within ten years, through French translators such as Serge Poltoratzky, Xavier Marmier, and Prosper Mérimée, Pushkin's name appeared in the Western press.[2] Pushkin's *A Captive in the Caucasus* (*Kavkazskii*

1 Lawrence Venuti, *The Translator's Invisibility: A History of Translation* (London: Routledge, 1995).

2 Yuri Druzhnikov, *Prisoner of Russia: Alexander Pushkin and the Political Uses of Nationalism* (London and New York: Routledge, 2018).

 https://doi.org/10.11647/OBP.0340.33

plennik, 1822) and other poems on liberty were translated and received attention from both the French police and the readers. Pushkin's 'The Gypsies' ('Tsygany', 1824) directly inspired Prosper Mérimée's novel *Carmen* (1845); Mérimée had previously made a prose translation of the Russian poem. The most enthusiastic European advocate for Russian literature, the diplomat and critic Eugène-Melchior de Vogüé, praised Pushkin as "Pierre le Grand des Lettres"; he considered his poetry so good as to be untranslatable.[3] This French admiration for Russian literature and for Pushkin, in particular, is especially important because, for nineteenth-century Ottoman Turkish society, French was the main language of transmission of European literary fashions.

When Pushkin travelled to Turkey, Turkish literature was experiencing a late and troubled Westernisation; it was still too early for the Ottoman Turkish literary community to understand Russian literature. Interestingly, Pushkin appeared aware of the problematic Ottoman reception of Western culture, which he compared with the analogous Russian experience. In the fifth section of *Journey to Erzurum*, he compared the conflict between Moscow and Kazan with the conflict between Erzurum and Constantinople (Stambul, in Russian; modern Istanbul). In his poem 'Infidels are Praising Stambul Nowadays' ('Stambul giaury nynche slaviat', 1830), he portrayed the Turkish capital and its pro-Western ruler, the *padishah*, as out of sync with their largely conservative nation. If he had observed it, he could have said the same for the Ottoman Turkish literary society based in Istanbul, which was trying to adapt Western literary forms and become a part of Western literature.[4] Their still-limited audience was also not ready to encounter Russian literature, much less prior to the emergence of Gogol, Turgenev, Dostoevsky, and Tolstoy.

Pushkin in Turkey

In 1878, the year that Dostoevsky began working on *The Brothers Karamazov*, the Ottoman-Turkish author Ahmet Mithat (1844–1912) founded a pro-Western periodical, *Translator of Truth* (*Tercüman-i Hakikat*). This journal would publish both Russian and European literature in translation, and it was the first Turkish forum to mention Pushkin: his short story 'The Snowstorm' ('Metel'', 1831) was serialised in the journal in early October 1880, translated via German by a certain Mehmet Tahir. Pushkin did not reappear until 1889, when in his *Universal*

3 David Baguley, 'Pushkin and Mérimée, the French Connection: On Hoaxes and Impostors' in *Two Hundred Years of Pushkin*, Vol. 3, *Pushkin's Legacy*, ed. by Robert Reid and Joe Andrew (Amsterdam and New York: Rodopi, 2004), pp. 171–91. For more on De Vogüé's legacy, see Elizabeth Geballe's chapter in this collection.

4 Özlem Berk, 'Translation and Westernisation in Turkey (From the 1840s to the 1980s)' (unpublished doctoral thesis, University of Warwick, 1999), http://wrap.warwick.ac.uk/4362/1/WRAP_THESIS_Berk_1999.pdf.

Dictionary of Important People and Places (*Kamus-ül alâm*), the Albanian-Ottoman writer, Şemseddin Sâmi (also known as Sami bey Frashëri; 1850–1904) mentioned him briefly: "Pushkin—a famous Russian poet; born in 1799 in Petersburg and died in 1837, he wrote several theatrical pieces, and also poems; his works have been widely translated into European languages".[5] Sami's dictionary is thought to be a free translation from the celebrated French lexicographer Marie Nicolas Bouillet's *Dictionnaire universel des sciences, des lettres et des arts* (1854); if so, it indicates that Turkish critics accepted French evaluations of Pushkin's status uncritically.

In 1889, at the Eighth International Congress of Orientalists in Stockholm, Ahmet Mithat met Ol'ga Sergeevna Lebedeva (1854-??), a Russian orientalist and translator trained at Kazan University.[6] During a previous visit to Istanbul, probably in 1881, Lebedeva had tried to publish her own Turkish translations of Pushkin, but, as memories of the recent war with Russia in 1877–78 were still bitter, government officials had unfortunately refused her permission to do so.[7] Mithat invited her back to Istanbul again and, in his journal, he published her translations of 'The Snowstorm', 'The Queen of Spades' ('Pikovaia dama', 1834), and her own short biography of Pushkin (1890). For the next several years, she translated Pushkin, Tolstoy, Lermontov, and others under the pseudonym of Madam Gülnar. As part of Istanbul's intellectual community, in 1892 she even encouraged the daughter of the Hungarian consul (pen name Madam Nigar), to translate some pieces of Russian literature from German and publish the first poem by Pushkin to appear in Turkish. In 1895, Lebedeva published a short *History of Russian Literature*, which included her Pushkin biography. Ahmet Mithat, in an accompanying note, commented that Pushkin was "the reformer

---

5 Quoted by Vladimir Aleksandrovich Gordlevskii, *Izbrannye sochineniia. Iazyk i literatura II* (Moscow: Izdatel'stvo vostochnoi literatury, 1961), p. 514. I cite Russian specialists on Turkish literature in this essay because Ottoman literature in the unreformed script has not yet been thoroughly researched by modern Turkish historians of Russian literature. All translations from Russian or Turkish are my own, unless otherwise indicated.

6 Olga Lebedeva's biography after 1909 is blurry. For more information on Lebedeva, see Hülya Arslan, 'Kültürlerarası İletişimde Örnek Bir Çevirmen Kimliği: Olga Lebedeva', *Littera*, 16 (2006), 133–35; Altan Aykut, 'Türkiye'de Rus Dili ve Edebiyatı Çalışmaları Rus Edebiyatından Çeviriler (1884–1940) ve Rusça Öğrenimi (1883–2006)', *Journal of Ankara University DTCF*, 46:2 (2006), 1–27. These two articles give no death date for Lebedeva, but another source states: "The last residential archive to list her address is found in St Petersburg dated 1913. Unfortunately, from that date information about Olga Sergeevna Lebedeva ceased to exist. What became of her fate thereafter is unknown". See Türkan Olcay, 'Olga Lebedeva (Madame Gülnar): A Russian Orientalist and Translator Enchants the Ottomans', *Slovo*, 29:2 (2017), https://doi.org/10.14324/111.0954-6839.065.

7 Aleksandr Iosofovich Shifman, *Lev Tolstoi i Vostok* (Moscow: Izdatel'stvo Nauka, 1971).

of Russian language and thought; he has found his way among the immortals of world culture and has been widely translated into French and English".[8]

In 1891, Sultan Abdul Hamid II had awarded Lebedeva a medal for her services to culture; during her last years in Istanbul, she concentrated on translating Tolstoy. She returned to Russia in 1896. Her translations of Pushkin were for a long period the only ones available in Turkish, apart from one small stanza translated from French in 1894 by the author Abdullah Cevdet (1869–1932) and two poems translated or paraphrased directly from Russian by an army officer, Celal Enisi (or Ünsî) in 1896.[9] By 1899, the journalist Ali Kemal (1867–1922), great-grandfather of former English Prime Minister Boris Johnson, was living in Paris where he wrote an article titled 'Poem and the Poet: Who is Pushkin?' in which he reiterated the European view of the poet: "[i]n Europe, they say that Pushkin is the Byron and Goethe of Russia". This article also contained an abridged prose translation of *The Bronze Horseman* (*Mednyi vsadnik*, 1833), but without a title.[10] Until the First World War, translations from Pushkin paused again; several novels such as Ivan Turgenev's *Smoke* (*Dym*, 1905), Maksim Gorky's *Mother* (*Mat'*, 1911), Lev Tolstoy's *Anna Karenina* were translated (usually via French) and serialised in newspapers. But in 1917, another journalist, Ahmed Ağaoğlu (1869–1939), "wrote an article about Russian literature, in which he gave much space to Pushkin".[11] Ağaoğlu, born in Azerbaijan, was educated in France, later working as a journalist and teacher in Russia, before emigrating to Istanbul in 1909. He taught Russian and Turkish history at the Darülfünun (the former name for Istanbul University) in 1912. Turkish Modernist and nationalist authors from different social backgrounds were now beginning to manifest particular interest in Russian literature and the Revolutions of 1905 and 1917. During the postwar occupation of Turkey by the British, French, Italian, and Greek armies, nationalists were among the leading groups of intellectuals to support republicanism and Westernisation. Later, most of these intellectuals would ally with the national independence movement led by Mustapha Kemal Atatürk (1881–1938), future president of Turkey. Mutual support between Kemal's loyalists and the Bolsheviks resulted in a continuing friendship between Soviet Russia and the Turkish Republic. The mildly

8 Ol'ga Lebedeva (Madame Gülnar), *Rus Edebiyatı* (Russian Literature) (İstanbul: Adadoryan Publishing, 1895). The book was transcribed into the Latin alphabet by Enis Mutlu Atak in 2013; my citations are from this unpublished transcription.

9 It is hard to determine the original Russian titles of these prose translations because they are paraphrased in old Turkish script without additional information. Even the translators' biographies are obscure.

10 For further discussion of Lebedeva, Celal Enisi, Ali Kemal, and other translators from Russian to Turkish active in this period, see Ali İhsan Kolcu, "XIX Asır Türk Edebiyatında Puşkin", *Türk Edebiyatı*, No: 269, March 1996, pp. 44–46; and also Türkan Olcay, "Cumhuriyet Dönemi Öncesi Rus Edebiyatından Türkçeye Yapılan Çeviriler Üzerine", *Litera: Journal of Western Literature* 18 (2005) ISSN 1304-0057, pp. 41–55 (esp. 51) https://ceviribilim.com/2006/05/06/cumhuriyet-donemi-oncesinde-rus-edebiyatindan-turkceye-yapilan-ceviriler/

11 Gordlevskii, *Izbrannye sochineniia*, p. 515.

Westernised Russian literary canon with its Socialist Realist themes was seen as a model for Turkish modernisation. One such supporter of modernisation, and a future member of parliament, the author Celal Nuri İleri (1881–1938), commented during a visit to Soviet Russia: "[a]h, how I wish that we Turks had just one Pushkin, Lermontov, Gogol, Tolstoy or Turgenev!'[12]

But such feelings were not reflected in actual translation activity. Not until 1925 was there a new translation of Pushkin; an individual writing under the pen name 'Necmettin' produced a partial prose translation of his narrative poem 'The Gypsies'. In 1930, two stories from *The Belkin Tales* (*Povesti Belkina*, 1830)—'The Station Master' ('Stantsionnyi smotritel'') and 'The Undertaker' ('Grobovshchik')—were translated by a certain Hasan Şükrü. And in 1932, another future parliamentary deputy, Hasan Ali Yücel (1897–1961), the future Minister of National Education, compared Russian literature (specifically, Pushkin's writing) with Turkish in a textbook. Much as Pushkin had attempted, through Mikhail Lomonosov, to align Russian culture with a classical cultural identity, Turkish intellectuals of the interwar period were eager to connect with their nation's Ancient Greek heritage.[13] Pushkin's keenest promoter at that time was the translator and diplomat Samizade Süreyya (1898–1968), who collected his own newspaper articles about the writer into a monograph, *Alexander Pushkin: The Great Poet and His Works* (*Aleksandr Puşkin: Büyük Şair ve Eserleri*).[14] He may be considered the first Pushkin scholar in Turkey. In 1933, he published the first Turkish translation of *The Captain's Daughter* (*Kapitanskaia dochka*, 1836), followed a year later by translations, probably made via English, of 'The Snowstorm' ('Metel''), 'The Shot' ('Vystrel'), and 'The Squire's Daughter' ('Baryshnia-Krest'ianka').[15] Samizade Süreyya was the first to publicly advance the idea that translating Russian literature would help to regenerate Turkish literature:

> We Turks don't know Pushkin. [...] We know little about Russian literature, Russian culture, Russian art [...] from a literary point of view, I don't believe that we are on the same creative level. We have a great need

12 Ibid.

13 Monika Greenleaf mentions that Pushkin admired Lomonosov's comments on the Greek heritage of Russian (*Pushkin and Romantic Fashion* [Stanford, CA: Stanford University Press, 1994], pp. 62–63). See also Saliha Paker's 'Changing Norms of the Target System: Turkish Translations of Greek Classics in Historical Perspective', *Studies on Greek Linguistics: Proceedings of the 7th Linguistics Conference* (Thessaloniki: The Aristotelian University of Thessaloniki, 1986), 411–26, which focuses on the period between 1866–1970. Gürçağlar comments on Ottoman-Turkish writers' eagerness to integrate with Greek culture and Hellenism (p.52). The poet Yahya Kemal (1884–1958), who introduced the trend of neo-Hellenism in Turkish, may have had common ground with Pushkin.

14 Samizade Süreyya, *Aleksandr Puşkin: Büyük Şair ve Eserleri* (Ankara: Akba Publishing, 1937).

15 Kar Fırtınası (Istanbul: Hilmi Publishing, 1934).

> for translation and transfer. Why shouldn't we use Russian literature for our needs? This literature is closer to our soul and taste in an artistic perspective, and superior to Western literature.[16]

At that time, Pushkin was not yet a part of the Soviet revolutionary iconography. The celebrated poet Nazım Hikmet (1902–63), who visited Soviet Russia in 1922, returned a convinced Communist with an affection for Vladimir Maiakovskii and the Futurists (who famously dismissed Pushkin and other canonical authors). Hikmet's writings do not mention Pushkin specifically. But by the 1930s, Pushkin was frequently referenced by openly anti-Soviet Turkish poets, like Behçet Kemal Çağlar (1908–69) and Mehmet Emin Yurdakul (1869–1944), who both compared themselves to the Russian poet.[17]

In 1937, the centenary of Pushkin's death, when he was already a Soviet icon, Turkish newspapers published enthusiastic articles and news about the celebrations in Soviet Russia. Cultural figures such as the critic Nurullah Ataç (1898–1957), the author Sadri Ertem (1898–1943), the teacher and politician Kazım Nami Duru (1875–1967), and the author and translator Yaşar Nabi (1908–81) all published articles and books about Pushkin. Sadri Ertem, a Socialist Republican, had recently visited Soviet Russia. His article, 'My Tovarishch Pushkin', reflected his impressions.[18] Duru's monograph, *Pushkin*, provided a detailed biography of the author and translations of his poems as well as extracts from articles published in Russia, England and France.[19] The biography of Pushkin published in the same year by Samizade Süreya was named *Aleksandr Puşkin*;[20] a third, by Hasan Ali Ediz (1905–72), was concisely named *Puşkin*.[21] Ediz was the leader of the (banned) Turkish Communist Party; he also published translations of 'The Queen of Spades', *Dubrovskii* (1832) and *Egyptian Nights* (*Egipetskie nochi*, 1835). But the critics were not satisfied with these publications; Ataç commented harshly about the lack of Turkish translations of Pushkin in a 1937 article:

> Thank God, the newspaper *Les Nouvelles littéraires* reached Istanbul on 8 February and our newspapers could write about Pushkin on 10 February. People who don't know the background will say, 'How good that we have many people that have read works of this Russian poet!' [...] Reds,

16 Samizade Süreyya, *Yüzbaşının Kızı* (Ankara: Akba Publishing, 1933) p. 4.

17 Çağlar asserted that the new generation of writers were as talented as Pushkin, Dostoevsky and Baudelaire, but the critics were unable to see their own skills as equal. See 'Behçet Kemal Çağlar cevap veriyor', *Kurun*, 30 March 1936, p. 6.

18 Ertem's impressions of Russia had to wait a long time—until 1989—to be printed: *Sovyet Rusya Hatıralarım* (*My Memories of Soviet Russia*) (Istanbul: Tarih ve Toplum Publishing, 1989).

19 Kazım Nami Duru, *Puşkin* (Ankara: Ulus Publishing, 1937).

20 Samizade Süreya, *Aleksandr Puşkin* (Ankara: Akba Library, 1937).

21 Hasan Ali Ediz, *Puşkin* (Istanbul: Resimli Ay Publishing, 1937).

> Whites, everybody says 'You have to read Pushkin', good, but how will we find him to read? Please go to the bookstores and ask for Pushkin translations, if you find any, please buy two copies and send me one of them [...] Even in French, it is hard to find Pushkin.[22]

This criticism, from a critic who was himself a translator from French, effectively showed the continuing neglect of Pushkin translations and scholarship in 1930s Turkey. But at least during the centenary year, Turkish audiences were informed about the importance of Pushkin in world literature and especially in the Soviet Union. Yaşar Nabi, writing a few days before Ataç, argued that Pushkin's foundation of the modern Russian language had opened the way for Dostoevsky and Tolstoy; he included his own translations of 'Exegi monumentum' (1836) and 'Echo' (1831) in the same article.[23]

The interwar period witnessed radical changes for the publishing sector in Turkey. This industry was not well modernised or even organised during the early twentieth century. The reading public and the number of printed books were still very limited. Publishers had quickly adapted to the reformed alphabet (introduced in 1928) and the government's literacy drive, but as they were few and confined to the big cities (İstanbul, Ankara, and İzmir), their effectiveness was limited. Then, in 1939, the government intervened and organised the First Turkish Publishing Congress, and the Ministry of National Education under Hasan Ali Yücel decided to establish a dedicated imprint for translated world classics. The process of symbolic and actual capital accumulation of national culture via translations was in force. These books, published and sold in special bookstores, and also distributed by the government to all the schools in the country, would help to create a reading public and also support the Westernisation of national literature.[24] The government acted as a specialised publisher until the 1960s. In 1939, the ministry issued a list of projected translations, including Russian classics.[25] Besides Denis Fonvizin, Mikhail Lermontov, Dostoevsky, Anton Chekhov, and Tolstoy, the Ministry of Education published eight books by Pushkin during the next fifteen years: *Boris Godunov* (1943, originally published 1831), *The Captain's Daughter* (1944), 'The Queen of Spades' (1944), *Belkin Tales* (1945), *Dubrovsky* (1945), *Little Tragedies* (1946; *Malen'kie tragedii*, 1830), *The History of Pugachev* (1949; *Istoriia Pugacheva*, 1834),

22 Ataç, Nurullah, 'Puşkin', *Son Posta*, 12 February 1937, p. 12.

23 Yaşar Nabi, 'Puşkin'in edebi hüviyeti', *Ulus*, 10 February 1937, p. 6.

24 Şehnaz Tahir Gürçağlar, *The Politics and Poetics of Translation, 1923–1960* (Amsterdam and New York: Rodopi, 2008). Gürçağlar's work and Berk's work are the best available studies of Turkish literary modernisation through translations; this period has not yet been studied from the perspective of sociology of translation, but Kader Konuk's *East West Mimesis: Auerbach in Turkey* (Stanford: Stanford University Press, 2010) also provides a general background of the time.

25 For more on Hasan Ali Yücel and his Translation Bureau, see Hülya Arslan's essay in the present volume.

and *Selected Articles* (1953). Also in 1951, Henri Troyat's 1946 *Pushkin* biography was published. But no poetry anthologies were included in the programme. Oğuz Peltek, who translated both books by Pushkin and Troyat's biography, commented that Pushkin's poetry was not available in French:

> As for the translation of his poems, it has been often said that Pushkin is untranslatable. He is the founder of both the Russian language and poetry. [...] Troyat wishes that one day a poet will appear to introduce Pushkin into French.[26]

The idea of the untranslatability of poetry, and of Pushkin's poetry especially, was then widespread. But successful translations of French poetry did exist; so the real reason for the absence of Russian poetry may be that Russian literature, in general, was internationally received as a prose literature. The newspapers praised Pushkin as a poet, but they published his prose without translating his poetry.

Fedor Dostoevsky	Year	Aleksandr Pushkin
	1943	*Boris Godunov*
'Another Man's Wife and a Husband Under the Bed' 'An Honest Thief'	1944	*The Captain's Daughter* 'The Queen of Spades'
'A Gentle Creature'	1945	*The Tales of Belkin* *Dubrovskii*
'A Little Hero' *The Adolescent* 'A Weak Heart' 'A Christmas Tree and a Wedding'	1946	*Little Tragedies*
Crime and Punishment 'The Village of Stepanchikovo'	1948	
	1949	*The History of Pugachev*

26 Henri Troyat, *Puşkin*, trans. by Oğuz Peltek, 2 vols (Ankara: Ministry of Education Publishing, 1951–54), I (1951), p. 4.

Stories	1950	
	1953	*Selected Articles*
Notes from the Underground	1955	
Demons	1958	
The Brothers Karamazov	1963	

Table 1: A comparison of Dostoevsky and Pushkin translations commissioned and published by the Turkish Ministry of Education.

These books were reprinted several times before 2000 by the ministry.[27] A lost opportunity and a very tragic event related to Pushkin's poetry was the murder of Sabahattin Ali (1907–48), a poet, novelist, and translator from German into Turkish. A friend of the Socialist poet Nazım Hikmet, in 1946 he co-translated Pushkin's *The Captain's Daughter* with the Jewish-Russian émigré translator Erol Güney (1914–2009) for the Ministry of Education. Then, in 1949, at a time when the Turkish government was repressing Socialist opinions, he tried to escape to Soviet Russia through Bulgaria. He was killed at the Bulgarian border. The motive for this murder remains unclear; it is possible that his polemical articles had irked a powerful government figure. Movingly, Ali's suitcase was found to contain only two books: a volume of Goethe, and a German translation of *Eugene Onegin*.[28] Ali may have planned to translate the latter into Turkish. In a commemorative poem by the poet Sabri Soran, Ali's image is linked with Pushkin's:

> Your glasses are broken
> On one side lies a murderous stick
> On the other Pushkin,
> Now that book can't talk with you,
> That wind will never blow again
> And your grey hair is covered in blood...
>
> Stars are in another world
> And Pushkin lies in his blood.[29]

27 This table is adapted from Sabri Gürses and Mehmet Şahin, 'Dostoevsky in Translation: Past, Present and Future Prospects', in *Zur Geschichte der Übersetzung in der Türkei. Themen und Perspektiven*, ed. by Faruk Yücel and Mehmet Tahir Öncü (Berlin: Logos Verlag Berlin, 2021), pp. 47–66.

28 From the police photo of the contents of Ali's last travel bag, the book cover resembles Ullstein Verlag's 1946 Vienna edition of Friedrich von Bodenstedt's 1854 German translation of *Onegin*.

29 "Gözlüğün kırık / Bir tarafta katil bir sopa / Bir tarafta Puşkin, / Artık o kitap bir şey söylemez sana, / O rüzgâr esmez artık / Ve kan içinde bembeyaz saçların...

Sabahattin Ali's death served as a warning for the poet Nazım Hikmet. Two years later, when the latter suspected that his life was in danger, he escaped Turkey for Russia. The 1950s continued to be marked by censure and repression in Turkish publishing. The 1960 military coup created a relatively democratic atmosphere, which lasted until the military memorandum in 1971.[30] During this decade, publishers felt more able to introduce Soviet Russian prose and poetry. Although the translator (and leader of the Turkish Communist Party Zeki Baştımar (1905–74)) translated *A Journey to Erzurum* in 1961, Pushkin did not receive much attention. In 1972, the Socialist poet and translator Ataol Behramoğlu (b. 1942) published an anthology of retranslations of all Pushkin's novels and stories as *Complete Works* (*Bütün Eserleri*).[31] *The Captain's Daughter* was republished as *Great Rebellion* in 1978, a title change indicative of Pushkin's rebellious image in Turkish culture at that time.[32] Like their peers in some Latin American and other underdeveloped countries, leftist Turkish intellectuals hoped to resolve all their society's conflicts and problems with a Soviet-style Socialist revolution. The next military coup in 1980 ended these political fantasies and again, as after the previous change of government, many books were proscribed and the publishing sector stopped producing them.

Behramoğlu exemplifies the outsider status of literary translators from Russian in Turkish society at this time. A radical leftist like his friend, the poet Azer Yaran (1949–2005), he had chosen to study Russian at university. He belonged to the Workers' Party of Turkey (TİP) and the literary magazine which he produced referred directly in its title to the nineteenth-century Russian activists known as 'narodniki', which he translated as *Friends of the People* (*Halkın Dostları*). After the Military Memorandum of 1971, he was forced to live abroad, in London and then Paris; in 1972, invited by the Soviet Writers' Union, he moved to Moscow for two years. In 1974 an amnesty was declared; he returned to Turkey and started publishing the literary magazine *The Militant* (*Militan*). After the 1980 coup, Behramoğlu returned to Paris again. Finally

/ Yıldızlar başka bir dünyada / Ve kan içinde Puşkin.' Sabri Soran, 'Sabahattin Ali'ye', *Başdan*, 26 (28 January 1949), p. 4.

30 The Turkish history of military coups is legendary: between 1950–2000 every decade experienced some form of military intervention in the nation's life. During the first coup in 1960, the army actually took control, and tried and hanged the prime minister. Turkey's Social Democrats regard this first coup as democratic or secular, defending the republican ideals; subsequent coups are regarded as reactionary. The so-called 1971 Military Memorandum was a coup, but rather than force change on the streets, the military forced the government to resign. Then, in 1980, the military took the government down by force. When, in 1990, there was no coup, people were surprised.

31 Ataol Behramoğlu, *Bütün Eserleri*, 2 vols (Istanbul: Cem Publishing, 1972).

32 By Oda Publishing, 1978. The translator's name, Şefika Şükrüoğlu, is probably assumed; Oda Publishing has since the 1990s produced many plagiarised versions of foreign classics ascribed to non-existent translators. See footnote 46 below.

resettling in Turkey in 1992, he started working as an academic at the Russian Studies department of Istanbul University. During this last period, he published collections of his translations from Russian poetry (including Pushkin), and a master's thesis on Pushkin's realism. In 2007, the Russian Federation awarded him its Pushkin Medal for his contribution to the dissemination and study of the Russian language and culture.[33] His original, politically motivated interest in Russian literature had shaped his career. The long title of his first collection of Pushkin poems in 1996 reflects this realisation: '*I have erected a monument not made by human hands*'— the first line of Pushkin's famous poem 'Exegi monumentum'. In some ways, Behramoğlu, like Ahmet Mithat before him, used his work as a translator of Russian to define his own literary self-image.[34]

Besides Behramoğlu, other translators now showed an interest in Pushkin's poetry. In 1987, author Tomris Uyar (1941–2003) translated *Mozart and Salieri* (*Motsart i Sal'eri*, 1832) and the *Little Tragedies* from English.[35] An anthology of Pushkin's poetry, translated by Mustafa Öztürk (b. 1964), was brought out under the title 'The Gypsies' ('*Çingeneler*') in 1990.[36] In the following years, several more Pushkin anthologies appeared. The first Pushkin biography to be translated from Russian (in 2000) was authored by Vasilii Kuleshov, a scholar at Moscow State University.[37] The year 2003 marked a turning point for Pushkin's poetry in Turkish, with two translations of *Evgenii Onegin* published simultaneously. Azer Yaran's translation avoids rhyme, while the co-translation by Bashkir translator Kanshaubiy Miziev and Turkish poet Ahmet Necdet is both rhymed and metrical.[38] Yaran specialised in Russian poetry, having translated Sergei Esenin, Aleksandr Blok, Marina Tsvetaeva, and Boris Pasternak among others. His *Onegin* culminated his professional dedication to Pushkin, following his versions of *The Bronze Horseman*, 'The Fountain of Bakhchisarai',

33 In fact, a reporter and a historian from Turkey were also awarded the medal. See Указ Президента Российской Федерации от 29.11.2007 г. № 1599, http://www.kremlin.ru/acts/bank/26560.

34 See also Cemal Demircioğlu's article, 'Translating Europe: The Case of Ahmed Midhat as an Ottoman Agent of Translation', in *Agents of Translation*, ed. by John Milton and Paul Bandia (Amsterdam and Philadelphia, PA: John Benjamins, 2009), pp. 131–59. What Midhat achieved for the Turkish reception of pre-Communist Russian literature, Behramoğlu continued for Soviet Russia and the Russian Federation; it is interesting that the Soviet and post-Soviet notions of the Russian literary canon are continuous.

35 Aleksandr Pushkin, *Mozart ve Salieri*, trans. by Tomris Uyar (Istanbul: De Publishing, 1987).

36 Aleksandr Pushkin, *Çingeneler*, trans. by Mustafa Öztürk (Istanbul: Damar Publishing, 1990).

37 Vasilii Ivanovich Kuleshov, *Puşkin*, trans. by Birsen Karaca (Istanbul: Multilingual Publishing, 2000). Kraca happened to be Kuleshov's student at MGU.

38 Aleksandr Pushkin, *Yevgeni Onegin*, trans. by Azer Yaran (Istanbul: YKY Publishing, 2003); *Yevgeniy Onegin*, trans. by Kanşaubiy Miziev and Ahmet Necdet (Istanbul: Everest Publishing, 2003).

and 'The Gypsies' in 1995. In that same year, the poet and editor Enis Batur had complained (like Nurullah Ataç before him) that translations of foreign poetry into Turkish were too few and that Turkish poetry could not expect to be globally recognised until it contained works of world literature such as *Evgenii Onegin*:

> We still haven't been able to host *Paradise Lost*, Góngora, Petrarch, Goethe, Leopardi, *Les Fleurs du Mal, Eugene Onegin*, or Mallarmé in our language. We still do not know the great living poets of our time such as Ashbery, Zanzotto, Eich, Jaccottet, Thom Gunn, or Deguy. Which works from this century have we translated that have left a deep effect on poetry: Do we know Valéry, Auden, Hesse, Hofmannsthal, Jakobson, Paulhan in the context of *ars poetica*?[39]

Batur's tone may have been exaggerated, but for the first time in Turkey, Pushkin's place in the international literary hierarchy was fully acknowledged.

Unfortunately, both translations of *Onegin* proved problematic: Yaran's translation was linguistically over-stylised and the Miziev-Necdet translation had oversimplified the poem for the sake of rhyme; their translations betrayed critical misunderstandings. I have previously analysed these issues in 2006, suggesting that Nabokov's strategy for translating *Onegin* without rhyme is preferable for transferring the precise meaning of the Russian original;[40] I used Iurii Lotman's and Vladimir Nabokov's commentaries for a renewed perspective upon Pushkin, tested in my own non-rhyming translation.[41] Batur's complaint, therefore, sparked three new translations within an eleven-year period (had Sabahattin Ali lived to attempt his *Onegin*, there could have been four within a half-century).

Overall, the history of Pushkin translations in Turkey reveals that, despite moments of enthusiasm, Pushkin's Turkish reception is conflicted. He has been hailed as Russia's greatest poet, and her first modern prose writer. But his image is mostly perceived through the prism of accounts by other Russian prose writers such as Gogol, Tolstoy, or Dostoevsky; even the popular *The Captain's Daughter* is not praised as a masterpiece like *White Nights* (*Belye nochi*, 1848). Dostoevsky's 1880 'Pushkin Speech' has been translated several times into Turkish since 1964; and in 1973 it was even retranslated with the title 'The Dead End of the West' ('Batı Çıkmazı') because Dostoevsky's praise of the uniquely Russian quality in

---

39 Enis Batur, 'Şiir ve Konvertibilite', in *e/babil Yazıları* (Istanbul: Yapı ve Kredi Publishing, 1995).

40 Sabri Gürses, 'Çevirmeni çevirmek: Nabokov'un Eugene Onegin çevirisi ve Türkçe Onegin çevirileri' ('Translating the Translator: Nabokov's Translation of Eugene Onegin and Turkish Translations of Onegin') (unpublished master's thesis, Istanbul University, 2006).

41 Aleksandr Pushkin, *Yevgeni Onegin*, trans. by Sabri Gürses (Istanbul: Çeviribilim Publishing, 2015); 2nd edn (Istanbul: Alfa Yayıncılık, 2016). This translation was shortlisted in 2018 for an award from the Russian Institute of Translation.

Pushkin chimed with the anti-Western, anti-imperialist, or anti-capitalist aura of that decade.[42] Gogol's and Tolstoy's praise for Pushkin as the father of Russian literature became gospel. But even this praise is understood to refer to Pushkin's prose; his poetry remains barely known in Turkish.

The peak of Pushkin's reception in Turkey was his centenary year, 1937. Press coverage then primarily focused on his image in European literature, his romantic biography, and his reception in Soviet culture. This was when diplomatic relations between the Turkish Republic and Soviet Russia were still positive. Radio Moscow even made a live Turkish-language broadcast, featuring musical compositions based on Pushkin's works.[43] Soviet Pushkin, the poet who had anticipated the birth of the USSR as a democratic, free state, seemed also to be accepted and promoted in Turkey by the Turkish press.[44] This may explain why Pushkin was less popular in Turkey than Dostoevsky and Tolstoy, who appeared more religious and conservative. The promotion of this 'Soviet' Pushkin faltered when Soviet-Turkish relationships deteriorated after Kemal Atatürk's death in 1938. Subsequently, as the new generation of translators from Russian, such as Ataol Behramoğlu, continued to promote this Socialist-leaning Soviet avatar of Pushkin, the poet's image in Turkey became still more secular and revolutionary.

Besides the books published by the Ministry of Education up to 1954, Pushkin was commercially available only through retranslations of *The Captain's Daughter*, which appeared to favour political dissidents. The most prestigious literary translator from Russian of the time, Nihal Yalaza Taluy (1900–68), retranslated *The Captain's Daughter* (*Yüzbaşının kızı*) in 1960. As we have seen, younger translators (of Behramoğlu's generation) perceived Pushkin through Soviet eyes; they focused on the image of Pushkin as a revolutionary poet, a perception fed by his clashes with Tsar Nikolai II. While not necessarily a distortion of Pushkin's real identity, this impression was imbued with the Cold War's political aura. Meanwhile in the USA, Vladimir Nabokov was trying to isolate and refute the Soviet image of Pushkin and Russian culture. In his own 1964 version of *Eugene Onegin*, he aimed to create a free-spirited, European, cosmopolitan, non-prudish image of Pushkin. But, Enis Batur aside, Turkish translators and commentators on Pushkin seem to have accepted the Soviet image almost uncritically—a reception legacy that lingers today.

---

42 Fedor Dostoevsky, 'Pushkin Speech', translated from English by Ülker Bilgin (Istanbul: Dergah Publishing, 1975).

43 'Moskova Radyosunun Türkiye için konseri' ('Radio Moscow is giving a concert for Turkey'), *Türkdili*, 11 February 1937, no 10163, p. 1. The programme was listed in the newspaper *Ulus* and it included pieces from *Ruslan and Ludmila*, *Boris Godunov*, *The Prisoner of Caucasus*, etc. 'Bu akşam Sovyet radyoları Türkçe neşriyat yapacaktır' ('Tonight Soviet Radios Will Be Broadcasting in Turkish'), *Ulus*, 11 February 1937, p. 4.

44 See Jonathan Brooks Platt, *Greetings, Pushkin! Stalinist Cultural Politics and the Russian National Bard* (Pittsburgh, PA: University of Pittsburgh Press, 2016).

This is probably one of the reasons why, when a Turkish translation of *Pushkin's Secret Journal 1836–1837* appeared in 2000, it aroused conflicting opinions.[45] This journal was published in English by Mikhail Armalinsky while he was an immigrant in Minneapolis; he asserted that it was given to him by someone in Russia and it included Pushkin's meditations on his sexual history.[46] How this book found its way from Minneapolis to Istanbul to be translated is another mystery, but while the Turkish media welcomed the book's obscenities, Behramoğlu harshly criticised it, contesting its originality. Whether this was because the book was a fake—which it was, and which therefore, as a specialist, he had to reject—or because he found the depiction of Pushkin as a happy author of erotica unacceptable, it is hard to say: the answer is probably a combination of the two. Prior to this book's publication, Pushkin was seen as an unlucky, cuckolded husband-poet; in 1937, an anonymous article called 'Pushkin and his Wife' encouraged women to spit in Pushkin's wife's face, suggesting: "O women! You should clean up the dismal memory of Pushkin's wife".[47] But an article from the same year by Ataç mentioned that Pushkin had had one hundred and thirteen lovers; this was intended as a compliment.[48] Solomon Volkov mentions that in the Soviet period, Pushkin's authorship of erotic poems was officially forgotten.[49] Thus we may say that *The Secret Diary*, even if fake, inaugurated a humanisation of Pushkin's image.

As we have seen, the translation history of Pushkin in Turkish reveals dedicated, highly visible translators anxious to transfer Pushkin's style and language into Turkish. This is the bright side of the story. Unfortunately, alongside this history of original translations from Pushkin, there is also a dark side: today, fake and plagiarised versions of Pushkin's prose abound in the Turkish literary market. Plagiarism is a timeless issue, but these mass plagiarisms started in 2005 when the Ministry of National Education made one hundred canonical literary texts mandatory reading on school curricula. This list included several works by Dostoevsky, Tolstoy, Gogol, and Pushkin, and mercenary publishers seized their opportunity to publish fake, plagiarised 'translations' of these classics.[50] Up to

45 Aleksandr Pushkin, *Secret Journal 1836–1837*, trans. by Mikhail Armalinsky (Minneapolis: M.I.P. Company, 1986); *Gizli Günce*, trans. by Cansel Rozzenna / Munire Yılmaer (Istanbul: Çiviyazıları Publishing, 2000).

46 Richard A. Gregg, 'Secret Journal 1836–1837 by A. S. Pushkin', *Slavic Review*, 46:3–4 (1987), 642–43, https://doi.org/10.2307/2498154.

47 'Puşkin ve karısı,' *Anadolu*, 14 February 1937, p. 5. Signed anonymously as Çimdik.

48 'Amerika'da Puşkin hakkında çıkan bir kitap', *Ulus*, 3 April 1937, p. 4. Signed as N.A., aka Nurullah Ataç.

49 Solomon Volkov, *Romanov Riches: Russian Writers and Artists Under the Tsars* (New York: Alfred Knopf, 2011).

50 There is considerable literature on this topic, including Mehmet Şahin, Derya Duman, and Sabri Gürses, 'Big Business of Plagiarism under the Guise of (Re) Translation: The Case of Turkey', *Babel*, 61.2 (2015), 193–218; Mehmet Şahin, Derya Duman, Sabri Gürses, Damla Kaleş and David Woolls, 'Toward an Empirical

forty different editions of *The Captain's Daughter* are now for sale, few of which are based on the original text. These artefacts litter the translational ecology; readers must carefully check the origins of any translation. Actual translators are faced with fewer readers and fewer sales, and readers are usually left without guidance especially in bookstores, online or not. Hopefully, this will not prevent prestigious publishers from commissioning and printing original retranslations. A complete translation of Pushkin's oeuvre is currently in progress.[51]

Conclusion

In conclusion, the millennium witnessed an unexpected improvement of Pushkin's image in Turkey. In 2002, Nobel laureate Orhan Pamuk wrote a novel about the city of Kars (the only foreign city that Pushkin ever saw). The main character is also a poet and the narrator depicts the Russian occupation during the nineteenth century and at one point mentions that "thanks to the new occupants the house in which Pushkin stayed during his visit to Kars [...] had been saved from demolition".[52] Surprisingly, this novel, which develops like a Turkish version of Dostoevsky's *Demons* and which parodies political conflicts in Turkey, has since inspired literary tourism to the city. Today people visit Kars to see the preserved Russian buildings and urban layout. The house where Pushkin stayed there has been turned into a museum; since 2016, the construction of another museum in Erzurum is in progress with the official support of the Russian consulate. A small Pushkin Museum opened in 2019 in the Southern seaside city of Antalya, a favourite holiday destination amongst Russians. Since the dissolution of the Soviet Union, the translator of Russian literature is less of an outsider in Turkish society. And as the number of Russian citizens living and working in Turkey has reached almost a hundred thousand, today, more than two hundred years after he journeyed to Erzurum, Pushkin has become an enduring symbol of Russian presence in Turkish culture. At least, it seemed so until the Russian occupation of Ukraine. Since then, the Russian cultural image may not have been cancelled as in the West, but it has certainly lost its glamour.

Methodology for Identifying Plagiarism In Retranslation', in *Retranslation Perspectives on Retranslation: Ideology, Paratexts, Methods*, ed. by Özlem Berk Albachten and Şehnaz Tahir Gürçağlar (New York and London: Routledge, 2018), pp. 166–91; and Sabri Gürses and Mehmet Şahin, 'The Shifting Value of Retranslations and the Devaluing Effect of Plagiarism: The Complex History of Dostoevsky (Re)Translations in Turkish', *Paralleles*, 35:1 (April 2023), https://www.paralleles.unige.ch/en/tous-les-numeros/numero-35-1/gurses-sahin.

51 This project includes my translations. A complete anthology of Pushkin's literary prose was published by Alfa Publishing in 2022; the volumes containing Pushkin's poetry are currently in preparation.

52 Orhan Pamuk, *Snow*, trans. by Maureen Freely (New York: Vintage Books, 2005), p. 318.

Those Russian citizens already living in Turkey have now been joined by Russian deserters and Ukrainian refugees, and it has become hard to praise Pushkin or any other writer on social media or in public without a reference to the war. In March 2022, poet Ataol Behramoğlu made a gentle attempt to criticise Russia's actions with a reference to his Pushkin Medal. He asked President Putin to end the invasion and stop two brother-countries from killing each other: "I see and understand that NATO and the whole Western block has targeted the Russian Federation... and I am sad about the cancelling of Russian culture [...] but no one can understand and accept the invasion," he said.[53] This call was of course met with silence; in March 2023, when Behramoğlu was invited to the Pushkin jubilee of the Russian Consulate in Ankara, he made no reference to his appeal, nor did he repeat it. The celebration was attended by eight Russian scholars, who had travelled expressly from Russia for the occasion, yet the Turkish press did not cover it. Sadly, the liberalisation of Russian literature has stopped, and the image of the translator from Russian will, in Turkey as elsewhere, be determined by the disposition of future Great Powers.

53 'An Open Letter from Ataol Behramoglu to Putin', 15 March 2022, https://turkiyenews.com/an-open-letter-from-the-author-ataol-behramoglu-to-putin/. The original text is here (there is no official Russian or English version of the text): 'Ataol Behramoğlu'ndan Putin'e açık mektup', Cumhuriyet, 14 March 2022, https://www.cumhuriyet.com.tr/turkiye/ataol-behramoglundan-putine-acik-mektup-1915678.

Uzbekistan

From Russian to Uzbek (1928–53): Unequal Cultural Transfers and Institutional Supervision under Stalinist Rule

Benjamin Quénu

Sen qancha tillarda sayraysan mag‘rur
Sozing yuksalajak yana baland, shan![1]

You proudly sing in so many languages
Your saz will rise again, glory!

(Oybek, 'Pushkin', 1936)[2]

During the Republican Conference on Questions of Literary Translation, held in 1952 in Tashkent, the poet Asqad Muhtor (1920–97) attacked the dramatist and poet Maqsud Shayhzoda (1908–67), who was already under pressure from a harsh personal campaign, accusing the latter of filling his translations of Pushkin

1 The current Uzbek Latin script has been used throughout this chapter, regardless of whether the original document was written in Arabic, early Latin, Cyrillic or present Latin script. This is a mark of respect for contemporary Uzbek research, which uses this convention. Conversely, the Uzbek names and words quoted in Russian-speaking documents follow the LoC transliteration.

2 Muso Oybek, 'Pushkin', in Oybek, *Mukammal asarlar to'plami* (*Complete Collected Works*), ed. by Naim Karimov, 20 vols (Tashkent: Fan, 1975–85), II (1975), pp. 38–39. According to this edition, the first publication of the Uzbek text dates back to 1955. Nonetheless, a Russian translation was published in 1937. See Muso Aibek, 'Pushkin', *Literaturnyi Uzbekistan*, 1 (1937), p. 144. Unless otherwise indicated, the author of this chapter is also the translator into English of both Uzbek and Russian texts.

 https://doi.org/10.11647/OBP.0340.34

and Maiakovskii "with Arabic and Persian words foreign to the Uzbek people".[3] This case vividly highlights two distinctive aspects of translation practice at the end of Stalinist rule. As a supervised professional activity, its accuracy was subject to firm control, which could potentially be weaponised against translators. Moreover, in the context of the Cold War and campaign against cosmopolitanism, literary translations from Russian were used to redefine the Uzbek language itself. In this situation, cultural transfers were acquiring a very specific meaning.

Since 2010, the Western historiography of Soviet translation practice has been re-invented. For instance, by focusing on translation as a social activity, Ioana Popa has revealed its contradictory uses: instrumentalised in the soft-power policy of the Soviet Union abroad, and at the same time exploited by writers and translators as a means of resistance or as an alternative form of consecration.[4] More recently, Natalia Kamovnikova has demonstrated how translation created a professional cadre that was simultaneously an autonomous community, thus empowering its members, the translators.[5] This renewal should be connected with debates within the historiography of creative unions. Meant to supervise, foster, fund, and even nurture the creative workers, these organisations were the interface between the demands of the Party and those of Soviet intellectuals. While early works exclusively focused on control exercised over creativity, more recent historiography has highlighted the construction of professional identity within the institution, as well as the agency of these recognised specialists.[6] The case of translation from Russian to Uzbek allows scholars to look beyond these paradoxical—yet not incompatible—dynamics. Different discourses

---

3 Asqad Muhtor, 'Respublikanskoe Soveshchanie po voprosam khudozhestvennogo perevoda', *Literaturnyi Uzbekistan*, 6 (1952), 84–122 (p. 86).

4 Ioana Popa, *Traduire sous contrainte, littérature et communisme, 1947–1989* (CNRS Éditions: Paris, 2010).

5 Kamovnikova highlighted the role of translation seminars in this process in Natalia Kamovnikova, *Made Under Pressure: Literary Translation in the Soviet Union, 1960–1991* (Amherst and Boston, MA: University of Massachusetts Press, 2019), pp. 196–269.

6 On the Soviet Writers' Union, see John and Carol Garrard, *Inside the Soviet Writers' Union* (New York: Free Press, 1990); Cécile Vaissié, *Les ingénieurs des âmes en chef : littérature et politique en URSS (1944–1986)* (Paris: Belin, 2008); and Carol Any, *The Soviet Writers' Union and Its Leaders: Identity and Authority under Stalin* (Evanston, IL: Northwestern University Press, 2020). On the agency of musicians within the Union of Soviet Composers, see Kiril Tomoff, *Creative Union, The Professional Union of Composers, 1939–1953* (Ithaca, NY and London: Cornell University Press, 2006). On the Soviet Writers' Union of Uzbekistan, see Ingeborg Baldauf, 'Educating the Poets and Fostering Uzbek Poetry of the 1910s to Early 1930s', *Cahiers d'Asie centrale*, 24 (2015), 183–211; Benjamin Quénu, 'Culture et politique dans l'Ouzbékistan soviétique de la Grande Terreur au Dégel (1937–1956): l'Union des Écrivains de la RSS d'Ouzbékistan, une expérience de cogestion du pouvoir et de construction des imaginaires politiques' (unpublished doctoral dissertation, Paris-10 Nanterre, 2019).

on translation practices, translation choices, and the unique place of Russian literature in the Uzbek cultural landscape emphasise how the supervision of translation practices has assisted in the construction of a multi-ethnic Soviet culture. In this essay, I will examine some of the collaborations and the conflicts between the agents involved.

The Premises of Institutional Supervision (1932–35)

In pre-Revolutionary Central Asia, translations formed part of Muslim cultural reform, which was carried out by a wide variety of intellectual movements usually grouped under the term *Jadidism*, and therefore highly valued as a means of reclaiming art and civilisation as weapons against the colonial oppressor. Uzbek translations were scarce, but Tatar and Ottoman translations were distributed in Jadid bookshops.[7] The Uzbek term for novel, 'roman', was first used as late as 1912 after the translation of Daniel Defoe's *Robinson Crusoe* (1719) into Azeri.[8] After the 1917 Russian Revolution, Jadid writers and translators worked with proletarian writers on Russian to Uzbek translations. Literary journals played a key role in the transmission of ideas and practices between different generations. For instance, during the 1920s, Muso Tashmuhammad o'g'li, commonly known by his pen name Oybek (1904–68), then a promising young poet from the anti-Imperialist circle 'The Star' ('Yulduz'), and the fiercely anti-Soviet Abdulhamid Sulaymon o'g'li, better known by his pen name Cho'lpon (1893–1938), the most influential writer of his generation, both contributed to the Uzbek-language literary journal *The Face of the Earth* (*Yer Yuzi*, 1925–31). During the year 1926, Oybek translated Maksim Gorky's 'Song of the Falcon' ('Pesnia o sokole', 1894) as 'Lochin Qushi Qo'shig'i', while Cho'lpon translated Nikolai Gogol's 'The Overcoat' ('Shinel'', 1842) as 'Shinel', in addition to many short stories from a wider cultural landscape.[9]

In 1932, the Sredazbiuro, the main board of the local Communist Party, based in Samarkand, ordered the dissolution of existing literary associations, and the formation of a creative union to supervise the production of literature in Uzbekistan.[10] This directive had little effect on these associations but quickly led to the formation of the Uzbek Soviet Writers' Union (Soiuz Sovetskikh Pisatelei Uzbekistana, SSPUz), which held its first congress in March 1934. However, from

7 Adeeb Khalid, *The Politics of Muslim Cultural Reform: Jadidism in Central Asia* (Berkeley, CA: University of California Press, 1998), p. 109, p. 117, p. 169.

8 Khalid, *The Politics of Muslim Cultural Reform*, p. 127.

9 S. Mamajanov, *O'zbekistonda badiiy tarjima tarixi* (Tashkent: O'zbekiston SSR Fan Nashryoti, 1985), p. 6, p. 116.

10 'Postanovleniia Prezidiuma i prikazy Sredazbiuro VSSP', Tashkent, O'zbekiston Respublikasi Markaziy Davlat Arxivi (O'zRMDA), R 2356, o.1, d. 2, fol. 2r.

its very beginning, the SSPUz showed little interest in supervising translation activity, and did not even create any section specifically dedicated to it.[11]

By contrast, the USSR Union of Writers (SP SSSR), the federal institution, not only set up a translation division, but soon divided it into sections dedicated to specific linguistic areas. In Uzbekistan, commissions and evaluations were shared out among the sections, which were grouped by literary genre (poetry, prose, theatre), and many translations into Uzbek were randomly distributed, whether from Russian or from another language. Translations from Uzbek to Russian were much more centralised as, regardless of genre, they were placed under the control of the Russian literature section. They even benefited from systematic publication in the Russian-speaking press of the Uzbek Soviet Writers' Union 'Literary Uzbekistan' ('Literaturnyi Uzbekistan', 1935–41), which met approximately bimonthly during this time. Translations into Russian, the dominant language and thus a powerful instrument of legitimation for a dominated culture, were already formalised, although they were, at least in Uzbekistan, controlled by the periphery instead of the dominating centre.[12]

By contrast, during the mid-1930s, the SSPUz still exercised little control over Russian-to-Uzbek literary translations. Nor did the translators working from Russian to Uzbek receive commissions unless they were writers themselves, resulting in a loss of professional recognition and material advantages. As for the commissions, most of them did not directly emanate from the Soviet Writers' Union, but from magazines, some of which were the publishing arm of the Union, like *The Literature of Soviet Uzbekistan* (*O'zbekistan Shora Adabiyoti*, 1933–34) and its many sequels. Others were much more autonomous, like the successors to the above-mentioned *Yer Yuzi*, the most important of these being *The Flower Garden* (*Guliston*, 1935–41), and *The Fist* (*Mushtum*, 1923-), the Uzbek satirical magazine, sometimes erroneously compared to the Russian *Crocodile* (*Krokodil*, 1922–2008).[13]

In this loose institutional context, until the mid-1930s, Uzbek translators enjoyed great freedom in their choices. Cho'lpon was even able to use the very act of translating as a subtle act of protest in *Mushtum*. In his translation of the short stories of Boris Cheprunov, a local Russian novelist, he emphasised the hidden meaning of his animal fable, *Miyoviddin Mirzo* (1935).[14] Cheprunov discreetly criticised Soviet power: his fable was ostensibly set during the so-called 'tyranny

11 'Stenograficheskii otchët I-go respublikanskogo s"ezda Soiuza pisatelei Uzbekistana'. O'zRMDA, R 2356, o.1, d. 2a.

12 As Pascale Casanova has demonstrated, translation into a dominant language—what she calls the world language—*adds value* to the translated text instead of devaluing it. See Pascale Casanova, *La langue mondiale: traduction et domination* (Paris: Le Seuil, 2015), p. 14.

13 See S. Mamajanov, '20 yillar O'zbek tarjimachiligi', in *O'zbekistonda badiiy tarjima tarixi* (Tashkent: O'zbekiston SSR Fan Nashryoti, 1985), pp. 6–29.

14 Sherali Turdiev, 'Boris Cheprunovning fojiali qismati', *O'zbekiston adabiyoti va san'ati*, 51 (2007), 2 (p. 2).

of the khans' (the Uzbek khanate of Kokand). Indirectly, however, it attacked the excesses of Soviet power, and its anti-colonial sentiment echoed Cho'lpon's own sentiments. Cheprunov would later be critiqued for his anti-Soviet tendencies, denounced as an Uzbek nationalist—although he was Russian—and shot.

Plays generally developed from collaboration between a theatre director and a translator. For example, Qodiriy's translations of Gogol's two-act comedy *The Marriage* (*Zhenit'ba*, 1832) as *Uylanish* (1935) and Chekhov's *The Cherry Orchard* (*Vishnevyi sad*, 1904) as *Olchazor* (1936), were the fruit of his artistic cooperation with the director Kamol Ilham in the Uzbek National Academic Dramatic Theatre (O'zbekiston Milliy akademik drama teatri).[15] Two now almost forgotten literati who were trying to reach the most respected ranks via their translation activity, Sanjar Siddiq and A'zam Ayub (Aiupov in some documents), were involved in many of these translations, of both Russian pre-Revolutionary and Soviet playwrights. For instance, Siddiq translated Nikolai Pogodin's play about Soviet industrialism *My Friend* (*Moi drug*, 1932) as *Mening do'stim* (1934), and Nikolai Gogol's *The Government Inspector* (*Revizor*, 1836) as *Revizor* (1935). Cho'lpon judged this latter play opaque to a non-speaker of Russian, thus advocating for a target-oriented translation, and showing his acute awareness of the linguistic risks associated with repeated contact with the Russian language.[16]

This tireless translation of the Russian classics should not obfuscate Uzbek writers' wider interest, predating the Revolution, in European literature and theatre. Despite their anti-colonial views, Muslim reformists had long studied modern European drama in order to promote their own ideology.[17] From this perspective, translation activity helped to accumulate cultural capital, a process which continued after the 1917 Revolution. The first play translated into Uzbek in Soviet Tashkent was the German dramatist Friedrich Schiller's *Cabal and Love* (*Kabale und liebe*, 1784), as *Makr va muhabbat*, directed by Kamol Ilham in the theatre later named after Hamza in 1921. The translator, the poet Shamsiddin Sharafiddin o'g'li, known as Xurshid (1892–1960), had been a contributor to the local Jadid press, including journals such as the appropriately named *Translator* (*Tarjimon*) and *The Mirror* (*Oyna*), since the beginning of the First World War. Schiller had been popular in the Russian Empire since the nineteenth century. He remained part of the Soviet patrimony, as he was long considered a poet of emancipation, with the social aspects of his works highlighted by Gorky.[18] Xurshid thus easily found a Russian translation on which to base his own. The playwright's popularity in Uzbekistan was therefore facilitated by his works'

15 Naim Karimov, 'Abdulla Qodiriy—tarjimon', *Jahon adabiyoti*, 4 (2014), 89–95 (p. 89).

16 Abdulhamid Cho'lpon, 'Ko'lagada qolg'onlar to'ghrisida', *Qizil O'zbekiston*, 10 May 1935, 4 (p. 4).

17 Khalid, *The Politics of Muslim Cultural Reform*, pp. 129–33.

18 Edmund Kostka, 'The Vogue of Schiller in Russia and in the Soviet Union', *The German Quarterly*, 36:1 (1963), 2–13 (10).

previous circulation in the Russian and Soviet Empire and by the Marxist analysis of his plays, besides local anti-colonial reinterpretations of his call for freedom. His reputation was so high that Ayub, probably influenced by the success of the play on the stage in Moscow since 1930, wrote a new translation for the Hamza Theatre in 1935.[19]

The extensive use of Russian as an intermediary language during this period illustrates the quest to expand cultural capital, as well as reinforcing the dominant position of Russian. Cho'lpon translated *Hamlet* for the Uzbek director Mannon Uyg'ur in 1934, while Sanjar Siddiq staged Goldoni's *The Mistress of the Inn* (*La locandiera*, 1753) as *Mehmonxona bekasi* (1935), and Lope de Vega's *Fuenteovejuna* (1619) as *Qo'zibuloq qishlog'i* (1935). The interest in the latter was connected to the rise of Spanish studies in Moscow. Sanzhar Siddiq used the translation that had been published some weeks before by Sergei S. Ignatov, who was both translating and analysing Spanish classics from a Marxist perspective.[20] Although such translations were related to Muscovite publications and interests in this way, they were not the result of any top-down Soviet translation policy. The case of *Fuenteovejuna* therefore indicates the intensity of the cultural exchanges between the centre and the periphery, rather than any attempt to supervise: translators appropriated the dominant culture for their own needs and did not limit themselves to Russian literature. Using the concepts coined by Casanova in her 'Consécration et accumulation de capital littéraire, la traduction comme échange inégal', one could say they conscientiously used a "translation-accumulation" strategy, completing the intensive "translation-consecration" policy led by the SSPUz and *Literaturnyi Uzbekistan*.[21] The pre-Revolutionary anti-colonial translation strategy here melded with the Soviet desire to become the legitimate heir and custodian of world literature.[22]

The Uzbek language was not at this time very standardised. In 1932, the Fifth Plenary Session of the Uzbek Communist Party voted on a first normative measure, standardising the language used in translations of Marxist-Leninist classics, imposing Russian words for many political concepts, replacing the Turkish 'jumhuriyat' with 'respublika', and making Russian technical terms like 'doklad' (report) mandatory, and thus reinforcing Russian-language dominance

19 Sotimboi Tursunboev, *Jahon teatri tarixi* (Tashkent: O'zbekiston Respublikasi olii va O'rta Maxsus Ta'lim Vazirligi, 2008), p. 269.

20 Ludmilla B. Turkevich, 'Status of Spanish Studies in the Soviet Union', *Hispania*, 41:4 (1958), 485–90 (p. 485).

21 Pascale Casanova, 'Consécration et accumulation de capital littéraire. La traduction comme échange inégal', *Actes de la Recherche en Sciences sociales*, 144 (2002), 7–20 (p. 9).

22 On Soviet claims to mediate world culture, see Katerina Clark, *Moscow, the Fourth Rome: Stalinism, Cosmopolitanism, and the Evolution of Soviet Culture, 1931–1941* (Cambridge, MA: Harvard University Press, 2011), pp. 9–11.

in strategic publications.[23] Nonetheless, despite the publication of a very short Russian-Uzbek dictionary in Kazan in 1934, these measures barely affected literary translation.

Translating Pushkin, an Act of Allegiance? (1935–37)

The first firm institutional supervision of literary translations from the Russian language arose in 1936, as a result of the Pushkin jubilee decreed in 1935. Russian literary historiography has thoroughly emphasised the jubilee's scope and significance within Russian culture, but has conversely overlooked its significance on both the Soviet and global scales. Yet, from the start, the basic structure of the All-Soviet Committee dedicated to the Pushkin jubilee reflected a determination to involve the Soviet peripheries in the celebration, as half of its members represented Soviet Socialist Republics. Sadriddin Ayni (1874–1954), who is usually considered a founding father of both the Uzbek and the Tajik novel, was one such member.[24] At this time, he was still influential in the Uzbek Soviet Writers' Union, which he encouraged to establish its own Jubilee Commission. From 1936, writers and translators met more frequently under the supervision of the SSPUz. Their main role was to decide which of Aleksandr Pushkin's works should be translated, and by whom. They organised strict plans, orders, publication objectives, and evaluations of all drafts submitted.[25] Unfortunately, the surviving documentation of their efforts is sparse and poorly conserved. The existence of such a commission, however, demonstrates that translations were now subject to the same procedural control as creative works. For the first time, the act of translating was planned and directed from above, and local institutions were enlisted to fulfil the demands of a central policy. The jubilee had deep institutional consequences, as it established a model for other All-Soviet jubilees, each of which must now also be directed by a committee specific to each republic, and composed of high-ranking and district-level Party officials, writers, and composers.[26] Translations were still not centralised, but there was such a succession of special events one after another that the

23 William Fierman, *Language Planning and National Development: The Uzbek Experience* (Berlin: Mouton de Gruyter, 1991), p. 158.

24 *Vlast' i khudozhestvennaia intelligentsiia, Dokumenty CK RKP(b) VKP(b), VChK - OGPU - NKVD o kul'turnoi politike 1917–1953*, ed. by Andrei Artizov and Oleg Naumov (Rospen: Moscow, 1999), p. 219.

25 'Protokoly zasedanii komiteta pro provleniiu stoletnogo iubilieia so dnia smerti Pushkina, spisok proizvedenii, izdavaemykh Gosizdatom na uzbekskom iazyke', Tashkent, O'zRMDA, R-2356, o. 1, d. 13, fol. 14r. .

26 'Sostav iubileinogo komiteta Lermontogo', Tashkent, O'zRMDA, R-2356, o. 1, d. 63, fol. 75r.

exception became the norm, and a *de facto* permanent supervision prevailed. The celebration of Pushkin was followed by the jubilees of the Georgian poet Shota Rustaveli (which was prepared from 1935 to 1938), of Vladimir Maiakovskii (1939–40), and of Mikhail Lermontov (1938–41) respectively, with each occasion involving its own translation commission.[27] Meanwhile, the all-Soviet millennium of the Armenian epic poem 'The Daredevils of Sassoun' ('Sasna Tsrer') was commemorated in 1939.[28]

The jubilee model was not exclusively used for promoting classic Russian literature. Moreover, every translation of selected samples of literature from the multinational Soviet Union had an Uzbek counterpart: for instance, there was the preparation for the jubilee of the Timurid (considered Uzbek) poet Alisher Nava'i, whose works were due to be translated into all languages of the Soviet Union until the war intervened.[29] Historians have thoroughly debated the Stalinist policy of promoting Russian classics, often characterising it as a means of producing a shared cultural medium while fixing standards of *kulturnost'* ('cultural level'), thus implying a struggle against 'cultural backwardness'.[30] Taken with these examples from other Soviet Republics' cultures, in the Uzbek context this Stalinist policy appears during the mid-1930s more as an experiment in a multinational culture than an assertion of Russian cultural imperialism. The

27 'Postanovleniia Soveta Narodnykh Komissarov Uzbekskoj SSR, protokoly zasedaniia komisii po provediniiu iubileia velikogo gruzinskogo poėta Shota Rustaveli (7 aprelia 1935–13 fevralia 1938)', O'zRMDA, R-2356, o. 1, d. 8, fols 1r-22r; 'Stikhi M.Iu. Lermontova, namechanye dlia perevoda na uzbekskii iazyk', O'zRMDA, R-2356, o. 1, d. 63, fols. 134r-137r; 'Protokol n°5 Zasedaniia Pravleniia Soiuza Sov. Pisatelei Uzb. 31-go marta 1940', O'zRMDA, R-2356, o. 1, d. 63, fols. 64r-65r.

28 'Postanovleniia Prezidiuma Pravleniia Soiuza Sovetskikh Pisatelei o sozyve iubileinogo Plenuma SSP SSSR v gorode Erevane v sviazi s prazdnovaniem 1000 letnego arm'ianskogo narodnogo ėposa "David Sasunskii", protokol zasedaniia iubileinoi komissii (27 avgusta-9 sentiabria 1939)', O'zRMDA, R-2356, o. 1, d. 50.

29 During the 1930s, Soviet orientalists and Uzbek writers declared the fifteenth-century Turkic poet Alisher Nava'i the official founding father of Uzbek literature, thus consolidating a long process of nationalisation begun by the Jadids. On the role of orientalists, see Marc Toutant, 'De l'indigénisation soviétique au panturquisme académique, Un cas de transfert culturel ambigu', *European Journal of Turkish Studies*, 22 (2016), 2–21 (2–3); Boram Shin, 'Inventing a National Writer: The Soviet Celebration of the 1948 Alisher Nava'i Jubilee and the Writing of the Uzbek History', *International Journal of Asian Studies*, 14.2 (2017), 117–42; on the specific role of writers in this nationalisation, see Benjamin Quénu, 'Culture et politique dans l'Ouzbékistan soviétique', pp. 220–57. The translation planning is recorded in 'Postanovlenie Soveta Narodnykh Kommisarov Uzbekskoi SSR o xode podgotvoki k 500 letnomu iubileiu Alishera Navoi', O'zRMDA, R-2356, o. 1, d. 49, fols. 36r-37r.

30 On global Soviet policy, see Terry Martin, *The Affirmative Action Empire: Nations and Nationalism in the Soviet Union, 1923–1939* (Ithaca, NY and London: Cornell University Press, 2001), pp. 126–32.

Russian model nevertheless affected writers' statuses and writing practices, and Russian literature remained the main referent. When the poet Hamid Olimjon (1909–44) and the novelist G'afur G'ulom (1903–66), both promoters of Socialist Realism, became the principal translators of Maiakovskii for the latter's jubilee, Hamid Olimjon was soon called "the Uzbek Maiakovskii", while G'afur G'ulom, head of the committee that had organised the translation, immediately borrowed the Soviet poet's famous percussive style for his own poetry.[31] In the same way, the quality of the prose of Abdulla Qahhor earned him the title of the "Uzbek Chekhov", an association that he encouraged further in his assertion that Chekhov was his 'domla'—his 'master'.[32]

Although strongly encouraged by central authorities, Pushkin's jubilee celebrations themselves soon acquired an ambiguous significance. Although they may initially have been conceived as a demonstration of allegiance and as promotion of Russian culture, the discourse and choices of early translators of Pushkin's works cast doubt on such an interpretation of the ceremonies. The first Uzbek translator of Pushkin's poetry and novels, Cho'lpon, was still openly anti-colonial. He chose to translate *Boris Godunov*, where the titular usurper's path to power is soaked with the blood of the Tsar's true heir, at the time he was publishing his *Night* (*Kecha*, 1936), an historical novel set during the 1916 Central Asian revolt against conscription.[33] As for the young lyrical poet Usmon Nosir (1912–44), he expressed mild criticism of contemporary Soviet policy. He translated Pushkin's poem 'The Fountain of Bakhchisarai' ('Boqchasoroy fontani', 1936), a choice certainly dictated by the Asian setting of the plot.[34] Oybek's political stance was ambiguous. Although he had participated in proletarian circles, he was an outspoken admirer and defender of more suspect writers, including Qodiriy and Cho'lpon, and was therefore also regarded with suspicion.[35] He opted to translate Pushkin's masterpiece, *Evgenii Onegin* (1825–1832). Drafts of his translation, kept in his former home (now a dedicated museum), show his lengthy research process. Oybek separated all individual alphabetical characters of his draft in order to allow for word

31 'Protokol n°5 zasedaniia Pravlenia Soiuza Sov. Pisatelei Uzbekistana, 31 marta 1940 g.', O'zRMDA, R-2356, o. 1, d. 63, fol. 64r.

32 Abdulla Qahhor, *O'tmishdan Ertaklar* (Tashkent: Yosh Gvardiya, 1976), p. 41.

33 Shawn T. Lyons, 'Resisting Colonialism in the Uzbek Historical Novel "Kecha va Kunduz (Night and Day)", 1936', *Inner Asia*, 3–2 (2001), 175–92 (176).

34 Aleksandr Pushkin, *Boqchasoroi Fontani*, trans. by Usmon Nosir (Tashkent: Gosizdat, 1936).

35 Muso Oybek, 'Cho'lpon, shoirni qanday tekshirish kerak', *Qizil O'zbekiston*, 17 May 1927, p. 2; Muso Oybek, *Abdulla Qodiriyning ijodii yo'li* (Tashkent: O'zbekiston Fanlar komiteti nashriëti, 1936); Adeeb Khalid, *Making Uzbekistan, Nation, Empire in the Early USSR* (Ithaca, NY and London: Cornell University Press, 2015), pp. 334–36; Benjamin Quénu, 'Culture et politique dans l'Ouzbékistan soviétique', pp. 95–98.

changes and permutations.[36] In key passages, the drafts offer evidence of his search for the right words and metrical accuracy. Although he placed himself under pressure, the result was indisputably successful, and set high standards for future versions. His accuracy demonstrated both professionalism, fidelity to the source author, and loyalty to Soviet power. The final version is not a literal translation; Oybek had to find an adaptation strategy to express the freedom of his interpretation. Like many others, he wrote a poem dedicated to Pushkin prior to the jubilee, which is quoted in the epigraph to this chapter, above. Like Cho'lpon, he did not praise Pushkin as the genius who gave birth to the Russian literary canon.[37] Instead, he emphasised Pushkin's struggle, as a poet, against an unfair political regime. This part of the Pushkin cult was certainly not new, as the Russian intelligentsia had cast him as a model of resistance since the middle of the nineteenth century.[38] It also had specific contemporary resonances in 1937 when it was published in Russian.[39] In this poem, Oybek portrayed Pushkin as a multilingual poet "crushing" tyranny—resisting tyranny with his verse—by opening an imaginary country to the reader. Oybek ended the poem with some distinctly ambiguous lines of verse: "The free homeland reads you with felicity / You proudly sing in so many languages / Your saz will rise again, glory!"[40] The "free homeland" referred to the Soviet Union, but also to Uzbekistan, and these lines clearly indicated that its ultimate identity was supranational, poetry itself. Moreover, the last verse bore a strong intertextuality with Cho'lpon's 'I play my saz again' ('Yana o'ldim sozimni', 1934).[41] Oybek attributed the saz, or traditional lute, to Pushkin, merging him implicitly with Cho'lpon, who had been his first translator; Oybek had already compared them in an earlier article.[42] As Cho'lpon seemed vulnerable when the poem was first published in Russian, this

36 Oybek uy-muzeyi, KP-7735.

37 Muso Oybek, 'Pushkin', in Oybek, *Mukammal asarlar to'pladi* (*Complete Collected Works*), II (1975), pp. 38–39 (p. 39). The Uzbek original was published only after the death of Stalin, which confirms this assumption.

38 Ol'ga Murav'ëva, 'Obraz Pushkina: istoricheskie metamorfosy', in *Legendy i mify o Pushkine*, ed. by Maria Virolainen (Sankt-Peterburg: Akademicheskii proekt, 1995), 106–28 (118–22); Marina Zagidullina, *Pushkinskii mif v kontse XX veka* (Cheliabinsk: Cheliabinsk State University Press, 2001); Stephanie Sandler, *Commemorating Pushkin: Russia's Myth of a National Poet* (Stanford, CA: Stanford University Press, 2004); Marina Zagidullina, 'At the crossroads between the elite and the masses cults: Pushkin's Middle Path in Russian culture', *Neohelicon*, 46 (2019), 183–97.

39 Muso Oybek, 'Pushkin', *Literaturnyi Uzbekistan*, 1 (1937), p. 142.

40 "Ila seni o'qir bu erkin Vatan / Sen qancha tillarda sayraysan mag'rur / Sozing yuksalajak yana baland, shan!". The last word, "*shan*", is also present in both Oybek's poem and Cho'lpon's.

41 Abdulhamid Cho'lpon, 'Yana o'ldim sozimni', *Yana o'ldim sozimni* (Tashkent: G'afur G'ulom nomidagi Adabiyot va san'at nashriyoti, 1991), p. 119.

42 Muso Oybek, 'Cho'lpon, shoirni qanday tekshirish kerak', *Qizil O'zbekiston*, 17 May 1927, 2 (p. 2).

was a bold move: although the translation of Pushkin was strictly supervised, Oybek had developed a strategy of resistance in his metadiscourse, using a coded language, which shed more light on his own translation. Meanwhile, Ayni, the actual organiser of the Pushkin jubilee, went even further, and allowed himself to publicly mock the vacuity of censorship in his eulogy written in Tajik:

> Censorship tried with all her might to hide
> The poet's marvellous treasure from the light
> But who will hold back the vividness of the years
> Who will capture the fragrance of spring?
> The pages blackened by censorship
> From mouth to mouth flew lighter than a bird
> The poet's lips cannot be sealed.[43]

Familiar with double discourse, Ayni might have been evoking his own poetry here, in a subtly subversive way.

As translation became more professionalised, the question of evaluating translation quality also arose. The Uzbek reception of the conclusions of the First All-Soviet Congress of Translators, held in Moscow in January 1936, indicates some criteria for this appraisal. The conclusions of this inaugural event, where prominent writers and translators shared their theories about the best way to achieve translation accuracy, were discussed in Tashkent in early February. A speech by the prominent orientalist Evgenii Bertel´s, already famous for his 1935 study of the Persian poet Ferdowsi, about translation issues specific to Turkic and Persian languages failed to raise much interest, perhaps because his thesis was not new in Uzbekistan.[44] This display of loyalty on the part of suspect specialists trying to use ideological criteria to justify their work did not encounter much support in Tashkent. Writers and translators paid much more attention to the discourse of the former Acmeist poet Mikhail Zenkevich, now working exclusively as a translator. As Zenkevich defended the interests of translators as a corporation, Uzbek translators demanded the same professional recognition.[45] They also discussed at length the ideas of Aleksandr Smirnov, a Shakespeare specialist, who defined the accuracy of a translation by the similarity of the

43 The poem was first issued in its Russian translation: "Tsenzura vsemi tselami ot sveta / Ukryt' stremilas' divnyj klad poèta. / No kto uderzhit virkhia bujnyi let? Kto aromat vesennyi v plen voz'mёt? Tsenzuroi zachёrnennye stranitsy / Iz ust v usta leteli legche ptitsy. Na rot pevtsa ne nalozhit' pechat'". Sadreddin Aini, 'Pushkin', trans. by Banu, *Literaturnyi Uzbekistan*, 1 (1937), 53–56.

44 On Zenkevich, see E. E. Zemskova, 'Strategii Loial'nasti:diskussiia o tochnosti khudozhestvennogo perevoda na Pervom vsesoiuznom soveshanii perevodchikov 1936 g.', *Novyi filologicheskii vestnik*, 4 (2015), 70–83 (p. 74).

45 'Protokol zasedaniâ prezidiuma Uzsovprosa, tezisa k dokladam P. Zenkevicha "Perevodchik i Izdatel'stvo", M. Lozinskogo "Iskusstvo Stixotvornogo Perevoda" i A. Smirnova "Zadachi k sredsvta khudozhestvennogo perevoda"', O'zRMDA, R-2356, o. 1, d. 12, fols. 6r-17r.

effect produced on the reader, a perspective one would call target-oriented in modern Translation Studies, which recalls and predates Western research on the "principle of equivalent effect" formalised by Émile Victor Rieu in 1953, as well as Eugene Nida's 1964 notion of "dynamic equivalence".[46] Smirnov's views were warmly received in SSPUz; opposing voices relied on source-oriented translation discourses. These debates encouraged local theories, and a few months later, Sanjar Siddiq elaborated his own criteria of accuracy in *The Art of Literary Translation* (*Adabiy tarjima san'ati*, 1936).[47] Unlike those in the Soviet centre, Uzbek translators set ideology aside during these debates, where scientific and aesthetic criteria dominated.

The Effect of the Great Terror (1937–38)

One year later, the Uzbek intelligentsia was seriously affected by the Great Terror, especially those former Muslim reformists who had contributed to the building of Socialism.[48] Translation activity was affected in many ways. First, prominent writers accused of nationalism tended to use their translation efforts as a defence strategy. Cho'lpon had no other option, since he lacked influential protectors. Until late 1937, the literary critic and journalist Rahmat Majidiy (1906–86), and the editor-in-chief of the SSPUz magazine, Aleksandr Kartsev (1901-?), who was also (from 1935) in charge of the Culture and Propaganda Department of the Central Committee in Uzbekistan, had defended him. Kartsev, as editor-in-chief of *Literaturnyi Uzbekistan*, commissioned the translation of long extracts from his masterpiece *Night*.[49] During the spring of 1937, external pressure mounted and the journal's editorial board was heavily critiqued; the Uzbek Soviet Writers' Union banned Cho'lpon. On 7 and 8 April 1937, having endured a harsh session of self-criticism, Cho'lpon tried to dismiss the accusations of nationalism being levelled at him. A document held in the State Archive summarises his intervention, rather than providing a full transcript (because Cho'lpon defended himself in Uzbek, while the stenographer was Russian); but his core argument can be readily deduced. He stressed that his activity as a translator proved his loyalty to the Party, since he was the first Uzbek translator of Pushkin, whose jubilee had just occurred, and (more surprisingly) since he

46 Émile Victor Rieu and John Bertram Phillips, 'Translating the Gospels: A Discussion Between Dr. E.V. Rieu and the Rev. J.B. Phillips', *The Bible Translator*, 6:4 (1955), 150–59; Eugene Nida, *Toward a Science of Translating* (Leiden: Brill, 1964), pp. 120–45.

47 S. Mamajanov, *O'zbekistonda badiiy tarjima tarixi*, pp. 33–34.

48 'Spisok lits podlezhashchikh sudu voennoi kollegii verkhovnogo suda Soiuza SSR 28-go marta', *Repressiia 1937–38, Dokumenty i materialy T.1*, ed. by Naim Karimov (Tashkent: Sharq, 2005), pp. 215–22.

49 Abdulhamid Cho'lpon, *Nochi* (*roman*), *Literaturnyi Uzbekistan*, 2 (1937), 52–128.

was the first Uzbek translator of *Hamlet*.[50] These facts indicated that he was not a bourgeois nationalist. This defence, based on the Soviet myth of the friendship of peoples, proved inadequate. Not only was Cho'lpon's exclusion from the Writers' Union upheld, he was later arrested too. Nonetheless, his defence was observed with interest by his peers; it showed that translation was, from this date onwards, seen as a legitimating activity in its own right. Russian classics, and particularly those by Pushkin, were included in a wider range of prestigious European literary works for translation.

The case of the young poet Usmon Nosir (1912–44), arrested and deported in 1938, follows the same pattern. It is not known if his translation activity was taken into account as an extenuating circumstance in 1938 during his expulsion from the Uzbek Soviet Writers' Union, but it was presented as the main argument for his rehabilitation when this was discussed in 1942. The evacuation of key resources and figures had put the Writers' Union in a strong position, so the members of the Presidium of the Uzbek Soviet Writers' Union, from Hamid Olimjon to G'afur G'ulom, risked sending Maqsud Shayhzoda to plead his case before the Military Court of the Central Asian District (SAVO).[51] They began by composing a collective letter, flattering Nosir's lyrical skills: "From 1933 to 1938, Usmon Nosir was one of the most talented and progressive poets of our time [...]". They minimised his faults: "But with time, around 1935–1936, themes full of black sadness and inconsolable despair, inspired by the social environment he frequented, began to dominate his work". To counterbalance this, once again, the clinching argument was the quality of his translation from two classic Russian authors commemorated across the Soviet Union during the late 1930s: "In addition to poetic composition, Usmon Nosir also worked as a translator. His translations of Pushkin's 'Fountain of Bakhchisarai' and Lermontov's 'Demon' are particularly noteworthy".[52] This attempt failed, as Usmon Nosir died before the commission was held, but it shows how Uzbek elites had integrated translation practices into their discursive strategies during the Great Terror. This contribution to the friendship of peoples, itself a construct intended to keep the Soviet Empire united, thus became the ultimate evidence of loyalty.

The Great Terror had immediate consequences for both translators and available translations. An immediate menace was the execution of numerous skilled linguists and translators—some also prominent writers, like Cho'lpon and the novelist Abdulla Qodiriy, as well as Sanjar Siddiq and A'zam Ayub. As elsewhere in the USSR, translations made by an arrested translator were suppressed on suspicion of ideological flaws. By contrast, original creative

50 'Stenogramma vystupleniia Cholpana na sobranii pisatelei 7–8 aprelia 1937', O'zRMDA, R-2356, o. 1, d. 29, fols. 1r-14v.

51 Benjamin Quénu, 'Culture et politique dans l'Ouzbékistan soviétique', pp. 382–85.

52 'V voennuiu prokuraturu SAVO—O tvorchestve poèta Nasyrova Usmana', O'zRMDA, R-2356, o. 1, d. 98, fols. 22r-24r.

writing by accused individuals simply ceased to be published; this differential between suppression and interruption underlined the comparably high status of the translator. A few days after the executions of early October 1938, Glavrepertkom (the central Soviet commission for approval of theatrical repertoires) suppressed all plays translated by "bourgeois nationalists" recently sentenced to death.[53] Not only had Uzbek literature lost the works of Qodiriy and Cho'lpon, the founding fathers of entire literary genres (especially the historical novel), it was also deprived of translations of plays previously recognised as part of the Soviet patrimony and '*kulturnost'*'. Both Gogol's *The Marriage* and Shakespeare's *Hamlet*, which had been great successes on stage, were removed in Tashkent and in provincial theatres. Lev Slavin and Nikolai Pogodin's plays, although considered as perfect samples of Soviet culture, also disappeared from the stage just after their translators were condemned. The purge culminated in the expulsion from the Hamza Theatre of the director Mannon Uyghur (1897–1955), who had produced most of these plays.[54]

Three years later, the Uzbek Soviet Writers' Union took advantage of a moment of thaw to constitute a commission, led by the writer and scholar Maqsud Shayhzoda, to supervise the rapid production of new translations.[55] Aiming to fill these gaps, Shayhzoda prioritised the retranslation of classic texts, but he faced difficult choices. As the condemned translations had been attacked for their alterations, he promoted strict accuracy, applying this rule equally to his own translations, which adhered to the original as closely as possible. This strategy was supposed to protect the translators for whom he was responsible, and therefore himself, from accusations of disloyalty; and to distinguish new retranslations from the previous, condemned versions. Abdulla Qahhor, Maqsud Shayhzoda, Oybek, and G'afur G'ulom were all closely involved in this process, but it took a decade for the Uzbek theatrical repertoire to recover from this crisis; nor was it the last to occur. As a result, the target-oriented theory that prevailed until the late 1930s was lost.

European playwrights, translated via Russian as an intermediary language, were even more problematic. The case of *Hamlet* is relevant: the 1933 translation by Mikhail Lozinskii (1886–1955) could no longer be used because Cho'lpon had worked on it; while the very poetic 1939 version by Anna Radlova (1891–1949) departed too drastically from the original. Therefore, no safe literary translation was available in Russian. Maqsud Shayhzoda had to wait for Boris Pasternak's 1940 translation, which was praised for its accuracy, to produce his *Hamlet*. He was interrupted by war, but this first attempt had a strong influence over his

53 Tashkent, Institut Isskustvoznaniia im. Hamzy ANUzSSR, T(M) I90 325/22, *Materialy po istorii uzbekskogo teatra*, T. 2, fol. 3r.

54 See Ildar Mukhtarov, 'Mannon Uygur: Episodes From A Career in The Theatre', *San'at*, 3–4 (2007), 71–76.

55 'Protokol n°6 zasedaniia Pravleniia Soiuza Sovetskikh Pisatelei Uzb., 21-ogo maia 1941', *Postanovlenie i Protokoly zasedanii Pravleniia Soiuza Sovetskih Pisatelei Uzbekistana*, O'zRMDA, R-2356, o.1, d. 84, fol. 13r.

own writing, especially the play *Jalaliddin* (1944), which included numerous speeches to the audience, extensive stage directions, and a long soliloquy.[56] When he finally translated *Hamlet* in 1948, Maqsud Shayhzoda opted for literalism, as a guarantee of ideological rectitude, whereas Cho'lpon had preferred concision, deliberately eliding some passages.[57] This is paradoxical, as Pasternak defined his own version as a "free translation" to avoid any accusation of formalism.[58] The ideological rectitude of any translation was thus acquiring a very different meaning in both the Russian centre and the Uzbek periphery: translations into the dominant language were expected to be an act of creation, while translations into a dominated language were expected to adhere as closely as possible to the original.[59]

In 1938, at the peak of the Great Terror, the question of accuracy was at the centre of the defence of Lidiia Sotserdotova, a translator of contemporary Uzbek literature since 1930. She was the translator of Qodiriy's *Obid-Ketmon* and *Scorpion from the Altar* (*Mehrobdan Chayon*, 1928), both commissions by the Uzbek Soviet Writers' Union; her versions had even appeared in *Literaturnyi Uzbekistan*, the Union's official Russian-language organ.[60] She was now accused by her peers of translating both incorrectly. Sotserdotova argued that she had been ordered to translate these works, while also emphasising her professional practices: "I strove for accuracy in translation. I did not hide nor change the political tendencies of any author".[61]

Professional skills could therefore be opposed to ideological accusations with some expectation of success, since Sotserdotova escaped punishment.

The SSPUz reacted to the vacuum created by the Great Terror of 1938 by commissioning new translations, but did not reinforce its control over the process. This institution was too disorganised by the attacks—its president, Hamid Olimjon, was even accused of being a German spy just before the outbreak of war—to muster sufficient human resources.[62] Therefore, translation

56 Maqsud Shayhzoda, *Jaloliddin Manguberdi Tarixiy drama* (*Urganch: Xorazm nashr matbaa, 2022*); Maksud Shaixzade, *Dzhalaleddin*, trans. by Vladimir Lipko, O'zRMDA, R-2356, o. 1, d. 109, fols. 66r-112v.

57 Muhammajon Kholbekov, 'Shekspir bepoyon' ('Boundless Shakespeare'), *O'zbekiston adabiyoti va san'ati gazetasining*, 9 (2009), 4 (p. 4).

58 Susanna Witt, 'Between the Lines', in *Contexts, Subtexts and Pretexts: Literary Translation in Eastern Europe and Russia*, ed. by Brian James Baer (Amsterdam: John Benjamins, 2011), pp. 149–70 (p. 165).

59 The condemnation of literalism as a formalist approach and the evolution toward free translation in translations into the Russian language have been described in Natalia Kamovnikova, *Made Under Pressure: Literary Translation in the Soviet Union, 1960–1991*, pp. 171–86.

60 See Abdulla Kadirii, 'Berdi-tatar', *Literaturnyi Uzbekistan*, 1 (1935), 40–47.

61 'Ia stremilas' k tochnosti perevoda, zamaskirovaniem ia ne zanimalas' i nikogda ne naviazyvala avtoram politicheskikh tendentsii', 'Protokol n°1 sobraniia russkoi sekcii s aktivnom ot 19-go oktobria 1937', O'zRMDA, R-2356, o. 1, d. 27, fol. 3r.

62 On the last attack upon Hamid Olimjon, see Charles David Shaw, 'Making Ivan Uzbek: War, Friendship of the Peoples, and the Creation of Soviet Uzbekistan,

activity remained mostly the preserve of dilettantes. Abdulla Qohhar (1907–68) even noted in 1939 that forty works by his beloved Anton Chekhov had been translated by amateurs. Instead of criticising the lesser quality of the translations, he rejoiced at their large-scale dissemination, since they proved Uzbek readers' enthusiasm for the Russian author.[63]

The Birth of the Translation Section (1940): Between Control and Agency

The Great Terror had created a need for new translations from Russian, and turned accuracy in translation into a survival strategy. But it did not mark a foundational moment in the imposition of institutionalised supervision. A dedicated section, with extended powers to command and evaluate translations, was put in place much later, during 1940. The context in Uzbekistan resembled a political thaw, as the Uzbek Soviet Writers' Union had already reintegrated some banned writers at a junior level, and was even, very unusually for this period, beginning to use the language of rehabilitation.[64] The Uzbek Committee for Artistic Affairs, an offshoot of the Uzbek Sovnarkom (Council of People's Commissars, the body that effectively ran each Soviet republic), reinstated Mannon Uyg'ur to the Theatre Hamza and commissioned him to produce *Othello,* translated by G'afur G'ulom. The play was less susceptible to misinterpretation than *Hamlet*, and approved Russian translations were available.[65] The Committee for Artistic Affairs even agreed to pay G'afur G'ulom a second time (after Mannon Uyg'ur rejected his first translation), for a total of thirty-five thousand roubles. This was a colossal amount of money (even for Moscow), given that the usual salary for the translation of a play at this time was around one thousand roubles.[66]

As the Uzbek Sovnarkom was funding translators intensively, certain prominent writer-translators took the initiative to organise centralised supervision of translation activity within the Soviet Writers' Union to manage such funding; and to ensure it was used for translations both from Russian to Uzbek and from Uzbek to Russian. Hamid Olimjon, as First Secretary of the SSPUz, endorsed this initiative. The process was divided into two steps. First,

1941–1945' (unpublished doctoral thesis, University of Berkeley, 2015), pp. 126–27.

63 Abdulla Qahhor, 'Chekhovdan o'rganaylik' ('Let Us Learn From Chekhov'), *Qizil O'zbekiston*, 14 July 1939, p. 3 (p. 3).

64 O'zRMDA, R-2356, o. 1, d. 58, fols. 52r-55r ; Marc Élie, 'Ce que réhabiliter veut dire. Khrouchtchev et Gorbatchev aux prises avec l'héritage répressif stalinien', *Vingtième Siècle. Revue d'histoire*, 107:3 (2010), 101–13 (p. 102).

65 On *Othello*, see Jill Warren, 'Acculturating Shakespeare: The Tactics of Translating His Works under Stalin in the Light of Recent Theoretical Advances in Translation Studies' (unpublished doctoral thesis, University of Nottingham, 2015).

66 'Prokol n°7 Zasedanii Kollegii Upravleniia po delam iskusstv pri SNK UzSSR ot 20/XII-40 g', O'zRMDA, R-2087, o. 1, d. 54, fols. 1r-54r (10r-11r).

in February 1940, the SSPUz organised a competition for the best translation from Uzbek to Russian, with a focus on short stories. Other competitions would follow before an official translation section was established; the juries for these competitions were intended to become its future board, which would regularly and uniformly evaluate the translations.[67] The promoters emphasised the need to attract more professionals to work as translators, and to use the competitions as training, with the help of a strict peer-review process. To ensure their appeal, the competitions were generously funded, with a first prize of three thousand roubles, and a second prize of two thousand, both of which were substantial sums in comparison with usual wages.[68] The development of institutional supervision for translations was therefore more about seduction than coercion of applicants. In this new context, translation had become a high-value activity, both symbolically and materially. The jury was comprised exclusively of professionals, some of whom were both prominent authors and translators, like Oybek, Abdulla Qohhar and Maqsud Shayhzoda, president of the jury, or Mirzaqalon Ismoiliy (1908–86), a writer and translator from Russian to Uzbek who had been active since 1928. Other members included the Ukrainian dramatist Sofia Levitina (1891–1957), whose plays had been translated into Uzbek, and I. I. Vilenskii, a forgotten local Russian poet and novelist who was briefly in charge of the Russian section on, and editor-in-chief of, *Literaturnyi Uzbekistan* (1940–41).[69] Uzbek speakers dominated, and ideological restrictions were as minimal as possible.

The second step was the reorganisation of the whole structure of the Uzbek Soviet Writers' Union, including the formal creation of a translation section in May 1940. As expected, the academic Maqsud Shayhzoda, who had supported Olimjon during the latter's election as first secretary, was appointed as head of this section.[70] Jury members who held another institutional role, like Oybek, Qahhor, Vilenskii, and Levitina, were not full members, but retained an important role in decision-making (apart from Vilenskii, whose career was soon ended). The newcomers were mainly translators from Russian to Uzbek, such as Maqsud Davron, who was also a translator of French literature, and Sobir Muhamedov, who was translating Vassili Ian's *Gengis Khan* (1939, awarded a Stalin Prize in 1942).[71] As for translators from Uzbek to Russian, the section

67 'Protokol n°2 Zasedaniia Pravleniia Soiuza Sovetskikh Pisatelei Uzb. 16-go fevralia 1940', O'zRMDA, R-2356, o. 1, d. 63, fol. 58r-v.

68 Ibid.

69 I. I. Vilenskii was editor-in-chief of *Literaturnii Uzbekistan* until his novel *Piandzh shumit* (*The Sound of the River Piandzh*) was condemned and cancelled. 'Protokol n°14 zasedaniia Pravlenia Soiuza Sov. Pisatelei Uzbekistana, 30-go sentiabria 1940 g.', O'zRMDA, R-2356, o. 1, d. 63, fols. 126r-129r; 'Protokol n°5 zasedaniia Pravlenia Soiuza Sov. Pisatelei Uzbekistana, 6-go aprelia 1941 g.', O'zRMDA, R-2356, o. 1, d. 84, fols. 19r-20r.

70 Protokol n°8 Zasedaniia Pravleniia Soiuza Sovetskikh Pisatelei Uzb. 16-go maia 1940', O'zRMDA, R-2356, o. 1, d. 63, fol. 96r.

71 'Tematicheskii plan na 1941 g.', O'zRMDA, R-2356, o. 1, d. 86; fol. 1r.

recruited Vladimir Lipko (1912–80), a Ukrainian poet-translator, who was at that time translating Alisher Nawai's poetry in preparation for this national hero's jubilee, and Sotserdotova.[72] The latter's election to this board was a significant development. Everyone was aware at this time that she was the main translator into Russian of Abdulla Qodiriy.[73] Moreover, most of the members knew that she helped his family after his arrest, and even tried to intercede with the NKVD, writing to Stalin that he was no enemy of the people.[74] Her selection as a member of the board was therefore an implicit rehabilitation of Qodiriy. It is also further evidence that the institutionalisation and centralisation of translations cannot be considered as a coercive policy. Translations from Russian were the priority, as shown by the composition of the section and its first commissions, which consisted of 136 carefully chosen Lermontov poems.[75] Nonetheless, while translations from Russian were numerous, the Uzbek Soviet Writers' Union also inaugurated a training course on translations from Uzbek to Russian, and the journal *Literaturnyi Uzbekistan* published almost 200 translations of Uzbek literary texts in half a decade.[76]

The full publication schedule for 1940 gives a picture of the situation on the eve of the war. The Uzbek Soviet Writers' Union ordered the publication of 423,000 volumes of translated literature (47%), and 478,000 volumes of Uzbek literature (53%). In less than a decade, translated works had almost overtaken the local production.[77] This situation clearly shows the dominance of the Russian language in this cultural exchange, but it cannot be compared to extreme examples of Russian cultural hegemony, as in Estonia.[78] Within the category of Russian literature (380,000 volumes representing 90% of translations into Uzbek), the classics of the nineteenth century predominated. The works of Pushkin, Tolstoy, Lermontov, and Goncharov had a print run of 15,000 copies each. Party-approved contemporary Soviet novels such as Mikhail Sholokhov's *And Quiet Flows the Don* (*Tikhii Don*, 1925–32), translated by Sharif Rizaev as *Tinch oqar Don* (1938–42), and Nikolai Ostrovskii's *How the Steel Was Tempered*

72 'Protokol n°8 Zasedaniia Pravleniia Soiuza Sovetskikh Pisatelei Uzbekistana', 16-go maia 1940, O'zRMDA, R-2356, o. 1, d. 63, fol. 93r.

73 'Protokol n°1 sobraniia russkoi sektsii s aktivnom ot 19-go oktiabria 1937', O'zRMDA, R-2356, o. 1, d. 27, fols 1r-8r.

74 Habibulla Qodiriy, 'Qodiriyning so'nggi kunlari. Khotira qissaning davomi', *Yoshlik*, 6 (1989), 36–55 (36–37).

75 'Stikhi M. Iu. Lermontova, namechanye perevoda na uzbekskii iazyk', O'zRMDA, R-2356, o. 1, d. 63, fols. 134r-137r.

76 'Protokol n°16 Zasedaniia Pravleniia Soiuza Sovetskikh Pisatelei Uzbekistana, 30-go sentiabria 1940', O'zRMDA, R-2356, o. 1, d. 63, fol. 128r.

77 'Tematicheskii plan na 1941 g.', O'zRMDA, R-2356, o. 1, d. 86, fols. 1r-9r.

78 During the early Sovietisation of postwar Estonia, Russian translated literature exceeded 60% of the production. See Daniele Monticelli and Anne Lange, 'Translation under Totalitarianism: The Case of Soviet Estonia', *The Translator*, 20:1 (2014), 95–111 (p. 100); see also Anne Lange and Aile Möldre's essay in the present volume.

(*Kak zakalialas' stal'*, 1934), translated by Olimjon as *Po'lat qanday toblandi* in 1941, enjoyed the same circulation (10,000 copies) as the most widely printed contemporary Uzbek fiction. Maksim Gorky's works were the exception, with seven novels each printed in 20,000 copies. The Uzbek Soviet Writers' Union was thus following the centralised policy of translation development emphasised by the USSR Writers' Union at that time.[79]

Nonetheless, translated Soviet-Russian literature was still less widely printed than Uzbek contemporary writers or even nineteenth-century literature. For instance, the works of Ayni, founding father of both Uzbek and Tajik literature, enjoyed a very high print run, especially for the second edition of *The Slaves* (*Qullar,* 1934)—of which there were 15,000 copies. Only the poetry of Olimjon, who ran the SSPUz, enjoyed a similar print run, and with Ayni he dominated the contemporary literary landscape. Moreover, the plan included a newfound 'Uzbek literary classics' category. The nineteenth-century poets Muqimiy and Furqat, praised for their criticism of pre-Revolutionary powers, were printed in runs of 20,000 copies, equalling those for Gorky's works.[80] Interestingly, translations of Marxist-Leninist staples were not particularly supported. For instance, former Soviet Commissar for Enlightenment Anatolii Lunacharskii's translated works had a print run of just 5,000 copies, like the numerous translations of Azeri and Persian poets, whose appearance in translation can be interpreted as an affirmation of the Uzbek language in a traditionally bilingual context.[81] In this literary landscape, Uzbek folklore and literature remained prominent, while absorbing challenges from the translations, mainly from Russian. Publication policy strove for balance, aiming to intertwine federal and national literary traditions, with translations informing a global quest for Soviet cultural legitimacy.

In Wartime: Reshaping the Institution, Promoting Uzbek Literature

Wartime and evacuation led to profound institutional changes, as elements from the USSR's core were transferred towards the safe margins of the Soviet Empire. To prevent a takeover by powerful evacuees, Olimjon, as First Secretary of the SSPUz, resorted to large-scale recruitment and the promotion of apparently

79 A complete fascicle of the collection of the Uzbek Soviet Writers' Union consists of the instructions issued by the central Soviet Writers' Union concerning the 'reorganisation of the section of artistic translations' from 1939 to 1940; Postanovlenie Biuro natsional'nykh komissii SSP SSSR ob uporiadochenii dela khudozhestvennykh perevodov s iazykov narodov SSSR, perepiska po voprosu podgotovki kadrov', Tashkent, O'zRMDA, R-2356, o. 1, d. 51, fols. 1r-18r.

80 'Tematicheskii plan na 1941 g.', Tashkent, O'zRMDA, R-2356, o. 1, d. 86, fol. 3r.

81 Ibid., fol. 8r.

loyal colleagues. For this reason, in early January 1942, Svetlana Somova (1915–89) and Sotserdotova both gained full membership of the Uzbek Soviet Writers' Union. The Presidium elected Somova unanimously after flattering reports from both her reviewer, the freshly evacuated Russian writer Vladimir Lugovskoi (1901–57), who was already writing about Socialist Central Asia (and whose works were always quickly translated into Uzbek), and Olimjon himself.[82] Her work as a poet, including her major poem cycle about the city of Tashkent in 1941, was barely mentioned, while her academic writing and translations were heavily emphasised (she was the Russian translator of Hamid Olimjon, Oybek and Ayni). Although she was born in Leningrad, she had spent all her childhood in Central Asia, completing her higher education at the State University of Central Asia (SAGU), like most Uzbek writers of her generation. The circumstances of Sotserdotova's election are less detailed, as the document has been redacted; yet it is clear that the main argument in favour of her integration was her translation into Russian of Ayni's *The Slaves* and 'Uzbek classics'. Fearing that Uzbek literature could be subordinated during the evacuation, the Presidium of the SSPUz promoted these two translators regardless of their political antecedents and social backgrounds. Their appointments resulted in a change of priorities within the section, which henceforward aimed to promote Uzbek literature while mobilising the masses for the war effort, rather than translating Russian classics.

Six months later, evacuation was realised on a mass scale. The Uzbek Soviet Writers' Union remained, and Olimjon, although still First Secretary, was obliged to share the position with Isai Lezhnev (1891–1955), a *Pravda* journalist known for his aggressive stance during the Great Terror. Lezhnev took the unilateral decision to create new sections, and to reallocate the positions to empower evacuees. Some local writers therefore had to suffer a huge loss of authority, especially ethnically Russian and Ukrainian authors like Vladimir Lipko; but translators enjoyed an expanded section with four directors' posts.[83] Temur Fattoh (1910–63), Somova, Lev Pen'kovskii (1894–1971), and Aleksandr Il'chenko were placed in charge. The composition of this section is worth noting. First, it was the only such committee where locals were in the majority, Il'chenko being the sole evacuee (from Ukraine). Two worked primarily as translators of Uzbek literature, especially the work of Alisher Nava'i, into Russian, thus confirming the directional shift in translation policy. Thirdly, Somova became the first woman appointed to a directorial position in the whole Uzbek Soviet Writers' Union. Clearly, translation activity enabled women to gain positions of power in the highly masculine world of the Uzbek Soviet Writers' Union—the other route being a career within the Party, like Oydin Sabirova's (1906–53).

82 'Protokol n°1 Zasedaniia Pravleniia Soiuza sovetskikh pisatelei Uzbekistana 20 ianvaria 1942 g.', O'zRMDA, R-2356, o. 1, d. 93, fol. 2r.

83 'Protokol n°9 Zasedaniia Pravleniia Soiuza sovetskikh pisatelei Uzbekistana 5 iunia 1942 g.', O'zRMDA, R-2356, o. 1, d. 93, fols. 26r-30r.

This female poet and novelist had been a member of the Executive Committee of the SSPUz since its foundation, and she had gained prominence providing ideological training for Party cadres during the postwar years. Nonetheless, a translation career was no guarantee, especially for the wives of powerful writers: Zul´fiia Israilova (1915–96), better known as Zulfiya, despite her widely praised work as a translator of numerous Russian classic and contemporary poems, and her celebrated original poetry, received no influential appointments during her husband Hamid Olimjon's lifetime.[84] As for Kibriyo Qahhorova (1914–96), born Fayzullaeva, she had been a military translator before her wedding with Abdulla Qahhor in 1945, and started a career as a literary translator after the war. Nonetheless, she remained overlooked until the 1960s, not even being a member of the SSPUz.[85] Qahhorova still translated major works from Russian to Uzbek, and from Uzbek to Tajik, working both alone, as she did to translate Gorky's *Mother* (*Mat'*, 1906) (translated as *Ona* (1950)), and in collaboration with her husband, as she did on Tolstoy's *War and Peace* (*Voina i mir*, 1869). Its publication under the title *Urush va tinchlik* was serialised: she took part in the translation from 1947 onwards, and translated the fourth and final part alone.[86]

Hamid Olimjon had ensured that the translation section remained in the hands of local people. He was therefore able to promote Uzbek productions, although these were sometimes published in Russian before Uzbek. In 1943, his own play *Muqanna* was performed in both languages, and directed by Solomon Mikhoels (1890–1948), who had been evacuated to Tashkent with the Moscow State Jewish Theatre. While translations from Russian to Uzbek were numerous during the war, SSPUz also tried to promote Uzbek literature on a larger scale, with support from local Party officials. Translation activity was not understood only as receptiveness to world culture, especially Russian authors, but also as a way to transform Uzbek literature into the pearl in the Soviet crown with the help of the evacuees' work and connections. Hamid Olimjon's death in a car accident (a genuine accident as far as we know) in 1944 did not stop this effort, and the newly promoted Oybek stepped up this policy.[87] The evacuees themselves were not willing to impose Russian aesthetic standards upon Uzbek literature. In July 1942, examining issues with translation from Uzbek to Russian, the critic

84 The edition of the complete works of Zulfiya recorded no less than ninety-three translated poems, most of them from Russian (nine by Pushkin, six by Anna Akhmatova), others from 'brother' or friendly nations. Zul´fiia (Israilova), *Asarlar* (*Works*), ed. by Salohiddin Mamajonov, 3 vols (Tashkent: G'afur G'ulom nomidagi Adabiyot va san'at nashriyoti, 1985), II (1985), pp. 271–529.

85 Kibriyo Qahharova, *Chorak asr hamnafas* (Tashkent: Yosh Gvardiya, 1987), pp. 16–18.

86 Lev Tolstoy, *Urush va tinchlik*, trans. by Abdulla Qahhor and Kibriyo Qahharova (Tashkent: Adabiyot va san'at nashryoti, 1979).

87 As the assassination of Solomon Mikhoels in 1948 was disguised as a car accident, the death of Hamid Olimjon might be suspected of following the same pattern, but there is no evidence nor even any widespread rumour of it.

and editor Kornelii Zelinskii (1896–1970) insisted on the need to preserve the "national colour" of local literature, claiming Uzbek literature should remain "faithful to the traditional form" at all costs. Others criticised G'afur G'ulom for borrowing too much from Maiakovskii, claiming that it resulted in the loss of his own style after Shayhzoda had noted the specific translation issue of his poems repeating the same sentence or word in both Uzbek and Russian to emphasise the unbreakable bond between the people.[88] Finally, personal taste and affinity played a stronger role in the choices of translation. The rhythm of publication and the needs were too high for the Writers' Union, let alone the Party, to control the entire process. For instance, Oybek had a friendly relationship with Anna Akhmatova, and translated her 'Courage' ('Muzhestvo', 1942) as 'Mardlik'. Here again, he showed some ambiguity. 'Courage' is not only a war poem, but also an ode to the emancipating power of the language in a devastated cultural landscape. This was clearly a preoccupation that Oybek shared, as highlighted by his many attempts to correctly translate key passages of the poem in his draft, as well as his emphasis on the freedom of the language.[89]

Postwar: The Art of Passive Resistance (1945–49)

War had favoured the diversification of translation but also the promotion of a discreet cultural nationalism. The Uzbek Soviet Writers' Union enjoyed extensive autonomy until the last day of 1944, when the Party reaffirmed its control. Then the power struggle in the Politburo between Andrei Zhdanov and Georgii Malenkov led some local Party members to intervene in cultural policy to compete with one another, just as they did in Moscow or Leningrad.[90] Peace

88 'Protokol Zasedaniia Prezidiuma SSPUz 13-go iulia 1942 g.', O'zRMDA, R-2356, / o. 1, / d. 93, / fol. 31r, O'zRMDA, R-2356, o. 1, d. 93, fol. 33r.

89 The draft is kept in the collections of the Oybek House Museum. (There is no corresponding reference number.) See also Anna Akhmatova, 'Mardlik' ['Courage'], trans. by Muso Oybek, in Oybek, *Mukammal asarlar to'pladi*, 20 vols, XVII (1981), p. 210 (p. 210). In Russian, these last verses are "I my sokhranim tebia, russkaia rech', / Velikoe russkoe slovo. / Svobodnym i chistym tebia pronesem, / I vnukam dadim, i ot plena spasem / Naveki!" ("And we will preserve you, Russian speech, / Great Russian word / We shall carry you out pure and free / And give you to our grandchildren, and save you from prison / Forever!"). In Uzbek, these verses read: "Lekin seni saqlaymiz, rus tili, bir zum—/ Unutmaymiz, bu so'z ulug', boy. / Gard yuqtirmay erkin, go'zal, seni eltamiz, / So'ylar senda nabiralar, asoratdan biz, / Quqtarurmiz seni adabiy!" This can be back-translated as follows: "But we will preserve you, Russian language—even for a moment / We shall not forget you, great and plentiful word / And shall deliver you immaculate, free and beautiful, / Our grandchildren will speak within you, and we shall from captivity, / Save you forever!"

90 Denis Babichenko, *Pisateli i tsenzory: Sovetskaia literatura 1940-kh godov pod politicheskim kontrolem* (Moscow: Rossiia molodaia, 1994).

had not even been signed when Party members regained the initiative over the cultural field, including Iskhak Razzakov (1910–79), better known as the First Secretary of the Communist Party of Kirghizia (1950–61). Razzakov had spent all his early academic and political career in Uzbekistan. In 1945, as head of the Agitprop Department of the Uzbek Communist Party, he passed a resolution reaffirming Party control, allocating several tasks to the Uzbek Soviet Writers' Union, and announcing new financial measures. Having first congratulated the institution, he next accused it of several shortcomings, including neglecting translations, especially from Russian:

> The Bureau of the CK KP(b) and the SNK UzSSR jointly note that the work of the Uzbek Soviet Writers' Union retains major shortcomings. The Writers' Union does not mobilise its writers sufficiently for sustained work, does not develop literary criticism to any great extent, does not solve the problem of the lack of attention paid by writers and young literary cadres to their political and ideological education, does not take care of translations into Uzbek or Karakalpak of the great Russian writers, nor does it take care of the study, especially by young writers, of the classic works of Russian literature.[91]

In fact, since the evacuees had returned to Moscow or Leningrad, the translation section no longer existed, as the Soviet Writers' Unions was not able to afford it. The new resolution did solve the problem by allocating huge financial resources as well as new privileges to the Writers' Union. Next Razzakov commissioned translations of Pushkin, Lermontov, Gogol, Nikolai Chernyshevskii, Ivan Turgenev, Nikolai Nekrasov, Tolstoy, Chekhov, Gorky, Maiakovskii, Aleksei Tolstoy, and Sholokhov. Nonetheless, he did not abandon the promotion of Uzbek culture, as he also commissioned a large 'Anthology of Uzbek Literature'.[92] He also planned to reinforce the power of the Writers' Union over the Karakalpak territory by increasing translation from Karakalpak to Uzbek and Russian, soon commissioning a translation of the ancient Uzbek epic poem *Forty Girls* (*Kyrk-Kyz*) to be made by Svetlana Somova. It was published as *Sorok devushek* in 1949.[93]

---

91 'Postanovlenie Sovnarkoma UzSSR i Central'nogo Komiteta KP/b/Uz o rabote Soiuza Sovetskikh Pisatelei Uzbekistana (tov. Razakov).', O'zRMDA, R-2356, o. 1, d.102, fols. 2r-11r.

92 Ibid., fol. 7r; see also *Antologiia Uzbekskoi poezii*, ed. by Muso Aibek, Vladimir Lugovskoi, and Svetlana Somova (Moscow: Gosizdat, 1950).

93 The Karakalpak Autonomous Republic enjoyed a limited autonomy inside the Uzbek Soviet Socialist Republic, as well as limited privileges for the Karakalpak nationality. In 1946, the Uzbek Communist Party, supported by the Uzbek Soviet Writers' Union, reassessed its authority over the Autonomous Republic by deflecting the Zhdanov resolutions against the Karakalpak Communist Party and the local Writers' Union. See 'Protokol Zasedaniia pisatelei Kara-Kalpakii sovmestno s rabotnikami iskusstva i partiino-sovetskim aktivom', O'zRMDA, R-2356, o. 1, d. 111, fols. 12r-41r.

The Uzbek Soviet Writers' Union's response to Razzakov is meaningful. During the meeting it held to determine how to apply the Party's resolution, it welcomed Sergei Borodin (1902–74), a Russian author famous for his historical novel *Dmitri Donskoi* (1941; awarded a Stalin Prize the same year), as an envoy from the all-Soviet Writers' Union Plenum. Instead of supporting the Party line, Borodin suggested the creation of a "section dedicated to the popularisation of Uzbek literature throughout the USSR" instead.[94] Not only was Borodin, as a former evacuee, eager to promote Uzbek literature, but this viewpoint also enjoyed some support from the all-Soviet Writers' Union. Others, like the academic and Russian-Uzbek translator Jumanyoz Sharipov (1911–2007), embraced the Party line, and emphasised the section's future role in translating most Russian classics, starting with Tolstoy's *War and Peace*. The section finally compromised between these two positions. It was named very neutrally as "Translators' Section", and was entrusted to President Oybek's right-hand man, Shayhzoda, soon seconded by Nikolai Ivashev, known for his translation into Russian of G'afur G'ulom's short stories and Oybek's novels. A balance between languages and objectives was therefore established, and the newly founded section commissioned translations of Russian classics, as well as translations from Uzbek to Russian. The Presidium of the Uzbek Soviet Writers' Union had thus formally respected the Party's resolution while keeping the promotion of Uzbek literature as a priority.

Shayhzoda only occupied the key role as chairman of the section for a year before becoming involved in a major political scandal. His play *Jaloliddin*, which was acclaimed as patriotic during the war, was re-evaluated and condemned as an apology for feudalism. On 5 October 1946, Oybek was obliged to dismiss him as head of the translation section, appointing in his place another personal friend, the poet and translator Mirtemir Tursunov (1910–78), known simply as Mirtemir, who remained in charge until his own downfall in 1949 (when Oybek was fired as SSPUz director and excluded from the Academy of Sciences). Mirtemir did not change the section's policy, but reinforced the intergenerational transmission of skills. He entrusted the direction of a large collection of Chekhov's short stories to Abdulla Qahhor, regarded since the mid-1930s as the best Uzbek Chekhov specialist.[95] The Uzbek Soviet Writers' Union survived the publication of Zhdanov's resolutions condemning Leningrad journals for printing Anna Akhmatova, and even the NKVD officer Aziz Niallo (1904–93), who had played a key role in the repression during 1938, avoided criticising the President Oybek and Zulfiya for their translation of Akhmatova.[96]

94 'Protokol n°1 zasedaniia Pravlenia Soiuza Sov. Pisatelei Uzbekistana Tashkent, 6 sentiabria 1945', O'zRMDA, R-2356 o.1, d. 104, fol. 1r.

95 'Protokol n°10 zasedaniia Pravlenia Soiuza Sov. Pisatelei Uzbekistana Tashkent ot 10 oktiabria 1946', O'zRMDA, R-2356, o.1, d. 110, fol. 16r-21r.

96 Andrei Vladimirovich Stanishevskii, better known under his revolutionary name Aziz Niallo (Niallo standing for 'no Allah'), had been the head of the commission

Aziz Niallo then switched to attacking the more vulnerable young Russian writers of Uzbekistan, without succeeding in triggering a purge.[97] The strength of the Uzbek Soviet Writers' Union and its new networks inherited from the war, since Oybek's participation in the Presidium of the all-Soviet Writers' Union, were therefore a sufficient protection for writers and translators. In 1947, they even allowed Oybek to challenge the Tashkent Soviet Academy of Sciences, which had not yet issued the Russian-Uzbek encyclopaedic dictionary that the translators needed.[98]

Facing a Second Stalinism and the Cold War (1949–52)

The situation shifted in 1949. Stalin considered Uzbekistan too autonomous, and removed the head of the Party, who had protected the Uzbek intelligentsia, via a subtle policy of promotion.[99] The new Uzbek Party officials were all hardliners, like Mavlyan Vahabov (1908–91), a propaganda specialist promoted to Secretary of the Tashkent Obkom in 1950, a position he merged in 1951 with the direction of the Ministry of Culture.[100] Their competitions with each other generated an ideological overreach, which led to a new wave of repression, destroying both the Academy of Sciences and the SSPUz. Whereas translation activities had been a marginal issue during the Great Terror, they were a central concern of this second wave. The 'Republic's Conference on Questions of Literary Translation', held in Tashkent in 1952, shows a clear transformation in the discourse.[101] First, it raised active local political issues: the first speaker, Asqad Muhtor, attacked

in charge of examining the loyalty of the Uzbek Soviet Writers' Union in 1937–38. In 1938, having dismissed Majidiy and Alekseev in May, he was very reluctant to stop the purge process and tried to arrest some survivors, like Hamid Olimjon. His activity can be tracked in the letters he sent to the Soviet Writers' Union in Moscow. See *Mezhdu molotom i nakoval'nei. Soiuz sovetskikh pisatelei. Dokumenty i kommentarii.* I (1925-iiun' 1941 g.), ed. by Valentina Antipina, T. Domchareva, and Z. Vodapianova (Moscow: Rosspen, 2011), pp. 793–96.

97 'Zasedanie Russkoi Sektsii Soiuza Sovetsikh Pisatelei Uzbekistana 30 oktiabria 1946 goda', O'zRMDA, R-2356, o. 1, d. 120, fols. 1r-40v.

98 'Stenograficheskii otchët Obshche-gorodskogo sobraniia pisatelei Soiuza Sovetskikh Pisatelei Uzbekistana', 16 sentiabria 1946 goda, O'zRMDA, R-2356, o. 1, d. 112, fols. 6r-42r (15).

99 The First Secretary, Usmon Yusupov, who dismissed all of the charges against Uzbek intelligentsia, was recalled to Moscow, as were all high-ranking officials. See Claus Bech Hansen, 'Power and Purification: Late-Stalinist Repression in the Uzbek SSR', *Central Asian Survey*, 36:1 (2017), 148–69 (p. 148).

100 'Mavlian Gafarovich Vakhabov', *Obshestvenie nauki v Uzbekistane*, 3 (1991), 55–56.

101 'O masterstve perevoda, Respublinskoe soveshchanie po voprosam khudozhestvennogo perevoda ; iz doklada A. Mukhtara', *Zvezda Vostoka*, 6 (1952), 84–91.

prominent translators within the Uzbek Soviet Writers' Union, most of them close to Oybek like Shayhzoda or Mirtemir, and finally Oybek himself. Weakened, the former chairman of the SSPUz was now a target. His translations of Pushkin were, once again, at the centre of the debate. The question had been revived by the accusations in Russia against Isaak Nusinov and Mark Azadovskii, two academics who had been condemned for connecting the works of Pushkin to European literature rather than erroneously reframing him as a poet of pure Russian genius, as Russian nationalism demanded.[102]

By attacking Shayhzoda, Asqad Muhtor transposed Russian ultra-nationalism into the linguistic engineering of Uzbek. Just as Pushkin had been disconnected from any foreign roots, the Uzbek language had to be 'cleansed' of words of Persian origin, while Arabic-derived words were now too religious to be used. Whenever possible, words of Turkish origin or Russian borrowings were to be substituted. This linguistic programme crystallised in the condemnation of Shayhzoda's works, including his literary translations, as he was using a lot of them. Asqad Muhtor invoked the authority of Stalin, accusing some "Uzbek Marrists", like G'ulom Karimov, of "anti-scientific views"—that is to say, of having "falsely presented" the Arabic language as the "main literary language in Muslim lands during a long period". The Georgian-born comparative linguist Nikolai Marr had dominated Soviet linguistics until 1949, when Stalin condemned his theories, especially the "japhetic theory", which presumed a unity between languages through a shared origin. During the Cold War, Stalin replaced the Marrist quest for a universal language with Russian exceptionalism.[103] While the japhetic theory postulated that Caucasian languages were related to Semitic languages, Asqad Muhtor extended his accusation to all kinds of linguistic areas: having promoted the Turkish epics and, therefore, implicitly postulated a unity between Turkish languages and cultures, Hamid Olimjon himself was accused of having spread this theory. Shayhzoda appeared as the last link in the chain, having "applied Marrist theory in his translations of Pushkin, Shakespeare, and Maiakovskii" by using Persian and Arab words in his translations. Therefore, Shayhzoda was both a Marrist and an accomplice of the USSR's Cold War enemies, especially Iran. Furthermore, his lexical choices rendered him a "corruptor" of the language. Translation, in a key defining moment for the Uzbek language, had become the site of a death

102 Efim Etkind, *Bozhestvennii glagol. Pushkin, prochitannyi v Rossii i vo Frantsii* (Moscow: Iazyki russkoi kul'tury, 1999), p. 455.

103 The japhetic theory of Marr, supposing the existence of proto-languages, dominated Soviet linguistics until 1949, when Stalin rejected his theories, boosting the former's opponents. International observers interpreted this condemnation as an imperialist turn in Soviet linguistic policy. See Sébastien Moret, 'Marr, Staline et les espérantistes', in *Un paradigme perdu: la linguistique marriste*, ed. by Patrick Sériot (Lausanne: UNIL, 2015), 199–214 (p. 206); on the rise of Russian exceptionalism authoritatively grounded in classics, see David Brandenberger, *National Bolshevism* (Cambridge, MA and London: Harvard University Press, 2002), pp. 197–213.

struggle between the supporters of an ethnic linguistic nationalism, which was very close to Russian nationalism, and the supporters of a more open linguistic landscape.

Study of lengthy extracts from back-translations demonstrated that Mirtemir's translations were inaccurate, as he did not respect the exact lexicon of the original: literalism as a guarantee of ideological rectitude was once again a distinct feature of the Uzbek literary landscape, although it had been banned from translations into the Russian language. The difference of status between languages was therefore increasing. Oybek, whose translation of *Eugene Onegin* was very accurate, was more difficult to attack, so his work was quickly condemned as not poetic enough. In the dual context of the Cold War and of the centre's attempt to control the periphery, translation activity was no longer a sufficient guarantee of ideological probity. The argument for accuracy, once invoked as a defence, was once again weaponised against translators. Pressure increased on Shayhzoda. In August, the case of the former right-hand man of Oybek was finally transferred to the NKVD.[104] Already accused of idealising the feudal past, Shayhzoda was now tarred with Pan-Islamism. Two months later, he was arrested, then sentenced to twenty-five years in a strict-regime labour camp.[105]

In addition to this requirement for rectitude, the speakers at the 1952 conference clearly demonstrate that two policies had been abandoned: the promotion of Uzbek literature, but also the promotion of the minorities of the USSR. Only translations from Russian and from foreign literatures into Uzbek were discussed. In fact, these were produced slowly. Complaints about productivity soon escalated. The Gosizdat (Soviet state publishing house) representative pointed out that the 1951 plan for publishing output was not yet fulfilled. For example, in March 1952, at the time of the conference, Abdulla and Kibriyo Qahhor had still not completed the second volume of their translation of *War and Peace* (*Urush va tinchlik*), while Mirtemir had promised to deliver his manuscript of Nekrasov's poem, 'Who is Happy in Russia?' ('Komu na Rusi zhit' khorosho?', 1866) before May 1950, yet he ultimately would not translate it until 1953 (as 'Rusiyada kim yaxshi yashaydi'), after Stalin's death.[106] As accuracy had become a strictly enforced requirement, and a potential weapon wielded

104 Rahmatulla Otaqo'zi, better known as Uyg'un, and Vladimir Milchakov, were at this time ruling the SSPUz. They sent thirty documents to the NKVD accusing him: 'Spisok materialov vydannykh organam', O'zRMDA, R-2356, o. 1, d. 109, fols. 1r-2v.

105 Shayhzoda was also the first former member of the SSPUz to be released from a labour camp after the death of Stalin. See Naim Karimov, *Maqsud Shayhzoda, Ma'rifiy—biografik roman* (Tashkent: Sharq, 2009), pp. 179–80, pp. 199–200.

106 A. Khodzhanov, 'O masterstve perevoda, Respublinskoe soveshchanie po voprosam khudozhestvennogo perevoda; iz vystupleniia A. Khodzhanova', *Zvezda Vostoka*, 6 (1952), 91–96 (p. 92).

against translators, the latter had become more prudent and thus slower in delivering their work, waiting instead for the repression to cease.

After critiquing translations from Russian to Uzbek, the speaker for Gosizdat pointed out the lack of translations into Uzbek of books awarded Stalin Prizes from foreign countries, especially oriental ones. Translations of literatures from other Soviet Republics, once a priority, were barely mentioned. 'Friendship between the peoples' was thus no longer understood as a pillar of federal culture, but as the core of the Soviet soft-power project abroad, with Uzbekistan its Eastern vanguard. At the same time, the promotion of Uzbek literature through new Uzbek-to-Russian translations, a policy which had resisted the Great Terror and even, paradoxically, benefited from the immediate postwar years, completely disappeared. During the 1952 conference, even Mikhail Sal'e (1899–1961), translator of the *Babur-nama*, the memoirs of the founder of the Mughal Empire, which had become a canonical text of Uzbek literature during the 1930s (its translation into Russian consecrating this process) did not utter a single word to promote translations from Uzbek to Russian.[107] Instead, he prudently commented on an anthology of Chekhov in translation edited by Abdulla Qohhar and published almost one year earlier. The balance between the promotion of Russian culture and the construction of a national one was disrupted, and, at least during late Stalinism, morphed into Russian hegemony.

Conclusion

Rather than linear development from a liberal to a fully supervised activity, the interaction between the institutionalisation process and the nature of Soviet multinational culture appears to be the result of small- and large-scale intricate power struggles, in the course of which the Soviet multinational model was constantly redefined, both in the centre and in the Uzbek periphery. In the Uzbek case, translations from Russian never outnumbered local creations,

107 From the late 1920s onwards, the categorisation of many Central Asian cultural figures as Uzbek in the interests of building a national culture was a major concern for both Soviet orientalists and Uzbek writers, whether Muslim reformists or proletarians. Abdurrauf Fitrat (1886–1938) included Babur in Uzbek literature in his essay 'A Global View of Uzbek Literature Since the 16th Century' ('XVI asrdan so'ngra o'zbek adabiyotiga umumiy bir qarash', 1928). His arrest did not interfere with the process: three years after the Great Terror, Hamid Olimjon officially identified Babur as the founding father of Uzbek prose. See Abdullarauf Fitrat, 'XVI asrdan so'ngra o'zbek adabiyotiga umumiy bir qarash', in Fitrat, *Tanlangan Asarlar* (*Selected Works*), ed. by Ozod Sharafiddinov, Naim Karimov and others, 5 vols (Tashkent: Ma'naviyat, 2000–2010), II (2010), pp. 55–61; 'Stenograficheskii otchët po obsuzhdeniiu romana *Sviashchonaia krov'* i p'esa Do'stlar', O'zRMDA, R-2356, o.1, d. 88, f. 1r-4v. On Fitrat, see Edward Allworth, *The Preoccupations of 'Abdalrauf Fitrat, Bukharan Nonconformist: An Analysis and List of His Writings* (Berlin: Das Arabische Buch, 2000).

but the difference of status between the two languages is highlighted in many other ways. First, the Uzbek Soviet Writers' Union executives tried to pay equal attention to translations from Russian as to translations into Russian, in order to consecrate Uzbek literature in the dominant language. Meanwhile, they appropriated Soviet policies and funding for their own purposes, using translations to accumulate cultural capital in a way that recalls the anti-colonial concerns of the Jadids decades earlier. Not only did they promote their emerging national literature through translation, but they tried through translation to appropriate works considered part of world cultural heritage, as well as writings by other ethnic minorities. This strategy was successful during wartime, and even supported by some Party officials, but it was harshly repressed between 1949 and 1952, when translations from Russian clearly dominated the cultural landscape, in line with the Russian nationalism promoted in the centre. The inequality of cultural transfers is also clearly illustrated by the changes in translation aesthetics. While translations into Russian disqualified literalism and were increasingly oriented towards 'free translation' when the USSR asserted itself as a major power, translations from Russian to Uzbek, once target-oriented, shifted to a source-oriented approach at the end of the 1930s and to a strict literalism during the postwar period, with small discrepancies viewed as political faults. Writers posed a subtle resistance to this evolution: praising (like Oybek or Ayni) the translated works in ambiguous ways; deliberately choosing (like Cho'lpon) anticolonial novels to translate; or simply delaying the translation process (like Abdulla and Kibriyo Qahhor). Others, like Asqad Muhtor, instrumentalised this evolution to nurture linguistic nationalism. The extent of the Thaw in 1950s Uzbekistan must now be considered in the light of translations, with a possible return to a target-oriented aesthetic of translation highly significant in the context of what came before.

Vietnam

Translation of Russian Literature in North and South Vietnam during 1955–75: Two Ways of 'Rewriting' the History of Russian Literature in Vietnam

Trang Nguyen

Introduction

The two decades between 1955 and 1975 form an exceptional period in Vietnamese history. During this time, the North and South regions of Vietnam were divided into two different political regimes. When North Vietnam was building Socialism, following the political path of the Soviet Union, the South was occupied by the United States army. The Republic of Vietnam was built in the South under US influence. The Vietnam War between these entities raged for twenty years. The Vietnamese people in the North wanted to liberate the South, unify North and South Vietnam, and achieve national independence. Not until 1975, when the Communists defeated the Republic of Vietnam, were their aims achieved. The United States subsequently withdrew all its troops from South Vietnam. This unique historical context has, naturally, affected the reception of foreign literature, and particularly its translation. Foreign literature, including Russian, reached readers in North and South Vietnam primarily through translations. As leading theorists have argued, the connection between target texts and target cultures in translation can reveal criteria for a translation strategy as well as for understanding the history of the source literature. Any analysis of the translation picture at a given time therefore cannot ignore cultural or political contexts, power discourses, or the connection of translations to the target cultural

 https://doi.org/10.11647/OBP.0340.35

context.[1] This essay contends that while the translation of Russian literature in North Vietnam favoured works that were consistent with the Socialist discourse pursued by the latter, translation activity in the South constructed an alternative literary canon which reflected both the political biases and artistic tastes of South Vietnamese readers. Thus, the first part of this chapter will analyse the historical reception of Russian literature in North Vietnam, in the context of ideological flow. In the second part, I will delve into the factors governing the curation of translation in South Vietnam and how Russian literature was 're'-written there, as demonstrated by selected translations. Finally, I will conclude with a comparison of the history of Russian literature through translation in South and North Vietnam, referring to the unique context of the period 1955–75.

Translating Russian Literature in North Vietnam

In North Vietnam, no literature rivalled Russian in terms of either number of translations or influence over readers. Between 1955 and 1975, when North Vietnam was building Socialism and supporting the South against the United States, the Soviet Union provided material support. It is thus difficult to deny the influence of both Soviet ideology and Russian culture on North Vietnam. In 1957, North Vietnam and the USSR signed an agreement for cooperation in the field of cultural friendship. Cultural exchange between North Vietnam and the Soviet Union was continuous and efficient. Many North Vietnamese intellectuals were trained in the Soviet Union. For example, Phan Hong Giang (1941–2022), who translated Anton Chekhov's stories, Ivan Bunin's *The Life of Arsen'ev: Youth* (*Zhizn' Arsen'eva. Iunost'*, 1930), the Avar-language poet Rasul Gamzatov's *My Dagestan* (*Dir Dag"istan*, 1970) and many other works, studied in Moscow State University's Faculty of Philology from 1960 to 1964. Do Hong Chung (1934–91), who translated Aleksandr Pushkin's poetry and prose and Chekhov's short stories into Vietnamese, was a classmate of Phan Hong Giang at Moscow State University. Hoang Thuy Toan (b. 1936) graduated from the Moscow State V.I. Lenin Pedagogical Institute in 1961. He translated Sergei Esenin's poetry, Pushkin's plays, and Lev Tolstoy's short stories, and in 2012 he became the first director of the Vietnam-Russia Literature Fund, a bilateral organisation founded to promote mutual translation and co-operation between the two countries.[2] Hoang Ngoc Hien (1930–2011), a translator of Vladimir Maiakovskii's poetry and comedy, defended his doctoral thesis at Moscow State University in 1959.

1 See Maria Tymoczko, *Enlarging Translation, Empowering Translators* (Manchester: St. Jerome, 2007); Edwin Gentzler, *Contemporary Translation Theories*, 2nd edn (Clevedon: Multilingual Matters, 2001).

2 For more on the Fund's activities, see 'Translated Works Bring Vietnamese, Russian Literature Closer', *Nhân Dân*, 26 July 2016, https://en.nhandan.vn/translated-works-bring-vietnamese-russian-literature-closer-post43966.html.

In addition, Doan Tu Huyen (1952–2020), who studied at Voronezh University, and Thai Ba Tan (b. 1950), a Moscow University of Foreign Languages alumnus, are present-day translators in North Vietnam. Their educated grasp of Russian culture and literature helped them to bring Russian intellectual culture closer to North Vietnamese readers.

During these two decades, approximately three hundred works of Russian literature were translated into Vietnamese in North Vietnam.[3] Many Vietnamese readers sensed that the 'Russian soul' resonated with their own spiritual life. Nguyen Thi Ngoc Tu (1942–2013), the internationally prize-winning Vietnamese author, wrote: "I have never been to Russia, but Russia has come to me through books. Rivers, streets, landscapes, and people, typical characters of Russian life in the works of great authors such as Tolstoy, Gorky, Turgenev are so close that just by closing my eyes I could imagine them. In each work, each author gives me a new horizon and new rays of light as well as nourishing my soul".[4]

However, when sketching literary translation from Russian in North Vietnam over a twenty-year period, it is important to emphasise the compatibility of translation and political ideology. North Vietnamese ideologues realised that Russian literature was inspirational for fulfilling the task of building Socialism and sustaining South Vietnam's war of resistance against America. Thus, at the Fourth Congress of the Soviet Union of Writers on 25 May 1967, Nguyen Dinh Thi (1924–2003), a well-known poet and composer who served as General Secretary of the Vietnam Writers' Association from 1958 to 1989, summed up: "'At present, in the trenches, the underground classrooms, the factories or on the fields, that Soviet literature that the Vietnamese consider a wonderful creation of human talents has become the spiritual weapons of our Vietnamese people".[5] In 1989, when recapitulating the history of translated literature in Vietnam, the celebrated translator Thuy Toan realised that "in just the past forty years, since the agreement on cultural cooperation between Vietnam and the Soviet Union was signed in 1957, the Literature Publishing House has published one hundred books by Russian and Soviet authors. Many works were reissued and retranslated."[6] The compatibility between the translation of Russian literature and political ideology and the discourse of power is evident from the texts that were selected for translation. Pushkin was the best-known Russian writer

3 See Thi Quynh Nga Tran, *Tiếp nhận văn xuôi Nga thế kỉ XIX ở Việt Nam* (*The Reception of 19th century Russian Prose in Vietnam*) (Hanoi: Vietnam Education Publishing House, 2010), p. 73. All translations from Vietnamese are my own unless otherwise indicated.

4 Thi Ngoc Tu Nguyen, 'Kỉ niệm tháng Mười' ('Celebrating October'), *Tạp chí Văn học* (*Journal of Literary Studies*), 5 (1977), 142–43 (p. 143).

5 Dinh Thi Nguyen, *Công việc của người viết tiểu thuyết* (*A Novelist's Work*) (Hanoi: Literature Publishing House, 1969), p. 20.

6 Thuý Toàn, *Không phải của riêng ai: dịch văn học, văn học dịch* (*Not Anyone's Own: Literary Translation, Translated Literature*) (Hanoi: Literature Publishing House, 1999), p. 49.

in North Vietnam. His work was most frequently translated during the two decades of the conflict. In the minds of Vietnamese readers, Pushkin is "our loyal friend in the cause of struggle for social and human renewal".[7] His novellas *The Captain's Daughter* (*Kapitanskaia dochka*, 1836) and *Dubrovskii* (*Dubrovskii*, 1841) particularly appealed to Northern Vietnamese readers, especially when land reform, collectivisation and agricultural cooperation were carried out in their country. In the words of one scholar, both novellas "explore many issues about the relationship between peasants and aristocratic landlords, the oppression and struggle, and consider the peasant movement as a high expression of the people's power".[8] On the relationship between the translation of Pushkin's work and political discourse, Nikolai Nikulin suggests that "the atmosphere of social reforms in Vietnam has strengthened Vietnamese readers' interest with Pushkin. They are especially interested in works expressing the desire to love freedom, containing the motif of protest against social domination and evil, [which are] showing sympathy for the oppressed".[9] Besides seeking a spiritual fulcrum for resistance against the Americans for national integrity and the foundation of a workers' state, Northern Vietnamese leaders and intellectuals enthusiastically welcomed the works of Lev Tolstoy and Nikolai Gogol. Gogol's 'Taras Bulba' ('Taras Bul'ba', 1835) and Tolstoy's *War and Peace* (*Voina i mir*, 1869) reached Northern readers in both French and Russian versions. According to Tran Thi Quynh Nga, 'Taras Bulba' touched Vietnamese people because this work "praises the patriotic heroism and indomitable spirit of brave people in the cause of defending the country".[10] Le Son (1937–2020), a researcher and translator, commented favourably on Gogol's "very realistic description of life".[11]

In the 1960s, translators such as Cao Xuan Hao (1930–2007), Nhu Thanh (1925–2020), and Hoang Thieu Son (1920–2005) studied Chinese, English, and French versions of *War and Peace* in order to bring Tolstoy's novel to North Vietnamese readers, beginning with the first published version in 1961. It was not until 1979 that the Vietnamese version of this novel was published, in full,

7 Lien Luu, 'Thiên tài Pushkin và tiểu thuyết lịch sử Người con gái Viên Đại uý' ('The Genius Writer Pushkin and His Historical Novel *The Captain's Daughter*'), *Tạp chí Văn học* (*Journal of Literary Studies*), 6 (1994), 38–41 (p. 41).

8 Thi Quynh Nga Tran, *Tiếp nhận văn xuôi Nga thế kỉ XIX ở Việt Nam* (*Reception of 19th Century Russian Prose in Vietnam*) (Hanoi: Vietnam Education Publishing House, 2010), p. 63.

9 N. I Nikulin, 'Tác phẩm của Pushkin ở Việt Nam' ('Pushkin's Works in Vietnam'), in *Văn học Việt Nam và giao lưu quốc tế* (*Vietnamese Literature and International Exchange*) (Hanoi: Vietnam Education Publishing House, 2010), pp. 701–10 (p. 707).

10 Thi Quynh Nga Tran, *Tiếp nhận văn xuôi Nga thế kỉ XIX ở Việt Nam*, p. 65.

11 Son Le, '*Taras Bulba*, tiểu thuyết lịch sử của Gogol' ('*Taras Bulba*, Gogol's Historical Novel'), *Tạp chí Văn học* (*Journal of Literary Studies*), 11 (1963), 24–28 (p. 27).

in four volumes (by Cao Xuan Hao).[12] *War and Peace* was especially significant to Northern Vietnamese people because what they read as its populist ideology chimed with the political ideal that their government pursued. When approaching *War and Peace* in Russian translation, the important North Vietnamese essayist Nguyen Tuan (1910–87) commented that "there has never been an indictment against a war of aggression which was longer, greater, or of superior artistic value".[13] In addition, in 1963 and 1964, Nhi Ca and Duong Tuong completed their joint translation of *Anna Karenina* (*Anna Karenina*, 1877) from French in a three-volume edition, using both the Russian and Chinese versions for comparison.[14] In 1970, a team of translators including Phung Uong, Nguyen Nam, Ngoc An, and Moc Nghia translated Tolstoy's *Resurrection* (*Phục sinh; Voskresenie*, 1899) from Russian. *Anna Karenina* had been presented to Northern Vietnamese readers as a work focusing on the issues of a new society, such as women's liberation and marriage.[15] *Resurrection* instilled belief in the rebirth of North Vietnam after suffering and wars. Explaining why Tolstoy's works were admired by his compatriots, the novelist Nguyen Minh Chau (1930–89) claimed that Tolstoy had "reached the heights of national spiritual values, even touching the souls of ordinary people of other countries".[16] Nguyen Minh Chau also stated that during the 1968 Khe Sanh Communist campaign against the US army, one copy of *War and Peace* was passed around all the soldiers. They forgot injuries from bombs and bullets, distracted by discussing Tolstoy's characters.[17] On why *Anna Karenina* appeals, its translator Nhi Ca has commented that "many Vietnamese readers considered the picture of the past in *Anna Karenina* as an image of society similar to Vietnamese society before the August Revolution.

---

12 *War and Peace* was translated as *Chiến tranh và hòa bình* by Cao Xuan Hao and several other translators (Hanoi: Literature Publishing House, 1976–79). A South Vietnamese version, also in four volumes with the same title, was published in Saigon (later Ho Chi Minh City) by the translator Nguyen Hien Le (1912–84) (Saigon: La Boi Publishing House, 1968).

13 Nguyen Tuan, 'Tolstoy', in *Nguyễn Tuân toàn tập* (*Nguyen Tuan's Collected Works*), ed. by Nguyen Dang Manh, 5 vols (Hanoi: Literature Publishing House, 2000), V (2000), pp. 661–85 (p. 676).

14 In 1944, the publisher Đời nay (Today's Life) printed an incomplete translation of *Anna Karenina* by Vũ Ngọc Phan (1902–87) as *Anna Kha Lệ Ninh* (a Chinese pronunciation of Anna Karenina with reference to Vietnamese phonetics). The Khai Trí (Mastermind) publishing house printed six volumes of *Anna Kha Lệ Ninh* co-translated by Vu Ngoc Phan and Vu Minh Thieu in 1970.

15 Tiếng dân (The Voice of the People) Press published Hoa Trung's translation of *Resurrection* (as *Phục Sinh*) on 9 July 1927.

16 Minh Chau Nguyen, 'Tác dụng kì diệu của tác phẩm văn học' ('The Magical Effects of Literary Works'), *Tạp chí Văn nghệ quân đội* (*Military Arts and Culture Magazine*), 8 (1983), 134–39 (p. 134).

17 Minh Chau Nguyen, 'Tác dụng kì diệu của tác phẩm văn học', p. 135.

The novel helps readers identify the evil face of the old regime, believe in the new regime, in the nation's future, and in the future of humanity".[18]

Since their preference was for epic inspiration and revolutionary heroism, North Vietnamese translators did not attempt to translate Fedor Dostoevsky's fiction for another twenty years. Dostoevsky is arguably a more individualistic writer. Contradictory personalities like Raskolnikov were not what North Vietnamese readers were looking for at that time. Therefore, although Cao Xuan Hao completed his translation of *Crime and Punishment* (*Prestuplenie i nakazanie*, 1866) in 1962, it was rejected, apparently on the grounds that Raskolnikov made a poor role model for Vietnamese youth. It appeared in print almost twenty years later. Cao Xuan Hao translated this work as *Tội ác và hình phạt*; nevertheless, when printing it, the publisher (Hanoi's Literature Publishing House (NXB Văn học)) changed this title to *Tội ác và trừng phạt*. *Hình phạt* in Vietnamese is a noun equivalent to 'punishment' (or indeed *nakazanie* in Russian). *Trừng phạt* in Vietnamese is a verb meaning 'to punish'. Moreover, *trừng phạt* in Vietnamese refers to the legal penalties meted out to criminals. The translator's preferred phrase, *hình phạt*, can mean both 'formal punishment suffered by the wrongdoer'; but also 'self-imposed, psychological suffering experienced by the perpetrator of the crime'. A subtle difference, but Cao Xuan Hao's formula evoked a psychological dimension of the concept of 'punishment' which Dostoevsky certainly intended to convey, and which his publisher chose to ignore. The furious translator called the title "a huge grammatical error" ("một lỗi ngữ pháp kếch xù"); fortunately, in 1985, soon after its publication, the wording was corrected.[19]

Northern intellectuals already recognised the artistic value of Dostoevsky's work, but the eligibility for translation seemed to be predetermined by the perceived need for national rather than personal inspiration. Nguyen Tuan rated Dostoevsky as a "creative genius" whose works "are profound utterances about love, happiness, justice and truth".[20] As we have seen, Cao Xuan Hao's translation could not be published in the 1960s due to the Soviet regime's existing prejudices against Dostoevsky, which in turn prejudiced its reception by intellectuals and the ruling elite in North Vietnam. As Marc Slonim commented, "radical and socialist intellectuals and critics never ceased quarrelling with

18 Nhi Ca, 'Lời giới thiệu Anna Karenina' ('Introduction to The Novel Anna Karenina'), in Tolstoy, *Anna Karenina*, trans. by Nhi Ca and Duong Tuong (Hanoi: Literature Publishing House, 1978), pp. 3–33 (p. 20).

19 Cao Xuan Hao, 'Về người biên tập' ('About Editors'), *Lao Dong* online journal, https://web.archive.org/web/20071109154315/http://www.laodong.com.vn/Utilities/PrintView.aspx?ID=3214. Interestingly, as in the case of the simultaneous translation of *War and Peace* in North and South Vietnam, in 1973 Truong Dinh Cu produced the first South Vietnamese edition of the novel, as *Tội ác và hình phạt*.

20 Nguyen Tuan, 'Dostoevsky', in *Nguyễn Tuân toàn tập* (*Nguyen Tuan's Collected Works*), ed. by Nguyen Dang Manh, 5 vols (Hanoi: Literature Publishing House, 2000), V (2000), pp. 499–519 (p. 516).

Dostoevsky. They did not deny his artistic genius, yet they could not accept his political and religious views, and this contradiction led to all sorts of conflicts and discussion".[21] Cao Xuan Hao himself, an academic linguist as well as a translator, had a successful career as Professor of Linguistics at Hanoi University.

When searching for works suitable for political discourse about the nation, Northern Vietnamese readers were drawn to officially promoted Soviet literature. According to statistics compiled in 2005 by the scholar Vu Hong Loan, the four most widely translated Russian authors in North Vietnam were Maksim Gorky, Il'ia Ehrenburg, Boris Polevoi, and Mikhail Sholokhov. Twenty-two of Gorky's works were published, and were continuously re-translated.[22] His novel *Mother* (*Mat'*, 1906), was retranslated and (re)published six times: in 1946 by the Women's Publishing House, again in 1955 by the People's Publishing House, thirdly in 1966 by the Education Publishing House, and then three more times up to 1984 by the Literary Publishing House.[23] Its translators were To Huu, Hoang Quang Gi, Ngo Vinh, Nhi Mai, Do Xuan Ha, and Phan Thao. Among them, To Huu was simultaneously a poet and a politician, in charge of crucial functions in the Vietnamese political system.

In North Vietnam, writers of underground/censored literature, like Boris Pasternak or Aleksandr Solzhenitsyn, were barely translated at all. Fiction about private life, or clandestinely published texts with negative perspectives on the Soviet regime, were also almost completely excluded. Thanks to its selective content, Russian literature became a spiritual pillar for its Northern Vietnamese readers, affirming their belief in the Socialist regime and their determination to fight the US army for the unification of North Vietnam and South Vietnam. The following statement by Pavel Korchagin, the hero of Nikolai Ostrovskii's *How the Steel Was Tempered* (*Kak zakalialas' stal'*, 1934) became a motto for North Vietnamese youth for many decades:

> Man's dearest possession is life, and it is given to him to live but once. He must live it so as to feel no torturing regrets for years without purpose, never know the burning shame of a mean and petty past; so to live that, dying, he can say: all my life, all my strength were given to the finest cause in all the world—the fight for the Liberation of Mankind.[24]

The admiration felt by Vietnamese youth generally—and by North Vietnamese young people in particular—for Korchagin's testament is mentioned in a diary

21 Marc Slonim, 'Dostoevsky under the Soviets', *The Russian Review*, 10 (1951), 118–30 (p. 118).

22 Hong Loan Vu, 'Văn học Việt Nam tiếp nhận Văn học Xô viết' ('The Influence of Soviet Literature on Vietnamese Literature') (unpublished doctoral thesis, HCMC University of Education, 2005), p. 44

23 See Hong Loan Vu, 'Văn học Việt Nam', p.44.

24 Nikolai Ostrovskii, *How the Steel Was Tempered*, trans. by R. Prokofieva, 2 vols (Moscow: Foreign Languages Publishing House, 1952), II (1952), p. 105.

by Nguyen Van Thac (1952–72), who, like many students in North Vietnam, volunteered to fight in the Southern battlefield and died aged just twenty:

> His [Pavel Korchagin's] life was a continuous springtime. That was the life of a young Party member, the life of a Red Army soldier. I want to live like that. I wish to devote my whole life to the Party and the class and live firmly against the storms of revolution and private life.[25]

Dang Thuy Tram, a Hanoi doctor who also died in the war of resistance against the US, wrote in her own diary that soldiers under fire were still discussing Pavel Korchagin.[26] Now I shall turn to the South Vietnamese reception of Russian literature, which was also significantly politically inflected, if in a different direction.

Translating Russian Literature in South Vietnam

From 1955–75, from the seventeenth parallel inward (that is, from the provisional military demarcation line between North Vietnam and South Vietnam established by the Geneva Accords (1954)), the government of the Republic of Vietnam was established under Ngo Dinh Diem's presidency with support from the United States. This government was politically opposed to that of North Vietnam. This historical and political context greatly influenced the South Vietnamese translation of foreign literature in general and Russian literature in particular. First, due to the presence of the US Army, South Vietnamese culture was deeply influenced by America and the West. Thus, for these two decades, South Vietnam was receptive to foreign literary works, including Russian. In addition, Western-educated South Vietnamese intellectuals who were fluent in foreign languages selected their own canon of commercially distributed world literature to develop the reading tastes of the South Vietnamese public. Among them, Nguyen Hien Le (1912–84), mentioned above as a translator of *War and Peace*, was a translator, writer, and researcher in philosophy and history. Do Khanh Hoan (b. 1934) was educated at the Universities of Saigon, Sydney, and Columbia (New York), becoming Head of the English department at Saigon University before emigrating to Canada after reunification. He is perhaps best

25 Van Thac Nguyen, *Mãi mãi tuổi hai mươi* (*Twenties Forever*) (Hanoi: Youth Publishing House, 2005), p. 119.

26 Thuy Tram Dang, *Nhật ký Đặng Thuỳ Trâm* (*Dang Thuy Tram's Diary*) (Hanoi: Vietnam Writers Association Publishing House, 2005), p. 115 and p. 136. Interestingly, this diary was translated into Russian as the result of another bilateral Russian-Vietnamese friendship initiative and published in Moscow in July 2012 under the auspices of the Russian Academy of Sciences. See 'Dang Thuy Tram diary to be published in Russia', *Saigon Online*, 26 August 2011, https://www.sggpnews.org.vn/dang-thuy-tram-diary-to-be-published-in-russia-post59866.html.

known for translating Homer into Vietnamese, but also translated Russian and Western literature. Nguyen Huu Hieu (b. 1940) was a lawyer and translator credited by some scholars with introducing Russian literature to South Vietnam, particularly through his translations of Pasternak and Dostoevsky (via French).[27]

A second historical factor was the war itself, which plunged Southern, like Northern, society into turmoil between 1955 and 1975. Consequently, Southern Vietnamese readers were inclined towards philosophical fiction, exploring literary pathos in the hope of finding humanist explanations for suffering. Nguyen Hien Le, when reading Dostoevsky, discovered "extraordinarily intense emotions, terrifyingly honest souls, and the entangled problems of an indescribable interior".[28] Southern Vietnamese readers also empathised with "the experience of living with the true values of life on the metaphysical and social philosophical level" that Pasternak described.[29] And a third, political factor manifested in the Republic of Vietnam's sharp opposition to the Socialist regime in North Vietnam. Therefore, when approaching Russian literature, some Southern readers tried to choose censored literature that 'lifted the veil' on the Socialist regime. Dissident writers such as Solzhenitsyn, Pasternak, Vladimir Dudintsev, Andrei Siniavskii, and even Andrei Sakharov were of particular interest to readers and critics. Nguyen Nam Chau (1929–2005), a professor at Hue University, a writer, researcher in literature and philosophy, and translator, considered Dudintsev and Pasternak as "plaintiff[s] who sided with the humanists against materialistic communism."[30] Regarding Pasternak, the political thinker Hoang Van Chi (1913–88) explained that "[u]ntil now, there has been no reliable book describing the October Revolution and the living situation of the Russian people correctly and objectively. Today, the world can learn many more valuable things from *Doctor Zhivago*."[31] When reading Solzhenitsyn's *An Incident at Krechetovka Station* (*Sluchai na stantsii Krechetovka*, 1963), some readers shared that "after reading the book, one can feel more poignantly than ever,

27 For more on Nguyen Huu Hieu's cultural importance, see Thanh Duc Hong Ha, 'Nguyễn Hữu Hiệu Reads Dostoyevsky', in *Practice Oriented Science UAE-Russia-India: Materials of International University Scientific Forum October 12, 2022* (UAE, 2022), pp. 38–46, http://ran-nauka.ru/wp-content/uploads/2022/10/Practice-Oriented-Science-October-12.pdf#page=31. Nguyen Huu Hieu wrote interpretative introductions for his own translations.

28 Hien Le Nguyen, 'Dostoievski, một kẻ suốt đời chịu đau khổ để viết' ('Dostoevsky, a Man who Suffered All his Life to Write'), *Bách khoa Journal*, 82 (1960), 41–49 (p. 42).

29 Dinh Luu Vu, 'Thân thế và sự nghiệp Pasternac' ('Pasternak's Background and Career'), *Journal of Literature*, 83 (1967), 21–28 (p. 27).

30 Nam Chau Nguyen, 'Pasternak và Sholokhov hai chứng nhân, một thế giới' ('Pasternak and Sholokhov, Two Witnesses, One World'), *Asian Culture Magazine*, 19 (1959), 17–24 (p. 19).

31 Van Chi Hoang, 'Nhận định về vụ Pasternak và tác phẩm Bác sĩ Zhivago' ('Comments on the Pasternak Case and *Doctor Zhivago*'), *Asian Culture Magazine*, 10 (1959), 17–23 (p. 22).

when thinking about the prisoner status of every individual human being—whether favoured or persecuted—in the Soviet regime".[32]

Thus a combination of American influence, Vietnam's recent history, and complicated international politics largely shaped the South Vietnamese reception of Russian literature, which focused on its political, artistic, and philosophical aspects.[33] According to Tran Trong Dang Dan's statistics, over the twenty years until July 1976, translated fiction in South Vietnam included 57 titles from German literature, 58 from Italian, 71 from Japanese, 97 from British English and 273 from American English, 499 translated from French, 358 from Taiwanese or Hong Kong authors, 120 books from Russian literature, and 381 translated from other languages.[34] This demonstrates the comparatively important position occupied by Russian literature within South Vietnam's literary translation system. However, most translations from Russian were made via English and French versions. In South Vietnam, almost no intellectuals during the period were fluent in Russian; moreover, most considered Russian literature as a subgroup of Western literature. It is therefore unsurprising that they discovered Russian literature via indirect translations from Western languages. In the following section, I shall discuss the Southern Vietnamese reception of Tolstoy, Dostoevsky, and both Communist and dissident Soviet writers of the twentieth century. Where relevant, I will contrast this reception with attitudes to the same writers in North Vietnam.

In combination, these criteria of artistic value and Western influence on the reading tastes of Southern Vietnamese audiences ensured that the profile of nineteenth-century Russian literature in translation differed from that which was available in North Vietnam. While the latter selected Pushkin and Gogol for translation, seeking fiction that would reflect their national spirit and epic inspiration, South Vietnam translated more books by Dostoevsky, Tolstoy, and Chekhov. The selection of texts in North Vietnam reveals a characteristic of translation that Maria Tymoczko has emphasised in her suggestion that translators unearth "the embodied and situated knowledge related to cultural configurations and practices, a kind of habitus, of both the source and the target texts and cultures, before embarking on a translation task to establish

32 Thanh Binh Nguyen, 'Vài nét về Solzhenitsyn và tác phẩm *Bất ngờ tại ga Krechetovka*' ['About Solzhenitsyn and *An Incident at Krechetovka Station*'], in Aleksandr Solzhenitsyn, *Bất ngờ tại ga Krechetovka* [*An Incident at Krechetovka Station*], trans. by Le Vu (Saigon: Journey Publishing House, 1973), pp. 57–58 (p. 58).

33 Thi Phuong Pham, *Văn học Nga tại đô thị miền Nam 1954–1975* [*Russian Literature in the Southern Urban during 1954–1975*] (Ho Chi Minh City: Publishing House of HCMC University of Education, 2010), p. 22.

34 These figures are derived from statistics compiled by Trong Dang Dan Tran, *Văn hoá, văn nghệ nam Việt Nam, 1954–1975* [*Culture and Art in South Vietnam during 1954–1975*] (Hanoi: Culture and Information Publishing House, 2000), p. 427.

a translation strategy".[35] According to Southern Vietnamese readers, these works represented the pinnacle of Russian literary art recognised by the West. When establishing parameters for literary excellence, the celebrated writer (and translator of *Wuthering Heights* into Vietnamese) Nhat Linh (1906–63) invoked Tolstoy, Dostoevsky, Gogol, and Chekhov. He classified the latter as, like Shakespeare, Western literary talents.[36] This reflects how "the process of [cultural] enrichment operates by diverting a central patrimony in various ways, through the importation of canonized texts and literary techniques".[37]

Dostoevsky was the most translated writer in South Vietnam. This is in contrast with North Vietnam, where he was not translated at all. In the 1960s, translations of *Notes from Underground* (*Zapiski iz podpol'ia*, 1864), *The Gambler* (*Igrok*, 1866), *Crime and Punishment* (*Prestuplenie i nakazanie*, 1866), and *The Eternal Husband* (*Vechnyi muzh*, 1870) appeared, and remained in print throughout the 1970s. *Crime and Punishment* was translated by Truong Dinh Cu (1920s-) and published in 1973 by Khai Trí (Mastermind) Publishing House. Khai Trí was a large book-selling business active in Saigon from 1952 to 1975. In 1973, Ly Quoc Sinh published another translation of this novel, as *Tội ác và hình phạt*, with Nguon Sang (Source of Light) Publishing House. *The Brothers Karamazov* (*Brat'ia Karamazovy*, 1881) reached Southern readers through two versions with the same Vietnamese title (*Anh em nhà Karamazov*) in the same year (1972): one by Truong Dinh Cu, published by An Tiem Publishing House, and the other by Vu Dinh Luu (1914–80), from Nguon Sang. Thus, although translation in North Vietnam did not focus on Dostoevsky (as we have seen, Cao Xuan Hao's translation of *Crime and Punishment*, although completed in 1962, could not be published until 1982), in the South his novels constituted not only a literary pinnacle, but a philosophical authority. For Southern Vietnamese readers, "[Dostoevsky] lived and wrote about the great problems of our time. The world he described was [also] chaotic, including full of signs of revolution and messianism," as Ngoc Minh Nguyen wrote in his 1972 introduction to *Demons* (*Besy*, 1872; *Lũ người quỷ ám*).[38] Moreover, Southern translators credited Dostoevsky as the originator of the *nouveau roman*. Vu Dinh Luu commented that "the *nouveau roman* [...] was formed from techniques signalled by Dostoyevsky, then Kafka and Malraux."[39] Pham Thi Phuong argued that the *nouveau roman* greatly influenced the writing style of Southern writers such as Duong Nghiem

35 Tymoczko, *Enlarging Translation*, p. 227.

36 Nhat Linh, 'Đọc và viết tiểu thuyết' ('Reading and Writing Novels'), *Văn hoá ngày nay* (*Journal of Today's Culture*), 3 (1961), 8–10 (p. 9).

37 Pascale Casanova, *The World Republic of Letters*, trans. by Malcolm DeBevoise (Cambridge, MA: Harvard University Press, 2007), p. 223.

38 Ngoc Minh Nguyen, 'Lũ người quỷ ám trong con mắt người Việt Nam (thay Lời giới thiệu *Lũ người quỷ ám*)' ('*Demons* in Vietnamese Eyes (Introduction)'), in Dostoevskii, *Demons*, trans. by Nguyen Ngoc Minh (Saigon: Nguon Sang, 1972), pp. vii-xiv (pp. ix-x).

39 Dinh Luu Vu, *Thảm kịch văn hoá* (*Cultural Tragedy*) (Saigon: An Tiem, 1966), p. 50.

Mau, Nha Ca, The Uyen, Duy Lam, and Thao Truong.[40] It motivated writers to go beyond the stereotype when describing the (in)coherence of a character's psychology. For example, a character in the renowned novel *Tuổi nước độc* (*The Age of the Poisonous Water*) by Duong Nghiem Mau (1936–2016), Ngac, exists in a state of overwhelming post-traumatic mental strain, gradually losing hope and becoming estranged from reality. In short stories such as *Trong lòng bàn tay* (*In One's Palm*), *Một giấc mơ* (*A Dream*), the same writer describes his characters as suffused with pangs of conscience, inhabiting a world strewn with insecurity and absurdity. The parallels with Dostoevsky's novels are obvious. Dostoevsky's oppositional dyads (freedom and violence, the individual and society) aroused particular interest among Southern readers in their quest for solutions to contemporary problems. Huu Hieu Nguyen realised the connection between Dostoevsky and Buddhism and Existentialism, which made Dostoevsky a vastly influential pillar for Southern writers.[41] Christians identified with Dostoevsky in his desire to believe in the Messiah, love, and forgiveness. Buddhists welcomed Dostoevsky's project of abandoning the rational and civilised West for the gentle Eastern home. The translator Nguyen Huu Hieu identified the tolerant Buddha with the positive characters in *The Brothers Karamazov*, Father Zosima and Alesha.[42] Scholar Pham Thi Phuong concluded that the Southern intellectuals and writers "can see in the ideologist Dostoyevsky [sic] problems that they seek to investigate, such as (i) the tragedy-afflicted status of humans, requiring succour through affection inflected by religion, promoting anti-violence and friendly beliefs or ideologies; (ii) beliefs or ideologies about returning to one's roots, including the roots of national identity".[43]

Works by Tolstoy that were translated in South Vietnam include *The Kreutzer Sonata* (*Kreitserova sonata*, 1889), 'The Death of Ivan Il'ich' ('Smert' Ivana Il'icha', 1886), and *War and Peace*. Many translations of *War and Peace* (*Chiến tranh và hoà bình*) have appeared in Saigon, such as the 1969 version by Nguyen Dan Tam (Southern Publishing House) or Nguyen Hien Le's 1968 version from La Boi (Buddhist Scriptures) Publishing House. These same works by Tolstoy, as we saw above, appealed to Northern Vietnamese readers for their "positive attitudes and military focus", consistent with Communist political discourse. Meanwhile, Southern readers welcomed Tolstoy's prose rather for aesthetic reasons. Translator Nhat Linh called *Anna Karenina* "the novel of the century",

40 Pham Thi Phuong, *Văn học Nga tại đô thị miền Nam 1954–1975*, p. 95.

41 See Thanh Duc Hong Ha, 'Nguyễn Hữu Hiệu Reads Dostoyevsky'.

42 Huu Hieu Nguyen, 'Dostoevsky', in Dostoevskii, *Anh em nhà Karamazov* (*Brothers Karamazov*), trans. by Vu Dinh Luu (Saigon: Nguon Sang, 1972), pp. i-iii (p. ii).

43 Pham Thị Phương, 'Sự "trưng dụng" tư tưởng F. Dostoevsky của văn nghệ đô thị miền Nam 1954–1975' ('The "utili[s]ation" of F. Dostoevsky's Thought in South Vietnamese Urban Literature 1954–1975'), *Tạp chí Khoa học ĐHSP TP Hồ Chí Minh/ Ho Chi Minh City University of Education: Journal of Science*, 10 (2015), 118–28 (p. 124).

revealing the "mysterious life of the soul".[44] Editor and translator Tran Phong Giao (1932–2005) pointed out that Tolstoy's interest in Asian characters and thought evoked the spirit of charity and nonviolence.[45] Chekhov also appealed to Southern readers principally for his short stories. His plays, however, were not translated since audiences preferred *Cai luong* (traditional Vietnamese folk opera). Soviet critics similarly neglected Chekhov, although Westerners praised him.[46] In the 1960s and 1970s, several of Chekhov's short stories were translated and published in various journals and anthologies.[47] Chekhov was highly appreciated by Saigon readers for his ability to "subtly observe life", as one translator summarised the Russian author's skill.[48] The translator and scholar Do Khanh Hoan (b. 1934) commented that Chekhov was "the single most important influence on the development of the modern short story".[49]

For Southern Vietnamese readers, the major twentieth-century authors of Russian literature were three Nobel Prize-winning writers: Boris Pasternak, Mikhail Sholokhov, and Aleksandr Solzhenitsyn. They particularly valued Pasternak, whose works were censored and could not be translated in North Vietnam. There were three Southern Vietnamese editions of the translation of *Doctor Zhivago* (*Doktor Zhivago*, 1957).[50] The rapid, repeated translation of Pasternak's work has proved Saigon culture could react to global world literary events despite the war. On 23 October 1958, Pasternak was offered the Nobel Prize.

---

44 Nhat Linh, 'Đọc và viết tiểu thuyết', p. 10.

45 Phong Giao Tran, 'Vài cảm nghĩ xuôi dòng' ('Some Streams of Thought'), *Tạp chí Văn / Journal of Literature*, 128 (1969), 79–84 (p. 80).

46 This is how Pham Thi Phuong explains the contrast between Chekhov's absence from North Vietnam and his presence, at least, as a writer of short fiction, in South Vietnam. See Pham Thi Phuong, *Văn học Nga tại đô thị miền Nam 1954–1975* (*Russian Literature in Urban South Vietnam, 1954–1975*) (Ho Chi Minh City: Publishing House of HCMC University of Education, 2010), pp. 106–07.

47 These journals included *Tap chi Bach Khoa* (*The Encyclopedia Journal*), *Nguyet san Van hoa* (*Monthly Journal of Culture*), and a special issue devoted to Chekhov in *Tap chi Van* (*Journal of Literature*), 53 (1966). In the 1970s, translations of Chekhov's short stories continued to appear in *Tap chi Van* and also *Tap chi Chan hung Kinh te* (*Journal of Economic Revival*), including a collection of fourteen short stories translated and introduced by Do Khanh Hoan. The same collection by Do Khanh Hoan was published as a separate volume by Ba Vi Publishing House in 1973, and reprinted in 1974 with a circulation of 2,000 copies.

48 Do Khanh Hoan, 'Lời giới thiệu Truyện ngắn Chekhov' ('Introduction to Chekhov's Short Stories'), in *Collection of Chekhov's Short Stories* (Saigon: Ba Vi Publishing House, 1973), pp. i-iv (p. iii).

49 Do Khanh Hoan, 'Lời giới thiệu Truyện ngắn Chekhov', p. ii.

50 These were Van Tu and Mau Hai's 1957 co-translation of the novel, published by Mat tran bao ve tu do van hoa (Frontline of Cultural Freedom Protection Publisher); and a 1974 version by Nguyen Huu Hieu published as *Vĩnh biệt tình em* (*Goodbye my love*) by To hop Gio (The Winds) Press. In 1975, this was reissued as *Bác sĩ Zhivago* (*Doctor Zhivago*) from Hoang Hac (Flamingo) Press.

In the Saigon media, an article about the Russian author appeared immediately.[51] In it, Luu Nguyen analysed for Saigon readers Pasternak's reluctance to refuse the Nobel Prize, the hostility of the Soviet regime towards him, the plot of *Doctor Zhivago*, Pasternak's biography, and his novel's enthusiastic reception in the West. Luu Nguyen's review also introduced the concept of the 'free world', as a global unity which supported and contended for Pasternak, in contrast to the prohibitions and very harsh political judgments imposed by the Soviet government. He cited the opinions and arguments of famous European scholars, and public excitement (especially in Sweden) about the power and significance of *Doctor Zhivago*. Of Pasternak, Luu Nguyen wrote, "[t]his writer [...] voiced that which made people on the other side of the Iron Curtain understand the deep feeling of a Russian under Lenin's regime".[52] In the same year, two of Pasternak's poems were translated from the original Russian.[53] In the following years, articles about Pasternak and his work continued to appear.[54]

Like Pasternak, Solzhenitsyn also intrigued South Vietnamese readers and critics for his artistic achievements, especially the Nobel Prize, as well as for his opposition to the Soviet government. His works reached Saigon even before he received the Nobel Prize. In 1963–64 excerpts from *Matryona's Place* (*Matrenin dvor*, 1963) and *One Day in the Life of Ivan Denisovich* (*Odin den' Ivana Denisovicha*, 1962) appeared in two South Vietnamese literary journals.[55] Between 1969 and 1973, his work continued to feature in many journals. Most of his works (*One Day in the Life of Ivan Denisovich*, *Matryona's Place*, *For the Good of the Cause* (*Dlia pol'zy dela*, 1963), *The First Circle* (*V kruge pervom*, 1968), *Cancer Ward* (*Rakovyi korpus*, 1966), *The Gulag Archipelago* (*Arkhipelag GULAG*, 1973), and *An Incident at Krechetovka Station*) were translated into Vietnamese in multiple editions. At that time, there were two different translations of *The First Circle*.[56] The translation of *The Gulag Archipelago* was published in 1974 in two of the largest journals in Saigon, namely *Tap chi Song Than* (*Journal of The Tsunami*) and *Tap chi Dan chu* (*Journal of Democracy*), the latter edited by Nguyen Van Thieu, who served as President of the Republic of Vietnam from 31 October 1967 to 21 April 1975. These two journals simultaneously published *The Gulag Archipelago* with two main motivations: boycotting bribery of the authorities and the military, and attacking the Communist system. *The Gulag Archipelago* was the most impressive and influential of Solzhenitsyn's works in South Vietnam, such

51 Luu Nguyen, 'Pasternak', *Bach Khoa Journal*, 46 (1958), 48–58.

52 Ibid., p. 55.

53 They were published in *Tap chi Pho thong* (*Journal of General Knowledge*) 5 (1958).

54 In journals including *Van* (*Literature*), 83 (1967), *Van hoa A Chau* (*Asian Culture*), 10 (1959), *Que huong* (*Homeland*), 12 (1960).

55 *Tap chi Bach Khoa* (*The Encyclopedia Journal*) and *Tap chi Van* (*Journal of Literature*).

56 These were Hai Trieu's 1973 version, *Tầng đầu địa ngục* (*The First Circle of Hell*), published by Dat moi (New Land); and Vu Minh Thieu's 1971 *Vòng đầu* (*The First Circle*)) from Ngan khoi (Distant Offshore) press.

that Southern readers used the word 'Gulag' to describe everything related to slavery and suffering. One of his translators, Nguyen Van Son, commented that "Solzhenitsyn is a witness who honestly narrated what he saw, heard, and lived in the ostensible Communist paradise."[57]

Compared with Pasternak and Solzhenitsyn, the conservative Socialist Realist author Mikhail Sholokhov was less widely translated in South Vietnam. Discussions on Sholokhov in South Vietnam often concentrated on his political bias. One 1959 article indicted Sholokhov as an advocate of a barbaric policy opposed to life, dignity, and love for humanity (i.e. as a writer loyal to the Soviet regime).[58] The debate continued even after Sholokhov was awarded the 1965 Nobel Prize for Literature. As a result, Southern readers became curious about this writer. *Virgin Soil Upturned* (*Podniataia tselina*, 1932) was translated in 1963 and reissued in 1964 and 1967. The novel *They Fought for Their Country* (*Oni srazhalis' za Rodinu*, 1975) and two collections of short stories by Sholokhov were also translated. However, no South Vietnamese publisher commissioned a translation of Sholokhov's best-known novel *And Quiet Flows the Don* (*Tikhii Don*, 1928–40). This could be explained by the opposition of the Southern government to North Vietnam's Socialist regime, Sholokhov's association with Socialist Realism, and Southern Vietnamese identification of Sholokhov's novel with its author's personal politics.

Conclusion

Translation history shows how North and South Vietnam formed their own impressions of Russian literature. The political context, cultural influences, and ideology during a very complicated historical period determined the respective translation orientation of North and South Vietnam. For twenty years, Russian literary works chosen for translation and introduction served as a spiritual pivot, inspiring people in North Vietnam to believe in and admire the cause of Socialist construction. Any approach to literary history dominated by political discourse is necessarily somewhat one-sided. The South Vietnam translation programme revealed Russian literature as a sub-canon of Western literature, principally valuable for its aesthetic and philosophical models amid turmoil. Contemporary Russian literature, especially prose by Soviet dissidents, appealed to the Southerners since it revealed the secrets of a political regime which the Republic of Vietnam considered as an enemy. On the contrary, in North Vietnam Soviet Socialist Realist texts by Ostrovskii and Sholokhov—reviled in

---

57 Van Son Nguyen, 'Lời người dịch' ('Translator's Foreword'), in Solzhenitsyn, *Ngôi nhà của Matriona* (*Matrena's Place*) (Saigon: Youth Publishing House, 1974), pp. 7–8 (p. 7).

58 Nam Chau Nguyen, 'Pasternak and Sholokhov—Two Witnesses to One World', *Journal of Asian Culture*, 19 (1959), 61–73 (p. 63).

the South—were foci for ideological sentiment and political patriotism; North Vietnamese readers viewed even nineteenth-century Russian literature through the same political lens. Both the translator and the text are ontologically bound in specific cultural and political contexts that to a large extent determine, implicitly or explicitly, translation processes. The canons of Russian literature, reflected through translation in North and South Vietnam respectively, shows that "writing the history of literature is a paradoxical activity that consists in placing it in historical time and then showing how literature gradually tears itself away from this temporality, creating in turn its own temporality, one that has gone unperceived until the present day".[59] This essay has shown how several important Vietnamese translators served to canonise Russian literature in their nation.

59 Casanova, *The World Republic of Letters*, p. 350.

NORTH AND SOUTH AMERICA

Brazil

Translating Russian Literature in Brazil: Politics, Emigration, University and Journalism (1930–74)

Bruno Baretto Gomide

In 1959, the well-known Brazilian critic Antonio Candido (1918–2017) published an important study on the formation of Brazilian literature.[1] Candido chose to explore the period from the end of the eighteenth century to the middle of the nineteenth, during which the Brazilian literary system was formed. I intend to draw on Candido's thoughts in this chapter to present a "decisive moment" in the translation of Russian literary texts in Brazil during a somewhat later period: from the beginning of the 1930s to the mid-1970s, when a densely interconnected network took shape, linking the publishing market, cultural journalists, translators born in Brazil, translators of emigrant origin, academia, and readers. During this period, many questions concerning the translation of Russian literature originating in previous decades were solved, and many of the critical and translational procedures that would inform later practices and conceptions were created.[2]

These four and a half decades encompass several important stages which will form the basis of my analysis in this chapter: the early 1930s witnessed the first direct translations of a collection of novels and short stories for the Iurii Zel'tsov translation-publishing series (known as the Russian Authors' Library). Zel'tsov

1 Antonio Candido, *Formação da Literatura Brasileira: momentos decisivos* (Belo Horizonte and Rio de Janeiro: Itatiaia, 1993).

2 Candido himself was also an important intellectual figure in the professionalisation of Russian Studies in Brazil, writing essays that related Brazilian and Russian literary texts, collaborating in the creation of the area of Russian Studies at the University of São Paulo, and acting as PhD supervisor to Boris Schnaiderman (whose legacy I will revisit in this chapter).

 https://doi.org/10.11647/OBP.0340.36

was a Jewish-Russian immigrant from Riga who, in Brazil, adopted the name Georges Selzoff. The next period saw large-scale production of translations, with a turning point in the final years of World War II and the Getúlio Vargas dictatorship (1937–45); debate over the so-called 'French' paradigm, questioning the role of Paris as a mediator of the Russophone 'Republic of Letters' (to paraphrase Pascale Casanova);[3] the emergence of several proposals and initiatives for the professionalisation of translation; the commissioning of the seminal collection of Dostoevsky's works by the publisher José Olympio; the debate over Vladimir Maiakovskii's translations made in Argentina; a shift in the relationship between translations of Russian prose and poetry, and the rise of avant-garde movements in Brazilian culture in the 1960s, notably Concretism and Tropicalism; the integration of this Brazilian translation scene within a transnational network of translators, especially of Russian poetry (such as Robel and Ripellino);[4] and finally the critical and translational influence of Boris Schnaiderman (1917–2016), from the creation of the Russian Literature course at the University of São Paulo (USP) to his professorial thesis ('livre-docência'), in 1974, which was an annotated Portuguese translation of Fedor Dostoevsky's short story, 'Mr. Prokharchin' ('Gospodin Prokharchin', 1846). This thesis was a milestone in the professionalisation of Slavonic Studies in Brazil. It was the first translation of a full-length Russian literary text in a Brazilian (or Latin American) university. Consequently, its completion will serve as the final date for the case I propose to discuss.

I begin with the year 1930, a significant one for the formation of modern Brazil. The first presidential term of Getúlio Vargas (1882–1954) initiated a series of structural reforms in politics, the economy, education, and culture, as well as in the publishing market, especially with the creation of a national Brazilian book industry.[5] The number of readers expanded significantly, despite the country's traditionally low literacy rate. The expansion of the public education system at primary and secondary levels and the creation of the first modern universities in Rio de Janeiro and São Paulo were important factors in increasing literacy. In addition, difficulties in importing European books, due to the First, and especially the Second, World Wars, stimulated the process known as 'import substitution', which hastened the development of an internal market for books in Portuguese. Georges Selzoff's 'Russian Authors' Library (Bibliotheca de Autores

3 Pascale Casanova, *La République mondiale des Lettres* (Paris: Seuil, 2008).

4 Léon Robel (1928–2020), translator of Gennady Aigui, Solzhenitsyn, and other Russian and Soviet writers; Angelo Maria Ripellino (1923–78), Italian Slavist and translator.

5 Laurence Hallewell, *O livro no Brasil: sua história* (São Paulo: Edusp, 2005); see also Johan Heilbron and Gisèle Sapiro, 'Outline for a Sociology of Translation: Current Issues and Future Prospects', in *Constructing a Sociology of Translation*, ed. by Michaela Wolf and Alexandra Fukari (Amsterdam and Philadelphia, PA: John Benjamins, 2007), pp. 93–107.

Russos)' series is a good indicator of the new state of affairs: within two years of its foundation (1930–32) it had published more translations of Russian literature than had appeared in the entire previous half-century (ten in total, up to 1929). Moreover, they were direct translations from Russian—a complete novelty in Brazil. The publisher's catalogue mixed nineteenth-century "classics" (Fedor Dostoevsky, Lev Tolstoy, Nikolai Gogol and Anton Chekhov), popular authors from the 1910s and 1920s (such as Leonid Andreev), and so-called "Soviets" (Il'ia Ehrenburg). The publisher's focus was on novels, novellas, and short-story collections, probably because Selzoff commissioned new translations from the original (which was theoretically more feasible with short texts).

The transliteration of authors' names and the translations of the titles of works in the 'Russian Authors' Library' was still dictated by French practice, noticeably the double 'f' in the endings of names, including the publisher's own. The Selzoff/Zel'tsov name variation is a clear example of the translational tensions of the period. The editor chose a French spelling with the dual aim of making the project more familiar to Francophile readers, but also to avoid police surveillance, always alert to Russophone names. There was widespread concern in the government and in various sectors of society about the spread of Communism, which in that period was fundamentally and almost exclusively associated with 'Russia' (as the Soviet Union was known). This fear had been evident since 1917, but since Vargas came to power in 1930, installing a centralising, modernising government, Soviet influence was actively resisted. Intellectuals and left-wing groups were for obvious reasons especially targeted, but there were periodic police raids on recreational or Russian religious associations (or those from elsewhere in Eastern Europe). The Modernist poet Carlos Drummond de Andrade (1902–87) commented ironically on the police's methods:

> Of the police searches in the homes of people whom the government suspect, perhaps none is more ridiculous than that concerning books in their libraries. Eighty or a hundred dog-eared works are lined up on a modest shelf, with pencil marks indicating the long hours of study and the reader's dialogue with the author. Two policemen touch these books with disheartened curiosity: they would perhaps want to find pornographic prints, which would distract them from this inconvenience [...]. But none of that. They are cold texts, in incomprehensible languages and bearing obscure names: as some of these names end in -ov, -ovsky and -insky, let's take them to the police chief, and the citizen will go too, just in case.[6]

---

6 Carlos Drummond de Andrade, 'Livros assassinados' in *Revista do Globo*, 9 June 1945, 12–58.

Drummond's account points to genuine and often arbitrary persecution, but it may obscure the fact that relations with Russian literature, both for the government and the police, were more ambiguous than this purely repressive operation allows us to suppose. An indicator of the complexity of the issue is the considerable diffusion of Russian literary texts, in French, Portuguese, and Brazilian translations, in law schools, and even among officials of the police and judicial systems: Dostoevsky, above all, was a very well-known author among police officers, prosecutors and judges. Selzoff made translations working with one or more Brazilian writers using the 'crib' or 'podstrochnik' method, in which Selzoff wrote an initial semi-literal version of the Russian text in Portuguese, after which other translators prepared the literary version. This process was entirely compartmentalised as Selzoff was not able to write in literary Brazilian Portuguese, while the Lusophone translators did not know Russian. This widely internationally accepted arrangement would reappear in Brazil three decades later, used by Schnaiderman and the so-called 'Concrete poets'.[7] In the latter case, however, the parties involved shared all aspects of the translation: Schnaiderman was a competent literary author and essayist, and the brothers Haroldo and Augusto de Campos had studied Russian with him.

Selzoff/Zel'tsov's publishing initiative must be evaluated against the background of the circulation of Russian literature in Brazil. This regional phenomenon was part of a transnational process, simultaneously in dialogue and in competition with the French translational paradigm that had emerged during the Russian novel's surge in popularity at the end of the nineteenth century. Various literary polysystems proceeded at varying degrees of distance from Paris: the German polysystem operated with relative independence from its early years; the Anglo-American one quickly detached itself from the French meridian;[8] the Italians achieved a remarkable degree of boldness and

7 This refers to the Brazilian Concretista movement, which proposed, following Ezra Pound, the superiority of the illuminating fragment over longer writings, especially in the creation of a 'paideuma', or series of works, which emphasised innovation. Intensity is better than distension: *non multa sed multum*, as the Latin proverb appropriated by the Concretistas states. The brothers Haroldo and Augusto de Campos, Bruno Schnaiderman's long-term collaborators on various translations from Russian, were leading Concretistas.

8 Pieter Boulogne, 'Europe's Conquest of the Russian Novel. The Pivotal Role of France and Germany', in a special issue *of IberoSlavica* on 'Translation in Iberian-Slavonic Exchange', ed. by B. Cieszynska (Lisbon: CLEPUL, 2015), 179–206; William B. Edgerton, 'The Penetration of Nineteenth-Century Russian Literature into the Other Slavic Countries', in *American Contributions to the Fifth International Congress of Slavists*, 2 vols (The Hague: Mouton & Co., 1963), I (1963), pp. 41–78.

independence in the second half of the 1920s;[9] while in the Iberian Peninsula and Latin America, the process was just beginning.[10]

The Brazilian readership was largely French-speaking. Russian literary texts were read in French translations that began to arrive in Brazilian ports in 1887.[11] Due to the ubiquity of these editions, which were of considerable symbolic prestige, practically no new Brazilian translations were made. The few existing ones, such as a version of Tolstoy's *Kreutzer Sonata* (*Kreitserova sonata*, 1889) by the prestigious publisher Garnier (Rio de Janeiro, 1890), were based on French intermediary texts, or, in some cases, on Portuguese or Spanish ones, also in turn usually based on French versions. French translational mediation is a phenomenon that has been surprisingly little studied, despite its cruciality for Latin American reception studies. There are three main gaps in scholarship: firstly, in relation to the publishing market itself, the intricacies of decisions made by the publishers involved (Plon, Hachette and others), sales strategies, and reader responses. Secondly, the careers of the main translators involved are little-known. Finally, further analysis of the translations themselves is required, based on the theoretical corpus provided in recent years by Translation Studies. It would also be worth reassessing the role of certain fundamental mediators, such as that of Eugène-Melchior de Vogüé (1848–1910), who was immensely important both for Brazilian literary criticism and for the motivation behind various strategies in the publishing market, including the three factors mentioned above.[12]

Most of what has been written about Russian literature in Brazil is based on a corpus of criticism and translations generated by a tiny group of Parisian

---

9 Laurent Béghin, *Da Gobetti a Ginzburg: diffusione e ricezione della cultura russa nella Torino del primo dopoguerra* (Brussels and Rome: Brepols Publishers/Istituto Storico Belga di Roma, 2007).

10 George O. Schanzer, *Russian Literature in the Hispanic World: A Bibliography* (Toronto: University of Toronto Press, 1972); Hélène Harry, 'La Russie en Argentine. Réception, diffusion et appropriation des idées russes dans l´Argentine des années 1920' (unpublished master's thesis, University of Rennes, 2006); Dina Odnopozova, 'Russian-Argentine Literary Exchanges' (unpublished doctoral dissertation, Yale University, 2012).

11 Bruno B. Gomide, *Da estepe à caatinga: o romance russo no Brasil, 1887–1936* (São Paulo: Edusp, 2011).

12 There is little scholarship on de Vogüé. The best sources are Michel Cadot, *Eugène-Melchior de Vogüé le Héraut du Roman Russe* (Paris: Institut d'Études Slaves, 1989); and Magnus Röhl, *Le roman russe de Eugene-Melchior de Vogüé* (Stockholm: Almqvist & Wiksell, 1976). For a recent account, see Anna Gichkina, *Eugène-Melchior de Vogüé, ou comment la Russie pourrait sauver le France* (Paris: L´Harmattan, 2018) and Pierre-Jean Dufief, 'Le Roman Russe de Vogüé et le dialogue des cultures', in *Les intellectuels russes à la conquête de l'opinion publique française:une histoire alternative de la littérature russe en France de Cantemir a Gorki*, ed. by Alexandre Stroev (Paris: Presses Sorbonne Nouvelle, 2019), pp. 271–82, and Elizabeth Geballe's essay in the present volume.

publishers. A famous case of how "bad translations can generate good criticism"[13] is the 1935 critical revision of the very important Brazilian author Machado de Assis by critic Augusto Meyer (1902–70), who radically reassessed the former's critical reception by citing the translation of *Notes from Underground* (*Zapiski iz podpol'ia*, 1864) by Ély Halpérine-Kaminskii (1858–1936).[14] Meyer refuted the traditional image of Machado as a sceptical, ironical author, on the model of Anatole France, instead framing him as an inhabitant of the same universe of fragmented consciousness, radical psychological introspection and unstructured language that Meyer identified in Dostoevsky's novella. As is well documented, the two most famous causes in the dispute that started in the 1920s—involving French intellectuals such as Gide—against the *belles infidèles* are linked to Dostoevsky: the adaptations of *The Brothers Karamazov* (*Brat'ia Karamazovy*, 1880) and *Notes from Underground*, which were reassembled by the translators and transformed into quite different texts.[15] *Alma de criança* (*Child's Soul*) was for a long time the title given to *Netochka Nezvanova* (1849), after the French *Âme d'enfant*. Publishers also tried to attract readers with seemingly new texts. Texts such as *O Tirano* (*The Tyrant*) and *Ensaio sobre o burguês* (*The Essay on the Bourgeois*) could trick buyers since they were, respectively, re-titlings of Dostoevsky's *The Village of Stepanchikovo and its Inhabitants* (*Selo Stepanchikovo i ego obitateli*, 1859) and *Winter Notes on Summer Impressions* (*Zimnie zametki o letnikh vpetchatleniiakh*, 1863).[16]

Selzoff's project can be understood from an international comparative perspective as part of a constellation of similar proposals that materialised in editorial projects aimed at translating or retranslating Russian literature against the hegemony of the first waves of French translations. This approach is evidenced by the efforts of Argentine translators from the magazine/publisher Claridador towards various book series showcasing translations of Russian literature, such as 'Proa' (Barcelona), 'Slavia' (Turin) and 'Les jeunes russes' (Gallimard/NRF, Paris), all printed in the late 1920s and early 1930s. A number of factors facilitated these projects: the original translations, already half a century old, were becoming outdated; the political impact of the Russian Revolution; the existence of new Soviet critical editions; the 'Modernist' demand for new translations, which would resonate with current literary trends; and

13 Adel Ramilevna Fauzetdinova, 'Translation as Cultural Contraband: Translating and Writing Russian Literature in Argentina or How "Bad" Translations Made "Good" Literature' (unpublished doctoral dissertation, Boston University, 2017).

14 Augusto Meyer, 'O Homem Subterrâneo', in *Textos Críticos*, ed. by João Alexandre Barbosa (São Paulo: Perspectiva, 1986), 195–99.

15 More about Halpérine-Kaminskii can be found in Stroev, *Les intellectuels russes*, pp. 284–87.

16 Vladimir Boutchik, *Bibliographie des ouvres littéraires russes traduites en français* (Paris: Messages, n.d.); Vladimir Boutchik, *La littérature russe en France* (Paris: Librairie Ancienne Honoré Champion, n.d.).

the availability of a translation workforce, made up of emigrants and 'fellow travellers'.

In Brazil, the translation of Russian literature was closely linked to the injunctions of macro-politics, especially the fluctuations of anti-Communist waves.[17] The relationship between anti-Communist discourse and Russian literature was complex. Initially, a complete division was established between literature before and after 1917. The latter was invariably proscribed by right-leaning pundits. As for the former, there was a wide range of reactions, ranging from the radical differentiation between the 'classical' Russian literary text and Bolshevism to the detection of continuity between these two phenomena. These reactions need to be taken into account in order to understand the choices faced by both editors and translators in the Ibero-American world, at both macro- and micro-textual levels.

Paralleling the efforts of certain sectors of Brazilian culture and politics to curb the circulation of translated Russian texts, there were many attempts to finance and encourage the latter by the Soviet cultural propaganda agencies. In the 1930s and 1940s, VOKS (the All-Union Society for Cultural Relations with Foreign Countries), the Foreign Commission, and representatives of other Soviet cultural agencies worked hard on exercising their soft power with dispatches of books and other material. Some of these texts were published in translation in books and periodicals across the Latin American continent. The poet and translator David Vygodskii, for example, sought to build, from 1926 onwards, a network of contacts with various Latin American intellectuals, including Brazilians; he used this network to effect important exchanges that resulted in several translation experiments both into Russian and Spanish and Portuguese.[18] Certain works produced in the Soviet Union were sent to contacts (journalists, writers, intellectuals) who disseminated them in several Latin American countries. Alternatively, depending on how favourable the political context was, these texts could be sent directly to bookshops. The periodical *La Literatura Internacional*, rich in Soviet literature, could be found on sale in the capitals of Chile, Uruguay, Cuba, Mexico and Colombia during the 1940s. At that time, no sustained attempts were made by the USSR to disseminate Russian texts in Brazil, mainly because Portuguese was the language of the latter. It was much more practical, from the Soviet point of view, to translate books, articles

17 Rodrigo Patto Sá Motta, *Em Guarda contra o Perigo Vermelho: o Anticomunismo no Brasil (1917–1964)* (São Paulo: Perpectiva/Fapesp, 2002).

18 Bruno B. Gomide, *David Vygódski, Um sismógrafo da crítica literária russa* (Campinas: Mercado de Letras/LETRA, 2021). On Soviet cultural propaganda and soft power, see: Sophie Coeuré, *La grande lueur à l'Est: les Français et l'Union soviétique, 1917–1939* (Paris: CNRS, 1999); Michael David-Fox, *Showcasing The Great Experiment: Cultural Diplomacy and Western Visitors to the Soviet Union, 1921–1941* (Oxford: Oxford University Press, 2014); Ioana Popa, *Traduire sous contraintes: littérature et communisme (1947–1989)* (Paris: CNRS, 2010).

and periodicals into Spanish, the language common to most countries in the region, and to hope that Brazilian readers, generally literate in Spanish, would come into contact with them indirectly. That this did often occur is evidenced by Brazilian used bookstores, where to this day one can find Spanish translations of works by Mikhail Sholokhov, Aleksandr Fadeev, and other Soviet writers from this period. Soviet agencies considered Argentina a key strategic centre for the diffusion of literary and political texts across the continent, thanks to its huge emigrant community and powerful publishing market. The translator Lila Guerrero (1906–86) sent a letter in May 1943 to Aleksei Tolstoy, via the Foreign Commission in Washington, which shows the level of friendship at that time between Soviet cultural authorities and Latin American translators.[19] Agreements made in the 1960s between the Russian Department at USP and several Soviet academic institutions facilitated the acquisition of Russian-language critical and literary texts in Russian, which could then be translated for scholars, and sometimes also for the wider publishing market.

There were two Russian "fevers"[20] at either end of the first Vargas era: the first in 1930, when the so-called Brazilian 'October Revolution' transferred power to the Gaucho political group from the southernmost state of Rio Grande do Sul. The second occurred in 1945, when a coup deposed Vargas, ending an authoritarian period. Between 1930 and 1935, the Vargas regime had alternated constitutional and pseudo-constitutional government, with more or less permanent police surveillance of Russophone activity. Sixty-three literary translations from Russian were published, almost all of them mediated through a third language, except for Selzoff's series. The texts used for translation were, in the vast majority of cases, late nineteenth-century French versions. The most translated texts were those which could command commercial interest, such as Tolstoy's *Anna Karenina* (1878) and Dostoevsky's *Crime and Punishment* (*Prestuplenie i nakazanie*, 1866).

Maksim Gorky, Dostoevsky, and Tolstoy, in that order, were the most frequently translated authors, followed, on a rapidly descending scale, by Chekhov, Andreev, and certain 'new' authors, such as Boris Pil'niak, Fedor Gladkov and Fadeev. New work by the latter was greeted positively in Brazilian newspapers and magazines, although it was rare for such reviews to specifically acknowledge translation issues. The translators of these books were either first-time fiction writers (Brazil experienced a surge in novel writing after 1930) or names now shrouded in total obscurity. Several translations were either anonymous or pseudonymous, like the Communist militant Leôncio Basbaum's 1931 translation of *The Brothers Karamazov* (for the Americana publishing house),

19 Letter from Lila Guerrero to A. N. Tolstoi, 16 May 1943. Archive of the Inostrannaia Komissiia, RGALI, Fond 631, opis 11, delo 404, 'Materialy po Iuzhnoi i Tsentral'noi Amerike' (n. 5).

20 I borrow this term from the translator and critic Brito Broca, in his *Ensaios da Mão Canhestra* (São Paulo: Polis, 1981).

signed "Raul Rizinsky". Basbaum justified his pseudonym as a screen against possible police repression, but also because he lacked confidence, as an amateur, in his own translatorial skills.

Between 1935 and 1937, Russian matters were further sensitised in the aftermath of the Communist insurrection of 1935—a military uprising partially financed by Moscow[21]—and by the counter-decree issued by the strongly anti-Soviet Estado Novo dictatorship on 10 November 1937.[22] These events halted the spread of Russian literature and its translations. There was heated discussion about the continued viability of Russian literature in Brazil, exercising both sides. Belisário Penna, for instance, then a member of the far-right party Ação Integralista Brasileira (Brazilian Integralist Action), clamoured against the "Russian Jews", "Communist delinquents", who were "stooges of Russian literature".[23] Despite such extremism, Russian literature continued to be translated and published after 1935. However, Soviet literature—or 'modern Russian literature', a rather euphemistic expression—had virtually disappeared. Soviet authors, including Gorky, were only published between 1930 and 1935, which demonstrates the stricter exclusion of 'suspicious' authors and the practical impossibility of producing new translations. From 1936 onwards, readers of Brazilian translations had access only to the nineteenth-century classics, mainly Dostoevsky and Tolstoy. During this period the publishers of translations were largely motivated to cash in on successful film adaptations of Russian novels, such as *Anna Karenina* or *Crime and Punishment*.[24]

At this time of uncertainty for the Brazilian intelligentsia, Dostoevsky emerged as a middle ground for all sectors of the Brazilian political and ideological spectrum. In mid-1935, the first critical interpretation of a Russian writer to be published in Brazil appeared: the monograph *Dostoiewski* by the Catholic essayist Hamilton Nogueira (1897–1981). At the same time, and perhaps paradoxically, Dostoevsky was being read voraciously by various leftist groups, including card-carrying Communists. In part, the ideological

21 On the 1935 uprising, see Daniel Aarão Reis Filho, *Luis Carlos Prestes, um revolucionário entre dois mundos* (São Paulo: Companhia das Letras, 2014).

22 See Lúcia Lippi Oliveira, Mônica Pimenta Velloso, and Ângela Maria de Castro Gomes, *Estado Novo: ideologia e poder* (Rio de Janeiro: Zahar, 1982).

23 Belisario Penna, 'Momento brasileiro', *Correio da Manhã* (Rio de Janeiro), 17 December 1935, 2.

24 One good example of this is the director Josef von Sternberg's 1935 film version of *Crime and Punishment*, starring Peter Lorre as Raskolnikov, screened across Brazil in the first half of 1936. Two translations of the novel were published at this time: one by a mysterious 'Ivan Petrovitch' (Rio de Janeiro: Ed. Guanabara) and the other by J. Jobinsky (Rio de Janeiro: Pongetti). In fact, both books plagiarise a previous translation by the Portuguese writer Camara Lima, which had been serialised in the Rio de Janeiro newspaper *A Manhã* in 1925–26. See Denise Bottmann, 'Um curioso às voltas com uma curiosidade histórica', *Cadernos de Tradução*, 3 (2017), 214–48.

appropriation was made possible by the existence of certain translations, for example, the aforementioned 'Ensaio sobre o Burguês', read as an anti-capitalist manifesto. Dostoevsky's ecumenical character was one of the reasons why the publisher José Olympio, from 1944 to 1960, published an edition of his complete works.

Times became difficult for editors of Russian literature from late 1937 onwards. With the consolidation of the Estado Novo dictatorship, numerous intellectuals were imprisoned or co-opted into the state machine and abandoned their Russian interests.[25] As a result, Russian literature ceased to be translated. 1938 was the first year in that decade when no new translations of Russian literature appeared. In the following two years (1939–41), the height of the Vargas dictatorship, only three translations appeared (of Dostoevsky and Tolstoy). From mid-1942, as a result of complex and (to some extent) contradictory geopolitics (since many members of the Vargas government sympathised with European fascism), the Brazilian Estado Novo aligned itself with the Allied Powers. War was declared on the Axis nations, and troops were sent to Italy in mid-1944. In a surprising turnaround, the Vargas regime ended up on the same side as the hated Communists. The Red Army's victories were celebrated in the newspapers, to the undisguised relief of many democratically minded intellectuals. Translating and publishing Russian literature became an Aesopian way of eroding the Estado Novo dictatorship. "Men advance through the steppes that filled Tolstoy's soul and Gorky's melancholy eyes with poetry", as one typical article said of Soviet military manoeuvres.[26] The translation that most clearly announced the arrival of a new period was the two-volume edition of *War and Peace* (*Voina i mir*, 1867), translated by Gustavo Nonnenberg for the Globo publishing house in Porto Alegre in the Southern state of Rio Grande do Sul. The translator, perhaps paradoxically, prepared the text from a German edition, which makes it the first and only Brazilian translation of Russian literature made from German, and not French or English.

This unprecedented number of new translations was closely associated with two great historical events: at a national level, the overthrow of the Vargas dictatorship, and at a global level, the end of the war. Russian literature, in criticism or translation, tends to be described in epic terms. The battle of Stalingrad became the great narrative of the period, its major text, and a metaphor present more or less explicitly in all critical and editorial initiatives. The entire process was conceived strategically and on a grand scale, pitting the idea of 'humanism' against 'barbarism' in both the exaggerated aspect and the notably 'red' tone of the initiatives. All this led to a flood of new translations from Russian. Never had so much Russian literature been published in Brazil as

25 Sérgio Miceli, *Intelectuais e Classe Dirigente no Brasil, 1920–1945* (São Paulo: Difel, 1979).

26 Anon., 'O contraste de dois mundos', *Diretrizes. Política, economia, cultura* (Rio de Janeiro), 11 June 1942, 8–24.

in the two years between 1943 and 1945. There were more than eighty volumes of literary texts (if those on history, literary criticism and journalistic texts were included, the number would increase considerably). There were some reprints of texts published in the 1930s, but most were newly issued. At an average of three and a half books a month, this equated to almost one release a week over this two-year period. In 1944 alone, two editions of *The Brothers Karamazov* were brought out by two of the most important publishers in Brazil, Martins and Vecchi, with José Olympio also preparing its own edition. The most published author during the 1943–45 period was Dostoevsky, with seventeen titles, closely followed by Tolstoy (fourteen), and Gorky (eight), accounting for almost half the total volume of translations, confirming these writers' prominence among the reading public and in the critical and editorial imagination of the period. Within this explosion of Russian literature, a special place may be assigned to Soviet literature, which now became very popular, despite having been almost completely ignored during the previous decade. Of the more than eight dozen works published, sixteen were by writers active after 1917. A similar yearning for diversity can be seen in the impressive series of short-story anthologies released between 1944 and 1945, which involved many professional and first-time translators, as well as new fiction writers, who used translation to supplement their incomes.[27]

At the same time, there was growing commentary in the press about the quality of the translations. First, critics and reviewers pointed out the need to expand knowledge of the Russian language in order to work from the original. The critic José Carlos Júnior, who came from Paraíba in the northeast of Brazil, reading Tolstoy in the French editions that arrived in the port of Recife, had mentioned this language problem as early as 1887, when the first Russian texts were arriving.[28] Half a century later, still confronted with the same problem, a São Paulo journalist stated that it was impossible to write about an author—in this case, Dostoevsky—whose language was unknown to critics.[29] Another way of trying to deal with the limitations was to criticise the amount of historic French intermediation: two Modernist critics, Ronald de Carvalho (1893–1935) and Mario de Andrade (1893–1945), disapproved of the incomplete, Frenchified Dostoevsky available in Brazil.[30] They also decried the dominance of indirect translations, targeting Portuguese versions ("poor little brochures sold to us in

27 Bruno B. Gomide, *Dostoiévski na Rua do Ouvidor: a literatura russa e o Estado Novo* (São Paulo: Edusp, 2018).

28 José Carlos Júnior, 'Apontamentos Esparsos', *A Quinzena* (Fortaleza), 15, 26 August 1887, 1–3.

29 'Dostoiewski e o regresso eterno', *Correio da manhã* (Rio de Janeiro), 6 November 1932, 1.

30 Ronald de Carvalho, 'O claro riso dos modernos', *O Jornal* (Rio de Janeiro), 5 February 1924, 1.

Lisbon")[31] for special attack, as well as unscrupulous editors and the "horrible translations" that they published. The term most frequently used by critics of available Russian translations was 'mutilation' (*mutilação*). This generated a symbiotic relationship between this word, traditionally used in various global contexts to indicate the hubris or limitations of some translators of Russian literature, and the political context of the end of the Estado Novo dictatorship. 'Condemned Books' is the title of an article by critic and translator Valdemar Cavalcanti (1912–82), who criticised the political and editorial mutilations to which books, especially those on Russian themes, were subjected.[32]

In addition to institutional precariousness and political pressures, there were very concrete practical problems. Schnaiderman recalled his first attempts at translation, in the 1940s, when there was just a single dictionary—Russian/French, not Russian/Portuguese—available to consult at the National Library in Rio de Janeiro. In fact, the great difficulty of obtaining Russian material for translation, even in later periods, should always be taken into account when studying the decisions that guided the preparation of editions or anthologies and those authors selected for translation. The parameters were set by foreign translations that circulated in Brazilian territory and by networks of contacts able to send copies of texts obtained in North American or European libraries; many of these packages were randomly confiscated at customs, further stymieing translators' efforts to access the original text.

There were efforts to improve the low quality of translations with ambitious projects. The main such attempt was the edition of Dostoevsky's *soi-disant* complete works by the publisher José Olympio in 1944, the most ambitious project by the most important publisher of the period.[33] The result pleased everyone and was praised in the newspapers. It boasted illustrations by celebrated Brazilian graphic artists (Oswaldo Goeldi, Axel Leskoschek and others). These images continued, on the other side of the Atlantic, the expressionist tradition of illustrating Dostoevsky, which was common in Central Europe in the first decades of the century. The illustrations in the 1944 edition have often been described as the best intersemiotic translation of Dostoevsky ever made in Brazil.[34]

The literary translations for Olympio's edition were made indirectly, at least in the early stages of the collection, by figures such as the trusted but obscure

31 Silvio Julio, 'Traduções novas?', *Correio da manhã* (Rio de Janeiro), 16 August 1944, p. 2.

32 Valdemar Cavalcanti, 'Livros condenados', *Leitura* (Rio de Janeiro), May 1945, p. 31.

33 José Olympio's Dostoevsky collection was labelled 'complete works' but many were missing, such as *The Diary of a Writer*.

34 Boris Schnaiderman, following Jakobson, examined this as a case of intersemiotic translation in his article 'Osvaldo Goeldi e Dostoiévski', *Revista da USP*, 32 (1996–97), 166–69.

Costa Neves, the 'Dostoevskian' novelists José Geraldo Vieira (1897–1977) and Rosário Fusco (1910–77), and also Rachel de Queiroz (1910–2003), one of the exponents of the new literary scene, who left some very interesting accounts of the joint translations that featured: a process that was both meticulous and messy, rigorous and improvised, involving a number of intermediary languages (French, English, Spanish and Italian) and always with reference to, and possible comparison with, the most recent Soviet critical editions. The translation of *The Idiot* (*Idiot*, 1868) published by Vieira in 1949 represents the most interesting case of 'success' in this wave of indirect translations. Vieira, a Modernist writer from São Paulo who had studied Dostoevsky's work academically for many decades, managed to find a Portuguese lexis in tune with the Russian author's poetics and to produce a text with an undeniable Dostoevskian flavour. In the early 1960s, when the José Olympio project was completed, Schnaiderman retranslated some of the translations that had been made in the original thriving period of publications. Olympio himself was fully aware of the limitations of indirect translations in the first phase of his project, but claimed that he had not been able to find an immediate remedy, due to a lack of suitable translators: around 1940, as we have seen, Russian-language experts were not good translators, and the good translators did not know Russian.

Another important moment in the maturation of translation methodology in the mid-1940s was the debate in São Paulo over the widely-circulated Argentine translations of Vladimir Maiakovskii, which had become the Latin-American Russian poetic Ur-text. Their translator, Lila Guerrero, was born in Buenos Aires to a Russian family and had spent much of the interwar period in Moscow.[35] When these translations were published, a more direct 'horizontal' dialogue about Russian literature took place between Brazilians and Argentines for the first time. Brazilians commented on production in their neighbouring country, not necessarily mediated by the critical production that came from Europe, especially France. Candido reviewed Guerrero's book of translations rigorously, considering it superficial and propagandistic, with an exaggerated emphasis on Maiakovskii compared to other Russian poets.[36] In a subsequent article, Candido played a Modernist-inspired joke. He created a pseudonym, "Fabrício Antunes", who questioned Candido's ability, since he knew no Russian, to comment on Guerrero's translation.[37] This incident inspired many proposals for better translation practice, which would be trialled in the following years.

The pioneering work of Selzoff and the dispute over Guerrero's translation points to the importance of writing by Russian exiles in the production of literary

35 Lila Guerrero, *Antologia de Maiacovski: su vida y su obra* (Buenos Aires: Claridad, 1943).

36 Antonio Candido, 'Notas de crítica literária—um poeta e a poesia', *Folha da manhã* (São Paulo), 11 March 1943, p. 5.

37 On Candido's game of pseudonyms, see Gomide, *Dostoiévski na Rua do Ouvidor*, p. 296.

translations.[38] This process would have been impossible without the presence of Russian-speaking emigrants, mainly Jews. In this sense, the history of the translation of Russian texts is, to a large extent, the history of port cities like Riga or Odesa, and their relationships with the migratory processes triggered by the Soviet and Nazi regimes. In the context of the 1940s and 1950s, one could mention other key names, such as Tatiana Belinky (1919–2013) and Paulo Rónai (1907–92),[39] Jewish emigrants from, respectively, Riga (arriving in São Paulo in 1929) and Budapest (coming to Rio de Janeiro in 1939). Both were leading figures in the process of professionalising the translator's work, with quality contributions to the translation of Russian texts, and particularly Russian-language short stories, although Belinky also published an excellent translation of Nikolai Gogol's *Dead Souls* (*Mertvye dushi*, 1842).[40]

The work on Russian literary translation took systematic shape thanks to another emigrant, Boris Schnaiderman. Despite some recognition of his importance as one of Brazil's major twentieth-century intellectual figures, his work has not been thoroughly studied. There is, for example, no critical assessment of his translations. His career, which is little known in international Slavonic Studies, provides some insights into important issues in the field, such as studies on exile and diaspora, the professionalisation of Slavonic Studies, and the processes of cultural transference in Russian texts. Born in 1917, Schnaiderman emigrated from Odesa in 1925. Russian was his mother tongue, but he did most of his schooling and literary training in Brazil. This was a special linguistic situation for the future translator, and he called his bilingualism "schizophrenic". Schnaiderman drew analogies between his trajectory and that of the great translator Lev (or Leone) Ginzburg (1909–44), also from Odesa, who emigrated to Italy as a child. This parallel with Ginzburg was always very important for Schnaiderman, and he also maintained contact with the translators and Slavists Ettore Lo Gatto (1890–1983) and Angelo Maria Ripellino. It is perhaps best to understand Schnaiderman's critical and translational path not as a binary (the Brazil-Russia bridge), but as a triangle with Italy as the third vertice. This bond was also important to Schnaiderman because of a personal experience: he had fought as an artillery sergeant on the Monte Castello front

38 For recent scholarship on exilic literature, see Galin Tihanov, *The Birth and Death of Literary Theory: Regimes of Relevance in Russia and Beyond* (Stanford, CA: Stanford University Press, 2019); *Redefining Russian Literary Diaspora, 1920–2020*, ed. by Maria Rubins (London: UCL Press, 2021); Annick Morard, *De l´émigré au déraciné. La "jeune génération" des écrivains russes entre identité et esthétique* (Paris, 1920–1940) (Lausanne: L'Age d'Homme, 2010).

39 Paulo Rónai, *A tradução vivida*, 4th edn (Rio de Janeiro: José Olympio, 2012); on Rónai, see Ana Cecília Impellizieri Martins, *O homem que aprendeu o Brasil: a vida de Paulo Rónai* (São Paulo: Todavia, 2020); Tatiana Belinky, *Transplante de menina* (Rio de Janeiro: Moderna, 2003).

40 N. Gógol, *Almas Mortas*, trans. by Tatiana Belinky (São Paulo: Abril Cultural, 1972).

in World War II. He embarked with the Brazilian Expeditionary Force in mid-1944, soon after delivering to Vecchi his translation of *The Brothers Karamazov*, under the pseudonym of Boris Solomonov. He used this same pseudonym for five other texts which he translated in the immediate postwar period, by Tolstoy, Aleksandr Pushkin, and Aleksandr Kuprin. Schnaiderman followed a very characteristic Ibero-American tradition of resorting to pseudonyms, often to protect the translator politically and preserve him from direct criticism of his (often rushed) translation. Schnaiderman's use of a pseudonym is meaningful, however. By transforming his patronymic (Solomonovich) into a surname, he only partially concealed his identity. One aim of this approach was to ensure he could claim copyright for his translations in the future. During the war, he began writing his only novel, *War on the Quiet* (*Guerra em Surdina*), released in 1964, which was inspired by recent Brazilian fiction (authors such as Graciliano Ramos, Clarice Lispector, and Guimarães Rosa) and by Russian war narratives (mainly by Isaak Babel and Tolstoy). Thus, this translator was also an experienced prose fiction writer.

From 1956, Schnaiderman began to publish in the prestigious 'Literary Supplement' of the *O Estado de São Paulo* newspaper, as well as in other periodicals. There, he reviewed Russian writers already familiar to Brazilian readers while introducing a series of other unknown or semi-unknown names, such as Aleksandr Grin, Velimir Khlebnikov, Osip Mandel'stam, Valentin Kataev, Konstantin Paustovskii, Iurii Olesha, Konstantin Fedin, and Babel. In a characteristic move for the period, his newspaper articles led him to be invited to teach Russian at the University of São Paulo, initially as open courses in 1960 (in a typical post-Sputnik environment), and, from 1963, with the implementation of the undergraduate course in Russian Language and Literature. Schnaiderman was central to the translation and introduction of important Russian-speaking theorists such as Eleazar Meletinskii, Mikhail Bakhtin, Iurii Lotman, Viacheslav Ivanov, and the Russian Formalists, above all through his relationship with Roman Jakobson, who visited Brazil in 1968 to deliver a series of lectures. The Russian Language and Literature course at University of São Paulo was created alongside a course in Literary Theory, which brought Russian Studies closer to the areas of linguistics and translation.[41] Schnaiderman was a unique figure in the context of Latin America at that time, uniting in his career academic activities, translation practice, and scientific and cultural dissemination. Schnaiderman's style was academic yet accessible to the common reader, thus transcending the almost universal division between professional Slavists and popularisers.[42]

41 More on this subject can be found in Bruno B. Gomide and Rodrigo Alves do Nascimento, 'Slavic Studies in Brazil', *Slavic and East European Journal*, 64 (2020), 31–39.

42 An example is Schnaiderman's *Turbilhão e semente: ensaios sobre Dostoiévski e Bakhtin* (São Paulo: Duas Cidades, 1983) (*Whirlwind and Seed: Essays on Dostoevsky and Bakhtin*), which brings together both published and unpublished articles.

In the following decades, he wrote several books, always preoccupied with translation. One of them focused on translation exclusively: *Translation, An Excessive Act* (*Tradução, Ato Desmedido*, 2010).

Translation was thus both a theoretical and concrete feature of Schnaiderman's work from his earliest journalism, which consisted of texts either written exclusively on the topic or commenting on it tangentially. A key point was his criticism of existing translations of Russian literature in Brazil. One of the main threads deals with the specific difficulties of poetic translation. Schnaiderman was already pointing to the partnership process that, at the beginning of the following decade, would develop between himself, the brothers Haroldo (1929–2003) and Augusto de Campos (b. 1931). The various outcomes of this collaboration are discussed in newspaper articles such as 'Maiakovskii Reprinted in Russia' ('Maiakovsky republicado na Rússia', *O Estado de São Paulo*, 8 April 1961), 'A Paradox of Maiakovskii' ('Um paradoxo de Mayakovsky', *O Estado de São Paulo*, 6 May 1961), 'Letter to Tatiana Iacovleva' ('Carta a Tatiana Iacovleva', *O Estado de São Paulo*, 29 September 1962), and 'Two Russian Themes' ('Dois temas russos', *O Estado de São Paulo*, 16 November 1963). These articles consider theoretical problems related not only to translation, but also translated poetry. In some articles, the voices of other authors help to partially communicate ideas original to Schnaiderman, as in 'Modern Art in the Soviet Union' ('Arte moderna na União Soviética', *O Estado de São Paulo*, 3 September 1961), which contains an extract from the autobiography *People, Years, Life* (*Liudi, gody, zhizn'*, 1960–67), by the Soviet writer Il'ia Ehrenburg (which Schnaiderman would partially translate). Here Ehrenburg comments on the avant-garde's relations with Soviet culture. In the same vein, 'Translation and Style' ('Tradução e estilo', *O Estado de São Paulo*, 21 March 1964) is a note on Theory and Criticism of Translation, published by the University of Leningrad, in which the critic and translator Efim Etkind (1918–99) "attacks the translations which seek to achieve an average style, that is, lean, correct, tidy, but without greater boldness, in the transposition of the stylistic peculiarities of an author [...]". Etkind states that, to overcome these deficiencies, modern theoretical conceptions on literary translation based on comparative stylistics need to be more effectively disseminated.[43]

Thus, Schnaiderman's partnership with Haroldo and Augusto de Campos represented a kind of confluence of views on the translation process. Schnaiderman was certainly inspired by the bolder conceptions of his interlocutors. However, praise for the dynamic and radical aspect of the literary text was already embedded in the comments on Russian literary prose that he had been making throughout his career. Schnaiderman laments, in the trajectory of several Soviet writers, the replacement of boldness with more traditional

43 For more information on Schnaiderman, see Bruno B. Gomide, 'Pormenores violentos: Boris Schnaiderman crítico', *Literatura e Sociedade*, 26 (2018), 22–36; and Bruno B. Gomide, 'Boris Schnaiderman: questões de tradução nas páginas de jornal', *Estudos Avançados*, 26 (2012), 39–45.

styles. The initial hundred texts written by Schnaiderman at the turn of the 1950s and 1960s, defending literary Modernism and the need to incorporate contemporary thinking into the translation, are enough to place him among important commentators on these themes.

The *Modern Russian Poetry* (*Poesia Russa Moderna*) anthology, published in 1968 by Schnaiderman and the de Campos brothers, who were exponents of the Concretist movement, followed a similar volume dedicated exclusively to Maiakovskii. It is certainly the most successful translation experiment of Russian poetry in Latin America.[44] This period was a golden age for Russian poetry anthologies globally, thanks to the favourable environment created by improvements in communication during the Thaw period, and by the interest in critical and theoretical experimentation in Russia at the beginning of the twentieth century, especially in the connection between Futurism and Formalism.[45]

The Campos brothers were instrumental in raising the discussion and practice of translation to a more sophisticated level in Brazil, and the importance of their contribution to Translation Studies has been increasingly evident on the international scene. The anthology's impact was unprecedented, with a very positive assessment made by a transnational network of scholars and translators of Russian poetry. Roman Jakobson, Iurii Ivask, Victor Terras, Léon Robel, and Angelo Maria Ripellino, among others, made glowing comments. In Brazil, the anthology was widely accepted by the public and reprinted several times, always including new translations. The book achieved the greatest success possible for poetry translators, being read as an original work, on the same level as the best Portuguese-Brazilian poetic production of the period. It also connected translated texts with contemporary musical language of the period, at a time of intense artistic and cultural activity: the translators strategically used excerpts from Brazilian popular songs to recreate Russian verses; in turn, the anthology inspired new work from popular composers. Schnaiderman continued to translate Russian poetry until the end of his life, always with collaborators. Poems by Iosef Brodskii, with Nelson Ascher, and by Gennadii Aigi, with Jerusa Pires Ferreira, stand out. Schnaiderman was one of the international pioneers in the dissemination of Aigi, having participated in congresses dedicated to the discussion of his work.[46]

44 *Poemas de Maiakóvski*, ed. by Boris Schnaiderman and others (Rio de Janeiro: Tempo Brasileiro, 1967).

45 See Gabriela Soares da Silva and Tiago Guilherme Pinheiro, 'Convergências da poesia russa moderna na América Latina dos anos 1960: Nicanor Parra, Boris Schnaiderman, Haroldo e Augusto de Campos', *El jardín de los poetas*, 10 (2020), 154–99.

46 *Guennadi Aigui, Clamor e silêncio*, ed. by Boris Schnaiderman and Jerusa Pires Ferreira (São Paulo: Perspectiva, 2010).

Dostoevsky was the writer around whom, historically, the most elaborate proposals of translation theory and practice in Brazil were woven. A final comment on Schnaiderman's technique may help us to understand the process of densification of the translation network that took place between the 1930s and 1970s. His work as a critic and translator sought to emphasise issues of aesthetics and language in Dostoevsky. His 1944 version of *The Brothers Karamazov* was highly praised by critics, especially because it was the first translation of an important literary work made directly from the Russian, but Schnaiderman always maintained that he himself was dissatisfied with it. He had felt obliged to produce an elegant and fluent text, incompatible with the irregularities and roughness of Dostoevsky's own text. Contemporary examination shows many merits in his translation, including some excellent solutions to difficult stylistic and terminological problems. Schnaiderman would never again attempt such an intense task. He remained firm in his intention to resist the verbose pathos characteristic of certain sectors of Latin American culture. He was very taken by the ideas of the Brazilian concrete poets, as mentioned above. Deviating from his desire to translate Dostoevsky's 'great novels', Schnaiderman produced most of his Dostoevsky translations in the early 1960s, consciously opting for shorter works: *Netochka Nezvanova*, *Notes from Underground*, *The Gambler* (*Igrok*, 1866), 'The Crocodile' ('Krokodil', 1865), 'The Eternal Husband' ('Vechnyi muzh', 1870), and *Winter Notes on Summer Impressions*. Afterwards, these translations passed through considerable revisions and underwent important changes by Schnaiderman, who saw translation as a process and an open text, subject to modification and improvement.

It is worth commenting on one book that brings together Schnaiderman's two main fields, criticism and translation: *Dostoevsky the Artist* (*Dostoiévski artista*), which includes two essays by Leonid Grossman, 'Dostoevsky the Artist' ('Dostoevskii khudozhnik'), and 'Materials for a Dostoevsky Biography' ('Matierialy k biografii Dostoevskogo'), translated by Schnaiderman in 1965. I believe this to be the first critical philological text about a Russian thinker translated in Latin America. The reasons why this book was published in Brazil may help us to understand some of the goals of Schnaiderman's translation work. First, the book questions the very genre of Dostoevsky's biographies. His "hectic" life was commented on to exhaustion in the Brazilian press.[47] Grossman's painstaking research helped to reduce and to contextualise a series of traditional Dostoevskian mythemes of suffering.

Schnaiderman wanted to provide a bibliography on Dostoevsky that would be independent from the French market, given that the translated texts traditionally available in Brazil were by emigrants residing in France, such as Henri Troyat, André Levinson, and Nikolai Berdiaev. The Brazilian version of

47 Giuliana Teixeira de Almeida, *Pelo prisma biográfico: Joseph Frank e Dostoiévski* (São Paulo: Desconcertos, 2020).

Grossman's essays was inspired by the book of the same title, *Dostoevsky Artista*, translated by Bompiani publishing house in Milan in 1961. Seven years later, Grossman's full-length 1965 biography *Dostoevskii* was published in Italian translation in Rome.[48] Schnaiderman was also interested in seeking a quality critical text written within Soviet Russia itself, that is, one that would frame a Russian writer in terms of current literary debates internal to the Soviet Union. Schnaiderman also helped to strengthen the theory and practice of translations of essays and literary criticism, which were still relatively rare in Brazil. This was the only translation of a complete book of essays by Schnaiderman (though he would later translate some shorter texts by theorists like Ivanov or Lotman).

Translators of Dostoevsky have often tried, at some point in their careers, to translate at least one of his 'five elephants', the key long novels. Schnaiderman, in a way, took the opposite route: he began with Dostoevsky's final novel and ended his cycle of translations with a short story, at that time relatively little studied by researchers outside Russia. I refer to 'Mr. Prokharchin', which Schnaiderman translated and commented on in his professorship thesis, presented at the University of São Paulo in 1974. This was Schnaiderman's last complete translation of fictional prose by Dostoevsky—and the first scholarly translation of Russian literature made at a Brazilian university. Afterwards, the text was published in a book called *Dostoevsky Prose Poetry* (*Dostoiévski Prosa Poesia*).[49] The translation of the short story is accompanied by an extensive critical essay that analyses the composition of the original alongside Schnaiderman's own translation decisions. Like other works by Schnaiderman, parts of this translational and essayistic project were printed in newspapers as works-in-progress. The translation he made for the thesis aimed to recreate Dostoevsky's complex and difficult style, noting its phonic aspects; the resulting effect (as Schnaiderman recalled on several occasions in lectures and talks) prompted the Concretist poet Décio Pignatari to call it a "brutalist" translation. Schnaiderman later reached the conclusion that he might have overcomplicated Dostoevsky's style. The version published in book form recreates the translation that was published in Schnaiderman's thesis, reducing the so-called brutalism. In correspondence with Paulo Rónai, one of the members of his thesis evaluation panel, and a leading specialist on Balzac and French literature, Schnaiderman engaged in an important dialogue about possible ways of translating the discontinuous text of Dostoevsky.

---

48 This would be Antonella di Amelia's translation, published as *Dostoevskij* (Rome: Samona e Savelli, 1968). Grossman's works were little translated elsewhere in the world: one exception was a 1940s French translation of his study of Balzac's reception in Russia, *Balzac en Russie* (Paris: O. Zeluck, 1946). His biography of Dostoevsky came out in English only in the mid-1970s, as *Dostoevsky. A Biography* (London: Allen Lane, 1974).

49 Boris Schnaiderman, *Dostoevsky Prose Poetry* (*Dostoiévski Prosa Poesia*) (São Paulo: Perspectiva, 1982).

His 1974 translation of 'Mr. Prokharchin', therefore, closes the arc begun in the 1930s. In this work, the elements existing in previous decades are condensed, rearranged and appear in a more complex and sophisticated way: the tense dialogue with 'French' conceptions of translation; Modernist, or even avant-garde, criticism of past conceptions of literary writing; the desire for an original participation at the level of international Slavonic Studies; the modulation of the bilingual and traumatised voice of the émigré translator; the need to establish bridges with the wider readership and the publishing market; the connection between academia and journalism; and, last but not least, the fight against concrete obstacles for the circulation of translations of Russian texts in Brazil—the delimitation of a possible canon in a country that was, in 1974, still going through the worst period of military dictatorship. The paradigm of simultaneously rigorous and creative treatment in the translation of Russian texts proposed by Schnaiderman provided theoretical and practical parameters for subsequent generations of translators, inside and outside the University of São Paulo.

Colombia

Pale Fire of the Revolution: Notes on the Reception of Russian Literature in Colombia

Anastasia Belousova and Santiago E. Méndez

Introduction[1]

It is well known that Russian literature has a considerable presence in Latin America: Maria Nadyarnykh once evoked a "Latin American cult of Russian literature".[2] Nevertheless, Russian-Colombian cultural relations can be

1 The authors express their sincere gratitude to Rubén Darío Flórez, Anastassia Espinel Souares, and Irina Luna for sharing with us their memories and impressions. Our research was supported by a Russian Science Foundation Grant held by V. S. Polilova at Moscow State University, 'Svoe i/ili chuzhoe: problema metro-ritmicheskikh zaimstvovanii v istorii i razvitii russkogo stikha' (grant no. 19–78–10132), https://rscf.ru/project/19-78-10132/.

2 Mariia Nad'iarnykh, 'Kul't russkoi literatury v Latinskoi Amerike', in *Russkaia literatura v zerkalakh mirovoi kul'tury: retseptsiia, perevody, interpretatsii: Kollektivnaia monografiia*, ed. by M. F. Nad'iarnykh, V. V. Polonskii and A. B. Kudelin (Moscow: IMLI RAN, 2015), pp. 897–942. See also George O. Schanzer, 'La literatura rusa en Uruguay', *Revista hispanoamericana*, 17 (1952), 361–91; George O. Schanzer, *Russian Literature in the Hispanic World: A Bibliography* (Toronto: University of Toronto Press, 1972); Iuliia Obolenskaia, *Dialog kul'tur i dialektika perevoda: Sud'by proizvedenii russkikh pisatelei XIX veka v Ispanii i Latinskoi Amerike* (Moscow: MSU, 1998); Bruno Gomide Barretto, *Da Estepe à Caatinga: O romance russo no Brasil (1887–1936)* (São Paulo: Editora de Universidade de São Paulo, 2011); Dina Odnopozova, 'Russian-Argentine Literary Exchanges' (unpublished doctoral thesis, Yale University, 2012); Adel Ramilevna Fauzetdinova, 'Translation as Cultural Contraband: Translating and Writing Russian Literature in Argentina' (unpublished doctoral thesis, Boston University, 2017); Alfredo Gorrochotegui

 https://doi.org/10.11647/OBP.0340.37

characterised as unsuccessful in the broader context of Russian presence in Latin American cultures. Through a case study of this failed intercultural dialogue, this chapter aims at identifying the factors that have contributed to its failure. The relationship between the two cultures began in the nineteenth century, when Soledad Acosta de Samper, then one of the most important figures in Colombian literature, responded to the works of Nikolai Gogol in her polemic against Realism *à la* Zola.[3] José Asunción Silva, the leading representative of Colombian Modernism, dedicated an enthusiastic review to Lev Tolstoy (1893).[4] In the twentieth century, however, literary relations between the two cultures did not progress as much as one might have expected: Russian literature did not seem to arouse much interest among Colombian translators and writers. The situation began to change only in the last decades of the twentieth century thanks to the efforts of translators, both Colombians and the representatives of the diaspora: Henry Luque Muñoz (Bogotá, 1944–2005), Marina Kuzmina (Moscow, 1937–Bogotá, 2018), Jorge Bustamante (b. Zipaquirá, 1951), Rubén Darío Flórez (b. Pijao, 1961), Irina Luna (b. Moscow, 1953), among others.

The role of institutions, both formal and informal, and of diasporas in intercultural exchange is central to the contemporary humanities, particularly Translation Studies. The latter carefully describes the social aspects of literary interactions (translators, editors, critics, and other institutions).[5] The genealogy of this approach can also be traced back to Russian formalism. An example is the recent book by Giuseppina Larocca on "Russian traces" in early twentieth-century Florence, in which the researcher draws on Boris Eikhenbaum's ideas about the social environment of literature ('literaturnyi byt') and transfers them to the comparative context.[6] As we will demonstrate below, the relatively

Martell, 'Gabriela Mistral y la literatura rusa. Una aproximación a la influencia de Lev Tolstói, Máximo Gorki y Leonid Andreiev en su vida y obra (1904–1936)', *Escritos*, 25 (2017), 135–63; Jordi Morillas, 'La recepción de F. M. Dostoievski en el continente iberoamericano. Una visión panorámica', *Estudios Dostoievski*, 2 (2019), 23–37.

3 Alfredo Hermosillo, 'Gógol en *El Historiador palmesano, Revista de España, La Iberia* y *El Imparcial*', in *Traducción y cultura. La literatura traducida en la prensa hispánica (1868–98)*, ed. by Marta Giné i Solange Hibbs (Berna: Peter Verlag, 2010), pp. 335–40 (p. 339).

4 José Asunción Silva, *Obra completa*, ed. by Eduardo Camacho Guizado and Gustavo Mejía (Caracas: Biblioteca Ayacucho, 1977), pp. 273–75; Rubén Darío Flórez, 'Lev Tolstoi v latinoamerikanskoi literaturnoi traditsii. Kolumbiiskii poet Khose Asuns'on Sil'va o tvorchestve L'va Nikolaevicha Tolstogo', in *Dukhovnoe nasledie L. N. Tolstogo v sovremennykh kul'turnykh diskursakh: Materialy XXXV Mezhdunarodnykh Tolstovskikh chtenii* (Tula: TGPU, 2016), pp. 5–11.

5 Susan Bassnett, 'The Translation Turn in Culture Studies', in *Constructing Cultures: Essays on Literary Translation*, ed. by Susan Bassnett and André Lefevere (Clevedon: Multilingual Matters, 1998), pp. 123–24.

6 Giuseppina Larocca, *L'aquila bicipite e il tenero iris: Tracce russe a Firenze nel primo Novecento (1899–1939)* (Pisa: Pisa University Press, 2018).

superficial character of the reception and translation of Russian literature in Colombia was determined by the lack of an adequate social environment (institutions and diaspora) resulting both from the specificity of the Colombian cultural situation and from the country's unique relationship with Russia during the Cold War. At the same time, we argue, the Soviet international educational project (epitomised by the Peoples' Friendship University, founded in 1960) and generalised processes of globalisation have gradually increased direct engagement with Russian literature, in particular the number of translations.

Thus, the fate of Russian literature in twentieth-century Colombia was not determined by any intrinsic aspect of the literary works themselves, for, as David Damrosch has shown, the processes of reception and appropriation of a text by another culture are intricate: "[these processes] do not reflect the unfolding of some internal logic of the work in itself but come about through often complex dynamics of cultural change and contestation".[7] Similarly, in Pascale Casanova's "world republic of letters", literary and artistic processes are closely linked to international politics (through the formation of national states, imperial expansion and colonialism), while also representing a field in which specific literary mechanisms can be discerned:

> This world republic of letters has its own mode of operation: its own economy, which produces hierarchies and various forms of violence; and, above all, its own history, which, long obscured by the quasi-systematic national (and therefore political) appropriation of literary stature, has never really been chronicled. Its geography is based on the opposition between a capital, on the one hand, and peripheral dependencies whose relationship to this center is defined by their aesthetic distance from it.[8]

Looking at the difference between the rise of Russian literature in the second half of the nineteenth century and the still-precarious state of Colombian culture in the same period, we will try to illuminate the consequences of this encounter between two literatures at different stages of evolution and with very different relations to artistic centres in the West. Their failed dialogue will not only reveal the differences in the development of both literatures, but also encourage more general discussion on the dynamics of reception and adaptation in that "world republic of letters".

Thus, this chapter offers a first outline of the history of translation and reception of Russian literature in Colombia—a history which is unique and interesting precisely because of its limitations compared to other Latin American countries. The first section of our chapter reviews the cultural

7 David Damrosch, *What Is World Literature* (Princeton, NJ: Princeton University Press, 2003), p. 6.

8 Pascale Casanova, *The World Republic of Letters*, trans. by M.B. DeBevoise (Cambridge, MA and London: Harvard University Press, 2004), pp. 11–12.

situation in Colombia and analyses examples of Russian literature's reception in the twentieth century (Ramón Vinyes, the Los Nuevos group, Luis Tejada, León de Greiff, and Gabriel García Márquez); the second part summarises the history of the Colombian-Soviet Cultural Institute, its publications and related cultural activities; while the third and final part examines the work of Colombian translators of Russian literature.

The Colombian Cultural Situation and the Reception of Russian Literature

Carlos Rincón's View on Colombian Cultural Idiosyncrasy

National literatures have their own timescale. The reception of a foreign literature within a national literature depends on the maturity of the latter and its willingness to accept external influence. The maturity of a literature can be estimated through an economic metaphor: the solidity of its internal literary market. Casanova argued that a necessary process for the consolidation of a nation's literary market, and for its integration into the world republic of letters, was the prior accumulation of "literary capital"[9] (mirroring the Marxist idea of the "primitive accumulation of capital"). In the following sections, we will outline the conditions that made Colombian literature less receptive to the influence of Russian literature, that is, with less "literary capital" than other nations whose relations with Russian culture were more fertile. Carlos Rincón suggests where to find answers to this problem. He follows the history of the country's cultural institutions—including its literature—in relation to the nation's own history. Rincón attributes the difficulties faced by grammarians, poets and journalists in consolidating a national literary canon to Colombia's failure as a modern nation-state.[10] In his understanding of the relationship between the construction of a nation-state and the emergence of its cultural institutions, Rincón follows Doris Sommer, who has devoted a famous study to the narratives she calls "foundational fictions".[11] These narratives portray romances between characters from different social strata (for example, between a *criollo* and an indigenous woman), whose union symbolises the social pact necessary for state consolidation and the promise of national fecundity. Thus,

9 Casanova, *World Republic*, p. 37.

10 Carlos Rincón, *Avatares de la memoria cultural en Colombia. Formas simbólicas del Estado, museos y canon literario* (Bogotá: Editorial Pontificia Universidad Javeriana, 2010), p. 52.

11 Doris Sommer, *Foundational Fictions: The National Romances of Latin America* (Berkeley, CA: University of California Press, 1991).

the evolution of Colombian literature, from the nineteenth century onwards, could be seen as a series of attempts to consolidate their nation.

The Colombian cultural scene of the second part of the nineteenth century was dominated by the notion that their capital, Santa Fe de Bogotá, was the "South American Athens".[12] This surprising revival of classicism in the late nineteenth century was accompanied by a conservative defence of Catholicism and Hispanism, which, at the same time, contrasted with the country's precarious cultural situation. Illiteracy levels were very high; consequently, the reading public was sparse. The fact that literature and other cultural expressions were so dependent on formal political institutions indicates, from the outset, that Colombia was not a modern state. One of the preconditions for the emergence of Symbolism in France was the relative autonomy of French literature in relation to political institutions. This was not the case in Colombia. David Jiménez points out that the nineteenth-century literary journals were inevitably associated with one of the two parties vying for power: the Liberal and the Conservative.[13] Thus, literary critics—if we can speak of literary critics in that context—were political partisans before they were readers.

Literary historians are less unanimous in their assessment of what happened to Colombian literature and literary criticism at the turn of the century. According to Jiménez, the emergence of Baldomero Sanín Cano (1861–1957), the Modernist literary critic, friend of the great Modernist poet José Asunción Silva, and believer in "the autonomy of art and literary criticism", indicates real progress.[14] Rincón, however, held the view that "[the] central phenomenon of the history of Colombian literature at the beginning of the second half of the twentieth century is its absolute deprivation of any aptitude, of any power to establish literary or aesthetic standards".[15] Although he details how first in the 1930s, with the Liberal Republic (a period of liberal political and social reformism, which began with the presidency of Enrique Olaya Herrera, in 1930),[16] and later in the 1950s, with the emergence of the Barranquilla Group (a literary association organised around Ramón Vinyes, including Gabriel García Márquez, the writer Álvaro Cepeda Samudio, the painter Alejandro Obregón, and others), writers began to deplore the impoverishment of the country's intellectual and literary scene, Rincón insists that the fault lies with Colombian cultural institutions and actors who not only deny this precariousness, but refuse to address it.[17]

12 Rincón, *Avatares de la memoria cultural*, p. 55.

13 David Jiménez, *Historia de la crítica literaria en Colombia, 1850–1950* (Bogotá: Universidad Nacional de Colombia, 2009), p. 22.

14 Jiménez, *Historia de la crítica literaria*, pp. 24–25.

15 Rincón, *Avatares de la memoria cultural*, p. 87. All translations from Russian and Spanish are our own unless otherwise indicated.

16 Antonio Caballero, *Historia de Colombia y sus oligarquías* (Bogotá: Crítica, 2018), pp. 313–16.

17 Rincón, *Avatares de la memoria cultural*, pp. 86–87.

Rincón stresses that Colombia has also been partially isolated from the cultural dynamics of the region. While in the 1930s the dominance of the two great classics of Colombian literature (*María* (1867) by Jorge Isaacs, and *The Vortex* (*La vorágine*, 1924) by José Eustasio Rivera) was just beginning to be doubted, there was no concerted challenge to Realist literature. Meanwhile, the rest of Latin America (Cuba, with Alejo Carpentier; and Argentina, with Jorge Luis Borges) was forging a radical new poetics, leaving behind not only local movements and localised Realism, but even Anglo-American Modernism.[18] The reception of Russian literature developed analogously. While Santiago, Buenos Aires, Mexico City, Lima, and Havana formed foci of Russian culture during the twentieth century, Bogotá was not included. Besides those Colombian cultural idiosyncrasies identified by Rincon, immigration was an important factor in this difference. Colombia has historically been a rather closed country, resistant to immigration, including by Russian-speaking Jews, causing Russian literature to flourish elsewhere in Latin America. When the racist and philoFascist politician Luis López de Mesa was Colombia's Foreign Minister (1938–42), he banned Jews from entering the country.[19] While some major Colombian authors praised Russian literature,[20] in most cases their response was rather superficial. They reveal a lingering fascination with the Russian Revolution and with nineteenth-century Russian literature, which was understood through the lens of the Revolution. But this reflected light of revolution, or its 'pale fire' (to borrow a Nabokovian phrase), failed to develop into a genuine reception. This failure can be attributed to the political twists and turns of the twentieth century.

Some Episodes in Reception

One of the most interesting and profound examples of the reception of Russian literature in Colombia is the case of Los Nuevos. This association emerged in 1925, when it began publishing its eponymous journal. Its members were young intellectuals who welcomed the 'red flood' of the Russian Revolution and embraced Socialist ideas. Among them were the journalist, writer, and future president Alberto Lleras (1906–90), the historian and politician Germán Arciniegas (1900–99), the writer Jorge Zalamea (1905–69), and the poets León de Greiff (1895–1976) and Luis Vidales (1904–90). Their movement combined a left-leaning desire for political change with demand for avant-garde literary renewal, leading its members to fantasise about distant Russia. As Lleras wrote:

18 Ibid., p. 84.

19 Azriel Bibliowicz, 'Intermitencia, ambivalencia y discrepancia: historia de la presencia judía en Colombia', *Les Cahiers ALHIM*, 3 (2001), https://doi.org/10.4000/alhim.535 (para. 13 of 20).

20 See, for instance, Jorge Zalamea's comments on Russian literature discussed below.

> The Russian Revolution, the triumph of Socialism that had been judged implausible, for the first time constituted in a strong government [...] exerted an almost irresistible attraction [...]. The first declarations of Los Nuevos in their journal reflected the anxiety, uneasiness, and vital anguish of a generation that did not see the way but thousands and thousands of kilometres away, in Russia, where everything seemed possible.[21]

And:

> [...] we saw appearing a red dawn over the destruction of the war, which pointed to the golden onion domes of the Kremlin and, like Luis Tejada, we thought that Lenin was going to decide our destinies and those of the universe, vertiginously.[22]

Los Nuevos played an important role in Colombian history as the cradle and the intellectual centre of liberal modernisation during Colombia's Liberal Republic period (1930–46). Some of its members frequented the Marxist circle organised by Silvestre Savitsky (1894–1954) in 1923.[23] Born in Cali, southwest Colombia, to Slavic émigré parents, Savitsky returned to Latin America in 1920 after spending some time in Russia where he participated in the Civil War. In Bogotá he set up a dyeworks where young intellectuals who wanted to learn news about Soviet Russia gathered. In 1925 he was arrested, accused of conspiracy, and deported to Mexico. After Savitsky's deportation, Lleras published his article 'Memories of a Conspirator', which began: "The Russian Bolshevik, Sawinsky [sic], arrested yesterday by the police, was found to have a list of Colombian communists [...]. The police believe they have discovered a wide-ranging conspiracy".[24] The episode allowed Lleras to describe his own encounter with Russian literature, since it is Russian literature, as he ironically asserts, that really turns one into a Nihilist:

> At that time I learned that beyond the seas, initiated by a series of patriarchs whose books are in my library and who can be taken to court, Russia, an old and nebulous country, full of cold and sweet and good men, had a revolution. Also, if I remember correctly, there had been a group similar no doubt to the one that today has just burst among us, of more or less fateful characters, who went to purge their torturing obsessions of regicide in the ergastula [in Roman times, a sort of slave

21 Alberto Lleras, *Memorias* (Bogotá: Tauris, 2006), p. 215.

22 Alberto Lleras, *Antología*, ed. by Otto Morales Benítez (Bogotá: Villegas, 2007), pp. 38–39.

23 Lazar Jeifets and Víctor Jeifets, *América Latina en la Internacional Comunista. 1919–1943: Diccionario biográfico* (Buenos Aires: CLACSO, 2017), pp. 632–33.

24 Lleras, *Antología*, p. 98.

> prison] of Siberia. Its name, nihilism, caught my spirit. And it was only natural that after all those years, a rabid desire to be a nihilist arose in my mind from that exotic and pernicious influence.[25]

The real conspirators are not characters like Savitsky, he argues, but Russian writers: "One of them was called Tolstoy, and he was crazy. Another one was called Gorky, and he had consumption. The third one was called Andreev, there was also Gogol... and the one after him..."[26]

Los Nuevos' fascination with Russian culture, which they read and interpreted from the standpoint of the Revolution, is evident in texts published in the groups' journal.[27] The most quoted Russian authors are Fedor Dostoevsky,[28] Maksim Gorky and Leonid Andreev. Jorge Zalamea's article 'Figures of Russia'[29] ('Figuras de Rusia') (signed 'J. Z.'), a kind of commentary on Andreev's novel *Sashka Zhegulev* (1911), describes the connection between Andreev's characters and the Revolution thus: "Russia is full of them [Andreev's heroes]. Yesterday's Russia, Tsarist Russia, which cries out now and then from the light and shadows but cries out desperately, tragically. Today their victory seems to be approaching".[30] In his essay 'The Mystical Spirit'[31] ('El espiritu místico'), Lleras explores the mysterious Russian soul, quoting Gorky and Dmitrii Merezhkovskii:

> The literary country of snow and of melancholic and stupid mujiks is, in the end, the one that possesses the most mystical sense. The Russian peasant that Gorky tells us about, kneeling before a Jewish icon or before one of the schism that opens the Catholic Bible or who reads the Lutheran pages, is nevertheless the one who carries more in his soul the oppressive anguish of any religiosity. He is a mystical peasant, essentially mystical, like the Indians of the Khali temples. Besides, the Russian people have a feeling of fatality, oppressive, hard, that floats around in the pages of any writer. And piety, piety that can become criminal in the paradox

25 Ibid., p. 99.

26 Ibid., p. 101.

27 A total of five issues of this journal appeared between June and August 1925. In this chapter, we cite the facsimile reproduction of all issues, published as an annex to Enrique Gaviria Liévano, *'Los Nuevos' en la historia de Colombia: una generación militante (1925–1999)* (Bogotá: Academia Colombiana de Historia, 2010), pp. 199–418. We refer to this edition as '*Los Nuevos*'.

28 For example, Víctor Manuel García Herreros published in *Los Nuevos* excerpts entitled 'The Comic in Dostoevsky' ('Lo cómico en Dostoievsky') and 'Porphyre Petrovich Speaks' ('Dice Porphyre Petrovich') (pp. 284–86, pp. 288–89). These excerpts are presented as diary entries and parts of a novel in progress 'Diary of the Poet Tulio Ernesto' ('Diario del poeta Tulio Ernesto'), pp. 280–89.

29 *Los Nuevos*, p. 333–35.

30 Ibid., p. 335.

31 Ibid., pp. 293–94.

> of Russian sentiment, is among the factors that would make it easy to propagate a religious revival.
>
> Russia exercises over Europe a sure dominance in literature and music, the two arts which, with architecture, are the basis of the mystical sense.[32]

The only translated Russian text we find in *Los Nuevos* is the short story 'The Laugh'[33] ('Smekh', 1901) by Andreev. The fifth and final issue of the magazine announced the publication of work by major new writers, barely known to the general public.[34] They included Aleksandr Blok, Vladimir Maiakovskii, and Vladimir Korolenko, but as the journal was suspended, these translations never appeared.

The most artistically interesting Russia-related publication in *Los Nuevos* is probably 'Diary in Zigzag'[35] ('Dietario en zig-zag') by Ramón Vinyes (1882–1952). Vinyes was a Catalan poet, writer, playwright, and bookseller who arrived in Colombia in 1913 and spent most of his life in the Northern port city of Barranquilla. He became one of the major members of the mid-century circle of journalists and writers known as the Barranquilla Group, including Gabriel García Márquez (1927–2014), who pays tribute to him in *One Hundred Years of Solitude* (*Cien años de soledad*, 1967). Here Vinyes appears as "the wise Catalan", "the man who had read everything". In short articles for *Los Nuevos*, Vinyes imagines Russia in Dostoevskian terms: "In all the sordid taverns of the world you will find a Russian consumptive prone to relapse".[36] He shows Russia as a land of shadows and sorrow.[37]

Vinyes was undoubtedly the only person in Colombia of his time who knew both nineteenth-century and contemporary Russian literature in such depth. In Barranquilla in 1917, he founded the journal *Voces*[38] (1917–20), one issue of which published translations of several Russian poets[39] with an explanatory essay by Vinyes entitled 'Russian poets' ('Poetas rusos').[40] In the essay, a Russian friend, "Nikolas Voynich" (we have not yet been able to establish his identity), offers the narrator a brief overview of Russian poetry and prose (mentioning Merezhkovskii, Skitalets, Nadson, Shchepkina-Kupernik, Ostrovskii, Miatlev,

---

32 Ibid., p. 294.
33 Ibid., pp. 374–77.
34 Ibid., p. 399.
35 Ibid., pp. 232–33.
36 Ibid., p. 232.
37 Ibid., p. 233.
38 In this chapter we cite the reproduction of all issues, published as *Voces, 1917:1920: edición íntegra*, ed. by Ramón Illán Bacca, 3 vols (Barranquilla: Universidad del Norte, 2003). We refer to this edition as *Voces*.
39 Number 18, 1918.
40 *Voces*, I, pp. 482–86.

Goncharov, Grigorovich, and others). The connection between Russian literature and the Revolution is again emphasised. Vinyes argues:

> Everything is revolutionary in Russia. When we recall Tolstoy's theatre [...]: it is revolutionary. 'The Power of Darkness' hallucinates. When we recall Gorky's theatre: it is revolutionary. 'The Lower Depths' gives chills. Pisemsky's theatre is revolutionary. 'Baal' is a violent satire against the upper classes. Ostrovskii's theatre is disturbing: 'The Storm' is revolutionary. Her poets, her musicians are revolutionary; her novelists are revolutionary [...] Her philosophers are revolutionary. [...] All writers of Holy Russia are revolutionaries. The restlessness of their life gives to their works this rough and dark stamp that characterises them, that shows them men without peace, homeless, neurasthenic and possessed like this poor priest in Andreev's novel, in whom faith has died for excess of faith, and who has to seek death to free himself from the oppressive adversarial darkness that envelops him.[41]

The fifth issue of *Voces* from September 1917 contained Vinyes' review of Grigorii Aleksinskii's book *Russia and Europe* (probably referring to the French edition published in Paris in 1917).[42] Vinyes comments: "Gloomy kings, wrathful princes, murderous popes. A sombre procession parades through the book. The figure of Tsar Nicholas I gives shivers. Russia appears to us once again deeply red, as its novelists and poets tell us".[43] A note on Dostoevsky was published in the October issue of the magazine.[44] In 1922, Vinyes also published an essay on 'Russian Theatre During the Revolution'.[45] It is likely that Vinyes, rather than Savitsky, determined the perception of Russian literature by *Los Nuevos*. After the closure of *Los Nuevos*, Russian literature continued to appear in *El Gráfico*, which brought out between 1925 and 1941 twelve short stories by Anton Chekhov and Arkadii Averchenko.[46] Felipe Lleras Camargo, director of *Los Nuevos*, continued the line of Socialist criticism in the newspaper *Ruy Blas* (1927–28).[47] Effects of their exposure to Russian literature and culture on the aesthetic projects of each of the members of *Los Nuevos* proved diverse, as shown by the example of two writers, Luis Tejada (1898–1924) and León de Greiff.

41 Ibid., p. 486.

42 Ibid., pp. 141–42.

43 Ibid., p. 142.

44 Ibid., p. 226.

45 Ramón Vinyes, *Selección de textos*, ed. by Jacques Gilard, 2 vols (Bogotá: Instituto Colombiano de Cultura, 1982), I (1982), pp. 136–37.

46 Paula Andrea Marín Colorado, 'Cuento, traducción y transferencias culturales en la revista colombiana ilustrada El Gráfico (1925–1941)', *Íkala* 23:3 (2018), pp. 521–34 (p. 524).

47 On 1920s magazines and journals, see Jineth Ardila Ariza, *Vanguardia y antivanguardia en la crítica y en las publicaciones culturales colombianas de los años veinte* (Bogotá: Universidad Nacional de Colombia, 2013).

For Tejada, perhaps the most original and important journalist in the country's history, aesthetic-literary relationships were interdependent with political ones. Tejada, like Maiakovskii, saw the integration of Futurism and Communism as a way to create a radical new world, abandoning the old social order and stale aesthetic conventions. In his essays from *El Espectador* (a newspaper founded by one of his maternal relatives), some passages are reminiscent of the Russian Futurists' motivations, tropes, and language:

> Simple movement, speed alone, is already the starting point of the road towards madness: those who rapidly go by automobile feel a certain frantic joy, a certain hilarious, vocal spiritual incoherence bordering on madness; and if the automobile did not, as it happens, maintain a relatively continuous, orderly, graduated, harmonious march, which, in a certain way, aligns itself to the uniform rhythm of the stars; if the automobile could, within its speed, jump, go backwards, march suddenly in a lateral direction, or suddenly fall to the ground to stand up again; if the automobile could dance without abandoning its speed, all those who were inside it would definitely go mad.[48]

Tejada believed that the proletarian revolution must entail an artistic revolution. He challenges both grammarians and oligarchs, whom he felt were essentially one and the same:

> [...] every unforeseen conjunction of words, outside of the grammatical moulds, implies the existence of a new idea, or at least, it indicates an original perception of life, of things. That is why in times of intense spiritual upheaval, in times of revolution, when everything is subverted or destroyed, grammar jumps to pieces, along with millenary institutions. Every profound social change has repercussions on grammar, subverting and renewing it as well [...]. Aleksandr Blok, Sergei Esseim [sic], Andrei Belyi, Maiakovskii, all the extraordinary poets of present-day Russia, who have determined the course of what is already called 'The Russian Renaissance', had to invent a language in order to express their ideas and sensations, full of penetrating originality.[49]

Tejada accompanied his poetic reflections on the surprising beauty of the locomotive or the bullet with explicit political agitation: some of his best writings aim to glorify Soviet political leaders. 'Prayer For Lenin Not To Die' ('Oración para que no muera Lenin', 1924) is a text that in its fusion of Christian theology and revolutionary frenzy suggests Aleksandr Blok's poem 'The Twelve' ('Dvenadtsat'', 1918). In Tejada's poem, global revolution appears as a cosmic

48 Luis Tejada, *Gotas de tinta*, ed. by Hernando Mejía Arias (Bogotá: Instituto Colombiano de Cultura, 1977), pp. 150–51.

49 Ibid., p. 323.

cataclysm creating a new world. Tejada calls Lenin—whom he had already described elsewhere as "[an apostle] of the futurist credo of equality"[50],"the sublime hyperborean Christ of slanting eyes, of sloe-coloured beard, of simple and enigmatic step".[51] We do not know how Tejada's later career would have developed, since his premature death at twenty-six occurred in 1924, the same year when his prayer for Lenin appeared. However, his friend and disciple Luis Vidales became arguably Colombia's best (and practically only) avant-garde poet. Vidales and his Soviet sympathies will be discussed below. Conversely, Tejada's contemporary, the poet De Greiff, understood Russian literature in weak, superficial terms. De Greiff, associated with Los Nuevos, was famous for creating his own literary *alter egos*, rather like the Portuguese poet Fernando Pessoa. One such, Sergio Stepansky, wrote several poems, including 'The Tale of Sergio Stepansky' ('El relato de Sergio Stepansky', 1931) and 'The Song of Sergio Stepansky' ('La cancion de Sergio Stepansky', 1931). The first opens with an epigraph attributed to Erik Fjordson, another of De Greiff's poetic pseudonyms: "I bet my life, I barter my life" ("Juego mi vida, cambio mi vida"), which becomes a leitmotif in the text.[52] The main character of the poem is vaguely reminiscent of the Russian 'superfluous man' type, a brilliant but idle young individual whose talents and abilities are underemployed by society. The poem has little to do with Russia and its literature, besides its title, the somewhat Onegin- or Pechorin-esque *ennui* of the main character, and the Dostoevskian lines "I am exchanging my life for a frank halo/of an idiot and a saint".[53] 'The Song of Sergio Stepansky', written in 1931, shows even more superficial Russian influence (referring to vodka!).[54]A slightly later example of Russian influence appears in a 1946 article by the journalist and novelist José Antonio Osorio Lizarazo (1900–64), 'A New Anniversary for Maxim Gorky'.[55] The affinity between Gorky's sentimentally inflicted Socialist Realism and the aesthetic project of Osorio Lizarazo, who was interested in creating a Colombian version of the Socialist Realist novel, is evident in Osorio Lizarazo's expressed belief that Gorkian narrative, which focuses on the suffering of the impoverished and disadvantaged, is pertinent to the Colombian reader who sees his or her own problems reflected in it. We can assume that Osorio's literary works, and in particular his magnum opus, the novel *El día del odio* (*The Day of Hatred*), published in 1952, had a very similar

50 Ibid., p. 187.

51 Ibid., p. 280.

52 León de Greiff, *Obra poética. Variaciones alrededor de nada y poesía escrita entre 1930 y 1936, Fárrago y poesía escrita entre 1937 y 1954*, ed. by Hjalmar de Greiff, 3 vols (Bogotá: Universidad Nacional de Colombia, 2004), II (2004), pp. 303–06.

53 De Greiff, 'El relato de Sergio Stepansky', *Obra poética* (II), p. 305.

54 De Greiff, 'Canción de Sergio Stepansky', in *Obra poética* (II), pp. 135–37.

55 José Antonio Osorio Lizarazo, 'Un nuevo aniversario de Máximo Gorki', in Gorky, *Novelas y crónicas*, ed. by Santiago Mutis (Bogotá: Instituto Colombiano de Cultura, 1978), pp. 546–55. This essay was originally published in 1946.

objective: to shock readers into political awakening, through empathy with the written experience of pain.[56]

Also relevant here is a curious passage from Gabriel García Márquez's memoir, *Living To Tell The Tale* (*Vivir para contarla*, 2002). García Márquez recounts a journey to Bogotá he made aged fourteen. During the trip, the young Gabriel meets a passenger whom he calls 'an inveterate reader' because he always sees him reading.[57] Investigating the passenger's belongings, he is overwhelmed by one book in particular: Dostoevsky's *The Double* (*Dvoinik*, 1846). In the end, the inveterate reader—whom we later learn was the national director of scholarships at the Ministry of Education—gives García Márquez the book as a gift.[58] The passage has an interesting textual precursor: earlier in his memoir, García Márquez tells an anecdote about a dead senator's overcoat possessing supernatural powers—an anecdote that could well have come from the pen of Dostoevsky or Gogol.[59] García Márquez owed his acquaintance with Russian classical literature to his friendship with Ramón Vinyes. However, this story provides an alternative origin.

Clearly, in the late 1910s and 1920s Colombian intellectuals were fascinated by Russia. Nevertheless, their interest rarely transcended cultural stereotypes of the previous century, thus failing to produce original interpretations (the prematurely deceased Luis Tejada excepted). Even if change had been possible in the 1940s, shifting political conditions made it unfeasible. Here we turn to what may be the most important milestone in the history of Colombian-Russian literary relations: the creation and development of the Colombian-Soviet Institute.

The Colombian-Soviet Institute (1944–48; 1960-)

In 1944, at the end of World War II, the Colombian-Soviet Cultural Exchange Institute (Instituto de intercambio cultural colombo-soviético)[60] was founded in Bogotá. Although officially presented as an initiative of Colombian intellectuals and artists, promoted by the Soviet Embassy, it was probably the result of a coordinated Soviet cultural policy. The Institute for Russian-Mexican Cultural

56 The authors would like to thank Miguel Alejandro Acosta, who introduced them to this relationship between Osorio Lizarazo and Gorky through his unpublished research for the National University of Colombia's Research Seminar in European Literatures.

57 Gabriel García Márquez, *Vivir para contarla* (Barcelona: Random House, 2002), p. 212.

58 Ibid., p. 219.

59 Ibid., p. 211.

60 In the documents we have consulted, the Institute is referred to by several names: Instituto colombo-soviético (Colombian-Soviet Institute), Instituto de Intercambio Cultural (Cultural Exchange Institute), etc. In the following pages, we use various names, according to context.

Exchange, the Chilean Institute for Cultural Relations with the Soviet Union, as well as the Italian 'Associazione per i rapporti culturali con l'Unione Sovietica' were founded in the same year, which is difficult to interpret as mere coincidence. The Colombian Institute's founders included important representatives of politics and culture: the poet De Greiff; his brother, the musicologist, poet and translator Otto de Greiff (1903–95); the historian, journalist and Minister of Education, Germán Arciniegas (1900–99); the future President of Colombia Alfonso López Michelsen (1913–2007), who was also the son of the current President; the writer, politician, and newly appointed rector of the National University of Colombia Gerardo Molina (1906–91); literary critic and essayist Baldomero Sanín Cano (1861–1957); writer, journalist, and Minister for Education Jorge Zalamea Borda; his cousin, the writer and journalist Eduardo Zalamea Borda (1907–63), who was also Gabriel García Márquez's first editor; and poet and essayist Luis Vidales, one of the founders of the country's Communist Party. The project was welcomed by President Alfonso López Pumarejo (1886–1959), who represented the Liberal Party. During his first presidential term (1934–38), López Pumarejo established diplomatic relations with the USSR. During his second term, in 1943, there was an exchange of ambassadors. Thus, the establishment of the Institute continued the rapprochement between the two countries during the Liberal Republic (1930–46). Many of the founders of the Institute had belonged to the Los Nuevos group in the 1920s and had Russophile and Sovietophile interests. In the next part of this section, we will consider the biographies of Miguel Adler (1904–70) and Lisa Noemí Milstein (1910–76), who played an important role in the Institute's operations after its establishment.

Miguel (Misha) Adler worked at the Institute until 1945.[61] Of Jewish family from Nova Sulitza, Bessarabia, he studied in Odesa and spoke perfect Russian. Adler arrived in Peru in 1924, where he studied philosophy and collaborated on editorial projects with the outstanding Marxist philosopher José Carlos Mariátegui (1894–1930). He married Noemí Milstein, who was born in Mogilev (now part of Belarus) and settled in Peru around 1928. She was also part of Mariátegui's circle; with Adler, she translated from German and Russian in *Amauta* (a Quechua word for 'master', 'instructor'), a journal with avant-garde and Socialist themes and sympathies. Mariátegui founded the journal in 1926. Three years later, Adler and Milstein co-founded their own journal, *Repertorio Hebreo* (*The Jewish Catalogue*), which ceased after a few issues. Only months after Mariátegui's death in 1930, the couple were expelled from Peru as suspected communists, moving first to Cali, Colombia, and later to France. There Adler studied anthropology with Paul Rivet. In 1936, Adler and Milstein arrived in Tuluá, Colombia. After living in several Colombian cities, where they founded

61 Lazar Jeifets and Víctor Jeifets, *América Latina en la Internacional Comunista*, p. 39. On Adler and Milstein, see the book their grandson wrote about them: Claudio Lomnitz, *Nuestra América. Utopía y persistencia de una familia judía* (México: Fondo de Cultura Económica, 2018).

Jewish schools as well as the anti-Fascist Hebrew journal *Nuevo Mundo*, they eventually became the central figures of the Colombian-Soviet Institute in Bogotá. As Claudio Lomnitz recounts:

> [...At] the institute Russian classes were offered, taught by Miguel and Noemí, and both also translated from Russian into Spanish and vice versa [...]. For his work teaching Russian, translating and other tasks, Misha [Miguel Adler] received a salary from the [Soviet] embassy.[62]

Between 1945 and 1946, Adler left the Embassy and the Institute and in 1947 founded a new journal, *Grancolombia*: "a genuine advocate of the country's Hebrew community".[63] Among its contributors were Sanín Cano, Vidales, and Arciniegas, the same intellectuals who had belonged to Los Nuevos and who later re-appeared among the founders of the Colombian-Soviet Institute.[64]

In 1945, the Institute published a translation of Nikolai Mikhailov's book *El país de las grandes realizaciones* (*The Country of Great Achievements*; the original Russian title: *Nasha strana*, 1945; no translator named). Eduardo Zalamea Borda wrote in his prologue:

> Mikhailov's work is a book that is clearly necessary. Even more: I would dare to affirm that today it is indispensable. Perhaps yesterday it was not so markedly the case, but in 1945 there is no country in the world that can afford the foolish luxury of ignoring the USSR and its position among the nations and its future and potential.[65]

Mikhailov's book was a form of Soviet propaganda, showcasing the natural beauty and achievements of the USSR in various domains: its territory, mineral resources, industry, agriculture, transport, population, and the friendship between Soviet nations. It contained numerous photographs as well as the text of the USSR's Constitution and of its national anthem. Also in 1945, the Institute published Nina Potapova's *Elemental Russian Language Manual for Spanish Speakers* (*Manual elemental de lengua rusa para españoles*; no translator named). The Institute's own *Colombian-Soviet Journal* launched in 1946.[66] In its first issue, Sanín Cano published an article entitled 'Soviet Russia Is Not a Totalitarian Country'.[67]

---

62 Ibid., p. 226.

63 Ibid., p. 241.

64 Ibid., p. 242.

65 Eduardo Zalamea Borda, 'Prólogo', in N. N. Mijailov, *El país de las grandes realizaciones* (Bogotá: Instituto de Intercambio Cultural Colombo-Soviético, 1945), pp. 5–8 (p. 7).

66 A very similar project was launched the same year in Mexico: Ángel Chávez Mancilla, 'La revista *Cultura Soviética* en el marco de la Guerra Fría cultural en México (1944–1954)', *Signos históricos*, 24:48 (2022), 428–59.

67 Baldomero Sanín Cano, 'La Rusia soviética no es país totalitario', *Revista Colombo-Soviética: órgano del Instituto Cultural Colombo-Soviético*, 1 (1946), 3–7.

Yet the Institute's vigorous activity, aimed at establishing cultural relations (extending to exhibitions, lectures, and chess competitions), and which was supported by prominent intellectuals, was interrupted. The Bogotazo riots, in which up to three thousand people were killed, began in 1948, after the assassination of the Liberal politician Jorge Eliécer Gaitán (1903–48). The riots were initially blamed on the Communists, and therefore diplomatic relations with the USSR were severed and all cultural ties were suspended. Nevertheless, during the 1950s, relations between the two countries were not completely stagnant. For example, Jorge Zalamea played an active role in the World Peace Council, one of the main means of cultural exchange between Latin America and the East during the Cold War. In 1954, Sanín Cano received the International Stalin Prize for Strengthening Peace Among Peoples, which was awarded to him during a ceremony in the Colombian city of Popayán.

Although Colombian diplomatic relations with the USSR were not restored until 1968, the work of the Colombo-Soviet Institute resumed in the 1960s. This resumption belonged within a broader process: following the success of the Cuban Revolution (1959), Soviet authorities seized the opportunity to establish the Soviet Association for Friendship and Cultural Relations with Latin America (SADIKS) in 1959. Its chairman was the famous Soviet composer Aram Khachaturian (1903–78), who visited Colombia in August 1960. SADIKS actively promoted cultural exchanges with Latin America. In March 1960, Jorge Zalamea, who would receive the Lenin Peace Prize in 1968, announced in the national press the relaunch of the Institute. In May of the same year, its new headquarters opened in the historic centre of Bogotá. The Communist-oriented newspaper *Voz de la Democracia* described it thus:

> The Institute thus initiates its activities in the capital of the Republic announcing, among its work, language classes, music services, cinema, conferences, round tables, literature and the issue of monthly printed bulletins. [... It] is a clear demonstration of the broad interest existing within the most diverse social strata for knowing and approaching the great cultural, economic, artistic and scientific achievements of the people of the USSR.[68]

According to Daniel Llana Parra, between 1963 and 1970, Jorge Zalamea, Jaime Mejía Duque, Hernando Salcedo, and José Ariza, among others, gave lectures on Russian literature and Cuban cultural policy at the Colombian-Soviet Institute.[69]

---

68 'Inaugurada Sede del Instituto de Intercambio Cultural Colombo-Soviético en Bogotá', *Voz de la Democracia*, 7 May 1960, p. 2.

69 Daniel Llano Parra, *Enemigos públicos: contexto intelectual y sociabilidad literaria del movimiento nadaísta, 1958–1971* (Medellín: Universidad de Antioquia, 2015), p. 75.

In 1968, the writer Germán Espinosa (1938–2007) gave a long speech about Pushkin's poetry, later published in *El Siglo*.[70]

Another activity of the Institute was the distribution of scholarships for studying in Russia, typically at the newly founded Peoples' Friendship University (Universitet druzhby narodov, Moscow). These scholarships and study visits to the USSR partially increased cultural exchange and resulted in some new translations of Russian literature during the following decades. From 1960 until the early 1990s, the president of the Colombian-Soviet Institute was the Communist politician, Rafael Baquero (recipient of the Soviet Order of Friendship of the Peoples in 1982). The poet Luis Vidales was the vice-president of the Institute and, like his predecessor Jorge Zalamea, received the Lenin Peace Prize in 1983. Other prominent collaborators of the Institute in the 20th century included the poet José Luis Díaz-Granados (b. 1946), and the academic Alfonso Cuéllar Torres (1940–2004). After the collapse of the Soviet Union, the Institute was renamed the León Tolstoi Institute. Its current president, the writer, translator and university professor Rubén Darío Flórez (b. 1961), was awarded the Russian government's Druzhba Order (Order of Friendship) in 2010. Despite the Institute's decades of work, dating back to the 1940s, and although Russian is currently taught at both the León Tolstoi Institute and the National University of Colombia, these institutions, lacking influence or political clout, have not been able to produce significant cultural change. Most Colombian translators of Russian literature trained outside Colombia.

Translators of Russian Literature in Colombia

Since we have already discussed the writers and, in part, the readers, we will now present brief biographical information about the translators thanks to whom Russian culture appeared on the cultural and artistic scene in Colombia. Henry Luque Muñoz (1944–2005), born in Bogotá, lived in Moscow with his wife Sara González Hernández (1950–2021) from 1978 to 1988. They both worked at the Soviet publishing house Progress, which published Russian books in translation into several languages. On his own or in collaboration with Sara Hernández, Luque published several anthologies of essays on classical Russian literature: *Following the Russian Classics: Pushkin, Lermontov, Gogol, Chekhov* (*Tras los clásicos rusos: Pushkin, Lérmontov, Gógol, Chejov*, Progress, 1986), *Two Russian Classics: Turgenev, Saltykov-Shchedrin* (*Dos clásicos rusos: Turguéniev, Saltikov-Schedrín*, Progress, 1989), a translation of Gogol's Petersburg Tales (*Cuentos petersburgueses*, Norma, 1994) and a monograph, *Heaven's Eroticism: An Introduction to the Social History of Modern Russian Literature* (*El erotismo del cielo.*

70 Germán Espinosa, *Ensayos Completos. 1968–1988* (Medellín: Universidad EAFIT, 2002), pp. 106–21 (p. 106, fn. 1).

Una introducción a la historia social de la literatura rusa moderna, Manigraf, 1999).[71] The theme of Russia is abundantly present in Luque's own poetry.

Jorge Bustamante García was born in Zipaquirá, a small town near Bogotá, in 1951. He is a translator, poet and essayist, although in Russia he studied geology at the Institute of Mining and Petroleum in Moscow and then at the Patricio Lumumba Peoples' Friendship University.[72] Even though he has lived in Mexico for a long time, he has published many translations of Russian poetry of the twentieth century in Colombia: *Five Russian Poets: Blok, Sologub, Gumilev, Akhmatova, Mandel'shtam* (*Cinco poetas rusos: Blok, Sologub, Gumiliov, Ajmátova, Mandelstam*; Norma, 1995); *Selected Poems* (*Poemas escogidos*; Norma, 1998), by Anna Akhmatova, a selection of which he had already published in Mexico in 1992; *Ten Twentieth-Century Russian Poets: Sologub, Maiakovskii, Esenin, Blok, Pasternak, Akhmatova, Mandel'shtam, Tsvetaeva, Brodsky, Tarkovskii* (*Diez poetas rusos del siglo XX: Sologub, Maiakovski, Esenin, Blok, Pasternak, Ajmátova, Mandelstam, Tsvietaieva, Brodsky, Tarkovski*; Trilce, 2002). He has also published an essay *Russian Literature at the End of the Millennium* (*Literatura rusa de fin de milenio*; Ediciones sin nombre, 1996) in Mexico.[73] Jorge Bustamante García is mainly interested in translating and anthologising the poetry of the so-called 'Silver Age', particularly the work of Anna Akhmatova.

Rubén Darío Flórez was born in Quindío in 1961. A philologist, he graduated from the Peoples' Friendship University and received a degree in philological studies from the State Moscow University. He is a poet, translator, and university lecturer. He has published an anthology of Pushkin's poetry[74] and has also translated an autobiographical prison novel by Nikolai Bukharin, *How It All Began* (*Vremena*, 1994; *Cómo empezó todo*, 2007). He has translated other twentieth-century and contemporary poets. Flórez has worked for the Colombian Embassy in Russia. Until 2023 he was a professor in the Department of Linguistics at the National University of Colombia, and Editorial Director of the Faculty of Humanities at the same university. Currently he is President of the León Tolstoi Institute.

Eduardo Rosero Pantoja studied philology at the Peoples' Friendship University in the 1970s.[75] Upon returning to Colombia, he joined the Linguistics Department of the National University of Colombia, where he has taught Russian ever since. He has translated and interpreted many Russian folk songs

71 'Henry Luque Muñoz', *Enciclopedia de la Red cultural del Banco de la República*, https://enciclopedia.banrepcultural.org/index.php/Henry_Luque_Mu%C3%B1oz.

72 Jorge Bustamante García, *Enciclopedia de la literatura en México*, http://www.elem.mx/autor/datos/4563.

73 'Jorge Bustamante García', *Sílaba*, https://silaba.com.co/perfil_autor/jorge-bustamante-garcia/.

74 Alexander Pushkin, *El habitante del otoño*, trans. by Rubén Darío Flórez (Bogotá: Casa de Poesía Silva, 1999). It was published in Spain by Pre-textos in 2000.

75 Eduardo Rosero Pantoja, 'La traducción de canciones rusas', *Revista Universidad de Antioquia* 340 (2020), 90–93 (p. 91).

and, in addition to publishing his own works, he has published several translated poems by Pushkin, Mikhail Lermontov, Evgenii Evtushenko, and others on his personal blog.[76]

Alejandro González Puche was born in Bogotá in 1961. He studied at the Russian Theatre Academy in Moscow (GITIS) in the late 1980s and worked as a theatre director in Russia.[77] He is presently a professor in the Department of Performing Arts at the Universidad del Valle (Cali, Colombia), having previously been the head of that department between 2011 and 2015. Together with Chinese Ma Zhenghong, also a theatre director (and an alumna of the Russian Institute of Theatre Arts (GITIS)), he has published a new translation of Anton Chekhov's *The Seagull* and *Uncle Vanya* in "Colombian Spanish" (Universidad del Valle, 2021).[78] Previously, they had translated and published the volume *Sixteen Unpublished Lectures of Mikhail Chekhov* (*Dieciséis lecciones inéditas de Mijail Chejov*, 2017).

Most of those profiled above undertook study trips to Russia in Soviet times and, upon their return, decided to bring Russian culture to the Colombian context. As we pointed out above, those who focused on the humanities were sparse. Notably, their main focus was on classic Russian literature and its smaller forms (poetry, short stories, drama). They aimed to translate the Russian cultural canon rather than seeking texts that might appeal to a specifically Colombian context. The next group of translators includes Russian women who settled in Colombia after marrying Colombian visitors to the Soviet Union and who decided, once settled in Colombia, to use their academic background to strengthen Russian-Colombian cultural ties.

Marina Valentinovna Kuzmina de Cuéllar (1937–2018) was born in Moscow. She studied at the First State Pedagogical University of Foreign Languages and continued her postgraduate studies in philosophy, Latin American literature, and English at Peoples' Friendship University. After coming to Colombia, she taught Russian literature.[79] She offered courses on literary theory and Russian literature at the National University of Colombia. There, together with a group of undergraduate students, she founded the research group 'Yasnaia Poliana' and a journal with the same name. Kuzmina has always focused on the relationship

76 Eduardo Rosero Pantoja, *No me lo estás preguntando....*, https://eduardoroseropantoja.blogspot.com/.

77 'González Puche, Alejandro', *Universidad del Valle, Departamento de Artes Escénicas*, http://escenicas.univalle.edu.co/docentes/nombrados/item/8-gonzalez-puche-alejandro.

78 'La gaviota y el tío Vania de Anton Pavlovich Chejov', *libreriasiglo.com*, https://libreriasiglo.com/artes/81067-la-gaviota-y-el-tio-vania-de-anton-pavlovich-chejov.html#.X8eDLGQzarc.

79 *Variaciones: seis ensayos de literatura comparada*, ed. by Patricia Simonson (Bogotá: Universidad Nacional de Colombia, 2011), p. 235.

between literature and socio-political phenomena.[80] She has translated the philosopher Aleksei Losev's monograph *The Dialectics of Myth* (*Dialektika mifa*, 1930; *Dialéctica del mito*, Universidad Nacional de Colombia, 2002); published an original study on the relationship between French and Russian Symbolists,[81] and co-edited a volume on Tolstoy.[82] She has also translated a short anthology of poems by Lermontov[83] and has written articles on Pushkin, Nikolai Gogol, Chekhov and others.[84]

Anastassia Espinel Souares was born in Cherepovets, USSR, in 1970. She holds a PhD in history from the Institute of Latin America of the Russian Academy of Sciences. She came to Colombia in 1998 and, since then, has taught history at the Universidad Industrial de Santander and the University of Santander. In 2005, she completed a biography of Catherine the Great in the popular series 'One Hundred Personalities/One Hundred Authors' for the publishing house Panamericana. Espinel Souares mostly translates short stories from the Silver Age by, for example, Bunin, and Valerii Briusov. She also writes historical novels and children's books.

Another translator and publisher is Irina Luna. She graduated from the Moscow Pedagogical University with a degree in Spanish and English. In Colombia, where she settled in 1979, she studied Spanish linguistics at the Caro y Cuervo Institute. In 2014, with Santiago Pinzón, she founded the publishing house Poklonka, the only one of its kind in Colombia, which aims to publish contemporary Russian literature.[85] Poklonka has published an anthology of contemporary Russian women's prose (2014), as well as novels by Boris Akunin, Andrey Kurkov, Viktoriia Tokareva, Tat'iana Tolstaia and others. Most of the translators who work with the publishing house are not Colombian (for example, the Cuban Marcia Gasca and the Argentinian Alejandro Ariel González). As an independent publishing house, Poklonka has received financial support for at least two projects from Russia's Institute for Literary Translation (Institut Perevoda).

---

80 Fabio Jurado Valencia, 'Entre la estética y la semiótica: los trabajos de Jarmila Jandova y Marina Kuzmina', *Literatura: teoría, historia, crítica* 22:1 (2020), 309–19 (p. 316).

81 Marina Kuzmina, 'Simbolistas franceses en Rusia', *Variaciones: seis ensayos de literatura comparada*, ed. by Patricia Simonson (Bogotá: Universidad Nacional de Colombia, 2011), pp. 153–80.

82 *León Tolstoi: La dialéctica del alma*, ed. by Marina Kuzmina and others (Bogotá: Universidad Nacional de Colombia, 2011).

83 Marina Kuzmina, 'Mijail Lermontov: el astro nocturno de la poesía rusa (antología poética)', *Mijail Lermontov: el genio rebelde*, ed. by Marina Kuzmina (Bogotá: Universidad Nacional de Colombia, 2012), pp. 83–122.

84 Marina Kuzmina, 'Nikolai Gógol: su risa, sus lágrimas', *Yasnaia poliana. Revista de literatura rusa* 1 (2010), pp. 7–18; Kuzmina, 'Antología', *Yasnaia poliana. Revista de literatura rusa*, 2 (2012), pp. 73–75; Kuzmina and Clara Galindo, 'Editorial', *Yasnaia poliana. Revista de literatura rusa* 3 (2013), pp. 4–6; and so on.

85 'Poklonka Editores', https://www.poklonka.co/.

Our brief summary of notable Colombian translators from Russian reveals several important aspects. On the one hand, it includes former Colombian university students who returned from the Soviet Union imbued with a literary outlook typical of the Soviet cultural environment, which they later reproduced in Colombia too. Contrastingly, it also lists several female translators with academic degrees in humanities, whose education is similar to that received by the first group during their sojourn as foreign students in the Soviet Union at much the same time. Finally, a new trend is set by the publishing house Poklonka, which expands its focus from classical Russian literature to include contemporary Russian culture.

Conclusion

Our analysis of the reception of Russian literature in Colombia reveals an interesting correlation. Firstly, we find evidence that superficial influence from Russian literature, as in the work of León de Greiff's pseudonymous Sergio Stepansky, produces schematic and stereotyped interpretations of the Russian theme. Even a knowledgeable writer such as Ramón Vinyes is not immune to this influence. Secondly, however, for those who eschew common stereotypes, like the members of Los Nuevos or the writer Osorio Lizarazo, 'Russianness' appears strongly linked to ideology. These writers fantasised about Russia, or rather the USSR, as the birthplace of the people's revolution. Thus, literature became subordinated to political aspirations.

Several factors might explain why Russian literature failed to take root in Colombian cultural life. First, the absence of a Russian diaspora hindered the advent of Russian literature and the dissemination of Russian culture. Crucially, Russian-speaking Jewish émigrés were not represented in the country due to the anti-immigration policy pursued by Colombia's government during World War II. Furthermore, the political environment was not conducive to Eastern European cultural influence; the persecution of Communist militants and the overall anti-Soviet spirit caused suspicion of any pro-Russian element. Finally, most Colombians who attended Soviet universities studied medicine and engineering rather than the humanities. After returning to Colombia, they were neither qualified nor likely to promote Russian culture and literature among their compatriots.

However, occasionally Russian literature did interest the cultural elite. Firstly, there are the extraordinary examples of Luque Muñoz, Bustamante and Flórez, who visited Russia and discovered its literary heritage, inspiring them to engage in translation and teaching activities upon their return to Colombia. There were also native speakers of Russian, such as Anastassia Espinel Souares, Irina Luna and Marina Kuzmina, who, after settling in Colombia for family reasons, established stronger literary connections between the two cultures. Unlike countries such as Mexico or Argentina that have professional translators such as Selma Ancira, Alejandro Ariel González or Fulvio Franchi, in Colombia Russian literature has mainly been translated by poets.[86] Only recently, with the establishment of the publishing house Poklonka, has the situation improved. As this chapter has demonstrated, the contrast between Colombia's approach to Russian literature and that of other Latin American countries not only illustrates different stages and strategies of reception of Russian culture. It also allows us to define cultural boundaries between Spanish-speaking countries. Importantly, it highlights the diversity of cultural situations in the Ibero-American countries, where multiple connections with external cultures (French, English, etc.) are often more intense and important than the interlinguistic links within the same language. This confirms Damrosch's suggestion that the reception of a literary work or a literary tradition within a particular nation depends not primarily on the inherent characteristics of the work, but rather on the historical and cultural settings of the destination culture.[87]

86 For more on Selma Ancira, see Rodrigo García Bonillas's essay on Mexico in this volume.

87 Damrosch, *What Is World Literature?*, p. 6.

Cuba and the Caribbean

The Last Soviet Border: Translation Practices in the Caribbean during the Cold War

Damaris Puñales-Alpízar

In recent Cuban culture, two movies illustrate how deeply the Soviet presence affected the island's social landscape over at least three decades. *Sergio & Sergei* (directed by Ernesto Daranas Serrano, 2017), and *A Translator* (*Un traductor*, directed by the brothers Rodrigo and Sebastián Barriuso, 2018), address, from different perspectives, the complicated yet rich relations between Cubans and Soviets between the 1960s and the 1990s, and the role that Russian language and literature played in Cuba's daily life. When *Sergio & Sergei* was first screened, the viewing experience was cathartic for local audiences. The film, which contains scenes in Russian with Spanish subtitles, represented an identity marker for many Cubans aged forty or older, for whom the Soviet Union and the Russian language had formed part of their sentimental and formal education. These generations belong to what has been called the Soviet-Cuban sentimental community.[1] The movie, inspired by actual events, tells the story of Sergio, a Cuban amateur radio operator who unexpectedly contacts the last Soviet

1 My article 'Cuba soviética: el baile (casi) imposible de la polka y el guaguancó' ('Soviet Cuba: The (Almost) Impossible Dance of the Polka and the Guaguancó') coins the term 'Soviet-Cuban sentimental community' to refer to Cubans born between the 1960s and the 1980s, who were exposed to Russian language and Soviet culture as no other generation. Such exposure provided them with a sense of belonging and cohesion. See Damaris Puñales-Alpízar, *La Gaceta de Cuba*, 1 (Jan-Feb 2010), 3–5, https://www.academia.edu/4342328/Cuba_sovi%C3%A9tica_el_baile_casi_imposible_de_la_polka_y_el_guaguanc%C3%B3. This topic is later explored more thoroughly in Puñales-Alpízar, *Escrito en cirílico. El ideal soviético en la cultura cubana posnoventa* (*Written in Cyrillic: The Soviet Ideal in Post–1990 Cuban Cultural Production*) (Santiago de Chile: Editorial Cuarto Propio, 2012).

 https://doi.org/10.11647/OBP.0340.38

cosmonaut, Sergei Krikalev, who is in orbit during the final months of the Soviet Union's existence.[2] In *A Translator*, the relationship between Soviets and Cubans is depicted in a different light. As in *Sergio & Sergei*, it is inspired by historical events that portray how ordinary lives are touched by history. The movie follows Malin, a professor of Russian literature and language at the University of Havana, who lost his job when Russian ceased to be taught after the end of the Soviet Union. He finds alternative work as a translator for those victims of the Chernobyl nuclear accident to be treated in Cuba.[3] As both films demonstrate, the Russian language was a unifying element that provided many Cubans with professional opportunities and a sense of belonging to a specific community. Taking these two films as its starting point, this chapter will explore the impact of Russian language and culture on Cuban society, arguing that translation practices within the Socialist bloc became a geopolitical instrument.

A Soviet Doorway to Latin America

After the Cuban Revolution of 1959, the island's geographical and historical proximity to North America made it a strategic territory for the Soviet Union. Until then, the latter had maintained different degrees of relationships with and interests in Latin America and Hispanic culture. But once aligned with the Socialist bloc, Cuba transformed into the westernmost border of the Soviet Empire, part-fulfilling its long-sought intentions to spread Socialist ideology into the American and African continents.[4] Many obstacles hampered the developing interactions

2 In May 1991, just a few months before the USSR disintegrated, the cosmonaut Sergei Krikalev arrived at the MIR space station. He remained there until March 1992, when Boris Yeltsin finalised agreements between public and private entities from all over the world to allow for Krikalev's safe return to Earth. But the country the cosmonaut had left no longer existed when he returned to the planet. See Claire Barrett, 'Cosmonaut Sergei Krikalev: "The Last Soviet Citizen"', in *History Net* (12 June 2020), https://www.historynet.com/cosmonaut-sergei-krikalev-the-last-soviet-citizen.htm.

3 The Ukrainian-Cuban programme Children of Chernobyl provided humanitarian and clinical aid; it began on 29 March 1990. It is estimated that in twenty years of medical assistance to victims of the disaster in Ukraine, some 21,000 children were treated in Tarara, the children's camp-cum-medical facility outside of Havana. The programme operated at full capacity until the year 2000, and although patients continued to arrive in the following decade, numbers were much fewer than in previous years. For more information on this topic, see: Desmond Boylan, 'Chernobyl victims treated in Cuba', *Reuters* (23 March 2010), https://www.reuters.com/news/picture/chernobyl-victims-treated-in-cuba-idUSRTR2BZRV; and Prensa Latina News Agency, 'Tarara: The Story of Chernobyl Children in Cuba', *Escambray* (27 August 2021), http://en.escambray.cu/2021/tarara-the-story-of-chernobyl-children-in-cuba/.

4 For further discussion about Cuba and USSR's involvement in the wars on the African continent, see Orlando Freire Santana, 'La otra cara de la intervención en

between the two nations, such as language barriers, geographical distance, and cultural and economic differences. To overcome them, both the Soviet Union and Cuba inaugurated a new chapter in their international relations by creating new institutions and programmes to foster mutual cultural and ideological understanding while also facilitating Soviet access to Latin America. In this way, from 1959, Cuba became the epicentre of geopolitical operations for Socialism, for which ideological dissemination through culture, and especially literature in Spanish translation, played one of the most active roles. The new direction that translation practices took after 1959, especially after Fidel Castro declared the Socialist path of his government in 1961, configured an alternative literary system on a global scale by facilitating the presence of Soviet culture in Latin America.[5] Cuba became the natural doorway through which the Soviets could gain access to that continent. Many Latin American intellectuals' fascination with the Cuban Revolution, together with the amount of resources that the Soviet Union poured into the region, allowed a very dynamic exchange between regional artists and intellectuals with Eastern Europe in general via the USSR.

Soviet Culture in Cuba

The triumph of the Cuban Revolution and Castro's rapid alliance with Soviet Socialism implied a shift in the geopolitical struggle between the Soviet Union and the United States for political and economic control in Latin America. Cuba, as the newest member of the Socialist bloc, found itself stranded: it did not share a language with either of these rivals. Spanish-language specialists from Eastern Europe were called in to help solve this problem. Most came from the Soviet Union, where many citizens of Spanish origin had been living since the Spanish Civil War. From 1936 onwards, many Spaniards had sent their children to the Soviet Union to protect them from Franco's troops.[6] Those *children of the war* (*los niños de la guerra*), as they are historically known, became the first translators to

África' ('The Other Face of Cuban Intervention in Africa'), in *Cubanet* (1 December 2010), https://www.cubanet.org/htdocs/CNews/year2010/Nov2010/29_C_2.html.

5 In April 1961, shortly after the US invasion of Cuba, Fidel Castro made explicit the Cuban Revolution's Socialist agenda, which he had previously denied. For more information see Fidel Castro Ruz, 'Discurso pronunciado en las honras fúnebres de las víctimas del bombardeo a distintos puntos de la República, el día 16 de abril de 1961' ('Speech Given at the Funeral Honors of the Victims of the Bombing in Different Parts of the Republic, on April 16, 1961'), http://www.cuba.cu/gobierno/discursos/1961/esp/f160461e.html.

6 It is estimated that between 1937 and 1938, some three thousand Spanish children had been evacuated to the Soviet Union, besides "educators and auxiliary personnel who accompanied the minors on the expeditions, the pilot students who were going to study at the Soviet aviation schools and the crew of the Spanish ships that were in that country or sailing towards it when the war". After 1939, the number of Spanish exiles to the Soviet Union declined drastically. See: Alicia Alted

work on Russian/Spanish translations, the first linguistic links between Cubans and Soviets post-1959.[7] A significant number of this cohort, including Arturo Carrasco, María Cánovas, José Santacreu, Francisco Roldán, Venancio Uribes, Aurora Kantoróvskaia, Clara Rosen, José Vento, Julio Mateu, and Isabel Vicente became translators. Many of their translations felt odd to Cuban readers, given the linguistic distance between the translators—raised and educated in the Soviet Union, and therefore unfamiliar with the Spanish spoken in Spain—and the readers on the island who in many cases found the translations to be too 'peninsular', rather than Cuban.

Almost simultaneously, Cuba created new university curricula for the study of Eastern European languages, new language schools opened, the educational system implemented the teaching of Russian as part of its regular curriculum, and even a radio programme (Russian Language by Radio/Russkii iazyk po radio) started teaching Russian to the general population. At the same time, thousands of Cuban students went to the Socialist bloc to learn languages, while students from those countries travelled to Cuba to learn Spanish. One of the first groups of Cubans that went to the Soviet Union left the island in 1961: a thousand young peasants travelled there as part of an agreement between the two countries that would allow Cubans to learn the Russian language and agricultural techniques.[8]

Unlike many other islands in the Caribbean, Cuba has never been a multilingual space. For many decades, translational tasks were performed individually by intellectuals, poets, and cultural agents; these were fundamental

---

Vigil, 'El exilio español en la Unión Soviética' ('Spanish Exile in the Soviet Union'), *Revista Ayer*, 47 (2002), 129–54.

7 See Verónica Sierra Blas, *Palabras huérfanas, los niños y la Guerra Civil* (*Orphan Words, Children and the Civil War*) (Madrid: Taurus, 2009). Carlos Aguirre offers some insights into the role that these "children of the war" played in bringing Latin American and Russian cultures closer together. See Carlos Aguirre, 'Dionisio García: De "niño de la guerra" a traductor de *La ciudad y los perros* al ruso' ('"Child of the War" to Translator of *The City and the Dogs* into Russian') (30 January 2016), https://blogs.uoregon.edu/lcylp/2016/01/30/dionisio-garcia-de-nino-de-la-guerra-a-traductor-de-la-ciudad-y-los-perros-al-ruso/.

8 In June 1961, a meeting of the International Union of Students took place in Havana. In the closing speech, Fidel [Castro] said: "The Revolution aims to expand the plans of cultural exchange and in relation to this we express our proposals to the Komsomol (Union of Leninist Communist Youth of the Soviet Union). We propose that Komsomol send us a thousand young Soviet peasants, not to teach them agricultural sciences, since we do not believe that our agriculture is so developed that we should act as teachers, but they could come to get to know our agriculture and learn Spanish. And, for our part, we are ready to send a thousand of our young peasants to the Soviet Union to study agricultural sciences and the Russian language there"'. Blas Nabel Pérez Camejo, *Cuba-URSS. Crónica* (*Cuba-USSR. A Chronicle*) (Moscow/Havana: Progress/Editorial Progreso, 1990), p. 254. All translations from Spanish in this chapter, unless otherwise noted, are my own.

not only to establishing relations with non-Spanish-speaking countries but also as a cornerstone in the foundation of the nation. From the end of the eighteenth century onwards, Cuban intellectuals always made a visible and constant effort to bring knowledge and literary creations from other languages into Spanish. At the same time, these efforts informed and influenced the island's literary production and shaped the road for the birth of a national literature into the global scene. Even with all their limitations, such practices of translation allowed, as Pascale Casanova describes when explaining the circulation of World Literature, for limited contact between Cuban and international literary production.[9] As Casanova states: "[t]he construction of national literary space is closely related, [...], to the political space of the nation that it helps build in turn [...] [i]n the case of 'small' countries, the emergence of a new literature is indissociable from the appearance of a new nation".[10]

Soon after Fidel Castro took power in 1959, translation practices became for the first time an institutionalised and centralised activity facilitating the circulation of literatures that, until then, were only rarely known in Cuba. Many of the actions promoted by the new government aimed to create a literate citizenship while, at the same time, enabling access for new potential readers to books and other cultural materials, especially after the national literacy campaign of 1961. According to Casanova: "[s]ince language is not a purely literary tool, but an inescapably political instrument as well, it is through language that the literary world remains subject to political power".[11] This explains, in part, how Cuba entered an international Socialist literary circuit that was, to a certain degree, parallel to the global literary market.

Given the precarious situation of the publishing industry in Cuba at the time and the reallocation of those scarce publishing resources for educational purposes, the support of the USSR was fundamental for providing Cuban readers with new books and a new ideology. Very soon, Cuban bookstores saw a flood of publications of Soviet origin in Spanish. The experiences and translation practices put in place in 1918 in the USSR, when Maksim Gorky founded the World Literature publishing house in Petrograd, were fundamental to speeding up the translation tasks between Cuba and the Soviet Union. Among those practices was the translation from a wide array of languages, the training of cohorts of professional translators, and the addition of didactic prefaces to

9 Maria Khotimsky offers a thorough explanation of the actions taken by Gorky to provide the Soviet reader with a wide variety of world literary works, in her article 'World Literature, Soviet Style: A Forgotten Episode in the History of the Idea', *Ab Imperio*, 2013:3 (2013), 119–54, https://muse.jhu.edu/article/531927. Gorky's publishing house only lasted until 1924.

10 See Pascale Casanova's sections on 'Literary Nationalism,' and 'National versus International Writers', in *The World Republic of Letters*, trans. by M.B. DeBevoise (Cambridge, MA: Harvard University Press, 2004), p. 85 and p. 104 respectively. See also pp. 103–15 for further discussion.

11 Casanova, *The World Republic of Letters*, p. 115.

translated works, normally written from a Socialist ideological perspective. Cuban literature was widely published and distributed in the Soviet Union. For instance, in 1960, print runs of a Russian translation of a poetry collection by the Cuban poet Nicolás Guillén totalled two hundred thousand copies. That year, twelve thousand copies of translations of Soviet literature into Spanish were sent to Cuba; two years later, in 1962, that number reached a million copies. Between 1959 and 1962, Cuban publishing houses printed about forty-seven Soviet titles, in a total of five million copies.[12]

In *The World Republic of Letters*, Casanova states that "political domination is often exerted by linguistic means [which] implies a condition of literary dependency". Such linguistic dependency is reinforced by different methods: "the effectiveness of consecration by central authorities, the power of critical decrees, the canoni[s]ing effect of prefaces and translations by writers who themselves have been consecrated at the centre [...] the prestige of the collections in which foreign works appear, and the leading role played by great translators"[13]. In the case of Cuba, however, the prefaces and translations had not only the effect of canonising certain literary works but also of enforcing ideological standards. Besides suffering most of Casanova's conditions of dependency listed above, Cuban authors lacked access to wider publication opportunities. Soon after 1959, all publishers became state-owned; thus, all publications had to be approved by the government. Therefore, any Cuban author wishing to stay on the island had to adhere to state policies regarding literature and culture. Gaining international visibility was only possible via the publishing houses in the Socialist bloc, mainly in the Soviet Union. As Damrosch notes, "[a] culture's norms and needs profoundly shape the selection of works that enter into it".[14] Cuban authorities saw culture as a means of ideological education; they followed Damrosch's principle by favouring works which aligned with Socialist models and ideas.

To help spread knowledge about Cuba in the Soviet Union, the two governments signed an agreement to jointly publish, between 1975 and 1980, a ten-volume collection of Cuban literary works in Russian translation. This was part of a more ambitious and comprehensive agreement:

> In June [of 1975], the USSR and the Republic of Cuba signed the first five-year plan for cultural collaboration. The relations between the two 'brother' countries started to have a planned basis, and to consider all perspectives, not only in the area of economics but also in the culture. In particular, an agreement between Goskomizdat and the Cuban Book Institute provided for publication in the USSR over five years

12 Pérez Camejo, *Cuba-URSS*, p. 300.

13 Casanova, *The World Republic of Letters*, p. 115.

14 David Damrosch, *What Is World Literature?* (Princeton, NJ: Princeton University Press, 2003), p. 26.

> of a 10-volume collection of Cuban literature. Soviet readers thus had the opportunity to learn about the best works of Cuban poetry, prose, and journalism, not in separate publications, but a compilation with a specific historical-literary order; the best Soviet specialists provided the translations of the Cuban authors.[15]

However, no such volume was ever published: Pavel Grushko and Yuri Girin, two leading Russian translators and specialists on Cuban culture and history, when specifically asked about these publications, stated that they had never heard of them.[16] Blas Nabel Pérez Camejo also informed us that '"the result was the separate publication of some books on Cuban literature, starting with José Martí".[17] Many other Cuban books were translated into Russian. Meanwhile, the number of Spanish-language publications on the island by Russian and Soviet writers continued to rise. Several titles became widely known, either by being sold and read or through citations in different cultural media, such as movies or soap operas. Among the most popular Soviet titles were *Seventeen Moments of Spring* (*Semnadsat' mgnovenii vesny*, 1969), a novel by Iulian Semenov, Nikolai Ostrovskii's *How the Steel was Tempered* (*Kak zakalialas' stal'*, 1934), and Aleksandr Beliaev's 1929 science-fiction novella, *Amphibian Man* (*Chelovek-amfibiia*). Semenov's novel became widely known thanks to the television series which it inspired, transmitted for the first time in Cuba in 1973; Ostrovskii's tragic Bildungsroman was broadcast as a radio soap opera there from the late 1960s to the early 1970s, while *Amphibian Man* was known in its 1962 movie version, often aired on Cuban TV.[18] Other novels, such as Gorky's *Mother* (*Mat'*, 1906), Boris Polevoi's *A Story about a Real Man* (*Povest' o nastoiashchem cheloveke*, 1947) and Mikhail Sholokhov's *And Quiet Flows the Don* (*Tikhii Don*, 1925–40), appeared on high-school curricula.

On 7 November 1980, the popular Cuban magazine *Bohemia* inaugurated a new feature, 'What Is Read?' ('¿Qué se lee?') highlighting the top ten bestselling books (fiction and non-fiction).[19] A quick examination of this section allows us to determine some of the most popular Soviet books among Cuban readers during the ensuing decade. Some of these were Ukrainian author Iurii

15 Pérez Camejo, *Cuba-URSS*, p. 354.

16 Pavel Grushko and Yuri Girin, email to the author, 1 January 2022.

17 Blas Nabel Pérez Camejo, email to the author, 5 January 2021.

18 For a more detailed account of all Soviet novels broadcast as TV series, see 'Novelas literarias que llegan al éter' ('Literary Novels that Reach the Ether'), *Televisión Cubana*, 9 July 2014, https://www.tvcubana.icrt.cu/secciones/seccion-historia/1293-novelas-literarias-que-llegan-al-eter; and Julio Cid, 'Shtirlitz-Tijonov: una dupla única' ('Shtirlitz-Tikhonov: A Unique Duo'), *Televisión Cubana*, 27 October 2018, https://www.tvcubana.icrt.cu/seccion-en-pantalla/3908-shtirlitz-tijonov-una-dupla-unica.

19 The National Book Distribution Company and the Culture and Science Publishing provided this information for the magazine.

Dol'd-Mikhailik's *Alone on the Battlefield* (*I odin u poli voin*, 1956; translated as *A solas con el enemigo*); Vladimir Bogomolov's *The Moment of Truth* (*Moment istiny*, 1973) which enjoyed fourteen weeks in the top ten, and Aleksandr Vek's *Volokolamsk Highway* (*Volokolamskoe shosse*, 1944; published in Spanish as two separate books: *Los hombres de Pánfilov* and *La carretera de Volokolamsk*), which stayed for five weeks on the bestseller list. We might note that all three books are on military topics. Overall, between 1959 and 1990, literature from Socialist countries (mostly from the Soviet Union) played a major function in the formation of the national literary system.

Fiction books were not, however, the only materials translated from Russian circulating in Cuba and the rest of Latin America during this period. To connect with more readers, the Soviet Union promoted the circulation of popular magazines on the continent, such as *Sputnik*, *New Times*, *Soviet Woman*, *Misha*, *Moscow News*, *USSR*, and *Soviet Literature*. All these magazines widely circulated in Cuba from the 1960s to the 1990s. Many Cuban magazines also spread Soviet culture: *Signs* (*Signos*) in Villa Clara and *Santiago*, in Santiago de Cuba, devoted special issues to Soviet literature. To a lesser extent, popular non-literary magazines such as *Bohemia*, often included literary pieces from Socialist intellectuals. On a regular basis, *Bohemia* included information about frequent visits by Soviet intellectuals, scientists, and political figures to the island. *Mondays of Revolution* (*Lunes de Revolución*), during its short life (1959–61—it was shut down by the government because of political disagreements) published information from the USSR and other Socialist countries.

Johan Heilbron and Gisèle Sapiro provide a useful theoretical framework to better understand the role of literary translations, the different levels of relations involved in Socialist translation practices, and the circulation of cultural goods within the Socialist bloc:

> To understand the act of translating, one should in a first stage analyse it as embedded within the power relations among national states and their languages. These power relations are of three types—political, economic and cultural. [...] In these power relations, the means of political, economic and cultural struggles are unequally distributed. Cultural exchanges are therefore unequal exchanges that express relations of domination.[20]

In the case of Cuba and the Soviet Union, the greatest weight was given to the ideological function of literature in translation for aligning nations despite widely different cultures, languages, and histories. The selection of works

20 Johan Heilbron and Gisèle Sapiro, 'Outline for a Sociology of Translation: Current Issues and Future Prospects', in *Constructing a Sociology of Translation*, ed. by Michaela Wolf and Alexandra Fukari (Amsterdam and Philadelphia, PA: John Benjamins, 2007), pp. 93–107 (p. 95).

for translation depended upon the cultural and editorial policies of both the country of origin and of reception; often the translators chose texts aimed at fostering a Socialist identity designed to create a new society based on Soviet Socialist criteria.

Between 1959 and 1990, thousands of books from other Socialist countries, such as Bulgaria, GDR, Romania, and Poland, were translated into Spanish and circulated in Cuba through a network of bookstores, libraries, and educational curricula. Four genres and topics were particularly favoured: poetry, Socialist Realism, science fiction, and detective novels. Thus, they modelled the literary genres considered desirable in a Socialist country.[21] The first translations of Soviet-Russian literature into Spanish to circulate in Cuba were made mainly by intellectuals of Hispanic origin—the *children of the war* referred to above. However, Cuban intellectuals and poets, who in many cases worked together with Russian translators, also played a very active role in the translation processes and in spreading Russian culture into the Hispanic world. To mention just two examples: *Russian and Soviet Poets: A Selection* (*Poetas rusos y soviéticos. Selección*), published in 1964 by Cuban writer Samuel Feijoo after spending four months in the Soviet Union, was a well-curated selection of Soviet poetry, with ten thousand copies printed. *Five Writers from the Russian Revolution* (*Cinco escritores de la Revolución Rusa*),[22] a volume edited by Roberto Fernández Retamar, was published in 1968.[23]

A review of magazines dedicated to the cultures of the Eastern bloc and to Asian Socialist countries shows clearly that they intended to unite the diverse nations of the Socialist world. The introductory sections common in books

21 Literary works were not the only texts translated into Spanish from different Socialist languages (the Russian language, given the economic and ideological weight of the Soviet Union, being predominant). Much information from the Socialist bloc circulated in Cuba. Moreover, every Cuban ministry had Soviet advisers; most pedagogical, military, and economic data exploited in Cuba from the 1960s to the 1990s originated in the Soviet Union or other Socialist countries.

22 The volume includes both poets and prose writers: Aleksandr Blok, Vsevolod Ivanov, Victor Shklovskii, Isaak Babel and Vladimir Maiakovskii.

23 Russian translator and literary critic Daria Sinitsyna provides an excellent analysis of the ideological-literary production from both Cuban and Soviet poets of the time in her article 'Thirsty for More Homeland: The Vision of Cuba/USSR in Committed Soviet and Cuban Poetry', in *Trasatlantica. Poetry and Scholarship*, 1 (2012–13), 42–52. Rafael Pedemonte offers a detailed study of the cultural agents who facilitated the exchange between the two countries in his article '"De Cuba a Seván no existe distancia: / Ha sido abolida por la poesía": el rol de los escritores y la consolidación de los lazos cubano-soviéticos (1959–1971)' ('"From Cuba to Seván There Is No Distance:/It Has Been Abolished by Poetry": The Role of Writers and the Consolidation of Cuban-Soviet Ties (1959–1971)'), in *Asedios al caimán letrado. Literatura y poder en la Revolución cubana* (*Sieges of the Literate Cayman. Literature and Power in the Cuban Revolution*), ed. by Emilio J. Gallardo-Saborido, Jesús Gómez de la Tejeda and Damaris Puñales-Alpízar (Prague: Carolina University Press, 2018), pp. 97–111.

translated into Spanish and the graphic composition of these publications functioned as paratexts that courted the reader to accept a culture presented as essentially familiar. In all cases, these similarities were mostly reduced to representing so-called anti-imperialist liberation struggles and constructing a new society. The effort to create a heroic cultural community among the Socialist nations, while putting into circulation other literatures that remained outside the international literary system, strove to unite countries and histories that had little in common. European Socialist nations and Cuba were connected, above all, by their commitment to Socialist construction. This intention to forge Socialist brotherhood was part of a political and ideological project that grew increasingly powerful in Cuba starting in the mid-1960s, enhanced by translation and publishing practices.

Newly created cultural institutions and policies in the Socialist bloc—such as literacy campaigns and the strong financial support given to book production—tried to challenge the concept of a bourgeois urban elite monopolising both the production and enjoyment of (high) culture. In the same way, the circulation of literature from Socialist countries exemplified an effort to create a new literary world map that defied the canons traditionally imposed by European and North American literature. Efforts launched from the epicentre of Socialism in Moscow attempted to extend the reach of a contemporary literary production that had often gone unheard in the dialogue of World Literature. For the first time, much of the literature produced in peripheral zones found itself circulating alongside and competing with more central literatures. In this sense, translation played a fundamental role in configuring a new literary order and putting Socialist countries' literary production into circulation and knowledge. Membership in the Socialist bloc facilitated a flow of works and authors that otherwise would never have happened, while allowing literature from minority languages and areas to reach realms and readers entirely out of their geographical or economic range. The translator's practice ceased to be an individual craft and became a social, collective labour, giving literary translation geopolitical weight. In most Socialist countries, translation departments and teams were created over the years, which led not only to the professionalisation of the translator but above all to the systematisation and regulation of a practice that until then had largely been in the hands of individuals or specific groups. Regardless of state policies, however, these translation departments were in many cases made up of prestigious intellectuals who put their talent, training, culture, and their own tastes into the translated works. This process enriched the final translated product and often influenced decisions on what to translate. Thus, we must analyse translation not as a mechanical task that only followed instructions according to the Socialist ideology but as a symbiotic and complex activity in which translators also added their personal and cultural touch.

Since early 1959, the Cuban government had prioritised culture; in addition to the literacy campaign of 1961 and other institutional and legal initiatives of that period, the state heavily subsidised the book industry. This made prices very affordable and increased the number of publications; precedence was given to all forms of knowledge disseminated from within the Socialist bloc. According to the *Catalog* of the Arte y Literatura publishing house—the main publisher of foreign literary works in Cuba—this organisation published a total of 1989 titles from its foundation in 1967 until 2004.[24] Until the 1990s almost 23% (that is, 453 titles) of its publications came from the Socialist bloc. In *Bibliography of Soviet Authors: Books and Brochures Published in Cuba (1959–1977)* (*Bibliografía de autores soviéticos. Libros y folletos publicados en Cuba (1959–1977)*), Ernestina Grimardi Pérez lists the number of Soviet titles published in that period: 450 titles in 17 years, an average of about 27 new titles per year.[25] Twenty-eight different publishers were responsible for producing these books. These numbers include not just literary works, but titles from almost all areas of knowledge. Nevertheless, none of these statistics considers books published in Spanish by other Soviet publishers, such as Progress (known as Progreso in the Hispanic world), Raduga, or Mir, for example, which were distributed through local Cuban publishing houses; nor does it count books from other Socialist countries.

These institutionalised practices of translation were common in all Socialist regions, where priority was given to re-structuring society. As Thomson-Wohlgemuth has shown, similar processes also happened in the German Democratic Republic.[26] The goal, not only for the GDR but for all Socialist countries, was to provide a comprehensive education for members of the nascent Socialist society. To this end, the creation of new institutions and cultural infrastructures was promoted to guarantee universal access to high-culture literature, not necessarily exclusively Socialist. As already mentioned above, the antecedent to these practices can be found in Russia at the beginning of the twentieth century. One of the main goals of the World Literature Publishing House, founded by Gorky in 1918, was to provide the Soviet reader with the best of global literary production while at the same time offering accurate paratextual information about the work to be read. The same trend—adding historical and social explanations as an introduction to literary works from a Socialist perspective—was followed by other Socialist publishers during the twentieth century.

In Socialist countries such as Cuba, following the example of the Soviet Union, translation practices had several functions. These were all-important and sometimes, at first glance, contradictory. Their goals were:

24 *Catálogo de Publicaciones* (Havana: Editorial Arte y Literatura, 2004).

25 Ernestina Grimardi Pérez, *Bibliography of Soviet Authors: Books and Brochures Published in Cuba (1959–1977)* (*Bibliografía de autores soviéticos. Libros y folletos publicados en Cuba (1959–1977)*) (Havana: Ministerio de Cultura, 1977).

26 See Gabriele Thomson-Wohlgemuth, 'A Socialist Approach to Translation: A Way Forward', in *Meta: Journal des traducteurs/Meta: Translators' Journal*, XLIX:3 (2004), 498–510.

1. to create a universal literary consumer, capable of enjoying the literature of the world;
2. to educate people about a specific model of society;
3. to reach out to different regions of the world to spread Socialist influence;
4. to seek a balance in the circulation of World Literature that would allow literatures from peripheral areas or minority languages to have a certain international presence while promoting literary production in those same areas.

Historically, in many societies, literary translation has played a central role in developing the local literary system. But as we show, the dynamics created during the processes of literary translation within the Socialist bloc—although not only there—were explicitly intertwined with the ideological intentionality of such tasks during the cultural Cold War.

All Cubans Learned Russian

Many years of teaching and learning Russian, and the many programmes and institutions created with this goal, ensured that Cuba had one of the highest Russophone populations in the Western hemisphere. Other factors also contributed, such as mixed marriages between Cubans and Soviet emigrants. And although the times of widespread Russian instruction are long gone, there are still Cubans who can recognise, at the very least, the letters of the Cyrillic alphabet. Others still retain some knowledge of the language, even if it is rusty from lack of use. However, despite widespread instruction in Russian, it never became a lingua franca in Cuba for various reasons—among them, Cuba's strong Spanish linguistic and cultural history, the geographical distance between the two countries, the lack of an effective Russian occupation of Cuba, and the concerted efforts made by Cuban cultural agents and institutions to maintain cultural independence. For most Cubans, some phrases in Russian became familiar and part of the daily speech, such as '*net*' ('no'), '*tovarishch*' ('comrade'), and '*konets*' ('the end'). Also, titles of Soviet movies and TV series entered common conversations in a process of re-semantisation by which such phrases were incorporated into the Cuban context, acquiring new and broader meanings. In a society that put great emphasis on reading and the production and circulation of books,[27] the book as an object became the bearer of a highly

27 After the Cuban Revolution of 1959, the government created new institutions and approved new laws to promote book production, such as the National Press House (1959–62); the Department of Literature and Publications of the National Council [of Culture] (1959–62); the National Publisher of Cuba (1962–67);

symbolic value—a "symbolic good", to use Bourdieu's term[28]—of belonging to an erudite group. Buying and accumulating books became a popular hobby, especially given that other hobbies were harder to support. But buying and accumulating books did not always mean reading them. Thus, many literary references of Socialist origin found their way into Cuba's culture, popular speech, and social imaginary not from the knowledge provided by reading, but from their inclusion in other forms of cultural production, such as radio, soap operas, or movies in what Itamar Even-Zohar has described as "indirect readers".

The direct consumption of *integral texts* has been, and remains, peripheral to the largest part of 'direct,' let alone 'indirect,' consumers of 'literature.' All members of any community are at least 'indirect' consumers of literary texts. In this capacity we, as such members, simply consume a certain quantity of literary fragments, digested, and transmitted by various agents of culture and made an integral part of daily discourse. Fragments of old narratives, idioms and allusions, parables and stock language, all, and many more, constitute the living repertoire stored in the warehouse of our culture.[29] In this sense, Soviet culture became a 'living repertoire' within Cuban culture, and found its way, directly and indirectly, into Cubans' daily lives.

Cuban translated editions of Socialist books comprised tens of thousands of copies, sometimes up to a hundred thousand; as a result, even if they were not read, these titles were part of the bibliographic heritage of many Cubans. Socialist literature in translation was more a reference than a direct source, and its influence was often mediated by its use in non-literary media. Although Soviet literature was published in Cuba on a massive scale by both Cuban and Soviet publishers, the popularity of many titles was made possible by their inclusion in other cultural forms, such as television and radio soap operas, movies, or plays. This might never have happened had they not been part of literary discourse in the first place. According to André Lefevere, translation has

---

Revolutionary Edition (1965–67); Casa de las Américas (1959); and the Union of Writers and Artists of Cuba (1961). For more information, see Jacqueline Laguardia Martínez, 'Industria editorial cubana: evolución y desarrollo' ('Cuban Publishing Industry: Evolution and Development'), in *Memorias. Feria Internacional del Libro de La Habana* (*Memories. Havana International Book Fair*) (Havana: Editorial Científico-Técnica, 2012), pp. 160–97. For example, between August 1960 and early April 1962, the National Press House printed 14,497,956 books; 26,463,600 brochures; and 22,579,882 magazines. See Pamela Maria Smorkaloff, *Literatura y edición de libros. La cultura literaria y el proceso social en Cuba, 1900–1987* (*Literature and Book Publishing: Literary Culture and the Social Process in Cuba, 1900–1987*) (Havana, Editorial Letras Cubanas, 1987), p. 140.

28 Pierre Bourdieu, *Capital cultural, escuela y espacio social*, trans. by Isabel Jimenez (Mexico City: Siglo XXI Editores, 2013).

29 Itamar Even-Zohar, 'The Literary System', in *Poetics Today*, 11:1 (Spring 1990), 27–44 (p. 36).

four specific purposes: communicating information, circulating cultural capital, entertaining, and convincing the reader to follow a certain course of action.[30] But these four functions are not the only ones possible. In the case of Socialist translation, as we suggest here, we might add a fifth or at least complicate the fourth: dissemination of Socialist ideology while providing a model of citizenship and society—or, in other words, circulating ideological capital.

Notes for a Conclusion

The arrival of Socialist revolution in Cuba allowed translation practices to become a political and ideological instrument. The material translated from Soviet Russian into Spanish was not limited to literary and scientific knowledge alone but, above all, pointed to a way of thinking about and understanding reality, a way of planning and trying to create a new society. We agree with Heilbron and Sapiro in describing the movement of world translations as irregular: "translation flows are highly uneven, flowing from the centre toward the periphery rather than the reverse [...] communication among peripheral languages very often passes through the intermediary of a centre" (96). We can conclude, however, that the dynamics driven by the Soviet Union not only sought to compete in the international market of cultural goods but mainly to challenge it by creating new ways of putting in circulation literary production from places left out of an international book market dominated by the West. As Susanna Witt notes, "[l]iterary translation in the Soviet Union may well be the largest more or less coherent project of translation the world has seen to date—largest in terms of geographical range, number of languages (and directions) involved and time span; coherent in the sense of ideological framework (given its fluctuations over time) and centralized planning".[31]

In this sense, the dynamics of translation created between the Soviet Union and Cuba defies the description that Heilbron and Sapiro have provided about the flows of translations. They have said: "[w]hile the dominant countries 'export' their cultural products widely and translate little into their languages, the dominated countries 'export' little and 'import' a lot of foreign books, principally by translation" (96). However, as demonstrated in this chapter, during the years of intense relations between Cuba and the Soviet Union, Cuban authors saw their literary works circulating in the (alternate) international book

30 André Lefevere, 'Translation Practice(s) and the Circulation of Cultural Capital. Some *Aeneids* in English', in *Constructing Cultures. Essays on Literary Translation*, ed. by Susan Bassnett and André Lefevere (Clevedon: Cromwell Press, 1998), pp. 41–56 (p. 41).

31 Susanna Witt, 'Between the Lines: Totalitarism and Translation in the USSR', in *Contexts, Subtexts, and Pretexts: Literary Translation in Eastern Europe and Russia*, ed. by Brian Baer (Amsterdam: John Benjamins Publishing Company, 2011), pp. 149–70 (p. 167).

market as never before or after. Although the number of publications of Soviet origin that circulated on the island was larger than the number of Cuban literary works translated into the Russian language, there was clearly an intention to reach quantitative equality between translations originating in each nation.

Although the effects of the influence of Soviet literary presence in Cuba have been fading since the 1990s, the door that the exchange between the two countries opened has allowed for a lasting flow of translating efforts and enterprises, sometimes at the individual level, both in Russia and in Cuba and Latin America. Almost six decades later, the remnants of Soviet presence in Cuba have been reduced to a cathartic afternoon in the cinema. But such a nostalgic moment ends once the audience steps back outside into a reality in which the Russian language and Socialist ideology are becoming more and more undefined and blurred. Its influence, however, was undeniable in the development of Cuban literature. Genres such as science fiction and detective novels were born and enriched because of the contact with Soviet literary works and until today we can find a considerable corpus where traces of Russian culture are evident.[32]

32 Many scholars have worked on the influence of the Soviet culture in Cuba. An essential bibliography would include Raúl Aguiar's article 'El futuro pertenece por entero al comunismo! Influencias del cine de ciencia ficción de la URSS y de otros países del este en el imaginario literario cubano' ('The Future Wholly Belongs To Communism! Influences of Science Fiction Cinema from the USRR and Other Nations on the Cuban Cultural Imaginary'), *Kamchatka*, 5 (2015), https://doi.org/10.7203/KAM.5.4619; Jacqueline Loss's study *Dreaming in Russian: The Cuban Soviet Imaginary* (Austin, TX: University of Texas Press, 2013); my own monograph *Escrito en cirílico* (2012), developed from my doctoral dissertation, 'Nieve sobre La Habana: El ideal soviético en la cultura cubana postnoventa' ('Snowing on Havana: The Soviet Ideal in post-1990 Cuban Culture') (University of Iowa, 2010), on Russian and Soviet influence on post-1990 Cuban cultural production; and José Miguel Sánchez's articles 'Lo que dejaron los rusos' ('What the Russians Left'), *Temas*, 37 (2004), 138–44 and 'Marcianos en el platanal de Bartolo: Análisis de la historia y perspectivas de la CF en Cuba' ('Martians in the Bartolo Plantation: Analysis of the History and Perspectives of SF in Cuba'), *StarDust* (2002), http://www.stardustcf.com/articulos.asp?arti=30; and Isabel Story's monograph, *When the Soviets Came To Stay: Soviet Influence on Cuban Culture, 1961–1987* (London and New York: Lexingon, 2020). There are also a number of useful unpublished doctoral dissertations on this topic, including Magdalena Matuskova, 'Cuban Cinema in a Global Context: The Impact of Eastern European Cinema on the Cuban Film Industry in the 1960s' (unpublished doctoral thesis, University of California, Los Angeles, 2017); and Vladimir Smith Mesa, 'KinoCuban: The Significance of Soviet and East European Cinemas for the Cuban Moving Image' (unpublished doctoral thesis, University College London, 2011).

Mexico

Three Stages in the Translation of Russian Literature in Mexico, 1921–2021[1]

Rodrigo García Bonillas

Introduction

This chapter offers an overview of the translation of Russian literature in Mexico during the century between 1921 and 2021. It develops three case studies of key figures in the intercultural process in question, in an attempt to provide a long-term vision of specific connections between Russian and Mexican literature from the 1920s almost to the time of writing. My methodological approach is 'microhistorical' insofar as my research seeks to expose the socio-cultural conjunction of personal experiences (essays, memoirs, interviews); infrastructure (state institutions, publishing houses, grants, prizes); and works (editions, collections).[2] Furthermore, this essay seeks to perceive all of these cases through the lens of the "sociology of translation".[3] The nature of each case study reveals characteristic stages of the uneven translation field from Russian

1 This research was carried out in the framework of my doctoral project 'Moscú por venir. Nueve escritores iberoamericanos en viaje al cosmos soviético (1920–1959)' ('Moscow to Come. Nine Ibero-American Writers on a Journey to the Soviet Cosmos (1920–1959)'), funded by the German Academic Exchange Service (Deutscher Akademischer Austauschdienst) and carried out at the University of Potsdam (Germany).

2 Jeremy Munday, 'Using Primary Sources to Produce a Microhistory of Translation and Translators: Theoretical and Methodological Concerns', *The Translator*, 20:1 (2014), 64–80, https://doi.org/10.1080/13556509.2014.899094.

3 Johan Heilbron and Gisèle Sapiro, 'Outline for a Sociology of Translation: Current Issues and Future Prospects', in *Constructing a Sociology of Translation*, ed. by

 https://doi.org/10.11647/OBP.0340.39

into (Mexican) Spanish. Firstly, its embodiment as a state and ideological undertaking, in Vladimir Maiakovskii's view of the cultural enterprise organised by the Mexican intellectual José Vasconcelos (1882–1959) during the latter's service as Rector of the National University of Mexico (1920–21) and Secretary of Public Education (1921–24), which stands as the major transformation of education and culture in post-Revolutionary Mexico.[4] Secondly, I will show translation as a conflation of diplomacy, literature, and travel, through the experience of author Sergio Pitol (who contributed to the 1955 Mexican edition of Maiakovskii's travelogue and also published an essay on José Vasconcelos). Finally, we will encounter translation as a professionalised contemporary task, methodically accomplished by Pitol's 'pupil', Selma Ancira. These three cases are distributed in the beginning, middle, and the end of the period studied; for each stage, I attempt to consider the most relevant agents that participated in the translation or circulation of Russian literary works in Mexico.[5]

Due to the relatively limited number of translators from Russian into Spanish in Mexico, the most important figures are easily distinguishable. For example, in the volume of interviews *By Trade, Translator. An Overview of Literary Translation in Mexico* (*De oficio, traductor. Panorama de la traducción literaria en México*, 2010), the only two translators from Russian into Spanish included are Ancira and Tatiana Bubnova.[6] Ancira, in turn, refers there to Sergio Pitol as her predecessor.[7] As we will see later, there were more translators working in this field besides Ancira and Bubnova. But by comparison with other Hispano-American metropolises (Madrid, Buenos Aires, or, after the Cuban Revolution, Havana) Mexico City did not play a prominent role in the direct translation of Russian literature into Spanish during the last century. Literary translations, either directly from Russian or indirectly through another European language, were typically, with few

---

Michaela Wolf and Alexandra Fukari (Amsterdam and Philadelphia, PA: John Benjamins, 2007), pp. 93–107, https://doi.org/10.1075/btl.74.07hei.

4 The National University of Mexico became the National Autonomous University of Mexico in 1929. The Secretariat of Public Education, created by Vasconcelos in 1921, is the official name for Mexico's Ministry for Education. It encompassed the fields of arts and culture until 2015, when the National Council for Culture and the Arts, formerly dependent on the Secretariat of Public Education, became a ministry in itself: the Secretariat of Culture.

5 For a regularly updated list of active translators of Russian literature in Mexico: 'Personas: Traductores', *Enciclopedia de la Literatura en México*, (n.d.), http://www.elem.mx/autores/f/1/a/tipo/3/tipo_lengua/INT/lengua/76.

6 Russo-Mexican scholar Tatiana Bubnova is the main translator and introducer of Mikhail Bakhtin in Mexico and, to an extent, in the wider Spanish-speaking world. I chose Ancira's case study instead of Bubnova's on account of the diversity of translated authors; the number of works translated from each author; and the wider network in terms of editions, institutions, and geographical zones.

7 *De oficio, traductor. Panorama de la traducción literaria en México*, ed. by Marianela Santoveña and others (Mexico City: Bonilla Artigas Editores and Consejo Nacional para la Cultura y las Artes, 2010), p. 280.

exceptions, disseminated in Mexico by foreign publishing houses during the first half of the twentieth century. In Mexico's National Library catalogue, for instance, one can find pre-1950 editions of Tolstoy from publishers J. S. Ogilvie (New York), E. Dentu (Paris), Perrin (Paris), América (Madrid), Naucci (Barcelona), Biblioteca Nueva (Madrid), or E. Bauza (Barcelona). In Dostoevsky's case, there are (rather fewer) editions from Espasa-Calpe (Madrid), Nelson (Paris), Bossard (Paris), Delamain & Boutelleau (Paris), or América (Madrid). In the second half of the twentieth century, Mexican institutions like Fondo de Cultura Económica or Editorial Siglo XXI adopted this task. Also, during the Cold War era, literary, political, and economic works of Russian origin circulated widely, but these were translated in the USSR through publishing houses like Ediciones en Lenguas Extranjeras (Izdatel'stvo Literatury na Inostrannykh Iazykakh), Editorial Progreso (Progress), or Editorial Raduga (Raduga). Even today there are no Mexican institutions or universities that hold departments, programmes, or chairs for the study of Slavic philology or for the professional training of translators from Slavic languages into Spanish, while these academic platforms can be found in other Ibero-American cities (São Paulo,[8] Buenos Aires,[9] Madrid, among others).[10] Similarly, no Mexican publishing house is (yet) specialised in translating Russian literature into Spanish.

Nonetheless, it cannot be said that Mexican literature or Mexican writers were not receptive to Russian literature, or that Mexico did not play a significant role in key events of Russian and Soviet history. Such events include the establishment of diplomatic relations in 1924 between the Soviet Union and Mexico (the first country in the Americas to recognise the former); political and cultural exchanges realised by individuals like Aleksandra Kollontai, Maiakovskii, Diego Rivera, Sergei Eisenstein, José Mancisidor, José Revueltas, David Alfaro Siqueiros, Victor Serge, and Efraín Huerta; and the granting of political asylum to Lev Trotskii (which ended fatally). Despite the relative scarcity of channels

8 "In that time [1960s] Prof. Boris Schnaiderman established the Graduation Course of Russian Language and Literature at the Philosophy, Literature and Humanities Faculty of the University of São Paulo, originally free, but officially recognised in 1963. In 1994 the Postgraduate Program of Russian Literature and Culture was recognised by University of São Paulo authorities [...]". See Milan Puh, 'Estudos eslavos no Brasil: Constitução de uma área', *Revista X*, 15:6 (2020), 674–97 (p. 680), https://revistas.ufpr.br/revistax/article/view/76848/42236. All translations are my own unless otherwise indicated. For more on Boris Schnaiderman, see Bruno B. Gomide's essay in this volume.

9 Such as the Chair of Slavic Literatures at the University of Buenos Aires.

10 So far, the first attempt in this direction has been the Russian Literature Seminar organised in 2021 by Mexican translators and scholars Mar Gámiz and Alfredo Hermosillo, and hosted by the Octavio Paz and Nikolai Gogol Extraordinary Chairs at San Ildefonso College (part of the National Autonomous University of Mexico) in Mexico City. See 'Seminario en Línea: Literatura rusa. Panorama crítico: desde sus orígenes hasta hoy en traducción al español', *Colegio de San Ildefonso* (2021), http://www.sanildefonso.org.mx/literaturarusa/.

for publication, Russian literature found various ways of circulating in Mexico, both in commercially run and publicly funded publishing houses. Moreover, at a crucial moment in Mexican history, Russian literature and Soviet strategy were a key inspiration for Mexican cultural agents, in particular for Vasconcelos, whose policies during the 1920s in the National University of Mexico and the Secretariat of Public Education forged institutions and programmes after the most turbulent years of the Mexican Revolution (1910–20):[11] firstly, the literacy plan launched during his time as Rector of the University; then, the creation of the Secretariat itself, which had diverse objectives, such as founding public schools and libraries, the reading-promotion campaign, updating educational programmes, arts patronage, or the publication of the book series 'The Classics'.

Post-Revolutionary Mexico

In his foundational essay 'On the Marvelous Real in America' (1949/1967; see note 13), Cuban writer Alejo Carpentier outlined an East-West axis in order to unravel the concept of the "marvelous real" as a cultural feature of Latin America where the extraordinary breaks into everyday life.[12] After confessing his lack of comprehension of China and the Islamic region (in particular, Iran), Soviet Russia was the first region where he was able to understand the local culture. The overlapping of European referents—and, to a lesser extent, of certain interventions in Russia by Latin American actors like the Venezuelan revolutionary Francisco de Miranda—enabled Carpentier to access certain Russian cultural milestones:

> On the way back from my long voyage, I found myself in the Soviet Union where, despite my inability to speak the language, my sense of incomprehension was entirely alleviated. [...] Pushkin made me think of *Boris Godunov*; I revised an unmusical French translation about thirty years ago at the request of a singer who had to play the role at

11 While 20 November 1910 is the exact date of the beginning of the Mexican revolution (coinciding with L. N. Tolstoy's death), the end is harder to identify with precision. Most historians date it around 1920. See Jaime Torres Bodet, *León Tolstói: su vida y su obra* (Mexico City: Porrúa, 1965), p. 9.

12 Later, in the 1975 lecture 'The Baroque and the Marvelous Real', Carpentier pointed out the differences between the 'marvellous real' as a cultural phenomenon and the 'magical realism' as the name of an artistic current coined by the German art critic Franz Roh in the mid-1920s. Furthermore, Carpentier also integrates the Latin American *Boom* in his conceptual history of the American baroque. Carpentier qualifies here the 'marvelous real' as the "unusual" or "unwonted" ("insólito"). Alejo Carpentier, 'The Baroque and the Marvelous Real', in *Magical Realism. Theory, History, Community*, ed. by Lois Parkinson Zamora and Wendy B. Faris, trans. by Tanya Huntington and Lois Parkinson Zamora (Durham, NC, and London: Duke University Press, 1995), pp. 89–108.

> the Columbus Theater in Buenos Aires. Turgenev was Flaubert's friend [...]. I discovered Dostoevsky in an essay by André Gide. I read Tolstoy's stories for the first time around 1920, in an anthology compiled by the Mexican Department of Education.[13]

In Vasconcelos's lecture campaign during the 1920s, Tolstoy was one of the three main contemporary writers championed; the other two were Benito Pérez Galdós (Spain) and Romain Rolland (France).[14] This is why some of Tolstoy's work was disseminated throughout Mexico and beyond, and why Carpentier obtained an anthology of his writing (presumably, his short stories, as we will see later). Like many other intellectuals from Latin America, Carpentier encountered Russian literature mainly through French intermediaries, whether writers, translators, or essayists. With France perceived as the centre of the "world republic of letters" at the turn of the nineteenth century, as Pascale Casanova asserts (following Fernand Braudel),[15] Russian literature started flowing into Latin America through French channels. Tolstoy's novels were introduced to Brazil indirectly, through the translation into Portuguese of French diplomat Eugène-Melchior de Vogüé's study *The Russian Novel* (*Le Roman russe*) (1886).[16] In the Spanish-speaking world the Spanish novelist Emilia Pardo Bazán's *The Revolution and the Novel in Russia* (*La revolución y la novela en Rusia*, 1887) stands as the pioneering work in this field. Unlike de Vogüé, Pardo Bazán did not understand Russian and her lectures about Russian novels were based on French translations; she also relied on de Vogüé's book as one of her main sources.[17] Nevertheless, the

---

13 Alejo Carpentier, 'On the Marvelous Real in America', in *Magical Realism*, pp. 75–88 (pp. 79–80). Parkinson Zamora and Faris explain in their 'Editor's Note' that "Part of ['On the Marvelous Real in America'] served to preface Carpentier's first novel, *El reino de este mundo* (*The Kingdom of this World*, 1949); we have translated an expanded version of that prologue, which was published in 1967 in a collection of Carpentier's essays, *Tientos y diferencias* (*Approaches and Distinctions*)" (pp. 75–76).

14 Claude Fell quotes Vasconcelos: "If we examine contemporary intellectual production, we find three major figures that the University advertises to attract public attention, three visionaries whose doctrines should flood the Mexican soul: Benito Pérez Galdós, Romain Rolland, and Leo Tolstoy." See Claude Fell, *José Vasconcelos. Los años del águila (1920–1925). Educación, cultura e iberoamericanismo en el México postrevolucionario*, trans. by María Palomar (Mexico City: Universidad Nacional Autónoma de México, 1989), p. 34.

15 Pascale Casanova, *La república mundial de las letras*, trans. by Jaime Zulaika (Barcelona: Anagrama, 2001), p. 23.

16 Bruno Gomide, *Da estepe à caatinga: O romance russo no Brasil (1887–1936)* (São Paulo: Universidade de São Paulo, 2011), p. 17. See also Elizabeth Geballe's essay in the present volume.

17 Francisca González Arias, 'La condesa, la revolución y la novela en Rusia', *Bulletin Hispanique*, 96:1 (1994), 167–88 (p. 168).

sources of many of Pardo Bazán's less original ideas were not always explicitly identified, and this provoked harsh attacks on her book.[18]

During the 1920s, the first cultural institutions created after the Mexican Revolution set in motion a major transformation of educational and artistic fields. Soviet and Russian thought had a significant impact on the Mexican intellectual José Vasconcelos (1882–1959), and consequently on the wider cultural enterprise.[19] After the foundation of the Ministry of Public Education during Álvaro Obregon's presidency (1920–24) on 10 October 1921, Vasconcelos took office as Minister of Education. His work was so challenging that it has since been considered a "cultural crusade".[20] For a long time, Vasconcelos gained the epithet '*El Maestro*' (both 'teacher' and 'master').[21] Sergio Pitol, who met Vasconcelos in person, also pointed out:

> José Vasconcelos was the main source of the Revolution's national and international prestige: the nation's educator, an apostle of printed literature, a thinker, and, above all, the creator of an authentic and extraordinary cultural Renaissance in the country, an effort where all his gifts and distinctions came together. Even now, we are immensely indebted to the cultural renewal movement he undertook seventy years ago. Education at all levels and diffusion of books stood as a national cause during that period.[22]

In the high tide of post-revolutionary cultural transformation, Vladimir Maiakovskii visited the Americas. Maiakovskii was the first outstanding figure of Russian literature to travel to Mexico and write about it.[23] In his travelogue

---

18 This point is thoroughly exposed in Cristina Patiño Eirín, '*La revolución y la novela en Rusia*, de Emilia Pardo Bazán, y *Le roman russe*, de Eugène Melchior de Vogüé, en el círculo de la intertextualidad', in *Estudios sobre Emilia Pardo Bazán. In memoriam Maurice Hemingway*, ed. by José Manuel González Herrán (Santiago de Compostela: Universidad de Santiago de Compostela and Consorcio de Santiago de Compostela, 1997), pp. 239–67. See also Margaret Tejerizo's essay in the present volume.

19 See Fabio Moraga Valle, 'Las ideas pedagógicas de Tolstói y Tagore en el proyecto vasconcelista de educación, 1921–1964', *Historia Mexicana*, 65.3 (2016), 1341–404, http://www.scielo.org.mx/scielo.php?script=sci_arttext&pid=S2448-65312016000301341#fn25.

20 The word 'crusade' was used by Vasconcelos himself (both in a political and religious sense) and it became commonly associated with his work in the early 1920s and to the educational programme he designed. See Fell, *José Vasconcelos*, p. 19, p. 83, p. 119, p. 228; Christopher Domínguez Michael, 'José Vasconcelos, padre de los bastardos', in José Vasconcelos, *Ulises criollo*, ed. by Claude Fell (Madrid: ALLCA XX, 2000), pp. 984–1066 (p. 1006, p. 1011, p. 1013).

21 Sergio Pitol, 'Ulises criollo', in Vasconcelos, *Ulises*, pp. xix-xxxiii (p. xx).

22 Ibid., p. xxiv.

23 See Luis Mario Schneider, *Dos poetas rusos en México: Balmont y Maiakovski* (Mexico City: Sepsetentas, 1973); William Richardson, *Mexico through Russian Eyes*,

My Discovery of America (*Moe otrkytie Ameriki*, 1926), he briefly addressed the subject of the circulation of Russian and Soviet literature in Mexico.[24] Maiakovskii could not understand Spanish. Hence, whatever he read about US-American or Mexican poetry would have been translated by someone else. However, some sarcastic comments on Mexican poetry and poets appeared in *My Discovery of America*. He was surprised to find that the translation of Russian literature in Mexico was a recent phenomenon:

> Russian literature is liked and admired, although largely by hearsay. They are now translating (!) [seichas perevodiatsia] Lev Tolstoy and Chekhov, and of newer things I have only seen Blok's *The Twelve* and my *Left March*.[25]

Most of the Spanish translations of Tolstoy circulating in Mexico in the years before Maiakovskii's journey to the Americas came from publishers based in Madrid, Barcelona, Valencia, or Buenos Aires. There were some exceptions. *Kholstomer: The History of a Horse* (*Kholstomer*, 1886; *Kolstomero*) appeared from the Mexican publishing house Ballestá in 1910, the year of the rise of the Revolution, while *Two Old Men* (*Dva starika*, 1885; *Los dos viejos y otros cuentos*) was edited by Cvltvra in 1922, with an essay by Dominican intellectual Max Henríquez Ureña. Cvltvra was an editorial project that was created in 1916 as a consequence of the armed conflicts during the 1910s and the necessity of editorial independence from Spain.[26]

For comparison, Anton Chekhov's writings were available from the Madrid-based Calpe publishing house (soon to merge with Espasa to become the influential publisher Espasa-Calpe) and other Spanish publishers. In 1922, Calpe published an anthology of Chekhov stories translated directly from Russian by Saturnino Ximénez, as *Historia de una anguila y otros cuentos* (*The Eel and Other Stories*).[27] N. Tasin (the pseudonym of Naum Iakovlevich Kagan)[28]

1806–1940 (Pittsburgh, PA: University of Pittsburgh Press, 1988), pp. 127–40.

24 I deal extensively with Maiakovskii's trip to Mexico in *Guerras floridas. Viajes poéticos de Vladímir Maiakovski y Efraín Huerta entre México y Moscú* (Xalapa: Universidad Veracruzana, 2021).

25 Maiakovskii, *My Discovery of America*, trans. by Neil Cornwell (London: Hesperus, 2005), p. 18.

26 The information about Cvltvra comes from Freja I. Cervantes Becerril's entry 'Cvltvra', *Enciclopedia de la Literatura en México*, (2018), http://www.elem.mx/institucion/datos/1512.

27 The first short story of this anthology is 'The Fish' (in Russian, 'Nalim', literally, a burbot). The Calpe anthology can be read online: Anton Chekhov, 'Historia de una anguila y otras historias', *Wikisource* (2021), https://es.wikisource.org/wiki/Historia_de_una_anguila_y_otras_historias.

28 See Tatiana Gritzai Bielova, 'N. Tasin y la España de la Edad de Plata', *Repositorio Institucional de la Universidad Complutense de Madrid* (2020), https://eprints.ucm.es/id/eprint/59312/.

and the Mexican intellectual and diplomat Alfonso Reyes co-translated Chekhov's *Ward No. 6* (*Palata No. 6*, 1892; *La sala número 6*), also published by Calpe in 1919.[29] During the 1920s, Reyes was Mexican Ambassador to France. Maiakovskii met Reyes in Paris before the former's journey to the Americas; they discussed Mexican art, as Maiakovskii reported in *My Discovery of America*. He described Reyes as a "novelist", although by that point the only fiction Reyes had published was the short story collection *The Oblique Plane* (*El plano oblicuo*, 1920). Might they have talked about Chekhov's *Ward No. 6*? I have not yet found any Mexican-oriented edition prior to 1925.

In 1923, under the imprint of the National University of Mexico, a volume of Tolstoy's *Selected Short Stories* (*Cuentos escogidos*) appeared in the former's book series 'The Classics' (Los Clásicos) with its distinctive green covers. The name of the translator is not given; only the following footnote is added to the first short story:

> From the translations published in this volume, the following ones were done directly from Russian: 'Two Deaths' [*sic*], 'Polikushka', 'The Death of Ivan Il'ich', 'Where Love is, God Is', 'How Much Land Does a Man Need?' [translated into Spanish as 'Pakhom el mújik', that is, 'Pakhom the Muzhik']. The versions of the other short stories included were carefully reviewed and checked against the Russian text.[30]

This series was conceived and promoted by José Vasconcelos, following what he considered the most essential books for educating the Mexican reader:

> In the same way that the Russians edit at that time the most relevant works of the human spirit and the artworks of their novelistic literature, Vasconcelos ascribes an ambivalent vocation to his editorial policy: to choose 'essential' books and to open the national spirit to the most recent currents of thought.[31]

It was meant to be the first attempt in Mexican history to create a state-run corpus of 'universal' works to be distributed *en masse* among the Mexican population at a low price. Besides Tolstoy's *Selected Short Stories*, an edition of the Gospels (Evangelios, 1923) included Tolstoy's 'What Is the Gospel?' (*Kratkoe izlozhenie Evangeliia*, 1883; '¿Qué es el evangelio'),[32] while *Exemplary Lives* (*Vidas ejemplares*,

29 Herón Pérez Martínez, 'Alfonso Reyes y la traducción en México', *Relaciones. Estudios de Historia y Sociedad*, 14.56 (1993), 27–74 (pp. 35, 70), https://www.colmich.edu.mx/relaciones25/files/revistas/056/HeronPerezMartinez.pdf.

30 Lev Tolstoi, *Cuentos escogidos* (Mexico City: Universidad Nacional Autónoma de México, 1923), p. 4.

31 Fell, *José Vasconcelos*, p. 485.

32 Cortés Bandala includes the titles of Tolstoy's writings, which appeared as an appendix to Juan de Valdés and Casiodoro de Reina's translation of the

1923), written by Romain Rolland, featured a *Life of Tolstoy* (*Vie de Tolstoï*, 1911; *Vida de Tolstói*) together with Rolland's lives of Beethoven (1903) and Michelangelo (1907). Other authors in the series (there were seventeen in total) included works by Homer (three volumes), Aeschylus, Euripides, Plutarch (two volumes), Plato (three volumes), Plotino, Dante Alighieri, Johann Wolfgang von Goethe, and Rabindranath Tagore.[33] It is not clear whether Maiakovskii had these editions in mind when he wrote about the Mexican translations of Tolstoy in the making back then, but, given the scope of Vasconcelos's project, it is highly likely that he meant some of the green 'Clásicos' editions, which local intellectuals probably presented to him as part of the new reading campaign. The Mexican painter Diego Rivera was Maiakovskii's guide during his Mexican journey. In his company, the Soviet poet visited Rivera's murals at the Secretariat of Public Education in Mexico City. This building used to be Vasconcelos's office until 1924 and also the epicentre of Mexican 'muralism': some of the masterpieces of this nationalist, state-funded and internationally acclaimed public art movement were painted on its walls. The Secretariat itself sponsored the works. Maiakovskii considered it "the world's first communist mural".[34]

In its turn, the reading campaign spearheaded by Vasconcelos had been inspired by the projects of Maksim Gorky and Anatolii Lunacharskii.[35] Years later, Vasconcelos evoked that time:

> In cafes and in humble diners we spent long hours discussing Lenin's methods or the novelties in education that Lunacharskii had introduced. I copied one of them when I had to direct education in Mexico: the edition of [literary] classics [...][36]

Gospel: 'What Is the Gospel?' ('¿Qué es el evangelio?'), 'What Does the Gospel Announce?' ('¿Qué anuncia el evangelio?'), 'God's Kingdom' ('El reino de Dios'), 'The Evil's Temptation' ('La tentación del maligno'), 'Bible and Gospel' ('Biblia y Evangelio'), 'Do Not Resist the Evil, Forgive' ('No resistáis al mal, perdonad'), 'All as Brothers' ('Todos hermanos'), 'The True Life' ('La verdadera vida'), 'Be like Children' ('Sed como los niños'), 'Jesus and the Sinner Woman' ('Jesús y la pecadora'), 'Conclusion' ('Conclusión'). The translator's name does not appear in this edition. See Yazmín Liliana Cortés Bandala, 'Análisis del proyecto editorial vasconcelista (1921–1924)' (unpublished master's thesis, Universidad Nacional Autónoma de México, 2009), p. 210.

33 For an electronic facsimile edition of the books: 'Clásicos verdes', *Gobierno de México* (1921), https://www.conaliteg.sep.gob.mx/clasicos_verdes.html?fbclid=IwAR0iqrs-9KsLhu0d9itYn2ZggVpbEKFpZcn1q0A7uXQFOhrQ5yeRUPUqbr0. See also Fell, *José Vasconcelos*, p. 490.

34 Maiakovskii, *My Discovery*, p. 17.

35 See Fell, *José Vasconcelos*, p. 21; Cortés Bandala, 'Análisis del proyecto', pp. 148–59.

36 Vasconcelos, *La creación de la Secretaría de Educación Pública*, ed. by Carlos Betancourt Cid (Mexico City: Instituto Nacional de Estudios Históricos de las Revoluciones en México, 2011), pp. 19–20, https://inehrm.gob.mx/work/models/inehrm/Resource/493/1/images/vasconcelos.pdf. Also quoted by Cortés Bandala, 'Análisis del proyecto', p. 148.

With regards to Soviet-era literature, Aleksandr Blok's 'The Twelve' ('Dvenadtsat', 1918) was published in 1922 by Cvltvra, in Salomon Kahan and Gabino A. Palma's translation and prologue, collected in the same volume with *The Song of the Hawk* (*Pesnia o sokole*, 1895) and *The Song of the Stormy Petrel* (*Pesnia o burevestnike*, 1901) by Maksim Gorky. This is probably the Blok edition to which Maiakovskii refers. Kahan himself published two versions of poems by Maiakovskii—'Our March' ('Nash marsh', 1918) and 'March to the Left' ('Levyi marsh', 1918), also co-translated with Gabino A. Palma—and an article, 'Russian Poetry of the Revolution versus "Aesthetic" Poetry (On the Occasion of Maiakovskii's Poems)'.[37] Kahan's translations and this article appeared in the August issue of Vasconcelian magazine *Torch* (*Antorcha*),[38] one month after the Russian poet left Mexico. It is therefore plausible that Maiakovskii and Kahan had met, or at least that a mutual acquaintance had informed Maiakovskii about Kahan's translation of 'The Twelve'.

The initial print run of Vasconcelos's Classics series was between twenty and twenty-five thousand copies per title. It was a large number by Mexican standards of that time,[39] and it allowed the still largely illiterate Mexican population mass access to so-called 'universal literature' through public libraries. Nevertheless, in the case of books imported and translated from other languages and cultures, the source editions and their translations were not always clear. Copyright was often violated: "The first volumes of 'The Classics' series (Homer, Aeschylus, Euripides, Plato, Plutarch, Dante) were published using translations from Spain and a little bit [*sic*] pirated".[40] If Lunacharskii's policies were "copied", translations were often used without paying attention to copyright, due to the urgency of the task.[41]

Sergio Pitol

My second case study is the dissemination of Slavic and Russian Literature in the Spanish-speaking world by Mexican writer and diplomat Sergio Pitol

37 Maiakovskii, 'Nuestra marcha', 'Marcha a la izquierda', both trans. by Salomón Kahan and Gabino A. Palma in *Antorcha. Revista Mexicana de Cultura Moderna*, 2:1 (August 1925), 21 and 21–22 respectively; and Salomón Kahan, 'La poesía rusa de la Revolución frente a la poesía "estética" (con motivo de los poemas de Vladímir Mayakofsky)' in *Antorcha. Revista Mexicana de Cultura Moderna*, 2:1 (August 1925), 17–20. See also Schneider, 'Dos poetas rusos', pp. 24–28.

38 Claude Fell, 'Un premier bilan culturel de la Révolution mexicaine: la revue *La Antorcha* (1924–1925) de José Vasconcelos', *América. Cahiers du CRICCAL*, 4–5 (1990), 97–110, https://www.persee.fr/doc/ameri_0982-9237_1990_num_4_1_973.

39 For information on the print run of the series: Fell, *José Vasconcelos*, pp. 488–89.

40 Claude Fell, 'L'État, le livre et la lecture au Mexique, au lendemain de la révolution', *América*, 23, 37–50 (p. 44).

41 Cortés Bandala also discusses this point: see 'Análisis del proyecto', pp. 131–32.

(1933–2018) in the last decades of the twentieth century.[42] Pitol belonged to the so-called Mid-Century Generation, during which the country's modernisation also affected its literature, towards the end of the 1940s. This generation was a turning point in relation to Mexico's Revolutionary ideology in the cultural realm:

> Interest in the revolutionary strife and related social topics had started a definitive decline in the diverse artistic spheres—painting, music, literature. [...] 1950 [...] was a crucial year, we can say that it was a watershed in Mexican culture. It is the moment when certain openly avant-garde lines start to be strongly defined at the expense of the nationalist discourse that marked the previous decades.[43]

After his unsuccessful campaign in the presidential elections in 1929, Vasconcelos went into exile. The members of the Mid-Century Generation matured in an era of political change during the 1930s and 1940s. The nationalist policies conducted by President Lázaro Cárdenas (1934–40) were reversed by Miguel Alemán's openness to foreign capital investment and his efforts to modernise the country in the early 1940s.

Pitol was born in the city of Puebla in 1933 and spent his childhood within a bilingual community of Italian immigrants in the state of Veracruz. Contact with foreign languages and literature played a significant role for him during these years. Before coming of age, he moved to Mexico City and, some years later, he entered the National Autonomous University of Mexico to study law. There, in university circles, he met some of the intellectuals and artists who would form the Mid-Century Generation. In 1955, Pitol and some of his colleagues published Elvira Nieto's translation of the Mexican section of Maiakovskii's travelogue in the left-wing magazine *Course* (*Cauce*). Nationalist ideologues harassed them for this publication since, in *My Discovery of America*, Maiakovskii harshly criticised Mexican reality.[44] This situation was symptomatic of the intergenerational conflict prevalent in the intellectual field during the 1950s. At the end of that

42 See *Victorio Ferri se hizo mago en Viena. Sobre Sergio Pitol*, ed. by Teresa García Díaz (Xalapa: Universidad Veracruzana, 2007).

43 My information about the Mid-Century Generation comes from: Armando Pereira's article 'La generación del medio siglo: un momento de transición de la cultura mexicana', *Literatura Mexicana*, 6:1 (1995), 187–212 (p. 192, pp. 196–97), https://revistas-filologicas.unam.mx/literatura-mexicana/index.php/lm/article/view/178/178.

44 For more research on this episode and the short life of *Cauce*, see Mario Alberto Carrillo Ramírez Valenzuela, 'El traductor en fuga. La práctica traductora y el pensamiento traductor de Sergio Pitol' (unpublished master's thesis, El Colegio de México, 2019), pp. 24–25, https://repositorio.colmex.mx/concern/theses/vq27zn76k?locale=es; and José Luis González Baena, 'El episodio *Cauce*: nacionalismo, guerra fría y literatura en México, 1955', *Revista Iberoamericana*, 87: 276 (2021), 835–51.

decade, Pitol published his first collection of short stories in Mexico: *Enclosed Time* (*Tiempo cercado*, 1959).[45] In 1960, he joined the diplomatic service and went to live abroad for the next twenty-eight years.

Pitol's most celebrated publications between the late 1950s and the 2000s comprised Spanish translations of dozens of literary masterpieces written originally in English, Italian, Polish, Chinese, Hungarian, and Russian. In addition to translating Chekhov, Boris Pil'niak, and Vladimir Nabokov, he wrote several essays about Russian writers and a book of memoirs devoted to his Russian experience, *The Journey* (*El viaje*, 2000),[46] in which he conflates his personal experience with certain dramatic episodes of Russian history (for instance, Marina Tsvetaeva's biography). In 2005, Pitol received the Cervantes Prize—the most important literary award in the Spanish-speaking realm—for his literary achievements. That year he published the autofictional book *The Magician of Vienna* (*El mago de Viena*), his last masterpiece and the final volume in his internationally acclaimed *Trilogía de la memoria* (*Trilogy of Memory*).

Pitol's case is exceptional for Mexico in that he combines the activities of translation and writing, impressing Spanish-speaking readers with his high-quality work.[47] In this sense, his essays build a bridge with the linguistic communities from which he translates. In 1989, for instance, he included notes on Pil'niak in his collection of essays *The House of the Tribe* (*La casa de la tribu*), edited by the Mexican publishing house Fondo de Cultura Económica. There, Pil'niak is portrayed as "the first and most original great narrator of the Revolution".[48] His narrative is deeply analysed by Pitol not only in terms of plot and historical context, but also in terms of its style and structure. Therefore, a reflection on these topics made by one of the greatest Mexican narrators of the last century exposes the internal mechanisms of Pil'niak's narrative. Pitol's knowledge of this mechanism was obtained not only from close reading, but also from translating some of Pil'niak's works. Ultimately, this sort of knowledge would influence his own writing: "I do not know better teaching to structure

45 Sergio Pitol, *Tiempo cercado* (Mexico City: Editorial Estaciones, 1959).

46 For the English version of the book, see Sergio Pitol, *The Journey*, trans. by George Henson (Dallas, TX: Deep Vellum, 2015).

47 Other writers of the Mid-Century Generation also translated relevant works of literature from French, English, and German: "Juan García Ponce translated, to name a few, Herbert Marcuse and Pierre Klossowski; Salvador Elizondo translated James Joyce, Malcolm Lowry, Ezra Pound, Ernest Fenollosa, Paul Valéry; Tomás Segovia translated Victor Hugo, Gérard de Nerval, Rimbaud and Bonnefoy; Ulalume González de León translated Lewis Carroll, e.e. cummings, Elizabeth Bishop; Esther Sellingson translated E. M. Cioran and Robert Musil" (see Carrillo Ramírez, 'El traductor en fuga', pp. 23–24).

48 Sergio Pitol, *La casa de la tribu* (Mexico City: Fondo de Cultura Económica, 1989), p. 51.

a novel than translation", he said once.[49] The affinities between the works he used to translate as a 'freelancer' and those that influenced his writing led the Mexican poet and translator Francisco Segovia to this conclusion:

> [...] he surely proposed the works [to be translated] to the editor, and not the other way around. This explains that Pitol became very soon not only the translator, but also the promoter of a series of writers little-known, poorly known, or [completely] unknown in the Spanish-speaking world, especially some Slavic-language writers from Eastern Europe, and more particularly Poland.[50]

Pitol worked at the Embassy of Mexico in Moscow from 1977 to 1980.[51] In Russia, he learned the language, wrote short stories, and started translating Pil'niak's *Mahogany* (*Krasnoe derevo*, 1929) and Chekhov's *The Shooting Party* (*Drama na okhote*, 1884).[52] His immersion in Russian culture led him to meet intellectuals like Viktor Shklovskii, "whom he visited many times",[53] and to deliver an impressive corpus of lectures on literature and theory: Russian Formalism, Angelo Maria Ripellino's essays on Slavic literature, Mikhail Bakhtin's *Rabelais and His World* (*Tvorchestvo François Rabelais i narodnaia kul'tura srednevekov'ia i Renessansa*, 1965), as well as every major Russian author. After he moved to Czechoslovakia in 1983 to serve as Ambassador for Mexico, Pitol increased his knowledge of Slavic literatures and languages. In *The Journey* he recalls:

> When I arrived at Prague, I looked for a Russian teacher. A formidable Czech lady was recommended to me. I read literary texts, I talked with her in that language and we did translation exercises.[54]

During his time in Prague, Pitol published his translations of Chekhov's *The Shooting Party* (*Un drama de caza*, 1985) and Pil'niak's *Mahogany* (*Caoba*, 1987) with the Spanish publishers Alianza Editorial and Anagrama respectively. As one of Mexico's most widely translated authors himself, Pitol's own work was already available in Russian by the 1980s. In the Soviet Union, one of his short stories 'Amelia Otero' (1959) was translated for the 1982 volume *Mexican Short Stories* (*Meksikanskie rasskazi*), which included fiction by Juan Rulfo and Juan José

49 Quoted by Francisco Segovia, *Detrás de las palabras* (*reflexiones en torno a la tramoya de la lengua*) (Mexico City: El Colegio de México, 2017), p. 107. Luz Fernández de Alba pointed in this direction (Carrillo Ramírez, 'El traductor en fuga', p. 127).

50 Segovia, *Detrás de las palabras*, p. 103.

51 Carrillo Ramírez, 'El traductor en fuga', p. 50.

52 Alejandro Hermosilla Sánchez, *Sergio Pitol: las máscaras del viajero. Caleidoscopios, lentes fractales y territorios asimétricos de la literatura mexicana: la danza en el laberinto* (Xalapa: Universidad Veracruzana, 2012), p. 74.

53 Carrillo Ramírez, 'El traductor en fuga', p. 50.

54 Sergio Pitol, *El viaje* (Mexico City: Era, 2000), p. 9.

Arreola, Elena Poniatowska and Rosario Castellanos, and even Vasconcelos.[55] Three years later, the Soviet publishing house Raduga published another anthology, *The Mexican Novel: The 1980's*, where Pitol's novel *Floral Games* (*Juegos florales*, 1982) was included with three stories by the authors Carlos Fuentes, René Avilés Fabila, and José Emilio Pacheco. The foreword to the anthology states that Pitol "during his diplomatic service, [...] lived in many European countries, dedicating himself to literary translation".[56]

In 1988, Pitol left diplomatic service and moved back to Mexico permanently. There he finished his translation of Nabokov's *The Defence* (*Zashchita Luzhina*, 1930; *La defensa*), published in 1990 by Anagrama, with whose founder, Jorge Herralde, Pitol had a good relationship. Over the next decade, he kept writing and received several important literary awards, including the National Prize for Arts and Sciences (Literature and Linguistics) from Mexico in 1993, and the Mazatlan Prize for his book *The Art of Flight* (*El arte de la fuga*, 1996) in 1997. Both his fiction and non-fiction were praised; his translations were well received in Mexico, Spain, and other Spanish-speaking countries. In terms of the quality of his versions, the diversity of the languages which he translated from, and the wide-ranging impact on his readers, Pitol represents an unusual type of translator in Mexican literature. In this respect, Mario Alberto Carrillo Ramírez's thesis (see note 44) presents a comprehensive history of Pitol's translations based on Itamar Even-Zohar's polysystem theory and compares Pitol's "scarce reflexions on translation" with those of other relevant Mexican translators (most of them, central figures of the Mexican literature from the twentieth century): Aurelio Garzón del Camino, Alfonso Reyes, Octavio Paz, Juan García Ponce, and Salvador Elizondo. However, extensive research on Pitol's translation techniques from Russian into Spanish is yet to be undertaken.

In a point-by-point comparison between the Russian text of *Mahogany* and Pitol's translation, we note that Pil'niak's prose style is often enhanced in Pitol's version with more elegant vocabulary, the use of additional words to translate a single term, and occasional additions to the original. For instance, this sentence from *Mahogany* reads:

> [E]ti krendeli ukrashali byt so dnei vozniknoveniia Rusi, ot pervykh tsarei Ivanov, byt russkogo tysiachelet'ia.

Vera T. Reck and Michael Green translate the sentence into English this way:

55 *Meksikanskie rasskazi*, ed. by Vera Kuteishchikova (Leningrad: Khudozhestvennaia Literatura, 1982).

56 *Meksikanskaia povest', 80-e gody: sbornik*, trans. by M. Bylinkina and others (Moscow: Raduga, 1985), p. 3.

> [T]hese sugar cakes have adorned everyday life from Russia's very beginnings, from the time of the first Tsar Ivans, the everyday life of Russia's thousand years.[57]

Pitol translated the same passage in a very peculiar way:

> [T]ales especies han sido el condimento de la vida rusa desde sus orígenes, desde los tiempos del primer zar Iván y han engalanado un milenio de vida nacional.[58]

I will try to render here Pitol's into English as literally as possible:

> [S]uch species have been the spice of Russian life since its origins, since the time of the first Tsar Ivan, and they have embellished one millennium of national life.

Some of Pitol's lexical choices are inaccurate: "species" avoids a precise equivalent for the Russian-baked product "krendeli" while "have been the spice" is more awkward than "have adorned" (the latter being closer to the original, although it is likely that he had tried here to hint at the *krendel*'s salty taste). The plural "Ivans" is also lost in Pitol's translation; thence, the historical reference to multiple rulers is compressed by the translator's focus on just one Tsar with that name, perhaps the notorious Ivan IV (the Terrible). He introduces an alien word ("engalanado", that is, "embellish", more semantically related to "ukrashali") in the last phrase, while the adjective "Russian" ("russkii") is not reiterated, but translated as "national". Other passages from Pitol's Spanish version of *Mahogany* also betray his grandiloquent personal style.

Pitol's fame increased after receiving the Cervantes Prize in 2005. From 1992 onwards, Pitol held a researcher position at the University of Veracruz's Institute of Linguistic-Literary Research, where he taught at the Department of Spanish Literature.[59] In 2007, the University launched the 'Sergio Pitol, Translator' ('Sergio Pitol Traductor') book imprint, which now includes twenty Pitol translations. Authors translated in this series include Jerzy Andrzejewski (twice), Jane Austen, Kazimierz Brandys (twice), Chekhov, Joseph Conrad, Tibor Déry, Ronald Firbank, Ford Madox Ford, Robert Graves, Witold Gombrowicz (twice), Lu Hsun, Henry James (three times), Malcolm Lowry,

57 For the Russian text, see Pil'niak, *Krasnoe derevo* (Berlin: Petropolis Verlag, 1929), p. 7. For the English version: Pil'niak, *Chinese Story and Other Tales*, trans. by Vera T. Reck and Michael Green (Norman, OK and London: University of Oklahoma, 1988), pp. 103–50 (p. 117).

58 Boris Piln'iak, 'Caoba', in *Pedro, Su Majestad, Emperador*, trans. by Sergio Pitol (Xalapa: Universidad Veracruzana, 2013), pp. 95–160 (p. 97).

59 Carrillo Ramírez, 'El traductor en fuga', p. 51.

Luigi Malerba, and Pil'niak.[60] According to articles and reviews analysed by Carrillo Ramírez, Pitol's reception as a translator differs radically. Some scholars like Rodolfo Mendoza, who manages the imprint,[61] consider Pitol an accurate translator because he conveyed the essence of the original; others, like Agustín del Moral, argue that Pitol's style overshadows the original text. Taking into account Lawrence Venuti's translation theory and his reflections on the "invisibility of the translator", Carrillo Ramírez concludes: "[t]o Del Moral, Pitol is a translator that becomes visible in his translations, while to Mendoza [...] he becomes invisible".[62] In view of the passage from *Mahogany* analysed above, Del Moral's opinion seems apt.

Ancira's Russian 'Odyssey': 1984–2021

My third case study concerns the industrious translation endeavour of Selma Ancira (b. 1956), which has now been maintained for forty years and which includes more than seventy titles, making her today's most prominent Russian-to-Spanish Mexican translator. Many of Tolstoy's and Tsvetaeva's complete works are now available in Spanish thanks to her labour.[63] Her translation corpus includes books by Aleksandr Pushkin and Nina Berberova, Osip Mandel'stam and Mikhail Bulgakov; and a personal anthology: *Capricious Landscape of Russian Literature* (*Paisaje caprichoso de la literatura rusa*, 2012), published by Fondo de Cultura Económica.[64] In an essay praising Ancira, Segovia observes her exceptional situation in the landscape of literary translation:

> [N]o translator that I know has had the fortune of earning a living by translating just what pleases him or her. [...] Usually, those who translate for pleasure do not translate professionally, and those who

60 For the series catalogue, see 'Libros. Catálogo general. Sergio Pitol Traductor', *Universidad Veracruzana*, (n.d.), http://libros.uv.mx/index.php/UV/catalog/series/SP.

61 For Mendoza's testimony on the conception of this collection, see Diego Salas, 'Entrevista con Rodolfo Mendoza, director de la colección Sergio Pitol Traductor', *Tierra Adentro*, (2016), https://www.tierraadentro.cultura.gob.mx/entrevista-con-rodolfo-mendoza-director-de-la-coleccion-sergio-pitol-traductor/. There Mendoza claims: "As far as I know, there is no other collection, at least in Spanish, devoted to the work of a single translator, although we have such skilled translators in Spanish".

62 Carrillo Ramírez, 'El traductor en fuga', p. 81; Lawrence Venuti, *The Translator's Invisibility: A History of Translation* (London: Routledge, 2008).

63 See Óscar Garduño Nájera, 'El punzante camino de la traducción: Selma Ancira', *Nexos* (2019), https://cultura.nexos.com.mx/el-punzante-camino-de-la-traduccion-selma-ancira/.

64 *Paisaje caprichoso de la literatura rusa*, ed. and trans. by Selma Ancira (Mexico City: Fondo de Cultura Económica, 2012). For the catalogue of Ancira's translations: 'Perevody', *Selma Ancira*, (2010), http://ancira.ucoz.ru/publ/.

> translate professionally do not choose what to translate. That is what is extraordinary about Selma: even though it helps her to survive [financially], her work is not governed by necessity, but by pleasure.[65]

Segovia compares Ancira's journey from Russia to the Spanish-speaking world and back (since her labour has also been recognised in Russia) as a form of odyssey. The Homeric allusion is particularly appropriate because Ancira's second language for translation purposes is Modern Greek. She received the Pushkin Medal in 2008 for her "great contribution to the study and preservation of cultural heritage";[66] Spain's National Prize for the Work of a Translator in 2011 for the entirety of her translations;[67] and the Tomás Segovia Translation Prize in 2012 for her "dissemination of literature" and her "career as a translator".[68]

Born in Mexico City in 1956, Ancira studied Russian Philology at the State University of Moscow and Modern Greek Language and Literature at the University of Athens,[69] and received her doctorate from the first of these universities, with a thesis on Dostoevsky.[70] In the early 1980s, she started translating Russian literature into Spanish. Her first published translation was Marina Tsvetaeva, Boris Pasternak, and Rainer Maria Rilke's *Letters from the Summer of 1926* (*Cartas del verano de 1926*), which the renowned Mexican publishing house Siglo XXI edited in 1984 (this translation had later editions). After graduating, she had offered Arnaldo Orfila, founding editor of Siglo XXI, her translation of the book by Tsvetaeva, Pasternak, and Rilke.[71] His acceptance marked the first step in her successful career.

Ancira claims Pitol as one of her leading mentors: "... [he] was cultural attaché in Moscow when I was studying [there]. When I told him that I was translating, he was incredibly generous: he gave me advice that I still take into consideration, he supported me, he guided me".[72] In 1988, she moved to Barcelona, where both the location (between Russia, Greece, and Mexico) and the active publishing industry suited her work. As a professional translator,

65 Segovia, *Detrás de las palabras*, p. 97.

66 Iurii Nikolaev, 'Medal'iu Pushkina nagrazhdena meksikanskaia perevodchitsa Selma Ancira', *RIA, Novosti*, 23 October 2008, https://ria.ru/20081023/153686793.html.

67 'Selma Ancira, galardonada con el Premio Nacional de Traducción', *El País*, 23 November 2011, https://elpais.com/cultura/2011/11/23/actualidad/1322002807_850215.html.

68 Marta Eva Loera, 'Selma Ancira recibe el Premio Tomás Segovia', *Universidad de Guadalajara*, 26 November 2012, https://www.udg.mx/en/noticia/selma-ancira-recibe-el-premio-tomas-segovia.

69 'Selma Ancira', *Enciclopedia de la Literatura en México*, (2018), http://www.elem.mx/autor/datos/2533.

70 Guadalupe Alonso Coratella, 'Selma Ancira: "Cada libro te pide algo distinto"', *Milenio* (2019), https://www.milenio.com/cultura/laberinto/libro-pide-distinto-selma-ancira-traductora-tolstoi.

71 See Garduño Nájera, 'El punzante camino de la traducción'.

72 Ibid.

Ancira moves between languages and spaces for the sake of the quality of her versions. Rather than achieving mere mechanical transfer from one language to another, Ancira insists on capturing "details", often travelling to the country of the source language to research the diverse aspects involved in each project.[73] From 2007 to 2015, Ancira also co-organised the International Congress of Russian Literature Translators in Iasnaia Poliana, where translators of Russian literature into various languages met on several occasions to discuss their work.[74]

Ancira's career is therefore a case study in both methodical and heuristic translation, which through professionalisation and institutional support enabled her to devote themselves to lengthy projects. For instance, most of Tsvetaeva's writings have already been translated by Ancira into Spanish, and published mostly in Spain, but often in Mexico too: *The Poet and Time* (*Poet i vremia*, 1932; *El poeta y el tiempo*, 1990); *The Devil* (*Chert*, 1935; *El diablo*, 1991); *Earthly Signs* (*Zemnye primetye*, 1922; *Indicios terrestres*, 1992); *My Pushkin* (*Moi Pushkin*, 1937; *Mi Puskin*, 1995); *History of a Dedication* (*Istoria odnogo posviashcheniia*, 1932; *Una dedicatoria*, 1998); *The Tale of Sonechka* (*Povest' o Sonechke*, 1937; *La historia de Sónechka*, 1999); *A Captive Spirit* (*Plennyi dukh*, 1934; *Un espíritu prisionero*, 1999); *Natalia Goncharova* (*Natalia Goncharova*, 1929; *Natalia Goncharova*, 2006); and *A Living Word about a Living Man* (*Zhivoe o zhivom*, 1932; *Viva voz de vida*, 2008).[75]

In contrast with Pitol, Ancira rarely writes about her own translations.[76] Some examples of her own writing, however, can be found. Her brief "Translator's Note" to *A Captive Spirit* is a good example of her sharp insights into literature:

> Marina Tsvetaeva's literary style is concise and sonorous. It pulverises words, swaps forms, plays with the music of language. And it is precisely music that her controversial use of dashes recalls. For her, the dash is a way to make her ideas more emotionally precise. It is a pause, a sign that is equal to the silence in the musical score. Educated in the universe of sounds, what happens in the prose and poetry of Marina Tsvetaeva is what happens in vocal scores, where syllables are separated with dashes in order to fit together with the cadence of melody.[77]

Hence, what appears to be a technical comment is revealed as a discussion of the musicality of writing. Firstly, Tsvetaeva's use of the dash—with which Ancira

73 See ibid.; Juan Carlos Castellanos C., 'Selma Ancira y su arte de la traducción', *20 Minutos* (2019), https://www.20minutos.com.mx/noticia/844835/0/selma-ancira-su-arte-traducci-oacute-n/.

74 Santoveña (ed.), *De oficio*, pp. 166–67.

75 For this list: 'Katalog perevodov proizvedenii M. I. Tsvetaevoi', *Selma Ancira*, (2010), http://ancira.ucoz.ru/publ/spisok_po_avtoram/rus/404/5-1-0-17.

76 Segovia, *Detrás de las palabras*, p. 101.

77 Selma Ancira, 'Nota de la traductora', in Marina Tsvetaeva, *Un espíritu prisionero*, trans. by Selma Ancira and Ricardo San Vicente (Barcelona: Galaxia Gutenberg and Círculo de Lectores, 1999), p. 33 (p. 33); see Santoveña (ed.), *De oficio*, p. 15.

has long been familiar and which her editors used to reject—is here explained to prepare the reader for the Russian poet's unconventional punctuation;[78] and, secondly, this theme serves to remind the reader of those features lost in every translation: the original "melody", "sound", "music", "cadence", "melody", etc. But even more than a technical comment or a brief theory of Tsvetaeva's punctuation, Ancira's remarks are a rhetorical device to make the reader trust the translator's expertise and acuity, to share her sense of closeness to the late author, and to show that a written text can sound like a musical score—and, eventually, come to life through the voice. Let us look at an example from Tsvetaeva's 'A Captive Spirit':

> Andrei Belyi—tabu. Videt' ego nel'zia, tol'ko o nem slyshat'. Pochemu? Potomu chto on—znamenityi poet, a my srednikh klassov gimnazistki.
>
> Russkikh—i detei—i poetov—fatalizm.[79]

Ancira translates this passage into Spanish thus:

> Andréi Bély era un tabú. Verlo era imposible. Sólo se podía oír hablar de él. ¿Por qué? Porque él era un poeta famoso—y nosotras—alumnas de clases secundarias.
>
> Fatalismo —ruso—de niños—y de poetas.[80]

Meanwhile, in an English version by J. Marin King, one finds:

> Andrei Bely was taboo. You can't see him, only hear about him. Why? Because he is a renowned poet, and we are secondary school girls in the middle grades.
>
> The fatalism—of Russians—and children—and poets.[81]

On the one hand, in the Russian version we can observe the typical use of the dash for the ellipsis of the verb "byt'" ("to be") in the present tense (i.e. in nominal predicates). While King decides to avoid the ellipsis by adding the verb ("we *are* secondary school girls", italics mine), Ancira keeps it ("nosotras—alumnas de clases secundarias"). On the other hand, both King and Ancira

78 Ancira stated recently: "For example, little by little I'm giving back to Tsvetaeva the dashes that the editors took from me. [...] Because they took Tsvetaeva's dashes from me and left me with fifteen percent of them". See Santoveña (ed.), *De oficio*, p. 215.

79 Marina Tsvetaeva, 'Plennyi dukh (moia vstrecha s Andreem Belym'), *Russkaia klassicheskaia literatura*, http://tsvetaeva.lit-info.ru/tsvetaeva/proza/plennyj-duh-1.htm.

80 Tsvetaeva, 'Un espíritu prisionero', in *Un espíritu prisionero*, pp. 97–171 (p. 101).

81 Marina Tsvetaeva, 'A Captive Spirit', in *A Captive Spirit: Selected Prose*, trans. by J. Marin King, pp. 99–169 (p. 101).

translate the dashes of the last sentence into their target languages and adapt the declension of the genitive adjective ("russkikh", that is, "of Russians") and nouns ("detei" and "poetov", that is, "of children" and "of poets"). King even retains the coordinating conjunction typical of Russian ("and children—and poets"). In this brief comparison we can see that Ancira (similarly to King, although with unique final decisions) chooses to maintain both some syntactic structures specific to the Russian language (the verbal ellipsis of the verb "to be" in the present tense) and the stylistic use of the dash in Tsvetaeva's work. Her translation presents the Spanish-speaking reader with a prose style that does not exclude or neutralise particularities from Russian, while remaining highly efficient as a literary device in the target language.

Conclusion

The translation of Russian literature in Mexico or by Mexicans has changed in most respects during the last century, except one: there is still no national facility for training professional translators from Russian into Spanish. This fact has shaped the dissemination of Russian literature in Mexico during this period. In post-Revolutionary Mexico, translations of Russian literature were often carried out via an intermediate language, like French, or else imported from publishing houses in Madrid, Barcelona, or Buenos Aires. This dependence on foreign institutions and expertise, nonetheless, did not prevent Mexico from enjoying a significant reception of Russian literature and figures. For political reasons, Russian writers were prominent during the 1930s and 1940s. This did not necessarily guarantee personal safety from Stalinist attack or economic security: some—like Serge between 1941 and his death in 1947—struggled to make a living in Mexico and to survive Stalinism. On the other hand, Vasconcelos's admiration for Tolstoy had a long-term impact: as late as 1965, the Mexican poet and civil servant Jaime Torres Bodet dedicated an essay to Tolstoy, *Leo Tolstoy: His Life and Work* (*León Tolstói: su vida y su obra*), in which he recalled his "Master", Vasconcelos: '"[w]hen Vasconcelos (whose footprint in Mexican education will be indelible) founded the Secretariat of Public Education, he professed an unrestrained admiration for Tolstoy. He ordered Tolstoy's name to be inscribed on his office's frieze".[82]

Later in the twentieth century, Sergio Pitol's essays and translations inaugurated a new approach to Russian literature. Texts directly translated from Russian ceased to be only discrete intellectual productions by Spanish or Mexican translators. For the first time, they acquired a new role as constituent elements within new fictions that are now considered among Mexican 'classics' of recent

82 Torres Bodet, p. 75. Torres Bodet was Vasconcelos's personal secretary at the Secretariat of Public Education during the early 1920s and would himself assume the role of Secretary during the 1940s.

decades: from *The House of the Tribe* to *The Journey*. Pitol's autobiographical texts often include fragments of his own translations. In a Borgesian turn, Elizabeth Corral suggests that some translated fragments from Nabokov or Pil'niak form an inseparable part of Pitol's *The Journey*.[83] While Pitol learned to translate from Russian in a stay motivated by professional reasons, Ancira is the one of the first relevant Mexican translators to obtain a university degree in philology in order to translate from Russian. Pitol's fame as a translator owed much to his existing celebrity as a writer. Selma Ancira, by contrast, belongs to a time where translators are becoming noteworthy in their own right. She made her name in the publishing industry, enabling her to dedicate time and energy to her long-term projects. After years of translating for both public and commercial publishing houses, since 2009 her work has been honoured with prizes and grants: for instance, the grant by the National System of Art Creators in the area of Translation, which the Mexican government awarded her three times in 2009, 2014, and 2017. This generous grant has a duration of three years in each case and enables the holder to develop an artistic project within that period.[84]

Through these three case studies, I have traced the slender thread in the transfer of literature from Russia into Mexico throughout the last century. Further research on this topic should consider case studies of translators less visible than those described here, either because they are less productive (Ancira's diverse and prolific output naturally attracts more attention), or because of the lack of institutional platforms. In this respect, the Russian Literature Seminar from August 2021 to March 2022 was the first attempt to bring together translators from Russian into Spanish with specialists on Russian literature from both sides of the Atlantic, within a Mexican framework. Some Mexican translators like Alfredo Hermosillo, Mar Gámiz, Indira Díaz, and the Colombian-born Jorge Bustamante García, participated in this Seminar; most of them have lived in Russia for a long time and have published translations of their own. It is likely that a new stage in the translation of Russian literature *in* or *out of* Mexico is now in the making, characterised by intensive collaboration and exchanges with fellow translators in Latin America and Spain.

83 Elizabeth Corral states: "[...] [Borges] forecasts joyful times when translation would be considered worthwhile in itself. For Pitol, that day came long ago. [...] Here, the translation, the foreign voice, is incorporated organically and harmonically into Pitol's writing, it turns into an essential element of the new textual weave, with which the condition desired by Borges is surpassed." 'Sergio Pitol, traductor', *Literal Magazine*, 11 (2012), https://literalmagazine.com/sergio-pitol-traductor/.

84 For the official results of the National System of Art Creators since its foundation in 1993, see 'Sistema de Apoyos a la Creación y Proyectos Culturales. Resultados: Sistema Nacional de Creadores de Arte', *Secretaría de Cultura*, (n.d.), https://foncaenlinea.cultura.gob.mx/resultados/resultados.php.

The USA

Contemporary Russophone Literature of Ukraine in the Changing World of Russian Literature: Andrey Kurkov and Alexei Nikitin

Catherine O'Neil

Introduction

The present chapter was first completed in 2021, before the full-scale Russian invasion of Ukraine on 24 February 2022. The discussion of the direction of Russophone Ukrainian literature is now more speculative than before, as it will only be possible to assess the issues raised in this chapter after the war is over. Nonetheless, eventually, the full-scale war that began in 2022 will be a milestone for changes in the reception of Russian-language literature in translation. Indeed, major changes in the choice of texts to translate and market demand are occurring as we speak. I have tried to preserve what is relevant in this analysis and have updated the rest in light of the ongoing war.

If 'classical' Russian literature of the nineteenth century retains its relevance and cultural authority in the rapidly changing world of publishing and the book market, contemporary Russian-language authors, or 'Russophone' authors, as they are now called, have a more complicated landscape to negotiate. The term 'Russophone', applied to Russian-language writers outside the territory of the Russian Federation, has come into circulation as a result of the efforts of several scholars.[1] The situation surrounding Russophone writers in Ukraine has been

1 See Kevin M. F. Platt, 'Introduction: Putting Russian Cultures in Place', in *Global Russian Cultures*, ed. by Kevin M. F. Platt (Wisconsin: University of Wisconsin Press, 2019), pp. 3–17; Maria Rubins, 'A Century of Russian Culture(s) "Abroad":

 https://doi.org/10.11647/OBP.0340.40

particularly dynamic since 2014, and has developed in a number of directions since the full-scale invasion. As the war continues and Russian speakers move all over the world, 'Russophone', not 'Russian', is becoming the most accurate way to describe this group of writers, including those who left Russia in 2022 and those who remained.[2]

The case of two contemporary Russophone writers from Ukraine, Andrey Kurkov (b. 1961) and Alexei Nikitin (b. 1967), reveals several factors at play. Firstly, the rapidly shifting linguistic situation in their home country regarding Ukrainian and Russian language usage has resulted in the domination of the native book market by Ukrainian-language writers and created a more precarious domestic position for Russophone writers. At the same time, the world's attention on Ukraine as a result of the current war has led both to greater international interest in Ukraine and demand for Ukrainian literature and art. Since Russian remains the better known of the two languages in the West, the Russophone writers are more accessible for translation. In addition, the changing market for international authors in translation as a result of the globalisation of the book market has opened up opportunities for lesser-known literatures—for example Ukrainophone Ukrainian literature—to gain an English readership, and the small size of the market for literature in translation means Russian-language texts are competing with more languages for fewer print runs. The careers of Kurkov and Nikitin provide a useful contrast, as they are prominent prose writers with very different publication experiences both at home and abroad. The discussion will focus on their reception in the US—quite established, in Kurkov's case, but just starting (or, perhaps, restarting) in Nikitin's—against the background of Translation Studies and the history of book marketing in the United States.[3] Both are Kyiv-based novelists who have, until recently, consistently written in Russian.

The Unfolding of Literary Geography', in *Global Russian Cultures*, pp. 21–47; and Marco Puleri, *Ukrainian, Russophone, (Other) Russian. Hybrid Identities and Narratives in Post-Soviet Culture and Politics* (Berlin: Peter Lang, 2020).

2 Kevin Platt and Mark Lipovetsky have argued that the term 'Russophone' should apply to Russian citizens who have left Russia in response to recent events. Their repositioning is already proving controversial, at least in the short term, as it may cause Russian writers to enjoy disproportionate prominence before Western audiences, space that should now arguably be allotted to non-Russian writers, especially Ukrainian ones. See Platt and Lipovetsky, 'The Russophone Literature of Resistance,' *World Literature Today* (March-April 2023), 38–58.

3 Kurkov's books sell steadily, more so in the UK than in the US, but he has a regular following in both countries. Since the war began, Kurkov's novel *Grey Bees* has become a success in both the UK and the US. To date, only one of Nikitin's novels has appeared in English, *Istemi*, translated by Anne Marie Jackson in 2013 and reissued as *Y.T.* in 2016. His most recent novel, *The Face of Fire* [*Ot litsa ognia*, 2021], translated by Dominique Hoffman and Catherine O'Neil, will be published by the Harvard Ukrainian Research Institute (HURI) in 2024.

The Book Market for Literary Translation in the US

The US book market has a well-established reputation for being at once massive and insular. In the sea of profits the industry makes, translation is an insignificant blip: for example, during 2009–10, "the US [bestseller] lists show a clear lack of translations, as well as of English-language literature from outside the country".[4] It may be hoped that this situation has altered since 2010, not least because of the rise of Amazon and its promotion of high-quality translations in its Amazon Crossing imprint.[5] Given the sheer numbers of the US population and, consequently, the enormous size of its market, even a small segment of that market amounts to meaningful cultural significance for 'niche' literature, including Russian writing: in 2009–10 the number of books produced in the US was double that of any other national book market, including those of such famously "reading nations" as the UK and Russia.[6] Of course, financial concerns govern the book market in the US, as they do so much else in American life: due to the "extreme liberalization" of the book market in the US, "cultural goods appear primarily as commercial products that must obey the law of profitability".[7]

Yet even the US requires products with 'symbolic' rather than economic value. As Johan Heilbron and Gisèle Sapiro have argued (following Pierre Bourdieu), market data are not sufficient to determine the 'value' of cultural products, such as books; small presses, small print-runs and 'cult' authors

4 Ann Steiner, 'World Literature and the Book Market', in *The Princeton Sourcebook in Comparative Literature*, ed. by David Damrosch and others (Princeton: Princeton University Press, 2009), pp. 316–24 (p. 321). Much of the global demand for translated books is from English into other languages: the low proportion of translated titles in UK and US book production (less than 4% in the early 1990s) can be contrasted with that of other countries: Germany and France (14–18%), Italy and Spain (24%), Greece (35–45%). See Johan Heilbron and Gisèle Sapiro, 'Outline for a Sociology of Translation. Current Issues and Future Prospects', in *Constructing a Sociology of Translation*, ed. by Michaela Wolf and Alexandra Fukari (Amsterdam and Philadelphia, PA: Benjamins Translation Library, 2007), pp. 93–107 (p. 96). Perhaps the situation has changed since the 1990s, but the influence of English books in foreign markets is likely still outsized compared to translation from other languages.

5 Regarding Amazon Crossing, see Ed Nawotka, 'Translations Pay Off for Amazon,' *Publishers Weekly*, 8 November 2019, https://www.publishersweekly.com/pw/by-topic/industry-news/publisher-news/article/81707-translations-pay-off-for-amazon.html. By 2016, Amazon Crossing, like a 'whale [jumping into] a koi pond' had taken up to 10% of all translation projects. See Angel Gonzales, 'Amazon's Turning Foreign Fiction into English, Irking Literary World,' *The Seattle Times*, 23 April 2017, https://www.freep.com/story/tech/2017/04/23/amazon-expands-its-literary-horizons-translations/100750020/.

6 Steiner, 'World Literature and the Book Market', p. 318.

7 Heilbron and Sapiro, 'Outline for a Sociology of Translation', p. 98.

influence literary reception as much as—if not more than—bestsellers.[8] Thus, even in the profit-driven US market, an academic and cultural elite promotes other value systems to counteract economic ones: "a sizeable share in the import process of foreign literatures arise[s] from the specific cultural logic which prevails in the area of small-scale circulation seeking for peer recognition rather than commercial success".[9] Academic publishers and small, independent presses, although struggling commercially, still seek highbrow books of sophisticated literary quality to supplement the bestsellers in their lists. The problem is more about promoting the books to the target readership. Readers in the US are perceived as predominantly monolingual and easily put off by intrusive and challenging foreign language names and allusions. The "invisible [that is, unrecognized] translator" in Lawrence Venuti's famous formulation is a by-product of this demand to suppress the 'foreign': "A fluent translation is written in English that is current ('modern') instead of archaic, that is widely used instead of specialized ('jargonization'), and that is standard instead of colloquial ('slangy')".[10] Venuti goes so far as to describe the resultant Anglo-American-centred subject, lulled into self-satisfied comfort by the "givenness" of English as the norm, as a psychologically impaired human being:

> the financial benefits of successfully imposing Anglo-American cultural values on a vast foreign readership [produce] cultures in the United Kingdom and the United States that are aggressively monolingual, unreceptive to the foreign, accustomed to fluent translations that invisibly inscribe foreign texts with English-language values and provide readers with the narcissistic experience of recognizing their own culture in a cultural other.[11]

The lamentable situation of current book markets and readerships is something US scholars, teachers, writers, and translators have been addressing for decades—long before the rise of Amazon and the devastation of the Covid pandemic, which I will discuss below. In this sense, the uphill battle waged on behalf of 'symbolic' capital rather than profit-based capitalism is one in which Americans have been wearily engaged for years. Nearly twenty years ago, US scholar Kevin Platt addressed the Russian academic community in North America with his article: 'Will the Study of Russian Literature Survive the Coming Century? (A

---

8 Books, and art in general, can be thought of as 'symbolic capital' whose value is separate from its economic impact. See ibid., p. 95.

9 Ibid., p. 100.

10 Lawrence Venuti, *The Translator's Invisibility: A History of Translation* (London and New York: Routledge, 1995), p. 4. Venuti here describes the translator's invisibility as "a weird self-annihilation, a way of conceiving and practicing translation that undoubtedly reinforces its marginal status in Anglo-American culture".

11 Ibid., p. 15.

Provocation)'.[12] Among other topics, Platt addresses the increasing difficulties in justifying—to university officials and potential students alike—the study of national literatures in isolation: "the kind of nationalist particularist ideology that supports the ideal of a separate and unique 'Russian' tradition is not only poorly based in reality, but often pernicious as well—a key weapon in the mobilizational arsenal of oppressive and repugnant political movements".[13] A similar analysis informs David Damrosch's account of the shift in the demands and subjects of the field of Comparative Literature: despite the apparent decline of traditional humanities, comparative studies, he claims, are thriving, due to "an expanding set of equally compelling needs, from the crises of migration and of the environment to the worldwide rise of inequality, together with violent conflicts that have the United States involved in an Orwellian state of perpetual war".[14]

The situation with Russian literature in the US is characterised by an additional feature beyond both the 'symbolic' value of 'great literature' and the economic value of bestsellers. The political priorities of Cold War agendas simultaneously privileged and funded the study of Russian while separating the field of 'Slavic Studies' (however conceptualised) from other national literature or comparative literature departments. However strong the humanities bent of the student of Russian and the programme in which they were studying, chances are high that some part of their education was funded by the government interested in 'winning' the Cold War.[15] The need to be politically relevant and a 'hot topic' in geopolitical entanglements still affects the marketing and publication in the US of literature from that part of the world.[16]

Meanwhile the Anglophone market for contemporary Russian-language books is often influenced by the reception of those books in Europe. German literary agent Thomas Wiedling owns a small business which is vitally engaged

12 Kevin M. F. Platt, 'Will the Study of Russian Literature Survive the Coming Century? (A Provocation)', *Slavic and East European Journal*, 50:1 (2006), 204–12. It is significant that Platt's more recent work focuses on Russian-language literature produced outside of Russia; he is one of the first theorists of the idea of Global Russian and Russophone Russian literature (see his *Global Russian Cultures*, 2019).

13 Platt, 'Will the Study', p. 206.

14 David Damrosch, *Comparing the Literatures: Literary Studies in a Global Age* (Princeton, NJ and Oxford: Princeton University Press, 2020), p. 4. Note that both Platt and Damrosch use political arguments to legitimise the study of literature, an inevitable feature of promoting classes, majors and disciplines in US universities.

15 See Chapter 5, 'Politics', in Damrosch, *Comparing the Literatures*, an excellent history of US governmental influence on education, including prioritising languages beyond those of Western Europe: "Though in principle the Title VI funding should have been well suited for comparative literature, its emphasis was on languages and regions far from the discipline's purview in that era" (pp. 86–87).

16 The politicised nature of academic funding for Russian-language and 'area studies' is under increasing scrutiny, as the scholarly field tries to grapple with its own complicity in the current war that will certainly reshape ideas about 'Russian' culture for generations. However, this is a topic for a different study.

with our topic: he represents many important contemporary Russian authors and Ukrainian Russophone authors, including Alexei Nikitin, and has helped to get them published in Germany, France and other countries, thereby facilitating their access to the English-reading public.[17] Wiedling observes that UK publishers will not usually consider non-English titles unless they have received acclaim in their home countries and/or been published in other European languages first. As for the US, Wiedling notes that a US publisher will not usually evaluate a work translated from another language unless it has already appeared in English in the UK. Discussions involving two of the best-selling contemporary Russian-language authors in the US, the Ukrainian Andrey Kurkov and the Georgian-Russian "publishing phenomenon" Boris Akunin (b. 1956), confirm Wiedling's views: both authors were able to penetrate the US market only after being published in English translation in the UK.[18]

Translation of the Classics and the Changing Field of Literary Studies

If contemporary authors such as Nikitin and the others represented by Wiedling's agency are struggling to find their English-language publishers, the tradition of Russian nineteenth-century literary classics seems, on the whole, to be alive and well in the North American book market and in academic programmes. Successful translators of Russian literature—that is, those who enjoy steady sales and are regularly offered contracts by publishers—typically translate nineteenth- or early twentieth-century works that are regularly taught, serialised, bought for book groups, or filmed. For example, most of the impressive number of books Marian Schwartz has translated are titles from the mid-twentieth

17 The list of authors Wiedling represents is impressive: besides Nikitin, it includes well-known authors such as Alexei Ivanov, Anna Starobinets and Leonid Yuzefovich (https://topseller.wiedling-litag.com). The discussion that follows is based on email correspondence and a Zoom conversation between myself, Nikitin and Wiedling in August 2021. The website's current page features Ukrainian Russophone writers and Russian-language literature against the war (https://wiedling-litag.com).

18 Kurkov has commented on his publication experiences in English in several places; most recently in a personal Zoom call with myself and his translator, Boris Dralyuk (20 August 2021). He made similar points in his keynote talk at the online ICCEES conference (5 August 2021) and his discussion with Boris Dralyuk about the translation of his 2018 novel *Grey Bees* [*Serye pchely*] ('Grey Bees,' online discussion with translator Boris Dralyuk, 24 February 2021). Stephen Norris similarly describes the path of Akunin via the UK publishers to the display table at his local Barnes & Noble—a place Norris had never seen a Russian writer before (Roundtable on 'The Akunin Project', ICCEES conference, 7 August 2021). I add more on Dralyuk later.

century or earlier.[19] A similarly prolific translating duo, the husband-and-wife team Richard Pevear and Larissa Volokhonsky, have translated or, more often, re-translated, over forty classic Russian novels. Their translations remain in print and thus dominate the academic market, despite their uneven critical reception.[20] Even so, the changing world of readership forces promoters of these 'timeless classics'—primarily university professors—to shift their focus: a chronological survey of Russian (or any) literature will not attract the students it once did. The need to address literature by contexts and themes, beyond country or language of origin, has driven publishers and professors alike to select the works they promote in other ways than 'Russian literature', or 'New Voices from Russia'.[21]

The shift away from national literatures as historical and aesthetic canonical 'givens' has resulted in growing interest in a broader range of texts being published, promoted, and taught in languages other than Russian from the post-Soviet space and in reduced attention to texts from Russia itself. It also affects the development of 'less commonly taught' language-learning in North America: more scholars and writers need to learn languages other than Russian to access these texts and, eventually, translate them. As noted above, the US government generously supports a wide range of languages *so long as they are considered strategic*, which since the rise of Vladimir Putin includes Russian and

---

19 See Marian Schwartz's list on Amazon Crossing, in Dennis Abrams, 'Two of the Season's Top Translators: On Russian Gangsters and a "Convincing Voice"', *Publishing Perspectives*, 15 September 2017, https://publishingperspectives.com/2017/09/translators-on-russian-gangsters-convincing-voice/. Her complete list of translations is huge and, in fact, does include quite a few titles of contemporary authors. (See: https://static1.squarespace.com/static/5aab07c78f513028aeeb545f/t/5f8eed9b4f171b204e3111ac/1603202459552/publicationsmaster+20oct20.pdf). However, it is her translations of Russian classics that get the steadiest sales for university courses.

20 For example, Frank Guan refers to their "decades-long, kudzu-esque campaign to choke out every field of Russian literature" ('Lost in the Fatherland. Dostoevsky's Russia as Curiously Modern After School Project', *The Baffler* [May-June 2019], 80–88 [p. 85])—yet he still cites them in his piece on Dostoevsky. However, in a recent survey on the (mostly) academic Slavic Studies listserv SEELANGS, a number of professors defended the Pevear/Volokhonsky translations, particularly of Tolstoy: "In particular, when Tolstoy repeats the same word and does not use a synonym, Pevear and Volokhonsky do the same thing" (Donna Orwin, SEELANGS post, 21 October 2021).

21 At the beginning of the 2021 academic year, a professor of nineteenth-century Russian literature at New York University sent out a plea to her friends on Facebook: "The updated version of Freud's question is: what do undergraduates want? Since I'm not qualified to teach any real favorites (vampires, sex), what is to be done? I'm soliciting advice from those who know the mysteries of the undergraduate mind: what 19th-c Russian lit class might students be likely to sign up for in spring 2022?" She adds: "I personally would love to teach a class on Turgenev and Goncharov, but it would have an enrollment of precisely zero". Post from August 2021. Quoted with permission.

other languages of the post-Soviet space. Of course, this is not primarily in the interest of literature. The trends that reduce the relevance of national literature departments and the sheer breadth and rapid development of literature produced in the regions and groups included in the field of Global Studies should be good news, ironically, for translators into English: if we cannot expect students to focus on one or two national literatures, more and more readers will rely on books in translation.[22]

In addition, for some languages in the post-Soviet region, Russian remains a bridge (or pivot) language for translation into English. This creates a situation necessitating either working with the Russian translator of a text or, to some extent, treating the Russian translation of the work as an original.[23] The trend to widen the definition of 'Russian' literature beyond the borders of the Russian Federation promotes inclusion of works produced by the Russophone diaspora: former Soviet states, the US or Canada, Israel. For languages other than Russian in these locales that have been gaining interest among readers, the need for good translators has grown, thus motivating translators from Russian to improve their knowledge of other languages and, more and more commonly, to work in collaboration with a native speaker.

Contemporary Ukrainian Literature

Within the broadening post-Soviet linguistic world, Ukrainian literature in particular is a blossoming field, drawing the interest of numerous scholars, students and translators. After decades languishing in isolation within Russian and Slavic Departments, the lone professors of Ukrainian literature and language now have a growing number of colleagues and students, as well as regular

22 Both Platt and Damrosch describe the decreasing focus on actual language proficiency in the new academy that rejects national literatures in favour of global studies: "language instruction begins to seem like a separate, speciali[s]ed function and is likely to wind up ghettoi[s]ed in a speciali[s]ed sub-department" (Platt, 'The Study of Russian Literature', p. 208). Damrosch similarly notes that the beleaguered graduate students in comparative studies, who traditionally needed to master three or four languages, now "feel increasing pressure to cut back intellectually": "Maybe there isn't time—or funding—to master that third language, still less to start a fourth?" (*Comparing the Literatures*, p. 6). The implications of the reduction in language experts for the business of translation have yet to be analysed.

23 This affects, among others, Kazakh writers, for whom Russian-speaking Kazakhs remain an intermediary. Yuriy Serebriansky, a Russophone Kazakhstani writer, described this phenomenon in a discussion of Russophone writers on Facebook (Naomi Caffee, moderator, 'Russophone Voices: A Conversation with Andrey Kurkov and Yuriy Serebriansky' [21 January 2021]). Note also Shelley Fairweather-Vega's work in this region, and the rise of a new translation network ('Turkoslavia') focused on Central Asian languages.

engagement with colleagues and literary circles in Ukraine. Since 2014, the book market in Ukraine has become more propitious for Ukrainian-language writers, a situation that is likely to continue after the war. Within the literary community of Ukraine, a number of major writers stand out, whose influence dominates both the domestic literary scene and the burgeoning academic field of Ukrainian Studies in the UK and North America: Oksana Zabuzhko (b. 1960), Iurii Andrukhovych (b. 1982), Sofia Andrukhovych (b. 1960) and Serhiy Zhadan (b. 1974), to name the most prominent. None of these towering figures in Ukrainian letters writes in Russian, and many writers whose first language was Russian and who originally wrote in Russian have been switching to Ukrainian for their literary work.[24]

This trend began in the aftermath of the Maidan protests in 2013–14 and the war with Russia that began in spring 2014 after Russian troops annexed Crimea and began the separatist war in Eastern Ukraine, the Donbas. Since the full-scale invasion in February 2022, the contention over language seems likely to become more acute. In the transitional time for the Ukrainian nation and its languages, Ukraine-based Russophone writers have lost their largest market—readers in the Russian Federation—and thus they need to find ways to be read both at home and abroad. Many Ukrainian readers remain bilingual in both languages but show a strong preference for reading in Ukrainian. Thus, the last ten years or so have seen an increased production of Ukrainian translations of Russian texts—something that was not considered necessary in the past as bilingualism among Ukrainians was taken as a given.[25]

After Maidan and the first stage of the Russian invasion in 2014, there was a danger that literature in Russian was on the way out of the Ukrainian literary scene. Indeed, in 2015 that seemed a possible outcome to the language wars that accompanied the political and military war. However, the two communities for the most part began to work more closely together: "[n]either attempts to build a high culture in Ukraine's territory exclusively in the language of the former imperial/colonial power [i.e., Russian] nor the spirited attempts to create a robust postcolonial Ukrainian culture that does not incorporate non-Ukrainophone cultural production would ultimately be successful".[26] In a 2020 article on the subject, Canadian Slavist Myroslav Shkandrij claims the "conversion trope"—where writers switch from Russian to Ukrainian as an act of patriotism—is losing ground to peaceful and mutual co-existence between the two language communities: "[t]his respectful interaction between citizens,

24 For example, Volodymyr Rafeenko and Olena Stiazhkina, both Russophone writers from Donetsk who relocated to Kyiv in 2015, now write entirely in Ukrainian.

25 On the Ukrainian reception of Russian literature, see the chapter by Lada Kolomiyets and Oleksandr Kalnychenko in this volume.

26 Vitaly Chernetsky, 'Russophone Writing in Ukraine: Historical Contexts and Post-Euromaidan Changes', in Platt, ed., *Global Russian Cultures*, pp. 48–68 (p. 58).

who speak whichever of the two languages they feel comfortable using, is an attractive phenomenon conveying that a single Ukrainian community exists with diverse constituents who understand each other, no matter what the language of preference".[27] In the academic English-speaking world, scholars are translating, analysing and teaching texts from both languages in political science, history, and literature courses.

Russophone Ukrainian writers will prove to be extremely important to the development of Ukrainian society; not only do they have access to more readers worldwide but they are codifying a new, specifically Ukrainian Russian that promises to develop into its own literary language.[28] Although there is still a divide about the status of Russian in Ukraine, the acceptance of Russophone Ukrainians is more likely to foster the development of civic society in Ukraine: "unlike the ethnic Ukrainians speaking Ukrainian who could readily fit into the ethnonationalist paradigm, Russophone Ukrainians had to look for other ways to conceptualize their relationship with the Ukrainian state and, thus, were in a more productive position to arrive at envisioning civic values as the core of the Ukrainian society".[29]

Kurkov and Nikitin, both Kyiv-based writers, are prominent in very different ways, but they share features that make comparison of their careers useful for discussion of Ukrainian literature written in Russian. (Odesa-based writers also include prominent Russophone writers, reflecting the predominance of Russian culture in that city's history.) Both are fluent in Ukrainian; but until 2022, they insisted that Russian was the only language in which they could write fiction. The full effect of the war still remains to be seen, but as of March 2023, Kurkov has risen to new prominence with awards and acclaim, and Nikitin has been included in the publishing list of the Harvard Ukrainian Research Institute (HURI), which previously only published books originally written in Ukrainian.

Andrey Kurkov: Non-Establishment Leader of the Literary Establishment

Kurkov was the first contemporary writer from newly-independent Ukraine in the 1990s to gain a wide readership abroad and to identify himself as Ukrainian, despite the fact that he writes in Russian: "since his earliest publications in the

27 Myroslav Shkandrij, 'Channel Switching: Language Change and the Conversion Trope in Modern Ukrainian Literature', *Journal of Soviet and Post-Soviet Politics and Society*, 23 (2020), 39–58 (p. 54).

28 It is "literature that can show us the path to undertake even while turning the gaze to the *other* 'Russian World'—and to the diversity of its *local* historical and cultural experiences" (Puleri, *Ukrainian, Russophone, (Other) Russia*, p. 22).

29 Anna Vozna, 'Towards World Russians? How Ukrainian Russophones Construct Boundaries from the Russian Federation', *eSamizdat*, XIV (2021), 121–36 (p. 125), https://www.esamizdat.it/ojs/index.php/eS/issue/view/26/24.

1990s [Kurkov] insisted that he considered himself a Ukrainian writer writing in Russian as opposed to a Russian writer living in Ukraine".[30] After the collapse of the Soviet Union and the establishment of Ukraine's independence in 1991, Kurkov became well-known for his darkly humorous 'Penguin' novels, *Death and the Penguin* (*Piknik na l'du*, 1995) and *Penguin Lost* (*Zakon ulitki*, 2002), as well as his other sardonic portrayals of former Soviet society in this very confusing period.

Kurkov has spoken and published widely about his writing and the development of his work.[31] In the 'Russophone Voices' talk, in which he and Russophone Kazakhstani writer Yuriy Serebriansky (b. 1975) discussed the changing landscape of Russian-language writing, Kurkov notes that when he began writing in the late 1980s, "Soviet Ukrainian literature was already dead" and "post-Soviet Ukrainian literature was not yet born". He describes a sea-change in the situation in contemporary Ukraine, where it seems people read more in Ukrainian now than in Russian. Not surprisingly, he pinpoints 2014 as the year when books in Russian lost a substantial number of readers in Ukraine because Russian was labelled the "language of the enemy". Although Kurkov speaks positively of the development of Ukrainian-language literature and clearly supports newer and younger writers of both languages, he also alludes in this discussion to a greater vitality and energy in Ukrainian-language literature and, by implication, a comparatively stagnant scene on the part of Russophone literature—with some notable exceptions, such as the vibrant Russian-language poetry scene in Odesa. His own contribution, he suggests, is his access to audiences and readers in the West, and he is justifiably proud of the dogged persistence that gained him his following in other languages. In 2020, he even stated, when describing the lower sales of Russophone-Ukrainian writers compared to Ukrainian-language writers in Ukraine: "[i]f I were not published abroad, I would be puzzled to answer the question 'for whom do I write?'". This comment suggests a strong feeling of disconnection from his homeland or home readership, despite his authority and prestige in Ukrainian literary society.

Since 2022, however, he has been one of the major international spokespersons for Ukraine. He is a tireless advocate for Ukrainian culture in all languages and is recognised as such by his countrymen. In spring 2019, he was commissioned to write a version of his novel *Grey Bees* for the acclaimed Theatre in Podil in Kyiv, where it has been performed several times, winning an award in 2020 for 'Best Play of the Year 2019'. His prominence in the Western press after the 2022 invasion of Ukraine and the tremendous success of *Grey Bees* in Ukraine and abroad has reinvigorated his work as a Ukrainian writer.

30 Chernetsky, 'Russophone Writing', p. 58.

31 In this discussion I draw primarily on Kurkov's comments made during a live panel discussion hosted by Facebook, 'Russophone Voices' (21 January 2021), and the 'Cabaret' he performed in London: 'Cabaret Extraordinaire. An Hour with Andrey Kurkov', https://www.youtube.com/watch?v=znofkoT0hNg.

Kurkov's novels *The Bickford Fuse* (2017) (*Bikfordov mir* (Kyiv: Kometko, 1993)) and *Grey Bees* (2019) (*Serye pchely* (Kyiv: Folio, 2018)), both translated into English by Boris Dralyuk, are more ambitious stylistically and serious in content than those of his novels to appear in English in the early 2000s, from *Death and the Penguin* to *The President's Last Love* (*Posledniaia liubov' prezidenta*, 2008). By his own admission, his first major influence was linguistically innovative Russian prose authors such as Boris Pil'niak and Andrei Platonov. *The Bickford Fuse* is his first novel, written in the 1980s, but was only translated into English in 2017, after the critical and financial success of his 'Penguin' novels. It is only in recent years that Kurkov has returned to a more serious style, a departure from the outlandish and comic, as evidenced in *Grey Bees*. He accepts that this move to more serious prose will change and possibly reduce his readership. It is striking that only in recent years has he staked his claim to a place in the Russian literary canon, whereas the books that gained him readership abroad were not, to all appearances, the product of distinct literary predecessors; rather they were pitched as absurd or comical, like some work by Franz Kafka or Nikolai Gogol. His current translator, Boris Dralyuk, is a staunch ally in Kurkov's current literary endeavours: Dralyuk discovered *The Bickford Fuse* after reading an academic article on it. By tackling this complex and prescient text about 'Soviet Man', Dralyuk broadened Kurkov's readership among more 'serious' readers of English. Their translation of *Grey Bees* won the 2022 National Critic Book Circle,[32] and his 2006 novel *Jimi Hendrix Live in Lviv* was listed on the longlist for the 2023 International Booker Prize.[33] Since the war began, Kurkov has completed a memoir in English, *Diary of an Invasion*, that has appeared in a number of European languages.[34]

Both Kurkov and Dralyuk have changed gears as a result of the war. Dralyuk has published several statements against the war; suspended the journal of Russophone literary translations, *Cardinal Points* (which he had co-edited with poet Irina Mashinski);[35] and focused more attention on promoting Ukrainian writers in the West. Originally from Odesa, Dralyuk has identified himself as a "Russophone Ukrainian"; he will likely continue to translate from both

32 Alexandra Alter and Elizabeth A. Harris, 'Ukrainian Author Andrey Kurkov among National Book Critics Circle Award Winners', *The New York Times*, 23 March 2023, https://www.nytimes.com/2023/03/23/books/national-book-critics-circle-award-2023.html.

33 Translated by Reuben Woolley (London: MacLehose Press, 2022), https://thebookerprizes.com/the-booker-library/prize-years/international/2023.

34 Andrey Kurkov, *Diary of an Invasion*, trans. by Boris Dralyuk (London: Mountain Leopard, 2022). (The US Edition was produced by Deep Vellum Press in April 2023.)

35 *Cardinal Points* was produced and funded since its foundation in 2010 by the Slavic Department at Brown University. Its archive may be viewed here: http://www.stosvet.net/cardinalpoints.html.

languages.[36] Among his current projects is a new journal of Russian-language anti-war literature, *The Fifth Wave*, edited by Russian writer Maxim Osipov, whose work Dralyuk has previously translated for the New York Review of Books Classics series.

Kurkov is a paradoxical figure: he is both a part of Ukrainian literary society and an outsider within it. He did not begin his career as a member of the rigid Soviet literary establishment; by his own account, his road to literary acclaim is a tale of stubbornness and determination. In a literary 'Cabaret' filmed at King's Place, London, Kurkov recounts his career to 2011 with generous doses of self-deprecating humour and musical interludes.[37] In his playful narration, Kurkov tells how he fulfilled all the roles in the book industry when beginning his career—that is, he was author, translator, agent, editor, and printing press all in one. Firstly, Kurkov sent hundreds of letters and chapter samples to publishers outside the Soviet Union; then he successfully raised funds to get his books published in Ukraine. In addition, he had to personally pay for and then physically unload the paper for the books (which had to be delivered from Kazakhstan). Finally, Kurkov oversaw the book production at a print shop in Kyiv. This summary does not do justice to the wealth of anecdotal detail recounting the deals he had to make, the not-quite-legal workarounds he both carried out and fell victim to, the complications he encountered, or the good-natured humour with which he tells this rather harrowing story. The main point of the story is that Kurkov was an outlier in the literary world even then, a self-made man, who launched his own career under extremely unpropitious circumstances.

Equally revealing in 'Cabaret' is Kurkov's account of his first publication in English, the novel *Death and the Penguin*. He sent a cover letter, synopsis, his CV and two chapters in English to thirty publishers in the UK and US. He received thirty refusals, including a memorable one he cites in full: "Dear Mr Kurkov, Thank you for your submission. Unfortunately, we only publish high-quality literature. We wish you good luck elsewhere". The letter in question came from Harvill Secker, who has since become his exclusive publisher in the UK. By his account, after spending two or three hours a day on this type of correspondence

36 For a lucid and concise statement of Dralyuk's views, see his recent series of tweets (17 May 2023) in response to a call by Ukrainian PEN for the separation of Russian and Ukrainian writers at public events: https://twitter.com/BorisDralyuk/status/1658870729956560896. PEN Ukraine's Executive Board statement 'We Respond to Our People' (17 May 2023) may be accessed here: https://pen.org.ua/en/my-vidpovidayemo-pered-svoyim-narodom-zayava-vykonavchoyi-rady-ukrayinskoho-pen.

37 'Cabaret Extraordinaire. An Hour with Andrey Kurkov'. There is no date on this film, but it must be between 2011 and 2013, as Kurkov states that the English translation of *Milkman in the Night* has recently come out [*Nochnoi molochnik*, 2011] and that *The Gardener from Ochakov* [*Sadovnik iz Ochakova*, 2013] is soon to be released.

for eighteen years, he finally signed a contract with a German press based in Zurich, Diogenes Verlag. Christa Vogel's translation of *Death and the Penguin* (*Picknick auf dem Eis*, 2000) became a bestseller in Switzerland, and then in Austria and Germany. From then on, Kurkov was able to sell the world rights to his books and publish them in multiple languages, including English.

Kurkov's earliest translator into English was George Bird, the father of one of his friends. Bird was a former MI5 linguist and very knowledgeable about Russia and the Soviet Union. He "interfered" with Kurkov's texts by shortening them and making them more palatable for a British reader; it had been common for British publishers to ask for cuts from Russian novels since the 1950s, in an attempt to "domesticate" them for the British public.[38] Subsequent translators of Kurkov's works, Amanda Love Darragh and Boris Dralyuk, have been contracted by the publisher rather than the author, following usual publishing practice in Europe. (In the US, it is frequently the translator who seeks the publisher and acts as an unpaid agent for the author.) Given Kurkov's excellent English, he is able to work with them effectively. In particular, his working relationship with Dralyuk has become a friendship.

While charismatic and popular, Kurkov does not quite fit either with the academic literary community or with readers of 'classical' Russian literature. Instead, by his own admission he is favoured by political scientists, historians, and journalists, who enjoy reading about current events through the filter of his novels. He has commented that his novels have different appeal for different national audiences: his path to Western readerships began with German translations of his books, popular among students first, and then "middle-class *belletristi* [writers and readers of fiction]". The French appreciated his "ironic philosophy", while his US fans are mostly in "political clubs, not book clubs".[39] His fame extends well beyond the West, with major fan bases in Japan and India. He is aware that he is a kind of 'ambassador' for Ukraine to other countries and is used to being called upon to explain his adoptive country to the world. As Ukraine takes an increasingly prominent place in world events and interest in the country grows, more Ukrainian writers are working in English or being translated into English, thus helping to relieve him of this rather lonely burden.[40]

38 Kurkov remembers Bird telling him about this practice himself. Personal call with author, August 2021.

39 Kurkov, 'Russophone Voices'.

40 Kurkov has spoken of this in private conversation and also in interviews. He pointed to the publication of three articles in the *Los Angeles Review of Books* by contemporary Ukrainian poets on different aspects of Ukrainian identity as a welcome addition to journalism about Ukraine. See Olesya Khromeychuk, 'How to Love Your Homeland Properly', *Los Angeles Review of Books*, 21 August 2021, https://lareviewofbooks.org/short-takes/ukraine-at-30-part-i-how-to-love-your-homeland-properly/; Sasha Dovzhyk, 'An Abundance of Emptiness' *Los Angeles Review of Books*, 23 August 2021, https://lareviewofbooks.org/short-takes/ukraine-at-30-part-ii-an-abundance-of-emptiness/; Iryna Shuvalova, 'The "Mova" I Live

Alexei Nikitin: Ukrainian-Russophone Literature in the Aftermath of Euromaidan

The other prominent Russophone-Ukrainian writer under discussion, Alexei Nikitin, has been as affected by Russian geopolitics as Kurkov, but in a dramatically different way. When Nikitin began writing and publishing in the late 1990s, he sought and received a sizeable readership and critical acclaim in the market best suited for his novels: the Russian Federation. Until 2014, a solid critical reception in the Russian market was the sign of success for Russophone writers in Ukraine, who had reason to believe very few people in their native Ukraine bought and read their books. Polina Lavrova, editor-in-chief of the Kyiv publishing house Laurus, mentioned Nikitin in an interview in 2015 in the context of how difficult it is to convince quality Russophone writers in Ukraine to sign on with Ukrainian presses. Since it was more prestigious and profitable to publish in Russia, Nikitin chose to go with the Moscow publisher.[41]

Nikitin made extraordinary inroads into the difficult realm of the Russian market, becoming an acknowledged and awarded literary newcomer on a scene crowded with great writers, both classic and contemporary. Before 2014, he was mostly read in Russia while less known in his native Ukraine. Nikitin typically answers the question about his readers very modestly. For example, when one interviewer asks: "Who are your readers? Where are you read more—in Russia or in Ukraine? Or maybe abroad [in the Russian diaspora]?" Nikitin answers:

In', *Los Angeles Review of Books*, 24 August 2021, https://lareviewofbooks.org/short-takes/ukraine-at-30-part-iii-the-mova-i-live-in/. The articles appeared in the *LARB* on the occasion of Ukraine's thirty years of Independence.

41 Polina Lavrova, 'The situation with the book market is not merely dire—it's practically hopeless' ['Situatsiia na knizhnom rynke ne prosto tiazhelaia—ona prakticheski beznadezhnaia'], in *The Price of a Question. 27 Interviews with Evhenii Stasinevych* [*Tsina pytannia. 27 interv'iu Yevheniiu Stasivychu*] (Kyiv: Laurus, 2016), pp. 75–82 (p.79). (Original in Russian; translation mine.) Six years after this interview, in 2021, Lavrova has a substantial catalogue of acclaimed books by both Ukrainian and Russian writers, including two by Nikitin (*Victory Park* and *The Face of Fire*). The problem for Ukrainian publishers remains, as in 2015, one of distribution: readers need to order directly from the publisher or from online Ukrainian megastores—which in turn requires a mechanism to find out about the book. So authors and publishers use Facebook and other social media for promotion. Annual book fairs such as the Kyiv Book Arsenal, as well as smaller fairs in L'viv and other regional centres, also help promote books—but here the pandemic did significant damage, both by shutting down the fairs in 2020 and by impacting the economy and reducing readers' budgets. The problem with Russian-language books is exacerbated by the fact that digital versions are pirated and authors and publishers rarely see profits from their sales. (From personal conversations with Lavrova, Nikitin and several members of the literary community in Kyiv.)

> I can't even give you an approximate answer. Probably, my publishers know more about this than I do, though I don't think even they have exact numbers. My Russian books practically don't end up in Ukraine at all. True, my Russian sales are not that huge either. Sales of foreign publishers are not much larger than Russian ones, but the English edition of *Istemi* sells in approximately 40 countries and you can find it in libraries around the world—from Canada to Australia. I would venture to say that most of my readers are on the Internet—but who are they? It's a mystery shrouded in fog.[42]

Nikitin's wry account of the ephemeral world of book sales reveals how little you can tell about the interrelation of acclaim with sales. The particular genius of Internet piracy in Russia is a separate topic, but it is generally known to be easy to lift Russian-language books online without paying either the author or the publisher.

Nikitin is and always has been a Ukrainian writer as far as the content and context of his fiction goes: all his works are set in Kyiv and all address central issues in contemporary Ukraine through the lens of history. Familiarity with Kyiv—indeed, an awareness of the city's centrality as the 'origin' of Rus—among Russian readers worldwide made his novels accessible and appealing to readers in the Russian Federation. Although each of his novels that came out in Russia was awarded or at least nominated for prestigious literary prizes, only one, *Istemi*, has appeared in English, first translated by Anne Marie Jackson in 2013 and reissued in 2016 under the title *Y.T.*. This is largely because of the timing of the release of his subsequent novels—just before Ukrainian and Russian cultural relations all but froze. The height of Nikitin's international recognition occurred in 2013–14, coinciding with the Maidan events. Three of his novels were published in Moscow and well-reviewed in the Russian-language press—*Istemi* (2011), *Mahjong* (*Madzhong*, 2012) and *Victory Park* (2013, the original title is in English)—and *Victory Park* received the prestigious 'Russian Prize' for 2014. The publication date of *Victory Park*, 2014, is somewhat deceptive, since the novel was circulated in manuscript to journals, newspapers, and prize-review boards. Thus, its reception and acclaim actually began in 2013, *before* the events of Maidan, the invasion of Crimea and the war in Donbas.

After 2014, many Ukrainian writers were dropped by Russian publishers. Via his Russian publisher, Ad Marginem, Nikitin was picked up by Thomas Wiedling's agency, most of whose authors (pre-invasion, at least) live in Russia. This in turn eventually helped to get *Istemi* and *Victory Park* published in other languages. *Istemi* (the title is the name of the protagonist's avatar in a strategy game), Nikitin's earliest full novel, came out with Ad Marginem in Russia in

42 My translation. 'Alexei Nikitin: I mythologize Kyiv and I do so consciously' ['Aleksei Nikitin: Ia mifologiziruiu Kiev, i delaiu eto soznatel'no'], interview with Elena Serebriakova, *Russkaia Premiia*, 19 May 2014.

2011; it was published in 2013 in Italian and English (the latter with Peter Owen publishers in Chicago).[43] *Mahjong* and *Victory Park* can be seen as a 'set': both are Kyiv novels, of about the same size (approximately 350 pages), and mix humour, tragedy and historical reflection about the city. However, *Mahjong* has not been translated into any language besides Ukrainian; instead, it became a runaway Internet seller the likes of which neither Nikitin nor his editors had seen before. There are hardly any paper copies of the novel in circulation anymore, but it continues to be available in digital form.[44] *Victory Park* appeared in French translation in Switzerland in 2017 and Italian translation in 2019.[45] The Swiss press, Noir sur Blanc, was founded by a Polish-Swiss couple who specialise in books from Eastern Europe. The Italian publisher Voland likewise (as the name suggests) specialises in Russian texts: Nikitin's novels appeared in the series 'Sirin'—that is, in the same press and by the same translator, Laura Pagliara, who had completed *Istemi* in 2013. *Victory Park* appeared in Ukrainian in 2016 (in the same Kyiv press that had published *Mahjong*, Fabula Publishers); however, a Russian edition only appeared in Ukraine in 2019, when Nikitin was able to publish it with Laurus Press. The international success of Nikitin's books is belatedly impacting his readership at home: he is becoming known in Ukraine, as it were, by arriving from abroad. For a self-professed homebody who only rarely bestirs himself to leave Kyiv even for a few days, Nikitin's situation is quite paradoxical.

After *Victory Park*, Nikitin wrote a novel that culminates with the violent events of 2013–14 themselves: *The Orderly from Institutskaia Street* (*Sanitar s Institutskoi*, 2016). This was his first novel to be published in Russian in Ukraine; significantly, it was published by a press that does not usually publish Russian-language works. Ukrainian literary scholar Vitaly Chernetsky notes that the

43 Nikitin, *Istemi*, Italian translator Laura Pagliara (Rome: Voland, 2013); English translator Anne Marie Jackson's version was reissued as *Y.T.* in 2016 (New York: Melville House).

44 Nikitin is at a loss to explain the very high sales of the digital version of *Mahjong* when it came out—in a typically self-deprecating joke, he supposed people bought it 'by mistake', thinking they were buying the actual game 'Mahjong'. Both *Istemi* and *Madzhong* were available in digital form on Amazon Kindle in 2011 and 2012. Soon after this, however, Amazon stopped publishing ebooks in Cyrillic. In addition, the Russian press Ad Marginem was not very forthcoming with Nikitin about the actual print run and how many copies were sold of the paperback. The topic of Russian language eBooks, their pirated distribution and sales, is beyond the scope of this paper. It is to be hoped that someone with greater digital savvy than this author possesses can investigate this further in the future. The Ukrainian translation of *Mahjong*, a hardcover edition, can still be found in Ukrainian bookstores, as can the Ukrainian translation of *Victory Park.* Oleksiy Nikitin, *Madzhong*, Ukrainian translation by Elena Yakimenko (Kyiv: Fabula, 2017).

45 *Victory Park,* French translation by Anne-Marie Tatsis-Botton (Lausanne: Noir sur Blanc, 2017); *Victory Park,* Italian translation by Laura Pagliara (Rome: Voland, 2019). I am currently working on an English translation of *Victory Park.*

response to the events of 2014 was a pivotal moment in the development of Ukrainian-Russophone literature, and that Russophone writers responded to these events mostly with nonfiction. Nikitin's *Orderly* was an exception to this, as it is fiction, so it is all the more important that it was the only Russian-language literary response to the events included in the five-year retrospective of political developments. In many ways, the novel is a significant moment in the movement of Ukraine's writers of both languages. His most recent novel, *The Face of Fire* (*Ot litsa ognia*, 2021), seems likely to become (and is already becoming) another major step in forging a 'horizontal comradeship' in the Ukrainian literary community: the Russian and Ukrainian editions appeared at almost the same time, and were presented together at the Kyiv Arsenal Book Fair in June 2021. The readership of this novel seems equally divided between Ukrainian and Russian speakers in Ukraine. It is currently being translated into English by myself and Dominique Hoffman and discussed in academic circles. Certainly, the English translations of both *Victory Park* and *The Face of Fire* will get an academic readership, but both books have the potential to appeal to much broader readerships. Since February 2022, Nikitin has been writing and participating in Ukrainian events centred on the war, but not as extensively as Kurkov and other writers with strong English skills. The publication of *The Face of Fire* in HURI's list in the US is an important event for clarifying the status of Ukrainian writers as Ukrainian first, no matter the language they write in.

Prospects for Future Translation Projects from Ukraine

On the whole, it is difficult and probably ill-advised to be optimistic about the future of the book market and the small place within it occupied by literary translation at this particular juncture.[46] Yet current trends—collaboration between translators and their authors, co-translation of texts, workshops and mentoring—invite an examination of what seems to be a large aspect of literary endeavours in general and Translation Studies in particular: a cluster of "imagined communities" of the type described by Benedict Anderson.[47] Venuti's lonely, "invisible" translator who attempts to create a work equal to and independent of the original is not gone, but (s)he is becoming rarer. Mentoring and collaboration in the field of literary translation helps to offset the difficulty caused by conflicting demands from the wider field, which requires translations from more and less known languages: native speakers of English can consult

46 For example, see the RusTrans interview with Marian Schwartz on 19 June 2020: http://rustrans.exeter.ac.uk/2020/06/19/how-can-literature-in-translation-survive-without-bookstores-the-coronavirus-crisis-blog-vii/.

47 Benedict Anderson, *Imagined Communities: Reflections on the Origin and Spread of Nationalism* (London: Verso, 1983).

and creatively pair with native speakers of the language being translated. Venues for workshops and professional advice, such as the University of Bristol programme in translation ('Bristol Translates') and the Association of Literary Translators in America (ALTA), offer platforms for discussing one's work.

Paradoxically, the devastating pandemic has broadened the already popular phenomenon of book groups and writer and translator workshops by forcing them online, thereby creating affordable and geographically inclusive venues. All of this produces more community-based readers, writers, and translators. Despite the obvious drawbacks of holding scholarly conferences online, the attendance of lectures and panels has shown, at least in some cases, that a larger-than-normal audience was reached and able to participate. Facebook itself—arguably more an 'imaginary' community than an 'imagined' one, given the self-replicating algorithms and targeted ads that keep one engaged mainly with like-minded people—is a forum for sharing and discussion of vital intellectual topics. In Ukraine, for example, Facebook is the main way to inform readers about publications and publish substantial reviews and commentaries. The data, of course, are not in yet, but there is reason to hope that literature as a 'symbolic' cultural product will not lose its value completely and English-language translation will continue its modest but essential work.

Russian Literature in the Anglophone Nations: An Overview

Muireann Maguire

> I bore you from the regions of the north
> Where ye first blossom'd, flowers of poetry!
> Now light your smiles and pour your incense forth
> Beneath our Albion's more benignant sky.
>
> —John Bowring (1821)[1]

> Finally, in reading the works of Tolstoi, Turgenev, Dostoevski, Gorki, Chekhov, Andreev, and others, what is the general impression produced on the mind of a foreigner? It is one of intense gloom.
>
> —William Lyon Phelps, *Essays on Russian Novelists* (1911)[2]

When John Bowring (1792–1872), a young wine merchant from Exeter in the English county of Devon, travelled to St Petersburg on business in 1819, he could hardly have known that he was about to inaugurate a new creative field: the translation of Russian literature into English. Although he lacked any literary qualifications, his apprenticeship in a merchant's office and his European travels had made him fluent in several languages, besides gaining "book-knowledge" of Russian and Hungarian.[3] When a friend at court, Friedrich von Adelung, the historian, linguist and quondam tutor to the future Tsar Nikolai I, provided

1 John Bowring, untitled poem, in Bowring, *Specimens of the Russian Poets*, 2nd edn (London: R. and A. Taylor, 1821), p. xxxvi.

2 William Lyon Phelps, *Essays on Russian Novelists* (1911). https://www.gutenberg.org/ebooks/5996.

3 Lewin B. Bowring, 'A Brief Memoir', in Sir John Bowring, *Autobiographical Recollections of Sir John Bowring*, ed. by L.B. Bowring (London: Henry S. King & Co., 1877), pp. 1–42 (p. 4).

 https://doi.org/10.11647/OBP.0340.41

Bowring with a helpful German crib—or bridge translation—of the latest Russian poetry, "the attraction was too powerful to be resisted", although as his son Lewin later noted, it was "no doubt detrimental to the prosecution of successful commercial pursuits".[4] The following year, Bowring's *Specimens of the Russian Poets* was published, the first ever English-language collection of Russian verse.

Bowring's 'Introduction' to his 'Russian Specimens' offers an interesting survey of the pre-Pushkinian players in Russian literature. (He can hardly be faulted for not including Pushkin, since the latter was in Crimean exile when Bowring visited Moscow; and known then only for *Ruslan and Ludmila* (*Ruslan i Liudmila*, 1820).) Lomonosov was identified as "the father of Russian poetry";[5] Sumarokov dismissed as an imitator of La Fontaine; the comedies of Von Visin [sic] were singled out for praise; and Derzhavin praised above all his contemporaries. Bowring translated poems by Kheraskov, Zhukovskii, Bogdanovich, Kapnist, Khemnitzer, Krylov, Dmitriev and Karamzin (whom he criticised for imitating Laurence Sterne on the grounds that "the peculiarities which characterize [Sterne] are only tolerable because they are original"),[6] among others. He added occasional insights into the personalities of these poets: "Krilov [sic] holds an office in the Imperial library in Petersburg. He is well known to the *bons vivants* of the English club. His heavy and unwieldy appearance is singularly contrasted with the shrewdness and the grace of his writings".[7] Of Karamzin, Bowring later wrote, "I found him an agreeable and intelligent man, but I remember nothing in his conversation that betokened a high order of intellect. It was his object to flatter the Emperor [...]".[8]

I expand on Bowring's *Specimens of the Russian Poets* because this slender anthology inaugurated not only the flow of Russian literature into the English language, but also an attitude to the field which would prove more enduring than the translations themselves. Bowring's critique, written from the sophisticated perspective of a religious and political radical (he was a Unitarian and a Benthamite), combined his personal view of Russian society as primitive and brutal, with sincere admiration for its writers' creations.[9] Although he dedicated the second edition of *Specimens* to Tsar Aleksandr I, his preface blamed Russian

4 Ibid., p. 5.

5 John Bowring, 'Introduction', in Bowring, *Specimens of the Russian Poets*, 2nd edn (London: R and A Taylor, 1821), pp. vii-xxxv (p. ix).

6 Ibid., 'Introduction', p. xv.

7 Ibid., 'Introduction', p. xvii.

8 Sir John Bowring, *Autobiographical Recollections*, p. 122.

9 For more discussion and criticism of John Bowring's role as an early translator of Russian literature, see Anthony Cross, 'Early English Specimens of the Russian Poets', *Canadian-American Slavic Studies*, IX:4 (1975), 449–62; Arthur Prudden Coleman, 'John Bowring and the Poetry of the Slavs', *Proceedings of the American Philosophical Society*, 84:3 (1941), 431–59; Miloš Sova, 'Sir John Bowring (1792–1872) and the Slavs', *The Slavonic and East European Review*, 2:2 (1943), pp. 128–44.

autocracy—and the rigid Russian system of social ranks—for the country's comparative backwardness. Bowring added hopefully: "Russia, full as she is of the materials out of which great minds are formed, may yet perhaps take her stand in intellectual eminence among the nations of Europe, at no distant period".[10] In other words, the translation of Russian poetry was part of a complex process of invitation, education, and inclusion—educating the British about Russian literature, while encouraging Russian writers to Westernise their social and political system in order to become full members of the European canon. Thus, Russian writers were represented at the very beginning of their translation journey into English as victims of their government; arguably, since the imperialist and anti-democratic trajectory of Putin's regime became obvious in the 2010s, this perception is once again dominant.

In two centuries since Bowring published his *Specimens*, the translation and reception of Russian literature in the Anglophone world has passed through three major stages: discovery, canonisation, and altruism. In this short essay, I will try to offer an overview of how these stages elapsed on each side of the Atlantic. I have focused on the United States and Great Britain, as the core regions from which most English-language translations have been exported to other Anglophone nations such as Australia and New Zealand,[11] South Africa,[12] and Canada.[13] (The Irish reception of Russian literature is covered separately in this

10 John Bowring, 'Introduction', p. xxv.

11 Russian influence on the Anglophone literature of Australia and New Zealand is under-explored; my own lack of expertise prevents me from expanding on it here. In New Zealand, university programmes in Russian or Slavonic Studies have been developing since the 1940s, and several of the contemporary writers most obviously influenced by Russian literature are also academics: one example is the poet Anna Jackson (b. 1964), who has written various lyrics responding to Vladimir Maiakovskii and Osip Mandel'shtam. See Jacob Edmond, 'No Place Like Home: Encounters Between New Zealand and Russian Poetries', *Landfall*, 213 (2007), 73–80 (esp. pp. 75–78). The New Zealand author Katharine Mansfield (1888–1923), who moved to England aged nineteen, drew on both Chekhov and Dostoevsky in her fiction; while another expat New Zealander, Dan Davin (1913–1990) modelled the plot of his first novel *Cliffs of Fall* (1945) upon *Crime and Punishment*. (On Davin, see Lawrence Jones, 'Strange Conjunctures: Three Russian Episodes in New Zealand Fiction', *New Zealand Slavonic Journal*, (1996), 45–52 (esp. pp. 48–52).) In Australia, the most prominent author overtly influenced by Russian literature may be Robert Dessaix (b. 1944), the novelist and Turgenev biographer. On the development of Slavonic Studies in both countries, see Peter Hill, 'Slavonic Studies in Australia and New Zealand During the Cold War and in the Post-Cold-War Era', *Transcultural Studies*, 9 (2013), 145–64.

12 See Jeanne-Marie Jackson, *South African Literature's Russian Soul: Narrative Forms of Global Isolation* (London and New York: Bloomsbury, 2015).

13 Russian influence on Canadian literature appears to be an under-studied subject, despite Canada's large Russophone diaspora.

volume.)[14] Traditionally, most comparative studies of Russian literary influence have focused on a single author, usually one of Phelps's "standard five" (see below) with the addition of Chekhov.[15] Such studies are unfailingly useful and enlightening; several essays in the present volume follow this pattern. Here, however, I try to isolate how the essential characteristics of 'Russian' literature were defined at different times in the USA and in Britain, and how sociopolitical and reputational changes in both nations have accelerated, or impeded, its reception.

The stage of discovery, from the 1880s to the 1910s, coincided with the global dissemination of Russian literature. Translators, educators, and critics who had independently discovered the aesthetic and philosophical value of Russian literature (whether in the original or in translation), subsequently imposed on themselves the task of making that literature available to as many of their compatriots as possible. These advocates included translators like Britain's Constance Garnett (1861–1946), who translated virtually the entire canon of late nineteenth-century Russian literature, mostly for the publisher William Heinemann, during her forty-year career; while in the US the work of Isabel Hapgood (1851–1928), Nathan Haskell Dole (1852–1935) and Leo Wiener (1862–1939) brought Tolstoy as well as other writers to Anglophone audiences for the first time. (Translations by the last-mentioned pair, although still frequently accessed as free online editions, are not noted for their quality, often because of the haste with which they were accomplished; Wiener, for example, translated twelve volumes of Tolstoy in two years.)[16] Marian Fell (1886–1935), an American citizen who spent much of her adult life in England, translated

14 No single article or monograph, as far as we are aware, studies the influence of Russian literature on Irish-born writers active prior to independence from Britain in 1922, such as George Moore, J.M. Synge, W.B. Yeats and G.B. Shaw. This is a significant lacuna in comparative literature.

15 Worthy examples—to make a very limited selection—include the following titles: Gilbert Phelps, *The Russian Novel in English Fiction* (London: Hutchinson's University Library, 1956); Helen Muchnic, *Dostoevsky's English Reputation, 1881–1936* (New York: Octagon Books, 1969); Glyn Turton, *Turgenev and the Context of English Literature 1850–1900*, which includes a close reading of Constance Garnett's Turgenev translations (London and New York: Routledge, 1992); Gareth Jones, *Tolstoi and Britain* (Oxford: Berg, 1995); and W. J. Leatherbarrow, *Dostoevskii and Britain* (Oxford: Berg, 1995). See also the Bibliography at the close of this volume.

16 For more on Wiener's intellectual contribution to US culture, see Susanne Klingenstein, *Jews in the American Academy, 1900–1940: The Dynamics of Intellectual Assimilation* (New Haven, CT: Yale University Press, 1991), esp. Chapter 1, 'A Philologist: The Adventures of Leo Wiener (1862–1939)', pp. 8–17. On Constance Garnett, see her grandson's biography *Constance Garnett: A Heroic Life* (London: Sinclair-Stevenson, 1991). A new life of Garnett by American journalist Jennifer Wilson is in preparation at the time of writing.

Chekhov's short stories for the major American publishing firm, Scribner's.[17] It is notable that Russian literature was never marketed as entertainment: a 1907 advertisement by the Boston publisher Dana Estes for a 'cabinet set' of Tolstoy's complete works in twenty-four volumes, translated by Wiener, made no effort to describe the contents of the volumes, apparently assuming that the target audience would recognise the intrinsic value of owning and reading Russian literature. Its one boast was that a biography of Tolstoy had been added, since the author's life "was as remarkable as his writings".[18] Tolstoy's name conferred literary value: a 1905 advertisement by the same publisher promised that a new novel by the German author Gustav Frenssen was "as popular as Dickens; as profound as Tolstoy" (a rather unfortunate equivalence, in view of Frenssen's later pro-Nazi sentiments).[19] Similarly, in the 1890s a British firm, the Walter Scott Publishing Company, offered an eight-volume set of 'Count Tolstoy's Works' at two shillings and sixpence per volume (or five shillings apiece if one opted for the luxury half-morocco binding, with gilt top). The set included both fiction and non-fictional works, with the option of adding moralistic essays such as 'If You Neglect The Fire, Don't Put It Out' as individual 'booklets'. The symbolic value of Russian literature as a source of both edification (if you actually read the novels) and of cultural cachet (if your work stood comparison with them) was thus, from their first appearances in the American and British literary fields, exceptionally great.[20]

Once translators had made Russian novels accessible, cultural advocates imbued them with symbolic value and, through criticism, citation, and emulation, embedded them in the Anglophone literary canon. This process is inextricable from the growth of Slavonic Studies in British and American universities between 1870, when the first lectures on the topic were delivered at Oxford, and 1946, when US donors established major interdisciplinary research institutions, the Davis and Harriman Centres, at Harvard and Columbia respectively. Important early advocates for Russian literature included, in the US, Willian Dean Howells (1837–1920) and William Lyon Phelps (1865–1943), and in the UK, Virginia Woolf (1882–1941) and Bernard Pares (1867–1949). Howells and Woolf

---

17 See Anna Maslenova, 'The Silhouette of a Translator: Marian Fell and Russian Culture', *Modern Language Review*, 118:4 (2023), pp. 434–57.

18 *The Publishers' Weekly*, 72:13 (28 September 1907), pp. 895–6 (p. 895). The volumes cost $1.50 each, or $72 for the entire set bound in morocco leather; equivalent to more than $2500 in 2023.

19 *The Publishers' Weekly*, 67:15 (15 April 1905), p. 1121.

20 For a study of how the popular British novelist Hall Caine sought to increase his own cultural capital through association with Tolstoy, see my 'Master and Manxman: Reciprocal Plagiarism in Tolstoy and Hall Caine', in *Reading Backwards: An Advance Retrospective on Russian Literature*, ed. by Muireann Maguire and Timothy Langen (Cambridge: Open Book Publishers, 2021), pp. 129–58, https://books.openbookpublishers.com/10.11647/obp.0241/ch6.xhtml.

exerted huge influence both as novelists and as critics.[21] Through their work, whether intended for students of literature or the intelligent reading public, Russian literature became a crucial section of the intellectual architecture of the twentieth-century Western mind. They made sense for readers and students of an otherwise incoherent programme of 'Russianness', extending from Tolstoy's crusading campaigns through Chekhov's almost actionless plays, Dostoevsky's hysterical protagonists, and a spectrum of radically intentioned political organisations, from the editorial committee of Aleksandr Herzen's journal *The Bell* (*Kolokol*, published in London 1857–65)[22] to the underground network of the novelist and former terrorist Sergei Stepniak-Kravchinskii, Constance Garnett's linguistic mentor. Thanks to critical interpretations, the Russian novel emerged from this mass of conflicting values to become metonymous with both psychological insight and social justice. Each critic picked at least one writer to champion. For Woolf, it was Dostoevsky; for Howells, Tolstoy; while Phelps, writing in 1911, helpfully picked "five standard writers" from among the many Russian authors "deservedly attracting wide attention": these were Pushkin, Gogol, Turgenev, Dostoevsky, and Tolstoy. He argued:

> Russian literature and American literature are twins. But there is this strong contrast, caused partly by the difference in the age of the two nations. In the early years of the nineteenth century, American literature sounds like a child learning to talk, and then aping its elders; Russian literature is the voice of a giant, waking from a long sleep, and becoming articulate.

21 On Howells's use of his role as a *Harper's Monthly* columnist between 1885 and 1892 to advocate for Russian literature, especially Tolstoy's writing, see Clare Goldfarb, 'William Dean Howells: An American Reaction to Tolstoy', *Comparative Literature Studies*, 8:4 (December 1871), 317–37. On how the Russian writer influenced his own novels, see Harry Walsh, 'Tolstoy and the Economic Novels of William Dean Howells', *Comparative Literature Studies*, 14: 2 (1977), 143–65. Phelps, a professor of literature at Yale, published his well-received lectures on the Russian novel in 1911. On Bernard Pares' achievements as an academic, diplomat, and translator of Russian, see Michael Hughes, 'Bernard Pares, Russian Studies and the Promotion of Anglo-Russian Friendship, 1907–14', *The Slavonic and East European Review* 78:3 (2000), 510–35. On how Woolf and her contemporaries received and critiqued Russian literature, and disseminated certain authors through Leonard and Virginia Woolf's publishing company, The Hogarth Press, see Peter Kaye, *Dostoevsky and English Modernism 1900–1930* (Cambridge: Cambridge University Press, 1999), and Helen Southworth, ed., *Leonard and Virginia Woolf, The Hogarth Press and the Networks of Modernism* (Edinburgh: Edinburgh University Press, 2010).

22 In an interesting example of diachronic influence, the Irish dramatist and critic Sean O'Faolain named his own countercultural, philo-European journal *The Bell* (1940–54) in honour of Herzen's publication. See Kelly Matthews, *The Bell Magazine and the Representation of Irish Identity* (Dublin: Four Courts Press, 2012).

Note the change in tone from Bowring's earlier reception of Russian poetry. The British translator had envisaged Russian literature as a post-Petrine edifice requiring the finishing touches of European influence; Phelps, an Ivy League professor who taught Yale's first course on the modern novel, argued that America needed to learn from the Russian novel. True, the latter was distinguished by both morbid melancholy and passive resignation: "no works sound such depths of suffering and despair as are fathomed by the Russians". But by situating the Russian novel within the Christian aetiology of humility and grace, Phelps argued that Russian psychology—exemplified in the work of Dostoevsky and Tolstoy—offered a model of spiritual perfectibility to Western readers.[23] Later critics, like Alfred Kazin, would argue that American literary Realism derived from the national reception of Tolstoy, as mediated by critics like Howells, John Macy, and Van Wyck Brooks; major writers like Theodore Dreiser and even Stephen Crane were firmly imprinted with Tolstoy's influence.[24]

Naturally, there was dissent. Henry James's famous "baggy monster" slur expressed his impatience with the length and psychological (sur)realism of Tolstoy and Dostoevsky. Russian aesthetic melancholy was ably lampooned in P.G. Wodehouse's 1920 comic novel *Jill the Reckless*, where one character experiences "the sort of abysmal soul-sadness which afflicts one of Tolstoy's Russian peasants when, after putting in a heavy day's work strangling his father, beating his wife, and dropping the baby into the city's reservoir, he turns to the cupboards, only to find the vodka-bottle empty".[25] But such criticisms lost force as the Anglophone book market on both sides of the channel ceased to be monolithically Anglo. The vast influx of Russian Jews before the 1917 Revolution into Western Europe and the USA, and the émigrés who left to escape the Communist regime, transformed the ethnic profile of both publishing and translation. Alfred Knopf Sr. (1892–1984), who would found Knopf, one of America's biggest publishers of translated fiction (especially Russian) was born into a Russophone family which had emigrated from tsarist Poland and Latvia; Thomas Seltzer, another pioneering publisher who translated Russian short stories for his own New York-based firm, was a Russian native. For Philip Rahv, the Ukrainian-born literary critic who helped define American fiction through his editorship of the *Partisan Review* during the 1930s and 1940s, "literature

23 All citations from Phelps in this section are from his *Essays on Russian Novelists* (1911), https://www.gutenberg.org/ebooks/5996.

24 Alfred Kazin, *On Native Grounds: An Interpretation of Modern American Prose Literature* (New York: Harcourt, Brace and Company, 1942), esp. p. 69 and pp. 177–79.

25 P. G. Wodehouse, *Jill the Reckless* (London: Herbert Jenkins, 1921), https://www.gutenberg.org/files/20533/20533-h/20533-h.htm. For an excellent and detailed exploration of how British modernism assimilated and ultimately rejected Russian literary influences, see Rebecca Beasley, *Russomania: Russian Culture and the Creation of British Modernism, 1881–1922* (Oxford: Oxford University Press, 2020).

began with Dostoevsky".[26] As Russophone émigrés became assimilated into Anglophone culture, so did their literature, assuaging that "hunger for culture", especially European culture, that typified American writers and critics of the early twentieth century.[27]

The second stage of Russian literary reception, that of canonisation, thus began in the 1920s and persisted until the canon became reified in the 1950s. Nineteenth- and early twentieth-century Russian literature in various translations were fully integrated into the Western literary canon. Tolstoy and Chekhov were taught in universities; multiple commercial publishers on both sides of the Atlantic cashed in by commissioning new translations of the classics; crucially, the 'Russian novel' had become a pit-stop on the road to intellectual self-discovery. The prevalence of Dostoevsky in twentieth and twenty-first century American letters is ubiquitous, and to a large degree undocumented.[28] His influence mid-century on Black authors was pronounced (it can be read most obviously in the title of Richard Wright's long-unpublished novel *The Man Who Lived Underground* (1940s; 2021)), as argued by Maria Bloshteyn and others.[29] Even today, popular, socially critical fiction like Zakiya Dalila Harris's *The Other Black Girl* (2021), a mildly comical novel about a young Black publishing assistant whose imposter syndrome is exacerbated by a hyper-efficient new colleague, appears to draw on Dostoevsky's *The Double* (*Dvoinik*, 1846). William Lyon Phelps's "standard five" had been reconfigured by mid-century as an 'ineffable four': a quartet of canonical writers, usually Tolstoy, Dostoevsky, Gorky, and Chekhov. Familiarity with their fiction was a prerequisite of educated status. Such was their ubiquity that, inevitably, publishers and translators tried to enlarge the canon by proposing newer, more contemporary Russian writers for membership, often by comparing their work favourably to that of one of the quartet.

An example of an unsuccessful attempt at canonisation is Mark Aldanov (pen name of Mark Aleksandrovich Landau, 1886–1957), a Russian-Jewish émigré

26 Mary McCarthy, 'Philip Rahv, 1908–1973', *New York Times*, 17 February 1974, p. 34.

27 Kazin, *On Native Grounds*, p. 168.

28 As in the case of English literature, academic studies of this topic tend to be piecemeal, by author or genre. Examples include Maria Bloshteyn's article 'Dostoevsky and the Beat Generation', *Canadian Review of Comparative Literature*, 28:2/3 (Summer 2001), 218–44; and Jesse Menefee, 'Dostoevsky and the Diamond Sutra: Jack Kerouac's Karamazov Religion', *Texas Studies in Literature and Language*, 53:4 (2011), 431–54, https://muse.jhu.edu/pub/15/article/455858). Benjamin Mangrum argues for the influence of Dostoevsky (particularly *Crime and Punishment*) on Patricia Highsmith's fiction in *Land of Tomorrow: Postwar Fiction and the Crisis of American Liberalism* (Oxford: Oxford University Press, 2018), pp. 85–97.

29 For an account of Dostoevsky's influence on the work of James Baldwin, Ralph Ellison and Richard Wright, see Maria Bloshteyn, 'Rage and Revolt: Dostoevsky and Three African-American Writers', *Comparative Literature Studies*, 38:4 (2001), 277–309. See also Dale E. Peterson, 'Richard Wright's Long Journey from Gorky to Dostoevsky', *African American Review*, 28:3 (Autumn 1994), 375–87.

writer of serious literary and historical fiction, often likened by critics to Tolstoy. When his novel *The Fifth Seal* (*Nachalo kontsa*, 1938; translated into English in 1943 by the Russian émigré Nicholas Wreden) was published by Scribner's in the US and Jonathan Cape in Britain, it was chosen as a Book-of-the-Month Club selection. Its excoriation of Stalinism briefly precipitated national controversy (this was still the era of tentative Americo-Soviet friendship, pre-McCarthyism). Both the club selection and the scandal jump-started sales; there were even inquiries from Hollywood. Nevertheless, in 1951 Scribner's stopped publishing Aldanov because of dwindling sales and consequent "heavy losses on each of his books". As a senior Scribner's editor confided to a colleague, "[t]here is a determined resistance in this country, at this time, to fiction the scene of which is laid in Russia and the characters of which are Russians".[30] Canonical status was not catching: the Ineffable Four, and a few other typically nineteenth-century authors like Gogol, Turgenev, and Lermontov, enjoyed market security and cultural status which could not easily be imparted to other Russophone authors, whatever their reputation at home. Only Solzhenitsyn, whose fiction sparked a bidding war between American and British publishers, seriously challenged the nineteenth-century authors in terms of sales and symbolic capital.[31] The most commercially successful novels in English translation in the early twenty-first century are genre fiction: the historical detectives of Boris Akunin, and horror-inflected science fiction by Sergei Lukianenko.

Despite the vagaries of sales, by the 1950s Russian fiction was firmly imprinted on the public imagination. The symbolic capital of certain authors, and their novels, was so great that the mere mention of the author's name—or book title—evoked a specific mood or philosophical conundrum. In Joseph Heller's iconic 1955 novel *Catch-22*, the hero, Yossarian, has worked out a self-preserving logic which, in his friend Clevinger's opinion, is equivalent to Raskolnikov's rationalisation of murder in *Crime and Punishment*:

> 'You're no better than Raskolnikov—'
> 'Who?'
> '—yes, Raskolnikov, who—'
> 'Raskolnikov!'

---

30 John Hall Wheelock, letter to H. Bartlett Wells, 1st May 1951. Box 203 'Author Files', Folder 5. Archives of Charles Scribner's Sons, Manuscripts Division, Department of Special Collections, Princeton University Library.

31 See Cathy McAteer, *Translating Great Russian Literature: The Penguin Russian Classics* (London and New York: Routledge BASEES series, 2021), pp. 132–36. Publishers who have continued attempting to revise and expand the canon of 'classic' Russian literature (for example, the Russian Library series produced until 2022 by Columbia University Press, in collaboration with the nonprofit Read Russia), have relied on non-commercial funding, such as subsidies from Russian state-sponsored organisations. For an overview , see 'The Russian Library', https://readrussia.org/russian-library/.

> '—who—I mean it—who felt he could justify killing an old woman—'
> 'No better than?'
> '—yes, justify, that's right—with an ax! And I can prove it to you!' Gasping furiously for air, Clevinger enumerated Yossarian's symptoms: an unreasonable belief that everybody around him was crazy, a homicidal impulse to machine-gun strangers, retrospective falsification, an unfounded suspicion that people hated him and were conspiring to kill him.[32]

Reference to Russian classics was not confined to literary fiction. In Ross MacDonald's 1950 private-eye caper *The Drowning Pool*, the narrator encounters a drunk boy sitting owlishly on a barstool after an unlucky night's gambling. He promptly labels him "Dostoevsky".[33] Other riffs on Russian literature in Anglophone fiction, highbrow and lowbrow, are legion.

The third and final category of literary reception is altruistic. Translators, publishers, and advocates, including literary critics, are marked by a sense of mission. Readers experience an almost orientalising pathos, provoked by paratexts (such as prefaces) which frame the authors as political martyrs or activists and their narratives as expressions of resistance or disaffection. While aesthetic appreciation and cultural capital remain significant factors in critical reception, the major criterion for publication is the intrinsic value of restoring—in translation—the voice of a writer who has been creatively silenced or even physically threatened in Russia. This dynamic motivated the independent publisher Ardis, established in Ann Arbor, Michigan by Russian specialists Carl and Ellendea Proffer in 1971, which published roughly 400 titles in both Russian and English over the next quarter of a century. By publishing a mixture of nineteenth-century writers and contemporary, banned Soviet authors (most famously Mikhail Bulgakov, but also figures who never gained significant visibility beyond Slavic Studies, such as Andrei Platonov and Fazil Iskander), Ardis acquired significant symbolic capital while 'rescuing' several generations of Soviet literature from total obscurity. At the time of writing, in the 2020s,

32 Joseph Heller, *Catch-22* (London: Vintage, 1994), p. 23. Later in the same novel, when on leave in Rome, Yossarian dodges through a nightmarish cityscape of drunks, prostitutes, and mass violence, where the agents of social order perpetrate disorder instead: even animals and children are savagely beaten. He thinks explicitly of Raskolnikov's dream of the horse beaten by the peasant (p. 475).

33 Ross MacDonald, *The Drowning Pool* (Milton Keynes: Penguin Random House, 2023), p. 121. In a more recent example, Jack Reacher, the drifter anti-hero of British-American novelist Lee Child's book series, reveals an unexpected fondness for both *Crime and Punishment* ("'a great story'") and *The Brothers Karamazov*, particularly Ivan Karamazov's condemnation of cruelty to children ("'Dostoevsky put his feelings in a book. I don't have his talent. So now I'm thinking I'm going to find these guys and impress on them the error of their ways in whatever manner my own talent allows'"). See Lee Child, *Without Fail* (London: Bantom, 2002), p. 340, p. 430.

altruistic reception is resurgent—in the midst of a general collapse in translation of contemporary Russian literature, it may be the only acceptable way to package writers from a politically discredited nation. Not only do the majority of publishers (both commercial and non-profit) currently refuse to accept Russian state subsidies for translations in the wake of Russia's 2022 invasion of Ukraine, causing this sector of the literary translation industry (which has never been commercially sustainable) to collapse, many critics now call for 'decolonisation' of the Russophone canon. Both critics and the academy are pivoting towards literature in other languages from the post-Soviet space.

These three categories of reception—discovery, canonisation, and altruism—are not mutually exclusive. Both publishers and critics frequently position newly translated Russian writers as brilliant or innovative (hence worth discovering), following in the tradition of Tolstoy or Gogol (thus attempting canonisation), and morally deserving (hence worthy of rescue).[34] Current critical trends, however, are forcing Anglophone publishers either to retreat to the ever-popular nineteenth-century classics, or else to curate new authors from a shrinking pool of Russian political dissidence, in the hope of premiering a new Solzhenitsyn or Brodsky. Rather like Chichikov's troika, Russian literature is launched on a new trajectory of translation—and its cultural ascendancy may be about to be dismantled.

34 Selected endorsements of contemporary Russian author Nataliia Meshchaninova's debut novel *Stories of a Life* (*Rasskazy*, 2017; translated by Fiona Bell, 2022), which appear on the website of her English-language publisher, the American independent firm Deep Vellum, follow this pattern. One critic canonises her with a comparison to Racine; the publisher identifies the aesthetic and critical value of Meshchaninova's narrative as a witness-text to "gender politics and abuse" in post-Soviet Russia; while her own moral integrity is signalled by her support for Russia's #metoo activism. See https://store.deepvellum.org/products/stories-of-a-life.

Bibliography

This bibliography is a partial record of key scholarly articles and monographs about the translation and reception of Russian literature into all global cultures. It is not all-inclusive, and more specific sources may be located within the individual chapters, including our regional overviews.

Australia

Anthony Pym, *Method in Translation History* (London and New York: Routledge, 1998).

Slobodanka Vladiv-Glover, 'Dostoevskii v Avstralii', *Dostoevskii: Materialy i issledovaniia* 20 (2013), pp. 167–80.

Slobodanka Vladiv-Glover, 'Dostoevsky in Australia', https://ausdostoevskysociety.net/history/.

Austria

Literary Translator Studies, ed. by K. Kaindl, W. Kalb, and D. Schlager (Amsterdam and Philadelphia: Benjamins Translation Library, 2021).

China

Mark Gamsa, *The Chinese Translation of Russian Literature: Three Studies* (Leiden and Boston: Brill, 2008).

Sin'mei Li, 'Perevody sovremennoi russkoi literatury v Kitae (seredina 1980-x–2010-x gody', *Vestnik Moskovskogo universiteta*, 9: 5 (2021), 195–204.

Mau Sang Ng, 'Ba Jin and Russian Literature', *Chinese Literature: Essays, Articles, Reviews* (*CLEAR*) 3:1 (1981), 67–92.

England *see* United Kingdom

France

Pieter Boulogne, 'Retranslation as an (un)successful counter-narrative: *Les frères Karamazov* versus *Les frères Karamazov*' ['Повторный перевод как (не)удачный контрнарратив: *Les frères Karamazov* vs *Les frères Karamazov*'], in *Slovo.ru: baltijskij akcent*, 13:1 (2020), 129–43. https://doi.org/10.5922/2225-5346-2022-1-8.

Pierre Bourdieu, 'The Social Conditions of the International Circulation of Ideas', in *Bourdieu: A Critical Reader*, ed. by R. Shusterman (Oxford: Wiley-Blackwell, 1999), pp. 220–28.

Pascale Casanova, *The World Republic of Letters*, trans. by Malcolm DeBevoise (London and Cambridge, MA: Harvard University Press, 1999; repr. 2007).

John L. Chamberlain, 'Notes on Russian Influences on the Nineteenth Century French Novel', in *The Modern Language Journal*, 33:5 (1949), 374–83.

Johann Heilbron and Gisèle Sapiro, 'Outline for a Sociology of Translation: Current Issues and Future Prospects', in *Constructing a Sociology of Translation*, ed. by Michaela Wolf and Alexandra Fukari (Amsterdam and Philadelphia: Benjamins Translation Library, 2007), pp. 93–107.

F. W. J. Hemmings, *The Russian Novel in France: 1884–1914* (London: Oxford University Press, 1950).

Leonid Livak, *How It Was Done in Paris: Russian Émigré Literature and French Modernism* (Madison, WI: University of Wisconsin Press, 2003).

A. McCabe, 'Dostoevsky's French reception: from Vogüé, Gide, Shestov and Berdyaev to Marcel, Camus and Sartre (1880–1959)' (unpublished doctoral thesis, University of Glasgow, 2013).

Daniel Simeoni, 'The Pivotal Status of the Translator's Habitus', *Target*, 10:1, 1998, pp 1–39.

Alexandre Stroev, ed., *Les intellectuels russes à la conquête de l'opinion publique française. Une histoire alternative de la littérature russe en France de Cantemir à Gorki* (Paris: Presses de la Sorbonne nouvelle, 2019).

Germany

Pieter Boulogne, 'Europe's Conquest of the Russian Novel. The Pivotal Role of France and Germany' in *IberoSlavica, A Peer-Reviewed Yearbook of the International Society for Iberian-Slavonic Studies*. Special Issue on 'Translation in Iberian-Slavonic Exchange, ed. by Hanna Pięta and Theresa Seruya (2015), 167–91. https://www.scielo.br/j/ct/a/g8MVPVQVqyYhHYjJ6pFdwLD/?format=pdf&lang=en.

Sigfrid Hoefert, *Russische Literatur in Deutschland: Texte zur Rezeption von den Achtziger Jahren bis zur Jahrhundertwende* (Tübingen: Max Niemeyer Verlag, 1974, rep. 2013).

Holland

Pieter Boulogne, 'The Early Dutch Construction of FM Dostoevskij: From Translational Data to Polysystemic Working Hypotheses', in *Translation and Its Others. Selected Papers of the CETRA Research Seminar in Translation Studies 2007*, ed. by Pieter Boulogne (2008), pp. 1–36. http://www.kuleuven.be/cetra/papers/papers.html.

Pieter Boulogne, 'The French Influence in the Early Dutch Reception of FM Dostoevsky's Brat'ja Karamazovy', *Babel* 55.3 (2009), 264–84.

Emmanuel Waegemans, 'Russische literatuur in de Nederlanden. Vertaling en receptie', in *Literatuur van elders. Over het vertalen en de studie van vertaalde literatuur in het Nederlands*, ed. by Raymond Van Den Broeck (Leuven: Amersfoort, 1988), pp. 57–61.

Emmanuel Waegemans and Cees Willemsen, *Bibliografie van Russische literatuur in Nederlandse vertaling 1789–1985* (Leuven: Universitaire Pers, 1991).

Ireland

Muireann Maguire, 'From Dostoevsky to Yeltsin: Failed Translations and Russian Literary Landings in the Irish Language', *Rus*, 11:17 (Dec 2020), pp. 6–43. https://www.revistas.usp.br/rus/issue/view/11828.

Mark Ó Fionnáin, 'Na Ceithre Máistrí: Chekhov, Turgenev, Tolstoy and Pushkin and the Translation of Russian into Irish', in *Representations and Interpretations in Celtic Studies*, ed. by Tomasz Czerniak, Maciej Czerniakowski and Krzysztof Jaskuła (Lublin: Wydawnictwo KUL, 2015), pp. 267–82.

Mark Ó Fionnáin, 'Opportunities Seized: From Tolstóigh to Pelévin', *Studia Celto-Slavica*, 9 (2018), 63–78. https://doi.org/10.54586/JMAU5002.

Lithuania

Dagnė Beržaitė, 'Dostoesvkii v Litve (Konets XX- nachalo XXI v.), *Dostoevskii: Materialy i issledovaniia* 20 (2013), 143–54. https://library.by/portalus/modules/rus_classic_prose/readme.php?subaction=showfull&id=1481283339&archive=&start_from=&ucat=&.

New Zealand

Irene Zohrab, 'Vospriiatie Dostoevskogo pisateliami i sviashchennosluzhiteliami Novoi Zelandii', *Dostoevskii: Materialy i issledovaniia* 20 (2013), 420–38.

North America

David Damrosch, *What Is World Literature?* (Princeton, NJ: Princeton University Press, 2003).

David Damrosch, *Comparing the Literatures: Literary Studies in a Global Age* (Princeton, NJ: Princeton University Press, 2020).

Clare R. Goldfarb, 'William Dean Howells: An American Reaction to Tolstoy', *Comparative Literature Studies* 8: 4 (1971), 317–37.

William Marling, *Gatekeepers: The Emergence of World Literature and the 1960s* (New York: Oxford University Press, 2016).

Rachel May, *The Translator in the Text: On Reading Russian Literature in English* (Evanston, IL: Northwestern University Press, 1994).

Lawrence Venuti, *The Translator's Invisibility* (London and New York: Routledge, 1995).

South Africa

Jeanne-Marie Jackson, *South African Literature's Russian Soul: Narrative Forms of Global Isolation* (London and New York: Bloomsbury, 2015).

South America

Bruno Barretto Gomide, *Da Estepe à Caatinga: O romance russo no Brasil (1887–1936)* (São Paulo, Brazil: Editora de Universidade de São Paulo, 2011).

Spain

Vsevolod Evgen'evich Bagno, *Emilia Pardo Basan i russkaia literatura v Ispanii* (Leningrad: Nauka, 1982).

Jordi Morillas, 'La recepción de Dostoievski en Pío Baroja', *Estudios Dostoievski*, 2 (2019), 118–30.

Lynn C. Purkey, *Spanish Reception of Russian Narratives, 1905–1939: Transcultural Dialogics* (Cambridge: Cambridge University Press, 2013).

United Kingdom (selected)

Susan Bassnett, 'Preface', in *Constructing Cultures: Essays on Literary Translation*, ed. by Susan Bassnett and André Lefevere (Clevedon, UK: Multilingual Matters, 1998).

Rebecca Beasley, *Russomania: Russian Culture and the Creation of British Modernism, 1881–1922* (Oxford: Oxford University Press, 2020).

Rebecca Beasley and Philip Ross Bullock, eds, *Russia in Britain, 1880–1940: From Modernism to Melodrama* (Oxford: Oxford University Press, 2013).

David Charlston, 'Textual Embodiments of Bourdieusian Hexis', *The Translator*, 19(1), 2013, 51–80. https://doi.org/10.1080/13556509.2013.10799519.

Peter Kaye, *Dostoevsky and English Modernism, 1900–1930* (Cambridge and New York: Cambridge University Press, 1999).

Cathy McAteer, *Translating Great Russian Literature: The Penguin Russian Classics* (London and New York: Routledge BASEES Series, 2021). https://doi.org/10.4324/9781003049586.

Jeremy Munday, 'The Role of Archival and Manuscript Research in the Investigation of Translator Decision-Making', *Target*, 25:1 (2013), 125–39.

Jeremy Munday, 'Using Primary Sources to Produce a Microhistory of Translation and Translators: Theoretical and Methodological Concerns', *The Translator*, 20:1 (2014), 64–80.

Carol Peaker, 'Reading revolution: Russian émigrés and the reception of Russian literature in England, c. 1890–1905' (unpublished doctoral thesis, University of Oxford, 2006).

Rachel Polonsky, *English Literature and the Russian Aesthetic Renaissance* (Cambridge: Cambridge University Press, 1998).

Wales (*see also* United Kingdom)

Samuel Jones, 'The "Vulgar Tongue" and the Russian Translations of T. Hudson-Williams', in *Proceedings of the Harvard Celtic Colloquium* 35 (2015), 129–49.

Author Biographies

Dr Sabina Amanbayeva is Associate Professor of English and Comparative Literature at Oklahoma City University. She teaches courses in World Literature, British Literature, and Russian language. Her research focuses on transcultural relations in the former Soviet region. She is currently co-editing an essay collection, *Transcultural Influences in Soviet and Post-Soviet Animation*.

Hülya Arslan graduated from the Department of Russian Language and Literature of Ankara University in 1988. She completed her master's degree at the Pushkin State Language Institute and her doctorate at Moscow State University. At present, she teaches at Yeditepe University, Department of Russian Language and Literature. Hülya has translated Pasternak's *Doctor Zhivago* (*Yapikredi Yayinlari*, 2014) and *A Story* (*Yapikredi Yayinlari*, 2020), as well as Dostoevsky's *Crime and Punishment* (*Kolektif Kitap Koridor Yayinları*, 2018) into Turkish. In 2016, her translation of Doctor Zhivago was longlisted for the Read Russia Prize.
Orcid: 0000-0003-3825-6581

Anastasia Belousova is Assistant Professor at the National University of Colombia and a Junior Researcher at the Institute of World Culture at Lomonosov Moscow State University. Her research interests revolve around the theory of verse and comparative poetics. She is part of the Comparative Poetics and Comparative Literature (CPCL) team (https://cpcl.info/).
Orcid: 0000-0002-0771-4271

Miquel Cabal Guarro is a literary translator from Russian into Catalan and Professor at the University of Barcelona, with a PhD in Linguistics and over forty published literary translations. He is Vice President of the European Council of Literary Translators' Associations and recipient of the 2021 Barcelona City Prize for the translation of Dostoevsky's *Crime and Punishment*.
Orcid: 0000-0001-7379-0494

Hiroko Cockerill is an Honorary Research Fellow at the University of Queensland in Australia. Her main research field is Translation Studies. Her research publications include *Style and Narrative in Translations* (St. Jerome, 2006) and *Futabatei Shimei no roshiago hon'yaku* (*Futabatei Shimei's Translations from Russian*) (Hōsei University Press, 2015).
Orcid: 0000-0002-5984-8300

Octavian Gabor is Professor of Philosophy at Methodist College, Peoria, Illinois. He works on Greek philosophy and has strong interests in Dostoevsky and the notion of personhood. His most recent translations are Andre Scrima's *Apophatic Anthropology* (Gorgias, 2016) and Constantin Noica's *The Romanian Sentiment of Being* (Punctum Books, 2022, with Elena Gabor).
Orcid: 0000-0003-2477-2542

Rodrigo García Bonillas holds a BA and MA in Literature from the National Autonomous University of Mexico. He completed his PhD at the University of Potsdam with a dissertation on travel literature of Ibero-American writers in the USSR. His latest book is *Guerras floridas. Viajes poéticos de Vladímir Maiakovski y Efraín Huerta entre México y Moscú* (Xalapa: Universidad Veracruzana, 2021).
Orcid: 0000-0001-7736-6156

Elizabeth F. Geballe is an Assistant Professor of Russian literature and culture in the Department of Slavic and East European Languages at Indiana University, Bloomington.

Sarali Gintsburg is a researcher at the ICS (University of Navarra). She holds an MA in Arabic philology (University of Saint Petersburg). She has authored over thirty scholarly publications, including many on Arab Studies.
Orcid: 0000-0003-2962-9534

Bruno Gomide is Associate Professor of Russian Literature at the University of São Paulo, Brazil, and a researcher at the CNPq. He has held visiting scholarships or fellowships at the IMLI, Pushkinskii Dom, Harvard, UC Berkeley, Glasgow University, and the EHESS.
Orcid: 0000-0001-9859-4449

Sabri Gürses graduated from Istanbul University's Department of Russian Language and Literature, where he earned his master's degree in Translation Studies with a dissertation on Nabokov's Pushkin and the history of Russian translations in Turkey. He received his PhD from Erciyes University with a thesis on Russian semiotics and Iuri Lotman. He is the editor of *Çeviribilim*, an online translation journal, and runs the Çeviribilim Publishing House. He is a postdoctoral researcher at Boğaziçi University. Besides retranslating Pushkin, Dostoevsky, and Tolstoy, he has translated twentieth-century Russian authors from Bakhtin to Nabokov into Turkish for the first time. In 2018, his translation of Eugene Onegin was shortlisted for the Read Russia Prize, which he won in 2020 for his Tolstoy translations.
Orcid: 0000-0002-6452-5426

Zsuzsa Hetényi is a Professor of Literature at ELTE, Budapest and a literary translator. She has received the Belletrist Prize (2020). She researches identity problems, emigration, and bilingualism in literature. Besides publishing over 650 academic works (including fifty edited volumes) she translates Russian and Russian-Jewish prose into Hungarian.
Orcid: 0000-0003-2144-9002

Tomi Huttunen (PhD 2007) is a Professor of Russian literature and culture at the University of Helsinki. His research interests include the history of Russian literature; the historical avant-garde; the history of translations of Russian literature in Finland; and late and post-Soviet Leningrad/St Petersburg literature and culture.
Orcid: 0000-0001-5054-8080

Marja Jänis (PhD 1991) was a senior researcher in the Savonlinna School of Translation Studies at the University of Joensuu (now University of Eastern Finland). Her interests include the history of Soviet theatre; translating drama for study and performance; the history of drama translation in Finland; and teaching translating and interpreting from Russian to Finnish (and vice versa).

Oleksandr Kalnychenko is Associate Professor in the Mykola Lukash Translation Studies Department at V.N. Karazin Kharkiv National University, Ukraine, and in the Slavic Languages Department at Matej Bel University in Banska Bystrica, Slovakia. He co-edited the Ukrainian version of *Handbook of Translation Studies* (John Benjamin, 2010-2021), and co-compiled *Anthology of Ukrainian Translation Thinking of the 1920s-Early 1930s* (Nova Knyha, 2011). His contribution to the present volume was supported by the NextGenerationEU programme under the Recovery and Resilience Plan of the Slovak Republic, Project no. 09I03-03-V01-00148.
Orcid: 0000-0001-7808-357X

Christina Karakepeli is a PhD student on the RusTrans project at the University of Exeter, writing her dissertation on how individual translators have shaped the Greek reception of Dostoevsky. She has a BA in Greek Language and Linguistics, and an MA in Translation Studies from the National and Kapodistrian University of Athens.

Mukile Kasongo is a Teaching Associate at the University of Birmingham. His main interests lie in the intersection of feminist translation, translation theory, linguistic hybridity, Francophone studies, Russian studies, African studies, and postcolonial studies.
Orcid: 0000-0002-3050-0044

Lada Kolomiyets is Professor of Translation Studies at the Taras Shevchenko University of Kyiv and the Harris Professor at Dartmouth College, USA. She is a widely published scholar on the history of translation and censorship in Ukraine, with a monograph, *Ukrainian Literary Translation and Translators in the 1920s-1930s* (Nova Knyha, 2015), numerous book chapters and articles.
Orcid: 0000-0002-8327-6672

Venkatesh Kumar received an Honorary Diploma from Rossotrudnichestvo, the Russian organisation for cultural cooperation abroad, for his efforts to familiarise India with the Russian language. The focus of his cross-cultural endeavours are Lev Tolstoy and Kothandapani Pillai, Venkatesh's diplomat-turned-literary translator grandfather, who is credited with translating Tolstoy's works into Tamil.
Orcid: 0000-0002-0802-7932

Anne Lange is a translator and Associate Professor in Translation Studies at Tallinn University. She has published on translation in Estonia in the context of cultural and intellectual history.
Orcid: 0009-0003-2269-201X

Muireann Maguire is Professor of Russian and Comparative Literature at the University of Exeter. Her research interests include nineteenth-century Russian literature, the translation and reception of Russian literature in Western Europe, and the representation of maternal subjectivity in fiction. Besides a newly minted passion for collecting vintage paperbacks, she is starting a new project about William Golding's reception of Tolstoy. She is currently completing a monograph about the history of literary translation from Russian in the US, provisionally titled *The Spectre of Nicholas Wreden: Translating Russian Literature in Twentieth-Century America, 1886-1986* (Bloomsbury Academic, 2025).
Orcid: 0000-0001-7615-6720

Cathy McAteer is a Postdoctoral Research Fellow at the University of Exeter for the ERC-funded project *The Dark Side of Translation: 20th and 21st Century Translation from Russian as a Political Phenomenon in the UK, Ireland and the USA* (RusTrans). Her main research interests are in the field of classic Russian and Soviet literature in English translation, specifically Penguin's Russian Classics. Her first monograph, *Translating Great Russian Literature: The Penguin Russian Classics* (BASEES Routledge series, 2021), is available in Gold Open Access. She is currently finalising her second monograph, *Cold War Women: Female Translators and Cultural Mediators of Russian and Soviet Literature in the Twentieth Century* (Bloomsbury Academic, 2024).
Orcid: 0000-0003-4998-0233

Santiago E. Méndez holds a master's degree in Literary Studies from the National University of Colombia. A former member of the research group in Comparative Literature *Contrapuntos* and of the editorial board of the student

journal *Yasnaia Poliana*, his interests include Russian literature, European Romanticism, Victorian literature, and visual culture.
Orcid: 0009-0008-9097-9182

Aile Möldre is Associate Professor in Publishing at Tallinn University. Her main research focus is twentieth-century Estonian book history.

Georgia Nasseh is Departmental Lecturer in Brazilian and African Portuguese at the University of Oxford. Her PhD research was concerned with issues of multilingualism, translation, and ethics in Angolan literature from the 1950s to 1970s, with an emphasis on the work of José Luandino Vieira. Her wider research is concerned with the literatures of the Global Sixties, anti-colonial and liberation movements in Portuguese-speaking Africa, and Cold War aesthetics. She is also Co-ordinator of the Oxford Comparative Criticism and Translation (OCCT) Research Centre, based in St Anne's College, Oxford.
Orcid: 0000-0002-7030-8241

Mark Ó Fionnáin teaches at the John Paul II Catholic University of Lublin, Poland. He has translated into Irish from both Russian (Kharms, Vvedenski, Pelevin) and Polish (Mrożek), as well as publishing various articles on the Gaelic languages and related issues of translation.
Orcid: 0000-0003-3345-8475

Catherine O'Neil is Professor of Russian Language and Culture at the United States Naval Academy. She received her Master's in Russian literature from the University of Toronto and her doctorate from the University of Chicago. She has written on Aleksandr Pushkin, Russian and European romanticism, and currently works on contemporary Ukrainian literature and Translation Studies. She has translated Alexei Nikitin's *The Face of Fire* (with Dominique Hoffman; Harvard Ukrainian Research Institute, 2024) and is translating *Victory Park.*

Pekka Pesonen (PhD 1987) is a Professor Emeritus of Russian literature at the University of Helsinki. His interests include the history of Russian literature and culture, especially modernism (symbolism), Russian contemporary literature and criticism. He recently directed an international project on 'St Petersburg / Leningrad: History—Narration—Present' funded by the Academy of Finland.

Anna Ponomareva is a Lecturer in Russian, Translation Studies and Comparative Literature at SSEES/UCL and Imperial College London. Her research addresses contemporary issues in translation theory; Russian language and literature; comparative literature and history of ideas. She is the author of several publications in Russian and English.

Dr Damaris Puñales-Alpízar, Associate Professor at Case Western Reserve University, has published *La maldita circunstancia. Ensayos sobre literatura cubana* (Almenara, 2020); *Escrito en cirílico. El ideal soviético en la cultura cubana*

posnoventa (Editorial Cuarto Propio, 2012); *Asedios al caimán letrado: literatura y poder en la Revolución cubana* (with Emilio J. Gallardo Saborido, and Jesús Gómez de Tejada; Karolinum Press, 2018); and *El Atlántico como frontera. Mediaciones culturales entre Cuba y España* (Verbum, 2014).
Orcid: 0000-0002-0732-7490

Benjamin Quénu holds a PhD in contemporary history. He teaches at the University of Paris-10 Nanterre and at the Nouveau Collège d'Études Politiques (NCEP, Paris). His main research interests include the intellectual and cultural history of Soviet Central Asia, war culture, and cultural transfers.

James Rann teaches Russian at the University of Glasgow. His research focuses on Russian literature and culture in the early twentieth century; he is the author of *The Unlikely Futurist: Pushkin and the Invention of Originality in Russian Modernism* (University of Wisconsin Press, 2020).
Orcid: 0000-0001-8397-4502

Susan Reynolds was Curator of Czech, Slovak and Lusatian at the British Library before moving to Research Services there. Twice awarded the English Goethe Society's Thomas Mann and Goethe Prizes, she has published translations of Erben's *Kytice* (Jantar, 2013) and the Adorno/Kracauer correspondence (Polity, 2020), and a chapter in *Racine's Roman Tragedies* (Brill, 2022).
Orcid: 0009-0005-5015-5443

Dr Ranjana Saxena is a Professor of Russian Literature at the Department of Slavonic and Finno-Ugrian Studies at the University of Delhi. Her academic interests are focused on Russian literature, Russian women's writing, feminist and gender issues. She has also extensively translated Russian literature into Hindi and English.

Claudia Scandura, Professor of Russian Language and Literature at Sapienza University in Rome, has authored numerous publications in Italian, German and Russian. She is currently focusing on Russian contemporary poetry and Translation Studies. In 2016, she received the 'Read Russia' Prize for her translation of Sergei Gandlevskii's poems, *La ruggine e il giallo. Poesie 1980-2011* (Gattomerlino, 2014).
Orcid: 0000-0002-2607-1953

Ilaria Sicari is a Marie Sklodowska-Curie postdoctoral research fellow based at Ca' Foscari University of Venice, with the project *Transnational Book Diplomacy beyond the Cultural Cold War: Toward a Socio-Cultural History of Tamizdat* (Horizon Europe, MSCA: TAMIZDAT, 101109157). Her actual research, which combines historical and socio-cultural studies with a digital approach, is devoted to the transnational production, circulation and reception of *tamizdat*, a topic within

which she deals since 2018. Currently, she is a visiting scholar at Stanford, where she is affiliated with the Center for Russian Eastern European and Eurasian Studies (CREEES) and the Center for Spatial and Textual Analysis (CESTA).
Orcid: 0000-0001-8643-0244

Elizaveta Sokolova (PhD 2001) is a literary translator from German into Russian. She has published extensively on German literature and Russian-German cultural interrelations; she is now Head of the Department of Literary Studies at the Russian Academy of Sciences' Institute of Scientific Information for Social Sciences.
Orcid: 0000-0002-7098-3589

Nikolay Steblin-Kamensky is a researcher at the Peter the Great Museum of Anthropology and Ethnography (Kunstkamera), St Petersburg, Russia. He has an MA in Ethiopian Studies from St Petersburg State University and an MA in Anthropology from the European University in St Petersburg. His academic interests are migration studies and Amharic literature.
Orcid: 0000-0002-2040-530X

Guzel Strelkova has worked in the Indian Department of Moscow Radio and in the Indian languages' department of the 'Mir' publishing house in Moscow. She has been Associate Professor of Indian Philology at the Institute of Asian and African Studies, Moscow State University since receiving her PhD in Philology there in 1991. Guzel teaches Modern and Medieval Indian Literature, and Hindi and Marathi as a second Indian language. She has published more than ninety articles on Indian Literature.

Ayesha Suhail is researching a PhD on 'Art and Ideology in Select Works of Leo Tolstoy'. Her areas of interest are nineteenth-century Russian literature, literary realism, the Orthodox Church, and life-writing. She has worked as an Assistant Professor at the Department of English and Teaching Assistant at Women's College, Aligarh Muslim University (AMU), India.

Dr Margaret Tejerizo was Senior Lecturer in Russian at the School of Modern Languages and Cultures, University of Glasgow. Currently she is completing a monograph entitled *The Theatre of A.P. Chekhov in Spain: 'Cries and Whispers'*. Her main research interests lie in cultural and literary relations between Russia and the Hispanic World.

Nguyen Thi Nhu Trang is a tenured Associate Professor and the Head of the Literary Theories Department at the University of Social Sciences and Humanities, Vietnam National University, Hanoi. Her research and teaching focus is on modern Russian literature. She has recently expanded her research to include cultural, urban, and migrant studies.
Orcid: 0000-0003-1615-3901

Zaya Vandan was awarded her PhD in Literature (2016) from Eötvös Loránd University (Budapest, Hungary). Her main research area is nineteenth-century Russian literature, focusing on the poetics and reception of Dostoevsky's works in Hungary and Mongolia. She specialises in the theory and practice of cultural translation within Translation Studies.
Orcid: 0000-0002-1698-9349

Yu Hang is associate professor at the School of Chinese Literature and Linguistics, Guangxi Normal University, China (2018-present) and a Fulbright Visiting Researcher at the University of California San Diego (2015-2016). Her research focuses on nineteenth-century Russian literature, especially Dostoevsky studies and Chinese-Russian literary relations.
Orcid: 0009-0006-6378-9581

Niovi Zampouka is a postdoctoral researcher at the Humboldt University of Berlin, holding a PhD in Slavic Studies which focuses on the Soviet translation of Modern Greek literature, and a literary translator from Russian into Greek. With research interests in Greek-Russian literary relations, world literature, translation and translingualism, her current work focuses on Greek literary communities in Ukraine and the Caucasus.
Orcid: 0000-0003-4177-8313

Index

About the Team

Alessandra Tosi was the managing editor for this book.

Maria Eydmans, Melissa Purkiss and Lucy Barnes proof read this book.

Lucy Barnes and Jennifer Moriarty indexed this book.

Jeevanjot Kaur Nagpal designed the cover. The cover was produced in InDesign using the Fontin font.

Cameron Craig typeset the book in InDesign and produced the paperback and hardback editions. The main text fonts are Tex Gyre Pagella and Noto. The heading font is Californian FB.

Cameron also produced the PDF, EPUB, XML and HTML editions. The conversion was performed with open-source software and other tools freely available on our GitHub page at https://github.com/OpenBookPublishers.

This book has been anonymously peer-reviewed by experts in their field. We thank them for their invaluable help.

Cover images:

1. Boris Pasternak, 2015 stamp of Albania, https://en.wikipedia.org/wiki/File:Boris_Pasternak_2015_stamp_of_Albania.jpg

2. Mikhail Bulgakov, 2016 stamp of Serbia, https://commons.wikimedia.org/wiki/File:Mikhail_Bulgakov_2016_stamp_of_Serbia.jpg

3. Hungary 1949, Mi 1040 B Block 14B souvenir sheet, 150th anniversary of the birth of Aleksander S. Pushkin (1799–1837), Russian poet, https://commons.wikimedia.org/wiki/File:Hungary_1949_Mi_1040_B_Block_14B_souvenir_sheet_(150th_anniversary_of_lhe_birth_of_Aleksander_S._Pushkin_(1799-1837),_Russian_poet).jpg

4. The Soviet Union 1964 CPA 3033 stamp, Soviet Writers, Nikolai Ostrovsky (1904–1936); illustration for the novel 'How the Steel Was Tempered', https://en.wikipedia.org/wiki/File:The_Soviet_Union_1964_CPA_3033_stamp_%28Soviet_Writers._Nikolai_Ostrovsky_%281904-1936%29._Illustration_for_the_novel_%27How_the_Steel_Was_Tempered%27%29.jpg

5. Romania 1949, Mi 1187–1188 stamps (150th anniversary of the birth of Aleksander S. Pushkin, Russian poet), https://commons.wikimedia.org/wiki/File:Romania_1949_Mi_1187–1188_stamps_(150th_anniversary_of_lhe_birth_of_Aleksander_S._Pushkin,_Russian_poet).jpg

6. The Soviet Union 1960 CPA 2392 stamp (Anton Chekhov and Yalta Residence), https://commons.wikimedia.org/wiki/File:The_Soviet_Union_1960_CPA_2392_stamp_(Anton_Chekhov_and_Yalta_Residence).jpg

7. Stamps of Germany (DDR) 1968, MiNr 1351, Maxim Gorki, https://commons.wikimedia.org/wiki/File:Stamps_of_Germany_(DDR)_1968,_MiNr_1351.jpg

8. Hungary 1949, Mi 1039 Stamp, 150th anniversary of the birth of Aleksander S. Pushkin (1799–1837), Russian Poet, https://commons.wikimedia.org/wiki/File:Hungary_1949_Mi_1039_stamp_(150th_anniversary_of_lhe_birth_of_Aleksander_S._Pushkin_(1799-1837),_Russian_poet).jpg

9. Stamp of India 1978, 150th Birth Anniversary of Leo Tolstoy (1828–1910), Writer, https://commons.wikimedia.org/wiki/File:Stamp_of_India_-_1978_-_Colnect_327117_-_150th_Birth_Anniv_Leo_Tolstoy_1828-1910_-_Writer.jpeg

10. DDR Stamp 1953, Famous Russian Writer Nikolay Gogol, https://commons.wikimedia.org/wiki/File:DDR_stamp_1953_Famous_Russian_Writer_Nikolay_Gogol.jpg

11. Stamps of Kazakhstan, 2014–021, https://commons.wikimedia.org/wiki/File:Stamps_of_Kazakhstan,_2014-021.jpg

This book need not end here...

Share

All our books — including the one you have just read — are free to access online so that students, researchers and members of the public who can't afford a printed edition will have access to the same ideas. This title will be accessed online by hundreds of readers each month across the globe: why not share the link so that someone you know is one of them?

This book and additional content is available at:
https://doi.org/10.11647/OBP.0340

Donate

Open Book Publishers is an award-winning, scholar-led, not-for-profit press making knowledge freely available one book at a time. We don't charge authors to publish with us: instead, our work is supported by our library members and by donations from people who believe that research shouldn't be locked behind paywalls.

Why not join them in freeing knowledge by supporting us:
https://www.openbookpublishers.com/support-us

You may also be interested in:

Reading Backwards
An Advance Retrospective on Russian Literature
Timothy Langen and Muireann Maguire (eds)

https://doi.org/10.11647/obp.0241

Twentieth-Century Russian Poetry
Reinventing the Canon
Katharine Hodgson, Joanne Shelton, and Alexandra Smith (eds)

https://doi.org/10.11647/obp.0076

Creative Multilingualism
A Manifesto
Katrin Kohl, Rajinder Dudrah, Andrew Gosler, Suzanne Graham, Martin Maiden, and Wen-chin Ouyang (eds)

https://doi.org/10.11647/obp.0206

www.ingramcontent.com/pod-product-compliance
Lightning Source LLC
Chambersburg PA
CBHW061112100726
47911CB00013B/504